Calendar of State Papers, Domestic series, of the reign of Charles I 1637 - 1638

Editor

John Bruce

Alpha Editions

This edition published in 2019

ISBN : 9789353927769

Design and Setting By
Alpha Editions
email - alphaedis@gmail.com

As per information held with us this book is in Public Domain.
This book is a reproduction of an important historical work. Alpha Editions uses the best technology to reproduce historical work in the same manner it was first published to preserve its original nature. Any marks or number seen are left intentionally to preserve its true form.

CALENDAR

OF

STATE PAPERS,

DOMESTIC SERIES,

OF THE REIGN OF

CHARLES I.

1637—1638.

PRESERVED IN

HER MAJESTY'S PUBLIC RECORD OFFICE.

EDITED BY

JOHN BRUCE, Esq., F.S.A.,

UNDER THE DIRECTION OF THE MASTER OF THE ROLLS, AND WITH THE SANCTION OF
HER MAJESTY'S SECRETARY OF STATE FOR THE HOME DEPARTMENT.

LONDON:
LONGMANS, GREEN, & Co.
1869.

CONTENTS.

	PAGE
PREFACE	vii
CALENDAR, 1637–1638	1
GENERAL INDEX	613
ERRATA	717

PREFACE.

The Calendar and Index contained in the present volume have run out to the full number of pages deemed desirable to be included in each of our publications; a brief note of the general character of the contents is all, therefore, that on this occasion we propose to give by way of preface.

This volume fairly launches us into that period in the reign of Charles I. to which may be applied a phrase lately grown into common use—the beginning of the end.

At the commencement of 1638, the ship-money writs, sent out for the fourth time in annual succession, again replenished the royal finances, but not to the same amount as in former years, although the machinery by which the tax was collected, and by which the government was enabled to watch the progress of the receipt, had attained its perfect working order.

In its own nature that machinery was equally simple and effective. Within the limits of his jurisdiction the sheriff was made personally responsible for the collection. His instructions from the Council, which he was taught to consider as a perfectly legal and authoritative warrant, were essentially comprised in two words,—demand, and (in case of nonpayment) distrain.

Scarcely more complex was the process by which the government was enabled to estimate the diligence of the sheriffs and their good will to this important service. Edward Nicholas, "always," as Lord Clarendon remarks (Hist. Rebell., ed. 1843, p. 371), "versed in business," and then one of the clerks of the council, was appointed to correspond with the sheriffs, and specially to watch their payments. Every Saturday, the Treasurer of the Navy, to whom the sheriffs remitted their money, made up his books, and sent to Nicholas a written account of all sums received by him under the current writs, and of the amount which remained unpaid from every county. Nicholas added a note of moneys reported to him by the sheriffs as collected but not then paid in, with a statement of the total amount received for that year, as compared with the similar sum brought in at the corresponding period of the preceding year.

These accounts were all directed to be submitted by Nicholas, week by week, to the personal cognisance of the sovereign at the customary meeting of the council held every Sunday—a direction which was punctually obeyed. The whole facts thus appeared at a glance. If any sheriff was found to be fainthearted or remiss, to be influenced by excuses for delay urged by persons assessed, or by the fear of legal proceedings, in case of distress, widely felt by the bailiffs,—if he did not duly render his accounts, or find means quickly to remit the money he had collected, oftentimes no easy task in the remote parts of the country— Nicholas was ordered to call him to account under the direct authority of the sovereign, and even under the imputation of disloyalty. He was referred to the simple wording of his instructions. He was ordered to pay in his amount by a certain day, or in default was directed to make his personal appearance before the Council. In important cases he was even summoned to appear before the King himself, to give account of his stewardship.

The present volume, like several of its predecessors, contains a continuation of the series of accounts rendered by the Treasurer of the Navy, and also of the correspondence between Nicholas and the sheriffs. In the latter we have the clearest disclosure of the real feeling of the country. In spite of the stringency of the system under which the money was collected, in spite of the exertions of an experienced official like Nicholas, and in most cases also of the sheriffs themselves, who were anxious to get through their unwonted and disagreeable task, the total sum received up to August 1638 fell short by thirty thousand pounds of the corresponding amount of the preceding year (one sixth of the whole amount). The collection was also accompanied by greater excitement among the people, by increased unwillingness to make the payment, and by more general dissatisfaction with the levy than had ever prevailed before.

Much of this disquiet, no doubt, arose out of the long discussion and ultimate decision of the suit against Hampden. Our volume does not contain a great deal that is directly connected with that subject. It was a case which official people not engaged in it were probably not very willing openly to notice. Such copies of the arguments of the counsel and judges as have been found, with several copies of an abridgement of the speech of the Attorney-General in support of the tax, probably prepared for the information of the friends of the government, have been thrown together into a volume by themselves, which is numbered CCCXCIV., and its contents are mentioned at p. 540.

The ultimate decision, given against the popular wish and feeling, was far from quieting the general dissatisfaction. Laws enacted for the security of freedom were believed to have been strained by the judges to the support of absolutism, and far greater regard was paid by the people to the arguments of the judges who were adverse to the Crown than to those of Lord Chief Justice Finch and his more pliant brethren, who were looked upon as mere creatures of the Court. Persons assessed who had been previously unwilling to submit to the tax still continued to evade its payment. There was a popular persuasion that, the judges having been divided in opinion, there would be some rehearing or appeal; and rumours were circulated that, under the circumstances, the King was unwilling that the payment should be enforced by distress or imprisonment. Officially the question was of course considered settled. Royal independence had been established by the judgment of the law. All the powers of the realm were now entirely at the command of the government. The Archbishop reigned supreme over the Church, and enforced his opinions upon opposers through willing agents and powerful tribunals, who acted with a severity which it is to be feared was congenial to the Archbishop's nature. The King by his success against Hampden was rendered in all ordinary circumstances independent of parliament. Nine years had elapsed since the last of those bodies was dissolved; it seemed as if the King might now reign for a long life without fear of having to meet any such troublesome assembly again. Such were the thoughts of those who looked only at the surface of affairs. There were others amongst those at the head of affairs, and even the Archbishop himself, who, at the very height and in all the pride of their success, could discern tokens of coming trouble. It approached probably sooner than any of them expected, and in a way which was not anticipated.

It was remarked in the Preface to our last volume, as a somewhat disappointing fact, that it contained but one paper which related to the Scottish difficulty. The cause appears in the volume now published. The King was not accustomed to take counsel upon Scottish affairs with his general council, which was a body essentially English, but only with one or two chosen persons, with whom he was closeted whenever tidings arrived from Edinburgh. These two persons are stated to have been Archbishop Laud and the Marquess of Hamilton. During the absence of the latter in Scotland as the King's commissioner sent to treat with the Covenanters, the Archbishop alone was the King's Scottish counsellor. Every step that was taken under this management was in the direction of increased trouble. In all England there were probably few persons less capable of understanding the character of the people of Scotland, or the strength of the feeling which had been roused in that country, than Archbishop Laud. As an opposition to what he esteemed to be a good and pious work he could only attribute the fervour and enthusiasm which pervaded all classes of the Scottish people to the influence of the father of evil, and, in conformity with his policy of "thorough," was of opinion that if some of those who had raised what he termed the "ill-favoured tumult" in St. Giles's Church on the 23rd July 1637 had been at once punished after the manner of Leighton or Prynne, the hostile feeling of the nation would have been borne down and overcome. The King ought to have understood the *perfervidum ingenium* of his fellow-countrymen more accurately. But Charles was as blind as the Archbishop, although from other causes. His personal preference for the English form of religious service, and his ever present consciousness of his own royal dignity, rendered him unwilling to abandon his designs until—such was the violence of the storm that he had raised—there was nothing left for him to abandon.

The business proceeded rapidly from bad to worse. The Scottish warlike preparations excited apprehension of an invasion of England, and the seizure of some of the northern keys of the kingdom—Carlisle, Berwick, or even Newcastle. Measures of defence became imperative. The King found it necessary to call a larger committee to his aid, and probably under their advice ultimately took the whole council into his confidence. On Sunday the 1st July, as we learn from Garrard (Strafford Corresp. II., 181), "his Majesty being in council told the Lords "that they could not be ignorant of the troubles in "Scotland; some wild heads have been the causers of it, "yet he would not proceed in rigour with them, but "show them mercy, if they went no farther; he said he "had given order to provide arms and munition to fortify "three towns upon the borders, and was resolved to send "my Lord Marshal to see it done." From this time our Calendar contains many valuable papers upon this subject, and especially with reference to warlike preparations. The guns were ordered to be withdrawn from Landguard Fort, from Harwich, and from some of the castles in the Downs, to be applied to the fortification of the northern towns. Hull was selected as a place of deposit for warlike stores. Colonel William Legge, Sir Jacob Astley and Sir Thomas Morton were sent into the North to inspect fortifications and hold musters of the trained bands, whilst in London preparations were making ready for an intended levy of men. Never was a country less prepared for war than England at that time. A few words of Sir John Heydon, Lieutenant-General of the Ordnance, by way of apology for his inability to make out certain returns desired by the Earl of Newport, the Master-General, will show the state of one important department of the public service. "The Surveyor is sick, the Clerk of the Ordnance

PREFACE. xiii

" restrained of his liberty, and one of his clerks absent,
" the Clerk of the Deliveries is out of town and his clerk
" absent, the Master-gunner dead, the Yeoman of the
" Ordnance never present, nor any of the gunners attend-
" ant." (Vol. CCCXCVII., No. 37.)

Such a state of things did not long continue. Alarm produced official exertion, and on every hand something was going on proportioned to the presumed necessity and the means at command.

The roads between England and Scotland were stopped, and letters were intercepted; the latter measure principally with a view to discover the correspondence believed to be carrying on between the disaffected in England and the Scottish Covenanters. The intercepted letters in our calendar, although they do not throw much light on that particular point, concur with others in giving reason to believe that the importance of the movements in Scotland, as bearing upon the condition of England, was thoroughly well understood on both sides of the Tweed, and that the presumed difficulty which the King would experience in raising an army in England to fight against the Scots was strongly felt by that people as an encouragement to perseverance in their revolt.

The navy also was called into service against the Covenanters. Its position at this time was somewhat peculiar. The King had for several years entertained the idea of making his second son, the Duke of York, Lord High Admiral. Child as he yet was—not quite five years old—his Majesty determined early in 1638 to take measures for carrying out this intention. In April of that year the existing commission to the Bishop of London and others as Lords of the Admiralty was put an end to, and the young Duke of York received his appointment for life; but in consideration of his tender years another grant of the execution of the office was at the same time made to the Earl of Northumberland, to be held by him during his Majesty's pleasure. Thus there were in fact two High Admirals; the Earl of Northumberland being the acting functionary under letters patent,* but the Duke of York the nominal holder of the office under a warrant actually executed but reserved in the council chest † until after the lapse of years the young Duke should be able to perform his duties. At the time of these appointments the ship-money fleet was lying in the Downs under the command of Sir John Pennington, the Earl of Northumberland being expected on board to take the command. Unfortunately he was almost immediately afterwards seized with fever. For many weeks his life was in great danger, which was increased by a partial recovery and relapse. It was not until the middle of August that the Earl's health was re-established.‡ The whole summer slipt away with the great fleet in total inaction. The despatch of a couple of ships to the westward upon an alarm that the Turks were in the Channel; the convoy of two ships laden with gunpowder into Dunkirk, passing through the Dutch fleet lying off that town;§ and finally the sending two ships to

---

* Dated the 13th April 1638, and entered on Rot. Pat. 14 Car. I., 38th part.

† See p. 351. The transaction is fully explained in an entry on the Council Register under the date of the 18th April 1638 (Vol. xv. Car. I. p. 141). The grant to the Duke of York was to "pass the privy-seal, and there stay without passing further, until his Majesty" signified his pleasure therein.

‡ It was upon this occasion that Waller wrote his lines "To the Earl of Northumberland on his sickness and recovery."

§ It appears from papers here calendared that Sir John Pennington received from Peter Ricaut, the merchant, 150*l.* for this business; what Windebank, who turned everything into money, was paid for procuring the King's authority for the use of the fleet in such a gross breach of neutrality, does not appear.

the North to intercept supplies of arms and ammunition which the Scots were procuring from Rotterdam and Bremen—these were the achievements of the fleet during the summer of 1638.

Another point on which there is considerable information in our pages is the rising in the Fens near Ely against the Earl of Bedford's drainage of the Great Level. The disturbance was at one time serious enough to give fear of general revolt of the inhabitants of that rude district. We here learn what measures were taken on the part of the Justices of Peace, and what relief was given to the complainants by a body of Commissioners of whom Attorney-General Bankes was one.

Most of the other current events of this period receive more or less illustration in our pages; and indeed it may be said of this as of all our previous volumes that there are few branches of inquiry, historical, local, biographical, genealogical, or what not, but are helped on by the information contained in these Calendars. The Index is designed to give the inquirer the greatest possible amount of assistance, and the Calendar itself is endeavoured to be so compiled that whilst avoiding redundancy, especially in our notices of formal documents, it should furnish the searcher with such information, and such amount of it, as would be most useful to him, without extending our notices to an unreasonable length. In some cases of peculiar importance or interest it will be seen that we have printed documents or a part of them entire in small type.

Mr. William Douglas Hamilton and Mr. Alfred Lowson still continue to render their assistance in this long and laborious work.

JOHN BRUCE.

2nd March 1869.

DOMESTIC PAPERS.

CHARLES I.

Vol. CCCLXXIII. December 1–15, 1637.

1637.

Dec. 1. Warrant to pay to Michael Oldisworth 1,400*l*. towards the charge of a masque at Whitehall on Twelfth night next. [*Docquet.*]

Dec. 1. The like to pay to Richard Snelling 357*l*. 4*s*. 9*d*., in full of 457*l*. 4*s*. 9*d*. for provisions delivered to the then Surveyor of the Navy, whereof he has only received 100*l*., as appears by certificate from Sir John Wolstenholme. [*Docquet.*]

Dec. 1. Grant to Edward Birkhead, of the office of one of his Majesty's sergeants-at-arms, with the fee of 12*d*. *per diem* during his life, in place of Robert Maxwell, deceased. [*Docquet.*]

Dec. 1. Licence for Sir Robert Carr to travel into foreign parts for five years. [*Docquet.*]

Dec. 1. Mincing Lane. 1. Officers of the Navy to Lords of the Admiralty. Concerning the Sovereign of the Seas, Mr. Cook conceives that if there be any intent of sending her to sea, Erith will be the fittest place for her moorings, in regard that her provisions are to come from London, and if it should prove a freezing winter she may fall into Tilbury Hope. But yet he concludes that St. Mary's Creek is more secure from ice, and that she may as soon be at sea from thence. He demands 100 men for her ordinary guard. The masters of the Trinity House deliver their opinions that Gillingham is the safest and most convenient place for the ship to be moored in; for the number of men they join with Cook, and hold it fit that a master constantly reside upon her. [1 *p.*]

Dec. 1. 2. Sec. Windebank to Sir William Tresham. Lady Tresham, your wife, has represented to his Majesty her necessitous condition by reason of the small exhibition you allow her for maintenance. His Majesty called to mind that, at your last being here, he enjoined you to take a present course for her relief, to which you promised conformity. Being much displeased that you had not yielded obedience, his Majesty commanded me to signify his pleasure that the 4,000*l*. which you received for her portion should be repaid into her own hands before Candlemas next, or otherwise that you leave your

1637.

VOL. CCCLXXIII.

employment there, and repair into this realm to live with her, and allow her a maintenance agreeable to her quality. [*Draft.* 1½ *p.*]

Dec. 1. 3. ―― Wharton to [Sir John Lambe]. You have seven times imprisoned me, and have not showed any cause, and you have very much impoverished me, and your pursuivants caused others to defraud me of 10*l.* 15*s.* of ready money out of my cupboard, the door of which they broke open. Quotes Whitgift, Andrewes, and Coke as to the illegality of the oath *ex officio.* [*Endorsed by Sir John Lambe,* "*Old Wharton's Letter.*" 1 *p.*]

Dec. 1. 4. Affidavit of George Brome, beadle of the College of Physicians, London, and Richard Bootwell, merchant tailor, of London. One Trigg, near the Custom House, who takes upon him to administer physic, was by Brome required to come to the college to answer before the president and censors, and Brome showed him a Council warrant to that effect, but he refused, and reviled Brome and also the warrant and the president and college. [½ *p.*]

Dec. 1. 5. Measurement of the banks of the marshes, North Somercotes, co. Lincoln, made by Thomas Bransby, Samuel Tottie, William Parker, and William Hinde. Total, 1,520 roods. [1 *p.*]

Dec. 1. 6. Receipt of Sir William Russell for 15*l.* paid by William Skipwith on behalf of Gervase Hollis, late mayor of Great Grimsby, on account of ship-money under writ of 12th August 1636. [¾ *p.*]

Dec. 1. 7. Similar receipt for 130*l.* paid by John Senior on behalf of Dennis Rolle, late sheriff of Devon, in full of 9,000*l.* charged upon that county by writ of 12th August 1636. [¾ *p.*]

Dec. 2. 8. Petition of Sir Thomas Thynne to the King. Petitioner being very sickly it will be very dangerous for him to travel this winter to his mansion house in the country. Prays leave to abide in London until Lady Day. [½ *p.*] *Annexed,*

> 8. I. *Certificate of Dr. William Harvey and Dr. Daniel Oxenbridge as to the state of health of Sir Thomas Thynne.* [½ *p.*]

Dec. 2. 9. Petition of Anthony St. Leger and Dame Barbara Thornhurst, his wife, relict of Sir Thomas Thornhurst, deceased, to the same. Pray for the establishment of an office for registering all ships and mariners void of employment, and a grant of the same to the said Anthony St. Leger, son of Sir Warham St. Leger. In consideration of such grant and certain payments to be made to the holder of the same, petitioners undertake to pay to his Majesty a rent of 300*l.* per annum, and to release all debts due from his Majesty to Barbara as executrix of Sir Thomas Thornhurst. [¾ *p.*] *Annexed,*

> 9. 1. *Petition of Dame Barbara Thornhurst to the King. His Majesty owed petitioner's late husband, Sir Thomas Thornhurst, 500l. for his services in the voyage to Cadiz, and 1,000l. for his services in the Palatinate and the Low Countries*

1637.

Vol. CCCLXXIII.

and at home, so as petitioner, being one of the co-heirs of Thomas Sherley, had been enforced to sell her inheritance for his maintenance in the same, and in this course Sir Thomas had lost his life at Rhé. Prays relief and satisfaction. [⅓ p.] Underwritten,

 9. I. i. *Reference to the Lord Treasurer to cause a true account to be made up of what is due to Sir Thomas, and to certify how the same may be satisfied. 4th June 1628. [¼ p.]*

 9. II. *Certificate of 85 shipowners and masters in favour of the proposal for erecting the registry office above proposed. [2 pp.] Written under the petition now calendared.*

 9. III. *Reference to the Lords of the Admiralty to certify their opinions. Whitehall, 2nd December 1637. [⅕ p.]*

Dec. 2.
Whitehall.

Lords of the Admiralty to [Montjoy Earl of Newport]. To permit Mr. Craddocke, William Pennare, and William Colthurst, owners, and John Heyes, master, of the Diamond, of London, of 160 tons, to supply the said ship with 16 pieces of cast-iron ordnance. [*Copy. See Vol.cccliii., fol.* 72 b. ¾ p.]

Dec. 2.
Whitehall.

Order of the Lords of the Admiralty on petition of John de la Barre, merchant. On 24th May 1633 the Lords gave order to Sir John Heydon that John Sulke might transport 20 pieces of iron ordnance, which belonged to his ship the Hope of Dantzic, which perished at Cromer. Mr. Browne, his Majesty's gunfounder, has stopped the said ordnance. Prays order for their transport. It was ordered that Mr. Browne was to see the petition, and send answer in ten days. [*Copy. Ibid., fol.* 73 b. ½ p.]

Dec. 2.
The Swiftsure, in the Downs.

10. Sir John Pennington to the Lords of the Admiralty. I have this day sent in for Chatham the Unicorn, whose victualling ends the 14th. We have no ships come out of France of late, only one who saith he stole away, and that there is a general embargo; neither have we any come out of Spain or the Straits. A small frigate of Calais took a Hamburgher that came from St. Lucar, bound for Dunkirk, her cargo being valued between 8,000*l*. and 10,000*l*. [*Seals with arms.* 1 p.]

Dec. 2.

11. Petition of William Garway, owner of the ship Mercury, to the Lords of the Admiralty. The Mercury is pressed for his Majesty's service. As she is almost laden, and chiefly with perishable goods, petitioner prays her release, that she may proceed for the Straits. [¾ p.]

Dec. 2.

12. Petition of William Courteen to the same. The Mary Rose, bound for St. Lucar, and having all her provision and part of her lading on board, on the 28th November was taken up for his Majesty's service. The ship is insured for Spain, and goods prepared there to be transported hither in the said ship. Prays order for her being freed. [½ p.]

Vol. CCCLXXIII.

1637.
Dec. 2.
Whitehall.

Lords of the Admiralty to the Officers of the Navy. We are informed that the Royal Merchant and the Swan are prepared for a voyage to the southwards, that the Mercury is laden with perishable goods, and that the owners of the Peter and Andrew have prepared 10,000*l.* worth of commodities, and that the ship is ready for sea. You are to discharge these ships if these allegations are true. P.S.—You are also to release the Mary Rose. [*Copy. See Vol. ccclii. fol.* 72 *b.* ½ *p.*]

[Dec. 2.]
Whitehall.

The same to the same. To send a list of such of the ablest gunners, boatswains, pursers, and carpenters in his Majesty's ships as you hold fittest to be removed to bigger ships, and also of such men as you think fit to be placed in such offices as they become void. [*Copy. Ibid., fol.* 73. ½ *p.*]

Dec. 2.

13. Petition of William Jones, of Ratcliffe, ropemaker, to the Lords of the Admiralty. By sample proffered by James Edwards, of London, merchant, petitioner bargained with Edwards for 80 winch of Russia and Holland cable yarn, and paid him 310*l.* in hand, but Edwards sent rotten and unserviceable stuff, such as is unfit to be employed, and if made up would endanger goods and lives, and refuses to take the same back. Prays that Edwards may be called to answer. [½ *p.*] *Underwritten,*

 13. I. *Order that James Edwards send the Lords his answer in ten days. Whitehall, 2nd December* 1637. [¼ *p.*]

Dec. 2.

Entry on the Admiralty register of the above petition and order. [*See Vol. ccclii., fol.* 73 *b.* ½ *p.*]

Dec. 2.
Westminster.

Nicholas to John Lord Poulett. Has read to the Council his letter of the 3rd of last month concerning his subscription to the fishing business. The Lords expect that he will not fail to pay in the whole sum in the next term to Peter Richaut. The Board was not pleased that he called the fishing a project, being a service tending very much to the good of navigation, especially as his Majesty had vouchsafed to call himself protector of that society. [*Copy. See Nicholas's Letter Book, Dom. James I., Vol. ccxix., p.* 164.]

Dec. 2.
Whitehall.

14. Thomas Jermyn to Sec. Windebank. The King's pleasure is that you make a reference upon this petition to the Lord Treasurer, the Lord Privy Seal, Lord Cottington, yourself, and Sec. Coke. The reason of this unseasonable haste is *Hannibal ad portas.* [1 *p.*]

Dec. 2.

15. Receipt of Sir William Russell for 45*l.* 7*s.* 9*d.* paid by Thomas Frampton on behalf of John Freake, formerly sheriff of Dorset, in part of ship-money charged upon that county by writ of 4th August 1635. [¾ *p.*]

Dec. 2.

16. Account by Sir William Russell of ship-money under writs issued in 1636. Total received, 184,491*l.* 5*s.* 9*d.*; remains, 12,123*l.* 1*s.* 10*d.* [1 *p.*]

DOMESTIC—CHARLES I.

Vol. CCCLXXIII.

1637.
Dec. 2. 17. Account by Sir William Russell of remains of ship-money under writs issued in 1635. Total, 8,508*l*. 11*s*. 2*d*.

Dec. 2. 18. Note of ship-money remaining in hands of sheriffs, on account of writs issued in 1636. Total, 200*l*.; which makes the total collected, 184,691*l*., and remaining 11,709*l*.

Dec. 2. See "Papers relating to Appointments in the Navy."

Dec. 3. 19. Petition of Richard Conquest, of Houghton Conquest, co. Bedford, to the King. There are two advowsons belonging to the church of Houghton Conquest, one called Houghton Conquest, the other Houghton Gildable, and two incumbents presentable, and yet but one church, which is at present vacant. Petitioner, being patron, prays that both these advowsons should hereafter be conferred on one minister. [½ *p.*] *Underwritten,*

    19. I. *Reference to Archbishop Laud, to take order for uniting the said advowsons. Whitehall, 3rd December* 1637. [½ *p.*]

Dec. 3. 20. Petition of Sir Philiberto Vernatti to the same. John Baptista van Lemens, taking notice of the Earl of Bedford's undertaking of draining the great level of Fens, and of petitioner's interest of 10,000 acres under the Earl, contracted with petitioner for 650 acres of the said 10,000 to be delivered at Christmas 1636, being one year after the Earl covenanted to finish his work of draining and to deliver the land to petitioner. The Earl having failed therein, van Lemens sues petitioner and threatens to arrest him. Prays reference to compose these differences, and that in the meantime petitioner may not be arrested. [*Copy.* 1 *p.*] *Endorsed,*

    20. I. *Reference to the Lord Treasurer, Lord Privy Seal, Lord Cottington, and the two secretaries, for the purposes prayed, and direction that petitioner should be freed from arrest until the King's pleasure were known. Whitehall, 3rd December* 1637. [⅓ *p.*]

Dec. 3.
Buckland. 21. John Button, late Sheriff of Hants, to Nicholas. Has received letters from the Lords to pay in the remainder of the ship-money, or attend the Board the first Sunday in Candlemas term. Has sent his servants to collect the money. Must be in London sometime in that term, and begs to be dispensed with till then. In the meantime will pay in what money he receives, and bring with him his rates and the sum of the clergy's tax. [¾ *p.*]

Dec. 3.
Custom House, Bristol. 22. Jo[hn] Dowell to Sir Henry Vane. I find many merchants have great quantities of powder by them which never issued out of his Majesty's stores, and that there are 46 retailers of powder in the city, and two or three mills going contrary to the proclamation. If you cause a commission to issue to examine the foresaid offences, and recommend the despatch of it to Mr. Cordall, I shall be enabled to give you a good account of my service. [*Seal with arms.* 1 *p.*]

Vol. CCCLXXIII.

1637.
Dec. 4. Grant of the office of one of the four tellers of the Exchequer to Robert Reade for life in reversion after Lawrence Squibb and Lawrence Swetman, the two first in reversion. [*Docquet.*]

Dec. 4. Grant for life in reversion to William Hill, son of William Hill, his Majesty's now ancient auditor of the Exchequer, of the office of one of the seven auditors of the Exchequer. [*Docquet.*]

Dec. 4. Grant of an almsroom in Trinity College, Cambridge, to John Peebles for life. [*Docquet.*]

Dec. 4. The King to Sir Alexander Denton, Sheriff of co. Buckingham. Licence to repair to London or any other place within the realm so often as his business shall call him. [*Docquet.*]

Dec. 4. Grant to Elizæus Burges, B.D., Archdeacon of Rochester, of the next prebend's place in the said church that shall fall void; his Majesty annexes a prebend's place in the said church to the archdeaconry of Rochester for ever. [*Docquet.*]

Dec. 4. Lease from Edward Trussell, clothworker, to John Power, merchant tailor, both of London, of the house in White Lion Court, near Fleet Street, in the parish of St. Bride's, lately in the occupation of John Berrington, to hold for 21 years. Consideration 20*l*. Annual rent 12*l*. Execution attested by John Ireton. [*One skin of parchment. See Case D., Car. I., No.* 20.]

Dec. 4.
Plymouth.
23. Nicholas Sherwill, Mayor of Plymouth, to the Council. There lately arrived in this harbour a Dunkirk prize taken at Rochelle from the Hollanders. We send their examination respecting a Spanish fleet from which they lately parted. They came purposely in here to sell their prize, as of late they have done three or four French, which begets an ill report of our place, and causes us to be ill received abroad. [*Seal of the town.* 1 *p.*] *Enclosed,*

> 23. I. *Examination of William Vanden Abele, of Dunkirk, purser of the St. John, of Dunkirk, and John Verhagen, of Dunkirk, pilot of the same, taken this day. On 7th December the said ship came from the Groyne with 37 other ships. The said ships had aboard 8,400 land soldiers, and 500 chests of plate, each of them as much as a man could bear. The General was a Spaniard, Don Lopes de Losse, and they were bound for Dunkirk. The St. John lost their company on Thursday last.* [½ *p.*]

Dec. 4. 24. Justices of Peace, Burgesses, and others of Westminster, 69 in all, to the same. The Woolstaple stairs has time out of mind been the usual place for landing goods for all the inhabitants of the said city. William Reynolds, wharfinger, endeavours to debar us of the same, and to take away the labour of the porters (120 in number). State the various inconveniences which ensue thereby; among them, that "the better sort remove into the Covent Garden and other places,

DOMESTIC—CHARLES I.

1637.
Vol. CCCLXXIII.

by reason of this and the like distastes." Leave the same to the consideration of the Lords. [1 *p.*]

Dec. 4. 25. Petition of Julian Fountnay, one of his Majesty's "Equiers" [equerries], to the Council. Sir Walter Titchborne, Sir Richard Titchborne, and Sir John Philpot had been indebted to petitioner 312*l.* for almost ten years, and by reason of a protection to Sir Walter and Sir Richard, petitioner remains unsatisfied. Sir Walter being lately deceased, petitioner prays the Lords to stay the renewal of Sir Richard's protection, and if petitioner be not satisfied to allow him to take the benefit of the law for recovery of his debt. [¾ *p.*] *Underwritten,*

> 25. I. *Order that this petition be shown to Sir Richard Titchborne, who is required to satisfy petitioner, by default whereof the Lords will grant such order as petitioner desires. Whitehall, 4th December* 1637. [¼ *p.*]

Dec. 4. 26. Sec. Windebank to Sir John Pennington. His Majesty is
Westminster. very well pleased with the diligence you used in putting the Bonaventure in a readiness. On receipt of this you are to give order to the captain to sail for the Groyne, taking the bearer (Mr. Scandaret) with him, and there to attend the Duchess of Chevreuse and bring her to England. It was very ill done of this bearer to communicate this secret business to Sir Henry Mainwaring, and his Majesty is very ill satisfied with it. But you did discreetly to make it known for your own justification and mine. The captain of the Bonaventure is to go, and not Sir Henry Mainwaring, for so is his Majesty's pleasure. You must charge Sir Henry from his Majesty not to divulge this secret at his peril. [1 *p.*]

Dec. $\frac{4}{14}$. 27. Elizabeth Queen of Bohemia to Sir Thomas Roe. Just now
The Hague. I receive yours of the 20th November. I have sent Colonel Ferentz's letter. By the next you shall have more lines from me. I hope by that time Hornec will be returned, who my son sent to the Landgravine and Milandre. By a letter I saw of his, I find he will not now be unwilling to have my son join with him; I would it were already done. As for the treaty, I am of your mind, that it will come to no great matter; yet if the King do not send an ambassador it will be taken as a great neglect, and I will write plainly to entreat him to send you. The Polish ambassador is gone. The French and Swedish ambassador did neither send to him nor visit him; only the Venetian did it. God knows why, for I dare swear he knew not himself, for after he had told me he would do as the others did, and let him alone at least a fortnight or three weeks, a sudden toy took him to do it. You know what discourses have passed betwixt the French ambassador and Rustorff; he is a good honest man, but ignorant of the affairs of Germany. The condition the Queen of Poland has signed to, in being content that that King should keep two volunteers, is the rarest article of marriage I ever heard; yet I like his plain dealing well. If he had married her you know

1637.

Vol. CCCLXXIII.

the article, I believe, would not have been in, but I doubt the effect had been alike. The Prince of Orange has a quartan ague. My Lord of Warwick sent his man over in an English bark with divers things to me. The Dunkirkers have rifled it and taken my letters, but yours escaped. [*Seals with arms.* 1½ *p.*]

Dec. 4.
Westminster.

Nicholas to Thomas Viscount Wentworth, Lord Deputy of Ireland. When I obtained a grant from the Lords of the Admiralty of the office of Ferriage in Ireland, they were certified by the Judge of the Admiralty that it was a particular belonging to the office of Lord Admiral of England. I never intended to hold it longer than till you should appoint me to dispose of it. What I did in it, was as well to prevent other suitors that endeavoured to get it to the prejudice of the Admiralty as to benefit myself, and it ever was my resolution to dispose of it as you shall please to command. [*Copy. See Nicholas's Letter Book, Dom. James I., Vol. ccxix., p.* 165.]

Dec. 4.
Westminster.

The same to William Clobery. The Lords of the Admiralty desire you to send particulars of your proposition for bringing in 100 tons of Barbary saltpetre yearly for the King's service. [*Copy. See Ibid., p.* 166.]

Dec. 4.
Whitehall.

28. Certificate of the Fishing Society of Great Britain and Ireland, that Thomas Bennit is sworn and made free of that society, and is employed for the Adventurers in the trade of fishing to the Isle of Lewis and other isles in Scotland, with request that he be allowed to proceed in his employment without molestation. [*Seal of the society attached.* ½ *p.*]

Dec. 4.
Whitehall.

29. Similar certificate for Bartholomew Brooke. [½ *p.*]

Dec. 4.
Whitehall.

30. The like for Henry Wright. [½ *p.*]

Dec. 4.
Whitehall.

31. The like for Robert Jegges. [½ *p.*]

Dec. 4.
Whitehall.

32. The like for Richard Crowther. [½ *p.*]

Dec. 4.
Whitehall.

33. The like for Humphrey Dewell. [½ *p.*]

Dec. 4.
Whitehall.

34. The like for James Wright. [*Imperfect.* ½ *p.*]

Dec. 4.
Melksham.

35. Godwin Awdry to Nicholas. If his Majesty and the Lords will settle the course which I shall set down, and appoint me a place to manage the business, I will take out of his Majesty's stores 200 lasts of powder at the rate of 18*d.* per lb., and pay such other fees as you spake to me of every year during my life, if so much may be spared. The course is too long to relate, but if the Lords appoint me to attend them I will not fail. [*Seal with arms.* ¾ *p.*]

Vol. CCCLXXIII.

1637.
Dec. 4.
Whitehall.

36. Statement of Nicholas, touching the annual consumption of gunpowder. The trained bands are estimated at 88,116 foot, of which number one-half are musketeers. If there be four musters annually, and every musketeer spend 1 lb. at each muster, the total will be 73 lasts 8 cwts. The consumption of the ships in ordinary is set down at 6 lasts, the extraordinary naval consumption at 15 lasts. Ireland is computed at 10 lasts, and the consumption by merchants at 50 lasts; making a total of 154 lasts 8 cwts. [*Endorsed are notes by Nicholas of a meeting of a committee upon the above subject.* = 1½ *p.*]

Dec. 5.

Petition of Thomas Killigrew to the King. About a year since, Edward Rawley, a servant of petitioner, at Newmarket, struck one of the harbingers, for which he was laid in prison. To release him, petitioner gave a 500*l.* bond for his appearance; since which he has robbed petitioner of 400*l.*, and fled the land. Petitioner prays to be released from his bond. [*Copy. See Vol. cccxxiii., p.* 206. ½ *p.*]

    I. *Note of his Majesty's pleasure, that the bond be delivered to the petitioner. Whitehall, 5th December* 1637. [*Copy. See Ibid., p.* 207. ⅙ *p.*]

[Dec. 5 ?]
This Tuesday night.

37. Christopher Gardyner to his brother Sir John Heydon, at his house, the Minorites [Minories]. Describes the progress of a chemical experiment, the ingredients used in which are expressed by signs. Send me Morinus. I will read him and give you my opinion of him. [1 *p.*]

Dec. 5.

38. Particular of gunpowder sold to merchants, masters of ships and chandlers, from 1st January 1636–7 to the 5th December 1637. Total, 164 lasts 1 cwt. and 78 lbs. [1 *p.*]

Dec. 5.

39. Receipt of Sir William Russell for 1,075*l.* 3*s.* 5*d.* paid by William Leigh, formerly sheriff of co. Gloucester, in part of 5,500*l.* ship-money under writ of 4th August 1635. [¾ *p.*]

Dec. 6.

Petition of Anne Stewart Lady Saltoun to the King. On certificates of the late Lord Treasurer Portland and of Sir Robert Heath, then Attorney-General, and with the advice of the Officers of the Exchequer, your Majesty, in lieu of petitioner's charges and for bringing up her children, granted petitioner a moiety of divers arrearages of rents. Petitioner has been at great charges in recovery of the same, but has received little benefit, and is likely to receive less hereafter, by occasion of divers questions arising upon her letters patent, and some mistake therein. Prays a rectification thereof. [*Copy. See Vol. cccxxiii., p.* 208. 1 *p.*] *Underwritten,*

    I. *Reference to the Lord Privy Seal and the Earl of Dorset, who, calling to them the two Lords Chief Justices and the Lord Chief Baron, are to certify his Majesty.* [*Copy. Ibid. p.* 209. ¼ *p.*]

Dec. 6.

40. Petition of Charles Dymoke to the same. Henry Earl of Stamford, in right of Anne his wife, as owner of Wildmore Fen,

1637

Vol. CCCLXXIII.

co. Lincoln, has laboured an improvement of the said fen, and agreed with petitioner that, in case he obtained it, petitioner should have a sixth part thereof. Since which the Earl, having interested the King therein, has, in his Majesty's name, procured 4,000 acres at the least, to petitioner's great loss. Prays the King to confirm petitioner's sixth part. [¾ p.]

Dec. 6.
Whitehall.

41. Order of Council on petition of William Bosvile and other tenants of the Earl of Lindsey. Petitioners complained against Nehemiah Rawson, prisoner in the Fleet, for opposing the work of Sir Anthony Thomas in the Fens near Boston, and obtaining means to get out of prison last vacation, which petitioners were by him put to great trouble by indictments and actions of trespass contrary to the order of the Board of 1st March 1636–7. The Lords ordered that Rawson should not be permitted hereafter to go out of the Fleet, and that the petitioners' damage should be satisfied out of Rawson's bond of 500l., which the Attorney-General was required to put in suit in his Majesty's name on behalf of petitioners. [1½ p.]

Dec. 6.

42. Petition of Thomas Cooke to the Council. Petitioner, supposing there had been leave given for building Long Acre, which is almost wholly built, took a lease of a little piece of ground there and built a tenement for his own dwelling. He is now summoned to answer his misdemeanour. Prays remittal of his offence upon reasonable fine. [½ p.] *Underwritten,*

    42. I. *Reference to the Earl Marshal and the Earl of Dorset, to give such order as they shall think fit, or to certify the Board. Whitehall, 6th December* 1637. [¼ p.]

Dec. 6.

43. Petition of William Wilkinson, porter, and Mary his wife, to the same. Petitioner, in March was twelvemonth, pulled down old tenements 30 foot square, and in their room erected a new building only 20 foot square, which he brought up to the roof. Petitioner, being warned not to finish his building, and also to attend the Lords, prays leave to finish the building. [½ p.] *Underwritten,*

    43. I. *Similar reference to that of the preceding petition. Whitehall, 6th December* 1637. [¼ p.]

Dec. 6.

44. Petition of Paul Prestland, of Market Deeping, clerk, to Archbishop Laud. Differences betwixt petitioner and his parishioners have risen concerning new framing and casting the bells and other rights of the church, and petitioner being sickly, and not willing to follow suits, prays a reference to Montagu Lord Willoughby and other eminent gentlemen next adjoining. [½ p.] *Underwritten,*

    44. I. *Reference to Sir John Lambe, to give the archbishop an account of petitioner.* W. CANT. *6th December* 1637. [¼ p.]

Dec. 6.

45. Petition of Thomas Brasier to the same. Petitioner, upon an unjust pretence, was brought into the High Commission, and being

1637.   Vol. CCCLXXIII.

unable to pay charges of defence, desired Sir John Lambe that he might be discharged, whereupon the archbishop imposed 30*l.* to be paid by him. Has paid 25*l.*, and prays discharge. [¾ *p.*] *Underwritten,*

  45. I. *Reference to Sir John Lambe. If he has no objection the archbishop is content that petitioner be discharged. 6th December* 1637. [¼ *p.*]

Dec. 6. 46. William Brissenden to [the Officers of the Navy]. Complaint of a great variety of ill-usage received by Brissenden at the hands of Capt. Seaman, in whose ship Brissenden was purser. The foundation of the maltreatment seems to have been that Brissenden had given information to the Officers of Navy of misconduct on the part of Capt. Seaman. [2 *pp.*]

Dec. 6. 47. Receipt of Sir William Russell for 74*l.* paid by Arnold Spencer on behalf of William Hearne, late bailiff of Godmanchester, being ship-money collected under writ of 12th August 1636. [¾ *p.*]

Dec. 7. Letters patent granting to Joseph Jackson the sole use of his invention of making, casting, and gilding the leaden seals used for the New Drapers for the term of 14 years, at the yearly rent, to be paid to the King, of 5*l.* [*Skin of parchment. See Case D., Car. I., No.* 21.]

Dec. 7. 48. Petition of John Cansfield to [the Commissioners for Recusants' Revenues]. Petitioner being a recusant convict, and having goods and lands, part in possession and other part in reversion after his mother's death, compounded for the same at 30*l.* per annum. His mother having died, the rectory of Thornton, co. York, came to Sir Francis Howard and Matthew Richardson for two lives upon certain trusts for the benefit of petitioner. Lionel Farrington, supposing petitioner had an absolute estate in the said rectory, caused inquisitions to be held, and compounded for two parts of the presumed value of the rectory and of the lands held by petitioner's mother. But those inquisitions having been set aside, and further progress resting between Mr. Farrington and petitioner, John Pulford, without informing the commissioners of the previous proceedings, has obtained some direction from them for proceeding upon the composition made by Mr. Farrington. Petitioner prays relief as against Mr. Pulford, and to be admitted to compound for his whole estate. [⅚ *p.*] *Underwritten,*

  48. I. *Reference to Sir Edward Osborne and the rest of the commissioners for the northern parts to settle petitioner's composition. London House, 7th December* 1637. [⅙ *p.*]

Dec. 7. 49. Statement somewhat in the nature of a brief in relation to the preceding petition and the interests of Pulford and Farrington in the recusancy of Cansfield. [½ *p.*]

Vol. CCCLXXIII.

1637.

Dec. 7. 50. Calculations by Sec. Coke concerning the provision and expense of gunpowder; similar, but with certain variations, to the paper on this subject by Nicholas, calendared under the date of the 4th inst. [2½ pp.]

Dec. 7. 51. Copy of the same by Sir John Heydon, with notes by him thereon written with black lead. [= 2 pp.]

Dec. 7. 52. Receipt of Edward Earl of Dorset for 150l., due to him under an assignment by Thomas Killigrew, of some payment out of the Exchequer. [¾ p.]

Dec. 8. Petition of Sir Cornelius Vermuyden and his partners in the draining of Hatfield Chase, in cos. York, Lincoln, and Nottingham, to the King. The King contracted with Sir Cornelius for draining the said waste and commonable grounds. He set on workmen and spent many thousand pounds; but by reason of opposition of the commoners he has been hindered perfecting the work, and has been ever since kept in suits for title. And, further, during the work, in the night and in times of floods, the banks have been cut, whereby 60,000l. loss has been sustained, and 150,000l. has been spent in law and in the work, which is twice the value of the lands allotted. Petitioners, nevertheless, stand charged to pay to the King arrears of rent ever since 1633, and also rents for time to come for lands which they have not in possession, and for lands which fall short in quantity, and for other lands which belong to the manor of Hatfield. Pray for a reference and relief. [*Copy. See Vol. cccxxiii., p.* 207. 1 p.] *Underwritten,*

    I. *Reference to the Lord Keeper, Lord Treasurer, and Lord Cottington, to examine and certify to the King. Whitehall, 8th December* 1637. [*Copy. See Ibid., p.* 208. ¼ p.]

Dec. 8. Petition of Percy Church, Groom of the Privy Chamber, to the same. There are some lords of lordships in Wales that pretend to take certain fines in the courts of great and quarter sessions, and divers tenants that have not enrolled their leases and fee-farms with the auditor of Wales. Prays grant of sums unjustly taken by the said pretended liberties, and arrears of rents which he shall discover. [*Copy. See Ibid., p.* 209. ½ p.] *Underwritten,*

    I. *Reference to the Attorney-General to consider and certify. Whitehall, 8th December* 1637. [*Copy. See Ibid., p.* 210. ¼ p.]

Dec. 8. 53. Edward Worseley to the Council. Complains of the continuance of the persecution to which he was subject by people that laboured with illusions, suggestions, and distracting sleights and tricks to fetch him into prison again. [*A letter similar to the one published in the last volume of this Calendar, under the signature of E. W., and dated* 19th October 1637. 2 pp.] Annexed,

    53. I. *The same "to Cottingam and his companions, formerly prisoners in the Marshalsea, but now lurking in their*

1637.

Vol. CCCLXXIII.

disguises and doing mischief in obscurity." 6th December 1637. [1 *p.*]

53. II. Edward Worseley *"to the more civil sort of Puritans that have put me to my thoughts and troubled me with their illusions for these twenty years."* 7th December 1637. [1 *p.*]

Dec. 8.
Westminster.
54. Sec. Windebank to Sir John Pennington. This morning yours of the 7th came to my hands. I find it very strange that you had not then received orders concerning the Bonaventure, seeing Scandaret, whom his Majesty employs in that business, had his despatch from me to you upon the 4th of this present. Recapitulates the directions given in his letter of the 4th inst. [*see No.* 26]. If the Duchess should not be come to the Groyne, upon the arrival of the captain of the Bonaventure, Scandaret has promised to give her notice of the ship, according to whose direction the captain is to govern himself. [*Seals with arms.* 1 *p.*]

Dec. 8.
55. [Capt. Walter Stewart to Nicholas.] Please to move my Lords that, since they have given order for my own pay, I may have order for that of my retinue, which is stopped by the officers. My general declared that I had his leave. [*Endorsed,* " *Nil.*" ½ *p.*]

Dec. 8.
56. Thomas Moncrieff to [John] Savile. Requests him to pay to Henry Malcolm 25*l.* 1*s.* 10½*d.* for the writer's fee, due at Michaelmas last. [½ *p.*]

Dec. 8.
57. Extract from the Register of the High Commission Court, touching the cause of Anthony Morse, late of Rodborne Cheney, Wilts. Morse had been questioned for incest with Frideswide Ball, daughter to his late wife, and, after various proceedings, had been enjoined penance. To avoid the same he had removed into co. Berks, and had been excommunicated. Frideswide Ball had confessed the fact, and had been enjoined penance. Morse had denied the charge of incest, and also a charge of antenuptial fornication with his present wife. [1½ *p.*]

Dec. 8.
58. Receipt of Sir William Russell for 195*l.* 16*s.* 2*d.* paid by John Walle on behalf of Walter Walle, formerly mayor of Hereford, ship-money under writ of 4th August 1635. [*Not signed by Sir William Russell.* ¾ *p.*]

Dec. 9.
Whitehall.
Lords of the Admiralty to Montjoy Earl of Newport. To send a list of the most expert gunners, such as, with advice of the Officers of the Ordnance and master gunner of England, he thinks fit to be placed master gunners in his Majesty's ships. [*Copy. See Vol. cccliii., fol.* 74. ½ *p.*]

Dec. 9.
Whitehall.
The same to the Master and Wardens of the Trinity House. To send a similar list of the most able gunners, boatswains, and carpenters. [*Copy. Ibid.* ⅜ *p.*]

Vol. CCCLXXIII.

1637.
Dec. 9.
Whitehall
Lords of the Admiralty to the Officers of the Navy. Send a letter addressed to the Earl of Westmoreland from some of his officers, and by him sent to the writers, complaining of an abuse of the purveyors, praying you to examine the same, and certify what you find to be the truth. [*Copy. See Vol. cccliii., fol.* 74. ⅓ *p.*]

Dec. 9.
Whitehall.
Commissioners of Saltpetre and Gunpowder to Lord Treasurer Juxon. We understand by petition of Sarah Collins and by the affirmation of Mr. Cordewell that there are 9 or 10 barrels of powder in his custody belonging to Mrs. Collins as executrix of her late husband. Pray him to order the same to be delivered to her, she giving security to transport the same into foreign parts. [*Copy. See Vol. ccxcii., p.* 71. ½ *p.*]

Dec. 9.
Burderop.
59. **William Calley to Richard Harvey.** For your bag of pistachios I have sent you a wooden bottle of metheglin. Let it have some time to settle. I desire to have Mr. Gunstone's whole piece of kersey. [*Seal with arms.* 1 *p.*]

Dec. 9.
60. Account of Sir William Russell of arrears of ship-money under writs in 1635. Total, 8,248*l.* [14s. 10d.?], reduced by Nicholas by allowances to 5,448*l.* 14s. 10d. [*Damaged.* 1 *p.*]

Dec. 9.
61. Examination of Dorothy Lee, widow, dwelling in Bloomsbury, taken this day. Examinate, before Bartholomew tide, about 6 o'clock at night, in a window in a staircase in Somerset House, took up a packet of letters, which she conceived to be letters of a madman who used to dispose letters in Somerset Yard directed to the Lords of the Privy Council. She carried them immediately to the shop of William Marshall in the Strand, and told the company there that she had found one of the madman's letters, and being asked how she durst open letters so directed, she said there was nobody's hand to them, and that once a week they were to be found cast in Somerset Yard. Either she or Robert, servant to Mrs. Thynne, who lodged in the same house, opened the letters and delivered them to a young man that served Mr. Marshall to read, and she then went up to Mrs. Thynne, to whom she related that she had found a madman's letter to light her tobacco, but Robert telling her that there was strange stuff in the letters, and that the King's Majesty was a Catholic, she, fearing she might be brought into trouble, earnestly entreated to have the letters back again, and promised a blind man, who had the letters, to restore them to him again as soon as she had showed them to Mrs. Thynne, but that she delivered them to Robert aforesaid, and told the blind man that she had burned them, that they should not importune her for them. Very shortly after she went into Yorkshire, and returned about three weeks after the beginning of last term, and then, hearing there was a warrant out for her concerning this business, she went to Lady Manners's maid, and asked her if she had not found any of the madman's letters, who delivered to her one which she now shows forth, and believes it was written by the same hand that wrote

1637.

VOL. CCCLXXIII.

those letters which she is now questioned about. [2 pp.] Annexed,

 61. I. *John Williams to his aunt, Mrs. Anna Colleton, at Eltham. Has been at Norwich, 100 miles an end, and is come home again, and boards himself in London. Has provided a ghostly father, Father Lambeth, one of the friars in Somerset House. He heard the writer's confession and the writer communicated. He is as yet unprovided of money to buy clothes, because his board is chargeable. Entreats her to send him money by the bearer. About Allhallowtide he shall sell his wood, and then she shall be paid. Desires to be remembered to his uncle and Mr. York. 6th October 1637.—P.S. Begs her to send him his books and some of her Catholic books.* [*Copy.* 1 *p.*]

Dec. 9. Examination o Walter Baker, servant to William Marshall, of the Strand, taken this day. Examinate persists in all that he said to the Council yesterday evening. The letter now showed him is not of the same hand with the letter which he read in his master's shop about the 16th August last. The letter so by him read seemed very sensible and composed with great malice, and in no sort to be suspected to be the letter of a madman. [½ *p. Written on the same sheet of paper as the preceding examination of Dorothy Lee.*]

Dec. 10. Whitehall. 62. Order of the King in Council. Taking into consideration the great mischief sustained through the pirates of Algiers, the King referred it to Lord Cottington, Mr. Comptroller [Sir Henry Vane], Sec. Coke, and Sec. Windebank, to advise of the best ways for abating the strength of the said pirates, and that such as they should know to be most experienced touching this affair, whether of the Turkey Company or of the Trinity House or otherwise, should be required to make propositions for effecting so a great work. [1½ *p.*]

Dec. 10. The Swiftsure, in the Downs. 63. Sir John Pennington to Sec. Windebank. Mr. Scandaret came hither on Friday night, and this morning they set sail. The Groyne fleet are arrived at Dunkirk, and have landed 4,000 soldiers, and some report 400, and others 700, chests of silver; but the Hollanders have taken two of their lags, in the one near 300 soldiers, in the other salt and other merchandize, but no treasure in either. At this instant the William has arrived here from the East Indies, and left the Jewel some 40 leagues from the Lizard, in a storm, but hopes she will be here to-morrow. [*Seals with arms.* 1 *p.*]

Dec. 10. Whitehall. 64. The Council to Sir William Widdrington. There being special occasion of your attendance on us, whereof you shall be further acquainted at your coming, you are to make your immediate repair before us in the company of this bearer, one of the messengers of the chamber. [*Copy.* ½ *p.*] *Prefixed,*

 64. I. *Jasper Heiley, Messenger of the Chamber, to Sir William Widdrington. Leaves the above copy warrant at Sir*

VOL. CCCLXXIII.

1637.

William's house at Blankney, co. Lincoln, that he may obey the same. *P.S.—Directions where Sir William may find Heiley or his fellow on his arrival in London.* [½ p.] *Annexed,*

64. II. *Sir William Widdrington [to Sir Dudley Carleton?] Requests to know the occasion of the Council's warrant, being altogether ignorant.* [¼ p.]

Dec. 11. Pardon to Henry Viscount Newark, Thomas Austen, and Henry Savage, for an assault upon Philip Kinder in the cloister of St. Peter's, Westminster, and other offences specified in an information in the Star Chamber by William Noy, late Attorney-General. [*Docquet.*]

Dec. 11. Presentation of Robert Field, clerk, M.A., to the rectory of Woking, void and in his Majesty's gift (*pro hac vice*) for want of suing forth of livery by James Zouch, his Majesty's ward. [*Docquet.*]

Dec. 11. Grant to Oliver Lloyd, Mathias Burges, and Thomas Barber, for the sole use of an engine for turning, working, and drawing all kinds of mills, drawing up of water, carriages and wheel works, for 14 years, rendering into the Exchequer a fifth part of the benefit that shall arise thereby. [*Docquet.*]

Dec. 11. 65. Petition of Sir Philiberto Vernatti, Sir John Ogle, John Gibbon, Katherine Bishop, widow, Philip Jacobson, and Marcellis Vanduren, on behalf of themselves and other participants within the level of Hatfield Chase, to the King. Petitioners purchased their lands long since from Sir Cornelius Vermuyden at a very dear rate, and have, notwithstanding, been constrained to lay scots amongst themselves to the rate of 23s. per acre, which not being sufficient to do the work, and the participants falling to difference amongst themselves, your Majesty, after several days' hearing, ordered a commission of sewers to commissioners named by the Lord Deputy of Ireland, to whom those parts were well known; since which that commission has been renewed to other commissioners, who have made unlawful sales of petitioners' lands at under values, by virtue of which petitioners are disquieted in their possessions, and infinite suits are likely to arise. Pray a reference for examination of petitioners' sufferings. [¾ p.] *Underwritten,*

65. I. *Reference to the Lord Treasurer, Lord Cottington, and Sec. Windebank, calling to them such of the judges and King's counsel as they shall think fit, to hear and determine these differences, or certify where the impediment lies. Whitehall, 11th December 1637.* [¼ p.] *Endorsed,*

65. II. *Appointment by the referees to hear this business. London House, 7th June 1638.* [¼ p.]

Dec. 11. 66. Copy of the same, with the reference and appointment. [1 p.]

DOMESTIC—CHARLES I.   17

1637.
Vol. CCCLXXIII.

Dec. 11. Another copy of the preceding petition, with the reference only. [See Vol. cccxxiii., p. 277. ¾ p.]

Dec. 11. 67. Petition of William Rokeby to the King. Your Majesty, by proclamation, heretofore commanded that no person having settled habitation in the country should make their residence in London during Christmas. The Council, by directions from your Majesty, have commanded all such to depart the town before the 12th of this month under certain punishments. Petitioner, having his abode in Yorkshire, has at this time his wife and children in town, where six of them have been visited with a disease called the rickets, as may appear from the annexed certificate, and are now under cure. Prays that he may not be prosecuted for his stay in town. [¾ p.] *Annexed,*

> 67. I. *Certificate of Sir Theodore Mayerne and Dr. Matthew Lister in verification of the above petition. Petitioner is described as of Skyers, co. York.* [½ p.]

Dec. 11. 68. Petition of Endymion Porter, a Groom of the Bedchamber, to the King. There was an ancient pier on the north coast, in co. York, called Filo [Filey?] Pier, which has been for many years defaced and ruined. There is a bay in the sea upon a plain firm sand, adjoining to the said pier, some five or six miles in compass, where 600 sail may ride safely, let the wind be in any quarter whatsoever (S.E. excepted), and at a low ebb has always about three fathoms water in all places, upon which coast many vessels are yearly cast away for want of a harbour there and a light to guide them into the bay, near which pier and bay there is a rock called Flamborough Head, 100 fathoms high, running near six miles in length, and so to Filo Bridge, under which rock Dunkirk[er]s and other robbers have usually lain and robbed his Majesty's subjects, not being to be discerned until ships passing that channel are within their command. Prays letters patent for a collection throughout England, Scotland, Ireland, and Wales, towards erecting a harbour at Filo and maintaining of a light there, and to grant the same to petitioner for 31 years, as the like were lately granted to Sir John Meldrum, and petitioner will pay into the Exchequer the yearly sum of 20*l*. [¾ p.] *Underwritten,*

> 68. I. *Reference to the Lords of the Admiralty for consideration. Whitehall,* 11*th December* 1637. [¼ p.]

Dec. 11. 69. Sir John Pennington to the Lords of the Admiralty. Ships
The Swiftsure, arrived from St. Lucar and Cadiz bring news of the arrival of the
in the Downs. plate fleet there on the 16th November, and that they brought with them 15 millions of plate, being but nine ships and two pinnaces, very poorly fitted. They took the Lemmond, of London, an English ship, as they came homewards, and brought her into Cadiz, wherein were between 30 or 40 passengers, the ship being bound for some of the plantations; Woolner master of her, that was lately boatswain of the St. Andrew. Young Whetstone was at Cadiz lading his ship

12.   B

1637.

Vol. CCCLXXIII.

when these came, and had done nothing against the French. All our ships that were [embargoed] in France are released. Mentions again the arrival of the Groyne fleet at Dunkirk and the ships from the East Indies, as mentioned in his letter to Sec. Windebank of the 10th inst. (*No.* 63), with this addition, that neither of them is so rich as was reported. [*Seals with arms.* 1 *p.*]

Dec. 11. 70. Rate made by Thomas Wood, Mayor of Bossiney, Trevena, and Tintagell, Cornwall, for collection of 36*l.* ship-money. Name of every person assessed with the amount charged. [1 *p.*]

Dec. 12. 71. The King to the Dean and Chapter of Canterbury. Limits
Westminster. the period for which they may demise their lands to twenty-one years, being a restriction of the power in that respect granted by a clause in chapter VI. of the statutes of the cathedral, confirmed by the King by letters patent dated 3rd January last. [*Office copy, from Rot. Pat.*, 13 *Car. I., pars* 15, *m.* 63. 2 *pp.*]

Dec. 12. Petition of the Farmers of his Majesty's Ironworks for the Forest of Dean to the King. Petitioners having been wounded in their reputations and damnified in their farm by the unjust practices of [John] Broughton and his complices, they acknowledge with thankfulness the King's permission that they may have the freedom of the laws for their vindication. The King having also given order for wood to be delivered to them for this next year, they pray a proclamation for restraint of the mines, which during this dispute by the unruly multitudes are violently in all disorder, and infinite quantities carried away to strangers' works. [*Copy.* See *Vol. cccxxiii., p.* 210. ¾ *p.*] *Underwritten,*

> I. *Reference to the Attorney-General to prepare proclamation as prayed.* Whitehall, 12th December 1637. [*Copy. Ibid., p.* 211. ¼ *p.*]

Dec. 12. Petition of Ann, wife of George Forster, to the same. Petitioner, about six months since, being with child, her husband went into Shropshire, leaving her altogether unprovided for, and is laboured by some of great power to dispose of his estate in such way as will be to the undoing of herself and children. Prays reference to the "good Lord Marshal" and the "good Lord Chamberlain," to cause her husband to assure a provision for her and her children. [*Copy. Ibid., p.* 211. ¾ *p.*] *Underwritten,*

> I. *Reference to the persons above mentioned, to determine these differences or to certify the King.* Whitehall, 12th December 1637. [*Copy. Ibid., p.* 212. ¼ *p.*]

Dec. 12. Lords of the Admiralty to the Clerk of the Signet. His Majesty's
Whitehall. pleasure is that you prepare a bill to authorize the sale of the Red Lion, and to cause the proceeds to be paid to the Treasurer of the Navy. [*Copy.* See *Vol. ccclii., fol.* 74 *b.* ⅓ *p.*]

DOMESTIC—CHARLES I.

1637.

Dec. 12.
Whitehall.
Commissioners for Saltpetre and Gunpowder to the Company trading to the East Indies. There is a quantity of saltpetre come out of the East Indies in your ships lately arrived; no part thereof is to be disposed of till it be viewed to see whether it may be useful for his Majesty. [*Copy. See Vol. ccxcii., p. 72.* ⅓ *p.*]

Dec. 12.
72. Officers of the New Corporation for regulation of aliens dwelling within three miles of London to Sec. Windebank. Our body consists only of tradesmen, amongst whom we hope there will be none to come under the charge of a provost-marshal. We conceive we have no use of such an officer, and have no power by our charter to make choice of any, or raise any salary for his support. [¾ *p.*]

Dec. 12.
Whitehall.
73. Henry Earl of Holland to Sir John Pennington. If the ships under your command be not otherwise directed for his Majesty's service, I entreat that one of them may waft over my two eldest sons to Dieppe. They are going to spend some time in France for their better education, and shall be at Dover on Saturday next to attend your appointment. [*Seal with arms.* 1 *p.*]

Dec. $\frac{12}{22}$.
St. Sebastian.
74. Prestwick Eaton to his brother-in-law [George Wellingham.] Sends beavers to be re-blocked. Wishes his sister to keep for him certain articles sent by Robert Sergeant, amongst them a bason and ewer, silver, a rich salt-cellar, a case of pictures, and a trunk of books. The damask bed sent to be dyed is inquired after. [2 *pp.*]

Dec. 12.
75. Receipt of Sir William Russell for 138*l.* paid by Sir John Ramsden, late sheriff of co. York, in full of 12,000*l.* ship-money for 1636. [¾ *p.*]

Dec. 13.
Letters patent for the institution of a voluntary office whither masters or others having lost goods; women for satisfaction whether their absent husbands be living or dead; parents for lost children, or any others for discovering murders and robberies, and for all bargains or intelligences may resort, if they please, for their better intelligence and satisfaction; and a grant of the same office to Capt. Robert Innis for 41 years, for execution whereof he is to receive such recompense as the parties will give. [*Docquet.*]

Dec. 13.
Warrant to the Judges of the Common Pleas to admit Jane, wife of John Bellasis (daughter and heir of Sir Robert Butler, deceased), being under the age of 21 years, by her guardian, to levy fines and suffer recoveries of the manors of Higham Gobion, co. Bedford, and of Temple Chelfin, Sacomb and Boxbury *cum* Chells, co. Hertford, with divers lands thereunto belonging; and is for the payment of the debts of her late father and mother. [*Docquet.*]

Dec. 13.
Warrant for payment of 150*l.* to George Kirke, gentleman of the Robes, for providing of masquing apparel for his Majesty's person. [*Docquet.*]

Dec. 13.
Grant to Sir Abraham Dawes, Mungo Murray, and George Duncombe, of 1,000*l.*, remaining of 2,0[00*l.*] imposed by the Commissioners

Vol. CCCLXXIII.

1637.

for Causes Ecclesiastical, as a fine upon Richard Murray, D.D., late guardian of the College of Manchester, for an offence of ecclesiastical cognizance, which fine upon the suit of the Earl of Annandale was by his Majesty's direction mitigated to 1,000*l*. The said Earl having agreed with the Archbishop of Canterbury to pay towards the reparation of St. Paul's the said 1,000*l*., the archbishop, at the nomination of the said Earl, has made Sir Abraham Dawes, Mungo Murray, and George Duncombe his deputies concerning the same fine. [*Docquet.*]

Dec. 13. The King to various Officers of the Exchequer. To make certificate to his Majesty, touching some particulars in question between the Earl of Berkshire and Dr. [James] Chambers upon their several patents. [*Docquet.*]

Dec. 13.
Whitehall. [Commissioners for Gunpowder] to Montjoy Earl of Newport, Master of the Ordnance. Warrant to deliver 12 barrels of powder at 18*d*. per lb. to Robert Russell, of London, chandler. [*Minute. See Vol. ccclv., No. 61, p. 5. ¼ p.*]

Dec. 13. 76. Answer of Edmund Bradshaw to objections of Robert Blake made against him at the Council Board. Blake's objections, as here stated, were that Bradshaw landed in Barbary without money; that he was brought to Blake's house and nourished by him; that he came into disgrace with the King of Morocco by using chemistry; and that whilst there he conversed with witches. Bradshaw disputes the accuracy of all these assertions. As to the practice of chemistry, he alleges that a chemical powder which he had, whilst in Morocco, was taken by Blake himself and by the Queen of Morocco. Blake was cured thereby of a flux, and the Queen received so much benefit that the King sent Bradshaw a Barbary horse in reward, and afterwards sent for more of the powder. Bradshaw denies all communication with witches, whom he ever abhorred, but states that some of the most learned sort of the people of that country repaired to him to confer about the said powder and other experiments in chemical art. He concludes by bringing counter-charges against Blake of misconduct in reference to the King's service. [1 *p.*]

Dec. 13. 77. Allegations of fishermen and traders in herrings at Great Yarmouth, in answer to a petition of merchants of London and owners of ships. The point in question was the propriety of Yarmouth being annually licensed to export five or six hundred lasts of herrings in strangers' bottoms. The contents of the petition of the merchants of London have been already stated in our calendar under the date of November 29, 1637, No. 78. [1¾ *p.*]

Dec. 14.
My lodging,
on Clerkenwell
Green. 78. R[obert] Innes to [Sec. Windebank]. "About the time of the Morocco ambassador's arrival, I went to Mr. James Maxwell upon the Old Exchange, to entreat him to move his Majesty to send me for the merchants to Morocco, in respect I had spent some time in Turkey. After I had spoke with Mr. Maxwell, there came a

Vol. CCCLXXIII.

1637.

Scottish man to me, seemed a master of a bark, and asked if that gent. I spoke with was Mr. Maxwell of the Bedchamber. I told him he was the man. His answer and discourse to me, 'I wonder that those Scottish men that are about the King will not move his Majesty that we be no more troubled in the government of our kirk of Scotland.' After my replication he went two turns and spake little, and then he said to me, 'How long have you been out of Scotland?' I told him fourteen years. He answered, there were as hardy bold lads now in Scotland as cunning in England, and that the Duke of Buckingham was a bonny flower standing in the morning but down before night. Ten days after, I met with one that goes by the name of Capt. Nepper [Napier], a Scottish man, in Gray's Inn. After salutation, asked one another what news. He told me that it was not well done the King should press the government of the Church of England to Scotland, with other discourse intending to that effect, which I did not heed nor desire to hear. Some few days after, I met this same man in the Common [Covent] Garden. In discourse he was praising of the Bishop of Lincoln. I asked him if he was known to his lordship; he told me very well, and he was often with him, and his lordship had promised to benefice his son, who is a divine. I asked Mr. Nepper how he came acquainted with the Bishop of Lincoln; he told me that he was of kindred to Mr. Linton, and so was known to his lordship by that means. I began to recollect myself concerning this my former relation, and I desired Mr. Nepper to go to the Cross Keys Tavern and I would give him his morning draught, which he did, and after I had demanded several questions concerning his projects, for he is a busy projecting man, and lives by that means, yet wary and secret, as seems always to me; but after a cup, two or three, he fell in praise of the Bishop of Lincoln, and withal asked me if I had gotten any good at Court, [since] my coming from the Venetian service. I told him I was one attendant. His answer was, he would tell me a secret of State, which was told him by a gent., and one that was one of the greatest and wisest statesmen in this kingdom; I told him I was his servant to command to secrecy. Then said Mr. Nepper, 'Be assured there is no good now here for Scottish men, as the government goes.' I asked his reason; he said the Bishop of Lincoln told him of one general rule of State done by the State here, that was begun when he was Lord Keeper, that any Scottish man that had any suit, notwithstanding of the King's gift, the ministers of State should keep them up while they did shake and pinch their business before they had it, that it should not be worth the uptaking, otherwise the ministers of State would find delays while the Scottish had not breath to stay longer by it in a sinistrous form; thus he concluded." [2 *pp.*]

Dec. 14. 79. Statement of William King, prisoner in Newgate, as to the cause of his imprisonment. He bought of Richard Gladding a parcel of manuscripts, which he gave to Lord Leppington to peruse, one of which, concerning the succession to the Crown, Lord Leppington

Vol. CCCLXXIII.

1637.

deemed to be "factious against the State." King requested Lord Leppington to hand it to Sec. Windebank, in hope of a reward. But the Secretary sent him to prison, where he has remained three years, having no maintenance but the city allowance of a ½ of bread one day and ¼ the next, with the stones and straw for a bed, till of late the keepers, taking commiseration upon him, suffered him to lie on a bed. [1 p.] Annexed,

> 79. I. *Statement of the result of examinations taken by George Long in relation to the above subject. Papers were shown to have been purchased by King from Gladding and Ling, who were committed to prison, and there remained some time until bailed to appear before the Lords on warning. 15th December 1637.* [⅔ p.]

Dec. 15. Grant of the office of sergeant-at-arms to Francis Langston, with the fee of 12*d*. per diem during his life, with all other profits, as William Griffeth lately held the same. [*Docquet.*]

Dec. 15. 80. Petition of the Gutstring-makers to the King. Many families by that trade have lived plentifully, and with that commodity served the artists of at least sixteen several societies of this kingdom, who must of necessity use these strings, as by the annexed appears, and, besides, they transported abundance beyond seas, wherewith they furnished a great part of Christendom. Frauds lately used have brought the commodity into disrepute, insomuch that, many families are brought to misery. For prevention of further misery petitioners were advised to petition for an incorporation, which was prepared by Attorney-General Noy, and the same lies at the Great Seal. Pray a command to the Lord Keeper to pass the same under the Great Seal. [¾ p.] Annexed,

> 80. I. *Certificate of pewterers, turners, braziers, spectacle-makers, needle-makers, pin-makers, watch-makers, founders, weavers, and hat-makers, who all must of necessity use gutstrings in support of the petition for incorporation* [1 p.]
>
> 80. II. *The like of his Majesty's drummers.* [1 p.]
>
> 80. III. *The like of Nicholas Laniere, master of his Majesty's music, and Thomas Day, master of the children of the chapel.* [⅓ p.]
>
> 80. IV. *The like of merchants who have usually bought gutstrings for transport for foreign parts.* [½ p.]
>
> 80. V. *The like of the supervisor of the customs as to the quantity of lutestrings, catlings, and other strings entered for export since 1st June last.* [¾ p.]

Dec. 15.
Whitehall.

81. Order of Council. Jason Grover, carrier of Ipswich and Yarmouth, being in custody of a messenger, upon complaint that he had transgressed the proclamation published and patent granted to Mr. Witherings, for settling the letter office, it was thought fit (in

1637.

Vol. CCCLXXIII.

regard the Lords had not time to settle the business) that Grover should be discharged upon bond of 200*l*. to appear in Hilary term next, to answer such things as should be objected against him. [1 *p*.]

Dec. 15. 82. Petition of Ralph Moore, Henry Symonds, Stephen Awdly, Edward Giles, and David Watkins, hour-glass makers, to the Council. For many years petitioners have bought merchantable hour-glass vials ready for use at 7*s*. the gross, and 7*s*. 6*d*. at the doors, brought home to the houses; but now Sir Robert Mansell having a grant of the sole making of glass, he or some under him have raised the price to 9*s*. the gross, whilst the ware is so bad that petitioners often lose one dozen in four. Pray relief. [1 *p*.] *Annexed*,

> 82. I. *Order of the Council that a copy of the above petition be delivered to Sir Robert Mansell, and that he or some person appointed by him attend the Board the second sitting after Twelfthtide next to answer thereto. Whitehall, 15th December* 1637. [*Copy.* 1 *p*.]
>
> 82. II. *Rough minute of contemplated arrangement between petitioners and Sir Robert Mansell and John Dalby.* 3*rd February* 1637-8. [½ *p*.]

Dec. 15.
Great Boughton, near Chester.
83. Francis Emerson and Robert Stranke to Samuel Cordewell, powder-master to his Majesty. Complain of the neglect of their work as saltpetremen within the hundred of Bromfield, co. Denbigh, both by the late high constables, John Rogers and John Wynn, and by the present high constables, Roger Griffith and Gough Greene, and by the magistrates, Sir Thomas Powell, Sir Thomas Middleton, Mr. Trafford, Jarrett Eaton, Mr. Meredith, Dr. Floyd, and Richard Floyd. Several tons of liquor had been lost by the non-supply of carriages for its conveyance from Holt to Great Boughton. [2¼ *pp*.] *Annexed*,

> 83. I. *Commissioners for Saltpetre to Sir John Bridgeman and the Council of the Marches. Recite the above complaint. Direct that the said justices of peace and constables be brought before the Council of the Marches, and that either the saltpetremen receive recompense, or that the Council certify whom they conceive to be faulty.* [*Draft by Nicholas.* 1⅓ *p*.]

Dec. 15.
Bristol.
84. James Dyer to Nicholas. There is a commission for examination of impositions laid within the city. We conceive that to be the ground of it, but the commissioners will not let us see it. They are Fox and Powlett, men of mean quality, who have a messenger to attend them, but commit witnesses as they please and threaten them, and keep them in custody until their leisure serves. The like course was never heard of. In a friendly way I desired a sight of the commission, but my friend Powlett told me no such fellow nor companion as I was should see it. I told him that I knew him well,

Vol. CCCLXXIII.

1637.

and held myself no companion of his, nor he fit for my society. He and his fellow commissioner give out that I shall be sent for. Pray, if occasion require, that I may attend the beginning of the term, and upon your letter. I shall prove that a commission of that nature was never heard of to be done with such insolence. [*Seal with arms. 2 pp.*]

Vol. CCCLXXIV. December 16–31, 1637.

1637.

Dec. 16.
Nottingham.

1. Justices of Peace for co. Nottingham to the Council. It was the ancient course that the hundreds of Newark, Hatfield, South Clay and North Clay, wherein the now sheriff dwells and most of his estate lies, paid the moiety of all payments against the hundreds of Bingham, Rushcliffe, Broxtow, and Thurgarton a-Leigh, where we live, but our sheriff pretending that there are in these last-named hundreds 34 towns more than the other, and not weighing the goodness of their towns, has laid more upon them by almost 500*l.* than upon the other. State a variety of circumstances why this should not have been the case, and crave redress. [*2 pp.*]

Dec. 16.
Whitehall.

2. Notes by Nicholas of business to be transacted by the Lords of the Admiralty. Order upon Sir Thomas Roe's letter touching the Dean of Windsor's complaint against Thomas Thornhill. Consider references from the King, of the petitions of Anthony St. Leger and of Lady Ouchterlony. Consider Mr. Browne's petition. The Dutchman, owner of 20 ton of Barbary saltpetre, will not appoint any to join in appraising it, so it lies still in the Custom House. Officers of the Navy attend to give an account of the state of the Prince and the Merhonour. Sign Davison's deputation. [¾ *p.*]

Dec. 16.
Whitehall.

Lords of the Admiralty to Thomas Viscount Wentworth, Lord Deputy of Ireland. Mr. Crane, surveyor of marine victual, has paid in that kingdom for pipe-staves bought this last year the imposition of 3*l.* a thousand. Forasmuch as the said imposition was made since the contract made with the surveyor, his Majesty is pleased that such sums as Crane has paid shall be repaid him out of the revenue of that kingdom. Pray that the same be paid, with the money due for victualling ships employed on the coast of Ireland last summer. [*Copy. See Vol. cccliii., fol.* 75. ¾ *p.*]

Dec. 16.
Whitehall.

The same to the Officers of the Navy. To make an estimate as well of his Majesty's ships in harbour, as of the salaries of officers and other works usually placed upon the ordinary of the navy, for one year from 1st January 1637[-8] to the last day of December 1638, deducting what may be spared by reason of ships to be set forth next year at the charge of the counties. [*Copy. Ibid., fol.* 75. ¼ *p.*]

Vol. CCCLXXIV.

1637.
Dec. 16.
Whitehall.
Lords of the Admiralty to the Master and Wardens of the Trinity House. We have sent you a petition presented to his Majesty by Lady Ouchterlony and Thomas Talbot, concerning the erecting of lights or flames for sea marks at Flamborough Head, and at the square at the mouth of the Humber. To certify your opinion. [*Copy. See Vol. cccliii., fol.* 75 *b.* ⅓ *p.*]

Dec. 16.
Whitehall.
The same to Montjoy Earl of Newport. About twenty tons of saltpetre, being by a Dutch merchant bought in Barbary of English factors, after his Majesty had contracted for all that should be made there, is unladen and put into the Custom House, London. As his Majesty's gunpowder-maker complains that he wants saltpetre to keep his mills in work, we pray you to order the Officers of the Ordnance to appoint persons to set an indifferent price on the said saltpetre, that we may take order for payment and for delivery thereof, to be made fit for his Majesty's use. [*Ibid., fol.* 75. ⅔ *p.*]

Dec. 16.
Another copy of the same. [*See Vol. ccxcii., p.* 72. ¾ *p.*]

Dec. 16.
Burderop.
3. Sir William Calley to Richard Harvey. Thanks him for having paid 8*l.* to Lady Cambell, and intending to "call for it again to Mr. Felix Long." If he can obtain leave for arresting John Titchborne, Sir William should have great hope to get his satisfaction. Urges Harvey to stay where he is for one year at least; if not, and he will return to Sir William, he shall live with him as his friend so long as they shall live together. [*Seal with arms.* ½ *p.*]

Dec. 16.
4. Petition of John Donne, clerk, to Archbishop Laud. Since the death of his father, lately Dean of St. Paul's, there have been many scandalous pamphlets published under his name which were none of his; one entitled "Juvenilia," printed for Henry Seale; another by John Marriott and William Sheares, entitled "Ignatius his conclave," as also certain poems, by the said Marriott, of which abuses they have been often warned by petitioner, but they profess suddenly to publish new impressions. Prays the archbishop to stop their further proceedings. [¾ *p.*] *Underwritten,*

> 4. I. "*I require the parties whom this petition concerns not to meddle any farther with the printing or selling of any the pretended works of the late Dean of St. Paul's, save only such as shall be licensed by public authority and approved by the petitioner, as they will answer the contrary at their peril, and of this I desire the Dean of the Arches to take care.*—W. CANT." 16th December 1637. [¼ *p.*]

Dec. 16.
5. Certificate of [the Officers of the Ordnance] of the quantity of gunpowder issued yearly by that office. It states the quantity issued for several years past, and gives the medium or average. Total, 128 lasts 13 cwt. 81 lbs. [5½ *pp.*]

Dec. 16.
6. Copy of the same [in the handwriting of Sir John Heydon], with the addition of a memorandum that the preceding certificate

VOL. CCCLXXIV.

1637.

was presented to the Lords of the Admiralty on the 18th inst., and a list also of the forts surveyed by Capt. Coningsby. [3 *pp*.]

Dec. 16. 7. A paper of memoranda and calculations apparently connected with the preparation of the preceding certificate. [1 *p*.]

Dec. 16. 8. Account by Sir William Russell of ship-money for 1636. Total received, 184,802*l*. 5*s*. 9½*d*.; outstanding, 11,812*l*. 1*s*. 10½*d*. [1 *p*.]

Dec. 16. 9. Account of ship-money for 1636 remaining in the hands of sheriffs 150*l*., which makes the total collected 184,952*l*., and in arrear 11,448*l*. [½ *p*.]

Dec. 17. Whitehall. 10. Order of the King in Council. Upon petition of Henry Lambe, and notice of the hard conditions offered to him in a certificate of the commissioners appointed to view the river from Bury St. Edmunds to the river Ouse (*see Vol. ccclxv., No. 47*), his Majesty appointed the first Sunday in Hilary term for hearing this business in his own presence, and required the commissioners to attend his Majesty with the depositions, and also to give notice to such gentlemen who are the cause of the said hard conditions to attend to give reasons for their so doing. [1¼ *p*.]

Dec. 17. Whitehall. 11. Similar order. The Lords, by letters of 2nd October, sent with the ship-money writs, gave directions that the sheriffs should return to the Board, within one month after the assessment made, a certificate of what is set upon each parish, and particularly upon every clergyman, which has been performed by few of the sheriffs. It was ordered that Nicholas should let them know that his Majesty takes it as a great neglect that they have not returned the said certificate, and wills them to do it forthwith, as also to certify to Nicholas every fortnight the progress of the business. It was also ordered that Nicholas should keep a book concerning the same, and all the letters, and every Sunday give an account of the state thereof. [1¼ *p*.]

Dec. 17. Whitehall. 12. The Council to the Sheriff of co. Lincoln. We send you a petition read at the Board in the name of Sir Anthony Thomas, John Worsop, and others, undertakers of the drained lands beyond Boston, and others interested therein, desiring that those lands may be spared from assessment to ship-money, till the same shall yield some considerable profit. His Majesty being inclined to give encouragement to the undertakers of such works, has commanded us to require you to give account what those drained [lands are] which petitioners complain of to be charged as aforesaid, what sum is laid upon the same, and what profit the same may now yield, with the reasons of your proceedings herein, that his Majesty and the Board may give further order herein. [*Copy.* 1 *p*.]

[Dec. 17.] 13. Petition of John Bartlett, stationer, to the Council. Petitioner has of late been called into the High Commission for buying and

1637.

Vol. CCCLXXIV.

selling schismatical books, as Dr. Bastwick's "Litany," Mr. Burton's "Appeal," and others. He has now unburthened his conscience in a free confession of the whole truth, and desires pardon. Petitioner is very poor, and has a wife and six children, and a father, 84 years of age, all depending upon him. Prays the Lords to accept his bond not to deal in such books hereafter. [1 p.] *Underwritten,*

> 13. I. *Statement in the handwriting of Sir William Becher of what "Sir John Lambe saith." That Bartlett was articled against*—1. *For buying and divulging schismatical books, as those of Prynne, Bastwick, &c.* 2. *For receiving the Scottish News and causing several copies to be written thereof. Upon examination touching the first he said he was not bound by law to make any answer, but upon admonition from Sir John Lambe he has since fully confessed. For the Scottish News he utterly denied to disclose the man who brought it, but confessed it was a Scottish man who used to come to his shop, and Sir John Lambe saw the Scottish News (of which Bartlett caused five copies to be taken) in a Scottish hand, and in that same hand some of the schismatical stuff which Bartlett had divulged, so Sir John conceives that there was familiar correspondence betwixt Bartlett and the Scottish man, and that if he be well handled now, after some punishment, he will discover the Scottish man's name and where he may be found, and Sir John conceives it to be of consequence to get so much from him.* [1 p.] *Written under the petition,*
>
> 13. II. Negatur. *Their Lordships leave the petitioner to the ordinary course of justice.* [2 lines.]

Dec. 17. 14. Order of the King in Council. Recites the facts stated in the above petition and the report of Sir John Lambe. It was ordered that Bartlett should by warrant from the Board be committed to the Fleet until he give better satisfaction as touching the premises, and more particularly touching the said Scottish man, and that the Earl of Stirling and Sec. Windebank should take a strict examination of Bartlett, and that the High Commissioners should communicate to them the examinations already taken; and that by all ways and means, as to the Earl and the Secretary should seem fitting, they should find out the whole truth, and particularly the name and abode, lodging, and person of the said Scottish man, and to report to his Majesty or the Board. [1½ p.]

Dec. 17. 15. Petition of Hugh Rigby, guardian to Gilbert Ireland, his Majesty's ward, to the Council. Petitioner on Sunday last petitioned the Board for stay of proceedings of the citizens of Chester against the inhabitants of Gloverstone for the levies of ship-money until the hearing of the cause before the Lords upon the country's certificate, which the Lords thought not fit unless petitioner could manifest how far he had proceeded upon the same. States the proceedings which

VOL. CCCLXXIV.

1637.

have taken place under the reference to the Earl of Derby and the Judges of Assize (*see Vol. ccclvii., No.* 144), and prays that the citizens may be ordered to forbear imprisoning the poor inhabitants and seizing their goods until the cause be heard. [⅔ *p.*]

> 15. I. *Order of the King in Council that petitioner should attend the issue of the hearing appointed the 4th February next, being now near at hand, and that in the meantime no surcease of the proceedings mentioned in the petition needed to be had. Whitehall, 17th December* 1637. [¾ *p.*]

Dec. 17.
Boston.

16. Sir Anthony Irby, Sheriff of co. Lincoln, to the Council. I am enforced to complain of Sir Walter Norton, who last term sent for Wyatt Parkins, my under-sheriff, and told him that he hoped I had not engaged him to assist me in the ship business, and advised him that, if he were clear of it, he should not meddle with it, for he knew I should procure me many enemies by it. It will be impossible for me to answer his Majesty's expectation without the assistance of the country ministers and my own officers, especially the under-sheriff. How far the discouragement of so near an officer may cause neglect in the more inferior, I leave to your consideration. Wha tothers he has or intends to dissuade, I rather fear than know. My request is that you would send for Sir Walter, that you may know what he intends by it, as also who they be that will be my enemies for doing his Majesty's service. [*Seal with arms.* 1 *p.*]

Dec. 17.
The Bonaventure, [Plymouth Sound].

17. Capt. Henry Stradling to Sec. Windebank. I have received order from Sir John Pennington to transport for the Groyne Mr. Scandaret, a servant of her Majesty, and there to receive on board the Duchess of Chevreuse. I have used my best endeavour to get thus far, where I have been forced to stop to furnish myself with a pilot. At this instant I am ready to set sail with a fair wind. Before I had command for this voyage I received an order from my admiral that whensoever I should meet with any ship belonging to Dunkirk I should do my best to bring her to him, or leave her in custody of the captain of one of his Majesty's forts, that satisfaction might be made to Mr. Breams for busses taken from him by men-of-war of Dunkirk. Going on shore at Plymouth, I had intelligence of a Dunkirk prize there, which I have delivered to Capt. George Bagg, lieutenant of the fort at Plymouth, with order to detain her until he receive command from the Lords of the Admiralty. I have sent the examination of those that have the command of her. [*Seals with arms.* 1¾ *p.*] *Enclosed,*

> 17. I. *Examination of John Verhagen and William Vanden Abele, belonging to the Conception, of Dunkirk, Philip Valencia, captain, lately in his Majesty of Spain's service, taken before Capt. Henry Stradling, 17th December* 1637. *They came in company with the Spanish fleet from the Groyne, bound for Dunkirk, about the 21st November last, and put into Plymouth with a Dutch prize laden with salt, called the St. John, of Agersfloate, of* 200 *tons, bound for Dunkirk.* [¾ *p.*]

VOL. CCCLXXIV.

1637.
Dec. 17.
Burderop.

18. Sir William Calley to Richard Harvey. I send four collars of brawn, two dozen of hogs' puddings (half white, half black), and a fat young swan, directed to Mrs. Porter. I and my wife have been much indisposed. Present my love and service to good old Mrs. Porter. We hear that Portugal is revolted from the King of Spain, that they have murdered all the Spaniards in the Castle of Lisbon, and that the Duke of Braganza has proclaimed himself King. Write me what you hear thereof. [*Seal with arms.* 1 *p.*]

Dec. $\frac{17}{27}$.
The Hague.

19. Colonel Thomas Ferentz to Sir Thomas Roe. In reply to letter of Sir Thomas of the 20th November (*see Vol. ccclxxii., No.* 7), full of noble zeal, wise discourse, and discreet conclusions. The writer's profession consists rather in doing well than in speaking wisely, but trusting in Roe's wisdom he is emboldened to reply. Doubts not that much good would result to the common cause if the West India Company could be set on foot in England, but doubts whether the present disposition of affairs will permit it. It is confirmed on all sides that the Swedes are treating, driven thereto by the force of the imperial arms and the disunion of their leading men. If despair of retaining the Swedes were to compel the French to unite with Great Britain, the treaty might be renewed, but if they can make peace otherwise, they will treat till the day of judgment without coming to any conclusion, accommodating themselves in that respect to the humour of your nation, which likes to come near the fire but not to burn the foot. Explains the state of things in reference to the Prince Elector's going in person to the army of the late Landgrave, that Roe might judge whether any good was likely to result from that step. States the contents of the will of the late Landgrave, his appointment of his widow to the regency of his states, and subsequent proceedings which it could not be doubted would terminate in a peace, of which the writer states the proposed terms. Hopes the affairs of the Prince Elector are not desperate, but they must have assistance. His Highness prepares himself to seek the issue of his business in an honourable death. He wishes to use a few jewels which remain to him in equipping himself better than has been done in England, and to die like a Prince at the head of a few gentlemen who think as he does. The Prince has not been wanting in will, nor in resolution, but in friends. [*French.* 4 *pp.*]

Dec. 17.
Haling.
[Hayling?]

20. Christopher Gardyner to his brother, Sir John Heydon. Reports upon the progress of a chemical or alchemical experiment in which the writer and Sir John were jointly interested. Sir John has underscored with black lead the passages deemed most important. [*Seal with arms.* 1½ *p.*]

Dec. 18.

Letters patent for the erection of office of muster-master within the city of London, and a grant of the same to Capt. John Fisher, gentleman pensioner, during his Majesty's pleasure, with the like fees as are paid to the muster-master of Kent. [*Docquet.*]

VOL. CCCLXXIV.

1637.
Dec. 18. Warrant to pay to the Earl of Denbigh, master of the Wardrobe, 1,612*l.* 11*s.* 0*d.*, to be paid to Mary Shackspeare, widow of John Shackspeare, his Majesty's bit-maker, deceased, in regard of her present necessities, in full of a debt of 1,692*l.* 11*s.*, for wares by him delivered for his Majesty's service in the stables, whereof there has been already paid unto her 80*l.* [*Docquet.*]

Dec. 18. Licence for George Lord Chandos, Baron of Sudeley, to travel into foreign parts for three years. [*Docquet.*]

Dec. 18. Whitehall. 21. The Council to Sir William Widdrington. Another copy of the letter already calendared under date of the 10th December instant; see Vol. ccclxxiii., No. 64., but with the present date. [½ *p.*] *Written on the same sheet of paper,*

    21. I. *Jasper Heiley to the same. Another copy of the letter already calendared under the date of the 10th December instant, as above referred to, No. 64. I.* [½ *p.*]

Dec. 18. Mincing Lane. 22. Officers of the Navy to Lords of the Admiralty. The King's master shipwrights conceive, from Capt. Pett's relation, that it is his Majesty's pleasure to have the Prince and the Merhonour rebuilt of the same moulds and dimensions that now they be. If the Merhonour be rebuilt at Chatham, which will save the charge of transporting her to Woolwich, there may be saved 3,000*l.*, by leaving some parts of her hull; and the like to the amount of 3,500*l.* in the case of the Prince, out of which latter sum the charge of transporting her to Woolwich is estimated at 1,500*l.* Our opinion is that the shipwrights can now build new ships of the like burthen better than either of them. The Prince cannot be rebuilt under 14,000*l.*, besides the savings before mentioned, nor the Merhonour under 6,000*l.* We advise, if his Majesty resolve to build another ship as great as the Prince, to build her totally new, and to take the benefit of what can be saved to build the Merhonour. [1 *p.*]

Dec. 18. 23. The same to the same. According to your letter of the 25th November last (calendared under that date), we find the account of the ships employed last summer for cordage, as in the abstract here enclosed, which being very exorbitant in some of them, we have thought fit to suspend their boatswains for the present, leaving them to your consideration. [1 *p.*] *Enclosed,*

    23. I. *Abstract of account of cordage above-mentioned. Four boatswains, Robert Lowndes, Jonathan Countrey, Abraham Sampson, and Thomas Norgate, had been suspended absolutely, and three others until their captains certified as to the expense.* [1 *p.*]

Dec. 18. 24. John Brown, his Majesty's gunfounder, to the same. Answer to petition of John de la Barre, praying for permission to export

1637.

certain ordnance, stated to be cast of foreign iron, not to be vendible in England, to belong to Dantzic, and to a ship of which John Sulke was master. Respondent hopes to be able to prove the very contrary of every one of these alleged facts; sets forth his own patent, dated in October 1635, whereby, in consideration of 12,000*l.*, the King granted him the sole making, vending, and transporting of iron ordnance and shot; and prays that he and de la Barre may be left to the law. [$\frac{2}{3}$ *p.*]

Dec. 18.
The Swiftsure, in the Downs.

25. Sir John Pennington to the Lords of the Admiralty. We cannot hear what is become of the Jewel; only I spake with a master of a ship that came from Malaga, who told me that he was aboard of them off the Wight, and that they had wine from him, and came along with him near Beachy, where he left her this day seven-night at night; since which time I have heard nothing of them. Except she be put back for the Wight, I fear she is cast away. The William is yet here, and cannot get wind and weather to bring her up, though I have assisted them with men and other provisions. Strong northerly winds. [*Seals with crest.* 1 *p.*]

Dec. $\frac{18}{28}$.
Madrid.

26. Christopher Windebank to his father, Sec. Windebank. The speedy journey of Mr. Fanchau [Fanshaw], secretary to the ambassador, gives me leave only to let you understand that I am as dutiful and ready to obey you, as I may be thought undutiful and negligent. This week I begin my journey for Italy, hoping you will send me one word of comfort in a letter to Florence or Ciena [Sienna]. The annuity you allow me will not find me meat and drink, therefore with my Lord [ambassador's] leave, I have taken up of Mr. Write [Wright] 100*l.*, with which, though my lord thinks I shall not be able to pass, yet I will husband it as sparingly as may be, and give you account. P.S.—I entreat you for your own honour's sake not to suffer me, your son, to perish, who never intended to stain it, as the effect will make good. [1 *p.*]

Dec. 18.

27. John Nicholas to his son, Edward Nicholas. It is ill news the increase of the sickness, and that it is come so near you. The weather being now grown sharp will, I hope, purge the air. I will send for Jack and Ned both before Christmas, and will return them the morrow after the holidays. I received 20*l.* of the Dr. [Matthew Nicholas, sent by Edward Nicholas to build the brewhouse destroyed by fire, *see Vol. cclxiii., No.* 44], and 5*l.* 0*s.* 4*d.* which my cousin Pitt sent you. Will send him two geese, two turkeys, two capons, and two Muscovy ducks. P.S.—Service to Sir Charles Herbert. [1$\frac{3}{4}$ *p.*]

Dec. 18.
Montague [Montacute].

28. Sir Robert Phelipps to Sir Dudley Carleton. My neighbours, the late constables of the hundred of Tintinhull, have preferred a petition to the Council, which I shall desire you to further. The contents are true, and the poor men have been no way faulty in his Majesty's service. If any fault has been, it was in Mr. Basset. If their petition may not be fully granted, or if any complaint come

1637.

against these poor men by Basset, I desire a reference to the Bishop of Bath and Wells. [¾ p.]

Dec. 18.
Barbican.

29. John Earl of Bridgewater to Sir Dudley Carleton. I pray you give expedition to the business which this enclosed letter concerns. [*Seal with crest. Endorsed as "Touching corn in Pembrokeshire."* ⅓ p.]

Dec. 18.
Office of Ordnance.

30. Estimate by the Officers of the Ordnance for 102 pieces of brass ordnance assigned the 7th December for the Sovereign of the Seas, his Majesty being aboard the same day, and the master and officers then attending and receiving his commands. Total amount, 24,447*l*. 8*s*. 8*d*. There was a former estimate of 20,592*l*. 13*s*. 6*d*. for 90 guns, which was superseded by the present. [3 pp.]

Dec. 19.
Whitehall.

Lords of the Admiralty to the Mayor of Bristol. Notwithstanding the proclamation against making gunpowder, there are powder mills in Bristol, and amongst others, the mill belonging to Baber still makes gunpowder. We require you to search what gunpowder mills are in your city, and to suppress them; and if you find any of the owners refractory, you are to bind them over to answer their contempt. [*Copy. See Vol. ccclii., fol.* 76. ½ p.]

Dec. 19.

31. Petition of Priscilla Titchborne, wife of John Titchborne, D.D., to Archbishop Laud. Petitioner was formerly married to Gawen Cotchett, of London, who died about 3½ years since, and left petitioner about 700*l*. in chattels. Before her marriage with Dr. Titchborne it was agreed that, in regard he could not make a jointure, he would not intermeddle with her estate for her life, and petitioner agreed that at her death she would leave him a great part thereof. Forthwith after their marriage, the Dr. and Nevill and John Titchborne, his sons, practised to seize on her whole estate, and mortgaged a house of hers for a debt of 100*l*. of John the son to Robert Titchborne. Last summer, Dr. Titchborne, falling sick, made a deed of gift of all petitioner's estate to his son Nevill, who by virtue thereof has seized even upon her wearing apparel, and is now about to sell her house. Prays relief. [¾ p.] *Underwritten*,

31. I. *Direction to Sir John Lambe to call the parties before him and make some peaceable end between them if he can, and if not, to call them into the High Commission Court, either upon fresh articles or upon additionals to those already therein against Dr. Titchborne for dilapidations.* 19*th December* 1637. [¼ p.]

Dec. 19.
The Cathedral, Bristol.

32. Dr. Edward Chetwynd, the Dean, with the Chapter of Bristol, to the same. Having understood his Majesty's pleasure that we should forbear granting any further estate either to Sir William Morgan, or to the tenants of Banwell, we have held it our duty to signify our readiness to subscribe thereto. Having had conference with our bishop, we hold it not good manners to prescribe unto our Sovereign or superiors, but rather for our parts submit the whole business to his Majesty. [*Seal with arms.* 1 p.]

Vol. CCCLXXIV.

1637.
Dec. 19.
Deptford.

33. John Hollond to Nicholas. Sends him, in answer to his inquiry, a statement of the wages paid per mensem to boatswains, gunners, and pursers, serving in harbour, on board the Swallow and the Ninth Whelp. The allowance made to pursers for maintaining lights on board the Admiral is 20s. per mensem, and that to surgeons for medicaments is 7l. 10s. for a ship of the third rank for eight months, and 3l. for a ship of the 5th rank for 12 months. The common man's pay is always 15s. per mensem. [1 p.]

Dec. 20.

Petition of Philip Burlamachi to the King. In 1632 the King let the alum works to Sir John Gibson for 31 years, from December 1637, at the rent of 12,500l. The works since that time are so improved that for the last four years petitioner has paid to the patentees 15,000l. a year, and is ready to pay that rent to the King for 7, 8, or 10 years, if he would resume the work into his own hand, or take a lease from Sir John Gibson, giving him 1,000l. per annum, which is received from the sub-contractors, wherein the King shall do no wrong, but only prevent the sub-contractors from encroaching upon his profit. Moreover, at the end of the term, in lieu of 1,800l. stock now upon the work, his Majesty should have a stock of alum worth 20,000l., by which means English alum should be sold and compared beyond seas to Romish alum, to the great increase of price and augmentation of the revenue. [*Copy. See Vol. cccxxiii., p. 212. 1 p.*] *Underwritten,*

    I. *Reference to the Lord Treasurer and Lord Cottington to consider and certify. Whitehall, 20th December 1637.* [*Copy. See Ibid., p. 213. ¼ p.*]

Dec. 20.

Petition of Sir John Shelley to the same. Petitioner is descended of an ancient family in Sussex, where for some ages past they have had convenient possessions. Having matched his eldest son with the good liking of the King and Queen, his said son is deceased, and left an infant of 10 months of age, who, if he be a minor at petitioner's death, will be your Majesty's ward. His mother being a stranger born, and this child petitioner's only hope, he prays a grant of the wardship if it shall happen. [*Copy. Ibid. ¾ p.*]

Dec. 20.

Petition of Edward Earl of Dorset to the same. Certain islands on the south of New England, viz., Long Island, Cole Island, Sandy Point, Hell Gates, Martin's [Martha's?] Vineyard, Elizabeth Islands, Block Island, with other islands near thereunto, were lately discovered by some of your Majesty's subjects, and are not yet inhabited by any Christians. Prays a grant thereof, with like powers of government as have been granted for other plantations in America. [*Copy. Ibid., p. 222. ½ p.*] *Underwritten,*

    I. *Reference to the Attorney-General to prepare a grant. Whitehall, 20th December 1637.* [*Copy. Ibid. ¼ p.*]

Dec. 20.
Whitehall.

Lords of the Admiralty to Thomas Wyan. There is remaining in your hands of the great wreck at the Isle of Wight about 811l. 18s. 4½d., and of reals of eight about 5,717 and a half. We pray

1637.

VOL. CCCLXXIV.

you to change the reals into sterling money, and to pay the same, with the 811*l*. 18*s*. 4½*d*., into the Exchequer. [*Copy. See Vol. ccclii., fol.* 76. ½ *p.*]

Dec. 20.
Whitehall.

34. Sec. Windebank to Attorney-General Bankes. His Majesty has given license to Lady Jane Bacon and Lady Cramond to remain in London with their families for six months, and has commanded me to require you to forbear to inform against the said ladies in the Star Chamber or elsewhere. [1 *p.*]

Dec. 20.

35. Sir Thomas Walsingham to Sir Dudley Carleton. The bearer, James Randall, of Leigh cum Spelherst [Speldhurst ?], is returned for not finding arms in Sir Leonard Bosvile's company. He has submitted himself, and entreats that he may be discharged from further attendance. [1 *p.*]

Dec. 20.

36. Account of Isaac Pennington, of London, merchant, of moneys put into his hands by way of trust by his cousin Sir John Pennington before his going to sea, as also of moneys since received by appointment of Sir John. It runs from April 1637 to this day. Total receipts, 4,644*l*. 19*s*. 4*d*.; payments, 1,417*l*. 4*s*. 0*d*. [1 *p.*] *Annexed*,

> 36. I. *Further account in explanation of an item in the above account of* 1,200*l*. *paid to the accountant's cousin, Thomas Pennington.* [⅓ *p.*]

Dec. 21.

The King to Thomas Viscount Wentworth, Lord Deputy of Ireland. To consider a petition of Edmund Fitzgerald, an orphan, and former letters, decrees, and orders on behalf of his ancestors, and finding his allegations true, to take order for recovery of his Majesty's right to the wardship of the petitioner. [*Docquet.*]

Dec. 21.

Presentation of Guy Carleton, clerk, M.A., to the rectory of Caythorpe, in the diocese of Lincoln, now *de jure* void and in his Majesty's gift. [*Docquet.*]

Dec. 21.
My lodging.

37. Lionel Wake, junior, to [Richard] Harvey. Please to pay the bearer 700*l*. for Sir Peter Paul Rubens. I send the *carta de poder* [letter of attorney], of which take a copy, and when you assign me a time I shall give receipt for 1,500*l*. [1 *p.*]

Dec. 21.
Dorset House.

Funeral certificate, by William Ryley, of Anne Countess of Northumberland, daughter of William Earl of Salisbury, and wife of Algernon Earl of Northumberland. She departed this life at Dorset House in Salisbury Court, Fleet Street, London, on Wednesday, 6th December 1637. Her body was conveyed thence on the Saturday following to Sion House, and there stayed three nights, and was from thence brought to Petworth, and there interred in a vault in the chancel. She had issue by the said Earl four daughters, Katherine, Dorothy, Anne, and Elizabeth, all very young. [*Copy. See Vol. ccclx., p.* 3. 1¼ *p.*]

Dec. 21.

38. See Papers relating to Appointments in the Navy.

VOL. CCCLXXIV.

1637.
Dec. 21. Petition of Richard Greene, sewer to his Majesty, to the King. 3,383*l*. 11*s*. 11½*d*. is due to Simon Greene, supplicant's father, and John Greene his brother, for provisions brought by them into his Majesty's stable and granary since his coming to the Crown, and 3,032*l*. 3*s*. 3½*d*. in the last five years of King James's reign. Petitioner prays a grant in satisfaction of the said debts to be raised by prosecution by the petitioner at his own charge, out of benefit due to his Majesty upon undue importation or exportation of any goods, or for goods prohibited, or for lading or unlading any goods at times or places not warranted, or for fines upon compositions before trials upon informations thereupon exhibited. [*Copy. See Vol. cccxxiii., p.* 214. ¾ *p.*] *Underwritten*,

    I. *Reference to the Lord Treasurer and Lord Cottington, who if they find that his Majesty has formerly granted these particulars to others for satisfaction of debts, that then they take the like order for granting the same to petitioner. Whitehall, 21st December* 1637. [*Copy. See Ibid., p.* 215. 1 *p.*]

Dec. 22. Petition of Henry Jermyn to the same. Divers new improvements in the soke of Somersham, co. Huntingdon, are leased to petitioner for three lives, at 20*l*. per annum. Prays a grant of the same in fee-farm in socage, reserving the said 20*l*. per annum. [*Copy. See Vol. cccxxiii., p.* 262. ⅕ *p.*] *Underwritten*,

    I. *Reference to the Lord Treasurer to certify the value of the reversion after the estates in being, and what his Majesty's interest in the same is worth. Whitehall, 22nd December* 1637. [*Copy. Ibid.* ⅕ *p.*]

    II. *Reference of Lord Treasurer Juxon to the Surveyor-General to certify the values above mentioned. London House, 27th December* 1637. [*Copy. Ibid.* 4 *lines.*]

    III. *Sir Charles Harbord, Surveyor-General, to Lord Treasurer Juxon. The improvements mentioned in this petition were made for her Majesty's use, Somersham being parcel of her jointure, and are granted by her Majesty to petitioner's father (and by him assigned to the petitioner) for 60 years, if three lives live so long, at 20l. per annum, and her Majesty has power to renew the estate during her life. The improvements contain 1,100 acres, and appear to be worth 400l. per annum over and above the rent, and I conceive the inheritance thereof in reversion to be worth 1,500l. 30th December* 1637. [*Copy. Ibid.* ⅕ *p.*]

    IV. *His Majesty having seen this certificate, grants the petitioner the improvements in the petition mentioned, reserving the rent of 20l. per annum, and the Attorney-General is to prepare a bill accordingly. Whitehall, 3rd April* 1638. [*Copy. Ibid.* ⅕ *p.*]

Vol. CCCLXXIV.

1637.
Dec. 22.
Westminster.
Nicholas to Godwin Awdry. If he will come up presently after Twelfthtide the Lords will hear his proposition (*see Vol. ccclxxiii., No.* 35). [*Copy. See Nicholas's Letter Book, Dom. James I., Vol. ccxix., p.* 167.]

Dec. 22.
London.
39. Receipt of Lionel Wake, junior, for 700*l.* paid by Endymion Porter, by his servant Richard Harvey, for Sir Peter and [*sic*] Paulo Rubens, by letter of attorney from him dated $\frac{13}{23}$ November last, in Antwerp. [½ *p.*]

Dec. 22.
40. See "Papers relating to Appointments in the Navy."

Dec. 23.
41. Petition of James Levinston [Livingstone] to the King. His Majesty's progenitors, being seized as in right of the Crown in the forest of North Petherton, in Somerset, upon false information granted away the same under the name of a manor or park, without reservation of any fee-farm rent. Prays a grant of the said forest at the yearly rent of 20*l.* [*Copy.* ¾ *p.*] *Underwritten,*

> 41. I. *His Majesty, in consideration of petitioner's service to him performed, grants him the said forest, as desired. The Attorney-General is to prepare a draft of a patent for his Majesty's signature.* [*Copy.* ¼ *p.*]

Dec. 23.
The Swiftsure, in the Downs.
42. Sir John Pennington to the Lords of the Admiralty. The East India ship, the Jewel, which has been so long missing, arrived here yesterday in safety, and set sail this morning for the Thames; she has [been] miraculously preserved, for she rode seven or eight days upon the coast of France in very f[oul] weather, where she lost all her cables and anchors, and after lay, driving to and again, in the sea, to [this] present that she got near Dover, from whence [she was] relieved. I received a command the 28th October last, for staying ships belonging to Dunkirk, for repaying Mr. Breames, of Dover, for his busses taken from him; whereupon I gave warrant to my captains that wheresoever they should meet any Dunkirkers to bring them to me, or to put them [in safe custody] into some of his Majesty's harbours. Advises the Lords of the detention of a Dunkirker by Capt. Stradling, of the Bonaventure (*see this Vol., No.* 17). [*Damaged.* 1 *p.*]

Dec. 23.
Mincing Lane.
43. Kenrick Edisbury to Nicholas. We had another letter yesterday from Mr. Cook, touching the riding of the Sovereign, being now in more fear of the ice, which made him lay out another anchor of 39 cwt., and so she rides by four great cables and anchors, which he hopes will hold her fast; he has sent out also for spars to shut off the ice. He writes also that there is no likelihood of any wind during this frost to stem the tide, to carry the ship lower in the river, and that men and victuals cannot be so suddenly got for that design, and desires to have victuals sent down for her ordinary company. We have given warrant accordingly for victualling 100 men for six weeks. The victualler demands allowance of sea-victuals for that ship, or that his Majesty pay for transporting it to the ship.

1637.   Vol. CCCLXXIV.

I am in hand to make an estimate for her and the Prince. Recommends that the bearer, Mr. Broad, who had command of the Roebuck last voyage, may have the place again in her next employment; Sir John Pennington has written to him to take the charge of master's mate in the Swiftsure, the mate Gayney being sick. [¾ p.]

Dec. 23.
Whitehall.
Lords of the Admiralty to Thomas Lambert, Henry Willoughby, John Topp, and George Howe. Complaint is made by the Dean of Windsor, rector of Knoyle Magna, Wilts, that Thomas Thornhill, late saltpetreman, upon pretence of digging for saltpetre, has overthrown the pigeon-house belonging to the rectory, to which complaint Thornhill made answer, that his work was not the cause of the fall of the pigeon-house. We require you to view the place, and hear such workmen as you shall think good to speak with, or as the Dean or Thornhill shall bring to you, and to make certificate of the truth. [*Copy. See Vol. cccliii., fol.* 76. ⅗ *p.*]

Dec. 24.
Licence to Sir William Russell, Baronet, and Francis Russell, his son, for preservation of his Majesty's game in divers places near Newmarket. [*Docquet.*]

Dec. 24.
Warrant to all Admirals and other officers not to stay any ships employed into Newfoundland, the whole continent whereof his Majesty hath lately granted to the Marquis of Hamilton and others. [*Docquet.*]

Dec. 24.
44. Petition of Lambert Osbolston, clerk, to Archbishop Laud. Petitioner is much afflicted with rumours spread abroad by Mr. Kilvert, that petitioner should, in some weekly letters of his to the Bishop of Lincoln, contrary to honesty and good manners, presume to asperse your Grace, and is to be publicly questioned in the Star Chamber for the same. Petitioner protests that he never had the least intent to wrong your Grace in any letter he wrote in his whole life, and does not doubt, but if he might see those particular letters he should be able to satisfy you therein. Prays to be preserved from public suits in law, which will ruin him, whether he be guilty or no. Protests, that although he has spoken sometimes freely unto your Grace, yet hath he ever as much honoured you, and written often unto his friends of your extraordinary favours to all scholars and clergymen, than any other man of his rank in all the kingdom, and appeals to those letters he wrote to the Bishop of Lincoln, if such poor weekly scribbles be extant. Beseeches your Grace, with a reflection upon this good and blessed time, to take petitioner into your charity and protection. [*Endorsed by the Archbishop.* 1 *p.*]

Dec. 24.
London.
45. John Grant to the same. After great praise of the archbishop's integrity, both for public justice and religion, he presents to him certain collections and commentations of divine writ which strongly reprove mistakes, and direct the lovers of truth into the holy "sabboth of God." His suit is that they may have the archbishop's favour and approbation. The author is a lover of the arch-

VOL. CCCLXXIV.

1637.

bishop, and desires that in this labour he may be concealed, but the truth published. [1 p.]

Dec. 24. Nicholas to the sheriffs of 39 counties who have not returned certificates of their assessments for shipping. To the same effect as a similar letter calendared under date of 30th January 1636–7; subjoined is a list of the counties in England to which, with all the counties in Wales, copies of the letter were sent. [*Copy. See Nicholas's Letter Book, Dom. James I., Vol. ccxix., p.* 169.]

Dec. 24. 46. Brief declaration of the account of the farmers of the customs for one year ending this day. The rent for one year was 150,000*l.*; against which were to be set various payments and allowances, which amounted to 186,873*l.* 0*s.* 7½*d.*, leaving the accountants in surplusage, 36,873*l.* 0*s.* 7½*d.* [1 *p.*]

Dec. 24. 47. Account of John Geddes of his receipts and disbursements upon the work of North Somercotes Marsh, since the 11th March last. His receipts had been 491*l.* 3*s.* 2*d.*; his disbursements, 517*l.* 13*s.* 3*d.* The balance of 26*l.* 10*s.* 1*d.*, owing to him, was this day paid to him by Endymion Porter. [= 9½ *pp.*]

Dec. 25. 48. The patentees of the parish of Stepney alias Stebunheath for the sale of tobacco, to Peter Boddam, of Upper Shadwell. Licence to sell tobacco, Boddam paying 30*s.* for a fine and 7*s.* 6*d.* quarterly. [1 *p.*]

Dec. 25. 49. Declaration of the account of Archbishop Laud (by Sir John Lambe, his attorney), as collector of tenths of all benefices and spiritual promotions, granted to the King within the diocese of Lincoln. The whole sum to be accounted for was 7,844*l.* 13*s.* 8¾*d.*; allowances and payments into the Exchequer amounted to 1,616*l.* 14*s.* 7¾*d.*, so that the arrear was 6,227*l.* 19*s.* 1*d.* [1 *p.*]

Dec. 26. 50. Petition of Julian Fountnay, one of his Majesty's equerries, to the Council. Recites petition of the 4th inst. (*see Vol. ccclxxiii., No.* 25), wherein he prayed satisfaction against Sir Richard Titchborne, and the order that the said petition should be shown to Sir Richard, and he be required to give the satisfaction prayed. Petitioner has been himself, and sent many times to Sir Richard's lodging, to show him the same, but he keeps out of sight; wherefore petitioner prays for leave to take the benefit of the law. [¾ *p.*]

Dec. 26.
Whitbourne.
51. Bishop Coke, of Hereford, to Archbishop Laud. I have sent by the bearer my account concerning his Majesty's instructions for this diocese, and had sent them sooner but that I purposed to send them by him, not suspecting any offence by that delay. I beseech your Grace take it in good part; hereafter I will not incur the like. I send also enclosed a note how I stand in the Court of Arches, and can get no sentence or release, notwithstanding I have acknowledged myself to be liable to so much as you have awarded, and have already paid one part of it, but am still drawn on in as much charges

1637.

VOL. CCCLXXIV.

as if I had maintained a suit. I beseech you that I may find some final end in it. The bearer, Christopher Pritchard, parson of Thornbury, was presented by his Majesty, and thereupon instituted, inducted, and read his articles in the church-porch of Brockhampton; but has been so deluded these six or seven years, that he could never get possession of the same farther than the church-porch. What has been the cause of so long delay he can best inform you, and how both he and I have been deluded by Mr. Barnaby, the patron, who has embezzled it to his own private use, notwithstanding it is apparent that it is a presentative thing. I beseech you to give direction to this poor man, who is much wronged. The business of Hampton is a matter of such equity, that I would beg no further help in it but to get indifferent judges, which our juries in this country, and many gentlemen, in any business against the Church, and specially against the Bishop, are much doubted to be. [*Seal with arms.* 1 *p.*]

Dec. 28. Grant of 2*s.* per day for keeping his Majesty's garden doors at Whitehall to Henry Middleton, during life, upon surrender of a like grant to Edward Birkett. [*Docquet.*]

Dec. 28. Grant of the offices of distiller of sweet herbs and waters and the keeping of his Majesty's library to the same, during life. [*Docquet.*]

Dec. 28. Grant of the office of serjeant-at-arms to the same, with the fee of 12*d.* per diem during life, as Evan Owen, deceased, lately held the same. [*Docquet.*]

Dec. 28. Warrant to the Lord Treasurer and Under Treasurer of the Exchequer, to give order to the Society of Soapmakers of London, for payment of 2,000*l.* lent by the late Society of Soapmakers of Westminster to the Duke of Lennox, as also for 7,000*l.* to the said duke in satisfaction of tallies for 9,000*l.* levied at the Exchequer upon the said Society of Soapmakers of Westminster, upon the profit of 6*l.* upon each ton of soap answerable to his Majesty for the year from the 2nd February next coming, out of such moneys as they are to advance to his Majesty upon their letters of incorporation, next after Sir John Harby shall be satisfied his assignment of 12,000*l.*, which several tallies were assigned to the duke in part payment of 22,000*l.* in consideration of his surrender to his Majesty of the priory of St. Andrew's in Scotland; the said officers of the late Society of Westminster, having surrendered their letters of incorporation, and being not liable to the payment of the said 9,000*l.* to the duke, and the 2,000*l.* so lent unto him being in part of the 9,000*l.* payable upon the said tallies. [*Docquet.*]

Dec. 28.
Whitehall. Proclamation touching the corporation of Soapmakers of London. Recites letters patent of the 22nd May last, whereby the King incorporated Edward Bromfield, then Lord Mayor of London, and divers others, by the name of the Soapmakers of London, providing that they should sell soap made of whale oil at 3½*d.* per pound, and that made of oil olive, being the best crown soap, at 4½*d.* per pound. All

Vol. CCCLXXIV.

1637.

making of soap except by license of the company is strictly forbidden, and all persons are also strictly forbidden to import any soap from foreign parts, or to sell potashes to any persons whatsoever, save to the said society. [4 pp.]

Dec. 28.
Westminster.

52. The King to the Lords of the Admiralty. Recites the ship-money writs, and that the King was to lend ships to those places which could not provide them; whereupon the Lords were authorized to direct the Officers of the Navy to prepare ships for that purpose, the Treasurer of the Navy was also authorized to receive the money from the counties, and thereout to make the necessary payments upon estimates signed by the Lords. [35 lines on parchment.]

Dec. 28.

Petition of Sir Walter Roberts and other Commissioners of Sewers and owners of the Upper Levels, and of Wittersham Level, in Kent and Sussex, to the King. Some of the commoners of the said Upper Levels, in June 1635, complained of a decree made by the said Sir Walter Roberts and other Commissioners of Sewers, and the Lords giving way thereto the said decree was repealed, and the charge of certain works decreed laid upon Sir Walter. The results having been very injurious, and petitioners being able to show that the lands may be better preserved, and navigation maintained and bettered, with less charge than the country is now at, petitioners pray that, in respect of the consequence of the work and the contrariety of opinions, the King would hear the matter himself. [Copy. See Vol. cccxxiii., p. 217. 1⅓ p.] Underwitten,

    I. *The King will hear this business at the Council Chamber in Whitehall, on the first Sunday in Hilary Term next, at one of the clock in the afternoon. Whitehall, 28th December 1637.* [*Copy. Ibid.* ¼ *p.*]

Dec. 28.

53. Sir John Lambe to Archbishop Laud. Report on a reference of a cause between the inhabitants of Reculver and those of the chapelries of St. Nicholas and Herne, touching the repair of the church of Reculver. Recites various decrees of former archbishops of Canterbury, that the inhabitants of the chapelries should contribute to such repairs; also that the church of Reculver, with its two steeples, is an ancient and necessary sea mark, and the repair will cost about 877*l*. Sir John thinks that the archbishop should cause the inhabitants of the chapelries (being in his own diocese) to contribute rateably to the said repairs, and should also desire the assistance of his Majesty or the Council, because the steeples of Reculver are such needful sea marks, and because, if the archbishop put it to any ordinary law suit, the steeples will in all likelihood be down. [2¼ pp.]

Dec. 28.
Westover.

54. John Ashburnham to Nicholas. Sent his man to Andover to wait the coming of the carrier, expecting to have heard from Nicholas, but the man returned without any news of the carrier. Kept his day with Mr. Cobbe, but an anticipated hindrance stayed

1637. VOL. CCCLXXIV.

their progress in the examination of the particular of a farm for which the writer was in treaty for Nicholas. He enters into various points of the bargain, one of which was that half the purchase money, which he estimated at about 3,000*l*., would be required next term. He was anxious to know if Nicholas was provided, but resolved that if he liked the other conditions that should not scare him. [*Seal with arms.* 1 *p.*]

Dec. 28.
Haling.
[Hayling?]

55. Christopher Gardiner to Sir John Heydon. Further report of his alchymical experiment alluded to in previous letters, with notes thereon written by Sir John Heydon in black lead. [*Seal with arms.* ¾ *p.*]

Dec. 28.

Minute of warrant to Sir William Uvedale, Treasurer of the Chamber, to pay to William Railton, one of the keepers of the Council Chamber, twenty nobles for moneys disbursed for one year ended in August last. [*Draft. See 31st January* 1637-8. 4 *lines.*]

Dec. 29.
Whitehall.

56. Order of the Lord Keeper and two Lord Chief Justices under the statute for prizing wines. Canary wines and Alicant were to be sold at 81*l*. the pipe, Muscatels at 18*l*. the butt, and at 12*d*. [per quart?] by retail; Sack and Malaga at 16*l*. the butt in gross and * * the quart retail; the best Gascogne and French wines at * * the ton, and Rochelle wines and other small and Th * * at 15*l*. the ton and at 6*d*. the quart, and that none sell at other than these prices during the next year, whereof the C[lerk of the] Crown is to take notice, and to see the same proclaimed in Chancery. The Lords further order that the Attorney-General shall draw up a declaration of these prices for his Majesty's signature, to be published throughout England, but allowing some additional price from places which are remote, so as the same does not exceed [a penny] in the quart, or 4*l*. in the ton for the land carriage. [*Damaged.* 1 *p.*]

Dec. 29.
Doddington.

57. Sir Thomas Delves to the Council. I lately received an order from you, for repayment of 6*l*. 13*s*. 4*d*. assessed upon Sir Thomas Aston for ship-money when I was sheriff for co. Chester, for profit of his farm of French wines. I have long since paid over the same, and have my discharge, although I have not received so much by reason of defects in the gathering, and there being given me in account divers distresses, which the constables have still in their hands. Being out of office, I do not conceive that I have any power to levy the same elsewhere, and I hope you do not intend I should pay it out of my own purse, being warranted by his Majesty's writ, and imposed by the privity of the gentlemen of the country in the country's right. [*Seal with arms.* 1 *p.*]

Dec. 29.
Whitehall.

Lords of the Admiralty to Montjoy Earl of Newport. William Garraway and others, owners of the Mercury of London, a new ship of 300 tons lying in the Thames, are to be permitted to furnish their ship with ordnance out of the founder's store. [*Copy. Vol. cccliii., fol.* 76 *a.* ⅖ *p.*]

Vol. CCCLXXIV.

1637.
Dec. 29.
Mincing Lane.
58. Officers of the Navy to Lords of the Admiralty. Since the receipt of your letter touching a complaint made by the Earl of Westmorland, for nonpayment for timber marked by his Majesty's purveyor in his woods in Kent, we have written to John Wale, purveyor at Maidstone, who confesses that he marked some timber on the Earl's ground, for which there is due 15*l.* 15*s.*, which we will see satisfied if the earl send to our meeting house in Mincing Lane. The purveyor about three weeks since made the King debtor for this parcel of timber, and since that time the moneys have not been demanded, which makes the fault of the purveyor somewhat the less. [1 *p.*]

Dec. 30.
Warrant authorizing Giles Penn to be his Majesty's consul at Sallee, and to execute that office by himself and his deputies in Morocco and Fesse [Fez], during his Majesty's pleasure, with such allowances as consuls in other parts of Turkey have from the merchants, or otherwise as Penn and the merchants shall agree upon. [*Docquet.*]

Dec. 30.
Westminster.
59. Warrant to the Lord Treasurer and the Chancellor of the Exchequer, and to the farmers of the customs upon wines. To grant a bill for importation, free of duty, of 50 tuns of French wines brought over by Mons. Bellievre, ambassador from France, for his provision. [*Copy.* 1 *p.*]

Dec. 30.
Docquet of the same.

Dec. 30.
60. Petition of William Nicoll and John Benfield, moneyers, prisoners in the Fleet, and of all the rest of his Majesty's moneyers, to the Council. Thomas Thornton, about two years since being provost of the moneyers, for defrauding his Majesty, detaining great sums of money from his fellow moneyers, and sundry other misbehaviour in his place, after two or three hearings, finding he should be thrust out, voluntarily gave up his place. Notwithstanding this, some of the officers have lately offered to put in Thornton as an overseer of the moneyers, who because they refused to accept him (the company being bound to make good all losses) Nicoll and Benfield were committed, and by habeas corpus bailed, and the next day carried before some of the Lords of the Council and committed to the Fleet. The whole company of moneyers knowing that the re-admission of Thornton would tend to his Majesty's prejudice and the loss of the moneyers, pray the Lords to free the prisoners and grant the moneyers relief. [*Signed by all the 33 moneyers.* 1 *p.*] Annexed,

> 60. I. *Order of Council that a copy of the above petition be delivered to some of the principal officers of the Mint, who are to answer thereto by the first sitting in Council after Twelfthtide. Durham House. 30th December 1637.* [1 *p.*]
>
> 60. II. *Sir Thomas Aylesbury, Sir William Parkhurst, Sir Ralph Freeman, Henry Cogan, and Andrew Palmer, officers of the Mint, to the Council. Answer to the above petition. They have no intention to put any man upon the*

1637.

VOL. CCCLXXIV.

moneyers, but only to bring them into order, and compel them to do their duty, which they have much neglected, to the dishonour of his Majesty and the scandal of the whole office. At the last pix fault was found for the ill-fashioning of the moneys, and justly, being notorious through all the kingdom. The officers give a long statement of the course they adopted to work an improvement. They stopped the moneyers' allowance of 1d. in the pound, and finding that ineffectual, they sometimes stopped all their wages, but they continued to work so ill that whole "journeys" were sent down to be molten again. Still things got worse and worse, and the officers found it necessary that some one well skilled in the mysteries of the moneyers should be daily with them. No man could be found so fit as Thomas Thornton, but when he went amongst them they put him out, and brought accusations against him, which were scandalous and full of untruths. Thereupon the officers committed Nicoll and Benfield, and on a hearing before the Council they were sent to the Fleet, where they spend upon the common purse, and give out that it shall cost them thousands before they will yield. The Mint, 8th January 1637-8. [3½ pp.]

60. III. *Petition of William Nicoll and John Benfield to the Council. Have very lately and by accident heard that the officers of the Mint are to make answer this day. For the present they are unable to give satisfaction. Pray the Lords to prefix a day when all the moneyers may attend, and that in the meantime petitioners may walk about with a keeper to prepare themselves.* [⅔ p.]

Dec. 30.   61. Information of endeavours used by the Justices of Peace of the four aggrieved hundreds of the co. Nottingham, to induce the sheriff to reform the wrong complained of in his assessing a surcharge of ship-money upon them, in such manner as to save that side of the country wherein the sheriff lives, which gave occasion to a suspicion of partiality. Presented to his Majesty and the Board by Sir John Byron. [¾ p.]

Dec. 30.   62. See "Papers relating to Appointments in the Navy."

Dec. 30.   Petition of Edmund Fortescue and Benjamin Connant to the King. In Devonshire and Cornwall are many creeks to which belong divers boats continually employed in fishing, by which a quantity of uncustomed goods are conveyed aboard ships bound to foreign parts and from such as have returned home, and also succour and supply given to pirates, and many escapes of felons. Pray letters patent for 21 years, authorizing petitioners to take yearly from every owner and master of such boats a bond of 40l., to be forfeit upon every such unlawful act as aforesaid, with power to seize all uncustomed goods, and for petitioners to take such fees as the Attorney-

1637.

Vol. CCCLXXIV.

General shall think meet, petitioners paying 20*l*. yearly during their grant. [*Copy. See Vol. cccxxiii., p.* 219. 1 *p.*] *Underwritten,*

> I. *Reference to the Lord Treasurer and Lord Cottington, who, calling to them the Attorney-General, are to certify. Whitehall. 30th December* 1637. [*Copy. Ibid.* $\frac{1}{6}$ *p.*]

Dec. 30.
Whitehall.

Lords of the Admiralty to Montjoy Earl of Newport. Robert Clement, Edward Fenn, and others, owners of the Flemish-built ship Love, of London, of 150 tons, are to be permitted to furnish their ship with ordnance from the founder's store. [*Copy. Vol. cccliii., fol.* 77. $\frac{1}{2}$ *p.*]

Dec. 31.

Petition of Thomas Pott to the King. You granted petitioner a reference to the Lord Treasurer and Lord Cottington, respecting the office of collector of the silk weavers for two lives, in lieu of Kirby [Kirkby?] Park, co. Lincoln, which was sold for 1,000*l*. by Sir Humphrey May, Chancellor of the Duchy, in the 8th year of the reign, and the money paid into the Exchequer. Your Majesty having granted away the said collectorship to Mr. Rawlin, petitioner prays a grant of the forfeiture of a bond of Mark Brand in 1,000*l*. for payment of customs concerning the importation or exportation of goods of this kingdom since January last. [*Copy. See Vol. cccxxiii., p.* 220. $\frac{3}{4}$ *p.*] *Underwritten,*

> I. *His Majesty grants petitioner's desire, and the Attorney-General is to prepare a bill for signature. Whitehall,* 31*st December* 1637. [*Copy. Ibid., p.* 221. $\frac{1}{4}$ *p.*]

Dec. 31.
Whitehall.

63. The Council to Archbishop Laud. His Majesty and the board are informed of the fear of ruin of the church of Reculver, and that there is a difference depending before you, between the inhabitants of Reculver and those of the chapelries of St. Nicholas and Herne, who shall contribute to the repair. The said church and steeples are ancient sea marks, wherefore this case can admit no delay. His Majesty has commanded us to signify that you proceed with expedition, and give order therein. [1 *p.*]

Dec. 31.

64. Attested copy of the same. [*Does not agree with the original as to the signatures.* 1 *p.*]

Dec. 31.

65. Sir Thomas Delves, late Sheriff of co. Chester, to the Council. Presents an account of his particular ratings of the clergy, whom he charged rateably as he found them in the King's Books, but afterwards made deductions in various cases, the nature of which he explains. Every living is stated, with the name of the incumbent and the amount charged upon it. [$1\frac{1}{2}$ *p.*]

Dec. 31.
The Swiftsure in the Downs.

66. Sir John Pennington to the Lords of the Admiralty. The Dunkirkers have taken a small English hoy, wherein were 13 or 14 English horses, reported to belong to the Earl of Holland, and have carried her for Dunkirk. There was also one of the King of Spain's men of war cast away within the Splinter, riding under the fort,

Vol. CCCLXXIV.

1637.

and an English ship of Milbrook laden with wine. I cannot hear that any of our ships embargoed in France are yet released, only those at Bordeaux. Divers vessels are at Dover laden for Rouen and other ports, but they dare not send them away. [1 p.]

Dec. 31. 67. Appointment by Archbishop Laud, of Sir John Lambe, to gather up the tenths of the clergy in Lincoln diocese, and to pay them into the Exchequer. [½ p.]

Dec. 31. 68. Brief of the account of Sir William Russell for ship-money during the year ended this day, with his payments thereout. The charge against him amounted to 202,340l. 2s. 3d., and the payments to 196,266l. 6s. 5¾d., so that there appeared to be a balance of 6,073l. 15s. 9¼d. in the hands of the accountant. But there remained unpaid of the ship-money for 1635, 1,023l. 12s. 3d.; for 1636, 4,536l. 12s. 4d.; and for 1637, 6,907l. 6s. 4d.; total arrears 12,467l. 10s. 11d., which left a balance owing to the accountant of 6,393l. 15s. 1¾d. [2 pp.]

[Dec.] 69. Petition of the Company of Wine Coopers of London to the King. A petition has lately been exhibited to your Majesty by the Company of Vintners of London, desiring that the wine coopers might be restrained from buying and selling wines, upon a surmise that they have lately intruded into that trade. Petitioners show that they are a company consisting of many thousand poor men that are commanded upon all occasions to serve the King, and they have their freedom of the city by ancient custom, and have a long time used to buy and sell wine both by wholesale and by runlets. Pray that their ancient and accustomed freedom may not be taken away from them upon a bare surmise, but that they may be heard before the King or referred to the Council, and that in the meantime they may not be bound by an order stated to be annexed. [1 p.]

[Dec.] 70. Petition of Paul Micklethwaite, D.D., master of the Temple, to the same. In the Temple there are consecrated places which, upon the foundation of the church, being dedicated to the church, still belong thereunto, as the churchyard, cloisters, and others. By colour of the late King's grant of the manor of the Temple to the two societies there, some of the said consecrated places are withheld from the church. Long since there was usurpation of the same places by one Spenser, and by his attainder the manor with the usurped places came to the crown. By writ or commission from the crown, temp. Edward III., redress was then made. Prays that a similar course may again be adopted. [1 p.]

[Dec.] Copy of a portion of the preceding petition. [*See Vol. cccxxiii., p.* 278. ¼ p.]

[Dec.?] 71. Petition of William Pickering to the same. Petitioner being censured in the Star Chamber, to be imprisoned during the King's pleasure, to pay 10,000l. for a fine, and undergo corporal punishment, in Michaelmas term last the King gave order for his enlargement

Vol. CCCLXXIV.

1637.

and declared that he would remit his fine, and directed Sec. Windebank to signify the same. Prays for a privy seal to discharge the fine, and that the bond entered into for his appearance on the hearing may be delivered up. [½ p.]

[Dec.] 72. Petition of **Richard Clay**, goldsmith in Cheapside, to the King. On petition of Hester Rogers, widow, John Rogers, clerk, and petitioner Richard Clay, protection was granted to all the said persons for one year, which will expire 16th March next. The debt of 3,200l. due from the King to the said Hester (the nonpayment whereof gave occasion to the said protection) being still unpaid, petitioner prays for a renewal of the same for another year, to commence from the said 16th March. [1 p.]

[Dec. ?] 73. Petition of the **assessors and collectors of ship-money in St. Giles's-in-the-Fields, Middlesex**, to the Council. Petitioners made a rate in 1636 for levying 230l. ship-money, and have paid to the sheriff 200l. The persons named in the schedule annexed refuse payment, and have no distress, living out of Middlesex. Pray that they may be called before the Council. [⅔ p.] *Annexed,*

    73. I. *List of defaulters. Among them occur, Thomas Bendish, 13s. 4d.; Lady Carew, wife of Sir Edmund Carew, deceased, 4l. 10s.: Sir Edmund Lenthall, 2l.; John Child, one of the collectors, who will not come to account, 4l. 10s.* [1 p.]

Dec. 74. Petition of **Sarah Collins**, widow, to the Lords of the Admiralty. Her late husband kept Chilworth Mills. His Majesty having disposed of the same to make powder, upon clearing petitioner's house there were found nine barrels and a half of powder. Samuel Cordewell, having undertaken to make powder for his Majesty's use, petitioner prays the Lords to permit her to dispose of the said 9½ barrels. [½ p.]

Dec. 75. Petition of **William Portington**, lieutenant of the horse for Middlesex, to the Commissioners for Buildings. Upon an order for demolishing sheds in Long Acre, a tenement of petitioner's, fronting the street, was presented as a shed, and petitioner was warned to render reasons why it should not be demolished. A shed is a leaning to something to bear up the roof, whereas this roof bears itself, and at its first erecting as a tenement it was built for one, and has long continued without enlargement, and is inhabited by persons of good conversation, as appears by certificate annexed. Prays that it may still stand, or that petitioner may be permitted instead thereof to build a fair house, adding three feet of ground to the front. [1 p.] *Annexed,*

    75. I. *Certificate of inhabitants in and near Long Acre as to the nature of the premises above mentioned, which had been a house for 16 years past.* [1 p.]

VOL. CCCLXXIV.

1637.
[Dec. ?]

76. Petition of the Mayor and Aldermen of Colchester to the Council. Petitioners lately received a letter from the Lords, dated the 2nd inst., commanding petitioners to require all the owners and masters of ships belonging to their port, who have used to trade to Newcastle, forthwith to go to fetch coals for the supply of London, and to examine the practice of the masters and owners in forbearing to use their trade. We sent for the masters and owners, and found that in the last summer some of them made eight or nine voyages, and all those who have ships big enough still go, and those who have small vessels so soon as the summer comes on will go on with their calling. [1 p.]

Dec.

77. Charles Louis, Prince Palatine, to Sir Thomas Roe. I find by yours and Cave's letter, that my not going to the Hessen troops is much blamed in England, where I see they would have me in action, so it be without their expense. States a variety of reasons why it could not have been, one being that the Hessians "would not put themselves out of the possibility of receiving the Emperor's grace, by engaging in a new and (as Milandre told Horneck) very desperate cause, without an assistance which might enable them to continue the war." To have gone as a volunteer with that small army of 3 or 4,000 men would neither have been honourable nor profitable for me, for it is hardly able to subsist without an addition of strength, without which they will lose both Cassel and Ziegenhaim. I have again offered them to levy troops and join with them; if they refuse, it is a certain sign that they will content themselves with an uncertain peace. The Landgrave of Darmstadt is content to abandon all his pretensions for the damages he has received during the war, but with these conditions: 1. That Landgrave Maurice's sons of his second wife should confirm the agreement concerning Marburg: 2. Quit their troops: 3. Restore East Friesland; which conditions the government at Cassel have accepted *ad ratificandum*. Sir Thomas Ferentz will acquaint you more at large with these matters. There is no time lost yet, if they do not play the fools or the traitors in accepting a peace for their own private ends; and to go to an army where you are not sure of the officers' good intentions, without a competent strength, had been a hazard to no purpose. You shall see I will shun none where I may get honour, for rather than be idle this next year I will pawn everything I have to my shirt. Now I am in treaty for Meppen, where I may make my rendezvous; it is the Prince of Orange's advice; but speak not of it until it be in more forwardness. The States will not send to Hamburgh, until they hear that the plenipotentiaries of the other confederates are arrived there. I wonder what should make them so slack? Here they want no pressing. I wish nothing more than to have you sent to Hamburgh; I should think your being there ambassador would be as advantageous for my cause as a little army; especially since the Duke of Lunenburg has fallen out with Gotha, and I know that Duke William of Weimar would be glad of any opportunity to return to the good party. I pray let the archbishop know this, by

Vol. CCCLXXIV.

1637.

which he may see how necessary it were the King should send a well affectioned man ambassador to Hamburgh. If that cannot be obtained, I shall beseech the King to give you leave to come over to stay with me for a while, the Queen shall do the same, if it be not inconvenient to you, or hindrance to your fortune in England. P.S.—I congratulate the augmentation of your family. Concerning my private business, let me know directly what to do, and I will do it speedily. As I had finished this letter, Horneck returns from Milandre, who shows all willingness to join with me, so that that conjunction must be taken in England for granted, and I make it so to the King. But really it is yet *in longis terminis*, for before we meet about the conditions much time will be lost. [¼ pp.]

Dec. 78. Sir Thomas Walsingham to [Michael Oldisworth, Secretary to the Earl of Pembroke and Montgomery, Lord Lieutenant of Kent]. The bearer, Mr. Sherman, being returned a defaulter for arms in Sir William Barne's company in Kent, I find that his father left him houses in Greenwich, which are let out to others, who ought to stand charged with arms, and not himself, for that he dwells in Middlesex. I could do no less but signify so much unto you, desiring that he may not be troubled by any messenger in this case. *Underwritten,*

> 78. I. M[ichael] Oldisworth to [Sir Thomas Walsingham]. *My Lord formerly commanded me to state to Sir William Becher, that where a deputy-lieutenant shall signify that the party complained against has conformed, his Lordship is well satisfied.* [1 p.]

Dec. 79. Certificate of seven prisoners in the Marshalsea that Alexander Hamilton committed for murder or suspicion thereof had such favour of the Marshal, Bartholomew Hall, that he usually walked abroad at his pleasure with his keeper, when poor debtors that were confined only for their fees could not have a keeper for one day to procure their enlargement by the space of five months. Sometimes Hamilton went out with the Marshal's wife, and sometimes with the Marshal and his wife, to make merry, and sometimes he left his keeper when abroad and came home to the prison alone. At the time of his escape he with his keeper attempted to pass through the lodge as formerly, but the turnkey denied him passage, whereupon Hamilton, with his keeper, went to Mrs. Hall's door that opens into the prison, and there they were let out through Hall's house, and never came more into the prison. [1 p.]

Dec. 80. Memorandum that Arthur Cundall has within four or five years erected divers sheds in Palace Yard, Westminster, near Parliament Stairs, upon new foundations, which are now become dwelling houses, and has continued them notwithstanding orders for demolishing them, and a warrant to the sheriffs of London and Middlesex last year to the same purpose. [½ p.]

DOMESTIC—CHARLES I.

VOL. CCCLXXV. UNDATED 1637.

[1637 ?]

1. Observations by Secretary Coke on the Statutes or Articles of Eltham, for the regulation of the King's household, and how far they affected various suggested alterations proposed to be made at this time. [4½ pp.]

2. Orders under the King's hand for the establishment of government in the Court, collected out of the ancient ordinances of the King's House, and commanded to be duly observed. [*Copy.* 16½ pp.]

3. Observations of the Avenor upon the Articles of Eltham so far as they relate to the management of the royal stables. [2 pp.]

4. Copy orders established for regulation of the Office of the Robes, with suggestion of [Sir Bevis Thelwall], Clerk of the Robes, that in conformity with the same orders all bills upon the office should be checked by himself as clerk, as well as by Mr. Kirke, the Gentleman of the Robes. [1 p.]

5. Another copy of the orders established for regulation of the Office of the Robes, with comments of [Sir Bevis Thelwall] on the results of the breach of the rule that his signature should be required to tradesmen's bills as well as that of the Gentleman of the Robes. [*Copy.* 2 pp.]

6. Report of a Commission appointed to inquire concerning the observance of the orders established for regulation of the Office of the Wardrobes and Robes, stating the nature of the question in dispute, as to the signature of the clerk, and the explanations in reference to the same given by the clerk which had been satisfactory to Mr. Kirke. [3¼ pp.]

7. Information of Sir Bevis Thelwall, Clerk of the Great Wardrobe, in reference to certain breaches of his Majesty's orders for regulation of that office, and the misconduct of two of the officers named Thomas Ripplingham and [William ?] Ripplingham. [¾ p.]

8. Petition of Robert Tias to the King. His grandfather and father lived in the office of clerk and under-clerk of the Great Wardrobe, during the reigns of Queens Mary, Elizabeth, and 18 years of King James I., and petitioner has been educated therein. Thomas Ripplingham being dead, who was in reversion after Sir Bevis Thelwall, now Clerk of the Great Wardrobe, petitioner prays a grant to succeed Sir Bevis. [½ p.]

9. The Avenor's reasons for not swearing to the parcel for the expense of the stable. The compositions are received and issued by the purveyors and garnitors, who are, therefore, the fittest men to swear to the parcel. [½ p.]

10. List of carriages attending the King and Queen upon removals. [*Endorsed, "Carts are now used." Among the persons provided for on the Queen's side are her Majesty's dwarfs, her monkeys and dogs, and "the billiard board." 3 pp.*]

[1637?]

Vol. CCCLXXV.

11. Number and description of servants appointed to attend on Prince Charles and the Princess Mary below stairs, with their wages and diet. [¾ p.]

12. Petition of four grooms of the Queen's Chamber to Sec. Windebank. Were behind of their wages one half-year, due six years since, amounting to 73*l.*, for which her Majesty lately sent Sir Thomas Stafford to the Commissioners of the Treasury. Petitioners have no other allowance but this fee of 2*s.* a day; the gentlemen-ushers and others having two or three fees apiece, were lately paid all due to them. [⅔ p.]

13. Minute of warrant for Francis Phillips, Auditor for Northampton, Rutland, and other counties, to be received and lodged as he travels up and down on his Majesty's service. [⅓ p.]

14. Account of fees paid for Lord Carnarvon on his creation as Viscount and Earl. [¾ p.]

15. Petition of John Gaspar Wolffen, his Majesty's servant, to the King. When Mr. Burlamachi made up his accounts, by an error he took 270*l.* of petitioner's moneys, and gave it to his Majesty in his accounts. On complaint to the Council, the business was referred to four Aldermen, who found that the 270*l.* was to be allowed by the King to Mr. Burlamachi or else paid to petitioner. Urgently prays payment. [1 p.]

16. Declaration [by Philip Burlamachi?] of the state of the business concerning the King's jewels pledged in Holland. Job Harby having been met in his endeavour to settle the accounts and redeem the jewels by unanticipated demands on the part of Philip Calandrini, at variance with his accounts previously rendered, an appeal had been made to the Courts of Law in Holland. Burlamachi insists that without litigation all the difficulties would be cleared up by the production of the original contracts. [*French.* 3¼ pp.]

17. Information of some person whose name is not stated, probably addressed to Sec. Coke, respecting the abuse of transportation of gold and coin by aliens from several ports, masters and owners of ships called "skippers." These persons omit to account in the customer's books for goods brought in by them, and transport great store of coin received from merchants, to be delivered to their factors in foreign parts. Prays him to signify the same to his Majesty. [½ p.]

18. Petition of Jacob de Leau, factor, to the King. Petitioner is questioned for transporting money into France. He only, according to his commission, consigned the same to John Parrett of Dover, merchant, who, without his privity, transported the same to Michael Huse, factor, at Calais. Petitioner received no more profit by the same money, but only his accustomed salary of 6*s.* 8*d.* per cent. Prays that he may be clearly acquitted. [1 p.]

VOL. CCCLXXV.

[1637?]

19. Petition of "the most distressed Charles Lord Stanhope" to Archbishop Laud. His father left him estated in the office of Postmaster General of England, and gave him the less estate during his mother's life. Having surrendered his patent, his means are so small and his debts so great that he cannot live in quiet for the outcry of his creditors, and his mother during her life keeps three parts of his estate from him, and will part with nothing to relieve him. Petitioning the King, he was appointed to apply to the Secretaries of State. Sec. Coke answers him that the King long since said that his mother had money enough. Prays the archbishop to speak to Secs. Coke and Windebank, to present his petition to his Majesty, that he may receive the arrears of his fees, to enable him to free himself from the clamours of his creditors. [½ p.]

20. Observations by Sec. Windebank for recalling the patent formerly granted to Mr. Witherings to be Postmaster for foreign parts. The principal grounds assigned are;—the inconvenience of suffering such an office to remain in the hands of a person who is no sworn officer. Suspicion that his patent was surreptitiously obtained. No signed bill was found. Persons who hold the office of postmaster abroad are of so great quality that they disdain to correspond with a man of his mean condition. Some satisfaction may be given him, but he has very much enriched himself upon the place. He is said to be worth 800*l.* a year in land. The office of Postmaster General being now vested in the Secretaries, the carrying of letters is a business of state. If Witherings shall insist upon his patent, his Majesty may sequester the place into the hands of the Secretaries. [2¼ pp.]

21. Petition of Thomas Cole to Secs. Coke and Windebank. John Lord Stanhope, being Master and Comptroller General of the Posts, appointed Thomas Clarke, and petitioner after his death, to be post of London for the packet; viz., from London to Waltham northwards and to Dartford southwards. In November last Clarke was suspended and has since died. Prays appointment according to the grant of Lord Stanhope. [⅔ p.]

22. Duplicate of the same. [⅔ p.]

23. Printed bill, which announces that the Count de la Tour and Tassis, General Hereditary of the Post of the Emperor and of the King of Spain in his Low Countries, Burgundy, &c., undertakes not only to perform the agreement made between the said Count and Thomas Witherings and William Frizell in 1633, but to improve it by expediting the mail in sundry particulars which involved a reduction in the time for conveying the letters to and from London and Antwerp and Brussels from 4 or 5 days to 2 or 3, and to and from Naples to 18 and 19 days instead of 23 and 24, with a proportionate reduction in all intermediate places. [2½ pp.]

24. Petition of John Wytton, Deputy Postmaster of the Court, daily attending your Majesty, to the King. For his wages of 10s.

[1637 ?]

Vol. CCCLXXV.

per diem there is due to him about 1,400*l*., neither has he allowance of diet or horsemeat or any other perquisites, the nonpayment whereof has brought him much into debt. Some of his creditors have petitioned the Lord Chamberlain to have the benefit of the law against him. He has granted the request unless petitioner give satisfaction by the middle of Michaelmas term. Prays that the Lord Treasurer may make present payment of what is due to petitioner, and meanwhile that he may have a protection, [1 *p.*]

25. Certificate of Richard Wakeman. There was a petition, subscribed the 19th June last, at the request of Mr. Witherings, Postmaster, desiring his Majesty to continue him in the execution of that place. We were abused by his pretending that some great persons intended to obtain the office of his Majesty, to the prejudice of merchants and trade. Although we are not aggrieved by Mr. Witherings in the dispatch of letters for foreign parts, or in their postage, yet we believe the office of Postmaster being under the supervision of the Secretaries of State the merchants shall have no cause to complain, but rather receive favour by the speedy conveyance of their letters. [*The paper runs in the plural number, but has only one signature.* ⅔ *p.*]

26. Petition of John Castlon, Postmaster, to Sec. Windebank. John Bulwer has lately petitioned for leave to sue petitioner for 10*l*. 10*s*. which he pretends to be due. Petitioner can make it appear by an acquittance under Bulwer's hand for 3*l*. 10*s*., and otherwise, that there cannot be above one quarter's rent due to Bulwer, viz., Midsummer quarter 1637, and that petitioner ought not to pay that in respect of agreements unfulfilled by Bulwer. [⅔ *p.*]

27. Petition of David Francis, late Post of Northop, to Secs. Coke and Windebank. There is 90*l*. in arrear to petitioner for execution of the said place, as appears by the last account of Lord Stanhope to the auditors. Has been three months in town soliciting payment, and received fair promises from Mr. Witherings, but now he absolutely says petitioner shall have none, so that he is like to be imprisoned. Has spent near his whole estate in coming to town to solicit for his father's arrears, who was Post of Chester 60 years. Prays order to receive part with the rest who are in the privy seal, otherwise he is like to perish by the prosecution of his greedy creditors. [⅔ *p.*]

28. Petition of Richard Scott, innkeeper of Stilton, co. Huntingdon, to Secs. Coke and Windebank. For some few years past the place of Post of Stilton, being in the high north road, has been executed by a deputy, who keeps an alehouse there, the Postmaster living twelve miles distant, and his deputy no ways able to receive gentlemen and travellers, much less noblemen, whereby the posts are forced to travel at unseasonable times and are not fitted with able horses. Petitioner being an innkeeper in the town, both able and willing to give noblemen and gentlemen entertainment, prays that he may serve his Majesty in that place. [1 *p.*]

[1637?]

Vol. CCCLXXV.

29. Petition of Thomas Parks, Postmaster from London to Barnet, to Sec. Windebank. Has executed that office about six years, which has stood him in 180*l.*, without any neglect, as Mr. Railton can inform you, and has received but two years' pay at the rate of 20*d.* per diem. Notwithstanding his diligence, Mr. Witherings endeavours to bring in another, and has already taken from petitioner the through posts' place of Charing Cross, which cost petitioner 63*l.* 6*s.* Prays order to Witherings to deliver petitioner his orders and confirm him in his place. [1 *p.*]

30. Petition of Anthony Penniston to the King. Francis Ewens was indebted to petitioner 600*l.*, and held a lease of Herriotts, co. Radnor. Petitioner being indebted to your Majesty extended the lease and had it assigned to him. Living in London, petitioner appointed one Phillips to receive the profits and pay your Majesty's rent, and afterwards assigned the lease to Mr. Joyner, but Phillips having made some default, one Wynne procured a new lease. Prays reference to the Commissioners of the King's revenue as Prince of Wales to vacate the new lease. [¾ *p.*]

31. Petition of Sir Basil Brooke to the same. The 5,000*l.* which his Majesty had accepted in satisfaction of damages done by petitioner in the Forest of Dean had been paid more than half a year. Sir John Wintour, hoping to procure a like defalcation, had used means to stay the pardon granted to petitioner, though it had received the King's signature nine months since, and Mr. Mynne's pardon had been long since sealed and delivered to him. Petitioner has yielded up his patent, and delivered possession of the iron works. Has been at great charge by his long attendance in these infectious times. Prays that his pardon may be speedily sealed. [1 *p.*]

32. Petition of the same to the same. Petitioner paid 5,000*l.* for the fine laid upon him jointly with Mr. Mynne. Mr. Mynne, having paid 7,000*l.*, presses petitioner, upon point of partnership, to pay him 1,000*l.* and 332*l.* 16*s.* interest, and upon that pretence has seized upon 2,000*l.* partible between them, by reason of the wire works which they hold in partnership. As his Majesty best knows upon what grounds their pardons were granted, petitioner prays him to declare his pleasure concerning the money paid by them severally. [1 *p.*]

33. Proposition for taking a new farm of Dean Forest upon terms more advantageous to the King. [*It is the proposition (slightly varied) of John Broughton, already calendared in Vol. ccclxi., No.* 48 I. 1 *p.*]

34. Sir Baynham Throgmorton to Endymion Porter. I am bold to present you an account what I did with my Lord Chamberlain. When I had informed him of the abuse committed by the farmers of the iron works in the Forest of Dean, he told me he would by no means countenance them in any dishonest thing, but else, because they chose him for their protector, and for his brother's sake that made them the grant, he should be willing to do them all courtesy.

Vol. CCCLXXV.

[1637?]

I perceive he is willing things may be examined, and as they prove against them, which I am sure will be foul, he would not meddle with it. My occasions hasten me into the country. I desire you will be a friend to us in this business, which being neglected our poor forest is ruined. The bearer, Mr. Bainbridge, is able to inform you of all particulars. [1 p.]

35. Petition of John Williams, prisoner in Newgate, to the Council. Has remained in prison for five years for being one at the depopulation of the Forest of Dean. Prays enlargement, not having wherewith to maintain himself in prison, with his wife and poor children. [⅔ p.]

36. Petition of Henry Earl of Huntingdon to the King. Was Lieutenant of your Majesty's late Forest of Leicester for life by gift of King James, which forest, about ten years since, was disafforested. Your Majesty thought petitioner worthy of recompense, whereupon he was to have received 400 acres out of the forest, but before the Earl of Marlborough, then Lord Treasurer, and the other referees, made their certificate, the ground was disposed of. Subsequently, at the suit of your subject's late wife, he was to have been recompensed by the lands of Sir Miles Hobart, deceased, if the same should fall to your Majesty, as they did, yet your Majesty was pleased to dispose of the same otherwise. Sir William Faunt was sentenced in the Star Chamber, on 19th October last, at petitioner's suit, for writing a libellous letter, whereby your service was much prejudiced, for which he was fined 5,000*l*. Prays a grant of the said fine in recompense for the said office. [⅔ p.] *Annexed*,

> 36. I. *Statement of the profits of Lieutenant of the Forest of Leicester. Total, per annum, 336l. 9s. 1d. Besides which there were claims for compensation on a variety of other grounds which are here fully stated.* [¾ p.]

37. Petition of George Johnson, late woollen draper to his Majesty, to the King. Your Majesty granted petitioner a privy seal for 4,853*l*. 17*s*. 1*d*. for cloth by him sold, and caused payment of 2,000*l*. in part of the same, so that there remains 2,853*l*. 17*s*. 1*d*., for want of which he was enforced to take up large sums on interest, and since to give over his trade, and become keeper in Brogborough Park in the honour of Ampthill. Having disbursed more than the principal for interest, he shall by this means be certainly ruined, and his friends who are his sureties. Prays order for a tally upon the receiver of the iron-works of the Forest of Dean due at Christmas 1638, or upon the new increase of wines to be paid by Sir Abraham Dawes at Michaelmas 1638 for the remainder of the said debt. [1 p.]

38. Petition of George Lord Chandos, your Majesty's ward, to the same. Upon your Majesty's late inclosure of the Forest of Braydon in Wilts, the lords of manors adjoining improved their waste grounds. Petitioner having the manor of Minety, with 1,200 acres

[1637?]

VOL. CCCLXXV.

of waste, his late guardian, Alice Countess Dowager of Derby, and his present guardian, Henry Earl of Manchester, have endeavoured to improve the same, but found the greatest obstacle, that the manor being held in capite, petitioner's tenants refuse to consent unless he can procure ground allotted to them to be holden in socage. Prays order for alteration of the tenure of the said allotments, and reference to Lord Cottington, Master of the Wards, and the Attorney-General. [1 p.]

39. Petition of Endymion Porter, your Majesty's servant, to the King. The forest of Exmoor, in Devon and Somerset, is in lease from your Majesty for divers years to come, under yearly rents amounting to 48l. 13s. 4d. Prays a grant of the same in fee farm, in consideration of his long service, with a tenure in socage, and the liberty of disafforestation. [$\frac{2}{3}$ p.]

40. Petition of Thomas Jerves to Sec. Windebank. King's Sedgmoor in Somerset has been proved to be the King's inheritance, wherefore King James resolved to make it a leading case, but now of necessity it must be a redeeming case, and not be sold from the crown, if there might be a million given for it. Petitioner's request is, that for the love that he bears to the general good, he may have warrant to go down amongst the inhabitants in 26 manors near adjoining, that they may give their advice which way it may be advanced to his Majesty's profit and the general good. Petitioner doubts not to bring such an answer as will be very pleasing to his Majesty and all his subjects. [$\frac{1}{2}$ p.]

41. Offer made by Thomas Lord Arundel of Wardour to sell Wardour to the King. Will accept for it some reversion or office or annual pension, with the rangership for his life. His son Thomas desires not to have it; it is too great a house for his son William, and he must leave it for payment of debts and raising portions for younger children. His Majesty has about Salisbury great command of fallow deer in Clarington [Clarendon] Park, in Cranborne Chase, and in Grovely, yet has he no park of red-deer, nor any house of his own fit to entertain his Majesty or the Queen. [1 p.]

42. Petition of inhabitants of Bolingbroke, co. Lincoln, consisting of 19 townships, being free commoners in that part of Wildmore called the Earl's Fen, to the King. For approving their said common, petitioners have made and repaired two great drains, which cost them 2,500l., whereby the fen for all the summer season is laid usefully dry, but of late, by defects in the banks of the Witham and Hildick, which ought to be repaired by others, and by water coming from the East Fen, which is to be drained another way, the waters of the said rivers and fen have overflown some part of the said common, whereupon the undertakers for draining in this extreme wet winter time have procured commissioners being strangers to adjudge 600 acres of dry ground, and as many acres that are not five months in a year at all wet, to be surrounded.

VOL. CCCLXXV.

[1637?]

Pray that the noisome waters may be kept from surrounding petitioners' common, and that in the meantime the King will withhold his assent from taking away petitioners' common until fully informed of the truth. [¾ p.] *Underwritten,*

42. I. *Minute of answer that the King's intention was only for the improvement of wet grounds usually and hurtfully surrounded, and the Earls of Lindsey and Dorset were to certify. [Endorsed: "Earl of Stamford." ¼ p.]*

43. The King to certain persons to be therein named and appointed Commissioners of Sewers for a level in co. Lincoln. Recites letters of 15 March 1636–7, whereby directions were given to the then Commissioners of Sewers for that level concerning 1,000 acres intended for the poor, and 1,500 acres to be tied for the maintenance of the works, as also for draining the level. The King, intending that the directions in those letters should be pursued, appoints the persons now addressed Commissioners of Sewers for that level, and commands them to carry out the former letters in a way which is here set forth; and that, with reference to a complaint of the inhabitants of Bolingbroke, they were to certify the King, that he might give direction therein as should be just. [*Draft.* 2½ pp.] *Underwritten,*

43. I. *Robert Long to Mr. Peacock. This is the letter which I have drawn, and think fit to be presented by Mr. Kirke to to Sec. Windebank, for his Majesty's signature. [½ p.]*

44. The King to [persons to be named]. For a great sum of money paid by Sir Peregrine Bertie and Sir Philip Landen, deceased, we, in August 1636, granted them divers marshes in cos. Lincoln and Cambridge, which they were to embank, and to answer a fee-farm rent for the same. As yet, little benefit has been reaped from our grant, by reason of the opposition of persons who pretend interest in the said marshes. Desiring to avoid unnecessary suits, we require you to compose the said differences as you shall think fit. And we give you leave to signify that, as we shall take it to be an acceptable service from such as shall comply in performance of a work tending so much to our honour and the good of the realm, so we shall show our displeasure and use our power against such as shall refuse to accept our grace and favour herein. [*Draft or copy.* 1 p.]

45. Certain citizens of London to the King. There are 10,000 or 12,000 acres of fen lying in the Great Level in the Isle of Ely belonging to the King. Offer 16,000*l.* for the same. [⅓ p.]

46. Report of Joseph Butler and Jasper Heiley, messengers of the Chamber, employed by warrant of Sec. Windebank into the Great Level of the Fens, to apprehend persons found disturbing the works of draining. Near Wicken, co. Cambridge, they met Peter Jarvis, constable. He persuaded them not to adventure into Wicken, the people being prepared to resist, and those of Soame [Soham?], Burrack, and Sopham having agreed to help them. Ultimately, the

VOL. CCCLXXV.

[1637?]

messengers, with the constable and the minister of the parish, entered the town, the messengers being on horseback. The people came out with pitchforks and poles, and gathered round a place where great heaps of stones were laid. Amongst them, John Moreclack, a principal rioter, was charged to obey the Council's warrant. When the messengers approached him, he pushed at them with his pike. The people prepared to assist him, and the women got together to the heaps of stones to throw at the messengers, who were scoffed at and abused by the whole multitude. [1½ p.]

47. Paper endorsed "Answer to the Earl of Lincoln's petition." The question in dispute between the Earl and the answerers was the sufficiency of certain drainage of fens in Lincolnshire. The petitioners state their case in reply to the Earl, and give the names in the margin of persons who will prove their assertions. Much of the damage complained of by the Earl was set down to the peculiar wetness of the season, and other parts of it to the violent interruptions of the people, who threw down the banks and dammed up the works. [6¾ pp.]

48. Petition of John Liens to the King. In 1635, petitioner, being director of the work of draining Hatfield Chase, the adventurers made an agreement with the inhabitants of Sykehouse and Fishlake for damages sustained before petitioner was director, for payment of a great sum, which is all paid but 600l., and petitioner was induced to set his hand to the said agreement. The inhabitants now fall upon petitioner for the 600l. Petitioner is employed in draining the Eight Hundred Fen for your Majesty's service, under the Earl of Lindsey. Prays a protection for one year. [⅔ p.]

49. Petition of Henry Earl of Dover to the Council. States the circumstances under which a decree had lately been made against petitioner by the Commissioners of Sewers for some part of Yorkshire, for raising a mill-dam upon the river Don, about 20 years before, in the lordship of Conisborough, to the prejudice of the town of Mexborough. Petitioner prayed a reference to the judges, or the determination of the case by the Council. [*This petition was probably presented in May* 1637. *Subsequent proceedings in reference to the same subject are calendared in Vol. ccclv., No.* 166; *Vol. ccclvi., No.* 158; *and Vol. ccclvii., No.* 61. 1 p.]

50. Minute of an information that the miller of the King's fee-farm mills at Purfleet at every spring tide lets in so much water as drowns the meadow ground adjoining; also that the owners of the meadows, not keeping their ditches scoured, the water has not its free return. An order of the Board is desired for stinting the miller to the marks on two posts set up for that purpose, and enjoining the owners of the meadows to see to the scouring of their ditches. [⅔ p.]

51. Petition of Capt. Francis Wrenham to the King. Prays the King, by himself or his Council, to be informed in the equity of

Vol. CCCLXXV.

[1637?]

petitioner's cause, and in the interim to direct that no grant may pass of petitioner's 500 acres in Sutton Marsh. [½ p.] *Annexed,*

51. I. *Particulars of his case above alluded to. In 1630 he purchased 500 acres of Sutton Marsh. For recovery thereof, he was cast upon a suit which cost him 1,000l. Obtaining a decree from the Lord Keeper in July 1634, he was, for settling the land, ordered to pay 800l. above the purchase money. Being thus in possession under a royal grant, his first year's crop was swept away for an arrear of rent for 18 years under a grant of the late King; he had poor crops the two subsequent years; and now a claim had been set up to the land itself, under another grant from the Crown to the inhabitants of the Marsh, said to have been surreptitiously obtained by the contrivance of William Tipper, and by an arrangement with Mr. Wimberley,* [*Imperfect.* 1 p.]

52. The King to Attorney-General Bankes. Captain Thomas Whitmore has repaired our decayed copper mines in Cumberland, and Thomas Bushell has the sole working of our mines in co. Cardigan. They have found out a way to prepare ores holding silver so as by water they can separate the silver without melting. You are to prepare a grant to them of their invention for the term by statute limited, reserving the tenth part of the silver to be gained, and thereby also to constitute them Surveyors-General of all mines royal within England and Wales during the said term, with the fee of four nobles yearly, authorizing them to search for metals in any grounds within England and Wales, to the end that the silver therein may be separated according to their invention. [*Draft, probably of a suggested grant.* ⅔ p.]

53. Offer to discover concealed lands in co. Warwick belonging to the Prince, provided the proposer may have a lease of the same for 21 years. [*Endorsed by Nicholas, "Mr. Ashbourneham for Sir Charles Herbert."* ⅔ p.]

54. Articles to be inquired of within the archdeaconry of Buckingham, at the visitation of the archdeacon there this present year 1637. The articles are 53 in number, and run into a variety of minute particulars. Appended is the tenor of the oath to be ministered to churchwardens and sworn men. [*Printed at London, by T. P.,* 1637, 4to. 8 pp.]

55. The King to the [Bailiffs and Burgesses of Shrewsbury]. The parish church of [St.] Chad's, in Shrewsbury, being sometime a college of priests, and devolved to the Crown, the cure thereof ought to be served by two stipendiary curates, who receive their wages out of our Exchequer; but you, having possessed yourselves of the Easter book of that church, and some other things conveyed to you in trust, have appointed your curate to be preacher; and the late curate and preacher being preferred to a living, Richard Poole, clerk,

[1637 ?] Vol. CCCLXXV.

by colour of a popular election, has thrust himself into that place, having already two benefices in another diocese. By the advice of the Archbishop of Canterbury we have made choice of George Lawson, clerk, late curate of Mainstone, in the diocese of Hereford, to be curate and preacher of that church, and have directed the Bishop of Lichfield and Coventry to remove Richard Poole, and to admit and licence George Lawson; and we command you to yield ready obedience thereto. [2¾ pp.]

56. Account of the revenues settled on the church of St. Chad's, in Shrewsbury, the clear total being 65l. 16s. 8d.; also of the vicarage of Chirbury, anciently endowed but with 9l. 6s. 8d. per annum; but the rectory being vested in the bailiffs and burgesses of Shrewsbury, in trust for the free-school there, it was agreed that 50l. per annum should be settled on the vicarage, whereupon the said vicarage was endowed with the tithes of a township of that amount. [¾ p.]

57. Award of Archbishop Laud in a dispute between the Bishop of Hereford and the dean and chapter there, as to whether the bishop, having a right to visit the cathedral of Hereford and the peculiars of the said dean and chapter, the same right could be exercised by his vicar-general, registrar, and other officers, and how long the said visitation, when it should happen, should last. The archbishop determined the right in favour of the vicar-general and registrar, but limited the duration of such visitation to three months. [*Rough draft. Lat. 3 pp.*]

58. Judgment of Bishop White, of Ely, and other judges delegates, in a cause of appeal between Robert Viscount Kilmorey and Sir John Corbet, patron of the parish church of Adderley in Salop, and Edward Wolley, rector of the same church, respecting the rights of the chapel of the Holy Trinity at Shavington. The judges quashed the decision of the court below, and declared it lawful to perform divine service and administer sacraments in the chapel in question, the same being the private chapel or oratory of Viscount Kilmorey and other inhabitants of the house of Shavington. [*Latin. Not fully signed. One skin of parchment.*]

59. Opinion of Dr. Thomas Rives, the King's Advocate, concerning his Majesty's title to the prebend of Wetwang, co. York, for so much as concerns the union of it to the deanery of Christ's Church, in Oxford. It had been contended that the union was not good, inasmuch as the deanery was not a separate body, but only part of the aggregate body of dean and chapter. Dr. Rives was of opinion that by the Canon Law it sufficed if the thing to which the union was made was a benefice, which he contended the deanery was. [1⅔ p.]
Annexed,
    59. I. *Statement of the case for the prebend of Wetwang, showing by what acts the union above mentioned had been effected.* [1 p.]

Vol. CCCLXXV.

[1637?]

60. The Dean and Chapter of Canterbury to Archbishop Laud. Copy of a letter, the original of which is dated "April 1637," and is already calendared in Vol. cccliv., No. 175. [2 pp.]

61. Case, and opinion thereon, of Sir Edward Littleton, Solicitor-General, on the title to the prebend of Sutton-*cum*-Buckingham, [in the cathedral of Lincoln,] which was stated to have been surrendered to the Crown by the holder thereof in the time of Edward VI., and to have been granted out to a person designated as A. The Solicitor-General was of opinion that, if the prebend were presentative, A had no good title under his grant, and that the Crown might now present. [*Copy.* 2 pp.]

62. Another copy of the same. [2 pp.]

63. Notes on the text, "per me reges regnant," perhaps compiled with a view to a sermon. There are references to other texts of Scripture, to St. Augustine, Bellarmine, Bishops Andrewes, Buckeridge, and others. [3⅔ pp.]

64. Notes by Archbishop Laud, in the nature of a catalogue of papers entitled the "Second Bundle of Papers," consisting of 12 articles. They consisted of documents relating to religious matters in the reigns of Queen Elizabeth and James I. Endorsed by Sir Joseph Williamson, "King's power in the Church—new Discipline." [1½ p.]

65. Note of an order of the King in Council, that orders of 29th March and 30th May 1637 should be vacated, and that all rates made by the bailiffs and others of a town not named, by virtue thereof should be void, and that the nomination of the stipendiary ministers to certain parishes not named should remain as before the said orders were made. [⅓ p.]

66. Information or remembrance to the King, touching his Majesty's right to the impropriate rectory and right of presentation to the vicarage of Croston, co. Lancaster. The vicarage had been endowed above 200 years ago by the abbess of Sion. At the suppression it came to the Crown. A lease was granted for 99 years in the 30th Henry VIII., which is now nearly out. [⅔ p.]

67. Statement entitled "the estate of the vicarage of Berwick-upon-Tweed." The Dean and Chapter of Durham, being owners of the impropriate rectory, have let the same to laymen, and paid the vicar incumbent 20*l.* per annum. In the time of Elizabeth, the garrison being strengthened, the inhabitants subscribed for maintaining two able ministers. On the accession of King James he granted a pension of 20*l.* to each of the ministers, and of late both these pensions are conferred on the vicar, and are all his maintenance, except the payment from the dean and chapter; and the other minister is lately provided by the charity of the Mercers of London with 50*l.* yearly. It is suggested that royal letters should be pro-

[1637?] Vol. CCCLXXV.

cured to the Bishop and Dean and Chapter of Durham, requiring that the vicar be admitted tenant to the dean and chapter of the impropriate rectory, in place of the now tenants, William Rosden and John Saltonstall, paying the same yearly rent, and Rosden and Saltonstall being recompensed by the Commissioners for disposing of moneys given *in pios uses*. [2⅓ pp.] *Underwritten,*

> 67. I. [*Some one unnamed to Sec. Windebank?*] *Recommends that the Archbishop of York should be advised with, who would prove a great furtherer towards his Majesty and the Archbishop of Canterbury, and also with the dean and divers of the prebends of Durham.* [¼ p.]

68. Sir James Douglas to [Robert] Reed. His Majesty has considered that whereas the lecturer of Berwick has 60*l*. per annum, the vicar, Gilbert Durie, has only in stipend 20 marks, his other helps being only benevolence, whereof his Majesty pays 40*l*., which the vicar is willing to relinquish if the dean and chapter will receive him as tenant in place of William Rosden and John Saltonstall, as also the vicar will repay William Rosden the 400*l*. he disbursed. As for Saltonstall, he came unjustly by his lease, and has made yearly more profit by it than it cost him. [*Incomplete.* ⅔ p.]

69. Petition of Peter Walter, John Crispe, and Ralph [?] Masterman, styling themselves the four old vicars [of Lincoln], probably addressed to the ecclesiastical visitors on the suspension of Bishop Williams, setting forth various grievances and oppressions, chiefly in money payments, at the hands of the residentiaries of the cathedral. [1 p.]

70. Petition of Paul Hood, D.D., to the King. In the schedules annexed are expressed the great wrongs which Bishop Williams of Lincoln and Hamlet Marshall, D.D., have done to petitioner. Prays a reference for examination and redress. [⅓ p.] *Annexed,*

> 70. I. *Schedule of the injuries done to petitioner. Dr. Hood having the prebend of Kilsby, in the cathedral of Lincoln, and Hamlet Marshall, the chaunter [precentor], having the prebend of South Scarle, Marshall claimed Kilsby as annexed to his chauntership. The bishop arbitrated between them, and awarded in favour of Marshall upon certain terms, one of which was that he should resign the prebend of South Scarle to Hood. Hood had given up Kilsby, but could not obtain South Scarle.* [= 2 pp.]

71. Minute of his Majesty's desire that Sec. Windebank should put him in mind of recommending Sir John Monson to the Lords and Judges, that in the Bishop of Lincoln's cause they may give him a repair in reputation proportionable to the injuries he has suffered through the bishop's means for doing his Majesty's service. [⅓ p.]

VOL. CCCLXXV.

[1637?]

72. Minute of an application to be made to his Majesty. William Parkinson and others, having become very poor men through the Bishop of Lincoln's molesting them with a suit in the Star Chamber, because they would not forswear themselves against his Majesty, his Majesty promised them 100*l*. out of the bishop's fine. Thomas Lund, Cadwalader Powell, and George Walker, three others that were fined together with the bishop, have since done very good service to his Majesty in revealing several foul misdemeanours committed by the bishop, and discovering the conveyances of his estate, and are to do further service therein, it is suggested that his Majesty should remit to Lund, Powell, and Walker their fines, they paying Parkinson and others the 100*l*. [1½ *p*.]

73. Petition of the Dean and Chapter of York to the King. The King, for preservation of the solemnity of divine service in some of his cathedral churches, and for the good of the inhabitants of those cities, has required the mayors, aldermen, and their companies to frequent those holy places on Sundays and holy days with all due reverence, and that the mayors should not use the ensigns of their authority within his Majesty's cathedral churches. Pray the King to cast a similar gracious eye upon the cathedral church of York. [*Endorsed by Sec. Coke, "Doctor Stanhope;" and see Calendar notice of Vol. ccclxiii., No. 9.* ⅔ *p*.]

74. Theological treatise upon vows stated in the endorsement to have been propounded by Mr. White, of Dorchester, and to have been answered by Mr. Ironside, a minister. The only answer that here appears consists of two notes on the first page. [6¼ *pp*.]

75. Comments upon a book termed "The Direction." The author of it moves the writer's passion when he writes of Protestantism waxing weary of itself, and of some of their chiefs who allow what sometime they condemned, and especially in what he brings from "The Coal from the Altar," and out of "Sunday no Sabbath." He helps the Puritans to cavil against that which was so evidently spoken in "Sunday no Sabbath" against the Centurists. The State should look to this man, and Signor Coneo and Signor Gregorio [Panzani] should be thoroughly informed of his exasperating vein. Perhaps he thought to make the Archbishop of Canterbury take occasion to complain of the Bishop of Lincoln upon it; yet he gives even the Archbishop of Canterbury cause of exception to him, though he seems to flatter him. [⅔ *p*.]

76. Articles objected by the Commissioners for Causes Ecclesiastical against Thomas Colebeach, parson of Ludlow; Matthew Clarke, parson of Bitterley; Thomas Archley, curate of Hopton-in-the-Hole, Salop. These persons were charged with omitting to wear the surplice, omitting to bow at the name of Jesus, omitting to stand up at the reading of the creed, and admitting persons to receive the communion who did not kneel; also with various irregularities in solemnizing matrimony. [13½ *pp*.]

Vol. CCCLXXV.

[1637?]

77. Articles objected by the same Commissioners against Francis Saunders, late of Shangton, co. Leicester, and then of Stamford, co. Lincoln. He was charged that there having been in his house, or that of William Stafford, of Blatherwick, at Christmas time, a lord of misrule, he and others had appointed that the lord of misrule must have for a lady or Christmas wife, one Elizabeth Pitto, daughter of the hog-heard of the town; whereupon, defendant putting on a gown, and a shirt or smock for a surplice, read the words set down in the form of marriage in the Book of Common Prayer, putting a ring upon the finger of the woman, and going through the rest of the ceremony, and afterwards, at night, putting the parties into a bed together. Defendant was also charged with being a swearer and drunkard. [$4\frac{3}{4}$ pp.]

78. Statement of Henry Page, Vicar of Ledbury, co. Hereford, in reply to articles against him, before the same Commissioners. He altogether denies the inconformity with which he is charged, but admits that in his catechising there slipped from him the following irreverent words:—"Why might it not be as lawful to pull at a cart-rope as a bell-rope on a Sunday?" He submits to make any acknowledgment or submission, and charges the institution of the suit as an act of malice upon Thomas Cox of his parish, whom he had presented for living in open adultery. [$\frac{1}{4}$ p.]

79. Instructions for articles to be preferred against Dr. Holmes before the Commissioners for Ecclesiastical Causes. He is charged with almost all variety of clerical misdoing then alleged against inconformable clergymen. Amongst other things, with speaking "unreverently" in the pulpit, using these words, viz., "the drunken knave priest;" with never reading the Book of Liberty; with speaking very unreverently and rudely against the reverend bishops; with preaching for divers Sundays together "in the pew and in the pulpit four sermons in a day;" with baptising his own child without the sign of the cross; with being passionate, and speaking angerly in the church, and in the church in his anger calling the writer of the present paper "mutcha-vile;" with allowing strangers, after evening sermon on Sunday, to resort to his house, so as we can see he does but "hover with all the ceremonies;" and many other similar offences. [$2\frac{3}{4}$ pp.]

80. Information that George Buncle, a recusant, baptised his own child, using the ordinary words, and pulling a glass of water out of his pocket. Mrs. Ferrabosco, grandmother to the child, desired that it might be christened according to the rites of the Church of England. [*Endorsed*, "Dr. Wood's note.—His Grace would have Buncle called into the High Commission, and upon his answer it may be seen what is further to be done." $\frac{1}{3}$ p.]

81. Information of words spoken by Mr. Oldham, parson of Shipton Moyne, co. Gloucester, in preaching on the 20th and 23rd August. The words quoted are in derogation of the cathedral service and of pictures of the Saviour. He also complained of the

[1637?]

want of able counsellors; that the people were contented with the present ill-government; that pulpit-men upheld all, of whom as yet there was a good number, though they were daily cut off for toys and trifles. Speaking of the buying and selling of places, he said, "all things are to be sold at Rome." [⅔ p.]

82. Information by [Mr. Flamsteed?] of words spoken by George Catesby, living about Ecton, co. Northampton, or in Bloomsbury "towards the fields," with a view to the exhibition of articles against him in the High Commission Court. He expressed dislike to the surplice, derided bowing towards the altar, disparaged the High Commission Court, expressed dislike of the sentence against Prynne, approved Henry Burton's book, and disparaged Dr. Heylin's answer, threatened to stone William Churchman, priest, for having, as he said, committed idolatry in bowing towards the Holy Table, with many other offences of the like kind. [2½ pp.]

83. Rate made at Chingford, Essex, for payment of the account of John Burnett, churchwarden, for expenses about the church and chancel, for bread and wine for the communion, for maimed soldiers, for a new communion-table and rails. The total was 14l. 6s. 8d., but exceptions were taken to the charges for the table, rails, and other things, as being excessive, and bought without advising with the parish, wherefore the rate was made for 10l. 11s. 10d.. [Signed by twelve persons. 2 pp.]

84. Reasons assigned by the churchwardens of Beckington, Somerset, for refusal to remove the communion table from the place where it stands and has stood since the Reformation. [¾ p.]

85. Brief of money received by Sir Edmond Sawyer, and promised to be paid in the future in the forest division of Berks, towards repairs of St. Paul's. Paid 119l. 18s. 7d. Promised 111l. 6s. 8d. [2⅔ pp.]

86. Certificate of Inigo Jones, of the barks constantly employed to bring stone from the Isle of Portland for repair of St. Paul's, with the names of the masters and mariners, and application for their freedom from impressment. [1¼ p.]

87. Copy of part of a letter from Bishop Curle, of Winchester [to Archbishop Laud], on the cause of the waste of wood on the lands of the bishopric of Winchester. All the copyhold tenants of the bishopric pretend a custom that they may fell what timber they will. Another cause is the covenant in the leases to find timber out of the bishop's wood for repairing houses and mills. Sir Daniel Norton, for such reparation, has demanded 83 tons, and because I refused him he has cut down 40 oaks in my woods, the lease whereof expires at Michaelmas next. In renewing leases I have taken care to quit myself from that covenant. If his Majesty laid his command upon me that I should not renew any leases with that clause,

[1637?]

it would be an answer to the importunities of such tenants as press me. [*In the handwriting of William Dell.* 1 *p.*]

88. Brief in a cause [in the Court of High Commission], wherein James Finch was plaintiff, and Hugh Nordway *alias* Nordwell defendant. The question in the cause was which of the said parties was the father of an illegitimate child of Anna Wittam, a servant of James Finch. [*Imperfect.*=19 *pp.*]

89. Brief in a cause in the Court of Arches between Hugh Wynn and Morgan Williams as to the right to a particular seat and burial place in the church of Lanvuda [Llanvedw, co. Glamorgan?] [*Last sheet imperfect.* 22 *pp.*]

90. Description of the glebe lands of the rectory of Carlton Curlieu, co. Leicester, conveyed to the parson and his successors by Sir John Bale and other freeholders. [1 *p.*]

91. Petition of William Dillon, clerk, and doctor of law, to the King. Petitioner, having heard some speeches from Bishop Williams of Lincoln, concerning matters of state, derogatory to his Majesty's proceedings, and also being privy to some sinister actions of the bishop, yet because he was a man of great place, your subject his chaplain had been fearful and unwilling to disclose the same; but remembering a subject's allegiance, petitioner could no longer conceal the truth contained in articles stated to be annexed. Prays order for examination of the premises, and protection against the bishop's power, in the prosecution of this complaint. [⅔ *p.*]

92. List of witnesses in Dr. Dillon's cause against Bishop Williams of Lincoln. [1 *p.*]

93. Petition of Edward Hastler, rector of Bignor, in diocese of Chichester, to the Council. Upon the petition annexed, the Lords gave direction to Mr. Nicholas to declare to Lord Chief Justice Finch that no further proceedings should be taken in the said cause till his Majesty and the Lords were further informed. In regard the cause concerns the church in point of tithes withheld, and that his Majesty is patron of the rectory, petitioner prays appointment for a hearing. [⅔ *p.*] *Annexed,*

> 93. I. *Petition of the same to the same. William Pellet stands seised of 200 acres in Bignor, which heretofore was a park, but for 40 years has been arable and coppice, and by that means has become titheable. Petitioner being forced to sue in the Ecclesiastical Court for the tithe, Pellet procured a rule in the Common Pleas for a prohibition. Petitioner by his counsel gave satisfaction, and it was ordered, in the absence of the Lord Chief Justice, that no prohibition should be granted, yet shortly after petitioner was again warned to appear in the Common Pleas, and there being persuaded by his Lordship consented to a trial at Common*

VOL. CCCLXXV.

[1637?]

Law, but upon better advice, finding the church (in his Majesty's gift) like to suffer by going to such a trial, petitioner prays the Lords to take a course for stay of the trial and relief of petitioner. [1 p.]

94. Petition of Thomas Wheatley, Thomas Hill, and John Coggin to the Council. Richard Massey, clerk, having exhibited a petition against petitioners and other his parishioners, petitioners protest that they so much reverence Mr. Massey, their minister, his coat and function, that they are unwilling to publish his weaknesses, but desire the Lords to cast their eyes on a certificate annexed. Mr. Massey has vexed petitioners at the sessions for the county, at the assizes, in the Ecclesiastical Court at Lincoln, by supplicavit in the Chancery, in the High Commission Court and in the Star Chamber, and now at this Board, for one and the same cause. Touching his pretence that petitioners are actors of a division betwixt him and his wife, he has himself occasioned that discontent by questioning her in the Ecclesiastical Court for incontinency, at the sessions for murder, and at the assizes for felony, yet could never make anything appear against her, and keeps her without livelihood for her and his three children. She having a suit now depending for alimony, petitioners deposed therein, which has occasioned this complaint. Pray reference to the justices of assize to certify the truth. [1 p.]

95. Petition of John Bul, prisoner in Old Bridewell, to Archbishop Laud. Has been committed by your Commissioners a year, where he has endured many months' labour of beating hemp, to the afflicting of his weak body, and the being companion of all manner of rogues, to the vexation of his soul. Prays to appear before you to answer for himself. If he be a false prophet, it is your duty to deal with him as the word of God requires. It is his only desire to be brought to trial. His suit is that you would consider the doom of that man of sin which the prophet Isaiah denounces in his 14th chapter and 17th verse, "for he opened not the house of his prisoners." [1 p.]

96. Petition of Francis Whitaker, yeoman of the guard, to the same. Four years since petitioner lodged in his house for seven months James Rotherford, a Scot, parson of Covenham Mary, co. Lincoln, with his wife, three children, and a maid. Rotherford departed in petitioner's debt 20 marks, whereof 4*l.* petitioner lent him out of purse. Having in like manner deceived many others, Rotherford still skulks in obscure corners about London, under the pretended name of Dr. Rotherford, and is defamed to be a cheating and cozening companion, and of so lewd and incontinent a life as is not fit to be specified. Prays a sequestration to be awarded for recovery of the debt out of Rotherford's rectory. [⅔ p.]

97. Petition of Thomas Ridges, of Newport Pagnel, plumber, to the same. Bishop Williams of Lincoln granted petitioner

[1637?] letters of commendation to all parsons in the archdeaconries of Huntingdon, Leicester, Buckingham, and Bedford, that petitioner might be employed in repairing the roofs of the churches. By suspension of the bishop the letters commendatory are not of any effect. Petitioner, having provided lead and other materials, prays the archbishop to grant him similar letters of commendation. [⅔ p.]

98. Philip Pregion, son of John Pregion, late registrar of the diocese of Lincoln, to Archbishop Laud. Ever since his father's death, petitioner has executed the office of registrar, but by reason of the suspension of the bishop is now suspended from the same. Prays the archbishop to restore him to the said office, being the only means of livelihood of his mother and her eight children. [⅓ p.]

99. Petition of the parishioners of Allhallows Barking, near the Tower of London, to the same. Of late years our parish church has been repaired, and the communion table as before placed and railed about according to the laws and customs of the Church of England. Now there is a new font erected, over which certain carved images and a cross are placed, and also our communion table is removed out of its ancient accustomed place, and certain images placed over the rail which stands about the table, all which, as we conceive, tends much to the dishonour of God and is very offensive to us parishioners and also perilous. We have desired our doctor to give way, that the images might be taken down, yet he refuses so to do. Petitioners pray the archbishop to command that the images may be taken down, and the communion table be restored to its place. [1 p.]

100. Petition of Gabriel More, prebendary of St. Peter's, Westminster, to the Commissioners for that collegiate church. By our local statutes every prebend has his peculiar stall, according to which he is to have his precedence, which is denied to petitioner. By the same statute, all materials for repair of prebendaries houses are to be allowed by the college, which is likewise denied to petitioner. Prays to be righted in the premises. [⅔ p.]

101. Petition of Christopher Withins of Eltham to Sir John Lambe. Petitioner's wife having preferred articles in the High Commission, pretending cruelty and adultery committed by him, gained an order for receiving the use of 200l. for maintenance of herself and two children, and also that she should have half her household goods. All which has been performed. Further she demands 8l. costs, which she has received with interest. By reason of compounding a bond which she secretly took from petitioner for 200l., and pretending that petitioner has not performed his order, an attachment is granted against him, to his and his children's utter undoing, if you do not intervene. Prays enquiry as to performance of the order, and that the attachment may be dissolved. [¾ p.]

102. Petition of Thomas Webb, clothier, to the same. Petitioner was censured in the Court of High Commission, the cause being prosecuted ex officio, and costs and charges taxed at 80l. Upon

[1637?]

Vol. CCCLXXV.

repair to Archbishop Laud, he conceived the costs to be exceedingly over-taxed, and ordered the same to be moderated, the crime of petitioner not being great. Prays Sir John to shew him what lawful favour he can. [½ p.]

103. Petition of John Warren, shoemaker, of Olney, to Sir John Lambe. Is brought up to London by attachment for absenting himself from his parish church, for which he is heartily sorry. Purposes a full reformation and careful obedience to the canons of the church. His offence being out of ignorance, and no faction, and himself very poor, he prays stay of proceedings, and to appoint him to attend Sir John in the country. [½ p.]

104. Petition of John Downame, parson, the churchwarden, and others, of Allhallows-the-Great, in London, to the same, concerning the suit of Revell against Bryan and his wife. It is three years since Bryan's wife was first presented, which suit has cost the parish above 20*l*. The offences are so odious, so apparent, and against the church door, that it has brought much scandal to the parish. If Bryan and his wife commute, pray that the poor in their parish may be remembered, and that an end may be given to the suit this term. Signed by the parson, churchwardens, and nine others. [1 p.]

105. Petition of James Chadwick, clerk, rector of Stanley Regis, co. Gloucester, to the same. A sequestration of the rectory of Stanley Regis was referred to the Commissioners at Informations by the Archbishop of Canterbury. Petitioner has served the cure there three quarters of a year, and during that time has paid tenths, ship-moneys, procurations, and synodals, also eight groats monthly to the poor, and has not received any of the profits by reason of a pretended lease, there being due to him 40*l*. at least. Petitioner being unable to prosecute the suit, having spent 20*l*. in the keep of himself and horse nine weeks, besides paying 5*l*. to a curate during his absence, prays relief. [½ p.]

106. Petition of Robert Edmonds, of St. Martin's-in-the-Fields, to the same. Petitioner is molested by Mary Sheppard, wife of Richard Sheppard, for words confessed by him before Dr. Swalman, late official to the Archdeacon of Middlesex, being before him convented for adultery with Mary Sheppard, for which crime he had performed public penance, but she has not yet undergone any ecclesiastical censure. Prays that she may be cited to answer for her offence. [1 p.]

107. Petition of John Brewer and Richard Glover, churchwardens of St Katherine Creechurch, London, to the same. The Council appointed that a certificate should be made by the churchwardens of every parish, whether there were any selected vestry or no, whereupon John Bill, who, notwithstanding he was inhibited, officiated as churchwarden, made a return, which has occasioned a suit, long

Vol. CCCLXXVI.

[1637?] depending before you, as to whether all the men of the said parish or but some be a vestry. In respect of the unquietness that has been and is likely to be, for the relieved in short time will, being many, be assessors of the relievers, if all be a vestry, petitioners pray a reference to the Council, whence the ground of the suit arose. [$\frac{2}{3}$ p.]

108. Statement of changes in the tithes of Creeton and Castle Bytham, co. Lincoln, resulting from inclosure. [$\frac{1}{2}$ p.]

109. Indictment found against Thomas Newcombe, or Newcomen, parson of St. Runwalds, in Colchester, under a statute of the 1st Elizabeth, for not reading prayers and administering the sacraments according to the Book of Common Prayer. [*Copy.* 1$\frac{1}{4}$. p.] *Annexed,*

> 109. I. *Opinion of Sir John Lambe that the indictment could not be maintained. The charges against the defendant related to the position of the communion table, the minister's standing at the north end thereof, his causing the communicants to come to the rail to receive the sacrament, his refusing to administer to those who came not to the rail.* [*On the same paper is written what is apparently an extract from a letter of a sheriff, on the unwillingness with which a second payment of the ship-money was paid in his county.* 1$\frac{1}{2}$ p.]

110. List of benefices in the collation and presentation of the Archbishop of Canterbury, with the values thereof, arranged alphabetically, with several additions in the handwriting of William Dell, secretary to Archbishop Laud. [*A paper roll.* 4 pp.]

111. Account of tenths payable from various livings in cos. Leicester, Huntingdon, Hertford, Bedford, Buckingham, and Lincoln, probably those within the bishopric of Lincoln. They are arranged in deaneries. From the marginal notes it would seem that the account was originally prepared in 1616, but by subsequent additions and corrections of Sir John Lambe, one of which is dated in this year, it may be inferred it was used at this time, perhaps, by the Commissioners appointed to exercise episcopal jurisdiction during the suspension of the bishop. [79 pp.]

Vol. CCCLXXVI. UNDATED 1637.

[1637?] 1. Minute by Sec. Windebank of a reference made upon a petition to the King. His Majesty referred the same to the Archbishop of Canterbury, the Lord Treasurer, and the Bishops of Bath and Wells and of Oxford, who are to make choice of persons in the University of Oxford to peruse the statutes of [Wadham] College, and when

Vol. CCCLXXVI.

[1637?]

they shall be informed of what interpretations and additions are fit to be made to the same, that then, having first acquainted his Majesty, they shall ordain such things as shall seem necessary. [⅔ *p.*]

2. State of the case between the Archbishop of Canterbury and the Universities concerning visitations. Enumerates the several grounds on which the Universities claimed exemption, and the result, as already calendared under dates of 18th June 1636 and 30th January 1636-7. [1½ *p.*]

3. Orders made by the Dean and Chapter of Christ Church, Oxford, from their foundation under Henry VIII., for the good government of the students, signed by Dr. Brian Duppa as dean, and seven others. [*Latin.* 14 *pp.*]

4. Statement of the rights of the Dean and Chapter of Christ Church, Oxford, concerning their revenues, the right of the students concerning their stipends, and of the dean and chapter concerning improved rents of their lands, and their right of government over the students. Prepared in answer to a claim set up by the students for a share in the improved rents. [2 *pp.*]

5. Copy of the preceding. [4 *pp.*]

6. Extracts from the statutes of [Merton College, Oxford], relative to the election of officers, and appointment of accounts, with an exposition given of the latter of these by Archbishop Islip in 1351. [*Endorsed by Archbishop Laud as "Dr. Turner's paper." Latin.* ⅔ *p.*]

7. Particular, said in the endorsement to be by the Dean and Canons of Hereford, of such things as were in their new statutes enjoined them in their service in the cathedral of Hereford which were not required in the old, nor were ordinarily practised till the receiving of the new statutes. [*Underwritten is a memorandum written in or after* 1638, *explaining how the new statutes came to be given to that cathedral.* 1 *p.*]

8. Petition of the Regent and Professors of the Musæum Minervæ to the King. Petitioners are bound to uphold the Musæum which his Majesty has founded, and have maintained the same, and borne those debts and inconveniences which these times of mortality have cast upon them. Being now no longer able to prevent the discontinuance of their studies, they have no relief but his Majesty's goodness. They beseech him to command Sec. Windebank to peruse a remonstrance of the estate of the Musæum, and give him an account of their distress, and the means proposed for the conservation of the Musæum till God restore health to London. [⅔ *p.*] *Annexed,*

8. I. *Propositions offered to Sec. Windebank. First.—That persons who have promised moneys to the Musæum might be*

[1637?]

Vol. CCCLXXVI.

ordered to make present payment. Second.—His Majesty's letters not having taken effect, that he would bestow a proclamation for better notice of his favour towards the Musæum. Thirdly.—By the lottery granted to George Gage and others for bringing a river to London much money was collected, but, the undertaking failing, the money remains in deposito, to be disposed to Sir Edward Peyto and Colonel Hambleton upon the like project. It is proposed that either this money be employed for the building of an academy, or that another lottery may be granted for that purpose. The remainder of the paper relates to a grant of lands in North Wales, formerly solicited (see 30th March 1637, Vol, cccli., No. 39.) Those lands appear to have been discovered to be worthless, and a grant of other lands is solicited; but this part of the paper is imperfect; probably a leaf is wanting. [1¼ p.]

9. Suggestions from a person whose name does not appear, who, having read over during his holidays the Annals of Tacitus with the Annotations of Lipsius, published in small 4to. in 1619 at Geneva, points attention to certain passages which are termed seditious, and wishes the book to be suppressed. [*Endorsed:* "Sentences at Bugden." 1 p.]

10. Petition of Edmond Barker, messenger of the Chamber, to the Council. Has had in his custody Nathaniel Wickens, servant to Mr. Prynne, ever since 13th April last, and Thomas Aslin, a porter, ever since 31st May last, whom he has entirely maintained, and as yet has received no satisfaction. Prays order for their discharge out of his custody, and that he may receive satisfaction [½ p.]

11. Petition of Robert Raworth, printer, to Archbishop Laud. Has been 28 years and more admitted a master printer in London; printed St. Chrysostom, done by Sir Henry Savile; has suffered many afflictions in his later age. Prays to be admitted into the Society of Printers of London. [⅔ p.]

12. Petition of Bernard Alsop, stationer of London, to Sir John Lambe, Sir Nathaniel Brent, Dr. Duck, and the other Commissioners of the High Commission Court. Thomas Creed in 1593 was admitted a master printer. In 1615 he and petitioner became partners, and in 1616 petitioner purchased Creed's moiety, with his books and copies, and his art of a master printer, according to the custom of the Company of Stationers, for which petitioner paid 300*l.*, and from that time has employed himself in printing without molestation. Petitioner prays that he may be admitted a master printer according to the decrees in that behalf. [⅔ p.]

13. Petition of Arthur Nicholls to the same. Petitioner has spent much time in founding letters for the printers of London, and has great store cast. His employment of founding letters alone will

[1637?]

Vol. CCCLXXVI.

not maintain him. Since the archbishop has otherwise determined to dispose of the printer's place at Oxford, prays leave to be a printer in London, that he may make use of his own letters. [½ p.]

14. Cause of complaint of the same Arthur Nicholls. Being cutter and founder of letters for printers, he is three quarters of a year cutting the punches and matrices of one sort of letters, which are some 200 of a sort, after which they are six weeks a-casting; that done, some two months is required for trial, and then the printers pay him what they themselves list. For Greek, the printers promised him the doing of all the common work, which drew him to do 400 matrices and punches for 80*l.*, truly worth 150*l.* Further, they caused him to spend five weeks in cutting the letter for the small Bible, it being approved for the best in England; notwithstanding they put him off about it for 15 weeks, till Mr. Patrick Young came out of the country, all which time he kept his servants standing still. Prays the archbishop not to confine him to these miserable uncertainties; but promises, if he will grant his petition, he shall see more done in one year than was ever done in England for all kinds of languages, which will be for the good of the commonwealth, and his grace's particular content. [½ p.]

15. Draft of the decree of the Star Chamber for regulating printing and printers. This draft contains a large portion of the decree as ultimately passed on the 11th July 1637, and exhibits some of the many alterations which were made in it during the progress of its preparation. Some of the suggestions are in the handwriting of Sir John Lambe. This draft contains 18 articles; the decree as finally published contained 33. [10 *pp.*]

16. List by Sir John Lambe, prepared with a view to the selection of the 20 printers to be licensed under the new decree of July 1637, similar, but with important variations, to the list already calendared in Vol. ccclxiv., No. 111. Archbishop Laud has written upon this paper a contingent recommendation of Thomas Payne, the petitioner in the article No. 23, to succeed in the place of Jones. [1¼ p.]

17. Notes, stated by Sir John Lambe to be from the clerk of the Printers' Hall. They are principally in opposition to the regulation that stands No. 18 in the published decree, that all books should be new licensed before they were reprinted. It was stated that such a regulation would be to the utter undoing of the greater number of the Society of Stationers, principally by its hindrance to the current business of reprinting works long licensed. [1 p.]

18. Copy of the clause of the decree touching reprinting mentioned above, with marginal notes pointing out the anticipated inconveniences, and that the result would be that the books to which it applied would in consequence be printed beyond sea. There is added a branch of a subsequent article, which seems to have been omitted. [½ p.]

[1637?]

Vol. CCCLXXVI.

19. Petition of Henry Holland, stationer of London, on behalf of Richard Wills and others, mercers of Coventry, to Archbishop Laud. By the late decree of Star Chamber concerning printing, all haberdashers and other tradesmen are prohibited from buying or selling books. Petitioner, on behalf of Richard Wills and one Hancock, his master mercers, certifies that they have sold lawful privileged books, as bibles, psalters, psalm books, and other school books, to furnish that city and county, and more especially to supply the King's free school in Coventry and other allowed schools. Petitioner being persuaded that it was not the intention of the Lords in that decree to prohibit mercers from buying and selling such authorized books as aforesaid, prays that Wills and others, having a good assortment of lawful books in their shops when the decree came out, may be still permitted to carry on their trade. [$\frac{2}{3}$ p.]

20. Petition of John Norton, printer, to the same. Has been in partnership with Nicholas Oakes for eight years, in which time many differences have arisen between them. Oakes had de novo exhibited a petition to the High Court of Commission, importing the same matter which had been decided by the late archbishop, and of which there is now a suit depending at common law. To defeat petitioner of his right, Oakes has assigned over all his title of printing to his son John Oakes. The archbishop intending to establish those printers which shall be thought meet to continue, petitioner prays to be established instead of Oakes, and he shall do all right to Oakes by way of co-partnership, as shall be thought fit. [$\frac{3}{4}$ p.]

21. Petition of Nicholas Oakes, printer, to Sir John Lambe, Sir Nathaniel Brent, and Dr. Duck, commissioners for the printers. John Norton has petitioned the Archbishop of Canterbury to be master of a printing press, on the ground of his being petitioner's partner. Petitioner was to blame for having admitted him without the privity of the archbishop or of the Commissioners. Norton, wanting capacity himself for the government of a press, has aided a company of factious persons in erecting an unlawful press in a secret place, and secretly conveyed out of petitioner's house forms and letters which afterwards were discovered by the Company of Stationers, and defaced, to petitioner's disgrace and loss. Submits whether Norton, having infringed the decree made in the Star Chamber, ought to be tolerated to be a master printer. [$\frac{1}{2}$ p.]

22. Petition of John Norton, of London, stationer, to Archbishop Laud and Bishop Juxon. Petitioner served apprenticeship, afterwards as journeyman, in his Majesty's printing house, eight years, and since has practised as a master-printer 12 years, and has employed his whole estate in purchasing materials. The Society of Stationers have lately taken away his press, as they allege by order from his grace, whereunto he submits, although never guilty of printing anything offensive to church or state. Prays relief. [$\frac{3}{4}$ p.]

DOMESTIC—CHARLES I.

Vol. CCCLXXVI.

[1637?]

23. Petition of Thomas Payne to Archbishop Laud. Sets forth the investment of his savings of 150*l.*, in partnership with William Jones, printer, lately questioned in the High Commission, and prays that Jones's sin may not be petitioner's punishment. [*Similar to Vol. ccclvii., No.* 177. 3. ⅔ *p.*]

24. Notes upon the prerogative power of the Crown in regulating printing, and the way in which the same had been executed in past periods, with some particulars relating to the establishment of the King's printers. The number of correctors employed by them was four, at 50*l.* per annum; their capital stock was 6,000*l.*, and they had been at 1,500*l.* charge in the last translation of the Bible. [2 *pp.*]

25. The King [to all Judges and other Officers]. Having received very good testimony of the loyalty of Sir John Wintour, of Lydney, co. Gloucester, and the Lady Mary his wife, the King extends his special grace towards them, and directs that no indictment, presentment, information, or suit be preferred against them for matter of recusancy. [*Draft in the handwriting of Robert Reed.* ¾ *p.*]

26. Information concerning recusants. By 3 Jac. I., cap. 4, every recusant shall, after the first year of his conformity, repair to church constantly and receive the sacrament once every year, under various penalties; also by 3 Jac. I., cap. 5, every recusant shall, within one month after birth, bring his child to the minister of the parish to be baptized, under other penalties. There are within one county 300 persons who conform and never receive the sacrament, and 100 who never have their children baptized but by a popish priest. There is a penalty also upon marriages and the like neglect of the statute.— "The Queen's Majesty conforms." [⅔ *p.*]

27. Notes concerning the legal liability of recusants in the cases mentioned in the preceding paper. The person from whom these papers proceeded was apparently an applicant for a grant of the penalties. He offered to find out a sufficient number of persons liable to make the penalties amount to "great sums, if not over great." *Endorsed:* "Lionel Farrington." 1⅙ *p.*]

28. Extracts from the Statutes against Recusants, which refer to the cases mentioned in the last two preceding papers. [*Endorsed:* "For Mr. Hodgkinson." 1¼ *p.*]

Order of the Court [of Sessions for Middlesex], That no further proceedings be made against Sir Charles Smith, an indictment of recusancy having been preferred against him unknown to the court. [*See Vol. cclxv., No.* 84. ¼ *p.*]

29. Petition of the poor recusants of the southern and northern parts to the King. Your Majesty had accepted such recusants into grace as should submit themselves to composition, which petitioners had most willingly embraced; but the great charge of passing their

[1637?] Vol. CCCLXXVI.

grants is such that without further favour they can reap no benefit. Pray that the settlement of the fees may be referred to the Lord Treasurer and the Lord Cottington, calling to them the Vice-President of the North. [¾ p.]

30. Petition of Clement Pastorne [Paston?] to the King. Petitioner being a Roman Catholic born and bred, whose father dying has left him an estate so much engaged that he shall be enforced to sell the greater part of it, unless your Majesty grant him your protection, which is solely desired for payment of his father's debts, and then he will submit himself and his estate to your pleasure as other Catholics must do. [Endorsed by Sec. Windebank; "Sent by the Queen's Majesty:" delivered by Mr. Dorington. [½ p.]

31. Petition of Thomas Leke, priest, prisoner in the Clink, to the same. Petitioner is 70 years of age, and troubled with infirmities which endanger his life, as by certificate annexed appears. Has been known near 40 years for a dutiful subject, and has given satisfaction in the oath of allegiance. Prays order to the Council for his discharge, giving bond to appear. [⅔ p.] Annexed,

    31. i. *Certificate of Drs. John Gifford and William Gibbes. Vouch for the bodily infirmities of Thomas Leke.* [¼ p.]

32. George Moore, called La Croix, to the Queen. Has been arrested at Dover on suspicion of being a priest, which he is not, on account of certain rosaries which he had about him. Prays her Majesty to let Sec. Windebank have the King's direction to set the applicant at liberty. [⅔ p.]

33. Petition of Francis Perkins, of Ufton, Berks, a recusant convict, to the Council. Petitioner by reason of his recusancy is confined to within five miles of his dwelling. Albeit in letters patent granted above ten years since of his Majesty's two parts of petitioner's lands, and for which his Majesty has been duly answered 50*l.* per annum, there is some clause that may seem to imply such a licence, yet petitioner having urgent occasion to travel into Wilts, as also to London and Westminster, prays licence in manner agreeable to the statute. [*Underwritten. Nil.* ½ p.]

34. Petition of Francis Newton, one of the messengers, to the Council. Petitioner for five years has had a general warrant for apprehending jesuits, &c., which service he has performed, neglecting his other employments, and often endangering his life. He has taken 29 priests and jesuits, whose names are annexed. Some he carried to prison, others he kept in his custody, especially Henry Morse, whom he kept for 30 days, and indicted him the last sessions at Newgate, where he was found guilty of treason, but no allowance made to petitioner for his pains, or for entertainment of witnesses. In this employment petitioner has expended above 200*l.* From the Spanish ambassador's and divers other places, on Sundays and at other times, great multitudes of people issue forth from hearing mass. Prays a renewal of his warrant, and a grant of another warrant, as Mr. Crosse

[1637?]

Vol. CCCLXXVI.

had, to apprehend some of those who flock in such multitudes to and from mass; also an order for satisfaction for his pains and charges. [⅔ p.] *Annexed*,

 34. I. *List of the 29 priests and jesuits above mentioned.* [1 p.]

35. Thomas Lyddell, mayor of Newcastle-upon-Tyne, to his brother-in-law, Sir Henry Anderson. Has delivered Anthony, servant to Sir Robert Hodgson, understanding that the Lords had given order therein. Some men being stayed at Shields by the searchers, he went with Mr. Clavering to bring them up, and now sends their examinations. One of them will find no language but a little Latin, French, and Dutch. The writer persuades himself he is an Englishman and a jesuit. There is found in the ship great store of books, which Dr. Jackson has viewed, and many manuscripts, with abundance of pictures and popish relics. Of the others, one is an English youth who put his beads into the river, and is committed for refusing the oath of allegiance; the third is a Scotchman. In their gaol there is the other supposed priest, who was last sessions condemned in a premunire, one Gilbert Skelton, committed for denying to take the oath of allegiance, with two others. Sends up the letters taken with these men. Prays Sir Henry to move to get reward for the officers. This kind of service has been too much neglected in this place. Mr. Alvie has seen some of the manuscripts, and says that he who penned them was a good scholar. We endure great scarceness, being debarred of our trade. There are yet two Dunkirkers off this coast, and, that which is worse, the plague continues. Last week there were 21 houses infected, and 15 died in the fields and 12 in the town. [*Probably written in May* 1637. 2 *pp.*]

36. Copy of suggested Order of Council confirming an arrangement, that upon the death of Robert Moyle, appointed third protonotary of the Court of Common Pleas, the same office should be held in trust for his sons, Walter, John, and Robert for their lives in succession. This paper is stated to have been penned and perused by the Attorney-General. [¾ p.]

37. [The Council to Justices of Peace of co. Warwick.] Imperfect draft of letter, charging them to see that the possession of the Earl of Leicester of certain lands at Balsall should not be disturbed in the manner complained of by William Emott, servant to the Earl of Leicester, on behalf of his master. This letter was probably never sent, being superseded by some of those upon this subject which have been calendared in previous volumes. [⅔ p.] *Annexed*,

 37. I. *Copy of part of an indictment against Thomas Furley and Joan his wife, Martin Fisher, Edward Careles, John Careles, Francis Smith, Thomas Swan, John Samon, William Furley, Juliana Measie, Maria Nibbs, John Everts, Thomas Wigley, and John Tomson, for a forcible entry into certain lands at Balsall.* [⅔ p.]

[1637 ?]

VOL. CCCLXXVI.

38. Petition of Sir Richard Levison and Katherine his wife, and others the daughters of Sir Robert Duddeley, to the Council. Upon a petition of William Emott, on behalf of the Earl of Leicester his master, suggesting a late violent taking possession of part of the manor of Balsall, co. Warwick, as for petitioners, with a prayer of restitution, the Lords made reference to Sir Thomas Leigh and others, who have returned their certificate. Pray a day of hearing, hoping the Lords will rather settle than any way alter what possession petitioners have of the said manor, which they claim by the same title as his Majesty quietly enjoys the castle of Killingworth [Kenilworth]. [¾ p.]

39. Brief in a cause in the Court of Delegates, on behalf of Christopher Williams, against Henry Every and Francis Lippencott. Defendants were charged with having fraudulently removed nine tons of wood from the ship the Mary Margaret, part of 27 tons seized in the said ship under warrant of the Court of Admiralty. [6 pp.]

40. Similar brief in a cause in the Court of Delegates, on behalf of Humphry Seaward, against John Beere and Urith Shapcott. On the 20th May 1637 letters of administration of the estate of Robert Fowling, of Ottery St. Mary, intestate, were granted to the defendants. This case was an appeal against that judgment by Humphrey Seaward, who was cousin-german once removed to the deceased, and had a previous grant of administration for the better preservation of the goods of the deceased. [5½ pp.]

41. Similar brief in the same cause on behalf of Thomas Shapcott, husband of Urith Shapcott. [3 pp.]

42. Account of the tithes of certain lands from 1634 to 1637, the double value of which was in dispute in a suit in the Arches Court, of Lady Dinham against Browne and others. The single value was stated to be 20l. 19s. [¾ p.]

43. Minute of a request of the Commissioners for Exacted Fees, that Sir Henry Mildmay and Sir Richard Wynne, two of the same Commissioners, would move his Majesty to declare whether the commission should surcease their inquiry in consequence of the Courts of Westminster Hall having empanelled juries to enquire what fees had been taken during the last 30 years. [⅔ p.]

44. Note of what his Majesty's subjects pay for taking an oath in the various places here enumerated. The clerks take for administering the oath to Knights and Burgesses of the Parliament 2s. 6d.; persons admitted of the Train Band, on taking the oath of allegiance, pay 1s.; the Chamberlain of the city, when he gives the oath to any freeman, takes 3s. 4d.; the companies, when they admit any, and give them an oath, take the same sum. [¾ p.]

45. Charges made against the Clerk of the Enrolments in Chancery for taking fees not warranted by the statute of 23rd Henry VIII.,

with answers thereto. [*Endorsed by Sec. Coke* "*Mr. Henlei's answers.*" 1 *p.*]

46. Legal case as to the effect of a clause in an episcopal grant whereby J. C. was appointed the bishop's "commissary," with the opinions of Dr. Nicholas Steward, Dr. Arthur Duck, Dr. Thomas Gwynn, and Dr. Basil Woodd thereon. [2½ *pp.*]

47. Statement respecting a will of Luke Fisher, late of Wisbeach, who being worth 8,000*l.* had made a will after he had been seized with a fit and was in extremis. The writer wishes the circumstances to be privately suggested to the archbishop. If no one will do so, the writer as ordinary will petition either the King or the archbishop. [1 *p.*]

48. Note of Mrs. Kyme's desires to be presented to Sir John Lambe, to whom her cause in the High Commission against her husband is referred. She sets forth the particulars of her husband's misconduct towards her, and prays for a separation and alimony. [1⅔ *p.*]

49. Statement relative to the wardship of Hoe Games, grandson of Sir John Games, of Newton near Brecon. The wardship, having been first granted to Richard Gwynn, was, upon his retirement, committed to Dr. Gwynn. He being about to relinquish the same, the right was in contest between Dr. David Betton, to whom Catherine Games, second wife of John Games, father of the ward, then deceased, had made over her right, and Sir Walter Vaughan and George Vaughan. On the one side it was alleged that the Vaughans were not related to the ward, and on the other that Catherine Games had never been married to the ward's father. Both these assertions were in dispute. [2¾ *pp.*]

50. Statement of the case of John Belasyse, who had married Jane, the daughter and heir of Sir Robert Boteler, deceased, who was in ward to the late John Lord Boteler, who had left Lord Dunsmore and Endymion Porter his executors. Mr. Belasyse, to redeem the wardship, gave Lord Dunsmore and Mr. Porter a statute upon all his lands for 2,500*l.*, and was bound to make a variety of other payments which are here set forth. The lady's lands were worth 430*l.* per annum in possession and 370*l.* per annum in reversion, but she was only 18 years of age, and if she died before she arrived at 21 all was gone. [1 *p.*]

51. Petition of ———— to the King. That his Majesty would erect an examiner in every county to the purpose in the annexed paper expressed, and to grant petitioner the nomination of them, on an annual payment. [*Endorsed* "*Mr. Pitcairne.*" [1 *p.*] *Annexed*,

    51. I. *Proposal for establishment of an examiner in every county, for taking depositions of witnesses to be examined*

DOMESTIC—CHARLES I.

Vol. CCCLXXVI.

[1637?]

by commission in causes depending in the Star Chamber, Chancery, Exchequer, Court of Wards, Court of Requests, Duchy of Lancaster, and the Councils established in Wales and the North. [1½ p.]

52. Petition of Nicholas Page, clerk, to the King. Your Majesty heard the difference between the Earl of Berkshire and petitioner concerning his patent for his invention for drying malt with an oven to bake bread, and granted him liberty to prove his priority of invention at law. Petitioner is informed that your Majesty is, through the solicitation of the Earl, again to hear the said difference within few days, and to order a commission in the interim for examination of witnesses on both parts. Petitioner cannot suddenly be provided of commissioners, and draw up interrogatories, and bring in his witnesses, and is informed by his counsel that this way will be more tedious and far more chargeable than a trial at law. Prays either to be left to a trial at law, or to have longer time for choice of commissioners and examination of witnesses. [⅔ p.]

53. Petition of John Lord Pawlett to the same. About three years ago petitioner lent Sir John Philpot 1,000l., and for security took bond from Sir John, his eldest son Henry, and Sir Richard and Sir Walter Titchborne. Two years since Sir John died, leaving his son Henry his heir. Petitioner was forced to put his bond in suit, and prosecuted the parties to outlawry. Since then Henry Philpot has conveyed away his estate, and absents himself, knowing that on his death his estate, being entailed, is no ways liable, and Sir Richard and Sir Walter Titchborne have obtained a protection, whereby petitioner is in danger of losing his debt. Prays his Majesty to withdraw his protection from Sir Richard and Sir Walter Titchborne. [⅔ p.]

54. Probably proposed renewed Royal Protection to Sir Richard Titchborne. [1½ p.]

55. Petition of Richard Halford and Jane his wife to the Council. About five years since petitioner Jane lent Sir John Philpot on his bond and that of Sir Richard and Sir Walter Titchborne 500l. Sir John, dying, made over to Sir Richard and Sir Walter leases to the value of 600l. per annum, to discharge that and other debts, and yet no payment is made, Sir Richard and Sir Walter standing upon his Majesty's protection. Pray that Sir Richard Titchborne's protection may not be renewed. [⅔ p.]

56. Petition of Henry Whitney, notary public, to Sir John Lambe and the Doctors Advocates. The steward's place of the Commons now stands void. Prays the appointment for Geoffrey Whitney, petitioner's brother. [½ p.]

57. Petition of Captain Thomas Lindsay to the Council. Has been for almost six weeks in custody of two messengers for supposed

Vol. CCCLXXVI.

[1637?]

words which he never spake. Prays to be discharged, putting in security for appearance. [½ p.]

58. Petition of **John Mogridge**, yeoman of the leash to the Queen, to the King. His Majesty granted to Edward Wilkinson the reversion of the messenger's office in the Court of Wards after William Browne. Prays a like grant in reversion after Edward Wilkinson. [⅔ p.]

59. Petition of **John Smith** and **Mary his wife** to **Sir John Lambe**. There have been divers suits in law between Susan Radcliff alias Bright, who claims the said John Smith to be her husband, and petitioners, as well at common as civil law, and about half a year since she commenced a suit in the High Commission Court, which was referred to your worship to determine, "whether of the said two women should be the lawful wife of the said John Smith." Smith being a very poor man, petitioners pray licence to follow the said suit in formâ pauperis. [½ p.]

60. Petition of **Sir Robert Wolseley**, Clerk of the Patents in the Court of Chancery, to the King. Has been questioned before the Commissioners for Exacted Fees, and has given his final answer, with which they are not satisfied. Prays reference to the commissioners for regulating his fees upon such composition as they shall think fit. [⅓ p.]

61. Petition of **Thomas Crosland** of Quarmby, co. York, clothier, to **Archbishop Laud**. Prays him to peruse the petition annexed, and to order that it be read at the Council, and that the Lords will be pleased to refer the examination of petitioner's grievances. [½ p.] *Annexed*,

    61. I. *Petition of Thomas Crosland to the Council. For the space of 20 years petitioner has been vexed by suits, as well before the Council at York as in the King's Bench and elsewhere, by means of Edward North, William Penny, and others to the number of 20. They would never stand to any trials, and when petitioner has obtained references have contemptuously slighted them. They have thereby brought petitioner to ruin, and now threaten the destruction of his wife and children. Prays relief.* [⅔ p.]

62. Minute of Order of Council on a complaint of the **Earl of Suffolk** against **Sir James Ouchterlony**. Sir James Ouchterlony, deceased, assigned 87*l*. 9*s*. due to him upon bond by Thomas Talbot, receiver of Yorkshire, in trust for payment of 25*l*. to the lieutenant and gunner of the fort in Holy Island, and the rest to others, which bond Sir James, being a joint executor, has released, so that the trustees cannot recover it. It is ordered that the money shall be paid back by Sir James, if he has received it, if not that Mr. Talbot shall pay it. [*Underwritten by Nicholas*, "Mr. Talbot hath the money." ⅔ p.]

Vol. CCCLXXVI.

[1637 ?]

63. Notes of the judgment of the Court of Arches in a tithe suit between John Smith, a holder of lands in the parish of Rushden, co. Northampton, and Thomas Whitby, rector of the same parish, with notes of Sir John Lambe. [= 1¾ p.]

64. Proposal of certain persons, whose names do not appear, but who state that they have acquired a knowledge of military discipline in foreign service, for the reformation of the cavalry of England and Wales. They desire letters patent whereby they may be made his Majesty's servants, to assist the Lord Lieutenants, Deputy Lieutenants, Captains, &c., at their several musters, by keeping a list of all those " who are required to find," instructing them in horsemanship, providing them with useful arms, and training them according to the best discipline then in use. For their salary they refer it to his Majesty. [1½ p.]

65. Petition of Lady Lucy Grantham, widow, to the Council. Was sent for by a messenger for default of finding arms at the musters in Nottinghamshire, but by reason of continual suits which she has had since the death of her last husband, Sir Thomas Grantham, she has been very little in Nottinghamshire, where she has a small jointure by a former husband, and consequently never had notice that she was charged. Prays discharge upon submission and conformity hereafter, offering to give bond to bring a certificate of conformity from the Earl of Newcastle, Lord Lieutenant of that county. [½ p.]

66. Edward Viscount Wimbledon to the King. Remonstrance concerning means, without his Majesty's charge, for repairing his forts and castles, and especially Portsmouth. His Majesty has put the Navy in order. The Viscount beseeches him to consider the bulwarks, bastions and " rampiers " of the kingdom. It is a common " nationary " law that the defence of a people ought to be maintained by the common charge. Queen Elizabeth, in time of a general peace, fortified Portsmouth upon the freehold inheritance of her subjects. The Viscount sees no reason why the King should not lay a general charge over the whole kingdom for fortifying all places selected by the Council of State and War. No place deserves more charge to be bestowed upon it than Portsmouth, both by reason of its situation and its being the frontier town, as it were, upon the Low Countries, France and Spain. The Viscount hopes the King will be as well pleased to repair it as Queen Elizabeth was to build it, and by a judgment of Gascoigne, in 13th Henry IV., the King may charge his people, without the especial assent of the commons, to anything that may be for the benefit of the common people. Suggests that the money may be levied by tolls all over the kingdom. [2¼ pp.]

67. Minute of application from the Lord Warden to Sec. Windebank, that his Majesty may be moved to grant a special warrant for repair of the castles of Dover, &c. Reference will cause delay.

VOL. CCCLXXVI.

[1637?] Therefore it is desired that the Lord Warden and the Earl of Newport may depute such commissioners as they shall see cause, to be accountable as his Majesty shall appoint. Camber Castle being altogether unserviceable, should be sold for repair of the other castles, and the soldiers, about ten, may be added to the gunners in Dover Castle, there now being but 16. [⅔ p.]

68. A treatise by Sir John Borough, Keeper of the Records in the Tower of London, entitled "The Sovereignty of the Seas of England proved by Records, History, and Municipal Laws of the Kingdom; also a particular relation concerning the inestimable riches and commodities of the British seas." [pp. 98, besides the title page.]

69. The Council to the Officers of the Navy. Ten ships have been recommended as fit for the King's service (whereof two are to be sent to Sallee, and the rest to be employed on the English coasts). The officers are to sign charter-parties to the owners for payment of their charges as herein stated. They are also to contract with John Graves and Robert Trankmore for building two pinnaces for present service at Sallee. The Treasurer of the Navy is also prayed to engage himself for payment of the moneys before mentioned, for which he shall have allowance in his account of the country moneys for 1637. [*Underwritten is a list of the ten ships above mentioned. Written between 1st January and 25th March 1636-7. Draft. 3 pp.*]

70. Sir Henry Palmer and Kenrick Edisbury to the Lords of the Admiralty. Give account of fees and allowances granted to the Comptroller and Surveyor of the Navy at the institution of those offices, at which time a groat was of as much value as twelvepence at present. The payments to the former officer were 155*l.* 6*s.* 8*d.*, out of which he paid 13*l.* 11*s.* for his liberate poundage and fees in the Exchequer; the latter 145*l.* 6*s.* 8*d.*, with a similar deduction of 13*l.* 6*s.* All the officers have clerks borne in the ordinary, but it costs the comptroller and surveyor 30*l.* a year each for two clerks diet. Pray the Lords to consider the great expense they have undergone these last three years of extraordinary service. [1 p.]

71. [Sec. Coke to Algernon Earl of Northumberland.] The Prince Elector and Prince Robert go hence on Monday to embark the next day. His Majesty thinks it requisite that the Earl should see the Prince aboard, and receive him with such honour as is fitting for his Majesty's nephew. The Prince is to choose his own ship, but the Earl to carry the flag. When the Prince has landed at Goree or Flushing, the Earl is to take his leave, but Sir Henry Mervin may wait upon the Prince to the Hague. [*Probably written in June 1637. See Vol. ccclxii., No. 64. Draft.* 1 *p.*]

72. Sir Henry Marten to [Sec. Coke]. I received from Mr. Weckherlin, your servant, a translation of that memorial lately presented to his Majesty by the Dutch ambassador against [George] Henley, with this, that you would be glad to hear my opinion

[1637?] thereupon. The sum of all therein contained is this, that the letters of reprisal granted to Henley are not well grounded, because justice was neither denied nor delayed, which the ambassador proves thus, because Henley had a former sentence for him and a latter against him, and that latter pronounced by judges of great worth. The answer is easy, viz., that a sentence is not made just by the rules of the civil law or by domestic practice, but by reality of truth. If not supported with some reasons that may give satisfaction, a judgment is so far from justifying the wrong as that it adds further contumely. Henley does not require his goods because he had a former sentence, but because, being a merchant, he had by lawful trade purchased those sugars, which were upon the seas violently and piratically taken from him by a man of war of Holland. If the first sentence be void by occasion of any error, Henley is where he was, lawful owner of goods whereof he was wrongfully spoiled by a pirate, till somewhat can be shown to the contrary. [*Copy.* 2¾ *pp.*]

73. Reasons why [George] Henley's letters of reprisal should stand. These are in accordance with the preceding remarks of Sir Henry Marten. They proceed from Henley and his partner Augustine Phillips, to whom the letters of reprisal were granted. [1¼ *p.*]

74. The Lords of the Admiralty to Sir John Pennington. His Majesty has given licence to Colonel John Lesley to transport 500 men out of this kingdom to Dieppe. They are to have free convoy thither by ships under your command. [⅔ *p.*]

75. Form to be signed by the Lords of the Admiralty, approving an account rendered to them, and releasing the accountant. [*Draft.* ⅔ *p.*]

76. Fair copy of the same. [1¼ *p.*]

77. Petition of Job Harby, merchant, and the rest of the tin farmers, to the Lords of the Admiralty. They have freighted the ship Mary of 400 tons, Roger Martin master, for transportation of tin to the Straits. The said ship is chosen by the Officers of the Navy for next summer's expedition. There are in the Thames ships every way as fit for the said service. Petitioner is owner of one fourth of the Hercules, and the owners of the Mary are interested in the Industry and Unicorn, all three taken up for the same service. Pray warrant for discharge of the Mary. [⅔ *p.*]

78. Petition of John Reston, Keeper of his Majesty's prison at Dover, to the same. By their warrant to the Lord Warden, command was given for imprisoning seventeen Frenchmen upon suspicion of piracy, whereupon warrant was given to petitioner for their safe-keeping, dated 9th July 1636, and he kept 15 of them for seven months with diet and lodging. These Frenchmen had two shallops, which were ordered to be sold, and thereout the charge of their imprisonment to be paid. The said

VOL. CCCLXXVI.

[1637?]

shallops were sold by John Jacob, Sergeant of the Admiralty of the Cinque Ports, in whose hands the money remains. Prays order for payment thereout. [¾ p.]

79. Petition of John Reston, Keeper of his Majesty's prison at Dover, to the Lords of the Admiralty. Another petition to the same effect, with prayer for directions to the Lord Warden to examine petitioner's charges, and thereupon to give order for petitioner's satisfaction. [¾ p.]

80. Order of the Lords of the Admiralty. Sir Henry Marten, Judge of the Admiralty, having decreed before sentence given to Henley and Phillips that the moiety of the hides should be sold, we order the Registrar of the Delegates to issue a commission authorizing the petitioner Nicholas Polhill to dispose of the goods, and such part of the ship, the Golden Wolf, as amount to 4,966l., such proportion being decreed to Nicholas Polhill and partners. [*Copy.* ⅔ p.]

81. Nicholas Polhill to the King. Remonstrance of the various steps which had been taken in his suit against the Dutch of Rotterdam, till Sept. 1637, when Sir Henry Marten recommended to Sec. Windebank, that either his Majesty should grant Polhill letters [of reprisal] under the Great Seal, or should give the Lords of the Admiralty a special commission for granting the same. [1 p.]

82. Another statement of the same proceedings, but differing somewhat in the particulars mentioned. [1 p.]

83. Petition of Daniel Brames, Citizen and Clothworker of London, to the Lords of the Admiralty. A suit was lately depending before the Judges Delegates between Edward Carpenter, since deceased, and Captain Daniel Hardenburch of Middleburg, wherein the latter has been condemned in 750l. Petitioner, by advice of the ambassador of the States, became bail for the said captain, the States writing their letter to the said ambassador that the suit should be followed at the charges of their country. The suit was for freight of an English ship laden with Portuguese goods taken by the said captain, which goods were disposed of by the Admiralty of Zealand, who have power to call the parties who shared in the prize to contribute their parts towards satisfaction of the freight. Prays licence to bring his action against such shipping of Middelburg as shall come into any port of England for the said 750l., for satisfaction thereof to the widow of the plaintiff. *Annexed,*

 83. I. *The States to Sir [Albertus] Joachimi, their ambassador. Directing him to follow the said suit at the country's charge and peril. 5th January 1636.* [*Copy.* ⅔ p.]

 83. II. *Statement of the distribution of the goods contained in the prize brought in by Captain Daniel Hardenburch on the 26 May 1633, and adjudged by the Court of Admiralty of Zealand to be a good prize.* [1 p.]

Vol. CCCLXXVI.

[1637?]

84. State of account of John Crane, Victualler of the Navy, for extraordinary victualling this year. Total of the charge, 32,895*l*. 15*s*. 9*d*. Total of the discharge, 34,007*l*. 5*s*. 6½*d*. Surplusage, 2,224*l*. 19*s*. 7½*d*. of which 1,114*l*. 9*s*. 10*d*. is charged as the value of remains of victual, casks, &c., which ought to have been returned to the accountant, but were converted to private benefit. [1 *p*.]

85. Notes by Nicholas. To move his Majesty, from the Commission of the Admiralty, concerning the petition of William Felgate and others, retailers of gunpowder and munition for shipping (*see Vol. ccclxviii., No.* 112); and about the warrant for Mr. Ferris executing the place of cook in the great ship by himself or his deputy, which is not agreeable to warrants for officers in his Majesty's ships. [*Endorsed are various memoranda relating to the importation and sale of gunpowder.* 1½ *p*.]

86. Commissioners for Revision of Sentences given in the Court of Admiralty to George Fielding, Registrar of the Court of Delegates. To receive an appeal made by Gaspar Burt against Humphrey Hooke and Thomas Hooke, and to issue a munition for transferring the proceedings to the commissioners. [*Draft of warrant calendared under date of 3rd May* 1637. 1 *p*.]

87. Draft, in the handwriting of Nicholas, of the operative part of the above, or a similar direction in some other cause. [¼ *p*.]

88. George Rookes to George Rudolph Weckherlin. I pray you that effectual letters may be written from his Majesty to France, touching restitution to be made for ships and goods taken by the French since the conclusion of peace, viz., the James, the Benediction, and the Bride, to the value of 50,000*l*. [1 *p*.]

89. List of the master and the company of a ship not named; Richard Hussey, master. [1 *p*.]

90. Petition of John Jacobson Boyerman and others, owners of the Fortune of Hoorn, to the King. State the facts before calendared of the seizure of their ship by Thomas Gayner at Knockfergus; its arrest by petitioners at Plymouth; the claim to it set up by Don John de Nicolaldi and his brother Don Michael; the judgment of the Court of Admiralty in favour of petitioners; the appeal to the Lords of the Admiralty by the Spanish resident; and release of the ship by his Majesty. It is now added that the Lords of the Admiralty disagreed among themselves, and that the Earl of Lindsey, Lord Cottington, and Sec. Windebank, against the liking of the Earl of Dorset, and in the absence of Sir Henry Vane and Sec. Coke, upon a Sunday dedicated to the Holy Trinity, on which since the kingdom stood never any sentence was pronounced, revoked the sentence of the Admiralty, whereby petitioners are much damnified, besides the prejudice of the States General. Pray his Majesty to

[1637?]

Vol. CCCLXXVI.

command the cause to be reviewed. [*Endorsed by Sec. Coke as presented by the States Ambassador.* ⅔ *p.*]

91. Petition of Thomas Leddoze, of Weymouth and Melcombe Regis, merchant, to the Council. Last year petitioner and his partners set forth the Marigold from Weymouth to Lisbon, where the ship's boat was seized by one Alfera and six soldiers, who put to sea therein, but being followed in another boat by the master of the Marigold, a fray ensued, in which Alfera was wounded, and forced to relinquish the boat. Alfera having complained of his hurt, petitioner's ship and goods have been ever since detained, and the master, with three of his company, and one Mr. Lowe, have been imprisoned for nine months. Prays that means may be taken for their delivery, and restoration of their ship and goods. [1 *p.*]

92. Petition of Anthony Lowne, boatswain in the St. George, to the Lords of the Admiralty. For 12 years petitioner has been employed as boatswain without reproof, but of late he has been sent for by a messenger from Portsmouth, and examined by the masters of the Trinity House concerning expense of junks and other pieces of cordage, and for the same has been prickt out of victuals and wages. Being employed in the St. George for carriage over seas of the Prince Elector Palatine, in the said voyage, through extremity of weather, he spent three top-masts, and on many other occasions has been constrained to expend cordage for the safety of the ship. Is most sorrowful that he has incurred displeasure, and prays to be again admitted into victuals and wages, and to have leave to return to Portsmouth to attend his Majesty's service. [¾ *p.*]

93. Petition of Henry Butler, who executed the purser's place for two years in the Fifth Lion's Whelp, to the King. That ship being in convoy of the Prince Palatine's goods, was cast away, to the utter undoing of petitioner, having served eleven years, and in service lost the use of his left hand. Being destitute, he implores your Majesty's favour. Prays the next purser's place that shall fall void. [½ *p.*]

94. Petition of William Brissenden, purser of the Providence, to the Lords of the Admiralty. Has been 14 years in his Majesty's service. In the late expedition to Sallee he observed divers abuses committed by Edmund Seaman, captain, and William Bramble, master, of the said pinnace, the particulars whereof are annexed. By reason of some of the abuses the pinnace now in the Downs is destitute of beer. Prays that order may be taken with the captain and master for their abuses. [⅔ *p.*] *Annexed,*

- 94. I. *Objections against Capt. Edmund Seaman and William Bramble. The acts alleged are pillaging ships taken, sale of cables and other stores belonging to the Providence, and excessive consumption of the beer. Signed by William Brissenden.* [2 *pp.*]
- 94. II. *Duplicate of the same, signed by four other persons belonging to the Providence, besides William Brissenden.* [2½ *pp.*]

Vol. CCCLXXVI.

[1637 ?]

95. Certificate of John Wale, purveyor of timber for the Navy, in Kent, of the quantities of timber carried by certain hundreds in that county, from 1630 to 1636. [1 p.]

96. Paper by Nicholas, entitled, Concerning bringing in the Arrears of the Ship-money. Through the remissness of the sheriffs in execution of the writs of *certiorari*, commanding them to return into the Petty Bag Office the names of such persons as are in arrear, with the amounts due from them, little money has been brought in. It is therefore offered to consideration that the Attorney-General may appoint some person of trust to take every term a very strict account from the sheriffs, and if it shall appear that they have been remiss, or that they return false accounts, that they be made to pay a good part of the arrear. If the sheriffs were thus held strictly to their accounts, they would be more careful what answers they make, while the parties in arrear, being put to answer in the Exchequer, would grow wiser than to delay payment of so small a sum. If care be not taken to get in the arrears the business of shipping will in a short time be lost, for the arrears are more every year. [*Draft.* $1\frac{2}{3}$ *p.*]

97. Answer of Sir Thomas Hendley, sheriff of Kent, as to ship-money remaining unpaid in that county. [4 *pp.*]

98. Copy statements of William Chapman and others as to the inequality and injustice of the taxations for ship-money made in Shelton in 1636 and 1637. The larger holders had been taxed at 2d. and 2$\frac{1}{2}d$. an acre, and some of the poor tenants at 4d., 1s., and even 2s. 4d. an acre. [1 p.]

99. Return of John Higgins, one of the chief constables of the hundred of Huntington, co. Hereford, of persons who have not paid their ship-money in his division. Total, 19s. 2d. [1 p.]

100. Similar return of Walter Pember, the other chief constable of the same hundred. Total, 1s. [$\frac{1}{4}$ p.]

101. Lists of persons in the parish of Enfield who have been raised and of those abated for the ship-money by the sheriff of Middlesex, contrary to the assessment made by the parishioners. Among the latter are Sir Thomas Trevor, Baron of the Exchequer, Sir Nicholas Rainton, and Dr. Roberts, vicar of the parish. [2 *pp.*]

102. Note of sums abated and those increased in several of the writs for ship-money issued in 1637. [$\frac{2}{3}$ p.]

103. Note of ship-money paid in 1637 by the Lord Mayor, aldermen Andrew, Smith, Cramer, and Gerrard, and Sir Nicholas Rainton. The first three there were 10l. each, the next two 8l., and Sir Nicholas 12l. [$\frac{1}{2}$ p.]

104. Lists of the counties in England, with the sum charged on each for ship-money, in 1636–1637. Total, 210,600l. [1 p.]

Vol. CCCLXXVI.

[1637?]

105. Draft, by Nicholas, of an account of the receipt and expenditure of the ship-money in the years 1634-5, 1635-6, and 1636-7. [4 pp.]

106. Return of arrears of ship-money in co. Hertford for 1636. Gives names, places of abode, sums assessed, and the reason of non-payment. Many of the defaulters were very poor; many had gone into New England; and it is stated of many of the principal persons, as of Lord Falkland, Sir Thomas Reade, and Sir William Lytton, that the bailiff dare not distrain, for fear of being sued. [6 pp.]

107. Memorandum by Nicholas to obtain from Sir William Russell a certificate of the surcharge upon the ship-money in 1636, when several ships were kept longer than the writs required. [4 lines.]

108. Petition of John Combes, Thomas Harmwood, and Thomas Wolvin to the Council. Richard Freake refusing to pay his ship-money, the sheriff made a warrant for his committal, and petitioners carried him to prison, whereupon he brought an action against them. The judges, perceiving it was about ship-money, acquainted the Attorney-General therewith, who applied to the Lords, and Freake was sent for to the Board; after which there was a reference to Sir William Goring and Walter Bartellott, by whom petitioners were bound to appear before the Board. They attend, and have been enforced to expend 20l., although they have done nothing but in execution of the sheriff's warrant, as appears by the annexed certificate. Pray discharge from attendance. [*Probably presented on 17th February* 1636-7. *See Vol.* cccxlvii., *No.* 47. ½ p.] *Annexed,*

    108. I. *Sir William Culpeper, sheriff of Sussex, to the Council. Certifies the circumstances under which he signed the rate made by Combes, and sets forth the conduct of Freake which induced him to give warrant for his being taken to gaol. 3rd November* 1636. [1 p.]

109. William Walter, sheriff of co. Oxford, to [Nicholas]. Begs to be informed, by his brother Killigrew, what sum his collection should amount to before it be sent up. He must accompany it to London, that country not being a place where great trades are. [½ p.]

110. Account, by the said William Walter, of the assessment of co. Oxford for ship-money in 1636, showing how much was to be collected by him, and how much by Lewis Harris, his under-sheriff. [¾ p.]

111. Notes, relative to the overcharge in the assessment of ship-money by Sir Robert Banister upon Rowell [Rothwell] hundred in co. Northampton, respecting which various papers occurred in our last volume, pp. 39, 53, 97, 259, 350, 506. The minute facts of the disproportion complained of are here stated, and it is contended that

[1637?]

Vol. CCCLXXVI.

the composition for provisions for the King's household did not form a precedent for the assessment of ship-money. [1⅓ p.]

112. Account, by William Bassett, late sheriff of co. Somerset, of ship-money for 1636 remaining uncollected in that county. Total, 33*l.* 17*s.* 6*d.* [*MS. book.* 8¼ *pp.*]

113. Account of arrears of ship-money in the hundred of Nassaburgh, co. Northampton. The principal defaulter was Lord Fitz-William, who was in arrear in several places in this hundred, altogether amounting to 28*l.* 4*s.* 4*d.* [27 *lines on a slip of parchment.*]

114. Sir George Stonehouse, sheriff of Berks, to [Nicholas]. Pray inform Sir Dudley Carleton that the order for rates concerning Sunning Hill made by the Justices of Assize, and which the Lords gave order should stand, may be inserted into the order, for avoiding future trouble. This passage being in your time of attendance, Sir Dudley desires to receive instructions from you. [⅔ *p.*]

115. List, by Mr. Parrat, of persons in Norfolk who refuse to pay ship-money. Lady Peyton, executrix of Sir John Peyton, and Sir William Herrick are amongst the defaulters. [½ *p.*]

116. Minute of application to the Council to be made for Sir Francis Thornhaugh, sheriff of Notts, that a messenger be sent for Ambrose Wood and to the town of Newark, who had not fully paid their ship-money to Sir Francis. [1 *p.*]

117. Names of opposers of the distress taken from John Cartwright, all being of Aynho, co. Northampton, with a note of request by Robert Toms that he may have satisfaction for his trouble and danger. [*See Vol. ccclxvii., Nos.* 32, 33, 64–67. ½ *p.*]

118. Petition of John Burge, one of the late constables of the hundred of Chewton, co. Somerset, to the Council. Was employed by the hundred to obtain a reduction in the ship-money, in accordance with an ancient rate called Hinton rate. The Lords referred the matter to the then sheriff, the Bishop of Bath and Wells, and Mr. Mallet, late sheriff, and the hundreds refused to pay that which exceeded Hinton rate. Petitioner is heartily sorry now that he understands the Lords are displeased with his proceedings therein, and submits to pay the monies in arrear. Prays to be discharged, and that he may receive satisfaction from the hundred for the ship-money unpaid, and his charges. [1 *p.*]

119. Petition of the same, here called John Burges, to the Council. Last year, at the desire of the hundred, petitioner used means for easing the hundred of a great overcharge in the ship-money. In that business petitioner laid out 45*l.*, besides the loss of 20*l.* in his private employments. The hundred jury desired a rate to be made for payment thereof. Prays that the now constables may be ordered to make such rate. [¾ *p.*]

Vol. CCCLXXVI.

[1637 ?]

120. Petition of Sir Edward Littleton, late Sheriff of co. Stafford, to the Council. Petitioner paid in for ship-money for 1636, 2,700*l.* There is an arrear of 300*l.*, which petitioner cannot as yet levy, and is commanded to attend the Lords. Prays until Easter term next, for collecting the same. [½ *p.*]

121. Petition of Sir Edward Hussey, Sheriff of co. Lincoln, to the Council. Petitioner and the corporations of that county are charged to pay 8,000*l.* for ship-money. 6,700*l.* is already paid by petitioner, without the corporations. The rest he cannot get in in due time, without some course be taken with persons refusing. Some whole townships, and various persons whose names are underwritten, wholly refuse to pay, and divers constables, whose names are also underwritten, refuse to perform the service. Prays that a messenger may issue for the persons alluded to. [*Underwritten are the names of Leonard Brown, John Tolson, William Officiall, Thomas Burton, and William Slater.* ¾ *p.*]

122. Petition of inhabitants of Horncastle Soke whose names are underwritten, to Sir Anthony Irby, Sheriff of co. Lincoln. Wildmore Fen has always been within the said soke, which consists but of 13 townships, yet has been rated at 2*d.*, against 26 towns as good and great which pay 2½*d.*, this great tax having been laid upon Horncastle in respect of Wildmore Common. Since the common has been inclosed, the inhabitants of the soke are unable to pay ship-money according to ancient rates. Pray the sheriff either to tax the enclosed grounds with the soke, or to set such rates upon the 13 towns as may be equal with towns in other divisions. [*Signed by 38 persons.* 1 *p.*]

123. Petition of Sir Edward Wardour to the Council. In ship-money and other rates petitioner has always been rated at Westminster equal with any of his rank, and has readily paid. He has a little house, with 6 acres of land, at Chiswick, where he retires in the long summer vacation, where he is likewise rated equal with those who hold 20 times as much land. At Easter sessions twelvemonth petitioner having complained, it was ordered that he should be rated according to the proportion of land which he held there, but upon this last command for ship-money Richard Smeeth and some others rated petitioner at 40*s.*, while Mrs. Saunders, who holds 40 times as much, is rated but at 3*l.*, and Dr. Duck, who holds more than 20 times, at 45*s.*, and Richard Smeeth at 8*s.*, none of them being rated anywhere else for their personal estate. Prays that in ship-money and other rates he may be rated in Chiswick only according to the land he holds there. [⅔ *p.*]

124. Petition of Richard Nicholas, John Hatch, and Francis Hamond, collectors of ship-money for Pinner, Middlesex, to the same. Petitioners have collected part of the ship-money, and have demanded the residue, but could not obtain payment; whereupon the sheriff thought it not fit that petitioners should distrain themselves, because

[1637?]

Vol. CCCLXXVI.

they would get the ill-will of their neighbours, therefore he promised he would send down bailiffs to distrain, and appointed first one day and then another, but no bailiffs came, so they conceive he has no just cause to complain of petitioners. Pray discharge. [½ p.]

125. Petition of Jonas Hunt and John Lisley, collectors of ship-money in Paddington, Middlesex, to the Council. Petitioners have collected the medium proportion, and have several times demanded the residue. They gave direction to Robert Colkett, the bailiff, to distrain; and, notwithstanding they shewed him distress sufficient, he neglected the same, so that they are not defaulters. Pray discharge. [½ p.]

126. Petition of Sir William Russell, Treasurer of the Navy, to the same. The sheriff of Suffolk having sent up 600l. ship-money, petitioner's servant, Edward Fenn, asked John Dynes of Mincing Lane, glazier, being a neighbour, and a responsible man, to receive the money for petitioner's use, for his Majesty's service, which Dynes did. Dynes refuses payment. Prays the Lords to take order therein. [*Probably the petition mentioned in Vol. ccclxviii. No.* 12. ⅔ *p.*]

127. Petition of Richard Knighton, constable of Artlingborough [Irthlingborough] in co. Northampton, to the same. On complaint that petitioner had not paid Sir Robert Banister, the late sheriff, moneys received for ship-money by ten or eleven pounds, and had not paid between four and five pounds which he was assessed at, he had been sent for by a messenger. Has paid to Sir Robert the money received. Denford being much infected with the plague, Sir Robert wished him to forbear the collection. He did not deny payment of his own assessment, but being assessed at 16d. in the pound, and the townsmen but at 4d., he made complaint to Sir Robert, and found no redress. Prays discharge. [⅔ p.]

128. Return of Thomas Oxton, mayor of St. Alban's, of persons in arrear of their ship-money for 1636. Total, 13l. 1s. [1 p.]

129. Henry Mellor, mayor of Derby, to the Council. Sends particulars of assessment for ship-money taxed upon the clergy and inhabitants of that town. [1 p.]

130. Petition of John Hope, mayor of Derby, to the same. Petitioner was summoned to attend the Lords concerning ship-money, which he has punctually observed. On account of age and infirmities, prays he may be called before them and dismissed. [⅓ p.]

131. Petition of Thomas Welles, of Ashton, co. Northampton, to the same. Was maintained in a house belonging to his brother, John Welles, out of charity, but was assessed 18d. ship-money, and his brother 5s. 6d., for the same lands. The sheriff gave warrant to Thomas Cooper and Robert Toms to distrain, who took a horse from off the common, which being lent to petitioner, a maid-servant of his, without his knowledge, rescued the same. The Lords have

VOL. CCCLXXVI.

[1637?]

ordered the Attorney-General to prefer an information against petitioner in the Star Chamber, on which he attends. He submits himself, and prays that paying the 18d. he may be dismissed. [⅔ p.]

132. Petition of Francis Sawyer, of ——, in co. Northampton, to the Council. Petitioner has paid his own ship-money, and also that for friends who have refused the same. Nevertheless he has been complained of to the Lords by William Drury, a bailiff, a man of very ill fame, who has collected divers men's moneys, and kept them to his own use; and when he had distrained he restored no overplus, and has followed petitioner with unjust molestations. Prays reference to some of the justices of co. Northampton. [⅓ p.]

133. Petition of the Sheriff and Justices of Peace of co. Hereford, on behalf of themselves and others the inhabitants of that county, to the same. His Majesty, at several times of late, has required supplies of ship-money. We find the burden to be very heavy, which we conceive arises from the unequal distribution of the charge upon us as compared with other counties. The county is small, and the sickness so much dispersed as we are charged with 55l. a week to relieve one town, and it is lately begun in Hereford and other places. Pray the Lords to reduce the rate to a proportion suitable with other counties. [1 p.]

134. Petition of Sir John Shelley, of Michelgrove, Sussex, to the same. Has been appointed by Sir Edward Bishop, sheriff of Sussex, grand collector of ship-money for the rape of Arundel, whereas in the two precedent payments the sheriffs used the constables and other petty collectors for that purpose. To any employment that concerns his Majesty's service petitioner shall bring hearty devotion; yet, regarding the gout confines him to his house, and that his dwelling is in another rape, he represents the unfitness of the choice. Prays to be freed thereof. [See Vol. cccxliv., No. 10. ⅔ p.]

135. Petition of Justices of Peace, inhabitants, and freeholders of co. Flint to the same. The last two years, viz. 1635 and 1636, petitioners have been assessed 738l. 4s. 8d. and 16l. upon Flint for ship-money. Conceiving themselves overcharged, they became suitors that they might be relieved. The consideration of the premises was referred to Sir John Bridgeman, who has set down a new rate for Denbigh, Montgomery, and Flint, otherwise than was heretofore observed in the six counties of North Wales, wherein he had no reference. Pray letters of reference to the Lord President of the Marches of Wales and Sir John Bridgeman, to settle an indifferent rate for North and South Wales. [1 p.]

136. Petition of the inhabitants of the hundreds of Bruton and Norton Ferris, Somerset, to the same. State their previous complaints against Henry Hodges, formerly sheriff, for unequally taxing them in the business of shipping, the reference to the bishop of the diocese and the then present sheriff, and their order that petitioners should be eased; notwithstanding the said unjust tax laid by Mr. Hodges

[1637?]

Vol. CCCLXXVI.

still rests upon them, and they are threatened to have it levied. Pray to be eased, according to the order of the referees, of 80*l*., and that direction be given to the present sheriff to rate them equally. [10 *signatures*. 1 *p*.]

137. Petition of Pentecost Doddridge, late mayor of Barnstaple, to the Council. In the time of his mayoralty he received writ for levying 150*l*. ship-money, and made shift to pay in 138*l*. 8*s*., in gathering which he was forced to take away with his own hands goods from some, and imprison others. In consideration of his pains in his Majesty's service, prays that he may not be liable to the 11*l*. 10*s*. which is behind, the same being impossible to be gathered, as may be judged by the schedule annexed. [¾ *p*.] *Annexed*,

137. I. *Names of those who have not paid ship-money at Barnstaple. Among them is John Delbridge, dead, 3l.; Richard Delbridge, his son and executor, 10s.; and Martin Black, the vicar, who says he ought not to pay 15s.* [¾ *p*.]

138. Another petition of the same, on behalf of himself and the corporation of Barnstaple, to the same. States the receipt of 138*l*. 12*s*. [*sic*] out of 150*l*. as above, the collection of which had occasioned much grudging and repining, and many threats of actions for the distresses taken by his authority, as was already done to some former mayors. Complains of the unequal assessment of the town. The Council fixed it at 100*l*., but the sheriff took off 50*l*. from Exeter and thrust it on Barnstaple; and for the county rates on that place men of greatest worth are rated least, those who have a small tenement of 20*l*. being rated at 20*s*., whilst, in the south part of the county such persons pay 3*d*. or 4*d*. in the pound at the most. Pray them to accept petitioner's account, and to grant them relief in assessment and protection from actions for having taken distresses in the King's service. [1 *p*.]

139. Petition of Henry Kyme, messenger of the chamber, to the same. Petitioner was employed for Mr. William Stroud, of co. Somerset, for nonpayment of ship-money, in which journey he rode 250 miles in a tedious and bitter season. Prays order that Mr. Stroud may pay him his fees. [1 *p*.]

140. Petition of the Cinque Ports to the same. In ancient time, when the five ports were to find 57 ships, 15 days together, at their own cost, and afterwards as long as the King pleased, at his own pay, those boats which served were of so small burthen that they were managed by 21 men and a gromett or ship-boy, and there was allowed, and still is, when fifteenths or tenths are granted by parliament, a good proportion from the adjacent hundreds to help to support the ports. The sea has left Hythe, Romney, Lydd, and Winchelsea, and not a fisher-boat, save at Hythe, where they arrive a mile from the town. At Folkstone the sea has eaten up four parishes and the churches, and there is not any boat of service. The channel of Sandwich Haven swarves up so that no vessel of any

[1637?]

Vol. CCCLXXVI.

burden can come in; boats there be some that carry corn to London or fetch coals, but trade of merchandise there is none. The pier at Rye is of late supported and serves fisher-boats for the King's provision, and for the passage to Dieppe. The last supply they have with all cheerfulness performed, though it were very heavy in regard of their extreme poverty, and the extraordinary charge they are at in finding arms, and supporting the government of those poor places where none of any account would dwell but that they are constrained by a late order procured by the Lord Warden; but the posterity of such as have any estate forego their dwellings, because of the great charge, and so very poor men are fain to exercise the quality of justices of peace. Pray to be eased as much as conveniently they may, and that as they bear the brunt from the county, which is large, rich, and populous, so they may now help to ease them. [1 p.]

141. Petition of Richard Price, sheriff of co. Cardigan, to the Council. Endeavouring to levy the ship-money, he tried by all fair and gentle means, but could not receive one penny, so that he was compelled to distrain oxen, kine, horses, sheep, household stuff, and implements of husbandry, the which petitioner can get no money for, nor any man to offer for them one penny, though often set at sale. Prays directions what he shall do therein. [$\frac{2}{3}$ p.]

142. Petition of Joseph Rea, deputy bailiff of Westminster, to the same. Prays that he may remain in the messenger's custody until he shall pay or put in security to pay 100*l*. ship-money, remaining in his hands collected, the rest being already paid to the Treasurer of the Navy. About 400*l*. remains to levy, of 3,166*l*. assessed on Westminster for two years past. [$\frac{1}{3}$ p.]

143. Certificate of Ralph Pollard, mayor of St. Alban's, to the same. Has been very earnest with certain persons under-named for payment of their ship-money, but cannot obtain it, nor find any of their goods. The list which follows includes Sir John Jenyns, K.B., 4*l*.; Robert Sadleir, 10*s*.; Edward Bardolph, 25*s*. He has disbursed 11*l*. 10*s*.; and except the Board set some directions is like to lose it. [1 p.]

144. Certificate made by John Lake, constable of the hundred of Axton, Kent, that John Swane has done the King service. [4 *lines*.]

145. [Commissioners for Trade?] to the Council. Report on the proper provision of powder necessary to be supplied by the gunpowder maker. Mr. Meautys had collected out of the muster books that the number of trained men amounted to 98,957, of whom 54,117 were musketeers, and the horse 5,239. Their supply would take 94 lasts 3 cwt. 46 lbs. To these was to be added the supply of castles, of the navy, and of merchant ships, all which made up a total of 191 lasts 11 cwt. and 46 lbs., to which was to be added 100 lasts 13 cwt. and 46 lbs. for store in hand, making up 291 lasts 22 cwt. and 46 lbs. [*Draft.* 3 *pp*.]

146. Notes by Nicholas, to speak with his Majesty from the Commission of the Admiralty upon various matters connected with

Vol. CCCLXXVI.

[1637?] the price of gunpowder, the insertion of the Earl of Newport in the commission for sale of gunpowder, and an application of Bagnall, the saltpetreman, that he may dig for saltpetre in Woodstock House. [*See Vols.* cccxlvi., *No.* 72., cccxlviii., *No.* 6. 1 *p.*]

147. Draft of the same notes. [1 *p.*]

148. [Edward Nicholas] to [Richard Poole]. To prepare deputation to Tobias Atkins, to make saltpetre in Devon, Cornwall, Salop, and six counties in South Wales. [*Form of letter.* ½ *p.*]

149. Similar form of letter for Hugh Grove, for cos. Cambridge, Huntingdon, Rutland, and Lincoln. [½ *p*]

150. Similar form for Alexander Harris, for London and Westminster, and their suburbs within two miles in Middlesex, Kent, Surrey, and suburbs of Southwark. [½ *p.*]

151. Similar form for Nathaniel Sykes, for Essex, Suffolk, and Norfolk. [½ *p.*]

152. Similar form for Edward Thornhill, for cos. Hertford, Bedford, Northampton, and Buckingham. [½ *p.*]

153. Similar form for Francis Vincent, for Kent, Sussex, and Surrey. [½ *p.*]

154. Similar form for Richard Bagnall, for cos. Oxford, Warwick, Berks, Middlesex, and Hants. [½ *p.*]

155. Petition of Deputies for Saltpetre to the Commissioners for Saltpetre and Gunpowder. Mr. Cordewell, the powder maker, contrary to the contract made by you with us your deputies, refuses to pay for our saltpetre. Having laid out our estates in this service, having great store of petre on hand, and this being the time to make our provisions to go on with the work in winter, we are enforced to represent that, except our saltpetre be taken off our hands, and money paid for the same, we must strike our works, and discharge our servants, which will be to our extreme loss, besides the prejudice to the King's service. [⅓ *p.*]

156. Petition of Alexander Harris, Richard Bagnall, Edward Thornhill, and Nathaniel Sykes, Deputies for Saltpetre, to the same. His Majesty being to be served with saltpetre at a price certain, however materials of wages rise or fall, it was provided that your deputies should take carts and carriages at 6*d.* per mile for a ton, or a draught at statute wages of 14*d.* per day, which otherwise would have been four times so much; and likewise to take ashes and coals at reasonable prices, which last formerly could be procured for 13*s.*, 14*s.*, or 15*s.*; but now the corporation of shipmasters for coals stand upon an order that in some months they shall not sell under 17*s.*, and in others at 19*s.* Petitioners pray that they may take at price certain, a small proportion of coal out of each ship, as has been accustomed. [⅔ *p.*]

Vol. CCCLXXVI.

[1637?]

157. [Nicholas?] to the Commissioners for Saltpetre and Gunpowder. Report on the alleged non-fulfilment by Mr. Evelyn, the late gunpowder-maker, of his contracts. On investigation, it appears that he brought in gunpowder in proportion to the quantity of saltpetre supplied to him. By marginal alterations, Nicholas has converted this paper into the draft of the report from the Commissioners to the King, which is calendared under the date of 8th July 1637. [1½ p.]

158. Duplicate of the preceding draft report as originally prepared. [1½ p.]

159. A note by Nicholas of what a barrel and what a last of powder comes to at 1s. 6d. in the lb., all fees being paid. [2 pp.]

160. Account of gain made by the King on gunpowder issued this year. The cost had been 18,000l. There had been a gain on the amount issued for the fleet of 4,286l. 5s., and on that sold to the subject of 10,500l.; total gain, 14,786l. 5s. [1 p.]

161. Account of the cost and profit to the King upon the manufacture of gunpowder paid for at the rate of 7½ per lb., or 75l. per last, and sold at 18d. per pound; the profit was 105l. per last. [½ p.]

162. Similar account, in which the profit on 15½ lasts is shown to be 1,627l. 10s. [1 p.]

163. The Lords Commissioners for Saltpetre and Gunpowder to Montjoy Earl of Newport. To deliver six barrels of gunpowder to Richard Buggins, merchant, to be sent into France, and there to be sold on his Majesty's account. [*See Vol. ccclv., No. 61, calendared under date of 31 May 1637, in which this letter appears with the name of Bogan instead of Buggins.* 1 p.]

164. Petition of all the owners of ships belonging to Bristol to the Lords of the Admiralty. Petitioners, in obedience to the proclamation, take their provision of powder out of the store in the Tower; but their ships being long abroad, their powder grows dank. Pray warrant to repair their decayed powder. [½ p.]

165. Petition of Robert Davies to the Council. Was ordered by the Council, in February last, to give bond in 500l. never to make any gunpowder, since which time he never did; yet, upon wrong information, the officers of the Tower have seized upon saltpetre which he had before making the order. Prays that he may have for the same the price he paid for it. [½ p.]

166. Petition of Robert Light, saltpetreman, to the same. Two years since, by ignorance of his servants, he broke open the castle of Hardinge, co. Flint, to search for saltpetre, but with better advice none was taken within. Petitioner has justly suffered in the messenger's custody, and had his commission taken from him. Professes penitence, and prays discharge. [⅓ p.]

Vol. CCCLXXVI.

[1637?]

167. Petition of Deputy Lieutenants of co. York to the Council. Recite warrant from the Council to the Earl of Newport for 3½ lasts of gunpowder at 12d. per lb., for supply of magazine of co. York. The money was not then levied by reason of last year's infection. As the warrant was granted before the price of powder was raised, pray a renewal of the same at the same rate. [¾ p.] *Annexed,*

167. I. *The Council to the Earl of Newport. Warrant above mentioned. Whitehall, 30th November 1635.* [⅔ p.]

168. Minute of warrant to the Officers of the Ordnance to take up 20 tons of saltpetre in the custody of Mr. Fletcher, belonging to the Barbary merchants, and to deliver it to Mr. Cordewell, his Majesty's gunpowder maker, paying for the refined 3*l*. 3*s*. 4*d*. the cwt., and for the unrefined 45*s*. [¼ p.]

169. Form of warrant, probably proposed to be granted to a messenger, to attach all mayors and other officers of corporations who ought to collect his Majesty's casual revenues, but have not accounted for the same for 13 years last past, and safely to keep them until they give security to appear in the Exchequer, and pass their accounts, the messenger taking of every such corporation for expenses only 50*s*., and of the bailiff of every liberty only 20*s*. [26 *lines on parchment.*]

170. William Richardson to ——. States in what manner a clear profit of 2,500*l*. per annum might arise to his Majesty, payable out of the alum business. The works have for the last four years yielded the rent of 15,000*l*. per annum, with sufficient profit to the renter, Mr. Burlamachi, who is willing to continue them at the same rate. Without intimation of this advance, a grant has been procured, to commence at Christmas next, at 12,500*l*. per annum. Burlamachi has advanced the manufacture from 900 tons, 1,200, and 1,500, to 2,000 tons, and resolves, if he may have the works, to advance them to 2,400 tons per annum. His Majesty at the time of making the grant in reversion was a stranger to this improvement. It is fit the patentees in reversion should give his Majesty the 15,000*l*. per annum, or leave the works to his Majesty to dispose of to his best advantage. [1½ p.]

171. Petition of Sir Paul Pindar, Farmer of his Majesty's Alum Works, to the Council. Petition, which is recited in a letter founded upon it calendared under date of 26th May 1637. *Vol. ccclvii., No. 85.* [1 p.]

Vol. CCCLXXVII. Undated 1637.

[1637?]

1. Petition of Sir Edmund Verney, servant to his Majesty, to the King. About Lent last petitioner prayed for an office to enrol prentices throughout the kingdom, London and other privileged places excepted. The request did not appear unreasonable to the

Vol. CCCLXXVII.

[1637 ?]

Attorney-General, but some other person had then lately moved for a corporation for enrolling apprentices within three miles of London, whereupon petitioner prayed that he might have the office of enrolments in the said corporation, to which the King assented. Prays the King to signify the same to the Attorney-General. [¾ p.]

2. Account of the nature and duties of the office of King's Remembrancer of the Exchequer. [5 pp.]

3. ——— to Sec. Windebank. Three years since, the King granted me all felons' goods within the stannaries of Devon and Cornwall, paying therefore 10l. per annum for a certain term of years, whereas before his Majesty had but 4l. brought in upon account. Two or three days since Sir George Southcott, a tinner in Devon, cut his own throat, which will fall within my grant. Fearing that this may be procured from his Majesty by a strong hand if the personal estate should prove above 400l. or 500l., I am content to pay one half to the King, all charges defrayed. [⅓ p.]

4. Account of the payment by Sir William Brouncker, of the rent of 1,000l. per annum, reserved upon the farm of the issues of jurors from 1625 till 1637. [⅔ p.]

5. James Marquis of Hamilton to the King. Proposes to become farmer of the King's right to pre-emption of lead-ore in the Lower and Higher Peak, co. Derby, for 21 years, paying 20s. upon every fodder of such lead-ore, over and above all other duties. [½ p.]

6. Minute of the acceptance by his Majesty of this offer of the Marquis Hamilton above mentioned. [*Probably prepared in the way of anticipation.* 1 p.]

7. Petition of John Cottrell and Thomas Haward to the King. Petitioners having knowledge of 12,000l. in money and plate, and also of jewels to a great value, belonging to your Majesty, but concealed in six houses in London, Middlesex, and Surrey, pray warrant to search for and bring the same to such persons as your Majesty shall appoint, petitioners having a grant of one-fifth part of the money and plate, and for the jewels, the same to be left to your Majesty's consideration. [½ p.]

8. Petition of Thomas Hygate to Lord Cottington, Master of the Court of Wards. Petitioner having found an office after the death of Thomas Garret, has procured a particular ready to pass a grant under the seal of this court. In respect of his poverty, petitioner is unable to satisfy the accustomed duties to Lord Cottington besides the King's fine and other charges. Prays Lord Cottington to remit his fee. [1 p.]

9. Warrant to Leonard Joyner, a Messenger of the Chamber, deputed by the King's Receiver for Kent, Surrey, and Sussex, to demand rents, tenths, and all other profits in those counties, and upon non-payment to levy distresses for the same. [*Unsigned. 18 lines on parchment.*]

[1637?]

Vol. CCCLXXVII.

10. Minute of request of Walter FitzWilliam, that his Majesty's pleasure should be intimated to John Allington, Surveyor of the Customs of the Out Ports, that if he will take composition for his place he is not to put it off to any other but to FitzWilliam. [½ p.]

11. Petition of Peter Lambe, merchant taylor, to Sir John Lambe. Sir John, at the request of William Lambe, petitioner's brother, had given his hand to Capt. Crippes, in behalf of petitioner's obtaining a place in the Custom House, but the captain cannot admit petitioner without the consent of the farmers of the customs. Prays Sir John to procure the signature of the Lord Treasurer, and to second the same by his own. [⅔ p.]

12. Petition of John Porter, of Bristol, to George Lord Goring. Petitioner is known to Mr. Nicholas, Clerk of the Council, and taking notice that you, with others, are to be appointed farmers of the customs, prays to be appointed one of those that are to wait in the port of Bristol. [⅔ p.]

13. Petition of Joseph Taylor, his Majesty's servant, to the King. To move the Lord Treasurer to bestow upon him the next King's waiter's place which shall fall void in the Custom House, London. [*Endorsed by Sec. Windebank, as "From the Queen."* ⅔ p.]

14. Petition, termed relation, of Joseph Smith, of Rochford, Essex, to the Council. Petitioner made a composition for retailing tobacco, and paid a fine, and intends to pay the rents, yet he is very much hindered and abused by Peter Jervis and Thomas Wayte. Prays that they may be called to answer, that he may quietly enjoy his licence. [1 p.]

15. Petition of William Parker, of London, grocer, to the same. On 25th of August, Maperley and Francklyn, searchers for Spanish tobacco, came to petitioner's house, who gave them liberty thereof. Finding no tobacco, they attempted to break open a little storehouse for other commodities, without even requiring the key. Petitioner would not give way thereto in regard of their incivility, unless they would bring an officer, which they could not procure. To work their malice on petitioner, they have procured him to be brought in by a messenger. He made his voluntary appearance on Saturday last, but, not procuring hearing, was taken into charge of the messenger, and so remains. Being ready to give his appearance, prays that upon putting in sureties he may be discharged. [⅔ p.]

16. D[?]. Cunningham to Robert Read. That his Majesty may be satisfied that the thing required is neither newly charged nor superfluous, the surest way will be to procure a reference, mentioning his Majesty's favour to petitioner, and that Sir David Cunningham, Receiver-General, and Sir Charles Harbord, Auditor-General for that revenue, certify the true state of the business.—P.S. For Mr. Secretary's favour herein 50*l*., for your own 30*l*., which I will punctually pay upon passing the Privy Seal. [⅔ p.]

Vol. CCCLXXVII.

[1637?]

17. Statement of the case of Thomas Rookes, Searcher of Dover, and of the occasion of many suits between his father, George Rookes, and himself. The father, in the hope, as is alleged, of ousting his son from his searchership, and procuring a grant thereof to himself, had involved his son in such multitudinous litigation that he now prays that a surrender of his office might be accepted, and a new grant be made to two such persons as he shall nominate, or that he might be allowed to name a coadjutor. [1¾ p.]

18. Answer to George Rookes's allegations in reference to money transactions between himself and his son Thomas, from which it is endeavoured to be shown that George's pretences of money owing to him by Thomas are entirely untrue. [¾ p.]

19. Another statement of these transactions, from which it appears that George Rookes had procured a grant of the searchership to himself and Robert Edwards in reversion, after the death, forfeiture, or surrender of Thomas Rookes, and that subsequently the Marquis of Hamilton, on information of the transactions between Thomas and George Rookes, had procured a grant of the execution of the office during the existence of the former grants to Turberville Morgan and Hugh Lewis, who now prayed to be established therein. [1 p.]

20. Legal opinion, unsigned, that the grants of the Searchership of Dover, formerly made to Thomas Rookes and George Rookes, were both void, as granted in opposition to certain statutes, and not containing any clauses of non obstante; wherefore the King might make good his intention to grant the office to Morgan and Lewis. [¾ p.]

21. Minute of an application to his Majesty by Morgan and Lewis, that George Rookes, having obtained possession of the searchership by most false and sinister suggestions, for which he was being prosecuted in the Star Chamber, at the same time that the question of right to the office was at issue in another suit in the Exchequer, his exercise of the office might be stayed until the causes in the Exchequer and the Star Chamber were heard. [½ p.]

22. Another copy of the same. [½ p.]

23. Minute of an application to his Majesty by Turberville Morgan, from which it appears that, as against Morgan, Thomas and George Rookes combined, and obtained an order of the Council for establishing George Rookes in possession of the searchership. His Majesty had, on Morgan's application, made two several orders therein, but the Lord Treasurer, although protesting that he had as much care of Morgan and his business as if he were his brother, did not consider the King's order sufficient to annul the order of the Lords. The Treasurer therefore desired to have another order, in a form which he had directed, under which he considered he should be able to meet opposition. [1 p.]

24. Minute of another application from Morgan to the King, praying him to sign a warrant, perused and corrected by the Lord Trea-

[1637 ?]

Vol. CCCLXXVII.

surer, and the necessity for which (with reference to other legal proceedings) had become extremely urgent. The Queen also commanded Morgan to represent this to his Majesty, and that it is her suit to the King that he would sign the warrant. [1 p.]

25. Notes on the receipts from an imposition of 1½d. per lb. upon smalt or blue starch imported. They amounted to 1,875l. per annum. With reference to this item, either alone or in connexion with other receipts from the customs of potashes, there is added the following comment:—"There is a mere cheat, though neatly shrouded with a strain of wit. If my Lord Chancellor of Scotland have 1,500l. per annum, which I do not believe to be so, yet there is 2,500l. remaining to his own use and more, for he hath made his brags that he had 3,000l. per annum in the custom house, he thanked God for it." [½ p.]

26. The King to Attorney-General Bankes and Solicitor-General Littleton. Upon petition of Michael Holman and Richard Holman, scriveners, we have considered that by statute of 21st James I., every scrivener who should take anything for procuring the loan of money above 5s. for the loan of 100l. for a year, or above 12d. for making a bond or bill, should forfeit 20l., and endure imprisonment for half a year; by the severity of which law our said subjects, by taking what is freely bestowed upon them, will be liable to informers. We grant that our said subjects may take such gratuities as the parties willingly bestow, without incurring any penalty; which licence you are to prepare for our signature. [*Probably a suggested draft.* ½ p.]

27. The King to the Lord Treasurer. His Majesty having condescended to a contract made between the salt-masters of England and Scotland, whereby salt imported from Scotland was limited to 8,000 wey yearly, for which the impost is to be paid in Scotland, the Lord Treasurer is to charge all customers in England, that upon certificate of the Lord Treasurer of Scotland that salt imported is part of the said proportion it shall be suffered to be delivered within any part of this kingdom. [*Underwritten by Sec. Coke are the names of Robert Hamilton and John Thompson, masters of ships from Preston Pans, to whom, with other ships from Scotland, the above warrant was intended to apply.* 1 p.]

28. The King to the Council in Scotland. To consider certain inclosed papers, and if you find that any there have, contrary to law and our charter to the Association for Fishing, wronged that company or given occasion to discourage them, you are to see the goods and other things taken from them, and concerning which no suit is depending in the Court of Admiralty there, restored, and that the delinquents be exemplarily punished. But if it should appear that there is no just ground for the complaints alleged, you are to certify us of the informers. As to the ships cast away in Stornoway harbour, and concerning which a suit is now depending in the Admiralty Court there, our pleasure is that it be adjudged

[1637?]

in that court with equality and expedition; but, now that there are judges deputed by the council of the society of fishing, if any matter happen touching the fishing business in future, it shall be determined by such judges only, and not by the Admiralty Court there. Complaint is made that some who claim interest in the Western Islands exact from those of the association an excise or duty upon the fishings. You are to examine their rights and our interest, and either repress such proceedings, or report to us the state of their rights, and what may conduce to our ends in a work whereof we have taken upon us to be the protector. [*Draft. 2¼ pp.*]

29. Advertisement of the damage which will redound to the commerce of England by the employment of ships sailing under privileges conferred by the King of Poland, and trading between Spain, England, Dunkirk, and all the Northern Parts. These ships, called Polanders, last year received wools, hides, indigo, &c. at two-third parts the freight of our English ships. It is suggested that these ships should be prevented landing goods in England, except they pay whole composition, and should not enter our ports to deliver part and then carry away the rest; also that they should be debarred convoy to Dunkirk. [8¾ *pp.*]

Memorial of the Levant Company, setting forth the reasons for their levying about 2 per cent. in Turkey on all their own goods exported and imported; as also 2 per cent. on all strangers' goods laden in English ships. The question to which this paper specially applied was whether the latter duty, called strangers' consulage, was levied for the general benefit of the company, or specially for that of the English ambassador. [*See Corresp. of Levant Company, Vol. i., No. 94. 2 pp.*]

Another memorial, similar to the preceding, but containing some additional facts of a somewhat later date. [*See Ibid., Vol. i., No. 95. 3 pp.*]

30. Minute of a letter proposed to be written by [Archbishop Laud?] to a person addressed as "your Lordship." Urges him to favour the election of Edward Misselden, as deputy at Rotterdam for the company of Merchant Adventurers. His Majesty has declared himself very fair for him to the company. Misselden has a business there to perfect for his Majesty, and the business of the company in that place is in such state that they have almost lost their privileges and trade, and have been constrained to apply to Misselden for his help. The persons suggested in opposition to Misselden are all new men, but the company is in a storm which will not admit of a novice at the helm. [*Qu. if not in Misselden's handwriting. 1 p.*]

31. Notes by Nicholas of two Orders of Council. Petition of Ellen Rockley, widow, referred to Sir Richard Harrison, Sir Edmond Sawyer, Sir Robert Bennet, and others. Grig to pay the 5*l.* set upon

[1637?]   Vol. CCCLXXVII.

him by Lord Goring and the other Commissioners for Tobacco, not to sell any more tobacco without licence, and on payment of fees to be discharged. [1 p.]

32. Minute of suggestion of the above reference, the subject being about the sluice on the Thames for the bargemen. [7 lines.]

33. Note of another suggestion, probably in connexion with the above reference. [6 lines.]

34. [Sir Sackville Crow?] to the King. Remembrances concerning trade with Turkey. In April the Turkey merchants made complaint that the Grand Signior, by imprisoning the King's subjects, by levying money on their goods, by seizing their weapons of defence, and even by taking away the arms of the ambassador, had violated the articles of peace, so that they durst not trade any further. After various proceedings between the merchants and the Council, the merchants had ultimately ordered two ships for Aleppo, richly laden to the value of 200,000l., which had fallen down to Woolwich ready for the next fair wind. Submits these things to his Majesty for further direction, and especially as to whether, if these ships be permitted to sail without expostulation, it will not argue to these infidels an insensibility in the King to the high points of honour connected with the outrages complained of, and an "inanimosity" towards his subjects good. [1½ p.]

35. Petition of merchants of London trading to Spain and Portugal to the same. Have by former petitions set forth the losses they undergo by Turkish pirates, and the many injuries done to their factors beyond seas, contrary to the articles of peace, for which nobody on your Majesty's behalf claims remedy, nor petitioners cannot, for want of unity and government. Pray that the charter prepared by the Attorney-General, and debated at the Council Board the 20th June 1636, may be despatched, that petitioners may be united, and enabled to speak in defence of their general causes, like a nation, and like your Majesty's subjects. [⅓ p.]

36. Petition of Governor and Company of Merchants trading to the Levant to the same. About two years since your Majesty made choice of Sir Sackville Crow to be Leiger Ambassador to the Grand Signior, and petitioners advanced him a good sum of money for his setting forth, and provided presents, but for reasons allowed by your Majesty he did not proceed, and thereupon order was sent to Sir Peter Wyche to continue there till further order. About two months since petitioners entertained two great ships to go with cloth to Constantinople, whereof they gave notice to Sir Sackville Crow, who pretended that he would be ready to take passage. Pray that he may declare his resolution touching his going. [¾ p.]

37. Objections against the Deputy Clerk of the Market. Articles which set forth a variety of abuses to which the office was liable; amongst them, that the deputies yearly sent out their warrants

[1637?]

commanding the attendance of all persons using any kind of measures, met-yards, or weights. Some few had their measures and weights marked, but the most part paid 2*d.* or 4*d.*, and were dismissed. The same weights and measures were to be paid for again the next year, yet there was no uniformity in measures, but in each market the bushels, hoops, and pecks differed. If any of these fellows were indicted, they would come there no more; but next year "we shall have a new fellow, who will tyrannize on the country, and do as bad or worse than his predecessor." [2 *pp.*]

38. Reasons offered by the Glovers why the incorporation for which they had petitioned should be made to comprise seven miles and not three only, as contended for by the leather-sellers. Also, that tanned sheep skins, called Bazells, ought to be sealed. In the course of their arguments there is much information respecting the history and state of the trade in leather. [2¾ *pp.*]

39. Petition of the Masters, Wardens, and Commonalty of the English bay and say makers, woollen weavers, tuckers, fullers, combers, and tailors of Colchester, to the Commissioners for the business of the Strangers born using trades in this kingdom. His Majesty, on the petition of the citizens of London, having authorized the said commissioners to take care of the complaints of his natural-born subjects, and of the means to reform abuses tending to their prejudice, petitioners pray them to take knowledge of the many differences between petitioners and the Dutch bay and say makers dwelling in the same place, and of the prejudice petitioners suffer by the over-much liberty of the Dutch, and to give directions therein. [¾ *p.*]

40. Petition of the same to the same. Set forth in thirteen articles the regulations which they desire to have made for the government of the trade carried on by the Dutch bay and say makers, referred to in the preceding petition. [¾ *p.*]

41. Order made by the Commissioners for the business of the strangers upon a petition of the wardens and commonalty of the English bay and say makers of Colchester, complaining of the Dutch bay and say makers of the same town. The disputes between these rival manufacturers turned upon a variety of minute points in the practice of their several trades. These points are fully stated and adjudicated upon by the commissioners. [3½ *pp.*]

42. Answer of Samuel Vassall, of London, merchant, to the petition of the clothiers of Surrey and Hampshire. For 20 years he has been the sole English merchant who has traded to Ragusa, where he has vented cloth and kersies, to the relief of many thousands of poor people in England. In November 1636 the Ragusans, not buying his cloth and kersies as formerly, his servants despatched in the custom-house of Ragusa certain bales of kersies, to be transported to Belgrade and other places in Hungary. Whereupon the state of

[1637?]

Vol. CCCLXXVII.

Ragusa imposed a variety of penalties upon petitioner and his servants, which have driven him from that trade, and disenabled him to take cloth and kersies as formerly, and yet would do if he might be relieved in the premises. [¾ p.]

43. Suggestions of measures to be taken to prevent the false making of all sorts of merchandise, which in this land is unspeakable, and brings a confusion in trading, ruin to merchants, and great loss to the King's customs. The paper principally applies to woollen manufactures, and enforces the necessity of inspection and a seal. [=3 pp.]

44. Propositions for preventing abuses practised by persons making and selling unserviceable soap. The proposal is, that besides the corporation for making and sealing soap, there should be instituted another corporation for licensing such persons as alone should sell the same. [Endorsed by Sec. Windebank: "Soap. Lord Conway." 2½ pp.]

45. Abstract of affidavits made touching John Hardwick, William Howlet, Thomas Howlet, William Garret, Ambrose Brookes, Edward Moore, Timothy Langley, William Hester, and John Coldham, refractory soapmakers, who had opposed the officers in searching their houses. [2 pp.]

46. Petition of the Master, Wardens, and others of the Soapmakers of Bristol, now prisoners in the Fleet, to the Council. Petitioners have been called before the Lords concerning payment of moneys demanded by the commissioners for arrears for making soap in Bristol. Having shown how much they have been disenabled for payment thereof, and standing committed to the Fleet, they pray time for payment of what sum the Lords think fit, and that they may be discharged. [Underwritten are 11 signatures. 1 p.]

47. The Cutlers of London to the same. Reasons against the false allegations in Benjamin Stone's petition (see Vol. cccxli., Nos. 132-133), and why the Office of the Ordnance should not prove the swords sent in by the cutlers. Amongst other inaccuracies alleged against Stone and his petition, one is, "that the swords which he petitioneth to be received into the store, and pretends to be blades of his own making, are all 'bromedgham blades' and foreign blades, and for the bromedgham blades they are no way serviceable or fit for his Majesty's store." [1 p.]

48. Information as to the present state of the Company of Starchmakers. Starch was imported until Queen Elizabeth's time, paying 5s. the cwt., when certain persons, having learned the manufacture, petitioned that all "importance" might be barred, and that they would pay the 5s., and would make the commodity of bran and pollard, and not of pure wheat. A proclamation was thereupon published accordingly, and farmers were appointed for collecting the

[1637 ?]

Vol. CCCLXXVII.

5s. per cwt. This continued till about 20th James I., when the starchmakers were made a corporation, taking to farm the 5s. per cwt., and paying 2,000l. per annum for certain years, with future increase of rent, and with a clause of forfeiture for nonpayment. Upon that clause the corporation lies sleeping, and forfeited, not a penny paid to his Majesty, the manufacture being never so generally used and of such profit as at this time. [1 p.]

49. Petition of Captain Edward Popham, late captain of the Fifth Whelp, and of the company lately employed in her, to the King. The said pinnace being by order of the Earl of Northumberland, Lord General of the Fleet, appointed to convoy to the Brill three vessels laden with the Prince Elector's goods, was, on her return, lost at sea, about sixteen leagues from the coast of Holland, where, after extraordinary hazard, they at length were landed, having lost all their goods, those of the captain of the value of 200l. and those of the company of 120l., besides which loss the captain was at the charge of 100l. for clothing and maintaining 40 men in the Low Countries a full month before they could procure passage for England. Pray order that satisfaction may be given to the captain and the company. [¾ p.]

50. Minute of direction for the Farmers of the Customs to certify whether prohibiting mixtures of beaver in making hats called demicasters be prejudicial to his Majesty in his customs. Endorsed is a minute of a similar direction for the Muscovy or Russia Company to certify whether the above mixture were any prejudice to that company. [¾ p.]

51. Answers to objections made by the Farmers of the Customs to a patent for the sole manufacture of buckram, to be granted to Samuel Mason. The objections which are replied to are: 1. That the patent may trench upon the treaty with France; 2. That it may be prejudicial to the customs; and 3rd, that the patentee is not able to furnish the kingdom. [1 p.]

52. Petition of the French merchants trading in French wines to the King. Some English merchants trading in French wines, who buy wines from petitioners, have, upon mis-information, obtained an order from the Council, dated the 29th March last, against petitioners, who are threatened that it shall be put in execution, though petitioners were never heard in their defence. Pray the King to consider their reasons annexed, or refer the same to the Lord Keeper or Lord Privy Seal. [⅔ p.] *Annexed,*

 52. I. *Memorial or part of the answer which the French wine merchants make to the merchants of London. The charge against the French merchants was that they brought in falsified wines, and that they sold French wines for Rhenish wine.* [2 pp.]

53. Petition of the same to the same. The order of the 29th of March against petitioners above mentioned, if put in execution,

[1637?] Vol. CCCLXXVII.

would turn to the utter undoing of petitioners. Pray consideration of their reasons, and relief. [⅔ p.]

54. Petition of Richard Robinson of London, vintner, to the Council. About five months past there was sent to his house a pipe of medium "Canara" sack, which being found unwholesome, he returned to the merchant; yet he is now sent for, and detained in the custody of a messenger concerning the same. Prays discharge. [⅔ p.]

55. Petition of William Powell to the same. Upon complaint of Mr. Fison and Mr. Lambell, concerning the medium wines, petitioner has been sent for by warrant. According to the Lords' order he received four tuns of French wine and three pipes of Spanish, one of which was vendible, and he paid 19l. for the same, but the rest being unvendible he desired the merchants to take them again, and he would give them 40l. Prays they may take back the wines on the offered terms, or give petitioner time for payment, and that he may be discharged. [⅔ p.]

56. Petition of the inhabitants of High Holborn in the parish of St. Giles'-in-the-Fields, to the same. Richard Woodkeeper has taken a house at the upper end of Holborn, intending to convert it into a tavern, there being five taverns of late permission erected within a stone's cast one of another, who suffer great disorder by drinking in time of divine service. Pray reference to Lawrence Whitaker and Thomas Sheppard, the two next commissioners of the peace. [⅔ p.]

57. M. Barty [Bertie], and 29 other persons, to the same. The house which Richard Woodkeeper purposes to open as a tavern, as mentioned above, is most unfit, and if suffered will be very inconvenient. [1 p.]

58. Petition of poor distressed pinmakers to the same. Some few of our company have obtained a hall, and freedom thereunto, pretending the good of the commonwealth and the relief of petitioners, the which petitioners find nothing less by reason that they compel petitioners to use only English wire, which is so high priced and ill conditioned that it will scarcely pay for the materials, whilst they themselves make use of outlandish wire. Pray for a free trade as formerly. [¾ p.]

59. Petition of Joseph Rutland, yeoman of the chamber, to the same. In April 1633, the archers petitioned against Adam Crips, John Skingle, and Francis Tredway, brickmakers, for spoiling the fields adjoining to the city of London. It was ordered that they should dig no more earth nor make no more bricks there, and that they should enter into bonds to that effect to his Majesty. Crips and Skingle have forfeited their bonds, which petitioner obtained from his Majesty, with an order of Council of 8th April 1636, according to the brickmakers desires, who are willing

[1637?]

VOL. CCCLXXVII.

to give petitioner his charges and something for his pains, so as they may have their bonds, which are in the hands of Sir William Becher. Prays order that he may receive the bonds from Sir William Becher. [⅔ p.]

60. Petition of Edmond Phipps, Henry Harris, and Richard West, to the Council. The paper mills of which petitioners are farmers have been suppressed from working ever since 2nd September, by reason of this contagious time, so that petitioners cannot support themselves and families, being about 120 persons, much less pay rent, being 9l. per week. The Lords have ordered that some relief should be afforded them from the hundreds. Pray order that during the time their mills shall be suppressed they may be discharged from paying the weekly rent. [⅔ p.]

61. Petition of John Gaspar Wolffen, his Majesty's servant, to the King. Your Majesty gave leave to petitioner to make trial of his invention for brewing with a "charked" sea coal, which, as your Majesty has seen yourself, yields no smoke, and will do as readily, and within a little as cheap, as the ordinary way of brewing. Prays licence for brewers of Westminster and other places, questioned about smoke, who are willing to embrace the said invention, to continue in their brewhouses without molestation. [⅔ p.]

62. Names of the fellowship of brewers at Newcastle-upon-Tyne, with the dimensions of their mash tuns, 35 persons; with 20 others whose names only are stated. [1 p.]

63. Petition of common brewers lately licensed by Commissioners for brewing in Essex, being seventy-one persons, to the King. They have addressed themselves to fulfilling the King's pleasure, and have erected convenient offices in most parts of the county. They have also furnished good beer at more reasonable prices than the high rates of malt this dear year would afford, and have given large fines, and are willing to pay the rents yearly to his Majesty, yet the innkeepers and alehouse keepers, who had been furnished with beer from petitioners, being grown far in their debt, do now, in contempt of the proclamation, and contrary to all equity, fall afresh to brewing their own beer. Petitioners have procured letters, warrants, and subpœnas for punishing the delinquents, but have met with no reformation, but rather a scornful aggravation of their misery, by reason whereof the greater part of petitioners, who lived in good rank and fashion, and maintained good hospitality, are like to fall into incurable ruin. Pray relief. [1 p.]

64. List of 67 brewers in Essex who have paid their fines, and are bound to pay their rent. [⅔ p.]

65. Table signed by Capt. James Duppa, showing the number of brewers and maltsters in most of the counties in England and Wales,

Vol. CCCLXXVII.

with the amounts paid for their fines and yearly rents. Totals, 643 brewers, 132 maltsters; fines and rents paid 5,896*l.* 13*s.* 4*d.* [1 *p.*]

66. Table containing names of brewers and maltsters in several counties, with amounts due from them. [1 *p.*]

67. Petition of Henry Wentworth and Thomas Meautys, his Majesty's servants, to the King. Abraham Cornish, a butcher, pretending to be able to discover the abuses of butchers about London, in using the trade of butchers and graziers together, was allowed by the Attorney-General to prosecute against them in the Star Chamber, whereupon some have been lately sentenced. Upon a late petition of petitioners, offering to prosecute divers like offenders, the Attorney-General was commanded to proceed against such as they should discover, in which service petitioners employed Cornish. It is discovered that Cornish has abused the trust reposed in him, receiving money from delinquents to forbear prosecution, upon complaint whereof he was bound over to answer at the next sessions in Guildhall, being 29th June last. Cornish not appearing, his recognizance in 200*l.* and those of his two sureties in 100*l.* each are forfeit. Pray a grant of the benefit of the same. [1 *p.*]

68. Petition of Francis Brimon, of Southwark, starchmaker, to the Council. Has been brought up in the trade of a starchmaker under his father, who was one of the assistants of the company, but cannot obtain admission into the said company. Prays the Lords to give direction to the wardens and assistants for his admission, or to show cause to the contrary. [$\frac{2}{3}$ *p.*]

69. Adventurers in the Fishing Association, under the subordination of Philip Earl of Pembroke and Montgomery, to the Council. Divers noblemen and others are behindhand one or two payments, and others have paid in nothing at all, so that the association has been forced to take up money at interest, which has brought great loss to the adventurers in general. Pray the Lords to take some course whereby each particular subscriber may be required to bring in his money. [*See Vol.* cccxlix., *No.* 58. $\frac{2}{3}$ *p.*]

70. Petition of George Margetts, David Davisson, William Felgate, John Awle, and others, creditors for goods delivered to Peter Richaut for the herring fishing, to the Council. In March last the Lords referred the examination of the case of petitioners to Sir Paul Pindar, Sir John Wolstenholme, Alderman Garway, Alderman Abdy, and Thomas Jennings, who have returned their certificate. Pray that as money shall be paid in to Peter Richaut, treasurer for the fishing, it may be issued out to petitioners for payment of their debts. [$\frac{1}{2}$ *p.*]

71. Petition of the poor fishermen of the Thames to Francis Lord Cottington. Petitioners being compelled by the great oppression of

Vol. CCCLXXVII.

[1637?]

Mr. Warner to become supplicants to his Majesty for redress, Sunday next 2 o'clock was appointed for hearing their grievances. Being very poor men, friendless, and exposed by Mr. Warner's dealings "to much miseries," they implore Lord Cottington's assistance at the Board with hearts more submissive than their knees. [½ p.] Annexed,

71. I. *Articles of complaint by the fishermen of the Thames, against Nowell Warner, who having obtained a grant for the sole transporting of "lamperns" into Holland and Zealand, exercised the power which this grant gave him over the fishermen who caught the lamperns, so as to reduce the payment for the fish, and in effect to take from the fishermen their means of livelihood.* [1⅓ p.]

72. Petition of Carew Saunders and Robert Awbrey to the Council. When the Lords wrote to the Merchants Adventurers at Hamburgh, on behalf of the creditors of petitioners, to call before them William Gore, and to cause him to pay to George Knight such sums of money as Gore was indebted to petitioners, Gore promised to appoint a friend of his in London to peruse the accounts, but his friend refused, whereby the creditors, 250 in number, are much wronged. Also, William Williams, a merchant adventurer, resident at Hamburgh, who pretends to be a creditor of petitioners for 220*l.*, since their failing has obtained out of Gore's hands, by order of the Court of Merchant Adventurers at Hamburgh, all his debt with interest, which money George Knight required of him, according to the letter of the Lords, but he most contemptuously refused to obey. Pray for a privy seal similar to that granted in the case of Thomas Clutterbooke of Delft, for Gore and Williams to appear before the Lords. [1 p.]

73. Petition of John Spencer, mariner, to the same. About two months since the Gift of God, of London, lying at anchor in the Thames, was violently boarded and plundered. Two Spanish cloths of the value of 16*l.*, belonging to petitioner, were presently after seized by a constable living in Bishopsgate Street, under warrant from Sir Hugh Hammersley, and had been ever since detained from petitioner. Sir Henry Marten refused a warrant for their restoration, by reason that the pirates were removed out of the Marshalsea, whither he had sent them, and had had a trial at Newgate sessions, and till the rights of the Court of Admiralty were settled he neither could nor would give any warrant, as was desired. Petitioner prays the Lords to direct their own warrant to the constable to deliver petitioner his goods, or to require Sir Henry Marten to do for petitioner as he has already done for others in this very business. [1 p.]

74. Petition of Thomas Smyth to the King. The ballasting of ships in the Thames belonging to his Majesty, in June 1636 he demised the same to petitioner for a good sum of money, to be paid

[1637?] yearly. Petitioner has paid for wharfs, lighters, and other materials 6,000l., and is engaged for divers yearly payments, having bought out all pretenders. Yet divers masters of ships refuse to take ballast of petitioner, and take it of others. Against these delinquents petitioner has proceeded in the Star Chamber, but has been stopt upon a reference from his Majesty, which the defendants protract, and yet proceed in their former course of contempt, to the ruin of petitioner, unless the King give order therein. [$\frac{2}{3}$ p.]

75. Petition of Thomas Smyth to the King. Nathaniel Tompkins has conveyed away a deed wherein Humphry Streete acknowledged that his name in the patent for ballasting of ships was for the sole use of petitioner, by which means Streete challenges a power to ballast ships, whereby a great rent reserved to your Majesty is like to be lost, and petitioner to be undone. Prays reference to the Lords of the Council. [1 p.]

76. Petition of Mary Burrell, widow, to the Council. The Lords ordered that Ralph Eltonhead should bring in his lease and partnership which he holds of petitioner. In contempt he will neither give possession nor suffer any ballast to be carried for petitioner's profit, but only for his own. Prays permission to carry ballast at her own wharf, until the business between Mr. Eltonhead and Mr. Smyth be ended. [$\frac{1}{2}$ p.]

77. Richard Crettall to the same. Certificate that Mrs. Bruer, of Boxley, Kent, widow, sells annually to merchants 2,000 load of "fulling" earth; also that John Crettall, of Hawkhurst, clothier, offered Edward Paine, of Burling, Sussex [Birling, Kent?], 30s. per tod for his wool, which he declined, and afterward the same was taken at sea by the searchers of Newhaven. Prays that Paine may be sent for to know to whom he sold the wool. [$\frac{2}{3}$ p.]

78. Petition of Gregory Pearse, coachmaker, to the same. Petitioner sold a coach and furniture for four horses to a Spanish merchant, which he intends to bestow on a judge of the country of Banda, in Spain. The same is now stayed at the custom house for the Lords' warrant. The coach being made after the Spanish fashion is not vendible here. Prays warrant to transport the same. [1 p.]

79. Petition of Thomas Watson, of Barnet, and Ralph Gladman, of St. Alban's, bakers, to the same. Petitioners frequenting Barnet market to sell their bread, which was made answerable to the assize, the price of corn considered, yet Adam Reynoll and Thomas Marsh, the ale-conners, violently took the same away. Petitioners complained to the justices of St. Alban's, who took order for the examination thereof, yet the said ale-conners have since given away Watson's bread, and have complained to the Lords against petitioners, who are now attending in custody. Pray that they may be liberated, and that the crimes suggested against them may be examined by the justices of St. Alban's, where the offence is supposed to have been done. [1 p.]

VOL. CCCLXXVII.

[1637 ?]

80. Petition of merchants of London trading to the East parts to the Council. By encouragement from the Council and the city, petitioners have imported wheat and rye, but cannot now sell the same scarce for one third penny loss of the prime cost. Pray direction to the Lord Mayor and aldermen to settle some course that the corn may be taken off petitioners' hands, or that they may transport some part thereof to such places within the kingdom where they shall find vent for the same. [1 p.]

81. Petition of Sebastian Prevost and Edward Barker to the King. Persons take upon them without any lawful authority to get millstones in the High Peak, co. Derby, and for want of some one to look over them make them of the softest stone, which when they come to grind corn make it full of grit and sand. Pray for a grant for 14 years that none shall dig or make millstones in co. Derby without petitioners' licence, nor take away the same without being first marked by petitioners, and a fee of 13s. 4d. paid for every pair so marked. Petitioners will pay for the grant a yearly rent of 13l. 6s. 8d. [¾ p.]

82. Petition of Henry Lort to the same. Upon a certificate of some justices of peace, co. Pembroke, insinuating that petitioner had transported corn into other parts of the kingdom in this year in which they pretend an extraordinary dearth there, the Lords have given order to put petitioner out of commission of the peace. Petitioner's ancestors being English, and lately planted in that county, having bettered their estates there by increase of tillage, and petitioner having last term had conferred upon him by the Lord Chamberlain the office of custos rotulorum, the persons that have certified being petitioner's adversaries, and some of them in suit of law with him, have through envy misinformed the Lords. Petitioner will manifest that Pembroke is a great corn country, and that the inhabitants have been used to make their bread of barley, oats, and rye, of which sorts of grain petitioner has not exported any this year, and that wheat, which is little used by the common people there, has been sold by his agents to as many as would buy the same. Petitioner will also manifest that he has not transported any corn out of the kingdom, having only sent one small bark load of wheat to Bristol, and another to Beaumaris, which he sold under market price, having yet lying by him much more corn than the country will buy. Prays to be admitted to clear himself, and that in the meanwhile the order for putting him out of commission may be suspended. [*See Vol. ccclvii., No. 86, and Vol. ccclxiii., No. 59.* 1 p.]

83. Propositions for the good of the kingdom, and to raise a great benefit to his Majesty. It is proposed to institute a corporation for ordering the fishings, and to grant them the privilege for the sole fishing of pilchards and lampreys; to prohibit the letting of money at interest above the rate of 7l. or 8l. per cent.; to erect an office for registering moneys delivered by exchange or at interest, and a table to be kept of the rates and values of all coins; to bring the silver money to an equal value with gold, and to coin copper money. [1 p.]

[1637?]   Vol. CCCLXXVII.

84. [Nicholas Murford] to Mr. Sherwood. Narrates the history of the establishment of the manufacture of salt at Yarmouth, and answers the objections commonly urged against it. The writer insists that sufficient quantities of salt might be made for the service of the kingdom, and of a better quality than was made at Newcastle or Shields or in Scotland, and at less expense. [6 pp.]

85. Proposal for construction of a water tower, and the laying of pipes from Temple Bar to Charing Cross, and thence to Westminster, at a present cost of 1,000l. and 300l. per annum in perpetuity. [1 p.]

86. Petition of Colonels Lodowick Leslie and James Scott to the King. After much charges and pains, petitioners have attained to the art of improving ground, making Castile soap, raising water and weights out of pits, and keeping chimnies from smoking. Pray a patent. [⅔ p.]

87. The same to the same. Duplicate, save that the cure of chimnies from smoking is here omitted. [½ p.]

88. Petition of William Hinde, Stephen Mallowes, William Austin, and Henry Leake, inhabitants of the liberty of Paris Garden and the Clink on the Bank side, to the Council. About a year and three months ago petitioners exhibited their petition concerning a way leading through part of St. George's Fields into the liberty of Paris Garden and so to the Thames side, which, being very anciently the only way for cart and horse, is a very convenient passage for all persons, and is the passage for many of the Lords when his Majesty lies at Greenwich. This way was recovered by verdict against the borough of Southwark about 12 years since, and has been ever since quietly enjoyed, until certain innholders of the borough, envying petitioners, who are tenants by fine and yearly rent to his Majesty for their inns, and drawing the city of London to their part, chained up the way. Upon the former petition of petitioners the Lords ordered that the way should be open until by course of law it should be otherwise adjudged. Petitioners pray that it may continue open accordingly, or that the Lords will refer the hearing of the controversy to whom they shall think fit. [⅔ p.]

89. Petition of the Lord Mayor and citizens of London to the King. The 7th February 1636-7 your Majesty directed the Attorney-General to prepare a grant to petitioners of the offices of package, scavage, balliage, and portage, and that the hostage of merchant strangers, having anciently gone with the office of scavage, should be included in the book. Before any book could be prepared, a question of the hostage of merchant strangers was set on foot by the Earl of Holland and others, which question has ever since depended, whereby the Attorney-General forbears to pass the hostage with the other offices. Prays direction to the Attorney-General to prepare the book for signature according to former directions, and to resume the reference concerning hostage. [¾ p.]

VOL. CCCLXXVII.

[1637 ?]

90. Petition of Robert Hore, apothecary in the Old Bailey, to the Council. Has been 18 months a suitor to the Commissioners for Building, for licence to rebuild his house, with a small addition on new foundation, and, having lately obtained leave, has pulled down his house, and laid the foundation for a new one; but upon petition of his next neighbour, Mrs. Andrews, the works had been stayed by order of the Council until the Commissioners certify. Prays that the works may go forward, it being a great hindrance to petitioner, very dangerous to his neighbours whose houses lie open, and Mrs. Andrews having petitioned out of malice. [½ p.]

91. Notes concerning the inconveniences which arise from the division of authority in Exeter. The Close being under the jurisdiction of the clergy, became a place of shelter for malefactors, especially during the absence of the clergy on their benefices, and in time of war infinite multitudes of persons might be received there without controlment, whereby the whole city might be surprised. In the rebellion, temp. Edward VI., a principal cause of the rebels overthrow was their long stay to have surprised the city, which being ruled by one government was strong, and performed honourable service, whereas if there had been two temporal governments within the walls strife might have weakened the city, and made it a prey. [1 p.]

92. Petition of Samuel Isack, town clerk of Exeter, to the King. Is questioned in the Star Chamber for taking fees supposed to be innovated. The same are no other than time out of mind have been there taken. There being no table of fees, or other rule save custom, he knows not what he may demand. Prays reference to the Commissioners for Fees to regulate his fees. [⅓ p.]

93. Return of new erected houses within the last 34 years, also of divided houses, inmates, and those that receive the alms of the ward of Coleman Street. [*Probably should have been included in those brought together into Vol. ccclix. 11 pp.*]

94. Notice that T. S. intends to be a suitor to the Lord Mayor and Court of Aldermen for a lease in reversion of the garbler's place, which is for the cleansing of all spices, drugs, &c. within the kingdom. Sets forth his qualifications for the office. [1 p.]

95. Information that Richard Harris, John Parker, and William Ward have built in Covent Garden at least 100 houses, most of them small petty buildings, dangerous for infection. [½ p.]

96. Names of contributors and amounts of their contributions towards making the new sewer in Scotland Yard, who are behind in their payments. [1 p.]

97. Estimate, by Sir John Lambe, of the revenue of the bishopric of Lincoln, with the several sources whence derived; total, 1,936*l.* per annum. [1 p.]

[1637?]   Vol. CCCLXXVII.

98. Another paper of calculations relating to the same subject. [=½ p.]

99. Rental of lands and profits of the Bishop of Lincoln within the manor of Bugden. Total received, 310*l*; estimated value, 475*l*. [1 p.]

100. Information for his Majesty concerning encroachments upon the Thames near Wapping, Shadwell, Ratcliffe, and Limehouse. Upon a suit in the Exchequer Chamber, on the prosecution of the late Earl Carlisle, and the report of a commission, it was determined that Wapping Street was the place of the ancient Thames or Wapping wall, and that all houses between that street and the Thames were encroachments. Some questions being again raised, it is recommended that the question be referred for re-hearing to three or four of the Lords, with the Barons of the Exchequer, and some of the King's counsel. [1 p.]

101. Minute of application to the King to recommend to the Archbishop of Canterbury the despatch of a reference touching a pontage at the bridge of Berwick, whereby the King may be freed of 100*l*. per annum for the said bridge, and of 2,000*l*. granted by King James for building a church in that town. Also that the Earl of Stirling may signify to the Lords of Scotland the King's pleasure for hearing that business. [*See Calendar*, 27 *June* 1637, *p.* 244. ½ p.]

102. Petition of Walter Thomas, portreeve of Swansea, whereof the Lord Privy Seal is chief lord, to the Council. By warrant of 19th of April last, petitioner was sent for, and has ever since given daily attendance, lying at great charge in custody of a messenger. Prays to be called to answer, and if he shall free himself to be discharged, and have allowance for his damage. [¾ p.]

103. Petition of George Weatherheard to Thomas Earl of Arundel, Earl Marshal, and Edward Earl of Dorset, Lord Chamberlain to the Queen. Petitioner in January last took a lease of an old stable in Lincoln's Inn Fields, which he used as a stable, having been so employed above 50 years. The stable having of late time been let for a few months to a joiner, divers malicious persons seek to prove it a petty "oastrie," which they cannot do, petitioner living in a very eminent house in Chancery Lane near his stables, for which he pays 48*l*. rent to Sir Robert Rich, and is able to furnish a dozen beds, and to give security for goods of gentlemen that shall lodge in his house. Prays that he may not be troubled about the stables, or that the view thereof may be referred to Sir Henry Spiller and Lawrence Whitaker, Commissioners for Buildings. [1 p.]

104. Petition of Sir William Russell, Treasurer of the Navy, to the King. By a contract, and letters patent, dated 27th December 1632, your Majesty granted to William Collins and Edward Fenn,

Vol. CCCLXXVII.

[1637?]

in fee farm, to the use of petitioner, a garden next to Old Palace Yard, Westminster, of the yearly rent of 26s. 8d., and two tenements near Charing Cross, of the yearly rent of 3l. 10s. When the Great Seal was affixed to the letters patent, the Lord Keeper called petitioner and the patentees to promise by writing not to sell the said parcels but according to your Majesty's pleasure. Petitioner has paid into the Exchequer 20 years' purchase for the premises, from the sale whereof he has been restrained contrary to the contract and letters patent, whereby he is damnified 402l. 12s., besides interest for five years. For that a surrender is already made of certain woods in Bewdley, co. Worcester, of 12l. per annum, according to your Majesty's pleasure declared to petitioner in a warrant from Richard Earl of Portland, late Lord Treasurer. Petitioner prays that for 106l. 6s. 8d. in part of the said 402l. 12s. and the interest, the writing remaining with the Lord Keeper may be delivered to him, and that he may sell the said garden and tenements; and that for 296l. 5s. 4d. in full satisfaction, the Attorney-General may prepare a warrant either for repayment of the same, or for allowing him so much upon his accompt for last year. [1 p.]

105. Petition of Thomas Hicks to the Council. Petitioner has several tenements in St. Olave's, Southwark, and stands bound to discharge the parish from them, according to a book of orders. Most of the tenants are behind with their rent, and some refuse to pay, besides divers are idle persons, likely to bring great charge on the parish, the burden whereof will lie upon petitioner. Prays relief. [½ p.]

106. Republication of an Order of Common Council, that thenceforth, when every precinct has presented the names of their inquestmen at the time accustomed, that then the good men of the same inquest shall make choice of one of the most discreet to be their foreman, who shall be allowed by the alderman of that ward, or in his absence by the Lord Mayor. [*Broadside, printed by Robert Young, printer to the city of London.* 1637. 1 p.]

107. The King to Attorney-General Bankes and Solicitor-General Littleton. To prepare a commission for Thomas Doughtie, and such others as he shall nominate, to inquire concerning the encroachment upon the streets of London and other towns of sign-posts, rails, posts, bulks, benches, shopboards, and footsteps into houses, and also concerning cellar-windows, and stairs descending into cellars which are made habitations, tap-houses, and forges for smiths, with power to treat and compound with offenders, or to remove the said nuisances. [*Draft.* ⅔ p.]

108. Petition of Giles Penn to the King. Being employed in the business of Sallee, to discover his best knowledge for a way to suppress the Morisco pirates of that castle, what he made known has been followed by setting forth a fleet, in which petitioner expected

VOL. CCCLXXVII.

[1637?]

some good place, but was omitted without any reward, and with payment of less by 50l. than his expenses. Prays that the fleet, having been successful, and having now returned, he may be appointed agent or consul of Sallee and the kingdom of Fez. [½ p.]

109. Minute of a passport for Levine Brinkmary, a High German, lately discharged from the Gatehouse, to pass the seas. [¼ p.]

110. Petition of Anne Daniel to the Council. Petitioner's husband, Capt. Charles Daniel, now serving as a captain under the King of France, is desirous to have petitioner and their three children come over to him. Prays warrant for their free passage. [⅔ p.] *Annexed,*

> 110. I. *Capt. Charles Daniel to his wife. Though our pay be not well paid, yet have we no want of good wine and fair bread, and you shall always have half of what God and the fortune of the wars shall send us, wherefore I pray thee come over with your children to Treport near Dieppe.* [¾ p.]

111. Petition of Paul Marke to the Council. About a year since he defrayed the charges of the Polish ambassador, for which he received a warrant under the Privy Seal. Not being able to give satisfaction to his creditors, to whom he is much indebted, touching that business, for that he could not receive his money in such manner as might content them, he has been already arrested, and is again threatened to be put into prison. Prays that until payment he may have a protection. [½ p.]

112. Petition of Anthony Fortescue, agent in this court for the Duke of Lorraine, to the King. The arrest set forth by the parliament of Paris against the duke and the rest of the princes of the house of Lorraine has been here printed in English, and published with licence by Weckherlin, who pretends to be the King's servant. Prays the King not to permit the duke and other princes to be thus publicly abused by subjects of the King, authorized by one who pretends to be his servant. The fame of the King's justice in punishing so heinous an offence will invite all other sovereign princes to be most tender of his Majesty's honour. [1 p.]

113. Petition of Peter L'Espert, a poor French merchant and protestant, to the Council. For the last five years petitioner and his wife have inhabited in London, carrying on a small commerce with France. He is now threatened with arrest by certain tradesmen, also Frenchmen, who detain his goods, refuse to allow him competent time to sell his merchandize, and endeavour to buy up his small debts, to disable him from following his business. Prays a reference to the Attorney or Solicitor-General. [¾ p.]

114. The King to Thomas Earl of Arundel, Earl Marshal. The Lord Stafford, our ward, whose guardian you were, is lately deceased, by reason whereof the estate, which is now to descend to his sister,

[1637?]

Vol. CCCLXXVII.

may come into some distraction. We recommend to you the care of his mother and sister, and likewise of that estate. We also require the Master of the Court of Wards to be assistant to them as occasion shall require. And we shall be ready to give testimony of our particular care of the support of that ancient and noble house. [*Draft.* ½ *p.*]

115. Notes on the descent of the barony of Stafford upon the death of Henry Lord Stafford in 1637. His sister Mary, wife of Sir William Howard, was not only his sole heir, but was presumed to be heir general of Hervy Bagot and Millicent his wife, sister and heir of Robert Lord Stafford, temp., King John, by whom the ancient barony of Stafford came into this family; but this last claim was disputed by Roger Stafford, who claimed to be the son of Richard Stafford, a younger son of Henry Lord Stafford, temp, Edward VI. This paper is adverse to his right, and contends that if it were established it would be a question whether it might not be discontinued for want of competent living, as had been the case with others of the nobility. [2 *pp.*]

116. Questions touching Roger Stafford's title to the barony of Stafford, against Mary the Lady of Sir William Howard. If Roger Stafford shall prove that he is the only issue male of Henry Lord Stafford, only son of Edward late Duke of Buckingham, who was attainted 13 Henry VIII., then the question will be, whether the barony shall descend to the Lady Howard, as heir general of Henry Lord Stafford, to whom the ancient feudal place is descended, or to Mr. Stafford, as heir male of Henry Lord Stafford, who has no lands. [½ *p.*]

117. Justices of Peace of co. Dorset [?] to the Council. Certificate of the plots and abuses long offered to Sir Robert Willoughby by his lady and one Garnier, a French gentleman, both styling themselves the Queen's servants. We have known Sir Robert to be well descended, and one who lives in good repute, but the only gentleman in England that ever we heard of who is a stipendiary to his wife, who, under pretence of a grant from the King, disposes of all Sir Robert's lands, and having procured money as lewdly she and her friend consume it. It is thought they live a disgraceful life, having invested herself with her husband's estate, and committing many outrages, as in selling his goods, breaking up his trunks and chests, and embezzling his evidences, and so granting estates of his lands at her pleasure. [*Underwritten, ten signatures.* 1 *p.*]

118. Similar certificate, signed by ten tenants and neighbours of Sir Robert Willoughby. They give outrageous examples of the violent and disorderly conduct of Lady Willoughby. [1 *p.*]

119. Petition of Thomas Stebbranck and Susan his wife, to the Council. Upon a former petition, which is annexed, the Lords referred the hearing of matters between Richard Phillips, father-in-law of petitioners, and them, to Sir Edward Barkham and Ralph

[1637?] Vol. CCCLXXVII.

Freeman, aldermen of London, who find 81*l*. 7*s*. 8*d*. to be due to Susan from her father-in-law, and 50*l*. more due to her child; but petitioner being poor and Phillips very litigious, they pray that Phillips may be sent for by warrant, and course taken for petitioner's satisfaction. [*See Vol.* cccxl., *No.* 15. ⅔ *p.*] Annexed,

> 119. I. *Petition of Thomas Stebbranck and Susan Stebbranck to the Council. Petitioners set forth their various claims against Richard Phillips, who upon his inter-marriage with their mother-in-law undertook to pay petitioners and their child about* 200*l*. [¾ *p.*] Underwritten,
>
> 119. I. i. *Reference to Alderman Barkham and Alderman Ralph Freeman, to end the cause or certify.* [¼ *p.*] Annexed,
>
> 119. II. *Report of the referees above mentioned. They found that Susan Stebbranck was entitled, as administratrix of Edward Symmes, her brother, to* 41*l*. 7*s*. 8*d*., *being a sixth part of their mother's estate, which by an award had been assigned to the said Edward, and also that* 50*l*. *was to be paid to Susan Stebbranck's child. Phillips refused all terms of arrangement that the referees could devise, and added that he would answer it before the Lords himself.* [½ *p.*]

120. Petition of David Stott, Messenger of the Chamber, to the Council. Petitioner is born to an inheritance of 9*l*. per annum lying at Cloyden [Claydon] in Suffolk, but which has been detained from him these 11 years by one Brookes, guardian to Alexander Stott, upon pretence of a surrender from petitioner's grandfather, which petitioner suspects to be false. Has solicited the late and present steward of the manor to resolve him whether there were any such surrender, but in vain. Prays reference to Robert Sparrow, a magistrate of Ipswich, and Edmund Harvey, counsellor-at-law, to command Mr. Bacon, lord of the manor, and Mr. Chapman, the steward, to resolve whether there be any such surrender or no. [1 *p.*]

121. Petition of Francis Taylor, Messenger of the Chamber, to the same. Thomas Parker having been committed to petitioner's custody, after seven weeks made his escape, when petitioner was by warrant committed to the custody of David Stott, one of his fellow messengers. States a variety of circumstances which ended in the committal of Stott to Newgate, the recapture of Parker, and his detention in the Counter in Wood Street. Prays examination of the premises by any persons whom the Lords shall think meet, and petitioner will give security to perform their order. [⅔ *p.*]

122. Petition of John Apsley, executor of Sir Allen Apsley, to the same. About March 1636 his Majesty gave warrant for a commission for passing Sir Allen Apsley's accounts, which accordingly passed the Signet and Privy Seal; but upon petition of some of Sir

Vol. CCCLXXVII.

[1637?]

Allen's creditors it was stopped at the Great Seal, and since the Lords ordered petitioner to pass the same in the ordinary way of accounts in the Exchequer, which he cannot perform, because the accounts for 1626 and 1627 ought to be signed by four commissioners, but petitioner can obtain but three commissioners to sign them. Prays that the commission stayed at the Great Seal may proceed, or that they would move his Majesty for a new commission, or would give warrant for allowing the accounts between his Majesty and Sir Allen not yet allowed, in regard he cannot pass them by way of the Exchequer. [½ p.]

123. Petition of John Apsley, executor of Sir Allen Apsley, Edmond Morgan, Robert Haughton, John Holt, Samuel Dones, William Chatterton, Thomas Clarke, William Newman, and Richard Carter, creditors authorized by all the others, to the King. Great sums of money have been due to petitioners these many years for provisions for the Navy, delivered to Sir Allen Apsley, as by report of Sir John Wolstenholme and the other referees appointed by an order of 29th September 1630 appears. Having petitioned for satisfaction, they have been referred to the examination of Sir Allen's accounts with his Majesty, which are now signed by the Lord Treasurer and Lord Cottington, and are found by the auditors of the imprests, the years 1626 and 1627 being disallowed for want of a fourth signature, to be indebted to your Majesty above 200,000*l.* Pray a privy seal for allowance of the said two years' accounts by the three signatures already affixed, and of the rest of Sir Allen's accounts; and that in the interim a reseizure may be made of all lands made over from your Majesty to Sir Allen, which have been otherwise disposed of than to the satisfaction of the navy debts, for which they were first granted, and that afterwards the Lords may have power to re-grant those lands to the use of petitioners, with power to the Attorney-General to sue in his Majesty's name for all debts due to the executor of Sir Allen. [¾ p.]

124. John Apsley, executor of Sir Allen Apsley, to the Council. Answer to the petition of Allen, William, James, Lucy, and Barbara, children of Sir Allen. The petitioners had alleged that Peter Apsley, in 1632, granted an annuity of 100*l.* for 16 years, to be paid out of sundry tenements in the occupation of the said Peter, and which annuity was paid until about six months last past, when the answerer, John Apsley, purchased the inheritance, and the deeds of the same were detained by him, whereby petitioners were destitute of maintenance. John Apsley answers that the petition is contrived by Dame Lucy Franck, wife of Sir Leventhorpe Franck, late wife of Sir Allen, and mother of the petitioners, with her brother's friends and allies, to whom Sir Allen made over his estate in his lifetime by his said wife's instigation, in whose custody the pretended deed remains, and to whom the same annuity (if any be) is to be paid, and not to the petitioners. Since the grant, Dame Lucy is intermarried, and sequesters herself from her husband, and intermeddles with Sir

Vol. CCCLXXVII.

[1637?]

Allen's estate as though she were sole. The annuity was paid to Dame Lucy by the answerer (being willing to do her any office of friendship he might), but in consequence of various suits against him by the creditors, who alleged that by combination with Dame Lucy and Sir John St. John, her brother, he went about to conceal Sir Allen's estate, and defeat them of their debts, he now detains the same, and prays that petitioners may set forth the facts as to the said annuity. The answerer will stand to such order as may be thought meet. [¾ p.]

125. [Katherine Lady Huncks to Edward Viscount Conway.] When it comes to the point that I must either offend you or myself, I will leave the comforts and contentments of this world, and frame my will to yours. I am now at Mr. Palmer's. I never went to any place with so ill a will; but, dear lord, I hope, nay, I do assure myself, that when you are settled again you will call me home to you, that I may end my old years with you. I trust God will hear the old widow's prayers, which shall never fail you. [*Imperfect.* ½ p.]

126. Petition of Richard Delamain, his Majesty's servant, to the King. Your Majesty, in 1627, entertained sundry aliens for engineers at 100*l.* per annum during life. They are now departed these kingdoms, such as remain being only directors of the manufacture, and not versed in the mathematical part, which is specially requisite for the engineer for military works. In the late expedition for measuring forts and castles, petitioner was by Sir John Heydon employed in their stead. Prays to be admitted to one of the said engineer's places, that he may devote his life and studies to his Majesty's service, as also to fit up for the prince against he come of age sundry mathematical tractates, which for more than 15 years past petitioner has collected and reserved. [½ p.]

127. Petition of the same to the same. Sets forth his past invitations to foreign service, with proffers of 200*l.* per annum, which he had declined, reserving himself for employment by his Majesty. Also, that in 1633 he was presented to his Majesty by Sir John Heydon for employment under the ordnance, whereupon the King granted him a fee of 40*l.* per annum, which petitioner hoped in time to be augmented, his predecessor having had 100 marks per annum besides his fee, and the least skilled engineers receiving 150*l.* and 200*l.* The better to enable him to live, and to fit for the press those collections in the mathematics gathered during 16 years' observation and study, which may be helpful to the prince against he comes of age, petitioner prays a grant of Peter Burr's place and fee of 100*l.* per annum, his place of engineer of fortifications having been void by absence or death for more than seven years. Prays also for money for payment of workmen employed in raising those large instruments for his Majesty's sight and service which were used by his Majesty on the 11th July last, for the confirmation of some new propositions,

[1637?]

Vol. CCCLXXVII.

and instruments to be made for his Majesty's bedchamber and for the Great Ship, the charge of which amounts to 76*l*., exclusive of petitioner's expenses. [¾ *p*.]

128. Edward Nicholas to [John Ashburnham?]. Letter of thanks for favours conferred upon the writer's brother, whose gratitude he guarantees, and in connexion with meditated purchases by Nicholas. Treaty on foot with France and Sweden which will produce a war with Spain. Bannier, the Swedish General, has driven the Duke of Saxe to great straits, being gotten into his best towns. [*Imperfect.* 1 *p*.]

129. Petition of Judith Marsh, executrix of Gabriel Marsh, to the King. Gabriel Marsh, about January 1627, lent Sir Sackville Crowe 1,000*l*. Failing in repayment, Marsh, in 1631, obtained a judgment for the debt, which was subsequently defeasanced that Sir Sackville should pay 1,100*l*. on days now about six years past, but Sir Sackville has not paid any part thereof. Marsh died about November was two years, intending the said debt for the advancement of his only child by petitioner. Prays direction to Sir Sackville, who is speedily to depart on foreign service, to satisfy the said debt, or to secure the same before his departure. [¾ *p*.]

130. Petition of William King, prisoner in Newgate, to the Council. Was committed to prison by Sec. Windebank for a little treatise delivered to Lord Leppington. Has remained in most woeful thraldom 27 months. Expresses contrition, and prays enlargement on bail, or that he may be called to answer. [*Underwritten,* "*Nil.*" ¾ *p*.]

131. Petition of Captain Christopher Burgh to the Council. Petitioner having for many years been employed as a commander in his Majesty's service beyond seas, is lately arrested at the suit of one Underhill, to whom he became bound for one Jobson, now worth 100*l*. per annum. Petitioner's other creditors being willing to agree to a composition, Underhill refused, saying petitioner should die in prison; and being informed that petitioner was likely to have employment in his Majesty's service, answered it was not in his Majesty's power to release petitioner. Prays reference to Sir Robert Vernon, Sir Thomas Jay, and Thomas Jay, Esq., justices of peace and commissioners for discharge of unable debtors, to bring Underhill to a composition, or take order for petitioner's release. [1 *p*.]

132. Petition of [Elizabeth?] Countess of Carrick to the King. Two years since she acquainted your Majesty with her necessities by the Earl of Ancheron [Ancram], whose answer was that you were well pleased to relieve her, but not in that way she desired, since which time her necessities have grown so great that she has been forced to sell 100*l*. a year of her jointure, and is likely to be ejected out of her house for nonpayment of rent. Prays for the making of

Vol. CCCLXXVII.

[1637 ?] a baronet, or 1,000*l*. out of the Exchequer, Custom House, Court of Wards, or Privy Purse. [½ *p*.]

133. Betteris Tottenham to Dr. Clerke. Information respecting the suspected unchastity of Anne Trepelo. She was thought to have had a child by Thomas Simcocks. [*In the margin are questions by Sir John Lambe, with replies. Copy.* 1 *p*.]

134. The King to George Kensham, of Tempsford, co. Bedford. Understands that he has a daughter, his only child, of whose bestowing the King doubts not he will use that care that becomes a discreet father. Recommends to him Thomas, eldest son of Sir Francis Windebank, as a fit match for his daughter, both in regard of the place which his father holds and in respect of his education and disposition. For his fortune, though the King believes that can be no impediment, yet a servant so near the King's person cannot but improve it daily. Kensham would do well, therefore, to enter into treaty with Thomas Windebank before any other. [*Draft in the handwriting of Sec. Windebank.* 1¼ *p*.]

135. Catalogue of books chiefly relating to law and history. The handwriting of certain corrections and additions is thought to be that of William Prynne. [*Endorsed,* "*Note of my books.*" 5¼ *pp*.]

136. Petition of Lambard Cooke to the Council. Petitioner, first by his father and since by suretyship, being much in debt, he had mortgaged his lands, and the same are now extended by his creditors, but they are willing to consent to a present sale. His wife having a jointure in part of the estate, petitioner cannot dispatch until her brother, Sir John Wentworth, of Somerleyton, Suffolk, be first spoken with, and a new assurance drawn. In the meanwhile petitioner fears to be arrested, and therefore prays for a protection. [⅔ *p*.]

137. Note, partly in Spanish, of the arrest of Bartholomew Kellam, at Warrington. The pursuivant Wainright, without commission, apprehended him, and made oath that he was a priest, and that he had heard him say mass, which was false. They took from him his horse, his sword, and his money, and sent him to the prison of Lancaster on foot, 40 miles. [¾ *p*.]

138. Petition of Robert Reade and Percy Church, his Majesty's servants, to the King. There has been lately a rape and murder committed upon a maiden named Hoy, within the hundred of Rochford, Essex, by certain persons unknown. Pray a grant of the forfeitures of the lands and goods of the murderers, whom petitioners will endeavour to discover and cause to be indicted. [⅓ *p*.]

139. Petition of Valentine Clarke, one of the Grooms of her Majesty's Privy Chamber, to the King. There was 1,200*l*. due to petitioner's brother, Edward Clarke, as Groom of the Bed-chamber to the Queen, for which he had a tally struck for 500*l*., and a direction from the then Lord Treasurer to Sir Robert Pye for pay-

[1637?]

ment of the rest, but not one penny paid, by reason of his Majesty's more serious occasions. Prays, in satisfaction of the 1,200*l.*, to grant to petitioner the next reversion in the Statute Office for life, by which he may be better able to pay such of the debts of his brother as he stands engaged for. [*Endorsed by Sec. Windebank,* " *Clarke, recommended by the Queen.*" ½ *p.*]

140. Petition of Lady Dorothy Shirley, widow of Sir Henry Shirley to the King. It was my weak estate, my younger children's want of maintenance, and a too sensible memory of my late husband's promises to Lord St. Albans and others, to make my jointure competent, that moved me, by the Earl of Holland, to implore of your Majesty some benefit out of my son's estate during his minority, which was conceived as granted in a greater measure than asked, although the Court of Wards will neither understand nor admit it so, but makes their Court-orders to destroy your Majesty's bounty. Prays his Majesty to make his bounty appear mercy and pity towards her. The strict execution only of your Majesty's commands herein will make me find and feel your princely goodness. [1 *p.*]

141. Petition of Martha Wildman, widow, to the Council. Sir Edward Bishop being required to give petitioner satisfaction of 17*l.*, due to her husband from Henry Sherley, whom Sir Edward Bishop slew when he came to his chamber by appointment to receive moneys due to him, or else to attend the Lords, Sir Edward only shewed himself on the day prefixed, but protested he would be neither compelled nor persuaded to give satisfaction of half the debt. Prays that Sir Edward may be commanded to attend on a day prefixed, and not to depart until the Lords give an end to this just demand. [½ *p.*]

142. Petition of Sir Garrett Ransford to the King. In a former petition he discovered speeches uttered by Sir Nicholas Stoddart, which trench upon his Majesty's government, and vilify the Scottish nation, whereupon the Attorney-General required him and others to testify the said speeches. After petitioner returned to the Fleet from Mr. Attorney's Chamber, the deputy-warden, James Ingram, put petitioner in the porter's lodge in irons, and the next morning, when petitioner went to the sessions to testify in your Majesty's behalf, Ingram forced him to go through the streets with irons on, and afterwards committed him close prisoner to the Tower Chamber, the most loathsome room in all the prison. Prays that he may return to his wonted chamber, and have his former liberty of the house. [⅔ *p.*]

143. Petition of Nicholas Reyser, mariner, and part owner of the St. Peter, now in the Thames, to the Council. Two years since, being in a merchant voyage, he maintained a sea-fight, wherein his ship was burnt and nine of his men killed, and the greatest part of his estate lost. To avoid such inconveniences he has provided himself with a very sufficient ship, and procured letters of denization, willing to

Vol. CCCLXXVII.

[1637 ?]

live and die his Majesty's liege-man. Prays the Lords' warrant for purchase of ordnance, he putting in security not to alienate the same. [⅔ p.]

144. Petition of Robert Prentice and Sarah his wife, widow of William Brockett, on behalf of the same Sarah, and of Brian, Frances, Lucy, and Margaret Brockett, youngest children of the said William and Sarah, to the Council. William Brockett died seized of lands to the value of 200l. yearly, besides personal estate of 3,860l. The administration of Brockett's goods appertained to Sarah, for herself and the said younger children, but she being sickly relinquished the same to Thomas Brockett, the eldest brother, upon agreement that she should enjoy all the goods in her husband's house called Stockenden in Surrey, that Thomas should pay his father's debts, and the residue to his younger brothers and sisters, and in the meantime should pay the said Sarah 30l. per annum for their maintenance. But the said Thomas, persuaded by Samuel Cowley, had broken his agreement, had conveyed all his goods and lands to Cowley, and had withdrawn himself, thereby leaving the debts unpaid, and the younger children like to starve or be thrown on the parish. Thomas Brockett not having been heard of for two years, petitioners pray that Cowley may be called before the Lords to answer. [¾ p.]

145. Petition of Sir Robert Sharpey to the same. Presented his person to the Board, upon notice of a warrant for his apprehension. Has been examined, and declared his innocent intentions. Expresses contrition for his unadvised presumption. Prays to be freed from the custody of a messenger, and that his word may be taken for his appearance upon the least summons. [½ p.]

146. Petition of the same to the King and Council. Expresses contrition and prostrate submission for the obnoxious petition concerning lead mines in co. Derby. Has presented former petitions to the Council, and in particular to Lord Newburgh. Implores pardon, and craves the charitable intercession of the Lords. [⅔ p.]

147. Petition of Robert Partridge, of Colchester, weaver, to the Council. Petitioner is the only son of Robert Partridge, deceased, and Rose his wife, who after the death of petitioner's father intermarried with one Mr. Rosse, who died without issue by her, and lastly petitioner's mother died seized of lands and personal estate to the value of 1,000l., whereof petitioner took administration. But William Grange and Mary Grange, servants to petitioner's mother at the time of her death, pretending a will, petitioner was forced to commence a suit against them, whereupon they joined with William Lynne, a justice of peace, to conceal goods conveyed away by Grange. In his suit petitioner retained William Arwaker as his attorney and solicitor, who, understanding petitioner's right, offered petitioner 500l. for the same, which petitioner refusing, Arwaker set up one Collins as a claimant, and procured him to seal a lease to Arwaker, to try the title, Arwaker at the same time having petitioner's deeds

Vol. CCCLXXVII.

[1637 ?]

in his hands, which they threaten to burn and undo petitioner, with many other unjustifiable proceedings. Petitioner prays the Lords to send for Arwaker, Lynne, and William Grange, and give him relief. [1 p.]

148. Petition of George Faunt, executor, and nephew of Sir William Faunt, to Archbishop Laud. Sir William was lately fined in the Star Chamber 5,000l. to the King, and 2,000l. to Henry Earl of Huntingdon, which latter sum, with 50l. costs, the Earl has long since received. Sir William, having three daughters and no son, settled all his estate upon petitioner and his heirs male, but charged it with debts and legacies amounting to 12,000l., to be paid very shortly, or else the lands are forfeited. The personal estate is not above 8,000l., and cannot be suddenly collected, and the lands, which are not above 1,500l. per annum, are heavily charged. The fine of 5,000l., now mitigated to 4,000l., is granted to the Earl of Huntingdon, who intends to levy the same on Sir William's estate, to the utter ruin of petitioner's name and house. Perjury, forgery, conspiracy, and other offences have been mitigated from thousands to hundreds, and those hundreds installed at moderate yearly payments. Petitioner, intending to sue to his Majesty for relief, prays the archbishop's favourable assistance. [⅔ p.]

149. Petition of Richard Wisdom, prisoner in the Counter, Woodstreet, to the Council. Petitioner, formerly an inhabitant of Reading and of a competent estate, complains that Thomas Hull, of Godalming, had drawn away the affections of his wife, and caused petitioner to be laid in prison upon a feigned action. Prays order that they may be prosecuted in the High Commission ex officio. [*See order upon this petition, Vol. ccclv., No. 43.* ⅔ p.]

150. Petition of Alexander Harris, prisoner in the Fleet, to the same. Petitioner at the Council Board unadvisedly said that Mr. Evelyn in former years sold powder at above 13d. the lb., and vouched Mr. Covell to have affirmed it. Mr. Covell being produced said he bought it of Mr. Pigott, whereby it appears that petitioner's affirmation was untrue. Petitioner is sorrowful and repentant, and prays enlargement. [1 p.]

151. Petition of George Touchet to the King. Petitioner coming to some maturity of years, and finding his education, through his father's many troubles, very mean, thought to better himself by travel, and without licence got into France, but his health failing he returned again within five months, for which folly, and refusing the oath, he has now been two months in restraint. Prays liberty to take the air of the country on bail. [*See Vol. ccclxxi., No. 86., where there is a similar petition addressed to the Council. In the Calendar the name of the petitioner in that case is printed "Tucket," by mistake.* ½ p.]

152. Petition of Robert Rigge, of Fareham, to the Council. Upon a petition presented by petitioner, intimating some abuses of John Barton, collector for ship-money, according to your letters to Sir

[1637?]

Vol. CCCLXXVII.

White Beconsaw, the late sheriff, Barton, with much ado, on 12th August produced his accounts, whereby, it appeared, 1. that he had neglected to collect 14*l.* 9*s.* of persons of worth; 2. that he and his tenants, being rated at 6*l.* 10*s.*, he never paid the same; and 3. that he collected 3*l.* 3*s.* from persons whom he returned to be poor, and kept the money in his purse; but, hearing of your letters, he privately redelivered the amount to the persons from whom he had collected it. All which is submitted to your consideration. [⅔ *p.*]

153. Petition of Robert Rigge, of Fareham, to the Council. About January 1636–7 petitioner informed the Lords of the wrongs committed by John Barton, a collector of ship-money, as above mentioned. Upon the last assessment for ship-money, Barton's father, Mr. Badd, whose sister young Barton married, and Mr. Penford, who married Barton's daughter, being three assessors, in petitioner's absence raised petitioner's rate 10*s.*, whereupon, petitioner being also an assessor, and finding the sums to want 30*s.*, set 10*s.* upon Mr. Badd, and 20*s.* upon Barton, senior, who is conceived to be worth 20,000*l.* The sheriff was acquainted with the doing thereof, and appointed petitioner collector, who collected the amounts, and paid every penny with expedition. Mr. Barton, being informed that the Lords misliked petitioner's altering the rate, has now petitioned against him for that, and words supposed to be spoken, but denied. Prays that he may not suffer by Barton's malice. [½ *p.*]

154. Petition of Thomas Badd to the same. Petitioner being assessed to pay 3*l.* towards 50*l.* for ship-money for Fareham, Robert Rigge, the collector, of his own authority added 10*s.* more, and, under pretence that petitioner refused to pay, prosecuted him in the Star Chamber. It appeared that Rigge had wronged petitioner, and done disservice to his Majesty in the alteration of assessments, and thereupon he stands committed. As petitioner did not refuse to pay the money first assessed, nor the 3*l.* 10*s.*, after he knew that the sheriff had confirmed the same, petitioner prays order that the bill against him may be taken off the file. [¾ *p.*] *Annexed,*

> 154. I. *Certificate of John Button, late sheriff of Hants. When the assessment for Fareham was first delivered to me, I conceived the same to be the act of the assessors. Upon further examination I found Mr. Rigge had raised Mr. Badd* 10*s. As I had confirmed the assessment, I refused to alter the same, and wished Mr. Badd to pay the money, which he seemed unwilling to do, but tendered* 3*l. which the assessors had rated him to pay.* [¾ *p.*]

155. Petition of Robert Rigge to the same. Petitioner, being an assessor and collector of ship-money for the hundred of Fareham, and Mr. Badd having forborne to pay, and making a reserve, petitioner informed the Lords thereof, but upon certificate of the sheriff that he knew not of the alteration of the rate till he had

Vol. CCCLXXVII.

[1637?]

signed the same, the Lords committed petitioner to the Fleet, where he now is. As petitioner took great pains in collecting, and did not conceive he had done any injury, he prays enlargement. [½ p.]

156. Sec. Coke to Montjoy Earl of Newport. Minute of application for a gunner's place to be bestowed on William Bray, who had served Sec. Coke these many years. [⅓ p.]

157. The King to Thomas Earl of Berkshire. Letters patent for the exclusive use for 14 years of certain kilns for drying malt by the said Earl invented, paying into the Exchequer during the said term a certain proportion of the profits of the said invention. [*Copy.* 10½ pp.]

158. Petition of John East, graver, to the King. Your Majesty has granted the under-graver's place of your mint to Charles Greene and petitioner, for the life of the longest liver of them. The grant being not yet passed the Great Seal, Charles Greene is dead. Petitioner prays you to confirm the grant to him alone. [½ p.]

159. Petition of Sir Francis Dodington and Alice his wife to the King. Set forth various settlements made by William Hobby the elder and William Hobby the younger, of, amongst other things, a lease of the scite and monastery of Hayles. The petitioner Alice, being daughter of the younger William Hobby, claims certain interests in the said lease, in opposition to her step-mother, Mary, widow of Horace Vere, Lord Tilbury. Lady Tilbury insisted upon a decree made by Lord Chancellor Bacon, which is impugned as made by some undue course, and not to be found upon record. Pray the King to recommend a reviewing of the said decree, and a rehearing by the Lord Keeper. [1 p.]

160. Minute of petition of —— Harris to the King. Prays, in consideration of petitioner's many losses at sea, and payment of 100 marks of his predecessor's debts, that he may have the privilege of printing a book called "The Mouth of the Poor," the most necessary book that ever was published for relief of the poor, and that every parish in the kingdom may receive one of them at a reasonable rate. [½ p.]

161. Petition of Sir Bevis Thelwall, plaintiff in a cause in the Exchequer against Jeremy Brett, Dame Frances Worsley his wife, and Sir Henry Worsley, to the King. Petitioner having obtained a decree in the Exchequer against defendants, whereby, amongst other things, they were decreed to stop up the breach in Brading Haven, they had petitioned the King to review the decree as too strict against them. The King entered on the hearing, but referred the examination of two points to four of the Council. Forasmuch as the decree is grounded upon other weighty reasons, petitioner prays that the other points of the decree may also be referred to the said referees. [¾ p.]

Vol. CCCLXXVII.

[1637?]

162. Petition of Sir Richard Grenville to the Council. Petitioner is informed that the Lords and the Earl of Lindsey are offended with the writing of a letter to his Lordship, which was far from his meaning. His error proceeded from his pen and not from his heart. Prays the Lords to pass it by without further censure. [½ p.]

163. Statement of misdemeanours committed by Turberville Morgan in execution of the searcher's office of Dover, he being entrusted by Charles Powell, stated to be one of the most dangerous Papists in this kingdom. The offences charged are suffering condemned persons and uncustomed goods to pass from that port. [½ p.]

164. S. Lady Hay to Sir William Becher. Recommends a friend to Sir William's favour in business before the Council. [1 p.]

165. Sidney Lady Hay to Mr. Savile. To deliver her husband's half year's pension to the bearer, Nicholas Grise. [¼ p.] *Underwritten,*

> 165. I. *S. Lady Hay to Mr. Hails [Hales]. That she will make good to him (if need be) the payment to Nicholas Grise above requested, he being servant of the writer's cousin, Sir James Hay, and the above being Sir James's wife's hand.* [¼ p.]

166. Note of Dr. Farmery's mediation betwixt Richard Massey and Judith his wife. The parties were living apart on account of the violence of the husband, the wife having alimony allowed her for her separate maintenance. [1 p.]

167. Acknowledgment by Margaret Burrish, widow of Edward Burrish, late citizen and mercer of London, of the payment by Sir Henry Burton of 200*l.* and interest, being the amount of a debt secured by a mortgage of a close called Sheppard Close at Carshalton, Surrey. [*One skin of parchment. Imperfect.*]

168. Accounts of Endymion Porter, endorsed "My own papers." They consist of lists of linen, dated from 6th August 1637 to 1st March 1637–8, and an account of moneys expended by Porter's cash-keeper from August to November 1637. In the last-mentioned account occur the following items:—"Paid my master his sister Mrs. Crane, by my master's appointment, 15*l.*; paid for bringing a present of Venice glasses, 5*s.*; mending my master's scarlet coat at Oatlands, 1*s.*; given one that brought a present of Spanish melons to my master, 10*s.*; for four new shoes and two removes for the bay gelding and grey horse, 2*s.* 3*d.*; given my Lord of Holland's man that brought a haunch of venison to my master, 4*s.* 6*d.*; paid my master at the Bowling-Green, 5*l.* 3*s.*; paid Walter Buckhannon, the groom, for so much he lent my master at the Bowling-Green, 5*s.* 6*d.*;

VOL. CCCLXXVII.

[1637?] for postage of a letter out of Spain, from Mr. Charles Porter, 5s.; for 1 lb. of bees wax to wax my master's boots, 1s. 6d.; for the hire of a horse to carry Francisco, the Italian, to Woodhall, and for sending the horse back to London, 6s. 6d.; paid Thomas Lyle for a book of the antiquities of England, 4s.; a pair of black silk laced garters with roses for Mr. Charles, 18s.; lent Francisco, the Italian mountebank, by my master's order, to repay again at pleasure, 1l. [24 pp. of which about 13 are blank.]

169. List of debts owing by Thomas Earl Cleveland and Thomas Lord Wentworth to several persons named. Total, 19,200l. [½ p.]

170. Names of various persons, perhaps foreign merchants, with a small sum attached to each, perhaps in the handwriting of Sec. Coke. Endorsed upon a scale of prices for dyers of cloth and silk. [= 1¾ p.]

171. Note of money endorsed by Sir John Lambe as laid out by Barnwell's mother. The first and second items are—Imprimis: For the wedding dinner and for wedding linen and clothes for him and her, 65l.; item, money he had of me (being arrested the next morning after marriage), and for goods bought for them, 30l. [¾ p.]

172. Sec. Windebank to some one addressed as "Sir." His Majesty has understood that you have left your home with a purpose to transport yourself into foreign parts. It is his pleasure that you repair hither to London, and presume not to go out of England until you have yielded obedience to his former order in settling 1,000l. yearly to the use of your Lady and your children during your absence. [Draft. ¾ p.]

173. Petition of Captain Nicholas Mynn to the King. Having served six years under Sir David Drummond, General-Major to the Queen of Sweden, petitioner is come over for men to complete his colonel and his own company. Prays liberty to pass for Germany with 80 men. [⅓ p.]

174. Information that Henry Hilton, of Hilton, co. Durham, has disobeyed his Majesty's proclamation, and been absent from his own country these 23 years. He lies at Islington, at Lady Shelley's house. Also that Sir Robert Hodson, of Heyborne, co. Durham, who has been absent in like manner for 5 years, dwells in St. John Street. [½ p.]

175. Account of pells written by Richard Hamby, from Easter Term 3rd James I. to the like term in the 13th Charles I. [1 p.]

176. Establishment of the garrison in St. Mary's, Scilly, as it existed in this year. The total charge amounted to 1,828l., which was paid partly out of the Crown revenue from Devon and Cornwall, and partly out of the Exchequer. [1 p.]

DOMESTIC—CHARLES I. 131

[1637 ?]   VOL. CCCLXXVII.

177. List of title-deeds relating to various properties belonging to Lord Cottington. Amongst them are Fonthill, Hanworth, Frome Selwood, Kennington, rectory of Feltham, new park of Richmond called Istleworth [Isleworth], extents of lands of Sir Paul Fleetwood and Sir Richard Fleetwood, manor of Blewbury, and various grants of fen lands. [2 pp.]

178. Notes of offices which might be created and fees which might be granted without the concurrence of a parliament. [1¾ p.]

179–183. See "Returns made by Justices of Peace."

PAPERS RELATING TO APPOINTMENTS IN THE NAVY,

To Offices under the Rank of Captain,

DATED BETWEEN 1ST JULY AND 31ST DECEMBER 1637.

Date.	Office.	Nature of Document.	Reference to Document.
1637. Aug. 5. Oatlands.	Master-gunner of the Merhonour.	Appointment of Robert Bacon, late master-gunner of the Dieu Repulse.	Vol. cccliii., fol. 46 b. ⅓ p.
Aug. 5.	Master-gunner of the Dieu Repulse.	Minute of appointment of Gerard Dalby, late master-gunner of the Adventure.	Ibid., fol. 46 b. 3 lines.
Aug. 5.	Master-gunner of the Adventure.	The like of Nicholas Oliver, late master-gunner of the Second Whelp.	Ibid., fol. 47. 4 lines.
Aug. 5.	Master-gunner of the Second Lion's Whelp.	The like of William Copple.	Ibid., fol. 47. 4 lines.
Aug.	Gunner in the Merhonour.	List by Nicholas of suitors for appointment, and note of proposed removals of William Copley and Richard Wilkinson.	Vol. ccclxvi., No. 88. 1 p.
Sept. 30. Hampton Court.	Boatswain in the Antelope.	Lords of the Admiralty to the Officers of the Navy. To enter Thomas Severne, now boatswain of the Third Whelp, in place of William Weymouth, deceased.	Vol. cccliii., fol. 56. ⅓ p.
Sept. 30.	Boatswain of the Third Whelp.	The same to the same. To enter William Johnson in place of Thomas Severne. Minute.	Ibid. ⅙ p.
Nov. 14.	Ship-keeper in the Nicodemus.	Kenrick Edisbury to Nicholas. Recommendation of Hugh Hennys. "Although he has some imperfection in his hearing, the Master-[attendant] saith he may very well perform the business."	Vol. ccclxxi., No. 103. ½ p.

DOMESTIC—CHARLES I.

Papers relating to Appointments in the Navy.

Date.	Office.	Nature of Document.	Reference to Document.
1637. Nov. 18.	Purser of the Defiance in place of John Fletcher, who is so infirm as not to be able to execute the office in person.	Lords of the Admiralty to Officers of the Navy. Warrant to enter Francis Austin.	Vol. ccclxiii., fol. 66 b. ⅓ p.
Dec. 2.	Boatswain of the Nicodemus.	The same to the same. To enter Thomas Bowers.	Ibid., fol. 72 b. ½ p.
Dec. 2 [?] Whitehall.	Master carpenter in the next ship that shall be built.	Order of the same Lords on petition of Isaac Tyeth for Officers of the Navy to inform themselves of his sufficiency.	Ibid., fol. 74 b. ⅓ p.
Dec. 21. Wapping.	Appointment as boatswain.	Capt. William Rainsborough to Nicholas. Vouches for the sufficiency of John Robinson.	Vol. ccclxxiv., No. 38. ½ p.
Dec. 22. Mincing Lane.	Boatswain's deputy in the Nonsuch.	Kenrick Edisbury to the same. Recommends Edward Eldinge who served master in the Fifth Whelp when she was cast away. They will then place Robinson in some good ship in lieu of one of those suspended. [Seal with arms.]	Ibid., No. 40. ⅓ p.
Dec. 30. Trinity House.	Boatswains, gunners, and carpenters.	Master and others of the Trinity House to the Lords of the Admiralty. Send names of men best fitting for appointment.	Ibid., No. 62. 1 p.

RETURNS MADE BY JUSTICES OF PEACE,

From 1st July to 31st December 1637;

Most of them relating to Measures for the Relief of the Poor, taken in pursuance of the King's Book of Orders and the Instructions of the Council founded thereupon.

Date.	For what Place.	Nature of Document.	Reference to Document.
1637. July 4 Foots-Cray.	Hundreds of Blackheath, Bromley and Beckenham, Little and Lesness, and Ruxley.	Return by Justices of Peace of rogues punished and sent with passes to the places where they were born, apprentices put out, alehouses suppressed, and penalties distributed to the poor.	Vol. ccclxiii., No. 33. 1¾ p.

RETURNS MADE BY JUSTICES OF PEACE.

Date.	For what Place.	Nature of Document.	Reference to Document.
1637. July 7.	Milton, Teynham, Boughton, and Faversham, with the Isle of Sheppey, being the upper division of the lathe of Scray, Kent.	Certificate of Justices of Peace of children apprenticed (11), rogues punished (65), and fines levied (4*l*. 13*s*. 4*d*.), since last assizes.	Vol. ccclxiii., No. 64. 2¾ *p*.
July 8.	The rape of Chichester, Sussex.	Certificate of Justices of Peace. General return of comformity with the Book of Orders.	Ibid., No. 79. 1 *p*.
July 10.	Hundreds of Calehill, Chart and Longbridge, and the township of Ashford, Kent.	Similar certificate, with full lists of 26 apprentices bound, 61 vagrants removed, and sums received for fines which went to the poor.	Ibid., No. 100. 5 *pp*.
July 12. At the Assizes at Maidstone.	The west part of the lathe of Aylesford, Kent.	Similar certificate, with lists of apprentices and vagrants.	Ibid., No. 115. 1 *p*.
July 12.	The lower division of the lathe of Sutton at Hone, Kent.	Similar certificate, with list of 14 apprentices and number of rogues punished, 87.	Ibid., No. 116. 1 *p*.
July 13.	Rape of Hastings, Sussex.	Return of names of children apprenticed and rogues punished from 22nd February 1636-7 to this day.	Ibid., No. 122. 2½ *pp*.
July 13.	Hundreds of Kingston and Elmbridge, Surrey.	The like, with addition of alehouses suppressed. Ann Ward, daughter of Elizabeth Ward, of Talworth, had been sent to the late Lady Hill's almshouses.	Ibid., No. 123. 1½ *p*.
July 15.	Rape of Bramber, Sussex.	Certificate of Justices of Peace of conformity with the Book of Orders, and names of apprentices bound.	Ibid., No. 130. 1 *p*.
July 15.	Rape of Arundel.	The like with names of rogues punished.	Ibid., No. 131. 2 *pp*.
July 15.	Hundred of Copthorne and half-hundred of Effingham, Surrey.	Justices of Peace to Justices of Assize. Certificate of apprentices bound and rogues punished.	Ibid., No. 132. 1 *p*.
July 17.	Rape of Lewes, Sussex.	The like to the same. Similar return.	Vol. ccclxiv., No. 8.
July 18.	Hundreds of Godalming, Woking, Godly, Blackheath, and Wotton, Surrey.	The like to the same. Similar return. Under Haslemere, William Cobden was apprenticed to William Greenfield, of Kirdford, Sussex.	Ibid., No. 17. 3 *pp*.
July 19.	Hundreds of Radfield, Chilford, and Whittlesford, co. Cambridge.	The like to Sir John Bramston and Sir George Croke, Judges of Assize. General certificate of conformity with the Book of Orders.	Ibid., No. 20. 1 *p*.

RETURNS MADE BY JUSTICES OF PEACE.

Date.	For what Place.	Nature of Document.	Reference to Document.
1637. July 20.	Hundreds of Chieveley, Staploe, Flendish, and Staine, co. Cambridge.	Justices of Peace to Sir John Bramston and Sir George Croke, Judges of Assize. General certificate of conformity with the Book of Orders.	Vol. ccclxiv., No. 26. 1 p.
July 20.	Hundreds of Blofield and Walsham, Norfolk.	The like to the same. Similar certificate.	Ibid., No. 27. ¾ p.
July 20.	Hundreds of Coleridge and Stanborough, Devon.	The like to Justices of Assize. Certificate of apprentices bound and vagrants punished.	Ibid., No. 28. 1¾ p.
July 22.	Great Yarmouth.	Bailiffs and Justices of Peace to Sir John Bramston and Sir George Croke, Judges of Assize. There is yearly levied as a rate for the poor 525l. Sixty-five soldiers come from beyond seas have landed there since the last assizes, who were passed upon certificates to the places of their abode. General certificate on other points comprised under the Book of Orders.	Ibid., No. 37. 1 p.
July 24.	Hundred of Edwinstree and Odsey, co. Hertford.	General certificate of Justices of Peace on the points required under the Book of Orders.	Ibid., No. 48. 1 p.
July 24.	Wapentake of Staincliff and Ewecross, co. York.	Justices of Peace to Sir George Vernon and Sir Robert Berkeley, Judges of Assize. General certificate.	Ibid., No. 49. 1 p.
July 24.	Hundreds of East and West Flegg, Happing, and Tunstead, Norfolk.	Certificate of the like as to relief of towns overcharged with poor, punishment of servants misdemeaning themselves in alehouses at night, and points comprised in the Book of Orders.	Ibid., No. 50. 1 p.
July 25.	Hundreds of Clackclose, Freebridge 'Lynn, and Freebridge Marshland, Norfolk.	General certificate of the like.	Ibid., No. 59. 1 p.
July 26.	St. Albans, co. Hertford.	The like certificate of Thomas Oxton, mayor, and two Justices of Peace. State prices of corn.	Ibid., No. 64. 1 p.
July 26.	Hundred of Cashio and liberty of St. Albans, co. Hertford.	The like certificate of Justices of Peace. In the parish of Redbourn, out of 17 deaths, since the 1st March, 15 were of the plague.	Ibid., No. 65. 1 p.

DOMESTIC—CHARLES I.

RETURNS MADE BY JUSTICES OF PEACE.

Date.	For what Place.	Nature of Document.	Reference to Document.
1637. July 27.	Hundreds of Hertford and Braughing, co. Hertford.	General certificate of Justices of Peace. Hertford, Ware, and Hoddesdon have been grievously visited with the sickness. 186 vagrants punished since 11th May 1636.	Vol. ccclxiv., No. 73. 1 p.
July 27.	Half-hundred of Hitchin, the same county.	The like certificate. 57 vagrants punished; "a counterfeit Bedlam" and two disorderly persons, gleaners of corn in the night, punished in the house of correction.	Ibid., No. 74. 1 p.
July 28.	Hundreds of Chafford and Barstable, and half-hundred of Becontree, Essex.	The like certificate. 169 vagrants punished; four drivers fined 20s. a piece for driving cattle on the Sabbath day; nine persons fined 1s. for each Sabbath for not coming to church.	Ibid., No. 83. 1 p.
July 31.	Hundred of Wangford, Suffolk, including Beccles and Bungay.	The like certificate, containing the numbers of convictions and presentments certified at the assizes.	Ibid., No. 103. ¾ p.
July 31.	Hundred of Babergh, Suffolk.	The like certificate of Justices of Peace.	Ibid., No. 104. ¾ p.
[July.]	The east part of Kent, being part of the lathe of St. Augustine.	Similar certificate, with names of apprentices and of vagrants punished.	Ibid., No. 119. 1½ p.
[July.]	The Downish division of Pevensey rape, Sussex.	Justices of Peace to Sir Francis Crawley and Sir Richard Weston, Justices of Assize. Certificate of apprentices put forth.	Ibid., No. 120. ¾ p.
[July.]	Division of Sussex in which the Justices of Peace held their meetings at Uckfield.	Certificate of Justices of Peace, with list of apprentices bound, 46 rogues punished.	Ibid., No. 121. 1 p.
[July?]	Part of Bolton division in the hundred of Salford, co. Lancaster.	Justices of Peace to Sir George Vernon and Sir Robert Berkeley, Justices of Assize. Certificate of proceedings touching the poor, rogues, and wanderers, &c. The great trading in fustians and woollen cloth at Bury had given the inhabitants continual employment for their children in spinning.	Ibid., No. 122. 1¾ p.
[July?]	Bolton division in the hundred of Salford above-mentioned.	The like to the same. Similar certificate, with the same statement respecting the trade of Bolton as is contained in the preceding concerning Bury.	Ibid., No. 123. 4 pp.
[July?]	Kent.	Abstract of certificates of Justices of Peace returned in the summer circuit this year.	Ibid., No. 124. 1½ p.

DOMESTIC—CHARLES I.

Returns made by Justices of Peace.

Date.	For what Place.	Nature of Document.	Reference to Document.
1637. [July ?]	Sussex.	Abstract of certificates of Justices of Peace returned in the summer circuit this year.	Vol. ccclxiv., No. 125. 1¼ p.
[July ?]	Hertfordshire.	The like.	Ibid., No. 126. 1½ p.
[July ?]	Essex.	The like.	Ibid., No. 127. ¾ p.
[July ?]	Surrey.	The like.	Ibid., No. 128. ¾ p.
Aug. 1.	Hundreds of Haytor, Teignbridge, and Axminster, Devon.	Certificate of Justices of Peace of persons punished and apprentices bound out. In Holne, Nicholas Momford paid 10s. for ten oaths.	Vol. ccclxv., No. 12. 1 p.
Aug. 1.	Hundreds of Crediton, West Wonford, and West Budleigh.	Similar certificate.	Ibid., No. 13. 1 p.
Aug. 4.	Hundred of Blackburn, co. Lancaster.	Similar certificate that vagrants had been punished, apprentices bound out, and misdemeanours fined.	Ibid., No. 19. 1 p.
Aug. 29.	Division of Manchester, co. Lancaster.	Similar certificate of vagrants dealt with and alehouse-keepers suppressed since the last assizes.	Vol. ccclxvi., No. 56. 1 p.
[Aug.]	Warrington and Winwick, in the hundred of West Derby, co. Lancaster.	Certificate of Justices of Peace of presentments made to them respecting vagrants, offences, and the binding of apprentices up to 10th July last.	Ibid., No. 89. =1½ p.
[Aug. ?]	Rochdale, co. Lancaster.	The like certificate, but stating the names of all the persons punished or passed.	Ibid., No. 90. 3 pp.
[Aug. ?]	Division of Ulverstone, co. Lancaster.	The like certificate of general conformity with the particulars required by the Book of Orders.	Ibid., No. 91. 1¾ p.
[Aug. ?]	District in the hundred of [West] Derby, co. Lancaster.	Catalogue of all such as have been stocked and whipped, certified by the Justices of Peace.	Ibid., No. 92. 1 p.
Oct. 1.	Parish or district in Kent.	Certificate of Sir Walter Roberts, Sergeant Sir Ralph Whitfield, Sergeant Edward Henden, and others, of apprentices put out, with the sums paid, rogues passed, and fines levied.	Vol. ccclxix., No. 3. 2 pp.
Oct. 17.	Hundred of Leyland, co. Lancaster.	Justices of Peace to Sir George Vernon and Sir Robert Berkeley, Judges of Assize. Certificate of conformity to the Book of Orders.	Ibid., No. 94. 1 p.]

DOMESTIC—CHARLES I.

RETURNS MADE BY JUSTICES OF PEACE.

Date.	For what Place.	Nature of Document.	Reference to Document.
Undated. [1637 ?]	Upper and lower hundreds of Eyhorne and Maidstone, Kent.	Certificate of Justices of Peace of children apprenticed and due examination had of presentments of the borsholders of the said hundreds.	Vol. ccclxxvii., No. 179. 1 p.
[The like.]	Division of Howdenshire in the East Riding of co. York.	Similar certificate, with the names of vagabonds whipped.	Ibid., No. 180. 2½ pp.
[The like.]	Division of Hunsley Beacon in the same East Riding.	Similar certificate.	Ibid., No. 181. 2 pp.
[The like.]	Hundred of Ermington, co. Devon.	Similar certificate, with the additional account of fines imposed for misdemeanours.	Ibid., No. 182. 1 p.
[The like.]	Borough of Devizes.	Certificate of Mayor and others of apprentices bound at meetings at Candlemas and Whitsuntide.	Ibid., No. 183. 1 p.

TRINITY HOUSE CERTIFICATES,

FOR THE YEAR 1637.

In continuation of those for the year 1636, printed in the Volume of Calendar for 1636–7, p. 335.

Date.		Name of Ship.	Where built.	Tonnage.	Reference to Certificate.
1636–7.					Vol. xvii.
Jan.	3	Jane Ann and Judith, of London	Wapping	—	No. 140
Feb.	1	Shipwright, of London	Bursledon Ferry, Hants.	140	,, 141
Mar.	1	Charles, of London	Not stated	220	,, 142
1637.					
May	13	Ambrose, of London	The like	200	,, 143
,,	13	Assurance, of London	The like	250	,, 144
,,	13	New ship on the stocks	Wapping	220	,, 145
June	10	The Muscovia Merchant	Woodbridge	300	,, 146
,,	14	Love, of London	Not stated	300	,, 147
,,	14	Pennington, of London	The like	80	,, 148
,,	14	Æneas, of London	The like	400	,, 149
,,	24	Lady, of London	The like	100	,, 150
July	12	Golden Fleece, of London	Southwark	400	,, 151
,,	12	Swallow, of Colchester	Colchester	150	,, 152
,,	22	Mary, of London	Not stated	60	,, 153
Aug.	2	Dover Merchant	Rotherhithe	350	,, 154
,,	9	Advance, of London	Ipswich	250	,, 155
,,	23	Exchange	Ibid.	300	,, 156
,,	26	Mayflower	Ibid.	180	,, 157
Sept.	16	Prosperous, of London	Ibid.	210	,, 158
Oct.	2	Blessing, of London	Flanders	160	,, 159
Nov.	22	Mary Rose, of London	Horsleydown	350	,, 160
,,	29	Diamond, of London	Not stated	160	,, 161
Dec.	20	Mercury, of London	Limehouse	300	,, 162
,,	29	Love, of London	Flanders	150	,, 163

Vol. CCCLXXVIII. January 1–17, 1637–8.

1637–8.
Jan. 1.
Boston.

1. Sir Anthony Irby to the Council. In reply to letter of the Council of the 19th December, enclosing petition of Sir Anthony Thomas and the other adventurers in the drained lands beyond Boston, complaining of the assessment made upon those lands towards the ship-money. Sir Anthony explains at length the grounds of the assessment complained of, and refers for further explanation to a return enclosed. [*Seal with arms.* 1½ *p.*] *Enclosed,*

    1. I. *Return by Sir Anthony Irby, Sheriff of co. Lincoln, of the quantity and value of the lands drained in that county by Sir Anthony Thomas and others, with the names of the owners and tenants. The number of acres drained was 6,049, valued at from 8s. to 12s. per acre, and assessed to the ship-money at 52l. 10s.* 1637, December 5. [=2 *pp.*]

Jan. 1.

2. Copy of a portion of the above letter. [2 *pp.*]

Jan. 1.

3. Statement concerning certain dealings between [Gerance?] James and [Peter] Fawtrart, in relation to the rectory of Paulerspury, co. Northampton; endorsed by William Dell as received this day from Dr. Beale. [1½ *p.*]

Jan. 2.

4. Warwick Mohun, Robert Powlett, and Charles Foxe, commissioners under commission dated the 30th November 1637, for inquiry into illegal duties on exports and imports taken at Bristol, to the King. Report the opposition they had met with in the execution of their commission, especially from Richard Long, master of the merchants of Bristol, James Dyer, the town clerk of that city, and —— Bowcher, collector of the impositions laid upon merchandize. The particulars of the acts complained of are minutely stated. The commissioners had been completely baffled in their inquiries. Having committed the town clerk for his contempt of their authority and persons, he had forcibly escaped from the messenger. [*See upon this subject Vol. ccclxxiii., No.* 84. 2 *pp.*]

Jan. 2.
Whitehall.

Lords of the Admiralty to Lord Keeper Coventry. Certify that Sir Robert Mansell, Lieutenant of the Admiralty, had daily travelled about the affairs of the said office from 1st January 1636–7 to 31st December following. Pray order for 10s. per diem, amounting to 182l. 10s. [*Copy. See Vol. cccliii., fol.* 77. ½ *p.*]

Jan. 2.
Whitehall.

The same to the same. Similar certificate for Sir William Russell for the same period. Pray order for 6s. 8d. per diem, amounting to 121l. 13s. 4d. [*Ibid., fol.* 77 *a.* ½ *p.*]

Jan. 2.

5. David Stevenson to Leonard Pinckney, at Mr. Smith's in Salisbury Court. I have sent two set of tubs into the country, and they are aided there, but in Huntingdon they will neither let me have carts to carry tubs out of the town, nor into it. The mayor and Robert Bernard, the recorder, bade the constable charge no carts for me. I lie here and my men at great charges, and if such

1637-8.

VOL. CCCLXXVIII.

men as these, that should be the chief aiders of me in performance of the King's service, give such a light [slight?], the country will soon hear of it, and we shall have no service performed. [¾ p.]

Jan. 2.
Whitehall.

The Lords of the Admiralty to the Mayor and Recorder of Huntingdon. Complaint is made by David Stevenson, deputy for saltpetre in co. Huntingdon, that you will not let him have carts for carriage of his vessels, but that you have required the constable to charge no carts for the said service. We are not willing to send for you by a messenger until we have given you notice of the complaint; yet we require you to give assistance to our deputy, and reasonable satisfaction for the charges you have put him to by refusing to give him assistance, or else that you attend us within ten days after the receipt hereof. [Copy. See Vol. cccliii., fol. 78. ¾ p.]

Jan. 2.

6. Sir William Russell to Nicholas. This week I shall have the officers at Deptford to sign my account for 1637, so as I cannot be ready for the shipping of next year until after Sunday next. Great number of ships will be in the river from the Straits, out of which good election may be made. If the Lords will appoint Monday next, or any time after, we shall attend them. In the meantime, I pray procure warrant to auditor Bingley to take my accounts of '36 and '37, and I shall be ready this month to bring the state of those years' accounts for the ship-moneys from the shires. [1 p.]

Jan. 2.

7. Information of Philip Thomas and William Griffith, taken before Peter Heywood and George Hulbert, Justices of Peace for Middlesex. Being at the Castle tavern in St. Clement's, presently after the execution done upon Prynne, Bastwick, and Burton, there was in company one Joseph Huchens [Hutchinson]. Thomas asking Hutchinson if he had been to see Prynne and the rest suffer at Westminster, answered "No." Thomas replied, "The punishment they had was not more than they deserved." Hutchinson answered, "Thou art a most wicked fellow, that thou durst say so of them, for in my conscience they are as honest men and as good subjects as any the King has." [¾ p.] Annexed,

> 7. I. *Information of Edward Everard, taken as above. Examinant was present during the above conversation. Hutchinson said that Prynne was as good a subject as any the King had, besides many other speeches which examinant cannot now remember.* [½ p.]

Jan. 2.
Ipswich.

8. Henry Dade, Bailiff of Ipswich, to Sec. Coke. I have been entreated to certify my opinion of the petition enclosed. I suppose the same to be true, which also former examinations will verify. In case much weight be given to accusations of beggarly and angry women, few scolding differences shall be between them in the country but the Council will be troubled with a complaint of some

1637-8.

abuses offered to King or state, by one side or other. [1 p.] Enclosed,

 8. I. *Petition of John Dixon, of Ipswich, labourer, to Sec. Coke. Petitioner, out of charity, in August last entertained a poor woman in his house who was cast out in the streets. She continued in his house five or six weeks, in which time she got a key to open his cupboard door where his money was, which being discovered by Ann Dixon, petitioner's daughter, aged fourteen, and the woman questioned, she threatened to procure petitioner's daughter much trouble, and went to the bailiffs of Ipswich, informing them that the child had spoken words against the King, and that a neighbour had heard the words. The neighbour, being examined, denied the same; notwithstanding, because the complaint imported matter concerning his Majesty, the bailiffs committed petitioner's daughter to prison. The accuser soon after fled the town, and petitioner's daughter has continued fourteen weeks and is there like to continue, until you signify your pleasure. Beseeches directions for liberation of his daughter.* [1 p.] Annexed.

 8. II. *Certificate of Edmund Humfrey and seven others. That the woman who accused the daughter of John Dixon, immediately after the accusation, forsook Ipswich, and has not been seen there since.* [¾ p.]

Jan. 2.
Boston.

9. Sir Anthony Irby to Sir Dudley Carleton. I lately received a letter from the Council, to which I am commanded to give answer, which I have done by these letters (*see the present Volume, No. 1*), which I request you with speed to present at their next sitting. P.S.—There are two petitions enclosed. [*Seal with arms.* 1 p.]

Jan. 3.

10. Petition of Robert and Margaret Buckley, children of Sir Richard Buckley, late of Beaumaris, deceased, to the King. Petitioners, son and daughter of Sir Richard and Dame Ann his wife, which Ann has since intermarried with Thomas Cheadle, late servant unto Sir Richard, have been by Cheadle reported to be none of the children of Sir Richard, and working on the weakness of Dame Ann he had gained her to deny petitioners. To colour the practice, Cheadle bound petitioners, being then infants, to mechanic trades by contrary names, and threatened to punish them if they challenged their right names. Petitioner Robert, about two years since, repaired to Beaumaris to his mother's house to tender his duty and entreat means of livelihood, of which Cheadle having notice, gave command that no entertainment should be given him, and prosecuting his former threats imprisoned him, vowing to detain him until he should disclaim his name and birthright. Petitioners' elder brother has 2,000*l.* a year, and is childless; Dame Ann, his mother, 1,000*l.* per annum, and has no other son but petitioner and his elder brother.

1637-8.   VOL. CCCLXXVIII.

As petitioners can prove themselves legitimate, pray his Majesty to give power to Archbishop Laud, Lord Keeper Coventry, the Lord Privy Seal, and Sec. Windebank, to call before them Cheadle and Dame Ann, and certify the same, that order may be directed for petitioners' relief. [*Copy.* ¾ *p.*] *Underwritten,*

    10. I. *Reference as desired. Whitehall, 3rd January 1637-8.* [*Copy.* ¼ *p.*]

    10. II. *Memorandum by the above referees, appointing the 13th April next for hearing the business at the Council board. 23rd January 1637-8.* [*Copy.* ¼ *p.*]

Jan. 3.   11. Petition of William Carne to the King. His Majesty granted petitioner and Edward Carne his brother, for their lives, the office of receiver of the revenue of tobacco licences and portage thereof, with 200*l.* per annum fee, which his Majesty has sinced farmed to Lord Goring, but has allowed petitioner the 200*l.* per annum fee. Petitioner, being deprived of portage and other perquisites, prays his Majesty to recommend the consideration of his loss to Lord Goring, and to accept a surrender of the said patent, and grant the like to two such persons as Lord Goring shall nominate. [½ *p.*] *Underwritten,*

    11. I. *His Majesty accepts petitioner's surrender, and the Attorney-General is to prepare a new grant to Timothy Butts and Pierce Deare with the said fee of 200l. per annum and 20s. per cent. for portage. Whitehall, 3rd January 1637-8.* [½ *p.*]

Jan. 3.   12. Petition of Richard Corles to the King. By statute every escheator ought to return every inquisition taken by him into the Court of Chancery within one month after its date, under a penalty of 40*l.*; yet divers escheators by undue practice with the parties conceal the same. Prays for a commission to examine and compound with such offenders. [½ *p.*] *Underwritten,*

    12. I. *Reference to the Lord Treasurer and Lord Cottington to certify the conveniency of this request. Whitehall, 3rd January 1637-8.* [¼ *p.*]

    12. II. *Lord Treasurer Juxon and Lord Cottington to the King. Escheators serve but one year, every county having one. The Lord Treasurer is careful in nominating of the sufficientest and honestest sort recommended by the justices of assize. If petitioner can inform of any particular misdemeanour, that party may be proceeded against; but to grant a commission of inquiry against so many hundreds of persons will intimidate others to serve in that place, and is very "unseasonable."* [⅔ *p.*]

    12. III. *Minute of the King's pleasure that this business be proceeded in no otherwise than according to the preceding report. Windsor, 15th August 1638.* [⅓ *p.*]

VOL. CCCLXXVIII.

1637–8.
Jan. 3.

13. Entry of the appearance of Abraham Thorne, of London, merchant tailor, before the Council. He was to remain in custody of the messenger until discharged. [*Draft.* ⅓ *p.*]

Jan. 3.
Dursley.

14. Dr. Hugh Robinson, Archdeacon of Gloucester, to William Dell, Secretary to Archbishop Laud. States his proceedings in reference to an accusation brought before him against John Oldham, a parson in that neighbourhood, of having preached some erroneous doctrine. Mr. Hodges, an old gentleman in Mr. Oldham's parish, and patron of the parsonage, was referred to in proof, but pending inquiry Mr. Hodges died. Mr. Oldham is described as a little touched perhaps with preciseness by the neighbourhood of others, but of himself a weak-brained man, and thought to be crazy, certainly quickly overtaken with a little wine or beer. Mr. Hodges had before put him in the High Commission, but had withdrawn the suit as not being a competent witness, being patron of the living. The writer submits to the archbishop what he would have done with Oldham, whether he should preach contradictory to what had been articled against him, or that the business (wanting just proof) should die in silence. An unknown person who first stirred in this business the writer believes to be a younger son of Mr. Hodges, then a scholar at Oxford. [*Seal with arms.* 3 *pp.*]

Jan. 4.

15. Examination of Joseph Hutchinson, taken before Peter Heywood and George Hulbert, Justices of Peace for Middlesex. Examinant, one of the beadles of the New Corporation, had been at the tavern in St. Clement's churchyard, but the time when he could not tell. Some of his fellows were with him, but their discourse, or whether there was any speech about Mr. Prynne, he could not tell. [½ *p.*]

Jan. 5.

Demise to Sir Popham Southcott and to Periam Pole, for seven years from Candlemas next, of the duty of 6*d.*, payable by the makers of hard soap in Somerset, Dorset, Devon, Cornwall, and Exeter, for every dozen soap made and vended in those counties, rendering the yearly rent of 1,800*l.* The making or vending of any other hard soap in those counties is restrained, excepting Sir Richard Weston's Castile soap, and the hard soap made by them of Bristol and Bridgwater. [*Docquet.*]

Jan. 5.
Whitehall.

Lords of the Admiralty to Lord Keeper Coventry. Certificate that John Crane, Surveyor of Marine Victuals, has been daily employed in the said office, from 1st January 1636–7 to 31st December following. Order is prayed for payment of 5*s.* 4*d.* per diem, amounting to 97*l.* 6*s.* 8*d.* [*Copy. Vol. cccliii., fol.* 78. ⅓ *p.*]

Jan. 5.

16. Note-book by Nicholas of proceedings upon various special references, and especially of a committee for revising the regulations for government of the royal household; for businesses of the moneyers and the clothiers; the exportation of lampreys; the complaint that the city ships fitted out for the King's service were

DOMESTIC—CHARLES I. 143

1637–8.   Vol. CCCLXXVIII.

insufficiently supplied with men; the maintenance of ministers in Norwich; Sir John Tyrrell and Sir Henry Browne (*see 7th November 1637*); complaint of the merchants of Norwich against Witherings; and of various places against the assessments for ship-money; petition of Sir Lawrence Washington for settlement of his fees as registrar of the Court of Chancery (*see Vol. ccclxxii., No.* 26), and various others. These notes extend from this day to the 30th inst. [112 *pp., of which* 91 *contain writing.*]

Jan. 5. Whitehall. 17. Order of the Lord Privy Seal, the Earl Marshal, the Earl of Dorset, and Sec. Windebank, referees of a petition to the King of Nowell Warner, master of his Majesty's barges, respecting the exportation of lampreys, already calendared under date of 21st November 1637. After full hearing of all parties this day it was ordered by the referees that Warner should thenceforth take off from the fishermen 400,000 lampreys at 52s. per thousand, and no more, unless, finding the vent beyond sea to require a greater quantity, he shall think fit to take more at that rate. And if the fishermen take a greater quantity than 400,000, they are to sell them at home for the use of the company of the great fishing of Great Britain or otherwise in the markets, but not to transport any until after the 20th January, and then not in foreign bottoms, but according to the orders of the 14th March 1635–6 and the 22nd July 1636. It was also ordered that no person should be allowed to fish for lampreys but those that were of the corporation of fishermen, and such only of them as were fishermen. [*Draft, with alterations made by Nicholas.* 1¼ *p.*]

Jan. 5. 18. Copy of the preceding order, without the alterations made by Nicholas. [2¼ *pp.*]

Jan. 5. Whitehall. 19. The Council to Attorney-General Bankes. We send you a paper signed by Edward Woodfine and Richard Johnson, silkweavers, wherein they charge Thomas Sandiford, a silkweaver, with having uttered dangerous speeches. We pray you to send for the parties and examine them both in private and apart to discover the truth, and having so done to commit Sandiford, and certify us of your proceedings. [*Draft.* 1 *p.*]

Jan. 5. 20. Minutes of resolutions of the Committee of Council appointed to revise the regulations of the royal household. These resolutions principally relate to the opinions of the committee on some previous orders which were reconsidered at this time. Endorsed are brief notes by Nicholas of other points considered by the committee. [= 2¼ *pp.*]

Jan. 6. 21. John Toppe and George Howe to Lord Treasurer Juxon. According to directions, they had called to them able workmen and taken a view of the pigeon-house of the Dean of Windsor at Knoyle Episcopi, Wilts (*see Vol. ccclxi., No.* 8). They describe it as a very strong-built house of stone, the walls three foot nine inches in thickness. The servants of Mr. Thornhill dug for saltpetre in the house

1637-8.

Vol. CCCLXXVIII.

after Christmas 1635, and in the following January or February. The part of the house which is fallen down is the whole inner lining of one side, about 2½ foot in thickness. The ruin happened about Easter, after the digging, and did not take place by casualty of wind or tempest. Austin Golsbery, Mr. Thornhill's servant, told the workmen that they had dug too near the north side. The ground was dug beneath the foundation above a foot. Mr. William Willoughby concurs in this report, but does not sign it because his name was mistaken, Henry for William, in the Lord Treasurer's letter. [*Seal with arms. 2 pp.*]

Jan. 6. 22. Account by Sir William Russell of ship-money levied and in arrear under writs of August 1636. Received, 185,015*l*. 5*s*. 9½*d*.; unpaid, 11,599*l*. 1*s*. 10½*d*. [1 *p*.]

Jan. 7. Petition of Christopher Beresford, Feodary for co. Lincoln, to the King. Petitioner served King James in the said office eleven years, and has since served his Majesty, to the advancement of the King's revenues, for which service petitioner may have incurred the displeasure of some persons who may bring causeless suits against him, and so draw scandal to the service, and put him to great expenses. Also for that petitioner has had other employments in the Court of Wards and Liveries, for which he desires to rest secure, therefore he prays a pardon of all errors and offences by him done in the Court of Wards and Liveries, and to refer the consideration thereof to Lord Cottington, master of the said court. [*Copy. See Vol. cccxxiii., p.* 239. *½ p.*] *Underwritten,*

    I. *Reference to Lord Cottington, to certify his opinion. Whitehall, 7th January* 1637–8. [*Copy. Ibid. ⅙ p.*]

    II. *Francis Lord Cottington to the King. Petitioner is a person of good reputation and diligent in his office. There is no information or complaint against him. If your Majesty please to admit him to a composition, I know no inconvenience in it.* [*Copy. Ibid. ⅙ p.*]

    III. *Reference to Lord Cottington to compound with petitioner and give order to the Attorney-General to prepare a pardon as desired. Whitehall, 6th February* 1637–8. [*Copy. Ibid., p.* 240. *⅙ p.*]

Jan. 7. 23. Foulke Reed to Edward Viscount Conway and Killultagh. Mr. Kite holds possession of Ragley house, his sister and some of her children being there. He is not forward to examine the inventory of the goods left with Lord Brooke which afterwards came to him. Some walls in the house and outhouses, which were down, the writer has caused to be made up, that wandering people escaped out of infected places might not get in and lodge there. The park pales require to be repaired, having been much neglected from the beginning of Lord Brooke's lease. A large liberty some thereabouts have taken in using their guns in this time of Lord Brooke's lease.

1637-8.   Vol. CCCLXXVIII.

Some are to be indicted at the next quarter sessions. A fowling piece of Mr. Ems, one of Lord Conway's tenants, had been taken from another that shot with it at pigeons and has been detained upon the excuse of consulting Lord Conway before it were delivered. The two pigeon-houses at Ragley are both destroyed and the hernery. The sickness is in Inkberrow parish in two or three houses. [1½ p.]

Jan. 8. 24. Petition of John Leaver to Archbishop Laud. Petitioner about six months ago brought over 1,000 books, called the Practice of Piety, printed at Amsterdam, 800 whereof were delivered into the custody of Mr. Knight, registrar of the High Commission, and the other 200 to the Company of Stationers, by information of Philip Chetwind, unto whom of right the copy belongs. Beseeches that the said books may be delivered to Chetwind, who thereupon is content to surcease his suit against petitioner in the High Commission. [⅔ p.] *Underwritten,*

    24. I. *Reference to Sir John Lambe to give an account of this petition at his next coming [to Lambeth]. 8th January 1637-8.* [⅙ p.]

Jan. 8. 25. John Ashburnham to Nicholas. The writer explains, in reference to some estate for which he had been in treaty on behalf of Nicholas, why it had been declined, and urges him to prosecute his enquiries respecting Broadlands. One Godfrey used it a long time, and paid about 280l. or 300l. per annum rent for it, but he got infinitely by it. He left it the last Michaelmas, and Mr. Symbarbe [St. Barbe, described previously in this letter as living in the New Forest, and said to be an honest man,] has it now in his own hands, and by what I hear it may be worth about 400l. per annum. It is the best land in all our county, and my fingers itch to be dealing with it. The Dr. [Matthew Nicholas] had paid the writer a visit, and brought with him Edward Nicholas's son John, who is spoken of as a youth of very great promise. His other son Ned had lighted on a very ill schoolmaster. [*Seal with arms.* 1¾ p.]

Jan. 8. 26. Account by Sir William Russell of ship-money received and paid in his office during the years 1635, 1636, and 1637. Sir William had paid 17,125l. 12s. 4d. more than he had received, and was to pay 6,300l. more, making in all 23,425l. 12s. 4d., against which there were arrears during the three years mentioned, amounting to 20,870l. 19s. 3d. [1 p.]

Jan. 8. 27. Bond of William Frizell of London, gentleman, to Endymion Porter of St. Martin's-in-the-Fields, esquire, in 300l., conditioned for payment by Frizell of 104l. to John Hall of Milk Street in the parish of St. Lawrence in the Old Jury, which sum was secured by the joint bond of Frizell and Porter. [1 p.]

Vol. CCCLXXVIII.

1637–8.

Jan. 8. 28. Certificate of Roger Kirkby, sheriff of co. Lancaster, of his assessment of 4,000*l.* upon the said county. The borough of Liverpool was set down at 25*l.*, that of Lancaster at 30*l.*, and the parish of Manchester at 132*l.* 14*s.* 7*d.* The return states the names of all the clergy, with the amounts assessed upon them. [8 *pp.*]

Jan. 8. 29. Estimate of the charge of such a fleet of ships as was employed in 1637, for the like time, with the surcharge in arrear for that year; total, 197,905*l.* 12*s.* 4*d.* [1 *p.*]

Jan. 9.
Whitehall. 30. The Council to the Bailiffs of Ipswich. Ann Dixon was accused to have spoken words against his Majesty, for which she was committed to prison (*see this Vol., No. 8*). The accuser having fled, and a neighbour alleged to have heard the words having denied the same, Ann Dixon is to be set at liberty. [*Draft.* ¾ *p.*]

Jan. 9/19.
The Hague. 31. Elizabeth Queen of Bohemia to Sir Thomas Roe. I send Honywood into England about my own particular business. My son takes this occasion again to acquaint the King what has passed lately betwixt him and Milandre, which Honywood will inform you of; he can also clear your doubt why my son did not presently take that army to himself. You may freely speak to him of all things. The frost is such as we can hear from no place, so I can tell you nothing of Bannier. I think the treaty is so frozen at Hamburgh as it will die of cold. My fingers have at this present the same disease. [*Seals with arms.* 1 *p.*]

Jan. 9. 32. Officers of the Navy to the Lords of the Admiralty. We have according to direction examined the charge in the building and launching the Sovereign of the Seas, and enclose a brief extract thereof. [¾ *p.*] *Enclosed,*

32. I. *Certificate of the charge above mentioned. Total,* 33,846*l.* 5*s.* 4*d.* [2 *pp.*]

Jan. 9. 33. The same to the same. According to warrant of 2nd December last, we have considered of pursers, boatswains, gunners, and carpenters fit to be removed into greater ships, as also of able men to be preferred in their room, all whose names we present. [1 *p.*]

Jan. 9.
Whitehall. [Commissioners for Gunpowder] to Master of the Ordnance. Warrant to deliver one last of powder at 18*d.* per lb. to Edmund Beane, of London, skinner. [*Minute. See Vol. ccclv., No. 61, p. 5.* ¼ *p.*]

Jan. 9. Minute of similar warant for Robert Russell, of London, chandler, to receive 12 barrels of powder. [*Ibid.* 2 *lines.*]

About
Jan. 9.
Danbury. 34. Sir Humphry Mildmay, Sheriff of Essex, to Sir Dudley Carleton. I received yours the 6th inst. My man being at Walden with Banson, the bailiff of the hundred, this —— Hanchett, did this wrong to his Majesty's service, and for the mistake of his christian name that rascal the bailiff is to be blamed, and no man else. I have complained of them all in general for a nest of rascals; they have

VOL. CCCLXXVIII.

1637-8.

much of his Majesty's money in their hands. I have written to my brother Henry Mildmay, about Thomas Lathum. At the Council board, I hope to charge him with that he cannot answer, and yet I know his face is brass enough. On Friday next I go for London, and from thence to attend this his Majesty's service. P.S.—John Dinely on his way towards [the] Hague dined here the day before, and this day, waiting for a ship and wind, is ready at Gravesend. [¾ p.]

Jan. 9.
London.

35. Nicholas Murford to Endymion Porter, one of the Grooms of the Bedchamber. I should have been glad of your presence at some assemblies holden for the corporation of saltmakers of Great Yarmouth at Arundel House, where you were desired and expected by Lord Maltravers, our governor, and the assembly, that you might have taken the oath of an assistant, and have been possessed of such important matters as concern his Majesty's service in our salt design. It was concluded that for this year a proportion of work should be erected near the Thames, for the vent of the city of London, and every assistant to give his answer, whether "yea or no" he will undertake therein, and to what proportion. My extreme want of health permits me not to attend you, therefore I appoint a time for taking the oath. [*Seal with arms.* 1 p.]

Jan. 9.

36. Certificate of Robert Pope, Constable of the eastern part of the hundred of Bempstone, Somerset, that he had received 160*l*. shipmoney, and had made payment accordingly, and that Thomas Cake, his partner for the western part, had received 80*l.*, out of which he had only paid 26*l*. [¾ p.] *Underwritten,*

> 36. I. *Note by William Bassett, late sheriff of Somerset. I have often sent to Thomas Cake to pay his money, and give me an acknowledgment of arrears alleged to be in his hands, but cannot hear of him, and therefore desire your Lordships to take course with him.* [¼ p.]

Jan. 9.
Whitehall.

37. Notes by Nicholas of various resolutions come to at the Committee for the regulation of the Royal Household. [*Draft.* 2 pp.]

Jan. 10.

Warrant to Thomas Killigrew and Robert Read, of the real and personal estate of Francis Lockwood, accruing to his Majesty by reason he died a Romish priest. [*Docquet.*]

Jan. 10.

Grant to Edward Manning of the manors of Bradbury and Hilton, co. Durham, for 979 years, at the rent of 550*l.*, and the covenants contained in a grant by King James in the 14th year of his reign to Thomas Emerson for 1,000 years. The interest of which lease being come to Edward Manning, he had surrendered the same to his Majesty, to the end his Majesty would grant the same to him in his own name. [*Docquet.*]

Jan. 10.

Warrant for enstalling the first fruits of the bishopric of Bangor at the rate of 118*l*. 12*s*. 9*d.*, and of the archdeaconry of Anglesea,

Vol. CCCLXXVIII.

1637–8.
which the Bishop of Bangor holds in commendam, at the rate of 53*l*. 14*s*. (the tenths of both being deducted). The first payment to be made on the feast of St. Michael next, and the whole sums be paid within 4 years. [*Docquet.*]

Jan. 10. Grant of the office of one of the Auditors of the Exchequer to John Phelips, son of Francis Phelips, one of the present Auditors, when the same shall become void by death of the present seven officers and of William Hill the younger, who is first in reversion after them, [*Docquet.*]

Jan. 10. Warrant for payment of 265*l*. 7*s*. to William Boreman, his Majesty's locksmith, in full satisfaction for his making anew and altering all the locks of his Majesty's lodging and garden at Whitehall and of St. James's park, and making keys thereto. [*Docquet.*]

Jan. 10. Warrant of the Chief Justices of the King's Bench and Common Plea, the Lord Chief Baron, and the rest of the Judges and Barons, for rating such reasonable sum as they shall think fit to serve for a fine upon plaintiffs and demandants, defendants and tenants, after judgment, in all his Majesty's courts of record, to be paid to his Majesty. [*Docquet.*]

Jan. 10. Petition of Henry Birkenhead to the King. Your Majesty, in January in the third year of your reign, granted petitioner and Henry Birkenhead his son, and Thomas the petitioner's brother, the offices of prothonotary and clerk of the crown for cos. Chester and Flint. For establishing all fees belonging to the said offices in March 1636, your Majesty referred the examination of the same to the Justices of Chester and Flint, which they have accordingly done. Petitioner's suit is, that your Majesty would refer the consideration of the said judges' certificate to the commissioners for fees, who, upon due examination, may give warrant to the Attorney-General for preparing your Majesty's confirmation of such fees, that petitioner may enjoy the same without question hereafter. [*Copy. See Vol. cccxxiii., p.* 221. ¾ *p.*] *Underwritten,*

I. *Reference as prayed. Whitehall,* 10*th January* 1637–8. [*Copy. Ibid.* ¼ *p.*]

Jan. 10. 38. Book of names of all members of the Council present at their meetings on January 10th, 12th, 17th, 19th, 21st, 23rd, 24th, 26th, 28th, and 31st. The King was present at the meetings of the 21st and 28th. [32 *pages, of which* 19 *are blank.*]

Jan. 10.
Whitehall. 39. Order of Council. Recites petition of the merchants of Exeter and inhabitants of Barnstaple, complaining that by a privy seal issued in March last, a former privy seal, to exempt petitioners from paying the import of 1*s*. 4*d*. upon a Barnstaple single baize was restrained to the port of Barnstaple and the members thereof. Recites also a reference to the Lord Treasurer and Lord Cottington, their report dated the 9th January inst., and a certificate of Sir John Wolsten-

1637-8. VOL. CCCLXXVIII.

holme and Sir Abraham Dawes, farmers of the customs, dated 16th December last, upon consideration whereof the Lords held that the exemption in question should extend to Exeter and Dartmouth as well as Barnstaple, and directed a privy seal to be prepared accordingly. [*Draft.* 2⅔ *pp.*]

Jan. 10. 40. Order of Council. It appearing under the hand of Capt. Nathaniel Darell, lieutenant to the Earl of Danby, governor of Guernsey, that Henry Burton, clerk, according to directions from this board, was delivered the 16th December last a prisoner into Castle Cornet, in which service several sums of money had been disbursed by Roger Kirkby, sheriff of co. Lancaster, the Lords ordered that Kirkby be allowed the same in the Exchequer. [*Draft.* ¾ *p.*]

Jan. 10. Whitehall. 41. Similar order. The Governor, Assistants, and Fellowship of the Eastland Merchants by petition represented that divers of that company were questioned in the Star Chamber for exporting dollars which they took for payment of their foreign customs in places where they either trade not at all, or where their commodities vend slowly; the Lords, upon examination of their charter and the nature of such foreign customs, not only freed those particular merchants, but granted liberty for a future exportation of a limited proportion of dollars; whereupon they sought licence that each of their ships might carry out a dollar and a half per ton. The Lords recommend the examination of this proposal to the Lord Treasurer and Lord Cottington. [*Draft.* 1¼ *p.*]

Jan. 10. 42. The like. The Company of Coopers by petition showed that having time out of mind been accustomed to buy and sell wines in gross, the Company of Vintners now endeavour to suppress them, to their utter undoing, and therefore, according to his Majesty's reference, desired to be heard at the Board. The Lords appointed to hear them on the 19th inst., and ordered that the vintners should have a copy of the said petition and notice to attend. [*Draft.* 1½ *p.*]

Jan. 10. 43. Minute of a warrant to George Carter, messenger, to fetch before the Lords Robert Jason. [½ *p.*]

Jan. 10. Similar minute of a warrant to the Warden of the Fleet to take into his custody Simon Corbet. [*Written on the same paper as the preceding.* ½ *p.*]

Jan. 10. 44. Petition of Law[rence] Squibb, Ja[mes] Proger, and Ro[bert] Squibb, his Majesty's Officers for Cards, to the Council. Since the proclamation touching cards and dice, there have been divers abuses committed by some ill-disposed cardmakers of London, by selling cards unsealed, making bad cards, and putting the marks of French cardmakers both on their cards and binders. For reforming which abuses petitioners conceive it necessary that all the moulds for printing their "teats and varlets" be brought into his Majesty's

Vol. CCCLXXVIII.

1637–8.

office, and be there printed, it being the black of the "coat" cards, whereof enough may be done in three hours as will serve for a month's work for one man, the same course being held by the whole company when they were united, according to orders confirmed by the Lord Keeper and the two chief justices. Pray warrant for bringing in their moulds accordingly. [*Copy.* ¾ *p.*] *Endorsed,*

44. I. *Reference to the Attorney-General to send for some of the chiefest cardmakers, and to certify his opinion thereupon. Whitehall, 10th January* 1637–8. [*Copy.* ¼ *p.*]

44. II. *Attorney-General Bankes to the Council. I have conferred with the Company of Cardmakers, who are contented for a trial to bring in their moulds for one quarter of a year for printing their teats and varlets at the office, and according as they shall like thereof to continue longer. It is alleged by the cardmakers that there are some that by law ought not to make cards, who have instruments whereby they make the same deceitfully, and sell the same concealed; and therefore petitioners desire a warrant to search for such instruments, and to take all such as shall be found, which I conceive may tend to his Majesty's service.* 25th *January* 1637. [*Copy.* ¾ *p.*]

Jan. 10.

45. Robert Sumpter, mayor, and seventeen others, of Norwich, to the Council. The merchants and buyers of Norwich stuffs came lately before us, and made known their grievances in respect of the weekly carriage of letters from the city to and from London, and that they intended to manifest the same to the Board, and desired our letters therein. We inform you that their said grievances are conceived upon good grounds, and that the feared consequence likely to follow by the alteration of the ancient use of carriage of letters to and fro may be very dangerous, not only to the merchants and tradesmen in this city who have commerce with London, but in a more especial manner to the makers of stuffs, and to many thousands of poor who by them are employed, besides the great detriment which will thereby befall the common carriers. [1 *p.*]

Jan. 10.
Bristol.

46. William Jones, mayor of Bristol, to Lords of the Admiralty. Upon receipt of your letters of the 19th December, touching gunpowder mills, I made search, and could find but two, both which I have caused to be suppressed, by taking into custody the implements, in such sort as they are wholly disabled to work any more. [¾ *p.*]

Jan. 10.
Whitehall.

Commissioners for Saltpetre to all Mayors, Sheriffs, and other officers. There is much occasion for carriage of gunpowder from the powder mills at Chilworth to London, and likewise of saltpetre from London to the mills. We require you to assist Samuel Cordewell, his Majesty's gunpowder-maker, in taking up such carriages as he shall desire to use, he paying for the same after the rate of 6*d.* per mile, the price allowed by the saltpetremen for carriage of saltpetre. [*Copy. See Vol. ccxcii., p.* 73. ¾ *p.*]

VOL. CCCLXXVIII.

1637–8.

Jan. 10.
London.

47. Sir James Bagg to Nicholas. I was this morning to have delivered you the enclosed, but you were not stirring. Be informed by this relation from Sir Ed[ward] Seamour [Seymour] and Dr. Marten our judge, of the misdemeanours of Hawkins and the other, and have it amongst your remembrances for this day. In the afternoon, when I attend my Lords, I will inform of the business, and petition their aid. [*Seal with arms.* ¾ *p.*]

Jan. 10.

48. Estimate of Officers of the Ordnance of the charge of making a new foundry at Brenchley, Kent, for John Browne to cast ordnance for the Sovereign of the Seas; 1,000*l*. [¾ *p.*]

Jan. [10?].

49. Statement of the shares in which 12,000*l*. was to be raised during the present year by the adventurers in the drainage of the Eight Hundred Fen, for carrying on works of drainage from Bourn to Kyme, and from Kyme to Lincoln. The statement is signed by the Earl of Lindsey, Sir William Killigrew, and Robert Long. The two former, with the addition of the Earl of Dorset, Lord Willoughby, Peregrine Bertie, Sir Edward Heron, Sir Thomas Stafford, Sir Francis Godolphin, Sir John Brooke, Sir Dudley North, and Mr. Langton, were the adventurers assessed. [2 *pp.*]

Jan. [10?].

50. Copy of the same, unsigned. [2¾ *pp.*]

Jan 11.

51. The Council to Sir Henry Marten. We send you a petition of Jacob Braems, customer of Dover, wherein he shows that for his loss of fishing busses taken by Dunkirkers, upon our directions to Sir John Pennington, the 22nd October last, to make stay of any Dunkirk shipping he could meet with, Sir John has caused a Dunkirk ship to be stayed at Plymouth, two-thirds laden with salt, and in regard petitioner has had no reparations from the Dunkirkers, and his Majesty's agent at Brussels is in small hopes of obtaining any satisfaction, he prays that the said salt and ship may be delivered to him, in part satisfaction. We pray you to give such direction therein as may be agreeable to equity and justice and the proceedings in that court. [*Draft.* 1 *p.*]

Jan. 11.

52. Minute of appearance of Robert Jason at the Council board this day; he is to remain in the custody of the messenger. [¼ *p.*]

Jan. 11.
Wells.

53. Bishop Pierce, of Bath and Wells, John Malet, and William Bassett, late sheriffs of Somerset, to the Council. We certified on 1st August last, in a difference between Henry Hodges, late sheriff of Somerset, and the inhabitants of the hundred of Wellow, concerning 40*l*. due for the shipping, that we had ordered that Hodges should pay the said sum, and be relieved by the hundred when he should make proof of the delivery of his warrant imposing the same during his shrievalty. We have since received your letters of the 19th November last, with Hodges's petition and certain affidavits, and find that Hodges has now made proof of the delivery of the said warrant. We have therefore ordered that the said sum shall be

1637–8.

Vol. CCCLXXVIII.

paid by the hundred of Wellow and liberty of Norton St. Philip, and Hodges be discharged thereof. [1 p.]

Jan 11.
London.

54. Nicholas Murford to Nicholas. Similar in purport to his letter to Endymion Porter of the 9th inst. (No. 35). He solicits a determination on the part of Nicholas whether his more important business will permit him to take the oath and office of an assistant of the Corporation of Saltmakers of Great Yarmouth, and states generally what was concluded at the late meeting at Arundel House. [*Seal with arms.* 1 p.]

Jan. 12.

Warrant to the Exchequer for striking a tally, purporting a discharge to Michael Holman and Richard Holman, of 700*l.* paid by them to the Earl of Morton, receiver of moneys arising by the late commission for scriveners and brokers, in full of a composition made by them for offences committed in their trade, for which his Majesty has granted them his pardon. [*Docquet.*]

Jan. 12.

Similar warrant to give order to the Farmers of the Greenwax for payment of 1,200*l.* per annum to Sir Richard Wynn, treasurer and receiver-general to the Queen, for her use during her life, in lieu of so much of her greenwax as his Majesty has taken for prevention of disputes with sundry sheriffs and bailiffs about the collection of the said greenwax, which said 1,200*l.* per annum is to be paid in manner following; viz., by the Earl of Berkshire, particular farmer of the post-fines, 800*l.* thereof; by the said Earl and his brother Lord Howard for their joint farm, 300*l.*; and by Sir William Brouncker out of the issues of jurors, 100*l.*, residue thereof. [*Docquet.*]

Jan. 12.

The like to discharge the Queen and her Officers of all moneys paid to her use for nonpayment of respite of homage, commonly called *Exitus et Amerciamenta coram Baronibus*, notwithstanding the same is not comprised amongst the titles of the Greenwax granted to her by his Majesty. [*Docquet.*]

Jan. 12.

Petition of Sir Henry Willoughby to the King. Upon divers acts touching the Great Level in cos. Northampton, Norfolk, Suffolk, Lincoln, Cambridge, Huntingdon, and the Isle of Ely, acted by the Commissioners of Sewers, there was "accosted" [allotted] to the undertakers of that level 76 acres of petitioner's several enclosures in Medney and Southery in Norfolk. Petitioner dwelling in Derbyshire, near 100 miles from the said place, could not at the time attend the commissioners to give them satisfaction why no part of the said enclosures should be set out for draining, but doubts not to give them such satisfaction if your Majesty will refer the same to their further hearing. Petitioner can make it appear that Sir John Willoughby, his father, about 40 years since, drained the ground of Medney and Southery, and laid the same absolutely dry, after whose decease petitioner had the same decreed to him in the 1st James I., he undertaking to keep the same drained, so as

Vol. CCCLXXVIII.

1637-8.

now the same grounds cannot any ways be bettered by the acts of the undertakers. Prays reference to such of the commissioners as were not parties to the said allotments, calling unto them the Surveyor-General to do therein as justice shall require. [*Copy. See Vol. cccxxiii., p. 223. ¾ p.*] *Underwritten,*

    I. *Reference to the Earl of Bedford, Sir Charles Herbert, and the Surveyor-General as prayed.* [*Copy. Ibid. ¼ p.*]

Jan. 12.
Whitehall.

55. Order of Council upon a petition of the Governor, Assistants, and Fellowship of the Eastland Merchants. Petitioners showed that at the last parliament in Poland an edict was made prohibiting the importation into that country of cloth except of certain sizes, which the statute of 4th James I. does not allow to be made in this country. Petitioners have cause to fear confiscation will be made upon such as transgress, and therefore humbly pray a toleration for making cloth for the Eastland vent in Suffolk, Essex, and Norfolk, and also in North-country clothing and perpetuanoes. The Lords conceiving this business to be a matter of great importance, referred the same to the Lord Treasurer and Lord Cottington, who, calling to them the Attorney-General and some of the most able merchants, are to consult of the petitioners' request, and to consider what has been heretofore done by the Council Board or otherwise upon any important occasion for altering the size of cloths from what is required by the statutes, and with all conveniency, in regard the time of shipping approaches, to return a certificate to the Board. [*Draft. 2½ pp.*]

Jan. 12.
Whitehall.

56. Similar order. The Attorney-General having, by relation of Thomas Violet, exhibited an information in the Star Chamber against John Massingberd, of London, merchant, for transporting great quantities of gold and silver without licence, the Lords, at the suit of Massingberd, referred the examination thereof to the Attorney-General, and after he had certified the Lords how he found the case to stand, the Lords caused Violet and Massingberd to be called before the Board. Violet was not able to prove that Massingberd had transported any gold or silver other than for the East India Company, who have licences for transporting certain proportions yearly, and were found to have shipped many thousand pounds less than they might have done, Massingberd being their agent. The Lords thereupon ordered the Attorney-General that Massingberd be no further proceeded against in the Star Chamber upon that information. [*Draft, corrected in many particulars by the Lord Privy Seal. 1 p.*]

Jan. 12.

57. Another previous draft of the same order. [*1¼ p.*]

Jan. 12.
Whitehall.

58. Order of Council upon the complaint of the Company of Glaziers against Sir Robert Mansell and his contractors, in reference to the dearness, badness, and scarcity of glass, and the want of full size. Sir Robert Mansell answered that the dearness was the result of the rise in the price of all the materials; that the scarcity was occasioned by the mortality that fell amongst the workmen at New-

1637-8.

VOL. CCCLXXVIII.

castle during the late visitation, and since for want of shipping; and that as to the badness, he agreed that whatever proved nought in the making should be broken at the furnace, and when the cases came here the glaziers should have the disposal thereof, paying the contractor for so much as they take. These answers seemed reasonable, but the Lords having found by their own experience that glass was not so fair, so clear, nor so strong as the same was wont to be, ordered that Sir Robert should take effectual care in those particulars. It was further objected that Sir Robert had contracted for all his glass with Lancelot Hobson, so that the glaziers could have none but such as he thought fit, and that he cut the glass into quarries, and made a reservation at Newcastle of the best glass. It was thought fit that the contract with Hobson should be dissolved, and that the cutters should be recalled from Newcastle, and no more be cut there, with a variety of other regulations to ensure the glaziers a proper supply, and at reasonable price. [*Draft, with alterations by Nicholas.* 2½ *pp.*]

Jan. 12.
Whitehall.

59. First draft of the preceding, with a variety of alterations made by the Lord Privy Seal, who has written upon it a note to Nicholas in reference to the changes he had made. [2¼ *pp.*]

Jan. 12.

60. Order of Council on the complaint of Ralph Moore and other hour-glass makers against Sir Robert Mansell, on account of the badness and dearness of their glasses (*see Vol. ccclxxiii., No.* 82). Sir Robert having entirely refuted the pretences of these petitioners, the Lords held their complaints to be merely clamorous and causeless, and ordered that if they thereafter troubled the Board they should be committed to prison. [*Draft.* 1 *p.*]

Jan. 12.

61. The like on the petition of William Price, groom of the chamber, who showed that by order of 29th September last a former order was confirmed for reducing six new houses which petitioner had built in Holborn into one house, and also that the houses which Nicholas Hudson, shoemaker, had begun to build, should be reduced to stables for the use of the said house; and the governors of the hospital of St. Bartholomew were required to take such course that the said order should be accomplished, which the governors have endeavoured to do, but Hudson remains refractory. The Lords ordered that some of the governors of the hospital and Hudson attend the Lords on the 19th instant. [*Draft.* 1 *p.*]

Jan. 12.
Whitehall.

62. The like on the petition of John Tanner, merchant, who showed that about 18 months since the patentees for logwood contracted with the petitioner to bring in logwood for his use. Thereupon petitioner gave order in the Canary Islands to buy a parcel of that sort of wood, and about 12 tons is sent him in the Anne and Elizabeth, now in London. Entry is made in the Custom House, yet the said wood is seized at the Custom House, upon pretence of some contentions between the Earl of Ancram and the patentees, who now leave petitioner in this trouble. Petitioner has

Vol. CCCLXXVIII.

1637-8.

also received advice of eight ton more of the same wood now arrived in the Downs, which was sent for upon the same directions, and petitioner fears the like trouble may arise upon the same. He therefore desires leave to transport both the said parcels into foreign parts. It was ordered that copies of the petition be delivered to the Earl of Ancram and the patentees, and the Lords appointed to hear the business on the 19th instant. [*Draft.* 1¼ *p.*]

Jan 12. 63. Order of Council that the Attorney-General should consider a complaint by Edmund Conquest against Robert Jason, and examine the parties and the witnesses adduced by Conquest, and certify the Board what he finds to be the truth. [*Draft.* 1 *p.*]

Jan. 12. 64. The Council to Attorney-General Bankes. A petition having been presented to his Majesty in the name of the bailiffs and burgesses of Derby, praying a confirmation of their ancient franchises, with certain alterations expressed in a schedule annexed to the petition; according to his Majesty's pleasure, the Lords have considered the same, and think fit that the charter be renewed, with the alteration of a mayor instead of the bailiffs, and certain enlargements of jurisdiction here stated. The Attorney-General is to prepare a new charter accordingly. [2 *pp.*]

Jan. 12. 65. The same to the Lord Mayor of London. By several letters and orders of this Board, and particularly those of the 24th May and 7th July last, we took notice how negligently the then Lord Mayor and aldermen had performed his Majesty's commands and the directions of this Board concerning the shutting up of all such shops in Cheapside and Lombard Street as were not goldsmiths, and ordered that if the aldermen of the said wards or their deputies should not forthwith cause to be shut up every such shop they should be committed to prison. Nevertheless, we are informed there are at the least 24 houses and shops that are not inhabited by goldsmiths, but in some of them there are one Grove and widow Hill [Gill?], stationers; one Sanders, a drugster; Medcalfe, a cook; Renatus Edwards, a girdler; John Dover, a milliner; and Brown, a bandseller, do still inhabit. We pray your Lordship to acquaint the said aldermen and their deputies therewith, and that if they do not presently put our former directions in execution we shall give such further orders as shall teach them to know that the commands of this Board ought not to be slighted. [*Draft.* 1 *p.*]

Jan. 12. 66. The same to Sir Henry Marten. Frequent directions have been given by this Board for preserving the beds and broods of oysters, and for remedying the excessive exportation of them, whereby they are now grown so exceeding scarce as they are not to be had but at extraordinary rates. To the end some expedient may be found out to meet with and prevent this decay, we require you to advise with Sir Dudley Digges, Master of the Rolls, and some other of the chief gentlemen of Kent and Essex, and to find out what is the true cause of this great scarcity, and to consider what may be a fit remedy. [*Draft.* 1 *p.*]

Vol. CCCLXXVIII.

1637-8.
Jan. 12.
67. The Council to Sir John Bridgeman and the rest of the Council of the Marches of Wales. We send a petition of Thomas Bushell, employed by his Majesty for discovering silver mines in Wales, who, by reason corn is scarce in those parts where his Majesty's miners work, to prevent the clamour of the country, has contracted for 1,000 quarters of corn to be delivered out of Pembrokeshire for the benefit of the said miners, but without licence he cannot be permitted to bring the same away. We recommend the same to you, requiring you to grant him licence for the same, as you shall think fit, and so from time to time either from that county or any thereabouts, if he desire it. [*Draft.* 1 *p.*]

Jan. 12.
68. The same to Bishop Pierce, of Bath and Wells, and the sheriff of Somerset. We send you a petition of the inhabitants of the hundred of Abdick and Bulstone, in Somerset, showing that in all payments they are generally charged after the proportion of 3*l*. in money for every 100*l*., or 3 men for every 100 men, according to which proportion they ought to pay 240*l*. towards the 8,000*l*. charged upon that county for shipping. According to this ancient rate, petitioners, in September last, made their collection for shipping after the proportion of 240*l*., but the sheriff has charged them with 280*l*., thereby to ease the hundred of Milverton, where the under-sheriff's estate lies. We pray you to take this complaint into consideration, and, if you find cause, to relieve petitioners, but with this proviso, that what abatement is made upon the petitioners may be charged elsewhere in that county, that so the whole sum may be fully paid. [*Draft.* 1¼ *p.*]

Jan. 12.
69. The same to all Mayors, Justices of Peace, and others. Whereas John Oved, of Tewkesbury, and John Saxby and Edward Hoggate, of Evesham, co. Worcester, by petition represented that in the said towns and other places in cos. Gloucester, Worcester, and Warwick, all manner of corn is very scarce, and the poor people without some present relief, not able to subsist. There being great plenty of corn in Cornwall, Devon, and Somerset, which may very well be spared, we require you to permit Oved, Saxby, and Hoggate to transport from the said counties for supply of the country and poor aforesaid all manner of corn, provided they enter into bond not to transport it into foreign parts. [*Draft.* 1 *p.*]

Jan. 12.
70. Minute of warrant to the Warden of the Fleet to receive into his custody Sir Thomas Fernefold. [½ *p.*]

Jan. 12.
Whitehall.
71. Sec. Windebank to Attorney-General Bankes. His Majesty gives licence to Lady Elizabeth Hatton to remain in and about the city of London with her family for six months from the 1st December last. You are to forbear to prosecute her or any of her family in the Star Chamber or elsewhere. [1 *p.*]

Jan. 12.
72. Certificate of John Pitman, late constable of the hundred or Pitney, and John Boyce and Thomas Hannam, late constables of

1637-8.   Vol. CCCLXXVIII.

Langport, Somerset, that the tithing of Muchelney (being within Pitney), together with Langport, by order of William Bassett, late sheriff, were ordered to pay 20*l*. towards ship-money, viz., for Muchelney and Midney, 12*l*. 7*s*. 8*d*., and for Langport, 7*l*. 12*s*. 4*d*.; which sum of 7*l*. 12*s*. 4*d*. the constables of Langport have paid to Bassett, and the residue the constables of Muchelney and Midney, viz., Roger Waggett and Richard Banbury, refuse to assess, whereby the service cannot be discharged as required. [¾ *p*.] *Underwritten,*

> 72. I. *Note by William Bassett. Having no power to compel the said refusers to obey my warrants, I pray your Lordships to take such course with them as shall be thought fit.* [¼ *p*.]

Jan. 12.
Ipswich.

73. Edm[und] Poley and three others, to Archbishop Laud. We have received letters from your Grace and others of the Council, concerning a further collection to be made within Suffolk towards repairing St. Paul's. There have been divers great charges imposed upon that country, as, namely, the shipping and three rates for relief of those infected with the plague in Hadleigh, Kersey, and St. Edmund's Bury, besides ordinary charges, we thought it therefore an unseasonable time to put in execution your letters, and refer it to some other time, when we may perform it with more hope of success. We desire you to accept our excuse for the hundreds of Hartismere, Samford, Bosmere and Claydon and Stow. We promise to perform the service hereafter. [1 *p*.]

Jan. 12.

74. Minutes of proceedings of Dr. Samuel Clarke and Dr. Robert Sibthorpe, substitutes of the chancellor and commissaries of the Bishop of Peterborough for the visitation of his diocese. These minutes relate to the acts of the visitors in relation to Peter Farren and Francis Rishworth, churchwardens of All Saints, Northampton. On the 26th October 1637, Rishworth appeared before the visitors, and was admonished to rail in the communion-table, and affix a kneeling bench to the same; also to remove certain seats extending 13 feet downward from the east end of the chancel, and place the communion-table altarwise, close to the said east end; and also to observe diligently the gestures of the ministers and parishioners, as to whether they bowed at the name of Jesus, and whether the ministers bade holy days, and turned their afternoon sermons into a catechetical way of questions and answers, or preached according to their own fancies; and also whether the parishioners received the communion kneeling. On the 16th December 1637 both the guardians appeared before the visitors, and not having performed these directions, they were warned to execute the same, for the second and third time, urgently, more urgently, and most urgently. This day they appeared again, and the mandate not having been obeyed, they were both excommunicated. [3⅓ *pp*.]

Jan. 12.

75. Commissioners of Sewers to the Council. Certificate made at a general sessions of sewers, held at Glanford Brigg, in reply to a

Vol. CCCLXXVIII.

1637–8.

petition of John Bellasis and Sir Michael Wharton, complaining of the proceedings of the commissioners in drawing a new river, called Ancholme, through the lordships of Worlaby and Saxby, belonging to petitioners, and which stood not in need of draining. The commissioners show that they proceeded upon the verdict of a jury, that the lands in question were surrounded grounds, that Sir John Monson, with the consent of the inhabitants, undertook the draining of a tract of fens of which Worlaby and Saxby are a part, and that 5,827 acres were agreed to be granted to him in compensation. They further certify that the work is in good forwardness, and that the lands alluded to are "the most sunken and wettest" in the whole level. [*Signed by 12 commissioners. 50 lines on parchment.*]

June 12.

76. Legal case respecting a difference between the dean of a cathedral not named and the treasurer of the same cathedral. The dean gave notice to the treasurer not to pay over a certain share in the balance of his account to a particular prebend. The treasurer disregarded the notice, and paid over the money. The question was, whether the dean might proceed against him in the chapter, and compel him to bring in the money, or in default thereof suspend, and, if necessary, deprive him. [1 *p.*] *Underwritten,*

    76. I. *Opinion of Dr. Arthur Duck in support of the power of the dean.* 12*th January* 1637–8, [½ *p.*] *Annexed,*

    76. II. *Opinion of Dr. Basil Woodd upon the same case. Doctors' Commons,* 12*th January* 1637–8. [1 *p.*]

Jan. 13.

Petition of Thomas Jermyn, his Majesty's servant, to the King. The manor and park of Killfoord, co. Denbigh, were leased by Sir John Walter, Sir Thomas Trevor, and others, lessors for your Majesty's lands as Prince of Wales, for 99 years, reserving the old rent of 20*l.* per annum, and a new increase of rent of 20*l.* to be paid from Michaelmas 1626, in which grant there is a *nomine pœnæ* of 8*l.* for every month in which the rent shall be unpaid, and also another *nomine pœnæ* for enrolling the grant before the auditors of the county. The new rent of 20*l.* per annum is unpaid ever since the same was reserved, and the lease is not enrolled, whereby there are due both the said forfeitures, of the benefit whereof petitioner beseeches a grant. [*Copy. See Vol.* cccxxiii., *p.* 224. ½ *p.*] *Underwritten,*

    I. *Reference to the Attorney-General to prepare a bill accordingly. Whitehall,* 13*th January* 1637–8. [*Copy. Ibid.* ¼ *p.*]

Jan. 13.
Chester.

77. Thomas Throppe, Mayor, and 11 others, of Chester, to the Council. Answer to the letter of the justices of peace and gentry of co. Chester, complaining of the conduct of the citizens of Chester in assessing the inhabitants of Gloverstone with the city, and also in their assessments upon Sir Thomas Aston and the Bishop of Chester (*see Vol.* ccclxx., *No.* 67). In the present letter the citizens reply upon every point, but state that the Council had already referred these differences to the Earl of Derby and the judges of

DOMESTIC—CHARLES I. 159

Vol. CCCLXXVIII.

1637-8.

Chester, who had appointed to hear the same at the next assizes, until which time they conceive that they of the county needed not to have troubled the Council. [*Seal of the city.* 2 *pp.*]

Jan. 13. 78. Sir Francis Thornhagh, Sheriff of co. Nottingham, to the Council. Replies to complaints made by the southern division of the county against his assessment for ship-money, upon the ground that whereas heretofore the south and north divisions paid such taxations in equal moieties, the sheriff had unequally assessed the two divisions, to the advantage of the northern division in which he resided. In the present letter the sheriff denies that the alleged equal division applied to such payments as the ship-money, and shows by a statement of his proceedings, and the grounds of them, that he had endeavoured to make the assessment altogether fair and equal, which he asserts it to be. He offers proof of the facts stated by him, and contends that if, as the complainants asserted, the King's service would suffer in this matter, it would be by their unjust interruption, and not by his assessment. [1½ *p.*]

Jan. 13.
Doctors' Commons.
79. A further case, entitled "The Commoners Defence," in the matter in dispute between the dean and treasurer of a cathedral not named (*see this present Vol., No.* 76), with two further legal opinions thereon of Dr. Basil Woodd, both dated this day. [2 *pp.*]

Jan. 13.
Edinburgh.
80. W. Elphinstoun to Sec. Windebank. A letter of compliments and thanks. The writer was once an unworthy secretary to a good but unfortunate great princess. Thanks to the secretary for giving life to Mr. Croft's and the writer's Lancashire business. If obstacles occur prays him to have recourse to the fountain of piety and justice, whose graciousness will not permit the writer to suffer to extremity. [*Seal with arms.* 1 *p.*]

Jan. 13. 81. Notes by Nicholas of business to be transacted by the Lords of the Admiralty. Order to the Lord Deputy for setting forth ships for guard of the Irish seas this next spring. Fleet to be set forth for guard of the seas next spring. Peruse letters from the Officers of the Navy. Appoint deputy-boatswain in the Nonsuch. Consider Mr. Brown's answer to Delabarre's petition. Despatch three or four petitions of poor men. Sir James Bagg appointed to attend about his accounts. [*Margin by Lord Treasurer Juxon:* "*Respectuatur.*" Saturday fortnight peremptory.] Consider two complaints by saltpetremen. Petition of a Dutchman recommended by the States ambassador touching 20 tons of saltpetre. The Attorney-General is to give account of the business touching Capt. Tokeley against Mr. Hooper. [1 *p.*]

Jan. 13.
Whitehall.
Lords of the Admiralty to Montjoy Earl of Newport. To supply the John, of London, of 260 tons, with ordnance; Jeremy Drury and others owners, Thomas Flute master. [*Copy. See Vol. cccliii., fol.* 78 *b.* ⅔ *p.*]

Jan. 13.
Whitehall.
The same to the same. We are informed that the powder and other provisions formerly put aboard the Henrietta and the Maria are near spent. As it is his Majesty's pleasure that these pinnaces

Vol. CCCLXXVIII.

1637–8.

shall be continued for this year, viz., the Henrietta for guard of the Thames and Medway, and the Maria for guard of Portsmouth, we pray you to give order for a survey of remains, and to cause them to be supplied, the master-gunners indenting for what they shall receive. [*Copy. See Vol. ccliii., fol.* 78 *b.* ⅔ *p.*]

Jan. 13. Lords of the Admiralty to [Henry] Kyme. To repair to the dwelling house of John Sedcole, of Exping [Epping], Essex, and bring him before the Lords to answer matters to be objected against him. [*Copy. Ibid., fol.* 79. ⅓ *p.*]

Jan. 13. Whitehall. Order of the same Lords upon the petition of David Eliot, John Thompson, and five other sailors. Petitioners showed that they were last summer employed by Capt. Trenchfield, Mr. Clements, Mr. Willoughby, and other merchants of London, in the Discovery, under Capt. Man, and were promised their wages and the sixth part of goods taken in any prizes. The ship took four prizes of a very great value, but the merchants have not performed their agreement. Petitioners besought the Lords to call the merchants to show cause why they detain petitioners' right. The Lords ordered Sir Henry Marten to examine the truth of the complaint, and take order for petitioners' satisfaction. [*Copy. Ibid., fol.* 79 *b.* ½ *p.*]

Jan. 13. Whitehall. The same Lords to the Officers of the Navy. By reason of the infirmity of Mr. Fleming, Clerk of the Navy, divers persons have made suit to his Majesty, and some of them have procured a reference to us, to succeed in that office. We are desirous, when the place shall be void, to have it supplied with an able man. We pray you to certify to us the names of such persons as you conceive to be of most sufficiency to discharge the same. [*Copy. Ibid., fol.* 77 *b.* ½ *p.*]

Jan. 13. 82. John Crane to the Lords of the Admiralty. I have made provision for such a number of men for six months service at sea for 1638 as was employed for the last year. My suit is, that you will give order to Sir William Russell to make me payment of 10,000*l.*, upon the first moneys [that] shall come to his hands from the counties. [1 *p.*]

Jan. 13. 83. Account of gunpowder spent in 13 of the ships of the Fleet employed at sea in 1637. [1 *p.*]

Jan. 13. 84. See "Papers relating to Appointments in the Navy."

Jan. 14. 85. Receipt of W. Fotherby for 165 barrels of gunpowder containing 16,558 lbs., from Mr. Cordewell, from the powder mills at Chilworth, being the return of 175 barrels sent out of the East India Company's storehouse at Blackwall to be refined. [½ *p.*]

Jan. 15. Grant to Lawrence Squibb of the office of one of the two clerks of the Court of Wards and Liveries in reversion after Richard Chamberlain, Hugh Audley, and James Maxwell, upon surrender made by Francis Jenoure, who had the same office granted to him on 15th August 1630. [*Docquet.*]

DOMESTIC—CHARLES I.

1637-8.

Jan. 15. Vol. CCCLXXVIII.

Petition of the Warden and Officers of the Mint to the King. Your royal predecessors above 300 years since incorporated the warden, workmasters, moneyers, and other ministers of the Mint, and their charter has been confirmed and enlarged by succeeding kings. Of late years divers privileges have been broken and some lost, namely, the keeping a court where all actions concerning the several members of that corporation ought to be tried and their disorders regulated. For want of that court many great disorders have crept in. Pray that such court be renewed. [*Copy. See Vol. cccxxiii., p. 224. ¾ p.*] *Underwritten,*

> I. *Minute of the King's pleasure that the court above mentioned be revived, and Mr. Attorney-General is to take especial care in drawing up a confirmation or further grant of the charter. Whitehall, 15th January 1637-8. [Copy. Ibid. ¼ p.]*

Jan. 15. 86. Alderman Henry Andrews to Richard Fenn, Lord Mayor of London. In obedience to the late Lord Mayor's precept touching the shutting up tradesmen's shops in Goldsmiths' Row in Cheapside, I and my deputy caused the said shops several times to be shut up, and the then Lord Mayor in person did the like; yet finding some to continue the opening in part, the then Lord Mayor committed to prison John Bartlett, bookseller, and Roger Stoughton, haberdasher of small wares. Since, upon receipt of your precept, according to the Lords' command of the 12th inst., I went with my deputy and a constable and read unto them your precept, and shut up the shops of John Dover, haberdasher of small wares or perfumer of gloves, Renatus Edwards, girdler, and Roger Stoughton, and gave warning to the constable if he found any of their shops open, or they or their servants using their trades, that they should bring them before you. The inhabitants complain that they have sustained great loss by shutting up their houses, so that they are disabled to pay duties to the King, the city, or parish, except some goldsmiths do take their houses of them. [1¼ *p.*]

Jan. 15. 87. Alderman Sir George Whitmore to the same. Similar letter, differing in the names of those whose shops had been shut up. "The poor widow Gill [Hill], Grove, Sanders, and Medcalfe" are the persons here mentioned. [1¾ *p.*]

Jan. 16. 88. The Council to all Mayors and other Officers. In the Ann Mary, whereof John Butler is master, there is laden a good quantity of Castile or hard soap, which ship being now in the Thames, it is believed that the said soap will be landed here, contrary to proclamation. You are required to be aiding to Richard Charnock, who is appointed to make search for such soap laden in the said ship, and to seize the same for the use of his Majesty. [*Draft.* ¾ *p.*]

Jan. 16. 89. Copy of the same. [1 *p.*]

Jan. 16. 90. Minute of a warrant to the Keeper of Bridewell to set at liberty James Leveret, a gardener. [¼ *p.*]

Vol. CCCLXXVIII.

1637–8.
Jan. 16.
91. Philip Burlamachi to Sec. Windebank. Having intelligence from his friends in Paris of certain exceptions taken by the ambassadors to Burlamachi's account of sums received there on account of the Queen's marriage portion, he enters into a long explanation of the state of the account, with the sums received by him and the losses and deductions to which he had been subjected by the state of the exchanges and in other ways. If any one could prove that he had received a single *liard* more than he had accounted for, he is willing to be considered the most infamous man in the world. The aldermen and others to whom his account was referred by the Lords of the Treasury bore testimony that he had acted honestly and justly. Their report is in the hands of the auditors. Wishes that by direction of the King the secretary should write to the ambassadors, that, instead of throwing obstacles in Burlamachi's way, they should help his friends to procure payment of what has been declared due to him. [*French.* 4½ *pp.*]

Jan. 16.
Whitehall.
92. Minutes by Nicholas of resolutions agreed to at the Committee for the regulation of the Household. Amongst other things it was resolved that an oath should be taken by the clerks and sergeants according to a regulation of 31 Henry VIII., and that the hall should be kept at the King's three standing houses, namely, at Whitehall, Hampton Court, and Greenwich, but before this last order was established the King was to be moved that if he intended to restore other ancient orders of household, then the Lords conceived this for the hall fit to be revived. [2 *pp.*]

Jan. 16.
93. Kenrick Edisbury to Nicholas. Sends the draft of a letter proposed to be written by the Lords of the Admiralty to the Officers of the Navy, which Edisbury thinks may enable them to do his Majesty good service in examination of the boatswains' accounts. When Nicholas makes a list for the ships in the next fleet Edisbury would willingly advise with him before it be signed. He meant to be with him this day, but being sermon day at Court, and the ways tedious, he put it off till to-morrow. [¼ *p.*] *Written over the preceding,*

    93. I. *Draft of the proposed letter above mentioned, and which was written on the* 17*th inst.* [¾ *p.*]

Jan. 16.
94. Return by John Herne and George Long, Justices of Peace for Middlesex, of the names of such persons of honour as have continued in various places in the outskirts of the city of London since the 12th December last. Amongst the persons mentioned were the Earl of Elgin, Lady Magdalen Bruce, Lady Penelope Gage, and Lady Judith May, the ladies being all widows; these lived in Clerkenwell. In St. Andrew's, Holborn, were the Earls of Warwick and Southampton, the Viscountess Cramond, and John Pimme, Esq. In Islington was Edward Lord Herbert. In Essex House in the Strand were Lord Digby and Viscount Mandeville. In Clerkenwell was William Fairfax, who has his Majesty's warrant for stay. Many alleged by way of excuse that they had no country houses. [1⅔ *p.*]

1637–8.   Vol. CCCLXXVIII.

Jan. 16. 95. Information of William Blythe, taken before Attorney-General Bankes. John Evelyn, of Godstone, Surrey, and John Pigott, late of London, grocer, in December 1636 conveyed into a storehouse of Pigott's, in Dunning's Alley, Without Bishopgate, 110 barrels of gunpowder, made of English saltpetre, which properly belonged to his Majesty, and there secretly kept the same from December [1636] to April [1637], and then Evelyn and Pigott sold the same in the presence of Thomas Steventon and Barcock, a chandler. [*The Attorney-General has added that Blythe received this information from Robert Davis and did not know it of his own knowledge.* ⅔ *p.*]

Jan. 16. 96. Similar information of Robert Davis. He states that the gunpowder was brought into Pigott's storehouse by one Knightley and his servants, and that it was sold to one Jasper Selwyn, now searcher at Rye, with various other particulars more minute than those mentioned by Blythe. [*The Attorney-General has added that Davis received the gunpowder into Pigott's storehouse, and was employed therein by the appointment of one Brush, Mr. Evelyn's man.* ¾ *p.*]

Jan. 17. Proclamation declaring the seasonable times when warrants for
Whitehall. venison in the King's forests, chases, or parks are to be served. Male deer are not to be killed before the 7th July, being about the end of the fence month, or after Holy-rood Day; nor female deer before Holy-rood Day nor after the feast of Epiphany, commonly called Twelfth Day. [*Printed. See Coll. Procs., Car. I., No.* 218. 1 *p.*]

Jan. 17. Petition of William Clerk, gold-wire drawer, to the King. Your suppliant has been petitioner these four years for the copper manufacture, which through his great pains and expense of 1,000*l*. (to his utter undoing) he brought to perfection, since which time petitioner has endeavoured to save your Majesty's bullion in the manufacture of gold and silver thread; for which cause petitioner can neither be admitted to work in the office (as was proffered him before), nor yet have any silver for his money, but his doors and chests are broken open, his goods taken away in the house and street, and his servant imprisoned. By means whereof, for relief of his wife and family, he was forced to do some work, for which he craves a pardon, and prays "his barr" to work in the office as others have, and that his silver and goods may be restored to him. [*Copy. See Vol. cccxxiii., p.* 226. ½ *p.*] *Underwritten,*

> I. *His Majesty remits petitioner's offence, and directs the commissioners for manufacture of gold and silver thread to restore his goods, and take order that he shall have "a barr" in the office, he giving security to work no more underhand, and to pay his Majesty's custom.* Whitehall, 17*th January* 1637-8. [*Copy. Ibid.* 1 *p.*]

Jan 17. Petition of William Newton to the same. There is a field near Lincoln's Inn called Pursefield with the pightels, being his Majesty's

164　　　　　　　　　DOMESTIC—CHARLES 1.

Vol. CCCLXXVIII.

1637–8.

inheritance and in jointure to the Queen, for which there is answered to the Crown but 5l. 6s. 8d. yearly rent, and the same are in lease at the same rent for 47 years to come. Petitioner being interested in part of the premises, prays licence for building on the same 32 houses, to ascend with steps unto them, with necessary coach-houses and stables, with back and outhouses, and for making sewers and altering footways. [*Copy. See Vol. cccxxiii., p. 227.* ⅓ *p.*] *Underwritten,*

 I. *Reference to the Attorney-General to prepare licence as prayed.*
  Whitehall, 17th January 1637–8. [*Copy. Ibid.* ¼ *p.*]

Jan. 17. Petition of Robert Terwhitt, Thomas Lewis, and Cyprian Day to the King. Divers cities and towns in England and Wales, especially London and Westminster, stand in need of greater quantities of water, and in particular to prevent fires, and to keep the houses sweet and free from noisome smells, the causes many times of great infection. Also divers parts of London and Westminster stand in need of Thames water for such like uses. Pray licence to build water-works throughout England and Wales, paying to his Majesty the yearly rent of 50l., to commence from Lady Day 1640, by which time petitioners may have finished one or more of their works. [*Copy. Ibid., p. 227.* ¾ *p.*] *Underwritten,*

 I. *Reference to the Lord Privy Seal, the Earl Marshal, and Sec.*
  Windebank, who are to certify their opinions. Whitehall,
  17th January 1637–8. [*Copy. Ibid., p. 228.* ¼ *p.*]

Jan. 17.
Whitehall.

97. Order of Council. The Lords having heard the deputy and divers of the company of merchant adventurers of England, and likewise some of the chief merchants of Exeter and their counsel, touching a remonstrance presented by the merchant adventurers, that Spanish cloths made in the west country ought to be shipped from London only, and being not willing to shut up the trade of the outports altogether, commanded that the deputy and two others of the merchant adventurers and Mr. Ball, the Queen's solicitor (who is of counsel with the Exeter merchants), and two of the western merchants should meet together and consider how the trade of Spanish cloth may be best accommodated, and to accord amongst themselves all differences between this and this day sevennight, when they are again to attend this Board, and the Lords will take order for a final end of this business. [*Draft.* 1⅓ *p.*]

Jan. 17.
Whitehall.

98. Order of Council upon a petition of Calcot Chambre to the Lord Deputy of Ireland, and by him remitted hither. The question in the matter related to the best mode of administering the estate of Calcot Chambre, deceased, father of the petitioner, which estate was in the hands of James Fiennes and John Crewe as trustees for payment of the debts and legacies of the deceased. An offer had been made by Mr. Samford, brother-in-law to the petitioner, to pay all the debts and legacies in three years, with an allowance in the meantime of 300l. per annum to the petitioner, if the trustees would make over the estate to him for that time. Before the Lords a counter offer was made by Samuel Weale on behalf of Sir

1637-8.

VOL. CCCLXXVIII.

Philip Percivall. The Lords conceived Mr. Samford to be an unfit man to have to do with the estate of the deceased, and directed the trustees to meet Weale, and having set down his proposal in writing, to present the same to the Lord Deputy, to whom the Lords remitted the final decision of the business. [*Draft.* 2½ *pp.*]

Jan. 17.
Whitehall.

99. Order of Council. The Lords having heard the Attorney-General and the Recorder of London, with Sir Maurice Abbot and others, the committee of the city for setting forth city ships in 1636, touching an information exhibited in the Exchequer by the Attorney-General against Sir Christopher Clitherow, Sir Maurice Abbot, and others, being the said committee, and one William Bushell, thereby charging the committee and Bushell with setting forth three ships in 1636, furnished with less men, victuals, and ammunition, and which stayed less time at sea, than was required by the ship-money writ, to the private profit to themselves of 1,000*l.* and more. It appearing that Sir Christopher was then Lord Mayor, and that the other aldermen named were committees (amongst others) chosen for that service, without any benefit to themselves, and they offering to make it appear that they had paid in full for the said ships and had no money remaining in their hands, it was ordered that the committee should put into the Exchequer their answer, and that afterwards producing the charter-parties made with Bushell and the other persons who contracted for performance of the service, and showing full payment of the money for that service, the Attorney-General is not to proceed further against them, but he is to proceed roundly against Bushell and all other persons that contracted for any of the said three ships, who have any of the said moneys unduly remaining in their hands, or have failed in performance of his Majesty's service or of the said charter-parties. The Lords declared that the Attorney-General did very well to exhibit his information, as well against the committees as the contractors, for the Lords conceived that the committees had been too remiss in not taking more care to see better performance of their contract. [*Draft.* 2½ *pp.*]

Jan. 17.

100. The like. Divers examinations having been taken by the Attorney-General of misdemeanours charged upon Robert Jason, it was ordered that the Lord Chief Justice of the King's Bench receive from the Attorney-General such proofs as concern criminal offences, and proceed legally against Jason as he shall think fit. [*Draft.* ½ *p.*]

Jan. 17.

101. Similar Order. Sir Richard Ducie, late sheriff of co. Gloucester, being charged with levying the arrears of ship-money for the time of his sheriffalty, and required to pay in the same or attend the Board the first Sunday in next term, represented by petition that a good part of the arrears being levied, he hoped by the end of the next term to give a good account for the rest, and therefore desired to be spared his attendance until a week after Candlemas. The Lords granted Sir Richard time till the 11th February next. [*Draft.* 1 *p.*]

Vol. CCCLXXVIII.

1637–8.
Jan. 17.

102. Order of Council. John Button, late sheriff of Hants, being required to pay in the arrears of ship-money charged upon that county in the time of his sheriffalty, in regard he has but lately received warrant from the now sheriff to collect the same, and the sums being small and lying scattered through the county, desired that he might be spared till a further day. The Lords ordered that the moneys now in his hands be forthwith paid to Sir William Russell, and that if he pay not in all the arrears by the 11th February next, then to attend the Board. [*Draft.* 1 *p.*]

Jan. 17.

103. The Council to Attorney-General Bankes. Upon the 5th inst. we directed you to examine Thomas Sandiford, accused by Edward Woodfine and Richard Johnson to have uttered dangerous speeches (*see this present Vol., No.* 19). Upon consideration of your certificate we require you to cause Sandiford to be indicted at the King's Bench bar some time next term. [*Draft.* 1 *p.*]

Jan. 17.

104. Minute of a warrant to the Warden of the Fleet, to take into his custody Robert Jason and keep him close prisoner until further order. [½ *p.*]

Jan. 17.
Whitehall.

Lords of the Admiralty to Officers of the Navy. There are now kept aboard the Sovereign of the Seas, at Erith, 100 men, notwithstanding his Majesty, when he was last aboard her, commanded there should be but 60 during her being at Erith. You are to take order that, as soon as the weather breaks and the danger of the ice is passed, there be no more kept but only 60. [*Copy. See Vol. ccclii., fol.* 79. ⅓ *p.*]

Jan. 17.
Whitehall.

The same to the same. We have received certificate from you, touching the account of boatswains' stores in the ships employed last summer at sea, which you conceive to be very exorbitant from some boatswains, and therefore have suspended them, wherein you did well, but we are of opinion that the wastes in the rest of the ships are much more than ought to be, and that the boatswains embezzle the stores committed to their charge. We pray you to place some honest and able men in room of those boatswains suspended, and to send for the rest of the boatswains to examine their waste; also calling unto you about six of the prime men of the Trinity House, to return us a certificate whether the particular boatswains' accounts be allowable, or they fit to be punished for deceit or ill husbandry. [*Copy. Ibid., fol.* 79 *b.* ⅔ *p.*]

Jan. 17.

105. Petition of Giles Creech, cutler, to Archbishop Laud. Being for many years a reader of the Holy Scriptures, he did for the exposition of them unfortunately light on the acquaintance of Familists, Antinomians, Anabaptists, and the like, and was a disciple of Dr. Everard, sometimes lecturer at St. Martin's-in-the Fields, whereby he became infected with those pernicious doctrines, till a few years since, hearing a sermon preached on Palm Sunday before his Majesty at Whitehall he was moved to discern and soon after to detest all those damnable opinions, and thereupon abandoned

Vol. CCCLXXVIII.

1637-8.

the company of those sectaries. They, conceiving a mortal hatred against him for the said revolt, have caused Isabel Brodenton to accuse him in the High Commission Court of those very errors which they themselves taught him. Prays his discharge, being poor and in debt, and that he may avoid further molestation and follow his trade. *Underwritten,*

> I. *Reference to Sir John Lambe. If he finds the suggestions in the petition true, he is to give an account to the archbishop that further order may be taken.* 17th January 1637-8. [1 p.]

Jan. 17.

106. Paper endorsed by Archbishop Laud "The state of the 34 parishes in Norwich, and the maintenance for the ministers there; as it was then [*i.e.*, this day] presented before his Majesty." This paper was in connexion with a proposal that the King should allot the ministers 2s. 9d. in the pound as in London and in one parish of Canterbury, or 2s. 6d. as in the rest of Canterbury, or 2s. according to the course of the Canon Law and the practice in St. Clement's at Temple Bar and elsewhere in London. The pecuniary results of these various assessments as applied to the case of Norwich are here stated. [1 p.]

Jan. 17.
Farlsthrope.

107. Answer of John Hales, vicar of Farlsthorpe, co. Lincoln, to articles of Archbishop Laud respecting the value of his vicarage and the way in which it might be increased. Its then value was 20l. per annum. Certain sums of 15s. 6d., 13s. 4d., and 5s., were said to be detained from the vicar by James Carrington, the impropriator, Francis Hanson, and John Gartsyde, rector of Willoughby-in-the-Marsh, respectively. The yearly value of the impropriation was 8l. The vicarage might be augmented by payment of the tithes in kind. [1½ p.]

Jan. 17.
Mumby
Vicarage.

108. Answer of Humphrey Garrard, vicar of Mumby, co. Lincoln, to similar articles of Archbishop Laud. The vicarage was worth 15l. per annum. The tithe of a windmill in Mumby, worth 6s. 8d. per annum, was paid to the rectory of Hogsthorpe. There was no vicarage house. The vicar lived in the rectory, but had to keep it in repair. The impropriation was worth 80l. per annum; 60l. clear was paid to the owner, Margaret Litchfield, of Cambridge, widow, by Robert Paul, farmer. The vicarage could only be augmented out of the impropriation. [¾ p.]

Jan. 17.

109. Similar answer of Thomas Rockley, vicar of Huttoft, co. Lincoln. The vicarage was reputed worth 20 marks per annum. The benefit of tithe milk is detained from the vicarage, worth 10l. per annum. The impropriate rectory is worth 100l. per annum. It is in the hands of the Duchess of Buckingham. The best means to augment the vicarage is out of the impropriation. [1½ p.]

Jan. 17.

110. Statement of Philip Burlamachi in further illustration of his account of money received in Paris in part of the Queen's marriage

1637-8.

Vol. CCCLXXVIII.

portion, as explained in his letter to Sec. Windebank, calendared in this Vol. under date of the 16th inst., No. 91. [1 p.]

Jan. 17. 111. See "Papers relating to Appointments in the Navy."

Vol. CCCLXXIX.   January 18-28, 1637-8.

1637-8.

Jan. 18. The King to Lord Treasurer Juxon and Lord Cottington. To give warrant for delivery of 13,500 cords of wood to the farmers of the iron-works in Dean Forest for the present year, and for the setting out of a new "fellett" before the 10th February next, to contain the like quantity of 13,500 cords of wood for the next year, according to the draft of a privy seal agreed on by Sir Ralph Whitfield and Sir Charles Harbord. [Docquet.]

Jan. 18. The same to the President and Chapter of Lichfield. To elect Samuel Fell, D.D., one of his Majesty's chaplains in ordinary, to the deanery of that church, void by the promotion of John Warner, D.D., to the bishopric of Rochester. [Docquet.]

Jan. 18. 1. Petition of the Mayor, Burgesses, and Commonalty of Bristol to the Council. On a petition to the King, hereunto annexed, and his pleasure thereon, divers of petitioners have given security to attend the Board and not depart without leave. Since when they have appeared before the commissioners, and have been again examined, but not upon the body of the commission, but chiefly in what manner the commissioners behaved themselves at Bristol, with other impertinent matter not examinable by the commissioners. Amongst others, the commissioners examined Edmund Arundell, one of petitioners, and demanded of him whether he thought if due obedience had been given to the commission at Bristol the commissioners would have broken up any doors or locks, whereunto Arundell answering that he could not tell, he was by the Lord Mohun and others committed to the messenger, and is now in custody. Forasmuch as these proceedings of the commissioners are as unwarrantable as their former, no power being given them to imprison, petitioners pray that they and the commissioners may attend the Lords for hearing, and that petitioner Arundell may be enlarged, and the rest discharged of further attendance. [1 p.] *Annexed,*

> 1. I. *Petition of the Mayor, Burgesses, and Commonalty of Bristol to the King. Recite commission to inquire of certain alleged illegal payments on goods exported or imported imposed at Bristol, calendared under 30th November 1637, No. 87. Complain of the illegal and unwarrantable proceedings of Charles Foxe and Robert Powlett, two of the commissioners, in taking into custody witnesses ready to appear before them, fetching others out of their*

1637-8.

VOL. CCCLXXIX.

houses and keeping them prisoners until examination, and unless they would subscribe to what Powlett wrote, though they knew it not to be true, declaring them to be refractory, and thereupon detaining them in custody, with much other matter in relation to these disputes minutely detailed, especially that some of their body who were sent to London to complain of these proceedings had been attached by a sergeant-at-arms upon the misinformation of these commissioners. Pray for the discharge of those who are in custody, upon security for their appearance, and that the King would appoint a day to hear the premises. [Signed by Thomas Colston, Edmund Arundell, and seven others. ¾ p.] Underwritten,

1. I. i. Minute of the King's pleasure that petitioners are to attend the Lord Treasurer and Lord Cottington touching the discharge of such as are in custody, who are to be set at liberty upon security, and that his Majesty will be present at the hearing, and Sec. Windebank is to be attended to know what day his Majesty will appoint. Whitehall, 7th January 1637-8. [¼ p.]

Jan. 18.
2. Minute of his Majesty's further pleasure in reference to the above petitions from Bristol. The petitioners are to sign their names to their petitions, and signification is to be sent to them that his Majesty will hear the commissioners' complaints against them on Sunday next. [⅔ p.]

Jan. 18.
Long Acre.
3. Statement by John Lord Mohun of Okehampton, Warwick Mohun, Robert Powlett, and Charles Foxe, the commissioners before mentioned, of the particulars in which Edmund Arundell, one of the wardens of the Company of Merchants at Bristol, had been a wilful contemner of his Majesty's commission. [1 p.]

Jan. 18.
Wolveton.
4. Sir Thomas Trenchard and John Freke, late successively sheriffs of Dorset, to the Council. Your letters of 31st October last commanded us to collect the arrears of ship-money (see Vol. ccclxx., No. 73). State reasons why since its receipt they could collect only 56l. 19s. 11d., which they have returned to Sir William Russell. Beseech the Lords to spare their attendance, and that a new writ may be awarded to the new sheriff, returnable in Easter term next, for collecting the same arrears, and they hope thereupon to levy the same. [1 p.]

Jan. 18
Burdcrop.
5. William Calley to Richard Harvey. Has sent by Robert Whippe 4l. 7s. 9d. Felix Long is at Dr. Bing's, and is expected at Burdcrop before Monday. "My brother Danvers, coming lately from Littlecote, made such a relation of Mr. Popham's funeral as would make any man but a coward hug death to gain so stately an interment." [⅔ p.]

Vol. CCCLXXIX.

1637-8.
Jan. 18.
Aby.

6. Answer of Richard Coxall, vicar of Aby, co. Lincoln, to Archbishop Laud's articles respecting vicarages before mentioned. His vicarage is worth 60*l*. per annum, arising from tithes. There are detained from the vicar 44*l*. per annum, principally by the Earl of Lindsey and his servants. No impropriation is known. [1 *p*.]

Jan. 18.
Whitehall.

Lords of the Admiralty to Thomas Wyan, Deputy Registrar of the Court of Admiralty. His Majesty, by privy seal dated 13th January 1630-1, gave warrant to cause 200*l*. to be yearly paid out of the profits of the Admiralty to Edward Nicholas for his service. Wyan is to cause the said sum to be paid to him for the year ended the feast of St. Thomas last past. [*Copy. See Vol. cccliii., fol.* 80. ½ *p*.]

Jan. 18.
Whitehall.

The same to Attorney-General Bankes. Great sums of money have been accounted for as paid by his Majesty for freight of ships employed in his service since 1625. Howsoever his Majesty has paid the full sums without abatement, yet it appears that the owners of ships have not been fully paid. You are to draw up a commission, directed to Sir Edward Sawyer, Edward Nicholas, and both the auditors of the Imprest, authorizing them to examine upon oath such persons as have any ways had to do with such payments, for better discovery of the truth. [*Copy. Ibid.* ⅔ *p*.]

Jan. 18.

7. Separate examinations of John Brush, Hugh Knightley, Edward Barcock, and Thomas Steventon, taken before Attorney-General Bankes, in reference to 100 barrels of gunpowder and 60 barrels of brimstone sent to the storehouse of Jasper Selwyn, under-tenant of John Pigott, by direction of John Evelyn. [1½ *p*.]

Jan. 18.
Office of Ordnance.

8. Estimate by the Officers of the Ordnance of the expense and return of powder into his Majesty's magazine from the Triumph, the St. George, the James, the Unicorn, the Rainbow, the Vanguard, the Henrietta Maria, the Convertive, the Dreadnought, the Roebuck, the Swan, and the First Whelp. Total spent, 13 lasts, 16 cwt., 36 lbs.; total returned, 36 lasts, 13 cwt., 39 lbs. [1 *p*.]

Jan. 18.

9. Note that the last gunpowder sent into Ireland was in March 1629, being 20 lasts. [2 *lines*.]

Jan. 18.

10. Copy information brought into the Court of Star Chamber by the Attorney-General against Bishop Williams, of Lincoln, and 23 other persons. It charged the bishop and others of the defendants with having procured several of the defendants to swear falsely in certain depositions taken in past proceedings against the bishop, and especially in relation to a question of whether John Prigeon the elder was the father of a bastard child of Elizabeth Hodgson. It also set forth a paper of instructions stated to have been prepared by the bishop and his coadjutors as to how the witnesses might upon examination equivocate with the questions asked of them, and alleged various instances of false swearing in compliance with those instructions. It further charged the bishop with having executed fraudulent leases of his lands in order

1637-8.

Vol. CCCLXXIX.

to defeat the King of any fine to be imposed upon him, and to have pleaded those leases in the Exchequer in bar to writs of extent issued for recovery of the fine of 10,000*l.* imposed in Trinity term last; also with having attempted to corrupt Mr. Kilvert, who was employed as solicitor for his Majesty in endeavouring to levy the said fine; also with having appointed Vincent Brampton, who was a grocer and kept an alehouse, to be curate of Asgarby, co. Lincoln, of which place the bishop as prebend was bound to serve the cure, and that Brampton being questioned upon the subject by the justices of peace, answered that he got more by the ale than the altar, and had rather leave the church than his alehouse. [11 *pp.*]

Jan. 18. 11. List, certified by George Rigby, clerk of the peace, of badgers licensed at the several sessions of the peace for co. Lancaster held from the 17th April 1637 to this day. In all 217. [6½ *pp.*]

Jan. 18. 12. List, similarly certified, of all licensed alehouse-keepers within the same county. Total, 793. [12 *pp.*]

Jan. 19.
Whitehall.
13. Order of Council. After hearing Thomas Witherings and Jason Grover, the common carrier of Yarmouth and Ipswich, and their counsel, it was ordered that Grover and all carriers shall henceforth conform to the letters patent granted to Witherings of the letter office and the proclamation in that behalf. *But their Lordships declared that it should be lawful for any carrier that should receive the letters of merchants or others to be carried from town to town within the kingdom to use what diligence he may and to ride what pace he will, so as he do it without shifting or change of horses.* It was objected that Witherings took more for the carriage of letters within the kingdom than was usual; the Lords referred the consideration of all complaints of that nature to the Secretaries of State, praying them to take course for redress of such abuse. [*Draft. The clause which we have printed above in italic was struck out by the King, who wrote in the margin* "This clause to bee left out. C. R." 1¼ *p.*]

Jan. 19.
Whitehall.
14. The Council to the Lord Mayor of London. We are confident his Majesty's commands set forth by proclamations and book of orders for keeping the Lent season, Vigils, Ember week, and other fasting days are not unknown to you, and therefore we cannot but let you know that his Majesty is resolved to have this ensuing Lent and other fasting days well observed. We require you to use your best endeavours to give his Majesty satisfaction; but for furnishing ambassadors and ministers of foreign princes residing here, and the relief of sick and weak persons, we permit you (according to custom) to grant licence to kill all sorts of flesh (beef only excepted) to eight butchers, and to eight poulterers to utter flesh and poultry ware. [*Draft.* 1½ *p.*]

Jan. 19.
Whitehall.
15. Order of Council. Having heard the petition of John Tanner, merchant (*see previous order, Vol. ccclxxviii., No.* 62), and also the

VOL. CCCLXXIX.

1637–8.

Earl of Ancram, touching logwood ordered by Tanner to be brought from the Canary Islands, upon an agreement made with the patentees for logwood, and understanding that there is a privy seal granted to the Earl for seizing a certain quantity of logwood, and likewise patents passed to others to seize a further quantity, it was ordered that Edward Herbert, the Queen's attorney, shall examine whether the Earl and his agents have fully received his proportion of logwood, and whether the patentees have any right as yet to bring in any logwood, and thereof to certify the Board by Wednesday next come sevennight, and in the meantime the logwood mentioned in the petition to be put into safe custody. [*Draft.* 1½ *p.*]

Jan. 19. 16. Minute of warrant from the Council to the Warden of the Fleet, to set at liberty Simon Corbet, William Nicoll, and John Benfield, moneyers. [½ *p.*]

Jan. 19. 17. The like of similar warrant to Nicholas Pye, messenger, to fetch before the Lords John Poole, constable of the hundred of Ongar, Essex, and Thomas Poole and John Ting, constables of Fyfield, Essex. [½ *p.*]

Jan. 19. The like to Henry Kyme, to fetch William Stane and Amos Prielove, constables of the hundred of Harlow, Essex, and Josias Wood, constable of Roydon, Essex. [*Written on the same paper as the preceding.* ¼ *p.*]

Jan. 19. The like to David Stott, to fetch John Croft, of Stoke Milborough, Salop. [*Ibid.* ⅓ *p.*]

Jan. 19. The like to Francis Taylor, to fetch Marcus Adams and Robert Adams, his son, of Ryehill, in the hundred of Harlow, Essex. [*Ibid.* ½ *p.*]

Jan. 19. 18. Petition of Nevill Titchborne to the Council. You were pleased upon a petition of petitioner's mother-in-law, Priscilla Titchborne, concerning a difference between her and her husband and children, to order that they should give attendance at the second sitting after Twelfth Day. Petitioner has attended on his and his father's behalf 14 days. As his mother has not given attendance, he beseeches you to dismiss him, and, if there be cause, to appoint a day peremptory for the hearing. [*Underwritten,* "*Nevill Titchborne appeared the 19th January* 1637[-8]." ½ *p.*]

Jan. 19.
Bishopthorpe.
19. Archbishop Neile, of York, to Sec. Windebank. I give you thanks for many good offices, and amongst them for your relation of his Majesty's acceptance of my service in intercepting Fenwick's books and provisions for printing, and of his Majesty's well allowing my last year's certificate. I trouble you with my certificate for the year past, which I pray you to present to his Majesty. P.S.—I received my brother of Chester's certificate but yesterday. [*Good impression of seal.* ½ *p.*]

Vol. CCCLXXIX.

1637–8.

Jan. 19.
The Swiftsure, in the Downs.
20. Sir John Pennington to Lords of the Admiralty. The embargo in France continues upon all his Majesty's subjects in all parts of that kingdom except Bordeaux and Rochelle, and they are now so far out of hope of being set at liberty, that divers masters belonging to Dover have sent home to their merchants to have leave to come away with their men. [1 p.]

Jan. 19.
21. Answers by Robert Bennett, vicar of Hogsthorpe, co. Lincoln, to Archbishop Laud's seven questions about vicars. His vicarage is worth 10l. per annum, paid by the bishop, with a house, but without any tithes, fees, or offerings. The bishop is the owner of the impropriation. It is worth 90l. per annum, but farmed by John Harbie at 28l. per annum. [1 p.]

Jan. 19.
22. Account of moneys due to James Duart, his Majesty's jeweller, upon privy seals from 22nd April 1636 to this day; total, 4,175l., including 800l. for a fair-faced diamond in form of a heart set in a ring sold to his Majesty, which having been long due, Duart prays payment. [⅔ p.]

Jan. 19.
23. Dr. Thomas Rives to Nicholas. I requested you about the end of last term to inform the Lords Commissioners that I had given in articles against Capt. Buller. He has denied all, and I have no instructions to prove anything against him. This may turn to my reproach; but thus am I served upon every cause sent to me from the Navy. Let me receive a word from you what I shall do, for the party demandeth inquest and to be released, nor can I gainsay but it is fit he should. [*Seal with arms.* ¾ p.]

Jan. 20.
Grant of the office of Clerk of the Statutes to Adrian May and Richard May, his brother, after Thomas Hampson, who now holds the same. [*Docquet.*]

Jan. 20.
Pardon to Walker Denn for the manslaughter of John Bingham, upon certificate of Sir John Finch, Chief Justice of Common Pleas. [*Docquet.*]

Jan. 20.
Restitution of temporalities of the bishopric of Rochester to John Warner, D.D., bishop of that see. [*Docquet.*]

Jan. 20.
Warrant to Sir James Palmer to sell to Philip Earl of Pembroke and Montgomery, Lord Chamberlain, one suit of hangings of the story of St. Paul, containing 306½ ells of Flemish measure, for 804l. 11s. 3d., which sum Sir James is to disburse about the manufacture of hangings at Mortlake upon account. [*Docquet.*]

Jan. 20.
Warrant to pay to Francis Wethered, surveyor of his Majesty's stables, for repair of the stables at the mews and at Sheen, from 11th October 1636 to the 12th December 1637, 78l. 17s. 6d., according to particulars allowed by the Marquess of Hamilton. [*Docquet.*]

Jan. 20.
The like to pay to Dr. Steward, Clerk of the Closet, 105l., disbursed for necessaries for his Majesty's service in the closet in times of progress. [*Docquet.*]

Vol. CCCLXXIX.

1637–8.
Jan. 20. Warrant to Sir William Uvedale, Treasurer of the Chamber, to pay to George Porter, junior, one of his Majesty's trumpeters, in the room of Edward Juxe, deceased, the wages of 16d. by the day. [*Docquet.*]

Jan. 20. The like to Edward Johnson, another of his Majesty's trumpeters, in place of George Porter, the wages of 8d. the day. [*Docquet.*]

Jan. 20. The like to the Master of the Great Wardrobe, for allowance of a livery to Edward Johnson, in place of Edward Juxe, deceased. [*Docquet.*]

Jan. 20. Petition of the Six Clerks of the Court of Chancery to the King. Upon a petition of the Master of the Rolls, the King, by order of Council of 3rd December last, referred the matters therein mentioned to all the judges. Those matters are encroachments pretended to be made by petitioners upon the rights of the Master of the Rolls and other officers of that court, with grievances against the King's subjects in general, under the patent of incorporation granted to petitioners. Petitioners conceive they have a good answer, but as the particulars are very many, and will require much time in the debate of them, and petitioners are not willing to hold anything which may give just cause of offence, or to continue a contestation against the Master of the Rolls, they pray the King to grant a reference to the Lord Keeper and the Master of the Rolls himself, to settle the differences arising out of their patent. [*Copy. See Vol. cccxxiii., p.* 228. 1 *p.*] *Underwritten,*

i. *Reference as prayed; the Lord Keeper and Master of the Rolls to certify the King, and in the meantime the reference to the judges to be suspended. Whitehall, 20th January* 1637–8. $\frac{1}{6}$ *p.*]

Jan. 20.
Whitehall. 24. Minute of a warrant from the Council to the Warden of the Fleet, to take into his custody John Baker, and to keep him prisoner until further order. [$\frac{1}{2}$ *p.*]

Jan. 20.
Whitehall. Notes by Nicholas of business to be transacted by Lords of the Admiralty. Appointed to hear an appeal between Hooke and a Dunkirker. Appoint what ships shall be set forth this year for Ireland and England. Consider a letter of justices of peace of Cheshire, concerning abuses committed by saltpetremen in that county. The Trinity House certify that they cannot approve of William Godfrey to be a boatswain. Appoint a day for hearing the caulkers and shipwrights referred by the Council. Consider Dr. Rives's letter touching Capt. Buller. Sign estimate for victualling the Great Ship. Peruse Officers of Navy's letters on behalf of Jo[hn] Blounden, to be purser in Jo[hn] Wriothesley's place. [*See Vol. ccclxxviii., No.* 81. $\frac{3}{4}$ *p.*]

Jan. 20.
Whitehall. 25. Lords of the Admiralty to Lord Keeper Coventry. His Majesty's services in the Navy much suffer, for that all the officers of

1637-8.

Vol. CCCLXXIX.

the Navy are not in commission of the peace for Kent, Essex, Surrey, Middlesex, and Hants. We pray you to cause Sir William Russell, Sir Henry Palmer, Kenrick Edisbury, and Dennis Fleming to be forthwith put into the said commission. [*Copy.* ¾ *p.*]

Jan. 20. Another Copy of the same. [*See Vol. cccliii., fol.* 80 *b.* ½ *p.*]

Jan. 20.
Sherborne.
26. John Earl of Bristol to Sir John Pennington. I understand by my son the great obligation that he and I have to you for your friendship towards him. He has been thereby so much encouraged in the way of a seaman's life, that he inclines to settle himself to that course. I entreat you to continue your favour, by directing him what you shall judge fittest for him to do. I hope you will breed up a young man that you will find to bear an honest and grateful heart, and I shall much desire to show myself thankful to you. My inclination is to have him be a lieutenant, and not to leap too soon into the command of a ship, or else to continue this next year as a volunteer. But whatsoever you shall judge fittest, that I will approve of. [*Originally dated the 6th inst., but altered to the 20th.* 1 *p.*]

Jan. 20.
Wapping.
27. Master and Wardens of the Shipwrights Company to Nicholas. At a meeting in August last, with the master shipwrights, Mr. Pett the younger, and others, we advised the reforming of divers abuses, and amongst them the misdemeanours of certain persons using the trade of caulking. Some of that profession being discontented, attempted to get themselves incorporated, and at divers private assemblies collected moneys to withstand the writers. Upon notice thereof the writers sent for some of the principal, and caused a fine to be entered for two conventicles. The counsel of the persons fined justifying their proceedings, the writers desired Sir Henry Marten to compose the difference, but one hour before the time for hearing appointed by him a reference from the Lords of the Admiralty was showed to them, intimating their pleasure to hear that business. We are humbly thankful, and desire the Lords to appoint when the writers shall attend with their counsel. Desire to know the charge of the complainants, with three or four days to provide counsel. [*Seal with arms.* 1 *p.*]

Jan. 20. 28. William Bassett, late Sheriff of Somerset, to [Nicholas?]. William Dore, late constable of the hundred of Norton Ferris, having about 40*l.* ship-money in his hands, upon his refusal to pay the same, the writer commanded his bailiff to arrest him. Dore has absented himself, wherefore the writer desires Nicholas to move the Lords to compel him to render an account. [1 *p.*] *Annexed,*

 28. I. *The same to the same. Similar letter with the same request as against John Burge, late constable of the hundred of Chewton, who had collected* 63*l. and had neglected to pay the same.* [1 *p.*]

Vol. CCCLXXIX.

1637-8.
Jan. 20. 29. Petition of Robert Pope, late one of the constables of the hundred of Bempstone, Somerset, to William Bassett, late Sheriff. Henry Pope, of Locking, being assessed 8s. to the ship-money, and refusing to pay, the writer distrained one of Pope's beasts and tendered him the overplus, which he refused to receive, whereupon petitioner kept the beast on his pasture a quarter of year, and then Robins and two others with long staves entered the pasture and drove the beast away. [½ p.]

Jan. 20. 30. Richard Maud, James Partridge, Moses Brampton, and William Edwards, to Bishop Bancroft, of Oxford. Certify that the work done by Humphrey Smith in rebuilding the spire of the church of Witney (the nature of which is particularly stated) is well worth 200l., besides 8l. for overplus work beyond his bargain with the parish. [1 p.]

Jan. 20. 31. Answer of George Scortreth, vicar of Alford, co. Lincoln, to Archbishop Laud's seven articles about vicarages. The vicarage of Alford is worth 19l.; 16l. paid by Sir Charles Bolles, farmer of the parsonage, and the rest by three acres of pasture, two "cotcher houses," and fees, viz., for a marriage 12d., a churching 1d., no chrisom, burials for a man or woman 2d., a child 1d.; no mortuary. The impropriation is worth 80l. per annum, the owner thereof the bishop of the diocese.

Jan. 20. 32. Agreement entered into at a meeting in London between George Low, Deputy of the Fellowship of Merchant Adventurers of England, residing in London, and Lawrence Halstead and William Essington, committees appointed by the Court of the said Fellowship on the one part, and Thomas Knott and Thomas Foard, appointed on the part of the brethren residing in Exeter and in co. Devon, on the other part. The merchants of Exeter are to have free liberty to ship Spanish cloth from Exeter or any port in co. Devon. They shall not transport any such cloth but only such as shall be made in co. Devon. No merchant of Exeter shall buy any of the said cloth, but only in the market of Exeter. All persons of co. Devon thereafter admitted into the fellowship shall observe this agreement. [1 p.] *Annexed,*

> 32. I. *Draft order of the Council confirming the said agreement and directing that the same should be carefully observed. Inner Star Chamber, 24th January* 1637-8. [½ p.]

Jan. 20.
Burderop. 33. Sir William Calley to Richard Harvey. I perceive Mr. Long has procured, by means of a good friend, leave to arrest John Titchborne. Now we can seize on his person I hope to get my money. I understand Mr. John Popham is deceased, and that his debt is near 38,000l., for which his brothers are jointly engaged, but their father nothing at all, and besides all this, it is whispered that a great part of his wife's land is sold outright, and the rest mortgaged. I hear your master [Endymion Porter] was the cause of the great funeral

1637-8.

Vol. CCCLXXIX.

that was made for him, and that his only credit procured the disbursement of the charge, but that the father will pay the amount. [*Seal with arms.* ⅔ *p.*]

Jan. 21.
Whitehall.

34. Order of the King in Council. Upon hearing a petition of the corporation of Bristol, complaining of the undue proceeding of Lord Mohun and others in execution of a commission for finding out moneys illegally imposed in the said city, his Majesty appointed this day sevennight to hear the petitioners and the commissioners complained of, for so much only as concerns any proceedings of the said commissioners, but for the matter itself contained in the said commission, the same is to proceed as the commission directs, and in no sort to be spoken of at the said hearing. [1¼ *p.*]

Jan. 21. 35. Draft of the same. [1¼ *p.*]

Jan. 21.
Whitehall.

36. Order of the King in Council. On consideration of a petition from the ministers of Norwich complaining that most of them had no certainty nor competency for means of living, but by the voluntary courtesy of the people, it was ordered that the citizens and the ministers should set down how much each minister has of certainty belonging to him, and what is allowed by the voluntary contribution of the parishioners, and also the contents of each parish, in regard of houses, rates, and number of communicants. The bishop and the petitioners undertook to present an authentic act of submission to the judgment of his Majesty from all the ministers of the city, and the mayor and others were required to attend on the first Sunday after Easter with an act under the common seal of the city, expressing their similar submission, in the same manner as London has done. It was also ordered that all persons who claim to have the nomination of ministers should come prepared, at the same time, to show by what right they claim the same. [*Draft.* 2⅔ *pp.*]

Jan. 21.
Whitehall.

37. Similar order, on complaint from the merchants of Norwich and others trading in Norwich stuffs, alleging that their weekly letters have been interrupted and their carriers forbidden by Mr. Witherings, his Majesty's postmaster, to carry letters otherwise than to go along with their carts, which it was alleged would be very prejudicial to their trade. It was ordered that the carriers of Norwich, as was ordered on the 19th inst. for the carrier of letters of Yarmouth and Ipswich, should conform to the letters patent granted to Witherings of the letter office and to the proclamation on that behalf, and not presume to do or attempt anything contrary to the same. [*Underwritten by Sec. Coke,* "This is according to his Majesty's pleasure, as by the draft signed by his Majesty appeareth." 1 *p.*]

Jan. 21.

38. The Council to the Mayor of Wenlock. By our letters of the 25th October last, we required you to pay to Sir William Russell 302*l.*, arrear of ship-money, or attend the Board that term, in both which you having made default, we once more require you to pay in the said moneys or to attend the Board this term, which if you

VOL. CCCLXXIX.

1637–8.

neglect order shall be taken to bring you to conformity. Morton Briggs and John Reynolds *alias* Mason are assessed for their estates within your liberties and refuse to make payment; you are to require them to conform, and if they refuse, to bind them over to appear before the Board. [*Draft.* 1 *p.*]

Jan. 21.   39. The Council to [Sir Robert Pointz,] Sheriff of co. Gloucester. The inhabitants of Oldland and West Hanham, two hamlets in the parish of Bitton, have represented that 47*l*. 4*s*. being charged upon the whole parish for ship-money, you have appointed petitioners to pay one half, although the rest of the parish contains in value and land twice as much, and is of far greater worth in estate. We require you that the parish be rated and pay together, and not by several parts for the ease of any particular persons; and that indifferent assessors be appointed, some of the hamlets and some of the rest of the parish, so that every man be rated with equality. [*Draft.* 1 *p.*]

Jan. 21.   40. The same to the Marshal of the Admiralty and other officers. Complaint is made by the Ambassador of the United Provinces that a man-of-war of Zealand, whereof —— Regimorter is captain, being attending at Gravesend to transport Mons. de Gorpdet, ambassador from the States, into Zealand, is arrested at the suit of one Brames. You are to release the ship, without taking any caution from the captain or any other. [*Draft.* 1 *p.*]

Jan. 21. Whitehall.   41. The same to the Lords of the Admiralty. It being his Majesty's pleasure that the Swallow and the Ninth Whelp be employed in the Irish seas next year, you are to give order to the Lord Deputy of Ireland to have the same prepared for that service upon the charge of the revenue of that kingdom. [1 *p.*]

Jan. 21.   42. Draft of the same. [1 *p.*]

Jan. 21. Whitehall.   43. The same to Thomas Waterworth. Several persons inhabiting St. Giles-in-the-Fields, having been assessed for ship-money, refuse to pay their rates. You are to repair to the places of abode of the persons named in a list annexed, and to demand the money assessed, and having received the same to deliver it to the assessors to be paid to the sheriff; and if any deny to pay, you are to warn them to give attendance on the Board till they be discharged; and if they refuse to do the one or the other by Friday next, you are to bring them before us to answer their contempt. [*Draft.* ¾ *p.*]

Jan. 21.   Minute of another similar warrant to bring before the Lords John Child, one of the collectors of the money in St. Giles-in-the-Fields. [*Written on the same paper as the preceding.* ¼ *p.*]

Jan. 21.   44. The like to Edmund Barker. To fetch Thomas Coke, one of the constables of the western part of the hundred of Bempstone, Somerset, and Roger Wagget and Richard Banbury, constables within the tithing of Muchelney and Midney in the same county. [⅓ *p.*]

Vol. CCCLXXIX.

1637-8.
Jan. 21. Minute of warrant from the Council to Henry Davis. To fetch William Dore, late constable of the hundred of Norton Ferris, John Burge, late constable of the hundred of Chewton, and Henry Robins, of Locking, Somerset. [*Written on the same paper as the preceding. 4 lines.*]

Jan. 21. 45. Sir Edward Rodney to Nicholas. I received letter from the Lords of the Admiralty, dated 2nd May 1635, with instructions for better regulating my office for his Majesty's profit, and in obedience I recommended Dr. Gilbert Jones, chancellor of Bristol, to be judge of my Vice-Admiralty, Matthew King, of Uphill, mariner, to be marshal, and John Selwood to be registrar. Dr. Jones proceeded so far as to take out a warrant for a patent, and then grew frightened from the employment, as you may perceive by his letter to you. I now recommend John Baber, of Lincoln's Inn, counsellor, who will undertake the place without starting. The bearer is he whom I recommend for registrar. I have sent him to solicit these affairs, and to go on in the business of the wreck against Mr. Heale, who, as lord of the manor on the sea coast, keeps to his own use all Admiralty droits; as indeed all the other lords of manors do. [1 *p.*]

Jan. 21. 46. William Bassett, late Sheriff of Somerset, to the same. Since being with you last night, I find I have received but 450*l*., which shall be paid to Sir William Russell to-morrow or Tuesday, with which you may acquaint his Majesty. [*Seal with arms.* ½ *p.*]

Jan. 21. 47. Edward Harbert to George Gylden at Kingston. Certifies that under a warrant sent him as constable of Bletchingly, by the sheriff, he distrained Mr. Turnor's cattle for the ship-money for 1636, but the distress being forcibly rescued by Thomas Allingham and William Rooker, servants to Turnor, he returned the same rescue to Gylden. As for other moneys to be levied by distress he paid them all to Gylden excepting Henry Newdigate's 2*s*. and John Kellick's 10*d*., for which he accounts. [*Endorsed by Nicholas as delivered by the sheriff of Surrey.* ⅓ *p.*]

Jan. 22. Warrant to the Justices of the Common Pleas to admit William Whalley, son of Ralph Whalley, being under age, to suffer a common recovery of lands in cos. Leicester, Derby, and Warwick, one moiety to be disposed of for the payment of Ralph Whalley's debts, and the other to be charged with portions for his seven daughters, but to descend to his heir. [*Docquet.*]

Jan. 22. 48. Petition of Henry Richards to the King. In former times the inventories of the estates of deceased persons were made by appraisers, sworn to make a true valuation, who had allowance according to the sum whereunto the inventories amounted, after the rate of 8*d*., and sometimes 7*d*., in the pound, which good order being in these latter ages not observed, executors commonly make choice of their friends to be appraisers, by means whereof men's estates are undervalued, and chargeable and tedious suits ensue. Petitioner prays for the erection of an office general throughout England and

Vol. CCCLXXIX.

1637-8.
Wales, that a competent number of appraisers may be sworn, and that there may be annexed to the said office 3*d*. in the pound, and the office be granted to petitioner for 31 years, one moiety of the fee to be expended in performance of the duties, and the other moiety to be paid into the Exchequer, deducting the usual allowance to receivers of revenue. [¾ *p*.]

Jan. 22. Copy of the same. [*See Vol.* cccxxiii., *p.* 230. ¾ *p*.] *Under-written,*

    I. *Reference to the Attorney and Solicitor General to certify their opinions, whereupon his Majesty will signify his pleasure. Whitehall, 22nd January* 1637-8. [*Copy. Ibid.* 1 *p*.]

Jan. 22.
Derby.
49. Henry Mellor and John Hope, Bailiffs of Derby, to the Council. In obedience to the writ for assessing 175*l*. they have, though with much pressure and hardship, in regard of their long-continued affliction with the plague, and according to a later direction from the Board upon the remonstrance of their misery, paid to the Treasurer of the Navy 60*l*. in part of 120*l*., which by the second direction they were appointed to pay. State in what proportion that sum has been assessed on the several parishes. [1 *p*.]

Jan. 22.
50. Rowland Lewen, Sheriff of co. Carmarthen, to the Council. I have acquainted Thomas Vaughan, the late sheriff, and others my predecessors, with the tenor of your letters. Vaughan has informed me that of the 160*l*. specified as unpaid, there remains in his hands but 110*l*., and that the other 50*l*. is in the hands of Richard Thomas, late mayor of Carmarthen, who is accountable for the same. Vaughan, in the beginning of this Hilary term, has taken his journey to London to pay the 110*l*. [1 *p*.]

Jan. 22.
51. Petition of Mary Thomas to Archbishop Laud. The archbishop referred her former petition to Sir John Lambe, to call Jones and Payne before him, and settle some course whereby petitioner might have her annuity of 14*l*. per annum. Sir John demanded of Payne if he could pay the said annuity, which he denied to do. Sir John then demanded of Jones if he would pay the same. Jones answered that if Payne restored him his press and letters, and the archbishop granted him the liberty (which others not in the decree have) to print during his life, he being aged, he would not only pay petitioner her annuity, and give security not to print any unlicensed books, but also give satisfaction to Payne. Petitioner prays the archbishop to grant Jones's request. [⅔ *p*.] *Underwritten,*

    51. I. *Reference to Sir John Lambe.* "*If Payne refuse to pay the pension here mentioned, let him be suspended from the use of his press as well as Jones.*" 22*nd January* 1637-8. [1 *p*.]

Jan. 22.
My chamber at the Middle Temple.
52. Answer of the Mayor and Recorder of Huntingdon to the complaint of David Stevenson, saltpetreman, in the handwriting of and signed by Robert Bernard, the recorder. The complaint

1637-8.

Vol. CCCLXXIX.

was that they required the constable to charge no carts for conveyance of his liquor. The fact is denied in a detailed statement which relates the whole circumstances. The carts in Huntingdon were very few, and the owners so poor that their horses were almost starved, and they refused to work at Stevenson's price, which was but 3*d*. per tun. They offered him to provide carts out of the hundred; this he refused, and ultimately, after two days' delay, a cart was hired by the corporation, which had done all his carriage, and cost the town 12*d*. for every tun, over and above his 3*d*., which amount even he does not fully pay. [2¼ *pp*.]

Jan. 22. 53. Answer of John Hudson, vicar of Calceby, co. Lincoln, to Archbishop Laud's seven articles concerning vicarages. The vicarage worth 20 marks yearly, which arises chiefly from wool, lambs, and milk. Finds in the records of the registry of Lincoln that two parts of the tithe corn belong to the vicarage. The vicarage, being so mean a thing, is charged with ship-money and tenths. The impropriation belongs to Robert Phillips, heir of the person of the same name, late of Wispington, who is ward to the King, his committee being Susanna Phillips, his mother. The yearly value is 18*l*. Calceby is decayed by oppression in rents and unoccupied houses; might they be bettered, the vicarage might be better. [1½ *p*.]

Jan. 23. Petition of Sir Robert Knowles to the King. Petitioner has in cos. Oxford and Berks an estate for life, with remainder to his sons in succession in tail, in lands to the value of 800*l*. per annum, being the ancient inheritance of his family. He has also the manor of Giffords, and a tenement called Palmer's *alias* Rawlies in Suffolk, and two tenements in Esse *alias* Ash [Essen *alias* Ashen?] in Essex, in which he has a like estate for life with similar remainders. He is grown much indebted by reason of buying in his other lands of his uncle, the Earl of Banbury, and having divers children, sons and daughters, to provide for, is necessitated to sell some part of his estate, and no lands so fit to be sold, in respect of the remoteness, as these in Suffolk and Essex. Prays direction to the Judges of the Common Pleas to permit William Knowles, his eldest son (near upon 18 years of age), to suffer a recovery of the said lands to the use of petitioner and his heirs. [*Copy. See Vol. cccxxiii., p.* 231. ¾ *p*.] *Underwritten*,

    I. *Reference to the Attorney-General to prepare a bill accordingly. Whitehall, 23rd January* 1637-8. [*Copy. Ibid.* ¾ *p*.]

Jan. 23. Petition of William Newton to the same. Recital similar to that in petition of the same person, already calendared under date of the 17th inst., respecting Pursefield, near Lincoln's Inn. Prays grant of the premises in fee-farm at a rent of 200*l*. per annum. [*Copy. Ibid., p.* 232. ⅓ *p*.] *Underwritten*,

    I. *Reference to the Attorney-General, authorizing him to procure a particular of the premises in question, and thereupon to prepare a grant in fee-farm as solicited. Whitehall, 23rd January* 1637-8. [*Copy. Ibid.* ¼ *p*.]

Vol. CCCLXXIX.

1637–8.
Jan. 23.
Tuderly.
[Tytherley.]

54. Richard Whithed to Nicholas. On letter from the Council of 31st October last, concerning remains of ship-money in 1635, which was 82*l*. 5*s*. 4*d*., there has been paid in by Mr. Harwood 9*l*. 15*s*. 6*d*., and I have sent to pay in the rest. Of the money we now pay, Sir White Beconsawe has paid 10*l*. out of his own purse, and I shall pay near thirty, which falls on us because there were no acquittances given for money paid into the Exchequer on the *certiorari*; most pretending to have paid there, we know not whom to distrain. As for the money unpaid on the schedule, there is not one penny to be levied. [*Seal with arms.* 1 *p.*]

Jan. 23.
Hounstert.
[Hound Street?]

55. Jerome Harvey to his cousin, Richard Harvey. I would you be acquainted with the bearer, Mr. Wakeman, who deals for me in all my law business, and who may have some occasion to make use of you at this present for another neighbour of mine. I pray you do him what good you can. [*Endorsed by the person addressed as a letter of his uncle, Jerome Harvey.* ⅓ *p.*]

Jan. 23.

56. Notes by Nicholas of business wherewith the Lords of the Admiralty were to acquaint his Majesty:—I. With the list of ships employed last year for guard of the coast, and of those that are ready to be employed next summer. [*Margin:* "The list is signed."] II. With the Officers of the Navy's letter touching the Prince and Merhonour. [*Margin:* "The King will hear the Officers of the Navy himself about this."] III. To speak with the King about the Officers of the Navy's pay. [*Margin:* "The King will advise of it himself."] [¾ *p.*]

Jan. 23.

57. Lists of ships employed in 1637 and of those in readiness to be employed in 1638. In the second list the King has struck out the Triumph and the Defiance, and inserted the "Soueraine" in their place. [1 *p.*]

Jan. 24.
Inner Star Chamber.

58. Order of Archbishop Laud and Lord Keeper Coventry, referees of a petition of Sir John Tyrrell to the King, calendared under date of the 7th November 1637. The referees declared their utter mislike of the frame of the petition, as well in regard of petitioner's uncle as of Sir Henry Browne, cousin-german to old Sir John Tyrrell, and of Lady Eyres, being persons of quality, and the rather for that old Sir John Tyrrell by Sir Thomas Jervoise, his counsel, acknowledged himself to owe very much to them both for their care of his health and supply of his occasions. The counsel for petitioner insisting principally upon the ruins of the house at Herne, and the waste of timber on the lands in Essex settled upon petitioner by his uncle on petitioner's marriage, and the question and degree of that waste being disputed, the same was referred to the Lord Chief Justice of the King's Bench and Mr. Justice Croke, who were also to consider the propriety of young Sir John Tyrrell joining with his uncle in leases of the lands in settlement at an improved rent, and were recommended to make an amicable end of these differences if they can. As for old Sir John Tyrrell's living with Sir Henry Browne and the Lady Eyres, the

Vol. CCCLXXIX.

1637–8.

referees hold them to be persons of so much worth as they see no cause why he should remove from their company. The consideration of reparation to Sir Henry Browne for aspersions cast upon him by petitioner was reserved by the referees until they received the judges' certificate. [$2\frac{1}{2}$ pp.]

Jan. 24. 59–60. Two copies or drafts of the same order in various stages of preparation. [3 pp. and $2\frac{1}{3}$ pp.]

Jan. 24.
Inner Star Chamber.
61. Another order of Council on the complaint against Thomas Witherings by the merchants and others trading in Norwich stuffs, differing from that already calendared under the date of the 21st inst., No. 37. It was now ordered that for the better accommodation of the said merchants, it should be permitted to the common and known carriers of letters belonging to Norwich or any other town to carry the letters of merchants or others, travelling with the same letters the ordinary journeys that common carriers travel, and coming to London, Norwich, or any other town not above eight hours before the carts, waggons, or pack-horses, whereunto Witherings and others are to conform themselves. [*Draft.* 1 p.]

Jan. 24. 62. Similar order. Robert Coytmore, servant to Lord Strange, by petition showed that Mr. Tartaro, husband to the Viscountess Molineux, delivered him a note intimating the Lords' pleasure to hear this day the business in difference between his Lordship and Lady Molineux, but neither having the papers nor time to acquaint his Lord, he prayed for further time. The Lords appointed the 2nd May next. [*Draft.* 1 p.]

Jan. 24. 63. Similar order. The difference between George Mynne and Benedict Webb having been referred to the examination of Alderman Abdy, Capt. Crispe, Mr. Low, and Mr. Clarke, Mynne showing by petition that there had been some differences between him and Crispe, he desired that some one else be named in his place. The Lords ordered that the said differences be referred to Alderman Abdy, Alderman Garway, Mr. Low, and Mr. Clarke, who are to settle these differences or to return certificate to the Board. [*Draft.* 1 p.]

Jan. 24.
Inner Star Chamber.
64. Order of Archbishop Laud, the Lord Keeper, the Lord Treasurer, and the Bishop of Norwich, referees of the petition of Randolph Gilpin, parson of Barningham, Suffolk, against Maurice Barrough [Barrow] and other parishioners of Barningham. The order deals with suits in Chancery, in the Court of Arches, in the Court of Requests, and two suits at law between Gilpin and Barrow, all apparently arising out of a dispute about certain alleged customs in tithing. Minute directions are given as to what was to be done in all these several suits, and the referees charged Gilpin and his parishioners thenceforth to frame themselves to live in a more quiet and peaceable manner. [*Draft.* 3 pp.]

Jan. 24.
Inner Star Chamber.
65. Order of Archbishop Laud, the Lord Keeper, and Lord Treasurer, referees of a petition of Arthur Heron, vicar of Bardwell, Suffolk, complaining against Mr. Barrow, of Barningham, that he

Vol. CCCLXXIX.

1637–8.

having a fourth part of the land in the parish, the tithes whereof were worth to the impropriator 18*l*., and to the vicar 4*l*., did begin to impale the said lands and make a park for deer, much to the prejudice of petitioner and of St. John's College, Oxford, which had the patronage of the vicarage. Mr. Barrow denied that he had done anything towards making a park of the land, but if at any time he should employ it otherwise than it has been accustomed he would give the vicar as much as has been made of the same for seven years last past, which promise was directed to be drawn up as an order, and registered among the acts of the Council, for prevention of any damage to the said rectory and vicarage. [*Draft.* 1⅙ *p.*]

Jan. 24.   66. Order of Council. A certificate from the Commissioners of Sewers of co. Lincoln, about a new river, called Ancolme, drawn through the lordships of Warlaby and Saxby, the land of John Bellasis and Sir Michael Wharton, being presented at the Board, the Lords appointed to hear the same on Friday next. [*Draft.* 1 *p.*]

Jan. 24.   67. Order of the King in Council on the complaint of some of the justices of co. Nottingham against the sheriff of that county for over-assessment to the ship-money of the hundreds of Newark, Hatfield, South Clay, and North Clay (*see Vol. ccclxxiv., No.* 1), and the answer of the sheriff (*see Vol. ccclxxviii., No.* 78). It was ordered that the sheriff proceed in perfecting his assessment and levying the moneys according as he has begun, he having undertaken to pursue to the uttermost of his power the honour of his Majesty's writ, and the directions of the Council, which required that the moneys should be laid with as much equality as may possibly be discerned. [*Draft.* 2 *pp.*]

Jan. 24.   68. Order of Council. William Leigh, late sheriff of co. Gloucester, was required to collect and pay in 220*l*. arrear of ship-money under writ of 1635, or attend the Board on the first Sunday in this term. By letter of the 22nd inst. he desired that his attendance might be spared, and further time given. For matter of his attendance the Lords granted his request, and ordered that he should pay 110*l*. within six days after this term, and 110*l*. within six days after Easter term, which if he fail to do, he is to attend the Board. [*Draft.* 1 *p.*]

Jan. 24.   69. The Council to Sir William Russell. John Crane, victualler of the navy has made provision of victuals for a like number of men for six months for service for 1638 as was employed for the last year. Out of moneys first received upon writs issued in September 1637, you are to pay Crane 10,000*l*. [*Draft.* ¾ *p.*]

Jan. 24.   70. The same to Robert Taverner, messenger. To fetch before the Lords William Bridge and James Master, of Canterbury. [½ *p.*]

Jan. 24.   71. The same to Richard Woolfe. To seize all soap, potashes, lees, and other materials tending to the making of soap. [½ *p.*]

Vol. CCCLXXIX.

1637-8.

Jan. 24. 72. The Council to the Governor of the House of Correction in Middlesex. To take into his custody Alice Sheppard, and keep her prisoner until further order. [½ p.]

Jan. 24. 73. The same to the Warden of the Fleet. To set at liberty Sir Thomas Fernefold. [¼ p.]

Jan. 24. The same to the same. To set at liberty John Baker. [*Written on the same paper as the preceding.* ¼ p.]

Jan. 24. 74. Draft entry of the appearance before the Council of John Child. He is to remain in custody of the messenger until discharged. [¼ p.]

Jan. 24. 75. Minute of a pass to Michael Clarke and Charles Birne, of co. Antrim, to travel into foreign parts for three years, with proviso not to go to Rome. [½ p.]

Jan. 24. 76. Order of Council in the matter of the dispute between the Merchant Adventurers of England residing in London and the brethren of that company residing at Exeter. Recites the order of Council of the 17th inst. (*see Vol. ccclxxviii., No. 97*), and the agreement of the 20th inst. (*see this present Volume, No. 32*), both before calendared. The Lords approved the said agreement, and commanded that the same should be entered amongst the acts of the Council, that it might prevent further trouble to the Lords, and might serve to determine all future differences between the parties. [*Draft.* 1⅔ p.]

Jan. 24. 77. List of causes specially appointed to be heard in the Star Chamber this day. They were—the Attorney-General against John All and Francis Hunton; further hearing postponed until Wednesday next; Thomas Williams against Alice Mercer and others; fine of 50*l*. for false report; Thomas Browne against John Borrett and others; fine of 20*l*. for default of prosecution; Jonathan Rashleigh against Reignold Mohun. [1 p.]

Jan. 24. 78. Notes by Sec. Windebank, taken on the hearing of the first and second of the above causes. The charge against All and Hunton was that, being providers of biscuits for the navy, they bought bad meal and used the same in making their biscuits. The notes state some of the evidence against them. In the second case they give merely the names of some of the witnesses. [1¼ p.]

Jan. 24.
Waltham Hall. 79. Sir William Luckyn, Sheriff of Essex, to Nicholas. Sends for a copy of certain rates out of Mr. Lucas's book. On Saturday he hopes his endeavours will appear to the satisfaction of doubtful apprehensions. [*Underwritten is a note by Nicholas, addressed to "Francis," to let Sir William Luckyn's man take what notes he pleases out of the late sheriff of Essex's book. Seal with arms.* ¾ p.]

Jan. 25. 80. The Council to the Mayor and Aldermen of Chester. On consideration of your letter of 13th inst. (*see Vol. ccclxxviii., No. 77*),

1637-8.

Vol. CCCLXXIX.

we spare your appearance on 4th February next, but require some of you to give your attendance on the 4th May next, at which time we will hear the matters complained of. For the matter of Gloverstone, referred to the Earl of Derby and judges of Chester, we expect their certificate to be returned by the same time. [*Draft.* 1 *p.*]

Jan. 25. 81. Draft entry of appearance before the Council of William Stane, Amos Prielove, and Josias Wood, constables of the hundred of Harlow, Essex. [1 *p.*]

Jan. 25. 82. Names of those who will attend at Whitehall on behalf of Henry Lambe, touching his intended river. They are—Lord Rivers by Mr. Lea, his servant; Lady Rivers by Mr. Sheeres, her servant; Sir Roger North; Thomas Steward; Sir Edmund Moundeford; and Walter Cradock. [½ *p.*]

Jan. 25. Entry of the appearance before the Lords of the Admiralty of John Sedcole, who is to attend until discharged. [*Copy. See Vol. ccclii., fol. 81.* ⅓ *p.*]

Jan. 25. Chesterfield. 83. James Webster, Under-sheriff of co. Nottingham, to Nicholas. The late high-sheriff of co. Nottingham is fourscore years of age, and little able to go through such a weighty business as ship-money. I have sent up 30*l.* more, so that there remains now only 30*l.* of the 3,500*l.* charged upon the county, of which 30*l.* Newark is behind 20*l.*, whereof the Earl of Berkshire, as the late mayor telleth me, should pay 10*l.*, and the town is poor. Two chief constables, namely, Pocklington and Sharpe, I cannot procure to account for the remainder of their moneys received, and many other odd moneys there are yet behind, so that I have paid in more than is come to my hands; but I hope I shall have your help therein by your letters to the chief constables. The now sheriff has been at London, and is not yet come down, so that no warrant has been made since your last letter. [1 *p.*]

Jan. 25. 84. List, signed by John Button, late Sheriff of Hants, of persons in arrear for ship-money. Among the noticeable persons are, in Hurstbourne-Tarrant, Lady Constance Lucy, dead, 3*l.*; in Sidmonton, William Kingsmill, refuses, 2*s.* 11*d.*; in Shamblehurst, Sir Gerard Fleetwood, refuses, 17*s.*; in Twyford, Thomas Seymour, refuses, 10*s.*: there are 11 refusers in all. Total of arrears, 42*l.* 6*s.* 8*d.* [2½ *pp.*]

Jan. 25. Mincing Lane. 85. Officers of Navy to Lords of the Admiralty. Upon surveys of the hulls of the ships undernamed, since their return from sea, his Majesty's shipwrights estimate the charge in perfecting them again for sea, as follows, viz., the Unicorn at 307*l.*; the Expedition at 265*l.*; the First Whelp at 80*l.* 10*s.*; for the performance whereof we desire your warrant. [1 *p.*]

Jan. 25. 86. List of ten merchant ships fit to be employed in the King's service, with tonnage, ordnance, and masters' names. [⅔ *p.*]

VOL. CCCLXXIX.

1637-8.
Jan. 25. 87. Propositions by Capt. William Rainsborough for redeeming captives in Algiers. To get the captives by treaty being found impossible, and their redemption by money impolitic, the writer recommends the employment of a fleet to besiege them by sea, and thus to force them to deliver up the captives. He thinks ten good ships and six pinnaces would be requisite for the service, and if such a fleet were continued for three or four years their trade would be destroyed and their ships become worm-eaten and unserviceable. He suggests also that the maintenance of the suggested fleet would be very much to the King's honour in all the maritime parts of Christendom, and if haply the fleet took some of them that take the English, and sold them in Spain or Italy, English subjects might be redeemed with the money. [1½ p.]

Jan. 25. 88. Extract from the Register of the Acts of the Court of High Commission relating to a case against Toby Bullock and others, aldermen of Gloucester. Mr. Bullock appearing, it was made known to him that he and others were convented for entrenching upon ecclesiastical jurisdiction in making orders for the government of the hospital of St. Bartholomew in Gloucester, and under pretence thereof making a lease of the means thereof to an inconformable minister. Mr. Bullock answered that they had not exceeded the bounds of their letters patent, whereupon the court ordered that he should attend Sir John Lambe and Dr. Duck with the said letters patent and other writings as soon as they came to town, and should give into court the names of all that had any hand in making the foresaid orders. [*Attested copy.* 2½ pp.]

Jan. 25. 89. See "Returns made by Justices of Peace."

Jan. 26. 90. Order of Council on the petition of John Gray, messenger. Petitioner stated that having apprehended Mr. Lawrence, a priest, and seized upon a trunk and divers books in his lodging, which he left in a constable's charge, petitioner being commanded to bring the books to the Board on Tuesday last, and going upon the service, was arrested at the suit of one James Lindsey, keeper of the Counter prison in Southwark, and although petitioner acquainted the officers of his present employment, they carried him to prison. It was ordered that the trunks and books be delivered to the registrar of the High Commission, and the commissioners are to give account thereof to the Archbishop of Canterbury. It was further ordered that Lindsey should give his attendance on the Board on Wednesday next, and that he should take order that Gray may be brought thither at the same time. [*Draft.* 1¼ p.]

Jan. 26. 91. Similar order. The petition of Humphrey Rowse with a certificate of Thomas Meautys, to whom the Lords referred the difference between Rowse, Foster, and Robert Aspinall, being this day presented, it was ordered that the petition and certificate should be recommended to the Lord Chief Justice of the King's Bench, to take order for petitioner's relief. [1 p.]

1637-8. VOL. CCCLXXIX.

Jan. 26. 92. Order of Council. By order of the Board of the 17th inst., the Lord Chief Justice of the King's Bench was required to proceed against Robert Jason, concerning certain criminal offences by him committed. It was ordered that the Attorney-General should likewise proceed against Jason in the Star Chamber for other offences contained in the examinations taken or laid to his charge by Edmund Conquest and others. [*Draft.* ¾ *p.*]

Jan. 26. 93. The like on petition of Richard Beale, of London, merchant. Petitioner complained that Sir Edward Bromfield, late Lord Mayor, being required to make answer on the 6th December last to a complaint of petitioner about the business of shipping, had forborne to do so. It was ordered that Sir Edward should send his answer in writing to the Board on the 9th February next. [*Draft.* 1 *p.*]

Jan. 26. 94. The like. The difference between Henry Morgan and Blanche, his wife, on the one part, and Henry Lingen, son to the said Blanche, on the other, was by order of the referees of the 10th inst. appointed to be heard on the 2nd May next, and it was also ordered that Henry Morgan or his wife should deliver to Lingen, within 14 days after sight, copies of such grants as they pretend title unto, and the articles made between his father and her friends. Henry Morgan, by petition this day, desired that the hearing might stand, and that he might have a longer time for giving the copies desired. The Lords resolved to hear the differences at the time appointed, and gave petitioners a month to deliver the copies. They also ordered Lingen to bring up such writings by which he makes title, to the end, if there be cause, the counsel of Morgan may see them. [*Draft.* 1 *p.*]

Jan. 26. 95. The like. The Governors of St. Bartholomew's Hospital being by order of 29th September required to confer with William Price and Nicholas Hudson, for reducing the buildings in Holborn by them begun, into one single house, to be used for an inn and stables as anciently it was. They having returned a certificate that they could not settle the business, the Lords referred the further consideration thereof to Sir William Becher and Sir Dudley Carleton, who are to treat with Price and Hudson, and by the best ways they can to accommodate the business, so as Hudson's buildings may be joined to Price's, and all be reduced into one entire house, to be used for an inn, and that the buildings beside Hudson's house, towards Lincoln's Inn, may be turned into stables. If the said referees cannot settle the business, they are to certify in whom the fault is. [*Draft.* 1 *p.*]

Jan. 26. 96. The like. By certificate of 30th December last, signed by Nicholas Herne, Ottowell Meverell, physician to the hospital of Bethlehem, Nicholas Randy, treasurer, and Ralph Yardley, apothecary, it appears that Richard Farneham, prisoner in the said hospital, did not appear to be mad or lunatic, and they were of opinion he might have the liberty afforded to others in that house. It is

DOMESTIC—CHARLES I.   189

1637–8.   Vol. CCCLXXIX.

ordered that so long as Farneham behaves himself well he should have such liberty. [*Draft.* 1 *p.*]

Jan. 26.
Star Chamber.
97. Order of Council. By order of 23rd June last, upon hearing the difference between Samuel Preston, vicar of Roade, co. Northampton, and Stephen Hoe, the impropriator, it was directed that Preston should search at Lincoln among the records to make appear, if he could, that there had been a vicar presented to the said church. This day, upon a full hearing and upon reading a pretended endowment of a vicarage in Roade and such presentations as Preston produced, forasmuch as it did not appear that there was ever any vicar presented in Roade or ever received any tithes there, it was ordered that Preston should renounce his title to any vicarage there, and should deliver up his presentation to Hoe, and should be allowed 20*l.* per annum by Hoe for his two years, and by the rector of Ashton for his third year, and so interchangeably to be paid unto him for officiating the cure at Roade. [*Draft.* 1½ *p.*]

Jan. 26.
98. The like upon the petition of Robert Barkham, now prisoner in the Fleet for not performing the decree of the Commissioners of Sewers and the directions of this Board. Petitioner desired leave to commence a suit for lands which he pretends to be taken from him by the said commissioners, and that he might be freed from imprisonment. The Lords ordered that he should remain committed until he should conform himself to the decree of the Commissioners of Sewers. [*Draft.* 1 *p.*]

Jan. 26.
Star Chamber.
99. The like. The Lords being moved on behalf of John West, who has a suit in the Exchequer against Robert Jason, prisoner in the Fleet, that he might serve Jason with process *ad audiendum judicium*, and being further moved that Jason might go with his keeper to instruct his counsel for the said hearing, it was ordered that the warden of the Fleet permit Jason to be served with the said process and suffer him to repair to his counsel, and after the hearing to keep him close prisoner till further order. [*Draft.* ¾ *p.*]

Jan. 26.
Inner Star Chamber.
100. The like. The Lords having upon a reference from his Majesty on the petition of Samuel Baldock, clerk, heard the counsel of Baldock and of Dr. Jarvis, touching the rectory of Greenstead, Essex, and finding that there is already a judgment against Baldock's title, and a writ of error thereupon depending, the Lords therefore thought fit to leave the said differences to be determined by the course of law. [*Draft.* ¾ *p.*]

Jan. 26.
101. The Council to the Sheriff of co. Warwick. We send you a petition presented on behalf of the inhabitants of that county, to be spared a moiety of the ship-money charged upon them this year, in regard that Birmingham being visited last summer with the pestilence they relieved them by a weekly allowance. In respect that county is easily rated, and that the sickness has not been so great nor general there as in other counties which have had no abatement, you are to proceed in levying the full sum. [*Draft.* 1 *p.*]

Vol. CCCLXXIX.

1637-8.
Jan. 26.
Whitehall.

102. The Council to Humanitas Mayo, Thomas Webb, and Thomas Boyles, messengers. Divers abuses are already committed by ill-disposed persons of the company of makers of playing cards, whereupon we hold it very necessary that all moulds for printing "teats and varlets," as also for the Jews, scissons and dozens, be brought into his Majesty's sealing house, and all teats and varlets be there printed. We authorize you to enter into the houses of any of the said company you shall suspect, and there search for all cards defectively wrought and all the said moulds, and carry the same away to his Majesty's office for cards in Great St. Bartholomew's, delivering them with an inventory and the names of the owners, that further order may be taken; and if any person refuse to permit you to search, you are to call a constable to your assistance and break open doors or other places, and to apprehend all persons who hinder you, charging all mayors and other officers and subjects to assist you. [2 pp.]

Jan. 26.

103. The same to Attorney-General Bankes. We enclose a list of persons who make white starch of sweet corn, contrary to proclamation. We hold it requisite that some of them be punished for example to others. We pray you to send for some of the chiefest of them, and if upon examination you find cause, to proceed against them. [1 p.]

Jan. 26.

104. Draft of the above. [1 p.]

Jan. 26.

105. Draft entry of the appearance before the Council of Thomas Poole and John Ting, constables of Fyfield, Essex, who are to remain in the messenger's custody until discharged. [¼ p.]

Jan. 26.

106. Similar entry of the appearance of Robert Adams, on behalf of himself and his father, Marquis Adams, who being 87 years of age is not able to travel, but he is nevertheless to remain in custody of the messenger until discharged. [¼ p.]

[Jan. 26?]

107. Petition of Robert Barkham to the Council. On petitioner's last petition to the Lords, they prayed the Lord Chief Justice of the King's Bench and the Attorney-General to call before them petitioner and the parties prosecuting him, and to settle the differences, or certify the true state thereof, with their opinions concerning the submission offered by the petitioner. The Lord Chief Justice and the Attorney-General being attended by petitioner and the contrary parties, without considering the decrees according to the laws of sewers, treated with petitioner touching the submission, and certified their opinion therein. Prays the Lords to spare the commitment of petitioner, and to continue the reference to the Lord Chief Justice and the Attorney-General, that they may certify their opinions of the decrees in question, according to the laws of sewers. [¾ p.]

Jan. 26.

108. Petition of John Sedcole, of Epping, Essex, to the Lords of the Admiralty. Of late, petitioner was charged by the constables of Epping to carry a load of saltpetre, which he was not able to

1637-8.

Vol. CCCLXXIX.

perform, not being provided with a team. Further, he does not hold any lands in that hundred save 30*l.* per annum, which was leased out by petitioner's father to one in Epping, with condition that he should pay all duties and services which belonged thereunto; and lastly, that George Spranger, who has the said lease, went himself and his horse towards the last carriage that came. Prays consideration hereof, and promises to submit to what shall be ordered. [½ *p.*] Annexed,

    108. I. *Affidavit of petitioner in verification of the facts stated in the petition.* [½ *p.*]

    108. II. *Certificate of John Mott, constable, that he warned John Sedcole to take a load of saltpetre to the Swan at Stratford Loughton, which Sedcole refused.* 6*th January* 1637–8. [*Underwritten statement of Nathaniel Sykes that he had been much hindered by the refusal of Sedcole.* ½ *p.*]

    108. III. *Certificate of Cicely Warden and eleven other inhabitants of Epping, in confirmation of the preceding statement of John Mott. Sedcole is an inhabitant in our parish, and has a sufficient team of horses to have done the service.* [¾ *p.*]

Jan. 26.
Carlisle.

109. Sir Thomas Dacre, Sheriff of Cumberland, to the Council. I received the writ for shipping together with letters of instruction. I enclose a memorial of the proceedings thereof, and I shall labour to collect the moneys and pay the same over. [*Seal with arms.* ½ *p.*]

    109. I. *Memorial above alluded to, being a general statement of the way in which* 1,400*l. was assessed upon Cumberland.* [¾ *p.*]

Jan. 26.
Northampton.

110. Ro[bert] Weldon to [Sir John Lambe]. Wrote last week of Sir Richard Samuel's acts and threats. Since that, what he before menaced he has put in execution upon the constable of Bugbrooke. Himself alone, without calling any other justice of peace, bound the constable to good behaviour for not carrying Gare the next way to gaol, but suffering him to put in bail before Dr. Clerke, whereas I have seen the warrant, which was, that whereas he had refused to put in sureties for good behaviour (which he did not, but tendered very sufficient men) he should be imprisoned till he found security. Beseeches the person addressed to hear Gare himself, what was the pretended cause of his binding. The true reason was stated in the writer's last letter. He will tell you that Sir Richard thrice questioned him what he had to do with Sir Miles Burkitt, and when Gare would make no other answer than that he was not bound to tell his worship, he replied that he might as well tell him in plain terms that he would not tell him. This Sir Richard Samuel is a man so venemous against ecclesiastical jurisdiction, that when a brief for collection comes he demands whether an apparitor brought it, and if it came from ecclesiastical power his answer is *eo nomine*

1637-8.

Vol. CCCLXXIX.

that he will give nothing. This head standing upon Puritan shoulders, neither will obedience be performed nor truth extracted. It appears "to us" that had the examination of the business, that they are not only powerful in their multitudes, but one way or other they prevail upon those that are not of their garb. Details the alleged cunning of "one of them" upon examination. Having given Gare the information, "when he came to it" he endeavoured to direct all that he had formerly informed another way. In his answers he had nothing perfect save a lapwing's cry to divert that part of the second article concerning the prosecuting and cropping of the faithful from that meaning which himself had construed it in. His name is Barefoot. Never went we to church to speed any act but we had some complaint of wrongs or threatenings to some of the witnesses, and apparent insolencies of the defendant before our faces. I shall not be in London this term. My duty requires this poor service. Zeal to religion and the peace of the Church engage me in it, and were there no other reason, the clergy, relieved by that power God and his Majesty have conferred upon that court, have cause to be jealous of its honour. [*Endorsed by Sir John Lambe*, "Nothing to a brief if a paritor bring it. Whipt a minister in bed. Commission." 1¾ *p*.]

Jan. 26. 111. Sum by Sir Thomas Roe of the report of himself, Sir Kenelm Digby, Alderman Garraway and others, referees appointed by his Majesty upon a petition of the West Country merchants, concerning the pirates of Algiers and Tunis, as far as memory will help him, having no notes nor copy, one being presented to his Majesty, to which Sir Thomas refers, another to the Lords, which is lost, and his own copy, having produced him nothing but reprehension, he burnt. The proposal of the referees was to set out a strong fleet which should go "right down to Alexandria," when the Turks' ships were there laden, and should make prize of all men and goods; and should afterwards range the coast of Barbary, land among the villages, and make prisoners of all men, women, and children, and then return to Algiers and Tunis, and there exchange the prisoners taken, and so redeem English captives. If they refuse to exchange, then to go over to Majorca, Sardinia, and Spain, and to sell the Turks for money. Sir Thomas adds, at considerable length, the objections urged against this proposal, with the answers. [3 *pp*.]

Jan. 26. 112. Notes by Sec. Windebank of causes heard in the Star
Star Chamber. Chamber this day. They were Penkevill against Willes, in which Willes was fined 500*l*. to the King and 100*l*. damages to Penkevill. In a second cross bill Willes was fined 20*l. pro falso clamore.* In Pleydall against John Trinder, William Hay, and John Cull, the cause was dismissed. [⅓ *p*.]

Jan. 27. Warrant to pay to John Crane 730*l*. 15*s*., for victuals and other expenses before launching the Sovereign of the Seas at Woolwich, and since at her moorings in the river, and for rigging and fitting the Prince Royal at Chatham. [*Docquet*.]

Vol. CCCLXXIX.

1637–8.
Jan. 27. Grant to George Vernon, his Majesty's servant, of benefit accruing to his Majesty out of the estates of Sir Edward Bellingham, Sir Ralph Standish, and John Owen, who stand outlawed after judgment. [*Docquet.*]

Jan. 27. The King to the Provost and Fellows of King's College, Cambridge, declaring that the whole college of Clare Hall (the chapel and libraries excepted) shall be removed 70 feet lower to the west, and that such portion of ground as shall remain between Clare Hall and the south-west end of King's College shall be conveyed to them for enlarging the chapel yard of King's College, and that for supply of room for their building at Clare Hall the Provost and Fellows of King's College are to convey to them all that part of the Butt-close which lies northwards of the bridge and causeway in their college of Clare Hall, together with the said bridge and causeway, upon such rent to be reserved as the same are reasonably worth to be let. [*Docquet.*]

Jan. 27. Petition of Sir Richard Titchborne to the King. Acts of Parliament which provided for reformation of abuses in servants, in the first year of Queen Elizabeth were all repealed and reduced into a law whereby, amongst other things, it was provided that no servant should depart out of his service without a testimonial of his licence so to do, which was appointed to be registered, for which 2*d.* was to be paid; and it was also provided that no person which should depart out of any service should be received without showing such testimonial. By reason that no officer has been appointed for making those testimonials, the same are neglected, and the reformation intended by that act of Parliament is frustrated. Petitioner prays grant of the office of making the said testimonials for 21 years, at the rent of [*blank*], with liberty to take 2*d.* for every such testimonial; and that your Majesty will by proclamation require the observation of the said statute, and give warrant to the Attorney-General to prepare a book for granting the said office. [*Copy. See Vol. ccxxiii., p. 232. 1 p.*] *Underwritten*,

> I. *His Majesty being well persuaded of the petitioner, and desirous to confer a mark of favour upon him, refers the said petitioner to the Lord Treasurer, the Lord Privy Seal, the Earl Marshal, and Sec. Windebank, who are to certify their opinions, and what rent is fit to be reserved.* [*Copy. Ibid., p. 233. ¼ p.*]

Jan. 27. 113. The Council to the Sheriff of Somerset. The inhabitants of Bath Forum complain that for the service of shipping you have taken off 40*l.* from the hundred of Wellow and liberty of Henton and Norton, and laid the same upon the said hundred and the liberty of Hampton and Claverton, notwithstanding it has been ordered by this Board that the rates should stand until there be a general review of the rates through the whole county. We pray you to take order that the hundred of Bath Forum be assessed at no higher rate

1637-8.

Vol. CCCLXXIX.

than it was last year by your predecessor, until all the rates for the said county shall be settled, if, as alleged, it was so desired by the justices at Bridgwater. [*Draft.* 1 *p.*]

Jan. 27.
Whitehall.

114. Notes by Nicholas of business to be transacted by the Lords of the Admiralty. The Lords appointed to hear the differences between the shipwrights and caulkers. Officers of the Navy attend about the Prince and the Merhonour, and the list of ships for this summer. Sign papers and the estimate of the Ordinary. Consider whether any merchants [ships] shall be employed this year. Peruse answer of the recorder of Huntingdon to the complaint of Stevenson, saltpetreman. Sedcole, who refused to send his cart for saltpetre, attends in the messenger's custody. Appoint carpenter for the Vanguard. Awdry has a proposition to make for venting 200 lasts of powder yearly. Consider the master shipwrights' petition. [1 *p.*]

Jan. 27.
Whitehall.

Lords of the Admiralty to Thomas Viscount Wentworth, Lord Deputy. We have order from the Council for setting forth the Swallow and the Ninth Whelp for guard of the coast of Ireland, at the charge of the revenue of that kingdom. We therefore pray you to set forth the Swallow for eight months with 150 men, and the Ninth Whelp for twelve months with 60 men, to be ready for sea at the beginning of March next; and at the end of their employment to send us an account of the charge expended. We shall give warrant to Capt. Thomas Ketelby, whom his Majesty has appointed to go in the Swallow, admiral of all ships employed on that coast, and likewise for his lieutenant, and shall send a warrant for Capt. Owen to be captain of the Ninth Whelp. [*Copy. See Vol. cccliii., fol.* 81. 1 *p.*]

Jan. 27.
Whitehall.

The same to Robert Smith, marshal and water-bailiff of Ireland, Leonard Cross, Henry Wheeler, Thomas Canditt, and William Rolewright. An execution under seal of the Admiralty, dated 1st December 1637, on behalf of George Rodney, is issued to you to apprehend John French and Edward Bourke, both of Galloway [Galway], and to keep them in safe custody until 5,000*l.* be by them paid to George Rodney. In assistance of the said writ of execution, we charge you to use all diligence to apprehend French and Bourke, and them to keep in safe custody. And we pray the Lord President of Munster to give you his aid, and require all vice-admirals and others to be assisting. [*Ibid., fol.* 81 *b.* 1 *p.*]

Jan. 27.
Whitehall.

The same to Montjoy Earl of Newport. The captain of the fort at Milton, near Gravesend, informs us that his store of provision is near spent. We pray you that a survey be taken of the remains of gunners' stores in the said fort, and an account of the expenditure, and that the wants be supplied. [*Copy. Ibid., fol.* 82. ½ *p.*]

VOL. CCCLXXIX.

1637-8.
Jan. 27. Minute of a similar letter for supply of the fort at West Tilbury, near Gravesend. [*See Vol. cccliii., fol.* 82 *b.* 3 *lines.*]

Jan. 27. The like for Upnor Castle. [*Ibid.* 3 *lines.*]

Jan. 27. The like for Warham and Bay Sconces. [*Ibid.* 4 *lines.*]

Jan. 27.
Whitehall. Entry on the Admiralty Register that the Lord Treasurer, Mr. Comptroller, and Sec. Windebank signified his Majesty's pleasure that Thomas Barloe shall be the next clerk of the Acts of the Navy, to hold the same from the death, surrender, or other determination of Mr. Fleming, the present clerk. [*Ibid., fol.* 85. ¼ *p.*]

Jan. 27.
Whitehall. Order of Lords of the Admiralty in settlement of differences between the shipwrights and the caulkers. The number of apprentices was to be regulated by the ordinances of the corporation of shipwrights, the shipwrights were to endeavour to keep the caulkers in work, some of the caulkers were to be elected assistants of the corporation of shipwrights, and were to be employed on surveys, and both shipwrights and caulkers were to be obedient to the government of the corporation. [*Ibid., fol.* 87. 1½ *p.*]

Jan. 27. 115. Petition of his Majesty's Master Shipwrights to the Lords of the Admiralty. Petitioners have formerly received extra for their service at Portsmouth 6s. 8d. per diem, but of late the same is confined to 40l. per annum. Being again commanded down for that service, petitioners are denied by Sir William Russell the said part reward. Beseech that they may have encouragement to do the duties of their places. [¾ *p.*]

Jan. 27. 116. Officers of Navy to Lords of the Admiralty. We have made a list of the captains mentioned by you, and have against every name set what a month's pay comes to. The pay of Sir John Pennington, as vice-admiral, was 40s. per diem; Sir Henry Mervin, rear-admiral, 20s.; Capt. Rainsborough, 10s.; Capt. Walter Stewart and seven others, 8s.; five at 6s. 8d.; and others at lower sums down to 3s. 4d. The monthly pay for the whole 22 was 268l. 16s. 10d. [1 *p.*]

Jan. 27. 117. Propositions of Godwin Awdry, of Melksham, Wilts, referred to the Lords of the Admiralty, concerning the orderly managing of the magazines in England. The proposal was that the deputy lieutenants in every county should appoint a man to renew the county magazine, and should grant their warrants to the constables to collect, by rate, money to buy 2 lbs. of powder, 6 yards of match, and 24 bullets for every musketeer. This provision was to be delivered out annually to every trained man, and what remained over after musters might be sold to any that would buy it for shipping or other purposes. [1 *p.*]

Jan. 27.
Draycot. 118. Robert Wynne to Richard Harvey. Has left Mr. Bower on account of insufficient allowance, and is now with his sister at Draycott. Prays Harvey's assistance in procuring another place. Sir William Calley and his wife are both well. [1 *p.*]

VOL. CCCLXXIX.

1637-8.
Jan. 27.
119. Account rendered by Sir William Russell of arrears of ship-money due upon writs issued in 1635; total, 8,203*l.* 10*s.* 9*d.*; with a memorandum of Nicholas deducting certain allowances which reduce the arrear (as he states the sum) to 5,403*l.* 8*s.* 2*d.* [*Much damaged by damp.* 1 *p.*]

Jan. 27.
120. Similar account of money received and outstanding on account of writs issued in August 1636. Total received, 185,904*l.* 12*s.* 0½*d.*; outstanding, 10,709*l.* 15*s.* 7½*d.* [*Much damaged by damp.* 1 *p.*]

Jan. 28.
Whitehall.
121. Order of the King and Council. Sir Edward Bromfield, governor of the present company of soapmakers, and others of the said corporation, complained that there is lately imported about 2,000*l.* worth of foreign soap, contrary to proclamation, which the said governor and company desired might be confiscated. Upon hearing the persons that claim interest in the said soap, his Majesty and the Lords, conceiving their allegations that the said soap was consigned for foreign parts and not for England to be only pretences, ordered that the soap so seized should be proceeded against in the Exchequer, to be there legally cleared or condemned according to justice. [*Draft.* 1 *p.*]

Jan. 28.
Whitehall.
122. The like order. That no composition shall be henceforth taken for soap imported into this kingdom contrary to proclamation by those who have power to compound for prohibited goods, but that it shall be proceeded against in the Exchequer, and there adjudged confiscate, and of this the customers are to take notice. [*Draft.* ¾ *p.*]

Jan. 28.
123. Similar order. Upon 17th December last his Majesty appointed the first Sunday in Hilary term for hearing the business of making navigable the river that leads to the Ouse in Suffolk, and commanded the commissioners for viewing the said river, and such gentlemen that have interest therein, to attend at the same time. His Majesty now appoints to hear the same on the 4th February next. [*Draft.* ½ *p.*]

Jan. 28.
Whitehall.
124. The like upon hearing the complaints of Lord Mohun and others, commissioners for inquiry respecting certain sums of money illegally imposed in the city of Bristol, and several petitions presented from Bristol touching the undue proceedings of some of the commissioners. His Majesty and the Lords ordered that the Attorney-General should exhibit in the Star Chamber informations upon these several complaints, and use expedition to bring them to a hearing, the complaints of the commissioners being first heard, but both causes to be sentenced together. [*Draft.* 1⅔ *p.*]

Jan. 28.
125. The Council to Sir Anthony Irby, Sheriff of co. Lincoln. We have considered your letter of the 1st inst. (*see Vol. ccclxxviii., No.* 1), about rating the lands drained by Sir Anthony Thomas and other adventurers beyond Boston. We well approve the easy hand you have held in charging lands so beneficial to the owners, and

VOL. CCCLXXIX.

1637-8.
pray you to proceed accordingly, and to hasten the sending to the Treasurer of the Navy the sum charged upon that county. [*Draft.* 1 *p.*]

Jan. 28. 126. The Council to the Lord Chief Justice and the rest of the Judges of the King's Bench. We send a paper which Joseph Neale pretends is a true relation of his proceedings against William Benlowes, junior, and of the escape he made, as he alleges, by the permission of Sir John Lenthall. Because the business is foul we recommend its examination to you, and having by Mr. Fessant, a counsellor, or Mr. Barker, attorney for Neale, informed yourselves of the true carriage of the business, we pray you to cause inquiry to be made where Benlowes, junior, now is, and how he came to make his escape, and thereupon to take such order as the said Neale may be relieved for the misery he has endured. And if you cannot make a good end thereof, you are to return certificate to the Board with your opinions. [*Draft.* 1⅓ *p.*]

Jan. 28. 127. The same to the Sheriff of Kent. The parishioners of Dartford complain of being overrated towards the ship-money for this year, and for the great charge they are yearly at towards the removes of their Majesties, the smallness of the quantity of their marsh ground in respect of the hundred of Little and Lesness, with which they are equally rated, and for many other particulars they desire to be eased. We pray you to examine the allegations, and if you find them true, to give petitioners relief, provided that what you abate them be laid on some other parts of the county that may better bear it. [*Draft.* 1 *p.*]

Jan. 28.
London.
128. Sir White Beconsawe, late Sheriff of Hants, to the Council. By their letter of 19th November 1637 the Lords required various collectors of ship-money to pay to Sir White certain small sums of money in their hands or to appear at the Council Board. He certifies that the executors of Robert Newland had paid him 6*l.* 10*s.*, but that John Barton, William Brooke, Stephen Marsh, and Edward Coles had refused or omitted to pay their several amounts or to give bonds to appear. [*Nicholas has written in the margin that Stephen Marsh had since paid his amount.* 1 *p.*]

Jan. 28. 129. John Lord Poulett to Nicholas. I am sorry the word "project" in my letter to you gave the Lords so much offence, being used by me but as the phrase in which the business was presented to me. For that I desire the Lords pardon. For the money I am ready to pay as I promised it, by 10*l.* a year. If the Lords will have it otherwise, I must leave myself to their pleasures. Pray present this answer in the best sense. [*Seal with arms.* 1 *p.*]

Jan. 28. 130. Note by Nicholas of what ship-money had been levied under writs issued in October 1637; total 20,700*l.* [*The date, total, and footnote of figures are in the handwriting of the King. Discoloured by damp.* 1 *p.*]

Vol. CCCLXXIX.

1637–8.
Jan. 28.
131. Account by Sir Anthony Vincent, late sheriff, of 3,500*l*. ship-money charged upon Surrey in 1636. 3,200*l*. had been paid in. Of the remainder 54*l*. was due from Southwark, and 10*l*. 5*s*. 2*d*. from Guildford; 49*l*. 19*s*. 1*d*. was due from persons of whom no distress could be found, and 185*l*. 15*s*. 9*d*. was in course of collection. Among the persons from whom no distress could be found were Lord Monson, at Reigate, 8*l*., Sir William Slingsby for the same sum at Addington, and the Earl of Annandale, Stoke juxta Guildford, 15*s*. [3 *pp*.]

Jan. 28.
132. Information of Robert Toms and Thomas Cooper, bailiffs employed for collecting the arrear of ship-money by warrant of Sir John Hanbury, sheriff of co. Northampton. They state their ineffectual endeavours to distrain at Long Buckby. The constables refused to assist them, and when the informants distrained upon one person, women, boys, and children assembled with pitchforks and their aprons full of stones, exclaiming "Knock them down! Beat out their brains! Hang them rogues!" and they prevented their bringing the distress away. In another case of distraining they put the distress into the pound, but the pound was broken open and the distress taken away. Richard Hopkins, high constable, John Woodom [Woodham?] and John Dingley, constables, and Thomas Watts, thirdborough, were the persons principally complained of. [1 *p*.]

Jan. 28.
133. List by Richard Whithed, late Sheriff of Hants, of such persons as were assessed under writ of August 1635, and have no distress in that county; amongst them, under Wherwell, is William Stroud, who lives at Barrington, Somerset, 2*l*.; under Sparsholt, Adam Ayrie, vicar, principal of Edmund Hall, Oxford, 10*s*.; under Odiham, Lord Arundel of Wardour, 10*s*. [*Strip of parchment.* = 1 *p*.]

Vol. CCCLXXX. January 29–31, 1637–8.

Jan. 29.
The King to Thomas Viscount Wentworth, Lord Deputy of Ireland, requiring him to consider a petition enclosed presented to his Majesty by John Hadnett, and to take order therein. [*Docquet.*]

Jan. 29.
1. The Council to the Judges of the Great Sessions for co. Cardigan. The inhabitants of the division of Ywich Ayron [Uchayndre?] by petition showed that co. Cardigan consists of two divisions, Yss Aioron [Issayndre?] and Ywich Ayron, which for all accustomed taxes have time out of mind been equally charged, but the inhabitants of Yss Aioron complaining of being overcharged, it was referred to you to take order therein (*see Vol. ccclxx., No.* 84), which reference was read at the said sessions when none of the parties were there to make opposition. You then ordered that petitioners should bear

VOL. CCCLXXX.

1637–8.

two parts of three of all taxes, wherein they, finding themselves much overcharged, desire to be relieved. We pray you at the next general sessions to take a review of the business, and compose these differences as well for the future as the present. But it is to be understood that these differences shall in no sort hinder the sheriff to proceed in performance of that service, according to his Majesty's writ and the directions of this Board. [*Draft.* 1 *p.*]

Jan. 29. 2. Minute of a warrant from the Council to George Carter, messenger, to fetch Lewis Harris, late under-sheriff of co. Oxford. [*Draft.* ½ *p.*]

Jan. 29. 3. Entry of the appearance of Leonard Vow, of co. Leicester, who is to attend until discharged. [*Draft.* ¼ *p.*]

Jan. 29. The like of Barnaby Gouge, sent for by warrant this day. [*Draft. Written on the same paper as the last preceding.* 2 *lines.*]

Jan. 29.
Vale Royal.
4. Thomas Cholmondeley, Sheriff of co. Chester, to the Council. By letters of 29th November last, you sent me a petition of the town of Nantwich, whereby they complained to be overcharged for their ship-money. Those letters came not to my hands till 28th December last, when I had settled a proceeding in the service. Since then I have weighed the justice of their complaint, and find that that town is a great market town, and reputed the wealthiest part of the county. This, with other privileges they enjoy, moves me to conceive they are but proportionately rated with the rest of the shire, and more especially because my last predecessor, Sir Thomas Delves, a near neighbour to their town, an ancient justice of the peace of their hundred, and better knowing their estates than myself, set the same assessment which is now upon them. [1 *p.*]

Jan. 29.
Ludlow Castle.
5. Sir John Bridgeman, Chief Justice, and Sir Marmaduke Lloyd and Adam Littleton, Justices of Chester, to the same. Report of their examination and inquiries as referees of a petition of David Edwards, William Edwards, and Thomas Edwards, all of Rorington, Salop, complaining of inequalities in their assessment for ship-money and oppressive conduct of Sir Paul Harris, the sheriff, in connexion therewith. The referees find that the leading and important facts stated in the petition are true, that the assessment was made with the general inequality complained of, and that Sir Paul Harris did much miscarry himself, in that conceiving the assessment to be unequal he did not alter it; and also for his neglect in not making the re-assessment till about the end of July, having direction in that respect about the end of February before; and in not pursuing the same direction as he ought to have done, but slighting it, and casting down the letter, saying, "Let Sir John Bridgeman assess it himself!" and now he showed an order of Council whereby Sir John Bridgeman was required to assist or direct Sir Paul in the new assessment, of which order he gave not Sir John any notice until the 12th of January instant. [*Seal with crest.* 2 *pp.*]

VOL. CCCLXXX.

1637-8.
Jan. 29.   6. Petition of John Horne, clerk, to Archbishop Laud. The appeal brought by the pretended appropriator, Lady Whorwood, against petitioner for the vicarage of Heddington, Wilts, has been depending in the Court of Arches these six terms, petitioner's rich adversary meanwhile receiving the profits of the vicarage. Prays relief. [¾ p.] *Underwritten,*

> 6. I. *Reference to Sir John Lambe to show petitioner all lawful favour for expediting his business. 29th January 1637-8.* [1 p.]

Jan. 29.   7. Petition of Robert Young, printer, to the same. Has disbursed 600l. to purchase an interest in copies of English books and in divers other things, besides his engagement in printing books of the common law (by virtue of which patent only, divers presses have been erected), and has furnished himself with good letter and able workmen, and has kept three presses, and sometimes four, at work, without giving any offence to authority. By the last decree in the Star Chamber he is limited to keep only two presses, unless you see cause to the contrary. As petitioner is no way able to perform his own work with two presses in printing English books only, and has dealt with a corrector to attend the press for his other engagements, he beseeches he may continue his employment. [½ p.] *Underwritten,*

> 7. I. *Reference to Sir John Lambe to consider the petition and give the archbishop an account of it. 29th January 1637-8.* [¾ p.]

Jan. 29.   8. Account of Sir Philip Parker, Sheriff of Suffolk, in respect of 8,000l. ship-money charged upon that county in 1636-7. Sir Philip had paid in 7,900l., and was ready to pay in 48l. 5s. 8d. more. Of the remainder he craved allowance of 51l. 14s. 4d., being the amount assessed upon persons who had since died, or had removed out of the county, with the addition of 4l. 4s. 8d., a balance due from Ipswich. [1½ p.]

Jan. 29.   Entry of the discharge of John Sedcole, upon his submission, giving satisfaction to Nathaniel Sykes, saltpetreman, and paying messenger's fees. [*See Vol. ccclxiii., fol. 84 b.* ½ p.]

Jan. 30.   Grant of a pension of 100l. per annum to Mary, daughter of Katherine Lady Dyer, now wife of Edward Wardour, son of Sir Edward Wardour, to continue during her life, which pension was by King James granted to Richard Connocke during the lives of Philadelphia Carr, wife of Edward Carr, and of Robert Carr, their son, and afterwards the said Richard Connocke assigned the same over to Philadelphia and Robert Carr. Shortly after, the said Robert Carr dying, the said Edward Carr and his wife assigned the same to Sir Edward Wardour, who is to surrender his interest therein before this grant pass. [*Docquet.*]

Vol. CCCLXXX.

1637-8.
Jan. 30. Warrant to pay to Anne Smith, administratrix of Christopher Smith, deceased, late one of his Majesty's gentlemen harbingers, 544*l.* 19*s.* 8*d.*, disbursed by Thomas Mynne, his Majesty's knight-harbinger, and the said Christopher Smith, for accommodating the Duke of Chevreuse and other ambassadors extraordinary from the French King. For payment thereof his Majesty gave warrant in the first year of his reign, but no part thereof has been yet paid, as appears by certificate from Sir Robert Pye, auditor of the Receipt. Since which time Thomas Mynne has assigned all his interest therein to the said Anne Smith, as appears by his deed. [*Docquet.*]

Jan. 30.
Whitehall. 9. The Council to Clement Wastell. Divers blocks of tin melted into bars are ready to be embarked without paying customs or having licence from the patentees, contrary to his Majesty's proclamation. These are to require all mayors and others to be aiding to you to search for such bars, and if opposition be made, or any refuse to open shop, cellar, or other place where the tin may be supposed to be concealed, we require all mayors and others to see this warrant put in full force. [*Draft.* 1½ *p.*]

Jan. 30.
Whitehall. 10. The same to Dr. Morrison, Sir William Powell, Edmund Powell, Richard Okeley, John Williams, Dr. William Griffith, John Ashenden, and John Powell. To give attendance on the 15th February next, to testify in a complaint made by Dr. Dillon against Bishop Williams, of Lincoln. [*Copy.* 1 *p.*]

Jan. 30. 11. Minute of a warrant from the Council to Thomas Welch, messenger, to fetch before the Lords Thomas Wells, of Ashton, co. Northampton, and John Cleypoole, of Northborough. [*Draft.* ½ *p.*]

Jan. 30. The like to Thomas Richbell, messenger, to fetch John Woodom [Woodham?] and John Dingley, constables, and Thomas Wats, thirdborough of Long Buckby, co. Northampton. [*Draft. Written on the same paper as the above.* 4 *lines.*]

Jan. 30. The like to Nicholas Golsborough, messenger, to fetch William Taylor and George Wilson, late constables of Warkworth, co. Northampton. [*Draft. Ibid.* 4 *lines.*]

Jan. 30. 12. Entry of appearance before the Council of William Bridge and James Master, aldermen of Canterbury. They are to remain in custody of the messenger until discharged. [*Draft.* ½ *p.*]

Jan. 30.
Westminster. 13. Robert Earl of Lindsey to Nicholas. Mordecai Hunton, William Green, William Blunston, Henry Luddington, William Middlecote, Sir George Hennage, Anthony Fulwood, Thomas Ward, Richard Fillingham, and Barnaby Gouge, by me returned for not showing arms in co. Lincoln, have by their submission given me that satisfaction that you may spare their further attendance, your fees being paid. [¾ *p.*]

Jan. 30. 14. Minute of the discharge of the persons above mentioned. [*Draft.* ¼ *p.*]

VOL. CCCLXXX.

1637-8.
Jan. 30.
Whitehall.
Lords of the Admiralty to Officers of the Navy. It is requisite that one of his Majesty's shipwrights remain constantly at Portsmouth, now that a good part of the navy remains there in the winter, and often comes in thither upon occasion of any defect. You are to appoint some [one?] of the master shipwrights to repair thither and to reside there constantly, without changing by turns as of late they have used to do. And you may allow to the master shipwright that shall reside at Portsmouth the allowance that you did to the three that served by turn. [*Copy. See Vol. cccliii., fol.* 83 *b.* ½ *p.*]

Jan. 30.
Whitehall.
The same to the same. By privy seal dated 29th December last, we are to give order for the sale of the Red Lion, and to cause the proceeds to be delivered to the Treasurer of the Navy. These are to require you to make sale of the said ship accordingly. [*Copy. Ibid.* ⅔ *p.*]

Jan. 30.
Whitehall.
The same to the same. The Merhonour is to be brought into the great dock at Chatham, to be there opened and searched, and if she be found fit she may be cut down and brought to have but two decks and a half. We require you that the said ship be brought into dock, and there opened and searched, as Capt. Phineas Pett shall direct. [*Copy. Ibid., fol.* 84. ⅓ *p.*]

Jan. 30.
Whitehall.
The same to the same. The Prince is to be rebuilt at Woolwich by Capt. Phineas Pett, who has undertaken to bring her about for [from?] Chatham to Woolwich at a less charge than that expressed in your letter of the 18th December last (*Vol. ccclxxiv., No.* 22). You are to give assistance to Captain Pett. The charge of rebuilding, you, with the said captain, are to set down in an estimate and return the same to us. [*Copy. Ibid.* ½ *p.*]

Jan. 30.
The Swiftsure, in the Downs.
15. Sir John Pennington to Lords of the Admiralty. We have had such miserable foul weather for these fourteen days or three weeks, that there has been very little stirring. The new Holland admiral (Martin Harpenson Tromp) is here with 20 sail of tall ships and two pinnaces, but as yet has met with none of the Dunkirkers, though they daily take their ships. There was a Holland man-of-war of 28 pieces of ordnance cast away last week upon the Horse, in coming down over the Flats. [1 *p.*]

Jan. 30.
16. Presentment of the Gentlemen Harbingers and the rest of their fellows to [the Committee for revising and settling the regulations of the Royal Household?]. Set forth a variety of difficulties which they meet with in the execution of their duty during progresses, and pray that for prevention of future inconveniences they may have a list of all such noblemen, gentlemen, and others as accompany the King and Queen, expressing how they may be provided for, and with what number of beds and horses every one shall be appointed to wait on his Majesty. [1 *p.*]

Jan. 30.
Whitehall.
17. Minutes by Nicholas of resolutions of the Committee for regulating the Royal Household, as to carriages, herbergage, and ordering the hall. [3 *pp.*]

Vol. CCCLXXX.

1637–8.
Jan. 30.
18. Statement of the number of carriages allowed on their Majesties' removes in time of progress. The number allowed by the book was 257, but the service according to the present practice numbered 406. Of the overplus number his Majesty pays for 110; the rest, being 39, were for the service of divers lords and ladies over and above the King's allowance. [⅓ p.]

Jan. 30.
19. List of the several officers and offices of the household to be provided with lodgings in time of progress. [1 p.]

Jan. 30.
See "Papers relating to Appointments in the Navy."

Jan. 31.
Presentation of Robert Dove, clerk, M.A., to the rectory of Merwood *alias* Marwood, Devon, void and in his Majesty's gift by lapse. [*Docquet.*]

Jan. 31.
Warrant to Sir William Uvedale, Treasurer of the Chamber, to pay to George Lovell, one of the Grooms of the Chamber in ordinary to the Queen, in place of Robert Smithick, deceased, 2s. by day during his life, to commence from 6th June last. [*Docquet.*]

Jan. 31.
Warrant to pay to Peter Sainthill 300*l.*, in recompense of his pains in advancing his Majesty a revenue out of the hard soap made in the western parts, and in executing a commission whereby he has brought the soapmakers to pay 6*d.* upon every dozen of hard soap. [*Docquet.*]

Jan. 31.
Warrant, under the signet, to the Sheriff of Surrey and keeper of the prison of the White Lion, in Southwark, to deliver Walter Feasey, a condemned prisoner there, to Capt. Roger Horton, to be transported into the parts beyond the seas, either to serve in the wars, or in some of his Majesty's plantations. [*Docquet.*]

Jan. 31.
20. Petition of William Berkeley, his Majesty's servant, to the King. It may concern your Majesty to know the number and quality of such foreigners as reside or resort into England, and that your Majesty would erect an office of registering the names of all strangers, except ambassadors with their servants, and merchants, and to prevent deceit in them who have their secret ends why they would not register their names, that your Majesty would prohibit all persons to lodge strangers without a ticket from the registrar, the said ticket to be renewed yearly upon a payment of one shilling. Petitioner prays a grant for his pains in settling the said office and the management thereof, of one-third part of the profit, being accountable to your Majesty for the remainder. [½ p.] *Underwritten,*

20. I. *His Majesty requires the opinion of the Attorney or Solicitor General as to the legality of the proposal, and what may fitly be done therein. Whitehall, 31st January 1637–8.* [¼ p.]

20. II. *Reference of the Solicitor-General to the farmers of the customs to certify him what they conceive of this proposition.* [3 lines.]

VOL. CCCLXXX.

1637–8.

20. III. *Sir John Wolstenholme and John Harrison, farmers of the customs, to Solicitor-General Littleton. We think it fit that his Majesty should know the number and quality of all strangers residing and resorting in the kingdom. Hitherto there has not been any order taken whereby to know the same, and we conceive the granting of this suit can be no way prejudicial to the customs, as having no relation thereunto.* [*Copy.* ¼ *p.*]

Jan. 31.
21. Petition of the widow and orphans of Clement Harby, late one of his Majesty's tin farmers, to the King. Clement Harby and Thomas Symonds for divers years traded as partners. Their debts being called for, Symonds pretended differences in account. Upon several bills exhibited in Chancery and the Exchequer, Symonds procured the accounts to be referred to Sir William Russell and Sir Maurice Abbot, who committed the examination of them to two accountants. Clement Harby drew up an account in which Symonds was made indebted in 1,500l. The accountants invented a new way of accounting, by which they made Clement Harby indebted to Symonds 14,277l. 4s. 5d., which account the accountants drew Sir William Russell and Sir Maurice Abbot to subscribe. By means of Sir Job Harby, brother to Clement, a review was obtained of the account, and all the differences between them were reduced to 156l. 10s.; but Symonds has procured a second reference to Sir William Russell, Sir Maurice Abbot, Alderman Garraway, Alderman Abdy, and William Cockaine. These commissioners prosecute the new way of account, and Symonds being a merchant continually on the Exchange, and having great kindred and alliance in the city, the poor petitioners are likely to suffer much. Pray that some of the Council, calling Mr. Robert Blake, now residing here for the King of Morocco (who was formerly acquainted with the said accounts), the said commissioners, and such other merchants as the Lords think fit, may determine these differences. [¾ *p.*] *Underwritten,*

21. I. *Reference to the Lord Privy Seal, Lord Cottington, and both the secretaries, as also such merchants whom the Lords shall think fit, to settle a quiet and peaceable end.* Whitehall, 31st January 1637–8. [¼ *p.*]

21. II. *Appointment to hear the parties on the 20th March* 1637–8. Whitehall, 14th March 1637–8. [¼ *p.*]

Jan. 31.
22. Copy of the same, without the appointment for the 20th March. [1 *p.*]

Jan. 31.
23. Petition of Nowell Warner, master of his Majesty's barges, to the King. Recites former reference to the Lord Privy Seal, the Earl Marshal, the Earl of Dorset, and Sec. Windebank, and order of the King in Council, on their report (*see Vol. ccclxxviii., No.* 17), that the same should stand in force for settling the things therein ordered. The fishermen, not regarding the said order, have since petitioned the

1637-8.

Vol. CCCLXXX.

Council table for redress, without mentioning the same. Prays that the same order may be established, so that petitioner may be at quiet. [⅔ p.]

Jan. 31.   24. Petition of John Child to the Council. Petitioner showed that, being last year appointed one of the collectors of ship-money in St. Giles's-in-the-Fields, he collected divers sums. The sheriff desired that all the collectors might meet and make a joint account for all the money collected. Petitioner was ready so to do, but George Hope, another of the collectors, pretending that he had spent 8l. at the vestry or tavern in making the assessment, refused to pay his money to the sheriff, intending to detain the same for his expenses. Yet Hope and others, upon pretence that there was money in petitioner's hands, complained to the Lords of petitioner, and he has been ten days in custody of a messenger. Petitioner, in regard that he had done his Majesty good service in this business, prayed his discharge without payment of his fees, and that the hearing of the matter might be referred to Alderman Abell. [¾ p.]

Jan. 31.   25. Order of Council on the preceding petition. That the business should be referred to the then sheriff, and if it shall appear that petitioner has been unduly complained of, the Lords order that Hope and the others shall pay the charges of his being taken into custody. But if the complaint against him be found true, then he is to bear the charges himself, and the sheriff is to certify how far Child has been to blame, that further course may be taken. It was also ordered that Child be discharged from custody. [Draft. 1½ p.]

Jan. 31.
Inner Star
Chamber.
26. Order of the Archbishop of Canterbury and the Lord Keeper, referees of a petition of William Bennet, curate of Maddington, Wilts. Having heard the petitioner, and likewise Sir Giles Estcourt, who has an estate of three lives in the impropriation of Maddington, and Sir Edward Hungerford, who is lord of the fee, and finding that Sir Giles has covenanted to allow petitioner 20l. per annum so long as he shall officiate the cure at Maddington, and that by his lease he is tied to allow a sufficient curate to officiate, which implies a sufficient maintenance, the referees ordered that Sir Giles should pay the said curate all the arrears of the 20l. per annum due at Michaelmas last, and from that time 20l. per annum. And if Sir Giles shall fail to make payment, then the curate is to attend the Lords, who will take a course for his relief. The Lords, pressing Sir Giles to add 10l. per annum to the curate's allowance, Sir Giles desired time to consider, to the end he might see how the curate would deserve it. Sir Edward Hungerford, at the Lords' motion, offered to allow (after the term granted to Sir Giles) 40l. per annum, besides the benefit of the Easter book. The Lords rendered him thanks, and ordered that his offer should be registered in the Council book. [Draft. 1 p.]

Jan. 31.
Inner Star
Chamber.
27. Order of the Archbishop of Canterbury, the Earl Marshal, and the Bishop of Winchester, referees of a petition of Edward Wickham, of Swalcliffe, and William Wickham, of Abingdon, pretending to be

Vol. CCCLXXX.

1637–8.

kinsmen of William [of] Wickham, heretofore Bishop of Winchester, and founder of New College and of Winchester College. After hearing counsel on behalf of the petitioners, and of Viscount Say and Sele, acknowledged to be of kin to the founder, and of Dr. Pinck and Dr. Harris, wardens of New College and of Winchester College, the referees declare that, however the parties petitioning make sundry specious arguments, the nature of which is here stated, yet, considering the answer of the defendants, they find no sufficient ground for the plaintiffs' kindred, and order that the colleges shall proceed in their elections without any obligation of kindred to the founder of the plaintiffs or any other; nevertheless they recommend the petitioners to the electors in respect of their name and in memory of so worthy a founder, when they shall be as eligible as others and as hopeful to make able men. [*Draft with additions of the Earl Marshal and Archbishop Laud, and signed by the former.* 1½ *p.*]

Jan. 31.
Inner Star Chamber.

28. Entry on the Council Register that Mr. Blake, understanding of a complaint made against him to the Lords by Capt. Bradshaw, came of himself and gave the Lords such full satisfaction in the presence of the captain, as the Lords not only approved well of the said Blake, and declared that they esteemed him worthy of the trust reposed in him by the Emperor of Morocco, but also ordered that Bradshaw should be forthwith committed prisoner to the Fleet for aspersions unjustly cast on Blake. [*Copy under seal.* ⅗ *p.*]

Jan. 31.

29. Minute of a Warrant to the Warden of the Fleet to take into his custody Capt. Edmund Bradshaw. [¼ *p.*]

Jan. 31.
Inner Star Chamber.

30. Order by the Archbishop of Canterbury, the Lord Keeper, and the Lord Treasurer, referees of a petition of Simon Lowth, rector of Dingley in the diocese of Peterborough. Petitioner complained of an enclosure made by Sir Edward Griffith at Dingley, which was very prejudicial to the Church, and that certain propositions made by the chancellor of the said diocese for ending the difference had once been condescended unto by Sir Edward, but were then forsaken. With consent of all parties a reference was made to the Bishop of Peterborough to settle the difference, certain lands of Sir Edward, which formerly belonged to St. John's of Jerusalem, being left so far exempt from tithes as the law exempts them. [*Draft.* 1 *p.*]

Jan. 31.
Whitehall.

31. Order of Council on petition of the Mayor and Aldermen of Canterbury, who stated that the Jersey spinners in the said city, being in number above 1,000, are by reason of great importation of yarns from Turkey made of camels' hair, whereof tammies, mohairs, grograms, and other stuffs are woven, fallen into great decay, being almost reduced to beggary, to the great burthen of the said city. It was ordered that the mayor and aldermen may transport into foreign parts one ton of Jersey or worsted yarn yearly for three years, paying customs and duties for the same, and if no inconvenience be found therein, the Lords will renew the licence for a longer time. [*Draft.* 1¾ *p.*]

Vol. CCCLXXX.

1637-8.
Jan. 31.
Inner Star Chamber.

32. Order of Council upon complaint of the high sheriffs of divers counties that the collectors appointed by them to collect the ship-money do most of them neglect or refuse to deliver accounts of their proceedings, whereby they not only detain the money they have levied, but have so puzzled the collections as without some course be taken to compel them to clear their accounts the sheriffs cannot proceed in levying the arrears. It was ordered that all collectors be required, within six days after sight of this order, not only to pay to the sheriff who gave them warrant all moneys in their hands, but also to give the sheriff an exact account how much every person in their parish was assessed, how much they have paid, and how much is due; and if any collector neglect, the sheriff or his messenger may take him into custody and bring him to answer before the Board. [*Draft.* 1½ *p.*]

Jan. 31.
Inner Star Chamber.

33. The like upon examination of John Ting, constable of Fyfield, Essex, who was convented before the Board concerning an answer made by him, in the name of the parish, upon a warrant of the sheriff requiring an assessment to be made for ship-money payable under the writ issued in September last. Ting confessed that he wrote the answer, and set the churchwardens' names underneath it. The parishioners never met to agree about the business of shipping, but he spake with the parishioners as he met with them. The answer followed a copy of the like answer made by the parish of Hatfield, brought from that place by George Taylor, a butcher. Ting was committed close prisoner to the Fleet, and Mr. Attorney was to proceed against him. [1⅛ *p.*]

Jan. 31.

34. Minute of warrant from the Council to the Warden of the Fleet to take into his custody Thomas Poole and John Ting, and that they speak not to each other. [¼ *p.*]

Jan. 31.

The like to the Keeper of Newgate for William Stane, Amos Prielove, and Josias Wood. [*Written on the same paper as the preceding.* 2 *lines.*]

Jan. 31.

35. Order of Council upon petition of Robert Stracey, collector of ship-money for Ryehill hamlet in the hundred of Harlow, Essex. Petitioner complained that Marcus Adams, being assessed at 14s., refused to pay, whereupon two of the sheriff's servants, assisted by Stracey, distrained one of Adams's bullocks, which was sold at 3l., and the overplus tendered to Adams and refused. Since then Adams has let his land and sold his stock to his son, Robert Adams, who pretends the bullock was his, and has brought an action of trespass in the Common Pleas against petitioner only, leaving out the sheriff's servants. It was ordered that Marcus Adams and Robert his son be required to cause the action to be withdrawn, and that they accept the overplus above mentioned, and give petitioner satisfaction for their unnecessary trouble, or that they stand committed to the Fleet till further order. [*Draft.* 1⅓ *p.*]

VOL. CCCLXXX.

1637–8.
Jan. 31.
36. Entry of the discharge of Robert Adams of further attendance upon his undertaking for himself and Marcus, his father, an aged man, to perform the above order. [*Draft.* ¼ *p.*]

Jan. 31.
37. Order of Council on the appearance before the Board of Sir Humphrey Mildmay, late sheriff of Essex, to give account for his not paying in the arrears of ship-money for 1635. The Lords ordered that he should levy the arrears, and pay them to Sir William Russell by the first day in Easter term next, or else attend the Board from time to time until discharged. [*Draft.* ⅔ *p.*]

Jan. 31.
Minute of a similar order for Sir Anthony Chester, sheriff of co. Buckingham. [*Draft. Written on the same sheet as the preceding. 2 lines.*]

Jan. 31.
Inner Star Chamber.
38. Order of Council. The Lords taking notice that proclamations, books, &c. printed by his Majesty's printer have been accustomed to be paid for out of moneys in the Hanaper in Chancery, by warrant of the Lord Keeper, and that divers of them are usually delivered unto messengers for the use of the Council, some for the use of his Majesty's chapel and closet, some for the Queen, the Prince, and the other royal children, so that the Lord Keeper is many times doubtful of giving allowance of the printer's bills, it was ordered that the printer deliver no books, proclamations, &c. for the use of the Council table but upon a warrant under the hand of one of the clerks of the Council; nor for the King's chapel but upon a warrant under the hand of the Dean; nor for the closet but upon a note from the Clerk of the Closet; nor for the Queen but upon warrant from the Earl of Dorset; nor for the Prince or any of the royal children without a note from their governors; and for such proclamations, &c. as he shall deliver into the Crown office he shall take the hand of the Clerk of the Crown. And if he shall deliver anything contrary to this order, he is not to expect payment for the same. [*Draft corrected by the Lord Privy Seal.* 1 *p.*]

Jan. 31.
Inner Star Chamber.
39. The Council to [George] Bingley, Auditor of the Imprest. Divers sums of money were collected by sheriffs by ship-money writs issued in 1635, all which were by special commission directed to be received and issued by Sir William Russell. You are to take and audit the account of Sir William Russell, and also the account of the Lieutenant of the Ordnance, and of the Surveyor of Marine Victuals, of the charge for setting forth and furnishing the fleet employed for guard of the seas in 1636. And whereas we are informed that all the ship-moneys under the said writs were not fully paid to Sir William Russell, you are to set upon the head of the sheriffs so much of the sums charged upon them as shall appear on the oath of Sir William Russell, who is accountant for the whole of the said moneys, to be unpaid to him. [*Draft.* 1½ *p.*]

Vol. CCCLXXX.

1637-8.
Jan. 31.
Minute of a similar warrant to take Sir William Russell's account under the writs issued in 1636. [*Written on the same paper as the preceding. 2 lines.*]

Jan. 31.
40. Charge against Sir William Russell in respect of ship-money received by him for the year 1635, being 199,700*l.*; and for the year 1636, being 196,400*l.* Sir William was charged with the whole sums directed by the writs to be levied, and was left to discharge himself by showing any deficiency in the amounts remitted by the sheriffs, and by setting forth his payments out of the moneys that came to his hands. [10 *pp.*]

[Jan. 31.]
41. Brief of the account of Sir William Russell of moneys received and issued in setting forth to sea sundry of his Majesty's ships in the year 1636, with the charges of weighing the Anne Royal sunk at Tilbury Hope. The total charge was 202,024*l.* 0*s.* 5¾*d.*; the payments and sums charged to the accountant, but remaining unpaid, exceeded the charge by 16,183*l.* 6*s.* 10¼*d.* [2 *pp.*]

[Jan. 31.]
42. Similar brief of the account of John Crane, the victualler, for 1636. The charge was 43,017*l.* 5*s.* 6*d.*, and the accountant in surplusage 6,092*l.* 3*s.* 8*d.* [1 *p.*]

[Jan. 31.]
43. Similar brief of the account of Sir John Heydon, Lieutenant of the Ordnance, for the year 1636. The total charge was 13,169*l.* 9*s.* 8*d.*, and the account was in surplusage 18,242*l.* 15*s.* 9¾*d.* [1¼ *p.*]

Jan. 31.
44. The Council to Edward Earl of Dorset and Henry Earl of Holland, Lord Lieutenants of Middlesex. There have been heretofore disorders committed on Shrove Tuesday by apprentices, who join with dissolute persons who abound in Westminster and the suburbs of London. We pray you to give order for strong watches to be kept, and also a number of the trained bands to be mustered on Shrove Tuesday next, in such places as may best serve for preventing any tumults which may be attempted. [*Copy.* ⅔ *p.*]

Jan. 31.
45. Minute of a letter of the Council to the Lord Mayor of London, of like tenor to one sent on 12th February 1636-7, to muster the trained bands on Shrove Tuesday, for prevention of riots. [*Draft.* ⅓ *p.*]

Jan. 31.
Whitehall.
46. The Council to the Sheriff of Kent. Complaint has been made from the Dean and some of the prebends of Canterbury, that notwithstanding an order of the Board, dated 25th January 1634[-5], the constables of the hundred of Westgate, by reason, as they allege, of the warrant you have given them for assessing the said hundred, have not only rated the clergy and other inhabitants within the precincts of the cathedral, but appointed persons to collect the sum so rated. You are to take order that the clergy belonging to the said church may assess themselves and the inhabitants within the precincts of the said church and close of Canterbury, but you are also to

Vol. CCCLXXX.

1637-8.

take care that the sum assessed amounts to the full sum of the rate expressed in the said order, and that the money be paid over to you in ease of the city. [*Draft.* 1 *p.*]

Jan. 31. 47. The Council to Sir John Poole and Sir Thomas Prideaux, Justices of Peace for Devon. Divers complaints have been made against the licensed brewers of St. Mary Ottery by Richard Cook and Emanuel Ford. We require you to call before you the said brewers and Cook and Ford, and return certificate to his Majesty's commissioners for brewing and malting, how you find the same. [*Draft.* ¾ *p.*]

Jan. 31. Minute of a similar letter for Lancelot Rea, complaining against a brewer of Cheltenham, directed to Sir John Prettyman, Timothy Gates, and Richard Barkley, Justices of Peace for co. Gloucester. [*Draft. Written on the same paper as the preceding.* ¼ *p.*]

Jan. 31. 48. The Council to the Mayor of Harwich. By writ issued in 1636, 20*l.* was assessed for ship-money upon that town, which sum you have hitherto forborne to pay. We command you to cause the said 20*l.* to be paid to the sheriff of that county by 2nd March next, or that you attend the Board to give account of your proceedings. [*Draft.* 1 *p.*]

Jan. 31. Minute of a similar letter to the Mayor of Hertford, for 55*l.*, assessed upon that town in 1636. [*Draft. Written on the same paper as the preceding.* 2 *lines.*]

Jan. 31. 49. The Council to the present and late Sheriff of Dorset. We understand there is 16*l.* 13*s.* behind of the ship-money under writs in October 1636 from the tithing of Frome Whitfield. We are informed that the said tithing paid last year with the hundred of the George [St. George], and pays with the said hundred to all payments except church and poor, yet now the same doth rather choose to pay with Dorchester, for that they are lower rated there, which will cast too great a burthen on the hundred, and disturb all the rates there long since assessed. You are to take order that Frome Whitfield be rated with the hundred of the George and not with Dorchester, and to give warrant to your immediate predecessor to assess all money unpaid accordingly, and that you the late sheriff pay the same with all expedition to the Treasurer of the Navy. [*Draft.* 1 *p.*]

[Jan. 31.] 50. Statement of the claim of Dorchester to the tithing of Frome Whitfield, which consists of two great farms in the hands of Lady Ashley and William Coker. From similarity of phrase this paper seems to have been used in the preparation of the preceding letter. [½ *p.*]

Jan. 31. 51. The Council to the Sheriff of Berks. We send you a petition of the parishioners of Sunninghill, complaining that, by an order of the Board of the 11th October last, the parishioners of Cookham and Binfield charge the inhabitants of Sunninghill towards the business

1637-8.

of shipping at a far higher rate than last year or than they are able to bear. We require you and Sir Richard Harrison, the late sheriff, to do therein according to the writ, for it is not his Majesty's pleasure that any should be charged above their abilities for the ease of those that are better able to bear it. [*Draft.* 1 *p.*]

Jan. 31. 52. The Council to Archbishop Neile, of York. We have considered the examination of William Stephenson, whom you committed for refusing the oath of allegiance, and find the manner of his refusal so full of disloyalty, as we pray you to take order that he be kept close prisoner till, upon conference with the judges about him at the next assize, you and they shall resolve of a further course to be taken with him. [*Draft.* 1 *p.*]

Jan. 31.
Whitehall.
53. The same to the Bailiffs of Maldon, Essex. There is yet 10*l.* in arrear of your ship-money for 1636. We require you to cause the same to be paid by the 2nd March next, or else that you attend the Board, and do not depart till you be discharged. [*Draft.* 1 *p.*]

Jan. 31. 54. The same to the Bailiff of Blandford, Dorset. To pay 25*l.* in arrear for 1636, before the first day of Easter term next, or otherwise to attend the Board. [*Draft.* ¾ *p.*]

Jan. 31. 55. The same to Bishop Davenant, of Salisbury, and the Judges of Assize for the Western Circuit, or any two of them, whereof the Bishop to be one. Sir Giles Estcourt, having purchased the churchyard belonging to the parish of St. Edmund in Salisbury, being, as he alleges, a lay fee, differences have arisen between him and the churchwardens. We require you to compose the same if it may be, or otherwise to certify the true state of the matter and your opinion. [*Draft.* 1 *p.*]

Jan. 31. 56. The same to Sir Robert Pointz, the present, and Sir Richard Ducie, the late, Sheriff of co. Gloucester. We have received your letter of the 17th inst. touching the rate assessed on the parish of Kempsford, with another petition from the inhabitants of that parish complaining of the hard hand that is still carried upon them, contrary to what your predecessor thought fit, notwithstanding he had the like certificate that you have. We send you the petition enclosed, praying you with your predecessor sheriff to reconcile the rates complained of if you can, or jointly to certify your opinion. [*Draft.* 1 *p.*]

Jan. 31. 57. The same to the Mayor of St. Albans. There is an arrear of 30*l.* from your town for ship-money for 1636. You are to pay the same by the 2nd March next, or attend the Board at that time. [*Draft.* ½ *p.*]

[Jan. 31.] 58. Petition of the inhabitants of Sleaford and Folkingham Sessions in Kesteven in co. Lincoln to the Council. The custom for raising public assessments in that co. has been to cast the whole sum into 14 parts, whereof Lindsey bears 7, Holland 3, and Kesteven 4. But Sir Anthony Irby has made his assessment thus: on Lincoln,

1637-8.

VOL. CCCLXXX.

with the members, 193*l*. 6*s*. 8*d*.; Grimsby, 15*l*.; Boston, 70*l*.; Grantham-cum-Socâ, 200*l*.; Stamford, 60*l*.; and on the body of the county, 7,566*l*. 15*s*. 7*d*.; of which sum, 2,161*l*. 18*s*. 9*d*. is imposed on the sessions of Kesteven, which with the sums imposed on Grimsby and Stamford, corporations in that division, is a surcharge of 161*l*. 8*s*. 6*d*. [*sic*]. The sheriff acknowledges the custom for assessment, but alleges that by the Lords' instructions he was first to assess the corporations, and then to divide the rest on the body of the county. Petitioners conceive that the meaning of the Lords was not to interfere with the ancient way. Pray that the 161*l*. 8*s*. 6*d*. may be taken off, and that the 260*l*. may be made up to four parts of 14 of the sum charged on the county. [*Copy. 2 pp.*]

Jan. 31. 59. The Council to [Sir Anthony Irby], Sheriff of co. Lincoln. Send the above petition. The Lords never intended to break the ancient use of assessing, and when sums set on corporations have been used to be in ease of any division, that custom should be still carefully pursued. [*Draft. 1 p.*]

Jan. 31. Clement's Inn. 60. William Thornton to Sir Edward Hussey. The Lords reading our petition, took off the surcharge of 161*l*. 18*s*. 9*d*. from Kesteven, and ordered as we desired. I shall not get the order till Monday next, nor a letter therewith to be sent to the sheriff. [*1 p.*]

Jan. 31. Whitehall. 61. The Council to the Lords of the Admiralty. It is his Majesty's pleasure to put to sea 22 ships of his own, and seven merchant ships. They are to take order for present preparing the said ships for eight months' service, to be all ready to put to sea by the 20th April. [*1 p.*]

Jan. 31. 62. Draft of the same. [*1 p.*]

Jan. 31. 63. Minute of a warrant to Sir William Uvedale to pay to George Ravenscroft, one of the keepers of the Council Chamber, 20 nobles for moneys by him disbursed for one year. [*Draft. ½ p.*]

Jan. 31. 64. Minute of a pass for Lieutenant Simon Jonson to repair into the Low Countries with his wife and his son, John Jonson. [*Draft. ½ p.*]

Jan. 31. 65. Entry of the discharge of James Master and William Bridge, aldermen of Canterbury, from further attendance on the Board. [*Draft. 3 lines.*]

Jan. 31. 66. Entry of appearance before the Council of Roger Wagget and Richard Banbury, late constables of Mutcheney [Muchelney] and Midney, Somerset, who were to remain in custody of the messenger until discharged. [*Draft. ¼ p.*]

Jan. 31. 67. Entry of the appearance of Henry Robins, of Hutton, Somerset, who is to remain in custody of the messenger until discharged. [*Draft. 4 lines.*]

Jan. 31. 68. Minute of warrant from the Council to Thomas Waterworth, messenger, to fetch up John Turnor, of Bletchingley, Surrey, Thomas Allingham and William Roker, his servants. [*¼ p.*]

DOMESTIC—CHARLES I. 213

Vol. CCCLXXX.

1637–8.
Jan. 31.
Whitehall.

Lords of the Admiralty to Officers of the Navy. Recite letter from the Council of this date, before calendared, and require the Officers of the Navy to prepare for service at sea, to be ready on the 20th April next, the Sovereign, the St. Andrew, the St. George, the Victory, the Charles, the Reformation, the Nonsuch, the Leopard, the St. Dennis, the Garland, the Entrance, the Antelope, the Adventure and the Expedition, the Providence, the Eighth Whelp, the Tenth Whelp, the Greyhound, the Roebuck, the Swan frigate, the Nicodemus frigate, and the Fortune pink, all those being King's ships; and also the Lewis, the Charles, the William and Thomas, the Recovery, the Exchange, the Reformation, and the Dolphin, being merchant ships. [*Copy. See Vol. cccliii., p. 82 b.* 1⅔ *p.*]

Jan. 31.

69. Attorney-General Bankes to Nicholas. Send me the return made from Hallingbury Magna, Essex, concerning the rate for the last shipping money, and other information touching the same, as was delivered to you by the sheriff of that county. [¾ *p.*]

Jan. 31.
Whitehall.

70. Robert Earl of Ancram to the same. I pray you to answer for me to the Lords, if I be called on for this logwood business to-day, that Mr. Herbert, to whom the Lords referred the examination, is so taken up with the Queen's business that he desires it may be put off to give the Lords his answer till about the latter end of next week. [*Seal with arms.* 1 *p.*]

Jan. 31.

71. Sir White Beconsawe to the same. There was an order from the Council, dated the 19th November 1637, to require arrears should be paid by collectors appointed in 1634. Stephen Marsh, being one of them, did not pay in 6*l*. 4*s*. accordingly, but is now willing to do so if it may be done. [*Endorsed is a memorandum that the money had been received from Marsh by Sir White.* ¼ *p.*]

Jan. 31.
Widdrington.

72. Sir William Widdrington to the same. I sent you an account of my proceeding in the ship-money last year. Upon Sunday last I received a letter from one of the messengers of the Chamber, with a copy of a warrant from the Board to command my appearance. I intend to wait on the Lords so soon as I can, considering the time of the warning and the remoteness of my abode, of which I desire you to acquaint the Board, lest I may be thought to neglect the warrant, it being of so old a date. I have written to desire the Earl Marshal, the Earl of Northumberland, and my Lord Chamberlain in the like kind. [*Seal with arms.* 1 *p.*]

Jan. 31.

73. List of causes to be heard in the Star Chamber this day. The Attorney-General *versus* John All and Francis Hunton; the same *versus* Mary Baker and others for erecting buildings contrary to proclamation, whereby the springs of water running to Whitehall and to Somerset House are putrified [*Margin, by Sec. Windebank:* "Mrs. Baker fined 1,000*l*.; the houses to be demolished"]; Thomas Browne *versus* John Borrett and others; the Attorney-General on the relation of Lord Sherrard *versus* Sir Henry Mynne for scandalous speeches of Lord Sherrard and his lady, and provocation to duels; Sir Richard Wiseman, Dame Susan his wife, and Diana his daughter

Vol. CCCLXXX.

1637-8.

versus John Stone and John Elmes, for scandal of the plaintiffs and provoking Sir Richard to fight; Henry West *versus* Martin Joyce and others. [1 *p.*]

Jan. 31.
Star Chamber.
74. Notes by Sec. Windebank of the proceedings this day in the first of the preceding causes. These are notes of the evidence for the defendant All and of the opinions of the judges. They were unanimous that there should be "no sentence." [1½ *p.*]

Jan. 31. 75. Bond of Thomas Cake, of Huntspill, Somerset, to the King, in 100*l.*, conditioned for payment to the sheriff by the last of February of ship-money in arrear to be by Cake collected in the hundred of Bempstone. [*Seal with arms.* ¾ *p.*]

Jan. 31. 76. Similar bond of Henry Robins, of Hutton, Somerset, in 50*l.*, for payment to Robert Pope, late constable of the hundred of Bempstone, the ship-money assessed upon him, and to give Pope full satisfaction for the herbage of the distress by him taken of Robins, and other charges as the sheriff shall award. [¾ *p.*]

Jan. Presentation of Luke Skippon, M.A., to the rectory of Tavistock *alias* Tawstock, in diocese of Exeter, in his Majesty's gift *pro hac vice*, by lapse, simony, or otherwise. [*Docquet.*]

Jan. Grant of an almsroom in Canterbury, void by the death of William Wotton, to John Winter for life. [*Docquet.*]

Jan. The like of an almsroom in Worcester, void by the death of George Williams, to Griffith Aboven for life. [*Docquet.*]

Jan. Grant to William Bosvile of the benefit of a bond of 500*l.* entered to his Majesty by Nehemiah Rawson and William Duncombe, conditioned for performing the orders of the commissioners of sewers for co. Lincoln, touching Sir Anthony Thomas's drainings near Boston, which he having broken to the great damage of Bosvile and others, tenants of the Earl of Lindsey, the Council thought fit they should be relieved out of the same bond. Bosvile may sue in his Majesty's name, and having levied the 500*l.* he is to satisfy himself and the other tenants of the Earl for their damages, and the overplus thereof he is to pay into the Exchequer upon just account, for performance whereof he has entered into a bond of 500*l.* [*Docquet.*]

Jan. Pardon to Thomas Higham of a fine of 100 marks, imposed upon him by the justices of the King's Bench, for striking a coachman, which fine was mitigated to 40*l.* But before the rule of mitigation was entered, the judgment for 100 marks was hastily entered and could not be amended. [*Docquet.*]

Jan. Grant, whereby his Majesty establishes a yearly pension of 1,200*l.* for ever, upon the Order of the Garter, and declares that the same shall be paid yearly to Sir Thomas Roe, Chancellor of the Order, out of the customs upon wines brought into the port of London; the pension to be employed by the Chancellor in discharge of the annual fees and pensions, payable according to constitutions made by the

1637-8.

VOL. CCCLXXX.

Sovereign and knights in full chapter. Account is to be yearly given of the moneys received and disbursed on St. George's day, and is to be examined within four days by the chapter or by three or more of the knights. His Majesty having had rents advanced by the present farmers of the duties on wines, for some time this pension cannot be paid according to his Majesty's appointment. In the meantime he authorizes the Lord Treasurer to take order for payment of the same out of some other of his Majesty's customs. [*Docquet.*]

[Jan. ?] 77. Petition of Sir Richard Strode *versus* Sir John Strode and his Confederates to the King. Petitioner had a gracious promise from your Majesty long since for a hearing in the Star Chamber, which he has diligently followed to get, but as yet cannot obtain it, as by copies of petitions annexed appears. Petitioner has the title of right heir to lands of great value, which, contrary to common law and decree of Chancery twice confirmed, have about 20 years been kept from petitioner to his damage of above 15,000*l.*, by the frauds sufficiently proved in the Star Chamber, where Sir John Strode will not confess what large gifts he paid in Lord Bacon's time for getting such strange things done in Chancery. The best of your Majesty's progenitors used to show once in their times the splendour of their justice and mercy at the hearing of some one cause in the Star Chamber, when neither of them ever had greater occasion than your Majesty has in this cause to maintain by your royal prerogative the equity of one of the chief fundamental laws of this kingdom, yet by the practice of Sir John Strode contemptuously disobeyed for above 20 years. Prays appointment of one hour in next Easter term for hearing this case. [¾ *p.*] *Annexed,*

    77. I. *Petition of the same to the same. Petitioner complains of the oppression and vexation to which he has been subjected by Sir John Strode during a litigation of 35 years in Chancery and 20 years in the Star Chamber. Sir Richard states that he had done good service to the King's content in Parliament and in the Commonwealth, and also with the hazard of his life in ordering the King's soldiers as he was commanded. Prays that his cause in the Star Chamber may be the first cause of next Easter term.* [*Copy.* ½ *p.*] *Underwritten,*

    77. I. i. *Minute of the King's pleasure that the cause be heard in Easter term without fail. Whitehall, 12th December* 1635. [*Copy.* 3 *lines.*]

    77. II. *Petition of the same to Lord Keeper Coventry, presented 30th November 1637. Recites the King's pleasure for hearing petitioner's cause in the Star Chamber in last Easter term was twelvemonth, and prays that Sir John Strode's delays may no longer put it off, Sir John being a very old man, grows weaker and weaker, but in his oppression against petitioner stronger and stronger. Prays for a hearing in the then next Hilary term.* [*Copy.* ⅓ *p.*]

Vol. CCCLXXX.

1637-8.
[Jan. ?]

78. Petition of the Gentlemen of the Privy Chamber in Ordinary to the King. Whereas it has pleased your Majesty to appoint commissioners for ordering your royal house according to the most ancient government thereof, and seeing that of all places that of the gentlemen of the Privy Chamber is most changed, we offer to your consideration seven particulars in which it is presumed that there require various alterations. They principally relate to the privacy of the Privy Chamber, the establishment of the precedency of the petitioners, allotting them places in chapel, permitting them to pass and repass with his Majesty on certain public occasions, assigning them lodging in the palace, and other similar privileges. [1 p.]

Jan.

79. The Master and Wardens of the Company of Mercers, of London, to the same. We have called a court of our company, to whom we imparted your letter of the 24th December [1637?], commanding that John Jemmat, clerk, receive no further salary for preaching at Berwick. The court in compliance ordered that a course should be taken for cessation of the said salary. A lease having been passed to Jemmat of tithes in Northumberland, some time will be requisite for avoiding thereof, for which a legal course will be requisite, which is ordered by the company, who yet have deferred to make any new election until Jemmat be fully outed by avoidance of his lease. [$\frac{2}{3}$ p.]

[Jan.]

80. Petition of the Merchants of Norwich and others trading in Norwich stuffs to the Council. There has long been a constant trade betwixt London and Norwich in sundry sorts of stuffs and stockings made in Norwich and Norfolk, which trade has always been maintained by the merchants of Norwich employing their stocks in buying the wares of the makers and sending them up weekly in carts by common carriers to London, whence they are dispersed into all parts of this kingdom, and also exported to foreign parts; in which intercourse of trade we always had our letters safely and speedily carried by our common carrier, by a horseman, not in manner of postage by change of horses, but as is usual by common carriers, and for little or no charge to us. Of late Mr. Witherings has intercepted our letters and molested our carriers, forbidding them to carry any of our letters otherwise than to go along with their carts and no faster. Petitioners explain how the sending their letters by this new way of postage will be very detrimental to their trade, which is further elucidated in certain reasons annexed. Pray that they may enjoy their ancient course of conveying letters by their common carriers. [$\frac{3}{4}$ p.] *Annexed,*

 80. I. *The reasons above alluded to, ten in number, and entitled, " Things considerable on the behalf of the merchants in Norwich, London, and elsewhere, concerning the weekly carriage of letters."* [1 p.]

[Jan.]

81. Petition of the same to the same. Petitioners on Sunday last attended the Board, and there tendered the preceding petition, which

1637-8.

Vol. CCCLXXX.

by reason of other weighty occasions could not then be read; yet our complaint being then offered to the Board, his Majesty being present, it was ordered that our common carriers should carry our letters as formerly, so it were by one horse and not in manner of postage by taking fresh horses, and we conceived the same would have been entered accordingly; but finding it altogether contrary we pray the Lords to intercede with his Majesty that the order may be entered as pronounced. [½ p.]

[Jan.] 82. Petition of Thomas Witherings to the Council. About three weeks since the posts of Norwich and Yarmouth petitioned to be released, which was granted with proviso that they should attend after the holidays, and in the meantime be conformable to the grant of the letter office by bond, which bond Grover, of Ipswich, has already forfeited. On the hearing, Mr. Hieron, counsel for the posts, cast an aspersion upon petitioner that he should say they ought not to be heard by your Lordships, which petitioner denies, and doubts not to clear himself of everything else that shall be objected to him. As the posts continue to carry letters contrary to petitioner's grant, he prays the Lords to consider the great charge he has been at in settling the conveyance of letters through England, Scotland, Ireland, and other parts beyond seas, and not to suffer the posts to continue carrying letters. [⅔ p.]

[Jan.] 83. Petition of Jason Grover to the same. Petitioner about two months ago, riding on one of his pack-horses with his pack, was arrested by the procurement of Mr. Witherings, postmaster of England for foreign parts. Petitioner remained in the messenger's custody 16 days before he came to this Board, when it was ordered that he should attend to be heard the first week in Hilary term, and in the meantime petitioner was permitted to follow his vocation. But on the 11th inst. there came a messenger and summoned petitioner to attend on Wednesday then next, all which he has punctually observed, yet Mr. Witherings threatens that he will not leave petitioner worth a groat. [¾ p.]

Jan. 84. Petition of the Bailiffs, Aldermen, Burgesses, and Commonalty of Great Yarmouth, to the same. His Majesty by warrant of the 12th instant, in contradiction to a former warrant of the 3rd inst., signified his pleasure that the salt at Yarmouth should be delivered to petitioners at 50s. per wey, but that petitioners for the matter of freight and waste should submit to such an allowance as his Majesty should award, upon which uncertainties the fishery dare not adventure, since they have offered 21s. per wey for freight and waste, which they can prove to be a very large allowance from Newcastle to Yarmouth. In regard the English contractors have not brought in any salt at all, and the Scottish refuse to deliver according to the order of Council of the 27th November, and his Majesty has commanded that petitioners make no provision of salt elsewhere, although they might be furnished with as much French salt for 6l. as the patentees will not sell under 14l., the poor fishery are in so great straight that

1637-8.

without your favour they will be utterly undone. Pray the Lords to settle the allowance for freight and waste, or else to permit the fishermen to go to sea and furnish themselves with salt where they best can. [⅔ p.]

Jan. 85. Remonstrance of the Governor and Company of the Merchant Adventurers of England to the Council, showing for what causes narrow-list coloured cloths, commonly called Spanish cloths, made in the west country, ought to be shipped from the port of London only. [1 p.]

Jan. 86. Answer and petition of the Merchants of Exeter to the allegations of those merchants of London that would have no Spanish cloth shipped out of any port of England save only from London. [*This and the preceding paper with the two which follow contain full statements of the arguments on both sides of the question, which was determined by the order of Council of the 24th inst., calendared in the present volume at p. 185.* 1 p.]

Jan. 87. Petition of Thomas Samford and 16 others, makers of Spanish cloth, of Tiverton, Cullompton, Kensbere [Kentisbeare], Broadhembury, Plymtree, Uffculme, and other parts of Devon, to Bishop Hall, of Exeter, and the Justices of Peace of the same county. Set forth the question in dispute between petitioners and the cloth merchants of London, and pray the persons addressed to be a means by letters to the Council for prevention of the engrossing project of the London merchants. [*Signed and sealed by the petitioners.* 1 p.]

Jan. 88. Bishop Hall, of Exeter, with Sir Edward Seymour, Sir George Chudleigh, and 10 others, Justices of Peace of co. Devon, to the Council. On behalf of the preceding petitioners, and deprecating on grounds fully stated any interference with the free trade which the western clothiers have so long enjoyed. [1 p.]

Jan. 89. Petition of Frances Jason and her two daughters, the unhappy mother of Robert Jason, now prisoner in the Fleet, to the same. Petitioner's unnatural son, in pursuit of his former intention, resolves to remain in prison rather than relieve petitioner and his sisters with their dues, having taken rooms in the Old Bailey, and there settled his family, and petitioner and her daughters heavily suffering through want. Prays relief. [½ p.]

Jan. 90. Duplicate of the same. [½ p.]

[Jan. ?] 91. Petition of Richard Mostin to the same. Petitioner being possessed of a tenement in Cororion, co. Carnarvon, worth 20l. per annum, for a term of years determinable on the lives of himself and his wife, who is still living, executed a mortgage for 30l. to William Griffith, which mortgage was assigned to Humfrey Jones, who afterwards advanced 50l. more. It ultimately turned out that the money advanced by Jones was really that of the Bishop of Lincoln, and the land was thereupon taken under an extent for the bishop's fine.

1637-8.

Vol. CCCLXXX.

Petitioner prays that he may continue tenant to his Majesty upon security to pay his Majesty's rent according to the rate. [1 p.]

Jan. 92. Officers of the Navy to the Lords of the Admiralty. According to directions, we present a particular of the fees belonging to our places, and which is really the value of all that accrues unto us; of so small consequence, considering the condition of these times and the great increase of our charge, as hath enforced our address to you to intercede to his Majesty for a better supportance. [1 p.]

Jan. 93. John Hill to Sir John Lambe. Communicates various particulars of a supposed simoniacal contract in relation to a presentation to a living, perhaps that of Shearsby. [1 p.]

Jan. 94. Articles objected by the Commissioners for causes ecclesiastical against Marie Noble, wife of Michael Noble, town clerk of Lichfield. Lady Eleanor Davies, from about Midsummer 1636 till near Michaelmas following, lodged at the Angel at Lichfield, and the said Marie Noble, with Susan Walker, wife of John Walker, clerk, resorted to the said lady daily, and had continual private conference with her, and took her to the cathedral, at first unto a seat in the quire where gentlewomen use to kneel and sit, and afterwards to a seat adjoining the bishop's throne, appointed for the wives of the bishop, dean, and canons, and although forewarned and a lock set thereupon, yet the said Marie kept the said seat for herself, and called it her own. At another time Mrs. Noble going into a seat appointed for the canons' wives, and meeting Margaret Twisden, now Mrs. Pelsant, at the entrance into the seat, she took her by the shoulders, and pulled her back again, and threw her about, and quarrelled and brawled there to the disturbance of the congregation. Lady Davies removed from the Angel to the house of John Walker in the Cathedral Close, and there wrote her book called "The Appeal to the Throne," and sent the same to the Bishop of Lichfield, and afterwards went into the bishop's throne and sat there, and said she was primate and metropolitan. She also with a pot of water, tar, and other filthy things, most profanely defiled the hangings at the altar of the cathedral, and said she had sprinkled holy water upon them against their next communion; and that Mrs. Noble and Mrs. Walker countenanced the same, and said that Lady Davies would better justify that filthy act than those that caused the hangings to be put up. Mrs Walker being required to put away Lady Davies out of her house, promised to do so, but did not; and being asked by Lady Weston, wife of Sir Simon Weston, wherefore Lady Davies would so wrong herself, replied that Lady Davies had but done her conscience, and that what she had done she would better justify than them that had set up the candlesticks and hangings, and said she would Mr. Latham was as well able to justify what he had done there as Lady Davies. [3 pp.]

Jan. 95. Note by Nicholas of public businesses left unfinished in January 1637-8. 1. Ships to be sent against the pirates of Algiers; the committee has not yet made report. 2. The business concerning

Vol. CCCLXXX.

1637–8.

castles and forts not yet taken into consideration. 3. Ting, constable of Fyfield, Essex, is prisoner in the Fleet and under the Attorney-General's examination. 4. Josias Wood, constable of the hundred of Harlow, Essex, prisoner in Newgate. 5. Mr. Solicitor is to give account what he has done in the business of starch. 6. Capt. Duppa is to answer complaint of the brewers of London, that they cannot have malt sufficient to make beer. [¾ p.]

[Jan. ?] 96. Sir Francis Asteley, Sheriff of Norfolk, to the Council. At a meeting at the Guildhall of Norwich on the 16th November 1637, the chief magistrates of that city and of the several boroughs of Great Yarmouth, Thetford, and Castle Rising, with myself, being present, the sum of 7,800*l.* charged upon the said county for ship-money was thus divided: Norwich, 400*l.*; King's Lynn, 200*l.*; Great Yarmouth, 220*l.*; Thetford, 30*l.*; Castle Rising, 10*l.*; and upon the body of the county 6,940*l.*, which last sum is assessed in the manner following. There ensues a statement of the amount charged upon every parish in the county, and how much thereof the clergyman was to pay on account of his ecclesiastical and how much for his temporal estate. [34 *pp.*]

[Jan. ?] 97. Return by Sir Anthony Irby of the assessment made upon the whole of the co. of Lincoln, exclusive of the city and the boroughs. In the return the several parishes are thrown into hundreds, and there is stated the name of the parish, the sum assessed upon it, the name of the clergyman, how much assessed upon him for his ecclesiastical and how much for his temporal estate, and where the rectory was impropriate the name of the farmer. [14 *pp.*]

[Jan.?] 98. Similar return by William Thomas, Sheriff of co. Carnarvon, of the assessment of the ship-money made upon that county. The parish and the amount to be levied are stated. It is added that the clergy in Carnarvonshire hold little or no lands or means temporal, and as for their spiritual they are very moderately taxed, being assessed but a third part of what the laity pay. [*Strip of parchment.* = 4 *pp.*]

[Jan.] 99. General statement of similar assessment for the hundreds and corporate towns in co. Northampton, certified by Sir John Hanbury, sheriff. Peterborough was assessed at 120*l.*, Northampton at 200*l.*, Daventry and Brackley at 50*l.* each, and Higham Ferrers at 36*l.* [1 *p.*]

[Jan.] 100. Certificate of Sir Robert Banister, late Sheriff of co. Northampton, that during his shrievalty he could not get the constables of Warkworth to make any assessment of ship-money, whereby he was enforced to endeavour to levy it by distress, but the constables refused to aid his bailiffs; since which time he is informed they have collected most part of the money and yet refuse to make payment thereof. Their names are William Taylor and George [Goodridge] Wilson. [*Underwritten is a confirmatory certificate from Edward Harrison, the bailiff employed to distrain.* 1 *p.*]

Vol. CCCLXXX.

1637–8.
[Jan. ?] 101. Petition of William Taylor and Goodridge Wilson, the constables mentioned in the last article, to the Council. On the complaint of Sir Robert Banister have been sent for by a messenger, in whose custody they remain. They are poor ignorant, illiterate men. They submit themselves very humbly, and pray the Council to remit their offence and discharge them. [1 p.]

[Jan. ?] 102. Notes of assignments of a pension or other payment of 50l. per annum out of Exchequer, granted by King James by letters patent of the 3rd November 1610 to John London, and by him assigned to Alexander Glover and John Rowden. [½ p.]

Vol. CCCLXXXI. February 1–12, 1637–8.

1637–8.
Feb. 1. Petition of the Sub-dean and Prebendaries of the King's collegiate church of St. Peter, Westminster, to the King. Petitioners, as well for keeping the scholars of the free school founded in the said church by his Majesty from straying into the town in the night season, as for the safety of themselves and other inhabitants within the close, as also for preventing disorders formerly committed, have ordered their porter to lock the gates of the close by ten o'clock, according to the ancient statute and laudable custom of all cathedral and collegiate churches. Some of the inhabitants pretending a late liberty of free ingress and egress at all hours, have thereupon attempted to break down the gates and have assaulted a servant of petitioners. Pray his Majesty to signify his pleasure that the inhabitants of the close and others shall conform to the said order. [*Copy. See Vol. cccxxiii., p. 234. ½ p.*] *Underwritten,*

> I. *His Majesty being highly displeased at these disorders, commands that the gates of the close shall be shut at 10 o'clock, and that the inhabitants shall conform to that order, and not presume to disturb "this court" or offer violence to the servants of the college, upon pain of severe punishment.* [*Copy. Ibid. ⅓ p.*]

Feb. 1. 1. Edward Bishop, late Bailiff of Wenlock, to the Council. In
Wenlock. answer to the Lords' letter of 21st January last (*see Vol. ccclxxix., No. 38*), 298l. 14s. 8d., part of the 302l. therein mentioned, was paid to Sir William Russell on the 9th January last. The residue, being 3l. 5s. 4d., Morton Briggs, John Reynolds *alias* Mason, and John Croft were certified for refusing to pay, since which Reynolds and Croft have paid, being 18s. 8d., which the writer has also paid to the Treasurer. The residue (2l. 6s. 8d.) due from Briggs he has been required to pay or enter bond to appear before the Council. He said that he would answer the matter, but would neither pay the money nor give any such bond. [1 p.]

Vol. CCCLXXXI.

1637–8.
Feb. 1.
Orchard
[Portman].

2. Sir William Portman, Sheriff of Somerset, to the Council. Has forborne to bind over certain collectors to appear, mentioned in a letter of the Lords, not knowing their names, and being assured by Mr. Hodges and Mr. Mallet, late sheriffs, that they would conform without further troubling the Lords. The Lords gave directions for a general review of the rates of the county, which is taken advantage of to defer payment of the last assessments. Suggests a direction of the Lords that no division should take the benefit of any review until they satisfy their rates now imposed. [*Seal with arms.* 1 *p.*]

[Feb. 1.]

3. Petition of the Company of Brewers of the city of London to the same. Lately petitioners made a contract with the Board of Green Cloth to serve his Majesty's household with 1,700 tons of ale and beer, amounting to 3,000*l.* per annum. But by reason there is a restraint of making malts without licence, petitioners cannot get sufficient malts, and also malts is grown so dear that most of petitioners are not able to brew any longer, to their utter undoing and that of many thousands of poor people. Pray that forasmuch as the fit season of making malts will speedily be past, and for want of malting much barley will be spoiled, and the merchants be discouraged from bringing in any more foreign corn for relief of the commonwealth's necessity, the Lords will recommend the suit of petitioners to his Majesty, that speedy course be taken for their supply and relief. [*Signed by 45 petitioners.* 1 *p.*]

Feb. 1.

4. Sir Henry Marten to Lord Chief Justice Finch. There is a rule given for a prohibition in a cause depending in the Admiralty between Thomas Flute, master of a ship, and Simon Plusher and John Dubois, Dutchmen. Flute will make known the state of his cause. Two things only I would recommend to your consideration : one, that Flute being circumvented in the delivery of a wedge of silver is like to be undone, and the other concerns the jurisdiction of the Admiralty and "states of merchants and masters of ships," betwixt whom bills of lading are almost the only evidence of authority to receive or deliver merchandises, the cognizance whereof cannot be denied to the Admiralty without great inconvenience. I know you and your colleagues will do nothing but right, and I hope you conceive that I have no other end but the desire to do his Majesty service and the commonwealth in the place which I hold. [*Copy.* 1⅔ *p.*]

Feb. 1.

5. Richard Wyan to Nicholas. By direction of Sir Henry Marten I send you the petition enclosed. Do what good office you can in it, for it concerns not only the ruin of a poor seafaring man, but a most dangerous breach in the jurisdiction of the Admiralty. If it be not prevented the prohibition will pass on Saturday. [¾ *p.*] *Enclosed,*

  5. i. *Petition of Thomas Flute to the Lords of the Admiralty. In January* 1636–7 *petitioner being master of the Jeremy,*

1637-8.

Vol. CCCLXXXI.

of London, then being at St. Lucar, received from Samuel Crocker, an English merchant resident there, a wedge or bar of silver consigned to John Parr, a merchant of London, and a letter directed to Parr with the bill of lading enclosed. The ship arriving in the Downs petitioner sent up his merchants' letters to London by his purser, who, according to use, gave notice upon the exchange where the merchants' letters brought in the said ship were, and there the merchants went and received their letters. But Parr being out of London his letters were intercepted and broken open, and the bill of lading came to the hands of Simon Plusher, a Dutchman, dwelling in London. Plusher pretended a letter from Parr, and ultimately sent John Dubois, a Dutchman dwelling at Canterbury, who received the silver out of the ship at Dover pier, delivered up the bill of lading, and gave a receipt for it for the use of Parr. Petitioner has been sued by Crocker in the Court of Admiralty and condemned to pay 290l. and 10l. costs. Petitioner on process of the Admiralty apprehended Plusher and Dubois, and the cause being ready for sentence they have moved in the Common Pleas for a prohibition to remove the cause from the Admiralty to Common Law. Petitioner prays the Lords to send to the Justices of the Common Pleas not to grant the said prohibition. [¾ p.]

Feb. 1.   6. Abstract of the petition of Thomas Flute to the Lords of the Admiralty above calendared. [¾ p.]

Feb. 1.
Aldermanbury.   7. Humphrey Oneby and Thomas Briggs to the Officers of Ordnance. Have made trial of divers bags of a quantity of Barbary saltpetre, only by seeing it burn. We cannot set any certain valuation upon it, but it is unrefined saltpetre of Barbary, of the same sort as has been formerly brought in from that country. [¾ p.]

Feb. 1.
Whitehall.   8. Sec. Coke to [Sir William Boswell?]. His Majesty has been informed that complaint was made to you by Madame and the Princesses of Phalsbourg, that the honour of the Duke of Lorraine, their brother and his Majesty's near kinsman, suffered much by the translation of an *Arrêt* of the Parliament of Paris into English, and the permission thereof to be published here. You may assure those princesses that no such thing was permitted by his Majesty's knowledge; no, nor with the knowledge of the State here, or any of his Majesty's Council. His Majesty gave present order for the imprisonment of the printers, who have continued in restraint at least twenty days. His Majesty's care has also taken this order, that there shall no such books be permitted to be printed without due examination, and hereof you will do well to give notice to those princesses, who, if they be herewith satisfied, will express their contentment, and desire the enlargement of the poor men, who otherwise

Vol. CCCLXXXI.

1637-8.

will be undone. This business reflecting upon your honest friend and servant Mr. Weckherlin, you will use therein the more care to make a speedy return. There is one Fortescue here, conceived to be a priest, but professes now to me that he is employed as agent for the Duke of Lorraine (see Vol. ccclxxvii., No. 112), though till this day I never heard of him, or of his employment. This man, though he confesses that this error was committed three or four years since, now on the sudden, when it was no more spoken of, presses it very much, by whose instigation I know not. No man shall be more ready to do those princesses right than myself, and I dare assure you that Weckherlin did herein mistake himself out of no ill affection, but by a little in these novelties complying with the time. [*In the handwriting of Weckherlin.* 1½ *p.*]

Feb. 1.   9. Petition of Edward Fenner, of Egerton, Kent, pailmaker, to Archbishop Laud. John Fenner, now prisoner in the Gatehouse, has many times endeavoured to persuade petitioner to separate from the Church of England, and once got him excommunicated. Further, Edward Fenner, father of the said John and Edward, since the imprisonment of the said John, dying, has made petitioner his sole executor. John not prevailing with petitioner to join him in separation has thereupon sought to molest him, and since the death of their father has threatened his undoing, and practised to raise suits against him. Prays that his brother may be restrained. [¾ *p.*] *Underwritten,*

> 9. I. *Reference to Mr. Kt. [Knight?] to take care that this petition be read in Court this present afternoon. 1st February 1637-8.* [¼ *p.*]

Feb. 1.   10. Petition of Richard Emery, bookseller, to the same. Your Grace with others of the Council made an order in the Star Chamber about Midsummer last, concerning brokers and others selling books that had not served apprentice to a bookseller. Yet divers persons in London daily buy and sell books to the great disenabling of those that have served their time. Desires an order therein for relief of petitioners and others of that society. [½ *p.*] *Underwritten,*

> 10. I. *Reference to Sir John Lambe to give an account of petitioner's suggestions, that further order may be taken. 1st February 1637-8.* [¼ *p.*]

Feb. 1.   11. Note of papers sent to the Attorney-General concerning the parishioners of Hallingbury Magna, Essex (see Vol. ccclxxx., No. 69). [*Endorsed,* "The papers are returned." ⅓ *p.*]

Feb. 1.   12. "Petitions and papers delivered over" this day [on change of the clerk of the Council in attendance]. [¾ *p.*]

Feb. 2.   Petition of Marie Viscountess Molineux, on behalf of herself and younger children, to the King. Richard Lord Molineux, her late husband, charged divers of his lands with an annuity of 100*l.* per

1637-8.   VOL. CCCLXXXI.

annum from his decease for the life of Cecil Molineux, his younger son, and also 100*l*. apiece for his two daughters, to be paid within a year after his death. Petitioner had for her jointure, amongst other lands, the tithes of Knowsley Barn, co. Lancaster, of the value of 100*l*. per annum; yet Lord Strange has, since her husband's decease, which is now almost two years, withheld the same from her, and the annuity for her son and portions for her daughters are also withheld from them. Out of respect to Lord Strange, into whose family her son is matched, and to prevent suits, petitioner addressed herself to his Majesty for relief. He referred the business to Archbishop Laud, the Lord Keeper, and Lord Treasurer, before whom petitioner produced her deed of jointure. It was pretended that Lord Strange's writings were in the country, whereupon the Lords gave him till before Michaelmas term to produce them, and directed speed to be used in raising the children's portions; none of which had been done, and Lord Strange had got the time for producing the deed enlarged until Easter term. Prays the King to direct a shorter day within a month after this term. [*Copy. See Vol. cccxxiii., p.* 235. 1 *p.*] *Underwritten*,

    I. *Minute of the King's pleasure that Lord Strange is to have his writings ready to be produced on the 14th March next, when the referees shall meet for determining this cause. Whitehall, 2nd February* 1637-8. [*Copy. Ibid., p.* 236. ¼ *p.*]

Feb. 2.   Petition of Samuel Whichcott, one of the clerks and attorneys of the Court of King's Bench, to the King. Upon a *quo warranto* prosecuted by the Attorney-General against Shrewsbury, the town being conscious of many miscarriages occasioned by the popular government, and fearing the forfeiture of their liberties, submitted themselves to your Majesty, and became petitioners for a new charter, which is drawing up. Forasmuch as the present town-clerk is an aged man, and petitioner is an inhabitant of the town, and by reason of education and practice in the law capable of the said place, he beseeches a grant of the reversion of the place, and warrant to the Attorney-General, that the same may be inserted in the new charter. [*Copy. Ibid.* ½ *p.*] *Underwritten*,

    I. *Reference to the Attorney-General to take special order that there be a sufficient grant to the petitioner inserted in the charter as desired. Whitehall, 2nd February* 1637-8. [*Copy. Ibid.* ¼ *p.*]

Feb. 2.
Kingston-upon-Hull.

13. James Watkinson, mayor, and nine others of Kingston-upon-Hull to the Council. The extreme distress of this town, by reason of the visitation of the plague ever since the 15th July last, and which still continues, constrains us again to address you. Upon our petition in December last, you directed your letters to the justices of peace of the three ridings of Yorkshire, requiring them to take order for a convenient contribution for relief of our visited persons, as also to the Vice-President and Council in the North for

1637-8.

VOL. CCCLXXXI.

such contributions from York and all corporations in Yorkshire as our condition required. The West Riding have ordered to be given but 200*l.* in all, the North Riding but 63*l.* 6*s.* 8*d.*, and the East Riding nothing at all, but have wholly withdrawn their former weekly relief of 60*l.* The corporations having given such very small benevolences and no weekly relief, all the sums thus given will not amount to that which we had before distributed over and above the assessments raised in this town, so that by discontinuance of the East Riding contribution of 60*l.* weekly, though a far greater sum would scarce have been sufficient, there being about 2,500 necessitous persons, who cannot be relieved under eighteenpence a head per week, the condition of this town is much more miserable than formerly. Therefore we are again forced to beseech you to enjoin the justices and corporations of Yorkshire to raise such additions to the said benevolences as may be reasonable, such supply to continue so long as the inhabitants shall be restrained of their liberty of commerce and trading, otherwise this town is in danger to be ruined, and the country endangered, if the necessitous persons should break forth into outrageous courses to purvey for themselves. [*Poor impression of corporate seal.* 2 *pp.*]

Feb. 2. 14. Application of Richard Paxford, gunner, for a supply of harbour stores for 16 ships about to remain in harbour. [½ *p.*]

Feb. 2. 15. W. Reade to Mr. Burden. Has not yet spoken with Hugh Lee, but his kinsman Mr. Gibson said he would be with Reade in Lent. Sends copies of letters patent, wherein the rectory of Queeniborough is granted. Begs him to show it to Sir John Lambe. It is worth two years' purchase more for the freedom of the tenure. Mr. Page, who is the owner of the rectory, is an inconstant man to deal with, therefore he must be taken "in the tip." The rectory will hold the rent Mr. Bennet informed you; it is the likelier to improve, as the townsmen are good husbands and the soil very good, albeit there be two sand fields, yet they are very profitable for corn. [½ *p.*] *Annexed,*

> 15. I. *Extract from the grant above alluded to. It is from the 10th part of Rot. Pat., 3rd Edward VI.* [*Latin.* ¾ *p.*]

Feb. 3. 16. Petition of Sir Henry Vane, Comptroller of the Household, to the King. By privy seal, dated 7th July 1630, you settled the savings upon the ordinary assignment of the house towards payment of the great surplusages owing in the same, by reason of extraordinary expenses for the Queen's marriage, and the entertainment of ambassadors. Whilst I was employed as ambassador extraordinary in Germany there was spent out of the ordinary assignment, contrary to the said privy seal, 6,719*l.* 18*s.* 8*d.* [*sic*], viz., for the prince, 1,512*l.* 2*s.* 6½*d.*; for Princess Mary, 3,828*l.* 11*s.* 6½*d.*; and for ambassadors and marriages, 1,369*l.* 4*s.* 7*d.*; all which was done by Sir Marmaduke Darrel, late cofferer, with consent of the Officers of the Greencloth, upon the

1637-8.

VOL. CCCLXXXI.

promise of the late Lord Treasurer and the now Chancellor of the Exchequer of repaying the same out of the Exchequer, which promise has not been performed. Prays order to the Lord Treasurer and Chancellor of the Exchequer that the 6,719l. 18s. 8d., and for the ensuing time all extraordinary expenses, may be paid out of the Exchequer according to the privy seal; and that particular persons who have debts owing to them upon the surplusage of your father's house may not by private suits get payment out of the Exchequer, as divers did in the time of the late Lord Treasurers Marlborough and Portland, before your servants be paid their wages, and the country their compositions, which irregularities tend to your great disservice and danger of paying the said debts twice, and also to the great disorder of your accountants, both in the household and Exchequer. [4 pp.] *Underwritten,*

 16. I. *Reference to the Lord Keeper, Lord Treasurer, and Lord Cottington to settle a course in this business, both for the time past and to come; and for the 6,717l. 18s. 8d., to arrange for petitioner's satisfaction as they shall think fit. Whitehall, 3rd February* 1637-8. [1 p.] *Annexed,*

 16. II. *Account of money paid out of the Exchequer to purveyors and others who had debts owing them in his Majesty's house upon their particular suits to Lord Treasurer Marlborough. Total,* 8,875l. 18s. 9d. [⅔ p.]

Feb. 3.
The King's Commission House, Fleet Street.

17. Copy order of the Commissioners for management of the King's Estate, as Prince of Wales, attested by Robert Tipper, their clerk. Orders having been made for the attendance of the mayor and burgesses of Newcastle-upon-Tyne, to compound for ground lying between high and low water mark of the said river, Mr. Liddell and Mr. Riddell, on behalf of the said mayor and burgesses, informed the Board that by several charters the said mayor and burgesses hold the said ground of his Majesty, with liberty to erect wharfs there, and the power of the conservancy of the river, upon preservation whereof depend the town and the coal trade, and that if any other should be admitted, upon any new composition, to obtain a pretence of a new title from his Majesty it would engage the town in a multiplicity of suits and overthrow the trade. It was ordered that if any person desire to compound for any part of the said ground, notice be given to the said mayor and burgesses. [1⅓ p.]

[Feb. 3.]

18. Statement of the title of the Mayor and Burgesses of Newcastle-upon-Tyne to the ground mentioned in the preceding article, of the purposes to which the same is put, and of the consequences which would result from any person being permitted to obtain any grant or hold an inquisition respecting the same. [1 p.]

Feb. 3.

19. Bill in the Star Chamber in the cause of Henry Jackson, of Newcastle-upon-Tyne, against the Mayor and Commonalty of Newcastle-upon-Tyne, Sir Thomas Riddell, Sir Peter Riddell, Robert

Vol. CCCLXXXI.

1637-8.

Shaftoe, Leonard Carr, Abraham Booth, Thomas Jackson, William Mills, Joseph Wray, Gabriel Clincard, John Thompson, and —— Matchett. The accusation against the defendants was that they had colourably preferred an indictment for forgery against William Mills, in order to protect him from punishment for forging a warrant in the name of Robert Shaftoe, then sheriff of Newcastle, under which warrant Robert Cooke was arrested, at the suit of John Robinson, on a plea of trespass. [*Copy.* 10 *pp.*]

[Feb. 3?]
20. Plea and demurrer of the Mayor and Burgesses of Newcastle to the bill of Henry Jackson, above calendared. They plead that they are not described in the said bill by their proper corporate title, and are therefore not bound to answer, and they demur on the ground that an indictment for forgery could be no colour of protection to Mills from question or punishment. [*Copy.* 5 *pp.*]

Feb. 3.
Whitehall.
21. Notes by Nicholas of business to be transacted by the Lords of the Admiralty. Consider Mr. Crane's account for victualling ships set forth in 1636. Appoint a carpenter for the Reformation in place of one lately dead. The purser of the Vanguard has surrendered his place; the Officers of the Navy recommend John Blounden to succeed him, being Mr. Edisbury's clerk. Mr. Awdry desires warrant for a last of gunpowder for Wilts. Consider Emerson's petition and Robert Stranke's affidavit touching saltpetre. Hear read a draft of your order touching ship carpenters. [*The Lord Treasurer has added "Mr. Clarke." ¾ p.*]

Feb. 3.
Whitehall.
Order of the Commissioners of Saltpetre and Gunpowder. There is a quantity of saltpetre in the hands of the East India Company, whereof there is occasion to make use for the King's service. Ordered that Samuel Cordewell and Mr. Blithe certify the true quantity, quality, and value of the same. [*Copy. See Vol. ccxcii., p. 74. ½ p.*]

Feb. 3.
Whitehall.
The Lords of the Admiralty to Montjoy Earl of Newport. We received order from the Council, dated the 31st January last, for setting forth 22 ships therein named. We pray you to give order that they be provided with ordnance and gunners' stores for eight months' service at sea, and that they be ready to put to sea by the 20th April next; the charge to be borne on the estimate for setting forth the great fleet next spring with the moneys payable from the counties. [*Copy. See Vol. cccliii., fol.* 85. ¾ *p.*]

Feb. 3.
Whitehall.
The same to Capt. Thomas Ketelby, of the Swallow. Appointment as admiral of the ships employed for guard of the coast of Ireland. [*Copy. Ibid., fol.* 86. ½ *p.*]

Feb. 3.
Whitehall.
The same to Capt. Richard Owen. Appointment as captain in the Ninth Whelp, employed on the coast of Ireland under Capt. Thomas Ketelby as admiral. [*Copy. Ibid., fol.* 86. ½ *p.*]

Feb. 3.
Whitehall.
Order of Lords of the Admiralty upon the account of John Crane, Surveyor of Marine Victuals. Allowance being demanded by him

1637-8.   VOL. CCCLXXXI.

for cask and biscuit bags expended in several of his Majesty's ships, of which the Officers of the Navy made question. It was ordered that the Officers of the Navy and the Auditors of the Imprest should certify what has been the practice concerning allowances of that nature, and attend the Lords with such certificates on Saturday next. [*Copy. See Vol. cccliii., fol. 86 b.* ½ *p.*]

Feb. 3.   22. Petition of Roger Dack, purser; Nicholas Spearman, boatswain; and John Fortescue, gunner of the Red Lion, to Lords of the Admiralty. Petitioners allege their long service, and that for better discharge of their duties they have had and have apprentices whom they have made fit for his Majesty's service. The Red Lion having become unserviceable, they pray for similar places in the next ship that shall be built, and that in the interim they may be allowed the like wages and victuals as they had in the Red Lion, and that their apprentices may from time to time be entered on board some of his Majesty's ships until petitioners be again employed. [¾ *p.*]   *Underwritten,*

22. I. *Reference to the Officers of the Navy to certify what is the practice touching present allowance in such case. Whitehall, 3rd February* 1637. [*Unsigned, and probably superseded by the order next calendared.* ¼ *p.*]

Feb. 3.   Order of the Lords of the Admiralty on the above petition. That petitioners should be appointed to the similar places that should first become vacant in ships of the second rank, or in the next ship of the second or third rank that should be built. [*Copy. See Vol. cccliii., fol.* 95. ½ *p.*]

Feb. 3.   23. Draft of the above order. [¼ *p.*]

Feb. 3.   24. Lord Chief Justice Finch to Archbishop Laud. He was very desirous to have waited on the archbishop and have given him an account of a business that happened in the Court of Common Pleas on the Thursday then last, but the Queen's Council, the ceremonies of Gray's Inn, which lasted till night, and illness had prevented him. There was a motion made by counsel for the last Lord Wotton's Lady, for a prohibition to stay proceedings in the High Commission Court against one that is incumbent of Pawlsbury [Paulerspury], or some such name in Northamptonshire. That which was alleged to induce the court to grant it was this. A former incumbent was convicted of simony, and so his institution and induction by law void, whereupon this present incumbent was instituted and inducted, against whom articles are exhibited in the High Commission to question and avoid his incumbency, as was alleged, merely as a superinstitution, and that they were denied a copy of the articles. So they made the ground of their motion double, one for denying the copy of the articles, the other for endeavouring to make the institution of the former incumbent good, which by the statute is made void. I assure myself you are very confident that no man ever sat on a bench that was more tender how he invaded the jurisdiction of other courts especially those of ecclesiastical cognizance; and for the High Commission court, I know (as I then openly said) that it is a court of a

1637-8.

high and eminent nature, and it behoved us to be very wary of granting prohibitions to stop that court, and it might well be the former incumbent was justly deprived, and this one deserves the same censure too. The court would not grant any prohibition nor make any order for stay of proceedings upon the merit of the cause, for that none, as I remember, was there to answer the motion. But in regard oath was made that they could not have the articles, and for that it was said unless some stay were for the present it would be too late to grant a prohibition, though there should appear just cause, the court made a rule for stay of proceedings till the articles might be had, in which case those of the court that are better experienced than myself said it was never denied. I have given you such an account as my memory in a business unexpectedly moved will give me leave. I was a little troubled at the motion, being the first that was ever made since I sat in that court, concerning any proceedings in that high court. [*Seal with crest.* 1¾ *p.*]

Feb. 3. 25. Sir William Parkhurst, Sir Abraham Williams, Lawrence Whitaker, Edward Norgate, and Capt. James Duppa, Commissioners for Brewing, to the Council. On the 2nd instant they received from the Lords a petition of the brewers of London preferred to the Council (*see No.* 3), alleging their want of malt, and the cause to be the restraining the maltsters to malt without allowance. The maltsters which usually furnish the city converted as much barley into malt before Christmas last as they could get at dear rates. Since their restraining barley is much fallen in price, and yet there is still a scarcity of barley in the eastern parts of the kingdom. Notwithstanding the restraint the greater part make malt underhand; so that the petition is rather clamorous than well grounded in that point. The true cause of their wants (if any such be) is the last frost, and after the breaking up of the frost, a flood of waters; during the former no one could malt, and during the latter the barges could neither go nor come. There is no fear but that after the fall of the waters their wants will be supplied. As for the importation of foreign barley, the commissioners conceive that, notwithstanding the restraint, the merchant will seek his profit, and they state that of late two merchants that brought in 1,000 quarters of barley desired leave to malt it and compounded for doing so, as the maltsters should have done, whereupon the commissioners conclude that that part of the complaint is as ill grounded as the former. [1 *p.*]

Feb. 3. 26. Examination of Thomas Hogan, of the order of St. Francis, calling himself Don Juan de Castro. He was designed chaplain to the Conde de Humanes, who was to have been ambassador here from the King of Spain, but he dying, Hogan became chaplain to the Spanish ambassador now here. He has been in England three years, and has been sometimes to present himself to the superior of his order here, but could never find him. Has not been in Ireland these 30 years. Has spent all his time in Spain, saving the time he has been in England. [½ *p.*]

VOL. CCCLXXXI.

1637–8.
Feb. 3.   27. Memorandum that Francis Creswick, Giles Elbridge, Thomas Colston, and Miles Jackson may be ordered to appear before the Council on the 13th inst. [½ p.] *Annexed,*

    27. I. *Nicholas to the [Mayor of Bristol?]. To warn the above-named persons described as merchants to attend his Majesty and the Council on 13th inst., touching matters in difference between them and William Murray. [Draft. ⅔ p.]*

Feb. 3.   28. Two papers against the right of the Wickhams of Swalcliffe to be regarded as of kin to William of Wykeham, the founder of New College and of Winchester College. One is entitled, "The arguments which disprove the pretence of the petitioners," and the other, "An answer to the presumptions and conjectures of the petitioners." [*Endorsed by Archbishop Laud as received this day.* 4¾ pp.]

Feb. 3.   See "Papers relating to Appointments in the Navy."

Feb. 4.   29. The King to Archbishop Laud, Archbishop Neile, of York, and
Westminster. to the rest of the Commissioners of the Court of High Commission. We are given to understand that divers disorderly persons have withdrawn themselves from their obedience to our ecclesiastical laws into several ways of separation, sects, schisms, and heresies, and being convented for the same or for other misdemeanours before you our commissioners, are grown to that obstinacy that some refuse to take their oaths, and others, being sworn, refuse to answer to the articles objected unto them. Now forasmuch as you are authorized by our letters patent, and your proceedings are not only according to the manner of the civil or canon laws, but with some relation also to the form of proceeding used in our Courts of Star Chamber, Chancery, Court of Requests, and Exchequer, therefore we declare and appoint that all persons legally called into our High Commission shall be enjoined to take their corporal oaths and to answer to such articles, and if any persons out of their perverse will shall refuse, and after monition shall persist in this obstinacy, every such person shall be declared *pro confesso,* and shall be held as confessed and convicted of all those articles, and these letters shall be a sufficient warrant in that behalf. [*Impression of the signet.* 1¼ p.]

Feb. 4.   30. Copy of the same. [3 *pp.*]

Feb. 4.   31. Petition of Hugh Rigby on behalf of Gilbert Ireland, his Majesty's ward, to the Council. Recites previous petition to stay the proceedings of the citizens of Chester against the inhabitants of Gloverstone, with the order thereon (*see Vol. ccclxxiv., No.* 15) and the subsequent letter of the corporation of Chester (*see Vol. ccclxxviii, No.* 77), on which, in order to wait the result of the reference to the Earl of Derby and the judges, the business was adjourned until the end of Easter term. Petitioner contends that this adjournment was unfairly procured, and a great prejudice to himself and the country, and prays that the reference to the Earl of Derby and the

1637-8.

Vol. CCCLXXXI.

judges may be enlarged so as to comprehend all the questions in dispute. [¾ p.]

Feb. 4. 32. Petition of Thomas Combes and the rest of the owners of the Exchange, of Southampton, to the Lords of the Admiralty. Having victualled and manned the said ship ready to set sail to Newfoundland, at a charge of 700*l.*, petitioners pray that she and her crew may be free from any press. [1 p.] *Annexed*,

32. I. *Names of the crew of the Exchange, 33 in number.* [¾ p.]

Feb. 4. 33. Declarations of Lewis Harris, formerly under-sheriff of co. Oxford, concerning the account of the arrears for shipping in the years when Sir Peter Wentworth and Sir Francis Norris were in succession sheriffs of co. Oxford. Harris strives to make it appear that the remissness in collection of the arrears in Sir Peter Wentworth's year was not his fault, but that of the sheriff, and he specially instances Lillingstone-Lovell, where Sir Peter Wentworth lived, the ship-money of which 9*l.* was still behind. States various other charges against Sir Peter Wentworth in seven articles, and in the last article prays to be discharged of the remainder of the account, having collected 1,200*l.* on the letter of the Lords. [1 p.] *Underwritten*,

33. I. *Reference to Sir Dudley Carleton and Nicholas to examine the accounts to be brought in by Harris and Robert French, under-sheriff of Sir Peter Wentworth; to reduce the same account and cause the same to be perfected, and represent the true state thereof to the Lords. Whitehall, 4th February 1868.* [⅔ p.]

33. II. *Appointment by Nicholas to hear the business on the 6th inst.* [¼ p.]

Feb. 4. 34. Copy [by the Dean of Windsor] of the estimate for repair of his dovecot at Knoyle Episcopi by the workmen whom the commissioners called to view the dilapidations caused by the saltpetremen. Total, 20*l.* 5*s.* [¾ p.]

Feb. 5. Petition of the Terre-tenants and inhabitants of co. Cambridge to the King. Recite order of the King and Council of 2nd September 1635, whereby the sheriff, who had rated the Isle of Ely at one-fifth part of the county instead of one-third, as in all former rates, was ordered to rate the isle according to the proportion of other public charges, which the next succeeding and the present sheriff have done. The inhabitants of the isle informing the King that they ought to bear but a fifth part, obtained a reference to the judges of assize and judge of the isle, who have appointed to hear the same on the 16th inst. The reference having been obtained without informing his Majesty of the whole facts, petitioners pray that he will add to the referees some of the Council who were present when the former order was made. [*Copy. See Vol. cccxxiii., p.* 237. 1 p.] *Underwritten*,

1637-8.

VOL. CCCLXXXI.

1. *His Majesty, calling to mind that he was present at the settling of the former order, confirms the same, suspends the reference to the judges, and directs that the sheriff shall proceed according to the former order. Whitehall, 5th February 1637-8. [Copy. See Vol. cccxxiii., p. 238. ¼ p.]*

Feb. 5. Petition of the Board of Gentlemen Pensioners to the King. When the Earl of Portland entered upon the place of Lord Treasurer there were four years' entertainment due to petitioners, two whereof he discharged; the other two are still behind. The same we presented to your Majesty about a year and a half since, and received a reference to the now Lord Treasurer, who advised us to find out something, and he would give us an assignment. We propounded the profits of your Majesty's soap at Bristol. We have divers times attended the Lord Treasurer therein, but have as yet received no certain resolution. Pray special direction to the Lord Treasurer for settling the same. [*Copy. See Ibid., p. 238. ½ p.*] *Underwritten,*

1. *Reference to Lord Treasurer Juxon and Lord Cottington to give petitioners satisfaction in this way if it may be done without prejudice to his Majesty's service. Whitehall, 5th February 1637-8. [Copy. Ibid., p. 238. ⅔ p.]*

Feb. 5.
Hereford.
35. Roger Vaughan, Sheriff of co. Hereford, to Nicholas. My ship-money accounts I hope you received of Richard Wootton, dated the 13th November, since which I received a writ out of Chancery, and there returnable 8th February, requiring me to certify the names and sums in arrear, all which I have done. I have paid Sir William Russell 3,254*l*. 13*s*. 8*d*.; the rest is on the mayor of Hereford's account (60*l*. 6*s*. 4*d*. excepted), which are the arrears in my charge, and the bailiff of Lempster's [Leominster's] account, being little more than 1*l*. [*Seal with arms. 1 p.*]

Feb. 5. 36. Order of Sir John Lambe, referee of the case of Edward Alston, charged in the High Commission with defiling the vestry and riding into the church of Edwardstone, Suffolk (*see Vol. ccclvii., No. 174*). In the matter of the vestry he has lawfully purged himself. For the other charge, it was in a great shower of rain, and without his command, that his horse was brought into the church; but he got up upon him in the church and used some indiscreet words to the sexton. Therefore it is fit that he acknowledge his fault in the church; but being an ancient gentleman, he desires to redeem his penance, and offers 20 marks towards the repairs of St. Paul's, which Sir John accepts, and further orders him to pay 6*l*. 13*s*. 4*d*. costs. [*Draft. 1¼ p.*]

Feb. 5. 37. Paper attributed in the endorsement to Sir Anthony Weldon. It consist of two parts, the first entitled "The way to remedy this abuse [in the unequal assessment of ship-money], by which neither sheriff nor high constable shall be left to their discretion;" the second, "To show that the abuse of imposing the ship-money by the sheriff

1637-8.

Vol. CCCLXXXI.

on the hundreds, and by the high constable upon the parishes, makes the discontent and burthen much greater than the charge itself." In illustration of both parts of his argument he gives the case of the hundred of Axton in Kent. [1¾ p.]

Feb. 6.
The Swiftsure, in the Downs.
38. Sir John Pennington to the Lords of the Admiralty. The wind blowing hard, the Holland admiral is here yet, only he has sent home his vice-admiral to fetch out a fresh fleet which is ready for him, and when they come, these are to go in. The Second Whelp has cut her main and mizen masts by the board riding at Dunkirk, but she has got no other hurt, and I have applied to the Officers of the Navy to send down new masts for her. There are at Dunkirk 31 sail of men-of-war, little and great, all new trimmed and tallowed, ready to come out, part of them being to carry two regiments of old Irish soldiers and Reformado captains for Spain, who are to be sent in a great fleet making ready for Brazil. They have lately brought into Dunkirk a merchant ship of Holland with 24 pieces of ordnance, whereof four or six were brass; she was homeward bound and rich. They report from Dover that our ships are set free in France. [1 p.]

Feb. 6.
Mincing Lane.
39. Sir Henry Palmer to Nicholas. Finding little success in our request to the Lords, and that [it] is impossible for us without better means to proceed, we desire that you would, at their next meeting, present this letter [the one next calendared], and contribute your best furtherance therein. Were it not that I foresee our ruin without relief, I should be most unwilling to prosecute it with so much importunity. [½ p.]

Feb. 6.
Mincing Lane.
40. Officers of the Navy to Lords of the Admiralty. Having found no redress in what we have often petitioned for, we daily find our business to increase so much as we are enforced to make known to you that we cannot, without better means, but foresee our ruin, growing daily into debt. We are suitors that you will either procure his Majesty to be sensible of our condition, or admit us to those ways of advantage which our predecessors had in times far differing from these, both in charge and trouble. But if it should appear to his Majesty a burthen to condescend to a continuing charge, yet we hope the issuing the country moneys lying upon us, it will appear reasonable that since we have undergone that business with much expense (this being the third year), we shall be taken into consideration. [1 p.]

[Feb. 6.]
41. Sir Peter Wentworth, formerly Sheriff of co. Oxford, to Nicholas. Prays Nicholas to procure that the writer may not be interested any further in collecting the arrears of ship-money, or that at the least Nicholas would suspend certifying anything respecting Harris's 7th article until Sir Peter had given an account how Harris had carried himself in the business. Nicholas had seen the worst Harris could lay upon Sir Peter's under-sheriff and himself, and nothing as yet that they could allege against him. P.S.—After

DOMESTIC—CHARLES I.

Vol. CCCLXXXI.

1637–8.

we parted from you Harris told me he had 90*l*. of our ship-moneys in hand, which he will now pay. [*Seal with arms.* 1 *p.*]

41. I. *Reasons for Sir Peter Wentworth not joining to collect the arrears. Alleges peculiar obstacles which stood in his way during his shrievalty, and imposed great difficulty in his then, two years after he had ceased to be sheriff, having anything to do with the arrears still outstanding.* [1½ *p.*]

Feb. 6. 42. Answer of Sir Peter Wentworth to the charges of [Lewis] Harris, contained in the seven articles of his declaration, No. 33 in this present Volume. Sir Peter strives to throw the blame of the non-collection of these arrears on Harris, and alleges that he himself did not interfere in the collection because he never had any letter or direction to do so. [*Draft.* 2 *pp.*]

Feb. 6. 43. Another copy of the same with various alterations. [2⅙ *pp.*]

Feb. 6. 44. Statement of the ship-money account of Thomas Wise, Sheriff of Devon. The whole sum was 9,000*l*. He had paid by Sir William Russell's order 1,500*l*.; will forthwith return 3,500*l*.; the corporate towns will return 1,280*l*.; the remainder, 2,720*l*., he will levy as soon as possible. [½ *p.*]

Feb. 6. 45. Receipt of William Batts for letters from the Council, directed to mayor of Hereford, bailiff of Maldon, mayor of Harwich, archbishop of York, bailiff of Blandford, and mayor of St. Albans. [¼ *p.*]

Feb. 7. 46. Thomas Thornhill to the Lords of the Admiralty. By desire of Mr. Morriloy, merchant, certifies that his saltpetre is worth 15*s*. or 20*s*. per cwt. more than Mr. Oneby and Mr. Briggs' last saltpetre was worth. [½ *p.*]

Feb. 7. 47. List of Lent preachers at Court from this day (Ash Wednesday) to the 25th March following (Easter Day); besides various bishops and deans, there are included in the list Drs. Thomas Lawrence, William Beale, William Heywood, John Blechinden, Gilbert Sheldon, and Benjamin Laney. [¾ *p.*]

Feb. 7. 48. Application of Capt. James Duppa, on behalf of the Commissioners for regulating the trade of Brewing, to the Council, for warrants to bring before the Board Christopher Chapman, of Harleston, and John Weeks, of Windsor, who had refused to appear upon the summons of the commissioners; and also for a letter to justices of peace near Long Stratton, to examine a difference between Robert Ward and the brewers in that place, and for a similar letter to justices of peace near Wallingford, in a difference between Edward Prichard and Frances Smith, of Wallingford. [1 *p.*]

Feb. 7. 49. Similar application for warrants against John Liney, John Coale, William Adams, and Richard Carpenter, of Bridgwater; and Jeremy Bally and Edward Bath, of Thame; also against Samuel Reynolds and Thomas Watts, of Westerham, Kent; and for a letter to justices of peace in differences between the brewers of Coggeshall and Richard Stowe. [⅔ *p.*]

Vol. CCCLXXXI.

1637-8.

Feb. 8. Warrant to the Judges of the King's Bench to levy issues and amercements upon indictments and other suits grounded on the common law, and to see the same employed for amending the ways where the offences were committed. [*Docquet.*]

Feb. 8. Grant to William Owen, for life, of the office of constable of Harlech Castle, co. Merioneth, with the fee of 50*l.* per annum, upon surrender of Thomas Stafford. [*Docquet.*]

Feb. 8.
Whitehall. Proclamation concerning kilns for drying malt and hops at a small charge. These kilns had been invented by Thomas Earl of Berkshire, and letters patent had been granted giving him the sole privilege of using his invention for 14 years. The present proclamation published the premises, and announced that all persons might compound with the Earl for his licence to use the said invention at a place in Fleet Street, near Temple Bar. [*See Coll. Proc. Car. I., No.* 219. 2 *pp.*]

Feb. 8.
Westminster. 50. The King to the Judges of the Common Pleas. We lately directed a privy seal to you to permit William Whalley, son of Ralph Whalley, to suffer a common recovery, that his father might sell lands for raising portions for his seven daughters, which hitherto you have forborne to do, by information given you by the brother of the said Ralph Whalley, that he is a debauched person and has diminished his estate by disorder. We have seen a certificate of neighbours of the said Ralph Whalley, that he has ever been a good husband, and always lived civilly amongst his neighbours, but has been unnaturally prosecuted by his brother, which has brought him into debt. We, conceiving that the said reports are raised by the brother merely in regard of his own right to the inheritance in case the said William die without issue, and understanding that the brother has a much more plentiful estate than the said Ralph, require you to pursue our command in our privy seal without delay. [*Copy.* ¾ *p.*]

Feb. 8.
Mincing Lane. 51. Officers of the Navy to Lords of the Admiralty. Having formerly moved you, upon complaints made of the prest-masters for pressing insufficient seamen, to send your warrant to the vice-admirals, deputy-lieutenants, and others, in all shires where there are any maritime towns, to enable them to press a proportionable number of mariners, gunners, and sailors, such as they know to be able and fit, which you seemed to approve of, and the rather because the magistrates and gentlemen of quality in many parts found themselves aggrieved to associate with such mean persons as our prest-masters. We now again present it to your consideration; which course if you think fit to make trial of, we will accommodate the vice-admirals of every county with prest and conduct money, which will free his Majesty of a great charge, and us of much clamour. [1 *p.*]

Feb. 8.
Mincing Lane. 52. Officers of the Navy to the same. We have had conference with the Trinity masters touching the expense of boatswains serving at sea the last year. They have returned us a very uncertain answer, which we enclose, observing by their opinions that

Vol. CCCLXXXI.

1637-8.

the excess of ten in the hundred in those ships nominated by them as most lavish, vizt., in the St. George, the Vanguard, the Convertive, the First Whelp, the Roebuck, and the Expedition, amounts to 9 tons 15 cwt. 1 quarter, which at 26*l.* 13*s.* 4*d.* per ton amounts to 240*l.* This is the best account we can give of the suspended boatswains' expense, wishing for this first time that it may be rather to correct than ruin them. [1 *p.*] *Enclosed*,

> 52. I. *Officers of the Trinity House to the Officers of the Navy. State the course of inquiry adopted by them on the subject of the boatswains' expenses. We find all their expenses to be very great especially. To find out every particular passeth our understanding. We conceive for the future ten per cent. may be a reasonable expense for ordinary wear and tear for six or eight months upon all their running-ropes, boat-ropes, buoy-ropes, and guess-ropes, casualties always excepted. Trinity House, 7th February,* 1637-8. [1 *p.*]

Feb. 8.
His lodging, Princess Street.

53. Sir Alexander Denton, Sheriff of co. Buckingham, to Nicholas. He has made such an approved division of the general sum of the ship-money into the hundreds, as that he hopes the Lords shall not be troubled with any complaints either from the gentry or other inhabitants. Those assessments which are distributed and confirmed in the towns (which are three parts of the county) are accepted as proportionably equal. That every particular man's assessment in those towns shall carry so just a distribution that none or very few shall have a cause to complain worth the admittance, has taken up his whole time in that county that has been so often troublesome to the Lords to regulate the just complaints of the inhabitants. In this he has endeavoured a reformation in general. The towns that have their assessments confirmed say they deny not to pay, but some desire time until the business betwixt his Majesty and the subject be decided, and others say they have not money to pay, in regard the restriction of the maltsters has taken away the benefit of venting their corn, which will not now sell to such a quantity as weekly will provide necessaries for their subsistence, so that he can receive so little a sum as is not worth the relation, nor has he any hope as yet to get any more upon fair terms. [2 *pp.*]

Feb. 8.

Nicholas to Richard Poole. To prepare a deputation from the Commissioners of Saltpetre to Alexander Harris, and —— Burroughs to be his assistant for working saltpetre in London, Westminster, and Southwark, and two miles compass. He is to bring in 6 cwt. of saltpetre per week, to continue for seven years. [*Copy. Nicholas's Letter Book, Dom., James I., Vol. ccxix., p.* 170.]

Feb. 8.

54. Petition of Bartholomew Boustfeild to Archbishop Laud. Presents in the annexed a declaration of his lamentable case, in which the archbishop will observe the unchristian malice of a punished offender, the abuse of the justice of the court, and the utter undoing of a poor innocent subject by the practice of a proctor and his client. Beseeches his consideration, and that he would

VOL. CCCLXXXI.

1637-8.

appoint Mr. Dell, or any other of his gentlemen, to take a more ample knowledge of petitioner's cause, especially of the first cause, wherein Morland was sentenced, upon which he is assured that the archbishop will grant him relief. *Underwritten*,

> 54. I. *Reference to Sir John Lambe, to peruse the petition and the paper annexed, and if any place be left for lawful favour to let it be shown. 8th February, 1637-8.* [1 p.]
> *Annexed*,
>
> 54. II. *Declaration above alluded to. Petitioner Boustfield having preferred articles against Austin Morland for blasphemy, his costs were upon some false suggestion reduced from 40l. to 10l., and Morland further procured a promoter to prefer many fearful articles against petitioner, which being heard in his absence, as he states, he was fined 500l. and 40 marks costs, he being a poor country tailor not worth 40 marks. He had now endured five years' suit in the High Commission, Chancery, and King's Bench, to his utter undoing.* [1 p.]

Feb. 8. 55. Reasons for granting the suit of William Bowyer and John Stretthay for a patent for an invention for making malt by a new way. It will save a great deal of wood, and also of straw; will make more wholesome malt and drink, and will be no way prejudicial, for that none shall be forced to use it. [½ p.]

Feb. 8. 56. Capt. James Duppa to Mr. Wild. Application similar to those of the 7th. inst., Nos. 48 and 49, for a letter from the Lords to Sir Anthony Drury, Robert Wilton, and John Buxton, justices of peace in Norfolk, to examine the differences between William Juby and John Valliet, against Robert and Edward Warne, all of New Burnham, Norfolk. [¼ p.]

Feb. 8. Memorandum that a letter from the Council was delivered to Mr. Keyme [messenger], directed to the present and late sheriffs of Dorset, touching the tithing of Frome Whitfield. [*See this Vol., No. 45. 3 lines.*]

Feb. 8. 57. Copies of two certificates, one dated this day, and the other on the 12th February 1635-6, signed by Dr. Arthur Duck and various other doctors of the civil law, and other persons connected with Doctors' Commons, that they had never known any commission of review granted in any cause of defamation. [*Endorsed by Sir John Lambe,* "For Mr. Andrew Wood." 1⅔ p.]

Feb. 9. 58. Petition of Randolph Church, one of your Majesty's gentlemen pensioners, to the King. Has for 16 years served as sergeant-at-arms, and since he left that place, in the place wherein he now serves; during which time he never received benefit by any suit, but he purchased some post places under Lord Stanhope, which he has executed by deputies for many years. But now Lord Stanhope, having surrendered his patent, petitioner's post places, to the value of 200l. per annum, are taken away, there being 650l. due to him for wages upon the said places; and now petitioner, being employed

1637-8.
Vol. CCCLXXXI.

in the prosecution of delinquents for converting timber to coal for making iron, and having expended much money therein, and being likely to bring great sums into the Exchequer, the means by which he should subsist are taken away. Beseeches some such satisfaction out of moneys brought into the Exchequer by his present service as may equal his places and arrears. [¾ p.] *Underwritten,*

> 58. I. *Reference to Lord Treasurer Juxon, to inform himself of the truth of the petition, and finding petitioner's services and losses to be considerable, to acquaint his Majesty therewith. Whitehall, 9th February, 1637-8.* [¼ p.] *Endorsed,*
>
> 58. II. *Lord Treasurer Juxon and Lord Cottington to the King. What loss petitioner has had by taking from him his places of postmaster, as likewise for arrear of moneys, the two Secretaries of State (now postmasters) can best give an account, as those who know your Majesty is noways chargeable touching the places nor with the arrear, but as the compositions are made. 5th July* 1638. [¼ p.]

Feb. 9.
Whitehall.
Lords of the Admiralty to [Montjoy Earl of Newport]. Thomas Withering and Edward Read, owners of the Fortune, of London, are to be permitted to furnish their ship with ordnance out of the founder's store. [*Copy. See Vol. ccclii., fol.* 87 *b.* ½ p.]

Feb. 9.
59. Petition of Richard Bagley to the King. Sir Richard Harrison, being lord of the manor of Hurst in Berks, and petitioner having a copyhold of inheritance in the said manor worth 10*l.* per annum, Sir Richard through vexatious suits about four years since enforced petitioner for peace sake to surrender his copyhold unto him for no consideration at all, but only with promise to surrender it again, if he did not help petitioner's son to his marriage portion of 2,500*l.*, which as yet he cannot get. Petitioner, who is a poor man, and by the hard prosecution of Sir Richard is utterly undone, having spent all his estate, which was worth 2,000*l.*, and is much indebted, prays a reference to Lord Cottington to treat of some relief. [*Copy.* ½ p.] *Underwritten,*

> 59. I. *Reference to Lord Cottington to send for Sir Richard Harrison to give answer to the complaint, and if he finds just cause to relieve the petitioner, and Sir Richard be refractory, to take order as he shall think meet. Whitehall, 9th February* 1637-8. [*Copy.* ¼ p.]
>
> 59. II. "*Let Sir Richard Harrison see this petition, and send me his answer thereunto forthwith in writing.*" 17*th March* 1637-8. [*Copy.* ¼ p.]

Feb. 9.
60. Petition of Philip Davies, clerk, Henry Demry and Abraham Cobb, churchwardens of Hill *alias* Hull, in the diocese of Gloucester, to Archbishop Laud. In obedience to your directions in your metropolitan visitation, we ordered the raising of the church railing

1637-8.

VOL. CCCLXXXI.

in the high altar or communion table in the said church, for doing which, with the necessary beautifying of the church, there were rates made by the churchwardens for the time being and the major part of the inhabitants, in which assessment Henry Heathfield, who is commonly reputed to be of that parish, was rated after the usual manner, his divers rates amounting to 28s. 6d. To avoid payment, Heathfield appealed to the Court of Arches, where the cause has depended eleven months. Pray for their better encouragement in performing your commands, in preserving the decency and ornaments of the church, to order the said cause to be speedily determined. [¾ p.] *Underwritten*,

    60. I. "*I desire Sir John Lambe, in case he finds the suggestions true, to take care that this cause may come to hearing with all convenient speed possible.* W. CANT." 9th February 1637-8. [¼ p.]

Feb. 9.   61. Copy of the above. [1 p.]

Feb. 9.   62. Petition of Thomas Sheylor, clerk, curate of Swallowfield, Berks, to Archbishop Laud. George Miller and Mary Phipps, wife of John Phipps, having a long time lived scandalously together, she apart from her husband in the house of Miller, petitioner and the churchwardens presented them at the visitation of the archdeacon of Berks on 5th October 1636, whereupon Miller and Mrs. Phipps were enjoined a purgation. They appealed to the Court of Audience, and made petitioner and the churchwardens parties, where the cause still depends, and they have not only proceeded in that vexatious course, but Miller has abused petitioner in violent assaults and vile language, the particulars of which are detailed. Prays relief. [¾ p.] *Underwritten*,

    62. I. *Reference to Sir John Lambe to award letters missive or an attachment for the party here mentioned to answer these misdemeanours in the High Commission Court.* 9th February 1637-8. [¼ p.]

Feb. 9.   63. Copy sentence of the Court of High Commission in the case of Laurence Snelling, rector of Paul's Cray, Kent. Defendant was charged that having been admonished by his ordinary to read the King's declaration for lawful recreations on Sundays, he had not done so, and that he had divers times omitted to read the Litany and wear the surplice and bow at the name of Jesus. It was ordered that unless he read the King's Book and did due reverence at the blessed name before the second court day of next term, he should be deprived. [*Underwritten is written a memorandum, probably in the handwriting of William Prynne, that Snelling was accordingly deprived, and continued so for divers years.* 5½ pp.]

Feb. 9.   64. List of causes to be heard in the Star Chamber this day. They were Thomas Browne versus John Barrett [Borrett?] and others [dismissed without costs;] the Attorney-General versus Sir Henry

Vol. CCCLXXXI.

1637–8.

Mynne, for scandalous speeches of Lord Sherard and his Lady; Sir Richard Wiseman and Susan his wife, and Diana their daughter, versus John Stone and John Elmes, for disgraceful speeches of the plaintiffs; Henry West versus Martin Joyce and others, for perjury; also a cause against William Anson and John Tomson, for refusing to furnish a light horse, and oppression by colour of a warrant from the Council. [1 p.]

Feb. 9.
Star Chamber.

65. Notes by Sec. Windebank of the case of the Attorney-General for Lord Sherard versus Sir Henry Mynne, heard at the Star Chamber this day. The charge was that Sir William Sherard having been created Baron Leitrim in Ireland, and being allied to the House of Lancaster on the mother's side, Sir Henry, at Oakham assizes, termed him a base Lord, a base informing Lord, a base fellow, a base informing fellow, and said that he would pluck the feathers off the proud peacock's tail. These words arose out of Lord Sherard's having procured Sir Henry Mynne's wife to be presented for a recusant. The words were addressed to Baron Trevor, the judge at the assize, being at dinner, and in the presence of Lord Campden, Sir Francis Bodenham, Sir Thomas Roe, Sir Henry Mackworth, and others, Mynne being in a passion. Lord Cottington proposed a fine of 1,000*l.*, which was concurred in by Mr. Justice Jones, Lord Chief Justice Bramston, Sec. Coke, the Earl Marshal, and the Earl of Lindsey. Sec. Windebank proposed to increase the fine to 1,500*l.*, and that the defendant should be put out of the Commission. The Earl of Dorset and Archbishop Laud would have added damages of 1,000*l.* to the relator. Ultimately the sentence passed as proposed by Sec. Windebank. [3¾ pp.]

Feb. 9.

66. Account of the numbers of the trained bands of all the counties of England and Wales. They are distinguished into foot and horse. Of the former the numbers of muskets and corselets are separately stated, and of the latter the numbers of lances, light horse, cuirasses, arquabusiers, and dragoons. The total numbers are: foot, 93,718, horse, 5,239. [3 pp.]

Feb. 9.
Whitehall.

Lords of the Admiralty to Capt. Thomas Kettleby, Admiral in the Swallow of all ships employed for guard of the coast of Ireland. The ships under his command were the Swallow and the Ninth Whelp. The instructions are similar, with some verbal alterations, to those which were given to Capt. Kettleby on the 21st May 1637. [*Copy.* See Vol. clvii., fol. 152 b. 3¾ pp.]

Feb. 10.

Petition of William Murray, one of the grooms of the Bedchamber, to the King. On 31st January, 30th Elizabeth, her Majesty, in consideration of lands of 150*l.* per annum to be granted to her by one Fludd and others, at the request of the then late Earl of Essex, contracted to grant to the said Earl rectories, parsonages, and such like, of the yearly value of 300*l.* per annum. Also, by another contract made between the said Queen and Sir Thomas Heneage, her Majesty, for 6*l.* per annum land to be by him conveyed to her, was

Vol. CCCLXXXI.

1637-8.

to grant to him in fee simple lands of that value. Under these contracts lands were procured from her Majesty in the names of Downing or Doding, of far greater value than was contracted for, whereby her Majesty was much deceived, and the grants of the said lands were void in law. Prays a grant of the lands conveyed to Downing or Doding in consideration of petitioner's service, and he will reserve 500*l.* per annum rent to your Majesty more than now stands in charge. [*Copy. See Vol. cccxxiii., fol.* 240. ⅚ *p.*] *Underwritten,*

    I. *Reference to the Solicitor-General to prepare a grant as prayed. Whitehall,* 10*th February* 1637–8. [*Copy. Ibid., fol.* 241. ⅙ *p.*]

Feb. 10.
Whitehall.
67. Report of Montjoy Earl of Newport, Sir Henry Vane, and Sec. Coke, appointed by the Council to consider of the provision of a requisite supply of gunpowder. They reported that the supply always to be in hand should be 300 lasts, the present store being 304 lasts 10 cwt. Towards the supply of this quantity the powder-maker undertook to supply 240 lasts per annum if provided with saltpetre. The saltpetremen contracted to furnish 180 lasts 12 cwt. per annum, and an import of 100 lasts per annum from Barbary was in treaty with the merchants trading to that country and the ambassador. The necessary annual expenditure of gunpowder was as follows: for the trained bands, 94 lasts 13 cwt. and 46 lbs.; for castles and forts, 6 lasts 22 cwt.; for the navy, 40 lasts; for merchants' ships, 50 lasts; supply of magazines, 100 lasts 13 cwt. 46 lbs.; total, 291 lasts 22 cwt. 46 lbs. (?). The referees recommend the return and examination of yearly accounts, with certificates from muster-masters. The supply of Ireland was provided for in that country under an establishment settled by the Lord Deputy. [*Copy.* 3 *pp.*]

Feb. 10.
68. Draft of the same. [3 *pp.*]

Feb. 10.
Another copy of the same. [*See Vol. ccxcii., p.* 74. 3¼ *pp.*]

Feb. 10.
Whitehall.
Order of the Commissioners of Saltpetre and Gunpowder. Samuel Cordewell, his Majesty's gunpowder-maker, shall receive the Barbary saltpetre, being about 20 tons, belonging to one Carolius [or Caralois in another place], a Dutchman, which being brought into Portsmouth, and there stayed, was afterwards brought to London and put into the hands of the farmers of the customs; and that Cordewell shall refine the same, for which he shall have the same allowance as he had for the last Barbary saltpetre, being 4*l.* 6*s.* 8*d.* the cwt. [*Ibid., p.* 78. ½ *p.*]

Feb. 10.
69. Account of what the saltpetre above mentioned cost in Barbary, and what has since been laid out upon the same. It was originally bought of Mr. Robert Blake and others who are termed "the renters" of the same. Total, 1,244*l.* 8*s.* 2*d.* [¾ *p.*]

VOL. CCCLXXXI.

1637-8.
Feb. 10.
Whitehall.
Notes by Nicholas of business to be transacted by the Lords of the Admiralty. Officers of the Navy are to attend about Mr. Crane's account. Consider the heads of a proclamation touching gunpowder. Peruse letters from the Officers of the Navy. Report to be made concerning sending ships to suppress the pirates of Algiers. Consider petition of Thomas Biggs, recommended by the Earl of Northumberland. Also the report of Sir Henry Marten on petition of Robert Jones. Move the King to give directions to the judges of assize to require obedience to the proclamation published in 1634 concerning preservation of grounds for making saltpetre, &c. Peruse Mr. Thornhill's letter touching the Dutchman's saltpetre. The owners of the Exchange, of Southampton, bound for Newfoundland fishing, desire her men may not be pressed. [*See this Volume.*, No. 21. 1 *p*.]

Feb. 10.
Whitehall.
Lords of the Admiralty to the Officers of the Navy. We understand by your letter of the 25th January last, that the Unicorn, the Expedition, and the First Whelp are necessarily to be repaired before they go forth to sea. You are to take order for the said reparation, and to cause the charge thereof to be borne out of the moneys to be this year paid by the counties. [*Copy. Vol. cccliii., fol.* 88. ½ *p*.]

Feb. 10.
Whitehall.
The same to Montjoy Earl of Newport. We are informed that the stores of provision in the Merhonour, the Triumph, the James, the Unicorn, the Defiance, the Rainbow, the Repulse, the Henrietta Maria, the Assurance, the Convertive, the Dreadnought, the First Whelp, the Third Whelp, the Mary Rose, the Moon, the Seven Stars, the Vanguard (at Portsmouth) are spent. A survey is to be taken of the remains, and an account how the provisions formerly delivered have been expended, and each ship is to be supplied with necessaries, the master-gunners indenting for what they shall receive. [*Copy. Ibid., fol.* 88. 1 *p*.]

Feb. 10.
70. John Stedman, Sheriff of co. Cardigan, to Nicholas. I had long since returned certificate of the ship-money assessed in this county, but that by a late difference about the inequality of taxing the divisions the ancient course was altered this year, which has begotten much unreadiness both of assessing and paying; for whereas the general charge in all taxes heretofore was equally laid upon two divisions called Ysairon [Issayndre] and Ywchairon [Uchayndre], upon petition to the Lords, and a reference to the justices of assize, the said course is ordered to be changed, and Uchayndre charged much higher than formerly (*see Vol. ccclxx., No.* 84), by which means the rates before in example becoming useless, the levies with much more difficulty and trouble to the sheriffs must be made, no man concerned assisting the service with the same willingness of payment as formerly. This necessity of my not stricter observance of the Lords' letter I desire you to represent to them, and to pray their direction for the better expedition of this service thus interrupted. [*Endorsed by Nicholas,* " Read, but

Vol. CCCLXXXI.

1637-8.

the Lords do not think fit to alter what the judges have set for the rates." *Seal with arms.* 1 *p.*]

Feb. 10.
North Mimms.

71. Sir Thomas Coningesby, Sheriff of co. Hertford, to Nicholas. On receipt of his commission he made warrants to the constables for warning every parish to assess certain sums of money, but the dispute above gave great delay, the general vote of the county being they would first hear what was determined at London. He then sent forth new warrants requiring the rates to be made by the 20th January by the petty constables, upon pain of commitment. Receiving very imperfect returns he repaired to the Lord Lieutenant, who advised him to proceed in performing the duty required of him. Since then most of the assessments have come in, but no levies made. Purposes with all expedition himself to assess the towns which have neglected, and will hereafter make no fail of due certificates to the Lords. [2 *pp.*]

Feb. 10.
Westminster.

72. Sec. Windebank to Sir John Pennington. His Majesty has commanded me to signify to you that you give order to the captain of the Providence to stand over to Dieppe, and there to expect the coming of Maurice Wynne, whom he is to receive on board and waft over with his company to England. He comes from the Earl of Leicester upon a special service of his Majesty, and with a charge of great value, and therefore the captain must be the more careful. [1 *p.*]

Feb. 10.
Nottingham.

73. Deputy Lieutenants of co. Nottingham to William Earl of Newcastle, Lord Lieutenant. We have received letters patent and proclamation for setting on foot the invention of the bow and pike, and by the bringers thereof are much pressed for a speedy putting the same in execution. But because the charge thereof will put the country to an excessive expense, and for that the proclamation bears date the ninth of his Majesty's reign, and the commission the tenth, we thought good to give you knowledge thereof, being very sensible how unwillingly the country, which is little and yet deeply charged with arms already, will receive this imposition. And we may conceive that the proclamation and letters patent having now slept for almost these four years, the Council have not thought the use of those arms so necessary for country people, and the rather in regard we have not heard that any county has put the same in practice. [*Seal with arms.* 1 *p.*]

Feb. 10.

74. Petition of Thomas Webb, clothier, to Archbishop Laud. Petitioner on Thursday last attended at the High Commission from 2 o'clock till night to have made his submission according to his censure, but was told afterwards by one of the registrars that it could not be done for want of a commissioner's hand to the order; howbeit petitioner has entered into bond, and is ready to make his submission next court. In respect that he has been long absent from his house, to the detriment of his workmen, beseeches that,

DOMESTIC—CHARLES I. 245

1637–8.   VOL. CCCLXXXI.

making his submission in the country, he may be released of his suspension. [½ p.] *Underwritten,*

> 74. I. *Reference to Sir John Lambe, to take order that this petitioner may make his submission upon the by-day, and that he may be despatched to follow his business with all convenient speed possible, "for I would not have a trading clothier kept too long from his company."* 10th February 1637–8. [*Endorsed by Sir John Lambe,* "Done 19th February 1637–8." ¼ p.]

Feb. 10.
Gresham
College.

75. John Greaves to Dr. [Peter] Turner, Professor of Geometry in Oxford and Fellow of Merton College. Approves the bargain made by the proctor's brother, Mr. Browne, for the purchase at Leyden of some printing types of probably an Eastern language. The only danger is that some are wanting. Mr. Bedwell when he bought Raphelengius's Arabic press found some characters defective, which he was never able to get supplied. Hopes now that Archbishop Laud has taken such care for furnishing the university with all sorts of types, and procuring so many choice MSS. of the Oriental languages, that some will endeavour to make true use of his noble intentions, and publish some of those incomparable pieces of the East, not inferior to the best of the Greeks or Latins. For this employment recommends Mr. Pococke, whom he praises in the very highest terms. Pococke desired once more to go into the East, and, to enable him to do so, wished the archbishop to bestow upon him some prebend or living *sine curâ*. The writer dwells on the honour it will be to the archbishop to employ such a man in foreign countries. The writer's brother will supply Pococke's place in his absence if the archbishop will protect him in his right to the next living in the gift of the Charter House. Mr. Petty desired to retain the writer in his Lord's service with an offer of 200*l*. yearly to have accompanied him to Italy, and thence to Athens. The writer explains in detail his own views and prospects and the grounds of his desire to visit Alexandria. Explains how he proposes to provide for the expense of such a journey, and especially his difficulties in respect to retaining his position at Gresham College during his absence. If he were at Constantinople he would take order that no ship should return without strictly observing the King's injunctions about Arabic books, and for such as are best and dearest, and may be worth the archbishop's acceptance. [1¾ p.]

Feb. 10.   76. Appointment by John Alford, of Offington, Sussex, of William Hawkins, of Westminster, to receive 52*l*. 10*s*. out of the Exchequer, being an arrearage of 30*l*. per annum payable there to Edward Alford, deceased, father of the said John. [*Seal with arms.* 1 *p*.]

Feb. 10.   77. Information of the misconduct of Thomas Ekins, Peter Hill, Thomas Jago, and Mark Hawkins, all of Dartmouth, who had boarded and rifled two ships cast on shore there, and then being in possession of the officers of Sir Edward Seymour, one of the Vice-

VOL. CCCLXXXI.

1637–8.

Admirals of Devon. The persons complained of declared that they did not care a pin for the Vice-Admiral's warrant, and threatened to throw his officers overboard. [*It appears from the endorsement that the paper was received from Sir James Bagg on behalf of Sir Edward Seymour. 2 pp.*]

Feb. 10. 78. Account by Sir William Russell of arrears of ship-money still outstanding for 1635. Total, 7,994*l*. 7*s*. 9*d*., or as rectified by certain deductions by Nicholas, 5,194*l*. 5*s*. 2*d*. [1 *p*.]

Feb. 10. 79. Similar account of arrears outstanding for 1636. Total received, 186,828*l*. 6*s*. 8*d*.; outstanding, 9,786*l*. 1*s*. [1 *p*.]

Feb. 10. 80. The like of sums received on account of writs issued in September last. Total, 8,814*l*., with an underwritten memorandum that the sheriff of co. York had delivered bills of exchange, payable between this and the 31st March, for 6,377*l*. 6*s*. 10*d*. [1 *p*.]

Feb. 10. 81. Account of moneys levied under writs issued in September 1637 and remaining in the sheriffs' hands. Total, 27,700*l*., which added to the sum paid to Sir William Russell makes 36,514*l*. [¾ *p*.]

Feb. 11.
The Swiftsure, in the Downs.
82. Sir John Pennington to the Lords of the Admiralty. Since my last no ships have arrived here from foreign parts The Second Whelp is come from Dunkirk, and in regard her masts were not come down, and a fair wind to carry her up for Chatham, I have sent her thither. Since the coming out of the Dunkirkers they daily pillage our small shipping that goes without convoy for France or Holland. The Holland men-of-war give a very great deal of respect to the King's pinnaces wheresoever they meet them. [1 *p*.]

Feb. 11. 83. Extract from the above of the passages concerning the pillage done by Dunkirkers and the respect shown by the Hollanders towards the King's pinnaces. [½ *p*.]

Feb. 11.
Waresley.
84. Sir John Hewett, Sheriff of co. Huntingdon, to Nicholas. According to instructions I assessed all the towns and sent out warrants to the constables and chief inhabitants of every town to make their particular assessments. After that, I appointed days until Christmas for receiving the assessments, hearing complaints, and removing the burthen laid upon poor people, which I found as general as heavy. Some 18 or 20 towns have not assessed as yet, so as I am destitute of a certificate answerable to the expectance of the Board. The causes I am ignorant of, but they are more backward than in my predecessor's time. About me it is through the oblique carriage of some. At St. Neots', a great town, Mr. Pain holds the third part of the lands, and refuses to pay according to the ancient and usual rates of that town. The best inhabitants have complained to me, and the constable dares not make the assessment until he lay Mr. Pain as he lift [list?], for fear he punish him some way hereafter, as he is a justice of the peace. Other towns take example

1637-8. Vol. CCCLXXXI.

by this not to assess. If it fall out the sheriff must assess the towns behind, the money will be long collecting. To quicken them I would desire some directions, and although I am upon some disadvantage, being a stranger in the county, yet I will not be wanting to use more than common endeavour to expedite the service. [*Seal with arms.* 1⅓ *p.*]

Feb. 11. 85. Petition of Andrew Bayly, clerk, to Archbishop Laud. William Bayly, petitioner's father, deceased, being official of Wolverhampton, a member of the free chapel of Windsor, and finding the organ there much decayed, and Emanuel Creswell, organ-maker, certifying that he could not repair the same, sent petitioner to Dr. Wren, then dean of Windsor, and now bishop of Norwich, to acquaint him therewith, who condescended that a new organ should be erected, and willed petitioner to use his name to the chiefest of the parish for their assistance therein, so that it was agreed that Creswell should erect a new organ for 140*l.* Creswell began to work upon the organ, but being in want of money to buy materials, procured 100*l.* of Henry Gough and 30*l.* of John Hawkins, and drew petitioner to be bound with him for the same, promising that he should first collect the same to make repayment thereof. Before the organ was perfected petitioner's father died, petitioner having only collected 41*l.* 10*s.* 0*d.*, and being remediless to collect the residue in regard that divers refused to pay. The interest of the 130*l.* petitioner has ever since paid (except 8*l.* only), and the said 130*l.* being unpaid, petitioner in Trinity term last was sued to judgment and execution upon his bond, and forced to absent himself and mortgage his land for discharge thereof, amounting to 200*l.* Prays order to collect such moneys as he has disbursed, and letters missive against such as refuse to pay. [*Endorsed by Sir John Lambe,* "I wrote to Mr. Latham, 11th February 1637-8." ¾ *p.*]

Feb. 12. Whitehall. 86. The King to the heirs or executors of John Wright, late clerk of the House of Commons assembled in the late Parliament. There was delivered to the Clerk of the Commons in the late Parliament the letters patent by us granted to the Earl of Holland of the office of Exchange, and a commission for executing a proclamation by us published concerning the same, which with other writings touching the business are remaining in your hands. You are to deliver the same to the bearer. [¾ *p.*]

Feb. 12. Petition of Thomas Killigrew, his Majesty's servant, to the King. About eight years since the King granted to Cicely Crofts, maid of honour to the Queen, and petitioner's late wife deceased, all mesne profits due to his Majesty by reason of any intrusion committed upon coal mines at Benwell in Northumberland from 13th of Queen Elizabeth until the 4th year of the present King. Cicely and petitioner have long prosecuted the King's title to the premises, but for some defect of form the court has directed a new information, to the further expense of petitioner, who has already disbursed 1,700*l.*

Vol. CCCLXXXI.

1637–8.

in the said suit. Prays the King to signify his pleasure for amending the said defects, and that the cause proceed to a final hearing. [*Copy. See Vol. cccxxiii., p.* 241. ⅔ *p.*] *Underwritten,*

    I. *Minute that the King, having resumed this business into his own hands, directs the information to be amended, and that the cause proceed to a final hearing, and hereof the Lord Treasurer, Chancellor, and Barons of the Exchequer are to take notice. Whitehall,* 12th *February* 1637–8. [*Copy. Ibid.* ¼ *p.*]

Feb. 12.

87. Petition of Ezekiel Wright, B.D., to Archbishop Laud. Petitioner has preferred articles in the Court of High Commission against Mr. Ward, Mr. Castle, and Mr. Cade, who are all instituted into the rectory of Dinnington. Petitioner, the last court day, moved by his counsel that defendant Ward should take out his commission to prove his defence and make all his proofs this vacation, returnable the first court day of the next term, which petitioner conceives was granted accordingly, yet the registrar seems doubtful of the archbishop's declaration in that particular, and Ward endeavours to delay the justice of the court. Prays the archbishop to signify his intention to the registrar. [¾ *p.*] *Underwritten,*

    87. I. *Reference to Sir John Lambe that on the by-day this commission be returned as is desired.* 12th *February* 1637[–8]. [1 *p.*]

Feb. 12.

88. Petition of Peter Farren and Francis Rushworth, churchwardens of All Saints, Northampton, to the same. On 16th December last, petitioners were by the ordinary's surrogate admonished to cancel in the communion table before the 12th January last, which petitioners were noways able to perform, by reason that during Christmas fit workmen could not be procured. Thereupon the surrogate excommunicated petitioners, who then had begun the said work, and shortly after the said excommunications they completed it. Praying to be absolved, and the surrogate refusing, they were forced to make their appeal to the Court of Arches, where by the information of the surrogate they cannot obtain their absolutions. Pray order to the Dean of the Arches for their absolution. [⅚ *p.*] *Underwritten,*

    88. I. *Reference to Sir John Lambe. If he finds the suggestions true, to take order that the petitioners be absolved.* 12th *February* 1637–8. [⅙ *p.*]

Feb. 12.

89. Petition of Sarah Cornwall, wife of Thomas Cornwall, late of Woodham Walter, Essex, to the same. Petitioner brought in marriage to Thomas Cornwall the yearly revenue of 140*l.* and upwards, part of which was lands of her own inheritance, the residue for life, together with a good personal estate, the greatest part of which Thomas Cornwall has wasted, and also prevailed with petitioner to join in the sale of the greatest part of her said estate of inheritance for 440*l.*, which was appointed towards the advance-

Vol. CCCLXXXI.

1637-8.

ment of three of her children by Bartholomew King, her former husband, which 440*l*., together also with 300*l*. more appointed by their said father, he has likewise consumed or disposed of from petitioner, and has leased out the remaining land of the petitioner at 70*l*. per annum, reserving the rent to himself. Further, about Midsummer last, he departed from petitioner out of the country to parts unknown, where he still remains, leaving petitioner neither provision nor maintenance for herself or her children. The tenants of her lands have now in their hands some rents, but refuse to pay the same to petitioner, whereby she and her children are altogether destitute. Prays relief. [⅚ *p*.] *Underwritten,*

    89. I. *Reference to Sir John Lambe, if he knows any way by the High Commission or otherwise for petitioner's relief, that he will give her his best directions.* 12*th February* 1637-8. [1 *p*.]

Feb. 12.   90. Kenrick Edisbury to [Nicholas]. The chiefest occasion of boatswain Mitchell's suspension was for a hawser that was sold out of the ship by Capt. Rainsborough's approbation, which he brought not to account, but since he paid Sir William Russell 6*l*. for the same. [½ *p*.]

Feb. 12.   91. William Letts, servant of Sir John Lambe, to his master. Reports on a variety of matters connected with Sir John's property, and about certain writings relating to Glendon House, which were in the hands of Mr. Fausbrooke, minister of Cranford, as administrator to the estate of Mr. Lane. The writer also describes certain property at Stoughton, for the purchase of which Sir John was in treaty. [1½ *p*.] *Endorsed,*

Roth[well?].

    91. I. *Particular of the lands at Stoughton with the terms on which they would be sold, with notes of Sir John Lambe thereon.* [1 *p*.]

    91. II. *Map of lands at Stoughton.* [=2 *pp*.]

Feb. 12.   92. Charges against Stanley Gower, rector of Brampton Bryan, co. Hereford, also against Sir Robert Harley, and against Richard Symonds, the schoolmaster of the said place. Gower is stated to have been guilty of all the customary irregularities. He never read the absolution nor the litany, seldom wore the surplice, and in his sermons inveighed against the superstition of places, and persuaded the people that the times were dangerous. Sir Robert Harley was said to countenance him, and Symonds, the schoolmaster, who was maintained by Sir Robert Harley, was a person of the same character, a suspended priest, driven out of North Wales. He was said to repeat Mr. Gower's sermons with comments in Sir Robert's house. They held private fasts, during which Gower prayed and preached *ex tempore* during the greater part of the day. [1¾ *p*.]

Vol. CCCLXXXII. February 13–23, 1637–8.

1637–8.
Feb. 13.

1. Petition of the Dean and Chapter of Durham to the King. Under letters patent they have held the benefit of the river **Tyne** *usque ad filum aquæ*, with salts and shores on the south side of the river, on which there are many salt-pans, and amongst other things a parcel of land called Jarrow Slake, overflown at every spring-tide. Very lately Thomas Talbot and Richard Allen have suggested that Jarrow Slake belongs to your Majesty as land drowned by the sea, and have obtained a grant of the same under a fee-farm rent of 5l. per annum. Pray reference as to petitioners' right, it being unfit for them, being scholars and men of the Church, to have suits in the law. [*Copy.* ⅚ *p.*] *Underwritten*,

    1. I. *Reference to Archbishop Laud, Lord Keeper Coventry, Lord Treasurer Juxon, and Sec. Windebank, to compose the differences as they shall think fit. Whitehall, 13th February 1637–8.* [*Copy.* ⅙ *p.*]

Feb. 13. Another copy of the same. [*See Vol. cccxxxiii., p.* 243. 1 *p.*]

Feb. 13.

2. Petition of Thomas Fountaine Lefever, Captain William Gibbs, Stephen Hawkins, Horatio Carey, sergeant-major, Lieutenant Henry Harris, Francis Le Fountaine, gent., Edward Panton, gent., and Lieut. John Gariney to the same. Notwithstanding your Majesty's manifold public edicts, your cavalry, being a prime nerve of your puissance, is altogether out of frame and unserviceable. Petitioners, who have gained experience in horsemanship in foreign wars, are ready to make an undeniable detection of the present defects in the said cavalry. Pray a reference to the Council of War for examination, and upon their certificate letters patent to confirm to petitioners the place to train up both man and horse, with a convenient annual salary from each trooper. [½ *p.*] *Underwritten*,

    2. I. *Reference to the Council of War to certify their opinions. Whitehall, 13th February 1637–8.* [¼ *p.*]

Feb. 13.

Petition of the Master Wardens and Commonalty of the Brewers of London to the same. Petitioners were first incorporated by Henry VI., and lastly in 21st of Queen Elizabeth, and their power was then limited to London and the suburbs and two miles from the same. Since which, petitioners and all other brewers within four miles of London had made a contract with your Majesty for the service of your household with ale and beer, which is hard to be performed. Petitioners have not power to govern the brewers within four miles of London, and the increase of buildings within that distance occasions the erection of more brewhouses, which ought to be subject to the same government as petitioners. Pray for a new incorporation with extension of limits and such powers as are mentioned in a schedule annexed. [*Copy. See Vol. cccxxiii., p.* 249. ¾ *p.*] *Underwritten*,

    I. *Reference to the Comptroller of the Household* [*Sir Henry Vane*], *who, calling to him the Attorney-General, is to prepare a bill for his Majesty's signature. Whitehall, 13th February 1637–8.*

Vol. CCCLXXXII.

1637–8.
Feb. 13. Another copy of the petition and reference last calendared. [*See Vol. cccxxiii., p.* 324. 1 *p.*]

Feb. 13. Petition of Sir Walter Roberts and other Commissioners of Sewers and owners of the upper levels of Wittersham in Kent and Sussex to the King. Your Majesty upon hearing the differences amongst the commissioners of the levels made an order on the 4th inst., that you would nominate commissioners and send down your own surveyor, who would certify the true state of the business. Because it will be almost impossible to nominate commissioners in Kent who are not interested in some of the levels, or in affection or affinity to some of the commissioners, petitioners pray that gentlemen may be nominated from other counties who are experienced in matters of this nature, or that six commissioners may be sent down besides the surveyor to execute the commission before Easter term, otherwise there will be a whole year lost. [*Copy. Ibid., p.* 242. ⅔ *p.*] *Underwritten,*

> I. *Sir Humphrey Stile, Sir John Manwood, Sir Robert Bell, and George Clapthorne are to be added to the commissioners appointed by the Board, and those seven or any four of them are to repair to the place and make a return before Easter term. Whitehall, 13th February* 1637–8. [*Copy.* ¼ *p.*]

Feb. 13. Petition of Henry Lord Burgevenney [Abergavenny] to the same. Petitioner's whole inheritance is so fast linked, that, without royal assent in Parliament, he cannot dispose of the same for payment of debts or preferment of younger children. Petitioner, at the request of friends of Lady Frances Nevill, late wife of Sir Thomas Nevill, deceased, petitioner's son, settled upon her a suitable jointure, and gave way that lands should be sold for payment of his son's debts, which took up that means which was intended for satisfying petitioner's proper debts, so as petitioner has done so much for his eldest son that he is able to do little or nothing for many young children, nor for payment of his own debts, unless your Majesty will lay a tie upon the mother and friends of petitioner's grandson, Henry Nevill, that he may not be bestowed in marriage without the royal assent and the privity of petitioner, to the end that he, receiving both his honour and whole fortune from petitioner, may out of his marriage portion contribute such sum towards payment of petitioner's debts and provision of his younger children as his Majesty shall think fit. [*Copy. Ibid., p.* 244. ¾ *p.*] *Underwritten,*

> I. *His Majesty conceiving the demands of petitioner most just and reasonable, considering that both the honour and fortune are wholly derived from him, and that the young gentleman is no ward, refers it to the Lord Privy Seal, the Earl Marshal, and Sec. Windebank, to take good caution from Sir Basil Brooke, who has married the mother of the young gentleman, and others, not to dispose of him in marriage, without the consent of the grandfather. Whitehall, 13th February* 1637–8. [*Copy. Ibid., p.* 245. 1 *p.*]

Vol. CCCLXXXII.

1637-8.
Feb. 13. Petition of Robert Earl of Lindsey, Lord Great Chamberlain of England, to the King. Your Majesty granted in fee-farm to petitioner the manor of Burrington, together with the forest or chases of Bringwood, Moctree, and Dervold, co. Hereford. The word "deforestations" was omitted in the warrant for the Attorney-General to draw petitioner's grant, the said word being necessary for satisfaction of purchasers and tenants. As there are no deer there, petitioner prays the insertion of the word. [*Copy. See Vol. cccxxiii., p.* 244. ⅓ *p.*] *Underwritten,*

  1. *Direction to the Attorney-General to insert the desired word. Whitehall, 13th February* 1637-8. [*See Ibid.* ⅙ *p.*]

Feb. 13. Petition of Thomas Jay to the same. Petitioner, with reference to his petition calendared under 29th November 1637, shows that the referees thereof had found that the office therein mentioned, that of weigher of goods on which customs were to be paid, would be an unnecessary burthen. He now shows that in Queen Elizabeth's time there was a surveyor to oversee the customers, collectors, and controllers, and in King James's time a supervisor was added, but the searcher has no superintendent over him. Petitioner prays, in respect of his long service, that if the Lord Treasurer find such an officer to be necessary, the same may be granted to petitioner with the same fees as the searcher receives. [*Copy. Ibid., p.* 245. 1 *p.*] *Underwritten,*

  1. *Reference to the Lord Treasurer and Lord Cottington to certify their opinions. Whitehall, 13th February* 1637-8. [*Copy. Ibid., p.* 246. ¼ *p.*]

Feb. 13. Petition of Francis Earl of Bedford, Henry Lord Maltravers, Edward Lord Gorges, and others, adventurers in draining the Great Level of Fens, to the same. Upon your Majesty's recommendation, and your assent to the Act of Sewers made at King's Lynn for effecting the said drainage, petitioners were encouraged to become adventurers in that vast work, and with the expense of very great sums of money, and after seven years' labour, have accomplished the same, as appears by four decrees of sewers. In pursuance of the law of Lynn the commissioners for the said level have set out 95,000 acres to be enjoyed by petitioners, 12,000 whereof are by petitioners set out for your Majesty, and a decree of sewers in accordance therewith has been presented for your assent, upon which the Attorney-General and the Attorney of the Court of Wards have reported that such decree may be prejudicial to your Majesty in point of tenure, so that the same law lies dead and fruitless. Pray assent to the decree, and a grant of the lands in free and common socage, not in capite or by knight's service. [*Copy. Ibid., p.* 246. 1 *p.*] *Underwritten,*

  1. *His Majesty much desiring the perfection of this work, and finding that, notwithstanding the judgments above referred to, the same is so imperfectly performed that the country and his Majesty remain much unsatisfied therein, and knowing the great advantage that would redound if the*

1637-8.

VOL. CCCLXXXII.

said level were made fit for culture, which petitioners have refused to undertake, commands the Lord Treasurer, calling to his assistance the Attorney, Solicitor, and Surveyor-General, to certify what is fit to be done for perfecting the level, which his Majesty desires and is resolved to accomplish. Whitehall, 13th February 1637-8. [*Copy. See Vol. cccxxiii., p. 247. ½ p.*]

Feb. 13. Petition of the Dean and Chapter of Winchester to the King. Petitioners being seized in right of their church of the manors of Overton, Alton, Stockton, and Patney, in Wilts, on the 20th June, 1st Edward VI., they granted the same to the King, in consideration whereof the said King on the 21st August in the same year granted to petitioners the rectories of Gresford, Crookehorne [Crewkerne], and Lawharne [Laugharne], which they have enjoyed accordingly, until the 21st November last Robert Brookes, clerk, surreptitiously obtained a presentation from the King to the last-mentioned rectory, and was thereupon instituted and inducted. Petitioners pray that they may be restored to their rights. [*Copy. Ibid., p. 248. ½ p.*] *Underwritten,*

> I. *Reference to the Archbishop of Canterbury, Lord Keeper, Lord Treasurer, and Sec. Windebank, to examine how the presentation to Brookes was procured, and to certify his Majesty. Whitehall,* 13*th February* 1637-8. [*Copy. Ibid. ¼ p.*]

Feb. 13. Petition of Sir Anthony Thomas to the same. Your Majesty having accepted from petitioner 1,200 acres of the lands drained by him near Boston, presented in acknowledgment of your favour and protection of his work, and having signified by Sec. Windebank, on 29th June 1635, that the said 1,200 acres should be granted to petitioner in socage at a rent to be settled by the Commissioners of the Treasury, who were to have regard to petitioner's great charge and time spent as the first mover in the Fen business. The setting down the rent was afterwards referred to Lord Cottington, but the lands lying within the honour of Bolingbroke, parcel of the Duchy of Lancaster, the rent was ultimately settled by decree in the Duchy Court at 150*l*. Prays directions to Lord Newburgh for drawing a grant to petitioner accordingly. [*Copy. Ibid., p. 250. ⅔ p.*] *Underwritten,*

> I. *Reference to Lord Newburgh, Chancellor of the Duchy, to give order for preparing a bill accordingly. Whitehall,* 13*th February* 1637-8. [*Copy. Ibid. ¼ p.*]

Feb. 13. Petition of Sir Cornelius Vermuyden on behalf of himself, his partners, and assigns in draining the level of Hatfield Chase and places adjacent in cos. York, Lincoln, and Nottingham, to the same. His Majesty contracted with petitioner for draining the said level, and in recompense thereof petitioner was to have one-third part and his Majesty another third part, which, in consideration of a very

1637-8.

VOL. CCCLXXXII.

great fine and increased rent, his Majesty contracted to grant to petitioner, who in pursuance thereof performed the said work. On the suit of petitioner the King gave order for passing the said lands by letters patent, but the same are not by the said letters patent sufficiently conveyed. Pray warrant to the Attorney-General to draw up a book for making a perfect estate in the law according to the contract to certain feoffees in trust for petitioner. [*Copy. See Vol. cccxxiii., p. 251. 1 p.*] *Underwritten,*

> I. *Reference to the Attorney-General to consider the petition and contract, and if the suggestions be true, to prepare a bill accordingly. Whitehall, 13th February 1637-8.* [*Copy. Ibid., p. 252. ¼ p.*]

Feb. 13.

Petition of Nicholas Crispe, his Majesty's farmer and servant, to the King. Petitioner having occasion to travel through the forest of Deane, found many parts of it not at all wooded nor fit to be incopsed or converted for the growth of wood, and lying altogether waste and unprofitable. Eight hundred or a thousand acres might be fitly enclosed, which might bring your Majesty a fine and a constant rent without prejudice to the iron mills or growth of timber or game. Petitioner made an offer for the said land, about a year past, to the Lord Treasurer, who referred the same to the consideration of Sergeant Whitfield, the Solicitor-General, and Sir Charles Harbord, the Surveyor-General, who reported that there were about 3,000 acres of the forest fit to be enclosed. Petitioner prays for a grant of so many acres as shall be found of that quality in fee-farm, at such rent as petitioner may have a pennyworth from your Majesty, and petitioner will at his own costs enclose the same and convert it into pasture. [*Copy. Ibid., p. 252. ¾ p.*] *Underwritten,*

> I. *Reference to the Lord Treasurer, the Earl of Holland, and Lord Cottington, who, calling to them the Surveyor-General, are to make a bargain with petitioner. Whitehall, 13th February 1637-8.* [*Copy. Ibid., p. 253. ¼ p.*]

Feb. 13.

Petition of Nicholas Crispe, Humphrey Slaney, and others to the same. Show that according to a reference on a petition, the nature of which does not appear, the Lord Privy Seal and the Earl of Dorset, having called the parties before them, have certified the true state of the business, and how disagreable both in equity and for matter of State the verdict is against petitioners. Pray that the matters in the certificate may be determined by your directions, and all proceedings on the verdict be stopped. [*Copy. Ibid. ¼ p.*] *Underwritten,*

> I. *His Majesty, finding that matter of State is concerned in this business, holds it not fit to be further proceeded in at common law, therefore all proceedings there are to be stayed, and the cause receive a final determination in some of his Majesty's Courts of Equity. Whitehall, 13th February 1637-8.* [*Copy. Ibid. ¼ p.*]

VOL. CCCLXXXII.

1637–8.
Feb. 13. Petition of Huett Leate, executor of Nicholas Leate, his father, and Richard Leate, his brother, both deceased, to the King. In 1623, at the importunity of the Turkey Company, who had the sole trading to Algiers and Tunis, an agreement was made at Constantinople by Sir Thomas Roe, English ambassador there, conditionally that the English should use a free trade thither, which by those of Algiers afterwards being distasted, James Frizell, consul there for the company, was enforced to give presents to the Bashaw and "Duan" for confirmation thereof, to the value of 2,905*l*., whereof 1,277*l*. 10*s*. he took out of the estate of petitioner's father, being then deputy of the company. In 1626 the Bashaw and Duan by an *avania* seized on the estate of Nicholas and Richard Leate, to the value of 5,000*l*., because a ship of the fleet at Cadiz took some goods out of a man-of-war of Algiers. For recovery of these sums petitioner's father and brother petitioned the Council, and had suits with the Turkey Company in Chancery, which petitioner has also prosecuted to his great charge, but not receiving any fruit he flies to your Majesty, and prays that, in regard Algiers and Tunis are towns with which the company have now refused to trade, but are places that will vent good store of cloth, a grant may be made to petitioner for some years of the sole trade thereto, and for information as to the equity of this petition that a reference be made to some of the Council, who may call before them Sir Thomas Roe. [*Copy. See Vol. cccxxiii., p. 254. 1 p.*] *Underwritten*,

    I. *Reference to the Lord Keeper, Lord Privy Seal, the Earl of Dorset, and Sec. Windebank, to certify the true state of this cause and their opinions. Whitehall, 13th February 1637–8.* [*Copy. Ibid., p. 255. ¼ p.*]

Feb. 13. Petition of Endymion Porter, Groom of the Bedchamber, to the same. Petitioner lately informed your Majesty that the dignity of baronet as it is now granted is not descendible, so that your Majesty may avoid whom you please, and retain those only that deserve your favour. Prays grant of the prosecution thereof, with such allowance for his discovery, labour, and charges as shall seem meet. [*Copy. Ibid. ¼ p.*] *Underwritten*,

    I. *Reference to the Attorney-General and the rest of his Majesty's learned counsel to certify their opinions of the business.* [*Copy. Ibid. ¼ p.*]

Feb. 13.
Whitehall. Lords of the Admiralty to Officers of the Navy. In your letter of the 8th instant (*see Vol. ccclxxxi., No. 52*) you are more apt to intercede for those boatswains that are most faulty than to certify what you find against such others as with our approbation you formerly suspended for their extraordinary waste. We require you to execute your office and duty on the boatswains of the six ships and pinnaces mentioned in your letter of the 8th instant, and to certify what is the excess of expense over 10 in the 100 in the rest of the ships whose boatswains you formerly suspended. It is time by due punishment to break off this custom of the boatswains' exorbitant wasting of stores. [*Copy. See Vol. cccliii., p. 88 b. ¾ p.*]

1637-8.

VOL. CCCLXXXII.

Feb. 13. Whitehall.
Lords of the Admiralty to the Lord Mayor and Aldermen of London. There is special occasion for 1,000 quarters of wheat for victualling his Majesty's ships appointed for sea next summer. We pray you to lend John Crane, surveyor of marine victual, that quantity out of the city store, he paying for the same such price as you shall agree for, or restoring at Michaelmas next the like quantity, which will be a great accommodation to his Majesty's service. [*Copy. See Vol. cccliii., fol. 89. ½ p.*]

Feb. 13. Whitehall.
The same to the Clerks of the Signet. It is his Majesty's pleasure that no grant of the office of governor of any of his Majesty's garrisons, nor of any office in the office of the Navy or Ordnance, shall henceforth be made for life, but to continue during his Majesty's pleasure only. You are to take care that no bill containing a grant of any such office, subordinate to the office of Lord Admiral or Master of the Ordnance, pass save in accordance with his Majesty's pleasure. [*Copy. Ibid. ½ p.*]

Feb. 13. Whitehall.
3. Order of the Committee for the affairs of the Household. Conceiving it very requisite for the furtherance of the business in hand for reformation of disorders in the Household expenses that an examination be taken of the accounts of former times, it is ordered that Sir Edmond Sawyer and Auditor Phillips shall examine all such parcels and accounts as they shall think fit to demand, from the 17th Henry VIII. until this present time, and certify in what particulars differences and irregularities have from time to time grown and increased. They are also to consider a paper presented to the committee for reforming divers abuses, signed by the Clerk of the Council, and certify what they think of the same. [*Draft. 1 p.*]

Feb. 13.
4. Brief notes and memoranda of Nicholas of the above order and of other matters transacted by the Commiteee on the Household at their meeting this day. [*½ p.*]

Feb. 13.
5. List of petitions and papers concerning the King's Household delivered over to Mr. Meautys this day. [*1 p.*]

Feb. 13. Whitehall.
Henry Earl of Holland, Chief Justice and Justice in Eyre of the Forests on this side Trent, to the Officers of the Forest of Salcey, co. Northampton. Dame Mary Crane, widow of Sir Francis Crane, having made suit for a licence to cut down so much underwood in Stoke Park, co. Northampton, whereof she is seized for life, as she shall have occasion to spend for her own use until she may agree with the reversioner to compound for the disafforestation, the Earl grants her licence accordingly, not exceeding ten acres, so that the said underwoods be sufficiently fenced for nine years, and provided she leave sufficient trees for standells. [*Copy. See Book of Orders concerning Forests, Vol. ccclxxxiv., p. 1. 1¼ p.*]

DOMESTIC—CHARLES I. 257

1637–8.

Vol. CCCLXXXII.

Feb. 13.
Whitehall.

6. Secretaries Coke and Windebank, Comptrollers General of the Posts, to all Deputy Lieutenants, Justices of the Peace, Mayors, and others his Majesty's officers. Warrant to assist Nicholas Compton, post of Shaftesbury, by taking up for his Majesty's service ten or twelve able horses, to be detained not more than two nights, and the owners to be paid such rates as Compton takes for the time of his own horses. [*Parchment, injured. 32 lines.*]

Feb. 13.

7. Petition of Charles Greene, bookseller, to Archbishop Laud. A few years since, petitioner had licensed a book entitled "New Canaan," but when some few sheets were printed it was stayed, and those sheets taken away by means of some of the agents of New England, which book is since printed and dispersed without being questioned. Of late the Wardens of the Stationers in their search after prohibited books took away about 400 of these, to petitioner's great damage, he being a young man and but a small time trading for himself, and they will not redeliver the same without your leave. Prays order to the Stationers to deliver the books to petitioner, or a reference to some person to report. [½ *p.*] *Underwritten*,

> 7. I. *Reference to Sir John Lambe to examine these suggestions, and give order to the Warden of the Stationers for delivery of the books if he see cause. 13th February 1637–8.* [¼ *p.*]

Feb. 13.
Heckington.

8. John Goodyeare, Bailiff of Aswardhurn, to Sir Anthony Irby. I spoke with Mr. Pointall and Mr. Carre, constables of Flaxwell and Aswardhurn, who have taken pains for the collection of ship-money, and when you send they will bring you the money they have got. The rumour in the country of the abatement makes men very loth to pay. If you let them have a special warrant to distrain, the rest would make more haste to pay. Some that now farm grounds, at Lady Day will be gone away, and then their assessment will not be gotten. [1 *p.*]

Feb. 13.

9–10. See "Returns made by Justices of Peace."

Feb. 14.

Writ out of the Exchequer addressed to Magdalen Johnson, widow, commanding her to fulfil and execute an order of the said court made on the 13th inst., the tenor whereof is to the present writ annexed. [*See Case E., Car. I., No. 1. Strip of parchment. 9 lines.*] *Annexed,*

> I. *Order of the Court of Exchequer, dated 23rd April 1629, made in a cause of the Mayor and Burgesses of Newcastle-upon-Tyne against Humphrey Johnson. After reciting various proceedings in the said court by English bill, it was ordered that a common brewhouse kept by the defendant at North Shields should be suppressed, and that the defendant should not by himself, or his servants, or otherwise, thenceforth keep any brewhouse or brew beer for sale at Shields or at any other place within the port save only at Newcastle.* [*Strip of parchment. 104 lines.*]

Vol. CCCLXXXII.

1637-8.

II. *Another order made in the same cause on the 25th November 1637. The court being informed that Magdalen Johnson, widow and relict of the said Humphrey, kept a common brewhouse at North Shields, where the same had been formerly kept by the said Humphrey, it was ordered that she should appear and show cause why she should not be restrained according to the above-mentioned order.* [*Strip of parchment. 61 lines.*]

III. *Another order made in the same cause on the 13th February inst., Magdalen Johnson not having shown cause according to No.* II. *It was ordered that she should be restrained as above mentioned.* [*Strip of parchment. 38 lines.*]

Feb. 14. 11. Orders by his Majesty made for the regulation of his Household. His Majesty having due to him by composition out of the several counties of the kingdom divers provisions towards the maintenance of his household, namely, beef, lambs, stirks, porks, hay, oats, &c., part whereof is many times remaining at the end of the year unexpended, and there being divers other provisions likewise necessary for the household for which he has no composition, but is forced to buy the same with ready money at the market price, it is his Majesty's pleasure that the said overplus (outcast and refuse fish only excepted) be sold towards buying the other provisions, the sale to be made in the counting-house before the Lord Steward, Treasurer, and Comptroller, or two of them at the least, with the rest of the officers of the Greencloth, and that the quantities and prices be entered on record, and be allowed as a sale in the parcel of the month. These orders also contain other regulations respecting keeping the accounts of the household. [1¼ p.]

Feb. 14. 12. Sir William Becher and Sir Dudley Carleton to the Council. Report made in pursuance of order of Council of 26th January last (*see Vol. ccclxxix., No.* 95). We have treated with Mr. Price and Nicholas Hudson touching the new buildings erected by Price in Holborn. After long treaty we brought Price to offer to pay Hudson the original money paid by him for his lease to the Hospital of St. Bartholomew, the new materials and buildings to be valued, and Price to have them accordingly, and the materials of the old buildings to remain to the use of Hudson, who should assign his lease to Price, and so the said buildings be finished as an inn as formerly by Price. This offer was not misliked by Hudson at first, but demanding time to consider he has since refused to accept the same. [½ p.]

Feb. 14. 13. Petition of William Davey to Archbishop Laud. Petitioner putting his eldest son to school, who had an estate of land left him by his grandfather, he was allured by William Artis, Robert Artis, John Southells, and others to marry the daughter of William Artis without the knowledge of petitioner, for which petitioner has

1637-8.   VOL. CCCLXXXII.

articulated against them in the High Commission, and they have fully confessed. Prays a day to be set for hearing the cause next term. *Underwritten,*

    13. I. *If the suggestions of this petitioner be true, Sir John Lambe is to appoint some day next term for the hearing.* 14*th February* 1637-8. [1 *p.*]

Feb. 14.   14. Petition of Edward Agas, clerk, curate of Hingham, Norfolk, to Archbishop Laud. Petitioner being appointed by the Chancellor of Norwich to officiate in Hingham, by reason that Robert Pecke, parson there, stands excommunicate for nonconformity, and finding divers of the parishioners very factious, in particular to forsake their own parish church and resort to others, one two miles and another five miles distant, petitioner acquainted the chancellor therewith, who required him to present some of the chief of them. Petitioner presented Isaac Picther and Thomas Taylor, whom the chancellor admonished to keep their own parish church, but they refusing to obey he sent out an excommunication against them, which being denounced by petitioner, Picther and Taylor appealed to the Court of Arches and got themselves absolved, and so continue still forsaking their own church, and to vex petitioner they made him a party in the Court of Arches. Prays that he may not be troubled for performing his duty. [½ *p.*] *Underwritten,*

    14. I. "*I desire Sir John Lambe to peruse this petition and give an account of it, for I shall not suffer my court to be made an instrument to trouble any man for doing his duty or informing his ordinary, if there be not other pregnant matter against him.* W. CANT." 14*th February* 1637-8. [¼ *p.*]

Feb. 14.   15. See "Papers relating to Appointments in the Navy."

Feb. 15.   16. The Dean and Chapter of Bristol to Bishop Skinner, of Bristol. The dean and chapter having been required by the bishop in the name of the archbishop to settle some provision for the future good of the cathedral out of the improvement of the manor of Peterston and parsonage of Banwell agree that 40*l.* shall be kept in their treasury to maintain the rights of their church, also that 20*l.* shall be yearly expended for repairs, also that for increase of the allowance of the quire 20*l.* per annum shall be allowed by the dean and chapter, and also the stipends of the dead offices of butler, caterer, and cook, amounting to 20*l.* more. [1 *p.*]

Feb. 15.   17. Separate informations of Elizabeth Potter, spinster, and Thomas Bell, with examination of Rachel Thorne, taken before Sir Nicholas Rainton, Justice of Peace for Middlesex. Rachel Thorne being at work with Potter and Bell, in the house of Joseph Dickson in Warwick Lane, referred to a rumour that the Queen's mother was dead, and said that she was a whore and a cutpurse whore, and that the Queen was a whore. Potter thereupon told her mistress,

VOL. CCCLXXXII.

1637-8.

when Thorne was arrested by a constable and carried to Bridewell. Potter verily believed Thorne was drunk. [2 pp.]

Feb. 15. 18. See "Returns made by Justices of Peace."

Feb. 16. 19. Petition of Thomas Brensford and other merchants, part owners of the Ann Mary, of London, to the Council. The Governor and Company of Soapmakers in January last seizing about 2,000 lbs. worth of soap brought from Marcellus [Marseilles] and consigned for Newhaven [Havre de Grace] in France, they moved to have the same confiscated. An order was made by the Council on the 28th January, that the soap should be proceeded against in the Exchequer, and there be cleared or condemned. The company have not brought any suit according to the order, but the soap is still kept in the Custom House. Pray order that the soap may be redelivered to petitioners, who will give good security to answer the suit, and return the soap or the value, if it be condemned. [¾ p.] *Annexed,*

> 19. I. *Order that the above should be showed to Mr. Lightfoot, of counsel with the Company of Soapmakers, to the end that the soap may be brought to a trial in the Exchequer, and that no unnecessary delay be used. Whitehall, 16th February* 1637-8. [*Copy.* ¼ p.]

Feb. 16.
Whitehall.

20. Order of Council. The Board was made acquainted by the Earl Marshal, Governor of one of the Associations of the Royal Fishings of Great Britain and Ireland, that he and the said company had lately, for payment of debts of the company and for stock for going on with the trade for the two years' partnership yet to come, made an order for 50*l.* per cent. to be paid by every adventurer. Most part of the adventurers refuse or neglect to make payment, and he desired the Lords to take order for reducing them to conformity, they having bound themselves thereunto by their first subscriptions. It was ordered that the adventurers should before Lady Day pay the said levy to Peter Richaut, treasurer of the company, or warrants should be directed to bring them before the Board. [*Copy.* 1 p.]

Feb. 16. 21. Sir Francis Godolphin, Governor of Scilly, to [the Council]. Until we shall be better fortified and our fort enlarged, which is at present so little as we can stow almost nothing within it, the late supply which we received out of the Office of Ordnance, together with our former remains, is as much as we can well dispose of, or shall well be able to employ with so few hands. If we should be assailed by an enemy, by reason our works lie now so undefensible, it would require a far greater number of hands than our small company together with the islanders amount unto to make good the place until we might be relieved from the main-land. Wherefore I conceive that on such exigent we might best be reinforced by some land companies, who must also bring their provisions with them, for our islands are no way able to afford them and us livelihood. Moreover, on timely intelligence of any such attempt, a squadron of ships

DOMESTIC—CHARLES I.   261

Vol. CCCLXXXII.

1637-8.

might be appointed to ride in our road, the better to frustrate such designs. Lastly, we are at present much necessitated by reason of our want of pay, there being near 2½ years due unto us, whereby we are much disenabled to make timely provisions out of the main for our livelihood, which is not to be gotten on these islands for such a company. [1 p.]

Feb. 16. 22. Copy of the above letter. [*Endorsed by Nicholas as received on the 21st inst.* 1 p.]

Feb. 16. Westminster. 23. Sec. Windebank to Sir John Pennington. You are to take order for transportation of these French gentlemen, her Majesty's servants, into France, in one of the ships under your charge, whose names are Mons. Jean Garnier, equerry and gentleman in ordinary of the Privy Chamber to her Majesty, Louis Garnier, his son, Mons. de St. Martin, two servants, and Mons. Montifaul, with two gentlemen of his company. They are to be accommodated with all things fit for persons of their quality. The choice of the ship is left to you. P.S.—I have received your letter, wherein you give me notice of the departure of the Providence for Dieppe. [1 p.]

Feb. 16. Chatham. 24. Officers of Navy to Lords of the Admiralty. Upon view of the hull of the Antelope, her bread-room is so defective that she cannot go to sea before she be dry-docked. We offer to your consideration, whether you hold it fittest for the Antelope to be dry-docked, or the Convertive to be made ready in her room. She is completely perfected in her carpentry and painted works for an eight or twelve months' voyage. [*Seal with crest and motto.* ½ p.]

Feb. 16. Chatham. 25. Henry Goddard to the Officers of the Navy. Communicates minute particulars of the defects in the bread-room of the Antelope, and suggests the employment of the Convertive in her stead. [¾ p.] *Underwritten,*

> 25. I. *Kenrick Edisbury to Nicholas. To move the Lords on the suggested change of the Convertive for the Antelope.* 17 *February* 1637-8. [¼ p.]

Feb. 16. 26. Answer of Edward Maria Wingfield, co-defendant with Sir Francis Bodenham and Robert Hall in a suit in Chancery, wherein John Guylett, of Keyston, co. Huntingdon, executor of Richard Guylett, his father, was the plaintiff. The suit related to the validity of leases of land in Keyston, granted by Sir James Wingfield, father of the said Edward Maria, on the 4th October 1622, and 1st July 1623, and 30th March 1634. [*The bill in Chancery in this case occurs Vol. cccxl., No. 26. Copy, last sheet damaged.* 19 pp.]

Feb. 16. 27. See "Papers relating to Appointments in the Navy."

Feb. 16. 28. See "Returns made by Justices of the Peace."

Feb. 17. Whitehall. 29. Notes by Nicholas of business to be transacted by Lords of the Admiralty. Consider a letter from Officers of the Navy touching

1637-8.

Vol. CCCLXXXII.

pressing mariners. The ships under Sir John Pennington are victualled but to the end of next month, and will come in at least ten days before their victuals end, which will be above a month before the time appointed for the new fleet to go out; consider whether (there being at present so many Hollanders, French, and Dunkirkers at sea) it be not better that the four ships with Sir John Pennington be supplied to the end of April. Consider draft letter of assistance which the shipwrights desire for the better ordering those of their corporation in the outports. Appoint a purser for the Henrietta pinnace. The East India Company are to be here to treat about the sale of their saltpetre. Letter from Officers of the Navy. [ ] *p*.]

Feb. 17.
Whitehall.

Lords of the Admiralty to Officers of the Navy. We are informed by Sir William Russell that the charge of building the Sovereign of the Seas is included in the certificate for 1636, and that part of the account for that service is put in the ledger for that year, and that the remainder is most proper to be entered in the same account. These are to authorize you to enter the said account accordingly, and the auditor of the imprests to give you allowance thereof, notwithstanding part of the service was not fully determined, nor part of the money paid, till the end of 1637. [*Copy. See Vol. cccliii., fol.* 89 *b.* $\frac{4}{5}$ *p.*]

Feb. 17.
Whitehall.

The same to all Admirals, Vice-Admirals, and others. To permit the Exchange, of Southampton, to proceed on her voyage to Newfoundland, and if you have already impressed any of her crew here enumerated, forthwith to discharge them. [*Copy. Ibid., fol.* 90. 1 *p.*]

Feb. 17.
Whitehall.

Order of Lords of the Admiralty upon the petition of Anthony Lownes, John Country, Henry Cowdall, Benjamin Jackson, William Brown, and Thomas Norgett, boatswains, showing that upon complaint of their lavish expense of cordage they have been examined by the Officers of the Navy and Masters of the Trinity House, that some of them have attended three months, and all have been pricked out of victuals and wages, proffering to make it appear that they have not been lavish, but submitting and praying to be again established in their places. It was ordered that the officers take bond with sureties of petitioners and the rest of the boatswains suspended, to be responsible for any of their stores wanting or misspent for the future, and thereupon to readmit them to their places, but they are to lose their wages and victuals for the time they were suspended. [*Copy. Ibid., fol.* 90 *b.* $\frac{1}{2}$ *p.*]

Feb. 17.
Whitehall.

Commissioners for Saltpetre to the Farmers and Officers of the Customs. By letter of 18th November last, we required you to put into safe custody such foreign saltpetre as arrived in London in a bark formerly stayed at Portsmouth, whereof Edward Capell was master. You are to deliver the same to Samuel Cordewell, his Majesty's gunpowder-maker. [*Copy. See Vol. ccxcii., p.* 77. $\frac{1}{2}$ *p.*]

Vol. CCCLXXXII.

1637-8.
Feb. 17.
Whitehall.

Order of the Commissioners for Saltpetre. Lucas Jacob is forthwith to deliver to Samuel Cordewell six barrels of East India saltpetre, brought thence by some of the Dutch East India Company, at 55s. the hundred, which Cordewell is to refine for his Majesty's service, and is to have 3l. 16s. 8d. per cwt. [*Copy. Vol. ccxcii., p. 78. ⅕ p.*]

Feb. 17.

30. Thomas Davies, his Majesty's barber, to the Commissioners of the Household. Having moved his Majesty for the rights that have belonged to the barbers to the King's predecessors, his Majesty promised him all that belonged thereunto, so that he could produce proofs. He presents a copy of a record whereby it is manifest that former Kings' barbers were sergeants of the Ewry, and had the sole disposing of the barbers' tents that attended the household. During Queen Elizabeth and King James's time William Ralph and Francis Bates were barbers for the household, and paid rent for the same to the sergeants of the Ewry, as appears by an affidavit of Bates's widow. Alleges other facts from which he infers that, there being no use of barbers under Queen Mary and Queen Elizabeth, the disposition of the barbers' tents continued with the sergeants of the Ewry, not as such sergeants, but as being the King's barbers. [¾ *p.*] *Annexed,*

> 30. I. *Copy, attested by William Ryley, of letters patent of 20th July, 25th Henry VI., whereby he granted to Robert Belley, sergeant of the Ewry, and Alexander Dover, groom of the Ewry, the barbers' tents at the gate of the royal house, to occupy the same with their servants, and to receive certain fees from Knights of the Bath and other knights, and all peers, on their creation, which fees are here set forth.* [*Latin.* 3½ *pp.*]

> 30. II. *Translation by William Ryley of the letters patent of Henry VI., calendared in the preceding entry.* [1 *p.*]

> 30. III. *Affidavit of Avis Bates, widow of Francis Bates, keeper of the barbers' tents and barber to the household. For rent of the tents her husband paid 10l. per annum to the sergeant of the Ewry. States how the rent was paid when her husband went the island voyage, and into Ireland with the Earl of Essex, and on another voyage attending the said Earl, on which last occasion the rent was paid by William Ralph, who was formerly her husband's master and afterwards his partner. Sworn, 17th February, 1637-8.* [1 *p.*]

Feb. 17.
St. Martin's Lane.

31. Sir Thomas Roe to Bishop Morton, of Durham. Received a copy of the bishop's book *De merito* by Dr. Cosin, and acknowledged the receipt. Presents the bishop with a letter from Mr. Dury, and one from Dury to the writer, from which the bishop may collect his state, and his constant resolution to pursue his business as long as God gives him bread to eat. Such a spirit the writer has never met, daunted with nothing, and only relying upon providence. Sends also

1637-8.

a letter from Paris. It is written from Pomerania to the King, that about the same time that Duke Bernard made his attempt to pass the Rhine, the Swedes under Bannier brake out of their garrisons and fell upon the imperial army, and slew 4,000, routing the rest, and that they have driven Gallas to forsake that province. Sir Thomas in Michaelmas term sent the bishop a great packet from Samuel Hartlib, correspondent of Dury, an excellent man and of the same spirit. If the bishop like his way, Hartlib will constantly write to him, and send all the passages both of learning and of public affairs, no man having better information, especially *in re literariâ*. Sir Thomas answers a question put to him by the bishop as to the opinions of the Greek church, by stating many particulars respecting Cyril, Patriarch of Constantinople, whom Sir Thomas knew in that city, and who sent King James a short symbol of their faith and doctrine; Sir Thomas has it at Cranford, and will send it to the bishop if he wishes it. To this symbol all the bishops of the Greek church adhere, and particularly Gelasius, Patriarch of Alexandria, a grave, saint-like man. Pope Gregory XIII. instituted a college at Rome for the education of young Greeks. In this college many Greeks have been bred up and taken the infection of the doctrine of Rome. Many of these have been sent into Greece to oppose the patriarch, and have corruptly got into some bishoprics. From such have arisen all the troubles of the Greek church, and the persecution of Cyril. Sir Thomas gives various details of the troubles of the Greek church arising out of Romish practices, and refers to several publications on the subject. Thinks the Brownists that live in England are proselytes of Rome and are maintained to raise a schism. No bishop in Greece dare avow the supremacy of Rome, or the infallibility of the Pope, for the people would stone them. [*Copy.* 3 *pp.*]

Feb. 17.

32. Petition of Richard Fortune to Archbishop Laud. Petitioner expended much money in seeking out three children of Gartwright Goodwin, *alias* Sanders, which she was delivered of in the time of her husband being beyond the seas, as will appear by the testimony of Dr. Thomas Somes and Sarah Heath, midwife, and others. Petitioner retaining Mr. Rowe for his proctor in the Arches against the said Gartwright, he without petitioner's knowledge agreed with her and solicited in her behalf for absolution, which was granted, the court not being rightly informed of her evil life, by which and the like means the court is evil spoken of, and the spiritual jurisdiction not had in such reverence as it ought to be. Beseeches warrant for Gartwright and Thomas Weekes, her father-in-law, who threatens to spend 200*l.* in her behalf, and in time of the suit kept her private that no process should be served upon her; and for Dr. Somes, Sarah Heath, and others, his witnesses, to appear before whomsoever you shall appoint to examine the business. [⅔ *p.*] *Underwritten*,

32. I. *Reference to Sir John Lambe to take such further order therein as he shall see cause. February 17th,* 1637-8. [¼ *p.*]

Vol. CCCLXXXII.

1637–8.
Feb. 17.
Tower Street.
33. John Goold to Nicholas. Recommends Mr. Alport that he may have the privilege of his place in serving the Navy with flags and ensigns, for which he has the late Lord Admiral's warrant and a further confirmation from the Lords of the Admiralty. An undeserving man seeks an usurpation or displacing of him. The writer's master [Sir William Russell?] is exceeding ill of the gout, or he would give a larger character of Alport's honesty and desert. [*Seal with arms.* 1 *p.*]

Feb. 17.
34. Account of Sir William Russell of ship-money received and in arrear under writs issued in 1636. Total received, 187,028*l.* 6*s.* 8*d.*; arrears, 9,586*l.* 1*s.* [*Damaged by damp.* 1 *p.*]

Feb. 17.
35. Similar account of sums received under writs issued in 1637. Total, 21,988*l.* 0*s.* 6*d.* [*Damaged by damp.* ½ *p.*]

Feb. 17.
36. Account of further sums on account of 1637 levied and in the hands of the sheriffs. Total, 19,750*l.*, which, added to the sum paid to Sir William Russell, makes the amount collected 41,738*l.* [*Damaged.* ¾ *p.*]

Feb. 17.
37. Duplicate of the above account, with an underwritten note by Nicholas that 200*l.* had been paid that week off the arrears of 1636. [*Damaged.* 1 *p.*]

Feb. 18.
Vale Royal.
38. Thomas Cholmondeley, Sheriff of co. Chester, to the Council. States in what manner he had proceeded to assess and collect the 2,740*l.* charged for ship-money on that county. He had followed the course of his last predecessor, but finding that if all the money assessed by him came in there would be surplusage of 70*l.* or 80*l.*, he had publicly made known that upon full levying of the money he would either restore the overplus to the high constables or abate the assessment to such as should be over-charged. He has collected and paid in 2,389*l.* 9*s.* 6*d.*, which is all he has received. Sends his assessment, with an account of sums he has abated. The service has gone on without murmur or reluctancy. For the clergy he finds no distinction of their temporal and ecclesiastical estates, nor can well make it without their great grievance, which he dare not press. The money uncollected shall with all diligence be called upon and paid in. [2¾ *pp.*] *Enclosed,*

38. I. *Assessment above mentioned, in which the amount charged on every parish and clergyman is distinctly stated, with how much has been paid and what is unpaid, and how much has been abated.* [18½ *pp.*]

Feb. 18.
Coggs.
39. Sir Thomas Penyston, Sheriff of co. Oxford, to Nicholas. When I received the letter of instructions from the Lords I sent forth the writs to the corporations, and having appointed a day of meeting, assessed them and gave them the first of this month for payment, but I have yet received no money from them. Presently after, at several days I called the constables and divers of every

1637-8.

VOL. CCCLXXXII.

parish before me at Oxford, Witney, and Chipping Norton, unto which places they all came, and I used the best reasons I could to persuade them to yield obedience, where receiving divers complaints of inequality in taxing the hundreds, and particularly in rating particular men, I have taken the rating of every town myself. It has been a work of very much labour and has required much time, yet I hope it will make the country more willing to pay, for I know that nothing more retarded the service than the unequal rating. Very shortly you shall hear again from me. [*Seal with arms.* 1 *p.*]

Feb. 18.
Putney.
40. Philip Burlamachi to [Sec. Windebank?]. I spoke this morning to the Lord Treasurer, who was of opinion that Monday was too near the end of the term, and that the auditors would not have finished their work. I pray you to let his Majesty understand this, that he may not be kept waiting. I hope that before Friday they will have done, and if that day or the Monday following pleased his Majesty, I would take care that everything should be ready. [*French.* 1 *p.*]

Feb. 18. 41. Copy of the same. [1 *p.*]

Feb. 18. 42. William Pierrepont, Sheriff of Salop, to Nicholas. Explains the reasons of his delay in sending up an account of his assessment. The money is to be paid to Simon Weston, John Studley, and others, merchants of Shrewsbury, who have undertaken the speedy payment of it. He sends an account of what each clergyman pays for his ecclesiastical livings and what for his personal estate. Very many complain that, their estates being at the utmost valued, they pay 1*s.* in the pound. He has laboured to have all rated with equality, and little less is to be collected to make up the 4,500*l.* [1¾ *p.*]

About Feb. 18.
43. Names of the Council of War, with a memorandum that a meeting was to be summoned for the 21st inst. at 8 o'clock, and that Sir Jacob Astley, the Earl of Portland, Sir Peter Osborne, Sir Francis Godolphin, and Mr. Henry Jermyn were to be desired to be there. The Council consisted of the Lord Treasurer, the Earl Marshal, the Earls of Dorset and Newport, Lords Wimbledon, Wilmot, and Cottington, Mr. Comptroller, Sec. Windebank, the Lieutenant of the Tower, and Sir John Heydon. [¾ *p.*]

Feb. 18. 44. Notes by Nicholas of Admiralty business with which his Majesty was to be acquainted. Upon advertisement from Sir John Pennington that there are divers Dunkirkers, French, and Holland men-of-war lately put to sea, which pillage his Majesty's subjects as they meet with them, the Lords have given order for supplying the ships with Sir John Pennington with victuals to enable them to stay abroad till some of the great fleet shall be ready to go forth. The Lords having also received certificate from the Officers of the Navy that the Antelope is defective, have given order for the Convertive to be set forth in her place. [¾ *p.*]

DOMESTIC—CHARLES I.   267

Vol. CCCLXXXII.

1637–8.
Feb. 18.
45. Certificate of Launcelot Worpson [?], mayor of Newark-upon-Trent, co. Nottingham, that on this day notice was given to the mayor and aldermen by Andrew Pawling, messenger of the Chamber, for their appearance in the Exchequer on the morrow of the Purification according to a warrant from Lord Cottington, at which time the corporation expressed that by a leave from his Majesty all escheats were granted to them. They also certified the names of the mayors for the last 13 years. [*Damaged.* ¾ *p.*]

Feb. 18.
46. See "Returns made by Justices of Peace."

Feb. 19.
Boston.
47. Sir Anthony Irby, Sheriff of co. Lincoln, to the Council. Replies to the complaint of the sessions of Sleaford and Folkingham, within Kesteven, that he had surcharged them in the ship-money 161*l*. 8*s*. 6*d*. more than the ancient rates of raising public payments, by which the county was divided into 14 parts, of which Kesteven bore four, and also that he did not allow them the benefit of their corporations to keep them in their proportion. Allows that he had laid Kesteven at 154*l*. more than last year, in which he contends that he had only followed the instructions of the Council in accordance with the practice of the first sheriff. The money was then paid without any question, and would be so now, but for the interference of Sir Edward Hussey, the mover of this petition, the last sheriff, a Kesteven man, who, succeeding the first sheriff, made alterations for the benefit of his own division. Complains of the conduct of Sir Edward in delaying to make his objection until the whole assessment had been completed, and also in writing a letter on the subject which was published at Sleaford on a market day to the prejudice of his Majesty's service. The writer makes no doubt that he shall obtain the money without disturbance or slackness if he may have the favour of the Lords. [*Seal with arms.* 1½ *p.*]

Feb. 19.
Boston.
48. The same to Nicholas. Sends up an account of his assessment, except upon two wapentakes, in one of which the constables were in London on the business of the fens, and in the other there was a great difference about altering the old rates by the last year's sheriff, which was referred to the justices of peace. As to the clergy, the Archbishop of Canterbury had sent a commission to divers doctors for easing their payments, and the writer had appointed Monday next for that business. He has received 1,500*l*., and has returned 1,000*l*. to Sir William Russell by John Gallard, receiver for co. Nottingham. Will send up the remainder as he receives it. Craves pardon for not returning fortnightly accounts by reason of the largeness of his county and the difficulty of ascertaining what was in his collector's hands. The petition of the Kesteven men has retarded the business and prevented the payment of 2,000*l*. [*Seal with arms.* 1 *p.*]

Feb. 19.
Whitehall.
Lords of the Admiralty to Officers of the Navy. To take order that the Antelope be had into dry dock and repaired, and that the

Vol. CCCLXXXII.

1637-8.

Convertive be made ready by the 20th April to go to sea in her place. [*Copy. See Vol. cccliii., fol.* 91. ⅓ *p.*]

Feb. 19.
Whitehall.

Lords of the Admiralty to Officers of the Navy. It is his Majesty's pleasure that one of the ships of the third rank appointed to be of the great fleet shall be fully furnished by the 20th inst. to go southwards. The officers are to cause one of the ships of that rank to be accordingly expedited, and to give notice to the Officers of the Ordnance which ship they prepare, that they may furnish her with what belongs to that office. [*Copy. Ibid., fol.* 91. ⅓ *p.*]

Feb. 19.
Whitehall.

The same to the same. The ships under Sir John Pennington are to be forthwith supplied with one month's victuals to make them able to stay abroad till the last of April next. You are to give order to the surveyor of marine victual to send the same to the Downs, and to put the charge, by way of surcharge, on some of the next estimates. [*Copy. Ibid., fol.* 91 *b.* ½ *p.*]

Feb. 19.
Whitehall.

The same to Montjoy Earl of Newport. We have appointed Richard Wilkinson to be master-gunner of the Nicodemus, which is to go to sea with the fleet. We pray you to give order that the gunner's store be delivered over to him. [*Copy. Ibid.* ½ *p.*]

Feb. 19.
Whitehall.

The same to the same. To allow Capt. William Rainsborough, of Wapping, mariner, William Juring, Mark Questwood [Quested?], and William Pulman, owners, and John Jobson, master of the Confidence, of London, of 200 tons, to supply their ship with 20 pieces of cast-iron ordnance. [*Copy. Ibid.* ¾ *p.*]

Feb. 19.
Whitehall.

The same to the Master, Wardens, and Assistants of the Company of Shipwrights. Order for reformation of abuses in their surveys, and in the entertainment of house carpenters and other unskilful persons. They are to cause their charter to be published and put in execution; to survey all ships in hand; to admit all persons who have served seven years, every one admitted taking his oath to be true to our Sovereign Lord the King, and giving bond in 500*l.* not to serve any foreign state without licence; to examine the number of apprentices, and whether they have been duly bound for seven years, and to punish all abuses therein. Lastly, all vice-admirals, mayors, and other officers are charged to be assisting to the master, wardens, and assistants in the execution of these orders and the punishment of all persons found disobedient. [*Copy. Ibid., fol.* 91. 2½ *pp.*]

Feb. 19.

Survey of decays of the pales of the Great Park of Windsor, with an estimate of the charges for repairs. 1,848 poles of paling are very ruinous. The repair will ask of new stuff 183 loads. The charge for felling will be 20*d.* per load, the carriage a like sum, and the charge for palers and labourers will be 8*d.* the pole. The timber may be taken within the Great Park, in Old Windsor woods, in Southbrooke and in Cramborne [Cranborne?] wood. [*Copy. See Book of Orders concerning Forests, Vol. ccclxxxiv., p.* 4. 1½ *p.*]

Vol. CCCLXXXII.

1637-8.
Feb. 19.
Mincing Lane.
49. Kenrick Edisbury to Nicholas. Upon Mr. Boate's removal to reside constantly at Portsmouth, he desires one of the shipwright's assistants to help him, which we cannot deny, the place requiring it. Young Peter Pett being at Woolwich, and Mr. Apslin not to be spared from Chatham, we must send his own son, who will not be willing unless we assure him the house at the dock, where he and his father dwelt, and which was settled at the first on his father, being keeper of the out-stores, now conferred on Augustine Boate. My desire is to put Stephen Danske, an ancient servitor and employed many years for a purveyor, for his deputy in his absence. If you have any mediation for any other I pray you stay it till Sir William Russell and I speak with you, for it is of great consequence to have an honest diligent man in that employment. [½ p.]

Feb. 19.
Cornbury.
50. Henry Earl of Danby to Sec. Windebank. So long as there was any likelihood that we might plead the justice of our complaint before the archbishop, I was silent, as more willing that my niece Carr should move commiseration by the merit of her cause and carriage towards her husband than by the mediation of any man. But since his Majesty has otherwise ordained, I must now entreat you to see this 1,000*l*. land so settled by Mr. Recorder, of my counsel, that those false friends who have been fatal to Sir Robert and his estate may not use their power to deprive the poor lady and her children. I beseech you that the suggestions of such as lay slanders upon the innocent may have no place in your heart; for I am so confident of her discreet carriage, and the true love she has signally showed her husband, that we will surrender even this remnant, if malice can produce any testimony against her. [*Seal with arms within the garter.* ¾ *p.*]

Feb. 19.
51. Account of the number of post-horses and the towns out of which they were charged to serve, in one day at Royston, by 4 o'clock in the morning. The number charged varied from 6 to 14 on every parish. The total number from 19 parishes was 200. [1 *p.*]

Feb. 19.
52. See "Returns made by the Justices of the Peace."

Feb. 20.
Newmarket.
53. Proclamation limiting the trade of making hats or caps to the members of the corporation of beaver-makers of London, prohibiting the importation of foreign beavers and other hats, and the intermixing of any hair or stuff with beaver in making hats. [*Copy.* 8 *pp.*]

Feb. 20.
The Swiftsure, in the Downs.
54. Sir John Pennington to the Lords of the Admiralty. Since my last here arrived two English ships from St. Lucar and Cales [Cadiz] that brought pretty store of silver, part whereof they have landed here, and with the rest and their goods are gone up for London. There came three other ships in their company from thence, which are all cast away in the channel; two of them Hamburghers, whose goods were consigned for Dover; the one was cast away in Plymouth

VOL. CCCLXXXII.

1637-8.
Sound, the other here at Bollaine [Boulogne], but their men and part of their goods were saved. The other, a Frenchman belonging to St. Malo, was cast away in Bigbury Bay between the Start and Plymouth, and neither men nor goods saved. I have been over with a convoy near Dunkirk, where I saw riding under the Splinter 32 sail of Spanish and Dunkirk men-of-war, divided into two fleets, for there are two admirals and two vice-admirals. [1 p.]

Feb. 20.
Christ Church, Canterbury.
55. Dean and Chapter of Canterbury to Archbishop Laud. Pray him to accept their acknowledgments for his late assistance in the business of the cess for the shipping, wherein the county made a second attempt upon them after the city received an order; and also for the stay of Sir George Tibball's [Theobald's] patent, till they may satisfy themselves that their church suffers no prejudice in his designs. These benefits suit well with the archbishop's constant vigilance for the church in general, and with his patronage of their cathedral. As the memory of them cannot but yet be fresh, so they beg him to believe that no iniquity of time shall blot them out. [¾ p.]

Feb. 20.
Richmond Park.
56. Robert Viscount Belhaven to Mr. Savile. To deliver to the Viscount's servant, John Portell, 27l. 7s. 6d., the half-year's fees for keeping the park of Richmond House, wardrobe, and gardens, due to the Viscount at Michaelmas 1636. [¾ p.]

Feb. 20.
57. Certificate of Sir John Borough, Garter King at Arms, confirming certain arms to John Wakeham, of Borough, Devon, attorney of the Common Pleas and one of the ancients of Lyon's Inn. [Copy. ½ p.]

Feb. 20.
58. Copies of two papers, one relating to French cards seized by Robert Lee and Robert Fryer on the premises of Edward Daniel, the other to a payment of 3l. 10s. made by Daniel to the same persons. [½ p.]

Feb. 21.
Whitehall.
59. Notes by Nicholas of business transacted this day at the Council of War. They relate to the importance and state of repair of Carisbrooke Castle, Sandham [Sandown] Castle, Yarmouth Castle, and Carew's Mount, all in the Isle of Wight, and also to the fortifications in the Islands of Jersey, Scilly, and Guernsey. [6 pp.]

Feb. 21.
Whitehall.
60. Order of the Council of War. Taking into consideration the certificate of the Earl of Newport touching the present state of the Isle of Scilly, and finding there is a difference in opinion touching its fortification, it was ordered that the Lieutenant of the Tower, the Lieutenant-General of the Ordnance, Sir Francis Godolphin, governor of the said isle, with Sir Jacob Astley, and Colonel Hamilton, should attend the Earl of Newport, and upon view of the plots of the said isle, and consideration of the said certificate, and of a letter of Mr. Bassett, lieutenant of the said isle, should agree what is best to be done. [Attested copy. ¾ p.]

Feb. 21.
61. Duplicate of the same. [¼ p.]

Vol. CCCLXXXII.

1637–8.
Feb. 21.
Whitehall.

62. Minutes of the whole proceedings of the Council of War this day, including the order above mentioned, and also an order on consideration of demands made by the Earl of Portland, governor of the Isle of Wight, Sir Peter Osborne, on behalf of the Earl of Danby, governor of Guernsey, and Henry Jermyn, on behalf of Sir Thomas Jermyn, governor of the Isle of Jersey. The same were referred to the Master and Officers of the Ordnance, who examining what provisions have been formerly issued to those isles, should certify their opinions of the same, and set down the charge of each of the said demands. Also a request to the Earl of Newport to certify how many engineers are under his Majesty's pay, what allowance they have, and whether they are men of experience. Also that the Lord Treasurer be desired to cause a certificate to be made of what money has been issued to the governors of his Majesty's castles and forts for reparations, and what account has been given thereof. [1½ p.]

Feb. 21.
Newmarket.

63. Sec. Coke to Sec. Windebank. His Majesty has perused the account of the ship-moneys, and is well satisfied with the care taken to hasten the proceedings in the city of London and to observe their days of meeting. The order to continue Sir John Pennington at sea, and the exchange of the Convertive for the Antelope, is approved. The result of your meeting at the Council of War is expected. The Lord Treasurer's resolution for Sir Arthur Hopton's provision is very acceptable, and assure him from me he shall not stay for his instructions. I send the re-credential for Lord Aston enclosed in my packet which Mr. Fanshaw should have carried. And because you do not specify what ship is appointed for Sir A[r]thur's transportation and to bring back his Lordship, I leave notice thereof to be given by yourself and Sir Arthur by the express to be sent by Withering, for whom I now send a letter of safe-conduct. [*Endorsed by Windebank*, "Answ[ered] 26, and sent another note of the ship-money." 1 p.]

Feb. 21.

64. [Captain] James Duppa to Mr. Wild. I pray cause a letter to be drawn for the Lords to sign, to be directed to Sir Robert Phillips and Thomas Lyte, to examine the complaints betwixt William Daw, brewer, and William Hawkins and Richard Brown, victualler, all of Ilchester. [⅓ p.]

[Feb. 21 ?]

65. Minute of a request for a similar letter to Sir Edward Broughton, and Edward Meredith and Garrod Eaton, Justices of Peace, co. Denbigh, to examine complaints between Thomas Pulford and Thomas Crompton. [⅓ p.]

Feb. 21.
Leicester.

66. Certificate of Daniel Morfin, Mayor of Leicester, that notice was this day given to the mayor, bailiffs, and burgesses of the said borough by Andrew Pawling, messenger of the Chamber, for their appearance in the Exchequer to pass their accounts of casual profits due to his Majesty. They certify that they hold the said casualties by demise from Samuel Knightley for certain years yet to come and under a yearly rent. [½ p.]

Vol. CCCLXXXII.

1637-8.

Feb. 21.
Office of Ordnance.
67. List signed by Officers of Ordnance of munition delivered out of that office for furnishing the Isle of Wight since the beginning of his Majesty's reign, with the present demand of the Earl of Portland, governor of the said isle, and an estimate of the charge thereof, amounting to 2,172*l*. 9*s*. 8*d*. [8 *pp*.]

Feb. 21.
68. Duplicate thereof. [8 *pp*.]

Feb. 21.
69–71. See "Returns made by Justices of Peace."

Feb. 22.
72. Petition of the Mayor, Aldermen, and Burgesses of Congleton, co. Chester, and of the tenants of the manor there, to the King. Upon petitions preferred to your Majesty on petitioners' behalf against William Bromhall, gent., for reinvesting your Majesty in the said manor gained out of your hands by the said Bromhall, your Majesty referred the said matter to the Lord Treasurer and Lord Cottington. Notwithstanding which, and that the referees have endeavoured to despatch the reference, Bromhall has delayed attendance upon the referees, so as petitioners are almost wearied out in prosecution of their suit. Pray recommendation to the Council, that Bromhall being called before them, order may be taken in the premises. [¼ *p*.] *Underwritten*,

> 72. I. *Reference to the Council to send for Bromhall, and upon hearing the differences between them to compose the same. Newmarket, 22nd February* 1637[-8]. [1 *p*.]

Feb. 22.
73. William Boteler, Sheriff of co. Bedford, to Nicholas. I sent you a recognizance of two men of Nether Gravenhurst, for refusing to make a tax upon their town. Since then I have been promised a rate from them by a gentleman who will see it performed. This recognizance will make these men tractable, and the example be good upon others. If you forbear the calling their names I think they will conform to reason without trouble to the Council. [*Seal with arms.* ¾ *p*.]

Feb. 22.
74. Memorandum, signed "Francis Browne," that Mr. Maperley has attached three barrels of powder in Browne's house for the use of his Majesty. [*Endorsed is the attestation* [?] *of two watermen at Bankside.* ⅙ *p*.]

Feb. 22.
75. Acknowledgment of Peter Fautrait [or Fautrart], clerk, M.A., that having obtained his Majesty's title to the rectory of Paulerspury, co. Northampton, upon lapse by simony, and being not able to make legal proof thereof, he compounded with the then incumbent, Gerance James, for 50*l*. Expresses his sorrow, renounces all claim to the said rectory, and promises to bring whatever instruments he has into the registrar's office of the High Commission. [½ *p*.]

Feb. 23.
76. Petition of Oswald Medcalfe, cook, to the Council. Having taken a house for certain years and entered into a bond to the landlord for the payment of 48*l*. a year, which house has been inhabited by cooks these 40 years; but being commanded by an order from

DOMESTIC—CHARLES I. 273

Vol. CCCLXXXII.

1637-8.

the Council not to continue there, but that goldsmiths should inhabit it, and divers goldsmiths having viewed the said house and utterly refused to take the same off petitioner's hands, by reason it stands in a very dark place unfit for goldsmiths; neither will the landlord himself take it into his hands, having a bond for payment of his rent. Prays order that he may keep open his shop as formerly. [½ p.] *Underwritten*,

76. I. *Order for petitioner and his landlord to attend the Board on Wednesday next. Whitehall, 23rd February* 1637–8. [½ p.] *Endorsed*,

76. II. *Reference to the Lord Mayor and such of the Aldermen as he shall think fit, to settle the business for petitioner's relief and indemnity, it not being intended that petitioner should suffer inconvenience by his conformity to the orders of the Board.* 28th February 1637–8. [¾ p.]

Feb. 23. 77. Petition of Alexander Harris, deputy saltpetreman for London, to the Commissioners for Saltpetre. Their deputation enables petitioner to take houses of other men wherein to work, and bestow his utensils, a thing more burdensome in London than in remoter parts. Petitioner has built a workhouse of his own, but presumes not to erect outhouses without leave, the want whereof has been exceeding chargeable for providing coals, hay, and ashes. Beseeches that he may erect an already framed barn, stable, and ash-house towards the fields of Ratcliff, where once before such stood, and build three tenements according to proclamation, to front upon Rosemary Lane, adjacent to the work, for so many of his most useful servants who night and day are employed. Petitioner's predecessor last year delivered little above three cwt. of saltpetre weekly. The place being conferred on petitioner at six hundred he has performed the same, and yet spared the old exhausted grounds, by finding out new earths, which were accustomed to be cast into the fields as waste, and for want of coverts never again procreated. Prays that his deputation may be for 21 years; and whereas his factors of Barbadoes and Virginia advise that saltpetre may be raised in those places, inhabited by the English, he prays the Lords to make him their sole deputy in those colonies. [¾ p.]

Feb. 23. 78. Form of warrant issued by Sir Thomas Penyston, Sheriff of co. Oxford, to the high constables in that county, directing them to assess and collect the amount of ship-money charged upon his district. Two copies of the assessment were to be made, one to be brought to the sheriff at the Star in Oxford at the next quarter sessions, the other together with the money therein expressed to be brought to him on the 18th April at the White Hart in Witney. [¾ p.]

Feb. 23. 79. Release of Peter Fautrait [or Fautrart], clerk, in which the circumstances stated in No. 75 are recited more fully. After receiving his composition of 50l., he left Paulerspury for seven years and lived in Jersey, where he held the rectory of Saint Brelade's. About

Vol. CCCLXXXII.

1637–8.

three months since he came again and challenged the rectory of Paulerspury, and sealed a lease to Thomas Staverton to try the title. He now released all right, and surrendered his presentation to be cancelled, and undertook that Staverton within two months should surrender his lease. [1 p.]

Feb. 23. 80. Attorney-General Bankes to [Sec. Windebank]. He had taken a surrender from Viscount Belhaven of grants of the site of the late monastery of Sheen, of a pension of 1,000 marks for life, of keeping Richmond House and park, and of the stewardships of the court leet and court baron of Richmond for life. [*Copy.* ⅕ *p.*] *Underwritten,*

> 80. I. *Queries as to which of the above particulars the King will grant to the Duke of Lenox.* [⅓ *p.*]

Feb. 23. 81. See "Returns made by Justices of Peace."

Vol. CCCLXXXIII. February 24–28, 1637–8.

1637–8.

Feb. 24.
Durham.

1. Lord Keeper Coventry to Sec. Coke. Baron Denham is fallen sick at Winchester. Upon consultation with Lord Finch, he resolves to set forward to-morrow, to be on Monday night at Salisbury, and so to undertake the remainder of the circuit if his associate continue ill and his own ability of body will permit him. If there shall be occasion to renew those commissions for the rest of the circuit (where the greatest shires and the greatest businesses will be), we have thought Sergeant Heath the fittest man. Sergeant Whitfield, his Majesty's other sergeant, is already in circuit as a practiser, and Mr. Heath in regard of his former employment will give speedier despatch than one that shall be suddenly put upon that course. It is not conceived fit to fix upon him without his Majesty's approbation, therefore I desire you would acquaint his Majesty, and as he shall direct I shall prepare the commissions and hasten other things, that his Majesty's service or the country's occasions suffer not. [1 p.] *Annexed,*

> 1. I. *Baron Sir John Denham to Lord Keeper Coventry. It has pleased God to visit me with an ague, whereby I am unable to travel or to despatch my business, and being of great years I am doubtful what prejudice may happen to the business of the circuit. I desire that if Lord Finch be able to come to Salisbury, he will be there on Monday next, where I will give him meeting if I be able, otherwise I entreat that the commissions may be renewed to Lord Finch and some of the King's counsel, that the service may not fail and the counties be disappointed. Winchester, 23rd February* 1637–8. [1 *p.*]

Feb. 24. 2. Petition of John Tyringham, son and heir of Sir Thomas Tyringham, deceased, to Archbishop Laud. Notwithstanding the award by the archbishop in the case of Anthony Tyringham and Edward

1637-8.

VOL. CCCLXXXIII.

Tyringham, petitioner's uncles, touching the parsonage of Tyringham and Filgrove, there remain some matters in dispute between petitioner and the present incumbent concerning the glebe lands belonging to the said parsonage. For discovery of the certainty whereof, petitioner, the incumbent, and their friends have used all diligence by search of ancient records and examination of witnesses, but by reason of the long union of the churches they cannot find out the same. Petitioner, to manifest his readiness to advance the revenues of the Church, and for avoiding all further differences, is contented to bestow upon those churches a third part of land more than the incumbent demands. Prays that the charge of re-edifying two houses upon the said parsonages (directed by the archbishop's award) may be bestowed upon one, and that the land petitioner is willing to settle may be appropriated to that house only, to remain for ever in satisfaction of all glebe lands pretended to belong to either of the said churches. [¾ p.] *Underwritten,*

    2. I. *Reference to Sir John Lambe to give the archbishop an account of the houses and glebe land by the beginning of Easter term. February 24th, 1637-8.* [1 p.]

Feb. 24.
Wells.

3. Bishop Pierce, of Bath and Wells, to Sir John Lambe. Acknowledges two letters concerning Roger Fort, excommunicated for non-performance of a penance for violation of a monument of a noble personage in the church of South Petherton, where he was churchwarden. Fort had appealed to the Court of Arches, and upon a statement of his case Sir John thought he must give him the benefit of his appeal. The bishop explains the facts, and that what had been done had been with the concurrence of the archbishop. His grace sanctioned a payment by Fort to St. Paul's by way of commutation. Since then Fort had one while declared that he would do his penance, and another while that he would commute. At one time he offered 100 marks, which was agreed to be accepted, and then he went to London, and on his return offered 20*l.* On Wednesday then last he had offered 30*l.*, and was to come again in a fortnight for an answer. Requests Sir John to confer with the archbishop and let the writer know his pleasure as to the acceptance of the 30*l.* [*Seal with arms.* 3 pp.] *Enclosed,*

    3. I. *Statement of the registrar of Bishop Pierce of the contents of the articles against Roger Fort and others, and of the subsequent proceedings. The charge against Fort was that he being churchwarden gave leave that a coffin should be taken up on purpose to have the lead, and that he caused it to be melted to be put to other uses and to save the parish. The coffin was that of a person of quality long since deceased. It was covered with a blue stone, and was lying near a fair monument of the late Earl of Bridgewater and his countess. The church doors were locked, and the coffin was dug out by Robert Fort, " beadman there," Richard Hebditch, the parish*

1637-8.

VOL. CCCLXXXIII.

clerk, and Edward Hebditch, his son, being present and consenting. Robert Fort, Edward Hebditch, Francis Boyce, and John Budchett lifted the coffin out of the grave, and the last two melted it, the bones of the deceased being returned into the grave. All the parties were ordered to do penance in the cathedral at Wells, in the parish church of South Petherton, and at Taunton, with white wands in their hands and papers on their heads declaring their offences. All of them performed their penances except Roger Fort, who stood excommunicated for not doing so, and had appealed as before mentioned. On the 11th January 1637-8 he appeared in the bishop's court and renounced his appeal. [2 pp.]

Feb. 24. 4. Certificate of William Clobery that so long as he should enjoy the saltpetre and custom farms of the King of Barbary he would deliver in the Thames all the coarse sort of Barbary saltpetre that should be there made for his use, at 45s. per cwt. ready money. And whereas there was due to him from his Majesty for the wages, victuals, freights, &c. of three ships taken for the expedition to Rochelle, 3,882l. 8s. 2d. principal, and 3,105l. 18s. 6d. for forbearance for ten years, in all 6,988l. 6s. 8d., he was a suitor to have 40 lasts of powder for satisfying thereof at 7l. 10s. 0d. per barrel, and he would pay the overplus in money. [1 p.]

Feb. 24. 5. Report of Bishop Pierce, of Bath and Wells, Paul Godwin, and Sir Robert Phelipps, respecting the asserted apparition at Minehead of "old Mr. Leakey," late of that place, who had died there above two years before. The report contains examinations of Elizabeth Leakey, wife of Alexander Leakey, son of the deceased, and also of Mr. Heathfield, curate of Minehead, of Elizabeth Langston, and of Eleanor Fluellin, all of whom alleged that they had seen the reported apparition, with observations on the whole case by the referees. They were of opinion that there was never any such apparition at all, but that it was an imposture devised and framed for some particular ends, but what they were they knew not. [*Endorsed by Archbishop Laud.* 12 pp.]

Feb. 24. 6. David Stevenson, saltpetreman, to all constables within cos. Cambridge, Huntingdon, Rutland, and Lincoln. Charges them by virtue of his commission and in his Majesty's name to assist the bearer in taking ashes and other materials for the service. Likewise that they provide carts and teams to carry materials for the service to the saltpetre-house in Huntingdon at the rate of 6d. per mile. [1 p.]

Feb. 24. 7. Account of Sir William Russell of arrears still outstanding of ship-money for 1635. Total, 7,796l. 17s. 9d., or, as rectified by Nicholas after certain deductions, 4,997l. 5s. 2d. [*Damaged by damp.* 1 p.]

DOMESTIC—CHARLES I. 277

Vol. CCCLXXXIII.

1637–8.
Feb. 24. 8. Account of Sir William Russell of sums received and outstanding on account of ship-money for 1636. Total received, 187,149*l.*; outstanding, 9,465*l.* 7*s.* 8*d.* [*Damaged by damp.* 1 *p.*]

Feb. 24. 9. The like of sums received on account of writs issued in September 1637. Total, 29,218*l.* 11*s.* 0*d.* [*Like damage.* 1 *p.*]

Feb. 24. 10. Account of sums remaining in the hands of the sheriffs under writs issued in 1637. Total, 15,850*l.*, which, added to the sum paid in, makes the total collected 45,068*l.* [*Like damage.* ¾ *p.*]

Feb. 24. 11. Similar account with other particulars signed by Nicholas. [1 *p.*]

Feb. 24. 12–14. See "Returns made by Justices of Peace."

[Feb. 26 ?] Lords of the Admiralty to Sir John Pennington. Lord Chandos and Lord Spencer are forthwith to repair into France, and desire to be transported in one of his Majesty's ships from Dover. You are to give order for a ship to attend at Dover and to transport the said Lords to Dieppe or to such place as they shall direct. [*Copy. See Vol. cccliii., fol.* 93 *b.* ½ *p.*]

Feb. 26. 15. Sec. Windebank to Lady Palmer. There has been a business lately in court concerning the education of a grandchild of my Lord your father, which though it reflected much upon his son, yet it has been a great advantage to you, whose moderation in matters of religion came thereby to be made known. That, being bred in the opinions of the Church of Rome, you should notwithstanding take care that your children be brought up, according to your former husband's will, in the religion of the Church of England, is a wisdom so rare that his Majesty is pleased to take notice of it, and will make demonstration of it to you upon occasion. For my part, besides that which concerns the public, I hold it a great honour that, in reference to Sir James Palmer, I am allied to so much goodness, and that it belongs to me to congratulate with you on his Majesty's gracious opinion of you. [*Draft.* 1 *p.*]

Feb. 26.
New College, Oxford.
16. John Windebank to his father, Sec. Windebank. Thanks for a variety of gifts, and amongst them for one special evidence of affection, with which the Secretary had not only enriched the writer but also adorned him; but in reference to which he did not so much glory in the gold as in the kindness. [*Lat.* 1 *p.*]

Feb. 27.
Newmarket.
17. The King to Sir Edward Kynaston. It is not unknown to you how long your son, Sir Francis Kynaston, has been employed in our service, and you may well conceive how much it will be to our dislike if his application to such courses as tend to our contentment in a public good should prove to his disadvantage in your estimation. We are persuaded that your affection as a kind father and your wisdom will induce you to perform at least as much as heretofore you have promised, and that the rather on our recommendation

1637-8.

you will take him into your favour and support him as the heir of your house and the pledge of your loyal service to us. [*Copy.* ⅔ *p.*]

Feb. 27.
Newmarket.

18. Sec. Coke to Sec. Windebank. I have acquainted his Majesty with your letter, and found him not satisfied with the assignment of the port at St. Anderos [Santander]; he knows it to be unsafe and too far within the bay, and not free for the ship's return. He would have the landing to be at the Groyne. For the Isles of Wight, Guernsey, and Jersey, the returns will be expected from the Officers of Ordnance. But for Scilly, when the works are found necessary, care must be taken to send carriages to mount the pieces, and to put it in defence against any surprise, and his Majesty wills the Lord Treasurer to supply what is necessary. The order you have taken with the letter post of Ipswich will reduce them to submit to his Majesty's order and service. The fair weather will keep us here till the end of next week. The Duke of Lenox went this morning for London, but your letter was delivered him before he took horse. The French ambassador is here with much contentment. [*Endorsed by Windebank as received on the 28th inst., and answered on the 5th March.* 1 *p.*]

Feb. 27.
Oxford.

19. Lewis Harris, late under-sheriff of co. Oxford, to Nicholas. I have enclosed the account of Sir Peter Wentworth, and what I have in my hands, and what I have collected and paid to the Treasurer of the Navy. As for the account of Mr. Walter, I have paid to the Treasurer of the Navy 1,600*l.*, but for perfecting thereof I cannot so suddenly do it, in regard that I am very much overcharged by him, and I want divers assessments which the constables have not yet brought in, so that my suit is that you would give me time till next term, and rather than his Majesty's service shall be neglected by the sickness of Sir Peter's under-sheriff, I will collect what I can of the arrearage of Sir Peter's account. Distresses I have in my hands, which so soon as I can possibly put off, I will pay in the 97*l.* upon Sir Peter's account. [1 *p.*]

Feb. 27.
Whitehall.

20. John Crane, Victualler to the Navy, to the same. By reason of the death of a kinsman I cannot wait on the Lords to-morrow to acquaint them with a hindrance to his Majesty's service by Sir John Leedes, in staying wheat bought near Shoreham, which I have ordered to be shipped to London or Portsmouth as the wind should best serve. Desires the Lords' letter to Sir John Leedes to let the wheat, which is 120 quarters, be sent away, and that he with his neighbour justices give furtherance to making provision of 200 quarters of wheat more at reasonable prices. I use no commission, and for what I buy I pay ready money. If I have not liberty to transport corn to such places where I am to use it, I shall not be able to put bread aboard his Majesty's ships. [*Seal with arms.* 1 *p.*] Enclosed,

> 20. I. *Sir John Leedes to John Crane. Explains the cause of the stay of the corn above alluded to. The outcry of the*

Vol. CCCLXXXIII.

1637–8.

poor in those parts, that they could neither have corn in the markets nor at farmhouses, was such that Sir John entered into an examination of the business, and found that William Avis and one Lawrence, both of Shoreham, had engrossed great quantities of corn and had sent away one ship-load. One sack of corn in two market days in Steyning was all the proportion sent thither, nor had the farmers sold any at their houses to the poor, though required. The 130 quarters exported was entered in the Customs book in the name of Mr. Alcock for London, but on the return of the ship she brought a certificate from Southampton, and that the corn was there sold for the private benefit of Alcock, Avis, and Lawrence, and no way expended for his Majesty's service. The corn now remaining was to have been exported to the same place and to the former benefit, Southampton not being a port to which Crane was authorized to export. This exportation will produce a scarcity, wheat, in respect of the small quantity of barley, being the only provision for poor as well as rich. Wappingthorn, 24th February 1637–8. [Addressed to Crane as "chief clerk of his Majesty's kitchen." 2 pp.]

20. II. *John Crane to Sir John Leedes. The export of the 130 quarters to Southampton was by Crane's order. The present service is for his Majesty; a bark is hired; the corn lies at Shoreham in some danger. If Sir John will give leave for it to pass, the writer promises him within a week after his Majesty's return from Newmarket to send him a warrant from the Lords for both these exports. Mr. Alcock's name was used in the business, but he had nothing to do in it for any particular of his own, but as the writer's principal man in his place for victualling the navy. Lawrence is not known to either of them. Avis is in fear of his life by the inhabitants of Shoreham, and also fears the breaking open the places where the corn is laid, which he prays Sir John to take care of. 26th February 1637–8. [¾ p.]*

Feb. 27.
Mincing Lane.

21. Officers of Navy to Lords of the Admiralty. Upon former information of the worm that did hurt to his Majesty's ships at Portsmouth, we caused the Triumph, the St. George, the St. Andrew, and the Swiftsure to be sheathed under water, and the rudders to be laid about with copper, as the East India ships use to be trimmed, to his Majesty's great charge, but notwithstanding most of them, after their employment at sea, are commanded to Chatham, and other ships sent to lie at Portsmouth. We mind you of what you warranted us to do, and pray you to order the Swiftsure, at the end of her service in the Narrow Seas, may be commanded to Portsmouth. [1 p.]

Vol. CCCLXXXIII.

1637-8.
Feb. 27.
22. Petition of Peter Fautrart to Archbishop Laud. States the effect of the two papers already calendared in reference to his presentation to Paulerspury (*see Vol. ccclxxxii., Nos. 75 and 79*), and that he is very poor and much indebted, and has nothing to sustain him, but a benefice in Jersey not worth 40*l*. per annum. Prays that he may be absolved from his excommunication and be released from the suspension *ab officio et beneficio*, and that his bond may be delivered up to him, and his fine, charges, and imprisonment released and he be dismissed, so that he may go and tend his cure at home. [⅔ *p*.] *Underwritten*,

> 22. I. *Reference to Sir John Lambe. If he find the suggestions true, and that petitioner have performed what is fitting, the archbishop is content that he have his absolution and dismission or any other lawful favour.* 27th February 1637-8. [¼ *p*.]

Feb. 27.
23. Petition of William Hill, clerk, to the same. In the metropolitan visitation of the Marches of Wales in 1636, by Dr. Owens and Mr. Nicholson, commissioners for the archbishop, upon complaint of petitioner the commissioners visited the parish church of Llanrhaiadr, in Kinmerch, co. Denbigh, where petitioner is vicar, and the same commissioners enacted that divers things which were amiss should be amended, and charged William Dolben, then churchwarden, to see the same performed, and to certify the performance to the Court of Bangor, or to appear before the archbishop at Lambeth. Dolben and many others whom he procured have certified that the act is performed, whereas the same is not fulfilled to this day. Prays letters to Dolben and others to appear at Lambeth to answer. [½ *p*.] *Underwritten*,

> 23. I. *Reference to Sir John Lambe to take order as he shall find just and fitting.* 27th February 1637-8. [¼ *p*.]

Feb. 27.
24. The same to the same. Petitioner, vicar of Llanrhaiadr, in Kinmerch, co. Denbigh, for twelve years, to the uttermost of his power waited upon his cure and observed all things concerning his canonical obedience. He shows that John Lloyd, one of the churchwardens of the said parish, came to petitioner, being in his vestments at the high altar to deliver the sacrament, and swore by God that he would make petitioner provide bread and wine, although contrary to the custom of the parish, and so deluded both priest and people with an empty flagon on the altar, without any wine or bread. And also that the said John Lloyd took an excommunication from the high altar after publication by the curate, so that he could not certify the same to the court, and for four years together has made himself churchwarden on purpose to domineer in the church and molest petitioner, so that he is driven to leave his parish and live in the parish of Llanvair, about four miles distant, where he hopes with the archbishop's licence to live, the rather that there are many English families in Llanvair, where petitioner hopes to do good service. Prays letters missive *ex officio* for Lloyd to appear at

1637-8.

VOL. CCCLXXXIII.

Lambeth to answer things to be objected to him. [¾ p.] *Underwritten,*

    24. I. *Reference to Sir John Lambe to give an account to the archbishop. 27th February 1637–8.* [¼ p.]

Feb. 27.   25. See "Returns made by Justices of the Peace."

Feb. 28.   26. Petition of Theophilus Earl of Suffolk to the King. Your Majesty having been pleased that moneys due to you from petitioner should be defalked out of such moneys as were due to petitioner from your Majesty, heretofore gave directions for the same, and for payment of such surplusage as should remain due to petitioner. Notwithstanding which, petitioner has not only not received any benefit of your Majesty's intended favour, but himself, his tenants, and lands are vexed under pretence of moneys due, although it has been made appear to the Officers of the Treasury that there is a surplusage due to petitioner. Prays order to the Lord Treasurer to make such defalcation, and to free petitioner from molestation. [¾ p.] *Underwritten,*

    26. I. *Direction to the Lord Treasurer as prayed. Newmarket, 28th February 1637–8.* [1 p.]

Feb. 28.   27. Order of Council. John Downes and Maurice Moseley, to whom the custody of the two daughters of Sir Richard Letchford was formerly committed, represented to the Lords that they could not provide them with clothing and other necessaries at the rate formerly allowed, being 20*l.* per annum apiece. Upon hearing Sir Richard Letchford now present, the Board propounded to Sir Richard that he should allow to each of them 30*l.* per annum, whereunto Sir Richard assenting, it was ordered accordingly. [*Copy.* ½ p.]

Feb. 28.
Whitehall.
   Lords of the Admiralty to all Vice-Admirals, Mayors, and other Officers. There is a Dutch ketch or pink, whereof Jaon Janson Steil is master, which is appointed to export oysters from Colchester or out of the Thames or Medway into the Low Countries for the Prince of Orange and his household. We require you to permit Steil to export the same for this one time only, notwithstanding any order given to the contrary. [*Copy. Vol. cccliii., fol. 93 b.* ½ p.]

Feb. 28.   28. Petition of Hugh Reeve, parson of Ampthill, co. Bedford, to Archbishop Laud. Petitioner has received the certificates of the christenings, burials, and marriages within cos. Bedford, Buckingham, and Hertford above twenty-eight years, and was appointed so to do by the now Bishop of Lincoln, and three preceding bishops, for the ease of those counties, the said certificates to be delivered into the Bishop of Lincoln's office at Buckden, according to canon. Beseeches that he may receive the said certificates as formerly. *Underwritten,*

    28. I. *Reference to Sir John Lambe.* "*If there be no just exception, I shall not be unwilling to grant what is here desired.*" *28th February 1637–8.* [¾ p.]

Vol. CCCLXXXIII.

1637-8.
Feb. 28.   29. Certificate of Dr. John Prideaux, Regius Professor of Divinity and rector of Exeter College, Oxford, with thirteen others of that college, of the good conduct of Philip Taverner, B.A., during his residence in Exeter College. [1 p.]

Feb. 28.   30. Acquittance of Hugh Baguley, constable, for 2l. 15s. paid by Thomas Earl of Berkshire for his castle and demesnes near Newark, parish of Stoke, for ship-money. [¼ p.]

Feb. 28.   31. See "Returns made by Justices of Peace."

[Feb. ?]   32. Petition of Richard Delamain to the King. Petitioner has employed sundry artificers for making up divers mathematical instruments by your Majesty's command, ever since he received a warrant at Oatlands in August last for metal which he could not have. These workmen have been in continual pay ever since, amounting to 5l. per week, which for six months comes to 120l., besides 3 cwt. of brass, 21l., taken up for making the great Octans spoken [about] unto your Majesty at Greenwich last summer, and for making your Majesty's great Universal Concave, lately presented to your view; which works, with the making up your silver instruments, petitioner was not able to undergo himself, but by the aid of sundry gentlemen, amongst whom Sir John Heydon has not been the least, and an eye-witness of the many labourers daily employed in your Majesty's house at the Minories about the same. Prays that he may receive the said 141l. for payment of many poor men yet unpaid, which shall satisfy petitioner for these inventions, which he presumes not to sell to your Majesty, but casts them and himself at your feet. [¾ p.]

[Feb.]   33. Petition of Theophilus Earl of Suffolk to the same. Upon former petitions of your subject signifying the decay of the castle of Dover and other castles under petitioner's survey, you gave order for means to advance the same, which have not taken effect. By letters patent for repair of the harbour of Dover, your Majesty heretofore granted an increase of duty of 12d. to be paid upon every pack of strangers' goods brought into or exported from Dover for three years to be ended the 19th of this February, which payment has continued without hindrance to trade, and the harbour been thereby sufficiently repaired and some surplusage in the hands of the receiver. For repair of the castles, prays order that the money in the receiver's hands, with such other money as shall be sufficient, may be issued and employed thereupon. [½ p.]

Feb.   34. Petition of Patrick Batty to the same. Your Majesty has often been petitioned on behalf of your tenants, the copyholders of the manors of Wavertree and Everton, co. Lancaster, to have the same granted in fee-farm, petitioner having spent much money in maintaining your right to the said manors against the citizens of London, who having purchased the manor of West Derby adjoining to the said two manors at the rent of 145l. per annum, which they pretend to be the rent of all the said three manors, and being about

1637-8.

VOL. CCCLXXXIII.

to obtain a renewal of their grant, intend to include the said two manors as one of their amendments. Pray warrant to forbear passing the same until certificate be made upon a petition referred to Lord Cottington and the Attorney-General on the 3rd March 1634-5. [½ p.] *Annexed*,

  34. I. *The King to Lord Keeper Coventry, Lord Newburgh, Chancellor of the Duchy of Lancaster, and Sir John Bankes, Attorney-General. Warrant above prayed for. February 1637-8.* [*Probably proposed form.* ½ p.]

Feb. 35. Petition of Thomas Barton, now prisoner in the Fleet, to the Council. Petitioner being served with a warrant from the Lords to appear concerning ship-money, made his repair to London, and having incurred your heavy displeasure, is most justly committed to the Fleet. Expresses great contrition and prays release. [½ p.]

Feb. 36. Petition of Eleanor Gibbins and Elizabeth Grove, widows, Thomas Harrison, William Parman, Edward Andrewes, William Gaudy, Thomas Worsley, and Richard Welbeck, licensed and incorporated beer brewers in Reading, to the Council. Reading being very populous, they are occasioned to often brewing, and to daily or weekly grinding of malt. The owners of the water corn-mills in Reading, called the Abbey Mills and St. Giles's Mills, paying a small farm rent to his Majesty, 20° Jacobi obtained a decree in the Exchequer against Christian Harrison, widow, John Grove, and Richard Minch, beer brewers, of Reading, all deceased, in these words, that the said widow, Grove, and Minch should pull down their horse-mills, and should erect no other within Reading. By this decree the owners of the said mills would restrain petitioners, who are farmers unto his Majesty and strangers to the said decree, from setting up horse-mills for their own private use, threatening petitioners with suits of law, alleging that petitioners are bound by that decree, which it is conceived binds only those made parties to the same. Petitioners hope they may set up horse-mills, the same being applied only to the service of their brewing. And the rather, that often by reason of floods, frost, or drought, the said water-mills cannot grind, as of late by reason of frost, which disabled petitioners to brew, insomuch as their grist could not be ground, which caused a murmur in the town, and many to want their weekly supplies. Pray that they may not be restrained from setting up horse-mills. [¾ p.]

[Feb.] 37. Petition of Francis Lippencott and Richard Mayne, of Exeter, to the same. By a complaint of merchants of Exeter that petitioners use two trades, viz., retailing and adventuring, petitioners are warned to appear before the Council on the next sitting after the 15th February, about which time there is a fair holden at Exeter, when petitioners have great sums to pay and receive. Pray for a month's further time. [*Answered "Nihil."* ½ p.]

Vol. CCCLXXXIII.

1637–8.
[Feb.] 38. Petition of Richard Mayne and Francis Lippencott to the Council. Another petition to the same effect as the preceding, but differently stated, and praying for three weeks' or a month's delay. [½ p.]

Feb. 39. Sir Thomas Cotton and Sir Robert Beville to the same. According to your letter dated 31st July last, we have used our best endeavours within the hundred of Normancross touching contribution towards the repairs of St. Paul's, London, and have received 8*l*. 14*s*. 6*d*.; we intend to send to the Chamber of London a particular certificate and to pay in the same there. [¾ p.]

Feb. 40. Petition of Henry Cowdall, boatswain of the Convertive, to the Lords of the Admiralty. The Convertive, formerly of the second rate, is of late fallen down to the third rate, and has no more allowance of cordage than ships of the third rate. Petitioner is complained of for lavish expense of cordage, and for the same these three months has been pricked out of victual and wages to his great disgrace. Vindicates himself against the charge, but is sorrowful for their displeasure, and prays them to restore him. [¾ p.]

Feb. 41. George Clarke to [the Commissioners for Saltpetre and Gunpowder]. I delivered your letter to the mayor of Bristol, who readily observed your direction, and has returned an account thereof by letter to you. The exchange of their old powder for new, with allowance, I hear nothing objected against. The city is very careful of the trained band, which consists of 300 men, directed by the State, which they have increased to 500. The charge of the powder is borne by the city, not by the trained soldiers. There are many retailers of gunpowder in the city, whose names I have collected, who were furnished by the powder-mills there and from Walter Parker, in Dorsetshire, who pretends he has a licence. He makes above 200 barrels a year. The trained bands of the country adjoining are supplied by the high constable of every hundred, the money raised by a hundred rate, which is very easily borne, but they appearing but at a general muster there is but little exercising. [1¼ p.]

Feb. 42. Petition of Jason Grover, the common carrier of Ipswich and Yarmouth, now prisoner in the Fleet, to Edward Earl of Dorset. Petitioner and the carriers of Norwich were lately questioned by Mr. Witherings touching the carriage of letters, and the Lords ordered a settled course, not only for the carriers of Norwich but for all other carriers, by order of 24th January last, to which order petitioner is willing to conform himself, but had no knowledge that the same was drawn up till the 10th February inst. And although petitioner has not broken the said order since the drawing up thereof, yet he with his two men were by Witherings' procurement for 17 days committed to a messenger and now to the Fleet, and cannot be discharged except petitioner will enter into bond to perform such order as Witherings has prescribed, which is contrary to the

1637-8.

VOL. CCCLXXXIII.

order of the Board. Prays that he may enjoy the benefit of the said order and not be punished before he has broken the same, nor compelled by Witherings to enter into bond, the order being a sufficient tie. [1 p.] *Annexed*,

    42. I. *Copy Order in Council of the 24th January 1637-8, calendared under that date, Vol. ccclxxix., No. 61.* [1 p.]

[Feb.]   43. [Sec. Windebank] to the Masters and Governors of the Turkey Company. His Majesty having a great desire to increase the knowledge of the Eastern languages, wrote his letters about four years ago that every ship returning from those parts should, at their own cost, bring some one or two of the Arabic books there to be had, and commanded the Archbishop of Canterbury to take special care of this business. His Majesty having lately spoken with the archbishop thereon finds that he has scarce received two books in these last two years. His Majesty has commanded me to require you to be more careful to satisfy his desires in this behalf. You shall do well to be careful of it, that his Majesty may see how willing you are to comply with his princely and just desires. [*Draft.* ¾ *p.*]

Feb.   44. Francis Earl of Bedford, Lord Lieutenant of Devon, to Thomas Meautys. Richard Please, John Brownescombe, Daniel Berrie, Henry Chichester, Christopher Hocking, Amias Paslowe, John Lea, Walter Palfreman, and John Dicker, have submitted to conform themselves at the next musters. I shall be contented that they be discharged from further attendance. [¾ *p.*]

Feb. ?   45. Particulars prepared by Sir Nathaniel Brent by way of instructions to Sir John Lambe for drawing up articles for the visitation of Merton College, Oxford. [*Endorsed and corrected by Sir John Lambe.* 2½ *pp.*]

Feb. ?   46. Articles objected in the High Commission against Richard Powell, clerk, vicar of Pattishall, co. Northampton. Many scandalous indecencies and profanations arising out of drunkenness are here charged against the defendant. Besides many great immoralities and extreme irreverence in the exercise of the duties of his ministry, it is imputed to him that he preached against ship-money, and that thereupon all his parishioners refused to pay the same, and many of them having been consequently distrained upon, the defendant in his next sermon inveighed against tyrannical princes that laid cruel and unjust taxes upon their subjects. It is also charged that he privately taxed the bishops for their pride and ambition. [14½ *pp.*]

[Feb.]   47. Collection of papers relating to a suit in the High Commission against Toby Bullock and others, who were charged with having encroached upon ecclesiastical jurisdiction in making orders for the government of the hospital of St. Bartholomew, in Gloucester, and, under pretence thereof, with having made a lease of the profits

1637-8.

Vol. CCCLXXXIII.

thereof, or a great part thereof, to an unconformable minister. The papers consist of the following :—

47. I. *Order of the Common Council of Gloucester that Toby Bullock and eleven others should survey the orders at the Bartholomew's and certify, that other laws may be made as cause shall be.* [¾ p.]

47. II. *Names of those appointed on the committee mentioned in the last article, and also of all the rest of the Common Council, with a copy of the certificate of the committee above mentioned, containing various suggestions of new orders.* [1¾ p.]

47. III. *Another copy of the certificate or report of the committee above mentioned.* [1 p.]

47. IV. *Extracts from the Minute Book of the Corporation of Gloucester, comprising :—*

47. IV. i. *Order of the Common Council that the committees for the Bartholomew's orders have power to draw orders for the government of the hospitals and present them to the House. 21st January* 1635–6.

47. IV. ii. *Order of the same for establishment of the orders for the good government of the Bartholomew's, King James's Hospital, and the Margaret's. 11th February* 1635–6.

47. IV. iii. *Another order to the same purport as the last. 23rd February* 1635–6.

47. IV. iv. *Order that the books of the new orders having been examined, one was delivered to John Ryce to be kept at the Bartholomew's, and the other to the stewards to be kept in the treasury of the city. 8th July* 1636. [*Altogether* 1⅓ p.]

47. V. *Archbishop Laud to the Mayor and Corporation of Gloucester, apprising them that having been informed of some things amiss at St. Bartholomew's Hospital, he required them to send him the books themselves or a true copy of the orders there, whether new or old. 4th June* 1636. [*Underwritten, memorandum that the old and new books were delivered to the archbishop at Oxford at the Act there.* ¾ p.]

47. VI. *Forty-two inhabitants of Little Dean to the Mayor, Aldermen, and Common Council of Gloucester. Mr. Wilse, the ancient tenant that holds the impropriation of Little Dean belonging to the hospital of St. Bartholomew, being grown very weak, petitioners pray that a grant of the same in reversion may be made to their present curate, Mr. Ridler, whom they highly praise. 12th December* 1636. [*Copy.* 1 p.]

Vol. CCCLXXXIII.

1637–8.

47. VII. *Thirty-three inhabitants of Little Dean to the Mayor, Aldermen, and Common Council of Gloucester. Their old curate is dead; pray them to appoint Mr. Ridler. Certify his conformity to the Church of England in every point. Little Dean, 21st December* 1636. [1 *p.*]

47. VIII. *Extract from the Minute Book of the Corporation of Gloucester that Walter Ridler shall have a lease of the parsonage of Little Dean for 21 years, if he live so long, at the old rent and the like covenants as Mr. Pleadall has Newnham, giving young Wilse 5l., and the bishop's approbation to be desired.* 23rd January 1636–7. [½ *p.*]

47. IX. *Copy minute from the Acts of the High Commission of the appearance of Toby Bullock before that court, when the cause why he and others were convented was made known to him, and he was ordered to attend Sir John Lambe and Dr. Duck, and to give in the names of all who had any hand in making certain orders for the government of St. Bartholomew's Hospital, Gloucester. This is a copy of the paper in Vol. ccclxxix., No. 88, calendared under the date of the 5th January 1637–8, with underwritten appointment of Sir John Lambe and Dr. Duck to hear the cause on the Saturday after the 7th February* 1637–8. [*Copy.* 1⅓ *p.*]

47. X. *Brief for the defence in the above cause. It states the effect of the letters patent, 27th July, 6th Elizabeth, and an Act of Parliament of 8th Elizabeth confirming the same, with the facts before stated respecting Mr. Ridler.* [2 *pp.*]

[Feb.] 48. Assessment of the shipping-mize in co. Merioneth. The amount assessed upon every parish and every clergyman is here stated, Hugh Nanney being the sheriff. [2 *pp.*]

[Feb.] Observations concerning the knighting of the children of Kings of this realm, the purport of which is to show that it has been usual for them to receive the Order of the Bath before that of the Garter. [2½ *pp.*]

Feb. 49. Brief notes, principally of various dispensations and presentations to ecclesiastical livings, procured by Archbishop Laud, between March 1634–5 and the present month. The following is a list of the persons to whom they relate:—

    Thomas Middleton, dispensation to hold Steynton, co. Pembroke, with Orchard, Somerset.
    Acceptus Frewen, the like to hold Stanlake, co. Oxford, with Warnford, Hants.
    Dr. Richard Bayly, presentation to deanery of Sarum.
    Dr. Dodd, ,, ,, Ripon.
    William Blower ,, West Ham, Essex.
    Declaration prohibiting all judges to meddle with ecclesiastical affairs without the approbation of the Archbishop of Canterbury.
    University of Oxford, grant to, enlarging the power of the Chancellor.

Vol. CCCLXXXIII.

1637-8.

Dr. James Halsey, presentation to Watton-at-Stone, co. Hertford.
Andrew Read, ,, ,, Howe Capell, *alias* Capella Hugonis [How Caple], co. Hereford.
Charles Keane, ,, ,, Foxholes, co. York.
St. John's College [Oxford], licence to purchase the township of Woodbevington and lands in Donington and Salford, co. Warwick, with legacies of 2,800*l*. and 900*l*.
Samuel Kynaston, presentation to St. Nicholas Yelford, co. Oxford.
William White, ,, ,, Wargrave, Berks.
William Brackstone, ,, ,, Widford, co. Gloucester.
John Burley, ,, ,, Stokenham, Devon.
Samuel Moyle, ,, ,, Roche, Cornwall.
Bishop of Winchester, grant of the office of his Majesty's chief almoner.
Dr. William Roberts, congé d'elire for bishopric of Bangor.
Thomas Jones, presentation to Tidcombe, Tiverton, Devon.
William Griffith, ,, ,, Llambedrocke [Llambedrog], co. Carnarvon.
Dr. Rawleigh, grant of the deanery of St. Borian, *alias* Burian, Cornwall.
James Hume, presentation to Tinmouth, co. Durham [Tynemouth, Northumberland?].
Dr. William Beale, ,, ,, Paulspurry [Paulerspury], co. Northampton.
Richard Mervin, ,, ,, Bratton, co. Wilts.
Thomas Nicolson, ,, ,, Ufford, co. Northampton. [Afterwards struck out.]
William Lyford, ,, ,, Sherborne, Dorset.
Dr. Micklethwaite ,, ,, Herstmonceux, *alias* Hurst Mounsey, Sussex.
Dr. John Warner, congé d'elire for bishopric of Rochester.
William Bray, presentation to a prebend in Canterbury Cathedral. [This entry is subsequently repeated.]
Samuel Bernard, ,, ,, Hollingbourne, Kent.
Francis Barrough, ,, ,, Langar, co. Nottingham.
Robert Brooke, ,, ,, Laugharne, co. Carmarthen.]
Edward Bullen, ,, ,, Sutterton, co. Lincoln.
Denys Prideaux, ,, ,, Honiton, Devon.
Edward Cookes, ,, ,, Brigham, Cumberland.
Daniel Whitby ,, ,, Theydon Mount, Essex.
John Gandy ,, ,, South Brent, Devon.

[Feb. ?] 50. Brief of evidence touching complaints of John Law, Richard Reeve, and John Foard and Sarah his wife, of the taking away from them of their moulds for printing playing cards. [1⅓ *p*.]

[Feb.] 51. Assessment of ship-money upon co. Pembroke. The amount charged upon every parish and clergyman is stated. Haverfordwest was assessed at 34*l*., Pembroke at 12*l*., Tenby at 15*l*. Certified by "Thomas Phellipes," sheriff. [8¾ *pp*.]

[Feb.] 52. Brief on behalf of Thomas Oliver against Richard Stamper in a cause of defamation. Stamper was accused of having set abroad reports that Oliver had attempted the chastity of various women at Arundel, where or near which the parties to the suit resided. [*Very much damaged by damp.* 37 *pp*.]

[Feb.] 53. Statement of the value of a barrel, a last, and 100 lasts of gunpowder at 23*d*. the pound. The amounts were respectively 9*l*. 11*s*. 8*d*., 230*l*., and 23,000*l*. [2 *lines*.]

[Feb.] 54. Extracts from the *Antiquitates Britannicæ*, in the life of Archbishop Warham, and from the Chronicle of Eadmer, which evidence,

Vol. CCCLXXXIII.

1637–8.

as stated in Archbishop Laud's endorsement, that the Archbishop of Canterbury appointed the preachers at Court, and that the King and the Queen were the archbishop's parishioners. [½ p.]

Feb. 55–7. See "Returns made by Justices of Peace."

Feb. 58. See "Papers relating to Appointments in the Navy."

Vol. CCCLXXXIV. 1637 to 1648.

Book of Orders concerning Forests.

The several entries appear in the calendar in the order of their dates.

Vol. CCCLXXXV. March 1–18, 1637–8.

1637–8.
March 1.
Melton Constable.

1. Sir Francis Asteley, Sheriff of Norfolk, to Nicholas. If the commands of the Lords of 2nd October have not been so punctually observed in returning the assessment made for shipping, were it known what pains befall me this present year (above my predecessors), the certificate thus late made will not be taken as a neglect, for I could not sooner finish the same. I have paid to the Treasurer of the Navy 2,514*l*. Every corporate town has received a particular writ, so as I expect their ship rates (being 860*l*.) to be by themselves paid. I have frequently urged diligence upon all the collectors. This county has been very backward this year. I have very lately put into some merchants' hands of Norwich 800*l*., to be returned up to the Treasurer of the Navy, and I understand of 300*l*. more to be ready in the hands of the collectors, which with some further augmentation shall be speedily sent up. Out of divers hundreds I have not yet received one penny, and the collectors but little, a note of which hundreds I have enclosed. I find much difficulty in causing the collectors to take distresses, and such as be taken few or none will buy. Countrymen combine together to bear name and property of one another's goods, which discourages the collectors, for fear of suits by mistakings. I shall to the best of my power work out these and other difficulties. [*The assessment sent up with this letter is probably that in Vol. ccclxxx., No. 96. Seal with arms.* 1¼ *p.*]

March 1.
Leicester.

2. Sir Richard Roberts, Sheriff of co. Leicester, to the same. In answer to your letter of the 27th January, I can yet make no certificate, for divers of the towns have not agreed on their assessments; others have undertaken to pay the money, but will make no assessments. Wherefore I thought it not good to stay till all were agreed, but made warrants out for the speedy collection of the money, which otherwise would have been driven off too long, and as soon as I can possibly get in the assessments I will make certi-

VOL. CCCLXXXV.

1637-8.

ficates. I caused 1,400*l*. to be paid to the Treasurer of the Navy last term, being more by 600*l*. than I had then received, and as yet I have not received so much. I am old, and could not travel this winter time, but now the days growing longer and warmer, I will abroad and get in what money I can against the next term. What to write once a fortnight I know not, but I find many of my officers and chief constables remiss and slack, which I must make good with my own diligence as well as I am able. [*Seal with arms.* ¾ *p.*]

March 1.
Mincing Lane.

3. Officers of the Navy to Nicholas. Upon notice of the Lords' exception at the demand of 800*l*. for travelling charges in the estimate for this present fleet, we consulted the account for last year's service, and find there has been paid to prestmasters and other ministers employed for despatching the service, 1,115*l*., whereof there was but 800*l*. allowed on the last year's estimate. Hereof we give you notice and desire you to satisfy the Lords, that the service being great, and part of the fleet fitted and paid at Portsmouth and other remote places, we cannot avoid this (among other) extraordinary expense, although if the fleet were fitted all at Chatham, or paid all at once, or in one place, a great part might be saved. For port beer and biscuit to admirals of fleets it has been paid for 20 years past and upwards. The Lords' pleasure shall be observed, but we conceive the demand rather too little than too much. [*Seal with arms.* 1 *p.*]

March 1.
Dover Castle.

4. Sir John Manwood, Lieutenant of Dover Castle, to Sec. Windebank. When I was at London I acquainted you with the defects in Dover Castle and the rest of the castles in the Cinque Ports, and your answer was, that upon a demonstration of the defects you would make it known to the Council and give assistance for speedy redress. I have now sent you the particulars of the present importancy, beseeching you to take it into your protection. The King's forts are unable to perform the duty they owe his Majesty, and so subject to receive affronts. A master of a ship at Dover, some four or five days since, met with the French fleet in two parts, eight by Plymouth and twenty-four by Portland. The admiral may be about 250 tons, most of the rest very small ships but full of men; I presume you have had the relation before. [*Seal with arms.* 1 *p.*] Enclosed,

 4. I. *Particular by Sir John Manwood of defects of ammunition in Dover Castle, whereof there is most urgent occasion of present supply; also of the reparations which are most necessary. Dover Castle, 1 March* 1637[-8]. [1 *p.*]

 4. II. *Similar particular by Increased Collins in relation to Moate's Bulwark, Dover. An extreme necessity for repair and a want of munition are represented in reference to every particular touched upon.* [1 *p.*]

 4. III. *Similar particular by Capt. Anthony Percivall with reference to Archcliff Bulwark, Dover, under his command. 28th February* 1637-8. [1 *p.*]

1637-8.

VOL. CCCLXXXV.

4. IV. *General certificate by Sir John Pennington and William Byng, captains, and Nicholas Lisle, deputy captain, respectively, of Sandown, Deal, and Walmer Castles, of their extreme state of dilapidation.* [¾ *p.*] Annexed,

4. IV. i. *Nicholas Lisle to Sir John Manwood. Since signature of the preceding certificate there had fallen down a principal piece of timber which supported the stonework of the outward gate. States other particulars of the condition of the castle. The soldiers, himself, his wife and family, besides the irksomeness of the rain, are in continual fear of their lives. Walmer Castle, 24th February 1637–8.* [*Seal with arms.* 1 *p.*]

4. V. *Particular certificate of Richard John Hippisley of the ruinous condition of Sandgate Castle and want of ordnance stores. 26th February 1637–8.* [1 *p.*]

March 1.
Dover Castle.
5. Sir John Manwood, Lieutenant of Dover Castle, to Sec. Windebank. Mr. Hempson has desired me to request, in case the King should grant his petition, that he only may have the transportation of moneys out of Spain for England and Flanders. The favours you do him he will be most thankful for, and present you with 500*l.* to buy a cupboard of plate. [*Seal with arms.* 1 *p.*]

March 1.
6–8. See "Returns made by Justices of Peace."

March 2.
9. Petition of Capt. Henry Bell, prisoner in the Gatehouse, to the Council. According to your directions in November last, petitioner sent to Sir William Becher the Elector of Brandenburgh's original letters of safe-conduct dated 1616, touching which report was to be made to you. Petitioner is now prepared to give full satisfaction as to the justness of his cause, and prays you to call upon Sir William for his report on the said letters, and to take petitioner's cause into a speedy hearing, or to refer the same to fitting persons. [¾ *p.*]

March 2.
10. Officers of Navy to Lords of the Admiralty. A survey has been taken of two of the ships to be set forth by the city of London, viz., the London and the Matthew. The London is conceived to be a good sailer and a stout ship, but the Matthew very unfit for his Majesty's service. The third ship, the Lewis, was formerly taken up by us for his Majesty, in place of which we have signified to the committees that they must provide another. We are of opinion that two middling ships were much better for the service than the London, that is of so great draught of water. All the great ships at Chatham are already graved, saving the Charles and the Leopard, which may be graved next week and ready to take in their victuals. The Sovereign of the Seas has much work as yet unperfected, which Capt. Pett has undertaken to see performed with all possible diligence. The St. George and the Constant Reformation are in preparation at Portsmouth, where we are going ourselves next week to pay the ordinary, and at our return shall be able to satisfy you of their forwardness. We are assured that the ships

stores are ready to be put aboard as soon as the ships are fit to receive them. We have despatched prestmasters to several counties, who we hope will do their duties, but we depend on one thousand sailors to be taken up about London, choice men, who, though with much difficulty, we hope to procure by the time that the ships are ready to go out. P.S. by Sir William Russell.—This letter was sent me to Deptford to sign, and my opinion is that in respect there are no ships in the river that may conveniently be had of about 400 tons, that the London should stand, and that the city may likewise have the Lewis, for I find there may another ship be had of 300 tons in place of her, and will be about 50 men less charge both for victuals and wages, whereby will be saved to his Majesty for eight months 800*l*. [= 2½ *pp*.]

March 2. 11. Copy of the preceding letter. [= 2 *pp*.]

March 2. 12. Articles of agreement between Endymion Porter, groom of the bedchamber, of the first part, William Ward of the second part, and Gerrard Wright, *alias* Herbert, of the third part, for draining marsh and surrounded lands in cos. Carmarthen, Pembroke, and Glamorgan, and the division of the lands so to be gained. Seals with arms of Ward and Wright, *alias* Herbert, and witnessed by William Risley and Fabian Phillips. [*Damaged by damp*. = 2 *pp*.]

March 2. 13–15. See "Returns made by Justices of Peace."

March 3. Grant to Sir Popham Southcott and Nicholas Southcott of the duty of 6*d*. per 12 lbs. of hard soap made in Somerset, Dorset, Devon, and Cornwall for seven years upon payment of the yearly rent of 2,500*l*. into the Exchequer; the making of all other hard soap in those counties being restrained, except Sir Richard Weston's Castile soap and the soap made in Bristol and Bridgwater. [*Docquet*.]

March 3. 16. Petition of Andrew Wood, clerk, B.D., one of the Senior Fellows of St. John's College, Cambridge, to the King. Mary Smith, of Warmingham, co. Chester, sued petitioner in Ecclesiastical Courts, upon pretence that he had uttered defamatory words against her, when indeed the words that he spake were uttered upon the command of the ecclesiastical judge in court, at an archiepiscopal visitation. That suit much hindered petitioner in his studies and service in his college, and withheld him many times from personal discharge of his cure; the cause depending before five of the judges delegates, four of whom *unanimi consensu* gave sentence for petitioner almost three years since. Since that time Mary Smith has importuned your Majesty to grant a commission of review, which was never done in any cause of pretended defamation, as by the underwritten certificate appears. Your Majesty having referred the granting of a commission of review to the Lord Keeper, petitioner prays that the

1637-8.   Vol. CCCLXXXV.

sentence of the judges delegates may be final. [½ p.] *Underwritten,*

16. I. *Copy certificates of Doctors of the Civil Law and others, that they had not known any commission of review in a case of defamation; being two of those already calendared under the date of 8th February* 1637-8. [¼ p.]

16. II. *Minute of the King's pleasure that if the commission of review be not yet issued, the Lord Keeper should make stay thereof until his Majesty's pleasure be fully signified. Newmarket, 3rd March* 1637-8. [*Copy.* ¼ p.]

March 3.
Inner Star Chamber.

17. Order of Council upon the petition of William Lewin, concerning the place of clerk to the Company of the New River, as also upon the petition of Sir William Middleton, governor of the said company, touching the said Lewin's fraud and misdemeanours. The Lords having considered the certificate of the Attorney-General, ordered that Lewin, being the clerk appointed by King James in the first charter granted to that company, be restored to his place until he be evicted by law. [*Copy or draft.* 1 p.] *Annexed,*

17. I. *Another copy or draft of the same order, but dated, apparently by mistake, 3rd May* 1637. [1 p.]

March 3.
Insula Vectis.
[Isle of Wight.]

18. Sir John Oglander, Sheriff of Hants, to Nicholas. My care and pains have been equal and more (by reason of my habitation in an island) than any sheriff's, for I have so ventured my person, because I would not disappoint the country about this service, that beyond expectation I have twice escaped shipwreck. I hope to pay by the 20th inst., at Portsmouth, near 4,000*l.* Our moneys rise "far more heavier," and therefore "more hardlier to be gathered, than that of Sussex." For, from Emsworth to Christchurch, all along the sea-coast, being 30 miles in length, the inhabitants (most fishermen) are so poor as they are not able to pay, and most of them have not whereon to distrain. Yet my endeavours shall overcome these difficulties. [*Seal with arms.* 1 p.]

March 3.

19. Petition of John Massam, victualler, to Archbishop Laud. Petitioner being much abused by William Fly, who, in November 1635, being then no apparitor, served on him a citation by a wrong name, and afterwards brought an excommunication to be published against him, pretending him to be of another parish than indeed he was, by advice of counsel petitioner brought his action against Fly, for which, in the Commission Court, he was ordered to stand committed till he released his action, which petitioner performed; yet, since his enlargement, there has been a monition executed on him to pay the said Fly 5*l.*, whereas there appears no order in court of his being condemned in any costs. Prays to be freed from the said charges. *Underwritten,*

19. I. *Reference to Sir John Lambe to take order for petitioner's relief as he shall find reasonable. 3rd March* 1637-8. [1 p.]

Vol. CCCLXXXV.

1637-8.
March 3. 20. Account of Sir William Russell of ship-money received and outstanding on writs issued in September 1637. Total received, 35,758*l*. 11*s*.; outstanding, 160,655*l*. 16*s*. 8*d*. [*Very much damaged by damp.* ¾ *p.*]

March 3. 21. Account of moneys levied and remaining in the hands of the sheriffs. Total, 12,300*l*., which makes the total collected 48,058*l*. [¾ *p.*]

March 4.
Durham Castle. 22. Bishop Morton, of Durham, to the Council. According to your directions concerning the mayor of Durham, which is, so to cess the inhabitants with an equality that the service be not disgraced, or the poor oppressed, or necessary clamour occasioned, these are to certify that the present cess, made by John Heighington, now mayor of Durham, has been made disproportionably in the most, and unworthily upon poor ones, because of his not observing your instructions. This neglect has caused the greatest clamour that I have hitherto heard of, wherefore my motion to your Lordships is that notwithstanding the cess be already made and most of it collected, yet, for the honour of his Majesty's equity, the mayor be commanded to make his cess anew according to that form which has been prescribed unto him. [*Seal with arms.* 1 *p.*]

March 4. 23. John Crane to Nicholas. I received warrant from the Officers of the Navy of 28th February last for putting victuals aboard seven merchant ships by 20th April for 900 men for six months. The time of year is so far past that victuals cannot be provided but at extraordinary prices, and pork hardly to be gotten. I pray that what is for this number of men may pass by way of account, or that you will treat with such as did the like service the years past, and know how they will do it, and at what rate. I will undertake it cheaper, if I may have ready money. I have received a former warrant for putting victuals aboard 22 of his Majesty's ships for 3,630 men for eight months, which I hope to perform by the 20th April, so that I may be furnished with the remainder of the moneys, being 19,799*l*. 11*s*. 4*d*., for which I crave warrant to Sir William Russell. I beseech you move his Majesty to grant me some increase of price for the victualling I am now to perform, in regard all provisions are at higher rates than have been known in the memory of man. [1 *p.*]

March 5.
Kelmarsh. 24. Sir John Hanbury, Sheriff of co. Northampton, to the same. Sends particular of his assessment, which he will suddenly return, and hopes in the next term to pay in a good sum of money. In the meantime desires the Lords to pardon his delay, not being yet perfectly recovered from a dangerous sickness. [¾ *p.*]

March 5. 25. Francis Lord Cottington to Sec. Windebank. Pain in his kidneys such and so continual that he is unfit for business and not able to endure a coach from thence to London, and besides, by a letter from Sec. Coke, he is commanded to entertain the Morocco ambassador for three or four days, and he will be there on Wednes-

1637-8.

VOL. CCCLXXXV.

day next. Before his coming from London he spake with the Attorney-General, and they agreed upon such principles as will free the Spanish ambassador in that business Windebank wrote of. Therefore Windebank will peradventure find no great necessity of the writer's assistance. [¾ p.]

March 5.   26. Dr. Richard Baylie, Vice-Chancellor, and other heads of houses in Oxford University to Archbishop Laud. The jurors (12 privileged and 12 freemen) impanelled by the University to inquire after misdemeanours impleadable in a court leet lately held in your name, have presented the conduit raised in the market-place at Carfax as a nuisance. We have deliberated upon the presentment, and acknowledge the same to be a just grievance. Our appeal unto you is unanimous, both university and city, beseeching you to order the same as you shall think fittest. [*Signed by* 21 *persons.* 1 p.]

March 5.   27. See "Returns made by Justices of Peace."

March 6.   28. Petition of merchants, owners, masters of ships, and mariners trading to Newcastle for coals to the King. In June last, petitioners informing the King of the practices of some few hostmen at Newcastle, and their combination for engrossing that trade into their own hands for their private gains, in selling bad coals by unjust measure, tending to the overthrow of petitioners and many thousands more, petitioners being ready to pay the King 12d. per chaldron more than formerly, provided they might have a free trade and just measure, and a power to govern their trade by way of a corporation or otherwise. On 24th June, after a hearing before the King at the Council Board, it was ordered that petitioners should have free trade and just measures, securing to his Majesty 3,000l. per annum for the new 12d. per chaldron, which they then did. Nevertheless, petitioners, by the practice of the Newcastle hostmen, have been hindered of a just measure and free trade, to the great grievance of the kingdom and the undoing of petitioners. Pray that some course may be taken for petitioners enjoying the benefit of the said order. [1 p.] *Underwritten,*

   28. I. *Reference to the Council to take such order therein as they shall find most conducing to his Majesty's profit and the general good of his subjects. Newmarket, 6th March* 1637–8. [¼ p.]

March 6.   29. [The Council?] to Humanitas Mayo, Thomas Webb, and Edmund Woodroffe, messengers. A commission has been granted to Sir Robert Rich, Sir William Parkhurst, Edward Johnson, Lawrence Lisle, and others, for discovery of offenders in buying and selling cards and dice unsealed, contrary to proclamation. You are to repair to the dwelling-houses of such offenders, or such as refuse to appear to be examined before the commissioners, first having warrant from the commissioners certifying the offenders, and to take them into custody and bring them before us, and all mayors and other officers and subjects are to assist you therein [*Copy.* 1 p.]

Vol. CCCLXXXV.

1637–8.
March 6.
Barbican.

30. John Earl of Bridgwater to Sec. Windebank. I enclose petition and certificate concerning the business between the Edwardses and Sir Paul Harris, but the certificate gives me so little satisfaction that I desire to have no more to do therewith than to present it to the Lords. I have likewise sent, sealed up, to the clerk of the Council such examinations as I lately received from Ludlow, but amongst them I have not one examination returned me of those I took in London and sent to the justices of Ludlow. My aim was to find out the truth, and I cannot but wonder that in the certificate there is no more particular touch of the personal estate of the Edwardses, which may be perhaps the greatest motive of all the business, nor any mention of a deed of gift made by John Edwards the elder, to John Edwards the younger, prosecutor of the petition, upon his first journey to London to petition for abatement of assessments, nor what is become thereof. John Edwards the younger, upon his examination by myself, confessed that there was such a deed. To what intention it was made I leave to the judgment of the Lords. P.S.—I have sent the first drafts of the examinations taken by myself in London. [*Seal with crest.* 1 *p.*]

March 6.
Suffolk House.

31. Theophilus Earl of Suffolk to the same. Last summer several French prizes were brought by Dunkirk men-of-war into Weymouth and Melcombe Regis, within my vice-admiralty of Dorset, and were there offered to sale, which the merchants would have bought in behalf of the French proprietors if they had had any order from the Board, and the proprietors would have made them satisfaction; of which they doubting, some of the prizes were carried away for Dunkirk, whereby the King lost his customs. If you move the Lords for an order that our English merchants may deal for prizes taken of either side, and some time be limited for proprietors to come in to make their claims, it will be a means that many prizes be sold in this kingdom, and it will much conduce to his Majesty's benefit, and be an ease to the proprietors in their losses. [*Seal with crest and garter.* 1 *p.*]

March 6.

32. Petition of Roger Bickton to Archbishop Laud. John Fathers, clerk, vicar of St. Stephen's, Cornwall, having committed offences punishable by the High Commission Court, has reported that if any one question him he shall lose his labour, for that upon appearance he will confess, and then he shall be dismissed; and so he reports that Prynne and Bastwick might have been, if they would have recanted, and thereby he deters every one from prosecuting him. Petitioner submits the offences of Fathers in articles, being ready to enter bond for proof in case Fathers does not confess. *Underwritten,*

> 32. I. *Reference to Sir John Lambe to award letters missive for the party complained of to answer the business in the High Commission Court. 6th March* 1637–8. [1 *p.*]

March 7.
Whitehall.

33. Order of Council on petition of Alice Malby, wife of Thomas Malby, against Mr. Coghill concerning an extent of Chalkwell in

1637-8.

Vol. CCCLXXXV.

Essex. It was ordered with consent of all parties that Coghill should have allowance of all debts due to him from Thomas Malby, with six per cent. for forbearance, and that the Solicitor-General and Mr. Hearn should cast up the amount, and should agree what term shall be leased to Coghill of the said manor for satisfaction of the said sums, reserving 30l. per annum to Thomas Malby, and 20l. per annum to Alice, the whole to remain to the survivor, whereupon the said term shall be conveyed to Coghill and the remainder be settled as formerly it was, which being performed, the arrearages of the 20l. per annum due to Alice by former agreement are to be paid to her by Coghill. And in case Mr. Solicitor and Mr. Hearn shall not agree, the Lords pray the Lord Keeper to settle the same. [*Copy.* 1½ *p.*]

March 7.
Newmarket.

34. Sec. Coke to Sec. Windebank. When I acquainted his Majesty with the account you sent of the slow coming in of ship-money, [he] thought it not sufficient to write to quicken the sheriffs, but required the sheriffs themselves near London who are most behind to appear before his Majesty and the Board on Sunday next, to [show] cause why they have not by distress or otherwise levied the moneys; considering the time for the fleet to set to sea comes on, and the necessity of moneys for preparations of all kinds. Hereof you must give notice to the Lord Keeper and the rest, that order be accordingly taken. Concerning the city ships his Majesty is satisfied with the report made by Sir William Russell, that the London should stand, and that the Lewis be consigned to them; also that another of 300 tons be taken up by the officers in her room; hereof you will give order to the Officers of the Navy. P.S.—Grover, the post of Ipswich, has by Sir Sidney Montague presented a petition of complaint against us, in the name of Witherings, but the answer is only a reference to the Board. I told him what the Board had ordered, yet he thought not fit to disappoint his client, though it might be taken ill to make references to the Board against the act of the Board itself. [1 *p.*]

March 7.
Passenham.

35. Sir Robert Banaster, late Sheriff of co. Northampton, to Nicholas. Amongst others I informed the Board of the slackness of Mr. Claypole and Mr. Barton in paying ship-money, neither of them as yet having showed their conformity. What order was taken with them? I would be sorry that I should not bring in part of my arrear this term. [*Seal with arms.* ⅓ *p.*]

March 7.

36. Montjoy Earl of Newport, Sir William Balfour, Sir Jacob Astley, Sir John Heydon, and Colonel James Hamilton to the Council. Certify their opinion of a report made by the Earl of Newport touching the Isles of Scilly, with the plans representing the manner of fortifying the same. They recommend the erection of a larger fort, sufficient to contain a sufficient garrison to defend the isles and to secure proportionable stores of victuals and ammunition. [2 *pp.*]

Vol. CCCLXXXV.

1637–8.
March 7. 37. Information of Leonard Guy. On the 6th inst. he went aboard the Patience, riding in the Thames against Rotherhithe, and demanded of George Pasfield, the master, two carpenters who had left their work aboard the Pembroke. Pasfield's answer was that he took no notice whether they were his men or not. Guy then pulled out the King's warrant and showed it to the master, and told him the King's hand was to it. His answer was a scornful one in reference to the warrant; he added that if the men would work he would pay them their wages, and he bade Guy get overboard, or else he would set him overboard. [1 p.]

March 8.
Whitehall. Lords of the Admiralty to [Montjoy Earl of Newport]. To permit Charles Deering and Thomas With, of London, and John Blith and Thomas Marsh, of Ipswich, owners of the Deliverance, of Ipswich, of 220 tons burthen, to purchase 20 pieces of iron ordnance. [*Copy. Vol. ccclxiii., fol. 94.* ½ *p.*]

March 8. 38. Petition of William Garret, stationer, to Archbishop Laud. About 1630, petitioner printed a book named "A Pattern of Catechistical Doctrine," and you commanded petitioner not to reprint the said book any more. William Sheares has now reprinted the same with petitioner's name and the year 1630, as if it were the old impression, of which petitioner gives notice, that you may proceed therein as shall seem fit. [¾ p.] *Underwritten,*

> 38. I. *Reference to Sir John Lambe to take order with the delinquent and to be sure to seize the books. 8th March 1637–8.* [1 p.]

March 8. 39. Four questions propounded to Archbishop Laud by Sir John Lambe, which have relation to the visitation of Merton College. 1. What is *uberius beneficium?* 2. Abuse in letting leases, and of the college stock. 3. Abuses in woods and wood sales. 4. Whether bachelors shall have voices in bestowing the ecclesiastical livings of the college. [¼ p.]

March 8. 40. Bond of William Shaw, junior, and Thomas Snelling, citizens and turners, to Humanitas Mayo, of St. Martin's in the Fields, in 100*l.*, conditioned for the appearance of Shaw before Lord Treasurer Juxon and Francis Lord Cottington, at all times whilst in custody of Mayo, as also for payment of Mayo's fees as a messenger. [1 p.]

March 8. 41. Certificate of Inigo Jones of the names of the crew of the Grace, of Weymouth, employed for transportation of stone from the Isle of Portland to London for repair of St. Paul's. [¾ p.]

March 8. 42–43. See "Returns made by Justices of the Peace."

[March 9 ?] 44. Robert Anwill to the Council. Details with great minuteness the circumstances of his voyage with William Prynne on his transportation from Carnarvon to the Isle of Jersey. The prisoner was handed over to the writer on the 9th October last, and after passing through many dangers, and being detained by tempestuous weather

1637-8. VOL. CCCLXXXV.

in many places for considerable time, they ultimately reached Jersey on the 18th January, when the writer delivered his prisoner into the custody of the Lieutenant-Governor. The writer left Jersey on his return on the 12th of February, and arrived at Southampton on the 23rd of the same month. He annexed a note of the charges he had been put to. [3 pp.] *Annexed*,

> 44. I. *Account of the charges above mentioned. The payment for the ship from Carnarvon Road to Jersey was* 40l.; *the diet of the writer of the above letter and his man for* 21 *weeks was charged at* 57l.; *the total charge* 106l. 10s., *besides his attendance, trouble, and danger.* [⅚ p.] *Underwritten*,
>
> 44. I. i. *Order of Council. Robert Anwill is to attend the Lord Treasurer, who will give fitting order for the sum to be allowed, and how it shall be paid.* Whitehall, 9*th March* 1637-8. [⅙ p.]

March 9. 45. Petition of Valentine Saunders to the Council. The late corporation of soapmakers of Westminster granted one share of 40 parts, containing 125 tons of soap, to Sir Henry Poore, Viscount Valentia. Lord Valentia by indenture sold petitioner one-fourth or quarter part of the said share, for which petitioner paid 300l. Petitioner at the instance of the corporation delivered the said indenture, on pretence to show the same to the Lords, and petitioner could never since procure the same. Since which time the King has given Sir Henry Compton and others for the use of the corporation 40,000l., to be paid by the soap-boilers of London by 4l. a ton for all soap by them made. Lord Valentia living in Ireland has appointed Sir Gregory Norton to receive the money due on his share, but Sir Gregory refuses to pay any part thereof to petitioner, and his indenture being kept, petitioner cannot take any course for recovery thereof. Prays that Sir Gregory may be ordered to attend and pay petitioner his fourth part of what Sir Gregory has received. [*Copy.* 1¼ p.] *Underwritten*,

> 45. I. *Reference to Sir William Becher and Nicholas to inquire what has become of petitioner's indenture, and to end the business if they can.* Whitehall, 9*th March* 1637-8. [*Copy.* ¼ p.]
>
> 45. II. *Appointment by Sir William Becher and Nicholas to proceed with the above reference on the* 24*th April* 1638. 17*th April* 1638. [½ p.]

March 9. 46. Sir Roger Twysden and others to [the same]. You have sent for George Rumney, of Tunbridge, for brewing against the proclamation. He is sorry for his offence and has promised conformity, and prays that in regard of his old age and late sickness he may be spared from attendance. [⅔ p.]

Vol. CCCLXXXV.

1637–8.
March 9.
Whitehall.

Lords of the Admiralty to Officers of the Navy. His Majesty is pleased that the London, in regard she has been so long in preparation, shall stand, and that the Lewis shall also be consigned to the city. But the committees of London are to take up a ship in place of the Matthew, to make the full number of tons. His Majesty's pleasure likewise is that you take up a ship of 300 tons in place of the Lewis, and send us a note of her name and burthen. If there be occasion, you are to assist the committees in taking up a fit ship in place of the Matthew, and to take care that the fleet be ready to put to sea by the time prefixed. [*Copy. See Vol. cccliii., fol. 94. ½ p.*]

March 9.
Whitehall.

The same to the Committees of London for setting forth ships. Give them similar directions respecting the London, the Lewis, and the Matthew. [*Copy. Ibid., fol. 94b. ½ p.*]

March 9.
Vale Royal.

47. Thomas Cholmondeley, Sheriff of co. Chester, to Nicholas. Since my letter of the 18th February last (*see Vol. ccclxxxii., No.* 38) I have received about 200*l.*, and am in good hope to receive the rest with such speed as that I shall ease both you and myself by including the whole in a final payment. In the meantime I have returned 120*l.* [*Seal with arms. ⅔ p.*]

March 9.

48. Sir Henry Marten to Sec. Coke. I received from Mr. Weckherlin, your servant, a translation of a memorial lately presented to his Majesty by the Dutch ambassador against George Henley, with this, that you would be glad to hear my opinion thereupon. The effect is, that the letters of reprisal to Henley are not well grounded, because justice is not denied nor delayed, which he proves, because Henley had a former sentence for him, and a latter against him, and the latter pronounced by judges of great worth. The answer is, that this kind of arguing passes not for good *in foro poli*, before the God of Heaven, nor *in foro juris gentium*, before the gods of the earth, sovereign princes and states; for there a sentence is not made just by the rules of the civil law, nor by domestic practice; reality of truth only, not fictions of law, have approbation. This kind of answer was not held satisfactory when the French gave sentence for them that took the Pearl, nor when they of Dunkirk and Brussels gave sentence in allowance of the tobacco, which they made prize against the English. A judgment not supported with reasons that may give satisfaction to another state is so far from justifying the wrong, as it adds a further contumely and scorn. By the law of nations, if the spoil cannot be justified, Henley must have his goods again, notwithstanding any argument drawn from their politic constitutions or local manner of judicial decision. Henley does not require his goods because he had a former sentence, nor think it just that he should lose them because the second sentence says there was an error in the former judgment, but because he, being a merchant, had by lawful trade purchased those sugars, which were upon the seas, far out of any territory of the States, violently taken from him by a man-of-war of Holland and brought in thither. Neither does Henley desire a sentence for his goods, but restitution of his own, and execution of justice against the offenders. Therefore, if the

1637-8.   Vol. CCCLXXXV.

first sentence be wrong, Henley is where he was, viz., lawful owner of the goods whereof he was wrongfully spoiled by this man-of-war, and this man-of-war is a pirate till somewhat be showed to the contrary. [3½ pp.]

March 9.   49. Copy of the same. [3½ pp.]

March 9.   50. John Crane to Lord Treasurer Juxon. By contract made with his Majesty the 20th February 1636-7 for victualling his Majesty's ships, it is agreed that the same should begin the 1st January 1635-6, and continue until 12 months' notice be given on either side, and thereupon the bargain to be void, and I am to serve his Majesty upon account. As all kinds of victuals are very dear, and are like so to continue, I pray you to take notice that longer than this year I shall not be able to serve his Majesty at the rates contracted for; and further acquaint his Majesty with the great loss that this year is likely to fall on me, for I shall lose about 100*l.* in the victualling of every hundred men for six months, which without his Majesty's favour will tend to the utter undoing of myself and thirteen children. [1½ p.] *Annexed*,

> 50. I. *Calculations showing the expense of victualling one man for 28 days upon the prices of 1636 and 1637, and also the same expense upon the prices of 1638. In the former case the cost was 19s. 11¾d.; in the latter, 23s. 2¾d.* [1¾ p.]

March 9.   51. Note of charges expended by John Edwards in following the business against Sir Paul Harris, late Sheriff of Salop. Total expenses, 57*l.* 8*s.* 6*d.*, with a claim for 40*l.* for damages occasioned by neglecting his other occasions to follow this business. [1 p.]

March 9.   52. Certificate of Sir Edward Wardour, Justice of Peace for Westminster, that John Brooke and Robert Brooke, sons of John Brooke, one of the Tellers of the Exchequer, and Daniel Witcherley, servant to John Brooke the elder, had taken the oaths of supremacy and allegiance before him. [*Seal with crest and motto.* ¾ p.]

March 9. Buckingham.   53. Certificate of Thomas Fowke, Bailiff, and John Nicholls, Deputy Steward of Buckingham. Notice having been given to the bailiff and burgesses of Buckingham by Andrew Pawling, messenger, for their appearance in the Exchequer, by virtue of a warrant of Lord Cottington to pass their accounts of casual profits due to his Majesty, they certify that they do not hold any casualties under their charter, and promise to appear in the Exchequer the next term, and to bring in a note of all the bailiffs' names since the first year of his Majesty's reign. [½ p.]

March 9.   54. Tabular account of weekly payments from the 27th October last to this day on various specified accounts, principally salaries or pensions, payable to persons connected with the royal household. The account has been carefully examined. [*Damaged by damp.* = 2 pp.]

March 9.   55-56. See "Returns made by Justices of Peace."

Vol. CCCLXXXV.

1637–8.
March 10.
Whitehall.

Notes by Nicholas of business transacted by the Council of War this day. Besides orders otherwise noticed, it was directed that the plot and certificate of the Earl of Newport and Colonel Hamilton, respecting the fortification of the Scilly Islands, should be shown to the King, and order be given as he shall think fit. [*See Vol. ccclxxxii. No.* 59. 1⅙ *p.*]

March 10.
Whitehall.

57. Order of the Council of War that all governors of his Majesty's isles, garrisons, castles, or forts, deliver to the Office of Ordnance an account of all ordnance stores received since the first year of the King, and how much thereof is expended, and in what manner, and what remains. The Master of the Ordnance is required not to deliver any further stores where such account is not rendered, nor without a receipt by indenture. [1⅔ *p.*]

March 10.

58. Copy of the same. [2¼ *p.*]

March 10.
Whitehall.

Resolution of the Lords of the Admiralty upon reading the letter of John Crane to Lord Treasurer Juxon, calendared in this present Vol., No. 50. As soon as the Lords should receive certificate from the Officers of the Navy and some of the Trinity House, as to the prices of victuals expressed in a paper presented by Crane, being a copy of No. 50. I., they will acquaint the King with the warning given by Crane, and attend his Majesty's further pleasure. [*Copy. See Vol. cccliii., fol.* 95 *b.* 3 *pp.*]

March 10.
Whitehall.

Lords of the Admiralty to Henry Kyme, messenger. To bring George Pasfield, master of the Patience, before them to answer matters to be objected against him. [*Copy. Ibid., fol.* 94 *b.* ⅔ *p.*]

March 10.
Taliaris.

59. (Unsigned) Sheriff of [co. Carmarthen] to Nicholas. The interval since my sheriffwick, in regard I have been the supply of another who should have executed your letters (I mean Sir Walter Vaughan) ought to excuse me, yet my pains have not been wanting in performing his Majesty's writ and the Lords' instructions, and about the midst of Easter term I hope to pay in the best part of the rate; the residue shall be collected with all speed. This poor country affords no commodity to make moneys of but a few cattle and sheep, which are not vendible till the beginning of summer, and therefore at this time of the year collections are most difficult; together with the moneys there shall be a certificate returned. [*Endorsed by Nicholas,* "Sheriff, as I think, of Carnarvon, without a name." *Seal with arms.* ½ *p.*]

March 10.

60. Recognizance of Robert Brace, of Cople, co. Bedford, yeoman, in 40*l.* for his appearance before the Council on the 18th inst., to answer neglects in not making an indifferent assessment upon the inhabitants of Cople towards ship-money. [*Signed by William Boteler, the sheriff.* 11 *lines on parchment.*]

DOMESTIC—CHARLES I. 303

Vol. CCCLXXXV.

1637–8.
March 10. 61. Account of Sir William Russell of ship-money received under writs of 1637. Total received, 39,004*l.* 10*s.*; unpaid, 157,409*l.* 17*s.* 8*d.* [*Damaged by damp.* 1 *p.*]

March 10. 62. Account of ship-money levied and remaining in the hands of the sheriffs under writs of 1637. Total, 15,200*l.*, which makes the total collected 54,204. [*Similarly damaged.* 1 *p.*]

March 11. Warrant to the Exchequer to discharge George Lord Goring of a recognizance of 22,400*l.*, upon condition that if Sir Sackville Crow, late Treasurer of the Navy, shall not within two months after the levying of certain tallies mentioned in the condition of the said recognizance deliver in his accounts signed by the Officers of the Navy, cleared of any debt to his Majesty, then Lord Goring to be liable for the full rents reserved for the wine licences. [*Docquet.*]

March 11. The like for payment of 2,831*l.* to Sir Sackville Crow for his charges about the disafforestation of the forests of Roche and Selwood, co. Somerset, to be raised by sale of lands assigned to Sir John Heydon for that purpose, or of lands remaining after 20,000*l.* shall have been satisfied to his Majesty for the disafforestation of those forests. [*Docquet.*]

March 11.
My house at Coggs.
63. Sir Thomas Penyston, Sheriff of co. Oxford, to Nicholas. Acknowledges the receipt of various letters urging payment of the ship-money, both that for the present year and the arrears due for past years, and ultimately of letters which informed him of a process issued out of the Exchequer for levying the arrears, which he was to execute. The last of these letters cast much blame upon him for not paying any part of the money for the present year. He replied that he had not received any money yet from any man in the county. From the corporations he has received neither money nor answer. Conceived the country to be more unable generally to pay this year than formerly, by reason of the multitude of poor people and the dearness of corn and all other provision, which was the chiefest reason that he had not yet more pressed the payment. If thereafter they should not pay, he would more earnestly call upon them. His greatest care was to spare the poorer sort. As this was a business of great trouble, and he had undertaken it all himself, without the assistance of his under-sheriff, he desired leave to take such time as might be most fit for raising the money with least inconvenience to the country. [*Seal with arms.* 1 *p.*]

March 11. 64. Petition of George Pasfield, master of the Patience, of London, to Lords of the Admiralty. Upon complaint of Leonard Guy that petitioner should speak contemptuous words against his Majesty's seal manual, petitioner was convented before the Court of Admiralty, where upon examination he was dismissed, as by the annexed order appears. Guy persisting in his malicious courses, has again complained unto you, whereupon petitioner has been sent for and been in custody of a messenger these five days. As petitioner is innocent

Vol. CCCLXXXV.

1637–8.

and is bound by charter-party to several merchants for a voyage to France and St. Lucar, and was to set forward the 10th inst., prays his discharge. [⅔ p.] *Annexed,*

> 64. I. *Order of the Court of Admiralty above referred to. After hearing Guy's accusation, the contradiction in his assertions, and the proofs of Pasfield, the Lords did not believe the accusation, and therefore dismissed Pasfield. 8th March* 1637–8. [2 pp.]

March 12. Entry on the Admiralty Register of the appearance of George Pasfield, master of the Patience, before the Lords. He was ordered to attend from time to time until discharged. [*See Vol. cccliii., fol.* 95. ¼ *p.*]

March 12.
The Swiftsure, in the Downs.
65. Sir John Pennington to the Lords of the Admiralty. The Spanish fleet rides yet under the Splinter by Dunkirk, attending a fair wind to carry them away. The new Holland fleet is not yet come out, neither can I hear any certainty that the French fleet is returned out of the Straits and gone in for Brest. Methinks we have a very great calm both of the French and Dutch, but how long it will continue I know not. We have received 28 days' victuals more. [1 *p.*]

March 12.
Westminster.
Nicholas to Lewis Harris, late Under-Sheriff of co. Oxford. Has acquainted the Lords with his letter of the 27th of February, but they will give no further time for perfecting his account. By his account for 1635 he alleged that there was in arrear only 446*l.* 11*s.* 10*d.*, whereof he says he has received 97*l.* 8*s.*, but there is unpaid to the Treasurer of the Navy full 500*l.* for that year. He and Mr. French would do well to look better to their accounts. The account was not satisfactory, for by it no man could tell who is behind. As for Mr. Walter's year, Nicholas was confident that Mr. Walter would make good whatsoever he had charged Harris withal, and the Lords will not be so trifled with any longer. Prays him to make up a perfect account and to set down in particular the names of persons behindhand. [*Copy. Nicholas's Letter Book, Dom. James I., Vol. ccxix., p.* 170.]

March 12. 66. John Nicholas to his son, Edward Nicholas. Arrangements as to his court-keeping. He purposes, when he has ended his court at Ramsbury, to go to Sir William Calley; is told he has not been well. Went that afternoon to the Bishop of Salisbury, who sets forth to London to-morrow. He is a good man, and has granted the writer a new lease *gratis.* Thinks Dr. Henchman will be his best friend in the chapter. Is rebuilding his kitchen at Winterbourne; hopes Edward Nicholas and his may long enjoy it; the writer's time is almost spent. Proposed transfer of Ned [Edward Nicholas's son] to a schoolmaster at Gillingham. Is sorry to hear that the sickness begins. Agues are very frequent in those parts. [*Seal with arms.* 1¾ *p.*]

Vol. CCCLXXXV.

1637-8.

March 12.
Lichfield.

67. Charles Twysden to Archbishop Laud. I have lately been at Coventry and viewed the addition of seats in St. Michael's church. The space left between the seats is nine feet at least. They are uniform and of an equal height, and may be removed in half an hour. The parishioners, by the churchwardens, request, that as there is morning prayer three times a week and a lecture on Wednesday, it would be troublesome and chargeable to remove the seats so often, which they must do to fit the congregation with seats, wherefore they desire leave to remove them but twice a month, except upon extraordinary occasion. Mr. Panting, the vicar, states that being lately in London he found the archbishop inclining thereunto, but the writer has given the churchwardens charge that the seats be removed every Monday morning until he understands the archbishop's pleasure. [1 p.]

March 12.
St. Peter's College, Cambridge.

68. Dr. John Cosin to Dr. Steward, Dean of Chichester and Clerk of the Closet. Gives him a full relation of that which had passed among the heads of houses at Cambridge concerning a sermon preached by Mr. Adams on the 25th June last in St. Mary's church. The scope of the sermon was to declare that confession to a priest was implicitly required by the text, St. John xx. 23, as necessary to absolution, without which there was no salvation. The writer quotes passages from the sermon in which this doctrine was strongly urged, and stated to be suggested in the liturgy of the Church of England. A copy of the sermon having been called for during the vice-chancellorship of Dr. Comber, there were no further proceedings until Dr. Brownrigg became Vice-Chancellor, when after various proceedings a form of submission and recantation was prepared by the Vice-Chancellor, and passed, but with great difficulty, and, as the writer insinuates, by management, in taking advantage of the absence of some of the members of the court known to be adverse to the form of recantation prepared. The speeches on both sides are stated. Mr. Adams had not recanted, and had withdrawn his intention to keep his act for his B.D. degree. [9 pp.]

March 13.

Petition of the Governor and Company of Silkmen of London to the King. By proclamation of 9th August in the 6th year of your Majesty's reign, it was commanded that no silks should be dyed before the gums were boiled off, and that no black should be dyed but Spanish black, which petitioners conceived was to prevent that sort of black silk called London silk or light weight, usually dyed on the gum, and by that means doubled or trebled in weight, which by petitioners' care is now wholly suppressed. At the time of that proclamation, and until a late hearing before your Majesty, there was a sort of silk called hard silk generally used, which was dyed upon the gum, but without increase of weight, which hard silk was no other than raw silk dyed into colours, and noway thereby weakened or corrupted, and was of most necessary use. At the said hearing, petitioners were charged with breach of the proclamation for dyeing hard silk, since which they have endeavoured to suppress the same. State the inconveniences and decay of trade which have

Vol. CCCLXXXV.

1637-8.

thereby arisen, and the diminution of 130,229 lbs. of silk imported and spent in the kingdom since the Christmas before the first hearing. Pray the King to declare his pleasure concerning the use of hard silk. [*Copy. See Vol. cccxxiii., p.* 255. ¾ *p.*] *Underwritten,*

> I. *Reference to the Attorney and Solicitor General, and Sir Abraham Dawes, to certify their opinions. Whitehall, 13th March 1637-8.* [*Copy. Ibid., p.* 256. ⅙ *p.*]

March 13.
Whitehall.

Lords of the Admiralty to [Montjoy Earl of Newport]. To permit David Goubard, of London, merchant, owner of the Henry Bonaventure, to purchase 12 pieces of cast-iron ordnance for the said ship out of the founder's store. [*Copy. Vol. ccclii., fol.* 95. ½ *p.*]

March 13.
Bedford House.

69. Francis Earl of Bedford to Thomas Meautys. I have received a certificate from Col. Pollard on behalf of Edward Poyntz, sent for as a defaulter at the last musters in co. Devon. He certifies that Poyntz had the arms he was assessed at for the parish of Bittadon, but the substitute of the soldier who was to serve with them made default, and further that Poyntz has been always ready in that kind, and therefore he conceives he may be discharged. [½ *p.*]

March 13.

70. Minute of application that Thomas Jones (a man of 30,000*l.* or 40,000*l.* estate, who has been six times bailiff) may be first mayor of Shrewsbury upon this new corporation. This may be done without disparagement to the now bailiffs, for the mayoralty may commence at Michaelmas, when the new sheriffs' [bailiffs'?] year will end. For this honour, Jones will give liberally to St. Paul's and will draw his friends to do the like. [½ *p.*]

March 13.

71. Archbishop Laud to Francis Cheynell, of Merton College, Oxford. Letters dimissory, whereby the archbishop gave licence to any bishop to confer upon Cheynell the sacred orders of the priesthood. [*Latin. Copy.* ½ *p.*] *Annexed,*

> 71. I. *Certificate of Sir Nathaniel Brent and eight Fellows of Merton College, as to the good conduct of Francis Cheynell during his residence as a Fellow in that college, and his conformity in doctrine with the Church of England. Merton College, 12th March 1637-8.* [*Latin. Copy.* ⅔ *p.*]

March 14.
Whitehall.

72. The King to Capt. John Weddell, Commander of the Fleet, whereof the Dragon is Admiral, employed by his Majesty to the Indies. We perceive that we were not deceived in our choice of you for the employment you are now upon, and as we trust you will crown your good beginning with success, so you may rest assured to find favour from us, and let not any rumour raised from such here as malign your employment beget any distrust of our continued esteem, or doubt that we will decline so hopeful an undertaking. That you and your adventurers may be the more confident, we have confirmed the commission we formerly gave to you and

1637–8.
Vol. CCCLXXXV.

them. As we formerly wished you to be careful not to prejudice the trade of our East India Company in the Indies, so we have now commanded that Company not to trade at Baticala or elsewhere on the coast of Malabar, or in the East Indies where they had none and you have settled factories. [*Copy.* 1 *p.*]

March 14.
Insula Vectis.
[Isle of Wight.]
73. Sir John Oglander to the Council. I beseech you to dispense with my attendance on the 18th March. The collectors are to bring in their moneys at Portsmouth on the 19th, and except I be there to give them receipts they will not pay. Likewise on the 20th, by order from Sir William Russell, I have to pay at Portsmouth 2,540*l.* for setting forth those ships there, which they earnestly expect. I have already paid, by order from Sir William Russell, to Steventon, clerk of the check at Portsmouth, 1,160*l.* I shall omit no opportunity that may conduce to the furtherance of this service, and, as my care and diligence have not been less than other sheriffs', so my pains and trouble, by reason of my habitation in an island, have been far greater. [*Seal with arms.* 1 *p.*]

March 14.
Insula Vectis.
[Isle of Wight.]
74. The same to Nicholas. Recapitulates the contents of the above letter, which he sends to Nicholas unsealed, to be delivered by him if he thinks fit. [*Seal with arms.* 1 *p.*]

March 14.
Boston.
75. Sir Anthony Irby to the same. Upon my return from Lincoln I give you a further account of my proceedings. I have received since I wrote last about 600*l.*; more I expect from Holland and Kesteven daily. The chief constables at Lincoln paid me what money was in their hands; very few they find to be refractory, but the hardness of the year makes very many slack, so as I am enforced to take it as they are able to pay. I have 1,000*l.* now in hand, which I am labouring to return. I have returned 220*l.* by Sir William Quadring. I have not yet fully done with the clergy. I have appointed another meeting upon Friday next for Lindsey with Dr. Tompson, whose long stay at London caused this delay. P.S.— I wrote in answer to the petition of the Kesteven men; let me hear something about it. [*Seal with arms.* ½ *p.*]

March 14.
76. Thomas Wyan to the same. The bearer, George Pasfield, was at a sessions for the Admiralty convented before the justices, and accused by Leonard Guy for speaking words against a warrant signed by the King. Upon full debate the bench acquitted Pasfield, finding Guy to be a malicious faltering fellow. I believe the Lords would not have further troubled this man if the complainants had informed them that he had before undergone his trial. Thus much at his request, being a stranger to me, I thought good to certify you. I have given him a copy of the Act of the Sessions, by which his dismission will appear. [1 *p.*]

March 14.
77. See "Returns made by Justices of Peace."

March 15.
Petition of the Master, Fellows, and Scholars of the College of St. John the Evangelist, Cambridge, to the King. The Bishop of

1637–8.

Vol. CCCLXXXV.

Lincoln, by indenture dated the 27th October 1632, granted to your orators all his books expressed in a catalogue, to secure your orators 100*l.* yearly during 10 years, for better furnishing the library of the college, or for augmenting the means of the keeper thereof, and notwithstanding no part of the sum secured has been paid. The bishop having been lately fined in the Star Chamber, the books with the rest of his goods are extended for payment of his fine. Pray that if his Majesty's Council finds that your Majesty's fine may be levied some other way, that then petitioners may have the said books in their library. [*Copy. See Vol. cccxxiii., p.* 256. ½ *p.*] *Underwritten,*

> I. *Minute that his Majesty, never intending that the fine set upon the Bishop of Lincoln should be in prejudice of petitioners, declares that the books of the bishop shall be reserved for the benefit of the said college. Whitehall, 15th March, 1637–8.* [*Copy. Ibid., p.* 257. ¼ *p.*]

March 15.

78. Petition of John Heron, farmer, to the Lords and Governors of the revenues and lands belonging to the Charter House. Petitioner being farmer of your island of Higney, the same within 70 years was a member of Woodwalton, co. Huntingdon, at which time Sir Henry Cromwell, being Lord of Woodwalton and Ramsey, and patron of both the livings, sold Woodwalton, reserving Higney, and tied the tenant and his successors to pay tithes to Ramsey (which is five miles from Higney), with all other taxations. Petitioner is oppressed with taxes by Ramsey, but is denied commonage with that town and abridged of his commonage with Woodwalton. Woodwalton being not two furlongs from Higney, petitioner has ever repaired to a seat in the church thereof, formerly built by your tenant, with consent of the parson, churchwardens, and townsmen, and now the Lord of Woodwalton assumes it to himself, by which means petitioner is destitute of a seat for himself and his family. Prays to be settled in the parish of Woodwalton, or else that you will command that he may enjoy the said seat or remove it to another part of the church. [1 *p.*] *Underwritten,*

> 78. I. *Reference to Sir John Lambe to consider to which parish Higney belongs, and if to Ramsey, then to require petitioner to repair thither once a year with his family to take the sacrament, and if to Woodwalton, then to settle him in a convenient seat in the church there, and if Higney does not belong to Woodwalton, yet to take a course that he may have a seat in the church there. Charter House, 15th March 1637–8.* [½ *p.*]

March 15.
Lamberton.

79. J. Renton to the Mayor of Berwick. The mayor having written to Renton respecting an assault committed by him, accompanied by 12 men weaponed, on Thursday, the 8th inst., upon Thomas Temple and his brother coming from Edinburgh, Renton replies with his version of the affair. It shows that there had been a previous question between Renton and Thomas Temple respecting

VOL. CCCLXXXV.

1637-8.

the detention by the latter of certain wheels belonging to Renton. Temple and John Foxton promised that the wheels should be delivered to Renton on the following day at the Bound Road, which promise was not fulfilled. Renton negatives the alleged assault and the weapons, but admits that "the people at the ploughing" seeing the meeting, some of them came with staves and gads "such as they use at ploughs." [*Copy.* 1½ *p.*] *Annexed*,

> 79. I. *J. Renton to John Foxton. Expected him that day at the Bound Road with the Temples and the wheels, but finds that he does not bide his word. Their next encounter shall be harder, for the writer will not be so easily satisfied.* [*Copy delivered to Foxton on 9th inst.* ½ *p.*]

March 16. The King to Thomas Viscount Wentworth, Lord Deputy of Ireland. Upon the Earl of Kildare's submission to an order of the Council there, for delivery of certain writings concerning lands in the earldom of Kildare to Lord Digby, he is to be released out of prison and the said writings are to be enrolled. [*Docquet.*]

March 16. Grant to the Countess Dowager of Carlisle during her life of a pension of 2,000*l.* out of the Exchequer, upon surrender of a like pension granted to the Earl of Northumberland for ten years, whereof eight are yet to come. [*Docquet.*]

March 16. Warrant to the Exchequer to give direction to Thomas Shadwell to pay to Richard Ledesham and Mary his wife 50*l.*, remainder of an escheat of 145*l.* which fell to his Majesty by the death of Sir Miles Hobbard [Hobart], which was due out of the Exchequer by an assignment of Lord Reay for his diet and lodging during his confinement at Greenwich. [*Docquet.*]

March 16. Petition of Charles Cary, younger son to the late Lord Hunsdon, to the King. Having lost 400*l.* per annum by the death of Mr. Dacres, which was the chiefest part of his livelihood, he is come into some debts, but hopes in time to come out of them if he might have liberty of going abroad to follow his business without fear of being arrested. Prays protection for one year. [*Copy. See Vol. cccxxiii., p.* 257. ¼ *p.*] *Underwritten*,

> I. *Reference to the Lord Keeper Coventry, Lord Privy Seal, and the two Lord Chamberlains of his Majesty's House to certify their opinions. Whitehall,* 16*th March* 1637[-8]. [*Copy. Ibid.* ⅙ *p.*]

March 16. Another copy of the said petition and answer, but the answer dated (as it is conceived by mistake) 16th March 1638, which would be 1638-9. [*See Ibid., p.* 264. ½ *p.*]

March 16. Petition of Nicholas Ivye to the King. There is a commodity of the nature of lead ore, and so called, but it is such as will not countervail the charge to make refined lead of, and one other thing called litharge, which is the dross of refined lead, both which are of little or no use in England, but are transported by Dutchmen, and

1637-8.

VOL. CCCLXXXV.

used for making or glazing tiles, earthen pots, and the like, upon the transportation whereof the duty paid to the Customs is $2\frac{1}{8}d.$ for every hundred. For that the said commodities are only transported by strangers, petitioner prays a grant of the sole power of transporting the same for 21 years, rendering his Majesty 4d. for every hundred, which is near double the custom that is now paid. [*Copy. See Vol. cccxxiii., p.* 268. $\frac{1}{3}$ *p.*] *Underwritten,*

1. *Reference to Lord Treasurer Juxon to certify his opinion.* Whitehall, 16*th March* 1637-8. [*Copy. See Ibid.* $\frac{1}{2}$ *p.*]

[March 16.] 80. Petition of Arnold Spencer to the Council. By letters patent petitioner many years since made the Ouse navigable from St. Ives to St. Neots, and thence to within four miles of Bedford. He has also proceeded far in making navigable the Stour from Sudbury to Manningtree, for which he pays yearly rents to her Majesty. There are also in hand divers other rivers in several counties to be made navigable according to the invention of petitioner, wherein petitioner has consumed most part of his estate. John Jackson has encouraged several base persons to break open some of petitioner's sluices built on the Ouse, promising that he will bear them out, which they have done accordingly. Prays that a course may be taken for punishing Jackson and his confederates. [$\frac{3}{4}$ *p.*]

March 16.
My house,
Bishopthorpe.

81. Archbishop Neile, of York, to the same. Upon receipt of your letters concerning William Stevenson's refusing to take the oath of allegiance, I sent for him, and imparted to him how you took his refusal to be full of disloyalty, and commanded him to be detained in close imprisonment. I again tendered the oath, with some persuasions to take it, which he refusing to do, I made warrant to the Keeper of York Castle to keep him close prisoner. When the judges of assize came to York I made the business known to them, and sent them a formal certificate of his refusal. Judge Berkeley, before he would put him to the exigent, sent for him to his lodging, and bestowed a great deal of labour to persuade him. Being in the public assizes required to take the oath, he took exceptions and refused, and the judge pronounced the judgment of *præmunire* against him, and recommitted him. I pray your resolutions whether he shall be continued in close imprisonment or not. He is thought to be a great agent for recusants of these parts, and for the priests that haunt this country, especially of George Fenwick, who has a long time exercised the Pope's jurisdiction in this province. The eyes of the country were upon our proceeding. Stevenson at his last being with me told me that there were more than a thousand in my diocese that would not take the oath, which I submit to your consideration, of how dangerous consequence the same may be to his Majesty and the State, and how necessary it is to purge the kingdom of the Pope's traitorous agents, that take upon them to exercise the Pope's jurisdiction within his Majesty's dominions, and sow the seeds of treason in the hearts of his Majesty's subjects. [*Seal with arms.* 2 *pp.*]

VOL. CCCLXXXV.

1637-8.
March 16.
82. **Kenrick Edisbury to Nicholas.** As soon as we came home from Ratcliffe, my wife made the mouth-water I told you of, which you will receive in a glass by the bearer. It must be made warm in a silver porringer, and then "garble" it in the mouth as hot as you can endure it. [*Seal with arms.* ⅓ *p.*]

March 16.
83. **Affidavit of Thomas Lloyd, of London.** Being in Radnorshire the summer last was twelve months, the winter following, and in summer last, he saw divers of Presteigne begging relief thereabouts, the chief constable and bailiff being unable to keep them in, and there died many of the sickness in that town. Deponent was at meetings of the justices of the peace, where he saw money paid which was collected for their relief, and being in the town a little before Michaelmas last, he found most of the inhabitants grown very poor. [*Endorsed,* * * "for a mitigation of ship-money." = ½ *p.*]

March 17.
Incorporation of about 70 brewers in Essex, with a restraint of all others. The Master Wardens and Fellowship are to have power to make ordinances. They are to admit into their corporation such only as shall be allowed by his Majesty or his commissioners. They are to take care that the malt and hops be wholesome, and that they keep the assize and gauge in their casks according to law. The master of the company is exempted from all offices in the county unless by direction of his Majesty or the Council. The yearly rent of 20s. is reserved to the Crown for ever, payable by the corporation above their compositions. [*Docquet.*]

March 17.
Congé d'élire to the Dean and Chapter of Ely, that see being void by the death of the late bishop. [*Docquet.*]

March 17.
Protection renewed to Sir Thomas Jervoise for one year. [*Docquet.*]

March 17.
Grant to Maurice Aubert, his Majesty's servant, of the benefit accruing to his Majesty as to the issues of the manor of Henhurst, Kent, by the outlawry of Thomas Wright, who, being seized of the said manor and outlawed, sold the same to Maurice Aubert, whereby the same became liable to answer his Majesty those issues. [*Docquet.*]

March 17.
84. **Petition of Henry Lee, of London, merchant, and Company, to the Council.** Petitioners have freighted the Philip, of London, for the Canary Islands, which, being ready to depart, has her men daily taken from her by the Officers of the Navy, by reason whereof petitioners suffer very much, in regard of the charge the ship stands them in, besides the loss of their market beyond sea. Pray that the ship's men may not be taken. [¾ *p.*]

[March 17.]
85. **Petition of Richard Harris, John Hosskisse, and others, assessors for ship-money in the time Sir Paul Harris was sheriff of Salop, to the Council.** Petitioners being assessors in the hundred of

Vol. CCCLXXXV.

1637–8.

Chirbury, have been complained of by John Newton, John Edwards the elder, lately dead, and John Edwards the younger, also by David Edwards, William Edwards, and Thomas Edwards, for taxing them at what the generality of the hundred thought reasonable, considering their great wealth, large possessions, great stock of cattle and money, and their penurious manner of living, and the poverty of the hundred in general, they having more riches than the whole hundred besides, being but three small allotments, and 128*l.* the sum to be levied. Petitioners have been most unjustly traduced, and pray a commission to examine witnesses to prove the reasons of their assessments. [1 *p.*]

March 17. 86. Sir Edmond Sawyer and Francis Phelips to [the Committee for the Affairs of the Household]. Report on the accounts of the household. They were threefold: 1. Those between the cofferer and the purveyors. 2. Those between the officers of the Greencloth and the sergeants of each office of the household. 3. The account of the cofferer to his Majesty for all moneys received. The writers set forth many imperfections and irregularities consequent upon this mode of accounting, and send certain forms which, if the committee pleased, might be substituted for them. [3¼ *p.*]

March 17.
Whitehall.
Entry on the Admiralty Register that George Pasfield was discharged, paying the messenger fees. [*See Vol. cccliii. fol. 97.* ⅓ *p.*]

March 17.
Whitehall.
Lords of the Admiralty to Officers of the Navy. We send you copy of a note of John Crane touching the prices of victual (*see this present Volume, No.* 50. I.), requiring you to certify whether those are the true prices of the said victuals, and whether, if the same had been provided in October and November in the years therein mentioned, the same might not have been had at easier rates. [*Copy. Ibid.* ½ *p.*]

March 17. Minute that a similar letter was directed to Capt. Thomas Best, Capt. William Rainsborough, Walter Coke, Anthony Tutchen, and John Totton [of the Trinity House]. [*Ibid., fol.* 97 *b.* 3 *lines.*]

March 17. 87. Another copy of statement by John Crane touching the prices of victual, referred to in the foregoing letters and already calendared in the present Volume, No. 50. I. [2 *pp.*]

March 17.
Aston.
88. Thomas Whitley, Sheriff of co. Flint, to Nicholas. My commission for the sheriffwick, with the writ and instructions for ship-money, I received in October last, but my patent with the writ of aid were imperfect, my name being omitted. Judge Bridgeman advised me to haste to London and acquaint the Lord Keeper therewith, which I suddenly effected, being 160 miles from my abode, and before I could perfect my business and reach home it was about the end of November. After I had received the county and gaol and settled the Crown business, I took order for the ship-money, and am very confident that before Michaelmas I shall pay in all. The poverty of our county being great I am enforced to travail oft, and

1637-8.

VOL. CCCLXXXV.

to send and write oftener, to hasten the payment, and yet have received very little. By the next I hope I shall give you an account of my first tax, and then " I will be paying in the money." [*Seal with crest.* 1 *p.*]

March 17.
London.

89. Thomas Atkin, Sheriff of Middlesex, to Nicholas. I deferred paying in the ship-money I had received till this afternoon, hoping to have paid in a greater sum, so as I came to pay it at Sir William Russell's house this afternoon, a certificate being sent away before of such moneys as came in this week. Give knowledge of 400*l*. paid in by me. P.S.—I shall be glad to see you at my house in Leading Hall [Leadenhall] Street. [*Underwritten by Edward Fenn, clerk to Sir William Russell*, "This 400*l*. was received after the certificate was sent away." ½ *p.*]

March 17.

90. Petition of Mary Woely, wife of Richard Woely, of St. Botolph without Bishopsgate, to Archbishop Laud. Petitioner brought unto her husband (to whom she has borne 12 children) 400*l*. in marriage and 30*l*. a year, which he still possesses, and has been his wife 28 years. For 2¾ years her husband has refused to live with her, having three times turned her out of his dwelling-house, she not knowing any just cause. He denies competent means, and would enforce her to take a chamber to live by herself, without any of her children, and upon such poor allowance as will not suffice, although he has 200*l*. per annum coming in by reason of the premises. Prays order that two of her children may live with her, and that her husband may allow competent means for her and them. [¾ *p.*] *Underwritten*,

    90. I. *Reference to Sir John Lambe to accord this difference in peaceable manner if he can, or else that the husband answer in the High Commission.* 17*th March* 1637-8. [⅛ *p.*]

    90. II. *Note by Sir John Lambe appointing to hear this cause on* 21*st inst. in Doctors' Commons.* [⅛ *p.*]

March 17.

91. Petition of Humphrey Smith, of Abingdon, Freemason, to the same. About two years past, petitioner and Thomas Harris and Robert Bryant, churchwardens of Witney, co. Oxford, agreed that petitioner should build up the spire of the said church (taken off by a sudden storm), in a substantial height and near to its former proportion, and the churchwardens promised to pay petitioner 200*l*., to be received as was agreed upon verbally. Having finished the same, he demanded his salary, which they deny your petitioner, there being 62*l*. arrear, alleging that the spire is not raised to its former altitude, which was impossible, in regard the lower part of the steeple under petitioner's work was falsely set, as appears under workmen's hands especially appointed by the Bishop of Oxford. Petitioner being out of purse 20*l*. by often bringing workmen to view and judge the work of the said steeple, besides petitioner's own expenses, is unable to wage law with

Vol. CCCLXXXV.

1637–8.

these refractory spirits of Witney, who have gathered 380*l*. towards the said repairs.. Prays that a course may be taken for his relief. [⅚ *p.*] *Underwritten,*

    91. I. *Reference to Sir John Lambe to give petitioner directions for recovery of his debt as he shall find just.* 17th March 1637–8. [⅙ *p.*] *Endorsed,*

    91. II. *Note by Sir John Lambe.* "*To advise whether action will lie in the Ecclesiastical Court, or to be called into the High Commission; against the churchwardens or inhabitants?*" [3 *lines.*]

March 17.   92. Articles of agreement between Philip Battalion, *alias* Shotbolt, of Yardley, co Hertford, and William Davenport, citizen and barber surgeon. The Earl of Berkshire has appointed Battalion his deputy to see to the setting up certain new invented kilns for drying malt, in co. Hertford. Battalion appoints Davenport as his agent to execute the said office for 14 years upon terms that the profits shall be shared between them. [*Executed by Battalion by the name of Philip Shotbolt. Seal with arms.* = 2 *pp.*]

March 17.   93. Account of Sir William Russell of ship-money received to this date under writs of 1637. Total, 42,163*l*. 15*s*.; leaving unpaid, 154,250*l*. 12*s*. 8*d*. [*Damaged by damp.* [¾ *p.*]

March 17.   94. Account of ship-money for 1637 levied and in the hands of the sheriffs, 14,850*l*. [1 *p.*]

March 18. Claverton.   95. William Bassett, Sheriff of Somerset, to Nicholas. Messengers were sent for the constables of the hundreds of Chewton, Norton Ferris, Bempstone, and Muchelney, but he has received no money, nor heard from any but those of Muchelney, who have paid all that was due. Neither does he hear of any reference about the difference of 12*l*. between the hundred of Tintinhull and the church liberty within that hundred, nor any order for money assessed upon Edward Philips in the hundred of Tintinhull, all which he desires to be satisfied in, for now he stands idle and knows not what to do or say. [*Seal with arms.* 1 *p.*]

March 18. Deptford.   96. Sir William Russell to the same. The following sums were received from sheriffs yesterday after making out the certificate, viz.: Middlesex, 300*l*.; Suffolk, 300*l*.; Cambridge, 1,000*l*. [*Damaged by damp.* ½ *p.*]

March 18.   97. Certificate of John Bayly, Samuel Cole, and Thomas Milner, prisoners in the Marshalsea, that William Leader, also a prisoner, a most turbulent fellow, daily raising seditions amongst the prisoners, spoke certain disparaging and filthy words concerning obtaining a privy councillor's hand to certain orders for regulation of the prison. [½ *p.*]

VOL. CCCLXXXVI. MARCH 19–31, 1637–8.

1637–8.

March 19. Presentation of Thomas Bayly, M.A., to the Subdeanery of Wells, void by resignation of the Bishop of Bangor and in his Majesty's gift, *pro hac vice*. [*Docquet.*]

March 19. The like of the same Thomas Bayly to a prebend's place in Lincoln, void by resignation of the Bishop of Bangor. [*Docquet.*]

March 19. Warrant for payment of 1,911*l*. 19*s*. 8*d*. to the Earl of Dorset, to be by him disbursed to divers artificers for work done for the Prince and the Duke of York for one year, according to a particular subscribed by the Countess of Dorset. [*Docquet.*]

March 19. Whitehall. Lords of the Admiralty to Sir John Pennington. It is his Majesty's pleasure that the Earl of Salisbury's two sons, being to return from France, shall be transported hither in one of the ships under your charge. You are to give order to some captain to stand over for Dieppe to receive them aboard on the 2nd of April next, and to transport them with their company unto such port in England as they shall appoint. [*Copy. See Vol. cccliii., fol.* 97 *b*. ½ *p*.]

March 19. Whitehall. 1. The same to Solomon Smith, Marshal of the Admiralty. Complaint is made by the States ambassador that a man-of-war belonging to the States, whereof Bastion Tieson is master, is by the Court of Admiralty arrested at the suit of Daniel Brames, merchant. It is his Majesty's pleasure the said ship shall be released. You are to take off the arrest and permit her to proceed on her voyage. [¾ *p*.]

March 19. Copy of the same. [*See Vol. cccliii., fol.* 97 *b*. ½ *p*.]

March 19. Whitehall. Lords of the Admiralty to all Admirals and others. The Philip, of London, Richard Hussey master, manned with certain men whose names are here stated, is ready to depart for [the Canary Islands]. You are to permit her quietly to proceed on her voyage, not taking out of her any of her men, or if you have impressed any discharging them. [*Copy. Ibid., fol.* 98. ⅔ *p*.]

March 19. Whitehall. The same to the Officers of the Navy. It is his Majesty's pleasure that there shall be 18 horses transported into the Low Countries for the Queen of Bohemia. You are to provide freight accordingly. They are to be sent under charge of the bearer, Mr. Armorer, his Majesty's servant. You are to take care that it be done at the easiest rates, and to put the charge on the next estimate by way of surcharge. [*Ibid., fol.* 98 *b*. ½ *p*.]

March 19. 2. Archbishop Laud to Bishop Wright, of Lichfield and Coventry. Acknowledges receipt of the bishop's account of his diocese. Had acquainted the King that the delay was but a slip of forgetfulness. His Majesty answered that the bishop had slipped in the same way before, and that he did not like that his commands should be so slightly regarded as to be so easily forgotten. The archbishop had also delivered to the Bishop of Bristol certain evidences concerning

Vol. CCCLXXXVI.

1637-8.

a survey of Abbot's Cromwell [Cromhall], which Bishop Wright had taken away with him to Lichfield, and had sent up to the archbishop to be handed over to the new Bishop of Bristol. But they did not include a counterpart of a lease of that place which the archbishop wishes may be looked for. The Bishop of Bristol also complains of leases granted of the farm and manor of Horfield, which had the effect of alienating the farm from the see of Bristol for "three lives upon three lives," which the archbishop is sure is no good church-work, and is contrary to the King's instructions. The Bishop of Bristol also complains that Bishop Wright had let a lease of the gate-house, being part of his mansion-house, to Dr. Jones for three lives, which if it proved good would alienate part of the bishop's house. Thirdly, that the vicarage of Fifehead, co. Dorset, had been annexed to the manor and let to one Newman, whereby the bishop is deprived of the right of presentation, and the pension paid by the vicar to the bishop is now paid to the tenant of the manor, "which is almost as bad church-work as the former." The archbishop hopes these things will not prove true. If they should, the King must be made acquainted with them, and course taken to right that see, which Bishop Wright should prevent. There is also a complaint of the new Dean of Lichfield concerning certain statutes made by the bishop at his last visitation. The right of the bishop to make these statutes is disputed, and no statutes can be binding unless they are under the broad seal. It is the King's pleasure that the bishop forbear to put those statutes upon the church, till the whole body of the statutes be revised by commissioners appointed by the King. The bishop is invited to give a fair and full answer upon these several points. [*Draft.* 1¾ *p.*] *Annexed,*

> 2. I. *Statement by Bishop Skinner, of Bristol, containing full particulars of his several causes of complaint against Bishop Wright, as above mentioned.* [*Endorsed as received by Archbishop Laud on the 27th February last.* 1 *p.*]

March 19.
Merton College.

3. Peter Turner to Archbishop Laud. By that part of the archbishop's letter which Mr. Vice-Chancellor communicated to the writer, it seemed doubtful whether articles would be exhibited at the college, to which every man would be sworn to answer, or whether every man would be left free to present whatsoever he knew to be amiss. The latter Mr. Vice-Chancellor liked the better. He likewise was casting how the visitation might be so ordered as that it might not appear who presented or gave information concerning any man, which he conceived might be accomplished in a way which is here described, and which was that informants should communicate privately with the commissioners in writing, and if they thought any facts material, the informants should in like manner bring in the proofs of their information. [1 *p.*]

March 19.
Trinity Hall.

4. Dr. Thomas Eden, Master of Trinity Hall, Cambridge, and Chancellor of Ely, to [Sir John Lambe]. Received letter from the

1637-8.   Vol. CCCLXXXVI.

Bishop of Norwich that the congé d'élire is to come down that week, by which he perceives there is like to be three visitations in one year, viz., a triennial visitation *sede vacante*, a metropolitical, and a primary. Had caused the archbishop's exhibition to be served on the archdeacon's registrar. He came presently to the writer to clamour and complain that they visited before their time and could not justify it. "I bade him be quiet and be gone, and so we parted." Wishes Sir John would consult with the Bishop of Norwich, and if need be with the archbishop, as to the time of this visitation and other points in connection therewith. [1½ p.]

March 19.
Tetbury.

5. William Chapman to [Sir John Lambe]. On Sunday, the 18th inst., according to your directions, I went to the parish church of Tetbury into my seat there, and took possession of it, the door being fast stopped up. Richard Talboys immediately after coming into the church, finding me and my brother in my ancient seat, required my absence; then showing him your seal and inhibition, he permitted me to sit (the minister being then in divine service), but with much discontent and unreverent demeanour he called me clown, and threatened me, and said to my brother, "What does this loggerhead do here?" Mrs. Talboys took "a mate" and set "him" in the midst of my seat, directly before my brother, to affront him from the sight of the minister, and sat upon "him," she leaning with the upper part of her body so hard upon my brother that he could not write the sermon. In the afternoon I came before the minister, and I found in my seat Thomas Talboys, son of Richard Talboys, and I desired him to open the door that I might come into my seat, and he would not, but constrained me to get over; then I required him by virtue of the seal to give place and go to his father's seat, and he said he would not, nor did not. [1 p.]

March 19.
Motcombe.

6. Sir John Croke, Sheriff of Dorset, to Nicholas. The multiplicity of complaints concerning inequalities of rates between the several divisions and subdivisions of this county, upon the in-hundreds and out-hundreds and several tithings, and by men's curious prying into their neighbours' estates, has occasioned my more than ordinary pains and trouble, which I have endeavoured to rectify, and has slacked hitherto the giving in of the account expected by the Lords. I have now received 1,000*l.*, which I will return to London about the beginning of the term. [*Seal with arms.* ¾ p.]

March 19.

7. Memorandum of William Whitledg and William Craft, bailiffs of Tewkesbury, that notice had been given to the bailiffs, burgesses, and commonalty of Tewkesbury by Andrew Pawling, messenger, for passing an account to his Majesty, which we do yearly in the Exchequer, and for which we have our *quietus est*, and we meddle with nothing more than is granted to us, and so we conceive we are not bound to account, but if by law we are, we promise to authorize Mr. Hill next term to do it. [½ p.]

1637-8.

VOL. CCCLXXXVI.

March 19. 8. Certificate of Inigo Jones of the names of the master and crew of the Barque, of Weymouth, employed for transportation of stones from the Isle of Portland to London for repair of St. Paul's. [*Damaged by damp.* ¾ *p.*]

March 19. 9. Similar certificate for the master and crew of the Swan, of Weymouth. [½ *p.*]

March 19. Whitehall. Henry Earl of Holland, Chief Justice and Justice in Eyre of the Forests on this side Trent, to Sir Charles Harbord, Surveyor-General. His Majesty is pleased, on the supplication of persons having lands in his forest of Rockingham, to accept a reasonable composition for the deafforestation of their several lands, retaining only the bailiwicks of Rockingham, Brigstock, and Cliff, or such part thereof as is meet to remain forest for the sustentation of his Majesty's game and his disport there. You are to view the said bailiwicks, and, with the advice of the officers of the forest, to set out by metes and bounds the said bailiwicks or such part thereof as you shall find meet to remain forest. [*Copy. See Book of Orders concerning Forests, Vol. ccclxxxiv., p.* 2. 1¾ *p.*]

March 20. Petition of Henry Duncomb to the King. By an ancient composition for finding a chaplain to perform service in the chapel of Thorpe, Surrey, there was allotted a house with a garden and a piece of land adjoining, and also the tithe of wool and lambs with other final [predial?] tithes arising in the said parish, with mortuaries and four loads of firewood yearly, and more if that should not prove sufficient, which composition has a long time been concealed, and the tithes with the piece of land unjustly detained by the parishioners, and only 20 marks yearly paid by them, to the great prejudice of petitioner and the church. Prays a reference to some of the Council for settling the tithes according to the composition, with damages for the time past. [*Copy. See Vol. ccclii., p.* 258. ⅓ *p.*] *Underwritten*,

    I. *Reference to Archbishop Laud, the Lord Privy Seal, and the Bishop of Winchester to compose these differences in such way as they shall find fit for relief of petitioner. Whitehall,* 20*th March* 1637-8. [*Copy. Ibid.* ⅙ *p.*]

March 20. Petition of Sir Theodore Mayerne, first physician to both their Majesties, Sir William Brouncker and Dr. Cadiman, physician to the Queen, together with the distillers of spirits, aqua vitæ, strong waters, vinegar, and "beeregar"-makers within London and Westminster, and 21 miles about, to the same. Divers petitions have been presented by distillers for obtaining several incorporations, and upon several references their differences have been fully debated. Now with unanimous consent they all jointly petition for one incorporation, with certain powers which are here briefly stated. Pray direction to the Attorney-General to prepare a bill accordingly. [*Copy. Ibid.* 1 *p.*] *Underwritten,*

    I. *Reference to the Attorney-General as prayed. Whitehall,* 20*th March* 1637-8. [*Copy. Ibid., p.* 259. ⅙ *p.*]

VOL. CCCLXXXVI.

1637–8.
[March 20.] 10. Certain articles concerning abuses committed by those that follow the calling of a porter. The porters of the city of London assumed to themselves, under the authority of an act of Common Council, the functions of a corporation, and levied a quarterly tax upon all porters, either admitted members of their body or otherwise, and upon non-payment imprisoned the persons making default, ruining some and driving others to despair. As a remedy for these abuses it is suggested that a commission should be issued to some worthy gentleman for providing an office for ordering the company of porters. [1 *p.*]

March 20. 11. The King to the Attorney-General. Form of suggested warrant for drawing a commission to be directed to Sir Henry Spiller, Ignatius [Inigo] Jones, Lawrence Whitaker, Richard Lowder, Nathaniel Snape, and William Gibbs for carrying out the purposes suggested in the preceding paper. [¾ *p.*] *Underwritten,*

    11. I. *Request of Sec. Windebank to the Attorney-General to certify whether his Majesty should be moved for such a commission as is mentioned in the preceding form.* 20*th March* 1637–8. [¼ *p.*]

[March 20 ?] 12. Another form of the preceding suggested warrant to the Attorney-General, in which Sir William Slingsby is added to the list of proposed commissioners. [½ *p.*]

March 20. 13. Officers of the Navy to the Lords of the Admiralty. They have examined the prices of the victuals mentioned in Mr. Crane's statement (*see Vol. ccclxxxv., No.* 50. I.), and report upon the difference in price between October and November in 1636 and 1637 and March 1637–8, which in most of the instances quoted was about one-fifth more, but they conceived the difference between these prices in October and November and March will [ordinarily] be about 20 in the 100. [1 *p.*]

March 20. 14. Officers of the Trinity House to the same. Report upon the
Trinity House. same subject as the preceding. They think the prices stated by Mr. Crane for 1636 and 1637 are true, and those for the present year rather under than over priced. If the provisions had been purchased in October or November last, there would have been gained upon every man's proportion of victuals for 28 days, 3*s.* 8*d.* [1 *p.*]

[March 20.] 15. [Referees of the petition to the King of the widow and orphans of Clement Harby (*see Vol. ccclxxx., No.* 21.) to Sec. Windebank.] Clement Harby and Thomas Symonds traded together as equal partners from 1624 to 1630, and settled two accounts, on both which a balance appeared to be due from Symonds to Harby. The latter made out a third account after the dissolution of the partnership, in which the balance against Symonds was stated to be about 1,500*l.* Symonds now rejected all these accounts, and made out new accounts from the beginning of the partnership

VOL. CCCLXXXVI.

1637-8.

disagreeing with the books of the partnership. The validity of these new accounts would be determined by the answers to four questions which are here stated. They refer to the propriety of certain partnership charges being thrown exclusively upon Harby, and also to the right of Symonds to throw aside the settled accounts which agree with the partnership books, as if he were not bound by them. The Secretary is prayed to take the advice of merchants on these questions, and then to make an end thereof. [*Unsigned.* 1¾ *p.*]

March 20. 16. Copy of the preceding paper. [1¾ *p.*]

March 20. 17. Another paper in which the four questions above mentioned are stated in a different way than in the preceding. [½ *p.*]

March 20. 18. Copy of the same. [½ *p.*]

March 20. 19. Estimate of the Officers of the Ordnance of the charge of munition for the 22 of his Majesty's ships appointed for sea. Total, 21,717*l.* 0*s.* 4½*d.* [1¾ *p.*]

March 20. 20. Duplicate of the same. [1¾ *p.*]

March 20. Whitehall. Henry Lord Holland to the Surveyor, Receiver, and Comptroller of the Castle and Honour of Windsor. Recites survey of the decay of the pales of Windsor Great Park, made by Sir Arthur Mainwaring and Sir Robert Benett, and calendared under the 19th February 1637-8. The persons addressed are to repair the said pales, and for that purpose, calling to them his Majesty's woodwards, are to cut down 103 loads of timber in the Great Park, 20 loads in Windsor woods, 10 loads in Southbrooke, and in Cranborne 50 loads, and to issue out of the receipts of the castle and honour of Windsor 92*l.* 2*s.* [*Copy. See Book of Orders concerning Forests, Vol. ccclxxxiv., p.* 6. 2 *pp.*]

March 21. Bisbrooke. 21. Edward Andrewes, Sheriff of Rutland, to Nicholas. About 28th February sent a letter by the Uppingham carrier, but it seems by the negligence of the carrier it came not to hand. Because Lyon Falkner stood pricked for this county and had his instructions come down, every one thought he should have stood sheriff. It was very late before his Majesty's writ came to the writer's hands, he then living in a remote country, and having not then any house in the county. Has taken as much pains and made as much expedition as lay in his power. All the county is assessed and he has received 300*l.*, and has given strict charge for bringing in the rest. By reason of their slackness, because of the dearth and scarcity of corn, he has been forced to use severity against them. He therefore beseeches his Majesty to have patience with him till Easter term, and then he engages himself to pay in 600*l.*, and the other 200*l.* as speedily as possible. [*Seal with arms.* 1 *p.*]

March 21. Insula Vectis. [Isle of Wight]. 22. Sir John Oglander, Sheriff of Hants, to the same. I will oftener render you an account of my endeavours in the service of ship-money, for I do not desire to be sent for by the Lords. By order of Sir William Russell, I paid on the 20th March last to Mr.

1637-8.

Vol. CCCLXXXVI.

Holt, the under-victualler at Portsmouth, 2,000*l.*; to one Tymbrell there, 300*l.*; and then and before to Mr. Steventon, clerk of the check, 1,400*l.*; total paid, 3,700*l.*; and I have here ready at Portsmouth and shall have very shortly to pay on further order from Sir William, 800*l.* I hope this will give content, professing I take more pains in this service than ever I did for any of my own. [*Seal with arms.* 1 *p.*]

March 21.
Rome, at St. Peter's.

23. Certificate of Giles Hervey, of the Society of Jesus, papal penitentiary, that Robert Powell, an Englishman, had visited the limits of St. Peter and St. Paul and the apostolic see, and had there made confession and been absolved by apostolic authority. [*A printed form, with blanks for the names and dates.* 1 *p.*]

March 21.
Dorset House.

24. Thomas Smith to Sir John Pennington. On Sunday last his Majesty declared in Council at Whitehall that he had made the Earl of Northumberland High Admiral of England, with which every one present seemed very well pleased, and according to custom applauded his Majesty's choice; however, we know that some look upon it with sore eyes, but it is no matter, *Honi soit qui mal y pense.* Our patent is drawing with all expedition, being as large as ever any admiral had, with this only difference, that whereas Nottingham and Buckingham had it for their lives, my Lord hath it only during pleasure, and until his Lordship shall deserve ill it shall never be taken from him. Informers begin to bestir themselves, and a great deal of knavery will be discovered; next week I will acquaint you with some of the particulars. An exact list of the ships is not as yet perfected by reason of a change. No captains are yet appointed, yet never more pretenders both to captains and lieutenants. Lady Norwich is lately dead, so that my Lord of Carlisle is newly entered upon a fair possession. The Countess of Banbury will shortly go over to France. I would know whether at your coming in you desire or not to have leave to send your ship about and to come overland yourself; as I know your mind, so I shall bestir myself both for your leave and for some ships to go out before the rest of the fleet. Yesterday the Morocco ambassador took his leave of his Majesty, and one of his Majesty's ships is to transport him, but he labours for two or three more to go for Sallee upon pretence that that town is again revolted from the King of Morocco, who will this spring come down with an army against it, and if his Majesty would but let some of his ships appear before that place the people will bind the governor in chains and deliver the town to that King, who is resolved to destroy all the Andalusians therein, or to disperse them, that they shall never be able to make head again. Best respects to your nephew, Dr. Ambrose, and Lieut. Fox, and my love to Mr. White. [3 *pp.*]

[March 22.]

25. Petition of the inhabitants of Presteigne to the Council. Their town has been grievously visited with the sickness for two years past, inasmuch as petitioners spent all they had, and have had relief out of the country until about Michaelmas, and now they

Vol. CCCLXXXVI.

1637-8.

are scarce able to subsist. There was cessed upon them yearly 12*l*. 8*s*. for shipping, which could not be collected. Pray that they may be spared from paying the same. [¾ *p*.]

March 22.

26. **Justices of the Peace for co. Radnor to the King.** By reason of the plague, the better sort of the inhabitants of Presteigne departed thence, and have not returned. The major part of those that now reside are fallen into extreme necessity, neither are their markets yet frequented. May it please your Majesty that the sum of 12*l*. 9*s*. for each of the last two years due towards the shipping may be remitted. [1 *p*.]

[March 22.]

27. **Petition of Evan Davies, late sheriff of co. Radnor, to the Council.** By writ and directions he was commanded to levy 490*l*. 10*s*. for ship-money, whereof Presteigne was charged with 28*l*. During his office he could not levy 12*l*. 8*s*. 10*d*., part of the 28*l*., in regard that the town was grievously visited with sickness, and the county paid about 400*l*. towards their relief. Petitioner has paid the 490*l*. 10*s*. except the said 12*l*. 8*s*. 10*d*. Prays that the bailiff of Presteigne or the now sheriff may account for the said 12*l*. 8*s*. 10*d*. and petitioner be discharged thereof. [½ *p*.]

March 22.

28. **Petition of Lawrence Squib, James Proger, and Robert Squib, his Majesty's Officers for Cards and Dice, to the same.** William Shaw the younger, merchant, has been of late with many dice-makers persuading them to sell him dice unsealed, but they refusing, and giving notice to petitioners, Shaw was sent for to be examined before the commissioners, which he refusing was committed to the custody of a messenger about the 6th inst., but the messenger giving him liberty, he not only persists in refusing to be examined, but endeavours to find associates to join with him for the overthrow of the card business, and to that end went to divers dice-makers. They refusing, he repaired to the card-makers, and amongst them could find none but Edward and Robert Fryer, who are refractory to his Majesty's proceedings, and now Shaw daily frequents Edward Fryer's house, where they consult and seek out other associates. In prosecution hereof he has taken a view of petitioners' contract, and has reported that he will spend 1,000*l*. to overthrow the business, and has made a vow never to buy cards or dice at the office, and that he will set 100 men at work for making dice beyond sea, and has used very unbeseeming language concerning petitioners. All which proceedings so harden the shopkeepers, that divers of them are resolved not to buy any cards or dice until the business be overthrown. Pray order for committing Shaw to the Fleet. *Underwritten,*

> 28. I. *Direction by Lord Cottington to Sir William Becher to draw warrant for commitment of Shaw and to get the Lords to sign it. 22nd March 1637-8.* [1 *p*.]

March 22.
Bisbrooke.

29. **Edward Andrewes, Sheriff of Rutland, to Nicholas.** Mr. Cave, of Stamford, has promised me to pay you 100*l*. ship-money received of Rutland. I would have returned 400*l*. or 500*l*. more if I could

1637-8.

Vol. CCCLXXXVI.

tell by whom securely to return it; if you can direct me I will take it very thankfully. [*Seal with arms.* ½ *p.*]

March 22. 30. Certificate of Thomas Fowke, bailiff of [Buckingham]. As I was informed that Henry Kyme in executing a warrant from the Council upon John Robyns, of Buckingham, was abused by Robyns and his wife, and Kyme's warrant taken from him and torn by the woman, Robyns and his wife are now for the said outrage in the gaol of Buckingham, where they shall remain until they find security for good behaviour and to yield their bodies when they shall be required to answer their contempt. [*Underwritten,* "This I will see performed; John Nicholls, deputy steward." ½ *p.*]

March 22. 31. Walter Walker, B.L., commissary and official of Bedford, in diocese of Lincoln, to Sir John Lambe. Release and surrender by Walker of his office of commissary of Leicester, granted to him by Bishop Williams, and of the officiality to the archdeaconry of Leicester, granted him by Dr. Pilkington, late Archdeacon of Leicester. [*Copy. Richard Kilvert one of the witnesses.* 1 *p.*]

March 23. Appointment of Capt. Richard Morison to be Captain of the Castle at Point Comfort in Virginia, void by the death of Capt. Hooke. [*Docquet.*]

March 23. Licence to Henry Lambe to proceed in making navigable a river leading from Bury St. Edmunds towards the river Ouse according to an order of Council of 4th February last, and a grant to him of the benefit of all water-carriage upon that river, except free liberty of water-carriage to all persons from the Ouse to Mildenhall, rendering to the Crown the yearly rent of 6*l.* 13*s.* 4*d.* [*Docquet.*]

March 23. Licence to Sir John Ashley for life to abide with his wife and family in such places in this kingdom and for such times of the year as he shall think meet, without incurring any penalty for the same. [*Docquet, originally prepared for John Ashley, Esquire, and Sir John Ashley, his son.*]

March 23. 32. Lords of the Admiralty to Sir John Pennington. Eighteen horses
Whitehall. are to be transported to the Queen of Bohemia under the charge of Mr. Armorer, his Majesty's servant, into the Low Countries in the Adventurer. To give order to some one of his Majesty's ships to convoy the said ship to the Brill. [*Official seal.* 1 *p.*]

March 23. Copy of the same. [*See Vol.* ccccliii., *fol.* 98 *b.* ⅓ *p.*]

March 23. 33. John Birtby, Robert Bickley, and Edward Powell to the
Hull. Officers of the Navy. There is an error in the warrant for impressing sailors in Hull, for that town and county are distinct from co. York and no member thereof, yet, for the advancement of the service, the mayor and his brethren are very forward to do what they can. Hull has been a long time much visited with pestilence, but that punishment is in good measure removed, not above 10 persons having died within a month past. We have prested as yet but

VOL. CCCLXXXVI.

1637-8.

27 men, of whom eight are of Hull, and the mayor has been careful to present none out of any infected place. Some will apply to you for discharge and relate the danger of the entertainment of people coming from thence, but this letter you may entertain for truth. It is not possible for us to gather the number of men enjoined. In Lincolnshire we could not get above 20 men, but hope for more on our return. The name of the mayor of Hull is James Watkinson. [1 p.]

March 23.
Westminster.

Nicholas to Jerome Earl of Portland, Governor of the Isle of Wight. Was commanded by the Council of War to send an order enclosed, to be communicated to the captains of all the castles and forts. [*Copy, with a memorandum underwritten, that similar letters were directed to Sir Thomas Jermyn, Vice-Chamberlain, governor of Jersey; to Henry Earl of Danby, governor of Guernsey; and to Theophilus Earl of Suffolk, Lord Warden of the Cinque Ports. Nicholas's Letter Book, Dom. James I., Vol. ccxix., p. 172.*]

March 23.
Edinburgh.

34. Resolutions of the Commissioners and Assessors of the Barons there present for the appointment of commissioners in every shire for procuring signatures to the Covenant, and directions to them how to proceed therein. The shires were to be convened for that purpose, and lists to be prepared of those who signed and those who refused. The presbyteries were also to be dealt with for the same purpose, and similar lists to be returned of the ministers who subscribed and refused. If the ministers refused to read it in the parish churches, the commissioners recommended that it should be read to the "well-set gentlemen of the parish," and a report to be returned on the 20th April next. Where the ministers celebrate the communion kneeling, that the gentlemen and their tenants forbear to receive the sacrament in those churches. [*Copy. Endorsed*, "Sir James Douglas." ⅚ *p.*]

March 23.

35. Another copy of the same in the handwriting of Sec. Windebank, with English words occasionally substituted for the Scottish terms used in the preceding. [1 *p.*]

March 23.

36. Examination of Stephen Marsh, aged 14. Being examined whether a certificate he carried be a true certificate or no, he says that his father-in-law, John Searle, a minister, who lives near the sign of the Maidenhead in Islington, wrote the same in his study, and brought it down before the writing was full dry, and enforced examinant to carry the same to divers ministers and others to gather money of them, and threatened to beat him if he refused; and that by this certificate and others to the same purpose he has gathered divers sums of Dr. Featley, Dr. Denison, Mr. Bray, the Archbishop of Canterbury's chaplain, and others, which money he delivered to his father-in-law. [*Copy, with an endorsed affirmation of Frederick Wigan, that Dr. Altingius is Divinity Professor at Groningen, and was tutor to the Prince Elector in 1626.* ⅔ *p.*] *Annexed*,

36. I. *Recommendation to all good Christians of this poor stranger, Dr. Altingius, a high German and sometimes a famous*

1637-8.

Vol. CCCLXXXVI.

preacher at Heidelberg. States what great dangers he had incurred from the hellish Jesuits, that he had preached twice before the King of Sweden, had a wife and ten children, and could not speak a word of English. Professes to be signed by Dr. John Prideaux, Dr. William Gouge, John Staltone [sic] in Aldermanbury, and Stephen Denison. [¾ p.]

36. II. *Similar recommendation of Dr. Lunensis, a famous preacher at Heidelberg, a very great scholar, learned in the oriental tongues, and now in banishment pro veritate Evangelicâ. Dated Oxford, 17th December 1637, and professedly signed by Dr. William [sic] Baylie, pro-chancellor, Dr. Richard Frewen, Dr. John Prideaux, Dr. Richard Holdsworth, and Josias Shute in Lombard Street.* [¾ p.]

March 23. 37. Certificate of Thomas Symonds, Mayor of Hereford, that Andrew Pawling, messenger, has summoned certain of the corporation who had been lately mayors to appear in the Exchequer for passing their accounts concerning his Majesty's casual revenues since 1625. *Underwritten,*

37. I. *Names of seven persons, being all past mayors of Hereford. One of them, Richard Veynall, is returned as dead.* [¾ p.]

March 23. 38. List of such orders made by the Council of War concerning accounts to be taken by the Office of Ordnance as were sent to the governors of the isles and castles following. [17 *in number, with receipt for the same of Henry Kyme, messenger.* 1 p.]

March 24. Petition of Richard Austen to the King. About six years since Robert Austen, petitioner's father, made his will, and bequeathed petitioner 120*l.*, and to Thomas, petitioner's son, 100*l.*, all which he willed to be paid to John Austen, one of the overseers of his will, and that petitioner should receive 9*l.* 12*s.* yearly for the use of the said 120*l.* until his son was of age, and then the overseer to purchase land or leases with the 220*l.* for the joint use of petitioner and his son. Petitioner with his three sisters, Elizabeth Belcher, Ann Hatchway, and Joan Blackgrove (all married), being executors of the said will, the said sisters with their husbands have combined with the overseers and got the estate, amounting to about 800*l.*, and deny to pay petitioner his 120*l.* or the 9*l.* 12*s.*, petitioner's said son being dead, and intend to swallow down the whole estate. Prays a reference to Sir Robert Jenkins, William Walter, Edward Dixon, and Henry Cornish to determine these differences. [*Copy. See Vol. cccxxiii., p.* 260. ⅔ p.] *Underwritten,*

I. *Reference as prayed. If referees cannot compose the differences they are to certify where the impediment is. Whitehall, 24th March 1637-8.* [*Copy. Ibid.* ¼ p.]

Vol. CCCLXXXVI.

1637-8.

[March 24.] 39. Commissioners for discovery of offences concerning buying and selling cards [and dice to a messenger not named]. Directions for the apprehension of [William Shaw the younger] under a warrant dormant of the 6th inst., for refusing to be examined before the said commissioners. [*Extract.* ⅓ *p.*]

March 24. Whitehall. 40. The Council to the Warden of the Fleet. To take into his custody William Shaw the younger, merchant, and to keep him safe prisoner until further order. [*Attested copy.* 1 *p.*]

March 24. 41. Copy minute of the above warrant as entered on the Council Register, attested by Nicholas. [½ *p.*]

March 24. Whitehall. 42. Lords of the Admiralty to Sir John Pennington. The Countess of Banbury being to repair to France, is to be transported thither in one of his Majesty's ships under your command. You are to give order for a ship to repair to Dover, and there to receive the Countess, this day sevennight, and from thence to transport her for Dieppe. [*Copy.* 1 *p.*]

March 24. Another copy of the same. [*Margin,* "Not sent."] See Vol. ccclii., fol. 99. ½ *p.*]

March 24. Whitehall. The same to Thomas Viscount Wentworth, Lord Deputy of Ireland. His Majesty having constituted the Earl of Northumberland Lord High Admiral, and required us to take the accounts of all Vice-Admirals, we pray you to appoint Robert Smith, Marshal and Water Bailiff of Ireland, forthwith to come over for England, his attendance being very necessary for the furtherance of that service. [*Copy. Ibid., fol.* 98 *b.* ⅓ *p.*]

March 24. 43. William Pierrepont, Sheriff of Salop, to Sir John Lambe. Received warrant from the Lord Treasurer, Sir John Lambe, and Dr. Duck. Never saw Dr. Clayton, nor knows any of his adversaries. If Edward Baugh can be found, will send him up or take good bond of him. The keeper of the prison at Ludlow said that Dr. Clayton was committed by order of the Council of the Marches for beating a man in the church. To the writer's man demanding Sir John's warrant sent to the writer, Dr. Clayton answered it concerned his life and he would keep it. The writer's servant desired to know wherein it concerned his life, but the Doctor would give him no other answer. The gentleman whom the writer desired to present his letter to Sir John said he would acquaint the Archbishop of Canterbury with it. Would like to know his grace's pleasure. [1 *p.*]

March 24. Newark. 44. Launcelot Thompson, Mayor of Newark, to Sir Francis Thornhagh. I think it will be never my fortune to see you at Fenton. This day I purposed to be there, but the gentle smith has pricked my horse that he is not able to stir. Nevertheless I have sent you by my son 66*l.* 13*s.* 4*d.*, and for the other 13*l.* 6*s.* 8*d.* (viz., Earl of Exeter, 3*l.* 6*s.* 8*d.*; Earl of Berks, 6*l.* 13*s.* 4*d.*; Squire Leek,

VOL. CCCLXXXVI.

1637-8.

3*l.* 6*s.* 8*d.*), I have demanded it, in the absence of their servants, and they say that their lords will pay it at London, as they did all the rest. Mr. Leek is not guilty of much money, neither hath he anything to distrain; you must return him as the other sheriffs did before, and they will make him pay. [*Seal with device.* 1 *p.*]

March 24. Fenton.
45. Sir Francis Thornhagh, Sheriff of co. Nottingham, to Nicholas. I have sent up to the Treasurer of the Navy 650*l.*, and about May Day or Whitsuntide I hope to send a good deal more, and about Lammas all the sum. Money is scarce in the country, and you know how I have [been] troubled about the assessment. I have neither spared care nor pains since I came down into the country. There is nobody denies, but only desire a little time. For the assessments, I have got a great sort, but they are imperfect. Within a month I hope to send them you reasonably perfect. [*Seal with crest and motto.* 1 *p.*]

March 24.
46. Milliner's bill for work done for Mrs. Olive Porter, the wife of Endymion Porter, from the 18th December 1637 to this day. Total, 22*l.* 12*s.* 11*d.* It includes suits of sky colour and "ezebelah" colour. [1½ *p.*]

March 24.
47. Account of Sir William Russell of ship-money received under writs issued in 1637. Total received, 45,131*l.* 15*s.*; leaving 151,282*l.* 12*s.* 8*d.* unpaid. [1 *p.*]

March 24.
48. The like under writs issued in 1636. Total received, 187,488*l.* 16*s.*; leaving 9,125*l.* 11*s.* 8*d.* unpaid. [1 *p.*]

1638.
March 25.
49. Master and Wardens of the Corporation of Brick and Tile Makers to [a messenger not named]. By virtue of warrant from the Council, we appoint you to bring before us on the 29th inst. Edward Norris and John Howard, of Epsom; William Carter and Thomas Browne, of Kingston; Edward Charlewood, of Leigh; Robert Moore, of Croydon; and John Mabank, of Brockham. [¾ *p.*]

March 25.
50. Account of the Farmers of the Customs and other duties upon currants and wines for one year ended this day. The rent due was 60,000*l.*, against which were set the surplusage on the last account, defalcations, and money paid into the Exchequer, amounting to 72,552*l.* 0*s.* 7*d.* [¾ *p.*]

March 25.
51. List of articles purchased on account of the Wardrobe for half a year ending this day. It includes a tennis suit, tennis silk hose, tennis garters, tennis socks, orders' ribbon, and gold and silver garters and roses, stags' leather gloves fringed with gold and silver, upper and under gloves, &c. [1 *p.*]

March 26. Kedleston.
52. Sir John Curzon, Sheriff of co. Derby, to Nicholas. I have been diligent in the service of ship-money since I received your letter. Many I have forborne upon their fair promises, they pretending want of moneys, but said they would pay it so soon as they could. I thought it a better course awhile to forbear them than to incense a

1638.

multitude, but I purpose to in it by one course or another shortly. P.S.—I purpose to be in London next term, to give you a further account of moneys received. [*Seal with arms, damaged.* ⅘ *p.*]

March 26. 53. Sir William Tresham to [Robert] Read. Let me entreat you to send by the bearer, Allfeires Standeven, a warrant for transportation of 300 men, in part of the 1,000 his Majesty has granted me, for the recruits of my regiment. [½ *p.*]

March 27. Petition of John Willmer, your Majesty's servant, to the King. Petitioner is indebted to your Majesty in 1,000*l.*, and has an extent against Robert Rookes, nephew to petitioner, for 700*l.*, upon his house and land. Rookes has leased the same at 4*l.* per annum for 21 years to Hercules Holiland, and since that has sold the fee simple, with certain copyholds, worth about 300*l.* per annum, to one Smyth, a mercer in Lombard Street. Smyth was warned by petitioner and some of his friends to beware before he paid his money, by reason there was an extent upon the house and lands for debts due to your Majesty, to which he answered in a scoffing manner, they should be paid by 4*l.* a year. The said house and lands lie in Sir Robert Quarilis' [Quarles's] walk near Havefrith [Havering] in the Forest of Essex, and were heretofore called the Purlieus, wherein divers of your red deer resort, and your Majesty may remember you gave petitioner command that a brace of stags should not be disturbed till you came from progress, for which you gave petitioner a buck at Theobalds. William Rookes, who left this house and land to the father of Robert, was not ancestor to these Rookes, but a kinsman, and was in default to Queen Elizabeth and to your Majesty. Petitioner prays a grant of the King's right and title to the said house and lands, and direction to Sec. Windebank to command the Attorney-General to know if this fall not to your Majesty by reason of the sale, and if so, to command Rookes and Smyth to let petitioner have it at the same rate as it is to be sold to Smyth, defalking the debt out of the purchase, whereby petitioner will be enabled to pay his debt to your Majesty, and settle himself there to preserve your deer as he has formerly done. [*Copy. See Vol. cccxxiii.*, *p.* 261. ¾ *p.*] *Underwritten,*

I. *Reference to the Attorney-General to certify the true state of the business.* Whitehall, 27th March 1638. [¼ *p.*]

March 27. 54. Hugh Nanney, Sheriff of co. Merioneth, to the Council. I have assessed upon the inhabitants of this county the sum commanded for ship-money and have appointed collectors to levy the same. The abler sort pay with alacrity, but the scarcity of money among the meaner sort causes some delay. I believe it is his Majesty's pleasure that his subjects shall be mildly dealt with, which makes me presume to levy the mize more leisurely of the poorer sort, but I shall have the money to pay in such time as shall be acceptable, for I can hear of none that are refractory. I

1638.
VOL. CCCLXXXVI.

send a schedule of the sums taxed upon every parish and clergyman. [¾ p.] *Annexed,*

  54. I. *Schedule above mentioned. The names of the several clergymen are mentioned.* 2 pp.]

March 27. 55. Duplicate of the foregoing letter. [¾ p.]

March 27. 56. John Nicholas to his son, Edward Nicholas. Details of family affairs. Was glad to hear that Edward had been able to ride to his country house. He was to blame at his being at his father's not to have expressed his desire how he wished his father's house should be set. If a reasonable charge would have done it, it should have been done. His brother [Dr. Nicholas] was there yesterday. He will endeavour to place Ned at Gillingham. Reports of Jack's forwardness in scholarship. Mr. Spratt has had a violent ague, and there have been 30 at the least in that parish have had the same disease this spring. Shall be glad to hear of Mr. Ashburnham's recovery. Desires to be remembered to Sir Charles Herbert. [2 pp.]

March 27. 57. Account signed by William Earl of Denbigh, Master of the Great Wardrobe, of moneys due to Charles Gentile, embroiderer. It consisted of three items : embroidery and stuffs employed for a masque in 1627, 227*l.* 7*s.*; embroidering a rich bed and canopy of green satin, with other furniture for her Majesty's bed-chamber against her lying-in in 1630, 675*l.*; and similar charges for a bed of tawny velvet in 1631, 771*l.* 16*s.* 3*d.* [⅔ p.]

March 27. 58. Bill of William Gomeldon and William Shepherd, both of Westminster, for payment on demand of 6*l.* to Richard Hamby under the penalty of 12*l.* [¾ p.]

March 28.
London. 59. Robert Blake to Sec. Coke. There being a meeting appointed this morning about Sir Job Harby and Mr. Symonds's business, I shall not be able to wait upon you with the enclosed note according to your direction, which was, to be put in mind thereof the next day the Lords sat, which I understand to be this day. I have been much troubled this night at the inhumanity of Mr. Pescod. It must needs be malice or some envious instigator (not policy) that moved him. He was the first man that crushed me heretofore, by treacherously imprisoning me when we were upon a treaty of a fair conclusion, and now again to attempt it, I being in so hopeful a way, grieves me not a little. Were I a man that refused to pay when I had it, he had [had] some reason ; but all men know that I have been of a contrary disposition. I seriously profess that as God blesses me with an estate (before my wife and children shall be provided for) he and others shall be satisfied to a penny, notwithstanding my losses were by the Dunkirkers and by Pescod's rigorous proceeding against me, not by any negligence or ill-husbandry of mine own. [*Dated* 1637 *by mistake. Seal with arms. Endorsed by Sec. Coke,* " Sir Edmund Verney, send for the man by a messenger." ¾ p.]

Vol. CCCLXXXVI.

1638.
March 28.
Northumberland.
60. Robert Bewick, Sheriff of Northumberland, to Nicholas. The Lords' letter of the 2nd October with the writ for shipping came not to hand until the 16th December. With that expedition I could I went on to effect that service, but for the greatness of a mighty storm of frost and snow, which lay long in this county, it was impossible to travel to effect that service against that time I was enjoined; and by reason thereof the goods of the country were brought to such weakness that no money could be made of them, nor as yet are fit to make any money upon, the inhabitants making a great moan for want thereof. Likewise it hath pleased God to visit the country with plague, by reason whereof the collectors dare not come amongst them, so that they are not able to give an account of their proceedings, nor I myself to make that certificate that the Lords require. That the moneys received are so very small is by reason of the want of the accounts from the collectors, who give me present hope that as soon as the markets begin to hold they will effect, which I hope the Lords will admit of for the present, and I will diligently endeavour to return such satisfaction as will both discharge their expectations and my own duty. [*Seal with arms.* 1 *p.*]

March 28. 61. See "Returns made by Justices of the Peace."

March 29.
Salisbury Court.
62. Algernon Earl of Northumberland to Sir John Pennington, Admiral of his Majesty's Fleet at sea. His Majesty having signified his pleasure that the Bishop of Angoulême, her Majesty's almoner, should have some vessel under your command to transport him to France, you are to cause a small vessel to repair to Dover Road, to take in the bishop, with his train and necessaries, and to transport him to Dieppe. [⅔ *p.*]

March 29. 63. Bishop Montagu, of Chichester, to Archbishop Laud. By Mr. Bray I sent you another part of my altar relations, as my between times of sickness would give me leave to transcribe; the rest, as I can despatch it, I will send after. In the last there is much of the Church's sacrifice faithfully related out of antiquity. I am but a narrator, and so the less offensive. I give you power to dispose of what I write as will fit the Church and State, for we are, I know, of the same religion, drive to the same end, though not the same way. So much I related to Mr. Bray and Mr. Beane, of Christ Church. The remains of my ague are worse than the ague [it]self, so that I cannot wait upon you as I would. I cannot learn that my Lord of Norwich is yet fully translated; till when, I suppose, there is no issuing my congé d'élire. God make me profitable to his Church, to which I can bring nothing but honesty and industry. [⅔ *p.*]

March 29.
Witchingham,
Norfolk.
64. Francis Neve to the Lord Mayor of London. Being given to understand that you require my answer touching a tenement of mine in Lombard Street, my desire is to satisfy you. My intent, ever since I knew his Majesty's pleasure and the order of Council, was, and is, that the same may be let to a goldsmith, but as it has been

1638.

Vol. CCCLXXXVI.

refused by many goldsmiths, and is by certificate adjudged, through the darkness thereof and the narrowness of the street where it stands, to be altogether inconvenient for a goldsmith's trade, I hope it is not his Majesty's pleasure nor the Lords' intent that I should be forced to discharge my tenant and to keep the house shut up, but that he may continue therein until the same shall be taken by a goldsmith, at which time he will avoid the possession. [⅔ p.]

March 29.   65. Information of Peter Law, of Berwick-upon-Tweed, taken before John Saltonstall, mayor, and William Grigson, alderman of the said borough. Thomas Temple, John Foxton, and George Temple, on the 8th instant, returning from Edinburgh to Berwick, riding to the Sturrilaw burn, John Renton, of Lamberton, with a sword drawn, and his man John Green with another, and eleven other men armed with swords, lance staves, forks, and other offensive weapons, came to assault them, and bid "Strike! strike!" and knock him down, for he was the said John Renton's prisoner, and he should go with him, and swore if he would not, he should go home on his "beer-trees." Deponent remonstrating, Renton said that Thomas Temple was his prisoner, and he would have him along with him, and caused one of his men to take away the horses belonging to Thomas Temple and George Temple with their saddles and cloak bags, but afterwards upon fair speeches used to Renton he caused bring back the horses, saddles, and cloak bags, and gave them liberty to go home to Berwick, on condition that Thomas Temple and Mr. Sleigh should meet Renton at the Bound Road the next day. [*Copy.* 1⅙ *p.*] *Annexed,*

> 65. I. *Information of John Foxton, taken the 9th of March instant, before John Saltonstall, mayor of Berwick. States the principal facts above mentioned, with the addition that Renton, in answer to the inquiries of the Temples and their company, said that Thomas Temple had done him wrong, and he was now his prisoner, and he would take him to Lamberton, and keep him till he had satisfaction. He states also that some of Renton's company gave divers blows with their swords, pike staves, and forks, but whether anybody was hurt he did not know.* [*Copy.* 1 *p.*]

March 29.   66. Information of Thomas Temple, taken this day before John Saltonstall and William Grigson. States the circumstances of the attack made upon him and his company. He was leading his horse down to the burn to give him water, when he heard one call "Strike! strike!" After remonstrance, he was told that if he would not go to Lamberton by fair means he would be made to go on his "beer-trees." Renton told Thomas Temple that if he had met him on Edinburgh "causey" he would have done as much. Upon Renton being told by Thomas Temple that if he had done him any wrong he might take course of law against him, he answered, "As for your laws in Berwick I will have naught to do with them, but I will

Vol. CCCLXXXVI.

1638.

take my own law at the Bound Road or wherever I meet you." In the struggle informant was thrust through the coat, and his brother was wounded in the right arm. Admits that they promised to meet Renton at the Bound Road on the morrow. [*Copy.* 1½ *p. Annexed,*

66. I. *Information of George Temple, taken the day and year and before the persons before mentioned. Confirms the statements of Thomas Temple.* [*Copy.* ¾ *p.*]

March 29. 67. Bond of Edward Baber, of St. Giles in the Fields, gentleman, in 100*l.* to the King, conditioned to appear before the Council to answer matters to be objected against him concerning making bricks. [*Seal with arms* ½ *p.*]

March 29. 68. First draft, in the handwriting of Sir John Lambe, of 30 articles to be inquired of the warden, officers, fellows, scholars, and chaplains of Merton College, Oxford, to be answered unto by every of them in writing. These articles inquire, with most minute particularity, as to whether the college statutes had been observed. [*Notes endorsed as to breaches of discipline and various financial matters, many of them affecting the warden, Sir Nathaniel Brent.* = 5½ *pp.*]

March 29. 69. Fair copy of the above. Signed by Dr. Richard Baylie, the Vice-Chancellor, Bishop Bancroft, of Oxford, Sir John Lambe, Dr. Gilbert Sheldon, and Dr. Arthur Duck, the commissioners for visitation. [6¾ *pp.*]

March 30. 70. Archbishop Neile, of York, to the Council. Thanks for their
Bishopsthorpe. letter of the 20th inst. William Stevenson is continued prisoner in such sort as the judges left him. You wish I could discover the truth of the affirmation of Stevenson, that he knew there were a thousand in my diocese that would refuse the oath. I know no other way than, as recusants come in my way (if you allow of that course), to require of them the taking of the oath, wherein I will do as you direct. [*Seal with arms.* 1 *p.*]

March 31. 71. Inigo Jones, John Herne, Lawrence Whitaker, and George Long, Justices of Peace for Westminster, to the master, wardens, and clerk of the corporation of the Brick and Tile makers of Westminster. By order of the Commissioners for Buildings, the writers are commanded to inform themselves of the truth of sundry complaints made against the corporation of the brick and tile makers, to the end the Council may be thereof certified. Divers persons have this day attended, but we, not willing to certify against you unheard, require your attendance on Monday next at the office of his Majesty's Works in Scotland Yard, and to bring with you your letters patent, your books of orders, and the oath by you administered to your members. [1 *p.*]

March 31. Henry Earl of Holland to Sir Charles Rich, Master in Chancery.
Westminster. Appointment, as the Earl's deputy, to adjourn all pleas of the Forest

DOMESTIC—CHARLES I.

1638.

Vol. CCCLXXXVI.

of Windsor in cos. Berks and Surrey. [*Copy. See Vol. ccclxxxiv. p. 8. ⅙ p.*]

March 31. 72. Commissioners appointed to survey the King's victualling houses at East Smithfield to Sir Charles Rich, Master in Chancery. Recite the contents of their commission under the Great Seal. Find that the houses have been much decayed by the neglects of Sir Marmaduke Darell, Sir Thomas Bludder, Sir Allen Apsley, and Sir Sampson Darell, former victuallers of the navy, and that Mr. Crane has expended in repairs 1,113*l*. 9*s*. 6*d*., and there remains to be repaired so much as will cost 820*l*. The houses are of great use for victualling the navy. A cage set near the great gate of the Mansion House by Thomas Foster is a great nuisance and fit to be removed; a variety of cottages and other encroachments which are here enumerated are nuisances of great danger to his Majesty's store of provision; and certain rooms in the possession of Robert Goodman and a house at the east end of the slaughter-house should be forthwith reduced into possession of the victualler. Signed by Sir Charles Harbord, Kenrick Edisbury, John Lightfoot, Justinian Povey, Nicholas Pay, Matthew Bankes, George Bingley, Richard Kynnesman, and Jo. Worfield. [1 *p*.]

March 31.
Coggs.
73. Sir Thomas Penyston, Sheriff of co. Oxford, to Nicholas. I will endeavour to satisfy his Majesty's expectation in speedy collecting of ship-money; the longest day I have given is in April. I took the longer time for more equal rating the county, and that it might be paid more willingly, for now they have sowed all their corn, which this year is very considerable in regard of the great price, and also all the land is settled for tenants, whereas at Lady Day many remove, which has caused much trouble in former years. All these excuses are taken away, and the greatest that will remain will be poverty (which is too apparent), but I hope the care I have taken in sparing the poor will much qualify that. One thing discourages men that are well affected to this payment, which is that bailiffs have distrained for ship-money due last year and the year before, when they showed an aquittance under the sheriff's hand. The complaint hereof has been made to me, which I intend this quarter sessions at Oxford to inquire further of. [*Seal with crest. ⅔ p.*]

March 31. 74. Information of Ralph Cox, one of the porters of the [palace] gate, taken before Sir Thomas Edmondes, Treasurer of the Household, Sir Roger Palmer, Sir Thomas Merry, Sir Richard Manley, and Sir Henry Knollys, &c. On Saturday, the 24th inst., there being a great rout of people running by the court gate at Whitehall beating a bailiff, the informant not knowing the cause, was careful to secure the fore gate; during which time a great ladder, usually hanging by the chapel, was carried into the back court by watermen, labourers, and boys, whom examinant knows not, whereupon he sent men to shut the back gate (newly opened to let out wood carried to Somerset House for the Queen's service) lest the ladder should be carried out; but the people in the street and those in the court who

1638.

carried the ladder pressed upon informant's servant, and beat him down, and so conveyed out the ladder. About an hour after, informant, supposing all had been quiet, heard a great noise in the street, whereupon he made all speed to shut the great fore gates, and having done that to shut the wicket, but, before he could effect that, one Locker pressed in at the little gate, having his sword naked in his hand, the scabbard being lost, and with him Mr. Carr, having his head and face bloody, but no weapon about him, who went together into the court, upon which informant shut all the gates, and so kept them until the tumult was appeased. Some of his Majesty's servants of good quality knocked earnestly to come in, unto whom informant denied to open the gates until they had warranted him that the tumult was over. P.S.—Did not call for the yeomen of the guard to assist him, lest by his absence some further mischief might ensue. [2 pp.]

March 31. 75. Certificate of William Roberts and two others, that Andrew Pawling at Monmouth gave summons to certain of the corporation who had been lately mayors to appear in the Court of Exchequer, for passing their accounts concerning his Majesty's casual revenues since the first year of his Majesty's reign. [½ p.]

March 31. 76. Account of Sir William Russell of ship-money received to this day under writs of September 1637. Total, 50,531*l*. 15*s*., leaving 145,882*l*. 12*s*. 8*d*. unpaid. [1 p.]

March 31. 77. Account of sums levied and remaining in the hands of the sheriffs. Total, 20,350*l*. [1 p.]

[March ?] 78. Petition of the Mayor, Sheriffs, and inhabitants of Newcastle-upon-Tyne to the King. The writs for ship-money for 1636 and 1637 came to the officers of the town, and also letters for payment of the amount, being 1,400*l*. But those for 1636 came in the great visitation of the plague, which continued both in that year and most part of 1637, during which the best sort of the surviving inhabitants remained with their families altogether in the country. The mayor, in 1636, could then make no cess, and many of the now inhabitants began to resort thither about the end of 1637. Yet the mayor, in 1636, has now proceeded to a cess for that year upon the now inhabitants, most of whom not then dwelling there, and having been assessed elsewhere, conceive themselves not chargeable; and in the meantime the mayor for 1637 can make no levy for that year. Pray that so much of the 1,400*l*. shall be remitted as shall be thought meet. [⅔ p.]

[March.] 79. Petition of the Governor and Fellowship of Eastland Merchants to the Council. John Stuart, of Coldingham, by petition to the King, desired to have a place of Surveyor-General for 61 years, to search and measure all deals and timber imported, pretending great abuses concerning the goodness, "skantling," and measure, and to have for his fee a halfpenny the whole board. His Majesty, on the 22nd No-

1638.   Vol. CCCLXXXVI.

vember 1637, referred the petition to the Attorney and Solicitor General, who, having heard the Eastland Company, and the companies of carpenters, shipwrights, joiners, and others, certified that the said companies denied that there were any such abuses, and therefore recommended that commissioners should be appointed to examine into the matter. A commission was accordingly granted, returnable the 4th of June 1638, and directed to Walter Fitzwilliams, Edward Trotman the elder, Francis Dynne, Edward Bosdon, Edward Ayscough, Jasper Manwood, Richard Willis, and Francis Smith. Petitioners having made it appear to the referees that there is no cause of reformation, for the buyer has free liberty to buy, take, or leave any sort of timber, they now set forth the inconvenience of the proposed office, and pray that some of the Commissioners for Building, and some of the Officers of the Navy and of his Majesty's Works, may be joined with the said commissioners, whereby a true examination may be had. [1 p.]

[March ?] 80. Petition of David Edwards, the father, William Edwards and Thomas Edwards, his sons, all of Rorington, Salop, husbandmen, to the Council. Recite their previous petition, complaining of an unequal assessment for ship-money imposed upon them by Sir Paul Harris, late sheriff of Shropshire, and informing the Lords of the several rates of ship-money imposed upon the gentry in that county. After Sir Paul Harris had been sent for, the Lords directed the Council of the Marches of Wales to examine the truth by witnesses, and to make certificate thereof, which was accordingly done at Ludlow by Sir John Bridgeman, Sir Marmaduke Lloyd, and Adam Littleton, and certificate sent up to London to the Lord President of Wales, and delivered to him on the 6th February last. The same being detained from the Lords, petitioners petitioned that it might be sent for; being still detained, they pray that a course may be taken to bring in the same, to be proceeded upon according to equity. [¾ p.] *Annexed,*

> 80. I. *Petition of the same to the same. The previous petition above mentioned, in which petitioners set forth what offence had been taken with them in their county because they had stated by way of contrast the rates at which persons of good rank and quality were assessed, and the rate of the assessment upon themselves.* [¾ p.]

[March ?] 81. Statement by Sir Paul Harris in reference to the inquiry at Ludlow into the above business of David Edwards and others, and the way in which it was conducted by Sir John Bridgeman and the other judges. It is asserted that but few of Sir Paul Harris's witnesses were heard, and that some of their statements were refused to be put into the depositions by Sir John Bridgeman upon the ground that they taxed himself. Sir Paul Harris's defence in the matter was that the assessors, and not himself, were responsible for the amount charged upon the Edwardses, upon which point all evidence was refused to be taken. [1½ p.]

VOL. CCCLXXXVI.

1638.
[March ?] 82. **Sir Edmund Sawyer to the Council.** Information that the sheriff of Berkshire having long since sent out his warrants for rating the ship-money, that for the hundred of Beynhurst was delivered to the high constable, William Foster, of Shottesbrook, tenant to Henry Powle. Foster appointed a day for the parishioners of White Waltham and Shottesbrook to make rates. Sir Edmund Sawyer and divers of White Waltham met. After waiting an hour and a half, the high constable came, but no one of his parish; and Mr. Powle will not yield to pay more than a fourth part of the sum the said parishes come to. The parishioners of White Waltham offered to make a rate for as much as they paid when Mr. Dolman and Sir Richard Harrison were sheriffs, but the high constable refused, and the rates are not yet settled. [½ p.]

[March ?] 83. **Petition of Sir John Lawrence, Nicholas Harman, and Sir John Abeale to the same.** Petitioners being appointed by the high constable, lately made a "ratement" for ship-money in Chelsea, according to the value of every man's estate there, following a ratement made last year by three justices of peace, and settled by the then sheriff. The present sheriffs, who are strangers to the place, at the instigation of some factious spirits, have struck out the names of several persons of quality who hold lands there to the value of 260l. per annum, and abated others who were duly assessed at 3d. in the pound, as all the rest were, except petitioners and some few others, who raised themselves to a higher proportion to spare the minister and some of weak estate. The sheriffs have cast these abatements wholly upon petitioners and the Countess of Devon and Sir John Fearne. Pray that the rate first made may be confirmed, or that the same may be equally raised *pro ratâ*. [¾ p.]

[March ?] 84. **Petition of Richard Robins, of co. Northampton, to the same.** Petitioner was, by the servants of the late sheriff, unequally assessed to ship-money; and being unwilling to pay, and the sheriff's servants coming to distrain a horse out of petitioner's team as they were bringing home corn in the harvest, petitioner's servants did not deliver the horse to them. The late sheriff's servants have complained to the Board, alleging that petitioner was assenting to the denial of the said distress. Prays a speedy time to be fixed for petitioner to answer. [½ p.]

[March ?] 85. **Petition of Sir Richard Letchford to the same.** Petitioner's two daughters were formerly committed by your order to John Downes and Maurice Moseley's tuition, who since have petitioned and got a further allowance of 30l. per annum for their maintenance. By reason of great losses, petitioner is no way able to give that allowance, neither did he ever promise the same. Besides, his children are greatly wronged, to his heart's grief, and are like to be ruinated, if you take not some speedy order. Prays the Lords to accept his submission, and let him have the comfort of his children, he giving caution that they shall not depart the kingdom without licence, and be ready to attend when required. [½ p.]

Vol. CCCLXXXVI.

1638.
March.

86. Petition of Morton Briggs, of co. Salop, to the Council. You have been certified (*Vol. ccclxviii., No.* 67) by the bailiff of Wenlock, co. Salop, that petitioner, being assessed at 2*l.* 6*s.* 8*d.* for ship-money for last year, contemptuously refused to pay, and desired to give bond for answering it, whereupon there was a warrant for fetching him up. The 2*l.* 6*s.* 8*d.* is part for small tithes for a mill, and part for some profits of limestone and ironstone from a waste land called the Clees. For that which is assessed on the mill, petitioner is ready to satisfy it; but for that which is chargeable on the limestone, the said waste land not being within the corporation nor any other township, as by ancient verdict appears, petitioner, finding the end of the bailiff to be an encroachment upon his right, apprehended, if he should pay, it might be evidence against him, wherefore he denied (not contemptuously) to pay the same when demanded, which was not till the 27th January last, although he was complained of before. Prays reference to the sheriff of the county to order the assessment according to the truth of the cause. [¾ *p.*]

[March.]

87. Petition of inhabitants of the soke or wapentake of Skirbeck, being but eight small towns, to Sir Anthony Irby, sheriff of co. Lincoln. Petitioners have been charged with great sums of money every year towards provisions of beefs and muttons for his Majesty's household, charges of arms and such like, and now towards ship-money, which last year amounted to 320*l.* These great charges they are disabled to undergo, by reason that several freeholds and 10,000 acres of common have been taken from them, being worth 5,000*l.*, the benefit of a moiety whereof belonged to petitioners. Pray the sheriff's assistance for mitigation of the said charge. [*Signed by 33 petitioners.* 1 *p.*]

[March ?]

88. Information as to unwillingness in Essex and cos. Oxford, Buckingham, Northampton, and, most of all, in co. Gloucester, towards the payment of ship-money. Though the sheriffs of those counties pretend to be true servants to the King, even Sir Robert Pointz, in co. Gloucester, has said, privately, that if he must commit all the refusers, and distrain all their cattle, there will not be found prisons or penfolds enough in the county to receive them. And the sheriffs of the other counties, and especially he of Buckingham, Sir Alexander Denton, privately listen very much to their kindred and friends near them, who, to speak very modestly, are known to be hollow-hearted to the King. It is doubted there will not be unanimity in the vote of the judges concerning the King's absolute right; but perhaps they may agree in condemning Hampden for this time, as having been defective in his plea, but without voting concerning the merits of his cause. [1¼ *p.*]

[March.]

89. Suggestions that Thomas Jones be the first mayor of Shrewsbury in the new charter, and that Shrewsbury should be made a county as Worcester is. A long and full statement of the case of the church of St. Chad, and the rival claims thereto of Mr. Poole and Mr. George Lawson, the one being a divine of the school of Perkins

1638.	and Dr. Downham, but without Greek enough to be thought worthy to be appointed head master of Shrewsbury school; the other a very able scholar, well read in the Fathers, Schoolmen, Councils, and History of all sorts, a great honourer of Archbishop Laud, and upon all occasions ready to plead for him and justify his proceedings. The archbishop having procured him to be presented by the King and admitted by the bishop, his appointment became a ground of disagreement, both sides of which are here stated with an evident leaning to the side of Mr. Lawson. [1¾ p.]
[March ?]	90. A breviate or statement of the case of the glovers of London who petitioned in May 1635 for an incorporation, but were opposed by the leathersellers and hucksters of leather. Various proceedings took place until June 1636, when they were dropped on account of the increase of the plague. It was now desired to revive the project. The frauds to which glovers were subject are explained, and reasons given for the use of a seal by which leather fit for glove-making was to be distinguished. [=3⅓ pp.]
[March ?]	91. Copy of a shorter paper on the same subject, which, according to the endorsement, was "given to his Majesty," the original remaining with the Attorney-General. [=1½ p.]
[March ?]	92. Draft of the same. [2⅔ pp.]
March.	93. Memorial of Sir William Becher of such businesses as were treated of in this month by the Council, and remained yet imperfect. 1. Letter to the Lord Mayor for more frequent provision of engines to shoot water for quenching fires. The Lords intimated that they would take order for like provision in the parishes out of the city liberties. 2. Warrant to the Lord Chief Justice and others to examine the late riot near the court, and to advise how the same shall be proceeded in. 3. Order to the Lord Chamberlain to present a list of the messengers extraordinary, that the Board may suppress such as are unnecessary. The list returned, but no further proceeding. 4. Report by the Earl Marshal and the Earl of Dorset concerning new-built houses to be demolished, and concerning the corporation of brickmakers; both referred to Commissioners for Buildings and justices of peace. [*Endorsed by Sec. Windebank*, "The Lords moved in all these businesses, 18th April 1638, at the Star Chamber." ¾ p.]
[March.]	94. Draft articles objected in the High Commission against William Pickering, of Stanton Lacy, Salop. They are, that being a layman he had taken in part of the churchyard, and made it into a hog-yard or pigstie; that he had enclosed and taken possession of part of a field or meadow, part of the glebe of the parish church, and had said that Dr. Clayton, the minister, was not a lawful minister, but that if any priest of the Church of Rome were there, he would let it go to the church; that he was a recusant of the papist religion and did not resort to the parish church; that he had caused Catherine Freeman, an excommunicated person, to be buried in the

1638.   VOL. CCCLXXXVI.

church of Stanton Lacy. [*An article charging him to be a common seducer of his neighbours to the Roman religion was struck out in the course of settling this draft by Sir John Lambe.* 6¾ *pp.*]

[March ?] 95. Answers of Bishop Williams, of Lincoln, to articles objected against him in the High Commission. These articles relate principally to his authorship and licensing of the book entitled "The Holy Table, Name and Thing, &c., printed for the Diocese of Lincoln," and to the handwriting of Lawrence Osbaldiston (the bishop's co-defendant) to a letter in which occurred the words, "To frighten you from answering the railing late pamphlet, &c." On the first point the bishop stated that he believed some bishops of Lincoln had styled themselves ministers of Lincoln, as for instance Robert Grosthead [Grossetête] in sundry of his epistles. He added that he believed he was not the author of the book then showed to him, entitled the Holy Table, &c., as before quoted. As to Osbaldiston's handwriting, he said he could not swear positively that the letter in question was his proper handwriting. [8½ *pp.*]

[March.] 96. Brief of the charges against the Bishop of Lincoln in another suit against him in the Star Chamber, with the names of the witnesses by whom they were proved. These charges relate principally to the bishop's alleged subornation of perjury in the previous suit in the Star Chamber, and the making conveyances and leases of his lands on purpose to defraud the King of any fine that might be imposed upon him. The principal witnesses who proved these charges were Dr. Walker, formerly the bishop's secretary and solicitor, and Cadwallader Powell, his steward. [3 *pp.*]

[March.] 97. Book of names of all his Majesty's servants and their servants in the Court below stairs, "anno xiiii^{to}," which began on the 27th inst.; no doubt prepared for the commissioners appointed to reform the King's household. The number of the King's servants here enumerated was 245; the number of their servants who are to continue 133; the number of servants to be dismissed 61. [21 *pp.*]

[March ?] 98. Brief on the behalf of Charles Whichcote, Roger Peard, and others against John Babington and others, proprietors of the Mary and Dorothy, of London. There was a claim for freight during a period of embargo. The Judge of the Admiralty awarded freight for eight months, and the present suit was an appeal against that judgment. [5½ *pp.*]

[March ?] 99. List of his Majesty's ships that are to be employed at sea this year, with a list of merchant ships to be employed in his Majesty's service, with the number of men in the King's ships, 3,590, and the tonnage, ordnance, and names of the masters of the merchant ships. [1 *p.*]

[March ?] 100. Account of moneys due to John Bancks, coachmaker to King James, by three debentures out of the wardrobe granted in 1615, 1616, and 1617, with the sums paid on account thereof. Total amount of debentures, 964*l.* 1*s.* 10*d.*; payments on account, 830*l.*; balance due, 134*l.* 1*s.* 10*d.* [1 *p.*]

Vol. CCCLXXXVI.

[1637?] March.
101. Certificate by William Ryley, Bluemantle, of the funeral of Mary Countess of Norwich, daughter of Thomas late Earl of Exeter, and widow of Edward Earl of Norwich, by whom she had issue one daughter, Honora, married to James late Earl of Carlisle, by whom she had one surviving son James, then Earl of Carlisle, who had married [Margaret], daughter of Francis Earl of Bedford. The Countess of Norwich was interred at Waltham. [*Draft, incomplete.* 1 *p.*]

March.
102. Fees and charges of Mal[achi?] Francis, sergeant-at-arms, for various journeys in pursuit of the defendant in a cause of Henry Fitzgeoffrey *versus* Elizabeth Bosse; total, 43*l*. 16*s*. 8*d*. [1½ *p.*]

[March?]
103. Petition of John Bishop to the King. Petitioner has spent much time, and all his means, in inventing and erecting an engine for bringing water out of the Thames to parts of the city which are destitute, and may by this means be conveniently supplied with pipes into their houses. Petitioner cannot make any use of his invention, nor set his engine on work, without licence from your Majesty, as well for laying his pipes into the river as for breaking the ground to lay pipes in the streets, all which he intends to do at his own charge, and without offence to any of the inhabitants. Petitioner prays a patent for 31 years for setting the engine on work, the work tending not only to his private benefit, but to the general good of that part of the city where he intends to prosecute it. [1 *p.*]

[March?]
104. Petition of William Joyce, one of the ordinary yeomen of the chamber, to the Council. Petitioner being commanded to show cause wherefore those five tenements he has afront the street in Long Acre should not be pulled down, states that they are not new erected tenements, but have been built and anciently inhabited well-nigh 20 years; neither did petitioner build them, but bought them of William Davis, citizen of London, believing that his Majesty's pardon granted in the first year of his reign, which he had sued out, would have secured them; neither has petitioner changed those tenements, or raised their rents, but only renewed their leases for petitioner's whole time unexpired, being only six years to come, his tenants being tradesmen who have entered into bonds to harbour no inmates. On their behalf petitioner prays the Lords to permit them quietly to enjoy their tenements for the said six years, and in the meantime to provide other tenements, from which they are now disabled by reason of the sickness and decay of trading in the two years last past. [½ *p.*]

[March?]
105. Names of all the alehouse-keepers and victuallers in co. Huntingdon licensed during the year 1637, certified by Augustine Neve, clerk of the peace. [6 *pp.*]

[March?]
106. List of badgers licensed within co. Lancaster; total, 289. [*Endorsed,* "More without licence." 3¾ *pp.*]

March.
107–113. See "Returns made by the Justices of the Peace."

Vol. CCCLXXXVII. April 1–17, 1638.

1638.
April 1.
1. Henry Dewell, Surveyor to his Majesty for the Highways, to the Council. Received warrant from the Lords the 19th May last, to require those who are behind for their work on the highways to reform it by Bartholomew day. I have endeavoured to fulfil the same. John Baker, surveyor of highways for the parish of St. Martin-in-the-Fields, being charged to mend the ways between the Mewsgate and Knightsbridge, and to remove rubbish which lies about the Mews, refuses to do any service at all, and in jeering words answered "that there are rich men in the parish who will have no tricks put upon them." [1 p.]

April 1.
Whitehall.
Lords of the Admiralty to all Vice-Admirals and others. At the request of the Prince of Orange, his Majesty having commanded that Jaon Janson Steil, of Maesland Sluis, in Holland, be licensed to export oysters from Colchester, or elsewhere on the English coast, into the Low Countries, for the provision of the Prince of Orange and his household, you are to permit the said Steil to export the same accordingly. [Copy. See Vol. cccliii., fol. 99. ½ p.]

April 1.
Whitehall.
The same to the same. To suffer the Charity of Southampton, with the 30 men undernamed, to proceed on a fishing voyage to Newfoundland without impressment. [Copy. Ibid., fol. 101 b. ⅔ p.]

April 1.
Whitehall.
2. Secs. Coke and Windebank to Philip Earl of Pembroke and Montgomery, Lord Chamberlain. We have appointed Richard Poole postmaster of the Court. We desire you to order that he may be sworn. [Copy. 1 p.]

April 1.
3. Dr. Richard Baylie, Vice-Chancellor of Oxford, Bishop Bancroft, of Oxford, Sir John Lambe, and Drs. Sheldon and Duck, Commissioners for the Visitation of Merton College, Oxford, to Archbishop Laud. Have taken the examination of the warden, fellows, and scholars that are of age of Merton College, to articles enclosed. Something is discovered, no fair dealing, in fines and leases, against the warden, which he denies, and must rest upon proof of witnesses, whereof some are at London, which we shall refer to your grace. To-morrow we shall call those that are detected in any faults, and so prorogue the visitation. The vice chancellor will write more particularly, and a more perfect account some of us shall be ready to give you at Lambeth. [Draft in the handwriting of Sir John Lambe. ½ p.]

[April 1?]
4. Orders upon matters complained of and found at the visitation of Merton College. The irregularities complained of were the following:—Selling their postmasters' places; diet not kept in the common hall; Newman and Nevill; lectures not read; lying out of college; not bowing with due reverence at coming in and going out of chapel; the college evidences not laid into the treasury; the chests of Bodley and Read not well kept; the money for the library not collected; twenty copies of Chrysostom's works given, in

1638.	Vol. CCCLXXXVII.

Mr. Warden's hands still; the masters converse with the bachelors and scholars; weekly accounts not taken; books borrowed out of the library not returned; postmasters want chambers, and the clerks and battelers have them; the college served wholly with double beer; reading the Bible neglected at meals in the hall; statute book not left in the library; speaking Latin neglected; leases not to be renewed for above 21 years; the upper part of the chapel to be paved with marble; leases renewed without notice to the fellows; college bakers to grind at the college mill; Liturgy partly omitted, as Te Deum, Benedictus, Magnificat, Gloria Patri, at the end of the psalm. [*After each of these irregularities a note is given of the order made thereon by the visitors. Draft in the handwriting of Sir John Lambe.* 1½ *p.*] |
| [April 1 ?] | 5. Notes of Sir John Lambe upon some of the preceding and other points raised during the visitation of Merton College, with attached list of eight persons, probably fellows of the college. [1¼ *p.*] |
| April 1. | 6. List of the Messengers Extraordinary appointed since the 23rd June 1625, with the dates of their appointments, and the special duty assigned to each. [2½ *pp.*] |
| April 2. | 7. Petition of Thomas Harding, clerk, rector of Souldern, co. Oxford, to the King. In Trinity term, 10th James I., a decree, passed by consent in the Court of Chancery, between John Weedon, then Lord of the manor of Souldern, and Thomas Norberie, clerk, a small freeholder there, and petitioner's predecessor and pretended patron of the Church, and other the freeholders and inhabitants, by which 40*s.* for every yard-land there, which comes far short of the worth of the tithes, was allotted to Norberie and his successors in lieu of the same. Petitioner finding the same to have been made without the consent of the ordinary, and to be very prejudicial to the Church, in Michaelmas term last preferred his bill into the Court of Chancery for a reversal thereof as to the tithes. Defendants in their answers pretend that any act done by a parson without the consent of his ordinary, if beneficial to the Church, is binding on the successors. Petitioner is advised that the ordinary not being party to the decree is sufficient ground for the reversal thereof; and that the pretence of the Church's good must be accounted feigned when "the succession" attempts to overthrow the decree. Petitioner has received no tithe these 18 months, and is no longer able to undergo the expense of this suit; wherefore he prays a reference to the Archbishop of Canterbury, the Lord Keeper, and the Lord Treasurer. [⅚ *p.*] *Underwritten,*

    7. I. *Reference as prayed.* Whitehall, 2nd *April* 1638. [⅙ *p.*]

    7. II. *Appointment by the referees to hear this business on the 2nd May next.* 3rd *April* 1638. [¼ *p.*] |
| April 2.
Oxford. | 8. Dr. Richard Baylie, Vice-Chancellor of Oxford, to Archbishop Laud. Gives account of the proceedings of the commissioners appointed to visit Merton College. They have sat in the hall taking |

1638.   Vol. CCCLXXXVII.

examinations and answers by candle till eight o'clock at night. The answers are, for the most part, of little consequence; those they take into consideration are such as discover neglect of the thrift and discipline of the house, wherein both the warden and fellows partake, and are both to blame. Explains the neglected state of their accounts, their negligence in studies, and that two or three are accused for bribery in admitting postmasters, and the sub-warden "insimulated" for selling woods by Maidstone to his kinsman for 120*l*., which were well worth 300*l*. The complaints against the warden are of more weight. They accuse him of neglect of accounts, of weakening discipline, of "guiling upon the college" in expenses in his lodgings. Near 1,000*l*. has been laid out in building and furnishing his house at Oxford and at London, and 50*l*. and 60*l*. a year charged for fuel in his lodgings. They accuse him, also, of corruption in selling college leases; getting some into his hands for nothing, some for a small value, and taking more for leases demised to others than has been accounted for to the college. Emildon and Penteland, in Northumberland, were leased to a friend of the warden's for 600*l*., although 2,000*l*. was offered by Ogle; and of the 600*l*. the warden divided 400*l*. between himself and the fellows, and 200*l*. to the college, where custom divides it equally. Thraces and Thrognolls, in Newington, although offered a rent of 420*l*., he overruled the company to take 300*l*.; at the same time he took of Mr. Trafford, the tenant, 700*l*., and for colouring the business, granted him an extension of his lease of Grancester [Grantchester?] Mills. The warden says that, at the same time, Trafford parted with Burmington, in Warwickshire, to Mr. Simonson, worth 30*l*. per annum. The warden confesses he got for Trafford's lease 100*l*. The writer suspects some fraud in this. Thanks the archbishop for mediating with the Lord Chamberlain for the writer's non-attendance, and for suffering him to provide for his kinsman's advancement. Mr. St. Giles shall have his money. The convocation shall despatch the particulars for degrees as the archbishop has directed precisely. Dr. Potter seems very weak, and much disheartened in himself. [3 *pp.*]

April 2.   9. Deposition of Peter Allibond, M.A., Fellow of Lincoln College. About July 1636, at the variation of Richard Newman, of Merton College, deponent heard Newman charge Richard Nevill, of Merton College, with fornication and pæderastia. [½ *p.*]

April 2.
Whitehall.   Lords of the Admiralty to Thomas Wyan, deputy registrar of the Court of Admiralty. His Majesty, by privy seal dated 13th January 1630-1, gave us warrant to cause 200*l*. to be yearly paid to Edward Nicholas, for his attendance in the affairs of the Admiralty. You are to pay him 50*l*. for one quarter ended at the feast of the Annunciation last past. [*Copy. See Vol. cccliii., fol.* 99 *b.* ½ *p.*]

April 2.
Whitehall.   The same to the Lord Keeper Coventry. Certify that Sir Robert Mansell, Lieutenant of the Admiralty, has daily travelled about the affairs of his office from 1st January 1637-8 to the 25th March

1638.

Vol. CCCLXXXVII.

following. Request liberate for payment to him of 10s. per diem, amounting to 42l. [*Copy. See Vol. cccliii., fol.* 99 b. ½ p.]

April 2.
Whitehall.

The like for Sir William Russell, Treasurer of the Navy, 28l., being 6s. 8d. a day for 42 days for his travelling charges during the like period. [*Copy. Ibid., fol.* 100. ½ p.]

April 2.
Whitehall.

The like for Kenrick Edisbury, Surveyor of the Navy, 35l. 8s., being 4s. a day for 177 days for his attendance on the affairs of the Navy from 1st September 1637 till the 25th March following. [*Copy. Ibid.* ½ p.]

April 2.
Whitehall.

The like for Sir Henry Palmer, Comptroller of the Navy, the like sum for his attendance in his office during the like period. [*Copy. Ibid., fol.* 100 b. ½ p.]

April 2.
Whitehall.

The like for Dennis Fleming, Clerk of the Navy, 32l. 10s., being 3s. 4d. a day for his travelling charges and boat hire during the like period. [*Copy. Ibid.* ⅔ p.]

April 2.
Whitehall.

The like for John Crane, Surveyor-General of Marine Victuals, 22l. 8s., being 5s. 4d. a day from 1st January 1637–8 till the 25th March following. [*Copy. Ibid., fol.* 101. ⅔ p.]

April 2.
Whitehall.

Lords of the Admiralty to Sir Thomas Miller, Chief Justice of the Marches of Wales and Judge of Chester. We send a complaint from divers justices of peace and gentlemen in Cheshire against Francis Emerson, our deputy saltpetreman in that and other counties, with his answer, and a complaint of Robert Strancke, assistant to Emerson, wherein we perceive that the first-mentioned complainants are somewhat averse to the service, rather because they have not been of late used to it (those counties having long lain still without being digged for saltpetre) than out of disaffection to a work of so good and great importance. We refer their complaint and the answer to you, to take such a course therein as his Majesty's work may proceed, and our deputy receive encouragement, putting those gentlemen in mind to observe what is required by his Majesty's proclamation, and to give our deputy their best assistance; and if any persons appear to be refractory, we pray you to certify to us their names and places of abode. [*Copy. See Vol.* ccxcii., *p.* 79. 1¼ p.]

April 2.
Charlton.

10. Sir Edward Dingley, Sheriff of co. Worcester, to Nicholas. Had sent the assessments [for ship-money], both of the laity and clergy, so far as he could. Has since paid Sir William Russell 100l., and has laid 100l. more to be suddenly paid, albeit not received. The constables plead poverty to be the cause of this delay, but he hopes to receive a good part in May next, and will see it paid himself if he may have liberty to come up and perform that service. [⅔ p.]

April 2.

11. Certificate of Nicholas Lisle, lieutenant of Walmer Castle under Captain John Mennes, the captain thereof. In the first year of his Majesty's reign there was received into that castle certain

1638.

Vol. CCCLXXXVII.

ordnance stores here particularized. They were indented for by Anthony Sanders, lieutenant to the late Captain Edmund Lisle, now both deceased. The remains of that supply had been taken by several surveyors, particularly by William Forster and Andrea Bassana, clerks of the Ordnance, 22nd January 1632. Since then there had been received three demi-culverins and one saker, all remaining. [⅚ p.] *Underwritten*,

> 11. I. *Certificate of Captain John Mennes, that at his entrance on the command of this castle in November 1637 he found not one piece of ordnance mounted, but four serviceable muskets and almost a barrel of powder, since expended, nor has there been any subsequent supply.* [⅙ p.] *Endorsed*,
>
> 11. II. *Particular of the present remains of ordnance stores by Nicholas Lisle.* [⅔ p.]

April 2.
Angram.

12. Ja. Moore, clerk of the peace, to Sir Robert Barkley, a judge of the Northern Circuit. The North Riding of co. York on the east part reaches to the sea, where mariners and fishermen live, and in other parts there are mines of lead, alum, and coal, which set many people on work; also there are many market towns, having many licensed alehouses, and many refractory people who brew without licence. In other parts, where the towns stand forth of the travelling roads, there is not above one or two in a town licensed, and in some towns none at all. I gave you at the last assizes a particular of all the licensed alehouses; I hereby give you a particular of the places and the reason, where most of them are licensed. It is the justices' care to lessen the number as they find occasion. [⅔ p.] *Enclosed*,

> 12. I. *Number of alehouses and brewsters licensed in Bulmer, Birdforth, Ryedale, Pickeringlythe, Langbaurgh, Allertonshire, Whitby Strand, Hang East, Hallikeld, Gilling West, Gilling East, and Hang West. Total, 1,239.* [2 pp.]

April 3.

Petition of Edward Chamberlaine to the King. Petitioner has for divers years past had the office of feodary of co. Worcester, and therein has done service without complaint, and was also appointed by the last master of the Court of Wards feodary in co. Leicester for a time, which he faithfully executed. For his good service in that place, and also in his employment for your Majesty in co. Northampton, as well for the ship business as for the forest there, he has drawn upon him the malice of ill-affected persons who may go about to question him in the Star Chamber; and also in regard petitioner has been escheator and deputy escheator of cos. Northampton and Leicester, wherein he gained for your Majesty many tenures concealed for many years; therefore, for his future encouragement in your service, he prays the protection of a pardon. [*Copy. See Vol. cccxxiii., p. 264.* ½ p.] *Underwritten*,

> I. *Reference to Lord Cottington, Master of the Court of Wards, to certify. Whitehall, 3rd April 1638.* [*Copy. Ibid., p. 265.* ⅙ p.]

1638.

Vol. CCCLXXXVII.

II. *Francis Lord Cottington to the King. Has never heard any complaint against petitioner, but on the other side that he had done good service to his Majesty, therefore thinks he may be admitted to a composition to a pardon. 5th April 1638. [Copy. See Vol. cccxxiii., p. 264. ⅙ p.]*

III. *Minute of his Majesty's pleasure that Lord Cottington shall compound with petitioner, and give order for preparing a pardon. Whitehall, 9th April 1638. [Copy. Ibid. ⅙ p.]*

April 3.
At the Sessions holden at Thirsk.

13. Justices of Peace of North Riding, co. York, to the Council. We have received an order concerning levying 300*l*. towards carrying ship timber in Durham. We have forborne levying it for these reasons. We conceive that we shall thereby be made subject to a contribution with that bishopric upon all like occasions, which we cannot learn was ever so heretofore, and we can make it appear that they aim at a greater proportion for the future. Weighing the great value of their coal and salt mines, with the fruitfulness of their county, it surpasses every way this part of Yorkshire. This county has ever showed good affection to his Majesty in all other payments, but this is so generally ill-relished that without extremity of distress it will not be paid, and we are not well satisfied how as justices of peace we can by law levy it. We likewise fear that if this be further pressed, it may do hurt upon other occasions for his Majesty's service. Lastly, we entreat that the voluntary act of a few, and that out of sessions, may not lay a new burthen upon all our inheritances. [*Seal of the Sessions?* 1 *p.*]

April 3.

14. Henry Freer and Samuel Clarke, constable, to the same. Certificate that upon request of Thomas House, who had taken the licence for brewing in Aylesbury, search had been made, and Robert Egleton, Mary Crofts, widow, and Griffin Pratt had been detected, some brewing and others selling strong drink. [½ *p.*] *Underwritten,*

14. I. *Captain James Duppa to Mr. Wild. Prays a letter from the Lords to Sir Thomas Sanders and Mr. Hackwell, justices of peace near Aylesbury, to examine the abuses of the persons above mentioned.* [¼ *p.*]

April 3.
Twinhill.

15. Thomas Collard to his cousin, Richard Harvey. Prays him to give assistance to Edward Luttrell, who married the writer's daughter, in a cause concerning the Barton of Northcott. He has a lease of 500 years, which came to him by the death of his uncle, Philip Ley, and was declared by Mr. Noy to be as good as could be made by the wit of man. His grandmother, Mrs. Ley, who was Juell's daughter and heir of Northcott, conveyed the inheritance to him, and now lately by corruption "they" have obtained two verdicts against him and outed him. If by Harvey's furtherance they could have the cause honestly tried, they should all have cause to pray for him. [1 *p.*]

DOMESTIC—CHARLES I. 347

Vol. CCCLXXXVII.

1638.

[April 3?] 16. Oath taken by a Freeman upon his admission to the corporation of brick and tile makers of the city of Westminster. [*Printed.* 1 *p.*]

[April 3?] 17. Another form of the same oath, containing the matter in the preceding, with some additions. The freeman was to swear not merely, as in the previous form, that he would "true faith and troth bear" to the King, but also to the corporation of brick and tile makers, with various other alterations which made this oath more comprehensive and stringent than the former. [*Printed.* 1 *p.*]

April 3. 18. See "Returns of Justices of Peace."

April 4. Whitehall. 19. Order of the King in Council. The consideration of the great scarcity of Newcastle coals being resumed in the presence of Mr. Morley, one of the contractors with his Majesty touching coals at Newcastle, on the one side, and Thomas Horth, of Yarmouth, with masters and owners of ships of Aldborough, Woodbridge, and Ipswich, traders to Newcastle, Sunderland, &c. for coals, on the other side, propositions were tendered by Horth and others that if they might have a free trade and just measure, "21 bolls to the chalder," as formerly, from March to August they would serve the city at 17s. the chaldron, and from August to October at 19s., and for the new 12d. per chaldron they would give his Majesty security for 10,000l. per annum. But if their proffers were not accepted, they were ready to let the men of Newcastle their ships at 10s. the London chaldron freight, provided they be tied to serve the city at the rates proffered, and to give as quick despatch to the ships as in the time of free trade. His Majesty required answer from Morley for the Newcastle men, but he craving time to advise thereof, his Majesty, approving well of the propositions, fixed the 2nd of May for the Newcastle men to bring in their answer. Further, his Majesty ordered that it should be registered to be his pleasure that at that time either a free trade should be ordered according to the conditions above specified, or else that the owners of ships should have such employment for their shipping as expressed in the second proposition. The masters and owners of ships were ordered by his Majesty in the meantime to despatch their ships to Newcastle, and taking in their full lading of coal at present prices, to return to the Thames where coals are wanted, and to sell the same at 19s. the London chaldron, for this voyage only. Copies of this order to be sent to the chief magistrates of Colchester, Ipswich, Harwich, Woodbridge, Aldborough, Yarmouth, Lynn, Boston, and Hull. [*Copy.* 3¼ *pp.*]

April 4. 20. Original paper of propositions stated in the preceding order to have been tendered at the Council by Horth and others. [½ *p.*]

April 4. Beverley. 21. Justices of Peace for the East Riding of Yorkshire to the Council. Acknowledge receipt of letter concerning relief of Kingston-upon-Hull. The magistrates of that place ought not to have complained against the writers, from whom they have received by way of contribution seven hundred and odd pounds, besides private

1638.

VOL. CCCLXXXVII.

benevolence. The East Riding is the least division of the county, and the contributions were not discontinued until the men of Hull themselves acknowledged a comfortable abatement of the burials, and until the writers found the great clamour of their own country concerning the levy, and that the collection of the ship-money was in hand. They were the more inclinable to withdraw it because the men of Hull prevaricated with them on the number of the poor to be relieved, and required double the allowances which the poor of the East Riding were contented with. They also considered the present calamity of their own country, so destitute of corn and hay that many farmers are compelled to leave great part of their lands unsown, and also some supposed mismanagement on the part of the magistrates of Hull, which is fully detailed. They are now informed that there have not died in that town above 25 persons of the plague in the last quarter of a year. [*Seal with crest. 2 pp.*]

April 4.
Guildford.

22. Sir Charles Howard and Sir William Elyott to the Council. Have examined the difference between Mr. Samuel Cordewell, his Majesty's gunpowder-maker, and John Warner, of Hamhaw in Surrey, wharfinger, concerning a barrel of gunpowder committed to Warner and not accounted for, as also for wasting some of his Majesty's saltpetre. Certify that the barrel of gunpowder was delivered to the "skoryer" of Hamhaw, who is son of John Warner, and that as to the wasted saltpetre, it was delivered to the servants of John Warner in very foul weather, and that the loss was occasioned by the circumstances of the voyage and consequent delay in landing, and by carelessness of the bargeman. [*Seal with arms. 1 p.*]

April 4.
All Souls' College, Oxford.

23. Dr. Gilbert Sheldon to Archbishop Laud. I have attended the commission for the visiting of Merton College. Dr. Duck will give you a particular account. Some smaller matters have been determined, but the warden is left to your mercy, whereof he will have great need. If I were conscious of so much carelessness of the main affairs of this college, or of such practising upon the company, to the wasting of the common stock and my own advantage, I should not have the face to endure a visitation, but should lay the key under the door and be gone. [1 *p.*]

April 4.
Radley.

24. Sir George Stonehouse, Sheriff of Berks, to Nicholas. I entreat your assistance in the resolution of a case to me doubtful, the rather because it has been examined as well by Sir Richard Harrison and Sir Edmond Sa[w]yer as by myself, and the settlement waived by them both. It is concerning the rates for Sonning hundred; whether I should make the assessments for ship-money according to the constant course of other payments, the values being unequal? I much desire that the Lords would give order in this matter, being assured it would prevent several petitions to them and much advance this service. [$\frac{2}{3}$ *p.*] *Encloses*,

24. 1. *Statement of facts in relation to the assessment above mentioned. Wokingham town, Wokingham parish, Arborfield, with Newland and Sandhurst, have paid all taxes*

1638.
Vol. CCCLXXXVII.

equally in fourth parts, but Sandhurst is unequal in value to the others. So also Sonning and Ruscomb with Wonersh have paid equally, but the latter are of much less value than Sonning. Shall not the value be considered in assessing the ship-money? [1 *p.*]

April 4. 25. Captain James Duppa to Sir Dudley Carleton. In the case of Thomas Bond, of St. Edmund's Bury, brought up by messenger, his Majesty has remitted his offence upon his submission. [¼ *p.*]

April 4.
Edinburgh.
Minutes by Sir James Douglas of business transacted this day by the Commissioners and Assessors appointed by the Covenanters at Edinburgh. 1. Lists were to be drawn up of all the heritors, freeholders, and ministers who have subscribed the covenant, and of those who have not, and the same to be reported on the 20th inst. 2. Synods, wherein bishops or any persons appointed and ordained by them were to be moderators, were to be attended by one of the presbytery, who was to desire that there should be a free election of a moderator, and if that proposal were refused, the requirer was to decline the moderator, and protest that all proceedings in that synod should be without prejudice to a lawful synod wherein the bishop did not moderate. 3. The commissioners were to advise the gentlemen of the shire to quit their creditors at the term ensuing, lest their remissness should be reputed to the time. 4. All gentlemen were to endeavour to keep his Majesty's peace, and to labour to compose all questionable matters. [*See Vol. ccclxxxvi., No.* 34. 1 *p.*]

April 4. Copy of the same in the handwriting of Sec. Windebank. [*See Ibid., No.* 35. 1 *p.*]

April 5.
Newcastle.
26. Sir Francis Howard, Sir Thomas Riddell, Sir William Widdrington, and Roger Widdrington to John Saltonstall, Mayor, and the Aldermen of Berwick-upon-Tweed. Conceive the riot committed by John Renton, of Lamberton, upon your neighbours in Berwick, greatly to reflect upon your town. Sir Francis Howard, one of his Majesty's commissioners, being presently to repair to Court, we think the informations should be sent up to London with him, who will acquaint the Earl Marshal and other the commmissioners now at Court. We doubt not but such order will be brought down by Sir Francis Howard as shall give redress. [*Copy.* ⅔ *p.*]

April 5.
Littlecote.
27. Nicholas Marten to Richard Harvey. I have already written what moneys I received; and for Mr. Hinward's 15*l.*, I was earnest with him betimes. I will do my best for your recovering your money, and desire to know if I shall have your parsonage at the rent that it was set for, viz., 18*l.* a year. [1 *p.*]

April 5. 28. Affidavit of John Deane, of Lyme Regis, beer-brewer. On 17th March he read to Nicholas Sommers and Thomas Carswell a warrant of Sir Abraham Williams, James Duppa, and Lawrence Whitaker, whereby according to his Majesty's proclamation they should desist from brewing or appear before Sir Abraham and the

VOL. CCCLXXXVII.

1638.

others on 5th April. They said they would brew in despite of deponent, and of them who subscribed the said writing, which they said was made under a hedge for ought they knew, to cozen the King and country. [⅔ p.]

April 5. 29. Account of ordnance and munition remaining in Archcliffe Bulwark, Dover, certified by Capt. Anthony Percivall. *Underwritten,*

> 29. I. *Memorandum that Capt. Percivall could give no farther account than from the time he entered upon command, being 24th May 1634.* [2 pp.]

April 5. 30. Account of ordnance and munition received and expended at Moates Bulwark, Dover, from the first year of the present reign, certified by Increased Collins, now captain. [1¼ p.]

April 6. 31. Petition of John Robinson, Vicar of Sunninghill, Berks, to the King. Before the King parted with the park of Sunninghill to Mr. Thomas Carew, his Majesty, when it was full stored with deer, gave to the vicar of Sunninghill 20s. for one lodge, and 3s. 4d. for the other, per annum, and the keeper, knowing the vicarage to be worth but 20 marks, allowed the vicar the going of a nag for nothing, and six or eight cows "for 6 a week." Since it came to Mr. Carew, notwithstanding, as it may be said, it has been disparked (for there are only some eight or ten deer kept to colour the keeping of the tithes from the poor vicar), the ground being let out to tenants in several parts, they not only deny the tithes due to petitioner upon the improvement of the lands, but also the former benefit allowed by his Majesty and the keeper, but and will only give him a mark, saying if he will have more, he must get it by law. Petitioner being unable to wage law, prays a reference to the Archbishop of Canterbury and the Lord Keeper, authorizing them to call the executors of Mr. Carew, and settle a course for relief of petitioner and his successors. [⅔ p.]

April 6. Copy of the preceding petition of John Robinson. [*See Vol. cccxxiii., p.* 263. [⅔ p.] *Underwritten,*

> I. *Reference of the same petition to the persons suggested by petitioner, who are to call all parties before them and settle an order for his relief. Whitehall, 6th April* 1638. [¼ p.]

April 6. 32. Petition of John Blanch, junior, to the Council, in behalf of his father, now prisoner in the Isle of Guernsey. Petitioner, *i.e.* Blanch, the father, has had divers references from the Lords against John de Quitville and others of that isle, and divers petitions on both sides have been preferred touching cautions. Petitioner and de Quitville are now agreed, but petitioner's other adversaries stand upon the interpretation of divers orders, and, namely, Peter Gosselin, Francis Tribert, and others, who by their practices detain petitioner prisoner to his great charges, some of the jurats combining with

DOMESTIC—CHARLES I.

Vol. CCCLXXXVII.

1638.

them to perplex him in his old age. Prays a reference to any two of his Majesty's counsel. [¾ *p.*] *Underwritten,*

32. I. *Reference to the Solicitor-General and Dr. Thomas Rives to certify their opinions. Whitehall, 6th April* 1638. [¼ *p.*] *Annexed,*

32. II. *Report of the referees. State the effect of various references from* 1632 *to* 1636–7. *The jurats should be required to give execution accordingly by a short day under some great pain; the Lieutenant-Governor should be required to see execution done, and Blanch forthwith set at liberty; and that the taxing of costs, damages, and imprisonment be referred to the Lieutenant-Governor.* 9*th April* 1638. [¾ *p.*]

April 6. 33. Indenture between Giles Carter, of Nether Swell, co. Gloucester, on the first part, William Courteen, of London, on the second, and John Moore, of Taynton, co. Oxford, and Anthony Hodges, of Broadwell, co. Gloucester, on the third part. Giles Carter demised to John Moore and Anthony Hodges the manor of Swell Inferior, *alias* Nether Swell, and the mansion house of the Boule, near the town of Swell, with the park called the Park, *alias* the Abbots Ward, in Nether Swell, and the barcarie or sheephouse called Garnour, and various closes of land adjoining, and the pasture grounds called Murden, for a term of 99 years, to be void upon payment by William Courteen to Giles Carter of 5,200*l.* in manner therein mentioned. [*Copy.* 2⅔ *pp.*]

April 7. Westminster. The King to Lord Keeper Coventry. To pass letters patent under the great seal in a form recited, granting to Prince James, the King's second son, the office of Lord High Admiral with all fees, emoluments, and privileges pertaining to the same, to be held by him for life. [*Endorsed,* "To be safe kept in the Council chest." *Skin of parchment. See Case E., Car. I., No.* 3.]

April 7. Eccleshall Castle. 34. Bishop Wright, of Lichfield and Coventry, to Archbishop Laud. In reply to the archbishop's letter (*Vol. ccclxxxvi., No.* 2), will put up the King's direction in the best storehouse age has left him, and endeavour to keep time with better memories. The Bishop of Bristol's thanks for the survey of Crumwell [Cromhall] is a new load of frivolous accusations. Is not a little comforted that ill-will has no worse to charge him with. For the counterpart of Crumwell he found none, therefore he left none. Gulliford offers his oath to the Bishop of Bristol's averment negatively. Thus that complaint is answered. The writer let no leases of Horfield not precedented by the former, both of farm and manor. He had got the quirk of three lives upon three lives by the end also, and Mr. Noy to boot for advice, but could make no good church work out of it. Leaves the archbishop to be satisfied by the learned, as the writer then was, and since has been, in his present see. He did not innovate anything, and all he did preceded his Majesty's instructions. The Gatehouse of St. Augustine's, Bristol, is a small

1638.

building far apart from the now palace, no way out of the one into the other ever known or conceivable. In his time the dean and chapter claimed it. He let a lease to try the title, but when it was yielded he revoked and cancelled it, and none of his will put in for it. The vicar of Fifehead's pension payable to the bishop he never received separately. He altered nothing concerning it. Some of his predecessors put it over as a dry and unimprovable rent, over and above the tenant's rent to be brought in by the lessee with his own money; for this as a courteous case he thought himself beholden and no injury. This is his answer. He has done nothing wherefore he should desire to prevent his Majesty's cognizance. As to the complaint of the new dean of Lichfield, were it not under the archbishop's hand he should hardly believe it. Not a syllable of it is true. Their statutes, not renewed since 1526, have grown very capable of reformation. He commended the work to the bishop, dean, and chapter's best care, adding that he desired they might be submitted to the archbishop for his Majesty's confirmation. Several drafts had been prepared, and the Bishop of Rochester took them to add something from the late statutes for Canterbury. Dr. Fell knows nothing of it but by hearsay; 'tis very strange therefore he should venture on such a complaint. Hopes the archbishop will have an ear for the writer's defence and justify him to his Majesty. [*Seal with arms.* 2 *pp.*]

April 7.
Burderop.

35. Sir William Calley to Richard Harvey. I have received the barrel of sugar, &c. We have had news lately here that the mutinous covenanters have taken the Castle of Edinburgh and have slain there 1,200 men, of 1,500 who stood for the King, the certainty whereof and of all other common news we expect to hear from you shortly, to whom I wish a good journey. I desire you to provide five or six dozen cork stopples; without them we cannot draw out our wine. [*Seal with arms.* ⅓ *p.*]

April 7.

36. Account of Sir William Russell of ship-money received under writs for 1637. Total, 52,451*l.* 15*s.*; unpaid, 143,962*l.* 12*s.* 8*d.* [1 *p.*]

April 7.

37. Account of ship-money for 1637, levied and remaining in the sheriffs' hands, being 17,800*l.*, making total collected 71,231*l.* [*sic*], which is 19,765*l.* less than on 8th April 1637. [1 *p.*]

April 7.

38. Inventory of ordnance and ammunition in Dover Castle at the entry of Sir John Manwood as lieutenant, 26th April 1637, with a note of articles since expended. [*Underwritten,* "I fear these accounts are not very perfect; at my coming to London I will bring a more perfect account if I can. John Manwood." 2 *pp.*]

April 7.

39. Names of witnesses to be examined according to his Majesty's commission touching abuses in payment of moneys for freight of ships [set forth by the city of London?]. [1 *p.*]

DOMESTIC—CHARLES I. 353

Vol. CCCLXXXVII.

1638.
April 9.
Whitehall.

40. The King to Edmund Earl of Mulgrave, K.G. Dispensation to excuse the Earl's attendance on the 22nd, 23rd, and 24th May next, the days appointed for celebration of the Feast of the Order of the Garter, and further, in respect of his age and weakness, to dispense with his attendance during his life, observing in his own house the rites and solemnities appointed by the canons of the order. [*Copy.* ¾ *p.*]

[April 9.]

The Lord Privy Seal and the Earls of Pembroke and Dorset, "the two Lord Chamberlains," to the King. Report on the petition of Charles Carey calendared under date of the 16th March last, p. 309. By the death of the late Lord Dacre a great part of petitioner's estate is gone from him. The creditors are not many, the debts small, and some are willing to lend petitioner time. The petitioner also shows care to give them satisfaction. Recommend the grant of a protection for a year. [*Copy.* See Vol. cccxxiii., p. 266. ⅙ *p.*] *Underwritten,*

    i. *Minute of the King's pleasure to grant the protection desired. Whitehall, 9th April [miswritten March] 1638.* [*Copy. Ibid.* ⅙ *p.*]

April 9.

Petition of Lady Ashley, widow, to the same. Petitioner has only one daughter, whom her deceased husband, Sir Francis Ashley, your Majesty's sergeant-at-law, at the special solicitation of the late Earl of Clare, married to his second and youngest son, Denzil Holles. At the time of this treaty petitioner and her husband were tendered divers matches with heirs to 3,000*l.* per annum and upwards. The Earl made use of Lady Elizabeth Hatton, to whom petitioner and her husband had committed their daughter, and promised to settle a large fortune on his son, but for the present gave him only lands in Cornwall worth 2,500*l.* Trusting to the honourable engagements of the Earl, and at the earnest solicitation of Lady Hatton, petitioner and her husband yielded to the match, which was accomplished about 11 years since. The Earl throughout his life manifested an extraordinary affection to his son, and took much delight in his company, and in effect declared a little before his death that he had settled upon him a greater estate than he had promised. The now Countess Dowager of Clare, more affecting her eldest son, kept her younger son from a timely knowledge of the danger of his father's sickness, and was unwilling that any person should put the Earl in mind of publishing his last will. And since his death she has set on foot an old will, made 39 years since, and cancelled many years ago, whereby the Countess and her elder son have possessed themselves of a great personal estate, and 6,800*l.* per annum which the Earl left at his death, and they attempt to carry off that estate which should come to petitioner's daughter and her issue (upon whom petitioner and her husband have settled the whole of their estate), and to keep from petitioner's son-in-law a personal estate due to him as executor to his grandmother. In dutiful observance of his mother he forbears to take any legal course, wherefore petitioner prays a

Vol. CCCLXXXVII.

1638.

reference to some honourable persons to settle such an end as shall seem just. [*Copy. See Vol. cccxxiii., p.* 266. 1¼ *p.*] *Underwritten,*

> I. *Reference of the preceding petition, and of another preferred to the King by the Countess of Clare, to the Archbishop of Canterbury, the Lord Treasurer, Lord Cottington, Sec. Windebank, and Lord Chief Justice Finch, to certify their opinion. Whitehall, 9th April* 1638. [*Copy. See Ibid., p.* 267. ¼ *p.*]

April 9.
New College, Oxford.
41. John Windebank to his father, Sec. Windebank. Having been intent on public duties, fears he may have neglected those of a private character. Cannot think his degree of Bachelor has been absolutely obtained until confirmed by his suffrage. [*Lat. Seal with arms.* 1 *p.*]

April [9].
42. Sir William Portman, Sheriff of Somerset, to Nicholas. The Lords' directions for review of the rates of the county have much retarded the service of shipping. Some places have been so backward that until they received some satisfaction from the gentlemen of the county upon their meeting for reconciling the rates, I could not from some hundreds get any assessments, from others no pay at all. Notwithstanding the Lords' order that the ancient rates should stand for the present year, and that no one should take benefit of the review for the present, yet in respect the gentlemen of the county upon their meeting at Wells in Easter week could not accord for settling the rates, but referred the same to be set again in August, such as expect ease or are refractory lay hold of the occasion for delay. I have returned to Sir William Russell to be paid next term 1,500*l.*, and have near 500*l.* more, which with additions will be paid about the middle of the term. The corporate towns answer that they intend to pay in by themselves. I have used all possible endeavours for getting in the assessments, but cannot yet obtain all. I have forborne to make return until I can receive the whole. Advertise the Lords of my most willing readiness for expediting the service. [1 *p.*]

April 9.
Bisbrooke.
43. Edward Andrewes, Sheriff of Rutland, to the same. You shall receive 200*l.* before the end of this month of my kinsman, Richard Andrewes, to whom please give acquittance. I trust you have received 100*l.* of Mr. Cave. I intend to see you about the latter end of the term and bring you some more money. [*Seal with arms.* ½ *p.*]

April 9.
Cambridge.
44. The President and Fellows of St. John's College, Cambridge, to Sir John Lambe. Letter of thanks for books given to, and others procured for, their library. [*Signed by Thomas Spell, president, and six other fellows. Seal with arms. Lat.* 1 *p.*]

April 9.
London House.
45. Lord Treasurer Juxon, one of the Commissioners for compounding for offences against the Forest Laws committed within the Forest of Rockingham, to the High Constables of the Hundreds

1638.   VOL. CCCLXXXVII.

within that Forest. The Commissioners having determined to meet weekly at London House, the persons addressed are to give notice thereof to all owners of lands within the forest, that they may attend, bringing with them particulars of the lands for which they desire to compound. The persons addressed are also to return lists of all owners of lands within their several hundreds, with the places where they dwell, and the quantity and value of their lands. [*Copy.* ¾ *p.*]

April 10. Petition of Richard Best and Rose his wife, daughter and heir of Richard Roos, deceased, cousin and next heir of Robert Roos, late of Ingmanthorpe, co. York, to the King. Upon petition of the said Rose and Christopher Roos her cousin, your Majesty referred them to the Earl Marshal, who required your Officers of Arms to certify touching the said petitioner's descent. The Officers of Arms have declared that Rose is next and immediate heir of the said Robert Roos, by reason whereof divers lands ought to descend, as by a case stated to be annexed appears. Pray the King to take an assignment of these lands, and reassign them to petitioners in fee-farm, at such rent as may be thought fit. [*Copy. See Vol. cccxxiii.*, p. 267. ¾ *p.*] *Underwritten*,

> I. *Reference to the Lord Treasurer and Lord Cottington, who, calling to them the Attorney-General, are to certify their opinions.* Whitehall, 10th *April* 1638. [*Copy. Ibid.*, p. 268. ¼ *p.*]

April 10. 46. Sir Thomas Coningesby, Sheriff of co. Hertford, to Nicholas.
North Mimms. At my last attendance at the Council table, time was given me to make return of his Majesty's moneys till the beginning of this term. For the 3,800*l*. charged on the county I have paid to the Treasurer [of the Navy] 600*l*., and have in hand only about 60*l*. The country's backwardness will appear in the examination of my proceedings; first, by my warrants in October for making the rates; secondly, upon their neglect to assess, by my warrants to the petty constables to make the same or be committed to prison, whereupon the rates were made, yet wanting the assistance of the chief parishioners, it begat a great deal of cavil upon particulars. For satisfaction I was enforced to give meetings to determine those exceptions and appoint under-collectors. My last warrants, to call in accounts, are not yet returned, but I expect them by a peremptory day next week. Finding the collectors cold in taking distresses I have employed my own special bailiffs therein, who find the meaner sort readiest to pay, but others backward until they be distrained. One testimony is as follows: On Monday last my bailiff requiring 3*l*. assessed upon Henry Coghill, of Aldenham, a man of great possessions in that place, and in purse ready for a purchase of 20,000*l*., he refused to pay, and gave charge to his servants not to suffer any distress, saying he would answer it at the Council table. My bailiff thereupon seizing a horse of his, a rescue was made by one Arthur, his bailiff, and another of his servants. This Coghill is a leading man

VOL. CCCLXXXVII.

1638.

on that side the country, and the neighbours' eyes are fixed upon the issue of this bold attempt. I had direction to receive 55*l*. in arrear last year from Hertford. Joseph Dalton, the then mayor, says there was 48*l*. received, but that he had lent out the money and cannot as yet get it in. The man, as reported, is going for New England, and for aught I perceive his conscience may serve him to take the money with him. For St. Alban's divers gentlemen inhabiting within the precincts have been overrated by the mayor and magistrates in ease of themselves. The complainants submit to pay proportionably, and are not noted for moneyed men, wherefore I shall proceed in relieving them, unless commanded to the contrary. [2 *pp.*]

April 10. 47. Remonstrance and petition of the Walloon congregation in Norwich to Bishop Wren, of Norwich. 1. Their predecessors at their entrance into your chapel, which was about the year 1566, found it more like a dove-house than a church, full of muck and ordure, the roof decayed and the windows broken. 2. They acknowledge no engagement to maintain the said chapel, much less to secure any of the bishops about dilapidations, but by way of thankful acknowledgment of their goodness in permitting them to make use of their chapel, they have voluntarily bestowed much cost upon it, and have left it well glazed and supported. 3. They never had any assurance of time in it, and therefore paid no rent for it, but it remained in the possession of the bishops, who had the keys of the west door, and made use of it, after it was repaired by the Walloons, for baptizing their children, ordaining English ministers, and other uses at their pleasure. 4. By your order they were warned out of the chapel and yielded up the keys about a year since, with 20 nobles by way of gratitude, neither did they carry out anything but their own. 5. By their removal the congregation have been put to the charge of 160*l*. to repair a poor little forlorn church granted them by the city's favour. Beseech you to hold them excused, although they secure you not about the dilapidations mentioned in your letter. 6. Your predecessors received satisfaction for dilapidations until you came to the see, since which time the congregation has expended 23*l*. in repairs. 7. There is no cause to fear sudden ruin. The beams will uphold the roof for 40 years to come. 8. The Walloons are a poor decayed congregation. [1½ *p.*]

April 10. 48. Thomas Smith to [Sir John Pennington]. Concerning your
Dorset House. nephew and Lieutenant Fox, I forgot to give you notice that the former is to be a lieutenant and the latter to have a Whelp, and yesterday the King in the presence of the Lord Admiral settled the list of captains, but their ships are not yet resolved upon. I hope to see you shortly, at which I exceedingly rejoice. Captain Carteret in the Convertive, and Captain Slingsby in the Expedition pinnace, will very shortly go out with the Morocco ambassador; they are to take him in at Portsmouth. Sir Henry Mervin has chosen the Victory, wherein he is to go Rear-Admiral, with some four smaller

1638.

Vol. CCCLXXXVII.

vessels to do the same you did last year; I pray God he do so well. The great ship is not to fall down these three weeks, because the Queen desires to see her, when she has her middle tier of ordnance upon her, and they will not be ready till then. Some lords and bishops lately come from Scotland bring no good news from thence, at which our Court is much troubled, insomuch that the installation of the Prince and the Feast of St. George are put off till September. P.S.—My lord has appointed your master to carry about the ship, because he conceives Lieutenant Fox will come in with you by land. [1⅔ p.]

April 10.
Loubnome.
[Lubenham?]
49. Richard Collins to Sir [John Lambe?]. Your letter came not until the 8th April. [An estate to which it referred] was sold to Mr. Coltman, of Fleckney, but for what sum we cannot learn. It was never let for above 8l. a yard land, but now he lets it to men in the town for 12l., in small patches of half or a quarter a yard. The dwelling-house he has pulled down, and his wife lives in the barn. The trees are about the bigness of a man's leg. A yard land is worth to sell about eight [s]core pounds. [1 p.]

April 10.
50. Certificate of Richard Bagnall, saltpetreman, Robert Sims, clerk, and two others, that Roger Houlderness, bargeman, received of Giles Baggs and Christopher Ring, coal merchants at Queenhithe, 12 chaldrons of coal to be carried to Pangbourne, Berks, but that he sold the same for a great profit, so that petitioner Bagnall was forced to buy coal and wood at unreasonable rates. [½ p.]

April 11.
Whitehall.
51. Order of Council upon a relation of the state of the Card business, with the reasons why it has not produced any benefit to his Majesty. The Lords declared that the officers ought to have all fitting assistance, and ordered the Attorney-General to take special consideration of the said relation, and to certify his opinion as to what he should think fittest to be done. [*Copy.* ⅔ p.] *Under-written,*

> 51. I. *Attorney-General Bankes to the Council. Conceives it fit to have a new proclamation wherein the points desired by the officers may be inserted, saving as to the embargo of ships and goods. By Statutes 3rd Edward IV. and 1st Richard III., the importation of foreign cards is inhibited, which statutes may be put in execution. For such cardmakers as have broken their contract, he conceives that they should not hereafter have benefit by the contract, but that the officers may be free from taking off their cards, and that the cardmakers should pay for sealing such cards as they make. 22nd May 1638.* [1 p.]

April 11.
52. Richard Fenn, Lord Mayor of London, and four other Aldermen to the Council. We have endeavoured to accommodate the difference between Oswald Medcalfe and his landlord, Francis Neve, dwelling in Norfolk, but could do nothing in it. Enclose letter from

Vol. CCCLXXXVII.

1638.

Neve, being that calendared under date of 29th March last, Vol. ccclxxxvi., No. 64. [¾ p.]

April 11.
Mincing Lane.

53. Officers of Navy and Auditors of Imprests to Lords of the Admiralty. Have advised concerning the demand of the Surveyor-General of marine victuals for the allowance of cask and biscuit bags expended in his Majesty's service. We have perused the Victualler's contract, and are persuaded that by reason of that exception specifying what cask the Victualler is to bear the expense of, if more be spent, the charge should be borne by his Majesty. State certain precedents of similar allowances. [1 p.]

April 11.

54. Petition of William Belke, clerk, to Archbishop Laud. John Belke, of Sheldwich, Kent, died intestate on 31st March 1633. He had two brothers, Gabriel and Michael, and a sister Elizabeth, all of whom died intestate in John's lifetime, but left issue. Sir Nathaniel Brent, your commissary, committed the administration of the goods of the deceased to Valentine Belke. On passing his account, there was a remainder of 1,500l. to be divided. It was proved by sufficient witnesses that the intestate intended the greatest part of his estate to petitioner, yet is there allotted by the commissary to the children of Gabriel Belke, 900l.; to the two daughters of Elizabeth, 560l.; and to petitioner, but 40l.; from which petitioner has appealed to the Dean of the Arches, but fearing that the adverse party will not be concluded by the Dean's sentence, petitioner prays that the cause may be heard in the Archbishop's presence. [*Endorsed*, "To show to Sir John Lambe." ¾ p.]

April 11.
Pensford.

55. John Locke to Richard Harvey, servant to Sir [*sic*] Endymion Porter. A friend of mine desires to farm your parsonage of Compton Dando. Having taken the tithes belonging to the vicar there, he will give 20s. more yearly than any man else can afford to do. [*Endorsed*, that this letter was answered by —— Munck the 30th April 1638, that he had engaged himself concerning Compton Dando, but that if they brake off, Locke's friend should have the refusing of it. ¾ p.]

April 11.

56. Answer of the President and College of Physicians, London, to petition of the Apothecaries to the Council. The delays complained of in the petition have arisen from the service of his Majesty and the sickness. Since the 6th February 1636, the apothecaries have never stirred. To the four grievances annexed to the petition the doctors answer: I. No fellow of the college keeps an apothecary in his house, although by law they might so do. II. In 40 years not above eight have been discommoned, and of these five are brought for judgment before the Star Chamber, whereby the Lords may discern whether the college had not good cause so to do. III. They never searched nor destroyed any drug but as by Act of Parliament is prescribed. IV. Unknown names are sometimes given to known things, lest the patient might suffer sometimes in his fame, and sometimes for other causes. This grievance is added, not that they

1638. VOL. CCCLXXXVII.

can be grieved therewith, but that they must show even before the Lords their respect to the college to be none at all. [¾ p.]

April 11. 57. Order of the Court of Exchequer, *ex parte* the King's Remembrancer. Upon motion made the 13th February last on behalf of the tenants of a close called Millgrove, and other lands in Hartpury, co. Gloucester, lately extended into his Majesty's hands for 1,100*l*. due by William Compton for arrearages of an annuity due to John Compton, convicted of murder, it was ordered that, for some imperfections in the said extent and inquisition, no further process should be awarded upon the same. Upon opening the cause by Mr. Lenthall, it is this day ordered that process shall proceed. [*Endorsed*, "Compton versus Underhill." 2 *pp*.]

April 11. 58. Information of William Mason, of St. Sepulchre's, London. Bryan Chadborne is a lodger in the house of informant's master, Richard Steevenson, a cook in Hosier Lane, London. Informant, William Gorway, Robert Coaker, and James Houlton being yesterday at dinner in informant's master's house in a drinking room in the yard, the tapster being in their company called Chadborne to drink with them, and after about half an hour's discourse he said that the King was a murderer, and that all the bishops and pastors of the kingdom were false prophets, and that a drunkard should sit with God in the kingdom of heaven. As the constable was carrying Chadborne to prison, a stranger said that Chadborne had been in Bedlam, Newgate, and the Compter. Being demanded what had provoked such words from Chadborne, informant said that Chadborne began to talk of the seven spirits mentioned in the Revelation, whereupon informant said why should he speak of such things, for he had no more judgment than a horse, and then Chadborne fell into a raging passion and uttered the said words. He was not drunk. [1½ *p*.] *Subjoined*,

  58. I. *Joint informations of William Gorway, Robert Coaker, and James Houlton, that the words charged against Chadborne were spoken in their hearing.* [½ *p*.]

April 11. 59. Examination of the said Bryan Chadborne. He denies that he spoke the very words he is charged with, but confesses that he said that the King would cut the throats of a thousand before he would lose his crown, and wherefore else does he send ships to the sea; further, he said that all the bishops and pastors were false prophets and had falsely translated the Bible. He is a tailor by trade. About six years since he was in Bedlam. [½ *p*.]

April 12. Petition of Mary Davenant to the King. Upon a sudden causeless and intolerable provocation given by one Warren, being a tapster or an ostler, he received a small hurt by William Davenant, petitioner's husband, which, by Warren's own neglect and by letting blood, of which he lost 10 or 11 ounces, was the cause of his own death. By the importunity of friends, in the absence of the said Davenant, and without having any testimony on his part, the coroner's inquest

1638.

VOL. CCCLXXXVII.

found the said offence within the statute of the late King. Afterwards the King, at the instance of his nephew Prince Charles Elector Palatine, granted letters of transportation on behalf of the said Davenant, which letters extend only to the safety of Davenant's life. His lands being held of some mesne lords who endeavour to prosecute him to outlawry to the ruin of petitioner and posterity, she prays them, her husband being still absent, to give a warrant for his pardon. [*Copy. See Vol. cccxxiii., p. 269.* ½ *p.*] *Underwritten,*

> I. *Minute of the King's pleasure to grant petitioner's husband, William Davenant, a pardon for his life, lands, and goods, and the Attorney-General is to prepare a bill for signature. Whitehall, 12th April 1638.* [*Copy. Ibid.* ¼ *p.*]

April 12. 60. Petition of John Earl of Annandale to the King. Richard Murray, D.D., warden of Manchester, and brother to petitioner, lately deceased, was fined by the Ecclesiastical Commissioners 1,000*l.*, which your Majesty appointed to be paid towards the repairs of St. Paul's. Petitioner for preserving his brother's estate had agreed with the Archbishop of Canterbury to pay the said 1,000*l.*, and had paid part and secured the remainder, whereupon your Majesty granted petitioner the said fine and extent in the names of Sir Abraham Dawes, Mungo Murray, and George Duncombe, and petitioner caused an extent to be sued out upon the estate of the said Richard Murray, but nothing was found to satisfy the fine but only the reversion of the advowson of Wigan after the death of the Bishop of Chester, so that petitioner will lose his 1,000*l.* unless your Majesty extend to him your grace. Prays that the said advowson may be secured to petitioner, or to Sir Abraham Dawes, Mungo Murray, and George Duncombe, or others whom he may appoint. [⅔ *p.*] *Underwritten,*

> 60. I. *Reference to the Attorney-General to certify. Whitehall, 12th April 1638.* [¼ *p.*] *Endorsed,*
>
> 60. II. *Attorney-General Bankes to the King. For petitioner's suit to your Majesty to secure to him the advowson of Wigan, so that your Majesty, your heirs and successors, will not by any title of prerogative dispose thereof after the avoidance of the same, I certify that the like was done by King James, in the 19th year of his reign, to Sir Walter Heveningham for one presentation. 28th April 1638.* [½ *p.*]

[April 12.] 61. Petition of Edward Hobbes to the Council. About five years since petitioner compounded with Charles Powell for his almsman's place in the cathedral of Bristol, and enjoyed the benefit thereof, until about four months since Powell made an unjust complaint that petitioner had detained the rent from him. Upon reference to the

1638.

Vol. CCCLXXXVII.

dean and chapter they have found it to be petitioner's right. Prays order that he may quietly enjoy the same. [½ p.] *Annexed*,

 61. I. *The Dean and Chapter of Bristol to the Council. They have examined the business between Charles Powell, their almsman, and Edward Hobbes, a reversioner by his Majesty's father's grant. Hobbes has received the stipend of 20 nobles per annum belonging to Powell's place, not by any trust, as in Powell's petition suggested, but by a fair contract upon consideration of money paid and service to be performed in that place in Powell's absence. Bristol, 12th April 1638.* [1 p.]

April 12.
Dorset House.
 62. Thomas Smith to Sir John Pennington. The 17th instant is the day for the Providence to be at Dover to attend Lady Newport. I know you are troubled that your ship goes to Portsmouth, and so am I. The Officers of the Navy pleaded the necessity. The Earl of Newcastle is made groom of the stole to the Prince, and his sole gentleman of the bedchamber, and though he shall not have the name of his governor, yet he shall have that superintendency. Doctor [Duppa], his tutor, is lately made Bishop of Chichester. Mr. Crane has given warning to the Lord Treasurer for breaking off the contract about victualling, pretending his inability to perform it at the former rate. There are others suing to do it at the same rate, so that Mr. Crane may be caught, as some ambassadors that I have known of Constantinople, who having desired to come home have after desired [offered?] good sums of money to stay. [*Seal with arms.* 1 p.]

April 12.
 63. Statement of abuses committed by John Reeresonn, Captain of a States man-of-war. He had invaded his Majesty's kingdom, battering it with ordnance, and landing 50 armed men. He had also broke down houses and windows and taken away his Majesty's subjects' estate to the value of 1,230*l*. [½ p.] *Underwritten*,

 63. I. "*Sir Henry Marten is desired to certify his opinion concerning this business, what may justly and fitly be done for the reparation of this wrong.* JOHN COKE." *12th April* 1638. [¼ p.]

 63. II. *Sir Henry Marten to Sec. Coke. Before I give my opinion give me leave to remind you that there is a noble ambassador here for the States, who professes himself zealous to do all good offices between this State and theirs, whether it were not very fit that these writings from Ireland should be delivered to the ambassador and an answer be procured, that the King may be enabled to give direction for further proceeding.* [1 p.]

April 12.
 64. Separate examinations of Thomas Welsh, *alias* Wood, of Compton Abdale, co. Gloucester, and of Thomas Mace, of the same place. Welsh stated that about Shrovetide, threshing at the house of Elizabeth Mace, the said Elizabeth said that what for ship-money

1638.

VOL. CCCLXXXVII.

and many other payments that came daily on, one upon another, she thought she should not be able to live. Examinant answered that the King must be served, upon which her son, Thomas Mace, replied, "If this be so, that the King must have all, I would the King were dead." Mace denied the words. His version was that Wood told his mother that he must go to the justices for some more relief. His mother answered that then she saw more trouble and money must be. Mace added, "God's will be done!" [*Endorsed that the matter was referred to the judges of assize.* 1 p.]

April 12. 65. Certificate of John Bigg and two others that Andrew Pawling, messenger of the Chamber, was at Bath that day, and summoned certain, who had lately filled the office of mayor, to appear in the Exchequer for passing accounts of his Majesty's casual revenues since the first year of his reign. [¾ p.]

April 13. 66. Petition of John Dod, clerk, rector of North Cadbury, Somerset, to the King. About seven years since petitioner being indicted by John Stone for money taken up of him at interest, was by him [drawn] to grant a lease to him of the rectory of North Cadbury for 49 years if petitioner should so long live, to the end that upon a redemise thereof to petitioner for his life, Mr. Stone might be secured for 350*l.* formerly lent and then paid to petitioner. Petitioner was drawn into that bargain in respect that Mr. Stone persuaded him that he might redeem it. Mr. Stone having received 500*l.* refuses to surrender the security to petitioner except upon such terms as would be petitioner's utter undoing. Prays reference to the Archbishop of Canterbury, the Lord Keeper, Lord Treasurer, and Lord Privy Seal to make a final order. [1 p.] *Underwritten,*

66. I. *Reference as prayed. Whitehall, 13th April* 1638. *Annexed,*

66. II. *Appointment by the referees of Friday, the first of June, for hearing this business. 9th May* [1638]. [¼ p.]

April 13. 67. Note of Vice-Admirals who have not accounted in the Admiralty. Earl of Lindsey for co. Lincoln from August 1628; late Earl of Suffolk for Northumberland, Cumberland, Westmoreland, and Durham, from the same time [*sic*]; the same Earl for Dorset since Michaelmas 1635; Earl of Derby for Chester and Lancaster since 30th March 1632; Earl of Nottingham for Sussex since 20th April 1632; Earl of Warwick for Essex since Michaelmas 1635; Viscount Chichester for Ulster from 10th October 1635; Earl of Pembroke and Montgomery for South Wales from 18th November 1635; Lord Maltravers for Norfolk, Cambridgeshire, and the Isle of Ely from 3rd December 1636; Sir James Bagg for South of Cornwall and Devon from September 1634, and a former account uncleared; Francis Bassett for North of Cornwall from 20th November 1636; Sir Edward Rodney for Somerset from 20th April 1632; Sir Thomas Walsingham for Kent from Michaelmas 1637; Francis Godolphin

1638. Vol. CCCLXXXVII.

for Scilly from April 1631; Sir Robert Loftus for Lempster [Leinster?] in Ireland from the date of his patent. [4¼ pp.]

April 13. 68. Notes of presentments for ecclesiastical offences made at the triennial visitation of the diocese of Lincoln by Commissioners of the Archbishop of Canterbury. The visitation extended from the 4th inst. to this day. By far the greater number of presentments were for incontinency, and very many of them for ante-nuptial offences of that kind. Among the other cases may be noticed—

> *Chenies.*—Richard Alleyne Smith [and] Richard Seyr, a bailiff, arrested Giles Gamon at the chancel door going to the communion.
> *Brill.*—Anne Godbeare, a recusant, buried in the night.
> *Newport Pagnel.*—Valentine Hall, famâ, sorcery, for stolen goods.
> *Bedford, Pauli.*—Thomas Waller, telling two of his neighbours they lied in ecclesiâ.
> *Caddington.*—Jo. Pryor, much absent from church, and when he does come it [is] much towards the end of prayer.
> *Flitton cum Silsoe.*—Ellinor uxor Tho. Bonner, threw away the communion bread when she had received it.
> *Woburn.*—Edmund Slingsby, not bowing at the name of Jesus and sitting with his hat on in the church.

[7¼ pp.]

April 14. The King to Sir William Russell, Sir Henry Palmer, Sir Henry Spiller, Sir Dudley Carleton, Inigo Jones, Edward Ayscough, Lawrence Whitaker, Kenrick Edgborough [Edisbury], Thomas Best, William Rainsborough, Walter FitzWilliams, Edward Trotman the elder, Francis Dynn, Edward Bosdon, Jasper Manwood, Richard Willis, and Francis Smith. Commission to inquire what frauds were practised in deal-boards and fir-timber imported into this kingdom, and to make certificate thereon into the Court of Chancery. [*See Coll. Sign Manual, Car. I., Vol. xiii., No.* 103. *Skin of parchment.*]

April 14. Petition of William Crowne and Thomas Addison to the King. Petitioners have found a way for breeding and feeding all sorts of wild fowls and taking them by the sea coast, so that the King's subjects may be served with a greater store of fowl and at more reasonable rates than they be now sold at. Pray letters patent for 14 years, for the sole use of breeding and feeding wild fowls upon sea creeks and navigable rivers, according to their way and call, with a rent to the King of 20 nobles per annum after the first year. [*Copy. See Vol. cccxxiii., p.* 269. ¾ *p.*] *Underwritten,*

> I. *Reference to the Attorney-General to prepare a bill for the King's signature. Whitehall, 14th April* 1638. [*Copy Ibid., p.* 270. ¼ *p.*]

April 14.
Chester.
69. William Earl of Derby with Sir Thomas Milward and Richard Prythergh, Justices of Chester, to the Council. Recite letters from the Council of 31st May last (*see Vol. ccclvii., No.* 144), and petition of Hugh Rigby on behalf of Gilbert Ireland (*see Vol. ccclxxxi., No.* 31), whereby a reference was made to the writers of the differences concerning the extent of "the Gloverstone" adjoining the Castle of Chester, and whether it lay within the county or city, and to which

1638.

Vol. CCCLXXXVII.

of them the inhabitants were chargeable for subsidies and such like payments. The Earl, assisted by the judges, finds that by the charter, whereby the city is made a county in itself, the Castle and Gloverstone are excepted, and that "the Gloverstone" extends from the castle to the stone called the Gloverstone, and that anciently it has been so reputed, and has paid all subsidies and other taxes as parcel of the county, till of late the city has compelled some of the inhabitants to pay with them. [*Seal with crest within the garter.* 2 *pp.*]

April 14. 70. Petition of Henry Folwell, tanner, of Pattishall, co. Northampton, to Archbishop Laud. Miles Burkitt, one of the vicars of Pattishall, being questioned in the High Commission Court for his inconformity and delinquencies, and supposing that petitioner should be produced as a witness against him, threatened him that he would utterly ruin him, and cause him to be indicted for erecting a house on his own fee simple, if he should testify against the said Burkitt. He has further caused petitioner by unjust information to be bound over to the sessions at Northampton, and said to Richard Mewe, one of his servants, that if he could not tax petitioner for stealing deer, or some other thing, it would be 100*l.* out of his way. Also that since petitioner has testified in a commission out of the High Commission Court, Burkitt has much molested him, to the utter undoing of petitioner and his family. Prays reference to some clergymen, justices of the peace of the said county, or to the commissioners assigned to examine the premises. [½ *p.*] *Underwritten,*

    70. I. *Reference to Sir John Lambe to take order for the poor man's indemnity.* 14*th April* 1638. [¾ *p.*]

April 14. 71. Account of Sir William Russell of ship-money for 1637. Total received, 60,851*l.* 15*s.*; unpaid, 135,562*l.* 12*s.* 8*d.* [1 *p.*]

April 14. 72. Account of ship-money for 1637 levied and remaining in the hands of the sheriffs. Total, 17,750; making 78,601*l.* as the total collected, which was 22,737*l.* less than on 15th April 1637. [1 *p.*]

April 14.
Kelmarsh.
73. Sir John Hanbury, Sheriff of co. Northampton, to Nicholas. Sends copy of the chief constables' assessment in their hundreds, and sends daily to them and for the petty constables to collect the money, and to make return of those who refuse to pay, that he may forward distresses. Such money as he shall receive he intends to pay in before the end of this term, and prays Nicholas's help in his excuse to the Council, for which he shall show himself very thankful. [*Endorsed by Nicholas,* "Trifling letter, and sends imperfect certificate." *Seal with arms.* ½ *p.*] *Enclosed,*

    73. I. *Copy of chief constables' assessment of ship-money as above mentioned. It does not state the sum assessed on the clergy, nor is it authenticated by the signature of the sheriff.* [= 2 *pp.*]

April 14.
Northumberland.
74. Robert Bewick, Sheriff of Northumberland, to the same. I have endeavoured by all ways and means to collect the ship-money,

Vol. CCCLXXXVII.

1638.

but am hindered by the poverty of the country, the raging of the plague in divers parts, and goods so poor, and some goods' that were distrained died. I have sent up all the moneys I could collect. Signify as much to his Majesty and the Council. Cannot yet certify his assessment, the warrants and schedules being in the collectors' hands. [*Seal with arms.* ½ *p.*]

April 14.
Heyghley.
75. John Newton, Sheriff of co. Montgomery, to Nicholas. I have sent enclosed two bills for payment of 300*l.* towards the ship-money. The remainder is in a fair way of collecting. When the fairs are past, which will be the end of May, I hope most will be paid. Particulars I shall shortly give you. [¾ *p.*]

April 14.
76. Petition of Mrs. Cooke, widow, and formerly nurse to some of the Earl of Manchester's children, to the said Earl, Lord Privy Seal. William Gilkes, who married petitioner's daughter, and John Vicke, were lately sued in the Arches by Edward Russell, upon pretence that they called him whore-master knave—words they never used; yet by the false testimony of three lewd idle, cheating, and beggarly fellows hired by Russell, the censure passed against them. Upon Tuesday next the court will tax their costs and enjoin them penance. They are very poor tradesmen of Banbury. If they should be enforced publicly to confess the speaking of such words as they never spake, it would be a great trouble to their consciences so long as they live. Prays the Earl to write to Sir John Lambe in their behalf to be sparing in taxing costs and enjoining penance. [*Underwritten, in the handwriting of the Earl of Manchester,* "My nurse's son is of a spiced conscience, made of a Banbury cake, and therefore I must desire you to pity him in his penance and spare him in his costs." 1 *p.*]

April 14.
77. Deed whereby Richard Steward, Doctor of Laws, and canon or prebendary of Worcester, resigned his prebend or canonry into the hands of his Majesty. [*Seal with arms. Latin.* ⅔ *p.*]

April 14.
Burderop.
78. Sir William Calley to Richard Harvey. I have bought the timber at Bupton of the Lady Pyle's man at 18*s.* per ton, for which Alexander Popham told you there was offered 22*s.* 6*d.* a ton. [1 *p.*]

April 14.
79. Information of Matthew Symmons of things observed in the Low Countries when he was over there in November last. It principally relates to English books printed in that country and imported into England. Amongst these are mentioned "Dr. Bastwick's things," printed by James Moxon, of Delft, and now of Rotterdam; the Scotch book called the English-Popish Ceremonies, many Bibles in 4to and fol. with notes; the News from Ipswich in Dutch, and intended to be printed in French, "to make the bishops' cruelty known to all nations;" a book called An Abridgement delivered to King James about 25 years since; a book concerning the proceedings of the last Parliament in Scotland; the Practice of Piety,

366   DOMESTIC—CHARLES I.

Vol. CCCLXXXVII.

1638.

printed by 10,000 at a time; the Poor Doubting Christian; the Soul's Humiliation; the Saint's Spiritual Strength; books of Dr. Preston and Dr. Sibbes; A Guide unto Sion; the New Covenant is going in hand; two great books against the altar and the Coal from the Altar; Lile's [Lilly's] Rules; Robinson's Justification of Separation is going in hand. All the shipmasters are engaged in this traffic, and they have a way, as they say, to cozen the devil. They strike upon the sands at Queenborough, and send away their passengers and deliver all their prohibited goods in some small boats, and then come off the sands without danger. [2 *pp.*]

April 15.
"My house in Salisbury Court."

80. Algernon Earl of Northumberland to Sir John Pennington. Warrant appointing him vice-admiral in the St. Andrew of all ships employed in the present expedition. [*Seal of the Earl attached. Parchment. 15 lines.*]

April 15.
The like.

81. The same to Captain John Mennes. Warrant for his appointment as captain of the Nonsuch. [*The like. 11 lines.*]

April 15.

82. Recognizance of Nicholas Hodgson, of St. Andrew's, Holborn, cordwainer, in 200*l.*, with John Morton, of the same parish, tailor, and Edward Johnson, of St. Martin-in-the-Fields, cook, as his sureties in 100*l.* each, for his appearance before the Lords in the Star Chamber on the 18th inst. [½ *p.*]

April 16.

Petition of George Earl of Desmond to the King. By the letters patent annexed to the last Book of Rates, it was signified that all foreign commodities brought into the kingdom might be again exported, so as the customs were first satisfied. In Bristol and other western ports some quantities of Irish leather, hides, and tallow have been imported, and the hides converted into leather and the tallow into candles in this kingdom, and have been afterwards exported, your Majesty's officers receiving customs for the same. Of late, upon question whether such articles might be exported, some seizures have been made, upon debate whereof in the Exchequer it is declared that it is in your Majesty to tolerate or prohibit such exportation. Petitioner prays a grant of the sole liberty of transporting the said commodities upon a certain payment for every dicker of hides or cwt. of candles. [*Copy. See Vol. cccxxiii., p. 270.* ¾ *p.*] *Underwritten,*

    I. *Reference to the Lord Treasurer to certify. Whitehall, 16th April 1638.* [*Copy. Ibid., p. 271.* ¼ *p.*]

April 16.

Petition of John Howston, your Majesty's servant, to the same. The manor or townships of Braithwell and Clifton, co. York, being of the ancient rent of about 14*l.* per annum, have been, under pretence of a grant from Queen Elizabeth, unjustly detained from the Crown for 60 years. Prays a grant of the same, with all arrears upon double the ancient rent. [*Copy. Ibid., p. 271.* ⅓ *p.*] *Underwritten,*

    I. *Reference to the Lord Treasurer and Lord Cottington to certify. Whitehall, 16th April 1638.* [*Copy. Ibid.* ¼ *p.*]

Vol. CCCLXXXVII.

1638.
April 16.
Insula Vectis.
[Isle of Wight].

83. Sir John Oglander, Sheriff of Hants, to the Council. By your letter of 4th April, I am required to free Winchester of 20*l*. of the 170*l*. ship-money laid thereupon. It was not myself, but you, who assessed Winchester at 170*l*., which was confirmed by the several corporations. In Michaelmas term, meeting the mayor in London, I told him if he would repair to the Board and solicit the taking off the 20*l*. before I had set the rates, I would go with him. His answer was he would not trouble you for so small a sum; whereon I promised him what I could collect above 6,000*l*. should be paid to him, with which answer I conceived he had been satisfied. Now, after the general assessments are made, and above 5,000*l*. collected and paid in to Sir William Russell, of which Winchester and some other corporations have not paid a penny, but pretend like poverty, I conceive it most difficult, and in a manner impossible for me, living in an island, and a stranger to the county, to effect; so I beseech you to suffer the same to stand for this year. What surplus I shall collect I will truly pay them. I hope you will not think it fit for me to pay any part of it out of my own purse. If the city be poor, the mayor is better able to bear the loss than the sheriff. [1 *p.*]

April 16.
Insula Vectis.
[Isle of Wight].

84. The same to Nicholas. I have paid at Portsmouth, by order from Sir William Russell, 5,060*l*., and was in hope speedily to have paid the remainder, had not this rubb fallen in the way. I conceive it cannot now be done, the rates being set, the money almost paid, and every place pretending the like poverty. I have written so much to the Lords, but leave it to you to make known by word of mouth my humble desires to their Lordships, or to deliver it. If Winchester this year may stand as it was set by the Lords, I promising to give them what surplusage I may collect above the 6,000*l*., not only myself, but Sir Arthur Mainwaring will thank you. [1 *p.*]

April 16.
Strand.

85. —— [?] Borthwick to Colonel Hugo Hamilton. The same day Mr. Bloome came here I was sent for to undertake the present employment for Scotland; neither was ever my mind to draw with such a one in one yoke, who will get no trust here of their best friends. I shall be careful of the business in Scotland, and hope to see you there, or it be long. I have put all letters in your kind cousin's hand, my Lady Seaton. You will find the two notes referred from William Morhead, and his bond for the money. P.S.—I desire to know how our business went on in Sweden. Mr. Inglish will send the letters you direct to me. [*Seal with arms.* ¾ *p.*]

April 16.
Taunton.

86. Roger Harvey to his brother, Richard Harvey, servant to Endymion Porter. Requires him to send by this carrier 4*l*. 10*s*. (to make up the 10*s*. at Hound Street, 5*l*.), which shall be allowed at our next. Hopes by the beginning of May to be able to travel. [½ *p.*]

April 16.
Office of the Ordnance.

87. Additional estimate for graving of 102 pieces of brass ordnance for the Sovereign of the Seas with the rose and crown, the sceptre and *tridens*, the anchor and cable, and a compartment under the

1638.

Vol. CCCLXXXVII.

rose and crown with this inscription: "*Carolus Edgari sceptrum stabilivit aquarum,*" the charge being 3*l*. per piece. [1 *p.*]

April 17.
Whitehall.

88. Order of the Lords Committees for the business of his Majesty's House, touching the several accounts of the House, made upon reading the certificate of Sir Edmund Sawyer and Francis Phillips, two of the auditors (calendared *Vol. ccclxxxv., No.* 86), and hearing the said auditors and the Officers of the Greencloth. In the mode of keeping all the three accounts, and in the transaction of the business relating to the compositions received from the counties, a variety of minute alterations were directed to be made in conformity with the recommendations of the auditors. [*Draft. Endorsed,* "Not to be entered." 2¾ *pp.*]

April 17.

89. Order of Council for redress of abuses of purveyors of timber and other provisions required for his Majesty's works, household, and other services. It is ordered that all purveyors who take up goods by virtue of any commission shall "blank" it according to law, and also keep a book stating the quantity, quality, place where taken up, and price of all goods, subscribed by the owner of such goods, and if any composition be accepted in lieu of the same. The book to be returned at the end of each year into the office whence the purveyor has his commission, for the inspection of his Majesty's subjects. [*Minute.* 1¼ *p.*]

April 17.

90. Petition of William Johnson, bailiff, William Allen, and Richard Dixon, to Archbishop Laud. Petitioners have been attached by warrant out of the High Commission Court upon an unjust information of William Richardson, vicar of Garthorpe, co. Lincoln, that they had arrested him by a writ out of the Court of Chancery upon New Year's Day, when he was going to read service at his parish church, pulling and "haling" and otherwise abusing him, to the wrong of his holy function. Concerning the time, it is acknowledged to be true, Richardson not living in his parish of Garthorpe, but on lands of his own in Saxby, which is a privileged place, where he kept himself all working days. The charge of pulling and haling is altogether denied. Richardson desired to be carried to an alehouse in Saxby, when he called for ale to the value of 2*s.* 8*d.*, and then desired to go to the other alehouse in Saxby, where he continued drinking and playing cards all day, and slept in his clothes till three or four o'clock the next morning, when he raised the house and enforced petitioners to carry him to Melton in an extreme dark season; whereupon petitioner Johnson required Dixon, in the King's name, to go along with him. Coming to Melton, Richardson was carried to his accustomed host, and then he fell a-drinking again till he and his company were drunk. At ten o'clock he entered bond to the sheriff and was set at liberty. Pray justice against Richardson, who has abused petitioners to their undoing. [⅔ *p.*]

April 17.

91. Petition of the before-mentioned William Allen and Richard Dixon to Archbishop Laud. Received order to make their appear-

1638. VOL. CCCLXXXVII.

ance before the next court day, which they have done ; but having no money to pay fees, the clerk of the office refused to enter their appearances. Being ready to make oath that they are not worth 5*l.*, pray that they may be admitted *in formâ pauperis*, and that you will review the schedule [petition] annexed. [¾ *p.*] *Underwritten,*

 91. I. *Reference to Sir John Lambe to take such order as he shall find just.* 17*th April* 1638. [¼ *p.*]

April 17. 92. Attorney-General Bankes to the Lord Treasurer and Lord Keeper Cottington. Sir Edward Stradling, Sir Walter Roberts, George Gage, and William Newce have sealed the counterpart of the indenture of covenants touching the aqueduct. They have entered bond of 14,000*l.* for payment of 7,000*l.* into the Exchequer in case of not performing the water-work within the time limited. [½ *p.*]

April 17. 93. Petition of Anthony Hopkins, brazier, to Richard Fenn, Lord Mayor of London. Petitioner warned Mr. Carpenter, brazier, before you for suing petitioner in the Spiritual Court for defamation about getting a woman with child, and Carpenter refused to refer it to you. Prays certificate to Sir John Lambe, that you found the cause to be more of malice and envy than otherwise. [½ *p.*] *Underwritten,*

 93. I. *The Lord Mayor to Sir John Lambe. Certifies that he had endeavoured to draw this difference to a final end, but could not get Carpenter to refer the same to him, and therefore was persuaded that it was more out of malice than for any other cause.* [½ *p.*] 17*th April* 1638.

April 17.
Ramsey.
 94. Sir Oliver Cromwell to [Sir John Lambe?]. John Heron of Higney endeavours to remove himself from paying dues to the parish of Ramsey, co. Huntingdon. Time out of mind the island of Higney has been a member of Ramsey. We desire that he may remain still of Ramsey. [⅔ *p.*] *Annexed,*

 94. I. *Extract from a record which states that the Abbot of Ramsey held the manor of Higney in Walton of the King in capite, and the messuage of the said manor.* [*Latin.* ⅓ *p.*]

April 17. 95. Certificate of Richard Hippesley, captain of Sandgate Castle. There has been no supply of munition to Sandgate Castle since he had the command, which was in the fourth year of the present reign. Gives account of what remains. [1 *p.*]

Vol. CCCLXXXVIII.   April 18–30, 1638.

1638.
April 18.   1. List of causes specially appointed to be heard in the Star Chamber. They were the Attorney-General versus Andrew Arnold and others; Richard Chafin versus William Martin and others; Sir Rowland Egerton versus Anne Mostyn, widow, and others; and the Attorney-General versus Richard Edwards and 11 others, apothecaries, for compounding ill medicines. The first cause was sentenced this day. The second and third on the 20th inst. Chafin was fined 500*l.*, *pro falso clamore*, and 500 marks damages to the King. In Sir Rowland Egerton's case, Mrs. Mostyn was fined 500*l.* to the King; Thomas Mostyn 500*l.* the like; Lewis Floyd, Peirce Fulke, Fulke Roberts, 100*l.* apiece; and David Thomas 200*l.* [2½ *pp.*]

April 18.   2. The Deputy Governor and others of the corporation of Soapmakers of London to the Council. John Garraway, merchant, has, according to the order of Council of the 6th inst., delivered to the officers of the corporation 14 chests of hard soap imported contrary to the proclamation. [½ *p.*]

April 18.   3. Petition of William Johnson to Archbishop **Laud**. Petitioner, being a bailiff under the sheriff of co. Leicester, arrested William Richardson, vicar of Garthorpe, neither of a Sunday nor in the church, but in the open fields, yet Richardson had procured an attachment against petitioner, and caused him to be kept three days in custody, notwithstanding he offered sufficient bond for his appearance. In obedience to this court he appeared the last court day and took oath to answer articles, and has daily attended the office to be examined, but not having money to discharge the fees, the officers there refuse to take his answer. Prays order to Mr. Knight that he may be examined, and his cause be referred to three of the commissioners. [¾ *p.*] *Underwritten,*

   3. i. "*I desire Sir John Lambe to peruse this petition, and give such further order to the Registrar of the High Commission Court as he shall see just cause.* W. CANT." 18*th April* 1638. [1 *p.*]

April 18.   4. Lord Chief Justice Bramston and Sir George Croke, Judge of the same court, to Archbishop Laud and Lord Keeper Coventry. Report on the matters between Sir Henry Browne and young Sir John Tyrrell. There is no considerable waste in the houses or woods, and old Sir John Tyrrell was indebted 1,000*l.* at the death of his lady, for which Sir Henry Browne stood engaged. For a peace between young Sir John Tyrrell and his uncle it was suggested that they should join in a lease of the lands upon terms here suggested, to which young Sir John consented, or to any other thing, to gain his uncle's favour, who seemed much displeased with him for this course. [*Copy.* 1 *p.*]

April 18.   5. Note of ship-money to be paid by Helsington, Watchfield, Nether Graveship, and Kendal Park, all in Westmoreland. [½ *p.*]

1638.

Vol. CCCLXXXVIII.

April 18. 6. Note of money received for fees in an office, probably of the Exchequer, between the first day of Easter term [13th inst.] and this day. Total, 8l. 3s. 6d. [¼ p.]

April 18. 7. See "Returns made by Justices of Peace."

April 19. Commissioners for Gunpowder to Mountjoy Earl of Newport. To issue out of his Majesty's stores 8½ lasts of gunpowder at 18d. per lb. to Thomas Frere, ammunitioner, for supply of ships and his own occasions in his shop. [*Minute. See Vol. ccclv., No. 61, p. 5.* ¼ p.]

April 19. 8. Memorandum of William Hill, mayor, and five others, of Bridgewater, that notice had been given by Andrew Pawling, messenger, to the corporation of that town, to appear in the Exchequer to pass their accounts of casual profits due to his Majesty. The said casualties were granted to them by charter, and confirmed by his Majesty, but the undersigned will appear in the Exchequer to answer matters objected against them, and to present a list of the mayors since the first year of his Majesty. [¾ p.]

April 20. 9. Petition of Richard Beale, merchant, to the Council. On 26th January 1637-8 the Lords ordered that Sir Edward Bromfield, late lord mayor of London, should send in a written answer to petitioner's petition, but his solicitor was taken sick, and so continues, and the order was not served by that day. Prays the Lords to appoint such time as they shall see meet for delivering the same. *Underwritten,*

 9. i. *Order that Sir Edward Bromfield send in his answer in writing, to be read at the board on Sunday, 29th April inst. Star Chamber, 20th April 1638.* [⅔ p.]

April 20. Whitehall. Lords of the Admiralty to Masters of the Trinity House. Send petition of Endymion Porter concerning erecting a harbour at Filey, near Flamborough Head, and keeping a light there. Pray them to certify what importance or convenience the same may be. [*Copy. See Vol. cccliii., fol. 101 b.* ⅓ p.]

April 20. 10. Petition of John Morton, of Ashwell, co. Hertford, to the Commissioners for Saltpetre. Petitioner having been a workman in the mystery of making saltpetre 28 years, has attained the knowledge of increasing and ordering the same, and is acquainted with the abuses and hindrances of the work. If dove-houses and dovecots may be ordered according to his Majesty's proclamations, petitioner will undertake to make as much more saltpetre for quantity, much better in goodness, and cheaper than otherwise can be, and to spare all dwelling houses and other places. Prays licence to search and view the dove-houses where saltpetre is to be gotten, with power to cause the same to be filled with mould. The dove-houses, which are the chief nurseries of saltpetre, are generally decayed through the kingdom, but petitioner will raise more of one hereafter than can be of six as now they are. [⅔ p.]

1638.

Vol. CCCLXXXVIII.

April 20. 11. Information of John Morton, of abuses committed by Edward Thornhill, deputy saltpetreman, within cos. Hertford, Bedford, Buckingham, and Northampton. He charges and discharges carts for money; he charges the country with carriage of coal in the winter time, and spares some for money, and makes the service more grievous to others. He oppresses poor people by digging their houses and bed chambers, and spoiling their clothes, and by sparing dove-houses increases carriages, and makes trade of his abuse of the country. Names of persons are stated, especially William Hurst and Clement Everard [Everett] of Ashwell, who could substantiate these charges. [$\frac{2}{3}$ p.]

April 20. 12. Statement of John Layer, Justice of Peace for co. Cambridge, of abuses practised by John Dallygood, of Walden, Essex, ashman, who took various sums of money of inhabitants of Wittlesford, Newton, and Thriplow, for release of their carts charged for fetching ashes out of Essex to Cambridge, and immediately charged other carts at Harston and Foxton to perform that service. The writer states, also, various other charges of extortion against the ashmen and saltpetremen, and especially against warrants issued in blank by David Stevenson, deputy saltpetreman for co. Huntingdon. [$2\frac{1}{4}$ pp.]

April 20. 13. Order of the Court of Exchequer. Recites order of the 13th February last upon motion made on behalf of the tenants of Millgrove and other lands in Hartpury, in the county of the city of Gloucester, being lands of William Compton, lately extended for arrearages of an annuity of 30l. granted by Walter Compton, father of the said William Compton, to John Compton, convicted of murder, a younger son of the said Walter, for his life, to begin after the death of the said Walter, and for 1,100l. for a forfeiture of a *nomine pœnæ* of 12d. a day for non-payment of the said annuity. It was then ordered that by reason of imperfections in the extent further process should be awarded. Recites also another order of the 11th inst., on the motion of Mr. Lenthall, whereby it was ordered that process should proceed upon the said extent, notwithstanding the former order, unless cause were shown to the contrary by that day sennight. This day the court was informed that the last order was entered so lately that the tenants had not had time to instruct counsel, and that William Underhill and Endymion Porter both pretend grants of the said arrearages and forfeiture; whereupon it was ordered that all sides should be heard this day sennight. [5 pp.]

April 20. Petition of Lionel Earl of Middlesex to the King. About ten years past your Majesty, in favour of the late Earl of Desmond, settled a course concerning the payment of a great debt which the earl owed to petitioner and Richard Croshaw, now deceased, which order was submitted to by the earl and Croshaw. Nevertheless, about Christmas last, a letter was got from your Majesty by the agents of the now Earl of Ormond, contrary to your settlement, by means whereof petitioner, who is so weak with grief and sickness that he is advised by his physicians not to travel so much as a day's journey from home, must travel into Ireland or lose his cause, it being im-

1638.

VOL. CCCLXXXVIII.

possible to commit his defence to an agent. Petitioner prays your Majesty to be rightly informed in the business, and to refer the same for examination. [*Copy. See Vol. cccxxiii., p.* 273. ½ *p.*] *Underwritten*,

  I. *Reference to the Lord Keeper, the Earl Marshal, Lord Cottington, and Sec. Windebank, to certify. Whitehall, 21st April* 1638. [*Copy. Ibid.* ¼ *p.*]

April 21.
Whitehall.
 14. Notes by Nicholas of business to be transacted by the Lords of the Admiralty. Sign estimates for setting forth the fleet this year. Consider draft commission for finishing the accounts and other businesses of the Admiralty. Resolve touching the certificate of the commissioners concerning the Chest at Chatham. The Dean of Windsor desires to know the pleasure of the Lords touching the certificate about his pigeon-house. Peruse petition of the solicitor and others employed to prosecute persons who claimed jurisdiction of Admiralty. Consider a complaint against Edward Thornhill, saltpetreman. To sign warrant for munition for the Mary Rose and First Whelp. [1 *p.*]

April 21.
Whitehall.
 Lords of the Admiralty to Montjoy Earl of Newport. To furnish with ordnance the Mary Rose and First Lion's Whelp to be set forth as an addition to the great fleet for guard of the seas. [*Copy. See Vol. cccliii., fol.* 102. ⅔ *p.*]

April 21.
Whitehall.
 The same to Robert Smith and Henry Kyme, messengers. To bring before the Lords Roger Holdernesse, a bargeman in Berkshire. [*Copy. Ibid.* ½ *p.*]

April 21.
Bisbrooke.
 15. Edward Andrewes, Sheriff of Rutland, to Nicholas. Has sent various sums towards ship-money, in all amounting to 650*l.*, leaving 150*l.* not yet received. [*Seal with arms.* ½ *p.*]

April 21.
Sarnesfield.
 16. Richard Monington to [Edward] Lord Herbert [of Chirbury]. Excuses delay in acknowledging favours by his hope to have been made happy by Lord Herbert's presence at Sarnesfield. The writer's wife, on her return from Troy, acquainted him that Lord Herbert desired the conveyance of all the writer's lands for payment of his debts might be sent up, which he will now receive. Since the sealing thereof the writer has not had the management of any part of the estate. He has by four inquisitions been questioned for not receiving the communion, but this deed being produced has always prevailed against the informer. [⅔ *p.*]

April 21.
 17. Account of Sir William Russell of ship-money received for 1637; total, 67,173*l.* 15*s.*, leaving unpaid 129,240*l.* 12*s.* 8*d.* [1 *p.*]

April 21.
 18. Account of ship-money for 1637 levied and remaining in the hands of the sheriffs; total, 12,600*l.*, making the total collected 79,773*l.*, which is 22,965*l.* less than on 22nd April 1637. [1 *p.*]

VOL. CCCLXXXVIII.

1638.
April 22.
North Somercotes.
19. Thomas Butler to Endymion Porter, Groom of the Bedchamber. Reports the state of farming operations upon Porter's land. Complains of Mr. Harber Newstead and Mr. Marrall. John Cutterice and the writer were in such straits for money, that they could not have ploughed and sown the land, but that Mr. Harrison, the minister of South Somercotes, tendering Mr. Porter's good, lent them 100*l*. The result, as the writer hopes, will be as good crops of oats and barley upon Porter's 500 acres as any in Lincolnshire. Prays him to give this courteous gentleman satisfaction for his 100*l*. [*Seal with crest.* 1¾ *p.*]

April 22.
20. Note of papers sent to Mr. Lightfoot touching soap. [½ *p.*]

April 23.
Petition of Thomas Tyrrell to the King. Petitioner had many years since made divers purchases in the manor of Hanslope, co. Buckingham, under the great seal, which he has quietly enjoyed ever since. Lately Sir Miles Fleetwood, upon untrue suggestions in relation to the Honor of Grafton, has got a warrant to compound with petitioner for the manor of Hanslope, to reduce the same again to the said honor, and without treating with petitioner has disposed of the greatest part of petitioner's estate, and has certified your Majesty that part of the forest of Salcey is included in the grant of the said manor, to the prejudice of your improvement of the said forest, whereas there is no such thing. Prays a reference to the Council. [*Copy. See Vol.* cccxxiii., *p.* 274. ⅔ *p.*] *Underwritten,*

I. *Reference to the Council as prayed.* Whitehall, 23*rd April* 1638. [*Copy. Ibid.* ¼ *p.*]

April 23.
Petition of Seuce [Susey?] Whitley, widow of Thomas Whitley, citizen and grocer, to the same. Your Majesty, on 30th January 1634–5, referred the examination of petitioner's then petition to the Court of Aldermen of London, to settle some course for her relief, whereupon Sir Edward Bromfield, Alderman Smyth, Alderman Wright, Alderman Abdy, and the common-sergeant, often met with the parties interested, and drew up a certificate of their proceedings, which was allowed by the Court of Aldermen, and ordered to be entered in their repertory, and to be performed. But hitherto petitioner has reaped no fruit, by reason there is no certificate to your Majesty showing on whom the fault lies. Prays your Majesty to command Sir Edward Bromfield and the rest to certify what they find due to petitioner. [*Copy. See Ibid., p.* 275. ½ *p.*] *Underwritten,*

I. *Minute of the King's pleasure that Sir Edward Bromfield and the rest make certificate to his Majesty as they did to the Court of Aldermen.* Whitehall, 23*rd April* 1638. [*Copy. Ibid.* ¼ *p.*]

April 23.
Petition of Sir Anthony Thomas to the same. Another copy of the petition already calendared under date of the 13th February last, with a similar reference underwritten, but dated this day. [*Copy. Ibid., p.* 276. ¾ *p.*]

Vol. CCCLXXXVIII.

1638.
April 23.
21. Sir William Becher, Thomas Meautys, and Sir Dudley Carleton to the Council. We have spoken with Mr. Windham and Mr. Savage, commissioners for licensing wine cask to be used by retailers of beer, as also with the brewers and vintners complaining of the restraint of using wine cask. The brewers in the country object to that monopoly as a breach of the agreement made with them on their compounding for licences to brew, the vintners that they shall not be able to vent their wine cask, and the brewers in London on two principal grounds, 1. As contrary to the promise made to them on their submitting to a payment of 4d. on every quarter of malt, for the use of his Majesty's household, and 2. That such a surcharge at this time, when coals and malt are so dear, will enforce them to break the composition with his Majesty. The writers state terms of composition offered by the commissioners. [2 pp.] *Annexed,*

    21. I. *Certificate of the Officers of Greencloth, in proof of the assertion of the brewers of London, that they were promised liberty to use wine cask when they submitted to the payment of 4d. on every brewed quarter of malt. 23rd April 1638.* [1 p.]

April 23.
Wrexham.
22. Sir Thomas Milward, Chief Justice of Chester, to Sec. Coke. Report on a complaint of Justices of Peace for Cheshire, against Mr. Emerson, the saltpetreman for that county, and Mr. Emerson's answer, with an accusation made by Robert Stranke against the justices of peace and constables for neglect in providing carriages. The justices' complaint against Mr. Emerson is, 1. That having to spend six tons of coal weekly, he did not make provision in summer, but compelled men to fetch them in the depth of winter, and 2. That his workmen dig in the lodging-rooms and under the beds of sick persons, placing their saltpetre tubs in the same rooms, and exact money to spare some. This last accusation I found to be true, but to have been committed without Mr. Emerson's knowledge, and he has since discharged the offenders, and promises to be very careful. Robert Stranke's accusation against the justices is an untrue calumny, and he deserves to be punished. All the justices are very willing to promote his Majesty's service in assisting Mr. Emerson, and for that purpose, instead of the three hundreds adjoining the saltpetre house being charged with carriages, a tax is to be laid upon the whole county, and all the coals are to be provided in summer; and Mr. Emerson has promised that the saltpetre water shall be carried at convenient times, so that hereafter I hope the work will be well supplied without any complaints on either side. [*Seal with arms.* ¾ p.] *Annexed,*

    22. I. *Sir William Brereton and four others, Justices of Peace for co. Chester, to the Council. Certify complaints preferred to them against the saltpetremen for those parts, which are extreme pressures upon the subject. The saltpetremen have likewise made their address to the writers for*

1638.

Vol. CCCLXXXVIII.

assistance for their further supply of coals in the depth of winter when no carts can pass without much difficulty. Represent the present state of this service, and attend further directions. *Castle of Chester, 9th January 1637-8.* [1 p.]

22. II. Statement of the grievances, ten in number, complained of at the quarter sessions on the 9th January 1637-8, and mentioned in the preceding letters. Their general nature is stated in the letters of Sir Thomas Milward, but they are here set forth more particularly. [2½ pp.]

22. III. Answers of Francis Emerson, Deputy Saltpetreman, to the grievances above mentioned. On the questions of carriage he throws the blame on the constables, with whom rested the power of executing the requirements of the saltpetreman as they thought best. On the other points he alleges that what was done was with the concurrence of the occupiers of the premises on which the operations of the saltpetremen were carried on. [2½ pp.]

22. IV. Articles of complaint by Robert Stranke, factor to Francis Emerson, in which he alleges neglect and opposition to the service on the part of the constables and justices of peace of the hundred of Broxton, co. Chester. [1 p.]

April 23.
Paris.

23. John Barter to [Richard] Harvey. Is astonished that he had not heard from Harvey for four months. Their moneys are done. Requests bills by the very next post. Doubts not to return the young esquire with satisfaction to his friends. He has been inclined to be a little coltish, and the writer fears he has a little colt's tooth in his head, but who could expect less from the liberty of his education? [*Endorsed,* Note of answer on the 25th April, and that a bill of exchange for 450 crowns 42 sous was inclosed. 1 p.]

April 23.

24. Extract from the Register of the Court of Arches of the introductory portion of articles exhibited in that Court by Sarah Coxe against Roger Fulwood, of Gray's Inn. [*Copy attested this day.* 1 p.]

April 24.
Whitehall.

25. Minutes of proceedings of the Commissioners for settling the orders of his Majesty's household. Taking into consideration the account concerning the stables, it is ordered that Sir Edmund Sawyer and Mr. Phillips, the auditors, and the avenor, and the two clerks of the avery, should confer together on the account of the avenor to be presented to the green cloth, and the oath to be taken to the parcels of such account, and should certify thereon to the Lords. It was also ordered that Inigo Jones should survey his Majesty's stables at the mews and elsewhere, and send estimates for repairs to the Lord Treasurer, who is to take order for repairing the same. [*Fair copy of draft. As originally prepared, the King's stables are enumerated as being at Hampton Court, Reading, St. Albans, and Sheen, as well as at the Mews.* [1⅔ p.]

April 24.

26. Nicholas's draft of the preceding minutes. [3⅙ pp.]

DOMESTIC—CHARLES I. 377

1638.
Vol. CCCLXXXVIII.

April 24.
27. Petition of Zachary Seaton, Rector of Aspley, co. Bedford, to Archbishop Laud. Is in all things conformable to the present government established in the Church of England, and has lately suffered exceeding loss in a fire in his house, but being called before Sir John Lambe, in his visitation for the archbishop in the diocese of Lincoln, and suddenly questioned for not reading the Book of Recreations to be used on the Lord's day, wherein petitioner not being then resolved upon an answer, he is suspended from his ministry. Prays the archbishop to absolve him, and to give him some some convenient time the better to inform his judgment. [½ p.] *Underwritten,*

27. I. *"I desire Sir John Lambe to consider of this petition, and if he find the petitioner intend really to inform his judgment, as is here suggested, to allow him such reasonable time as he shall think fitting. W. CANT." April 24th 1638. [¼ p.]*

April 24.
Enmore.
28. John Malet to Nicholas. Has endeavoured to collect the arrearages of ship-money for Somerset in the year of his shrievalty, but Mr. Hodges, the former sheriff, has wholly neglected the same. This winter quarter there have been no cattle upon the lands to distrain, but now his servants are busy collecting the money. Prays that a little more time may be allowed, and that Mr. Hodges may be enjoined to assist. [*Seal with arms.* ⅔ p.]

April 24.
Pensford.
29. John Locke to Richard Harvey, servant to Sir (*sic*) Endymion Porter. Formerly sent a letter concerning his parsonage. Prays an answer. [⅓ p.]

April 25.
Westminster.
30. The King to Dr. Geoffrey Swalman, Official to the Archdeacon of Middlesex. Writ out of the King's Bench to prohibit the Archidiaconal Court of which Dr. Swalman was the judge to compel Felix Wilson, one of the clerks of the King's Bench, and necessarily occupied in writing the writs thereof, to take upon him the office of one of the churchwardens of the church of Stanwell, Middlesex, whereof Bruno Ryves was vicar. [*Parchment. Latin. 27 lines.*]

April 25.
Chester.
31. Mayor, Sheriffs, and ten others, of Chester, to the Council. Not knowing what the Earl of Derby and the judges of Chester have certified touching the payment of ship-money by the Gloverstone, the writers pray that they may be heard by counsel concerning the city's right therein, and to answer to what in the letter in the name of some of the county has been objected. Others within the city, led on by the question raised by the Gloverstone, now refuse to pay ship-money with the city. The Bishop of Chester, who has no residence in the shire, and upon two former writs paid 20 nobles a time with the city, upon this last writ refuses to pay with the city, and has lately paid with the shire. So also the dean and chapter, having also upon two former writs paid 20 nobles a time, and having been told by the bishop that they might well bear that sum, and that they ought to pay with the city, yet Dean Mallory on this last

1638.

VOL. CCCLXXXVIII.

writ wrote unto the writer that, unless they would waive the rigid words of "assessing" and "demanding," and accept the 20 nobles as a free gift, they would leave the writers to their course, and they now refuse to pay with the city, and have lately paid with the shire. Pray directions of the Council that they may pay as they formerly have done. In the meantime the writers have sent up the sum apportioned upon them by the last writ, except the 20 marks which rest with the bishop and dean and chapter. [2 *pp.*]

April 25. 32. Attorney-General Bankes to the Council. Report on a petition of William Shaw the younger. Petitioner, being summoned to appear before the Commissioners for Cards and Dice, to testify his knowledge against other men concerning buying and selling cards and dice, he refused to take his oath before the Commissioners, whereupon, by warrant of the Lord Treasurer and Lord Cottington, dated the 6th March last, he was committed to a messenger. Afterwards petitioner spake opprobrious words against the business for cards and dice, and against his Majesty's officers, and that he would spend 1,000*l.* rather than the business should pass over thus, and that he would set 100 men at work beyond seas for making dice, and would never buy any at the office, and thereupon, by warrant of the Council, dated the 24th March last, he was committed to the Fleet, where he remains a prisoner. Petitioner has now submitted, and being a merchant, and having affairs beyond seas, desires his liberty, and also prays liberty for making "cource" [coarse?] dice, and transporting them, on payment of customs, as heretofore, the officers [for cards and dice] undertaking to furnish the merchant as he shall need at the same rates as themselves shall pay, but Shaw putting in security not to employ any beyond the sea for making dice, and not to do anything to the prejudice of his Majesty, or the said officers, or of the company. [*Copy.* 1 *p.*] *Pre-written,*

> 32. I. *Petition of Lawrence Squibb and others to the Council. Sets forth the alleged misconduct of William Shaw the younger, as above detailed, and prays the Lords to give order for his punishment.* [*Copy.* ¾ *p.*]

April 25.
Wells.
33. Bishop Pierce of Bath and Wells, with William Walrond and Patrick Goodwyn, Justices of Peace, to the same. Report on a petition of the inhabitants of Wells Forum against the city of Wells for procuring the inhabitants within the liberty of the Cathedral of Wells to join with the city in payments for ship-money. We find, 1. That the liberty of the cathedral is within the city of Wells, but not within the corporation, and always has been an exempt jurisdiction. 2. That the hundred of Wells Forum is not over-rated to the ship-money. 3. That the 60*l.* assessed upon the city lies chiefly upon shop keepers and handicraftsmen, and therefore we conceive it very reasonable that the inhabitants within the cathedral liberty should join in the payment of ship-money with the city for the ease of the same. [1 *p.*]

1638.
April 25.
Whitehall.

Vol. CCCLXXXVIII.

Commissioners for Gunpowder to Montjoy Earl of Newport. To issue out of his Majesty's stores 18 barrels of gunpowder at 18*d.* per lb. to Bartholomew Hitchins of Tower Street, ship-chandler. [*Minute. See Vol. ccclv., No.* 61., *p.* 5. ¼ *p.*]

April 25.

34. Petition of Elizabeth Adams, widow, and Andrew Hebb, to Archbishop Laud. According to your reference to Sir John Lambe and Dr. Duck concerning the complaint of petitioners against Adam Islip for imprinting their fourth part of the Turkish History, Sir John and Dr. Duck referred the cause to the Company of Stationers, who made choice of four of their Assistants to examine their books of orders and entrance concerning the said copy. Two of the referees have drawn up their report in favour of petitioners' right, but the other two, by long delay in favour of Mr. Islip, have encouraged him to go on printing the book. Pray order to stay the further imprinting, that the sheets already printed be brought in, and the cause be further heard. [⅔ *p.*] *Underwritten,*

 34. I. "*I desire Sir John Lambe to take present order for the doing of what is here desired, if he have no just exception to the contrary.* W. Cant." *25th April* 1638. [¼ *p.*] *Annexed,*

  34. I. ii. *Report of Nathaniel Butter, Thomas Downes, Samuel Man, and John Parkar, about the right to the Turkish History. It was entered in* 1612 *to Adam Islip alone, but to the same entry was annexed a subsequent record by Richard Collins, then Clerk of the Company, of the assignment of one half of the copy to George Bishop and John Norton. Islip asserted that the entry should have been limited to one impression, but that did not otherwise appear.* [1 *p.*]

April 25.

35. Petition of Richard Dixon to the same. Being a very simple poor man, he is much vexed by Mr. Richardson, clerk, because he was heretofore a witness against him in the High Commission Court in a most just cause. Petitioner being now summoned to answer to some unjust articles, and having little means beside the charity of the parish, he prays licence to answer Mr. Richardson *in formâ pauperis.* [¾ *p.*] *Underwritten,*

 35. I. *Direction to Sir John Lambe that if he find petitioner's suggestions true, he is to take order that he be admitted accordingly. 25th April* 1638. [⅛ *p.*]

April 25.

36. Sir William Russell to Nicholas. Henry Head, a merchant in London, having received from the Mayor of Plymouth 190*l.* ship-money, refuses to pay the money except I will give him a receipt not fit for me to give. Prays Nicholas to move the Lords to send for Head, and to order him to pay in the King's money and take such acquittance as I am ordered by the Lords and usually give. [½ *p.*]

Vol. CCCLXXXVIII.

1638.
April 26. Petition of Sir Henry Ferrers to the King. William Ferrers the elder, upon the marriage of William Ferrers his son with Jane daughter of Sir Peter Vanlore, by indenture dated 8th February 1620-1, covenanted within two years to purchase lands of the value of 300*l.*, per annum, and assure the same to William and Jane, and the heirs of the body of William the son, and for want of such heirs to the right heirs of William the son; and further, that he would leave to William the son, his heirs and assigns, other lands and goods which at the death of William the elder should be of the yearly value of 15,000*l.* William the son and Jane are dead without issue, Sir Peter Vanlore is dead, and William Ferrers the elder is also dead, leaving petitioner and Thomas Ferrers, a half-brother of William the elder, his executors. William the elder died without assuring any lands according to his covenants, the benefit of which in right belongs to petitioner, being next heir of William the son. Petitioner living far remote from the place where William the elder died, and not knowing of his death, Thomas Ferrers proved his will, got his estate into his hands, and by improper means concealed the amount from petitioner, and received rents to which petitioner was entitled. Further, petitioner having occasion for moneys, Thomas advanced the same out of the testator's estate, but pretending that he did so out of his own moneys he took bonds from petitioner for the amount. After various other proceedings, which are here set forth, and which had the effect (designed, as is suggested, by Thomas Ferrers,) of entangling the affairs and setting fast petitioner, Thomas Ferrers died, whereupon Judith his wife and sole executrix sued petitioner upon his bonds, which he contended had long since been satisfied out of the estate of William the elder. Petitioner now prayed a reference for examination of the facts to the Archbishop of Canterbury, the Lord Keeper, the Lord Privy Seal, the Lord Treasurer, the Earl of Dorset, or any three of them. [*Copy. See Vol. cccxxiii., p. 279. 2 pp.*] *Underwritten*,

I. *Reference as prayed.* Whitehall, 26*th April* 1638. [*Copy. Ibid., p.* 291. ⅙ *p.*]

[April 26?] Petition of John Bonnington and Peter Bonnington to the King. Francis Bonnington, uncle of petitioner, in the 28th year of Queen Elizabeth was found lunatic, and so has continued, being seized of lands in Basingfield, Kingston, Sutton, Bennington, and Keyworth, co. Nottingham, and Barrowcoat, Etwall, and Burnaston, co. Derby. Since the office Ralph Bonnington, deceased, petitioners' father, second brother and heir apparent of the lunatic (being in possession of the said lands), and petitioner John Bonnington, sold divers parcels of the said lunatic's lands, part to the now Earl of Kingston, and other parts thereof they mortgaged, for composing whereof petitioner John Bonnington has transferred all his interest in the said lands to petitioner Peter Bonnington, who might now settle the estate, much for advancing the family, and without wronging any one, if he were provided with money to redeem the mortgages,

1638.

VOL. CCCLXXXVIII.

which cannot be effected without the sale of part of the lands by the lunatic by fine, and in case the lunatic, who is now 85 years years of age, depart this life before the same be done, the family is like to lose lands which have remained in them and their ancestors many hundreds of years, and Peter Bonnington all his charges. Prays for a privy seal to commissioners authorizing them to take a fine of the lunatic and petitioners, to the use of the said Earl and his heirs, as to the lands in Basingfield and Keyworth, and as to the residue to the use of petitioner Peter and his heirs. [*Copy. See Vol. cccxxiii., p.* 291. ⅗ *p.*] *Underwritten,*

    I. *Reference to the Attorney-General and the Attorney of the Court of Wards to certify.* [*Copy. Ibid.* ⅙ *p.*]

April 26. 37. Attorney-General Bankes to the Council. Report on petition of one Fryar. He confesses the sale of some cards for his necessity, but submits himself, and craves pardon, being a very poor man. The officers for cards and dice desire he may give bond not to sell any cards or dice for the future, and they will see that he shall be set on work, and have 6*l.* per annum, so long as he shall work journey-work according to the direction of the Lord Treasurer. [*Copy.* ⅔ *p.*]

April 26. 38. Commissioners for granting licences for sale of tobacco to the same. We find that Edward Grigge has for more than three years vended tobacco in London without licence. We ordered that he should pay a fine of 5*l.*, and should either take a licence or enter into bond to sell no more tobacco by retail. Without submitting to our order, he departed, and continued to sell tobacco, whereupon we obtained a warrant that he may be brought before you, before whom he has said that he will answer it. [1 *p.*]

April 26. 39. The same to the same. In a similar case of Nathaniel Extill of London, who had for a long time sold tobacco without a licence, and was fined 20 nobles, which he refused to pay, and is now in a messenger's custody, but he regards it not. [⅔ *p.*]

April 26.
Portsmouth.
40. Sir John Oglander, Sheriff of Hants, to Nicholas. If Winchester must be abated any of the 170*l.*, he knows not where to lay it, especially when most of the money from the county is paid. He has paid in to Sir William Russell 5,600*l.*, and cannot procure one penny from Winchester, although he has appointed them three several days. A sub-collector, John Edwardes, of Weston Patrick, is, as Mr. Hyde, the high collector, informs him, the most obstinate man in the whole county. Desires he may be sent for by a messenger. Although he has paid in more money than any of his predecessors have done so early, yet the loss at the last will be much, for many are run away, others grown poor, and divers rated for coppices, on all of whom no distress can be laid, and if Winchester should be eased it will be impossible to make up the 6,000*l.* [2 *pp.*]

Vol. CCCLXXXVIII.

1638.
April 26.
Lambeth.

41. Order of the High Commission Court, refering the articles and answers of William Pinson, of Birmingham, attorney, to Sir John Lambe and Sir Charles Cæsar. [1¼ p.] *Underwritten,*

    41. I. *Order of the referees above mentioned appointing Wednesday then next for hearing this cause in the dining-room of Doctors' Commons.* 11 June 1638. [1⅔ p.] *Annexed,*

    41. II. *Articles additionals to be ministered by the Ecclesiastical Commissioners against William Pinson and John Rogers. Defendant Pinson was charged that from 1631 to 1636 he lived at Wolverhampton, and was inconformable to the Church of England, and very obstinate and perverse therein. That he maintained conventicles in his house, in which persons of other families assembled together, and Pinson made long extempore prayers, and repeated sermons, and expounded scripture, and that he went to the houses of other people where similar conventicles were held at set times. That he, together with his wife and her midwife, and other women, went to the church of Wolverhampton, that his wife might be churched, but being demanded by the priest why she did not wear a veil, she answered she would not, and being told by the priest that he was commanded by the ordinary not to church any but such as came thither reverently and lowly in their veils, she in the church, after prayers ended, scornfully pulled off her hat and put a table napkin on her head, and put on her hat, again, and so departed from the church. That ever since that time Pinson had threatened the said priest, being Hugh Davies, then one of the curates of Wolverhampton, to be revenged of him, and in consequence had stirred up and carried on against him various legal proceedings in the name of John Hopkins, upon a pretensed battery, and in the course of them procured him to be arrested in the churchyard of Wolverhampton, and to be dragged through the market-place; and further, because Davies prosecuted both defendants in the High Commission, they procured warrants against him for good behaviour, and brought him before Sir Richard Dyott and the quarter sessions, by whom he was dismissed.* [5 pp.]

    41. III. *Answers of the defendant Pinson to the preceding articles. He admitted that whilst residing at Wolverhampton he prayed with his family, and that he used to conceive a prayer, repeat sermons, and read and expound the scripture, and also that other persons who have by chance then come in, or who came to hear a repetition of a sermon, were sometimes present. He also admitted the other acts of inconformity charged against him, except that he denied that there had been any set times of meeting at*

1638.   VOL. CCCLXXXVIII.

one another's houses. He alleged that his wife went to be churched without a veil, as divers others had used to do, and that when Mr. Davies spoke to her she put on a veil, and put on her hat again, but that Mr. Davies refused to church her, and so she departed unchurched, to her and his grief. He enters into long detail respecting the legal proceedings charged against him, but alleges that what he did therein was legal and justifiable. 12*th April* 1638. [13½ *pp.*]

April 26.
Lambeth.

42. Sentence of the High Commission Court in a cause against John Andrews and Oliver Andrews, of Sudbury, Suffolk. The sentence recites the history of the church of St. Gregory with the chapel of St. Peter's, in Sudbury, which has been stated in past volumes of our Calendar, and the order made by the High Commission Court on the 18th February 1635–6, for the payment of the ancient allowances to the curates, such payment to be made by the defendants, who were the lay impropriators of the said church and chapel (*see Vol. of Calendar,* 1635–1636, *p.* 499). It was further stated, that the defendants had omitted to pay these allowances, and had endeavoured to bring another curate into St. Gregory's, without the sanction of the bishop. The previous order for payment of the allowances was confirmed, and the defendants were ordered to pay all the arrears. They were also declared to have taken upon them unlawfully to exercise ecclesiastical jurisdiction, and to have contemned the orders of this Court; wherefore they were fined jointly in 500*l.*, and were ordered to make a public submission *conceptis verbis* in this Court, which submission together with this sentence was to be published at Norwich and Sudbury. The defendants were also condemned in costs of suit. [12 *pp.*]

April 26.
Lambeth.

43. Order of the High Commission Court in a cause against Richard and Peter Whineates, Richard Forman, Thomas Gilbert, John Marten, William Pickering, William Robertes, Henry Croftes, and William Rose, of co. Derby. Defendants were ordered to put in bond to stand to such order as Sir John Lambe, Dean of the Arches, should set down, or in default thereof the cause to be reassumed in this court, and be sentenced according to the merits. [½ *p.*]

April 27.

44. Memorandum of Jonathan Saltern, Mayor, and three others of Bideford, that notice had been given by Andrew Pawling, messenger, to the corporation of that town, to appear in the Exchequer to account for casual profits due to his Majesty. The said casualties are granted to them by charter, and they are no escheators; nevertheless they will appear, in the next Trinity term, to answer matters to be objected against them, and will bring a note of the names of all the mayors since the first year of his Majesty's reign. [⅔ *p.*]

April 27.

45. List of causes to be heard in the Court of Star Chamber. They were: the Attorney-General against William and John Guise, and twelve others; the same against Richard Edwards and eleven

1638.

Vol. CCCLXXXVIII.

others; Alexander Dupper against James Freeze and three others; Francis Cufaud and two others against Anne and Thomas Doleman and Thomas Brent, for oppression and abuse of his Majesty's prerogative in the Court of Exchequer. [1 p.] *Endorsed,*

> 45. I. *Notes by Sec. Windebank of the sentence of the Court in the first of the preceding causes. William and John Guise, Edmond Baylis, and John Bradnock were fined from 300l. to 500l. As to John Langston, Lord Cottington suggested a fine of 1,000l. with imprisonment. Lord Finch, 2,000l. fine, incapable to hold office, and the pillory. This was concurred in by all the other judges, except Archbishop Laud, who desired the increase of the fine to 5,000l. The Lord Keeper agreed with the majority, and recommended "the reviving of the murder to the Lord Chief Justice." The sentence to be read at the Assizes.* [⅔ p.]

April 27.
Star Chamber.

46. Further notes of Sec. Windebank in reference to the first of the preceding causes. The case was one of riotously taking possession of lands belonging to a mill at King's Norton. In the riot, the leg of Guest, one of the persons in possession, was broken, and Richard Suger was killed. Francis Wheler, surgeon, gave evidence as to the breaking of Guest's leg. "If the skin had been broken the leg would have dropt off." [2 pp.]

April 27.

47. Petition of Thomas Noel to the Council. The ordering of the Countess of Castlehaven being by the Council committed to Lord Campden and others, his Lordship in his absence has committed the care of the Countess to petitioner. Before she was committed to his Lordship, she employed Rolfe, a scrivener, to put forth her money at interest, who lent the same to several persons in the annexed particular mentioned upon bond. Interest was paid by Rolfe and by Massey, who succeeded him, until November 1635, when petitioner demanded the moneys of the parties mentioned in the bonds. They affirm that they long since paid the same to Rolfe and Massey, who promise payment, but delay. There is 800l. principal debt, besides interest for 2½ years, being the greater part of the means of Lady Castlehaven, and petitioner has disbursed above 120l. for her maintenance. Petitioner prays the Lords to call Rolfe and Massey before them, and take order for payment of the money. [¾ p.] *Annexed,*

> 47. I. *Note of the sums of money lent at interest as above mentioned. Sir Robert Oxenbridge had 100l., Edward Popham 200l., William Blake 100l. Total, 800l. Underwritten,*

> 47. II. *Order of the Council. A copy of this petition to be delivered to Rolfe and Massey, and they to answer in writing, and attend the Council on the 19th of May. Inner Star Chamber, 27th April 1638.* [¼ p.]

Vol. CCCLXXXVIII.

1638.
April 27.
——eweit.
48. Robert Stratford to Edward Marten, at his chamber in Clifford's Inn. I have received your letter and writ. Send me by next post an attachment of privilege at my suit against Richard Poyner of Oxenhall, co. Gloucester. It is upon a bond of 20*l*. for payment of 10*l*. with interest. I suppose I may hold him to special bail. [⅔ *p*.]

April 28.
Whitehall.
49. The Council to all Mayors and other officers. John Paperill, lieutenant-colonel and principal engineer for his Majesty's fortifications, being commanded to take order for repairing Archcliff Bulwark, near Dover, you are to aid him in impressing in London a sufficient number of masons; also in the Thames and Kent, ships for carrying stone from the Isle of Purbeck, as also carpenters, workmen, and labourers, taking care that such wages be paid them as in like cases. [1 *p*.]

April 28.
Torrington Magna.
50. Memorandum of the Mayor and five others of Torrington, Devon, that notice had been given by Andrew Pawling, messenger, to the corporation of that town, to appear in the Exchequer, to pass their accounts for casual profits due to his Majesty. Such casualties are granted to them by charter; but they will appear next Trinity term to answer such matters as shall be objected against them, and will bring the names of the mayors who have held office since the first year of his Majesty. [⅔ *p*.]

April 28.
51. Affirmation of Edward Seymour and thirteen others that the tithing of Yarnfield, Somerset, has hitherto been taxed with the parish of Maiden Bradley, in Wilts, in all parish rates, until recently Sir Henry Ludlow, lord of the manor of Yarnfield, and some few others, having made a new rate for the maintenance of the King's Bench, maimed soldiers, and gaol and hospital, the lands of Sir Henry, in Yarnfield, were excluded, and the whole rate laid upon Bradley and certain lands of Edward Seymour, in Somerset. [*Copy. In the margin are some written contradictions of several of the principal assertions in this paper.* 1 *p*.]

April 28.
52. Answer of Edward Thornhill, deputy for making saltpetre in cos. Hertford, Bedford, Buckingham, and Northampton, to the complaints of John Morton, calendared under date of the 20th inst., No. 10. Thornhill denies that he ever took money for charging or discharging carts, or that he ever spared a dove-house that was worth working. He explains his practice in providing coals, and what price he pays for ashes. He denies that he ever oppressed any poor people, or dug anywhere but where he had warrant for, and refers to certificates annexed in contradiction to some of Morton's specific charges of corruption. Morton, about two years since, was detected for abusing the country, and taking bribes at Northampton, was set on the pillory, fined 40*l*., and lay three months in prison by order of the judges of assize. [2 *pp*.] *Annexed*,

> 52. I. *Certificate of William Hurst that he never gave Thornhill 20s. to discharge any cart. 26th April 1638.* [¼ *p*.]

Vol. CCCLXXXVIII.

1638.

52. II. *Similar certificate of Clement Everett, negativing the gift of any money.* 26*th April* 1638. [¼ *p.*]

52. III. *The like of John Clarke.* [¼ *p.*]

52. IV. *Certificate of John Pigge and two others that John Morton took a bribe of 20s. or 25s. of Lewis Clarke, of Roslingworth, for sparing his dove-house.* 26*th April* 1638. [¼ *p.*]

April 29. 53. Sir Edward Bromfield, late Lord Mayor of London, to the Council. Answer to the complaint of Richard Beale, merchant, touching his assessment to the ship-money, as to which see pp. 188, 371. He was rated at 20*l.* in the ward where he dwelt and where his uncle once lived, from whom, as his executor, he enjoyed house and estate of at least 30,000*l.* Being discontented at his assessment, he left his dwelling, and took a house in another ward. He was rated there at 6*l.*, which he readily paid. Being a very rich man, he was forced to pay the 20*l.*, but might have had the 6*l.* restored to him. [⅔ *p.*]

April 29. 54. Answer of the Churchwardens and 21 other parishioners of Clerkenwell to his Majesty's direction of 15th April inst. They gave notice of the said order to as many owners of estates as they could find, and also gave public notice in the church, after divine service, of a meeting to treat of the business on Sunday afternoon, 22nd April inst., when there assembled, of such as had estates of inheritance only 4, and of lessees of houses 19. The order of Council was then read. None of those assembled subscribed to the submission mentioned in the said order, but they are willing to set forth the truth of their cases when his Majesty shall give them leave to attend him by their counsel. [½ *p.*]

April 29. 55. Certificate of Robert Earl of Lindsey, Lord-Lieutenant of co. Lincoln. John Leger, of South Reston, returned for not showing a horse at the last musters, has promised reformation. The Earl desires that he may be discharged. [½ *p.*]

April 29. 56. Nicholas Martin to Richard Harvey. I have finished your uncle's tombstone. The chancel likewise is tiled. The glass windows in the aisle of the church are out repair. Gives account of moneys received. Offers a rent of 20*l.* for the parsonage at Compton. [1 *p.*]

April 29. 57. Notes, by Nicholas, headed as concerning shipping. It consists of memoranda made from time of alterations desired to be made in the ship-money writs. Most of them were made before the present date, and some were carried out in the writs issued in 1637. The last entry, which bears date this day, intimates that Winchester was, in future, to be abated 20*l.* of the 170*l.*, at which it was rated in the last writs. [2 *pp.*]

April 29. 58. Account of Sir William Russell of ship-money received for 1637. Total, 71,722*l.* 15*s.*; unpaid, 124,691*l.* 12*s.* 8*d.* [1 *p.*]

Vol. CCCLXXXVIII.

1638. April 29.	59. Account of ship-money for 1637 levied and remaining in the hands of the sheriffs, 11,058*l.*, making the total collected 82,780*l.*, which was 28,335*l.* less than on the same day of 1637. [1 *p.*]
April 30. Denbigh.	60. Edward Morris, Sheriff of co. Denbigh, to Nicholas. Sends certificate of the assessment of ship-money upon each parish and clergyman. Would have done so sooner, but that David ap John, one of the high constables of the hundred of Isaled, died, and had received 200*l.*, of which no account can be received of his executors. Without the Council set him in a way to seize upon what estate he has left, the money is like to be lost. [*Seal with arms.* ½ *p.*] Encloses,

      60. I. *Parochial assessment for ship-money in co. Denbigh, above mentioned.* [4 *pp.*]

      60. II. *Names of all the clergy, co. Denbigh, and the sums set upon each of them for ship-money.* [3¼ *pp.*]

April 30.	61. Philip Burlamachi to [Sec. Windebank]. Long explanation in reference to two points connected with the accounts between the writer and the King. The first relates to a payment to be made to a Mons. Aubret, at Paris. Burlamachi explains what advice he had given in reference to the mode of procuring payment, which was all the connexion he had had with that matter. The second point in the letter is, that the Earl of Leicester, the English ambassador in France, had taken exception to the accounts between Burlamachi and the King, on the ground that he had defrauded the King by omitting to account for a sum of 50,000 French livres received in Paris. The King had referred the examination of the business to the Lord Treasurer, Lord Cottington, the two Secretaries, and the Comptroller of the Household. Burlamachi repudiated the charge with great indignation, and trusted that the proofs he should produce before the referees on the Wednesday following would be such that the King would direct the Earl to show whence, how, and by whom he had received the sum in question. Burlamachi, at great length, combats the idea of his having been guilty of so great a fraud. [*French.* 4 *pp.*]
[April.]	62. Petition of Sir William Selby to the King. Recites former petition, calendared under date of 30th May 1637, whereupon the King, to enable petitioner to pay his and his late son's debts, amounting to 11,000*l.*, gave warrant to the justices of assize for co. Durham to permit William Selby, an infant, petitioner's grandson, by his guardian, to suffer a recovery of one-half of the moiety of the manor of Winlaton, co. Durham, which recovery is since executed almost one year since. But most of the moneys being to arise out of the sale of the coal mines, no man can make any gain by them but a free oastman of Newcastle-upon-Tyne; and there being very few free of that company that can dispend so much money, petitioner is like to receive no fruit; the debts must remain unpaid, and petitioner's friends who stand engaged for the same be undone. Prays that

Vol. CCCLXXXVIII.

1638.

such persons as shall buy the coal mines of petitioner may be admitted to trade as free oastmen of Newcastle, as petitioner is, by which means petitioner will soon find chapmen for the said mines. [⅔ p.]

[April.] 63. Petition of Sir Francis Kynaston, one of the esquires in ordinary of his Majesty's body, to the King. Your Majesty, considering the long expense of petitioner's time and means in your service, wrote to Sir Edward Kynaston, petitioner's father, recommending petitioner's courses to his father's favour, so as petitioner might be supported as the heir of his father's house (see Vol. ccclxxxiii., No. 17). Petitioner's father, coming to London instead of answering your letter, gives out that petitioner takes idle courses, and has been so chargeable that his father cannot do any more for him, and thereupon intends to go back into the country. Prays that his father may receive a command to set down in writing what he can object against petitioner touching any idle courses or unnecessary expenses; and that he may not depart from London till he has performed your Majesty's command. [1 p.]

[April.] 64. Sir Edward Kynaston to William Earl of Stirling and Sec. Windebank. In obedience to his Majesty's command, signified by their letter of the 20th inst., Sir Edward presents to them an answer to the King's letter from Newmarket. Since his son's serving in Court, over and above his own means, which were 170l. per annum, he has supplied him with many thousands of pounds of ready money. Touching his willingness to support his son as his heir, he has settled all the lands expressed in the indentures made at his marriage, and also all the writer's lands purchased since, so that after the writer's decease he will have all the writer's lands to enjoy, according to a decree in Chancery, made with his own assent. [1¼ p.]

[April ?] 65. Petition of the Master, Wardens, and Assistants of the Brick and Tile Makers of Westminster to the Council. Petitioners having been incorporated for regulating their trade, granted to his Majesty 6d. out of every 1,000 bricks and tiles, and directions were given to the Attorney-General to assist petitioners in putting in execution the laws and ordinances of the corporation. Nevertheless divers gentlemen and others take upon them to make bricks and tiles as for their own use, to be employed in their building, but really for sale, as Mr. Newton of Queen Street, whereby his Majesty loses his 6d. per 1,000, petitioners are beaten out of their trade, and the public suffer by bricks and tiles deceitfully made. Past proceedings having been ineffectual, and petitioners being so molested by the bricklayers that they cannot proceed in the orderly regulation of their trade, they pray the Council finally to settle the same. [¾ p.]

April. 66. Petition of the merchants, proprietors of the Judith of London, Edward Prince master, to the same. Petitioner's ship lately returning from Morlaix in France was stayed at Gravesend according to

1638.   VOL. CCCLXXXVIII.

the order concerning ships coming from infected places, and thereupon she fell back again into the Hope, where she still remains. The ship's company have continued in perfect health (as appears by the affidavit annexed), and whilst at Morlaix no one went ashore, nor any Frenchman came aboard, but they only loaded their ship with goods, long since provided by petitioners' factor. The ship has lain in the Thames since the 19th of March last, and was 14 days on her voyage homeward. Pray order for her release. [⅔ p.] *Annexed*,

> 66. I. *Affidavit of Edward Prince, master of the Judith. Departed with his ship and nine mariners about two months since from the Thames on a voyage for Morlaix, and has lately returned. During the whole time he and all his company have been in perfect health. 22nd March* 1637–8. [½ p.]
>
> 66. II. *Petition of Edward Prince to the Council. Similar petition previously presented.* [½ p.]

April.   67. Petition of Richard Bagley to Secretary Windebank. Petitioner having sustained his utter undoing through the oppression of Sir Richard Harrison, as stated in his former petition to his Majesty (see *Vol. ccclxxxi.*, No. 59), was referred to Lord Cottington, who directed him to show his petition to Sir Richard, and require him to send in his answer. After waiting three weeks in town for the answer of Sir Richard, he is directed by Lord Cottington to apply to you. [⅔ p.]

April.   68. Petition of Bruno Ryves, vicar of Stanwell, co. Middlesex, to Archbishop Laud. Time out of mind the vicars of Stanwell have yearly chosen one churchwarden and the parishioners another. Petitioner nominated Felix Wilson, Clerk of the Court of King's Bench, churchwarden for 1638, but he has served a prohibition upon Dr. Swalman, Official to the Archdeacon of Middlesex, to forbid him further to prosecute the nomination, grounding the prohibition upon his exemption as a servant to that court, a course altogether unjust in the case of electing churchwardens. Prays the Archbishop to consider how far the premises may intrench upon the honour and privileges of the church, and to take a course for redress. [1 p.]

April.
Old Jewry.   69. William Bassett, late sheriff of Somerset, to Nicholas. States the names of certain constables during his shrievalty and the sums due for ship-money by each of them. Desires Nicholas to take such course as may be best. [*Underwritten; names of the constables and sums unpaid.* 1 p.]

April ?   70. Thomas Earl of Arundel and Surrey, Earl Marshal, to all Justices of Peace and other officers of the King. To summon Edward Holt, executor of Richard Viscount Molineux of Maryborough in Ireland to appear in the Earl's Court Military in the Painted Chamber in the Palace of Westminster, on Wednesday, 9th May, to render their accustomed rights to Sir John Borough,

VOL. CCCLXXXVIII.

1638.

and the other officers of arms, especially for not bringing in a certificate into the office of arms after the death of the said viscount. [*Strip of parchment. 17 lines.*]

April.
Bristowe.
[Bristol.]
71. Richard Halford to [Sir John Lambe?]. I see by your letter that you have received 100*l.* of my brother Blunt, of which your servant Turner paid me 50*l.*, and Dr. Lake long since 38*l.*; the 12*l.* remaining, when I see Mr. Burdin, I shall have. My humble suit is in behalf of my kinsman Thomas Halford, parson of Edithweston, that you would afford him lawful favour in his cause. He is placed amongst a company of troublesome and perverse people. [⅔ *p.*]

April.
72. List of ships employed by his Majesty at sea between 20th April 1637 and 1st April 1638, with the tonnage, number of men, and names of the captains of the principal ships. In this list it appears which were the King's ships, which were merchant ships set forth by the King, which were set forth by the city of London, and which were the ships sent against Sallee, and how long the several ships continued at sea. [1⅔ *p.*]

April.
73. Note of the several employments of William Earl of Denbigh at sea between the 12th August 1626 and 19th March 1627-8. [⅔ *p.*]

April.
74. Extracts out of a review of the Council of Trent, first written in French by a learned Roman catholic, and afterwards translated into English by Dr. [Gerard] Langbaine, Provost of Queen's College, Oxford. These extracts consist of passages and references relating to the power of the popes. [4⅙ *pp.*]

April.
75. Note of Allegations forgotten at the visitation of Merton College; they relate to the loss sustained by not taking yearly the *status cistæ*; to the loosening of the college discipline by the warden's allowing the bachelors to proced an Act before their time; and to practises of Mr. Fisher at and since the visitation. [1¼ *p.*]

April.
76. Names of 20 brewers in and about London appointed to attend the Council. [⅔ *p.*]

April.
77. Petition of eighteen inhabitants of Royston to the Justices of Peace for co. Hertford. Thomas Haggar of their town, inn-holder, bearing himself so irregularly by authority of his office [as postmaster], abuses his protection, to the great grievance of the town and country; breaking open some of their doors in the night without constable; taking away their horses without their privity; extorting, bribing, beating, commanding, threatening countrymen that will not fee him, or do him service with their carts, or spend their money in tippling in his house; hindering poor men from coming to the market to sell their corn by taking their horses post when there is no cause; causing the horses to be double-posted; keeping them longer than the service requires; and misusing young colts and horses not fit for that service, whereby they are oftentimes spoiled, as also

1638.   Vol. CCCLXXXVIII.

taking more horses than need requires. State the consequences to their market, and pray relief. [2 *pp.*] *Annexed,*

77. I. *Affidavit of John Rutter, of Harleton, co. Cambridge, husbandman. His and other horses being taken up to go post to Ware, he seeing one of them released, said he feared there was underhand dealing, whereupon the postmaster's wife, and afterwards the postmaster himself, violently assaulted him so that he was forced to lie at Royston all night for his hurts to be drest, and was compelled to go to Ware after his horse, and had to pay charges for him, being paid only for one stage, although his horse had gone two, and was much wronged thereby. Haggar, his wife and servants, usually take money to free horses from going post, and then take other horses to do the service.* 20th April 1638. [1 *p.*]

77. II. *The like of Richard Amps, of Croydon, co. Cambridge, yeoman. States an instance in which Haggar having taken a horse to go post one stage from Royston, was taken on to Newmarket, and when brought back Haggar refused payment. Amps complained to Sir Robert Chester, since which, whenever Amps came to Royston, Haggar is ready to take his horse, and put an unreasonable load upon it.* 20th April 1638. [1 *p.*]

77. III. *The like of Robert Romball, of Royston, one of the chief constables of the hundred of Odsey, co. Hertford. Having to serve a warrant on Haggar for an assault, he compelled deponent to send on the packet. By taking money to excuse post horses the market of Royston is much wronged.* 23rd April 1638. [1 *p.*]

77. IV. *The like of Giles Royston, of Harleton, co. Cambridge. States another case of assault by Haggar's wife and Haggar himself on John Rutter, who seeing another man's horse released and his own taken remarked, "I fear there is a bribe."* 23rd April 1638. [1 *p.*]

77. V. *The like of Richard Knowleton, of Enfield, husbandman. States how three of his mares with foal were taken by Ibbitt, Haggar's deputy, when going to fetch a load of his Majesty's "carriage" at Theobalds. Deponent hired another horse to go in place of one of them, but never got one penny for the journey, and lost much of his horses' furniture.* 25th April 1638. [½ *p.*]

77. VI. *Separate statements, not upon oath, of John Thurloe, Edmund Sterne, Robert Philips, and Morris Gotte. They all adduce instances of alleged misconduct and oppression. Phillips was one of four that went out with warrants to warn country towns to bring in horses. In two days he warned about 200, most of which he believes the constables compounded for.* [¾ *p.*]

Vol. CCCLXXXVIII.

1638.
[April.] 78. Return by Sir Thomas Coningsby, sheriff of co. Hertford, of the amounts due for ship-money from the corporations in that county; St. Alban's, 120*l*.; Hertford, 55*l*.; and Berkhamstead, 25*l*. [⅓ *p.*]

April. 79. Answer of Henry Coghill of Aldenham, touching the paying of ship-money, in reply to the complaint of the sheriff of co. Hertford, for which see Vol. ccclxxxvii., No. 46. Aldenham lies partly in the hundred of Cashio and partly in that of Dacorum. The part which is in Cashio has on former occasions paid for ship-money 38*l*., and was so at first assessed by the present sheriff, but afterwards, by a second warrant, for the ease, as is stated, of his own tenants in Tiberstreet, which is that part of Aldenham which lies in Dacorum, he took from them 7*l*. 6*s*. 8*d*., and charged that money upon Aldenham in Cashio. This raised the assessment upon Coghill from 2*l*. 10*s*. 0*d*. to 3*l*., which being esteemed unjust, he and the other inhabitants refused to pay their amounts. He had tendered his tax of 2*l*. 10*s*., which had been refused. On behalf of the other parishioners and himself he prays that the tax may be as it formerly was. [1 *p.*]

Vol. CCCLXXXIX. May 1–7, 1638.

1638.
May 1. Demise to Sir David Cunningham for 21 years of a duty of 12*d*. payable to his Majesty upon every beaver hat and cap made by the Company of Beaver makers of London, with a moiety of the benefit of seizures of all foreign beaver hats imported, and of other profits arising to his Majesty upon their charter and contract. There is reserved a yearly rent of 500*l*. If the said duty be restrained by any Act of Parliament, Act of State, or otherwise, then the rent to cease. [*Docquet.*]

May 1. Petition of William Ryley, servant of your Majesty, and Edward Mabb, to the King. There are daily many great losses by fires about London, as by late experience has appeared. For prevention, petitioners present the propositions annexed, praying for a patent for 41 years. [*Copy. See Vol. cccxxiii., p.* 326. ¼ *p.*] Annexed,

> I. *Propositions touching the prevention of fire in London. The owners or inhabitants of houses in London, Westminster, or Southwark, paying* 12*d. per annum for every house, or after the rate of* 12*d. for every* 20*l. rent, shall have their houses re-edified in case of loss by fire. For security,* 5,000*l. shall be deposited in the chamber of London, and be permitted to accumulate at five per cent. until it attains* 10,000*l. There shall be kept a continual watch all night. Engines shall be kept in every ward. The watch shall call for the engines, and reserves of water shall be made*

1638.

Vol. CCCLXXXIX.

in convenient places. Various " conveniences" arising from the adoption of this course are enumerated, amongst them that 200l. per annum shall be allowed towards rebuilding the steeple of St. Paul's. [Copy. Vol. cccxxiii., p. 326. 1 p.]

II. *Reference to the Attorney-General to consider this petition and the propositions, and to certify his opinion. Whitehall, 1st May 1635. [Copy. Ibid. ⅙ p.]*

III. *The Attorney-General to the King. Reports that the propositions are reasonable, if petitioners be tied to their limitations; that no man be pressed to subscribe; that the buildings be not re-edified out of the 5,000l. to be lodged in the chamber of London; and that they be re-edified in convenient time; that the watches and engines and reserves of water be kept; and the 200l. per annum be paid to the repair of St. Paul's. 14th August 1638. [Copy. Ibid., p. 327. ¾ p.]*

IV. *Minute of his Majesty's pleasure to grant petitioners a patent, with the limitations stated. Whitehall, 16th October 1638. [Copy. Ibid., p. 328. ⅙ p.]*

May 1. 1. Petition of Francis Norton, prisoner in the Marshalsea, to the Council. Having received divers enormous wrongs by Richard Morris and Thomas Smith, of Brentford, he complained to Sir Edward Spencer and Sir Edward Littleton, the next Justices of Peace, for relief, but they found the abuses to be of so high a nature that by their authority they could not inflict any punishment on the offenders, whereupon petitioner had a purpose to proceed in the Court of Star Chamber, had he not been prevented by his adversaries bribing his attorney. Prays the Lords to send for Morris and Smith, and to take some course for his relief. [1 p.] Annexed,

I. 1. *Particulars of such grievances as petitioner has sustained of the parties named in his petition. The petitioner took a lease of a house in Brentford from Morris, but when the time came for him to be put in possession Morris refused to permit him to enter, and he and Smith, who was a constable, laid violent hands upon petitioner, tore off his clothes, and put him into the stocks. Among the witnesses whom petitioner referred to, to prove his case, was " Mr. Henderson, minister of Brentford." [1 p.]*

May 1. 2. Petition of William Anthony and John Foord, in the name of the Company of Tobacco-pipe Makers, to the Council. The company of tobacco-pipe makers being a dispersed fraternity without government, and most of them very poor, Richard Cox, complotting with two or three of the richer sort, under pretence of settling them in a set form of government, has engrossed the sole vending of tobacco-pipe clay, thereby enforcing the poor members to buy clay of him at his own prices, pretending the authority of a patent granted to one Foote, by King James I. Petitioners are not only compelled to

1638.

Vol. CCCLXXXIX.

buy their clay of Cox, but he causes the same, being of the nature of fullers earth, to be transported beyond seas, contrary to law, and to the utter ruin of 200 poor families. Pray the Lords to take such order that petitioners may have free liberty to buy their clay where and at what prices they best can. [1 p.]

May 1. 3. James Marquis of Hamilton to Sec. Windebank. To-morrow being the day appointed for hearing the coal business, the King will have it in his own presence. You are to advertise the Lords that the Council may sit at Whitehall. The Queen desired the King to give order for expediting one Tartaro['s] Privy Seal, of which I am commanded likewise to give you notice. [*Seal with arms.* ⅔ p.]

May 1. 4. Petition of John Chew, Postmaster of Bewdley, to Secs. Coke and Windebank. Petitioner is above 90 years of age, and has served postmaster above 30 years. There is due for his post wages in his stage towards the marches of Wales, begun 2nd June 1625, and ended this day, 471*l*. 4*s*. Divers of the postmasters have got their whole pay, and generally all of them their whole pay save the last five or six years. If petitioner were paid even with them he could the better stand to such abatement as is now propounded, which now will be his utter undoing. No man is so long behind, and no one more necessitated, having sold his estate to keep men and horses for this service. Prays relief. [1 p.]

May 1. 5. Answer delivered to Nicholas by the Clerk of the Check of the Guard, touching the orders of the household concerning the guard. The number of the guard depends upon the King's pleasure. What concerns the ushers is performed according to the book. The wages may be altered at the King's pleasure, according to the necessity of the times. If any orders be not observed, it shall be amended. [½ p.]

May 1. 6. Sir Thomas Penyston, Sheriff of co. Oxford, to Nicholas. I have received 800*l*. of ship-money, and expect every day to receive more. What I shall have received I will bring up myself next term. By some misreport, I hear his Majesty is much displeased with me, for not choosing, at the last county court, two verderers within the bailiwick of Woodstock. It was not at that time done because the writ had no return. It had been kept above five weeks before it came to my under sheriff. I entreat the Lords to mediate for me to the King. The next county court day I will see the writ executed with the best care I can. [*Seal with crest.* 1 p.]

May 1.
Northampton. 7. William Collis, Mayor, and eight others, of Northampton, to Richard Lane, Attorney-General to the Prince and Recorder of that town. Send the last week's bills of burials, and give a minute report of the number of houses infected. Misreports of the dangers in the town far beyond the truth. The country is restrained by persuasions from coming in to trade, the markets are decayed, corn and provisions come in scant, and the tradesmen, though with certificates for their clearness from infection, are not suffered to come to fairs

1638.

or markets or to trade abroad. Being a fair that day at Towcester, their tradesmen yesterday repaired thither, but Sir Hatton Farmer [Fermor] would not suffer them to enter the town. Upon their coming back, Sir Barnaby Bryan, Dr. Clark, and Mr. Edwards, three justices, wrote letters in their behalf, but Sir Hatton would not receive the letter, nor allow any Northampton men to come to the fair. These strict courses have made divers of the inhabitants flee abroad, and the day labouring men want means and work. P.S.—We have two felons in gaol, and would have a leet and sessions in Whitsuntide, or if a meeting may not seem convenient we pray you advise us some other way. [2 *pp.*]

[May 1.?] 8. Note by John Gyfford [one of the signers of the preceding letter, and the note probably enclosed in it]. The mayor was informed by the physicians, some to be of the plague and some of the spotted fever, yet the writer conceives them all of one disease, because they die within three or four days, and catch it one of the other. [5 *lines.*]

May 1. 9. Sir Francis Asteley, Sheriff of Norfolk, to the Council. Complains of Matthew Stevenson, Roger Reynolds, William Meek, and Thomas Dawson, chief constables, for neglect in the collection of ship-money. Also of Edward Holt and Edmond Hilton, attorneys-at-law, who had not paid, and encouraged others to stand out. Also of Henry Nowell, a clergyman, who after two months' delay complained of a rate set upon him for an impropriation which he had on lease. Sir Francis, after examination, declined to alter it. After some altercation, which is here repeated, and Nowell braving the sheriff in a great assembly, the sheriff committed him. He had not been in gaol above an hour before he wrote a submission; whereupon, out of respect for his profession, the sheriff discharged him, but he has not paid, and goes about boasting and encouraging others to withstand the payment. There are many more to be complained of, but he certifies these few, not desiring to draw up multitudes before the Lords. Prays the Lords to write to all the corporations, except Thetford, to make speedy payment. The parts of the county adjacent to them have an eye to them, and upon their delay are not so forward as otherwise. [2¼ *pp.*]

May 1.
London.
10. Agreement between Sir Basil Brooke, James Maxwell, Anthony Stanford, and Endymion Porter. Stanford having found out an invention to make perfect bar-iron without the use of Scotch coal, charcoal, pit-coal, or wood, out of raw-iron or bloom-iron, and being in hope also to make sow-iron or bloom-iron without the said materials, is resolved to petition the King for a privilege in his name and that of Bartholomew Bishop, for the sole practising of his invention. It is agreed that the whole benefit of the patent shall be equally divided betwixt the parties to this agreement. [⅔ *p.*]

May 1.
Publow.
11. Nicholas Marten to Richard Harvey. Rests upon Harvey's promise that he should be his tenant for the parsonage of Compton-Dando. Desires to be informed when he will be in the country,

Vol. CCCLXXXIX.

1638.

that he may get in what moneys he can. John Coxe, John Markes, and others say they have paid already. [1 p.]

May 1.
St. James's.

12. Roger Harvey to his brother Richard Harvey. Private letter relating to an advance of money by Richard to Roger, and various family disputes. [2½ pp.]

May 1.

13. Account by Richard Poole of saltpetre brought into his Majesty's store and delivered to Samuel Cordewell, the powder-maker, from 1st November 1637 to 1st May 1638. Total, 92 lasts 3 quarters and 27 lbs., of which 13 cwt. 2 quarters had been brought in by merchants, and the remainder by the saltpetremen. [1 p.]

May 2.

14. Petition of James Rawson, clerk, vicar of Milton Abbas, Dorset, and one of his Majesty's chaplains, to the King. Differences had arisen between John Tregonwell the younger and petitioner, about the rights of the church whereof he is incumbent. The said John Tregonwell and his father are possessors of the dissolved monastery of Milton Abbas, the demesne whereof, with the manor, glebe, and tithes, are worth 2,000*l*. per annum, of which petitioner has only a pension of 24*l*. in lieu of his whole vicarage. Petitioner, in respect of the smallness of his means, is altogether unable to wage law or defend his rights; wherefore he prays a reference to Sir Francis Fulford, Sir Walter Erle, Sir John Brune, Dr. Braddish, vicar of Piddletown, Mr. Rogers, vicar of Bere Regis, and Mr. Thomas Clarke, rector of Mappowder, to make a christian peace, or else to certify to the King what they find to be the truth. [*Copy.* ¾ *p.*] *Underwritten,*

14. I. *Reference as desired. Whitehall, 2nd May* 1638. [*Copy.* ¼ *p.*]

May 2.

15. Petition of James Zouch, your Majesty's servant, to the same. Without any just cause, petitioner has been menaced by Lord Mountnorris to be sued in the Star chamber concerning the settling of his own estate. Prays a reference to the Lords of the Council. [¾ *p.*] *Underwritten.*

15. I. *Reference as desired. Whitehall, 2nd May* 1638. [¼ *p.*]

May 2.

16. Petition of Thomas Knightley, rector of Byfield, co. Northampton, with the churchwardens, George Harries and William Wade, and the rest of the inhabitants, to the same. The hamlet of Trafford has ever been assessed for payments to the King, church and poor, at a third of that charged on the whole parish of Byfield. Sir William Wilmer, owner of the said hamlet, which is all pasture ground, has endeavoured, by chargeable suits, to make the same subject to the custom of tithing used in the common and arable fields of Byfield, and although in one suit he was non-suit, and in the other a verdict passed against him, Sir William threatens more prohibitions, and for four years has refused to pay to church or poor, and

1638.

VOL. CCCLXXXIX.

and wearied out petitioners with chargeable suits. Pray a reference to one or more of the Privy Council. [*Copy.* ½ *p.*] *Underwritten,*

16. I. *Reference to the Archbishop of Canterbury, the Lord Treasurer, and Lord Privy Seal. Whitehall, 2nd May 1638.* [*Copy.* ⅙ *p.*]

16. II. *Appointment of the referees for hearing this business at the Council Board, on 8th of June. 7th May* 1638. [*Copy.* ⅙ *p.*]

May 2. 17. Order of the King in Council. Recites a proposition made to the King and Council on the 4th of April last by the masters and owners of ships trading to Newcastle, Sunderland, Blyth, and other places for coals, with the order made thereon, for which see Vol. ccclxxxvii., No. 19. This day his Majesty, sitting in Council, having received the answer of Mr. Morley and the oastmen to the said propositions, and having heard all the parties, it was ordered that the said masters and owners of ships, giving security that they being made a corporation will supply London with ship-coals according to the terms of their said proposition, and will answer the new duty of 12*d.* upon every chaldron they shall load, according to the measure of 21 Newcastle bolls to the chaldron, for the space of ten years, that then they shall have a free and open trade at Newcastle as formerly, and the Attorney-General is to take a surrender of his Majesty's contract with the oastmen, who are to be relieved of all payments touching the 12*d.*, and is to prepare a charter of incorporation of all such merchants, masters, and owners of ships who shall use the trade for coals to Newcastle-upon-Tyne, Sunderland, Blyth, Nook, and Berwick, with a variety of powers which are here set forth. [*Copy.* 5½ *pp.*]

May 2. 18. Draft of the preceding, with corrections by Nicholas. [6 *pp.*]

May 2. 19. Petition of the owners of the ship the Margaret to the Council. Going to Newcastle to lade coals, and being enforced to lade with the contractors, they were assigned coals which are so bad that, being sold in London, the coal merchants refuse to pay for the same. Pray the Lords to enjoin the contractors to pay the damage, or take the coals at 19*s.* per chaldron, the price at which good coals are sold. [½ *p.*]

May 2. Whitehall. 20. Order of the King in Council on the preceding petition. Lawrence Whitaker, clerk of the Council in Extraordinary, Robert Dickson, Peter Heywood, and George Hulbert, justices of peace, are to survey the coals brought by the Margaret, now lying at a quay near Charing Cross, and to certify of what condition they are. [*Draft.* ⅔ *p.*]

May 2. 21. Order of Council made on complaint of Sir Francis Asteley, calendared under date of the 1st inst. Matthew Stevenson, Roger Reynolds, William Meek, and Thomas Dawson, chief constables, were to collect and pay the ship-moneys assessed upon their hundreds before the beginning of next term, and Edmond Holt and Edward

398   DOMESTIC—CHARLES I.

Vol. CCCLXXXIX.

1638.

Hilton were to pay their rates assessed upon them, or the sheriff was to bind them over to answer at the Board on the 27th instant. [*Draft.* 1 *p.*]

May 2.

22. Minute of a warrant from the Council to the Warden of the Fleet, to release Bartholomew Baldwin and George Goodson, they having paid their ship-money, co. Buckingham. [*Draft.* ½ *p.*]

May 2.

The like of a similar warrant to discharge William Heyburn, he having entered into bond for the ship-money in arrear in the time of Sir Anthony Chester's bailiwick. [*Draft, written upon the same paper as the preceding.* ¼ *p.*]

May 2.

23. Draft entry of minute of appearance before the Council of Robert Middleton, for his father Thomas Middleton, of Leighton, co. Lancaster, being sent for on account of default of arms. [4 *lines.*]

May 2.

The like of Thomas Roberts, of South Newington, co. Oxford, husbandman. He is to remain in custody of a messenger. [*Written on the same paper as the preceding.* 6 *lines.*]

May 2.

24. Draft minute of a pass from the Council for Sir Nicholas Biron, captain of a company in the Low Countries, Richard Winkfield, and Peter Robinson, to travel into the Low Countries with three servants. [¼ *p.*]

May 2.

25. Commissioners for licensing brewers to use wine-casks to the Council. Answer to various questions demanded of them. The brewers, who were heretofore contented to take licences, will not now discover themselves, being put in hope that they shall be at liberty to use wine-cask without payment. We would give 800*l.* per annum rent for London and four miles' compass. Other questions we cannot answer without seeing the contracts between the officers of the Green Cloth and the brewers. [⅔ *p.*]

May 2.
Wellow.

26. Sir William Portman, Sheriff of Somerset, to the same. Upon reference to the Bishop of Bath and Wells and himself of a petition of the inhabitants of the hundred of Abdick and Bulstone, concerning an alleged over-rate of 40*l.* to the ship-money, thereby easing the hundred of Milverton, the bishop and the writer had a meeting at Wells, and heard both sides. They found that in some rates Abdick and Bulstone paid after the proportion of three men, but to the composition they paid after the rate of three and a half men, or 3*l.* 10*s.* for every 100*l.*, which had been paid for ship-money in Mr. Hodges' and Mr. Malet's years, and that Milverton usually paid after the rate of 1*l.* on every hundred. Forasmuch as the bishop and Sir William could not accord this difference, the writer thinks that Abdick and Bulstone should stand charged with 280*l* for this time, for the present expedition of the service. Contrary to the assertion of petitioners, the writer has a great part of his estate lying in the hundred of Abdick and Bulstone, and no lands in Milverton, on

DOMESTIC—CHARLES I.

1638.

Vol. CCCLXXXIX.

which point he desires a reference to the judges of assize. [1½ *p.*] *Annexed,*

> 26. I. *Copy of the petition of the inhabitants of the hundred of Abdick and Bulstone to the Council above mentioned, and the contents of which are already stated under Vol. ccclxxviii., No. 68.* [1 *p.*]

May 2. 27. List of causes specially appointed to be heard in the Court of Star Chamber. They were:—the Attorney-General *versus* Richard Edwards and others; Alexander Dupper *versus* James Freeze and others; Francis Cufaud and others *versus* Anne Doleman and others; and John Blomer *versus* John Ruddle and others. [1 *p.*]

May 2. 28. Notes taken by Sec. Windebank on the hearing of the first of the causes above mentioned. The defendants were apothecaries, and the charges against them, promoted by the College of Physicians, were the falsification of medicines, resisting government and order, and contemning an order of the Lords, with the utterance of calumnious speeches against members of the College of Physicians. The present notes refer to the proceedings of this day, in which the Attorney-General stated the evidence for the prosecution, and the Solicitor-General summed up the case against the defendants. There is added in another sheet the continuation of the proceedings on the 4th inst., when Mr. Herne addressed the Court on the part of the defence, and stated the evidence on their behalf. [11 *pp.*]

May 2. 29. Book of notes made by Nicholas of proceedings of the Council at their several meetings during this month. They state the names of the members of the Council present on each occasion, and briefly indicate the several businesses considered and the orders made. The days on which the Council sat, and to which these notes refer, were the 2nd, 4th, 5th, 6th, 8th, 16th, 18th, 23rd, 24th, 25th, 26th, 27th, and 30th of the present month. [112 *pp., of which 27 are blank.*]

May 2. Deed, whereby the parsons, vicars, and curates of the places and parishes adjacent to the city of London submit the cause of their several churches concerning tithes, oblations, obventions, and other rights now depending before his Majesty, and all their right, title, and interest therein, to the arbitrament of his Majesty, promising obedience to whatsoever he shall order and determine concerning the premises. The deed is signed and sealed by the following persons: Daniel Featley, rector of Lambeth; Thomas Turner, rector of St. Olave's, Southwark; William Haywood, rector of St. Giles-in-the-Fields; Gilbert Wimberley, curate of St. Margaret's, Westminster; John Johnson, rector of St. Mary Matfellon, Whitechapel; Richard Dukeson, rector of St. Clement Danes; John Littleton, rector of St. George, Southwark; John Squier, vicar of St. Leonard, Shoreditch; James Archer, curate of St. Saviour's, Southwark; William Bray, vicar of St. Martin's-in-the-Fields; Henry Goodcole, curate of St. James, Clerkenwell; John Bloodworth, rector of St. Mary, Newington; John Maccube, curate of the Savoy; and

1638.

Vol. CCCLXXXIX.

Benjamin Spencer, curate of St. Thomas-in-Southwark. [*Nine seals with arms; one with a crest, one with initials, one with a merchant's mark, one with a fanciful device, and one without any impression. See Case E., Car. I., No. 4. Parchment. 10 lines.*]

May 3. Grant, whereby, in consideration of 250*l.* to be paid into the Exchequer, his Majesty disafforests the lands of Richard Derling and sundry others, lying within the forest of Deane, and grants them a pardon for offences against the forest laws formerly committed. [*Docquet.*]

May 3. Presentation of William Farrow, B.D., to the rectory of Knaptoft, co. Lincoln, in his Majesty's gift by lapse, simony, or otherwise. [*Docquet.*]

May 3. Grant to Thomas Edwards, his Majesty's servant, of the office of constable of Flint Castle, void by the death of Thomas Griffith, with the fee of 10*l.* per annum, to be paid by the receiver of the revenues of the principality of North Wales. [*Docquet.*]

May 3. 30. The Council to the Warden of the Fleet. To take [John Wragg, *alias*] Bonyragg, messenger, into custody, and keep him prisoner till further order. [*Draft minute.* ¼ *p.*]

May 3. The same to the same. Warrant for commitment of —— Meridale, prisoner, to the Fleet. [*Draft minute, written on the same paper as the preceding.* ¼ *p.*]

May 3.
Whitehall. 31. Similar warrant to a messenger not named, to fetch before the Lords, John Edwards, of Weston Patrick, Hants. [*Draft minute.* ¼ *p.*]

May 3. 32. Certificate and answer of the parishioners of St. Giles-in-the-Fields to an order of Council. Upon reading a late petition by their parson, amongst others, to his Majesty, concerning rights pretended to be withheld or prejudiced by new buildings, and for increase of maintenance, as also the order of Council made thereon, we, the parishioners whose names are underwritten, believe that all rights are duly answered; and if our parson means any duties detained in respect of houses, we are assured by counsel that none by law are due to him; and for any prejudice in respect of tithes of land lost by new buildings, we find that the old payments in lieu of tithes are continued, and we are satisfied that the profits arising by oblations and obventions, besides voluntary gifts, far exceed what the lands by tithes in kind could formerly yield. And as for the present maintenance, we conceive it competent, as being at least 200*l.* per annum, wherewith many reverend divines have lived contentedly, and to the relief of our poor. [103 *signatures.* = 2 *pp.*]

May 3. 33. Thomas Gardiner, Recorder of London, to Sec. Windebank. The [nine] persons undernamed being convicted prisoners in Newgate, are fit to be transported over seas for martial service, if his Majesty vouchsafe them mercy. Among the convicts, two were

1638. VOL. CCCLXXXIX.

indicted for breaking the house of Sir John Jacob, and stealing divers parcels of plate. One person named was a woman (Susan Austin), indicted for stealing two horses. [¾ p.]

May 3.
London.

34. Michael Stanhope to Dr. Lake, at his house at Leicester. I have received a letter out of Ireland, authorizing me to make choice of a King's advocate. If you think the place worth your pains, nothing remains but the procuring of my Lord of Canterbury's letter to the Lord Deputy. Direct to me at the castle at Dublin. [*Seal with crest.* 1 p.]

May 4.

35. Petition of the owners of the Margaret to the King. By certificate annexed, it appears that the coals complained of (*see* No. 19) are so bad that they are of little worth. Pray that Mr. Morley may pay petitioners for them at the prices they were sold at, with allowance for loss of their ship's time and the charge of lighters, wherein the coals have remained ten days. [½ p.] *Annexed,*

> 35. I. *Certificate of Lawrence Whitaker, Peter Heywood, and George Hulbert, justices of peace, that the sea coal in three lighters was very bad and unserviceable, very little better than dirt, and such as would neither burn nor cake. It was brought from Newcastle in the Margaret of Yarmouth, and is now lying at West's Wharf, near Charing Cross. The price paid at Newcastle was* 12s. *the chaldron;* 18s. *was charged in London.* [1 p.]

May 4.
Inner Star Chamber.

36. Order of Council. Upon consideration of the answer of the president and College of Physicians to the petition of the apothecaries, exhibited the 11th of April last, the Lords ordered that all matters in variance should be referred to the two Lord Chief Justices, and the other referees nominated in a former order of 8th January 1635; and if they can fall on any expedient that may accommodate all things, the clause in the order of the 8th January 1635, restraining the referees from meddling with the matters depending between some of the physicians and some of the apothecaries in the Star Chamber, shall be no impediment to an entire agreement. [*Copy.* 1¼ p.]

May 4.

37. The like. Upon petition of Marmaduke More, wherein he confesses some errors for which he besought the Lords to accept his submission, it was declared that, for the sake of the Earl of Suffolk, his Lord and master, the Lords are content to pass by the same, but ordered that More should pay to John Badcock all such costs as should be allowed him by Sir Dudley Carleton, and thereupon More to be released from imprisonment. [*Draft.* 1 p.]

May 4.
Inner Star Chamber.

38. The like. Upon hearing the Patentees or Commissioners for Wine-cask, and some on behalf of the Brewers within four miles of London, and having considered the answer of the patentees to propositions made to them (*No.* 25), it is declared very unfit to disturb the contract made with the brewers by way of composition for 3,000*l.* per annum upon any hopes of the patentees; but inasmuch as in

402 DOMESTIC—CHARLES I.

VOL. CCCLXXXIX.

1638.

their answer they allege the securing of the said composition to depend upon the consideration of the contract, it was ordered that they should attend the Treasurer and Comptroller of the Household at the Greencloth, and there see the contract; and if they can show a way to raise the rent of 3,000*l.* without using coercive power on the brewers the Lords will further consider their propositions; but they are to take care that they do not distemper his Majesty's service with the brewers. [*Draft.* 1½ *p.*]

May 4.
Inner Star Chamber.

39. Order of Council. On petition of the parishioners of St. Gregory's, London, and consideration of articles between them and the parishioners of Christ Church, concerning accommodating them in the west end of Christ Church, it was ordered that the parishioners of St. Gregory's should place only moveable pews in Christ Church, so that burials may not be hindered; that they should make use of the west doors only; that they should leave the church at St. John Baptist, 1641, in as good repair as they find it; that they shall have liberty yearly to bury ten of their parishioners within the west end of Christ Church; that the parishioners of both Christ Church and St. Gregory's shall submit to the Bishop of London for composing all differences; and lastly, that the churchwardens, common councilmen, and sidemen of both parishes shall subscribe to the aforesaid articles, and upon such subscription the keys of the west part of Christ Church shall be delivered to those of St. Gregory's. [*Draft.* 2¼ *pp.*]

May 4.

40. The like. Upon petition of Matthias Styles, B.D. and preacher of St. Gregory's, London, wherein he shows that by taking down St. Gregory's Church he is in danger of losing his livelihood, it is ordered that his pension and allowance shall be confirmed to him by the said parish, he continuing his preaching in the west end of Christ Church, and that the churchwardens of St. Gregory's shall take order for rating and collecting the same. [*Draft.* 1 *p.*]

May 4.

41. The like. Upon signification of his Majesty's pleasure by letter from the Earl of Dorset, that the hearing of the business between Thomas Tyrrell and Sir Miles Fleetwood, formerly referred to this Board, should be transmitted to the Lord Treasurer and Lord Cottington, It is Ordered that Mr. Tyrrell and Sir Miles shall attend at such times as the said referees shall appoint, and that they be prayed to hear the said business, and report to his Majesty. [*Draft.* [1 *p.*]

May 4.
Inner Star Chamber.

42. The like. The Lords being made acquainted that over the New Exchange, called Britain's Burse, there are divers families inhabiting as inmates, and that adjoining the wall of the court of Durham House there are sheds employed as eating rooms and for other uses, to the great annoyance of the inhabitants and danger of infection, It was Ordered that the Lord Privy Seal and Lord Newburgh, chancellor of the duchy, should call before them the inhabitants of the said places, and take order for their removal; and if they find any of the said persons obstinate, should certify their names. [*Draft.* 1 *p.*]

Vol. CCCLXXXIX.

1638. May 4. Inner Star Chamber.

43. Order of Council. On petition of Martin Bradgate, of London, merchant, that having intelligence from his factor in the Canary Islands of 600 quintals of logwood laden aboard the George for London for want of other goods, the rest of the lading being sugars and other rich commodities which would produce 2,000*l.* customs, the said petitioner prayed that he might be allowed to transport the logwood to parts beyond the seas. The Lord Treasurer was prayed to give order to take good security for the exportation of the logwood, regulations being made for its keeping whilst here, and a certificate to be produced of its landing in foreign parts. [*Draft.* 1¼ *p.*]

[May 4.]

44. Draft of a clause in the above order, in the handwriting of Lord Cottington, respecting the mode of keeping the logwood until its exportation. [6 *lines.*]

May [4.] Whitehall.

45. The Council to the Officers of Customs. To suffer Martin Bradgate to land and export the logwood above mentioned. [*Signed by the Council, but afterwards cancelled on some alteration of the terms.* 1 *p.*]

May 4.

46. Order of Council. On petition of the inhabitants of Wells Forum, touching the difference between them and the city, whether the cathedral of Wells should pay with the city towards the ship-money, the Lords referred the examination thereof to the bishop, with the two next justices of peace, who have returned a certificate. The Lords confirm the same, and require all parties to yield obedience. [*Draft.* 1 *p.*]

May 4. Inner Star Chamber.

47. The like. Edward Ferrers, owner of the mills of Hertford, and Edward Baynes, B.D. and parson of St. Andrew's, Hertford, by petition, submitted certain differences between them touching the tithes of the said mills, to be composed and ended by the Lords. Upon debate, and consideration as well of the yearly value of the said mills as of the charge Mr. Ferrers had been at in repairs, It was Ordered that there should be nothing paid for the time past, but for five years next ensuing Ferrers to pay five marks per annum, and afterwards 5*l.* per annum. [*Draft.* 1 *p.*]

May 4.

48. The like. Dame Mary Powell, wife of Sir Edward Powell, by petition, prayed the Lords (to whom the difference between her, Sir Edward Powell, and Sir Peter Vanlore, was referred by his Majesty) that their declaration that it was no way their meaning by their award to prejudice petitioner or the trust for her by the will of her deceased mother, might be entered in the Council Book. The Lords, before they would give way to this request, ordered Sir Edward Powell and his lady to attend on Wednesday next, with each of them one of their counsel. [*Draft.* 1 *p.*]

May 4.

49. The like. Michael Fawkes, by petition, desired a day to be appointed for hearing the question in difference between him and John Gibbon, for the possession of 200 acres of land lying in the

1638.

VOL. CCCLXXXIX.

level of Hatfield Chase, co. York, which were sold by the Commissioners of Sewers to petitioner's wife. The Lords appointed to hear the same at the first sitting in next term. [*Draft.* ⅔ *p.*]

May 4.
50. Order of Council. On a petition of many inhabitants of St. Martin's-in-the-Fields, it was shown that there is a passage down to the Thames, called Ivy Bridge, adjoining the Earl of Salisbury's house, which has been an ancient customary place for washing and watering the horses of his Majesty, the nobility, and others, but is now so far out of repair that it undermines the Earl's house, for which cause his steward has barred up the way. The vestry of St. Martin's having been applied to for a collection to repair the same, refused to grant the request. It was therefore desired that the Lords would order the justices and burgesses of the parish of St. Martin's to make an assessment for that purpose. It was Ordered that the justices of peace and burgesses of St. Martin's and the liberties of the Savoy and St. Clement's should make an assessment upon those persons who make use of the said passage for their horses, both for repairing and maintaining the same, and none are to have benefit thereby who shall refuse to contribute. [*Draft.* 1½ *p.*]

May 4.
51. The like. Sir John Corbet complained by petition that, having for his part conformed to the order of the Lords of 12th May 1637, made betwixt him, Sir James Stonehouse, and Peter Egerton (*see Vol. ccclvi., No.* 18), yet the wastes mentioned therein are not repaired by Mr. Egerton, nor security given by Sir James Stonehouse and his lady. It was Ordered that if the parties complained of shall not perform the said order before Michaelmas term, they shall be sent for to answer their contempt. [*Draft.* 1 *p.*]

May 4.
Inner Star Chamber.
52. Order of the Archbishop of Canterbury and the Lord Treasurer, referees of a petition of John Lowen, clerk, and others, and of the matter in difference between them and one Symes, touching a tenement in Birchen Lane, London, called the Bull. The referees understanding that the special verdict was not upon the whole case, Ordered that the business be again referred to a trial at law, and that the whole case be put in issue; and for the costs upon the trial past, that the same be ordered by the judges. [*Draft.* ⅔ *p.*]

May 4.
53. Order of Council. The corporation of Congleton, co. Chester, prayed the Lords to appoint a day next term for hearing a business between that town and William Bramhall, about a manor alleged to have been gained by Bramhall out of his Majesty's hands, which business was referred by his Majesty to the Lords. The first sitting in the next term was appointed for that purpose. [*Draft.* 1 *p.*]

May 4.
Inner Star Chamber.
54. Order of the Archbishop of Canterbury, the Lord Keeper, the Lord Treasurer, and the Lord Privy Seal, referees of the matter in difference between the Church and the City of Exeter. The referees being informed that the judges cannot make their report so soon as was expected, It was Ordered that time be given till the first sitting

1638.
Vol. CCCLXXXIX.

after All Hallows day next, when both sides are ordered to attend. [*Draft.* ⅔ *p.*]

May 4.
Inner Star Chamber.
55. Order of the Archbishop of Canterbury, the Lord Keeper, and the Lord Treasurer, referees of the business between Thomas Harding, clerk, rector of Souldern, co. Oxford, and the Lord of the manor and freeholders there. Appointment to hear the same on Tuesday next; and in case the Lords' occasions will not give leave for that day, the parties are to attend the day following. [*Sealed with the seal of the Council.* ½ *p.*]

May 4.
56. Draft of the preceding. [¼ *p.*]

May 4.
Inner Star Chamber.
57. Order of the Archbishop of Canterbury, the Lord Keeper, and the Lord Privy Seal, referees from his Majesty of matters in difference between Henry Morgan and Blanche his wife, and Henry Lingen, son to the said Blanche. With consent of the parties, It was Ordered that Mrs. Morgan shall, during her life, enjoy the house in Stoke Edith, co. Hereford, for her habitation, and shall be paid by Mr. Lingen 400*l.* per annum, and that Mr. Lingen shall have the manor of Stoke Edith and the rectory of Taddington [Tarrington?], co. Hereford, during his mother's life. [*Copy signed by the parties.* 2⅓ *p.*]

May 4.
58. Order of the Archbishop of Canterbury and Bishop Wren, of Ely, referees of a difference for matter of tithes and increase of maintenance between Joshua Meene, vicar of Wymondham, Norfolk, and Nicholas Andrewes, of Godalming, Surrey, and John Smart, citizen of London, lessees of the rectory. By consent of the parties it was agreed that Meene, besides his house, glebe, hearth-silver, pensions, Easter oblations, churchings, marriage and burial fees, should receive 17*l.* yearly, and Andrewes and Smart are to receive all the small tithes; which agreement the referees confirmed. [*Draft.* 1 *p.*]

May 4.
Inner Star Chamber.
59. Order of Council. The informations of Richard and Phillis Phillips, John Belcher, and Richard Mason, against Richard Dickson, are to be sent to the Solicitor-General, who is to examine Dickson, and certify his opinion. [½ *p.*]

May 4.
60. Draft of the preceding. [⅓ *p.*]

May 4.
61. Entry on Council Register of appearance of William Hockin, of Great Torrington, Devon. [*Draft.* 3 *lines.*]

May 4.
62. The like of Nathaniel Extill, of London, sent for by warrant for selling tobacco by retail, contrary to proclamation. He is to remain in custody of the messenger until discharged. [*Draft.* 5 *lines.*]

May 4.
63. The Council to Robert Taverner, messenger. To bring before the Lords Nehemiah Rawson, of Buckwood, co. Lincoln. [*Draft minute.* ⅓ *p.*]

VOL. CCCLXXXIX.

1638.
May 4.
The Star Chamber.
The Council to Warden of the Fleet. To take into his custody Nehemiah Rawson, to be kept prisoner till further order. [*Draft written on the same paper as No. 62. ¼ p.*]

May 4.
The like to Edmond Barker, messenger. To bring Maurice Thomson, Oliver Clobery, Oliver Read, and George Lewin, of London. [*The like, written on same paper as No. 63. 4 lines.*]

May 4.
The Star Chamber.
64. The like to Warden of the Fleet. To continue Alexander Jennings, who had used scandalous speeches in derogation of his Majesty's government, prisoner in the Fleet till further order. [*The like. ⅓ p.*]

May 4.
The Star Chamber.
65. The like to Robert Taverner, messenger. To fetch before the Board John Baker, surveyor of highways for St. Martin-in-the-Fields. [*The like. ¼ p.*]

May 4.
The like to Reignold Gunnell. To bring John Skill, of Great Sampford, Essex. [*The like; written on the same paper as the preceding. 3 lines.*]

May 4.
The like to Thomas Waterworth, messenger. To bring William Hickman, of Barnacle, co. Warwick. [*The like. Ibid. 3 lines.*]

May 4.
The like to James Naylor, messenger. To fetch Henry Nowell, clerk. [*The like. Ibid. 2 lines.*]

May 4.
The like to George Carter, messenger. To fetch John Edwards, of Weston Patrick, Hants. [*The like. Ibid. 5 lines.*]

May 4.
The like to Edmond Barker, messenger. To fetch William Mills, of Hamhaw, Surrey, junior. [*The like. Ibid. 3 lines.*]

[May 4 ?]
66. Petition of the Mayor and Aldermen of Newcastle-upon-Tyne to the Council. Upon complaint of many disorders committed on the Tyne, the Lords appointed some burgesses of that town to put in execution orders thought expedient for cleansing thereof. Petitioners have hitherto submitted themselves to your commands, and have not insisted upon any grant; yet, by experience, they find it breeds contempt towards petitioners, and will stir up further controversies. The government of the town, and also of the river, being by charter and prescription settled upon petitioners, they pray the Lords to restore to them their government of the river, they undertaking to manage the same with all care, or else to be accounted unworthy of their places. [⅔ p.]

May 4.
67. John Marlay, Mayor of Newcastle-upon-Tyne, and nine others, Commissioners for Conservancy of the river Tyne, to the same. Report of their proceedings from Michaelmas 1637 until Easter 1638. State the case of Nicholas Harrison and Christopher Fuller, to which the following order has relation. [1 p.]

May 4.
68. Order of Council. The Lords being informed that Nicholas Harrison, by appointment of Christopher Fuller, has begun to build

DOMESTIC—CHARLES I. 407

1638.

VOL. CCCLXXXIX.

a shore at Jarrow Slake, on the Tyne, and that Fuller being required by the Commissioners of Conservancy to surcease his work till he had shown good authority, or, according to former orders of Council, had given bond that the shore should be no prejudice to the river, he still proceeds with the building, and of late has suffered two ships to cast ballast there. It was Ordered that Fuller and Harrison forthwith cease the building until they show their authority, and give bond to perform the former order of Council; or, in case they remain refractory, the commissioners are to take bond for their appearance before the Lords on the first sitting day of next term. [*Draft.* 1⅓ *p.*]

May 4. 69. Sir William Becher and Edward Nicholas to the Council. Report on petition of Valentine Saunders, calendared under date of 9th March last (*No.* 45). Lord Valentia made over a fourth part of one share in the late soap business for 300*l.* to Valentine Saunders, by indenture, which is traced by the reporters to the hands of William Headlam, who gave it to Sir Richard Weston, and it cannot now be found. Sir Gregory Norton, who is authorized to receive the whole share of Lord Valentia, forbears to pay the fourth part, because this indenture is not extant. The reporters recommend an order that Sir Gregory pay the fourth part to Valentine Saunders, and be acquitted as against Lord Valentia for the same, and that Saunders give bond to repay the same in case the Lords within one year order the same. [¾ *p.*]

May 4.
Aston.
70. Thomas Whitley, sheriff of co. Flint, to the Council. States that he had assessed and given order to collect the 575*l.* ship-money for that county. Had received 350*l.*, which shall be paid to the Treasurer of the Navy by the last of this month, and on the 24th of June. The rest he hopes will be paid by the 14th July. *Enclosed,*

70. I. *Assessment of* 575*l. ship-money on the hundreds and parishes in co. Flint, with an account of how much was charged upon every clergyman.* [4 *pp.*]

May 4. 71. William Bassett, late sheriff of Somerset, to Nicholas. Alexander Middleton and Richard Harvey, late constables of the hundred of Abdick and Bulstone, having been very diligent in the levy of ship-money, are now sued by John Pine of Curry-Mallet, for levying money assessed and refused to be paid. Pray you afford them your assistance to the Lords for their relief. P.S.—Send me Mr. Phillips's order that I may demand his money, otherwise I shall never get it, the constables being willing to shift and delay. [*Seal with arms.* 1 *p.*]

May 4.
Canterbury.
72. The Deputy Mayor and Aldermen of Canterbury to the Council. On the 15th April the house of Henry Bartlam, a shoemaker of this city, was shut up, but some hours before it was known to be infected two men fled, one his son, Nathaniel Bartlam, whose person and attire are described, and the other a servant, and although search was made for them throughout the city, and warrants sent to all the coasts round about, and also to London and Oxford,

1638.

they have not been apprehended. Bartlam, who remains in a tent with his family, says that he heard lately that his son and the other were working in London, wherefore the writers had sent the bearer, a man of that trade, who knows them well, if you please to employ him. The Mayor is in London about his Majesty's affairs. [1 p.]

May 4. 73. Sir John Finch, Lord Chief Justice of the Common Pleas, to the Council. Report on the matter in question between the hundreds of Bath Forum and Wellow. Bath Forum pretends that Norton St. Philip's, which has usually borne half a man in the rates of the county, ought to be cast towards the ease of Bath Forum, whereas the sheriff has joined it to Wellow. It was proved on behalf of Wellow that the constant practice for 20 years before Mr. Hodges' time was for Norton St. Philip to pay with that hundred. I gave Bath Forum ten days to produce to the now sheriff a rate before Mr. Hodges' time, to demonstrate the practice, and if they failed I ordered that the sheriff's rate imposed this year should stand. Bath Forum has neglected to attend the sheriff, whereupon he has proceeded to levy his former rates. [1 p.]

May 4. 74. Order of Council. Recites the preceding report of Sir John Finch. The Lords, well approving what the Chief Justice had done, ordered that the rate set upon the hundred of Bath Forum for this year shall stand, and that all persons conform themselves thereto. [*Draft.* 1 p.]

May 4. Tottenham. 75. Sec. Coke to Lord Keeper Coventry. I have received the enclosed from the Earl of Dorset. The king's business for some foreign dispatches will not suffer me this day to attend at the Council Board. [*Seal with arms.* ⅔ p.]

May 4. 76. Edward Viscount Wimbledon to Nicholas. I have long solicited a supply of gunpowder for Portsmouth, which was deferred until account was made of the powder formerly received, which is now sent into the office of Ordnance. The garrison has lately been utterly destitute. I have been constrained to borrow out of the store for the Navy ten barrels. Solicit the Lords for a supply of six lasts, as has been accustomed. Sec. Windebank will further the dispatch thereof. [⅔ p.]

May 4. Salisbury. 77. Bishop Davenant of Salisbury to the same. It is above ten years since by order of Council I received into my custody certain arms belonging to Lord Arundel of Wardour. It was ordered that they should be scoured and looked to at the charge of the said lord. Nothing has been done to them as yet; and when I last spoke with Lord Arundel, his answer was, he took no further care of them, having given them to his Majesty. I first entreated Mr. Oldsworth (my Lord of Pembroke's secretary) and since yourself to acquaint the Lords. Pray move them, that as by their command I took the arms into my keeping, so by their direction I may deliver them up, before they be spoiled. [*Seal with arms.* ½ p.]

DOMESTIC—CHARLES I.

1638.

Vol. CCCLXXXIX.

May 4. 78. Bishop Skinner of Bristol to Archbishop Laud. Rejoinder to Bishop Wright of Lichfield's answer to Bishop Skinner's complaint (*see* 7th April last, No. 34). The Bishop of Bristol quotes passages from the Bishop of Lichfield's letter, and gives his own comment upon it in an opposite column. [2 *pp.*]

May 4. 79. Particular of premises in Chelmorton, co. Derby, formerly held by John Dale, who died on the 9th December 1622, at the yearly rent of 3*l.* 12*s.* 6*d.*, leaving William Dale, his son and heir, of the age of 8 years, with underwritten direction of Lord Cottington, Master of the Court of Wards, dated this day, for a lease of the premises during the minority to be granted to John Ince. [1 *p.*]

May. 4. 80. Another particular of the same, showing that the annual value of the premises over and above the said annual rent was 17*s.*, with underwritten minute, signed by Lord Cottington, of the sale thereof this day to the said John Ince for 7*l.*, subject to the yearly rent of 3*l.* 12*s.* 6*d.* above mentioned. [¾ *p.*]

May 4. 81. Particular of Tunsteed Hall, co. Derby, formerly held by Thomas Tunsteed, who died on 5th February 1623-4, at the yearly rent of 6*l.* 16*s.* 8*d.*, leaving Richard Tunsteed his son and heir, of the age of 4 years, with an underwritten direction of Lord Cottington, Master of the Court of Wards, for a lease of the premises during the minority to John Ince. [1 *p.*]

May 4. 82. Another particular, showing that the annual value of the same premises, over and above the said rent, was 1*l.* 6*s.*, with underwritten minute, signed by Lord Cottington of the sale of the same this day to the said John Ince for 20*l.*, subject to the said rent of 6*l.* 16*s.* 8*d.* [¾ *p.*]

May 5. Warrant to the Lord Treasurer to order the officers of the port of London to permit Viscount Belhaven to transport into Scotland, for his own use, 3 basins, 3 ewers, 24 plate trenchers, 2 great salts, 2 little salts, 3 bare cups, 1 little basin, 1 sugar dish, 2 tankards, 1 caudle cup with a cover, 1 porringer, 6 candlesticks, 1 pair of snuffers, 3 dozen of spoons, and three oval wine cups. [*Docquet.*]

May 5. Warrant to discharge Walter Long and Thomas Long of a fine of 2,000 marks imposed on Walter Long in the Star Chamber, in regard the same, according to his Majesty's pleasure, has been paid by Thomas Long to John Ashburnham, in satisfaction of so much due by his Majesty to him. [*Docquet.*]

May 5. Grant of an almsroom in the cathedral of Carlisle for John Moodie, void by death of Thomas Dunn. [*Docquet.*]

May 5. The like in Peterborough for George Day, in place of Richard Smith, deceased. [*Docquet.*]

May 5. Warrant to the Master of the Great Wardrobe to deliver stuff for liveries for the King's and Queen's footmen, littermen, coachmen, charioteer, and postilions. [*Docquet.*]

Vol. CCCLXXXIX.

1638.
May 5. Grant of denization to John Peterson Keier, mariner, Herman Parens, weaver, and John Nicholas King, born in foreign parts. [*Docquet.*]

May 5. 83. Parishioners of Lambeth to the King. They have authorized the churchwardens to present their general desire that their parson, for any rights pretended, may be left to the ordinary trial of law. And that his Majesty will excuse them from providing any increase of maintenance, their parson's living being worth above 200*l.* per annum in tithes, and no way impaired by new buildings, which yield by oblations and obventions more profit than the tithes formerly. [95 *signatures.* = 2 *pp.*]

May 5.
Whitehall. 84. Questions submitted to Serjeant Heath by his Majesty and the Committee of Trade upon a proposal to license all innkeepers to brew the beer and ale they sell in their own houses. The questions were, whether the innkeepers would voluntarily come in and compound for such licences, and pay a rent for the same, and how the permanency of such rent could be secured, and how those who refused to compound could be compelled to so do. [*Draft.* ⅔ *p.*]

May 5.
Whitehall. 85. Order of the King in Council. His Majesty being made acquainted that there is a certificate made by some of the officers of works and others touching the houses near Piccadilly Hall, which annoy the springs serving Whitehall and Somerset House, and that the certificate had been so carried that the Surveyor of Works had not been made acquainted therewith, which his Majesty finding to be a strange proceeding, ordered that the clerk of the Council should send for the certificate, and deliver it to the surveyor, who is to survey the said springs, and see whether a new way propounded for bringing the water to his Majesty's houses be fittest, or whether the way first resolved on, to demolish the buildings through which the water is to pass, can be made sufficiently good for that service, and thereof to return certificate. [*Draft.* 1¼ *p.*]

May 5. 86. The Council to Sir William Russell. The Mary Rose and First Whelp are added to the great fleet of 22 ships appointed to put to sea, and 1,394*l.* 5*s.* 4¼*d.* is requisite for powder, shot, and other munition for the said ships. You are out of the ship-money to pay the same to Sir John Heydon, Lieutenant of the Ordnance. [*Draft.* ½ *p.*]

May 5. 87. Draft minute for entry on the Council register, that Robert Middleton, son of Thomas Middleton of Leighton, co. Lancaster, having entered bond that his father shall show such arms at the musters as are charged upon him, was discharged from further attendance. [6 *lines.*]

May 5. 88. Bond of the said Robert Middleton to the King in 30*l.*, conditioned as above stated. [¾ *p.*]

1638.

Vol. CCCLXXXIX.

May 5.
Exeter.
89. Thomas Crossing, Mayor of Exeter, to the Council. A bark of this harbour, named the Prosperous, arrived on the 8th of April here from Morlaix, a place known to be infected with the plague, with a lading of linen cloth, since which time her company, both mariners and passengers, have continued in perfect health. At the request of the merchants, the writer prays order that the goods may be delivered ashore. [½ p.]

May 5.
90. Petition of Francis Waller to the same. Having been employed about his Majesty's business concerning New England, and having made oath before Sir John Michell of the disobedience offered against the king, as by the annexed testimonial appears, and having expended 20 nobles out of his own purse, petitioner prays the lords to let him have some relief, and to authorise him or some other to look after this business, and so call this proud disobedient constable to answer his contempt. [1 p.] *Annexed*,

> 90. I. *Affidavit of Francis Waller of Botley, mariner. By command of the Council, directed to the sheriff of Hants, for stopping the New England people's victuals, by command from the sheriff he went to James Alexander, high constable of the hundred of Mansbridge, the latter being a well-willer to the New England Company, desiring him to search according to command. The constable answered that he would search when he thought good, commanding deponent to be gone, or he would lay him by the heels, and the said constable kept away his warrant and order, whereby his Majesty's business was neglected and hindered. 5th May 1638. [½ p.]*

May 5.
91. Petition of Edward Henshawe, clerk, and Rebecca his wife, to Archbishop Laud. Petitioners exhibited a libel in the Court of Arches against Joan Maie, relict and executrix of Anthony Maie, executor of Thomas Maie, father of Anthony, of a legacy of 428*l*. 11*s*. 6*d*. bequeathed by the late Thomas Maie, and the cause being ready for sentence, Joan Maie has served them with a process of Privy Seal, and exhibited an information against them in the name of his Majesty's attorney, on behalf of Edward Maie, her son, his Majesty's ward, of whose person and estate she is committee, merely to weary out petitioners in that chargeable court. Pray order that, notwithstanding the said information, petitioner's cause may proceed to sentence in the Arches Court, or that the Archbishop would direct some course for petitioners more speedy and less chargeable remedy. [½ p.] *Underwritten*,

> 91. I. *Reference to Sir John Lambe to take order as he should find just.* 5th May 1638. [1¼ p.]

May 5.
92. Petition of Thomas King, vicar of Chishall Magna, Essex, to the same. Certain tithes given to the vicarage of Chishall Magna, by Adam Rumboll, and also the small tithes of the parsonage lands are detained from petitioner by Thomas Cooke, the impro-

1638.

Vol. CCCLXXXIX.

priator, and the evidences thereof were taken out of the church chest by the said Cooke, and are by him detained. Cooke has also divers times interrupted petitioner in divine service and sermon, and brags that he will make him fly the country, and has threatened divers who have been witnesses, that none dare testify the truth against him. Prays relief, and order that he may show his writings concerning his impropriation, and be further proceeded against in the High Commission Court or otherwise *ex officio*, in regard petitioner is a poor man, and the vicarage not worth 30*l.* per annum, while the impropriation is worth 200*l.* per annum. [¾ *p.*] *Underwritten,*

  92. I. *Reference to Sir John Lambe to take such further order as he shall find fitting. May 5th* 1638. [¼ *p.*]

May 5. 93. Petition of Thomas Whatman, on behalf of himself and the rest of the parishioners of Maiden Bradley, Wilts, to Sir John Finch, Chief Justice of the Court of Common Pleas, and Chief Judge of the Western circuit. Maiden Bradley lies in Wilts, and the tithing of Yarnfield, part of the same parish, in Somerset, but has always been taxed in all parish rates with Bradley. At Easter sessions 1636 in Wilts a rate made including both was confirmed, but a later rate has been made excluding Yarnfield, and including land of Edward Seymour in Somerset, whereby controversy has arisen. Upon complaint of Henry Parsons, one of the churchwardens of Maiden Bradley, at the last Easter quarter sessions, against Thomas Whatman, for refusing to pay the last rate, the court excluded all the said lands in Somerset from the said parish rate, though they lie within the said parish, and are nowhere else taxed, either to the King's Bench, Maimed Soldiers, Gaol, or Hospital. Prays the Lord Chief Justice to examine the premises at the next assizes, and in the interim to give directions to the sessions to forbear proceedings upon their last order. [¾ *p.*] *Underwritten,*

  93. I. "*I appoint to hear the matters in the petition myself at the next assise.* JOHN FINCH." *May 5th* 1638. [¼ *p.*]

May 5. 94. Agreement between Joshua Meene, vicar of Wymondham, and Nicholas Andrewes and John Smart, in accordance with terms stated in the order of the Archbishop of Canterbury and Bishop of Ely Calendared under date of 4th inst., No. 58. [⅔ *p.*]

May 5. 95. Sir John Curzon, Sheriff of co. Derby, to Nicholas. I received a letter from the Council, requiring me to review the assessments for ship-money of some particular townships. I made my assessments according to the usual course of the county, and charged no townships more than last year. Of these townships now complaining, none, except one, made complaint, but generally all the county complained of poverty and inability. Some of the townships now complaining had paid their moneys before they made this complaint, but are now provoked by Mr. Woolhouse, who the first year paid 10*l.* or 12*l.*, and is now charged but 5*l.* For the future the Judges

DOMESTIC—CHARLES I. 413

1638.   VOL. CCCLXXXIX.

of Assize, by command of the Council, have required the Justices of Peace to settle the rates of the county with equality, and to relieve those whom they see cause, and my warrant by the Lords letter was *pro hac vice tantum*. I desire you to acquaint the Lords with this much. [*Seal with arms.* 1 *p.*]

May 5. 96. Account of Sir William Russell of ship-money received for 1636; total 188,077*l.* 2*s.* 3*d.*, leaving unpaid 8,537*l.* 5*s.* 5*d.* Nicholas has added, that there was 588*l.* 6*s.* 3*d.* paid of the arrear of this year since the account of 24th March last. [1 *p.*]

May 5. 97. The like account of ship-money received for 1637; total 84,236*l.* 11*s.* 9*d.*, leaving unpaid 112,177*l.* 15*s.* 11*d.* [1 *p.*]

May 5. 98. Account of ship-money for 1637, levied and remaining in the hands of the sheriffs, being 7,300*l.*, making 91,536*l.* as the total collected, which is 8,756*l.* more than on 29th April 1637, and 22,079*l.* less than on 6th May 1637. [1 *p.*]

May 5. 99. Copy of a rule *nisi* in [the Court of Common Pleas?] for a prohibition in a cause in an ecclesiastical court, between the churchwardens of Wigston Magna, co. Leicester, and Sir John Lambe. [½ *p.*]

May 6. 100. Petition of the Churchwardens of St. Olave's, Southwark, in behalf of the whole parish, to the King. In obedience to an order of your Majesty and the Council made the 15th April last, petitioners, having assembled the parishioners, acquainted them with the petition in that order mentioned, and likewise with your Majesty's pleasure. The parishioners authorize us to pray your Majesty to refer our parson to the judgment of the law, whereunto we readily submit ourselves. [½ *p.*]

May 6. 101. Similar petition on behalf of the parish of St. George, Southwark. They pray to be spared any increase to the parson, and that he may be left to the ordinary trials and judgment of the law. [½ *p.*]

May 6. 102. The Churchwardens and Vestrymen of the parish of St. Thomas, Southwark (whose names, 17 in number, are subscribed), to the King. Certify that, in obedience to order of the 15th April, they had assembled together, and that the Corporation of London, governors of the Hospitals of Edward VI. of Christ, Bridewell, and St. Thomas the Apostle, are parsons of the rectory of St. Thomas in Southwark, and that all the profits of the same belong to them, and that they have elected ministers to serve the cure of the said parish church, and have made such allowance to the said ministers as has been agreed upon between them; and that in October 1627 the corporation elected Benjamin Spencer, clerk, to be minister, who still serves the said cure. [1 *p.*]

May 6. 103. Petition of the Parishioners of St. Leonard, Shoreditch, to the same. There are 400 acres of good ground which pay church

1638.

duties, besides orchards and gardens which pay tithe, and there is no abridgment of any tithes issuing out of any grounds upon which new buildings are erected, but rather an addition of profit to the vicar, by fees and Easter dues, and he has as much as any of his predecessors. If the vicar (who never yet demanded duty which was denied him) conceives any right detained from the church, it will require a decision at law. [*Signed by 51 petitioners.* = 2 *pp.*]

May 6. 104. The Churchwardens of St. Mary, Whitechapel, to the King. The parishioners under their hands have authorized us to return this their answer. Though they know your Majesty's wisdom and justice to be unparalleled by any prince in the world, yet they beg that they may not be pressed to any other way of determination of this matter than is afforded by your laws. Their minister's living is not incompetent, they being willing to secure him 400*l.* per annum. The increase of population has not increased his trouble, for the parishioners have built a new church at their own charge, and maintain two able churchmen to officiate therein. As buildings have been erected the minister's benefits have been enlarged. Within 60 or 70 years, it was not more than 70*l.*, now it is 400*l.* Ground built upon still pays the same amount in tithes. The greatest increase is of buildings erected upon Wapping Wall, not a place which formerly paid any tithe. Every house in the parish pays according to custom, and besides pays the Easter offering of 2*d.* for every communicant, and other fees. [$\frac{5}{6}$ *p.*] *Annexed,*

> 104. I. *Authority given by the parishioners of St. Mary, Whitechapel, to the churchwardens and vestrymen to answer his Majesty concerning the petition of the ministers.* [*Signed by 125 persons.* = 2 *pp.*]

May 6. 105. The Churchwardens of St. Clement Danes to the same. The parishioners humbly desired to be excused from making any such submission, and authorized us, the churchwardens, to report their said answer. [1 *p.*] *Annexed,*

> 105. I. *Names signed by themselves of parishioners of St. Clement Danes who authorized the churchwardens and vestrymen to give their answer to the King. 342 signatures; amongst them that of the Earl of Essex.* [9 *pp.*]

May 6. 106. The Churchwardens and Vestrymen of St. Martin-in-the-Fields to the same. The parishioners with one universal consent refused to submit, which we most humbly certify. [1 *p.*]

May 6. 107. The Churchwardens and Vestrymen of St. Margaret, Westminster, to the same. The same answer. [1 *p.*]

May 6. 108. The Churchwardens and Vestrymen of St. Giles-in-the-Fields to the Council. Certificate that the parishioners refused to authorize

1638.

Vol. CCCLXXXIX.

the vestrymen or churchwardens to return to his Majesty their answer, but answered they would make a "demonstrance" to his Majesty. [½ p.]

May 6. 109. Certificate of the Churchwardens and Vestry of the Savoy. The parishioners refused to return their answer in writing, or to authorize us to submit the matter in question. [½ p.]

May 6. 110. Authority of the Parishioners of Newington, co. Surrey, to their Churchwardens. To present to his Majesty that their church is endowed with glebe worth 40l. per annum, with tithes of 480 acres, worth 90l., besides other small tithes, oblations, and obventions, worth 40l., which they conceive to be competent, few country parish churches, as theirs is, being better provided, and the parson's predecessors living well and contentedly when the maintenance was far under. Concerning rights pretended to be detained, by which we believe to be meant our houses, we are informed that no payment is of common right demandable by law, nor was ever made in our parish, and that our case is not like that of London, the parsons there having little or no glebe or tithes. As for any loss of tithes of land by new buildings, which are few, ground built upon exceeds ten for one to the parson, by oblations and obventions. We pray that our parson may be left to the determination of law, the rather that our parish is over-burthened with poor. [85 *signatures.* 2 *pp.*]

May 6. 111. The Churchwardens and Vestry of St. Saviour's, Southwark, to the King. Set forth the state of the churchwardens in relation to the two ministers who serve the cure, and the parishioners who pay dues and tithes. The rectory of St. Saviour's, composed of St. Margaret's and St. Mary Magdalen's, was parcel of the inheritance of the Priory of St. Mary Overy, and since the dissolution has been leased by the crown to the churchwardens, for the use of the parish. Under the last lease the churchwardens were bound to pay a rent of 47l. 5s. 4d., to build a grammar school, to maintain a schoolmaster and usher, to pay 60l. per annum to two ministers, and to repair the chancel. Subsequently to the granting of this lease, the parish bought the freehold of the rectory for 1,500l., and the same was conveyed by letters patent to John Bingham, George Payne, John Treherne, and Philip Henslowe, as trustees. The patentees were bound by covenant to pay 20l. to the schoolmaster, 10l. to the usher, and over and above 30l. apiece to the two ministers. They now allow Mr. Archer, one minister, 50l. a year in money and dues; and Mr. Morton, the other minister, 30l. in money; the whole rectory not being worth more than 200l. per annum, and the parish owing 580l., borrowed to pay the 1,500l. for the letters patent. The churchwardens and vestrymen conceive themselves bound by the trust; and the parishioners having been assembled, beseech your Majesty to spare them from the required submission, and permit them to enjoy what they have purchased at so dear a rate. [=2 *pp.*]

1638.
May 6.
Whitehall.

Vol. CCCLXXXIX.

112. Order of the King in Council. Information was given that when the order of 15th April last touching the submission of 16 of the out-parishes in the suburbs of London unto his Majesty, as other parishes had done, was published in the church of St. Giles-in-the-Fields upon Ascension day last, George Winder, a messenger extraordinary of the chamber, in the midst of a great assembly of parishioners, in most insolent manner affronted Dr. Haywood, his Majesty's chaplain in ordinary, and parson of that parish, and Lawrence Whitaker, a justice of peace, when they persuaded the inhabitants to submission; whereby, and by his affirming untruths, the votes of the parishioners were diverted from giving satisfaction to his Majesty's proposition. It was Ordered that the Lord Chamberlain should call Winder before him, and examine him touching the said offence, and if found as it was informed, should take order for his punishment, either by taking from him the countenance of his pretended service, or otherwise. [This paper contains also the substance of the next two papers, as if it was originally intended that the whole three should form one order. *Draft.* 2 *pp.*]

May 6.

113. The like. Upon information that George Winder has erected divers houses in the parish of St. Giles upon new foundations, and having made a composition for them two or three years since has not paid the same, It was Ordered that Sir Henry Spiller and Lawrence Whitaker, commissioners for buildings, should survey the said buildings, and certify whether they have been all built upon new foundations or not, that the Lords may give order for demolishing the same. [*Draft.* 1 *p.*]

May 6.

114. The like. His Majesty and the Board having seen the answer made by the parishioners of St. Giles, wherein they refuse to submit to his Majesty for an increase to the maintenance of their minister, at present not much exceeding 100*l.* per annum, out of which the said parson pays for a house to dwell in, and to his curate and otherwise 60*l.*, It was Ordered that the Attorney-General, who is an inhabitant of the parish, advise with others of the parishioners to devise how the said maintenance may be raised to 200*l.* per annum, exclusive of what the parson pays out of it, or at least how a fit yearly addition may be added to the present means, and this to be done with all speed by such rates as the Attorney shall think most convenient. [*Draft.* 1 *p.*]

May 6.
Whitehall.

115. Order of Council. Sir Richard Wiseman by his petition complaining that he cannot proceed in the suit against him in the Star chamber by reason that he cannot have the processes of the court delivered to him without money, It was Ordered that if he will make affidavit of his poverty he shall be admitted *in formâ pauperis*, but if not the Lords will not admit of his pretences whereby to delay the proceedings of the court. Sir Francis Dodington and Mr. Leighton are ordered not to go out of town till they have been examined on Sir Richard Wiseman's part. His complaint

1638.

that he had been kept close prisoner five days longer than he ought to have been, the Lords are satisfied to be untrue. The order for his being freed, made on Friday morning last, was sent to him the same night. [*Draft.* 1 *p.*]

May 6.
Whitehall.
116. Order of the King in Council. Upon hearing matters in difference between the city of London and the new corporation, concerning restraining aliens, binding apprentices, and granting freedoms within the privileged places of Blackfriars, Whitefriars, Duke's Place, St. Bartholomew's, and Coleherbert [Coalharbour], his Majesty declared his resolution to maintain the new corporation in their privileges granted under the Great Seal, and ordered that the recorder of London and the two chamberlains of the new corporation should attend the Attorney and Solicitor General, who are to reconcile as many of the differences as they can, and particularly to settle a way, how a freeman of London may work within the new corporation, and a freeman of the new corporation within the city of London, and to ripen for his Majesty's further consideration such differences as they cannot reconcile. In the meantime all suits are to be stayed, and his Majesty requires the new corporation to proceed according to their letters patent and his proclamations, so as his service, and the good which he intends thereby to his people, may not be retarded. [*Copy.* 1⅔ *p.*]

May 6.
117. Draft of the same. [1¾ *p.*]

May 6.
118. The Council to the Bailiff of Blandford Forum, Dorset. The ship-money charged upon Blandford Forum for 1636, at which time W. Strechley was bailiff, is still unpaid, and yet he caused it, being 25*l.*, to be assessed upon the inhabitants, and might have received the same. We require you to let W. Strechley know that we command him either to levy the 25*l.* and cause it to be paid to Sir William Russell, Treasurer of the Navy, by the second Wednesday in next term, or that you bind him over to answer his contempt before us. [*Draft.* 1 *p.*]

May 6.
119. Draft entry on the Council Register of the appearance of Nicholas Burlace, sent for for default of musters at Berrynarbor, Devon. [4 *lines.*]

May 6.
The like of the appearance of Maurice Thomson, Oliver Clobery, and Oliver Read, of London, merchants, and George Lewin, of Redriffe, mariner, sent for upon complaint of the Guinea merchants. They are to remain in custody of a messenger till discharged. [*Written on the same paper as the preceding.* ½ *p.*]

May 6.
120. The like to Hugh Peachy, messenger, to fetch John Wiltshire, of Wilden, co. Bedford, and John Graienunce [Gray], of Milton, co. Bedford, constable. [*Draft.* ½ *p.*]

May 6.
The like to Edward Stockdell, messenger, to fetch John Starkeys and William Wright, of Latton, Essex. [*Draft, written on the same paper as the preceding.* ½ *p.*]

Vol. CCCLXXXIX.

1638.
May 6.   121. Richard Lane to Nicholas. Presents to him the condition of Northampton as it has been stated to the writer by the mayor and his brethren (*see* 1st May inst., No. 7). Desires the Lords' letters to the justices of peace of the county to take order that the town may be supplied with provisions fitting to relieve their necessities, as also with such contributions as may ease the heavy burden, and whereby their poor may be kept from straggling abroad, and some good order may be preserved. [⅔ *p.*]

May 6.   122. William Congham and Ambrose Money to Sir Hamon L'Estrange, Sir Francis Asteley, and John Coke. Acknowledge their offence in obtaining a patent for maintaining the quay in Wells Ducis, and their miscarriage towards the persons addressed; with their acceptance of the apology underwritten. [¾ *p.*]

May 6.   123. Minute of warrant of the Council to the Warden of the Fleet to set at liberty William Congham and Ambrose Money. [*Draft.* 1 *p.*]

May 6.
Gatcomb.   124. William Cox to John Malet, late Sheriff of Somerset. I sent to Higgins to receive an account touching the ship-money, and he has been about the country these five or six weeks, and has spent (he and a man) 40s., and can collect but 40s., notwithstanding he had extracts for at least 300*l.* The reason is, that upon the rumour of the judges' opinion no man will pay, but suffer their cattle to starve in the pound, or replevy, or wound them, if they see them taking any distress. Higgins was pierced in the back with a pike by a man whose name he cannot learn, as he was distraining, and has languished these ten days, and been like to die, otherwise he had come to London. I am persuaded I shall have the like account from others. I pray you acquaint Mr. Nicholas herewith, and know what course we shall take, for I see no other hopes but death, or what is as bad, perpetual suits, if we proceed in this kind. [*Seal with arms.* 1 *p.*]

May 6.   125. Certificate of 14 parishioners, including the late and present churchwardens, of Iver, Bucks, to Sir John Lambe, official of the Archdeaconry of Bucks, or to his commissary Dr. Roane. Hugh Lloyd, vicar of Iver, lately suspended for not appearing at the last visitation, was at that time prevented by a violent fever. [1 *p.*]

May 7.   Warrant to pay George Lord Goring 6,000*l.* with 189*l.* for interest, in satisfaction of two sums of 3,000*l.* paid to the Prince Elector Palatine in part of arrears of his pension of 2,000*l.* per annum. [*Docquet.*]

May 7.   126. Petition of Anthony Stanford and Bartholomew Bishop to the King. Petitioners have found out an invention to work iron of the first melting, known as raw iron, sow iron, or bloom iron, into perfect merchant iron or bar iron, without wood coals, stone coals, or pit coals (*see* 1st May inst., No. 10). Pray a grant for 14 years of

1638.   VOL. CCCLXXXIX.

the sole privilege of making iron their way, paying such moderate rent as your Majesty shall think fit. [¾ p.] *Underwritten,*

> 126. I. *Minute of his Majesty's pleasure that the Attorney-General prepare a patent as desired. Whitehall, May 7th, 1638.* [¼ p.]

May 7. Petition of Thomas Killigrew to the King. Your Majesty lately resumed into your hands a suit which heretofore you granted to Cicely Crofts, petitioner's late wife, who with petitioner prosecuted your Majesty's title thereunto in your Court of Exchequer [by information] exhibited by William Noy, late Attorney-General, against Sir Peter Riddell and others who have gained a great estate by intrusions into your coal mines at Benwell. The cause has received five hearings, and now a new information is ordered to be exhibited contrary to your Majesty's commands (*see* 12*th February* 1637-8, *p.* 247), for amending the defects and rehearing the cause. Prays a reference on the validity of the information to a committee of the Privy Council, and in the meantime a stay of the said order. [*Copy. See Vol. cccxxiii., p.* 292. ½ *p.*] *Underwritten,*

> I. *His Majesty will hear this business himself, and therefore commands a stay of entering the order mentioned in the petition, until he has declared his further pleasure. Whitehall, 7th May* 1638. [*Copy. Ibid.* ¼ *p.*]

May 7. 127. The Council to the Mayor of Colchester. You were required
Whitehall. to levy in Colchester 400*l.* for ship-money. We are informed you have neither paid any part thereof, nor given any account of your progress. We not only admonish you of your remissness, but require you to hasten the collecting of the said sum, and to pay the same to the sheriff, or the Treasurer of the Navy, by the first Tuesday in next term, or else that you attend the Board. [*Draft with underwritten memorandum, that like letters had been written to Maldon for* 80*l., to Thaxted for* 40*l., and to Harwich for* 20*l.* 1 *p.*]

May 7. 128. Draft entry on the Council Register of the appearance of William Baker, late surveyor of highways for St. Martin's-in-the-Fields, sent for on the complaint of his Majesty's surveyor of highways. He is to remain in custody of the messenger till discharged. [¼ *p.*]

May 7. 129. Pass under the Common Seal of the Council of the Society
Whitehall. of Fishing of Great Britain and Ireland, for William Upshire, of London, merchant, who had been sworn and made free of the said society, and was employed for the adventurers in the trade of fishing to the Isle of Lewis and other isles in Scotland. [*Signed by Nicholas.* ⅓ *p.*]

May 7. 130. The like pass for Hugh Cocke, of London, merchant.
Whitehall. [½ *p.*]

Vol. CCCLXXXIX.

1638.
May 7.
C. C.
[Coggs?]

131. Sir Thomas Penyston, Sheriff of co. Oxford, to Nicholas. Hopes his last letter may remove those ill opinions of his neglect and disaffection to his Majesty's service. He has 1,000*l*., and endeavours to return it, but his daily expectation of more denies him liberty to come up before next term, when he hopes to have a good addition to it. [*Seal with crest.* ⅔ *p.*]

May 7.
Stoughton.

132. Nicholas Stoughton, Sheriff of Surrey, to the same. I have received 1,450*l*., whereof I have paid to Sir William Russell, 1,150*l*., and to George Price by Sir William's order 300*l*., and there is near about 100*l*. remaining in my hands. The whole charge of the county being 3,500*l*., the boroughs of Southwark, Guildford, and Kingston are charged respectively 360*l*., 50*l*., and 81*l*.; what moneys they have received or paid in I know not. I cannot yet send you the parochial and ecclesiastical rates. Very many in divers parts of the county deny payment, and threaten the collectors with actions if they distrain them, whereupon the collectors forbear distraining, and desire to know how they shall be secured or saved harmless from such actions, and are not satisfied when they are answered that their warrant will secure them. I would therefore desire the direction of the Board herein, what shall be said or done to those collectors who refuse to distrain unless they be further secured, and what with the distresses; they cannot be sold, no man being willing to buy them. [*Seal with arms.* 1 *p.*]

May 7.
Waresley.

133. Sir John Hewett, Sheriff of co. Huntingdon, to the same. The country's averseness has caused my proceedings to be slow in getting money, a great part of which has been raised by distress, and that from several places and by small sums, which at last is come to about 500*l*., besides what I paid in before and what is in the collector's hands, noways doubting before this time to have brought it to 1,000*l*. Now of late the towns refuse to pay, and the collectors nor constables do obey my warrants, nor will come to give accounts of what is in their hands, but the bailiffs distrain, and one of them was told publicly by Oliver Jackson, a schoolmaster in Fenny Stanton, that neither he nor I had authority to distrain, and that they were fools to pay, and some there are that openly threaten to sue me, and I have been told by a constable to my face, they are not to pay now. Notwithstanding, I will not desist from distraining, and mean to bind over refractory persons, but without countenance and protection from the Lords, and some exemplary course to be taken with the contemners of the service, I shall not be able to do what I would. All my time I spend about it, and I have omitted all my own business, and stir not out of the country, but the success neither answers my pains nor expenses. [*Seal with arms.* 1 *p.*]

May 7.

134. John Nicholas to his son Edward Nicholas. Sends receipt for money received by Edward Nicholas of Mr. Byrch, and remitted through the writer to Mr. Lyttleton. Acquainted the bishop with Edward Nicholas's willingness to do him service, and that he would have waited on him but for sickness. He took it kindly, and has

1638.

Vol. CCCLXXXIX.

written to him. Edward Nicholas may do his country good, and especially that neighbourhood, who are much oppressed by the postmaster of Sarum, Roger Bedbury, the innkeeper of the Three Swans in Sarum. Sends copy of a warrant Bedbury has procured from the Secretaries of State. By virtue thereof he sends his warrants to the constables to bring in horses furnished, and to pay for their keep, and employs them, not in his Majesty's service, but to his own benefit. Leonard Bowles, one of the constables of the hundred of Alderbury, being required, brought in horses, and in his presence a minister coming to the postmaster to hire horses, he delivered to the minister one of them. The constable asked the postmaster wherefore the minister rode post, imagining he was not employed in his Majesty's service, to which the postmaster answered, he rode for a benefice, as he thought. If Edward Nicholas may prevent the postmaster's knavery, prays him to do so. Thanks for tobacco, and various details respecting a brother of Edward Nicholas, and respecting his sons, Jack who was at school at Winchester, and Ned at Gillingham. [*Seal with arms.* 2 *pp.*] *Enclosed,*

 134. I. *Roger Bedbury to the constables of the hundred of Alderbury. Recites warrant from Secs. Coke and Windebank, Controllers-General of the posts, dated 13th February last, for sending to Bedbury ten or twelve able horses from New Sarum or six miles compass. By virtue thereof requires the persons addressed to send on the 9th inst. six able horses with furniture, to be ready for his Majesty's service for two days and two nights at the charge of the owners. 5th May* 1638. [1 *p.*]

May 7. 135. Certificate of Henry James, Mayor, and three others of Totnes, that notice was given by Andrew Pawling, messenger, for the appearance of the corporation of that town in the Exchequer, to pass their accounts for casual profits due to his Majesty. The casualties mentioned are granted to that corporation by charter, and they are no escheators, but they are willing to take such lawful course in the premises as shall be fit. [½ *p.*]

May 7. 136. Certificate of Nathaniel Snape, Justice of Peace for Middlesex, that Roger Burgoyne, son of John Burgoyne, of Sutton, co. Bedford, had taken the oaths of allegiance and supremacy before him. [⅔ *p.*]

May 7. 137. Certificate of receipts and payments of the Court of Wards and Liveries between 1st March 1637-8, being the day of the last certificate, and 7th May 1638. Total received, 9,778*l.* 11*s.*; paid out, 9,311*l.* 18*s.* 3*d.* Among the payments were, 1,000*l.* to the Cofferer; to the Treasurer of the Household, 3,000*l.*; to the Prince, 2,500*l.*; pensions, 1,288*l.* 0*s.* 2*d.* The last were payments to the Duke of Lenox, the Countess of Anglesey, Lords Grandison, Willoughby, and Conway, Sir Thomas Edmondes, Sir Francis Biondi, Sir Benjamin Rudyard, and Thomas Bray. [¾ *p.*]

Vol. CCCXC.   May 8–24, 1638.

1638.
May 8.
Grant whereby his Majesty restores the ancient liberties of the honour of Peverell, cos. Nottingham and Derby, and declares that the jurisdiction thereof shall extend throughout the wapentakes of Broxtow and Thurgarton-a-Leigh, co. Nottingham. There shall be a high steward, a steward of the courts, two bailiffs, a chief sergeant-at-mace, and other officers to be appointed by the high steward. The Lord Goring to be the present high steward. A court of record to be held weekly for personal actions not exceeding 50*l*. The steward of the courts to make replevins of cattle or goods, distrained and unjustly detained. There shall be a gaol within the honour. [*Docquet.*]

May 8.
1. The Council to the Lord Mayor of London. Upon the late scarcity of coals, the same being at 26*s.* the chaldron in the Pool, his Majesty took order for a sufficient quantity to be furnished at 19*s.* the London chaldron, and required the oastmen of Newcastle to give the ships a speedy despatch. Complaint is now made by the masters and owners of the ships that the coalmongers in the city combine together and will not take off their coals but at under prices. We are by his Majesty's command to let you know that he expects that you forthwith take effectual order that the coals be taken off at a reasonable price and the ships despatched without further delay, or otherwise his Majesty will give order that the masters and owners shall be permitted to sell them to any such persons as will provide a way to take them off their hands. [*Draft.* 1 *p.*]

May 8.
2. Order of Council. Recites certificate of Justices of Peace appointed to survey the coals laden in the Margaret, already calendared under date of 2nd May, Nos. 19, 20. It was ordered that those who sold the coals at Newcastle take off the same at the prices they were sold at, and make satisfaction for the ship's time and the charge of lighters. [*Draft.* 1¼ *p.*]

May 8.
Whitehall.
3. The Council to the Lord Mayor of London and to the Officers of the Customs. The infection being very great at Morlaix, yet ships laden with linen cloth are at the present time arrived in the Thames, and others are expected from those parts. You are to give order that no such commodities be suffered to be landed, nor the seamen to come on shore until they have remained in the river full 40 days. [*Draft.* 1 *p.*]

May 8.
Whitehall.
4. The like to Robert Bateman, Chamberlain of the city of London. To issue out of moneys collected for repair of St. Paul's, 3,000*l.* to Michael Grigg, paymaster for the work. [*Draft minute.* ½ *p.*]

May 8.
The like to Michael Grigg. To receive the above-mentioned 3,000*l.*, and to pay carriages, workmen's wages, and other necessaries, according to warrant from Inigo Jones, surveyor of his Majesty's works. [*Draft minute, written on the same paper as the preceding.* ¼ *p.*]

1638. Vol. CCCXC.

May 8. 5. The Council to John Lisney, messenger. To fetch before the Lords John Bodington. [*Draft minute, dated* 1637 *by mistake.* ½ *p.*]

May 8. 6. Minute of pass from the Council for Roger Burgoyne, son of John Burgoyne, to travel into foreign parts for three years, with proviso that he go not to Rome. [*Draft.* ½ *p.*]

May 8. 7. Certificate of Henry Lide, Justice of Peace for Westminster, that Allen Henman, of Cambridge, had taken the oath of allegiance before him. [¼ *p.*]

May 8. 8. Minute of pass for Allen Henman similar to that for Roger Burgoyne. [*Draft.* ½ *p.*]

May 8. 9. William Pierrepont, Sheriff of Salop, to the Council. I sent up a month since 1,500*l.*, which is paid in to Sir William Russell, and the rest shall be paid with what speed I can. Many complain of unequal assessing, but most do it only to delay. Seeing the money was to be paid before 1st March I conceive I have no authority now to examine, but obey. Very many refuse to pay, most having only arable or meadow and living in other counties. I cannot have any distress till harvest, neither can attach their bodies. Many of the clergy desire only to pay where their glebe is, and where they live. Some whose times in their grounds ended in January are since gone out of the country; some are dead, and the executors refuse. I have often sent to the corporations, but have received none from them. The merchants of Shrewsbury promise to pay to Sir William Russell the next term 1,200*l.* [1 *p.*]

May 8. 10. The Nobility, Justices of Peace, and Gentry of co. palatine of Chester, to the same. Complain of the citizens of Chester having in their letter of the 13th January last (*see Vol.* ccclxxviii., *No.* 77) sought to blemish the writers in the opinion of the Council by traducing them. Reply on the various points raised in that letter, and especially respecting the assessment with the city of Sir Thomas Aston and of the liberty of the Gloverstone, and contend for the futility of the complaint of the citizens that they pay more than men of far greater estates in the county. Pray the Lords to move his Majesty that they may have full hearing upon all these points in his presence. [30 *signatures of the first men in the county. Seal with arms.* 2 *pp.*]

May 8. 11. John Batcock, of Hackhurst [Hawkhurst], Kent, tanner, to Marmaduke Moore. By Order of Council Moore was to pay to Batcock all such costs as he had lately disbursed. On payment of a competent sum Batcock hereby releases Moore. [⅔ *p.*]

May 8. 12. Certificate of the Auditors presented to the Committee for reformation of the household. After conference with the avenor and the two clerks of the aviary, the writers explain the nature and manner of the accounts of the said office, and state their opinion as to how far and with what modifications the existing arrangements should be confirmed by the committee. [2⅔ *pp.*]

Vol. CCCXC.

1638.
May 8.
13. Sir Thomas Trevor, Baron of the Exchequer, to Mr. Savile. Prays him to pay to his servant, Richard Winch, all moneys payable to Sir Thomas out of the Exchequer. [¼ p.]

May 8.
Taunton.
14. Roger Harvey to his brother, Richard Harvey. Acknowledges receipt of 4l. 10s. on May Day. Complains of some one whom he terms an "impudent, incestuous, epicurial atheist," as having devised matters against him; also of his mother, who devises matter against all her children save one viper who sucks her blood. [1 p.]

May 8.
Leicester.
15. William Heaward to [Sir John Lambe]. Reports various proceedings against ecclesiastical offenders in and about Leicester. The persons named are Mr. Hubbock, who has always been of a peevish disposition; Elizabeth Orson, whom Mr. Burden had enjoined her penance single in a white sheet; the midwife of Glenn, Amy Cooke; Mr. Willows's maid; Mr. Cotes, of Ailston; and John Angell. Suspicions that the registrar and Mr. Burden many times take mitigations and double fees, as much as they can get, and account to Sir John Lambe only for single fees. [1 p.]

[May 8.]
16. Information by [Sir Edmond Sawyer] of abuses practised by John Allen, purveyor and one of the grooms of the wood-yard, in reference to wood taken by him in 1635 for his Majesty out of Lord Craven's wood at Caversham, co. Oxford. The question is one of account. Allen is charged with having kept back 18 loads of wood for his own use, and also with having received too much from the King and paid Lord Craven too little. [1 p.]

May 8.
17. Answer of John Allen to the above information. He replies that the wood said to have been kept back was delivered at Windsor, except two loads lost at the wharf, and one which was burnt by the bargemen. He enters also into long details in explanation of the money account. [4 pp.]

May 8.
18. Certificate of William Cowper, late high constable of Hitchin, that he did not give Edward Thornhill any money for discharge of carts for saltpetre or coals (see 28th April last, No. 52). [=¼ p.]

May 8.
19. Similar certificate of William Papworth, another constable of the same hundred. [=¼ p.]

May 8.
20. Similar certificate of Thomas Papworth, another similar constable. [=¼ p.]

May 9.
Warrant for payment of 1,674l. 3s. 3d. to Charles Gentile, embroiderer to the Queen, for embroidering two rich beds against her lying-in, in 1630 and 1631. [Docquet.]

May 9.
The like for cancelling a recognizance of 200l. entered into by Thomas Weston and Richard White for payment of 160l. and 40l. according to a composition between the Commissioners for disafforesting lands and Thomas Weston for disafforesting the manors of Skreenes and Tichall, Essex, sold by Weston, the Earl of Portland,

1638.
VOL. CCCXC.

and the Countess Dowager of Portland to Lord Chief Justice Sir John Bramston; and for disafforesting of Dunmow Park, sold to Lord Maynard and Sir John Maynard; and for discharging Thomas Weston, Sir John Bramston, and Lord Maynard from the said 200*l*., his Majesty pardoning the same. [*Docquet.*]

May 9. The King to the two Chief Justices and the other Judges. To give strict charge in every county at the next assizes that the sheriffs deliver a perfect book of all such freeholders as they have, and that every bailiff deliver a note of all freeholders in their several hundreds and liberties to the Lord Treasurer. [*Docquet.*]

May 9. Royal Assent for Bishop Montague, of Chichester, to be Bishop of Norwich. [*Docquet.*]

May 9. Warrant for payment of 1,000*l*. per annum to John Hamilton during pleasure, to be by him disbursed for his Majesty's secret service, with revocation of a former Privy Seal for payment of 40*s*. per diem to the said John Hamilton for like service. [*Docquet.*]

May 9. 21. Copy of last preceding docquet. [½ *p.*]

May 9.
Westminster.
22. The King to William Baker. Recites grant of the 4th December 1635, whereby Robert Lindsey was appointed keeper of his Majesty's house at Newmarket for his life with the fee of 12*d*. per day, also keeper of the garden adjoining the same for the same term and with a similar fee. The said Robert Lindsey having surrendered those offices, the King now grants the said offices to William Baker upon the like terms. [*Skin of parchment much damaged.*]

May 9. 23. Draft entry on the Council Register of the appearance of John Bodington. He is to remain in the messenger's custody until discharged. [5 *lines.*]

May 9.
St. Mary
Magdalen's
College, Oxford.
24. Dr. Accepted Frewen to Archbishop Laud. Tubney is, as you write, a melancholy place, nor has your letter any whit amended it. By it I understand that you have designed me once more to be Vice-Chancellor [of Oxford]. Give me leave to plead my excuse. Dr. Potter is now, in the judgment of most here, perfectly recovered, and besides him we have many young governors in the university whose wits as they are fresher and their shoulders stronger than mine, so having never borne the office, they will take it as great a favour to be called to it, as I shall to be passed by. Two years I have already sate at the helm, little of it, I confess, in your time; I wish there had been more, I should not then be to steer now by a new compass, in the which no novice amongst the heads that is not as well skilled as myself. If this satisfy not I humbly submit, hoping that my readiness to obey my superior will teach others with whom I shall have to deal in my government to do the like. [1 *p.*]

Vol. CCCXC.

1638.
May 9.
25. Petition of the Company of Mercers of London to Archbishop Laud. John Poynter, preacher at Huntingdon, according to the provision of Richard Fishborne, mercer, deceased, being lately, by authority derived from your Grace, inhibited, petitioners thought it their duty, as intrusted with the managing of the pious uses of so noble a benefactor, to sue for the restitution of Mr. Poynter. Pray the same accordingly. [½ p.] *Underwritten,*

    25. I. *Reference to Sir John Lambe to give account whether Poynter were inhibited for any crime or because he came not in by a canonical way; and if so, how this business may be settled. 9th May 1638.* [¼ p.]

May 9.
26. Petition of William Cooper, priest, parson of St. Thomas the Apostle, in London, to the same. Petitioner lately implored your assistance against the churchwardens of his parish for refusing to bring in a true terrier of the glebes belonging to his parsonage, and found your Grace readier to assist him than he could expect. His cause is now depending in the Arches and in the Archdeacon's court. Prays a favourable word to the judges for their lawful assistance until the cause shall grow ripe for a higher court and judge. [½ p.] *Underwritten,*

    26. I. *Reference to Sir John Lambe and Mr. Archdeacon of London, to take order that a true terrier be brought in, and that they afford petitioner all lawful assistance. 9th May 1638.* [¼ p.]

May 9.
27. Bond of Henry Walpoole, of Skillington, co. Lincoln, to Archbishop Laud in 20*l*., for payment of 10*l*. towards repair of St. Paul's on 11th November 1640. [*Seal with arms.* 1 p.]

May 9.
28. Notes by Sec. Windebank of an examination of Capt. Steward respecting his having arrested goods belonging to the Spanish Ambassador. He was asked why he had done so. He answered, because the Ambassador arrested certain goods in Spain for which he had given security that they should be delivered in England. The Ambassador replied that this was no reason, for those goods were arrested in Spain by the judges there. The security that was given was good in Spain. [⅓ p.]

May 9.
29. Certificate of Sir Anthony Irby, sheriff of co. Lincoln, that Matthew Clarke and Thomas Knott, of Alderkirk, sued Robert Harris, chief constable for distraining them last year for ship-money, which much hinders the present service. [¼ p.]

May 9.
30. Order of the Quarter Sessions for Middlesex. On reading his Majesty's letters patent of 3rd January 1627-8, it appeared to be his Majesty's pleasure that John Chamberlain, of Lyndhurst, should not thereafter during 60 years be indicted for recusancy, and that if any indictments be that no process should be had thereon. It was ordered that his Majesty's pleasure should be obeyed. [*Copy.* ½ p.]

May 9.
Another copy of the said order. [*See Vol. cclxv., No.* 84. ½ p.]

1638. VOL. CCCXC.

May 9. 31. Bill of Thomas Stort, of Westminster, for payment of 17*l*. 4*s*. 10*d*. to William Davenport, citizen and barber surgeon, on the 29th September 1638. [⅔ *p*.]

May 9. 32. Certificate of Lawrence Whitaker, Justice of Peace for Middlesex, that Sir John Packington had taken the oath of allegiance before him. [¼ *p*.]

May 10. Licence for Thomas Brocas to reside with his wife and family in London or in such places of this realm as he shall think meet; granted upon certificate of Sir Simon Baskerville and William Goddard, Doctors in Physic, that he has been much afflicted with sickness. [*Docquet.*]

May 10. Safe-conduct for Giovanni Michaele Verani. [*Latin. Docquet.*]

May 10. Warrant to the Master of the Great Wardrobe for a livery or coat for Richard Eason, his Majesty's corn-sucker. [*Docquet.*]

May 10. Warrant under the Signet to Anthony Mould, licensing him to practise the curing of certain diseases in London or elsewhere, so long as he shall behave himself honestly and use no ill practice. [*Docquet.*]

May 10. The King to Thomas Viscount Wentworth, Lord Deputy. Recommends to him the speedy payment of arrears due to Sir John Ogle for himself and his officers and soldiers, by reason of his employment in Ireland, amounting to 1,464*l*. 11*s*. [*Docquet.*]

May 10. 33. Petition of the Moneyers of the Mint to the King. Your Majesty has directed the Attorney-General to draw up a charter of confirmation of such liberties as petitioners have always enjoyed. The neighbouring people to the places where petitioners live being offended at petitioners' privileges have endeavoured by complaints to the Greencloth to make petitioners liable to payments for lands by them enjoyed as other persons are, whereas these privileges are the greatest recompence for their service, petitioners having no more wages for their work from your Majesty than they have received these 100 years. Pray reference to some of the Lords of the Council as his Majesty shall think fit to consider the service done, with the wages received, and set down what immunities petitioners shall enjoy in respect of their lands. [½ *p*.] *Underwritten*,

> 33. I. *Reference as prayed to the Archbishop of Canterbury, the Lord Keeper, the Lord Treasurer, the Lord Privy Seal, and the Treasurer and Comptroller of the Household, to certify. Whitehall, 10th May 1638.* [¼ *p*.]
>
> 33. II. *Order of the first four of the referees, appointing the last Star Chamber day in Trinity term next for hearing this business. 23rd May 1638.* [¼ *p*.]

May 10. 34. The Council to Justices of Peace of co. Northampton. We understand from the Recorder of Northampton that, by reason the

1638.

VOL. CCCXC.

infection is much spread there, the country forbears to come to trade with that town, by which the markets are decayed, corn and provisions scant, and the tradesmen, although they go with certificates that they are clear from the infection, are not allowed to come to any fairs or markets, which strictness has forced divers of the inhabitants to fly abroad into the county towns, and the poor (there being no trade) cannot be long relieved without the help of the country. We therefore pray you at your next Quarter Sessions to take order that the town may be supplied by the country with all fitting provisions, and that some weekly contribution may be sent in during the continuance of the infection. [*Draft.* 1⅓ *p.*]

May 10. 35. The Council to the Warden of the Fleet. To set at liberty Thomas Crosse. [*Draft. Minute.* ½ *p.*]

May 10. 36. The same to Samuel Hill, messenger, to bring before the Board Matthew Clarke and Thomas Knott, of Alderkirk, co. Lincoln. [*Draft. Minute.* 1 *p.*]

May 10. 37. Minute of pass for Sir John Packington, of Westwood, co. Worcester, to travel into foreign parts for three years, with proviso not to go to Rome. [⅓ *p.*]

May 10. 38. Bond of William Baker to the King in 20*l.*, conditioned for his appearance before the Council to answer to whatsoever is objected against him. [⅔ *p.*]

May 10. 39. Instructions given by Algernon Earl of Northumberland, Lord High Admiral, and Admiral and General of his Majesty's fleet now setting forth to sea, to be duly observed by all officers and men in the said fleet provided for this expedition. This copy is addressed to Captain John Mennes, captain of the Nonsuch. Underwritten is a memorandum signed by Thomas Smith, that the Lord Admiral intended to have signed these instructions himself, but being prevented by sickness, his will is that Sir John Mennes should observe the same as carefully as if they had passed his own subscription, as also all such orders as should be issued by Sir John Pennington, Vice-Admiral of the Fleet, whom the Earl had commanded to take charge of the same during his absence. [5⅔ *pp.*]

May 11. Warrant to the Officers of the Household to allow to Sir John Winter, Secretary and Master of Requests to the Queen, 200*l.* yearly for wages and board wages. [*Docquet.*]

May 11. Westminster. 40. The King to the Treasurer and Under-Treasurer of the Exchequer. Warrant to pay to Sir Miles Fleetwood, receiver of the Court of Wards, 1,820*l.* 13*s.* 9*d.*, viz., 1,000*l.* borrowed by him at interest to enable the payment of 7,500*l.* mortgaged money, which with interest for 3½ years amounts to 1,289*l.* 9*s.* 9*d.*; 126*l.* 4*s.* 10*d.* disbursed in the year 1634 by Sir Miles Fleetwood and his servants when he made contracts with the tenants of the honour of Grafton, and 405*l.* 8*s.* 2*d.* disbursed by the King's command about suits in

DOMESTIC—CHARLES I. 429

1638. Vol. CCCXC.

the Exchequer between Sir Miles Fleetwood and Sir Francis Crane, late Chancellor of the Order of the Garter. [*Copy.* 1⅔ *p.*]

May 11. 41. Note of the sums specified in the above warrant as making up the total of 1,820*l.* 13*s.* 9*d.* [5 *lines.*]

May 11. 42. Minute for entry on the Council Register of the appearance of John Wiltshire, of Wilden, co. Bedford. He is to attend until discharged. [*Draft.* 4 *lines.*]

May 11. Similar minute of the appearance of John Gray, of Milton Ernest, co. Bedford. He is to remain in the messenger's custody until discharged. [*Draft, written on the same paper as the preceding.* 4 *lines.*]

May 11. 43. The like of Thomas Hall, of Bodicote, co. Oxford. [*Draft.* 4 *lines.*]

May 11. 44. Information of Lawrence Whitaker and request for a warrant to the sheriff of Middlesex, for demolishing a high fence or enclosure, being the beginning of a building contrary to the proclamations, in the fields at the back of Clement's Inn, near Louche's Buildings, which was twice forbidden by the Commissioners for Buildings, yet notwithstanding almost finished in the night-time. [½ *p.*]

May 11. Aston. 45. Thomas Whitley, Sheriff of co. Flint, to the Council. In answer to letter of the Council of the 25th April, received the 8th inst., states the contents of his letter to Nicholas of the 17th March last, calendared under its date, No. 88. Hoped Mr. Nicholas would have acquainted the Lords with what he had written, that he might have been freed from suspicion of negligence or disaffection to this service. Trusts very speedily to perfect the same, having now brought it to a good issue. [*Seal with crest.* 1 *p.*]

May 11. Lyme Regis. 46. Certificate by Anthony Ellesdon, mayor, and four others of Lyme Regis that notice had been given by Andrew Pawling, messenger, for their appearance in the Court of Exchequer, to pass accounts for casual profits due to his Majesty. Next term they shall be willing to take such lawful course for their answer as shall be meet. [½ *p.*]

May 11. 47. Francis Earl of Bedford, Lord Lieutenant of Devon, to Nicholas. Concerning Nicholas Burlace, charged with arms as a defaulter, upon certificate of Sir George Chidley and others, it appears that Mr. Burlace's estate in the lands chargeable determined upon his mother's death, so that he is to be cleared, and the arms to be levied upon those who have the estate in the land, stated to be a ward. So, for the present, his Majesty's service suffers, and the messenger's pains are unsatisfied. [*Endorsed,* "Enter a discharge." ¾ *p.*]

May 11. 48. Minute, for entry on the Council Register, of an order in accordance with the preceding statement of the Earl of Bedford, for discharge of Nicholas Burlace. [*Draft.* ½ *p.*]

Vol. CCCXC.

1638.
May 11.
49. Certificate of Alderman Sir James Cambell that Henry Chicheley, of Wimpole, co. Cambridge, had taken the oaths of allegiance and supremacy before him. [¼ p.]

May 11.
Whitehall.
Warrant of Henry Earl of Holland, Chief Justice and Justice in Eyre of the Forests on this side Trent. Whereas divers fines were set upon delinquents in the forests of Rockingham, Whittlewood, and Salcey, at the justice-seats on the 18th September 1637, and thereupon order given for issuing process, I have authorized Richard Batten to receive the said fines. [*Copy. See Book of Orders concerning Forests, Vol. ccclxxxiv., p. 11.* 1 p.]

May 11.
Taunton.
50. John Graunt to his cousin, Richard Harvey. The 10l. for which uncle Harvey had the writer's bill, he gave to the writer's wife at Michaelmas last; but, if Richard Harvey will have it, the writer will pay it at Christmas. You write also for a chest of linen of my uncle's. I protest I never had any. [*Endorsed*, "I wrote that I was content to forbear the money due upon his bill obligatory until Christmas next." ¾ p.]

May 11.
51. Certificate of George Lassells, late Sheriff of co. Nottingham. The Earl of Berkshire assessed to the ship-money in 1636, 10l. for the castle and lands he has in Newark, refuses to pay. Sir John Byron refuses to pay 3l. of his assessment. William Pocklington and George Sharpe, two chief constables, were collectors of ship-money, and refuse to give account. [½ p.]

May 12.
52. Minute, for entry on the Council Register, of the appearance of William Wright and John Starkeys, of Latton, Essex, potters. They are to remain in the messenger's custody until discharged. [⅓ p.]

May 12.
Cheeswick.
53. Francis Earl of Bedford to the Council. Has examined the account of William Hockin, son and executor of Christopher Hockin, for conduct money received by Christopher Hockin from the north division of Devon in 1627, and sums thereout expended for billeting soldiers returned from Rhé, and he has heard the objections thereto of Robert Yeo, deputed by the inhabitants of the said north division. Notwithstanding several orders for its settlement, Mr. Hockin's account stood open until he received an order of Council of the 13th April last, whereupon on the 30th April he repaired to Baronet Pollard and paid him 161l. 4s. 11½d. as the money remaining in his hands. Mr. Yeo showed that payments were alleged by Mr. Hockin to have been made which were not made, and insisted that the amount paid ought to have been 228l. 0s. 11d., and should have been paid nine years ago; wherefore he demanded on behalf of the inhabitants consideration for the forbearance and his charges spent on behalf of the country. The Earl adds that the King sent down money to repay the whole country, out of which Mr. Hockin, instead of 300l., received only 96l. 7s. 9d., which he paid out according to a warrant signed by Baronet Chudleigh, Sir William Stroud, and Sir Francis Glanville. By all which means the north division, being the poorest part of the

1638.   VOL. CCCXC.

county, and that where the greatest number of soldiers were billeted, suffered very much, as well by Mr. Hockin's indirect accounts as by not receiving their due proportion of the money transmitted by his Majesty. [= 2 *pp.*]

May 12. Commissioners for Gunpowder to Montjoy Earl of Newport, Master of the Ordnance. To deliver one last of gunpowder at 18*d.* per lb. to Thomas Frere, of Tower Street, ship-chandler, for supply of his shop. [*Minute. See Vol. ccclv., No.* 61, *p.* 6. ¼ *p.*]

May 12. 54. Account of Sir William Russell of ship-money for 1637. Total received, 89,926*l.* 1*s.* 9*d.*; unpaid, 106,488*l.* 5*s.* 11*d.* [1 *p.*]

May 12. 55. Account of ship-money for 1637 levied and remaining in the hands of the sheriffs, 6,900*l.* The total collected, 96,826*l.*, which is 25,263*l.* less than on 13th May 1627. [1 *p.*]

May 12. 56. Order of the Court of Wards and Liveries. By inquisition taken after the death of Richard Sankey the elder, in co. Lancaster, on 21st March 1636, his Majesty was entitled to the wardship of the body and a lease of a third part of the lands of Richard Sankey for the minority of Clare Sankey, cousin and next heir of Richard, and the ward was committed to Thomas Hawett. A third part having been chosen by Mr. Auditor for his Majesty's part, it is now ordered that the same shall be enjoyed in severalty by Mr. Hawett, and an injunction and writ of assistance are to be issued for quieting his possession. [2½ *pp.*]

May 12. 57. Certificate of Sir Francis Darcy, Justice of Peace for Middlesex, that John Offley, son of Sir John Offley, of Madeley, co. Stafford, had taken the oaths of allegiance and supremacy before him. [¼ *p.*]

May 12. Southwark. 58. The like of Richard Wright, Justice of Peace for Surrey, that James Furlong had taken the same oaths. [½ *p.*]

May 12. Funeral certificate by William Ryley, Bluemantle, of Mary Marchioness of Hamilton, wife of James Marquess of Hamilton and Earl of Cambridge, daughter of William Earl of Denbigh, and niece to George [late] Duke of Buckingham. She died at Wallingford House, near Charing Cross, on the 10th inst., and was buried at Westminster Abbey this day, in a vault with her grandmother the Countess of Buckingham. She had issue by the Marquess three sons and two daughters: 1. Charles Earl of Arran; 2. James; 3. William; Anne and Susan; all young. [*Copy. See Vol. ccclx., p.* 5. ½ *p.*]

May 12. 59. Herald's proclamation at the funeral of Mary Marchioness of Hamilton. [1 *p.*]

May 12. 60. Inscription on her coffin. [= ¼ *p.*]

May 12. London. 61. Certificate of Sir Theodore Mayerne. Lady Margaret Fleming has been long afflicted with an obstinate melancholy, with many very serious symptoms frequently recurring. It is very necessary that

1638.

she should have medical advice and assistance at hand, and that she should not leave town. [*Latin.* ¾ *p.*]

May 13. 62. William Boteler, Sheriff of co. Bedford, to Nicholas. I find so sudden and so general a backwardness in the King's service, that I must be enforced to trouble the Council Table with some delinquents; and if I find no better success hereafter I must repair to that Board for further directions. I lately sent a warrant to the constables and others of Tilsworth, pretending a special command to send them to the Council upon the 16th inst. If they appear, acquaint the Lords that the cause of their appearance is for disobeying my warrants, of which I have sent several, and could never have any answer until I sent this last warrant. Since then one of them came and brought a tax, but because they brought no money I refused the tax, and enjoined them to appear at Whitehall upon Wednesday next. I have also bound over John Gregory, of Eversholt, to appear on the 20th for refusing to collect and distrain. If the parties appear, and have respite to a further day, I doubt not before their second appearance they will give me satisfaction. If they do not appear, I desire there may be no notice taken of them until you hear further from me. [1 *p.*]

May 14. Petition of Sir Pierce Crosby, his Majesty's servant, to the King. Petitioner being by the Council on the 8th July 1636 committed until he should answer to an information exhibited against him by relation of the Lord Deputy of Ireland, upon suggestion that petitioner shunned to be served with process, where in truth the information being exhibited on the 5th July, petitioner appeared gratis on the 7th, and the complaint and order were not made till the 8th. Nevertheless, petitioner was apprehended by a sergeant-at-arms, and continued in restraint not only during his answer and examination, but until he entered bond of 2,000*l.* to appear at the hearing, albeit FitzHarris, the principal party charged in the information, was upon his answer and examination discharged without bond, having confessed the crime laid to his charge, whereas petitioner has cleared himself. Petitioner being indebted in England and Ireland, for which his friends stand engaged, was willing to sell part of his estate to free his sureties, and enable himself to follow his business, it being most necessary for his defence that he should have liberty. When he was to receive money of Sir Walter Crosby and others, the Lord Deputy sent for Sir Walter and required him not to proceed, saying it were to defraud your Majesty of a fine and himself of damages, which would be due on censure in the Star Chamber. Prays that his bond may be cancelled, and that he may sell land to the value of 4,000*l.*, there being left sufficient to answer more than can be conceived would be imposed upon him in the Star Chamber if he were guilty. [*Copy. See Vol. cccxxiii., p.* 293. 1⅙ *p.*] *Underwritten,*

> I. *Reference to the Attorney-General to inform himself whether, in case his Majesty license the sale desired, there may be*

sufficient estate left to pay such a fine as may probably be set in the Star Chamber if petitioner be found guilty, and to certify thereon. Whitehall, 14th May 1638. [Copy. See Vol. cccxxiii., p. 294. ¼ p.]

May 14. 63. The Council to Sir William Portman, Sheriff of Somerset. We hold it fit that the rate by you set upon the hundred of Abdick and Bulstone, being 280*l*., shall stand for this year, but in regard the Bishop of Bath and Wells and you could not agree in settling the same, we require you at the next assizes to desire the judges from the Board not only to settle the rate for the future, but also to examine the complaint made against you, and return a certificate to the Board. [*Draft.* 1 *p.*]

May 14. 64. The same to William Faldoe, messenger, to bring before the Lords Henry Ludlow, senior, of Tadley, Hants. [*Draft minute.* ⅓ *p.*]

May 14. Minute of pass for John Offley, of Madeley, co. Stafford, to travel into foreign parts for three years, with proviso not to go to Rome. [*Written on the same paper as the preceding. Draft.* ⅓ *p.*]

May 14. 65. Memorandum that William Hickman, of Barnaile [Barnacle?], co. Warwick, entered his appearance, with direction on the back to look out the petition for —— Watson, to be eased of ship-money. [= ¼ *p.*]

May 14. 66. Robert Benson, Clerk of the Peace within the West Riding of co. York, to Sir Robert Berkeley, Judge of Assize. The late clerk of the peace, two years since, made a particular certificate according to the Privy Council's letters, and I coming lately to the place cannot give such an account as you require. I believe there are about 2,000 alehouse-keepers licensed within the West Riding, and 500 more that brew without licence, most of them poor people, which otherwise would fall upon the parish. The country subsists chiefly by the trade of clothing, and the clothiers have their drink from the alehouse-keepers, and scarce one brews his own drink. Their servants drink a kind of small ale, about three or four quarts a penny. The west part of the riding is partly barren land, and replenished with clothiers that have spread themselves all over the country, as well in closes and parcels of waste ground as in towns. [1 *p.*] *Annexed,*

> 66. I. *The same to the same. More particular certificate of the number of alehouses licensed by the magistrates at the several sessions held in the West Riding since the 28th May 1637. The names of the magistrates are stated. At the first Sessions they were Sir Ferdinando Fairfax, Sir Henry Goodrick, Thomas Fairfax, William Mallory, Thomas Mauleverer, and George Marwood. Total alehouse-keepers about 2,500 licensed, besides unlicensed. Skipton, 14th May 1638.* [1 *p.*]

Vol. CCCXC.

1638.
May 14.
67. William Pierrepont, Sheriff of Salop, to Nicholas. I sent you long since what the several divisions and subdivisions in this county paid, and what every clergyman. I also sent a certificate about one Edwards, which my under-sheriff tells me he delivered to Sir Dudley Carleton. I request to know from the Board how to behave myself in these doubts. Hereafter, if anything be for me to know or to be done, acquaint my brother, Lord Newark, who lives in Dean's Yard, Westminster. [*Seal with arms.* 1 *p.*]

May 14.
68. John Nicholas to his son Edward Nicholas. I know not whether the bishop has yet heard from the Master of the Ordnance. He told me about a fortnight since that he had not from any man about it. He is now in visitation. Touching the postmaster, I will meddle no further if there must be such a business in it; but let the constable, or who else finds himself wronged, follow it and inform against him. It will be good service in any that shall do it, and good for your own understanding to know the ground of the warrant, and whether the postmaster may require the owner of the horse to pay for his meat two days and two nights. It may be my own case, for the constable has been with me for a horse. I put him off with good words, but how I shall do it again I know not; yet if it be too troublesome to you, I pray you meddle no further. [*Seal with arms.* 1 *p.*]

May 14.
London.
69. Receipt of Lionel Wake for 1,170*l.* received of Endymion Porter for Sir Peter Paul Rubens, by virtue of a letter of attorney concerning a privy seal of 1,500*l.* [⅓ *p.*]

May 15.
Licence to Edward Stanley to empark 500 acres of his own demesne lands within the manor of Bickerstaff, co. Lancaster, with free warren in all his lands, so as the same be not within any of his Majesty's forests. [*Docquet.*]

May 15.
Commission to William Earl of Newcastle to take into his charge Prince Charles, similar to the commission of James I. to Sir Thomas Chaloner, touching the charge of the late Prince Henry. [*Docquet.*]

May 15.
Grant to Adam Crosseley, Anthony Goddard, and Allen Calcott, his Majesty's footmen, of fines amounting to 260*l.*, imposed by the barons of the Exchequer on several sheriffs in Wales, touching false returns by them made upon his Majesty's process. [*Docquet.*]

May 15.
Whitehall.
70. The Council to the Mayor of Exeter, the Officers of Customs there, and others. Recites letter of 5th May inst., No. 89, and orders the release of the Prosperous, which arrived in Exeter from Morlaix in France on the 8th of April. [*Draft.* ⅔ *p.*]

May 15.
71. Minute of pass for the Conde d'Oniate et de Villa Mediana, ambassador extraordinary from the King of Spain, to embark at any port for his return to Spain, and that he be treated with the respect fit for a person of his rank, and be provided with carts, post-horses, &c. to the seaside. [*Draft.* ½ *p.*]

1638.
May 15.

Vol. CCCXC.

72. Minute for entry on the Council Register that John Edwards, sub-collector of ship-money in Weston Patrick, Hants, upon bond given to acquaint the sheriff with his proceedings in the execution of his warrant, and to observe such directions as the sheriff shall give him, was discharged. [*Draft.* ¼ *p.*]

May 15.

73. Minute of pass for Thomas Terrill, of Rye, to go into France with his sons William and Charles for three years. [½ *p.*]

May 15.

74. Certificate by Henry Michell, Mayor, and three others of Weymouth and Melcombe Regis, that the mayor had received notice by Andrew Pawling, messenger, for his appearance in the Exchequer to yield an account of casual revenues due to the King. The warrant bears date 21st December 1637, and was returnable *in Crastino Purificationis*, which words being blotted out no time of return appears. Heretofore they were summoned by the sheriff to the like effect. They are ready to answer in a legal way. [*Draft.* ⅔ *p.*]

May 15.
Twinhill.

75. Thomas Collard to his cousin, Richard Harvey. You write to me to be a means for 250*l.* which my son-in-law, Edward Luttrell, owes to my uncle Harvey. My uncle drew me to this match for my daughter, and persuaded me to give 500*l.* in marriage portion; Luttrell's suits in law have also cost me 300*l.*, and now I furnish him with 100*l.* for this trial next term. I beseech you to do your best in this trial, which if he gain there will be enough to pay you and every man. [⅔ *p.*]

May 16.

Warrant to the Master of the Great Wardrobe for delivering stuff for a livery to Peter Ireland, page of her Majesty's robes, in place of Hugh Pope. [*Docquet.*]

May 16.

Warrant to the Lord Treasurer to order the Officers of the Ports to suffer Margaret Douglas, wife of ―― Douglas, to transport several parcels of plate into Scotland for her own use. [*Docquet.*]

May 16.

Warrant to pay to Thomas Earl of Kelley 500*l.* as of his Majesty's free gift. [*Docquet.*]

May 16.

The like for installing the first-fruits of the bishopric of Ely after the rate of 1,921*l.* 8*s.* 6*d.* ob. qr., ½ qr., ⅓ qr. to be paid in four years, by the bonds of the bishop without sureties. [*Docquet.*]

May 16.

The like to pay to Thomas Powell, under-housekeeper of Nonsuch, and John Rogers, gardener there, 374*l.* 6*s.* 10*d.* for moneys disbursed about the said house and garden for six years last past, and for their yearly fees. [*Docquet.*]

May 16.
Whitehall.

76. The Lord Keeper, the Earl Marshal, and Sec. Windebank to the King. Report upon a petition of Lionel Earl of Middlesex (*see 20th April last, p.* 372). Find that the debt due on the 1st March 1627 from the Earl of Desmond to the Earl of Middlesex and Mr. Croshaw was stated and agreed to be 8,099*l.* besides charges,

Vol. CCCXC.

1638.

and that it was settled to be paid with future interest by 1,100*l.* per annum. The Earl of Middlesex complains that although the debt is not yet fully paid, yet by a letter procured for the Earl of Ormond, who married the Earl of Desmond's heir, the examination of the account is drawn over into Ireland. In our opinions it is not fit that a settlement made with care and pains upon your Majesty's reference, and with your privity and the consent of all parties, should be altered. But if the Earl of Ormond finds that the said settlement is not observed we think that whatsoever differences arise should be settled here. [*Draft.* 2 *pp.*]

May 16. 77. Order of Council. The master and owners of the Margaret, of Yarmouth, showed that according to the order of the 8th inst. they repaired to Mr. Liddell and others, the contractors for coals, to have satisfaction for the badness of the coals supplied to that ship, but that they refused the same. It was Ordered that the coals complained of be sold by Lawrence Whitaker and Peter Heywood, and that the contractors for coals, who by covenant were to send none but good and merchantable coals, are to make good the full price thereof, with such allowance for loss of the ship's time and charges as two indifferent men shall think fit. [*Draft.* 1⅔ *p.*]

May 16. 78. The like. William Castell, Francis Gregory, and Edward Saye showed that Richard Trowell and Edward Miller, &c., being, by orders of 7th March and 29th November last, to appear in the Court of Woodstock, and plead as Mr. Noy directed, or in default thereof judgment to be had according to the course of the court, Trowell and Miller would not appear, nor could petitioners obtain judgment. It was Ordered that if Trowell and Joan his wife, and Miller and Katherine his wife, should not, after warning given, appear the next court but one, the steward should proceed to judgment against them and direct execution to be awarded. [*Draft.* 1½ *p.*]

May 16. 79. The like. Sir Richard Wiseman having complained that the counsel assigned him by a former order refused to accept fees or be of his counsel, the Lords not only appointed but prayed and required Sergeants Henden and Warde to be of his counsel in the cause in the Star Chamber against him upon an information in the name of the Attorney-General. [*Draft minute.* ½ *p.*]

May 16. 80. The Council to the Sheriff of Middlesex. Recite information of the Commissioners of Buildings, respecting new buildings at the back of Clement's Inn (*see the* 11*th inst., No.* 44). It was Ordered that the sheriff see the same pulled down to the ground at the cost of the owners and builders. [*Draft.* 1½ *p.*]

May 16. 81. Order of Council. Recites petition of Dame Mary Powell, wife of Sir Edward Powell, praying for a day to be heard in the difference between her and Sir Edward (*see the* 4*th inst., No.* 48). The Lords appointed Friday the first day of next term. [*Draft minute.* ½ *p.*]

Vol. CCCXC.

1638.

May 16. Whitehall.
82. The Council to the Keeper of the Gatehouse. Warrant for commitment of John Starkeys and William Wright for giving ill language and reviling speeches against the collectors of ship-money in Latton, Essex. [*Draft minute.* ⅓ *p.*]

May 16.
83. The same to Henry Keyme, messenger. To bring before the Lords Henry Head, of London, merchant. [*The like.* ¼ *p.*]

May 16.
84. The same to the same. To bring John Watson, William Griffin, and Richard Baseley, of Fenny Compton, co. Warwick. [*The like.* ¼ *p.*]

May 16.
The same to Thomas Welch, messenger. To bring Joseph Carpenter and William Jeffes, of Priors Marston, co. Warwick. [*On same paper as the preceding. The like.* 3 *lines.*]

May 16.
The same to Robert Taverner, messenger. To bring Thomas Jeffes, George Jeffes, and Richard Woodfall, of Priors Marston. [*The like.* 4 *lines.*]

May 16.
The same to David Scott, messenger. To bring Edward Clarke, Edward Freeman, of Fenny Compton, and Edward Tompkins, of Bishops Itchington, co. Warwick. [*The like.* 4 *lines.*]

May 16.
85. Order of Council. William Pocklington and George Sharpe, two chief constables and collectors of ship-money in co. Nottingham, for 1636, being required by the sheriff of that year to give up their accounts, absolutely refused. It was Ordered that the sheriff should once again demand the same, and if they still refused he is to bind them over to appear at the Board. [*The like.* ⅔ *p.*]

May 16. Whitehall.
86. The Council to the Mayor of Bristol. By writ of 1637 you were required to levy 800*l.* ship-money upon the city of Bristol, and to pay the same to Sir William Russell. Although the time be long since expired, yet it appears by the account of Sir William that you have neither paid in any part thereof, nor, for ought we yet understand, so much as assessed or levied the same. We are by his Majesty's express command to let you know that the slackness of your proceedings so apparently shows your neglect and disaffection to this important service, that unless you pay in the sum charged by the last day of next term, we require you on the 24th of June next to give your attendance upon the Board, at which time, if you give not his Majesty better satisfaction, we shall take a course to make you more sensible of your duty. [*Copy.* ¾ *p.*]

May 16.
87. The like to the several Sheriffs for 1636 in arrear for ship-money. After recitals similar to those in the preceding letter; unless you pay the arrear by the last day of next term, we are to require you upon the 17th of June to give your attendance upon the Board. [*Draft.* 1 *p.*]

May 16.
88. List of the counties to the Sheriffs of which copies of the preceding letter were addressed. They are sixteen in number, and

VOL. CCCXC.

1638.

against each county is the sum then in arrear. Underwritten is a receipt for the same letters given by William Hewes, clerk of the check. [1 p.]

May 16.
Westminster.

89. Sec. Windebank to Hugh Peachy, messenger. Upon information made to his Majesty that, since the last commission of sewers held at Huntingdon, divers disordered persons in the great level of the fens have taken encouragement to interrupt the workmen employed by the Earl of Bedford in dividing his allotments, you are to make your speedy repair into the said great level, lying in cos. Norfolk, Suffolk, Cambridge, Huntingdon, Lincoln, Northampton, and the Isle of Ely, and there to apprehend all such persons as you shall understand to give any disturbance to the Earl's works, and to bring them before the Council. [*Seal with arms.* ⅔ p.]

May 16.
Lambeth.

90. Archbishop Laud to Dr. Accepted Frewen. I received your letter of May 9 (*see No.* 24), and take it extremely well that you are so ready to take upon you the troublesome place of the vice-chancellorship now a second time. If they who live under you be not as ready to obey you, as you have showed yourself to obey me, it will sooner or later prove their own harm. The truth is, I was in hope for Dr. Potter, but he is so full of an opinion that it will prejudice his health if not his life, that I am very loth to put the place to him or any man on such terms. I confess two years is enough for any man to bear that load, and therefore I am far from blaming you for making excuse. Besides mention of Dr. Potter, and your twice bearing the place, you put me in mind of some younger heads, which you conceive as fit for the place as yourself. I did not think of this latter part. I shall be ready to lay the load upon some younger head (the rather because these years will be fuller of trouble than ordinary, because of the statute concerning the examination of them which stand for degrees). I pray therefore send me word clearly, whether you had rather be spared. I protest you shall no way offend me, but I shall as readily admit of your excuse as you can wish me, and shall be as ready to serve your occasions either in the university or out of it, as if you had again submitted. [*Draft.* 1 p.]

May 16.

91. Petition of William Burton, Fellow of Merton College, to Archbishop Laud. Upon discovery of a false report made to your [our?] college by Mr. Fisher, sub-warden of the same, concerning waste committed by a tenant of the college at Basingstoke, upon woods there belonging to the college, and that the sub-warden moved the warden and company to deliver up a bond of 100*l.* which the tenant had given to make good the said waste, petitioner and Mr. Howson drew from the tenant a confession that the sub-warden had taken of him 5*l.* for sealing his lease, whereas not above 40*s.* was due by custom; and he further said that he would agree well enough with the sub-warden for his bond. Since the visitation the sub-warden has prevailed with the tenant utterly to deny what we have deposed concerning these speeches, and offered his oath thereupon. Prays that the credit of petitioner's depositions (to which

1638. VOL. CCCXC.

Mr. Howson's agree) may be supported by such means as the archbishop shall think fit; also that the college may be relieved, which has in this waste been damnified at the least 200l., and the tenant's bond of 100l. be paid out of hand or put in suit. [⅚ p.]

May 16. 92. Petition of William Hockin to the Council. Recites petition of the inhabitants of North Devon, respecting the accounts of Christopher Hockin, petitioner's father, for money raised many years ago upon the said inhabitants for conduct money of his Majesty's army. By a late order of Council the Earl of Bedford, Lord Lieutenant of Devon, examined all such accounts as petitioner had then in town, but petitioner could not then give answer without certain writings which were in the country. Prays that the Earl of Bedford may peruse the warrants lately brought up out of the country, and review the account and his certificate, and compose the difference, or certify the truth to the Council, and that petitioner may have his liberty upon security. [1 p.]

May 16. 93. Francis Earl of Bedford to Nicholas. Concerning the business
Bedford House. of the north division of Devon and Mr. Hockin, I desire to be spared, having drawn it to those heads in pursuit of the order that I conceive it fit for the Lords' final determination. [⅔ p.]

[May 16.] 94. Account of money disbursed by Robert Yeo in prosecution of the business against Christopher Hockin and William Hockin his son, for recovering the conduct money for the north division of Devon; total, 133l. 5s.; with underwritten memoranda that the same account was presented to the Earl of Bedford on 12th May 1638, and that the interest of 228l. 0s. 11d. found remaining in Hockin's hands amounts to 164l. 8s. [2¼ pp.]

May 16. 95. Memorandum of six Burgesses of Dorchester, that in the absence of the mayor and bailiffs notice had been given by Andrew Pawling, messenger, for the appearance of the mayor in the Exchequer to pass account for his Majesty's casual revenues. [½ p.]

May 17. 96. Sir Edward Osborne to the King. Since 2nd August 1634, which was my entrance upon the service of compositions with recusants in the northern parts, until 21st of March, I have raised out of that small number, which were left uncompounded at the Lord Deputy's departure into Ireland, 3,920l. per annum in rents, and in arrearages upon compositions the further sum of 6,284l., all which rents and arrearages are yearly paid to your Majesty. [Sec. Windebank has endorsed, "Delivered by me to his Majesty the 17th of May 1638." 1 p.]

May 17. 97. Petition of John Jennison, of Walworth, co. Durham, to the same. William Jennison, petitioner's brother, about six years since attended the Commissioners for Revenues arising by Recusants in the northern counties, to make composition for petitioner's recusancy (who durst not attend for fear of arrests), and condescended to a higher rate than petitioner's estate was able to bear, which was 30l.

1638.

VOL. CCCXC.

per annum, with arrears for three years, whereas petitioner's clear estate is not above 42*l*. per annum, and that only for life, which is all the means petitioner has for support of his mother, wife, and seven children, and payment of 1,000*l*. debt. Prays abatement, or order for the commissioners to relieve him. [½ *p*.] *Annexed*,

> 97. I. *Certificate of Ferdinand Morecroft (justice of peace and parson of Walworth) and five others, who vouch for petitioner as an honest and industrious man, and confirm the statement in his petition as to his means.* [⅔ *p*.] *Written under the petition,*
>
> 97. II. *Reference to the Commissioners for Recusants in the north parts to consider this petition and certificate, and take order for petitioner's relief.* Whitehall, 17*th* May 1638. [¼ *p*.]

May 17. Copy of the preceding petition without the certificate annexed, but with the King's reference. [*See Vol.* cccxxiii., *p*. 297. ¾ *p*.]

May 17. 98. The Council to Sir Thomas Leigh, late sheriff of co. Warwick. Send two petitions, one presented by John Orton, constable, wherein he charges William Hickman that he dissuaded him from executing warrants for ship-money, and that he would bear him out, and threatened him that he would undo him for doing his duty, and the other by Hickman, whereby he excuses himself. As the difference happened in your shrievalty, and you being on the place may better judge of the assessment and proceedings therein, we pray you to compose the said differences, or to certify in whom the fault lies. [*Draft.* 1 *p*.]

May 17. 99. Minute for entry on the Council Register of the appearance of Henry Head, of London, merchant. He is to remain in the messenger's custody until discharged. [*Draft.* 4 *lines*.]

May 17. 100. The like of the appearance of Henry Nowell, clerk. [*Draft.* 3½ *lines*.]

May 17. 101. The like that John Gray, late constable of Milton Ernest, co. Bedford, having entered into bond to pay to Robert [Henry?] Chester, late sheriff of that county, his arrears of ship-money, was discharged. [½ *p*.]

May 17. 102. Bond of John Gray in 30*l*. to the King, mentioned in the preceding article. [¾ *p*.]

May 17. 103. Thomas Coventry to [Capt. Charles Price?]. For Sir Richard Wiseman no plot can be discovered. One witness swears that Sir Richard said that he should be maintained in this business by a great man. Who that is appears not. The business will receive a public hearing. If anything more be discovered you shall partake. Lord Cottington's business is broken off upon point of portion, the demand being 6,000*l*., the offer 4,000*l*. His own addresses were rare; what he did was by his agents. I think it was never heartily meant. My brother Francis was married to Mrs. Cæsar on Thursday

1638.   Vol. CCCXC.

before Whit-Sunday. My Lord [the Lord Keeper] has settled upon him 300*l.* per annum out of an office at York, and 300*l.* more in reversion out of the same, but no land, but only to secure the 600*l.* in jointure to my sister in case she survive and the office fail; besides this, it is said that my brother is to have in money 1,000*l.*, but I am not satisfied of the truth of this. My sister brings in jointure and land of her own, in present and reversion, 800*l.* per annum. Mr. Alured, my Lord's secretary, is past all hope of recovery; not like to hold out many days. [1¾ *p.*]

May 17.
Mincing Lane.
104. Officers of the Navy to Nicholas. By reason of the Lord Admiral's sickness, we entreat you to move the Council to grant letters to the justices of peace of several counties for land carriage of timber bought for the use of the Navy, to be brought into his Majesty's yards this summer, which may be subject to damage if left in the woods, or at the water-side through fresh floods in winter. The quantity of timber to be carried from Kent, Sussex, Surrey, Essex, and Norfolk is stated with some particulars to be introduced into the solicited letters. [2 *pp.*]

May 17.
105. Memorandum of John Giggen, mayor of Wareham, and another, that notice had been given by Andrew Pawling, messenger, to the corporation of that town to appear in the Exchequer, to pass their account for casual profits. They further certified that the lords of the manor of Wareham claimed to have the casual revenues, and that their names were Thomas Haynes, John Harding, Robert Morton, John Fursman, and George Plucknett. [½ *p.*]

May 17.
106. Note of moneys disbursed by Dr. Richard Baylie, at the appointment of Archbishop Laud, from 16th July 1637 to 12th May 1638. Total, 124*l.* 6*s.* 4*d.* It includes carriage of fir-boards from London [to Oxford], 7*l.* 3*s.*; given to young Cotton by the archbishop's appointment for his journey to London, 10*s.*; and paid Mr. Richardson for framing and setting up the wainscot in the new library [at St. John's College], 50*l.* Dr. Baylie received the amount this day. [1 *p.*]

May 18.
Grant to Sir Richard Wynn of the prefines and postfines in co. palatine and city of Chester and county of Flint for 31 years, at the rent of 100 marks, upon the surrender of a grant to Griffin Lloyd for 21 years, at the rent of 20*l.* per annum. [*Docquet.*]

May 18.
Warrant to the Master of the Great Wardrobe to pay his Majesty's servants and artificers for service and wares delivered for the King's and Queen's stables. [*Docquet.*]

May 18.
Warrant to pay to Henry Weekes, paymaster of the works, 1,123*l.* 5*s.* 5*d.* upon account for work to be done in the new lodge at Hyde Park, according to an estimate of Inigo Jones and Thomas Baldwin, officers of his Majesty's works. [*Docquet.*]

Vol. CCCXC.

1638.
May 18. Warrant to pay to Henry Weekes 350*l.* for mending the brick walls and coping round about the court at Hampton Court, by estimate of Inigo Jones and Thomas Baldwin. [*Docquet.*]

May 18. A like to pay to Sir Philip Carteret 1,300*l.* to be employed in fortifying Castle Elizabeth in the Isle of Jersey. [*Docquet.*]

May 18. Grant authorizing William Watkins to discover and receive money heretofore collected in England and Wales by way of loan by virtue of privy seals, and still detained in the hands of the collectors, and to deliver the same to the Archbishop of Canterbury, to be employed towards repair of St. Paul's. The moneys collected in cos. Huntingdon, Lancaster, Surrey, Kent, and Carmarthen are excepted, having been formerly granted to Watkins. [*Docquet.*]

May 18. Protection for Philip Burlamachi and Pompeio Calandrini, of London, merchants, for six months from the 20th of May inst. [*Docquet.*]

May 18. 107. Order of Council. John Holles, Earl of Clare, complained that having impaled a parcel of his own land in Clement's Inn Fields, to lay materials in safety to frame a building to be erected elsewhere upon an old foundation, upon information to the Board that the enclosure was erected by night, and was intended to be a new foundation contrary to proclamation, warrant was given to the sheriff for demolishing the same; secondly, that his mansion being in Drury Lane, there were formerly adjoining to his garden two stables, which about February last were converted into two tenements, one by Seagood, the other by Turney, and chimneys erected, the smoke from which annoyed his garden and gallery. It was Ordered that Sir Henry Spiller and Inigo Jones, commissioners for buildings, should view the ground impaled, as also the tenements converted from stables, and return certificate of what they conceive fit to be done; also that the sheriff of Middlesex forbear to demolish the impaling till further direction. [*Draft.* 1¾ *p.*]

May 18. 108. The like. The mayor and others of Norwich showed by petition to his Majesty that the bringing of stuffs made of wool to Blackwell Hall in London to be searched, according to a proclamation lately obtained on petition of Christ's Hospital in London, and a report from the Lord Mayor and divers aldermen of the city, would tend to the overthrow of the trade, and undoing of many thousands of poor people, besides spoiling their wares, and great expenses in fees, carriage, and otherwise. His Majesty on the 10th instant referred the examination thereof to the Lords, who appointed to hear the same on Friday the first day of next term. [1½ *p.*]

May 18. 109. The Council to the Keeper of the Gatehouse. To release John Starkeys and William Wright upon their petition acknowledg-

1638.   VOL. CCCXC.

ing their error in reviling the collectors of ship-money in Latton, Essex. [*Draft minute.* ¼ *p.*]

May 18. 110. The Council to the Keeper of the Gatehouse. To take into his custody John Bodington. [*The like.* ¼ *p.*]

May 18. Whitehall. 111. The same to John Lisney, messenger. To bring before the Lords Edward Frodsham. [*The like.* ¼ *p.*]

May 18. 112. Draft entry on Council Register of minute of discharge of John Warde, of London, girdler, sent for by warrant for default in showing arms in Middlesex, on promise of future conformity. [¼ *p.*]

May 18. 113. Bond of Henry Ludlow, son of Henry Ludlow of Tadley, Hants, to the King, in 200*l.*, for the appearance of his father before the Council on 30th instant. [¾ *p.*]

May 18. 114. Petition of Christopher Hildiard to Sec. Windebank, Chief Postmaster of England. John Housman, postmaster of York, being bound to petitioner in a bond of 20*l.*, which was due the 29th November last, wrongfully denied payment thereof. His being postmaster privileged his person from arrest, but petitioner prayed licence to take legal course for recovery of his debt. [½ *p.*] *Underwritten,*

    114. I. *Order of Secs. Coke and Windebank that Housman should see this petition, and if he give not petitioner satisfaction in ten days petitioner might take his course in law against him.* Whitehall, 18th *May* 1638. [¼ *p.*]

May 18. Imbercourt. 115. Sir Dudley Carleton to Nicholas. Sets forth various formal difficulties in the drawing up of orders for regulation of the household, with the preparation of which Nicholas and he were charged by the Council. Solicits Nicholas's advice. [2 *pp.*]

May 18. Fenton. 116. Sir Francis Thornhagh, sheriff of co. Nottingham, to the same. I have sent up 500*l.* ship-money, as much as I could get in in a fair way. My forbearance has produced no other effects but refractoriness, but now I intend to proceed to distraining, which I hope will bring in the money more speedily, though not willingly. The arguments of Judge Croke and Hutton against the King for this ship-money have made men more backward than they would have been. It is reported that the King has expressed himself that he would have nobody distrained nor imprisoned. I pray write me what the Council would have done with those who refuse, that I may, as near as I can, satisfy the King's expectation, wrong nobody and keep myself out of danger. [1 *p.*]

May 18. Whitehall. Commissioners for Gunpowder to Montjoy Earl of Newport, Master of the Ordnance. To deliver 50 lasts of gunpowder at 20*d.* per lb. to William Greene, of London, merchant. [*Minute. See Vol. ccclv., No.* 61, *p.* 6. ¼ *p.*]

VOL. CCCXC.

1638.
May 19. Presentation of Brian Duppa, D.D. and tutor to the Prince, to the rectory of Petworth, void and in his Majesty's gift by promotion of the late Bishop of Chichester. [*Docquet.*]

May 19. Restitution of temporalities of the bishopric of Norwich to Richard, late Bishop of Chichester, he being elected and confirmed in that see. [*Docquet.*]

May 19. 117. Minute for entry on the Council Register of the appearance of Edward Frodsham. To remain in custody of a messenger. [*Draft.* ⅙ *p.*]

May 19.
Whitehall. 118. The like of discharge of Henry Nowell, clerk, curate of Great Plumstead, Norfolk, sent for by warrant for uttering contemptuous words against the business of shipping, upon his acknowledging his error and promise of conformity in all his Majesty's services. [*Draft.* ⅓ *p.*]

May 19.
Westminster. 119. [Sec. Windebank] to Sir John Pennington. His Majesty having occasion to employ the Mayflower, Anthony Leaming master, and the Providence, Thomas Stone master, both of London, in his special and important service, you are to stand with the whole fleet toward Dunkirk, and safe-conduct the said ships to that place, giving them assistance, and defending them in case of assault, and when this service has been performed you are to return into the Downs. [*Endorsed as* "Concerning transportation of powder." *Draft.* ½ *p.*]

May 19. 120. Account of Sir William Russell of ship-money received for 1637. Total, 93,596*l.* 1*s.* 9*d.*, leaving a remainder of 102,818*l.* 5*s.* 11*d.* [1 *p.*]

May 19. 121. Petition of Elizabeth Barnewell, wife of John Barnewell, to Archbishop Laud. Has been married to her husband two years, and borne him a child, notwithstanding which he has used her very hardly, accompanying with other women, and leaving her and her child unprovided for. Prays the archbishop to call her husband before him, or to refer the examination to such as may certify the truth. [¾ *p.*] *Underwritten,*

    121. I. *Reference to Sir John Lambe and Dr. Clerk as prayed.* 19*th May* 1638. [¼ *p.*]

May 19.
Burderop. 122. Sir William Calley to Richard Harvey. Gives him a variety of commissions for the purchase of livery cloaks, wine, sugar, almonds, olives, capers, salad oil, Dantzic sturgeon, a book or books of Foreign Occurrents, and 40*s.* or 3*l.* in single pence or twopences. [*Seal with arms.* 1 *p.*]

May 20. 123. Minute for entry on the Council Register of the appearance of Thomas Knott and Matthew Clarke, of Alderkirk, co. Lincoln. They are to remain in the messenger's custody until discharged. [¼ *p.*]

VOL. CCCXC.

1638.
May 20. 124. John Cutteris to Richard Harvey. Details various matters of business in relation to the management of lands of Endymion Porter. States particulars relating to Christopher Simpson, who had died in debt. Complains of the expenditure of Mr. Butler and Mr. Murrell, and anticipates with pleasure Harvey's visit to set things to rights. Hopes to see his master when the King comes his progress, for he comes within 30 miles of them. Requests Harvey to call for 10l. from John Weaskete [Waistcoat?], a scrivener, at the Naked Boy in Fetter Lane; old Mrs. Porter has the bill. [1⅓ p.]

May 20. 125. Fees for the knighthood of the Prince. The Earl Marshal in lieu of money was to receive the Prince's horse and furniture, the heralds 26l. 13s. 4d., and all the servants of the royal household in proportion to their station; for example the knight harbinger 3l. 6s. 8d.; the King's barber 1l.; the porters at the gate 1l.; the sergeant trumpeter 1l.; the trumpeters 2l.; the drum major 13s. 4d.; the coachmen 10s.; the jester 10s.; total, 78l. 6s. 8d. [1 p.]

May 21.
Westminster. 126. The King to Lord Treasurer Juxon, the Earls of Lindsey and Dorset, Lord Cottington, Sir Henry Vane, Comptroller of the Household, and Secs. Coke and Windebank, late Commissioners for the Admiralty. Commission appointing them commissioners for perfecting such business as remained unfinished in their time of execution of the office of Lord High Admiral of England, with authority to call to account all vice-admirals and others for any profits of Admiralty accruing since the death of George, late Duke of Buckingham, late Lord High Admiral, until the date of the letters patents lately granted of that office to Algernon Earl of Northumberland. [*Skin of parchment. 26 lines.*]

May 21. 127. Fees for the installation of the Prince as Knight of the Garter. The Dean of Windsor for his robe 40l., his fee 5l. 13s. 4d.; the Black Rod 40l.; Garter for his Highness's upper garment 60l., his fee 40l.; the canons 20l.; the choir and choristers 12l.; the poor knights 20l.; officers of arms 40l.; various gratuities to the servants of the household. [1 p.]

May 21. 128. Copy of the preceding, but without the gratuities to the servants. [⅔ p.]

May 21.
Taunton. 129. Roger Harvey to his brother, Richard Harvey. Mrs. Rowe is returned for recusancy. She lives sometimes in Dorsetshire, sometimes in Somerset, and sometimes by stealth in Devon, in papists' houses. She is now at Chideock to be near Plucknett, her brother-in-law, who follows the suit for her. She was no married wife, for her father gave her an estate of 30l. per annum, upon condition that if she married the writer's uncle Jerome it was to go to George Rowe and his children. Mr. Sturton and his wife are both living; he has passed away his farm to his daughter. My mother was here last night. I privately acquainted her with the letter sent in her name. It was written without her privity. There is the foulest matter

1638.

like to come against Snow that ever I heard of since I was born, a most incestuous thing. Although he be a base fellow, I will prevent the prosecution thereof if I can. [1 p.]

May 21. 130. Certificate of Henry Carter, churchwarden, and seven others of Priors Marston, co. Warwick, that George Jeffes of that place is 70 years of age, lame, and not able to ride on horseback or go on foot to London without danger of his life. [½ p.]

May 21. 131. See "Returns made by Justices of Peace."

May 22. 132. The Council to Dr. Robert Mason, chancellor of the diocese of Winchester, and to the Surrogate in the Consistory Court there. We send a petition of the parishioners of Gatcombe in the Isle of Wight, and likewise a certificate from you Dr. Mason, by which you will perceive that through the averseness of Mr. Worsley, lord of the manor of Gatcombe, the church there has become very ruinous, and in such decay that the minister in stormy weather must read the service in his seat. An assessment being made in the parish for repair of the church, Worsley not only refuses to pay the rates set upon him, but withholds also the church-house and a piece of land thereto belonging, which he has converted to his own use, and albeit he has been presented by the churchwardens, yet, being rich, he delays and wearies the parishioners with vexatious suits in such sort as the church runs daily to further decay. We recommend this business to your consideration, requiring you to take effectual order therein, so that the church may be repaired and the church-house and land restored, and that no man's potency or refractoriness should prevail to defer the course of justice. [*Draft.* 1⅓ p.]

May 22. 133. The same to [William Pierrepont] Sheriff of Salop. Francis Watson, of Church Aston, co. Salop, complains that the assessors of the ship-money in Great Bolas have, to ease themselves and friends, assessed some for one plough-land under 10s., some at 13s. 4d., and himself for less than two plough-lands at 5l. You are to call the parties before you, and if you find the allegations true, to cause a new assessment to be made. [*Draft.* 1 p.]

May 22. 134. The same to John Lisney, messenger, to bring before the Lords James Zouch. [*Draft minute.* 1 p.]

May 22. 135. William Cooke to Nicholas. Prays him to procure appointment for Richard Cooke, the writer's son, as boatswain's deputy in the Anne. Is indebted to Nicholas for his warrant for this voyage. He will give satisfaction for both. They wait hourly to be gone. [⅔ p.]
Tilbury Hope.

May 22. 136. William Calley to Richard Harvey. Wishes him to buy for the writer and his wife certain quantities of Holland, some of it for handkerchiefs, linen boot hose, linen socks, white gloves, a black tiffany hood, and an ounce of the best hard wax. The writer is almost out of conceit with "wafer." This day there is like to be a very
Burderop.

1638. VOL. CCCXC.

bloody battle between cocks at Marlborough. Mr. Hawkins the clothier died about Easter last, worth 10,000*l.* [⅔ *p.*]

May 22.
Burderop.
137. Sir William Calley to Richard Harvey. Further commission for six good table knives without a case. Underwritten are various memoranda by Harvey respecting the articles to be purchased for the Calleys, and on the fly-leaf are laid down five patterns of lace. [2 *pp.*]

May 22.
Taunton.
138. Roger Harvey to the same. When he made his last letter, knew not of his sister's sudden going for London. She comes by herself with the carrier. Her husband comes not these ten days. Hopes he will advise her. They have dealt very hardly with her at the old house. [¾ *p.*]

May 23.
Grant in reversion of the office of Filazer in the Common Pleas to John Ekyns, one of the clerks of that court, in consideration that John Bell, who married Agnes, late wife of John Milward, D.D., to whom the late King granted a pension of 100*l.*, payable out of the Exchequer in Scotland, in consideration of her husband's preaching the gospel in that kingdom, has released to his Majesty 1,000*l.*, being the arrears of the said pension. [*Docquet.*]

May 23.
Grant to Ralph Crathorne of the benefit of a bond of 400*l.*, entered into by George Thwing to the said Crathorne, in trust for William Clitherow, a Romish priest, condemned in a premunire, for payment of 200*l.*, who by his will disposed of the same for payment of his debts and legacies to his servants, &c., which the said Thwing refused to pay. His Majesty grants to Crathorne all his interest, to the intent he should pay the debts and legacies of Clitherow. [*Docquet.*]

May 23.
Pardon to Thomas Ashmole, attorney-at-law, of a fine of 100*l.* and other punishment imposed on him in Hilary term 1635, by the Court of King's Bench, for offences for which he was indicted, he having suffered imprisonment for the same ever since, and being utterly unable to pay his fine. [*Docquet.*]

May 23.
Grant to Sir William Waller and his heirs, in fee, of the castle of Winchester and forest of Westbeare, with coppice woods there and in Parneholt, Hants, upon surrender of a former grant thereof made to Jerome Earl of Portland and the Lady Frances his wife, and their heirs male in tail. [*Docquet.*]

May 23.
Warrant to the Earl of Holland, the Earl of Dorset, and others, feoffees in trust for the Queen's use, by an assignment from Sir John Walter, Sir James Fullerton, and Sir Thomas Trevor, of their interest in a remainder of an estate of 99 years in the manors of Somersham, Fenton, Bluntisham, Colne, and Earith, co. Huntingdon, to convey the same to Henry Jermyn, containing in all 1,125 acres, reserving a rent of 20*l.* per annum. [*Docquet.*]

Vol. CCCXC.

1638.
May 23.

139. Order of Council. By orders of the Board of the 7th of July, commissions were awarded to Mr. Justice Crawley, Sir John Jennings, Mr. Wingate, and Mr. Vaux, to examine what damage the freeholders of Caddington, cos. Hertford and Bedford, were like to sustain by enclosing the commons of that place, and also to certify what contempts had been committed against former orders. The commissioners had held many meetings, but had not certified. On petition of the freeholders of Caddington the Lords prayed the commissioners, if ready, to return certificate as desired, but no stop is to be made of any proceedings in that work. [*Draft.* 1¼ *p.*]

May 23.

140. The like. Robert Lewes, by petition, showed that in April last he presented a petition in the names of Thomas Smith and others, wherein they complained of Thomas Roberts, of South Newington, and Thomas Hall, of Bodicot, co. Oxford, for undutiful speeches against the Board in general and Mr. Comptroller in particular, whereupon Roberts and Hall were sent for by warrant, and proof made of the words spoken. It was now Ordered that Roberts and Hall upon payment of fees be discharged with this intimation, that if hereafter they behave themselves otherwise than becomes good subjects and civil men, the Lords will direct such a course as they shall be made better to know themselves. [*Draft.* 1¼ *p.*]

May 23.

141. The like. Arthur Morehead, master of his Majesty's free school in the Isle of Guernsey, by petition showed that Queen Elizabeth erected the said school, and gave unto it a certain church, churchyard and land belonging of old to the Friars Cordeliers, as also with certain rents of wheat out of her Majesty's own receipt, all which have since been taken away from the school, and are in the possession of the jurats of the said isle, their children and kinsmen, and part of the rents lost, and the rest in danger. The Lords prayed the Earl of Danby, governor of the isle, to consider these particulars and put the matter in some good way for redress, or else to certify the Board. [*Draft.* 2 *pp.*]

May 23.

142. The like. William Grimes and Agnes his wife, sister to Archibald Armstrong, late his Majesty's jester, by petition complained that Archibald 14 years since possessed himself of the estate of James Armstrong, his brother, to a great value, out of which there was given to Agnes 60*l.*, to her son 30*l.*, and 30*l.* more for the "crowner's" fees and his burial. Archibald, by the power and countenance of his coat and prince [place?], has hitherto detained the money from Agnes and petitioner Grimes, who for three years have in these parts and in Ireland waited upon Archibald, in hope by fair means to get satisfaction, and accordingly Archibald in Ireland promised to settle petitioner in 100 acres of land, part of 1,000 acres which his Majesty had bestowed on him, but now refuses. It was Ordered that Henry Lide and Peter Heywood, justices of peace for Westminster, call the parties before them and make a final end of the difference, or else certify the Board. [*Draft.* 1½ *p.*]

1638. VOL. CCCXC.

May 23. 143. Order of Council. Robert Lee, Richard Ford, John Watkins, and Nathaniel Musgrave, constables, &c. of Gravesend and Milton, Kent, showed by petition that they are prosecuted in the King's Bench by Walter Rugg, a waterman, who was apprehended for escaping from his Majesty's ships, being pressed for the service, and they doing nothing but what they had warrant for. The Lords Ordered Sir William Russell, Sir Henry Palmer, and the rest of the Officers of the Navy, to call the parties before them, and end their differences, if they can, or else to certify the Board. [*Draft.* ¾ *p.*]

May 23. 144. Like order. Recites report of the Dean and Chapter of Bristol upon a reference to them of a complaint made by Charles Powell, that Edward Hobbes detained a rent from him of 20 nobles per annum for an almsman's place belonging to the cathedral of Bristol (*see* Calendar for 12th April 1638, No. 61). It was Ordered that the dean and chapter see Hobbes quietly settled in the said place. [*Draft.* ¾ *p.*]

May 23. 145. Like order. On complaint of the Merchants Adventurers of Newcastle-upon-Tyne, touching impositions laid upon them at Rotterdam by the Merchants Adventurers of London, the Lords gave time to the Merchants Adventurers of London to bring from the three Lords Chief Justices such certificate as was required by two former orders. Such certificate not being yet returned, petitioners prayed that the moneys seized of them at Hamburgh and Rotterdam for the said impositions may be restored, and themselves be discharged from all charges laid by the Merchants Adventurers of London, other than the 8*l.* per annum anciently paid. It was Ordered that the Lords Chief Justices certify why they have not returned their certificate, and whether it has been through default of the Merchants Adventurers of London. [*Draft.* 1 *p.*]

May 23. Whitehall. 146. Like order. Edward Gregge, having been found a delinquent by vending great quantities of tobacco without licence, was thereupon fined by the Commissioners for Tobacco 5*l.*, and required to take out a licence, or enter bond to sell no more tobacco by retail. In contempt of the commission he refuses to submit, and having been convented before the Lords, It was Ordered that he should pay the fine set upon him by the commissioners, and enter into bond as they had directed, which being performed, and fees paid, he is to be discharged; but if he shall refuse, the messenger is to keep him in custody, and to acquaint the Board with his refractoriness at their next meeting. [*Copy.* 1¼ *p.*]

May 23. 147. Draft of the same. [1¼ *p.*]

May 23. 148. Like order. After reciting previous proceedings in relation to the matter in difference between the north division of Devon and William Hockin, executor of Christopher Hockin, of Great Torrington, and especially the certificate of the Earl of Bedford, calendared under date of the 12th inst., No. 53, It was Ordered that William Hockin should deposit in the hands of the Earl of Bedford the said

1638.

Vol. CCCXC.

228*l*. 0*s*. 11*d*. conduct money detained, as also 133*l*. 5*s*. expended in prosecution of this business. And whereas William Hockin pretends to have received out of the country, since the former hearing by the Earl of Bedford, divers material writings relating to this business, he is to attend the Earl therewith, who is prayed to take the same into consideration, and if he shall see cause to alter his former certificate, or allow back any part of the sums above mentioned, the Board authorizes him to cause the same to be allowed. [*Draft.* 2¼ *pp.*]

May 23.
Whitehall.

149. The Council to Lawrence Whitaker. There are divers books and writings belonging to Edward Frodsham now in his chamber in a turner's house near Charing Cross, which may much concern his Majesty's service. You are to repair to the same place, and having taken the same writings into your custody, you are to deliver the same to the Attorney-General. [*Draft.* ¾ *p.*]

May 23.

150. Order of Council. Recites the reference to Sir William Becher and Edward Nicholas of the difference between Valentine Saunders and Sir Gregory Norton, relative to the division of 125 tons of soap, and the report of the said referees, calendared under the date of the 9th March last, No. 45. It is Ordered that the parties above-named conform themselves thereunto, and that the Lords' directions therein be entered in the Register of Council Causes. [*Draft.* 1 *p.*]

May 23.

151. The Council to Edmond Barker, messenger, to bring before the Board Thomas Phelps, of St. Martin's, coachmaker. [*Draft minute.* ⅔ *p.*]

May 23.

152. Minute for entry on the Council Register of the appearance of Richard Bret, of St. Martin's, London, sent for, for not showing arms. On promise of conformity he was discharged. [*Draft.* ¼ *p.*]

May 23.

153. Order of Council. Recites order of reference to the Solicitor-General and Dr. Ryves of the matter in difference between John Blanche and Peter Gosselin, Francis Tribert, and others, and the report of the referees, calendared under its date of 6th April last, No. 32, I. It is Ordered that the jurats of Guernsey, within 14 days after sight hereof, give execution, and that the Lieutenant-Governor see execution done, and Blanche set at liberty, and also tax the costs and the charges of imprisonment sustained by Blanche, and see the same allowed to him. [*Draft.* 1¼ *p.*]

May 23.

154. Like order. The petition of John de la Barre about ordnance seized by John Browne, his Majesty's gunfounder, in answer to the objections of the said Browne, being read, it was ordered that the Earl of Newport and the Officers of the Ordnance examine the particulars, and if the allegations be true, take order for petitioner's relief. [*Draft.* ⅔ *p.*]

May 23.

155. Petition of Francis Newton, one of the messengers for apprehending Jesuits and seminary priests, to the Council. His Majesty

DOMESTIC—CHARLES I.

1638.   VOL. CCCXC.

referred to the Lords a petition stated to be annexed, that they might set down what allowances they thought fit for petitioner for his disbursements and services, and give order for payment, which reference he has been driven to forbear by reason that his house was visited with the sickness. [½ p.] *Underwritten,*

    155. I. *Reference by the Council to Sec. Coke, to set down such allowance as he thinks good. Whitehall, 23rd May 1638.* [¼ p.]

    155. II. *Report of Sec. Coke to the Council. I think fit to allow 200 marks besides the vestments which are given him by the Lords. 5th July 1638.* [¼ p.]

May 23.
Whitehall.

156. James Marquis of Hamilton to Sec. [Windebank?]. Notwithstanding the difference between Old Rookes and Mr. Morgan, concerning the searcher's place of Dover, has been ordered by his Majesty to be determined by law [*See Vol. ccclvii., Nos. 17 and 24*], I doubt in my absence Rookes will be busy, as formerly he has been, to procure some new reference. If any such thing happen, I earnestly entreat you to put his Majesty in mind what has passed. [½ p.]

May 23.
Vale Royal.

157. Thomas Cholmondeley, Sheriff of Chester, to Nicholas. When I wrote last I hoped to make a quicker address than yet I can do. The general bruit of the late arguments of those judges who have concluded against the ship-money is so plausibly received by those who were before too refractory and countenanced by some of rank, that I have found more difficulty in that poor remain yet uncollected than in all the rest. The service is so far advanced that I hope this little remainder will not be much noted. Herein I shall entreat your friendly advice as to one desirous to advance his Majesty's service without just grievance of the subject. [¾ p.]

May 23.

158. Answer of Francis Lord Mountnorris to petition of James Zouch (*see 2nd May inst., No. 15*). He never menaced Zouch to sue him in the Star Chamber concerning the settling of his estate, but Zouch being married to his daughter, with whom defendant gave 2,000*l.* in portion, he had, at Zouch's request, taken great pains for settling his estate and payment of his debts, and had disbursed divers sums of money to stop the cries of his creditors, and had received many thankful acknowledgments from him. There having been a long treaty for settlement of the differences between Zouch and his mother concerning the executorship of Sir Edward Zouch, writings were perfected between them on the 20th April 1638, in which Lord Wimbledon and George Duncombe, on the part of Lady Zouch, and defendant and Arthur Annesley his eldest son, nominated by petitioner, were made trustees. After the perfecting of which deeds Zouch sent by his servant to George Duncombe two other deeds, pretended to be made in February last, with intent to avoid the deeds betwixt him and his mother, whereupon Mr. Duncombe wished petitioner's servant to bid his master take heed thereof, for it might move a Star Chamber matter, but defendant never spake word

1638.

VOL. CCCXC.

thereof. Prays that for avoidance of unnatural suits those deeds may be produced, and order taken thereon. [1¼ p.]

May 23.
Andover.
159. Memorandum of William Blake, bailiff, and four others, of Andover, of notice given by Andrew Pawling, messenger, to the corporation of Andover, for their appearance in the Exchequer, to pass accounts for casual profits due to his Majesty. They promise to appear next Trinity term, and to bring a note of the bailiffs' names since the first year of his Majesty's reign. [⅔ p.]

May 23.
160. Certificate of George Long, Justice of Peace for Middlesex, that Anthony Hill, of Redlands, co. Gloucester, has taken the oath of allegiance before him. [⅓ p.]

May 23.
161. Acquittance of Nathaniel Hyde for 6l. charged upon Weston Patrick, Hants, for ship-money of that tithing, with memorandum endorsed that Hyde, being high collector, wrote that John Edwards might have his bond. [¼ p.]

May 24.
162. The Council to John Buxton. You will with this receive his Majesty's patent for your being sheriff of Norfolk. It has been expedited in regard of his Majesty's services, which, by death of the late sheriff, are left unfinished. Lest you should not suddenly receive the original instructions sent to your predecessor touching the shipping business, we send a transcript herewith, requiring you in his Majesty's name to employ your best diligence for speedy collecting the ship-money. [*Draft.* 1 p.]

May 24.
163. Minute for entry on the Council Register of pass for Clement Harby, son of Sir John Harby, to travel into foreign parts for three years, with proviso not to go to Rome. [*Draft.* ½ p.]

May 24.
164. Similar minute of the appearance of Thomas Phelps, of St. Martin's, coachmaker, sent for by warrant. He is to remain in the messenger's custody until discharged. [*Draft.* 3½ *lines.*]

May 24.
Whitehall.
165. Minute of proceeding before the Lord Great Chamberlain and the Earl Marshal. Alderman Andrewes promised that if Robert Gasset would pay him the money at which his goods extended by the alderman were appraised, he would deliver them back; also, that if Gasset would pay the 200l. principal he would quit the interest. [½ p.]

May 24.
166. Timothy Tournour and Mr. Sergeant J. Hoskyns to the Council. Report concerning complaint of destruction of woods by George Mynne. By Letters Patent of 26 July 1636, Mynne has power to convert into charcoal such woods as he then had or should buy within 12 miles of Whitland Abbey, co. Carmarthen, *non obstante* the statutes 7th Edward VI. and 1st Elizabeth. State the various purchases made by him of woods in that district, and recommend that Whitland Wood, being the stock timber in those parts, and the greater half being cut down, a restraint is necessary. P.S. by

1638. VOL. CCCXC.

Mr. Tournour.—This certificate was in London with Sergeant Hoskyns at the date and all Trinity term after, and because neither party demanded it he brought it back into the country where he died, and in September last Tournour received it of his servant. [1 p.]

May 24. 167. Lawrence Whitaker and Peter Heywood to the Council. In accordance with the order of the Board of 16th May inst., they used their best endeavours for selling the coals brought from Newcastle in the Margaret, of Yarmouth, and landed at the wharf of West, the woodmonger, near Charing Cross. Only West offered so much as 5s. per chaldron, and therefore to him they were sold at that rate. Mr. Morley, the contractor, having refused to choose any one to arbitrate as to compensation to Thomas Hardware, the owner of the ship, the writers appointed Anthony Bedingfield and Thomas Gooch to consider thereof. They were of opinion that 113l. 10s., less 18l. 15s. to be paid by Mr. West, ought to be allowed to Mr. Hardware for his loss. [1 p.]

May 24. Lambeth. 168. Archbishop Laud to the Sub-Warden and Fellows of Merton College, Oxford. I shall, at my first leisure, think upon such injunctions as shall be fit for the future government of that college; meanwhile, I require you to yield obedience to the injunctions given by my visitors by word of mouth. On the 2nd October I shall be at Lambeth, and give hearing to the whole business. Having given you this large warning, if any fail to make his just defence let him blame himself, for I shall then certainly proceed, and if any be concerned in his own particular, he must attend the hearing for himself. For complaints concerning the discipline and thrift of the house in general, I think it fit that some two or three fellows who are best acquainted with the business attend in the name of the rest, and I require both warden and fellows to attend at the time and place above mentioned. [*Copy.* 1 p.]

May 24. 169. Certificate of Sir Thomas Bludder, Justice of Peace for Surrey, that John Bill of London had taken the oath of allegiance before him. [½ p.]

May 24. 170. Certificate of George Palmer, Constable of Yaxley, co. Huntingdon, John Clarke and Thomas Russell, servants to Leonard Pinckney and David Stevenson, saltpetremen, and four others, that Henry Finnimore, with some six of his company, came to make a mutiny in the house of Richard Hart, whereby his Majesty's said officers were in danger of being killed. Pray the bench to take order with Finnimore before murder or manslaughter be committed. [¾ p.]

May 24. 171. George Palmer and Thomas Russell to ——. Send the paper last before calendared, and pray the person addressed to prosecute the matter therein mentioned. Finnimore's fellows were Christopher Langthorn, John Cooke, Richard Aslin, and others. [= ¼ p.]

Vol. CCCXCI. May 25-31, 1638.

1638.
May 25. Confirmation to the Weavers of London of their ancient charters, and extending the corporation throughout England and Wales. All weavers in London and Southwark, being free of other companies, to be translated to this. There are to be two bailiffs, two wardens, and 20 assistants, half broad silk and stuff weavers, and half narrow weavers and others, freemen of the company, besides six weavers of Canterbury to be added to the 20 assistants. William Haslopp to be clerk of the broad weaving trade for life, and after John Conliffe's death to be clerk to the whole company. Searchers and sealers to be elected by the companies of mercers and weavers, to search and seal all stuffs made of foreign materials, and to seal the good stuffs and to seize the bad. The making or importing of silk stuffs mixed with cotton, thread, worsted, and such like materials is inhibited. Stuffs made of foreign materials here imported to be of a stated breadth, and all silk stuffs to be sold by measure and not by weight. The weavers are to buy their silk raw at the best hand, and to put it forth to be dyed, but without any corruption. His Majesty pardons the weavers for taking a silver spoon of each person made free of the company, and they may take towards relief of the poor of the company and other charitable uses. An invention for weaving ribbons and laces in great looms, whereby much deceit is practised, is inhibited, as also such as carry stuffs, offering them to sell in the streets of London and Westminster. [*Docquet.*]

May 25. Indenture between his Majesty and the Company of Weavers, whereby they covenant to pay to his Majesty 8*d.* upon every pound, black or coloured, wrought by them into broad stuffs made of silk only, and aliens shall pay 12*d.* upon every pound for two descents, but after that to pay only as the English. The company to take a bond of 200*l.* of every person free of the company for paying the said duty to his Majesty, with various other regulations. [*Docquet.*]

May 25. Demise to George Earl of Kinnoul of the customs, subsidies of pondage, sums of money, and other duties, except imposts, payable upon the import or export of smalt, saffer, and potashes, and of all forfeitures for nonpayment of the same, for 31 years, at the yearly rent of 240*l.*, with such powers as were contained in a grant to Sir George Hay, late Chancellor of Scotland, which being not yet expired is surrendered by the said Earl as executor of the said late chancellor. [*Docquet.*]

May 25. Grant to George Earl of Kinnoul of an annuity of 1,500*l.* for five years, to be paid out of the customs. [*Docquet.*]

May 25. Licence for Thomas Howard to travel into parts beyond seas for three years. [*Docquet.*]

May 25.
Whitehall. 1. Order of the King in Council. George Henley and Augustine Phillips, of London, merchants, and Nicholas Polhill and his partners

1638.

Vol. CCCXCI.

complain that having obtained letters of marque against the subjects of the United Provinces, for reparation of their losses from the same, and having accordingly set forth several ships, some already at sea, and the rest ready to put forth, the same are now stayed by a command delivered in his Majesty's name from Sec. Coke to Sir Henry Marten, Judge of the Admiralty, whereby petitioners are put to a charge in keeping their ships of 850*l*. a month. His Majesty and the Board being very sensible of the extremity whereto petitioners are reduced, and finding by order of 25th April last that the letters of reprisal are granted upon very good reasons, which order they now again very well approve of, and his Majesty declaring that he caused Sec. Coke to stay the proceedings at the intercession only of the Ambassador of the States, it was ordered that the Principal Secretary of State shall make known to the Ambassador the sense that his Majesty and the Board have of petitioners' cases, and shall demand in what time he will procure petitioners satisfaction for their losses, and who shall bear the charge of this delay, and thereupon to make report to his Majesty or the Board. [*Draft.* 2 *pp.*]

May 25. 2. Copy of the same. [1¼ *p.*]

May 25.
Whitehall.
3. Order of the Archbishop of Canterbury, the Lord Treasurer, Lord Cottington, Sec. Windebank, and Lord Chief Justice Finch, referees of petitions of the Countess Dowager of Clare and of the Lady Ashley. Having been solicited by Lady Ashley that a commission might be issued forth for examination of witnesses, and the Countess Dowager of Clare and the Earl her son declining to join in such commission, we direct that Lady Ashley exhibit her bill in some court of equity against the Countess and her son, and set forth wherein she desires to be relieved. We further order that they shall forthwith appear and answer, and after a replication that a commission be awarded for examination of witnesses, after which we will proceed to consideration of the business, whereby to certify our opinions to his Majesty. [*Draft.* 1½ *p.*]

[May 25.] 4. Exceptions taken by Thomas Crompton, executor to Lady Vanlore, and trustee for Lady Powell, to an award made by the Lords' referees enumerated in the next article, who were appointed upon a petition to his Majesty touching matters in difference between Sir Edward Powell and Sir Peter Vanlore. The exceptions principally relate to interests in the estate of Lady Vanlore vested in the exceptant as trustee for Lady Powell. The referees seem to have made their award in ignorance of the legal interests of the exceptant. [1 *p.*]

May 25.
Whitehall.
5. Declaration of the Archbishop of Canterbury, the Lord Keeper, Lord Treasurer, and Lord Privy Seal. By their award, dated 5th July 1637, they ordered divers differences between Sir Edward Powell and Sir Peter Vanlore. They did not intend thereby in any sort to prejudice Sir Edward or his Lady in anything, and they

456 DOMESTIC—CHARLES I.

Vol. CCCXCI.

1638.
make this declaration in the presence of Sir Edward and his Lady and their respective counsel. [*Copy.* ¾ *p.*]

May 25.
6. Another copy of the same, but without date or the names of the makers of the declaration. [⅓ *p.*]

May 25.
7. Suggestion or first draft of the declaratory portion of the preceding paper. [¼ *p.*]

May 25.
8. Minute for entry on the Council register of pass for George Vane and Walter Vane, sons of Sir Henry Vane, Comptroller of the Household, to repair to their charge in the Low Countries under the States. [*Draft.* ½ *p.*]

May 25.
9. Like minute of appearance of John Skill, of Hempstead, Essex, sent for by warrant. He is to remain in the messenger's custody until discharged. [*Draft.* ¼ *p.*]

May 25.
10. The like of appearances of Thomas Jeffes for himself and his father George Jeffes, and of Richard Woodfall, of Priors Marston, co. Warwick. [*Draft.* 6 *lines.*]

May 25.
The like of Richard Basely, of Fenny Compton, co. Warwick. [*Draft. Written on the same paper.* 2 *lines.*]

May 25.
Whitehall.
11. Sec. Windebank to Capt. John Mennes. A Spanish gentleman, Don Juan de Palacio, is to pass into Spain with the Condé d'Oniate, the ambassador. On arrival in Spain he is to go in diligence to that King, on his Majesty's special affairs. After you have landed the ambassador you are to stay there with his Majesty's ship until Don Juan shall return, and to bring him back with his company. [*Copy.* ¾ *p.*]

May 25.
Sydenham.
12. Thomas Wise, Sheriff of Devon, to Nicholas. Sends various papers relating to a complaint of the parishes of Chudleigh, Bishop's Teignton, &c., against John Witchalse, for dividing the sum imposed upon his division of the hundred of Exminster otherwise than has been done in former payments. Wishes these papers tendered to the view of the Lords, and begs their direction. The question is, whether a sheriff, in pursuit of the general directions of the Lords, must follow the usual proportions, when both the deputy lieutenants and the justices at sessions have ordered new and reformed rates for raising money for the King's service. Gives a summary of his account for ship-money. The county paying 9,000*l.*, and 1,280*l.* borne by Exeter and the incorporate towns, 7,720*l.* is left to his particular care. Of this sum he has paid 6,430*l.* 7*s.* 2*d.*, and there is about 180*l.* or 200*l.* in hand. The reason of this backwardness he will, upon review of his notes, inform Nicholas. He has twice called upon Exeter and the towns to pay their amounts to the Treasurer of the Navy. [*Seal with arms.* 2 *pp.*]

May 25.
13. John Saltonstall, the Mayor, with the Bailiffs and Burgesses, of Berwick-upon-Tweed, to their fellow burgesses, Sir Robert Jackson, Thomas Widdrington, their recorder, Robert Fenwick, John Sleigh,

1638.   VOL. CCCXCI.

and John Rushforth. Letter of attorney whereby the corporation appointed Sir Robert Jackson and the others their deputies to answer the King's letter dated 26th March last, requiring them to surrender to his Majesty the houses in the palace in Berwick, with the storehouse near the wall towards the east end of the town, or otherwise to repair the same, and so keep them for the common good of the town. Sir Robert Jackson and the others are also authorized, according to instructions annexed, to petition his Majesty concerning his letter, and therein to specify the great burthen and charge of widows and orphans, relicts of the late dissolved garrison, and other poor people decayed for want of trading, and to do all other things concerning the premises. [¾ p.] *Annexed*,

> 13. I. *Instructions to Sir Robert Jackson and the others above named. We received his Majesty's letter above mentioned in a packet to Sir James Douglas. All the houses in the palace, except the brewhouse, malthouse, and storehouse, are in good repair, and are by the town granted by leases for many years to come, at yearly rents for the same, towards our common charge. Some of those houses are intended for a house for a schoolmaster for a free school, and the rest for good use for the town's best advantage. The repairs thereof have been very costly, as the Lord Governor's house, to Sir William Bowyer, three or four hundred pounds, and other part of the palace much near the like charge to Sir Robert Jackson, and for the storehouse and the rest we are now about the repairing thereof, so that his Majesty's desire shall be immediately fulfilled in one point, and for surrender thereof we cannot do it, in regard of the leases formerly granted. Therefore we crave his Majesty's favour that we may continue these houses.* [1 p.] *Annexed*,

> 13. I. i. *The King to the Mayor, Bailiffs, and Burgesses of Berwick-upon-Tweed. Our dear father granted you certain houses within the palace there, as also a storehouse for munition, pretending thereby the public good. We are informed that these premises neither are nor can be beneficial, but rather a burthen to the townsmen, if they should keep them in repair, by reason whereof they have for many years past neglected them. Finding that the houses may be converted to better use for the common benefit of the town, we require you, unless you can make it appear that they are necessary and of good use to you, and that you will sufficiently repair them, and be bound to maintain them hereafter, to make a surrender of them to us.* [*Copy.* ½ p.]

May 25.   14. Sir William Tressam [Tresham] to Sec. Windebank. Demand of a warrant for 300 men more of the thousand that his Majesty

1638.

Vol. CCCXCI.

granted for re-enforcing Sir William's regiment, Captain Douglas having transported the former 300. [⅔ p.]

May 25.
Aynho.

15. Reginald Burdyn to [Sir John Lambe]. I came hither last night, upon request of my now patron, to assist about the inventory of mine old patron's goods. I intend for Leicestershire on Monday, for that your courts are there next week. I sent up the commission of Bartholomew Audley of Hinckley. He will be deposed that by Mr. Walker he renewed his patent three times. Walker had 5l. a time for the two first, and 8l. and a bill for 40s. for the last, and his man Johnson had 20s. every time for writing his patent. Insley of Lutterworth procured an absolution for his wife from the Prerogative. I saw it in the hand of Mr. Toovey. I pray that Mr. Williamson be remembered to look after it, that I suffer not unawares. P.S.—My patron last night came from Wellingborough sessions, where he [met with] much opposition, and was hunted by the clamours of Dr. Watkins, Hans[lip?] and Drope. Dr. Sibthorp was there, and is coming up. He knew the matters and their extreme malice. [1 p.]

May 25.

16. Edward Gregge to the King. Bond in 100l. for payment of 5l. fine set upon him by the Commissioners for Tobacco, and not to make sale of tobacco by retail without licence. [*Seal with arms.* ⅔ p.]

May 26.

17. Petition of Henry Earl of Dover, Sir Abraham Dawes, Sir John Darton, and George Drywood to the same. Upon a former petition your Majesty promised that you would hear petitioners' cause about their few mines, in case after hearing in the Duchy Court they found cause to appeal to you. In regard that after the said hearing petitioners have had no better success than they expected, and that they intend to do special service to your Majesty about the preemption of lead ore, they pray that their cause may be heard in your presence, and that no new lease be granted either of the mines or pre-emption before that time. Petitioners will settle a good revenue upon the crown, as they only hitherto have endeavoured, and not Sir Robert Heath, whatsoever he pretends. [*Copy.* ⅔ p.] *Underwritten,*

    17. I. *Minute that his Majesty had appointed Wednesday 6th June for hearing this cause. Whitehall, 26th May* 1638. [⅓ p.] *Memorandum subsequently written by Sec. Coke,*

    17. II. *"Tuesday after term, at Greenwich."* [1 *line.*]

May 26.
Whitehall.

18. The Council to Sir John Bramston, Lord Chief Justice of the King's Bench. We send you petition of Hubert Hacon against his son John Hacon, who for many years has carried himself in a malicious and desperate way towards him, his son-in-law William Gawen and Katherine his wife, upon whom he threatens to make such tragedies as have not been seen, adding that God may do what he pleases with their souls, but he would take order with their bodies, all which being represented to you, you caused him to be committed, but being since liberated, his father is put in continual danger of suffering violence under the fatal hand of

1638.   Vol. CCCXCI.

his unnatural son. We pray you to call John Hacon again before you, and to direct that the strictest course may be taken to reduce him to obedience, and in the meantime that you cause him to be kept prisoner in safehold, that his father may be secured from danger and fear of so lewd a son. [*Draft.* 2 pp.]

May 26. 19. The Council to the Judges of Assize for co. Warwick. We send you informations of Richard Phillips and Phillis Phillips, with affidavit of John Belcher and Richard Mason, wherein they charge Richard Dickson with scandalous speeches against the King and his government, and also the Solicitor-General's report concerning Dickson. We pray you to cause Richard and Phillis Phillips and Dickson to be bound over to appear at the next Assizes, when, if you find the information true, then to proceed against Dickson according to his demerit, but if it be done rather out of malice than truth, to punish the informers. [*Draft.* 1 p.]

May 26. 20. The same to the Justices of Peace for Middlesex. It appears by certificate of the minister and others of the parish of the Savoy, that John Oakely about 13 years since was impressed in that parish to go in the voyage to Cadiz under Viscount Wimbledon, and in that employment received several wounds, whereby he is disabled to labour for his living. We pray you at the next quarter sessions to take order for his relief, by settling a yearly pension upon him. [*Draft.* ¾ p.]

May 26.
Whitehall. 21. The same to the Sheriff and Justices of Peace for co. Huntingdon, Commissioners for St. Paul's. Divers letters have been sent you touching the repair of St. Paul's, with little effect. We are very loath to attribute this backwardness to the disaffection of any of the gentlemen of that county, but rather that the want of some discreet person to solicit this business has been a main obstacle. We have therefore entreated Sir Capell Beadell to undertake this trouble, of whom we shall expect a due return of moneys collected into the Chamber of London, with certificates of those who have given. We pray you to deal effectually with clergy and laity to set their helping hands to so great a work. [*Draft.* 1 p.]

May 26. 22. The same to John Lisney, messenger, to bring before the Lords John Vaughan, High Constable of the hundred of Montgomery, and Rice-ap-Evan-ap-Owen, of the parish of Carno, co. Montgomery. [*Draft minute.* ½ p.]

May 26. 23. Minute for entry on Council Register of pass for Anne, daughter of James Van-Notten, a Dutchman, to go into the Low Countries. [*Draft.* ½ p.]

May 26. 24. The like for Captain Anthony Hill of Redlands, co. Gloucester, to travel in foreign parts for three years. [*Draft.* ½ p.]

May 26. 25. Petition of the beaver makers of London to the Council. You lately directed a proclamation for restraining the importation

1638.

VOL. CCCXCI.

of foreign hats, which is since published. By former proclamations for restraining mixtures with beaver and other enormities, the care of the same was committed to petitioners. They having no power to open a lock or door, pray warrant of assistance, as other companies have, that with the aid of a constable they may open any door or lock, and that offenders may be taken into custody of a messenger to answer before the Lords. [½ p.]

May 26. 26. Petition of Inhabitants of Moreclack [Mortlake] to Archbishop Laud. The vicarage of this parish lately falling void, you recommended Mr. Harrison to Edward Viscount Wimbledon as a fit man to be minister, of whom petitioners conceive you were misinformed. Had you known the manner of his life since his abode in the parish, as petitioners do, you would have thought him altogether unfit. Pray you to hear the allegations against Mr. Harrison. [¾ p.] *Underwritten,*

> 36. I. "*I desire Sir John Lambe and Dr. Rives to call the party complained of before them, and to give me an account what can be proved against him, either for life or learning, that further order may be taken as shall be fitting,* W. CANT." 25th May 1638. [¼ p.]

May 26. 27. Allegations rendered in answer to a petition of the Merchants of London and owners of ships, showing that the exportation of 500 or 600 lasts of herrings in strangers bottoms is no hindrance to navigation, but the great encouragement of the fishery, which is the seminary of seamen, and that the suggested medium is neither really intended by the London merchants, or of possibility to take effect, notwithstanding a willingness in Yarmouth men to comply with them therein. [2 pp.]

May 26. Chatham. 28. Kenrick Edisbury to Nicholas. The drafts to the justices of Kent, Hampshire, and Essex are exceeding well penned. I hope you make the like to Norfolk and Surrey. Your clerk's pains in transcribing shall be remembered. I have written to John Davies to send the purveyors, or Kyme the messenger, to attend you for the letters. I shall be in London about Thursday or Friday, being in our way to survey the hull of the Prince, lying in dry dock at Woolwich, and the shipwrights with us, to give them in their estimate for her new building. [⅓ p.]

May 26. 29. Account of Sir William Russell of ship-money received for 1637. Total, 97,216*l.* 1*s.* 9*d.*, leaving unpaid 99,198*l.* 5*s.* 11*d.* [1 p.]

May 26. 30. Account of ship-money received for 1637 levied and remaining in the Sheriff's hands, 6,550*l.*, making the total collected 103,766*l.*, which is 6,940*l.* more than on the 12th inst. [1 p.]

May 26. Burderop. 31. Sir William Calley to Richard Harvey. Pray you pay Lady Cambell 8*l.* for me, due the 17th inst., and take the money you

VOL. CCCXCI.

1638.

disburse for me of Felix Long; adds two gimlets and an oz. of hard wax to his former commissions. [¼ p.]

May 26. 32. Order of the Lord Treasurer and Lord Cottington (with direction from Sir Robert Pye) to pay to Balthazar Gerbier, his Majesty's agent at Brussels, 225*l*. for post of letters, intelligences, and other secret services for three quarters of a year ended 31st March 1638. [1 p.]

May 26. 33. Acquittance of Jacques de Nowell Perron, Abbot of St. Taurin and Lyre, Great Almoner to the Queen, for 200*l*., parcel of his annuity of 400*l*., for half a year ended at the feast of the Annunciation last, under a Privy Seal dormant, dated 10th August 1631. *Signed* "*Jacques du Perron, Evesque d'Ang^{me}* [*Angoulême*]." [⅔ p.]

May 27. Petition of the parson, churchwardens, and other inhabitants of Newington, Middlesex, to the King. The churchwardens of the said parish have time out of mind held, for the use of their church, five acres of pasture, in the said parish, yielding 5*l*. rent per annum, which land has for 14 years past been detained by Sir Francis Popham, who holds by lease from St. Paul's the manor of Newington. Sir Francis holds in that parish 300 acres of land as the demesnes of the lordship, the whole parish consisting but of 500 acres, for which he pays no tithe, but only 6*s*. 8*d*. per annum for his orchard, which is contrary to a proviso in the church lease, and also to the course held by the rest of the parish, who pay 18*d*. an acre in lieu of tithe, which makes not much above 15*l*. per annum for their part. Pray a reference to some Lords of the Council. [*Copy. See Vol. cccxxiii., p.* 298. ½ *p.*] *Underwritten,*

 I. *Reference to the Archbishop of Canterbury and the Lord Keeper.* 27*th May* 1638. [*Copy. Ibid.* ⅙ *p.*]

May 27. Whitehall. 34. Order of the King in Council, that no order of importance either concerning his Majesty's service, or the public, or which shall revoke any former order of the Board, shall be issued by any of the clerks of the Council, as an order, until the same has been first read and approved of at the board. [⅔ p.]

May 27. Whitehall. 35. Draft of the preceding, with an underwritten memorandum that it was read at the Board, the King present, at Greenwich, 3 June 1638, and approved of. [⅔ p.]

May 27. Whitehall. 36. Order of the King in Council. A certificate of Justices of Peace and other persons of quality in co. Chester presented in October last, touching differences between the county and city of Chester (see 29th October 1637, No. 67), being considered, the Lords were moved to hear that part which concerns the assessment of Sir Thomas Aston by the city for the farm of the French wines. It appeared by two Orders dated 3rd April 1636 and 14th May 1637 that the difference between the city of Chester and Sir Thomas Aston had been formerly twice heard and ordered, his Majesty being both times present, It was thereupon expressly Ordered that Sir Thomas Aston shall observe the said former orders, and shall not presume to

1638.

trouble his Majesty or the Lords any more with this business. [*Draft.* 1½ *p.*]

May 27.
Whitehall.

37. Order of the King in Council. Recites that the differences concerning the extent and liberties of the Gloverstone, adjoining the Castle of Chester, whether the same were taxable with the county or county of the city of Chester, were referred to the Earl of Derby, assisted by the Justices of Chester, who had made the certificate calendared under date of 14th April last, No. 69. Such certificate having been read and counsel heard, It was Ordered that the said certificate be confirmed and all persons be required to conform to the same. [*Draft.* 1¼ *p.*]

May 27.
Whitehall.

38. Like order. Upon consideration of a certificate from divers gentlemen of quality living in co. Chester (see 29th October 1637, No. 67), and hearing counsel on all sides, touching the question whether the bishop and the clergy of the cathedral ought to be assessed to ship-money and other public payments with the county or the city, It was Ordered that the Earl of Derby, assisted by the Justices of Chester, be prayed to hear the parties, and to certify to which of them the bishop and clergy ought to be assessed. [*Draft.* 1½ *p.*]

May 27.

39. The Council to the Sheriff of co. Nottingham. We have seen your letter of the 18th instant [No. 116] to Mr. Nicholas, desiring directions concerning those who refuse to pay ship-money, and marvel that having received so large power by his Majesty's writ, and so ample instructions from this Board, you should now propound any such question. We are, by special command from his Majesty, present in Council, to require you without any stop or delay forthwith to proceed in levying the remainder of the ship-money according to the said writ and instructions, and that you fail not to pay the same to the Treasurer of the Navy with all expedition. [*Draft.* 1 *p.*]

May 27.
Whitehall.

40. Order of the King in Council. Some differences between the societies of the two Temples and Dr. Micklethwaite, the master, were, upon a reference from his Majesty to certain Lords, by articles dated 16th May 1634, ordered and settled. A petition has been since presented to the King by Dr. Micklethwaite, touching other differences, as concerning consecrated places belonging to the Temple church, and other things pretended to be appertaining to the same. It was Ordered, that whatsoever is due by the articles of 16th May 1634 shall be paid to the master by the said societies respectively; and as concerning other differences, other than the point of visitation, which was not insisted upon, it was ordered that his Majesty's learned counsel, not being of either of the said societies, should prepare the same for the further hearing and final determination of his Majesty and the Lords. [*Draft.* 1 *p.*]

May 27.
Whitehall.

41. Order of Council. By order of the 22nd April last, the aldermen of every ward in the city of London, and the parson of every parish, were required to meet, and certify what the clear main-

1638. Vol. CCCXCI.

tenance of each of the said ministers is for the present, and of all the impropriations moderately valued, deducting tenths, pensions, procurations, and the like. It was likewise required that a moderate valuation should be made of the yearly value of houses and other things titheable in each parish, which certificate was to be presented to his Majesty on the first Sunday in June. His Majesty having been this day moved by the Archbishop of Canterbury to give the city and parochial ministers a further time to accommodate things amongst themselves, gave them till the first Sunday after Michaelmas, and left them at liberty to draw to an agreement amongst themselves, but so as it be left to his Majesty to add, or alter, and so establish what he shall think fit. [*Draft, damaged by damp.* 1⅔ *p.*]

May 27. 42. Order of Council. John Beck, John Slaney, and others, complaining not only of an unequal assessment for ship-money made for Hornchurch, Essex, by George Thorogood and others, but of the indirect carriage thereof, It was Ordered that a copy of the petition be sent to the said George Thorogood and William Ballard, who are, upon Wednesday next, to present their answer, and to attend the Lords. [*Draft minute.* ⅔ *p.*]

May 27. 43. Edward Viscount Wimbledon to Nicholas. Although I have been much abused by this fellow, yet out of charity I desire you to discharge him. [¼ *p.*]

May 27. 44. Minute for entry on the Council Register of the discharge of Thomas Phelps, coachmaker, sent for by warrant, but liberated upon the preceding note from Viscount Wimbledon. [*Draft.* ¼ *p.*]

May 27. 45. Certificates of S. Smethe, a clergyman, and Thomas Cooper, churchwarden, respecting the non-attendance of the wife of William Gutteridge, and other women, to perform an enjoined penance. The wife of Gutteridge, when served, said she had done no fault, and none would acknowledge. After Evening Prayer, when the clergyman had gone to his own house, they sent the churchwardens to him to say they were then in the chancel, but he had extraordinary business, and could not go to them. [½ *p.*]

May 27. 46. Another certificate of Thomas Garwood the younger [?], relating to the same business. [¼ *p.*]

May 28. 47. The King to Richard Lane, Attorney-General to the Prince, and to the Benchers and Gentlemen of the Middle Temple. For further advancing the subscription for the repair of St. Paul's, and being unwilling that posterity should look over the catalogue of those benefactors, and find no mention of your so noble a society in the contribution to so glorious a work, to the which you have a more immediate relation, your whole society being twice in a year, by the orders of your house, to repair together to that church, our pleasure is that you recommend this work to the members of your house in our name, assuring them that we shall take notice of their

1638.

Vol. CCCXCI.

several expressions as a sign of their zeal to religion and conformity to our royal example. And to that purpose you are to cause a book to be made, containing the names of every member of your house in their degrees, with the sum which each shall contribute, and return the same to our Council Board, from whence, after due consideration thereof, it shall be transmitted to the Chamber of London, to be there kept as a monument of your charitable dispositions. [*From an underwritten memorandum, and one endorsed, it appears that copies of this letter were sent to Rowland Wandesford for Lincoln's Inn, to Sir Edward Littleton for the Inner Temple, and to Sir John Bankes for Gray's Inn. Draft. 1 p.*]

May 28. Petition of Elizabeth Lady Morley, Henry Lord Morley and Monteagle, and Charles Parker, sons of William late Lord Morley and Monteagle and the said Elizabeth, to the King. About 16th James I., the said William late Lord Morley conveyed the manor of Great Hallingbury, Morley House, Morley Park, the chace or forest of Hatfield, a messuage called Haryes with Talboys woods, in Essex, to the use of himself for life, after to Lady Morley for her life, after to the petitioner Henry Lord Morley for his life, and after to the first son of petitioner Henry Lord Morley and the heirs males of his body, with remainders over to William Parker and petitioner Charles Parker, sons of William Lord Morley. In the 11th year of your Majesty's reign, petitioner and the said William Parker settled the said lands to the use of Lady Morley for life, afterwards to Henry Lord Morley, and after to William Parker and petitioner Charles Parker, and their heirs males successively; since which William Parker is deceased, and Henry Lord Morley has a son born named Thomas, an infant of two years of age. As petitioners before the last conveyance had power to disbar the infant Thomas from his remainder, and as there are lands to the value of 3,000*l.* per annum which are to descend upon him, and for that Henry Lord Morley is indebted to divers persons, petitioners pray that for raising 5,000*l.*, and settling 100*l.* per annum on petitioner Charles, your Majesty will direct your letters to the Justices of the Common Pleas, authorizing them to permit Thomas Parker to suffer a recovery of the said lands. [*Copy. See Vol. ccccxxiii., p. 299.* $\frac{2}{3}$ *p.*] *Underwritten,*

  I. *Reference to the Attorney-General to prepare a bill to the effect desired.* [*Copy. Ibid.* $\frac{1}{6}$ *p.*]

May 28. Petition of William Maurodd and Alexander Man, two of his Majesty's footmen, to the King. There was granted to Thomas Bird and Walter Paunsford, for three lives, by the late King, in the 16th year of his reign, a moiety of rents to the value of 240*l.* per annum, which were unjustly withholden from the Crown. In 20 years there is recovered but 20*l.* per annum, and the remainder is like to be lost to your Majesty. Your Majesty granted the other moiety to Arthur Begg, one of your cooks, but before the solicitor made ready the bill, Begg died, so that the suit now remains to your Majesty to

1638.

Vol. CCCXCI.

dispose of. Petitioners pray a grant of the last-mentioned moiety for three lives, paying to your Majesty 50*l.* a year rent. [*Copy. Ibid., p.* 300. ½ *p.*] *Underwritten,*

 I. *Minute of his Majesty's pleasure to be certified from his Attorney or Solicitor as to the state of this business.* Greenwich, 23rd June 1637. [*Copy. Ibid.* ⅙ *p.*]

 II. *Attorney-General Bankes to the King. Report which sets forth the grant to Bird and Paunsford, and that only* 20*l. per annum thereof had been recovered. We cannot advise your Majesty to grant away your moiety, as desired by this petition, but, as petitioners are willing at their own costs to recover the said rents, we submit whether your Majesty would grant them the arrearages of such rents as they recover, reserving a fourth part to your Majesty.* 11th May 1638. [*Copy. Ibid.* ⅓ *p.*]

 III. *Direction to the Attorney-General to prepare a grant to petitioners of so much of their desire as by the said certificate is advised.* Whitehall, 28th May 1638. [*Copy. Ibid.* ⅙ *p.*]

May 28. Petition of Elizabeth Shillitoe, widow of George Shillitoe, to the King. Petitioner's husband, having received a great portion with her, conveyed the manor of Seacroft, co. York, to petitioner for her jointure, but afterwards becoming indebted, the said lands with the rest of his estate were extended, and he became disabled to allow petitioner means to live. Her said husband being dead, petitioner was in hope to enjoy her jointure, but Robert Benson, an attorney of the Common Pleas, having got possession thereof, detains the same without right or title, and stirs up troubles against petitioner and scandal against her and her estate. Prays a reference to Lord Chief Justice Finch. [*Copy. Ibid., p.* 301. ⅔ *p.*] *Underwritten,*

 I. *Reference as prayed.* Whitehall, 28th May 1638. [*Copy. Ibid.* ⅕ *p.*]

May 28. 48. Minute for entry on the Council Register of a pass for George March, aged 12 years, son of Richard March of the Tower, London, to travel into foreign parts for three years, with proviso not to go to Rome. [*Draft.* ⅓ *p.*]

[May 28.] 49. Petition of Matthew Clark of Alderkirk, co. Lincoln, to the Council. Petitioner, with Thomas Knott his neighbour, upon certificate of Sir Anthony Irby, intimating that they sue Robert Harris, a chief constable, for distraining them last year for ship-money, is to his grief and charge fetched up by a messenger near 100 miles, and has been detained in custody these ten days. Conceives that Sir Anthony has much mistaken himself, for petitioner has always readily paid his assessment, was never distrained therefore, nor is, nor was there ever, any suit on petitioner's behalf. Prays order for enlargement, and that the Lords would consider his causeless and

VOL. CCCXCI.

1638.

chargeable sufferings, he giving bond to appear if it be proved that he has committed any offence. [½ p.]

May 28. 50. Minute of Entry on the Council Register of the discharge of Matthew Clark upon entering bond to pay such ship-money and other rates as shall be assessed upon him in future. [*Draft.* ¼ p.]

May 28. 51. Bond of Matthew Clark in 20*l*. to the King of the purport stated in the preceding article. [½ p.]

May 28. 52. Hugh Nanney, Sheriff of co. Merioneth, to Nicholas. States contents of a letter of his of the 27th March, sent by Foulk Salesbury, an alderman of Chester, which he supposes to have miscarried. Sends another certificate and schedule verbatim with the former, save that upon the death of his deputy-sheriff on the 5th April a great many complained of partiality in the assessors, whereby the poorer sort had been overcharged, in rectifying whereof he had great incumbrance, yet now he is in a fair way to perfect all. Pays some part of the money already collected. The rest he will levy with all possible speed. [1 p.]

May 28.
Bilboa.
53. George Wyche to Richard Harvey. Some few days past arrived there in good safety. Has had conference with Mr. Gyffard concerning a chest and certain things recommended to him by Mr. Porter. Sends his discharge. [⅔ p.] *Enclosed,*

    53. I. *George Gyffard to George Wyche. According to promise I now send you the relation of such things as I received for and from Mr. Porter. That which came from "ma^d" [Madrid] was stolen out of my chamber. What I received from "Loⁿ" [London ?] is all sent up, except two globes which await a proper conveyance. I had an "excommunion and paulina" read for the stolen articles in churches and other places where I suspected.* [⅔ p.]

May 29. Grant to Sir James Scott, gentleman of the Privy Chamber, of a pension of 13*s.* 4*d.* by the day, during his life. [*Docquet.*]

May 29. Grant to Sir William Stewart and George his son, for life, of a pension of 200*l.* per annum, upon surrender of a like pension granted to Sir William by the name of William Steward in the 4th year of his Majesty's reign. [*Docquet.*]

May 29. Licence for Charles Lord Ker, son of the Earl of Ancram, to travel beyond sea for three years. [*Docquet.*]

May 29.
Whitehall.
54. Order of the Committee for regulation of the Household. The cofferer and the rest of the officers of the Greencloth shall attend the Committee on this day sen-night, with the books signed from the first year of Queen Mary downwards, and likewise with a certificate of all diets of 21 dishes of meat and of 16, 10, 7, and 5 dishes of meat, both of the King's and Queen's side, that are now served, with what alterations have been since that time, and who are assigned to be sitters at the said diets or tables. [*Draft.* ½ p.]

May 29. 55. Rough draft of the same. [⅔ p.]

1638.
Vol. CCCXCI.

May 29. 56. Minute for entry on the Council Register of a Warrant, with general directions, and more especially to the messengers of the Chamber, for John Pyborne, Laurence Petty, Thomas Hodgson, and Thomas Freere, deputed by the Company of Soapmakers to seize all soap, lees, and other materials prohibited by proclamation, according to that exhibited the 21st of June last. [⅔ p.]

May 29. 57. The Council to the Warden of the Fleet, to take into his custody Francis Wilson. [*Draft minute.* ½ p.]

May 29. 58. Petition of the Sewers of the Chamber in ordinary to the Lords Commissioners [for regulation of the Household]. They had a grant of 7½d. a day and diet in the King's Court from the first foundation of the King's House, which has been continued until within these few years, which diet has been detained without consideration. Pray the Lords to consider the poor means they have, and to settle them in their former rights. [½ p.] *Underwritten,*

    58. I. *The Lords Commissioners desire Mr. Cofferer and the rest of the officers of the Greencloth to consider this petition, and to certify when petitioners' diet was taken from them, and wherefore. Whitehall, 29th May 1638.*

[May 29 ?] 59. [Officers of the Greencloth] to the Lords Commissioners for the Household. The King in the sixth year of his reign reduced his house to the reglement of the 44th of Queen Elizabeth, at which time the sewers having no diet were left out of the book signed by his Majesty for the establishment of his house. Since that time they have not had any allowance of diet or board wages. [*Unsigned.* ½ p.]

May 29. / June 8. Rome. 60. Christopher Windebank to his father, Sec. Windebank. The order I received from you in Spain brought me to Italy, where I have seen Florence, Naples, and Rome, where I have been extremely honoured by Cardinal Barbarini, whom I have visited twice. The want of your letters and of other necessaries for a journey has made me rely upon Mr. Weston. In Rome I have had 25l. of John Wilford. We go hence to-morrow to Venice. [1 p.]

May 29. Westminster. 61. Robert Reade to Nicholas. These two men are apprehended upon information given by this bearer, John Bradstreet, of misdemeanours usually committed by them and their associates, as, namely, the taking up of men and selling them like cattle to be transported beyond seas by such as have no licence to levy. Mr. Secretary desires you to examine them upon interrogatories, that according to the nature of their offences they may be remitted to the Lords or otherwise ordered. [⅔ p.]

May 29. Greenwich. 62. Endymion Porter to Richard Harvey. I would have you go to Mr. Railton, and receive the remainder of Sir Peter Rubens's moneys, which are now ready, and let Mr. Wake have them to make over to Antwerp for him. If you meet with Mr. Millington, I would

1638.

have you go to Wandsor [Windsor?] with him, and take an account of Campian, and see how everything there stands. [½ p.]

May 29.
Fenchurch Street.

63. Richard Harvey to [William] Langhorne. There was a bill of exchange of 700*l.* drawn upon you from Dublin, payable to Endymion Porter about 11th July last; his desire is to know when and to whom the money was paid. [Underwritten, copy receipt for the above 700*l.*, signed " *by appointment of Richard Woodward, Thomas Kinaston.*" ½ *p.*]

May 29.

64. Articles in answer to the allegations of Thomas Davies, his Majesty's barber, claiming the disposing of the barbers' tents for the service of the household, as formerly enjoined by his predecessors, barbers to his Majesty's ancestors (*see 17th February 1637-8, No. 30*). The answer contends that the record quoted by Davies proves that the disposing of the barbers' tents was not granted to Robert Bolley as barber, but as sergeant of the ewry. It asserts that in the 17th Henry VIII. the sergeant of the ewry and the King's barber were different persons, for that Godfrey Villers was then sergeant of the ewry, and Edmund Haran and Mr. Penne, barbers to his Majesty. In addition to much other matter it also appeals to an order of Lord North and Sir William Knollys, treasurer and comptroller of the household, dated 3rd May 1599, whereby William Raffe and Francis Bates, who then kept the barbers' tent allowed to follow the Court, were ordered to pay to the sergeant of the ewry 10*l.* per annum, retaining still the disposal of the said barber's place in the gift of the Lord Steward. [1½ *p.*]

May 29.

65. Petition of Thomas Farbeck, clerk, to Archbishop Laud. Petitioner is vicar of Ketton, co. Rutland, whereunto the church of Tixover, two miles distant, is united, and by ancient composition the vicar is to find a curate resident to officiate at Tixover. Richard Bullingham is farmer for three lives at a small rent of the rectory of Ketton, being the corps of a prebend in the cathedral of Lincoln, and receives out of the rectory 300*l.* per annum clear, while the vicarage is not worth above 26*l.* per annum, and one moiety of that is allowed to the curate of Tixover. There is reserved to the diocesan full power to augment the said stipend, as by an ancient composition in the church of Lincoln, hereunto annexed, appears. Prays that the Archbishop would command that some order may be taken for the augmentation of petitioner's poor vicarage. [⅔ *p.*]

Underwritten,

65. I. "*I desire Sir John Lambe to consider of this petition, and if there be any way left for the church's just relief I shall be very willing to give my best assistance.* W. CANT." 29*th May* 1638. *Annexed,*

65. II. *Extract from a roll of the time of Oliver Sutton, Bishop of Lincoln, who took possession of that see in* 1280, *in which are set forth the profits at that time of the vicarage of Ketton with the chapel of Tixover, to which is added a statement of the various sums received by the petitioner since his coming to the vicarage in* 1614. [1⅔ *p.*]

1638.
May 29.

Vol. CCCXCI.

66. Memorandum of Thomas Beeston, Mayor, and four others, of Portsmouth, that notice was given by Andrew Pawling, messenger, to the corporation of that town, to appear in the Exchequer, to pass their accounts for casual profits due to his Majesty. The said mayor and others certify that they have given order to their solicitor to pass their accounts that Trinity Term. [¾ p.]

May 29.

67. Note of fees paid on the funeral of the Marchioness of Hamilton, Countess of Cambridge, to the officers of the College of Arms. Garter received 15l., eight others 1l. 18s. each, and four 19s. each. Total received, 35l. [½ p.]

May 30.
Inner Star Chamber.

68. Order of Council. Philip Oldfield, clerk, rector of Lasham, Hants, by petition to his Majesty, which was referred to the Lords, showed that he had been rector of Lasham for 25 years, but by reason of a pretended lease for 99 years (20l. per annum only being reserved for the cure) he could never enjoy the full right of the church, and when by law petitioner attempted to void the lease, Sir Edmond Plowden, the now patron and assignee of the said lease, so multiplied suits upon petitioner, threatened his ruin, unjustly detained his body, beat his wife great with child, and insulted over his weak and declining estate, that neither friend, kinsman, nor servant dared be assistant to petitioner, who was forced to compound, and enter bond in 200l. not to trouble Sir Edmond. He therefore besought his Majesty to refer the hearing of this business. Upon hearing all the parties We Order Mr. Oldfield to bring an action of trespass against Sir Edmond for entering into some part of the parsonage of Lasham, and that Sir Edmond shall plead not guilty, and go to trial at the next assizes at Winchester, and shall admit the trespass, and give in evidence the lease of the said parsonage of 4th of Queen Elizabeth by William Guy, the incumbent, and Nicholas Pinke, the then pretended patron, and afterwards confirmed by Robert then Bishop of Winchester, and when the Lords shall be advertised of the result of the trial they will take further order according to his Majesty's reference. [*Draft.* 2⅓ p.]

May 30.

69. Petition of John Lassells and Elizabeth his wife to the Council. By order of the 10th May 1637, George Lassells, father of John Lassells, was ordered to pay, for relief of petitioners and their children, 20s. a week, and also for a future provision to settle a house and land of the yearly value of 34l. 13s. 4d. upon them and their children. For the non-performance of which order George Lassells was committed to the Fleet, and afterwards ordered to be kept as a close prisoner, and to be put in irons, and fed with such food as is appointed by law for prisoners upon a Statute Merchant, until he conformed himself to the order of the 10th May. The said George Lassells and petitioner, since the last order, have referred themselves for settling the matters aforesaid to Sir Robert Coke and Harbottle Grimstone, who have made this end, viz., that 100l. should be paid in hand to petitioners, and that Sir Robert Coke should become bound to John Coppinger, uncle of the said Elizabeth

1638.

Vol. CCCXCI.

for payment of 500*l.*, with interest at 8*l.* per cent., upon the 30th May next, which 100*l.* and bond have been delivered to Harbottle Grimstone until George Lassells shall have an order for his enlargement and a discharge of all the former orders. And the said referees have further ordered that petitioners may quietly remain in the house where they now dwell, at Elston in co. Nottingham, until payment of the said 500*l.* Pray the Lords to order the discharge of George Lassells, and the vacating of all former orders, as also to confirm the agreement of the said referees. [*Copy attested by Sir Robert Coke and Harbottle Grimstone. 3 pp.*]

May 30.

70. Order of Council. Recites the above petition, confirms the agreement therein mentioned, and Orders that George Lassells be forthwith set at liberty, and when the 500*l.* is paid, that the former orders be vacated, and the possession of the house at Elston be delivered up. [*Draft.* 1¼ *p.*]

May 30.
Inner Star Chamber.

71. Like order. Taking into consideration the petition of John Beck, John Slaney, and others of Hornchurch, mentioned under the 27th inst., No. 42, and hearing their counsel, and the counsel of George Thorogood, William Ballard, and others, also inhabitants of Hornchurch, concerning a rate factiously made by the latter at Chensford [Chelmsford], 15 miles distant from Hornchurch, upon a reference obtained from this board to the sheriff upon untrue suggestions, after a rate had been made by Beck, Slaney, and others at the constable's house at Hornchurch (the usual place of meeting for parish business), and been confirmed by the sheriff, and most part of the money collected, it appeared that the rate made by Thorogood and the others was unduly made, and by its inequality was probably designed to prejudice the service. It was Ordered that the former rate shall stand, and if Thorogood shall not obey the will of the Lords, and pay his rate, the sheriff is required to bind him over to answer his contempt at this board. The sheriff is to see this order put in execution, and to cause whatsoever has been levied upon the second assessment to be restored. [*Draft.* 1¾ *p.*]

May 30.
Inner Star Chamber.

72. Like order. The Lords having heard Mr. Walter, a Justice of Peace for co. Oxford, why he bound William Sessions, churchwarden of Churchill, co. Oxford, to his good behaviour, and finding that he had very good cause so to do, approved of his proceedings, and ordered Sessions to ask pardon of Mr. Walter for having unjustly complained of him to the board, and thereupon Mr. Walter shall be prayed to cause him to be released of his said recognizance. [*Draft.* 1 *p.*]

May 30.
Inner Star Chamber.

73. Like order. Upon hearing the differences between the said William Sessions, churchwarden of Churchill, co. Oxford, George Morecroft, parson of Kingham, and George Dadford of Churchill, touching the great decay of the church of Churchill, and finding that the money spent in such suits would be better employed in repairing the church, It was Ordered that the said differences shall

1638.

Vol. CCCXCI.

be referred to the Bishop of Oxford, who is to order a survey of the church, and to settle the rates towards the reparations, and in the meantime all suits are to be stayed. The Lords further enjoin the churchwardens and parishioners to stand to such order as the bishop shall make; and as Morecroft, being a clergyman, by refusal to pay the rate has shown himself more refractory than became a man of his calling, the Lords pray the bishop to enjoin him to be a leading man in payment of the rate he shall set upon him, and if he shall refuse the Lords will take a course to render him an example for his refractoriness. [*Draft.* [1½ *p.*]

May 30.
Inner Star Chamber.

74. Order of Council. The Landholders and Inhabitants of Whittlesey, in the Isle of Ely, co. Cambridge, having petitioned his Majesty about draining the Great Level of the Fens, and their right of common, his Majesty referred the same to the Lords, who Ordered that a copy of the said petition be delivered to some one of the undertakers of that work, and appointed to hear the same upon Wednesday 13 June next. [*Draft.* 1 *p.*]

May 30.

75. Like order. Thomas Leigh by petition represented that the difference between him and Anne Dale, his tenant, was upon her suit referred to Viscount Savage, the Lord Chief Baron, Roger Downes, Vice-Chamberlain, and Evan Edwards, Baron of the Exchequer at Chester. Upon 21st February following, in regard there was a suit by Dale at Chester for the same matter, which had come to an issue, petitioner desired it might proceed to a hearing, but that was denied, in regard the Lords were willing the referees should make an accommodation, but it was not their intention that any stay should be given to petitioner in his legal proceedings; yet, under colour of the said reference, the cause is deferred, and petitioner with-holden from his possession for two years since the expiration of Dale's lease, and bound by injunction from any proceeding at common law; by means whereof, and Dale's scandalising petitioner's title, he is deprived of taking fines to the value of 1,000*l.* of the rest of his tenants. Lord Savage and Roger Downes called petitioner and Dale before them, when Downes declared that Dale had no more colour for enjoying the tenement without consent of petitioner than any tenant of the said Downes had after the term was expired. Petitioner besought the board that the reference might be discharged, and the Lords appoint a time for a hearing, or that they should command Mr. Downes to proceed to a legal hearing. It was Ordered that the reference should be no longer in force, but that petitioner should be at liberty to seek his remedy by ordinary course of justice, and that Downes should without delay proceed to a legal hearing. [*Draft.* 1½ *p.*]

May 30.

76. Like order. The petition of the fishermen of the Thames, wherein they complained to his Majesty that Nowell Warner, master of his Majesty's barge, and patentee for transportation of lampreys, refused to give them satisfaction, and had broken the order of the 5th January 1637–8, calendared under that date, No. 17. The Lords,

1638.

finding the fishermen's complaint to be grounded upon no just cause, confirmed the said order, and required the fishermen to forbear to trouble the board any more with such causeless and clamorous petitions. [*Draft.* 1 *p.*]

May 30.
77. Order of Council. The Lords on 2nd May inst. appointed Friday 1st June to hear a complaint made to his Majesty by Winter Graunt, his Majesty's servant, about the manner of proceedings in the court of exchequer, one being in Latin at the common law, the other in English in the Exchequer Chamber. The Lords required the Attorney and Solicitor General to attend them at the hearing of the said cause. [*Draft.* ⅔ *p.*]

May 30.
78. Like order. Complaint has been made by Thomas Alden that although the Lords by orders of 24th November and 20th April last appointed the twelve governors of Crediton to pay him the arrearages of 12*l.* per annum for the time he served the cure of Exminster, amounting to 108*l.*, they refused unless he would give security to repay the same, which refractoriness of the governors the Lords could not but take notice of, so they again required them to pay the 108*l.*, with such costs for their delay as two justices of peace of Crediton should think fit, and if they refused or delayed to pay the same within 14 days after sight hereof, then the justices of peace were to bind over four of them to answer their contempt at the board. [*Draft.* 1 *p.*]

May 30.
79. Like order. The petition of Oliver Lloyd, for regulating aliens residing out of the limits of the new corporation, being read, the Lords commanded that an Act of Council should be entered to declare their utter dislike of the same, and that if Lloyd should presume to tender it again that it be cast out, as a thing absolutely rejected. [*Draft.* ½ *p.*]

May 30.
80. Like order. The difference between the Mayor, Aldermen, and Burgesses of Congleton and William Bramhall being appointed to be heard at the board this day, Bramhall attended, but the other parties desired a further day. The Lords appointed Wednesday the 6th June. [*Draft.* ⅔ *p.*]

May 30.
Whitehall.
81. The Council to Sir Richard Fenn, Lord Mayor of London. His Majesty having appointed his servant, Clement Laniere, to weigh all hay and straw to be sold within three miles circuit of London and Westminster, the said patentee by his petition complained to his Majesty that notwithstanding he had spent 300*l.* in endeavouring to settle that office for the public good, he is interrupted therein by directions from the Lord Mayor or the Court of Aldermen, and being unable and unwilling to undergo a suit at law with the city, he craved his Majesty for assistance, who commanded us to settle this business, or report our opinions. We earnestly recommend the business to your consideration, not doubting you will take such order therein as his Majesty shall not be further

DOMESTIC—CHARLES I. 473

1638.
Vol. CCCXCI.

troubled to interpose in a business wherein so general a good is concerned. [*Draft.* ¾ *p.*]

May 30. 82. Order of Council. The Dean and Chapter of St. Paul's, London, on behalf of themselves and their under-tenants in Caddington, complain that being by order of the board peaceably to enjoy the part of Caddington Wood by them enclosed, yet that Richard Turner and Jeremy Garsley (who were formerly committed to the Fleet, and on the 14th April, upon their submission, and bond of 200*l.* not to offend in like kind, were discharged), since their return home the servants of Turner and Garsley have again contemned the Lords' order, and Turner, reviling petitioners' tenants threatens to undo one who turned out their cattle, which are daily driven into the inclosures. By whose example William and Richard Bowse have lately thrown open the inclosures, carried away several burthens of bushes, and sown oats there, as to which petitioners' tenants say they stole oats there last year, and now sow them that they may after mow them. Petitioners desiring to be relieved herein, It was Ordered that the justices of peace next adjoining be required to send for Richard Clothier and Thomas Bengo, servants to Turner and Garsley, as also for William and Richard Bowse, and cause them to be all sent to the House of Correction, there to receive corporal punishment for such their insolences.. [*Draft.* 1½ *p.*]

May 30.
Inner Star Chamber.
83. Like order. Recite reference of the petition of young Sir John Tyrrell to the Lord Chief Justice of the King's Bench and Mr. Justice Croke, and their certificate, calendared under date of the 18th April last, No. 4. We confirm the said certificate, and, as concerning the aspersions laid by the petition on Sir Henry Browne, we find him faultless in all those things wherewith he is charged in the said petition, and hold the petitioner very much to blame to asperse a gentleman of so much honour and worth, and who performed towards old Sir John Tyrrell the offices of a very affectionate kinsman and real friend. [*Draft* 1½ *p.*]

May 30. 84. List of Causes appointed to be heard in the Star Chamber this day; viz., the Attorney-General against William Pickering and others, for speeches against his Majesty; the same against William Poe, for procuring counterfeit persons to personate men of value in sealing a bond of 200*l.*; the same against Robert Ryther and others, for combinations and conspiracies; Alexander Dupper against James Freeze and others, for coinage and other offences. [1 *p.*]

May 30. 85. Notes by Sec. Windebank of proceedings in the Star Chamber in the case of the Attorney-General against William Pickering Defendant, about a year and a half ago, meeting Francis Huberley, called him a beggarly knave, whereupon Huberley called him a beggarly papist. He replied, "I am a papist, and the Queen a papist, and the King a papist in heart and conscience." Dr. Clayton, D.D., stated that Pickering had several times affirmed that all Protestants were damned heretics and devils, and that the King's

1638.

VOL. CCCXCI.

Majesty is reconciled to the Bishop and Church of Rome. He enclosed a court, whereby he took in part of the churchyard, and uses it for a pig-sty. Lord Cottington proposed for sentence, " Stand in the pillory with a paper, and lose both his ears; 10,000*l.* fine; restitution of the sacred ground." Lord Finch added, " Whipping." Secs. Windebank and Coke, Mr. Comptroller, Lord Newburgh, the Earl of Dorset, and the Lord Chamberlain all concurred with their predecessors. The Lord Privy Seal suggested the additions of: " Stigmatised with a letter L; allowed law, the tongue bored with an awl; whipped." The Lord Treasurer agreed with the general vote of the court. The Archbishop of Canterbury: " With the highest sentence." The Lord Keeper: " With the general vote of the court, a special imprisonment, either during life or during the King's pleasure." $1\frac{2}{3} p.$]

May 30. 86. Minute for entry on the Council Register of appearance of Edward Tompkins of Bishops Itchington, co. Warwick, sent for by warrant. He is to remain in the messenger's custody until discharged. [*Draft.* $\frac{1}{4} p.$]

May 30. 87. The like of appearance of Henry Ludlow of Tadley, Hants. [*Draft.* $\frac{1}{4} p.$]

May 30. 88. Petition of William Cowthery, of Stratfield Turgis, Hants, to the Council. About 24 years ago petitioner, being possessed of a farm called South End in Stratfieldsaye, worth 50*l.* per annum, Richard Berry, then under-sheriff, under pretence to secure him harmless of Sir Richard Norton, then sheriff, by indirect ways outed petitioner and his tenants, and imprisoned them, where three died, and a fourth fled the country, leaving four distressed widows. The petitioner was no ways engaged whereby his lands should be extended, but the extent should have been executed upon the lands of William Cowthery of Basingstoke. Petitioner is much impoverished, and unable to wage law against his powerful adversaries, and Berry being since dead, petitioner has no remedy but against Sir Richard Norton. Prays reference to Lord Charles Powlett, Henry Sandis, Richard Tilney, and Edward Pitts. [$\frac{3}{4} p.$] *Underwritten,*

  88. I. *The Lords pray the Judges of Assize to call the parties before them, and to compose the differences, if they can. Inner Star Chamber, 30th May* 1638. [1 *p.*]

May 30.
Dorset House. 89. Algernon Earl of Northumberland to Sir John Pennington, Vice-Admiral aboard the St. Andrew. I lately gave order to the captain of the St. Dennis to be ready at Margate road to transport for Holland Colonel Goring, Sir Jacob Ashley, and two of Mr. Comptroller's sons. Colonel Goring having had some business at Court which has retarded his coming away, he fears the ship may be gone. In that case give order for some other ship of the fleet to

Vol. CCCXCI.

1638.

receive him on board, and transport him to such port in Holland as shall be most convenient for his landing. [*Seal as Lord Admiral.* ⅔ *p.*]

May 30. Chelsea House. 90. Henry Earl of Danby to Sec. Coke or Sec. Windebank. Being not well, I entreat you to deliver my knowledge upon a petition exhibited by one Sessions against William Walter and Mr. Moorecroft, clerk, all my near neighbours in co. Oxford. The cause is concerning an order made by the late Lord Chief Baron Walter, confirmed at the Quarter Sessions, and, as I verily think, both just and good; and for the persons, Mr. Walter is so well known to all the Lords that I need not express how much he is valued amongst us, neither is Moorecroft, in his quality, esteemed less worthy, either in the University where he was bred, or in the shire where he lives, being, in the opinion of the best, both free and far from those suggestions contained in Sessions' petition. [⅔ *p.*]

May 30. Sleaford. 91. Sir Robert Carr to Sec. Windebank. Desires to obey his Majesty's commands. To the best of his understanding had settled the yearly rentcharges which he spake of to his Majesty. Mr. Dallison framed the deed, and to the truth thereof the writer takes God to witness; nevertheless, if the form please not, he is willing to do what may reasonably be required. Returns "the licence" by the messenger. [*Seal with arms.* 1 *p.*]

May 30. Durham. 92. John Richardson to Sir Henry Vane, Comptroller of the Household. Heretofore I moved you to give directions to your bailiffs of Barnard Castle and Raby lordships, that the alehouse keepers within those liberties should have paid the fees due to the clerk of the peace by an ancient table of fees allowed by Bishop William James and others, which you promised you would do. Some of our justices, as Mr. Maxton and Hugh Wright, who are somewhat captious and covetous for their clerks to have 12*d.* apiece, which was never demanded nor taken in the county till within three years last, have opposed it. My grandchild, who is clerk of the peace, desires no more nor other fee than all his predecessors had in time of memory; and that order is confirmed by Mr. Chancellor, upon hearing the cause in Chancery. Now he is come up to petition the Lords to have it ratified, wherein I desire your furtherance. [*Seal with arms.* 1 *p.*]

May 31. Warrant to pay to Sir Philip Carteret 1,300*l.* upon account, to be employed in fortifying Castle Elizabeth in Jersey. [*Docquet.*]

May 31. Grant of a pension of 200*l.* to George Corrie, usher of the Privy Chamber, during pleasure. [*Docquet.*]

May 31. Indenture between his Majesty and Robert Earl of Lindsey, whereby, in consideration that the earl has undertaken to drain certain fens called the Great Level in co. Lincoln, he is to have 24,000 acres, and to assign 3,000 acres to his Majesty, also, in consideration that the said earl has undertaken to drain the Eight

1638.

Vol. CCCXCI.

Hundred Fen, his Majesty covenants, in case he perform the same within one year from the 22nd of February last, to accept of 1,500 acres in lieu of the said 3,000 acres. [*Docquet.*]

May 31. Warrant to the Ranger, Keepers, and other his Majesty's officers within Cranborne Chase, for preservation of the deer. [*Docquet.*]

May 31. Warrant to the Exchequer, for discharging the Marquess of Hamilton, Master of the Horse, of 400*l.* by him received for provision of horses for the King's and Queen's use, by Privy Seal, dated 12th February 1638, as of 500*l.* received for like provisions, by Privy Seal, dated 22nd March 1638, and for allowing him 26*l.* by him laid out by way of surplusage, and also for payment to him of 400*l.*, to be by him disbursed for like provisions hereafter, by way of imprest. [*Docquet.*]

May 31. Licence to the new Farmers of the Customs to compound with merchants for their customs upon goods brought into London and Dover, and from thence to be reshipped beyond seas, and to receive those compositions for their own use. [*Docquet.*]

May 31. Grant whereby his Majesty (on the certificate of divers Scottish shipmasters trading to London that it is the custom of other nations to have an appointed officer before whom merchants and masters of ships confirm their bargains for freight) appoints William Murray, his Majesty's servant, to execute that office between his Majesty's subjects of Scotland trading to London for 21 years, demanding therefore after the rate of one ton freight for every ship by him freighted, which is according to the order of other countries, with authority also to deal for other his Majesty's subjects and strangers who are willing to employ him. [*Docquet.*]

May 31. Warrant to pay 130*l.* to Martin Lumley for the rent of his house in Wood Street, London, taken up last winter for reception of Alcayde Taudar Ben Abdala, ambassador extraordinary from the Emperor of Morocco, where he resided for six months. [*Docquet.*]

May 31. Warrant to Sir Richard Norton for preservation of game, of hare, pheasant, partridge, heron, and other wild fowl in East Tisted, Hants, and within seven miles compass thereof. [*Docquet.*]

May 31. 93. Petition of Thomas Twisse, clerk, parson of Buscot, co. Berks, to the King. After long suit upon a general inclosure of lands in that parish, petitioner obtained a decree in Chancery that every parishioner should pay the parson certain moneys as rents out of their lands inclosed, in lieu of tithes, amounting in the whole to 140*l.* per annum, whereby the worth of the parsonage is augmented 100*l.* per annum; but by reason of the great charge in maintaining the church's right your subject was constrained to mortgage the said rents in lieu of tithes, and the two next presentations to the said church. All which being well known to Walter Hungerford, one that pretended great friendship, he often treated that

1638.   Vol. CCCXCI.

he might redeem the mortgage, and take it into his hands, to which your subject condescending, delivered the writings to the said Hungerford, and leased to him all the said rents in lieu of tithes during your subject's life, and also granted to him the two next presentations, wholly relying that at any time he would have accepted the moneys disbursed. But although he has received full four years' profit of the said rents at 140*l*. per annum, he refuses to release the premises, unless he may have full interest and 500*l*. besides; and, working on petitioner's wants, has got a lease from him of his glebe lands during life at a great under value, and having entangled petitioner by bonds, threatens to cast him in prison if he seek by any means to be relieved. Petitioner, bearing the name of parson only, discharges the cure, and pays ship-money and all dues, but Mr. Hungerford reaps all the profits. Having lived there 20 years in good credit, conformable to all the ceremonies of the Church of England, he is now like to be turned out and left destitute. Prays a reference for examination to any of the Council. [¾ *p*.] *Underwritten,*

> 93. I. *Reference to Archbishop of Canterbury, the Lord Keeper, and the Lord Treasurer. Theobalds, 31st May* 1638. [¼ *p*.] *Endorsed,*
>
> 93. II. *Order of the referees appointing Wednesday 24th October next for hearing this business at the Council table. 14th September* 1638. [¼ *p*.]

May 31.   94. Petition of John Rowdon, his Majesty's servant, to the King. Having been formerly a clerk in your Majesty's receipt, to one of the tellers there, he disbursed great sums of money by command of superior officers, for a great part whereof he never could get allowance or repayment, by which means his estate has been extended, and himself imprisoned in the Fleet 14 years. There is due to petitioner, in the name of John London, upon an annuity of 60*l*. per annum, 650*l*. Your Majesty, by a reference to the Earl of Portland, late Lord Treasurer, signified your pleasure to take order for what was then due to your petitioner, for the relief of his necessities, but as yet he has not received any benefit thereby. Prays order to the now Lord Treasurer for payment of the said pension and arrears. [½ *p*.] *Underwritten,*

> 94. I. *Reference to the Lord Treasurer and Chancellor of the Exchequer to take order for petitioner's relief. Theobalds, 31st May* 1638. [¼ *p*.]

[May 31.]   95. Petition of divers poor women, in behalf of their husbands in captivity in Algiers, to the King. Petitioners and their children are in extreme want, besides the insupportable miseries endured by their husbands in cruel bondage, being lately taken in a ship, the Mary, of London, bound to the southward. Petitioners having nothing at all towards their ransom nor their own livelihoods, the merchants who set forth the ship, although they have lost ship and goods, have consented to contribute 100*l*. towards the re-

VOL. CCCXCI.

1638.

deeming of them, which will cost about 800*l*. in all. Pray letters by way of brief for a collection in aid of the sum, to be contributed by the merchants, without which their poor husbands must end their days in Turkish slavery, and petitioners in miserable penury. [⅔ *p*.]

[May 31.] 96. Petition of divers poor women to the Lords of the Council. Similar to last petition. [¾ *p*.]

May 31. London. 97. Certificate of Nicholas Crispe, Humphrey Slaney, William Clobery, and John Woods, owners of the Mary, of London, at the request of the wives of James Bearblock and eleven others whose names are enumerated, mariners in the said ship. About August last the certifiers set to sea the said ship. After a long fight with three great Turks' men-of-war, divers of their men being hurt and one slain, they were at last taken near the island of Mathera [Madeira?] and carried to Algiers. We are willing to contribute towards their ransom 100*l*., the whole sum being put at about 800*l*. The master is a skilful man, and well experienced. [¾ *p*.]

[May 31?] 98. Petition of the distressed wives and children of many mariners, prisoners in Algiers and Tunis, to the Council. Upon their late petition to the Lords for the release of their husbands and fathers, you appointed that Captain Leate should ransom so many of the captives as were mentioned in a note by petitioners delivered to you, and that the captain should receive again the money out of such sums as may be collected in England. Since which you have ordered the contrary, and a stay is made in that proceeding, so that petitioners are still enforced to trouble you. Pray speedy order may be taken for redemption of the captives and relief of petitioners. [¾ *p*.]

May 31. 99. Order of the Archbishop of Canterbury and the Lord Keeper, referees of a petition of John Robinson, clerk, vicar of Sunning Hill, (calendared under date of 6th April 1638, No. 31,) against the heirs and executors of Thomas Carew, touching the tithes of the park there. In regard to which it was alleged against petitioner that 13*s*. 4*d*. had used to have been paid in lieu of tithes, and that the heirs were under age, and the executors in trust. It was Ordered that petitioner should bring his action at law upon the statute of Edward VI., for not setting forth tithes, against Mrs. Carew and Mr. Fisher, who should appear and plead, so as the matter may proceed to trial at the next assizes, and no advantage be taken on either side, but to insist upon the right only, whether there be such a rate or no, and admitting there be, whether it will bar the petitioner, the park being now employed for tillage and other uses. And the Lords referees this next term will consider how petitioner, in case the trial fall out against him, may be relieved. [*Draft*. 1 *p*.]

May 31. 100. The Council to Attorney General Bankes. We send you a certificate of commissioners appointed to view the condition of his

1638. Vol. CCCXCI.

Majesty's manor of East Smithfield, and of his Majesty's house there, employed for the service of the Navy, and in the possession of John Crane, surveyor of marine victuals, calendared under 31st March 1638, No. 72. Finding that there are matters mentioned in the certificate which are very fit to be rectified, we require you to take a course to compel those who have been the cause of the decay of the said house to repay the money expended in repairs, as also to make repair of the residue of the decays. We further pray you to take order for removing such cottages, cages, and other buildings as are built adjoining the said house or on his Majesty's waste there, as also to reform all other abuses mentioned in the certificate, so that the buildings may be entirely employed for the service of the Navy; and if you shall need the assistance of this Board we shall readily give it upon intimation from you. [*Draft.* 1½ *p.*]

May 31. 101. The Council to the Judges of Assize for co. Lincoln. The inhabitants of the sessions of Sleaford and Folkingham in the division of Kesteven, co. Lincoln, complain that although the custom long used for raising public assessments has been to cast the whole sum into 14 parts, whereof Lindsey bears seven, Holland three, and Kesteven four, Sir Anthony Irby, now sheriff, has charged them with 161*l.* 8*s.* 6*d.* towards the ship-money more than they ought to pay, and they desire that the settlement of the rates might be referred to the Judges of Assize (*see* calendar for 31st January 1637-8, No. 58.) We require you to call the parties before you, and so to settle the said rates that his Majesty's service may not suffer, nor the country have cause to complain, and of your proceedings therein to return a certificate. [*Draft.* 1½ *p.*]

May 31. 102. The same to Sir William Portman, Sheriff of Somerset. By petition inclosed, Thomas Crompton, gentleman, complains of being over-rated towards the ship-money for a glebe and tithes in Weston, Somerset, paying the first year but 7*l.*, from which he was raised the last year to 11*l.* 5*s.*, and this year to 12*l.* 5*s.* We pray you, finding the particulars to be true, to give order that petitioner be assessed equally according to his Majesty's writ and the Lords' instructions. [*Draft.* 1 *p.*]

May 31. Whitehall. 103. The same to Sir Anthony Vincent, late Sheriff of Surrey. We have seen your letter of the 20th inst. to Edward Nicholas, Clerk of the Council. We grant your request, and give you till Michaelmas next for paying in the arrears of ship-money in the year of your shrievalty, 1636; but we require you to make no default therein. [*Draft.* ½ *p.*]

May 31. Whitehall. 104. The same to Justices of Peace for Kent. For building and repairing his Majesty's ships there are 400 loads of timber, plank, and treenails provided; 200 loads to be brought from Warnham, Sussex, to Kingston-on-Thames; 200 loads more from Lunningston [Lullingston?] Park to Woolwich. We pray you to give order for teams for the carriage at the accustomed rates of 5*d.* per mile for

1638.

Vol. CCCXCI.

every load; but no carts are to be charged on the lathe of Aylesford and the seven hundreds which carry yearly the timber bought near Maidstone to the river Medway. [*Draft.* ¾ *p.*]

May 31.
Whitehall.
105. The Council to Justices of Peace for Essex. Similar letter for carriage of 800 loads provided in several places in that county to the Thames' side. The purveyor will inform you where the timber lies. [*Draft.* ⅔ *p.*]

May 31.
Whitehall.
106. The same to Justices of Peace in Sussex and Surrey. Similar letter for carriage of 200 loads, from woods near Grinstead and lands of Mr. Evelyn to Deptford and Woolwich. [*Probably one letter to each county. Draft.* ¾ *p.*]

May 31.
Whitehall.
107. The same to Justices of Peace for Norfolk. Similar letter for carriage of 800 loads for the frame of the ship royal "the Prince;" 500 loads to be brought from Boddenham Woods to Lynn, and 300 loads from Sir Miles Hobart's lands to Norwich. [*Draft.* ⅔ *p.*]

May 31.
Whitehall.
108. The same to Justices of Peace for Hants. Similar letter for carriage of 700 loads; 200 loads from Quarry Hill, the land of Sir John Jepson, to the Thames' side at Ham Haw, and 500 from several parts near Portsmouth, whither the said timber is to be brought. [*Draft.* ¾ *p.*]

May 31.
109. The same to Lord Chief Justice Finch. We have sent you the petition of James Robbins, purveyor for ship timber, and James Emery, contractor for conveying thereof, by which you will see that the Justices of Peace for Wilts (which shire was charged with the carriage of 500 loads) have been exceeding negligent in that service, and that particularly Sir Lawrence Hyde, and Robert Hyde, recorder of Salisbury, have been more peremptorily adverse (if it be as informed) than becomes men of their place, for which we should call them to a further account, but that finding you, of your affection to all matters concerning his Majesty's service, have given some order in that business, we refer the same to you, to take order that the moneys payable for the said service be forthwith satisfied, and that at the next assizes you call for an account how such order as you shall give has been executed. [*Draft.* 1½ *p.*]

May 31.
110. The same to Edward Stockdell, messenger. Whereas Richard Turner and Jeremy Garsley, of Caddington, co. Bedford, have, contrary to the order of the Board and their own bonds, caused their tenants to turn their sheep into the enclosure of the Dean and Chapter of St. Paul's, London, you are to bring them up, and deliver them to the Warden of the Fleet, there to be kept in prison till further order. [*Draft.* ¾ *p.*]

May 31.
The same to the Warden of the Fleet, to receive and keep Richard Turner and Jeremy Garsley above named. [*Draft minute written on the same paper as the preceding.* 3 *lines.*]

VOL. CCCXCI.

1638.

May 31. 111. Minute for entry on the Council Register of pass for John Bill, of London, gentleman, to travel into foreign parts for three years, with a proviso not to go to Rome. [*Draft.* ¼ *p.*]

May 31. 112. The like, of pass for Sir Edward Bishop of Parham, Sussex. [½ *p.*]

May 31. 113. The like, of pass for Sir Robert Honywood to go into the Low Countries with his lady and three children. [*Draft.* ½ *p.*]

May 31. 114. The like, of discharge of William Baker, of St. Martin's in the Fields, surveyor of the highways, sent for by warrant for default of mending the ways, upon submission and acknowledgment of his fault. [*Draft. 5 lines.*]

May 31. 115. Bond of Edward Shelley and Francis Union, both of St. Andrew's, Holborn, in 100*l.* to the King. Shelley having been attached by John Gray, messenger, to appear before the Council after 21 days warning, if he shall so appear within 21 days next ensuing, and attend till he be discharged, this obligation to be void. [*Draft. Signed, " By me John Gray."* ⅔ *p.*]

May 31. 116. Thomas Gardiner, Recorder of London, to Sec. Windebank. Certifies the names and cases of six condemned prisoners in Newgate, fit to be transported into some foreign plantation, if his Majesty vouchsafe to them that mercy. Among them are Lewis Rively, convicted of robbery in taking a hat from Thomas Lawes, and James Tobin, convicted of stealing 500*l.* from John Gresham, his master. [1 *p.*]

May 31. 117. Roger Downes and Edward Wrightinton to the Archbishop of Canterbury, the Lord Keeper, and the Lord Treasurer. According to an order of the 6th April last, we, the counsel for the Lord Strange and Lord Molyneux, attended Sergeant Whitfield and other of the counsel for Mons. Tartaro and the Lady Molyueux, his wife, concerning 100*l.* per annum annuity claimed by her for her younger son, and 1,000*l.* apiece claimed by her for her two daughters' portions. It was showed by Edward Holt, agent for Lord Molyneux, that the lands chargeable with these payments were of the value of 600*l.* per annum, and that they were subject to precedent charges, which are here enumerated, and which far more than exceeded the value of the lands. Nevertheless, Lord Molyneux offered that if Lady Molyneux will not out of her great estate maintain her said children till Lord Molyneux be of full age, being but two years, he would provide that for one of the daughters, Lady Strange, being her godmother, would keep her as she does her own daughters, and for the younger son that he shall be provided for according to his rank, without any great charge for the present, to the estate. For the younger daughter, being about five or six years old, her charge in her mother's hands for the present is not considerable. [= 1⅓ *p.*]

DOMESTIC—CHARLES I.

VOL. CCCXCI.

1638.
May 31.
London.

118. Peter Richaut to Sir John Pennington. At your last being in London, I had some speech with you concerning convoying to Dunkirk two small ships laden with powder, the Providence, of London, master Thomas Stone, and the Mayflower, of London, master Anthony Leamon. Since which time his Majesty has given you directions for convoying them into Dunkirk (see calendar for 19th May inst., No. 119). These ships departed from London about three days since, and, as I understand, are not further than Gravesend, being they have heard that between that place and the Downs there be some rogues which they fear may do them mischief. I entreat you to command a pinnace to Gravesend to convoy them to you. As soon as I understand the powder is in Dunkirk, I will desire you to accept 150*l.* for your care. [1¾ *p.*]

May 31.
North Somercotes.

119. John Gray, vicar of North Somercotes, co. Lincoln, to [Richard] Harvey, servant to Endymion Porter. Long detail of the facts respecting the tithes of the lately drained marsh of Somercotes. Before the embanking, the marsh was supposed to belong to North and South Somercotes, the inhabitants of both which places were joint commoners; but it was ever known, notwithstanding, to be only in the parish of North Somercotes, if in any parish. But an inquisition has been lately found whereby the marsh is found to be out of any parish, and to belong to the King by his prerogative royal, whereupon the tithes have been conferred upon the writer's vicarage, not as belonging to it as of right, but as a gift and annexation. In rating this new land for the tithe the writer has had consideration for the great charges of embanking, and has charged Mr. Porter's land at 7*d.* an acre, and Mr. Fortescue's part (which is now Mr. Porter's also) at 12*d.* An endeavour was now making by Mr. Cutteris, who intended to farm the Fortescue land, to bring it down to the same rate as Mr. Porter's land. Against this proposal the writer argues, and hopes that neither Harvey nor Mr. Porter will support it. [2½ *pp.*]

May 31.

120. Note by Nicholas for his servant Francis [Smith] to deliver the certificates concerning Wright and Wriothesley to Edward Goodfellow, with his receipt. [½ *p.*]

May 31.

121. An inventory of the Books of the Acts of Council and other papers in the Council Chest, taken the 23rd January 1635–6, with additions made up to the present day. [7 *pp.*]

May.
Whitehall.

122. The King to Sir Philiberto Vernatti and Capt. Thos. Whitmore. Recites letters patent of 12th December last, which granted to Vernatti and Whitmore the sole making of iron with sea coal, pit-coal, peat, and charcoal, not exceeding the fifth part of the ordinary expense, being a new invention, for 14 years. Also an indenture bearing even date with the letters patent, whereby it was stipulated that the iron was to be made into bars, and the King was to have the same at 12*l.* the ton, and in default of his Majesty buying he was to have 20*s.* the ton, and for so much as should be con-

1638.

VOL. CCCXCI.

verted into copper or wire 6s. 8d. the ton. Also reciting that whereas the King was now given to understand that the erection of forges would be necessary for the iron to be converted into bars, which, without a vast expense and length of time, could not be done, wherefore permission was given that Vernatti and Whitmore, during five years of the 14, might vent in blooms and raw iron, rendering to the King 5s. for every ton. [*Probably a suggestion only.* ¾ *p.*]

May. 123. Act of homage to the King performed by Matthew Wren, D.D., late Bishop of Norwich, on his appointment to the Bishopric of Ely. [*Parchment.* 17 *lines.*]

May? 124. Petition of Thomas Yonge to the King. In January 1633-4 petitioner was sworn examiner, only for your Majesty, in the Court of Star Chamber, in causes resulting upon your commission of fees, which he has performed without reward. In April 1636 your Majesty granted him the benefit of a bond of 1,000*l.*, forfeited by William Wall, of London, merchant, reserving to your Majesty an eighth part of what should be recovered. Having passed the said grant, and prepared the cause for trial in the Exchequer, the same was deferred till Easter term last, when Wall procured a reference to some of the Council, of purpose to prevent the trial. The certificate mentioned in Wall's petition is by him pleaded in the Exchequer in bar of the said bond, and, if proved, he would have small trouble to avoid the said debt, but being conscious of its invalidity, and not able to prove the exportation mentioned in his petition, he only intends to make use of the reference for delay, giving out that petitioner shall not get one farthing. Prays his Majesty to countermand the reference, and to direct that the trial may be had this term. [¾ *p.*] *Annexed,*

  124. I. *Order of the Court of Exchequer for deferring the cause of the Attorney-General versus William Wall, upon a bond for 1,000l., for the transportation of certain ends of logwood, from Hilary till Easter Term, to be then tried.* 13*th February* 1637-8. *Copy.* [1 *p.*]

  124. II. *Petition of William Wall, of London, merchant, to the King. Petitioner being a merchant of large trading has been charged, by a bill in the Court of Star Chamber, for importing certain quantities of logwood, and vending the same here, although he had entered into a bond of 1,000l. to transport 538 ends thereof beyond seas. The logwood, after being landed here, was exported and landed at Hamburgh, as by a certificate under the common seal of that town dated 4th September 1635 appears. Notwithstanding, petitioner, for avoiding suits, made full composition for all matters charged in the said bill; but, in spite of his composition, petitioner is now sued in the Exchequer upon the bond of 1,000l. by Mr. Yonge, who has obtained a grant from the King of the benefit thereof.*

1638.

VOL. CCCXCI.

Prays a reference to the Archbishop of Canterbury and the Lords Keeper, Treasurer, and Privy Seal. [¾ p.] Underwritten,

124. II. i. Reference as prayed. Whitehall, 13th April 1638. [Copy. 1 p.]

[May?] 125. Petition of Robert More to the King. By a proviso in the letters patent granted by your Majesty's father for the institution of the hospital of the Charter House, it was provided, that if any of the feoffees present any pensioner, and do not within two months' after his place fall void possess him therein, it falls by lapse into your Majesty's hands. There is a pensioner's place lately so fallen into your hands, and by your letter of the 22nd March you bestowed the first place that should fall void upon petitioner. Prays that by one of your servants you will signify to the master and other officers of the house that they receive petitioner into such place. [1 p.] Annexed,

125. I. *Petition of the same to the same. Petitioner was bred a scholar, and travelled in his youth in England, France, and the Low Countries, and followed his studies till he had tasted of the civil law, physic, and the art military, which he practised for a time in the Netherlands. He was employed by the late King, and ultimately taken into his domestic service, wherein, at his Majesty's command, he managed the estate of the late Earl of Holdernesse. On the death of his royal master and noble friend, his fortunes began to fail, and time has brought him at above* **70** *years of age to an end of all his means. Prays the King to admit him to the hospital of the Charter House, and with that view to write to the Feoffees and Commissioners. [Copy. Underwritten six Latin lines enforcing petitioner's request. ¾ p.]*

125. II. *The King to the Feoffees and Commissioners of the King's Hospital of the Charter House. To admit Robert More into the said hospital, and place him therein, according to his petition. Westminster, 22nd March 1637-8. [Copy. ½ p.]*

May. 126. Draft of the preceding petition of Robert More. [⅔ p.] Annexed,

126. I. *Extract from the Act of Parliament giving Thomas Sutton power to found an hospital, of the clause in a petition recited in the said Act relating to the appointment of master, preacher, schoolmaster, usher, poor men, poor children, and officers of the said hospital. [¾ p.]*

May. Appointment by Henry Earl of Holland, Chief Justice, and Justice in Eyre of the Forests on this side Trent, of Richard Lane, Attorney to Charles Prince of Wales, as the Earl's Deputy, to hear and determine pleas in the courts of the forests of Whittlewood and Salcey,

1638. VOL. CCCXCI.

in cos. Northampton and Buckingham, as also in the forest of Rockingham, co. Northampton. [*Copy. See Book of Orders concerning Forests. Vol. ccclxxxiv., p.* 12. 1⅓ *p.*]

May. 127. **The Council to the Bailiff of Blandford Forum.** We are informed that the ship-money charged upon the borough of Blandford Forum for 1636, at which time William Strechley was bailiff, being 25*l.*, was assessed and received or might have been received by him, or the collector appointed by him. We require you to let him know that we take notice of his great neglect, and admonish him to levy and pay in the said 25*l.*, "by the   of the next term," or that you bind him over to answer before us. [*Draft.* 1 *p.*]

May. 128. Assessment of ship-money for co. Flint, made 10th Dec. 1637, and forwarded at this time to Nicholas by Thomas Whitley, the sheriff. The total sum was 575*l.* This account states the amount assessed on every hundred, with the names of the high constables. [1 *p.*]

May. 129. Petition of two distressed widows, late yeomen's wives of his Majesty's Aumary [Almonry], to the Commissioners for the Household. Petitioners have sixteen debentures for 64*l.*, whereof some were due in King James's time, and the rest long since, besides their standing wages and creditors. Pray order for payment. [½ *p.*]

May. 130. Statement, addressed to the Council, of things desired by the parishioners of Christ Church to be added to the propositions offered by the parishioners of St. Gregory's, touching the use of the West end of Christ Church (see 4th May inst., No. 39). 1. In regard the parish of Christ Church contains between ten and twelve thousand souls, and the churchyard small, that those of St. Gregory's have no burial in their church or churchyard. 2. That some of the ablest men of St. Gregory's will be bound to perform the articles, or that the same may be confirmed by Act of the Council. [½ *p.*] *Underwritten,*

    130. I. *The Desire of St. Gregory's upon the above propositions, addressed to the Council.* 1. *As St. Gregory's has no place to bury their dead, and Christ Church yielded before the Lord Treasurer to St. Gregory's burying ten every year, that they may not be debarred, but restrained to such number as the Council think fit.* 2. *That the assurance given by the churchwardens and others of the better sort of St. Gregory's may be accepted, or that St. Gregory's may be concluded by some order of the Board.* [½ *p.*] *Annexed,*

    130. I. *Promise of the parish of St. Gregory's, subscribed by the Churchwardens and others, being the propositions or assurance above alluded to.* 1. *They promise to place no pews in the church.* 2. *To use the West doors only.* 3. *To depart at 3 years' end from St. John the Baptist* 1638. 4. *To leave the church as well repaired as they find it.* [*Attested copy.* = 2 *pp.*]

Vol. CCCXCI.

1638.
[May ?]

131. Notes upon the way in which Prince Charles ought to be knighted before receiving the Order of the Garter. The opinion of the writer is, that it would not be for the prince's honour that he should be made without solemnity as a carpet knight. [1 p.]

Vol. CCCXCII. June 1–14, 1638.

1638.
June 1.
Claverton.

1. William Bassett, late Sheriff of Somerset, to Nicholas. By letters of the 16th May he is required to pay in all the arrear, which appears to be 437l., before the last day of this term, or attend the Lords on the 17th inst. His attendance will do no service, for he has collected as much as he is likely to do without their especial assistance. His servant Boyce will pay in the amount, which will bring the arrear to 229l. 7s. 9½d., and there he is at a stand for want of assistance, having received no direction from the Lords since he waited on Nicholas, by reason whereof, and because he is appointed at a sessions at Wells, as a committee, with others, to equal the rates of that county, which falls out just at the same time with other business, he desires Nicholas to make his excuse, but send him his aid for levy of the residue of the money. P.S.—Alexander Middleton and Richard Harvey, late constables of Abdick and Bulstone, who are sued by John Pyne for taking distress in this service, solicit that they may receive some answer to their petition for relief, for they shall be informed this term of Mr. Pyne to go to trial, in which they much doubt they shall suffer, without the Lords' aid. Prays that his man may have an answer whether he shall be excused for appearance, for which favour he shall be ready to make acknowledgment. [1¼ p.] *Endorsed,*

> 1. i. *Two classified general statements of the amount in arrear, showing in what way the 229l. 7s. 9½d. is made up.* [2 pp.]

June 1.

2. Hugh Awdeley to Lord Keeper Coventry. Answer to a petition of Edward Nicholas. Many years past Mr. Awdeley compounded with Mr. Hunton for purchase of the manor and lands in Nicholas's petition named, and proceeded some way towards completion, when Sir George Wroughton, a creditor of Hunton, obtained an extent against the said premises for 2,200l. Afterwards Hunton and Mr. Cusse, in whom the [legal e]state of the same premises remained, represented that all the incumbrances could be compounded for at less than 2,000l., whereupon Awdeley himself agreed to pay 2,900l. for the premises as soon as the debts were compounded for. He also compounded with Sir Edward Baynton, who had an extent upon the lands, and thereby got into possession. In December last, upon affirmation of Mr. Cusse that the debts would be compounded for at less than 1,400l., a decree was made by the Lord Keeper that certain payments should be made to the children of Mr. Hunton,

1638. VOL. CCCXCII.

he having died, admitting that there would be sufficient to pay the same after the incumbrances had been discharged. But the incumbrances have not yet been discharged, and certain of them will require 2,600*l*. by way of composition, besides other judgments of great amount, and Awdeley is already out of purse 700*l*. Awdeley hopes the Lord Keeper will not think it fit that he should pay any money to the children until the incumbrances shall all be compounded. [=2½ *pp*.]

June 1. 3. Information of Thomas Mousdale, of Enfield, labourer, taken by Edward Atkins, steward of the manor, by direction of Lord Newburgh, Chancellor of the Duchy. Informant dwells in a cottage in Enfield near the Chase side, by the New River, and the same has continued a cottage for 12 years. About a month since he was warned by Richard Knowleton, headborough of Enfield, to attend the Commissioners for new erected cottages, at the Bull in Tottenham. He found three commissioners, who questioned him. He informed them that his cottage was ready to fall down to the ground. They replied that if he compounded he might build it up again. They required of him 3*s*. 6*d*. in money, whereof 12*d*. for making a bond to pay 20*s*. the 22nd May last, at the house of Humphrey Fulwood, in Covent Garden, and 2*s*. 6*d*. for the Barons of the Exchequer. When he had paid the 3*s*. 6*d*. they told him he had compounded only for what was past, whereupon he was sorry that he had paid them any money. Eight other cottagers likewise compounded. [½ *p*.] *Underwritten*,

> 3. I. *Information of William Barnes to the same effect. He compounded for himself and widow Clay.* [¼ *p*.]

June 1. 4. William Bowker and five others to [the Lords of the Admiralty].
Yaxley. Certify the great abuse committed by Henry Finnimore, who has of late been found a common barretor, and stands bound to good behaviour, being a man of an ill life and conversation. He, coming into the house of Richard Hart with Christopher Lanckton, John Cooke, Francis Bludwick and others, of purpose to make a quarrel, or rather a mutiny, with the constable, who was conferring about carriages for the saltpetre works, the said constable being "intercepted" and ever since going in danger of his life, could not at that time charge the carts desired, which was a great hindrance to the service. George Palmer, the constable, and George Russell and John Clarke, saltpetremen, can further testify. [¾ *p*.]

June 2. Notes by Nicholas of business to be transacted by the Lords of the Admiralty. Read the new commission. Directions for letters to call the Vice-Admirals to account. Sir James Bagg to attend about his account. [Margin by the Lord Treasurer, "*non comparuit*."] Complaint by Mr. Pinckney, a saltpetreman, and by Mr. Bagnall, against a clergyman. Consider proportions of saltpetre brought in by deputies. Petition of Capt. Doves, being the next article calendared. Consider Dr. Mason's petition, and Edward

Vol. CCCXCII.

1638.

Thornhill's answer to petition of John Morton. [*See* 21*st April* 1638, *No.* 14. ¾ *p.*]

June 2. Whitehall.
Order of the Lords of the Admiralty. By petition of Samuel Doves, Captain Robert Tokely, and Henry Careless, it was prayed that a commission out of date, formerly granted to Sir Edmond Sawyer, Edward Nicholas, Auditor Worfield, and Auditor Bingley, for examination of abuses in payment of freight for ships, might be renewed, and made returnable at Bartholomewtide, and that three other commissioners be added, with enlarged powers. The petition was referred to the Attorney-General, to certify his opinion. [*Copy. See Vol.* ccclⅲ., *fo.* 103. ½ *p.*]

June 2. Claverton.
5. William Bassett, late Sheriff of Somerset, to the Council. Reports the leading facts stated in his letter to Nicholas of the 1st inst., and prays direction and assistance in levying his arrears of ship-money, and to be spared his attendance on the 17th inst. [=½ *p.*]

June 2.
6. Account of Sir William Russell of ship-money for 1637. Total received, 99,432*l*. 1*s*. 9*d*.; unpaid, 96,982*l*. 5*s*. 11*d*. [=2 *pp.*]

June 2.
7. Account of further sums levied and in the hands of the sheriffs. Total, 6,140*l*.; making the amount collected 105,572*l*., being 31,887*l*. less than was paid in on 3rd June 1637. [1 *p.*]

June 2. Whitehall.
Order of Commissioners for Saltpetre, that a certificate of Edward Fotherby, storekeeper at Blackwall for the East India Company, addressed to —— Cordewell, that all the decayed gunpowder sent to the mills at Chilworth from the East India Company's powder house from 3rd January to 20th March last was 93 barrels, whereof there were returned from the mills 90 barrels on 29th April last, should be entered in the Book of Registry for saltpetre. [*Copy. See Vol.* ccxcii., *p.* 80. ⅔ *p.*]

June 2.
8. Certificate of Edward Finch, vicar of Christ Church, London, with Thomas Risdon his curate, and the churchwardens and 28 of the parishioners, amongst them Sir Thomas Fanshawe, as to the conformity of William Wickins, lately chosen steward of Christ's Hospital. [1 *p.*]

June 2. Burderop.
9. Sir William Calley to Richard Harvey. Thanks for his readiness to provide things desired. Wishes for a tierce of the best claret. Mr. Foster greatly abused them in the last tierce. [½ *p.*]

June 3. Whitehall.
Lords of the Admiralty to a messenger not named. To bring up Henry Finnimore of [Yaxley], co. Huntingdon, to answer matters to be objected against him, with general clause of assistance. [*Copy. See Vol.* ccclⅲ., *fol.* 120 *b.*]

June 4.
10. Receipt of Lionel Wake the younger, for 330*l*. in full of 3,000*l*. due by his Majesty to Sir Peter Paul Rubens, for pictures bought of him long since. [½ *p.*]

Vol. CCCXCII.

1638.
June 4.
11. Receipt of Edward Hodgson, clerk of Robert Bateman, chamberlain of London, for 40*l.*, being Sec. Windebank's second gift to the repairs of St. Paul's. [$\frac{2}{3}$ *p.*]

June 4.
Lambeth.
12. Archbishop Laud to all ecclesiastical persons within the archdeaconry of Buckingham. We have received information that many churches in that archdeaconry daily grow ruinous, especially in the plumbing and leads. We are not only by law to take care for upholding the churches, but by his Majesty's proclamation of the 11th October 1629 all bishops are commanded to take special care thereof. We commend to you Henry Awdeley of Buckingham, plumber, that you may employ him in repairing churches "defectuous" in the leads, he behaving himself civilly, doing his work substantially, and at as easy a rate as any other, and returning to us certificates of his repairs, and of all ruins and defects that shall continue unamended, that we may proceed against those in default. [*Seal removed. Parchment.* 34 *lines.*]

June 4.
13. Richard Bagnall to the Lords Commissioners for Gunpowder. Prays that the bargemen trading westward may carry coals from London to the nearest place by water to the saltpetre works, when required, which is not above one year in six or seven, and likewise carry saltpetre from any place near the works to his Majesty's storehouse at Broken Wharf, at the usual rates for his Majesty's carriages, vizt., from London to Wallingford and Burcot 5*s.* per ton, to Reading 4*s.* 2*d.*, to Henley 3*s.* 4*d.*, to Windsor 3*s.* 4*d.* [$\frac{3}{4}$ *p.*]

June 4.
14. John Cobham the elder to [Nicholas?]. Certifies that he, being of Rochester, chandler, and one of the aldermen of that city, had passed over his shop to his son William Cobham, with powder and shot and other wares; and that his son, before the proclamation was proclaimed at Rochester, bought certain powder of divers men in the same trade. [$\frac{1}{4}$ *p.*]

June 4.
Burderop.
15. Sir William Calley to Richard Harvey. Lady Calley wishes Harvey to buy her as much of the very best and richest black flowered satin, of the best work, yet fit for an ancient woman, as will make her a straight bodied gown, wherein she wishes Mr. Davison's advice taken, and that he should make it up after the fashion most used. The last bodies he sent her were very fit. This, with other articles for Lady Calley here enumerated, were to be put in a reckoning apart. [$\frac{1}{2}$ *p.*]

June 4.
Burderop.
16. William Calley to the same. His father having given him leave to turn Harvey over [for payment] to Felix Long, he orders a black satin gown, and a white satin waistcoat, with other things, for his wife, and a pair of gold colour silk stockings for himself. Is glad the plague is so little in London, but death has more than one dart. Anthony Hatte this day took his leave of the world. [*Seal with arms.* 1 *p.*]

Vol. CCCXCII.

1638.
June 5.
Heyghley.

17. John Newton, Sheriff of co. Montgomery, to Nicholas. There is an arrear of ship-money in Salop since the time of my being sheriff, which by a special letter from the Lords was transferred to be collected by the succeeding sheriff, Robert Corbett, who for that year had no other service to do in the ship business. He entertained the service, and collected a great part of the arrear, which in the whole was 200*l*. He has left 40*l*. uncollected, which I am required by the Lords to collect. I hold myself free from this service, and desire by your good means I may be so. I have inclosed a bill for 200*l*. for ship-money in co. Montgomery, which makes 500*l*. The service in that county is indifferently well taken, and the rest of the monies are collecting. Two towns are much visited with plague, Newtown and Llanidloes, yet I will use diligence to accomplish the service. [*Seal with arms. 1 p.*]

June 5.

Commissioners for Gunpowder to the Master of the Ordnance. Warrant to deliver one barrel of gunpowder at 18*d*. per lb. to Henry Rider of Guildford, chandler. [*Minute, Book of Warrants for Gunpowder. See Vol. ccclv., No. 61, p. 6. ⅕ p.*]

June 5.

18. Certificate of John Armistead, that being under-book-keeper to Ralph Clavering's part, he directed, on the 4th of April last, four tickets, every ticket for five chalder, all which were loaded aboard the Margaret, of Yarmouth, Clement Baker master. [*Underwritten is a confirmation of the above from the men who loaded the coals aboard the ship, to which the men, all marksmen, made a voluntary acknowledgment before John Marlay, the Mayor of Newcastle, and two others, probably aldermen. 1 p.*]

June 5.
Stratford.

19. [John Gaspar] Wolffen to Sec. Windebank. His Majesty three days ago gave me answer that he would order one of his chief secretaries to confer with me. But being troubled with gout, so that now and then I am not able to stir, I set down the sum of the business. Two years and a half ago the brewers at Westminster being in trouble about sea coal smoke, which annoys his Majesty's houses at Whitehall and St. James's, I offered them (with his Majesty's liking) a fuel which yields no smoke at all. Having seen a trial, they were very glad of it, and began to deal with me about it. But another device was offered them, with pretence that it should save more than half the coals. I took pains to demonstrate to them and to the King the impossibility of the pretended invention; yet was I fain to stay almost a year to see an end of it, which was such that his Majesty was much displeased with it. Two or three days after there was another device brought in by the Marquess of Hamilton's recommendation, and I was forced to stay for an end of it, which being no better than the former, his Majesty much disliked it. Now there is nothing left to the brewers except my fuel without smoke. All I desire of his Majesty at this time is to let the brewers know for certain that if they make smoke they shall not stay at Westminster, and that they may stay if they make no smoke. For that effect the fuel will serve them. They make a question if it will not be costly, and never would see the trial what the charges would be. Others who have

Vol. CCCXCII.

1638.

seen it will be glad to come in their room; the which, if it prove so, it might easily be brought to go farther than to Westminster. [=1½ p.]

June 5. 20. Petition of Roger Reeve to Archbishop Laud. On the last court day, upon the petition of William Richardson, who pretended that there were many suits depending between him and his parishioners, you referred all matters between them to Sir John Lambe, in case the parties on both sides would enter into a bond to stand to his determination. The suits against Mr. Richardson are now ready for hearing, and the suits against his parishioners have been entered only in hope to take off petitioner from prosecution against him. Prays that Richardson may take upon him *ad probandum* against petitioner and his other parishioners, or that they may be dismissed, with costs; and because the matters against Richardson are very foul that those causes may be heard next court day. [½ p.] *Underwritten,*

20. I. *Reference to Sir John Lambe to consider the above suggestions, and do as he shall find just. 5th June* 1638. [⅙ p.]

June 5. 21. Notes of Archbishop Laud taken upon the hearing of a cause in the Star Chamber against Sir Richard Wiseman, for taxing that court with injustice in reference to a former suit of his dismissed, and the Lord Keeper with corruption. The present cause was heard partly on the 1st inst., and partly to-day, when it was sentenced. These notes refer to the proceedings on both days. The slander was contained in two petitions of Sir Richard Wiseman to the King, in one of which he taxed the Lord Keeper with having received from him a bason and ewer and a sum of 220*l.* in money. The presentation of the bason and ewer were not disputed. It was a new year's gift. On its presentation inquiry was made if any suit were depending. The bearer answered, there were no suits, but Sir Richard had received many courtesies before. The Lord Keeper called for the book of causes, and looked upon it, and found none, yet he said, if it should be found otherwise the plate should be returned. A subsequent offer of silver plate was refused to be received, both by the Lord Keeper and by his Lady. The 220*l.* was stated to have been given by Sir Richard Wiseman to the Lord Keeper alone, who thereupon, as it was alleged, told Sir Richard that his cause was good, although it was afterwards "cast out of the court." This was denied and disbelieved. Sir Richard was sentenced to be fined 10,000*l.*, to be imprisoned, to pay 5,000*l.* damages to the Lord Keeper, 1,000*l.* to Mr. Justice Jones, and 1,000*l.* to John Thomson, servant of the Lord Keeper; if a knight, he was to be degraded; if a baronet, there was to be a *scire facias* against his patent; he was to stand in the pillory with papers, and [lose] both his ears; he was disabled from giving testimony, and a "whetstone about his neck." [8 *pp.*]

June 5. 22. Notes in another hand of one of the speeches delivered on giving sentence in the cause against Sir Richard Wiseman. [½ p.]

Vol. CCCXCII.

1638.
June 5.
[St.] Lawrence Ayott.
23. Thomas Reade to Sir John Lambe. Those refractory women of King's Walden, who were enjoined penance at your last Court at Hatfield, to acknowledge their faults before the minister and churchwardens in the chancel after prayers, not only please themselves in the contempt thereof, but address themselves to a further attempt either to trouble you with the continuance of clamour in casting blame where it should not be, or in appealing to the High Commission. [1 p.]

June 5.
24. Certificate of John Farnaby and four others, parishioners of Christ Church, London, of the conformity of William Wickins, steward of Christ's Hospital. [¾ p.]

June 5.
25. Rental of the manors of Aston-sub-Edge and Mickleton, co. Gloucester, for one half year, due to Endymion Porter at May day 1638; total, 144l. 15s. Among the tenants were Sir Nicholas Overbury, Thomas Southern, and Richard Canning. A chief rent of 5l. was payable to Sir Edward Fisher. [1 p.]

June 5.
26. Account rendered to Endymion Porter by Hugh Campion of the produce of wood sold in the manor of Allfarthing during 1638; total, 18l. 10s. [1 p.]

June 6.
Petition of James Earl of Carlisle and of the Trustees of the Estate of the late Earl of Carlisle to the King. Your Majesty, towards satisfaction of a debt of 21,320l. due to the late Earl of Carlisle, on 10th April 1636, at the request of the said Earl, granted to John Van Haesdonk 10,000 acres of marish ground at 20s. per acre, and 4d. rent, lying in cos. Norfolk, Suffolk, Kent, and Chester, which were found by inquisitions to be usually overflown at ordinary spring tides, and therefore belong to your Majesty in right of your crown, they being of the nature of deserted lands left and spewed out by the sea, and of the same soil and condition as the sea-shores. Van Haesdonk has embanked some part, and for gaining possession of the same has commenced a suit in the Exchequer. The opposers of your Majesty's title are much encouraged, and Van Haesdonk somewhat discouraged to proceed to a hearing, for that the Barons have discovered their doubt that marshes so usually drowned at ordinary spring tides do not belong to your Majesty, but such as are drowned at daily and neap tides. For clearing your Majesty's right, petitioners have drawn some reasons, and pray you to recommend the same to the serious consideration of the Barons of the Exchequer, and direct them to call unto them your counsel at law, and advise thereon. [*Copy. See Vol. cccxxiii., p. 302.* ⅚ *p.*] *Underwritten,*

> I. *Reference to the Lord Treasurer and Lord Cottington, calling to them the Barons of the Exchequer and his Majesty's learned counsel, to certify their opinions.* [*Copy. Ibid.* ⅙ *p.*]

Vol. CCCXCII.

1638.
June 6.

27. Sir John Manwood to Theophilus Earl of Suffolk, Lord Warden of the Cinque Ports. This morning is arrived from Dieppe the Count of Egmont, under the title of a French Baron. He is desirous to speak with the Spanish ambassador (who went hence on Monday last, and in probability is returned by a contrary wind this night,) by a second person, and has sent unto the Downs to see if he be there. This Count, being both by birth and fortune of one of the eminentest families of the Netherlands, retired into France out of Flanders about six years since, when the Duke of Arscot was arrested in Spain, but could never be induced to take arms against his Prince, so that in appearance he would treat of his reconciliation. Of this I made a discovery by an Irish sergeant-major, whose passport discovered him, who has importuned me not to discover him from being a French Baron. I beseech you open it to the King, that when his Majesty sees him he would not seem to know him, for his intention is not to discover himself till he comes to the King. He is about 37 years old, and has one of his sons with him. He goes to Canterbury to-night, and to-morrow towards London. The packet-boat is not come from Dunkirk, so that I can write no variety of news. Since routing the two French regiments by the Prince Tomaso, and the Duke de la Force's joining with Chatillon's army before St. Omer, both consisting of 10,000 horse and 35,000 foot, the lines of circumvallation are not yet perfected, but many strong forts built by the French upon their lines, and cannon upon them. This is French news. The Governor of Calais wrote that by the 20th of this month, N.S., they shall know where the Prince of Orange's designs are for. My occasions draw me to London to-morrow. [*Endorsed by Sec. Windebank*, "Sent to me by the Earl of Suffolk. 7th June." 2 *pp.*]

June 6.
Wilburton.

28. Sir Miles Sandys the elder to Sir Miles Sandys the younger. I have received letters this day by this messenger from the Council, requiring my present and personal attendance at the Board. You know the inability of my body. I pray you make my excuse. I cannot conceive of any other occasion but some suggestion from my cousin Isaac Barrow about the tumults in Wickham, where he dwells, which he suffered unpunished, and now would make show as if he stood in fear of his life, and that none would obey his warrants. It is believed in these parts that he can rule them all with a word of his mouth. So his son-in-law, Mr. Grimmer, curate of Wickham, could do in his absence, as Mr. Heiley, one of the King's messengers, after himself and two other messengers were by threats and force driven out of the town, told me. The question of speech about me may thus arise. One Barker, a labouring man, dwelling near me in Haddenham, came and told me of a great riot made at Wickham by hurling in my Lord of Bedford's works, and with all told me of treasonable speeches used by one Hovell of Bott Soham [Bottisham] against his Majesty, which Hovell dwells about two or three miles from Mr. Barrow. I told Barker that I dwelt in the Isle of Ely, and had not authority in the shire where these words were spoken, and

Vol. CCCXCII.

1638.

therefore required him to address himself to Mr. Barrow, the next justice. [*Details the proceedings before Mr. Barrow, which ended in the committal of Hovell to Cambridge Castle, and Barker being bound over by the writer to give evidence at the next assizes.*] Barker named Thomas Knock of Bott Soham who could also testify the same words spoken to him. I signified as much to Mr. Barrow, but cannot hear that Knock has been examined. If this were the occasion of the Lords sending for me, you shall do well to produce this letter. If there be any other occasion, upon notice I will express myself to them. P.S.—Whilst writing, word is brought by my Lord of Bedford's workmen, that the country rose up against him, both in Coveney and Littleport, by the example of Wickham men. I fear if present order be not taken, it will turn out to be a general rebellion in all the Fen towns. [*Seal with arms. 2⅔ pp.*]

June 6.　29. Answers by the Merchants of London to the reasons of the Yarmouth merchants for not delivering their herrings to the merchants of London at a medium quantity and price for seven years to come. The paper answered will be found in this calendar under date of 26th May last, Vol. cccxi., No. 27. [*2 pp.*]

June 7. Greenwich.　30. The King to the Mayor and others of Berwick-upon-Tweed. We are informed that there are certain grounds in the possession of Sir James Douglas, called Madlenfield, Coneygarths, and Batt, lying near the walls of Berwick, and enclosed by the town walls, Madlendyke, and the sea, in which grounds you put some of your cattle, under pretence of grazing under the wall ditches, and also impound the cattle of tenants of Sir James Douglas, which has not heretofore been done. Our pleasure is that you forbear to put your cattle into the said grounds, or impound those of the tenants of Sir James, till your claim to the said grounds shall be made good by law, to which our pleasure we expect your conformity. [*Draft. ⅔ p.*]

June 7. St. James's.　31. William Earl of Newcastle to the Council. In obedience to your commands of the 20th April last, I signified to my Deputy Lieutenants of co. Derby the complaint of divers townships of unequal assessments laid upon them in the business of ship-money, after the rate of their trained soldiers. They returned me this inclosed answer by which you may perceive the ground of that complaint, and the condition of him that has moved them to it, and that the justices of the peace have no intention to tie themselves to this rule, but where they conceive it may be done with equality and indifferencey. [*Seal with arms. 1 p.*] *Endorsed,*

  31. I. *Deputy Lieutenants of co. Derby to William Earl of Newcastle. At this time the townships above alluded to are principally stirred up by Mr. Woolhouse of Glapwell, to complain, who has got money of them to follow this business at the Council Board, having suits of his own which occasion almost his constant attending at London*

1638.

Vol. CCCXCII.

every term. We find no necessity that all the levies made by the justices should be regulated by the trained soldier, there being several charges raised by other rules, and these letters from the judges of assize to the justices of peace, to see that the assessments be made with equality and indifferency. The justices propose to see it done, and if there be cause will relieve the townships mentioned in the petition and all other places. 20th May 1638. [1 p.]

June 7. 32. Affidavit of John Hynde, of St. Clement Danes, and William Hart of St. Andrew, Holborn, that Andrew Ball, solicitor for George Onsloe, having seen a reference procured by Robert Lyham from the King to Lord Chief Justice Bramston and Sir George Croke, judges of assize for Suffolk, Ball, in a slighting manner, said, "Tush, I care not a pin for such references! I can have a hundred of them for 20s. apiece, and the King shall never know of them." And likewise said that the King never saw the said reference, nor knew of it, and many other words to that effect. [1 p.]

June 7. Petition of Nicholas Pescod, of Southampton, to the King. There has been a chargeable suit between petitioner and Richard Uvedale, concerning 1,000l. which Uvedale challenges to be due to him, on a promise which he alleges that petitioner made when Tuppin Scras and Uvedale were discoursing about Uvedale's adventuring 330l. in a ship with Scras, that whatsoever agreement Scras made with Uvedale, petitioner would see it performed, which petitioner utterly denies. There have been several suits brought by Uvedale first against Scras and since against petitioner, in Chancery, in the Court of Requests, in the Exchequer, and at Salisbury assizes before Lord Chief Justice Finch. Prays a reference for finally determining the matter. [*Copy. See Vol. cccxxiii., p.* 303. ⅓ *p.*] *Underwritten,*

    I. *Reference to the Lord Keeper, the Lord Privy Seal, the Lord Chief Justice Finch, and the Lord Chief Baron. Greenwich, 7th June* 1638. [*Copy. Ibid.* ⅙ *p.*]

    II. *Minute that his Majesty, for that this business has been already tried by the Lord Privy Seal, and by him referred to a trial at law, reserving the equity, and several trials had, some with him [petitioner] and some against him, that the Lord Privy Seal, calling to his assistance the two Lord Chief Justices, shall in open court hear the cause again in equity, and end the same, according to the merits. Whitehall, 19th January* 1638-9. *Copy. Ibid.* ⅙ *p.*]

June 7. Petition of Sir Edward Alford and Richard Dowdeswell to the same. Sir Francis Popham, being a person of a great estate, and very much bent to have his will in what he once undertakes, has multiplied so many vexatious suits against petitioners, and others for their sakes, for matters of little or no value, and therein uses such

Vol. CCCXCII.

1638.

unworthy instruments, and such undue means, that they foresee that by these oppressions they must suffer, even to their utter ruin, or yield to his will in all things, unless by your Majesty's interposing they may be relieved. Pray the King to cast his eye upon certain articles, or refer the examination thereof to persons of honour. [*Copy. See Vol. cccxxiii., p.* 303. $\frac{1}{3}$ *p.*] *Underwritten,*

I. *Reference to the Attorney-General to consider the petition and articles, and exhibit an information against Sir Francis Popham in the Star Chamber, if he find matter enough. Greenwich, 7th June* 1638. [*Copy. Ibid., p.* 304. $\frac{1}{6}$ *p.*]

June 7. Petition of Sir Peter Killigrew to the King. By order from the late King, the late Earl of Salisbury and Sir Julius Cæsar took in lease from petitioner's ancestors certain lands in Cornwall whereupon your Majesty's fort of Pendennis Castle stands, for a fine and at a yearly rent of 13*l.* 6*s.* 8*d.*, which land has since descended to petitioner, and the lease is near expiring. Offers for consideration whether his Majesty should not take the inheritance of the land for other lands to be given in recompense to petitioner, wherein, if the King be inclined to value petitioner's endeavour to serve him, it will much the more enable petitioner to continue the same. [*Copy. Ibid.* $\frac{1}{2}$ *p.*] *Underwritten,*

I. *Reference to the Lord Treasurer and Lord Cottington to inform themselves what parcel of land petitioner desires in exchange, and to certify the values of both, with their opinion. Greenwich, 7th June* 1638. [*Copy. Ibid.* $\frac{1}{6}$ *p.*]

June 7. Petition of Henry Alexander, second son to William Earl of Stirling and Mary his wife, one of the daughters of Sir Peter Vanlore, to the same. Petitioner's grandfather, Sir Peter Vanlore, bequeathed to all his grandchildren (daughters) 1,000*l.* apiece, to be paid at their days of marriage, and died, leaving Dame Jacoba, his then wife, and John Delate, his son-in-law, executors, the said John Delate being only named in trust for Dame Jacoba, who has since died, leaving Thomas Crompton her executor in trust for Lady Powell her daughter. Petitioner making demand "thereof," Thomas Crompton makes scruples in payment. To avoid a suit, prays a reference. [*Copy. Ibid., p.* 305. $\frac{1}{3}$ *p.*] *Underwritten,*

I. *Reference to the Earl Marshal, Mr. Comptroller of the Household, and Sec. Windebank, to settle an order for relief of petitioner. Greenwich, 7th June* 1638. [*Copy. Ibid.* $\frac{1}{6}$ *p.*]

June 7. Petition of Sir Peter Vanlore to the same. Petitioner is son and heir of Sir Peter Vanlore, deceased, one, whilst he lived, of great estate, who, being aged 80 years, made his last intended settlement of estate much (as was most just) for the advantage of petitioner and his children. Nevertheless, by mistake, or practice of others,

1638.

Vol. CCCXCII.

the writings were so penned that, contrary to petitioner's father's intention, Sir Edward Powell, who had married one of petitioner's sisters, is gone away with the greatest part of the estate, and petitioner is hardly able to subsist and bring up his children. Questions hereupon growing, Sir Edward obtained a reference to the Archbishop of Canterbury and the Lords Keeper, Treasurer, and Privy Seal. Their appointments petitioner attended with his counsel, but the referees could not hear the case by reason of their greater occasions. At another time, when petitioner could not procure his former counsel, and could only beg further time, an award was made, to which Lady Powell does not submit. Prays the King to hear the cause himself. [*Copy. See Vol. cccxxiii., p. 305. ⅔ p.*] *Underwritten,*

> I. Minute of his Majesty's declaration that he will hear the business in person on Sunday, the 17th inst., at Greenwich, at two in the afternoon. Greenwich, 7th June 1638. [*Copy. Ibid., p. 306. ⅙ p.*]

June 7. Lambeth.

33. Draft definitive sentence of the Court of High Commission in a cause against John Ward, clerk, rector of Dinnington [Dennington], Suffolk, and William Castle and Robert Cade, clerks. In 1624 the rectory of Dinnington became void by the death of Robert Wright, the incumbent. Sir John Rous, the patron, gave a presentation to Thomas Boswell, fellow of Pembroke Hall, Cambridge, provided he would reside at Dinnington, and otherwise left the presentation at his disposal. By the interference of Nicholas Bacon and Mr. Godbold (the latter an intimate friend of Mr. Boswell) 650*l*. was paid to Mr. Boswell, who thereupon handed over his presentation to Mr. Ward. He re-delivered it to Sir John Rous, and received from Sir John a fresh presentation, made out in Ward's own name, upon which he was instituted and inducted. Of the 650*l*. paid to Boswell, 400*l*. seems to have been advanced by Nicholas Bacon out of his own money, and the remainder was borrowed by him at interest. Shortly after Ward's induction, he procured Sir Lionel Tollemache to make arrangements with Nicholas Bacon for the gradual repayment of the money. But whispers of the simoniacal bargain got abroad, whereupon Castle procured a presentation from the King, which was quashed by payment to him of 260*l*. Cade also took certain collusive proceedings with the view of strengthening Ward's title, and Ward himself procured a coronation pardon from the present King. The Court deprived Ward of the rectory of Dinnington, and declared the church to be void. They pronounced Castle and Cade incapable of holding the same. They fined Castle 260*l*. to his Majesty, and condemned all the defendants in costs. Letters missive were also ordered against Sir John Rous and Nicholas Bacon, to call them to answer the premises in this court. [9¾ *pp.*]

June 7. Lambeth.

34. Order of the same Court in a cause against Richard Whineates and others of Chellaston, co. Derby. A petition having been read on

1638.

VOL. CCCXCII.

behalf of Vincent Oliver, prosecutor of this cause, reciting a former order, that unless the defendants appeared before Sir John Lambe, and gave bond for performing such order as Sir John should interpose, before a day limited, the cause should be resumed and sentenced here. The defendants not having observed that order, petitioner desired that the cause should go on, and the defendants be attached. The court referred the petition to Sir John Lambe and Sir Charles Cæsar. [1½ p.] *Underwritten,*

 34. I. *Appointment by the referees to hear this cause on Wednesday then next.* 11*th June* 1638. [¼ p.]

June 7. 35. Memorandum by the three Masters of Kingston-upon-Thames, that in the absence of the bailiffs notice had been given by Andrew Pawling for the said bailiffs to appear in the Exchequer to pass account for his Majesty's casual profits. [½ p.]

June 7. 36. Isaac Pennington to his cousin Sir John Pennington. He has transacted the business with Mr. Hawkins, having taken in the bill of exchange and protest, and written upon it an acknowledgment that he received 10*l.* of Sir John's free will and bounty, and not as a due debt. Sends underwritten a copy of the acknowledgment. [1 p.]

June 8. Grant to Sir James Palmer, his Majesty's servant, of the reversion of the demesne lands of the manor of Ogmore and Week, parcel of the duchy of Lancaster, in co. Glamorgan, now in lease for 21 years, at the rent of 16*l.* 19*s.* 0¼*d.*, to be holden of the duchy of Lancaster as of the manor of Enfield, Middlesex, in free and common socage, under the fee-farm rent of 16*l.* for ever. [*Docquet.*]

June 8. Pardon to Richard Nicholl, convicted of burglary, and of stealing 30 lbs. of tobacco and a petticoat from Matthew Gleane and Elizabeth Tompson, widow, of which he was convicted at the assizes for co. Chester, 7th April 1638. [*Docquet.*]

June 8. 37. The King to Sir William Balfour, Sir John Heydon, Sir William Becher, and Sir Francis Godolphin. We are resolved to have a fair trial what despatch may be made in the fabrique of our moneys by mills and presses (moved by Nicholas Briot), in comparison of the ancient way of the hammer, and to that purpose we commanded our pleasure to be signified on the 28th May last, and have since been moved on behalf of Briot, to proceed to this trial according to our commission in the 7th year of our reign, when Sir Robert Harley was our officer in the Mint. As the proceeding on that commision will not give such present despatch as we might expect, our pleasure is, that the first thing to be done shall be the trial of despatch according to our directions of the 28th May, and we require you to proceed therein without delay or further excuse on either party, and when this is done the commission shall be proceeded upon as desired on behalf of Briot. [1 p.]

June 8. 38. Petition of Roger Fullwood to the King. Judgment being given against petitioner and others for petitioner's forcibly taking

DOMESTIC—CHARLES I.   499

1638.   Vol. CCCXCII.

away Sarah Cox and marrying her, your Majesty has granted petitioner and all the rest your pardon. But the said Sarah and her friends desiring to question the said marriage, petitioner has agreed to give his consent to a nullity, at what time the Court of Arches shall require him. States the point at which proceedings in that court have arrived, and prays direction that the pardon may presently pass the seal, for if it be not forthwith despatched petitioner will be enforced to lie in prison all the long vacation. Petitioner will enter into a recognizance of 2,000*l.* to consent to a nullity of the marriage. [¾ *p.*] *Underwritten,*

> 38. I. *Minute of his Majesty's pleasure that the pardon for petitioner and Mr. [Richard] Bowen be no longer stopped, petitioner entering a recognizance as above mentioned. Greenwich, 8th June 1638.* [¼ *p.*]

June 8.
London.

39. William Clobery to Sec. Coke. When the King was last at Newmarket, I was with Mr. Comptroller about my Barbary saltpetre, who caused me to subscribe a note, the copy whereof is enclosed, and wished me to repair to him when his Majesty returned from Newmarket, and he would move his Majesty on my behalf for the 40 lasts of powder for my old debt. But since that time great pain of the stone has prevented me from waiting upon Mr. Comptroller. Now having a vessel come from Barbary which has brought 30,000 lbs. of petre, and the works being now well settled, as this bearer, my principal factor now come from thence, can inform you, and how he could have sold all my petre at a great rate to the King of Spain's agent, I am an humble suitor that you will confer with Mr. Comptroller, and that by both your favours with his Majesty I may have the said powder for satisfaction of my debt, by the rates of which powder and petre his Majesty will be a great gainer. Explains the inconveniences which the delay in payment had occasioned him. [1 *p.*] *Enclosed,*

> 39. I. *Copy note or undertaking above alluded to, and already calendared under date of 24th February 1637-8, No. 4.* [½ *p.*]

June 8.
St. Andrew,
in the Downs.

40. Sir John Pennington to Sec. Windebank. I am this instant returned from Dunkirk, where I have seen the two ketches with powder safely at anchor under the fort, within the Splinter. There were nine sail of Hollands men of war at anchor in the road, and five sail riding without, and some others plying to and again, but they did not offer to come near us. There were also eight sail of Dunkirk men-of-war riding within the Splinter. I spoke with nobody, but so soon as I had seen them out of danger came my ways. [*Seals with arms.* 1 *p.*]

June 8/18.
Rome.

41. Christopher Windebank to his father, Sec. Windebank. Apprises him that, by the advice of Sir William Hamilton, he had taken up 50*l.* to serve him and his servant to Paris, whither he is advised to go first, before he settles in any place, to get some cor-

1638.

VOL. CCCXCII.

respondent there to whom he may address his letters for England, and receive them from thence. Has given a bill for the money, which he received through Father John Wilford, who expresses himself the Secretary's servant. [=1½ p.]

June 8. Funeral certificate by William Riley of Anne, late wife of William Lord Howard of Effingham (eldest son of Charles Earl of Nottingham), and sole daughter of John Lord St. John of Bletsoe, who died on the 7th inst., and was buried this night in Westminster Abbey. She had issue by the said Lord, Elizabeth, their only daughter and heir, married to John Earl of Peterborough, by whom she has issue Henry Lord Mordaunt, aged 13 years, and John, aged 12, and two daughters, Elizabeth and Anne. [Copy, unsigned. See Vol. ccclx., p. 7. ½ p.]

June 9. Petition of Philip Earl of Pembroke and Montgomery, Lord Warden of the Stannaries, to the King. The stannary and duchy courts have many privileges confirmed by charters and allowed by the Star Chamber, Chancery, King's Bench, and other courts, yet the same have lately been impeached by writs of prohibition, habeas corpus, and injunction, and other writs out of the King's Bench and other courts at Westminster, in causes depending in the stannary courts between Prust and Pincombe, Dart and Redford, Sweet and Scoble, Grosse and Gaire, and Grills and Bligh, and bailiffs for arresting with stannary process, and tinners for suing in the stannary courts, have been sued at common law, namely, Matthew by Eveleigh, Blake by Tristram, Hole by Dearing, Turner by Clapp, upon pretence that no owners of tin works should have privilege of suing there, but only the labouring tinners; whereas, life, land, and limb only excepted, the same appertain to petitioner to hear and determine, with appeal to the Prince's Council, to the Privy Council and to your Majesty. For maintenance of the revenue of the Prince and the jurisdiction of these courts, petitioner prays the King to signify that there be no further procedings in the said causes, nor such suits prosecuted. [Copy. See Vol. cccxxiii., p. 306. ¾ p.] Underwritten,

  I. *Minute of his Majesty's pleasure that there shall be no proceedings in the courts at Westminster in any of the causes above mentioned, nor any such writs in cases of that nature, until his Majesty shall, in person, hear and settle the points touching the jurisdiction and privileges of the stannary and duchy courts.* [Copy. Ibid., p. 307. ¼ p.]

June 9.
Huntingdon.
42. William Earl of Exeter to the King. This night about seven of the clock, coming to mine inn at Huntingdon, I met with this good news, whereof this bearer brought me letters from Sir Anthony Mildmay and Sir Edward Montgomery, whereof I leave the report to their own letters, not doubting but that your Majesty will send thanks to them, to their good encouragement. I have written my

Vol. CCCXCII.

1638.

letters to meet me to-morrow by the way, and we may consult how to proceed further. In my opinion you shall not need to fear a general revolt, for though divers that look upon them do allow of their work, being glad of the reformation, knowing their intents to be no further, and in that respect will levy no arms against them, yet in my opinion they are otherwise touching their allegiance dutiful subjects, and in the end, if upon suppressing these tumults which grow upon the rage the poor people bear to these enclosures, you show a public reformation by law, the effect will be to your great honour, to the great contentment of your people, and the placing yourself and posterity in peace and security. [*Seal with crest within the garter.* 1 *p.*]

June 9. Notes by Nicholas of business to be transacted by the Lords of the Admiralty. Speak with Sir James Bagg upon his account; also with Sec. Coke about cask and biscuit bags. Consider Mr. Bagnall's paper touching a warrant to take up lighters or barges for carrying saltpetre and coals. Also certificate upon Mr. Dore's petition; also letter from the Chief Justice of Chester touching Emerson, the saltpetreman for that county. [*See 21st April 1638, No. 14.* ½ *p.*]

June 9. Whitehall. Order of the Lords of the Admiralty. Upon Mr. Attorney's certificate on the petition of Samuel Dove (*see 2nd June inst., p. 488*), it was ordered that the commission mentioned in that petition be renewed, with an addition of three commissioners, and that a messenger be appointed to attend the said commissioners. [*Copy. See Vol. cccliii., fol. 103.* ½ *p.*]

'June 9. Whitehall. The Lords of the Admiralty to Thomas Viscount Wentworth. His Majesty having constituted the Earl of Northumberland Lord High Admiral of England, has by special commission, dated the 21st May last, required us to call to account all vice-admirals for profits of Admiralty accrued from the death of the Duke of Buckingham to the appointment of the Earl of Northumberland. We therefore pray you to cause such an account of the profits in your vice-admiralty up to the 13th April last to be prepared and sent with the money due thereon into the High Court of Admiralty before the first November next, when we shall give order for the examination thereof. [*Copy, with underwritten memorandum that similar letters were sent to the following vice-admirals; viz., the Earl of Lindsey, for co. Lincoln; the Earl of Pembroke and Montgomery, for South Wales; Lord Maltravers, for Norfolk, Cambridge, and the Isle of Ely; Sir Edward Seymour and Sir James Bagg, for Devon; Sir Adam Loftus, for Leimpster [Leinster]; the Earl of Suffolk for Dorset, Northumberland, Cumberland, Westmoreland, and Durham; the Earl of Mulgrave, for co. York; the Earl of Nottingham, for Sussex; the Earl of Warwick, for Essex; the Earl of Derby, for cos. Chester and Lancaster; Viscount Chichester, for Ulster; Sir Lionel Tollemache [for Suffolk]; Sir George St. George,*

Vol. CCCXCII.

1638.

for Connaught; Sir Thomas Walsingham, for Kent; Sir James Bagg, for the south parts of Cornwall; Sir Edward Rodney, for Somerset; Sir William Guise, for co. Gloucester; John Griffith, for North Wales; and Francis Basset, for the north parts of Cornwall. See Vol. cccliii., fol. 103 b. 1⅔ p.]

June 9.
Whitehall.

The Lords of the Admiralty to Jerome Earl of Portland. We have received petition from Dr. Mason, judge of your Vice-Admiralty of Hants and the Isle of Wight, praying for a recompence for holding sessions of Admiralty and for other services. We conceive that the judge and registrar of every Vice-Admiralty ought to have their recompence out of that part of the profits of the Admiralty which pertains to vice-admirals. We spoke formerly to you at Oatlands to take order that the judge and registrar, as well as the King's proctor, might receive satisfaction for certain special services. We understand you have satisfied the proctor and registrar. We recommend to you Dr. Mason for a recompence answerable to his worth. [*Copy. Ibid.* 1 p.]

June 9.

Order of the said Lords. Recites demand of John Crane, Surveyor of Marine Victuals, for allowance of 270½ tons of cask at 12d. per ton, and for 531 biscuit-bags at 10d. a-piece expended in his Majesty's service in 1636, and that the demand had been referred to the officers of the Navy. Also reciting a report of the said officers dated the 11th April last, wherein they cited certain cases of similar allowances. The Lords declared that allowance ought to be given for all cask and biscuit bags spent in his Majesty's ships, over and above what is expended for water-cask and steep-tubs. [*Copy. Ibid.*, p. 106. 1⅚ p.]

June 9.

The like order. John Crane, Surveyor of Marine Victuals, in 1636 paid for 13 hogsheads of Irish pipe-staves, which he was constrained to buy of the East India Company for his Majesty's use, about 3l. a thousand for an increase of price, by reason of an imposition laid on that commodity, whereof he craves allowance. We hold it reasonable that, the imposition having been laid since his contract, the amount thereof should be allowed him. [*Copy. Ibid.*, p. 108. ⅔ p.]

June 9.

Order of the Commissioners for Saltpetre and Gunpowder. The East India Company shall have for all the saltpetre in their hands 4l. per cwt., which they are to deliver to Samuel Cordewell, his Majesty's gunpowder maker, who has undertaken to refine it at the same price as the last, according to order of 24th May; the East India Company to be paid on the 20th October next. [*Copy. See Vol. ccxcii.*, p. 88.]

June 9.
Office of Ordnance.

43. Account by Officers of the Ordnance of the proportion of artillery and munition for land service to attend an army of [*blank*] men. Some of the ordnance and shot, the account of which occupies 1½ p.,

1638.

Vol. CCCXCII.

is stated to be in store; the remainder, extending to 16½ pp., is classified under "Emptions," and priced at 7,247*l*. [17½ *pp.*]

June 9.
Office of Ordnance.

44. Duplicate of the preceding. [17½ *pp.*]

June 9.

45. **Justices of Peace for the Isle of Ely to the Council.** On the 4th inst. we had notice that there were 40 or 50 men gathered in a fen called Whelpmore, near Littleport, but common to Ely and Downham with Littleport, and that their assembly was appointed to throw down the ditches which the drainers had made for enclosing their fen ground from the common, which was left to the inhabitants of the said towns. We were also certified that the next day there should meet 600 men in the same place to a foot-ball play or camp, which camp should be called Anderson's camp, who should bring an hundred strong with him. We sent out warrants for some who were the chief movers of this action, and committed two of them to gaol. Whether it was by reason that the chief leaders were in ward, or of the great rain that fell on that day, there came none that day; but upon the next day there assembled out of Ely and Lakenheath about 200 men, throwing down the undertaker's ditches, but not hurting any man's person or goods. We sent out and apprehended four more of the chief of them, whom we also committed to gaol at Ely. The multitudes are dispersed, and we hear not of any more mutinous assemblies; but in Ely speeches are cast out that the gaol shall be broken open and the prisoners delivered, which makes us keep strong watch about it by night. And this we find, that our warrants that we send in his Majesty's name are resisted by some, neglected by others, and some that are charged to aid the constables make light of it, and refuse it, and that the people grow desperately careless, and nourish bad spirits among themselves, one town holding privy intelligence with another. We thought it our parts to let you understand in what condition we are, and leave it to your directions. [1 *p.*] *Enclosed,*

> 45. I. *Informations and examinations taken before the writers of the preceding letter, and in connexion with the subject thereof.* WILLIAM GOATES *of Littleport, informer, stated that meeting Robert Baxter of Littleport, labourer, Baxter told him there was a foot-ball play or camp to be holden in Whelpmore. Informer asked if it was Sayre's camp. Baxter answered, "No; it will be Anderson's camp." Informer replied, "Does Anderson mean to be hanged?" Baxter answered that Anderson would have the first blow at the ball, and would bring with him from Ely 100 men.* NICHOLAS SAYRE, *labourer, examined, said, on Monday last he was digging hassocks in the fen, and went from his work to throw down the ditch in Whelpmore which the undertakers made. On the same day he met Pollard, Wilson, and William Howson, who asked him if he came to play a game at foot-ball. Examinant replied, "What foot-ball?" They told him Anderson would bring a ball*

1638.

and meet the town of *Littleport* in *Burnt fen* to play at foot-ball. Thomas Cooke and Thomas Brooke went to Lakenheath, and David Smith and William Howson said, that Lakenheath men sent word that they would meet in Burnt fen to play at foot-ball. EDWARD ANDERSON, in opprobrious words, said that he would not leave his commons until he saw the King's own signet and royal assent, and that he would obey God and the King, and no man else: "for," he said, "we are all but subjects." And he asked if one might not be inspired (and why not he?) to do the poor good, to help them to their commons again. After he was committed to the constables to be carried to gaol, he said that he would come out of the same in spite of the justices. JOHN BRYCE. He went out of Ely with 30 or 40 men into Whelpmore, and met there 200 or thereabouts all of Ely, which, when they met together, flung in part of the ditch. They met 13 or 14 of Lakenheath men, but they did not anything. Names various persons who were there, and those who persuaded him to go. He carried a foot-ball. What became of it he cannot tell. JOHN IVES, being on Burnt fen looking for cattle, on the first day of the riot, states shortly what he saw of the throwing in the ditches. Cannot tell the names of any of them. WILLIAM GOATES said that Thomas Cooke stated that there were 100 throwing in the ditch at Whelpmore, and would be 600 the day following. THOMAS COOKE. He was in the fen, with two or three that live in Little London in Ely, whose names he cannot tell, though they live near to him. There were 100 men flinging down the ditch, and would be 600 on this day, whereof he was one, and further he would not confess. JOHN CRABB, the elder, deposed to communications between the rioters and the people of Lakenheath and Mildenhall. ROBERT AYRE. Jonathan Westwood told him, that if the justices sent so many to the gaol, it would be the means to have 1,000 people to rise. ROMAN KISBY saw John Bryse with a camping ball, and did camp the same some two furlongs into a great part of the town, and so camped the same back again, and so carried the same into Whelpmore. The same ROMAN KISBY, with HENRY LAVENDER, one other of the constables of Ely. They are altogether afraid to apprehend sundry persons, for they go weaponed with pitchforks and other weapons. LAWRENCE WORMSTEAD. He was going down into a fen called Redmore, and met between 30 and 40 men. Relates a conversation these men had about going to Littleport. One said the constables were gone thither to take some of the men that were in Whelpmore the day before, and therefore "let us go to Littleport, and if we can meet the constables with the men, we will take them from the constables, and bring them back again with us." [4 pp.]

Vol. CCCXCII.

1638.
June 9. 46. Bond of Walter Gyles of the precincts of St. Katherine, Tower Hill, tailor, and Augustine Bale, of St. Botolph Aldgate, butcher, and Francis Yonge of the precincts before mentioned, waterman, to the King, in 50*l*., conditioned that Walter Gyles shall not hereafter take up, entertain, billet, harbour, receive, or convey away any of his Majesty's subjects to parts beyond seas, save by lawful warrant. [1 *p.*]

June 9. 47. Account of Sir William Russell of arrears outstanding of ship-money for 1635; total 4,980*l*. 2*s*. 7*d*.; with underwritten memorandum that since making out this account Sir Humphrey Mildmay. late sheriff of Essex, had paid 117*l*. 15*s*., and that Sir Walter Norton, late sheriff of Lincoln, had paid over and above the charge on that county 45*l*. 15*s*. 6*d*. [= 2 *pp.*]

June 9. 48. Similar account of sums paid and remaining for 1636; paid 188,228*l*. 0*s*. 11*d*.; remaining 8,386*l*. 6*s*. 9*d*. [= 2 *pp.*]

June 9. 49. The like for 1637; paid 102,106*l*. 16*s*. 1*d*.; remaining 94,307*l*. 11*s*. 7*d*. [= 2 *pp.*]

June 9. 50. Account of ship-money for 1637, levied and in the hands of the sheriffs; total 5,300*l*., which makes the sum collected 107,406*l*. [1 *p.*]

June 9.
Insula Vectis. 51. Sir John Oglander, Sheriff of Hants, to Nicholas. It seems on my information to you Mr. Filder is sent for. I have sent up my clerk to justify what I writ to you. My request is that Mr. Filder may pay all his rates to the ship-money before he be released, and that my servant be suddenly discharged. [1 *p.*]

June 10.
Greenwich. The Commissioners for Saltpetre and Gunpowder to William Blythe. There is remaining under your charge four barrels of gunpowder, stayed on suspicion that either it was foreign powder, or powder embezzled out of his Majesty's ships. William Cobham has entered into bond to be answerable for the said powder for a year and a day. You are, therefore, to deliver the same to him. [*Copy. See Vol. ccxcii., p.* 81.]

June 10. 52. Petition of Thomas Whitmore, counsellor-at-law, to Archbishop Laud. Petitioner, by command of Lord Craven, was appointed to prosecute Ralph Clayton, D.D., in a judicial way before his Majesty's Commissioners for foul crimes, and petitioner has given security for that purpose. The doctor had day given till the last court to make his defence, whereof he failed, his excuse alleged being imprisonment. Prays that, as the doctor now lies in prison in Ludlow Castle, he has his liberty of drinking and rioting, and lives as it were in contempt of justice, and as petitioner is still bound as a prosecutor, you

Vol. CCCXCII.

1638.

would appoint a speedy day for hearing the articles and proofs. [½ p.] *Underwritten,*

    52. I. *Reference to Sir John Lambe to take order that the business be brought to a summary hearing, especially if the party complained of has had notice, and will not use means for his defence, nor for his liberty that he may make the same.* 10*th June* 1638. [¼ p.]

June 10.
Burderop.

53. William Calley to Richard Harvey. "Venison! Bah!" You know who said it. I like it as well, for which my father upbraids me with a mechanic taste. You may see how continued breeding at home has metamorphosed nature, and made my palate degenerate. I would entreat your master to bestow a warrant for a buck on me, out of Clarendon, Cramborne, or Grovely. P.S.—My brother Danvers has a little child that it is feared has the King's evil, and he desires to know whether his Majesty will touch any this progress, or whether he might not obtain so much favour as to have his child touched. She was so ill last winter that it troubles them to think on that time, till when, if there be no remedy, they must stay. [*Seal with arms.* 1 *p.*]

June 11.
Newmarket.

54. Deputy Lieutenants and Justices of Peace of co. Cambridge to the Council. According to your directions we met at Newmarket, and informed ourselves of all such riots as have this summer been made in our parts of co. Cambridge, and we certify that on the first day of June inst. two of us on the first hearing of such assemblies (made at Swaffham, Bulbeck, Burwell, and Wicken), having sent to the sheriff to give him notice, and having a jury of twelve sufficient men returned before them to inquire of the same, the said jury found only Thomas Shipp to be a principal man to raise the assembly made riotously at Burwell; which Shipp, upon his examination, taken before us this day, has confessed the same, and discovered divers of his company. For Shipp, we have sent him to the castle of Cambridge as a prisoner, for that he cannot find sufficient sureties for his appearance before you. Shipp named these persons of Burwell to be with him and of his company, viz., Richard Bulman, John Ormes, William Wyatt, Edward Crow, Ambrose Farrow, and Robert Gilbert, senior, with others whose names he remembereth not, in all 13 or 14, and that those named joined with him in casting down the ditches in four places of the ditches lately made by the Queen's officers. Shipp further said that John Pope, of Burwell, brought them victuals. For John Ormes and Robert Gilbert it is proved before us that they, being blamed for such riotous doing, answered that though other townsmen had given away their right, they would cast them down again. As for Wicken, we are informed that John Mortlock, Henry Dimock, John Ashford, and Thomas Key cast in some banks, but they said they did it in their own right of commonage, and that if his Majesty's royal assent were thereto, and his Majesty's proclamation in print were published, that

1638.
Vol. CCCXCII.

they might know his Majesty's pleasure therein that it should be taken from them, they would ditch it up again at their charges. And as for Swaffham, Bulbeck, and Bottisham we cannot learn justly of any riots. All is now quiet in these towns, as in all parts of our division of co. Cambridge. All the rest accused by Shipp we have given out warrants for apprehending and binding them over, according to your letters. [*Seal with arms.* 1 *p.*]

June 11.
Aston.
55. Thomas Whitley, Sheriff of Flint, to Nicholas. Has taken order with Thomas Pwlford, a drover, for payment of 150*l.* ship-money on the 12th, and 200*l.* by the 24th of this month. Wishes to hear of its receipt, and how his certificate of his proceedings was liked of by the Lords. [1 *p.*]

June 11.
56. Henry Lingen, Sheriff of co. Hereford, to Richard Wotton, over against St. Dunstan's church. When I began to collect the ship-money, I desired the justices of peace not to alter any constables till they had accounted with me, who promised they would not, but they have altered so many (I think a-purpose to hinder the service) that they have put me to a great deal of trouble. Some constables have collected most part of the money, and being discharged detain the money, and have lost (as they say) the assessments, so that I am mightily troubled, and the constables that are now made know not what their predecessors have received, the assessments being detained. Go to Mr. Nicholas, and desire him to move the Lords to write to the justices. P.S.—Sir Richard Hopton is the ringleader, and alters more than all the rest. Wishes Wotton to tell Vanley, the tailor, to be mindful of the writer's scarlet jacket against the assizes. [1 *p.*]

June 11.
57. Certificate of Harbottle Grimstone, Justice of Peace for Middlesex, that Marmaduke Darell of Fulmer, Bucks, had taken the oath of allegiance before him. [¼ *p.*]

June 11.
Certificate of Sir Richard Fenn, Lord Mayor, and the Aldermen of London, that in the Repertory of the Acts of the Court of Aldermen there appears an order of the 24th May last, upon an information exhibited in the Lord Mayor's court against Richard Turner, clerk to the Company of Barber Surgeons, for binding and making free Arthur Taylor, which cause was referred to Ralph Lathum, common-sergeant, and Clement Mosse, under-chamberlain. Upon hearing their report, it appeared to the court that Dr. Allott, living in St. John's College in Cambridge, and a rare practiser both in physic and surgery, heretofore admitted of the said company, wrote to the company that Arthur Taylor might be bound to some freeman of the company, and that by order of the company he was bound to Richard Turner, and turned over to Dr. Allott, and that at the expiration of his seven years, on the recommendation of Dr. Allott that he had truly served, he was made free of the company, and afterwards admitted a freeman of the city, Thomas Trevillian, the prosecutor in this case, being renter-warden of the company, and cognizant of the transaction. As no corruption or indirect dealing

Vol. CCCXCII.

1638.

appeared in Richard Turner, but much malice in Trevillian, the court ordered that no information in this cause should be received, and that all proceedings should be stayed. [*Attested by Hamlet Clarke. Seal imperfect. See Case E., Car. I., No. 5. Parchment.* 40 *lines.*]

June 11.
London.

58. Isaac Pennington to Sir John Pennington. Mr. Richaut has paid him 150*l.* on Sir John's account, which shall lie by till he knows Sir John's pleasure therein. On the morrow he is going to his country-house, where he has not been this fortnight. [½ *p.*]

June 11.

59. Inscription over the grave of Paul Viscount Bayning, who died this day in the 23rd year of his age. [⅙ *p.*]

June 12.

Petition of Dame Dorothy Maunsell, widow, to the King. Petitioner brought an action of debt upon a bond of 6,000*l.* against Sir Walter Maunsell, and thereupon had judgment at the Great Sessions in co. Carmarthen. Defendant brought a writ of error at the Council in the Marches, and there obtained a reversal of the former judgment. She is informed by her counsel that the reversal is erroneous, and that there is just cause to have a writ of error in the Court of King's Bench, but the Lord Keeper makes some difficulty thereof, except he were warranted by your Majesty. Prays the King to require the Lord Keeper to order the Lord Chief Justice and the rest of the Judges of the King's Bench to deliver their opinions to the Lord Keeper of what is agreeable to law in this case. [*Copy. See Vol. cccxxiii., p.* 308. ½ *p.*] *Underwritten,*

> I. *Direction to the Lord Keeper to require certificate from the Lord Chief Justice and other Judges of the King's Bench to the effect above mentioned. Greenwich,* 12*th June* 1638. [*Copy. Ibid.* ⅙ *p.*]

June 12.

Petition of Edward Ferrers to the same. Petitioner and his younger brother Thomas Ferrers had many years since dealing for great sums of money, and there growing some differences of account between them, Thomas Ferrers persuaded petitioner to give him a bond of 800*l.* till the accounts were cast up; whereas petitioner was indebted to him only in a small sum, which for many years he did not demand or so much as mention, knowing there were monies due to him from petitioner. Afterwards William Ferrers, the elder brother of petitioner, being of a great estate and very aged, settled his estate, and appointed petitioner and the said Thomas executors, but afterwards, by procurement of Thomas, William struck out petitioner, whereby petitioner's nephew, Sir Henry Ferrers and the said Thomas Ferrers became his executors, yet by his will he gave to petitioner a sixth part of his estate. After the death of the said William, Thomas got into his hands the estate of the said William, before which time he had also got into his hands the estate of William, son of the said William, of the value of 7,000*l.* or 8,000*l.* (out of which a good part is due to petitioner), and neither admitted Sir Henry to intermeddle, nor paid petitioner any part of what was due to him. Besides which, he owed petitioner for house rent and

1638.

VOL. CCCXCII.

dilapidations of a house at Bow. Being ill, Thomas made his will, and appointed his wife Judith executrix, after whose death, she finding the bond of 800*l.* and another bond of 100*l.* from petitioner and his eldest son, has put the same in suit, although there be much more due to petitioner than the penalties of the said bonds. Prays a reference to some of the Council. [*Copy. Ibid.* 1 *p.*] *Underwritten*,

> I. *Reference to the Archbishop of Canterbury, the Lord Privy Seal, Lord Newburgh, and the two Secs., to hear and determine these differences, or otherwise to certify. Greenwich, 12th June,* 1638. [*Copy. Ibid., p.* 309. ¼ *p.*]

June 12. Petition of Thomas Harrington to the King. Petitioner's father being possessed for years in lands of the Londoners' plantation in co. Londonderry, and being seized of lands in England, charged the same with payment of his debts and provision for petitioner and his younger children. Not being able to sell the lands in Ireland, the same having been long in question between your Majesty and the city of London, nor the lands in England on account of rent-charges which have come into infants' hands, and hindered to negotiate abroad for fear of arrest, petitioner prays for a protection for a year. [*Copy. Ibid., p.* 309. ⅓ *p.*] *Underwritten*,

> I. *Reference to the Council to give order for a protection if they find it fit. Greenwich,* 12*th June* 1638. [*Copy. Ibid.* ⅙ *p.*]

June 12. Petition of Sir John Harvey, Governor of Virginia, to the same. The colony of Virginia is in great want of powder, arms, and other munition. Your Majesty granted petitioner for his subsistence there as Governor for your Majesty an allowance of 1,000*l.* per annum, which has been in arrear until it amounts to 4,000*l.* Prays warrant to the officers of Ordnance to deliver to petitioner 150 barrels of powder, and 1,000 muskets and carbines out of the Tower of London, at such prices as your Majesty usually pays for the same, and that the sum may be deducted out of the said 4,000*l.* [*Copy. Ibid.* ½ *p.*] *Underwritten*,

> I. *Reference to the Lord Treasurer and Lord Cottington to certify their opinions. Greenwich,* 12*th June* 1638. [*Copy. Ibid., p.* 311. ⅙ *p.*]

June 12.
Whitehall.
Commissioners for Saltpetre and Gunpowder to Thomas Clee, brewer at Tower Dock. Six barrels of Barbary saltpetre were laid in a store-house belonging to you about eight years since, by one Knight, which is now bought for his Majesty's use. You are to deliver the same to Samuel Cordewell, his Majesty's gunpowder maker. [*Copy. See Vol. ccxcii., p.* 81. ½ *p.*]

June 12.
Whitehall.
The same to the Governors of the East India Company. We are content to give for the 20 tons of saltpetre in your hands after the

Vol. CCCXCII.

1638.

rate of 4*l.* per cwt., to be paid on 20th October next. We pray you to cause the same to be forthwith delivered to Mr. Cordewell. [*Copy. Ibid., p.* 82. ½ *p.*]

June 12. Entry on the register book of the same Commissioners of the appearance of Henry Finnimore. He is to remain in the messenger's custody until discharged. [*See Ibid.* ¼ *p.*]

June 12. Arundel House. 60. Thomas Earl of Arundel and Surrey, Earl Marshal, to the Clerk of the Signet, now attending. It is his Majesty's pleasure that you prepare a bill for his signature, authorising Sir David Cunningham, Receiver-General of the Revenue of Prince Charles, to pay to Sir John Borough, Garter, for knighthood of the Prince at Windsor, May 20, 78*l.* 6*s.* 8*d.*, and for his Installation at Windsor, May 21, 339*l.* 16*s.* 8*d.*, and 130*l.* in lieu of scarves, hats, and plumes of his Highness' colours due to the Heralds at the Installation. [*Draft.* ⅔ *p.*]

June 12. 61. Information of Thomas Porter, of Barking, Essex. The 11th inst., I being at Awdley in Essex, heard these words spoken by Mr. Gogney's son, the high constable for that hundred, vizt. One Mrs. Cole, of Cranham Hall, being in the tide-boat discoursing, touching the censure of Mr. Pickering, Mrs. Cole answered that if she were as the Queen she would quickly make away King Charles for dealing so hardly with that religion. Mr. Stone, a scholar, heard the same words, and dwells not far from Mr. Gogney. [⅓ *p.*]

June 12. 62. Table or list of 25 diets then served in the King's household. Distinguished by the number of dishes of which they were composed. [=1½ *p.*]

June 12. 63. Abstract of points settled by order of the Lords Commissioners touching the mode of keeping the accounts for his Majesty's household, and agreed upon by the officers of the household and the auditors. Signed by Sir Roger Palmer, Sir Thomas Merry, Sir Richard Manley, and Sir Henry Knollys, on behalf of the Board of Greencloth, and by Sir Edmond Sawyer and Francis Phelips, auditors. [2½ *pp.*]

June 12. 64. Copy of the same. [2¾ *pp.*]

June 13. 65. William Walter, late Sheriff of co. Oxford, to Nicholas. Acknowledges letter from the Lords requiring payment of his arrears of ship-money by the end of this term, or his appearance before the Lords on the 17th inst. The under-sheriff, whom it immediately concerns, received notice from the writer, of such letter. Presumes he will be ready to appear and make answer. Prays that it may be remembered that the writer's account has been made long since, with a distinct charge of the under-sheriff's and the writer's division in collecting, whereof the writer's part was brought in within the year, and his remonstrance against the employment of his under-sheriff, which he hopes will redeem him from the opinion of neglect in the service, and render his appearance fruitless. [*Seal with arms.* ¾ *p.*]

1638.
June 14.

Vol. CCCXCII.

66. Petition of Lady Theodosia Tresham, wife of Sir William Tresham, to the King. Petitioner's husband still refuses to obey your Majesty's commands, as knowing petitioner is not able to disburse money to pay fees due to your Majesty's officers, who should see your commands performed, but on receiving the portion of 4,000l. petitioner will not fail to do so. Prays the King to sign the signification of his pleasure thereunder written, without which she utterly loses her portion, her husband being ready to go into Flanders, where he enjoys 2,000l. a year by being colonel under the Prince of Orange. [½ p.] *Underwritten,*

> 66. I. *Suggested command of the King above mentioned, but not adopted. It does not differ very materially from the subsequent, except in expression.* [⅙ p.]
>
> 66. II. *Minute of the King's pleasure that Sec. Coke send for Sir William Tresham, and in his Majesty's name command him not to depart the realm until he has obtained his Majesty's licence, or before he has given satisfaction to petitioner. Theobalds, 14th June 1638.* [¼ p.]

June 14.

67. Petition of Henry Goche, D.D., to the same. Your Majesty accepted petitioner's service in Persia, by commending him to the Archbishop of Canterbury, who accordingly moved your Majesty on petitioner's behalf for the rectory of Pulham in Dorset, void during the wardship of the patron. Prays licence to hold the same together with the rectory of Cheadle, co. Stafford, until he can exchange one of them for some other living within distance, and in the meantime residing six months every year upon each. [¾ p.] *Underwritten,*

> 67. I. *Minute of the King's pleasure to be certified by the Archbishop of Canterbury or the Bishop of London his opinion touching petitioner's suit. Theobalds, 14th June 1638.* [¼ p.]

June 14.

68. Petition of John Barker, rector of Cleobury Mortimer, co. Salop, upon the presentation of his Majesty, to the same. Barkhill, Wirehill, and certain "binds" in the forest of Wire, and parcel of the parish of Cleobury, are now claimed by John Boraston, parson of Ribbesford, co. Worcester, who detains the profits from petitioner, to the wrong of your Majesty, by pretence of a composition made in the time of King Henry VIII., which petitioner is by counsel informed does not bind petitioner. Prays reference to the Archbishop of Canterbury and the Lord Keeper. [¾ p.] *Underwritten,*

> 68. I. *Reference to the Bishop of Hereford to compose this difference, if he can, or otherwise to certify to the Archbishop of Canterbury and the Lord Keeper. Theobalds, 14th July 1638.* [¼ p.]

June 14.

69. Petition of Francis Smith, aged almost fourscore years, to the same. Petitioner being long detained in prison for suspicion of being a priest, was enlarged by commiseration of the Council, at the

Vol. CCCXCII.

1638.

intercession of the Queen, with leave to reside where his physicians should direct, for recovery of his health, and that no pursuivant should molest him or those who received him. Petitioner repaired to the house of Bartholomew Fromonds at Cheham [Cheam] in Surrey, where the next day after his arrival, upon search made in the house by Francis Newton, John Gray, and Thomas Mayo, pursuivants, he was by them found, being then very sick, at which time Mr. Fromonds gave them 35s. to depart, and not affright his wife, who died shortly after. They departed, and promised not to molest Mr. Fromonds or petitioner, yet not long after they threatened to indict them both, unless petitioner would give them 5l., which he being not able to do they indicted petitioner for a priest, and Mr. Fromonds for harbouring him, and upon that indictment outlawed petitioner, he being ignorant of their proceedings, and procured Mr. Killigrew, your Majesty's servant, to beg the forfeiture of their estates, which grant, upon information to your Majesty, was recalled. Forasmuch as these pursuivants, out of their malice, are at this time contriving to engage some of your servants to beg them both again, petitioner prays your Majesty not to permit any such grant to pass, and to give order to the Lord Chief Justice of the King's Bench and Mr. Justice Berkeley and your Attorney-General to stop all future proceedings against them upon that cause, and that petitioner may go to his grave in peace. The witness who swore to the indictment is a perjured person, and Newton was adjudged to be thrown over the bar of the Court of Common Pleas, fined 20l., and sentenced to imprisonment during your pleasure for dishonest causes in that court. [$\frac{2}{3}$ p.]

June 14.

70. Lord Chief Justice Bramston, Sir William Jones, Sir George Croke, and Sir Richard Berkeley, the Judges of the King's Bench, to the Council. Report as to the conduct of James Franklyn, Keeper of Newgate, and William Raven, officer of the Lord Mayor, in permitting [Richard ?] Chambers, committed to Newgate for refusing to pay ship-money, and after several times remanded to the same custody, but by negligence permitted to remain at large. The judges declare that Franklyn had been guilty of great remissness and negligence, and Raven in fault in bringing back Chambers to the house of the keeper, and there leaving him without acquainting the keeper with his bringing the prisoner thither. [2$\frac{1}{2}$ pp.]

June 14.

71. Francis Earl of Bedford to the Council. According to order of the 23rd May last (see that date in calendar No. 148), reports that Mr. Hockin has showed him notes of sums allowed by Baronet Pollard, amounting to 21l. 10s. 9$\frac{1}{2}$d., which being deducted from 228l. 0s. 11d. there remains still 206l. 10s. 1$\frac{1}{2}$d. to be repaid to the North Division. With respect to the amount of charges, 133l. 5s., the Earl leaves it without alteration. Touching Mr. Yeo's affidavit of further charges, submits it to the Lords. Is suitor that the money may be repaid in the country, and that particular regard be had to the three towns of Holsworthy, Hatherleigh, and Torrington

1638.   Vol. CCCXCII.

which were longer burthened with the army than any other part of the country. [1 p.]

June 14. 72. Notes of votes or opinions of the Judges in the High Commission Court, delivered this day on finally settling the sentence against John Ward, William Castle, and Robert Cade. (*See the 7th inst., No. 33.*) Sir John Lambe has added who were present, and has given a separate list of those who voted for each point of the sentence. [3 pp.]

June 14. 73. Sir Robert Berkeley to Sec. Windebank. Upon signification of his Majesty's pleasure, he has examined whether Smith and Fromonds were maliciously indicted. It appeared, on credible affidavits, that Gray made offer for 5l. to have composed the business, and that if such a sum were given there should be a desisting from molesting them. But that Smith and Fromonds refused, and presently after refusal indictments were preferred against them. [*Seal with arms.* ¾ p.]

June 14. 74. Petition of Henry Finnimore to the Lords of the Admiralty. On complaint that petitioner hindered the saltpetre works at Huntingdon, he was sent for by warrant, and brought up by a messenger, in whose custody he remains. The complaint was made by three malicious persons, petitioner being innocent, and forward in his Majesty's service, as by annexed certificates appears. Expresses sorrow, and is willing to give Mr. Pinckney satisfaction. Prays discharge. [¾ p.]

> 74. I. II. III. *Certificates of Robert Edwards and various other persons that William Bowker, George Palmer, and Richard Hart. the informers against Henry Finnimore, are discreditable persons.* [=1¼ p.]
>
> 74. IV. V. *Certificates that Finnimore did not, on the occasion referred to by the informers, hinder the service of saltpetre, but rather furthered and helped it; that the saltpetremen and constables remained in the alehouse drinking and singing until twelve of the night before they departed, as will appear by the watchman; and that the fault was in the constables, who charged pack-horses, milne-horses, and butchers' horses, only used to carry packs and burthens, and unacquainted with drawing burthens.* [½ p.]
>
> 74. VI. *Certificate of Jasper Heiley, messenger, that being sent by the Board for Henry Finnimore about two months ago, for nonpayment of 8s. towards the musters, Finnimore tendered the money to the constables, but they would not take it, and one of them, George Palmer, said that Finnimore was worth 1,000l., and that he would not leave him until he had made him spend 500l., and that Palmer had other things against him which he should be sure to hear of. 14th June 1638.* [½ p.]

Vol. CCCXCIII. June 15-30, 1638.

1638.

June 15. Privy Seal for levying 6s. 8d. per yard for subsidy and 15s. per yard for impost, for "tabies" and other like stuffs, for that the property of tabbies, formerly rated at 5s. subsidy and 10s. impost, is now altered, being now made as broad again as they were, and of better value than broad taffety, which pays 6s. 8d. subsidy and 13s. 4d. impost. [*Docquet.*]

June 15. Privy Seal whereby his Majesty requires that the duty on foreign silver imported, which is 30s. per cent., be raised to 40s. per cent., in respect that his Majesty has licensed the merchants of foreign silver imported to transport two parts of the same, leaving a full third to be sent up to London to be coined, and to ship as much as they think fit in one vessel. [*Docquet.*]

June 15. The King to the Company of East Country Merchants, recommending Henry White, a freeman of London, to be admitted of their company. [*Docquet.*]

June 15. Warrant under the signet to the Master of the Great Wardrobe, for a livery to Hugh Pope, Groom of the Queen's Robes, in place of James Bardowe. [*Docquet.*]

June 15. A like to James Bardowe, now Yeoman of the Queen's Robes. [*Docquet.*]

June 15. Confirmation of Charter granted in the 11th year of his Majesty's reign to his Majesty's musicians, with some additions. [*Docquet.*]

June 15. Entry on the Admiralty Register of the appearance of Walter Rugge; he is to remain in the messenger's custody until discharged. [*See Vol. cccliii., p.* 108.]

June 15. 1. Inigo Jones to the Council. In regard that the water that serves his Majesty's houses of access is of so great importance, both for his Majesty's diets and all other necessary uses, the writer suggests to the Lords to give order for a proclamation or other writing to be read in the neighbouring churches prohibiting all persons to erect any building, dig any pits, or lay any laystalls, near the springs or conduit heads which serve any of his Majesty's houses, or to break up any of the pipes, or take away any of the water which passes through their grounds; in which also his Majesty's plumber be strictly charged to give notice of any abuse or nuisance, upon pain of punishment. [=1¼ *p.*]

June 15. 2. Examination of Mary Cole, widow, of Cranham Hall, Essex, taken before the Attorney-General. She is a Roman Catholic, and so has been for 12 years past. She has not been in any tide-boat or any other boat since Lent last. Never heard of Pickering, nor that he was censured in the Star Chamber. Denies the words imputed to her in the information of Thomas Porter, calendared under the date of 12th June inst., No. 61. Confesses that about Shrovetide last, falling out with Thomas Powter [Poulter], she said to him

1638. VOL. CCCXCIII.

that if she were a Queen, and he a King, she would hang him if she could. [½ p.]

June 15. 3. Receipt of Balthasar Gerbier, the King's Agent at Brussels, for 225l. for port of letters and secret services for three quarters of a year ending the 31st March 1638. [½ p.]

June 15. 4. Bill of charges of Ralph Hellyer, in connexion with an award, remaining in London 35 weeks, and paying scriveners and others for writings; total 47l. 2s. [*Endorsed by Nicholas, that Sir William Becher and himself taxed Mr. Ludlow to pay 30l. of the same, besides the 30l. ordered by the Earl Marshal and the Board.* 1 p.]

June 15.
Theobalds.
5. Philip Earl of Pembroke and Montgomery, Lord Chamberlain, to Sir Dudley Carleton. I have special occasion to use the books and records in the Council Chamber concerning his Majesty's Household and Chamber. Let my servant Oldisworth have the use of such as he shall think "conducible" to my service. For his re-delivery of them I will be answerable to you. [*Underwritten memorandum by Nicholas, that he delivered to Mr. Poole, upon this letter, the old Book of Eltham and the book signed by this King concerning Orders of Household.* ½ p.]

June 15. 6. John Cutteris to Richard Harvey. All things are as you left them. We could not send the horses according to promise, by reason they were so fat, till we had ordered them three or four days, and our purses so lean that we had not money to bear the fellow's charges. What Mr. Murrell says regard not; he will say anything to serve his own turn. Send me word what he says. [1 p.]

June 16.
Whitehall.
7. Order of the Lord Treasurer, Lord Cottington, and Sec. Winebank, referees of a petition of Sir Philiberto Vernatti, John Gibbon, and others, participants in the Level of Hatfield Chace. It was Ordered that the Lord Chief Justice of the King's Bench, Mr. Justice Jones, and Mr. Justice Berkeley, should take into consideration the particulars complained of, the exceptions of Mr. Gibbon, and the answers of the Commissioners of Sewers, and come prepared to give the Lords information concerning the same on Wednesday next. [⅚ p.] *Underwritten,*

> 7. I. *Appointment of the Lord Chief Justice and Mr. Justice Jones to consider the matters above mentioned on Monday then next, at Sergeant's Inn in Fleet Street. 8th December 1638.* [⅙ p.]

June 16.
London.
8. Leonard Pinckney to [Nicholas.] Henry Finnimore and he are agreed. Finnimore has given his bond for payment of 5l. on 1st July. [½ p.]

June 16. Entry on the Admiralty Register of the discharge of Henry Finnimore of Yaxley, co. Huntingdon. [*See Vol. cccliii., p.* 108. ¼ p.]

Vol. CCCXCIII.

1638.
June 16. Similar entry on the Register Book of the Commissioners for Saltpetre. [*See Vol. ccxcii., p.* 82. ¼ *p.*]

June 16. 9. Petition of Roger Hollings of Methley, co. York, to Archbishop Laud. On the last of May last you desired Sir Henry Marten to consider petitioner's petition then preferred, and to take order for payment of the legacies of 20*l.* apiece given by Grace Gomersall unto the three daughters of petitioner. Sir Henry Marten called the parties before him on 7th June inst. Nathan Akeroid, the executor, was willing that the legacies should be paid, but Francis Zacharie, the overseer, having the money in his hands, did not appear; whereupon Sir Henry stated that he had no power to compel the said Zacharie to come in, which properly belonged to Sir John Lambe, and willed petitioner to procure either an order against Zacharie or a reference to Sir John. Prays an order that Zacharie shall pay the said legacies to petitioner for his three daughters, he giving security. [⅔ *p.*] *Underwritten,*

    9. I. *Reference to Sir John Lambe to take such order as he shall find just.* 16*th June* 1638. [⅙ *p.*]

    9. II. *Appointment of Sir John Lambe to hear the cause on the* 25*th June inst.* [⅙ *p.*]

June 16. 10. Joan Crowne to Richard Harvey. Being ill, and in distress, she entreats him to disburse 5*s.* to redeem her trunk, and do other acts of kindness; also to answer an enclosed letter from her brother Roger. [1 *p.*] *Enclosed,*

    10. I. *Roger Harvey to Mrs. Joan Crowne in Tugfall's Alley near the Scotch Arms in Westminster. Her husband is at Bicknell. Would be joyful if things might fit well to her content, but wishes her to desist from her farther resolution. The writer's daughter, Ursula, died yesterday. St. James's,* 11*th June* 1638. [1 *p.*]

June 16. 11. Account of Sir William Russell of ship-money received and outstanding for 1637; received 107,511*l.* 5*s.* 1*d.*, outstanding 88,903*l.* 2*s.* 7*d.* [=2 *pp.*]

June 16. 12. Note of ship-money collected and remaining in the hands of the several sheriffs; total, 5,900*l.*; making the total paid 113,411*l.* [1 *p.*]

June 17. Petition of Humphrey Slaney, Nicholas Crispe, Abraham Chamberlaine, and William Clobery, merchants of London, to the King. Petitioners by former petition set forth their great losses by the French men-of-war in taking the Benediction, and by the owners of the ship in unconscionably prosecuting them at common law, seven years afterwards, upon which they got a verdict of 2,000*l.* upon pretence of the want of 12 men. Your Majesty referred the same to the Lord Privy Seal and the Earl of Dorset, and to call to them Sir Henry Marten. The referees found petitioners' complaints

1638.   VOL. CCCXCIII.

just, and declared that the business being settled by way of state, the subjects of both nations were to rest pacified, and being a case of great extremity the trial at common law was improper. Upon their certificate your Majesty declared that all proceedings at common law should be stayed, and that the cause should receive a final determination in some of your courts of equity. Thereupon petitioners entered their suit in the Court of Requests against the owners. Being this day to receive a hearing, the owners produced a petition by them preferred to your Majesty, whereupon, by misinformation, they had obtained your directions to stop proceedings in equity, and to go on at common law, whereby they intend to take execution to-morrow for the 2,000*l.* Petitioners pray that their cause may proceed to an end in the Court of Requests, and that the proceedings at common law be stayed according to the former order. [*Copy. See Vol. cccxxiii., p.* 311. 1⅙ *p.*] *Underwritten,*

    I. *Minute of the King's pleasure that these matters be examined by some of the Council, from whom he will be informed of the true state thereof. Greenwich, 17th June* 1638. [*Copy. Ibid., p.* 312. ⅙ *p.*]

    II. *His Majesty, having been informed of the state of this business, declares that he will appoint some time after his return from the progress to hear this business in person, at which time Sir Henry Marten shall be required to be present, and in the meantime all proceedings to be stayed. Greenwich, 26th June* 1638. [*Copy. Ibid.* ⅙ *p.*]

June 17. Petition of Thomas Killigrew, his Majesty's servant, to the King. Upon petitioner's former suit your Majesty declared that you would in person hear the matters in question between the Attorney-General and Sir Peter Riddell and others, on the 25th May last, at which time defendants neglected to give their attendance. Prays a reference as to the validity of the information to the Lord Keeper and Lord Privy Seal. [*Copy. Ibid.* ½ *p.*] *Underwritten,*

    I. *Appointment by his Majesty of Sunday the* 1st *July next for hearing this business, and that in the meantime the Lord Keeper and the Lord Privy Seal shall examine the validity of the information, and certify whether it will hold plea in a court of equity. The Queen's Attorney-General is to open the state of the business to the referees. Greenwich, 17th June* 1638. [*Copy. Ibid., p.* 313. ¼ *p.*]

[June 17.] Heading of petition of John Gibbon to the same. Blank left for this petition, but it was not transcribed. [*Copy. Ibid.* 2 *lines.*]

June 17. 13. Petition of John Browne, his Majesty's servant and gunfounder, to the same. Petitioner has cast the ordnance for the Royal Sovereign as far as the estimate will extend, there remaining 4 demi-

1638.

Vol. CCCXCIII.

cannons of 12½ foot long of 5,300 lbs. for the lower tier for the chase abaft, which will weigh in all 10 tons 12 cwt., amounting to 1,700*l*. Prays order to the Lord Treasurer to direct Sir John Heydon to pay petitioner the said 1,700*l*. out of money received for powder. [*Copy.* ½ *p.*] *Underwritten,*

  13. I. *Minute of his Majesty's pleasure that the Lord Treasurer give the order desired. Greenwich, 27th June* 1638. [*Copy.* ¼ *p.*]

June 17. 14. Agreement of Hubert le Sueur, sculptor, to cast for the King two statues of 5 foot 8 inches high, one of King James, the other of King Charles, for 340*l*., to be paid 170*l*. in hand, and the other 170*l*. when the work shall be finished and delivered to the Surveyor of the Works in March next. [*Attested by Inigo Jones.* ⅔ *p.*]

June 17.
Kingsthorpe.
 15. Dr. Samuel Clerke to Sir John Lambe. The sickness is sore at Northampton. The deaths in the last three weeks have been of the plague 26, 16, and 29. Before the last sessions the Prince's attorney and myself made a tax for the 5-mile towns, and at the sessions I got an enlargement, with much reluctance, over the whole county. The first was 48*l*. weekly, the second 100*l*. more, and the market is kept on Northampton Heath. In requital of my love and pains they now do what they list in the church service at All Saints in Northampton. Some very lately cut the rail or cancel that was about the Lord's board in pieces, and brought down the Lord's table into the middle of the chancel. I long since advised the mayor and his brethren that the Thursday lecture, and sermons on Sundays in the afternoon, should be forborne in these infectious times. They then raised a report of me, that I was about to starve their souls. You may do well to acquaint his Grace with so much of this as you please. The schismatical puritans now bring their appeals from the Audience, as, namely, the churchwardens of Towcester, for not presenting some 80 or 100 of their parish who refused to receive the blessed sacrament at the cancel at Easter last, and one Mr. Clerke (my namesake), of Eastcote, in the parish of Pattishall, for calling the Divine sermons porridge, and the long puritan sermons roast meat. Your cousin remembers her kind respects to you. [1 *p.*]

[June 18.] Henry Earl of Holland, Chief Justice and Justice in Eyre of all the Forests on this side Trent, to Richard Willis and James Crompe, his Majesty's Woodwards for co. Northampton. It appears that, notwithstanding the late repair of pales in the park of Grafton, there are places about the said park still decayed, which will want 70 oak trees to perfect the said reparations. You are to cause the specified number of trees to be felled within the forests of Whittlewood and Salcey, or one of them, causing the old pales, posts, and rails to be made to serve again as far as they may. [*Copy. See Book of Orders concerning Forests, Vol. ccclxxxiv., p.* 14. 1⅔ *p.*]

1638.
June 18.

Vol. CCCXCIII.

Lord Treasurer Juxon, Henry Earl of Holland, and Francis Lord Cottington, to Richard Willis and Thomas Beale, his Majesty's Woodwards of cos. Northampton and Rutland. For small decays of lodges, rails, and mounds in co. Northampton, there have been formerly allowances made of timber and money by your predecessors, upon a dormant warrant, which you have hitherto forborne to do, not having like warrant. We authorize you, as often as need shall require, calling to you two or more regarders of the forests where such want of repairs shall be, to take view thereof, and assign timber trees and money for the performance of that service. [*Copy. See Vol. ccclxxxiv., p.* 15. 1⅓ *p.*]

June 18.

16. Archbishop Laud and others, Judges of the Court of High Commission, to Lord Chief Justice Finch. There is lately issued out of the Common Pleas a writ of *ne admittas* to the Bishop of Norwich at the suit of Sir John Rous, original patron of Dennington, Suffolk. Certify that on the 14th inst. sentence had been given in the High Commision against John Ward for simony, and against William Castle and Robert Cade for presentations surreptitiously obtained from his Majesty to the support of the said simony. His Majesty has hereupon granted a presentation to a clerk of his own. We therefore pray you to revoke the said writ of *ne admittas*, to the end the church may not lie void, the cure of souls be unserved, and the King's presentation be hindered. [*Underwritten is a memorandum that a supersedeas was granted out of term and in the absence of the patron, by virtue whereof Mr. Wright held possession, and the profits for three years, and so long kept the patron in suit, causing him to spend* 400*l. Copy.* ⅚ *p.*]

June 18.
Originally dated ———.
from 'Uckfield,' but that was afterwards struck out.

17. ——— to the Mayor of some borough or city not named, ———. I am retained by Samuel Sampson to be of counsel with him concerning a suit begun against him upon a recognizance taken by your predecessor for his appearance, and he informs me that your town-clerk has denied him a copy of any of the proceedings against him, and yet that they urge him peremptorily to enter a traverse on Tuesday next before you. Argues the impossibility of his doing so, and prays the person addressed to order him a copy of the proceedings, and a further day to put in his traverse. [*Draft.* ¾ *p.*]

June 18. 18. See "Returns made by Justices of Peace."

June 19. Petition of Sir Pierce Crosby, his Majesty's servant, to the King. By reference on the petition annexed the Attorney General was left at no liberty to do anything for petitioner's relief (*see* 14*th May* 1638. *p.* 432), although petitioner offered him to assign lands to the value of 500*l.* per annum, to be made liable to a fine in case he should be censured in the Star Chamber. Prays order that Mr. Attorney shall take assurance of the said lands to be liable as aforesaid, and to cancel petitioner's bonds, whereby he may dispose of the rest of his estate for payment of his debts, freeing his sureties,

Vol. CCCXCIII.

1638.

and relieving his necessities. [*Copy. See Vol. cccxxiii., p.* 314. ¼ *p.*] *Underwritten,*

I. *Minute of the King's pleasure to license petitioner to dispose of part of his lands for payment of his debts to the value in the petition desired, if he can satisfy the Attorney-General that he has other lands worth* 500*l. per annum which will be liable to a fine in case he should be censured in the Star Chamber. And for the bonds in the petition mentioned, Mr. Attorney is to certify his Majesty whether any other defendant in like case has been bound to appear at the hearing. Greenwich,* 19*th June* 1638. [*Copy. Ibid.* ¼ *p.*]

June 19. Petition of John Persall, son of Sir John Persall, to the King. Petitioner about —— years since married the daughter of Robert Knightley, who in that space has not, until within 3 years last past, given unto her 10*l.* towards her maintenance in apparel, since which time he has given unto her 24*l.* per annum, a means very insufficient, not discharging her very diet. For which cause petitioner is enforced to supply that particular out of his own means, being but 50*l.* per annum, an amount also very insufficient, as also to defray charges of nurses, maintenance of children, and servants' wages, which charge far surmounting petitioner's present estate, the said Robert suffers, having before and since petitioner's marriage boasted that he would give 3,000*l.* with his daughter, so that petitioner might have estated upon her 300*l.* per annum, which petitioner's father cannot do, but offers in present and reversion 200*l.* per annum. Further, this unnatural conduct of petitioner's father-in-law towards his daughter has drawn on her such inconveniences that without speedy relief her life cannot avoid eminent danger. Prays reference to the Council to order this difference. [*Copy. See Vol. cccxxiii., p.* 315. ½ *p.*] *Underwritten,*

I. *Reference to Lord Privy Seal, Lord Cottington. and Sec. Windebank. Greenwich,* 19*th June* 1638. [*Copy.* ⅙ *p.*]

June 19.
Coggs Court.
19. Sir Thomas Penyston, Sheriff of co. Oxford, to Nicholas. My wife's great weakness has hindered my coming to London. I have not received in money above 1,200*l.*, which is paid to the Treasurer of the Navy. Three corporations are directed to pay in their money themselves, being 205*l.* I sent also to Sir Christopher Clitherow and Mr. Ridge, aldermen of London, to pay the Treasurer of the Navy 20*l.* apiece the 1st May, having good estates in this country, so that there is paid in and directions given for 1,445*l.* The country generally forbears to pay, and expects some declaration of the judges' opinion, but I have sent out new warrants to all the towns that have not paid, and will endeavour to get in all, which as I receive shall be sent up. [*Seal with crest.* ¾ *p.*]

June 19.
Greenwich.
20. Minutes of the Proceedings of the Commissioners for the affairs of his Majesty's Household, sitting as a Committee. Mr. Cofferer and the rest of the officers of the Greencloth were prayed to

1638.

Vol. CCCXCIII.

cause the clerks of the kitchen to attend the committee this day se'nnight, at their next meeting, and to bring with them the bills of fare of all the tables of ten dishes and upwards. It was ordered, that when the Lord Chamberlain shall dine or sup abroad in the Guard Chamber, then the gentlemen ushers daily waiters shall sit at his table, as they have used to do, and when his lordship shall have his table in his said chamber then the gentlemen ushers shall have their five dishes to themselves. The Lord Chamberlain and Mr. Treasurer and Mr. Comptroller are desired to bring to the next meeting a list of all his Majesty's servants fit to be sitters at tables in the King's house. [*Draft.* 1¼ *p.*]

June 19. 21. Memorandum of Francis Andrewes, that he this day repaired to Henry Cusse from Edward Nicholas, to desire him to go to Mr. Awdley, to tender himself as ready to seal the conveyance mentioned in the decree for settling Bushton [Bishopstone?], upon the passing which 520*l.* is payable to the children of Mr. Hunton, deceased. Mr. Cusse and the writer went accordingly to Mr. Awdley, who said that until all the debts were compounded he was resolved to sit as he is. [⅔ *p.*]

June 19. 22. Suggestions [by Sir John Lambe] for a division to be made by Archbishop Laud of the personal estate of John Belke, late of Sheldwick, Kent, deceased (*see* 11*th April last, No.* 54). The estate amounted to 2,001*l.* 9*s.* 10*d.* Of this sum it was suggested that 900*l.* should be allotted to Valentine, Thomas, Michael, Gabriel, and Anne, the five children of Gabriel Belke, brother of the intestate; 40*l.* to William, only son of Michael Belke, deceased, another brother of the intestate; 560*l.* to Anne and Frances, the two children of Elizabeth, deceased, sister of the intestate; 21*l.* 9*s.* 10*d.* allotted by Sir Nathaniel Brent for pious uses. [¾ *p.*]

June 19. 23. Certificates of Mary Wight and three others, in testimony that John Evans, footman to the Marquess of Hamilton, was at Chelsea in the afternoon of Easter Eve last. [¾ *p.*]

June 20. 24. Informations taken by the Attorney-General respecting words alleged to have been spoken by Mary Cole (*see* 15*th inst., No.* 2). THOMAS PORTER of Barking, Essex, gentleman, stated that William Godney said that Mrs. Cole, discoursing about Pickering, spake the words in question. WILLIAM GODNEY, gentleman, deposed that he heard John Lambard say that Mrs. Cole spoke the words alleged. RICHARD HASTLER, clerk, said that he heard John Browne affirm that Mrs. Cole, speaking with some of the servants in Mr. Petre's house touching marriages between protestants and papists, and one of the company demanding why it might not be, in regard the King had matched with a catholic, the said Mrs. Cole said, if she were as the Queen she would hang the King for dealing so hardly with papists. Browne related these words from Mark Heyward, Mr. Petre's gardner. JOHN BROWNE affirmed that Mrs. Cole used the words

1638.

Vol. CCCXCIII.

aforesaid, but he did not hear her; the relation was made to him about six weeks since. [1½ p.] *Underwritten,*

> 24. I. *Further examinations respecting the said words, taken the 23rd June inst.* THOMAS POULTER *stated that about three months [ago] Mary Cole, his fellow servant at Mr. Petre's house, discoursing with him, and being angry, used these words :—If she were a Queen she would hang the King—the Keeper she meant—God save the King! And her son, Roger Hepthrow, standing by, said, Mother, take heed what you say. The words were spoken all at one time. He did not hear her speak of Pickering.* ANNE SNOW *confirmed the account given by Thomas Poulter.* MARK HEYWARD *said that on the 2nd March Thomas Poulter and Mary Cole, servants in house to Mr. Petre, were discoursing about the powder treason, and Poulter, asking who they were that committed the same, she answered, "By God if I were the Queen I would have the King hanged." Then her son-in-law, Roger Hepthrow, said, "Oh mother! take heed what you say. I have known one hanged for a less word." Then she answered again, "As Christ save me, I meant the Keeper. I pray God bless me, and sweet Jesus bless the King!" Poulter and Heyward, being confronted, affirmed their examinations without variation.* ROGER HEPTHROW, *of Ockenden, labourer, is a papist. Married the daughter of Mary Cole. Was present at her discourse with Poulter. Heard her say, "If she were a Queen she would hang the King—the Keeper I mean—God save the King!" Examinant said, "Take heed, mother, what you say."* [2 pp.]

June 20.

25. Affidavit of John Brooke, Sir William Killigrew, and Robert Long, all described as of London. John Lyons, master-workman, and director of the Earl of Lindsey's undertaking for draining the Great Level, co. Lincoln, and the Eight Hundred Fen there, about January last obtained leave of the Earl to go into the Low Countries, upon promise to return in March or April. The Earl's undertaking hitherto depended upon Lyons's sole direction, and by reason of his absence the works have been much retarded. [⅓ p.] *Underwritten,*

> 25. I. *Memorandum of the Lord Treasurer and Lord Cottington, that having made his Majesty acquainted with the above affidavit, he had given them permission to allow the adventurers six months more to perform the draining of the Eight Hundred Fen. Fulham House, 5th July 1638.* [½ p.]

June 20.
Office of
Ordnance.

26. Additional estimate of the Officers of Ordnance for 102 brass pieces for furnishing the Sovereign of the Seas; total, 1,688*l*. 4*s*. 6*d*. [2 pp.]

Vol. CCCXCIII.

1638.
June 20. 27. A List of pieces of Brass Ordnance, with the weights, endorsed with this date, and probably connected with the preparation of the preceding. [½ p.]

June 20. 28. Similar shorter List, without the weights. [¼ p.]

June 20.
Westminster.
29. Nicholas to Sir John Pennington. My Lord Admiral is relapsed into his fever, and though his fits be but small the physicians advise him to lay aside the thought of all businesses, insomuch as now the place of Lord Admiral is totally managed by Mr. Comptroller, who I fear shall go admiral in the great ship when she goes to sea, but this is told me in secret. Viscount Bayning is lately dead of a fever. The judgment for the ship-money is now given for the King, and so entered, and the business goes on well and quietly. Mr. Mason, the famous master of fence, was Thursday last in the evening murdered by a Frenchman of the same profession and his associates. The Frenchman is fled to the French ambassador's house, but his servant is taken, and the fact is notorious. The Queen much importunes the King for the Frenchman's pardon. We hear that the Prince of Orange has received a great blow near Antwerp, where he has lost six pieces of ordnance and 1,500 men, which has almost quailed the States' hopes of taking that important city. There are various reports of the business in Scotland, which is kept here very secret; but I am told it is like to be all well composed. The King's progress holds, and he sets forward from Theobalds the 16th July, and about that time the Queen goes to Oatlands. I shall continue here this fortnight, and shall not fail to be at court every Sunday till the King be gone. Order is given for victualling eleven of your ships for six months, to begin the first of July next, but for what service none but Mr. Comptroller knows. Your preparation for shipping of landmen is, I suppose, at an end. [1 p.]

June 20.
St. Nicholas, Harnham.
30. Dr. Matthew Nicholas to Edward Nicholas, his brother. Thank you for the timely advertisement of the King's gests, by which I shall be prepared to give attendance, and perform that service which shall be required of me. I hope the business which oppresses you at other times will not [sic] then set you at liberty, when we should receive some benefit in the opportunity to enjoy your company. If you be required to attend his Majesty at Salisbury, I shall free my house of the widow, and account it best employed for your accommodation. If the Council meet here (as I imagine it may, because of the many Sundays the King comes hither,) I hope you then must attend. We talk here that my Lord's Grace [the Archbishop] will be here, whether there come any of the rest of the Council or not; and blessed is that man, and bishopped shall he be, that receives him under his roof. The orders you speak of have been put in execution long since. Two residentiaries are to give their attendance at prayers instantly twice a day for a whole quarter of a year. My quarter falls to begin at Christmas. Your advice in the injury I sustain about my stables accords to my own thoughts. I will only add this to what I have already done, get

1638.

Vol. CCCXCIII.

that claim to be recorded, and then I shall be at liberty to revive my right, if I see occasion, and prevent the prejudice of my successor by my quietness. Dr. Henchman is the only visible man in our church; the rest are contented to obscure themselves to give him light, and for their own ease derive on him all business. Dr. Steward is firm to him. Dr. Mason would gladly remember that he once set his hands on his shoulder to leap over his head, but his relation to Mr. Packer biasses him to the bishop. There is only Dr. Osborne, a constant man, but seldom here; the rest are his, or not their own, and I must follow the cry, or spend my mouth to no purpose on a singular scent. This is the power of the man, and I think he has sufficient malice, but I thank God I fear him not. The worst he can do is to charge the hospital with Harnham Bridge. That he endeavours with all his strength; and I, as much as I can, decline being seen in the business because I doubt the issue. Explains the cause of his father's desire to procure a renewal of his lease from the bishop, and comments on a purchase offered to Edward Nicholas by Mr. Paulet. Health of the writer's wife. His daughter Betty is grown much awry, and he doubts is liver-grown. [*Seal with arms. 2 pp.*]

June 21.
Whitehall.
Commissioners for Gunpowder to Montjoy Earl of Newport. To issue 12 barrels of gunpowder at 18*d.* per pound to Edmund Beane of Tower Street, London, ship chandler. [*Minute. See Vol. ccclv., No. 61, p. 6. ¼ p.*]

June 21.
31. —— to Mr. John Fleming, merchant of Edinburgh, at his house on the north side of the Weigh House in Edinburgh. Letter of intelligence, consisting partly of ciphers, expressed in numbers, and partly of written words, the greater number of which last are nullities. The letter is wholly written upon one page. At its four corners there are, 1st, a perpendicular line; 2nd, a horizontal line; 3rd, a horizontal line; and, 4th, a perpendicular line, which last occurs at the corner where the signature ordinarily stands. [1 *p.*]

June 21.
32. Copy of the preceding, disposed in numbered lines, and with the nullities underscored. [1 *p.*]

June 21.
33. Another copy, in the same state as the preceding. [2½ *pp.*] Annexed,

33. I. *Explanation of many of the numbers in the original. It is also here suggested, in another hand and in another ink, that the horizontal line above mentioned means "Antrim." If this is to be construed as if Randal Earl of Antrim were the writer of the letter, it seems unlikely.* [1 *p.*] *With the assistance afforded, sometimes by one and sometimes by the other, of these copies, the letter reads as follows, the orthography being modernized:—*

"Here's not a man of the English Council knows any passage of Scotland, except 56 [conjectured to mean the Archbishop of Canterbury or the Marquess of Hamilton], which they take all in ill part; the King and 66

1638.

Vol. CCCXCIII.

were lately shut up close together for half a day; and no packet comes from Edinburgh but is answered by them both. There do want arms for 20,000, with all provisions suitable. This is advanced upon the customs. Here is a speech that 81 [the Lord Lieutenant] hath promised to bring out of 171 [Ireland] 15,000 with furniture. It is thought he dares not set out nor attempt it. 201 hath much diffidence. Antrim will supply him with a ship or with two, but if yr [they?] come, no harm that way. 92 [the people?] are your sure friends, it's thought plenty gotten here; if more be, you and your brother shall have notice. The King and 56 comes to 247, and will not be known but that all the rest of 361 [Edinburgh] goes onward, and none of the Council in Scotland dare take notice of it. The protestants and the precisians and many others very tenderly remembering you, heartily desire that you receive no conditions of agreement but in a parliament, and you will find pardon with other the like conditions of peace of having 9 or 10 more makes 82 for their and your safety. The end of all is, 201 [Hamilton?] will promise anything at this hard pinch, which he cannot perform afterwards. The King cannot sleep for want of his friend Thomas [Wentworth?] who cannot come here. Say, if they condescend on any agreement with him for [in?] the name of three or four of the rest, all will be disappointed, and all your so happy work be spoiled. Wherefore clear the root and branch, for you are suspected by Will. and Tho. [Laud and Wentworth] and by 201 [Hamilton?] to have him for your correspondent 111 [which I believe not], and that you will have more use for your money than that. Protection unto 362 is denied, and much harm comes to him, with discontent among his neighbours. 102 you may withhold, seeing he doth so persist in your demands of his house. Nothing can either help or hinder you, but the great God, your assured friend, and mighty helper to all yours that be distressed."

June 22. 34. Petition of Mark Proudfoot, the King's servant, to the King. Prays for licence for 21 years for transporting 20,000 dozen pounds of tallow candles every year into places in amity with your Majesty, paying 3d. for every dozen pounds transported. And petitioner will every year bring into England a like quantity of tallow. [½ p.] *Underwritten*,

34. I. Reference to the Lord Treasurer and Lord Cottington. Greenwich, 22nd June 1638. [⅙ p.]

34. II. The Lord Treasurer and Lord Cottington to the King. The exportation of tallow is against the law, chiefly for that it is accounted munition, as that without which ships cannot be drest. And the care of not raising [the price of] candles has always been very considerable. The offer of petitioner to bring in tallow is not considerable, for from Ireland is now imported as much as can be spent, and from any other place it is presumed the petitioner will not bring tallow. Upon the whole the suit is very inconvenient, of ill consequence, and cannot be granted. 5th July 1638. [¼ p.]

June 22. 35. Sir Edward Bromfield and others, Governor and Assistants of the Society of Soapmakers, to [the Council]. Report on a petition of —— Lenning. Petitioner did not, as he pretends, give over his trade in obedience to commands of his Majesty, but having got ample estate by the trade, and purchased lands 44 miles from London, where he resides, about two years before his Majesty's grant to the

Vol. CCCXCIII.

1638.

late corporation of Westminster, he gave over his trade, and let his soap-house to John Rowell, one of the present society. Further, when his Majesty settled the trade, it was proposed that personal security should be given for performance with his Majesty. Petitioner offered to join, and was nominated, but afterwards refused, to the distraction of the business, alleging that he had renounced the trade, and had an estate, and would not adventure it with partners. Thirdly, he is of such a haughty spirit and turbulent disposition that he will trouble his Majesty's service and perplex the society. The writers are willing to admit his son, when he shall attain 21. [1 p.]

June 22. 36. The late Overseers of the Poor of St. Martin's-in-the-Fields to the Council. Certify names of persons who refuse or delay to pay the rate for relief of the poor. Have given them warning for attendance on your Lordships. [*Amongst the persons named are "Monsieur Amigoe," Mungo Murray, Paul Williams, who attended the Council, George Colt, William Carr, and "The Lord Choare."* 1 p.]

June 22. 37. Notes of various payments made to John Taylor, his Majesty's agent in Germany, upon privy seals dated from the 30th November 1633 to the 23rd April 1638, the last payment being made this day. [1¾ p.]

June 22. Commissioners for Gunpowder to Montjoy Earl of Newport. To deliver 12 barrels of gunpowder to Edmund Beane. [*Minute. See Vol. ccclv., No. 61, p. 6. 3 lines.*]

June 22. 38. Sir Theodore Mayerne to the Count d'Amont [Lord Livingstone of Almond]. Long letter of medical advice. He must not believe that the remedies he has used have been useless, although he has not yet experienced any benefit arising from them. Recommends him to use what he terms "spa waters," and especially to go to the waters of Knaresborough, which are sharp, vitriolic, and ferruginous, if in his own country there are no similar waters. Wishes him to drink these waters in increasing quantities, beginning with four glasses or 40 ounces by the day, and augmenting the amount day by day until he is able to take ten glasses or 100 ounces, which is enough to do him good, although some people run on to 120 or 150 ounces. Thinks he will be well pleased to get away some little distance from the place where he is, where it must be difficult for him to do his duty and to please all the world. May God protect and direct him. For the writer, he is devoted to the public good and the service of the King. [*Indorsed by Sec. Windebank. "Dr. Mayerne to my Lord of Amont, inclosed in the letter without name directed my Lord of Amont, which appears to be Levingston, the tailor; first intercepted coming." French.* 1⅔ p.]

June 23. Grant to the Marquess of Hamilton of Chelsea Place and the manor of Chelsea, to be held in socage, rendering 10*l.* per annum,

1638.

Vol. CCCXCIII.

which mansion house and manor were granted by the late King to the Countess of Nottingham, and to James Howard her son, since deceased, for 40 years after her decease. [*Docquet.*]

June 23. Grant to Robert Earl of Ancram, of power to find out ambergris within his Majesty's dominions, and to recover things out of the sea which belong to his Majesty, for 31 years, reserving to his Majesty a tenth part. Sir George Douglas and Degory Priske had the like grant in the 3rd year of the King's reign, for 31 years, whose interest in the same is now transferred to the Earl of Ancram. [*Docquet.*]

June 23.
Greenwich.
39. The King to Sir John Manwood. About two years since our Council, at the petition of the corporation of Dover, and upon certificate of the farmers of our customs, ordered that a boom should be made in the harbour of the said town, and the custody thereof be committed to the corporation. We now think fit to commit the custody thereof to Sir John Manwood, lieutenant of our castle of Dover, during the time of his lieutenancy, taking such droits as the commissioners of the harbour shall think fit, having respect to the custom of other countries, and when Sir John Manwood shall cease to be lieutenant, the said office shall be disposed of by the Lord Warden to the lieutenants of the said castle successively. [*Copy.* ½ *p.*]

June 23. 40. Edward Fenn to Nicholas. Received since the last certificate, of the late sheriff of Hertford, 77*l.* 7*s.* 8*d.*, and of the late sheriff of Worcester, 20*l.* [On account of ship-money for 1636. ¼ *p.*]

June 23. 41. Account of Sir William Russell of ship-money received for 1637; total, 108,471*l.* 5*s.* 1*d.*; outstanding, 87,943*l.* 2*s.* 7*d.* [= 2 *pp.*]

June 23. 42. Account of ship-money for 1637 levied by sheriffs, and not yet paid in, 6,250*l.*; which makes the total sum collected, 114,721*l.*, which is 29,499*l.* less than this time twelve months. [1 *p.*]

June 23. 43. Opinion of Mr. Thomas Tempest on the matters in difference between the companies of Merchant Adventurers of London and Newcastle. States the substance of the facts proved on both sides, and wishes the company of Newcastle to be acquainted therewith, that if they can add anything thereunto for further instruction it may be inserted. [1½ *p.*]

June 23. Lords of the Admiralty to Sir Charles Howard, Sir William Elliot, and Henry Weston, Justices of Peace for Surrey. We send you a petition of John Warner, of Hamhaw, wharfinger, complaining of Samuel Cordewell, his Majesty's gunpowder maker. We pray you to examine the said complaint, and certify your opinion of what is fit to be done. [*Copy. See Vol.* cccliii., *p.* 109. ¼ *p.*]

June 23. Copy of the same. [*See Vol.* ccxcii., *p.* 83. ½ *p.*]

Vol. CCCXCIII.

1638.
June 23.
44. Particular by Mr. Hill, of such works as are yet to do for the perfect draining of Bourne Level and the Eight Hundred Fen. [1 p.]

June 23.
45. J. P. to John Jemmat, minister at Berwick. I doubt not you have sympathized with me in my condition. I shall be glad sometimes to hear from you. Great expectation there is with us what issue the Lord will put to the great difference that is now raised betwixt the nation beyond you and me. You are placed as it were in the centre betwixt both nations, and no doubt have intelligence of more occurrences than is in other places. And as you have an advantage that way, so also to have your spirit affected and prepared according to occasions. Surely the Lord is working a great work, and when he pleases can want no instruments to effect it. Well will it be for us if we can keep close to him. Jeremy, Daniel, and others that have been most careful to keep their consciences tender have sped best in afflicting and trying times. If those times of temptation be at hand (as is conceived by many), then it concerns us to labour to get the church of Philadelphia's condition, and be within the promise of Him who is able to preserve. P.S.—Put Mr. Symons in mind of the 5l. I paid upon your motion to Mr. Letchford. [*Endorsed by Sec. Windebank.* "*First intercepted going.*" 1 p.]

June 23.
Burderop.
46. Sir William Calley to Richard Harvey. Acknowledges receipt of things formerly directed to be purchased, and orders currants, case pepper, nutmegs, ginger, cinnamon, mace, cloves, and Jordan almonds. [⅓ p.]

June 23.
47. See "Returns made by Justices of Peace."

June 24.
48. Order of the King in Council. On the complaints of the stuff weavers, exhibited to the board by divers aldermen against a clause in the charter granted to the weavers of London ready to pass the great seal, It was Ordered, that the clause inhibiting all mercers to put forth any silk to be made in stuff, unless they had served seven years to the trade of weaving, and were admitted to that company, be expunged; and that it should be lawful for mercers and others to put forth silk or yarn to any weaver that is a free brother of the said company, having been an apprentice to the trade; also that no merchant shall set any looms on work in their houses; and that the said stuffs shall be all brought to the public hall of the said company, to the end the King may not be defrauded of the duties. [*Seal of the Council attached.* 1 p.]

June 24.
49. Endymion Porter, of St. Martin's-in-the-Fields, to his servant, Richard Harvey. Letter of Attorney to receive his rents in the parish of North Somercotes, co. Lincoln, and to settle all accounts concerning the same. [*Seal with arms.* ¾ p.]

June 25.
The Court at Greenwich.
50. Sir Henry Vane, Comptroller of the Household, to Nicholas. Sends Jasper Selwyn to him, whose examination he desires Nicholas to take about the business of powder, upon the same interrogatories

1638.

Vol. CCCXCIII.

which were formerly taken in a like case by Mr. Attorney, and to bring the same to Sir Henry on the morrow afternoon at Whitehall. [*Seal with arms.* ⅓ *p.*]

June 25. 51. Examination of Jasper Selwyn. I agreed with John Pigott, of London, grocer, for 110 barrels of powder, and paid for them to John Evelyn, by the hands of William Bevis, his servant, which was about May 1637. The powder was sent to my storehouse by John Brush. Furthermore, the aforesaid John Pigott received of John Vincent, saltpetreman, divers hogsheads of petre, and sold them again, entering them in his book for ginger. [¾ *p.*]

June 25. [Edinburgh.] 52. [—— Borthwick?] to some unnamed persons whom he addresses "Noble Lords." Thanks for letters.

"As to the common business here in hand, concerning religion, there is nothing as yet done, but time delayed, and a great deal of money spent by the subjects in waiting so long at so high a rate as we live here in Edinburgh. The commissioner had a purpose .... to make some declaration of his Majesty's will by a proclamation, but hitherto has been stayed by reason that the petitioners are ready to protest that they rest not satisfied without a free general assembly and parliament, as the only way to settle this present combustion. The commissioner has been petitioned for those remedies, and replied, that some impediments being removed he would. This was found to be the destroying of the late covenant, at least a fair explanation of that part which seems to import unlawful combination, and this has spent the most part of the time since the commissioner came. Now they have cleared sufficiently that they intended no rebellion or combination for any other end but in defence of their religion and laws, and so this day they are to petition of new for a free general assembly and parliament, which if they be refused of it is like they will call both themselves, and settle the estate of the country the best may be, and so continue in possesion of what they think warrantable. There remains here of the nobility Rothes, Montrose, Eglintoun, Hume, Dalhousie, Weemys, Lyndsay, Boyd, Sinclair, Yester, Cranstoun, Montgomery, Fleming, Frissell, Forester, Elcho, Almond, Balcarres, Carnegy, Drumlanrig, Burley, Balmerinoch, Couper. [Besides these names there are added in the margin, "Cassilis, Lothian, Loudon, Johnston."] General Lesley, four commissioners from each shire for barons, and with them three, four, or five score of assessors of the gentry of each shire, and so of ministers and barons, so that there will remain, of the whole, betwixt three and four thousand in Edinburgh, with which the town may subsist and determine as occasion offers till the rest be advertised when need is. This I may say, all degrees goes on without fainting, and not a man is known to fall from their number, but daily coming in. There was never at any time such plenty of preaching and prayer as is now in Edinburgh. All the most able ministers are set a-work, preach every day in many places, and on the Lord's day three sermons in each church ordinarily, and so in all the halls and other great houses. God is not wanting with his blessings, for the obstinate are powerfully brought in by the ministers of the word. This last Lord's day the commissioner was earnestly solicited by the bishops to go to chapel, and hear sermon and the English service, which has been long in use there (the two former he was at Kinneil, where he heard Mr. Alexander Henderson and Mr. Richard Dickson). It was heard of in the town, but if the Bishop of Dunblane, who is dean of the chapel, had not gone and petitioned the commissioner that all should be discharged, and fled himself to Seatoun, it is like we should not been longer troubled with him and some others who stay privately about the abbey. So the commissioner went to Dalkeith on Saturday at night. It is true there was a guard strong enough put to the Castle of Edinburgh, and at the commissioner's desire was discharged. Only it is well looked to, and the town of Edinburgh

Vol. CCCXCIII.

1638.

keeps a strong watch in their town, about 150 musketeers. We hear much of English armies and ships to come, but we neither see nor fear anything that way." Acknowledges receipt of letter which " a kind friend " directed to John Smith, a direction which should be continued. " Show Mr. Morehead that I have spoken with James Douglas . . . but mind never to meddle with him more. . . . I found him altogether mad and without reason. . . . Render Sir John hearty thanks for his news. Lord Eglintoun assures me that he writes to him all occurrences here, and so I find it more convenient to write only to you."

[*Endorsed as intercepted.* 4 *pp.*]

June 25.
Lincoln's Inn Fields.
53. Felix Long to Richard Harvey. Sends a note for Mr. Malet's bond, and wishes Harvey a happy and prosperous journey. [¾ *p.*]

June 25.
Salisbury House.
55. William Earl of Salisbury to Denzil Holles. It has been made known to the Earl that Holles had caused divers timber trees to be felled, and others to be lopped, on the Earl's land at Damerham, contrary to the covenants of his lease. States the numbers of trees so dealt with, and that it is conceived that 250*l.* will not satisfy the wrong done. Could not have suspected such spoils from Holles, who has always professed such a respect unto the Earl. Lets him know that he expects satisfaction, and his answer whether he denies or acknowledges the premises *de facto*, and why he should not make due payment. Although Holles has not regarded the warning of the Earl's servant, wishes him to take notice of the covenants of his lease in future, or the Earl shall be enforced to seek the preservation of his inheritance by legal means. [*Copy.* 1 *p.*]

June 25.
55. See " Returns made by Justices of Peace."

June 26.
56. Petition of the Company of Weavers of London to the King. State the effect of their charters from the time of Henry II. to the present day, and complain that an infinite number of strangers, men of other nations, and especially Walloons, who are neither of the church nor have served for the trade of weaving according to the statute, daily come over, and prove very hurtful to the poor English weavers, whose bread they take out of their mouths, and tend to the utter destruction of petitioners. The strangers too are thrust up with their families in tenements of very small receipt in the city and suburbs, which are much annoyed with offensive and troublesome inmates, against the free usages of the city and the statutes of the land, and likely to breed contagious diseases. Pray order for reformation. [⅚ *p.*] *Underwritten,*

56. I. *Reference to the Commissioners for Trade to certify their opinion. Theobalds, 26th June* 1638. [⅙ *p.*]

[June 26.]
57. Note of the number of Dutch, French, and Walloons now exercising the trade of weaving in and about the city of London. Totals, Dutch, 95 ; French, 137; Walloons, 1,998. [⅔ *p.*]

June 26.
58. Bills of fare, according to the several seasons of the year, for the dinners and suppers of 10, 7, and 6 dishes, as they are usually served in the King's household. [7½ *pp.*]

VOL. CCCXCIII.

1638.
June 26.
Whitehall.

59. Order of the Commissioners for the affairs of the Household. Pray Mr. Cofferer and the rest of the officers of the Green Cloth to examine from the 17th Henry VIII., and to certify what diet has been allowed to the Master of the Jewel House, and why it has been retrenched. [*Draft.* ½ *p.*]

June 26.

60. See "Returns made by Justices of Peace."

June 27.

61. Order of Council. On further consideration of the objections made by those of Congleton, against William Bramhall, concerning his indirect procuring the manor of Congleton to be passed from the crown to the City of London, and afterwards to himself, It was Ordered that the Attorney and Solicitor General and the Attorney of the Duchy should examine the said matter, and if the obtaining appears to have been to the prejudice of his Majesty, and to the wrong of the ancient tenants in any considerable value, then the Attorney and Solicitor General are to advise of a legal course for recovering the same manor. [1¼ *p.*] *Underwritten,*

61. I. *Appointment by the Attorney and Solicitor General to hear the said matter on the 27th October. 28th June* 1638. [*Council Seal attached.* ¼ *p.*]

June 27.
London.

62. Thomas Viscount Somerset to Sec. Coke. Was commanded by the King to leave the enclosed petition with Sec. Coke, which through his interference will he doubts not receive a gracious reference from his Majesty. The King has promised to take the writer's long faithful service and great charge and expence into his consideration. Excuses himself for not taking leave personally of the Sec. Begs him to accept of a paper of reasons in favour of his petition. [1 *p.*] *Enclosed,*

62. I. *Petition of Thomas Viscount Somerset to the King. Petitioner is given to understand that your Majesty intends to disafforest the Forest of Deane, co. Gloucester, and to distribute the lands and woods thereof to such persons as you shall think fit. Prays, in consideration of his long and faithful service to your Majesty, as also to your father and mother, (for recompense whereof petitioner has not been importunate,) that you will bestow upon him* 4,000 *acres of the said lands to be disafforested, he paying for the same as it shall please you to appoint.* [1 *p.*]

62. II. *Statement of reasons to move his Majesty for granting* 4,000 *acres of the disafforested Forest of Deane to Viscount Somerset.* i. *He gave up his place of Master of the Horse without recompense, whereas all others that had places under the late Queen, your Majesty's mother, were restored to places or had other recompense.* ii. *He yielded to the*

1638.

Vol. CCCXCIII.

late Duke of Buckingham the patent he had of the Treasury of the Common Pleas, for which he had the King's word for a recompense. iii. *His quitting pensions of 600l. per annum with 4,000l. arrears for marsh lands in co. Lincoln, the rates of the purchase being far higher than any man would have given, and he not to receive any profit for 17 years.* [1 p.]

June 27. 63. William Calley to Richard Harvey. Mr. Davison will bring a bill of the writer's to Harvey. If Felix Long has no money of Sir William Calley's in his hands, prays Harvey to pay the amount. Wishes to have a fan of black feathers with a handle of either silver or otherwise, as is most worn. [*Seal with arms.* 1 p.]

June 27. 64–65. See "Returns made by Justices of Peace."

June 28.
Greenwich.
66. Proclamation to the people of Scotland. We neither were, are, nor by the grace of God ever shall be, stained with popish superstition, but are resolved to maintain the true protestant Christian religion, and we assure all men that we will not press the practice of the book of canons and service book, nor anything of that nature, but in such a fair and legal way as shall satisfy all our loving subjects that we neither intend innovation in religion or laws. And to this effect have given order to discharge all acts of Council made thereanent. And for the High Commission, we shall so rectify it, that it shall never impugn the laws, nor be a just grievance to our loyal subjects. And what is further fitting to be "agitat" in general assemblies and parliament for the good of the Kirk shall be taken into our royal consideration in a free assembly and parliament which shall be called with our best conveniency. And we take God to witness that our true meaning is not to admit of any innovations either in religion or laws, but carefully to maintain the purity of religion already professed and established, and noways to suffer our laws to be infringed. [*Printed. Broadside.* 1 p.]

June 28. 67. Statement by the Armourers of London of the lowest prices at which they can make armours, with the reasons of the prices, and why they cannot make them at the rates in the schedule formerly granted. For a cuirassier's armour, 5l.; for a harquebusier's, consisting of breast, back, gorget, and head piece, 40s.; for a harquebusier's armour, light, 35s.; for a footman's armour, unlined, 25s. The reasons for these prices being higher than those mentioned in the commission are: 1. Dearness of plate, coals, and victuals. 2. Many journeys before they can have order what to do. 3. These are the prices the King used formerly to pay. As to the prices in the commission, they were brought to them by many fair promises of enlarged and continual employment, which have not been fulfilled. [1 p.]

DOMESTIC—CHARLES I. 533

VOL. CCCXCIII.

1638.
June 28. 68. Copy of the paper calendared under date of the 19th inst., No. 22, relating to the distribution of the estate of John Belke, but with blanks for the sums to be allotted to each of the intestate's next of kin. [¾ p.]

June 28. 69. Petition of John Gibbon, on behalf of himself and other participants in the level of Hatfield Chase, to the King. Upon complaint of petitioners, who are fee-farmers unto your Majesty, of unjust sales of their lands contrived by commissioners of sewers (see Calendar for 11th December 1637, No. 65), there was a reference to the Lord Treasurer, Lord Cottington, and Sec. Windebank. The referees on the 16th June inst. entered on the hearing thereof, and appointed a time for further hearing, and commanded petitioners to deliver particulars to the commissioners, which petitioners did accordingly, and the commissioners desired time till Michaelmas term to answer the same, and had it granted. In the interim, the commissioners, on the 24th June inst., without informing your Majesty that anything had been done upon the reference, have obtained a direction transferring the examination from the referees to the Council Board. When the matter shall be examined by the referees, petitioners will be suitors to your Majesty to hear the same in person, but they pray that the reference may go on, and a certificate be first made, before there be any further order. [¾ p.] *Underwritten,*

 69. I. *His Majesty, understanding that the former referees have entered into this business, commands that the said reference shall proceed, any direction given to the contrary notwithstanding. Greenwich, 29th June 1638.* [¼ p.] *Endorsed,*

 69. II. *Appointment by the Lord Treasurer, Lord Cottington, and Sec. Windebank, to proceed with this business on Friday se'nnight; and they desire the judges mentioned in the order of the 16th June (see Calendar of that date, No. 7) to pursue the directions thereby given, and the commissioners of sewers to attend. Whitehall, 16th December 1638.* [⅓ p.]

June 28. 70. Sir John Lambe, Sub-collector and Receiver to Francis Bishop of Peterborough of all tenths payable to his Majesty by the clergy of that diocese, to the King. Sir John being accountable to his Majesty by reason of the said office, and divers persons in a schedule mentioned by their writings obligatory standing bound to him the said Sir John in the sums of money therein mentioned, Sir John assigns over the said writings and moneys to his Majesty. [*Copy.* 2⅓ pp.]

June 28. 71. G. T. [?] to ———. I have never been in a country where things go so slowly or stupidly as in this country. I seem to be in the middle of Spain. As a proof of it I will tell you a little of what is going on in Scotland, where the good people, under the mask of religion, are setting up an anarchy, and to that end refuse every-

1638.

thing that the King offers them, because they seem to be able to resist all that he can do against them. It is confidently asserted that they have more than 40,000 effective men armed *cap à pied*. They have four commanders, men of celebrity bred up in the wars of Germany. They have made all the people take an oath of fidelity to those of their covenant, as they term their rebellious league. They have set up three bodies of councillors, and one of war. They have taxed the whole country to maintain the war, and the King having sent a ship laden with munitions and other necessaries for the castle of Edinburgh, they have seized them, and distributed them amongst their soldiers, and taken possession of the castle and all the other strongholds of the kingdom. They make pretence to defend their liberty and religion from innovation, to hold a free parliament, to reform the church of England, to have the King reside with them six months every year, and to regain their ancient liberties, of which the King has of late deprived them, as they pretend. The King in this affair has gone on too quietly, and in the judgment of wise men has too much despised them, and shown such feebleness that his subjects begin to raise the head, and make little revolts and mutinies even in England. He has sent the Marquess of Hamilton to try to gain them over; which most people think very strange, knowing how little affection he has for the King's affairs, and the authority he might have with that people, being descended from their blood royal, and a man fit for their designs. At first they would not allow any one to speak to him alone, and when he prayed them to lay down their arms against the King, assuring them that the King would give them content, they flatly refused. They have also given him a guard, as it were of honour, but it is thought that if he wished to return this guard would let him know that he could not. From the whole proceeding the King sees evidently that they will not submit to reason by treaty, and has resolved to compel them by force. He is about to raise an army in Ireland, not daring to trust the English, who are greatly irritated against him by reason of the ship-money. This counsel, of raising an army in Ireland, has been suggested to him by the Archbishop of Canterbury and the Lord Deputy of Ireland, who govern him entirely, for he has never yet opened his mouth upon the subject to his Council of State, but strives to keep all close, which very much displeases them. They hold that the raising an army in Ireland is very dangerous; but I know not what better he could do, for in England everybody is discontented, and to raise an army here is to put a sword in their hands to defend themselves, for the party of the puritans is so numerous, and has such correspondence with the Scotch, that they begin already to break down the altars which the Archbishop had raised, bring accusations against the bishops, and demand the re-establishment of many silenced ministers, with a thousand other insolences. Such is the state of one little kingdom, which seems to be in profound peace and flourishing, but *latet anguis in herbâ*, and the least insurrection in Scotland would occasion great trouble in this country. Some think that in two or three

1638.

Vol. CCCXCIII.

months we shall see a revolt, but the difficulty is, that here they have neither soldiers nor commanders; in Scotland they have all. [*Endorsed as* "Writ by a Jesuit to his superior in France." *French.* 2¾ *pp.*]

June 28. 72. G. T. [?] to Messrs. Lamaghi. Letter upon the same subject as the preceding, and giving a detail of the same incidents, with some variations in phrase, and a few additional statements as of fact. Among the latter it is asserted that among the Scottish demands were the delivery of the Archbishop of Canterbury to them as a prisoner, the banishment of Mons. Con, whom they call the Pope's man, and of all catholics. It is added, also, that it was feared that if the King endeavoured to suppress them by force they would call in the Prince Palatine to be their King. On the morrow the writer intends to return to the country for some time, and after that to come back to London, to remain until the proper time for going to Italy. Hopes in passing to salute the person addressed, as he does in this letter, with his brother, "mademoiselle sa femme," Mons. Benagla, and all the house. [*French.* 2 *pp.*]

June 28. 73. Notes of Orders dated 24th November 1636, 25th July 1637, and this day, for Sir Henry Marten to examine and certify the whole loss and damages which Robert Powlett and company have suffered by Capt. T'Kint with the St. Peter of Rotterdam. [1⅙ *p.*]

June 29. 74. Account of Brass Ordnance weighed at Mr. Browne's new foundry, appointed for the Sovereign of the Seas: total, 55 tons 15 cwt. 2 qrs. 9 lbs.; with account of certain pieces for the same ship, and others for the Providence and the Expedition, cast but not proved. [1½ *p.*]

June 29. 75. Dr. Robert Sibthorpe to Sir John Lambe. Wishes all happiness to the married couple, and that a couple of those who, as Sir John says, danced at the wedding, were married. Northampton men continue still inveighing against idolatry, yet idoling their own inventions, insomuch that on the 21st inst. there was a preaching-fast by Mr. Ball in the forenoon and Mr. Newton in the afternoon, but neither of them prayed for any archbishops or bishops, nor used the Lord's prayer at conclusion of theirs before sermon, nor did they or the people use any of the reverend gestures or rites and ceremonies enjoined. How these things are like to be amended, except some higher hand vouchsafe to assist, he may perceive by the enclosed copy of a letter sent to Dr. Clerke, from a reverend man, a bachelor of arts of 16 or 17 years standing at the least, Sir Noake, Mr. Bacon's brother-in-law, and a chaplain, &c., wherein he will observe that if it take not, it is but Sir Noake, not his lord, nor so much as the doctor's chaplain, &c. If it take, and be ill taken, either Sir Noake was mistaken, or others mistook him, or at the least it must be others doing, not the lords, yet if others will not do it they are the wicked persecutors, and not he. But be it as it may the writer for his part is resolved, and so he thinks he has settled him to whom the letter was sent, except direct command come to the contrary

Vol. CCCXCIII.

1638.

Reminds Sir John of his promise to let the writer have a copy of the sentence in the High Commission against the Sussex churchwardens (he thinks of Lewes), for removing the communion table out of the cancelling, &c. It may concern the writer. Beseeches Sir John to give Mr. Knight some item that he may not favour Miles Burkitt, nor disfavour Gare or his proctor too much. His wife had some relation to a Burkitt, which inclines him to favour Mr. Miles. The assizes at Daventry were very small by reason that the gaol could not be removed from Northampton. There is no new commission come down, although the prince's attorney told Dr. Clerke that the Lord Keeper told him he had given warrant to put out Sir Richard [*Margin by Sir John Lambe:* "Sir Richard Samuell"], and the clerk of the peace told the writer that a warrant lay at the Crown Office, &c., but they expect some fees before they are willing to write so much as it comes to, and I believe somebody will be at some charges rather than it shall be long undone, only your assistance may be implored as formerly. P.S.—These Towcester men, on whose behalf the inclosed letter was written, were infected by Stoner, a lecturer, maintained by the Londoners, now gone to New England, and they have misapplied divers texts of Scripture against the communion table standing at the east, and their coming up to receive, with divers other disorders (not to call them blasphemies or profanations) which I will acquaint you with hereafter. [*Seal with arms.* 1¾ *p.*]

June 29.   76. See "Returns made by Justices of Peace."

June 30.   77. Petition of Thomas Bushell, your Majesty's servant, to the King. Upon information by petitioner that there were great quantities of ore which held silver daily transported beyond seas, contrary to law, and if generally suffered might redound to the prejudice of your mint, and frustrate your design in the silver-mines, you prohibited the transporting of any ore unwrought. Some persons who study only their private ends have petitioned to transport poor ore, under the cloak of charity, for supplying the country and miners with corn. Your mines royal can never be brought to perfection if any subject has power to transport ore, unless it be the servant whom your Majesty trusts for discovery of the same and preservation of your mint. Prays the King to authorize petitioner, and none other, to transport refuse ore that holds no silver, by approbation of the paymaster, to prevent clamour for corn and relief of the miners in danger of dearth, but to encourage the subjects to discover their mines by giving the tenth ton of ore to themselves. [½ *p.*] *Annexed,*

    77. I. *Copy order of the King prohibiting the transportation of any metal as it is drawn out of the mint. 15th October 1637.* [1 *p.*] *Written under the above petition,*

    77. II. *Reference to Sec. Windebank, to prepare a letter fit for his Majesty's signature, for the purposes mentioned in the said petition. Greenwich, 30th June 1638.* [⅙ *p.*]

DOMESTIC—CHARLES I. 537

1638.
Vol. CCCXCIII.

June 30. 78. The King to Thomas Bushell. Authorizes Bushell, and none other, to transport refuse ore in the terms prayed for in the preceding petition, and gives the tenth ton of ore to such persons as shall discover their mines. [*Copy endorsed by Robert Reade, Sec. Windebank's secretary.* ½ *p.*]

June 30. 79. Copy clause in the Charter about to be granted to the Weavers of London, which was objected to by the stuff-weavers, and ordered by the Council on the 24th June inst. (*see No.* 48) to be expunged. Certified by the Attorney-General, with annexed draft of a clause proposed to be inserted in its place. [= 1¼ *p.*]

June 30. 80. Copy clause to be inserted in the Charter to the Weavers, in lieu of the clause to be expunged, as mentioned in the preceding article. Certified by the Attorney-General. [¾ *p.*]

June 30. 81. Account of Sir William Russell of ship-money for 1637. Received 109,391*l.* 5*s.* 1*d.*; outstanding 87,023*l.* 2*s.* 7*d.* [= 2 *pp.*]

June 30. 82. Account of ship-money levied and in the hands of the sheriffs. Total 5,340*l.*, making the whole sum collected 114,731*l.*, being 33,468*l.* less than was paid in on 1st July 1637. [1 *p.*]

June 30.
Burderop.
83. Sir William Calley to Richard Harvey. You wrote me that low-priced Spanish cloth was falsely made now-a-days, but so is some Kentish also, for the livery cloaks now sent are made of hollow, bracky, and mill-washed cloth, and the bracks very botcherly mended. [*Seal with arms.* ½ *p.*]

June 30. 84–85. See "Returns made by Justices of Peace."

June. Grant to the Corporation of Bristol to hold a weekly court for trial of personal actions within that city belonging to the Admiralty, with an appeal from the same court to the Lord High Admiral or Judge of the Admiralty Court. [*Docquet.*]

June. 86. Account in the same handwriting and of a similar character to that inserted on 22nd June inst. relating to John Taylor. The payments here are classed under the heads of "King James," "King Charles," "Queen Mary" [Henrietta Maria], and "Sweet Waters," and at the bottom of each page is a statement of the amount due on each account up to Midsummer 1638. [4 *pp.*]

June. 87. Estimate for such provisions as are forthwith to be made for the King and Queen's service and their children. Amongst other things, linen for his Majesty's royal person, for the quarter to end at Michaelmas next, 260*l.*; apparel and other necessaries for the princesses, 300*l.*; trunk for his Majesty's linen and robes, and barehides for his Majesty's Bedchamber carriages, 66*l.*; furniture for a chapel and service books, 200*l.*; a bedstead and bedding for the Duke of York, 52*l.*; a robe of purple velvet, lined with taffety, &c., for the Chancellor of the Garter, 40*l.*; 480 ells of fine Holland for sheets for her Majesty, 288*l.*; two rich carroches lined with velvet,

Vol. CCCXCIII.

1638.

trimmed with gold and silver laces and fringes, for his Majesty; one great horse-saddle of velvet, embroidered with gold and silver, and fringed suitable; two pad saddles and six hunting saddles, all for his Majesty's own service, 2,400*l.*; a side saddle cloth and furniture of velvet, trimmed with gold and silver fringes, with buttons and loops, suitable for the Queen; the like for the Duchesse of Chevreuse; a side-saddle for the Groom of the Stool to her Majesty; two coaches of wrought velvet, trimmed with silk, for the ladies and maids of honour, and ten side saddles for them, 900*l.*; total, 9,608*l.* 6*s.* 8*d.* [2¼ *pp.*]

June.

88. Petition of Sir Lewis Pemberton to the Council. Petitioner, having occasion to reside for some time in London, took lodgings for himself, children, and servants in the house of one Sampson in Holborn. As it after happened, an extent was to be executed upon the said house and goods by the under-sheriff of Middlesex, of which petitioner and his children and servants, and also Sir Thomas Burton and other lodgers, taking notice, without giving any offence or resistance, they got quietly forth of the said house at the back door, the street door being shut upon them, before the gentlemen of Gray's Inn acted any violence. Upon information you committed petitioner to the custody of a messenger, and also the said Sir Thomas Burton and others, to answer their being in the house. Upon Sunday last at Greenwich you discharged Sir Thomas Burton. Prays, in that he is aged and sickly, that he also may be discharged. [⅔ *p.*]

[June?]

89. [The Council] to the King. On the petition of Ralph Massie, his Majesty referred the examination of great accounts and the composing of Massie's debts to us. We referred the preparation of the same accounts to Lawrence Whitaker and Robert Wolrich. His Majesty granted Massie a protection for one year. Massie has diligently laboured therein, but has not been able to bring the same to perfection by reason of the absence of Rolfe, who is principally chargeable in the said accounts, and Blake from Massie demands great sums, who has absented himself altogether, but both of whom are now about London. Whitaker and Wolrich, having also reported their inability to perfect the same accounts, we recommend to his Majesty to renew the protection to Massie for one year. [⅔ *p.*]

June.

90. William Bramhall to the Council. Answer to the offer of the town of Congleton, mentioned in an Order of Council of the 6th inst. With protestation of the untruths contained in the petitions of the said town, I answer that the intention of the offer is said to be that they might become his Majesty's immediate tenants, as formerly they were. The corporation neither are nor ever were such tenants, and those that are farmers thereof are no parties to the petitions, and are more willing to continue tenants to my brother, the Bishop of Derry, and myself, (being joint purchasers,) than to become tenants to the corporation, which may subsist for the future without having any interest in the demesnes and royalties of the manor, as well as

1638.

Vol. CCCXCIII.

they have done for 350 years. All the tenants gave their consent to petitioner's purchase by a voluntary attornment in 1629, and by payment of rent to Sir Thomas Fanshawe, petitioner's brother, and himself, for divers years. Besides 60 years' purchase paid to the city of London almost ten years since, and the interest thereof, and almost 400*l.* more spent in his defence, petitioner has been damnified by missing the office of Chief Remembrancer in the Exchequer in Ireland, and by being withdrawn from all employment, both in Ireland and this country, ever since his landing here two years ago, by the prosecution of the town of Congleton. Prays the pardon of the Lords for not accepting the offer of Congleton, whose aim therein is rather the private ends of particular persons than his Majesty's service or the good of the town. Besides that his brother is joint purchaser, petitioner, being drawn into a good deal of debt by the violent prosecution of Congleton, has been forced to charge the manor with encumbrances. [1¼ *p.*]

June. 91. Brief of the cause of the Justices of Somerset in defence of their Orders of Sessions against Edward Shoard and Thomas Whatman, and respecting the assessment of Maiden Bradley. The question was whether Yarnfield, a liberty in the parish of Maiden Bradley, was to be taxed with the hundred of Norton Ferris in Somerset, or with the hundred of Mere in Wilts (*see this Vol., pp.* 385, 412.) [2 *pp.*]

June. 92. Articles ministered in the Court of High Commission against Miles Burkitt, one of the vicars of Pattishall, co. Northampton. He is charged with not bowing at the name of Jesus, and disobeying an injunction of his ordinary to keep within the rails at the ministration of the sacrament, and to administer to none that would not come up to the rails; also with irreverent speeches against the Lord's Prayer, the Belief, the Ten Commandments, and the Virgin Mary, and with abetting Paul Ganner, one of the churchwardens of Pattishall, in the removal of the communion table into the body of the chancel. [*Endorsed, "Gare contra Burkitt."* 2⅙ *pp.*]

June. 93. Similar articles against William Warde, parson of Allesley, co. Warwick. Defendant was charged with having been for at least 12 years past a common frequenter of alehouses in Allesley, Coventry, and other towns, drinking with coblers, butchers, tinkers, pedlers, and the like persons of base condition in excessive manner. Being legally questioned before the then Bishop of Coventry and Lichfield for the crime of drunkenness, he received a canonical admonition, and was enjoined to preach a sermon in his parish church, and therein to acknowledge his vice of drunkenness and inveigh against its heinousness, since which he has frequented alehouses as usual. Instances are alleged of his excessive drunkenness during the performance of divine service, and whilst drunk of his playing at ninepins with a butcher on a Sunday afternoon, of his tumbling and wallowing in the highway, fighting with a cobler in the yard of an alehouse, tumbling from his horse on his return from Coventry,

Vol. CCCXCIII.

1638.

swearing at Mrs. Hemingham, and threatening, with a naked knife in his hand, to kill her dog; with a variety of other profanities and immoralities, concluding with his producing in this court a false certificate of his sober and quiet demeanour. [11 *pp.*]

June.   94. Bishop Wright, of Coventry and Lichfield, to Edward Archer, M.A. Appointment as coadjutor and curate of Endfield [Enville], co. Stafford; Anthony Fowke, the rector, being a lunatic. [*Latin. Parchment.* 31 *lines.*]

June.   95. Calculation as to the way in which 3,000*l.* on the 1st July next, and the like sum on the 1st August following, were to be paid by the shareholders in the Earl of Lindsey's works of drainage, in co. Lincoln. The contributors were: Sir William Killigrew for five shares; the Earl of Lindsey for four shares; the Earl of Dorset, Lord Willoughby, and Sir Edward Heron, two shares each; Peregrine Bertie, Sir Thomas Stafford, and Sir Francis Godolphin, for one share each. [⅔ *p.*]

[June ?]   96. Names of such persons as have of late years compounded with the Vestry of St. Martin-in-the-Fields to be excused from bearing offices in the said parish, with a suggestion, attributed in the endorsement to Mr. Hulbert, that if these sums were "repaired," and no more such fines taken, it would produce much good to the parish and his Majesty's service. [= 2 *pp.*]

June.   97–99. See "Returns made by Justices of Peace."

Vol. CCCXCIV.   June 1638.

PAPERS RELATING TO THE CASE OF SHIP-MONEY, Between The King And John Hampden.

1637.
Oct. 22.   1. Reply of Mr. Holborne to the argument of Sir Edward Littleton, Solicitor-General. [56½ *pp.*]

[Dec.]   2. The heads and chief pieces of the argument of Sir John Bankes, the Attorney-General. [1½ *p.*]

[Dec.]   3. Copy of the same. [1⅔ *p.*]

[Dec.]   4–5. Two other copies of the same. [3⅓ *pp.* and 3¼ *pp.*]

1637–8.
Jan. 27.   6. Argument of Sir Richard Weston, one of the Barons of the Exchequer. [18½ *pp.*]

Jan. 27.   7. Argument of Sir Francis Crawley, one of the Judges of the Common Pleas. [12 *pp.*]

1638.   Vol. CCCXCIII.

[April 14.] 8. Argument of Sir George Croke, one of the Judges of the King's Bench. [34½ pp.]

April 14. 9. Notes of the argument of Sir Thomas Trevor, one of the Barons of the Exchequer, and of the preceding argument of Sir George Croke. [3⅓ pp.]

June 9. 10. Argument of Sir John Finch, Chief Justice of the Common Pleas. [40 pp.]

PAPERS RELATING TO APPOINTMENTS IN THE NAVY,

To Offices under the Rank of Captain,

DATED BETWEEN 1ST JANUARY 1637–8 AND 30TH JUNE 1638.

Date.	Office.	Nature of Document.	Reference to Document.
1637–8. Jan. 13. Whitehall.	Deputy boatswain of the Nonsuch.	Appointment of Edward Elding.	Vol. ccclxxviii., No. 84. 1 p.
Jan. 13.	Copy of the same.	- - - -	Vol. cccliii., fol. 80 b. ½ p.
Jan. 17.	Boatswain in care of the King's pinnaces.	Masters of the Trinity House to Nicholas. William Godfrey, being young and inexperienced, they have advised him that he should go a voyage or two in a Straits-man before they could certify on his behalf.	Vol. ccclxxviii., No. 111. ⅔ p.
Jan. 30. Whitehall.	Master-carpenter of the Vanguard.	Appointment of Robert Morecocke, now master-carpenter of the Dreadnought.	Vol. cccliii., fol. 84 b. ⅓ p.
Jan. 30.	Master-carpenter of the Dreadnought.	Minute of appointment of James Benns.	Ibid. 4 lines.
Feb. 3. Whitehall.	Purser of the Vanguard.	Lords of the Admiralty to Officers of Navy. To enter John Blunden in place of John Wriothesley who has surrendered the said office.	Ibid., fol. 85 b. ⅓ p.
Feb. 3. Whitehall.	Master-carpenter of the Reformation.	The same to the same. To enter Thomas Day, now master-carpenter of the Antelope, in place of Maurice Boynes, deceased.	Ibid. ⅓ p.
Feb. 3.	Master-carpenter of the Antelope.	Minute of similar letter for Robert Boynes, in place of Thomas Day.	Ibid. 4 lines.
Feb. 3.	Lieutenant in the Swallow.	Appointment of Mr. Thomas Kettleby.	Ibid., fol. 86 b. ½ p.

Papers relating to Appointments in the Navy.

Date.	Office.	Nature of Document.	Reference to Document.
1637–8. Feb. 14. M[incing] Lane.	Steward's place in the Henrietta pinnace.	Kenrick Edisbury to Nicholas. Recommends Richard Cole to succeed John Somers, lately drowned. [*Underneath is a further recommendation, signed* "Henry Clerke."]	Vol. ccclxxxii., No. 15. ½ p.
Feb. 16.	Purser's place in the Henrietta.	Sir Henry Mainwaring to Sir Henry Vane. Certifies in favour of Thomas Baker, who had been 2 years steward in the Unicorn.	Ibid., No. 27. 1 p.
Feb. 17. Whitehall.	Master-gunner of the Nicodemus.	Appointment by the Lords of the Admiralty of Richard Wilkinson.	Vol. cccliii., fol. 89 b. ⅓ p.
Feb. 17. Whitehall.	Purser in the Henrietta pinnace.	Like appointment of Thomas Baker, in place of John Summers, deceased.	Ibid., fol. 90. ⅓ p.
Feb. 17. Whitehall.	Deputy-purser in the Roebuck pinnace.	Like appointment of Thomas Paradice, in place of John Fitzherbert, the purser.	Ibid. ½ p.
Feb.	Pursership in the Maria pinnace, void by death of the late purser.	Petition of Henry Butler to the Lords of the Admiralty. Sets forth past services. Was in the Fifth Whelp when she was cast away, and lost all he had. Prays appointment.	Vol. ccclxxxiii., No. 58. ½ p.

Returns made by Justices of Peace,

From 1st January 1637–8 to 30th June 1638;

Most of them relating to Measures for Relief of the Poor, taken in pursuance of the King's Book of Orders and the Instructions of the Council.

Date.	For what Place.	Nature of Document.	Reference to Document.
1637–8. Jan. 25.	Wapentakes of Skyrack and Barkston [Ash] in the west riding of co. York.	Return by Justices of Peace of of all children put forth during the year 1637.	Vol. ccclxxix., No. 89. 4 pp.
Feb. 13.	Oldham, co. Lancaster.	Certificate of presentments taken monthly before the Justices of Peace, from 26th September 1637 to this day, principally relating to the maintenance of the poor and other matters provided for in the Book of Orders.	Vol. ccclxxxii., No. 9. 2 strips of parchment = 4 pp.

DOMESTIC—CHARLES I.

Returns made by Justices of Peace.

Date.	For what Place.	Nature of Document.	Reference to Document.
1637-8. Feb. 13.	Liberties of Cartmell and Furness, co. Lancaster.	Certificate of all the presentments made to the Justices of Peace since the last assizes, 1637.	Vol. ccclxxxii., No. 10. Paper roll = 9 pp.
Feb. 15.	Three hundreds of Cottesloe, Bucks.	Similar certificate of presentments made this day.	Ibid., No. 18. 1 p.
Feb. 16.	Hundreds of Copthorne and Effingham, Surrey.	Similar certificate of presentments received since 15th July last.	Ibid., No. 28. 1 p.
Feb. 18.	Upper division of the lathe of Scray, Kent.	Certificate of Justices of Peace of children apprenticed, fines levied, and rogues punished, since the last assizes.	Ibid., No. 46. 2 pp.
Feb. 19.	Hundreds of Blackheath, Bromley and Beckenham, Little and Lesness and Ruxley, Kent.	Similar certificate, referring to all the above particulars.	Ibid., No. 52. 1 p.
Feb. 21.	Lathe of Shepway, Kent.	Similar certificate, but only of apprentices placed since the last assizes.	Ibid., No. 69. 1 p.
Feb. 21.	Lathe of Aylesford, Kent.	Similar certificate of apprentices placed and rogues punished.	Ibid., No. 70. 2½ pp.
Feb. 21.	Rape of Chichester, Sussex.	Certificate of Justices of Peace of attention to the points directed by the Book of Orders, with the number of children apprenticed.	Ibid., No. 71. 1 p.
Feb. 23.	Division of Bolton, co. Lancaster.	The like certificate of presentments made at the meetings of the Justices of Peace from the 28th August 1637.	Ibid., No. 81. 3⅙ pp.
Feb. 24.	The downish part of the rape of Bramber, Sussex.	The like certificate of performance of the requirements of the Book of Orders.	Vol. ccclxxxiii., No. 12. 1 p.
* Feb. 24.	Hundred of Manshead, co. Bedford.	The like certificate of vagrants punished since last assizes. States the number in every parish; total, 156.	Ibid., No. 13. 1 p.
Feb. 24.	Rape of Arundel.	The like certificate of attention to the Book of Orders, with lists of apprentices bound and rogues punished.	Ibid., No. 14. 1½ p.
Feb. 27.	Part of the wildish division of the rape of Bramber.	The like certificate, with names of apprentices and masters, and numbers of rogues punished.	Ibid., No. 25. ¾ p.
Feb. 28.	Hundreds of Elmbridge and Kingston, Surrey.	The like certificate, with numbers of apprentices put out, vagrants punished, and alehouses put down since the last assizes	Ibid., No. 31. 1 p.

Returns made by Justices of Peace.

Date.	For what Place.	Nature of Document.	Reference to Document.
1637–8. Feb.	Bury division, within the hundred of Salford, co. Lancaster.	Justices of Peace to Sir George Vernon and Sir Robert Berkeley, Judges of Assize. Certificate of proceedings upon the statutes for the poor, rogues, wanderers, &c. since the last assizes.	Vol. ccclxxxiii., No. 55. 2 pp.
Feb.	Hundred of Amounderness, co. Lancaster.	Return of presentments made to the Justices of Peace in sessions at Poulton at their meetings from 17th January 1636-7 to the 19th day of February 1637–8.	Ibid., No. 56. 21 pp.
Feb.*	Hundred of Broadwater, co. Hertferd.	Similar return of presentments at monthly meetings.	Ibid., No. 57. 2½ pp.
March 1.	Hundreds of South Erpingham and Eynesford, Norfolk.	Certificate of Justices of Peace of general conformity to the several points of the Book of Orders.	Vol. ccclxxxv., No. 6. ½ p.
March 1.	Borough of St. Albans.	Certificate of Ralph Pollard, mayor, and two Justices of Peace, of apprentices bound and rogues punished, and other acts done in conformity with the Book of Orders.	Ibid., No. 7. 1 p.
March 1.	Part of the hundred of Cashio, within the liberty of St. Albans.	The like of Justices of Peace.	Ibid., No. 8. 1 p.
March 2.	Hundred of Blackburn, co. Lancaster.	Justices of Peace to Sir George Vernon and Sir Robert Berkeley, Justices of Assize. Similar certificate.	Ibid., No. 13. 1 p.
March 2.	The same.	Certificate of the same, of presentments made at their meetings since the Summer assizes, 1637. [*Unsigned, perhaps superseded by the preceding.*]	Ibid., No. 14. 1⅛ p.
March 2.	Another division of the same county, the meetings being held at Rochdale.	Justices of Peace to Sir George Vernon and Sir Richard Berkeley. Particular certificate of presentments of various kinds made to them from the 5th September 1637 to this day.	Ibid., No. 15. 3¾ pp.
March 5.	Hundreds of South Greenhoe, Wayland, and Grimshoe, Norfolk.	Justices of Peace to Judges of Assize. Certificate of general conformity to the several points in the Book of Orders.	Ibid., No. 27. 1 p.
March 8.	Hundreds of Loes, Wilford, Thredling, and Plomesgate, in the liberty of St. Etheldred, Suffolk.	Justices of Peace to the sheriff. Similar certificate.	Ibid., No. 42. ¾ p.

* Really dated " 29th February," but the " 29 " was originally written " 19 ;" it was probably intended to be altered to " 20," the " 1 " was altered to " 2," but the " 9 " was forgotten to be corrected.

DOMESTIC—CHARLES I.

RETURNS MADE BY JUSTICES OF PEACE.

Date.	For what Place.	Nature of Document.	Reference to Document.
1637–8. March 8.	Hundred of Hitchin, co. Hertford.	Justices of Peace to the Judges of Assize. More particular certificate of the same kind as the preceding, with a special clause as to the necessities of the labouring men by reason of the dearth of corn and want of work. In Hitchin there were 180 poor families, many of whom having pawned and sold their goods, not only broke hedges and spoiled woods, but stole sheep in the night, and garbaged them in the fields and lived upon the flesh. . . . . And when they have work the wages are so small that they hardly suffice to buy them and their families bread, for they pay 6s. per bushel for "myscelyn" grain, and receive but 8d. for their day's work. Pray direction and assistance.	Vol. ccclxxxv., No. 43. = 2 pp.
March 9.	Hundreds of Edwinstree and Odsey, co. Hertford.	The like to the Council. Certificate of apprentices bound, with their names and those of their masters; punishment of vagrants, and penalties inflicted since the last assizes.	Ibid., No. 55. 1 p.
March 9.	Hundreds of Hertford and Braughing, co. Hertford.	Certificate of Justices of Peace, delivered at the general gaol delivery at Hertford to Sir Thomas Coningsby, sheriff. Certify names of apprentices bound and general conformity to the Book of Orders.	Ibid., No. 56. 1 p.
March 14.	Hundreds of Crediton, West Budleigh, and West Wonford, co. Devon.	Similar certificate of apprentices bound forth and to whom, and what offences had been punished since the last gaol delivery.	Ibid., No. 77. = 1½ p.
1638. March 28.	Various parishes in the wapentakes of Agbrigg and Morley, in the west riding, co. York.	Similar certificate of the names of 118 children apprenticed, with the names of their masters.	Vol. ccclxxxvi., No. 61. 3½ pp.
[March ?]	Various other parishes in the wapentakes of Agbrigg and Morley.	Similar certificate, with the names of 56 children apprenticed and those of their masters.	Ibid., No. 107. 3 pp.
[March ?]	Hundred of Normancross, co. Huntingdon.	Justices of Peace to the Judges of Assize. Certificate of general conformity to the Book of Orders, since the Lent assizes 1637; 50 vagrants punished and 30 poor children apprenticed. They had also given order that no person from London or other infected	Ibid., No. 108. 1 p.

Returns made by Justices of Peace.

Date.	For what Place.	Nature of Document.	Reference to Document.
1638.		places should remain in their towns without a certificate that such person had not been visited, and that no common feasts, wakes, whitsonales, stage plays, bear baitings, nor other meeting should be suffered.	
March.	Sussex.	Abstract of certificates of Justices of Peace for this county, delivered at the Lent assizes.	Vol. ccclxxxvi., No. 109. $\frac{3}{4}$ p.
March.	Surrey.	The like.	Ibid., No. 110. $\frac{1}{3}$ p.
March.	Kent.	The like.	Ibid., No. 111. 1 p.
March.	Hundreds of Reigate and Tandridge, Surrey.	Justices of Peace to Sir Francis Crawley and Sir Richard Weston, Judges of Assize. Return, in tabular form, of number of apprentices bound out and of rogues punished since the last assizes.	Ibid., No. 112. 1 p.
March.	Division of hundred of West Derby, co. Lancaster.	Certificate of Justices of Peace of such alehouses as have been suppressed since the last assizes.	Ibid., No. 113. 2 pp.
April 3.	Hundreds of Forehoe, Humbleyard, and Mitford, Norfolk.	Justices of Peace to the Council. Certify general conformity to the Book of Orders.	Vol. ccclxxxvii., No. 18. $\frac{3}{4}$ p.
April 18.	Ward of Kendal, Westmoreland.	The like to the same. Report their compliance with the directions of the Book of Orders, as appears by particular notes from the churchwardens and overseers. *Annexed,*	Vol. ccclxxxviii., No. 7. $1\frac{1}{4}$ p.
		Return for Barbon.	I. $\frac{1}{4}$ p.
		,, Beetham.	II. 1. 2. 3. = 2 pp.
		,, Burton in Kendal.	III., 1. 2. = 2 pp.
		,, Casterton.	IV. 1. 2. = $\frac{3}{4}$ p.
		,, Crook.	V. 1. 2. = $1\frac{1}{4}$ p.
		,, Crosthwaite.	VI. 1. 2. = $1\frac{1}{4}$ p.
		,, Firbank.	VII. = $\frac{1}{2}$ p.
		,, Grayrigg.	VIII. 1 p.
		,, Grestmere [Grasmere], including part of	IX. 1. 2. 4 pp.
		Ambleside,	IX. 3. 4. = 1 p.
		Langdale,	IX. 5. = $\frac{2}{3}$ p.
		Rydall.	IX. 6. = 1 p.

DOMESTIC—CHARLES I.

RETURNS MADE BY JUSTICES OF PEACE.

Date.	For what Place.	Nature of Document.	Reference to Document.
1638.		Return for Helsington.	Vol. ccclxxxviii., No. 7. x. 1. 2. 3. =1 p.
		,, Heversham.	XI. =1 p.
		,, Holme.	XII. 1. 2. =1 p.
		,, Hutton, New.	XIII. 1. 2. =1 p.
		,, Hutton, Old.	XIV. 1. 2. =1¼ p.
		,, Hutton, Roof.	XV. 1. 2. =1½ p.
		,, Kentmere.	XVI. 1. 2. =1 p.
		,, Killington.	XVII. 1⅙ p.
		,, Killington Firbank.	XVIII. 1. 2. 1¾ p.
		,, Kirby Kendal.	XIX. 1. 2. 3. 4. =4½ p.
		,, Lambrigg.	XX. 2 lines.
		,, Langdon.	XXI. ¼ p.
		,, Levens.	XXII. =⅙ p.
		,, Long Sleddale.	XXIII. 1. 2. =1¼ p.
		,, Lupton.	XXIV. 1. 2. =1½ p.
		,, Mansergh.	XXV. =¼ p.
		,, Middleton.	XXVI. =¼ p.
		,, Natland.	XXVII. 1. 2. 3. =1 p.
		,, Nether Graveships.	XXVIII. ¼ p.
		,, Preston Patrick.	XXIX. 1. 2. ½ p.
		,, Preston Richard.	XXX. =⅙ p.
		,, Sigswick [Sedgwick?]	XXXI. =¼ p.
		,, Skelsmergh.	XXXII. =1 p.
		,, Skelsmergh and Patton.	XXXIII. =½ p.
		,, Stainton.	XXXIV. =¼ p.
		,, Staveley (the three hamlets).	XXXV. 1. 2. 3. 4. =3½ pp.
		,, Strickland Kettle and Strickland Roger.	XXXVI. 1. 2. =1¾ p.
		,, Underbarrow.	XXXVII. 5 lines.
		,, Whitwell and Selside.	XXXVIII. 1. 2. 3. =2 pp.
		,, Witherslack.	XXXIX. 1. 2. =¾ p.

Returns made by Justices of Peace.

Date.	For what place.	Nature of Document.	Reference to Document.
1638.		Returns for Windermere, including part of Ambleside, and also Applethwaite, Undermilbeck, and Troutbeck.	Vol. ccclxxxviii., No. 7. XL. 1. 4 pp. XL. 2. 3. 4. = 2½ pp. XL. 5. 6. 7. = 2½ pp. XL. 8. 9. = ¾ p.
		Various returns, in which it is not stated to what places they apply.	XLI. 1–9. = 4 pp.
May 21.	Hundred of Cottesloe, Bucks.	Justices of Peace to Lord Chief Justice Bramston. Return of apprentices bound in the several parishes within that hundred.	Vol. cccxc, No. 131. Parchment roll.
June 18.	Norwich.	Robert Sumpter, mayor, and Thomas Cory, alderman, to Lord Chief Justice Bramston, and Sir George Croke, Judges of Assize. Return of pecuniary fines levied during the last year in cases in which the penalties are to be employed for the use of the poor. Total, 16l. 11s. 4d.	Vol. cccxciii., No. 18. = 2 pp.
June 23. Chichester.	Chichester rape, Sussex.	General certificate of Justices of Peace of proceedings for the last six months, as required by the Book of Orders.	Ibid., No. 47. 1 p.
June 25.	Hundreds of Chafford, Barstable, and the half-hundred of Becontree, Essex.	Justices of Peace to the Judges of Assize. Return of numbers of children apprenticed, vagrants punished, and other things directed by the Book of Orders, since the last assizes.	Ibid., No. 55. ¾ p.
June 26.	Hundred of Ongar and half-hundreds of Harlow and Waltham, Essex.	The like to the same. Return of number of children apprenticed and of rogues punished and passed.	Ibid., No. 60. ⅔ p.
June 27.	Hundreds of Milton, Teynham, Boughton, Faversham, and Isle of Sheppey, Kent.	Certificate of Justices of Peace of poor children bound apprentices and rogues punished since last assizes.	Ibid., No. 64. 2 pp.
June 27. Foots Cray.	Hundreds of Blackheath, Ruxley, Little and Lesness, Bromley and Beckenham, Kent.	The like certificate of presentments made at their meetings.	Ibid., No. 65.
June 29.	Hundred of Axton and Ville of Dartford, part of the lathe of Sutton at Hone.	The like certificate.	Ibid., No. 76. 2½ pp.
June 30	Hundred of Oxney, in the lathe of Shepway, Kent.	Certificate of Justices of Peace of apprentices put forth and unlicensed alehouse keepers punished.	Ibid., No. 84. 1 p.

Returns made by Justices of Peace.

Date.	For what Place.	Nature of Document.	Reference to Document.
1638. June 30.	Rape of Hastings, Sussex.	Certificate of Justices of Peace of apprentices put forth and rogues punished.	Vol. cccxciii., No. 85. 2½ pp.
June.	Hundred of Tendring, Essex.	Certificate by Sir Harbottle Grimstone of the numbers of apprentices bound, vagrants punished, and alehouses suppressed since Michaelmas 1637.	Ibid., No. 97. 1 p.
June.	The hundreds mentioned in the last three certificates.	Abstract of the last three certificates.	Ibid., No. 98. ⅔ p.
[June ?]	A division in the lathe of St. Augustine's, Kent.	Certificate of Justices of Peace of apprentices put forth, rogues punished, alehouses put down, and unlicensed keepers punished, from 1st Jan. 1637–8.	Ibid., No. 99. 2 pp.

Vol. CCCXCV. July 1–31, 1638.

1638.
July 1.   1. Notes by Nicholas of matters wherewith to acquaint his Majesty from the Commissioners for the Affairs of the Household. The commissioners have given order for various alterations in the household below stairs. What concerns the stables is left to be perfected when the Master of the Horse returns. The commissioners have also settled certain orders for the accounts which are to be inserted in the new book of orders for the future. They have also settled an order touching purveyors, and another concerning the diet of the gentlemen ushers daily waiters, allowing them five dishes, but they insist to have six, which the commissioners leave to his Majesty. The quarter waiters' diet is to be provided when the Lords meet at Michaelmas next. The King to be moved for an increase of their board wages. [1 p.]

July 1.   2. Affidavit of Charles Forbench, clerk, M.A. The Eastland merchants having respited their answer to his Majesty's letter for admitting Henry White of their company, deponent accompanied White, being his brother-in-law, to their assembly, in "respective" manner, entreating their answer. Sir Christopher Clitherow, master of the company, with some vehemency alleged that if his Majesty's letters should prevail in that kind they knew not where or of whom to raise moneys for defraying the expense of their assemblies, adding that such admittances were contrary to their oath and orders. White offered to pay whatsoever was due to the uttermost, not claiming any privilege in that kind by virtue of his Majesty's

1638.

Vol. CCCXCV.

favour. And deponent alleged the respect which the universities showed to satisfy his Majesty's missives, and offered to their consideration his Majesty's expression in the "perclose" of his letter, implying a requital or good turn. Sir Christopher replied, in an unseemly slighting manner, that they all knew well enough what the King's good turns were when they came to seek them, or words to that effect, and withal, taking advantage that some word in the King's letter was not effectual, said he could answer the King's letter well enough. Which speeches, so unrespectively and slightingly uttered in public, deponent conceives were in contempt of the honour of his sovereign, and therefore holds himself obliged in loyalty to disclose the same, being ready to verify his statement *in verbo sacerdotis*, or upon his sacramental oath. [⅔ *p.*]

July 2.
Maidstone.

3. Justices of Peace for Kent to the Council. Your letters of the last of May were delivered to us the 2nd inst., whereupon we gave order for the carriage of two hundred loads of timber from Lullingstone Park to Woolwich. As for the two hundred loads to be carried from Warnham in Sussex to Kingston upon Thames in Surrey, we desire you to excuse this county. We never had the assistance of any other county in any such service, it being likewise a thing unknown to go out of this county into another to carry timber from thence into a third. This county having also been of late much charged with carriages, we entreat you to ease us of that part of this burden. [*Seal with crest.* 1 *p.*]

July 2.

4. Petition of Sir Samuel Luke, of Woodend in the parish of Copehall [Cople ?] and diocese of Lincoln, to Archbishop Laud. Petitioner's house being distant from his parish church about a mile, and the way thither, especially in the winter, being so foul, and often such sudden inundations over the same that he cannot go thither, he beseeches you to license him and his wife, two men servants and a maid servant, to go to the parish church of Carrington [Cardington ?], where he has another house, or to Hawnes, where his father lives, or to Norrill [Northill], being the adjoining parish. *Underwritten*,

    4. I. "*I am content that a licence be granted as desired, provided petitioner and his family duly receive the Holy Communion at his own parish church, and discharge all other duties that are fitting.* W. CANT." 2nd *July* 1638. [1 *p.*]

July 2.

5. Thomas Barnard to —— Webb, secretary to the Duke of Lenox. The privy seal, mentioning the number and natures of the ordnance, with particular directions to my Lord [Newport], is the usual course, and his warrant to the officers of the Ordnance for delivery. The number and nature of iron shot must be likewise expressed, with the quantity of powder. If you procure a privy seal, and send it me, with the expedition you require, I shall serve you. P.S.—I shall be glad to receive your commands to-morrow at Greenwich. [1 *p.*]

Vol. CCCXCV.

1638.
July 2.
6. Certificate of George Fulbert. Eleanor, wife of Edward Browne, has taken the oath of allegiance before me. [⅓ p.]

July 2.
My house at the Old Palace.
7. Similar certificate of Sir William Brouncker. Humphrey Fitz-William, having occasion to travel into France, has taken the oaths of supremacy and allegiance before me. [⅓ p.]

July 2.
8. The like, of Peter Heywood, Justice of Peace for Middlesex. Walter Steckland [Strickland?] of Swinton, co. York, has taken the oath of allegiance before me. [⅓ p.]

July 2.
9. Presentment of the Grand Inquest at the Assizes holden at Bath. We present that corn is grown to an excessive rate, which we conceive not to be occasioned so much by scarcity as by other accidents, namely, by the great and heavy taxations by new invented ways, which is so heavy a burthen on the farmers as causes them to sell their grain at high rates to support their charge, by which labourers are not able to get sufficient sustenance, and is a cause of many thefts and felonies. Another cause is, by reason of a late practice of gathering great companies of unruly people at bull-baitings, under pretence of helping some poor man, who brews about 30 or 40 bushels of malt, and spends it all at one of those meetings, and there are many thefts committed after their departure. Also that of late there are come commissions into the country under the hand of the two Secretaries of State to all post-masters, for taking up such numbers of horses as the post-masters shall think fit, and the post-masters take into their stables 10 or 12 horses at one time, and keep them two nights, and then take in so many more, and if they have employment for any of them they pay the post price, otherwise they make the owners pay for their meat and dressing what rate they please, but some upon composition they release, which makes the burthen the heavier upon the rest. We beseech you to present this grievance to his Majesty. Also vagrants abound by the neglect of watch and ward. Also the saltpetremen, having removed their works into other counties, have pressed the inhabitants adjoining the coal-mines to carry, not only their saltpetre and vessels to places far remote, but their fuel also, which we present as a great grievance. [2½ pp.]

July 2.
10–11. See "Returns made by Justices of Peace."

July 3.
Petition of the Dean and Chapter of St. Paul's to the King. Your Majesty's predecessors granted to petitioners and the canons of the said cathedral by charters, immunities and privileges, not only in the country, but also within the city and suburbs of London, within their tenements, lands, and fees, which they thankfully acknowledge they have enjoyed and still do enjoy. Differences arise many times between the Dean and Chapter and Canons and the city of London touching rights belonging to the said church, and more may arise, if by your Majesty's accustomed piety they be not prevented. Petitioners, understanding the Lord Mayor and citizens to be suitors for

Vol. CCCXCV.

1638.

renovation of their charter, beseech you to give order to the Attorney-General to take care that no addition or alteration of any clause or word be made in the city charter which may prove prejudicial to the said church. [*Copy. See Vol. cccxxiii., p.* 315. ½ *p.*] *Underwritten,*

 I. *Reference to the Attorney-General, to be careful that nothing pass in the charter of the city, when renewed, that may tend to the prejudice of St. Paul's. Greenwich, 3rd July* 1638. [*Copy. Ibid., p.* 316. ⅙ *p.*]

July 3. Petition of Thomas Killigrew to the King. Your Majesty is entitled to the goods and chattels of Simon Jackson of Botsone [Bottisham?], co. Cambridge, lately convicted of the manslaughter of Isaac Heath, servant to Lord Rochford. Petitioner prays a grant of your Majesty's right to the said goods and chattels. [*Copy. Ibid., p.* 316. ¼ *p.*] *Underwritten,*

 I. *Reference to the Attorney-General, to prepare a bill accordingly. Greenwich, 3rd July* 1638. [*Ibid.* ⅙ *p.*]

July 3. Petition of Robert Smyth and Leonard Stockdale, relators in the Star Chamber, against the Company of Starchmakers, to the same. Petitioners, at their sole expense, discovered the insufferable abuses of the defendants, whereupon it was ordered by the Council, in presence of your Majesty, that Mr. Attorney should exhibit an information against them in the Star Chamber, which was done, and the cause ready for publication ever since Easter Term, and likewise petitioners offered an increase of your revenue, by good caution of able merchants, to pay 500*l.* the first year, 1,000*l.* the second, 3,000*l.* the third, and so to continue, whereas formerly you had only 200*l.* per annum, and the Earl of Ancram 600*l.* per annum at most *de claro*. The starchmakers made an offer to the Lord Treasurer and Lord Cottington, which, presenting the appearance of some improvement upon petitioners' offer, their Lordships thought fit petitioners' should be joined with the starchmakers in the latter propositions, whereupon the starchmakers elected petitioners' into their company. Petitioners, having no warrant to the contrary, did nevertheless not slack prosecution in the suit, which has caused so great a height of malice towards them that the starchmakers now continually labour to circumvent them by false imputations, and having got your warrant for a new patent, now endeavour to exclude petitioners from the company. Petitioners have expended near 1,000*l.* in prosecution of the cause in the Star Chamber, and in improving your revenue; but such is the malice of the starchmakers that, unless you protect them, they will be surely undone. Pray reference as to petitioners' service and reimbursement to such of your Council as you think fit, and they to certify what they shall think reasonable. [*Copy. Ibid., p.* 316. 1 *p.*] *Underwritten,*

 I. *Reference to the Archbishop of Canterbury, the Lord Keeper, the Lord Treasurer, and Lord Cottington, to take order for petitioners' satisfaction. Greenwich, 3rd July* 1628. [*Copy. Ibid., p.* 317. ⅙ *p.*]

DOMESTIC—CHARLES I. 553

1638.
July 3.

Vol. CCCXCV.

Petition of Roger Hollings and Katherine his wife, to the King. According to a reference heretofore made by your Majesty upon a petition of petitioners, plaintiffs, against Nathan Akeroid, defendant, Henry Garway, alderman, Edward Trotman, and William Armitage, three of the referees, have called before them the parties, and have endeavoured to mediate some end for relief of petitioners, but could not effect the same. Whereupon they have certified that the said Katherine was an orphan, and committed to Thomas Gomersall and Grace his wife, she being her own aunt, and that there is due to petitioners 320*l*., which they conceive ought to be paid by Akeroid, being the executor of Grace Gomersall, deceased, which he utterly refuses to do, but giveth forth in speeches that it shall cost hot-water, and that he will spend 500*l*. before petitioners shall have one penny from him. Pray a reference to Archbishop Laud and Lord Keeper Coventry, to make such order for payment of the said 320*l*., and for petitioners relief and quiet, as shall seem best. [*Copy. See Vol. cccxxiii., p. 318.* ½ *p.*] *Underwritten,*

I. *Reference to Archbishop Laud and Lord Keeper Coventry, as desired. Greenwich, 3rd July, 1638.* [*Ibid., p. 318.* ⅙ *p.*]

July 3.

Petition of the Merchants of London to the same. In regard there are many sorts of cloths and stuffs made in this kingdom, for the true making whereof there is no statute law, whereby the makers make them very deceitful, so that if other countries beyond the seas were not busied in wars, but had the benefit of peace, as we have, they would fall to making cloths and stuffs which would far excel ours, and be a great hindrance to the trade of this kingdom. Pray his Majesty to command certain able merchants in London to be committees of inquiry to examine the grievances of his Majesty's subjects which are more than the brevity of a petition can set forth, that they may inform your Majesty, and set down a course how it may be reformed, and that it may be your own proper business. [*Copy. Ibid., p. 319.* ⅓ *p.*] *Underwritten,*

I. *Reference to the Lord Treasurer and Lord Cottington, who calling to them the Attorney-General, are to certify their opinions. Greenwich, 3rd July, 1638.* [*Ibid.* ⅙ *p.*]

July 3.

12. Petition of Lady Carr, wife of Sir Robert Carr, of Sleaford, co. Lincoln, to the same. Petitioner since Michaelmas was two years has endured insufferable usages from her husband, whose wife she has been nine years, having living by him one son and three daughters, in all which time she has been a most loving wife, using all patience in hope of his future amendment. But such are his evil counsellors that have gotten possession of his present estate, that they maliciously cross all good agreement, subtilly practising their separation, to the ruin of them and theirs. Beseeches his

1638.

Vol. CCCXCV.

Majesty to hear her just complaint, or to refer the examination thereof to some of the Council. [⅔ *p.*] *Endorsed,*

I. *Reference to Archbishop Laud, the Lord Keeper, the Lord Treasurer, the Lord Privy Seal, and the Lord Cottington, to mediate some agreement if they can, otherwise to certify his Majesty where the impediment lies, with their opinions. Greenwich, 3rd July* 1638. [½ *p.*]

July 3.   Copy of the same. [*See Vol. cccxxiii., p.* 318. ½ *p.*]

July 3.
Leicester Castle.

13. Edward Lake to [Sir John Lambe]. Upon the 16th inst. the four months for this triennial end. Our course is to go on with the Archdeacon's jurisdiction, without expectation of a relaxation; yet, whether you would have it so now or no I pray let us know, as also your pleasure for the Archdeacon's visitation, for which it is necessary there should be new books of articles. There has been none this long time, saving those for this archiepiscopal visitation, the tenor whereof is much different from those for the Archdeacon's visitation. If there were no difference it now were necessary, for more than a third part of the towns had none this last visitation. I wrote to you, and desired William Heyward to bring your receipt of that 38*l.* which you received from me of Mr. Halford for St. Paul's, and William Heyward tells me that you said you acknowledged the receipt. I never had any note. [1 *p.*]

July 3.
Sampson's Place, formerly called Simson's Place.

14. Sir Archibald Douglas to Thomas Young, Clerk to the Signet in Scotland, Edinburgh. My soul and heart rejoice because I hear there is many men both religious and courageous in Scotland, our native land. May show a copy of this letter, but as yet not from him, except to his honoured friend Sir Thomas Hope. Will shortly send to them both unexpected good news. Will shortly bear his buff coat again as a commander at the wars, and will use his *Duo Gladii*, which is the true emblem of his name *Dall Glas*, and with the word of God, which is sharper than any two edged-sword, will go against the Lord's enemies. With much other rhapsodical matter, very similar to that written by his wife, Lady Eleanor Davies, now Douglas. [*Endorsed by Sec. Windebank as* "third intercepted going," *with an addition in pencil, in another hand,* "Dougle fooleries." 1 *p.*]

July 3.

15. Brief of the proofs of John Nicholas de Franchis [or Franqui] against Captain Walter Stewart, in a matter respecting ten chests of silver money, containing, 200,000 rials, received by Capt. Stewart at the Groyne on board the Victory, to be transported to England, and thence to Flanders. The chests in question were shipped, with others, by Bartholomew Barillaro, under a licence granted by the King of Spain to Francisco Maria Pichonotti. After they were on board the Victory, Barillaro assigned them to de Franqui, and Capt. Stewart signed a new bill of lading in the name of de Franqui. On arrival in England, Capt. Stewart delivered the ten chests to the Conde

1638.   Vol. CCCXCV.

d'Oniate, the Spanish ambassador, upon a certificate by Martin Lopez de Ivara, said to be a Spanish Secretary of State, that they had been confiscated by the government of Spain, on the ground that Barillaro had no right to assign them to de Franqui. On the other side it was contended that there had not been any confiscation, and that de Ivara was no Secretary of State, but a notary public. [*Endorsed are notes by Sec. Windebank as to the facts of the case.* 8 *pp.*]

July 4.   16. Petition of Mary Coffland to Archbishop Laud. Daniel Coffland, one of the pages of the Back Stairs to the Duke of York, was lawfully made sure to petitioner almost seven years since, with the consent of her father, Richard Lloyd, then of Lambeth, whereupon, almost two years since, he gave her 20s. to provide a wedding ring, and about April 29, 1636, he sent for her over to the Sun Tavern, Westminster, where he had provided a man, who he said was a Romish priest, (the said Daniel being a Roman Catholic,) to marry them. Petitioner suspecting that he was no priest, because he went in coloured apparel, Daniel, with many oaths, affirmed that he was a priest, and that he might lawfully marry them at that time, (it being about one or two o'clock in the afternoon,) and in that place, without danger of the law. Whereupon Daniel and petitioner were married by the priest, none other being present but William Brothers, a friend to Daniel. The marriage being solemnized, petitioner returned to her father's house, where, about eight or nine o'clock at night, her husband came, and asked her father's and mother's blessing, desiring them not to be angry, saying that he had kept their daughter long in hand, but now he had made her amends, for he had married her; but he earnestly desired that his marriage might not be divulged, lest he should lose his place. Thereupon her parents promised secrecy, and permitted them to accompany each other. But since the death of petitioner's father, by whom her husband hoped to have gotten a greater estate than her father was able to give, her husband has not only used her unkindly in words, but has also forsaken her, and denies her means for her livelihood, unless she will deny that she was married unto him. And because she claims him for her husband, he has served her with a process, upon an action of defamation, to appear before Dr. Mason, chancellor of Winchester. By all which unjust dealing, petitioner, being great with child, not only is defamed, but also for want of means cannot answer the law. Prays the Archbishop to cause her husband to associate with her, as becometh him, and to allow her alimony, and to stop the proceedings in the Ecclesiastical Court. *Underwritten,*

> 16. I. *Reference to the Bishop of Chichester, to speak with the Countess of Dorset concerning the party complained of, that upon signification of her Ladyship's pleasure (he being the Duke's servant) such course may be taken as shall be fitting. July 4th, 1638.* [1 *p.*]

Vol. CCCXCV.

1638.
July 4.
Dover.
17. J. Barter to Mrs. [Olive] Porter. Your son G. P. [George Porter] and his aunt Lady Newport arrived here an hour since, as the bearer will tell you. His aunt will not suffer him to come without her, who to-morrow morning will be coming towards you [*Seal with arms.* ¾ *p.*]

July 4.
18. See "Returns made by Justices of Peace."

July 5.
Westm[inster.]
19. Edmund Crowne to ——. On the 2nd inst. Sir Charles Herbert and Mr. Latch were in the Petty Bag Office looking for the filing or enrolment of the law of the sewers made in the 10th of James, whereby the said King was nominated undertaker for divers fens. The Attorney-General sent the same day to look for the law whereby his now Majesty is undertaker for the Eight Hundred Fen, but neither of them was there to be found. Upon some speeches about the necessity of enrolling the said laws, Mr. Haward, one of the clerks of the office, and the man that exemplified your law, desired me to inform my Lord that he would advise with his counsel whether it be not fit to enrol the exemplification, lest the law itself may happen to be embezzled off the file. You and Mr. Long, if you see cause, may give direction for the inrolment. [¾ *p.*]

July 5.
Herald's certificate of funeral of Paul Viscount Bayning, who died at Bentley Hall, Essex, on 11th June 1638. He married Penelope, daughter and sole heir of Sir Robert Naunton and Penelope his wife, daughter and sole heir of Sir John [Thomas?] Perrott, by [Dorothy] his wife, daughter of Walter Earl of Essex. Lord Bayning had issue by his said lady one daughter, named Anne, born 1st May 1637, and left his widow great with child. He was buried in a vault on the north side of the church of Bentley, Essex. His executors were his lady relict and Sir Thomas Glemham of Glemham Hall, Suffolk. [*Unsigned.* ½ *p.*]

July 5.
20. Affidavit of Richard Woodcock, of Westminster, yeoman. Being watchman of the prison of the Gatehouse, he was upon Wednesday night last about 12 o'clock required by Francis Whitney, a constable of Westminster, to open the gates, and receive the body of Jasper Heiley, messenger. He then saw Heiley show the constable a warrant, signed by Sec. Windebank, directed to Heiley, to apprehend John Mayo, clerk, bearing date the day aforesaid, requiring the constable to read the said warrant, and to repair to the house of Mr. Secretary for further satisfaction. The constable replied that he could not read it. Deponent answered that he was well assured that the warrant was signed by Sec. Windebank. Then Heiley said to the constable, "Now you have seen this warrant, surely you dare not commit me." The constable replied that he had a better warrant (showing his constable's staff) than Heiley had. And presently the constable, with divers of his watchmen,

1638.　　　　　　　Vol. CCCXCV.

thrust Heiley into the prison, giving deponent charge to keep him safe. Heiley did not give the constable any ill language, nor was Heiley distempered with drink. [1 p.]

July 5.　21–22. See "Returns made by Justices of Peace."

July 6.　23. Sir Henry Marten to [the Council]. Report on the true cause of the great scarcity of oysters. From returns of jurors at courts held to inquire into this matter, it is found that in Essex the scarcity arises by the taking the broods and spats of oysters, and the shells upon which the spats grow, from off the common oyster grounds, and carrying them into private "lannes" and grounds, where the spat and brood for the most part die; also by the extraordinary great quantity of oysters, and many times brood and all, taken and put up in barrels and sent to London; and that the corporations of Colchester and Maldon challenge the waters of Ponte and Colne, which are the best brooding places, to belong to them, and at prohibited times license men to dredge; and that the price is much enhanced by the transportation of oysters beyond seas, and to Hull and the north parts, and by fishmongers and others that go from London into Essex, and contract for all the oysters, and engross them into a few hands. In Kent, the reason of the scarcity is the numbers of oystermen there more than in former time, and the most part poor, unruly, and incorrigible; these men, violating all orders in dredging, have taken away the stock and nursery of oysters. To this is to be added the excessive transportation, under pretence of licences granted for oysters for the Queen of Bohemia and the Prince of Orange. For remedy the writer suggests an order of the board that no oysters should be taken from the grounds in Essex until they be come to some maturity, and in no week more than 1,000 half barrels; that no fishmonger buy oysters to sell again until they be brought to the common quay; and that a fitting proportion be set down for the Queen of Bohemia and the Prince of Orange. That letters be written to the vice-admirals to see this performed, and to the mayors of Colchester and Maldon, forbidding them to license any to dredge at prohibited times. [4½ pp.]

July 6.　24. See "Returns made by the Justices of the Peace."

July 7.
Greenwich.　25. Sir Thomas Jermyn, Vice Chamberlain of the Household, to Sec. Windebank. The King has commanded me to will you to go forthwith to the Lord Keeper, and to let him know that he suffer not Sir Henry Croke's pardon to pass the seal until his Majesty give further order. [¾ p.]

July 7.
London.　26. Edward Fenn to Nicholas. Since the last certificate, I have received of the bailiff of Bishop's Castle, Salop, 15l.; and of the Mayor of Hastings, 42l. 10s.; which is all the money that has come in this week. P.S.—The Sheriff of Carmarthen is in town, and will pay 300l. or 400l., as he says. [½ p.]

Vol. CCCXCV.

1638.
July 8.
Dover Castle.

27. Sir John Manwood to Theophilus Earl of Suffolk. There is news come of the French army quitting the siege of St. Omer, and that they burnt their quarters last night. Prince Tomaso and Piccolomini follow the rear of the French army. This is all I can write for the present, and this you may give to the King for news, for I believe he cannot have any fresher. I send enclosed the Lord Treasurer's warrant, which pray return if you find it fit that it may be obeyed. In the interim I will take all the care I can. [*Endorsed by Sec. Windebank.* 1 *p.*]

July 9.

28. John Nicholas, to his son Edward Nicholas. Hoped to hear of the time of his coming into the country, but the King's altering his progress hinders it. Is not ignorant of the necessity of his attendance during the Lords sitting in Council, yet the Lords will desire to recreate themselves at their country houses. I endeavour to make you in love with this place. I have almost fitted it for a habitation for one that may spend twice as much as I am able, and will leave it to you as soon as you will. Your mother and I will give over all worldly business, and live privately, for our time cannot be long. Details as to his wife's state of health. The doctor's wife looks every day for a good hour to be delivered. Jack and Ned both want new shirts and more bands. They have but three a piece, and at Winchester they wash but once a month. [*Seal with arms.* 1¾ *p.*]

July 9.

29. Statement of Gervase Clifton, that John Alured on the 4th inst. said these words concerning the Scots; that they were brave boys, and would make us all quake. And it being told they could not much avail to do us hurt, he said they would come to our faces, and that they did well; they would reform this land by a parliament as well as they have done theirs already, for the King would be forced to lay down his taxes by their coming into England. Being told they durst not invade us, he said the King would get nobody to fight against them, for they were our own nation and our own blood. [*Underwritten.*] "These words are not fit for any particular man to question in the Star Chamber, but if they be made known to the Lords of the Council they will give such direction therein as they shall hold fit." [*Endorsed by Sec. Windebank.* "This Alured dwells in Guilserland upon the borders of Scotland, and hath 4 or 500*l.* per annum." 1 *p.*]

July 9.
Grinewige
[Greenwich.]

30. Examination of John Alured. I hear say that I, discoursing with Mr. Clifton concerning the Scotch business, said that I heard that the Scotchmen stood upon having a parliament in Scotland, and could not be so content, but desired to have one here too; likewise saying they were mad boys. [½ *p.*]

July 9.
Clerkenwell.

31. George Long to Sec. Windebank. Declares his knowledge upon a difference between Thomas Izaack and Sir Thomas Reynell. After a decree in the Exchequer Chamber against Izaack, at the

1638.   Vol. CCCXCV.

prosecution of Sir Thomas, the former, by the mediation of Mr. Lenthall, one of his counsel, left with the writer 200*l*. for certain arrears grown due to Sir Thomas, which was paid him accordingly. There being further matter of account between them, it was arbitrated by Mr. Lenthall and myself that Izaack should pay Sir Thomas other 220*l*. in consideration of his charges, and that Sir Thomas should move the then Lord Treasurer Portland for a final discharge of the further account. [1 *p*.]

July 9.   32. See "Returns made by the Justices of the Peace."

July 10.   33. George Kirke to Sec. Windebank. Although I now be off
Ham[p]ton.   the stage of the Court, and can play no useful [part] to do my friends any service, yet I hope to appear again, to be either useful to you or some of yours, though not with the requital, yet with some acknowledgment. The thanks I give you at present is for procuring the letter of draining from his Majesty, which I understand was not without great difficulty, and that you are desired to speak with Mr. Long before you deliver it. Mr. Long is now in the place whither this letter is to be sent, and has the commission there, and expects the letter's coming, and if it be stayed till his return we shall lose the season. At his return I make no doubt but he shall give you satisfaction. The country desires nothing but what his Majesty in his former letters has directed, and the law of sewers has ordained; that is, that the undertakers should perfect the draining, the 2,000 acres should be set out for the poor, and 1,500 acres for maintenance of the work; all which I conceive was the substance of his Majesty's former letters and of this likewise. [*Seal with arms.* 1 *p*.]

July 10.   34. Thomas Butler to Richard Harvey. Hopes Harvey came
Somercotes.   well to London. Has sent up the four horses. Desires to hear how his master [Endymion Porter] approved of what was done in Harvey's journey. Has written for 200*l*., with which he entreats Harvey to make all the haste that may be possible, because of the necessity of the poor people. [*Seal with crest and initials.* 1 *p*.]

July 10.   35. See "Returns made by Justices of Peace."

July 11.   36. The King to Elizabeth Countess of Suffolk and Theophilus
Greenwich.   Earl of Suffolk. After consideration of a decree in chancery between Mr. Harding and you, and many contempts against that court, we were contented to hear your counsel against that decree, and expected that you would speedily conform yourselves to the determination we should make. We found the decree most just, and such as you the countess, as well by law and justice as for the respect you ought to bear to your own honour and to the honour of your deceased husband, are bound to perform. And you the earl, upon many considerations importing the honour of your father and mother, and most nearly reflecting upon yourself, have great reason to assist your mother, if her own estate be too weak, in the observance of that decree. In

Vol. CCCXCV.

1638.

confidence of your better conformity we forbore at the hearing to insist on that obstinacy which for the space of divers years had been showed in opposing that decree, aggravated with circumstances very scandalous to our justice, and only declared our order, with much favour to you, what ought to be performed. Yet we have not hitherto received any fruit of your obedience suitable either to your duty or to our expectation, and therefore we admonish you, without any further tergiversation or delay, that you apply yourselves to the speedy performance of that our order; which, if you refuse, we let you know that we shall not only resume the consideration of all former contempts, and take order for the punishment thereof, but shall for such an immediate affront against ourself take such course as may vindicate so great an injury against ourself and our justice. [*Copy.* 1½ *p.*]

July 11.   37. Petition of Thomas Valentine, rector of Chalfont St. Giles, co. Buckingham, to Archbishop Laud. Having been first suspended about three years since, by the Archdeacon's Court, for not reading the Book of Recreations on Sunday, and after, the book being read by his curate, absolved simply, and not *in diem*, and again suspended, about a year and a half since, by the same court for the same cause, and an act of sequestration of petitioner's benefice entered in the same court and executed about half a year since, petitioner having formerly moved your Grace you assured petitioner that he should stand right in your opinion, except some other matter appeared against him. As petitioner never made any opposition to the said book, he prays that the punishment he has sustained may satisfy, and that you will order that he may be absolved from the suspension and sequestration. *Underwritten,*

> 37. I. *Reference to Sir John Lambe. If he finds that petitioner seriously intends the satisfaction of himself in this particular the Archbishop will be content that the suspension and sequestration be released in diem, and that petitioner have twelve months time allowed him to the purpose aforesaid. July 11th, 1638.* [1 *p.*]

July 11.   38. Sir Henry Mildmay to Nicholas, near Egham. I thank you
Wanstead.   for letting me see the order made by the Lords before your hand went to it. But whereas it is written " to search from Henry VIII.," may you please, (if you may,) with your pen to put that out, and write " to search from the first of Queen Elizabeth." [¾ *p.*]

July 11.   39. Peter Heywood, Justice of Peace for Middlesex, to the Council. Francis Gerard, of the [*sic*] Harrow-on-the-Hill, has taken the oath of allegiance before him. [⅓ *p.*]

July 11.   40. Information of Car[ew ?] Stockwell. Being in the house of Christopher Hatton, of Kingsthorpe, co. Northampton, innholder, and upon a court day, William Walker, chief constable, prating and grumbling much against the ship-money, uttered these speeches :—
1. Being asked when we should pay our ship-money, he answered

1638.

that he hoped never, and his reason was, because it was stayed. And being questioned upon what ground, he jeeringly replied, because he thought they were ashamed of it. 2. He said that the ship-money was an intolerable exaction, burden, and oppression laid upon the land. 3. Believed that the ship-money here in England would cause the like stirs that were now in Scotland before it were long. 4. Said the King was under a law as much as any subject, and that he could do nothing of himself without his subjects. 5. He confessed that some judges had determined it to be law, but the best and most honest had not. 5. After much arguing the right and equity of the ship-money, with great stomach he told me that because I stood so much for it I should therefore pay for it in my tax and assessment, and for this purpose he rode over to Towcester, and there moved the high sheriff to have me raised, and because the under-constable, John Green, would not yield to his unjust motion, he told him, with reviling terms, that I had given him a bribe to lay me at an under rate. 7. In gathering the ship-money (to the bad example of the town and hundred) he suffered his corn openly and in the street to be distrained upon, and did not pay his tax till after his return from London, if it be yet paid. [*Endorsed by Sir John Lambe as delivered to him on the 17th November* 1638. 1 *p.*]

July 11.
Oxford.

41. Sir Nathaniel Brent, Warden of Merton College, to Archbishop Laud. At my coming to Oxford on Friday last, I found at the college two letters sent to us by you. This day I read them to the Fellows, and gave order (as the letters enjoined) that they should be fairly written into our register book. Other things required shall be most punctually observed. But concerning the time of our audit, you have been misinformed. Our last bursar's quarter ends on Friday night next before August, after which he has four weeks to make up his account. After this we are to make up our general accounts. This will require time, first to make it up, then to pass it by the approbation of the company, and last to copy and send it to your Grace. It shall be done with all speed. We have nominated three of our senior Fellows to wait on you at Lambeth the 2nd October next. These we hold fittest to give information concerning the discipline and thrift of the college, rather than three young men who have more passion than experience; and yet these also may come up if they please, and so it is declared to them. The choice of our officers has been made ever since I was warden according to our statute and our custom inviolably observed. [1 *p.*]

July 11.
Merton College.

42. Dr. Peter Turner to the same. According to your directions, when our sub-warden came home I gave him your letter to the company concerning the nomination of two or three fellows to prosecute the complaints exhibited in the visitation, together with the act made on publishing the said letter, requiring him from you to enter them both presently into the register, which he promised to do. This Wednesday morning, Mr. Warden called a meeting of

1638.

the fellows, in which he caused your letter to be read, and made a proposal whom they would nominate. Upon this proposal, together with the Warden's exceptions against the three formerly chosen (as men obnoxious to sundry complaints, and unacquainted with the discipline or husbandry of the College), they have nominated French, Fisher, and Gibbs (men that have made no complaints at all) to prosecute the complaints of other men, partly against themselves, partly concerning the general misgovernment, in which they find nothing to complain of, but *omnia bene*. Whether these men be not likely to prevaricate in the prosecution of other men's complaints, I leave to your consideration. The business of which I principally desired to inform you is, that at this meeting the sub-warden declared that he had entered into the register neither your letter nor the act made thereupon, and desired to know of Mr. Warden what he should enter. The warden wished him to enter your letter and this last act concerning the nomination of French, Fisher, and Gibbs, to which three (to make up a mess) they have added me. Which act of theirs, how far it crosses the act allowed by you and your direct precept to the sub-warden concerning the entry of the former act, I leave to you to estimate. [1 *p.*]

July 12.

43. Petition of Anne, wife of William Gilbert, to Archbishop Laud. Having been married 21 years, at her marriage her husband poor, not able to buy clothes for himself, yet had a reasonable portion with petitioner, and is by profession a cook. During most of that time they endeavoured themselves and gained above 100*l.* clear, which occasioned her husband to grow haughty and proud, insomuch that he would beat petitioner in such barbarous manner that she was enforced to run into the streets in the dead time of the night out of her bed, without any clothes to cover her, [through] the continuance of which violent usage petitioner is become a cripple, and her husband has now lately left her, destitute of all relief, and has made proclamations in sundry market towns that none should trust petitioner or relieve her. As her husband has much money at interest, prays order for him to allow her competent maintenance, or to admit her to sue him for alimony *in formâ pauperis*, and allow her some relief in the meantime. *Underwritten,*

43. I. *Reference to Sir John Lambe to take such further order as he shall find to be just. July 12th, 1638.* [¾ *p.*]

July 12.
Westover.

44. John Ashburnham to Nicholas. I am to receive 400*l.* out of the Exchequer, for which I have a tally upon the collectors of the diocese of Exeter, which tally I have left with Mr. Swettnam, into whose office the money is to be paid. I pray you to receive the said 400*l.* for me, and whatsoever acquittances you give I oblige myself to confirm. [¾ *p.*] *Annexed,*

44. I. *Memorandum to send to Mr. Swettnam, in Mr. Squibb's office, for the tally above mentioned.* [4 *lines.*]

July 12.

45–46. See "Returns made by the Justices of Peace."

1638.
Vol. CCCXCV.

July 13.
47. Sir Richard Fenn, Lord Mayor, and Thomas Atkin and Edward Rudge, Sheriffs of London, to [the Council]. "The petitioner," Richard Chambers, has paid all the ship-money which was assessed upon him, being 10*l*., and so we leave him to your Lordships further directions for his discharge. [½ *p*.]

July 13.
48. Sir John Lambe to Archbishop Laud. The bearer is a suitor for the poor rectory of St. Mary's in Stamford, worth about 12*l*. per annum. The Bishop of Lincoln has twice collated to it as by lapse, for we know not who is patron; nor will any be hasty to own it as patron, nor any to take it as parson, unless the parish shall like, and so contribute, because the means are so small. The last incumbent left it a year ago, and has gone into Ireland, and has there taken a good benefice. Before he went he delivered his instruments of collation and induction to the bearer, his fellow collegiate, thinking that that had been a sufficient resignation. But all these will well amount to a cession in law. If you will collate it to him *per cessionem* no more needs. If you had rather put off the imputation and question in law from yourself, I have drawn a presentation, and will stand to it myself, and pray you to do nothing in it but as ordinary, viz., to institute him at my presentation, that will defend it well enough. I understand by the registrar of Hertfordshire that Mr. Archer, parson of All Saints, Hertford, has been above a year gone, and not like to return; he stands suspended. So that if you will collate *per cessionem*, I make no doubt it will be well enough. Mr. Keeling promised me to procure the parson's resignation, which perhaps cannot be had so soon, and the church is at an ill stay the whiles. I [think] if a discreet man have it the parishioners will freely contribute. St. Mary's, Leicester, has been void many years, and so in lapse, and held by sequestration from me, worth 30*l*. per annum. If you will get the Lord Keeper to present Mr. Daniel, it may be now fittingly done, because I hear that the curate there that holds by sequestration has got a benefice in Rutland. I shall think of some more of them for you, that you may do good to the church in that diocese while your jurisdiction there lasts. [*Draft.* ⅘ *p*.]

July 13.
49. Copy of entry on the Register of the Court of Arches of the appearance of Thomas Valentine, rector of Chalfont St. Giles, co. Buckingham, who sought that he might be absolved from the sentence of suspension pronounced against him, and from the sequestration of the fruits to the said rectory belonging. The judge absolved him from the said sentence until the Feast of the Nativity of St. John the Baptist, and released the sequestration aforesaid until the same day. [½ *p*.]

July 13.
Boston.
50. Estimate of the charge of the several works [of drainage] to be done between Kyme Eau and Bourne during the remainder of this year. Total, 8,333*l*. [1⅓ *p*.]

July 13.
Henry Earl of Holland, Chief Justice and Justice in Eyre of his Majesty's forests on this side Trent, to all Officers of his Majesty's

Vol. CCCXCV.

1638.

forest of Shotover. Upon the application of the county of Oxford, the Earl gives licence to Richard Powell, verderer of the said forest, to dig and carry within the same so much stone and gravel as will be needful for mending the highway leading through the forest to the city of Oxford. [*Copy. See Book of Orders concerning Forests. Vol. ccclxxxiv., p.* 17. 1¼ *p.*]

July 14.
Burderop.

51. Sir William Calley to Richard Harvey. His wife and daughter have received their gowns. Desires Harvey to purchase two pair of linen socks and two codpiece points of musk colour silk, and bring them with him, together with other things specified in former letters. [*Seal with arms.* ½ *p.*]

July 14.

52. Account by Sir William Russell of ship-money for 1637. Total received, 110,078*l.* 15*s.* 1*d.*; leaving 86,335*l.* 12*s.* 7*d.* unpaid. [1 *p.*]

July 14.

53. Account of ship-money levied and remaining in the hands of the sheriffs. Total, 5,540*l.*; which makes the total collected 115,618*l.*, which is 32,581*l.* less than was levied this time twelve-months, being 15th July 1637. [1 *p.*]

July 14.

54. Notes upon the state of various churches in co. Bucks upon a visitation of that portion of the diocese of Lincoln. They are in continuation of those calendared under the dates of August 1637, No. 79, and 11 October 1637, No. 59. The churches dealt with are Stoke-Mandeville, Weston Turville, Buckland, Bierton, Quarrendon, Fleet Marston, Upper Winchendon, Ashenden, Wootton Underwood, Dorton, all visited this day; Brill, Oakley, Boarstall, Ludgershall, Waddesdon, visited the 16th inst.; and Hardwicke, Whitchurch, Pitchcott, and North Marston, visited the 17th inst.; and Hoggestone, Swanbourne, Mursley, and Drayton Parslow, on the 18th inst. [11 *pp.*]

July 14.

55. See "Returns made by Justices of Peace."

July 15.

56. "The Duke of Lennox's opinion." This is a pretended speech, the object being to dissuade the King from entering upon a war with his Scottish subjects. It professes to have been delivered at a sitting of the King's Council, and was popularly attributed to the Duke of Lennox; but this copy is endorsed by Sec. Windebank, who could not but know whether it was the Duke's or not, thus:—"D. of Lenox, his supposed speech." The pretended speaker's argument treats first of the uncertainty of war. "The worst of wars is commonly in the close . . . The most advantageous war that ever was waged, all reckonings being cast up, the conqueror has had little whereof to glory." He then deals with the unnatural character of a war between a sovereign and his subjects, and passes on to the asserted necessity of the proposed war as upholding the King's royalty. He cites Louis XI. of France and Henry VII. of England as having counted it no dishonour to yield to their subjects demands, though sometimes unjust and unreasonable. "These wise Kings

1638.

Vol. CCCXCV.

considered," it is added, " that the end of war is uncertain, the event various, and that he who commits one error in the war, especially when the seat of it is in his own kingdom, seldom lives to commit a second. We need not go far for instances. Richard II. and Edward II. will be fresh precedents for any that desire to buy experience thereof upon such dear terms they did." He then urges the King to remove the occasion. The wisest Kings have had their oversights in government, which a wiser day has taught them to recal. Secondly. If this like not, let time work it forth, by which means they will learn to endure the proposal with less regret. Thirdly. Cannot your Majesty remove the obstacles by degrees, turning the humour some other way? The things in agitation are not such as are worth hazarding a kingdom for the gaining of them. My advice to your Majesty is never to use war but where the end is either certain or probable peace, and when there is no way left but that only. [3¼ pp.]

July 15. 57. John Crane to the Council. I pray you give order to Sir William Russell to make me payment of 11,025*l*. 8*s*. 8*d*. in full of the estimate for this present year, which will enable me to discharge my credit for 2,828*l*., already disbursed for victuals put aboard his Majesty's ships, and for making timely provision for the ships his Majesty shall continue at sea for his winter service. [¾ *p*.] *Annexed*,

57. I. *Account by John Crane of the charge of victuals already delivered for the extraordinary service in the present year; total, 26,755l. 0s. 4d. 15th July 1638.* [1 *p*.] Written under the letter.

57. II. *Reference of the King in Council to the Lord Treasurer and the Lord Admiral, to give order therein as they shall find most convenient for his Majesty's service. Theobalds, 22nd July 1638.* [¼ *p*.]

July 16.
Waresley.

58. Sir John Hewett, Sheriff of co. Huntingdon, to Nicholas. It was the 12th July before I received the order of the Board of the 8th July which related to a letter of the 30th June, but which was not delivered me until the 12th July, and then by much enquiry, I received it of a servant of Sir Sidney Montagu's, that I am scanted of some of that short time allotted me to bring in the money, little or none being to be got but by coercive means. Some moneys I got by sending servants of my own to each particular town, and I would desire as much time as I should have had if the letter had come to me as to others, otherwise I will send up money already collected, and return such persons as neither obey nor regard my warrants. So cheap is the authority of the sheriff grown amongst them, that I am constrained, with my purse, person, and pains, to do that that none of my predecessors were put to; but with zeal and faithfulness to the service I shall effect it as soon as possible. P.S.—Send your letters to the Seven Stars in Fleet Street, over

1638.

VOL. CCCXCV.

against St. Dunstan's church, and they will come speedily to me. [*Seal with arms.* 1 *p.*]

July 16.
Coggs.

59. Sir Thomas Penyston, Sheriff of co. Oxford, to Nicholas. I received from the board a letter of the last of June, which I conceive might be mistaken in the direction, for the arrear of 2,400*l*. does not agree with what is paid by me. There are also other particulars which differ from what I have formerly written, which I only observe because I would not willingly take upon me the blame laid upon that sheriff of remissness in his Majesty's service. I have received upon my last warrants almost 300*l*. more, and find that divers towns have paid their money to the petty constables, who have kept it, which I purpose to enquire of, and commit such constables to prison. By these last warrants I required a particular answer of every man that denied, whereby the general reason of their nonpayment appears to be an expectation of another trial the next term, not conceiving the last to be a determination of the right. I intend to make collectors in every hundred, for ease of the country this harvest time, but all men refuse to take that employment. I desire to know what I shall do upon their refusal, for I do not conceive there is any power given me to compel them, neither can they distrain; and I want sworn bailiffs, who by the law are only to execute that service, for there is not one hundred in all the shire that belongs to the sheriff, being all granted to private men, who make the bailiffs themselves, and are in many places such poor and mean fellows as I dare not trust them, except the lords of the liberties may be answerable for their bailiffs. There shall no neglect be justly laid upon me, for I shall ever prefer his Majesty's service before anything that shall concern myself or mine. [*Seal with arms.* 1 *p.*]

July 16.

60. Report addressed to Francis Paulett, Recorder of Lynn Regis, Norfolk, of meetings of the Queen's tenants at Walton in Marshland, Walsoken, and Walpole in Norfolk, to treat with Commissioners appointed by the Queen for an improvement to be made for her Majesty by draining the marshes in the said parishes. The tenants generally declined to treat of any improvement, and claimed their rights of common, the precise nature of which in each manor is here set forth. [1¾ *p.*]

July 16.

61–64. See "Returns made by Justices of Peace."

July 17.

Petition of your poor subjects, the Inhabitants of the Isle of Portsea, to the King. Petitioners always have been commanded by the Lord Governor of Portsmouth and Isle of Portsea to do their service with persons and carts in the said town and island, and there are exercised in their arms at all commands, as also for keeping continual watch by the sea-side, which costs them above 27*l*. per annum, and which none other of his Majesty's subjects thereabouts are charged withal. For which cause they have been heretofore freed (until of late years) from doing any service elsewhere, the said

1638.

Vol. CCCXCV.

town and island being places of as great importance to be strongly fortified as any in the kingdom. But of late the constables of the hundred of Portsdown have commanded petitioners to serve with persons and carts in remote places, sometimes above forty miles from the said town and island, which is not only the impoverishing of your subjects, but makes them unable to perform service in the said town and islands. Pray order that they may not be commanded to do any service elsewhere than in the said town and island. [*Copy. See Vol. cccxxiii., p.* 320. ¾ *p.*] *Underwritten*,

> I. *Minute of his Majesty's pleasure that petitioners' shall enjoy their ancient privileges, and be not otherwise charged than they have been; and the Viscount Wimbledon, governor of Portsmouth and Isle of Portsea, is to take order in this business according to his Majesty's pleasure. Theobalds,* 17*th July* 1638. [*Copy. Ibid.* ¼ *p.*]

July 17.
Aynho.

65. Reginald Burdyn to [Sir John Lambe.] Acknowledges receipt of letter in which Sir John gives an overture of his coming down, and of various other matters relating to Leicester. The writer had returned an answer by Mr. Bankes, the new parson of Sharnford. Saw also his letter to Mr. Heaward, and has enquired of a house for Sir John at Leicester. The great house wherein Mr. Poultney dwelt is vacant, and is at the disposal of Mrs. Poultney, his widow, who lives with Sir Alexander Denton, her brother, who lives at Hillington [Hillesdon]. There is also the house where old Mrs. Hunt dwelt. The writer has spoken to Mr. Gipps, who has bought, and he is ready to pleasure you. All matters at the Leicester Assizes passed fair, saving that Mr. Gery of Barwell, who preached from Rom. xiii. of the higher powers, construed the words to be of temporal magistracy, to the exclusion of ecclesiastical magistracy, which I take to be a gross and pestilent error, and questioned him for it. [1 *p.*]

July 17.

66. Sir John Lambe to Archbishop Laud. The bearer is the curate of Kingston, that for three years has supplied the place (in Dr. Stanton's suspension time) out of which he had occasion to show his ability and discretion among so many malignant eyes that were upon him. It may please you to give order for licensing him. For the books of Dr. Cowell, I will get all brought in that can be had. I monished them before. If they be sold or gone they [the company of Stationers] may be severely punished for disobeying their own master and wardens and my monition. If they be brought into their hall, they promise to be accountable for them without diminishing of any (which the other side so much fear), and also to give a good account of all that have been seized and brought into their hall for these seven years, or longer, as you shall please, which I like well, for it is said many hundred pounds will not make them up, and so some good for Paul's by them that are able to pay, and well worthy if any be embezzled or seized as unlawful, and yet made benefit of. For this of Dr. Cowell, if the ill carriage had not been, the book had not been so much

1638.

Vol. CCCXCV.

prosecuted, much less persecuted, with such their eagerness. For my Lord of Norwich's Articles, I learn that two impressions have been here already, one his Lordship caused of 1,400, of which he took but 1,200, and left 200, which are sold, and they begot another stolen impression, so one of the wardens saith, who, with their hall-clerk and others of their company, I have sent to search and seize, who can do it better, and with less open noise, than the pursuivants. For much noise of seizing doth but make them more desired, and encrease the price, which is 18d. or 2s. now. His Lordship disavows the impression here as false printed in many places, and will reprint them, I hear, at Cambridge, and then he may suppress his own 1,200, if he has not sent them forth already. The articles I have perused, and as I have altered them may pass; but I hope his Lordship will peruse them better than I could have time, at 12 o'clock last night. The writer then enters at great length into a controversy at Norwich about a proposed inhibition of a pending archiepiscopal visitation. P.S.—The master and wardens are come. They now say that 1,400 were printed for my Lord, and since 500, whereof they have seized 354; the rest it seems are sold. [*Endorsed as relating to the Bishop of Norwich's Articles and Cowell's Interpreter. Seal with arms.* 2⅙ *pp.*]

July 17. 67. Extract of a part of the above letter relating to the visitations. [2½ *pp.*]

July 18. 68. Peter Heywood, Justice of Peace for Middlesex, to the Council. Thomas Stanton, of London, has taken the oath of allegiance before me. [¼ *p.*]

July 19. Milton Abbas. 69. Sir Francis Fulford, Sir Walter Erle, and Thomas Clarke, to the King. Report upon a reference of a petition of James Rawson, vicar of Milton Abbas, calendared under date of the 2nd May last No. 14. We find that the demesne lands being exempted, the parsonage is not worth above 120l. per annum, and that instead of 20 marks per annum, limited to the vicar by the letters patent, his maintenance is increased by the gift of Mr. Tregonwell to 30l. per annum, besides his house and garden, worth about 5l. per annum more, and he never heretofore complained. The chancel has always been repaired by Mr. Tregonwell and his ancestors; and the Bishop of Bristol lately, upon hearing the petitioner's pretended title to the chancel, ordered him to leave it to Mr. Tregonwell, and advised the vicar to reconcile himself to him, and not make any further claim. Lastly, the petitioner has not proved any of the oppressions complained of. Mr. Tregonwell's proceedings at law have been upon great occasions for assaulting his only son, a child not above 12 years of age, by a son of petitioner's in time of divine service in the church, of which the child is not fully recovered. We endeavoured to make an accord between the parties, but were not able to effect the same. [1 *p.*]

DOMESTIC—CHARLES I. 569

VOL. CCCXCV.

1638.
July 19.
Woodhall.
70. Endymion Porter to Richard Harvey. I have sent you the warrant for Mr. Banks. Let Daniel give the enclosed letter to Lord Edward Pawlett's man, and within these two days I will send you word what is to be done. [*Seal with arms.* ¾ *p.*]

July 19.
71. Extracts from the Principal Register of the See of Canterbury. of entries of releases issued this day to the Archdeacons of Buckingham and Bedford. [*Endorsed by Sir John Lambe as relating to releases of the visitations of those countries.* ½ *p.*]

July 20.
72. Petition of Sir John Manwood to the King. Upon your grant to petitioner of the custody of a boom at Dover harbour, and of receiving such droits as the Commissioners for that harbour should find fit. The Commissioners have expressed themselves as is hereunto annexed; but petitioner, in obedience to a command of your Majesty in a letter of the 17th inst., directed to the Mayor and Jurats of Dover, and in the last place to the Lieutenant of Dover Castle, did presently deliver the custody of the boom to the mayor. Albeit petitioner finds that neither your Majesty nor himself were clearly dealt withal in the information whereupon that order was obtained, the letter importing that petitioner had kept from your knowledge an order of Council whereby the boom was committed to the town of Dover, whereas that order was both informed and is mentioned in the grant to petitioner. For that neither petitioner, nor any one on behalf of the Lord Warden or Lieutenant of Dover Castle, were heard when the town obtained that order, petitioner beseeches your Majesty to take into consideration the disablement that your immediate officers in that castle and port shall receive to serve you in your Admiralty jurisdiction if the custody of the boom should remain in the hands of the corporation, as also how far it trenches upon their rights, the boom having, when the same has been used, been entrusted to the lieutenant of the castle. [1 *p.*]

> 72. I. *Certificate of the Commissioners for Dover harbour above referred to. It recites the appointment of Sir John Manwood as keeper of the boom, and declares it fit and reasonable that he should receive such droits for the same as are taken by the officers of Calais, Dieppe, Dunkirk, and other foreign ports where his Majesty's subjects trade, and that a table be forthwith made for the view of all persons whom it shall concern. Dover Castle, 20th July* 1638. [1 *p.*]

July 20.
73. Petition of John Wharton, close prisoner in the Fleet, to the Council. Petitioner has been close prisoner these three weeks, locked up in his chamber with a young man, and not suffered to have the presence of his wife or servant to help him in his great extremity. Being 85 years of age, he is so weak and sickly that of himself he is not able to get to bed, or to rise, or to turn himself in his bed, and by reason of his close keeping is much impaired in health. Prays for his liberty. [¾ *p.*]

Vol. CCCXCV.

1638.
July 20.

74. Archbishop Laud to Sir Nathaniel Brent, Warden of Merton College. I have received your letters of July 11th, but being sent by the Wednesday carrier they came so late to Croydon that I could not give answer till now. I read in your letters a promise of punctual obedience to mine, but see the contrary. You tell me you found two letters of mine at the College, and that on Wednesday last you read them to the fellows, and gave order that they should be written into your register book. But my letters required so much of the sub-warden before your coming, and I will have an account of him at Michaelmas, why it was not done accordingly. For if you be not at the College, the sub-warden shall not make bold with my commands, at his pleasure to do them or leave them undone, till your return. In the next place, you say, that the time of your audit is mistaken in my letters. If it be, the matter is not great, so that at your audit, whenever it is, all those things be done which my letters require, and of which I shall call for an account. Thirdly, you write you have nominated three of your senior Fellows to attend me at Lambeth the 2nd October next, and withal that they are three fitter men than the three which were named before. But my visitors here think not so, nor I either. For they who made no complaint themselves cannot be held fit to be prosecutors of other men's complaints, which perhaps they thoroughly understand not. But howsoever, they other three were first named, and at a meeting commanded by me, and therefore they three shall stand, yet with this indifferency, that they who are now named, or any other, shall have liberty to come if they please. And further, I commanded the registering of that act of the choice of those three, as well as of the registering of my letters, which yet (it seems) your sub-warden either refused or neglected to do. But I shall call him to an account for this, as well as for other things, at Michaelmas, and in the meantime I require this of you, that you see that act registered of the choice of the former three. For the choice of your officers, perhaps you have made them according to the words of your statute, and as custom has been in that house for these 40 years, which is but your own time and Sir Henry Savile's, if all that. But I am sure it is against the true meaning of your statute, and a very ill custom for the college, that any one man should be sub-warden so many years together, and live among his fellows like another head of a college in your absence. And therefore for this I refer myself to my former letters, and require you, that there be not only a choice, but also that a new man be chosen yearly, as I have directed, and that another be now chosen at your next election, which I take it is at the beginning of August, and then for other things I shall after settle them according to your statutes and that justice which belongs to a visitor. So for this present I leave you. P.S.—This I would have you and the fellows further know, that whosoever comes to prosecute the complaints shall not thereby have any testimony of their own taken off by the putting of this thankless office upon them. [*Copy.* 1 *p.*]

Vol. CCCXCV.

1638.
July 20.
London.

75. John Pym to John Wandesford, his Majesty's agent and consul at Aleppo.

> "I have passed thorough much variety of occasions since I last writt to you, and they afford me matter of excuse of several kinds, which will not leave any the least charge or touch of disrespect or forgetfulness to be laid upon me. Now being again to go into the country, where I have been for the most part of those two years last past, and it being a time which threatens great change and trouble, I have thought good now to salute you with this short letter, and to assure you that you have always had a place in my thoughts and affections of much estimation and respect, and that I think myself indebted to you for many kindnesses and expressions of love which I cannot deserve. How God will dispose of me I know not? If the public peace continue, I hope to write to you again in Michaelmas Term; if distemper and confusion do overwhelm us, in whatsoever condition I am, I shall live in a resolution, both by my prayers and endeavours, always to express myself your very assured friend and servant. Jo. Pym."

[*Seal with arms.* 1 *p.*]

July 20.

76. Archbishop Laud to Sir John Lambe. Authority to appoint a general apparitor for the diocese of Lincoln, during the suspension of the bishop. [¼ *p.*]

July 21.
Huntingdon.

77. Attorney-General Bankes to Sec. Windebank. We, his Majesty's Commissioners of the Great Level, have now spent almost four days in this service, and have by letter given account to the Lord Treasurer, that he may represent the same to his Majesty. In some things we desire his directions, and desire you to be a means for a despatch by this messenger. If my Lord Treasurer be not at court on Sunday, then we request you to open the letter to him, and to present the same to his Majesty, either privately or in Council, as his Majesty shall direct. When Mr. Surveyor-General and myself, on Tuesday sennight, waited upon his Majesty at Greenwich, touching this business of the Great Level, his Majesty took notice of complaints that men, whole townships and hundreds, were excluded from the possession of their lands and commons, whose grounds were not drained, and thereupon gave us directions to restore such possessions until the lands were adjudged drained, which directions we have observed, yet so as we admit none to this grace but such as make due proof that their grounds are not bettered by the Earl of Bedford's draining, and that they have the order of the court for it, and that they shall not pull down any hedges, but make a gap, and enter in a peaceable manner. This order is pursuing [pursuant] to the decree made touching this Great Level, 19th James, when King James was undertaker, and is agreeable to the rule of justice, and has given a great contentment. This inclosed warrant was couched by my Lord of Bedford's counsel; whereupon, after the court risen, the Commissioners sent for the messenger, because, under pretence of this warrant, he might apprehend such whom the court restored to the possession, and so impediment his Majesty's service. After consultation, we resolved not to acquaint his Majesty with it nor my Lord Treasurer, but to send it back to you, and request you to call in some other like warrants. I meet here with rumours that this undertaking for the Great Level is for

1638.

VOL. CCCXCV.

the benefit of some private suitors. His Majesty has by his letters declared that it is for himself, and I desire you to move him that it be so really, otherwise the work will be stifled in the birth, and receive many impediments. I write not to hinder his Majesty's grace towards the Earls of Exeter and Bedford, and their participants, who have expended great sums of money about these works, for his Majesty has declared that he will have a princely care of their interests. I cannot foresee when we shall end this session, but I shall attend this service until I see things settled, or his Majesty shall otherwise command. [*Seal with arms.* 1½ *p.*] *Enclosed*,

77. I. *Sec. Windebank to Jasper Heiley, messenger. Warrant to apprehend disturbers of any of the Earl of Bedford's works in the Great Level of the Fens, similar to that already calendared in Vol. cccxc., No. 89. Whitehall, 16th May 1638.* [*Sec. Windebank's seal impressed.* ½ *p.*]

July 21. 78. Edward Fenn to Nicholas. I have received this week upon account of ship-money 10*l.* of the bailiff of Maldon, and 35*l.* of the mayor of Plympton, which is all that is received since the last certificate. [½ *p.*]

July 22.
Brackley.
79. Dr. Robert Sibthorpe to [Sir John Lambe.] Had I been assured of your being at Brickhill Court or at Rothwell, I would have waited upon you. I send these lines to acquaint you with a new misdemeanour, or rather multiplied misdemeanours, in Mr. Miles [Burkitt], vicar of Pattishall, who having caused the communion table to be often brought down from the east end of the chancel, administered the communion disorderly out of the cancelling. The poor clerk, Henry Sutton, by the appointment of the other vicar, Mr. Powell, watched that it should not be carried down again, and to that purpose, after ringing a peal to Morning Prayer, sat in the church porch, from whence he was called upon occasion, and being watched as well as he watched others, no sooner had he turned his back but two horses which were in the churchyard went, or rather were driven, into the church, whereupon Mr. Miles, whose reverence to that holy place may be collected by his comparing it to a hogsty in his sermons, is so much incensed at this accidental profanation, that he turns the poor old clerk out of his office without his fellow vicar's consent. Hereupon the business was complained of to Dr. Clerke and myself. We enjoined Sutton penance for his neglect, and sent a note to both the vicars to receive him as formerly upon performance of his penance. These he delivered, but Miles rejected him, and in his stead elected John Bennet, a notorious puritan. Thereupon Miles was cited to answer his contempt, inhibited to prejudice Sutton, or to admit Bennet, &c. The inhibition was served upon Miles and Bennet. They contemptuously disobey it, and are cited to the next court, where perhaps suspension of Bennet and excommunication of Miles (being *judicialiter monitus*) may be their reward. But there is feared an appeal to the Audience, where Sir

Vol. CCCXCV.

1638.

Charles [Cæsar] may drive a good trade, if that place may be (as is boasted) the Asylum of the Brethren. I beseech you therefore to take notice of these practices, that conformity as well as inconformity may find patronage under his Grace's jurisdiction, and that these by ways may be prevented.—P.S. How Dr. Clerke has been used for meddling with this faction I have partly acquainted you, and leave the rest to him; I conceive it worth your hearing. [1½ pp.]

July 23.
Oxford.

80. Sir Nathaniel Brent to Archbishop Laud. It is a grief unto myself and others that you should conceive amiss of us upon private information given by those who are notoriously ill-affected. The sub-warden will be able to give you absolute satisfaction when he shall appear before you at Michaelmas. He long since registered all that was required of him; he did it at the first in papers, according to the custom of the college, and since in the register book. For choosing a new sub-warden every year, no man has made any question since we received your commands. But I much wonder that any man should inform that the present sub-warden lords it over his fellows. I assure you that he is an honest and a moderate man, every way conformable to the Church of England, extraordinarily well esteemed of in the university, both for his learning and preaching, and I wish that his accusers were in any near degree to be compared to him. I hope you will not conceive it either of him or others, until it appears how private informations can be made good by proof. When I called the fellows together to consider of your commands, we found that we were required to send up some to give information concerning the discipline and thrift of the college. We were all of opinion, except three or four of the younger sort, that the seniors were more fit for this employment than the juniors, who know least of the state of the college, and are, or at least some of them, the greatest corrupters of our discipline. But now that we understand your pleasure by your last letter of the 20th inst., we will accordingly conform ourselves. On Lammas Day, which is the time of our solemn meeting, and when in likelihood no man will be absent, your directions shall be made known. I humbly desire you, as before, not to think amiss of any of the company until the hearing, when it shall be made clear that the chiefest complainants are most notoriously malicious and perjurious. I am very sorry that I have cause to say so much. [1¾ p.]

July 24.

Petition of John Bell to the King. Your Majesty granted a filazer's place in reversion in the Court of Common Pleas to petitioner, in recompense of 1,000l. acquitted to your Majesty in Scotland, secured by a privy seal of that kingdom, of which reversions there are six before this, and half of them for two lives apiece, and therefore, it being so remote in expectation, is not worth, to be sold, 100l., besides the charge petitioner has been at in suing for the said 1,000l., and in passing of this grant, which is now stayed at the great seal, whereby petitioner is likely to be utterly undone, in regard he shall both lose this suit, being very small, but also his

Vol. CCCXCV.

1638.

charges, without your Majesty's favour in giving special directions to the Lord Keeper for passing it under the great seal, for which petitioner prays. [*Copy. See Vol. cccxxiii., p.* 321. ½ *p.*] *Underwritten,*

> I. *Reference to the Lord Keeper and the Earl of Stirling. If they find petitioner's allegations true, then the Lord Keeper is to pass the grant under the great seal. Theobalds, 24th July* 1638. [*Ibid.* ¼ *p.*]

July 24.
Faringdon.

81. Sir Robert Pye to [Robert] Reade. Letter in relation to transactions between the Earl of Antrim and his wife, the Duchess Dowager of Buckingham, on the one part, and the Duke of Lenox, who had married the Duchess's daughter Mary, on the other part. The writer assures Mr. Reade that a security given to some one not named was the best that Lord Antrim could make, after he had passed away for security of 10,000*l.* Bramshill and some other things. The whole transaction had been made known to his Majesty, and Sir Robert is confident that no danger or loss can be if the Duchess live until next term; and if she should die in the meantime, all will be secured by her consent and decree in the Court of Wards. [1 *p.*]

[July 25 ?]

82. Petition of Richard Knightbridge, M.A., and one of the Fellows of Wadham College, Oxford, to the Council. Petitioner being a young man desirous to see the universities beyond the seas for his preferment in learning, prays a pass for three years to travel. [*Underwritten a note by Robert Reade that petitioner had taken the oath of allegiance before him.* ½ *p.*]

July 25.

83. Bond of John Alured, of Charterhouse, in Sculcoates, co. York; Sir Frederick Cornwallis, of Brome, Suffolk; and Thomas Westrop, of Cornbrough, co. York, to the King, in 2,000*l.*, for the appearance of Alured before the Council upon 20 days' warning to be left at his house in Blackfriars, London, to answer such matters as shall be objected against him. [1 *p.*]

July 25.

84. Acknowledgment made by James Rawson, Vicar of Milton Abbas, Dorset, clerk, in the presence of Lord Chief Justice Finch, in open court at the assizes at Dorchester, of wrongs done by him to John Tregonwell the elder and John Tregonwell the younger, his son, in his petition to his Majesty, calendared under the 2nd May last, No. 14, and in accordance with the report of Sir Francis Fulford and others, calendared under date of the 19th July inst., No. 69. [1 *p.*]

July 26.
Westminster.

85. The King to Lord Treasurer Juxon and Francis Lord Cottington, Chancellor and Under-Treasurer of the Exchequer. We have appointed 200,000*l.* to be employed in our especial affairs of great weight and importance, by the order and direction of you the said Lord Treasurer, and of the Earl of Arundel and Surrey, our Earl Marshal, of Algernon Earl of Northumberland, our High Admiral, and of you our said Chancellor of the Exchequer, and of

1638. Vol. CCCXCV.

Sir Henry Vane and Secretaries Coke and Windebank. We command you, out of the receipt of our Exchequer, to pay all such sums, not exceeding in the whole the sum of 200,000*l.*, to such persons and for such our services as shall be ordered by you our said Treasurer and Under-Treasurer and the Lords of the Council above-named, or any three of you, whereof you our said Treasurer and you our Under-Treasurer be always two. [*Copy.* 1 *p.*] *Endorsed,*

85. I. *Lord Treasurer Juxon to Sir Robert Pye. To draw an order by virtue of the above privy seal for issuing to John Quarles, merchant,* 15,230*l. on account of the* 200,000*l. above-mentioned.* [*Copy.* ½ *p.*]

85. II. *Notes of various payments made on account of the said* 200,000*l., amounting altogether to* 58,292*l. In several payments to Sir John Heydon,* 17,303*l.; Mr. Comptroller, for secret service,* 1,000*l.; John Quarles, as above,* 15,230*l.; Marquess of Hamilton,* 5,000*l.; Sir Thomas Morton,* 295*l.; Mr. Pinckney,* 500*l; Sir John Heydon, for repair of the fort in Holy Island,* 129*l.; more to him for completing the arms, as by estimate dated 14th September* 1638, 8,835*l; more to John Quarles, on account, for providing 2,000 harquebuziers with pistols and carbines. Dated 30th September* 1638. [½ *p.*]

July 26. Copy of the above Privy Seal for the payment of 200,000*l.* [*See Vol. cccxcvi., p.* 1. 1½ *p.*]

July 26. 86. Another copy of the same. [1 *p.*] *Annexed,*

86. I. *Draft in the handwriting of Nicholas of a direction to the Clerk of the Signet, to prepare a similar privy seal, for payment of* 300,000*l., by order and direction of the Lord Treasurer, the Marquess of Hamilton, the Lord Deputy of Ireland, Lord Cottington, the Treasurer of the Household, and Sec. Windebank, or any three of them, whereof the Lord Treasurer or the Chancellor of the Exchequer to be always one.* [½ *p.*]

July 26. Copy of the above direction to Sir Robert Pye to pay to John Quarles (*No.* 85, I.) 15,230*l.* [*See Vol. cccxcvi., p.* 2. ½ *p.*]

July 26. Petition of Dame Mary Powell to the King. Petitioner's late father and mother, Sir Peter Vanlore and his lady, left to her a very good real and personal estate, intending the same or most part thereof should be in her dispose. Jointure she has none settled, unless about 40*l.* per annum, albeit 400*l.* per annum was promised. Her present and former allowance from her husband has been and is so mean that she cannot therewith provide necessaries of livelihood; his usage of her so unworthy that she suffers in mind and reputation. The trust reposed in him by petitioner's late mother, acknowledged under his own hand and seal, he has broken and turned to his own use, and he enjoys near 2,000*l.* per annum by petitioner and in her right, and she cannot enjoy so much as peace with him unless

576 DOMESTIC—CHARLES I.

Vol. CCCXCV.

1638.

she will submit to make him master of all her estate, which, though not *de jure*, yet *de facto* he exercises, for he receives and keeps great sums of money, as also divers deeds and specialties, from the executor of her late mother, who is only trusted to dispose of all that estate as petitioner shall direct under her hand, and not otherwise. Nevertheless Sir Edward takes upon him to compound debts and otherwise to do what he pleases. Her suit is that his Majesty will take the hearing of her many grievances into his own determination, and give some final order for petitioner's redress, and appoint some time for that purpose, and in the meantime some convenient maintenance to be allowed petitioner; and that all suits concerning "the state" [estate?], against the executor of petitioner's late mother and others commenced by Sir Edward may by command be stayed. [*Copy. See Vol. cccxxiii., p. 322. ⅔ p.*] *Underwritten,*

> I. *Minute of his Majesty's pleasure to hear this business in person on Sunday the 7th October next, at 2 o'clock in the afternoon, wheresoever his Majesty shall then be. Somerset House, 26th July 1638.* [*Copy. Ibid. ¼ p.*]

July 26. 87. Copy order of the Lord Treasurer and Lord Cottington for payment to John Quarles of the said 15,230*l.*, with underwritten memoranda of the several amounts by which the whole sum was paid, and of the names of the tellers of the Exchequer by whom the said amounts were paid. [= ½ *p.*]

July 26. Copy of part of the before-mentioned note of payments made on account of the said 200,000*l.* (*No. 85, II.*), containing the first payments made, amounting to 39,328*l.*, with an underwritten memorandum that the warrants for those payments were written by the Committee before Mr. Nicholas was appointed to attend to this business. [*See Vol. cccxcvi., p. 3. ½ p.*]

July 26. 88. Return of Robert Heallam, [constable] of Ware, co. Hertford, of those that have not paid to the ship-rate; total, 10*l.* 10*s.* due from thirteen persons, Robert Heallam being charged with 3*l.* 5*s.* Underwritten it is stated that none of these "refuse to pay," but "it has pleased God to withold his blessings from many of them, being farmers, that the earth has not yielded her encrease, as at other times, therefore they desire 'your worship' to spare them as long as you can." [¾ *p.*]

July 26. 89. Presentment of the Grand Inquest for Wilts at the assizes at Sarum. The jury received information from divers constables of hundreds and others that they were much oppressed by warrants sent out from the postmasters of New Sarum [Salisbury] and Shaston [Shaftesbury] for bringing in post horses under pretence of his Majesty's service, by reason whereof all the tithings within six miles of the said city and town were charged with great payments for the continual supply of horses, which being not able to supply they were forced to hire them at extraordinary rates. The jury knowing

DOMESTIC—CHARLES I. 577

1638.

VOL. CCCXCV.

the truth of the complaint present the same as a great burden, humbly craving the assistance of this court for redress. [1 p.]

July 26. 90. See "Returns made by Justices of Peace."

July 27. Warrant to the Master of the Great Wardrobe, to pay to his Majesty's servants, tradesmen, and artificers, for service and goods for his Majesty and the Queen in the stables, according to his Majesty's orders. [*Docquet.*]

July 27. A like, to the same effect, for the stables also. [*Docquet.*]

July 27.
Donington.
91. Henry Earl of Huntingdon to [Sir John Lambe]. I have been a suitor to you and the court that those seats which formerly belonged to my ancestors in the church of Loughborough might be allotted to me, whereupon, at Dr. Roane's visitation in May last at Leicester, he granted a commission, under the seal of the Archbishop, to Mr. Blount, Mr. Beverege, Mr. Foster, and Mr. Henry Robinson, who came to Loughborough, and appointed forth the places and dimensions of the said seats. Not long after I caused the seats which were placed there to be taken up, having provided timber for making them. Since which time Henry Skipwith has caused a seat to be placed there. I desire nothing but what is my right, and to enjoy those seats which many of the inhabitants will depose did belong to my predecessors. In all my time, which is 33 years since the decease of my grandfather, George Earl of Huntingdon, I was never so confronted, nor such an indignity offered to be put upon me. I beseech you to see me righted. [1 p.]

July 28.
Deptford.
92. Sir William Russell to Nicholas. I received yesterday a letter from my son Chicheley, sheriff of co. Cambridge, by which I understand that he was to attend the Lords to-morrow concerning the ship-money, which by reason of sickness he cannot do, and has desired that the Lords will excuse him. In which request I must join, well knowing that what he writes is very true. He has expressed in his letter his diligence in pursuing his Majesty's and the Lords' directions, and has endeavoured to the utmost of his power, but finds his county so backward and refractory that it has aggravated his sickness, for little or no moneys can be got but by distress and forcible means. He promises to attend the Lords next week, to give account of the service. In the meantime he has sent up 250*l*., with entreaty to you to acquaint the Lords that his Majesty has not any sheriff or subject that more truly affects the furtherance of his service, and is obedient to the Lords' commands. [*Endorsed by Nicholas* "To be read." ¾ p.]

July 28. 93. Account by Sir William Russell of ship-money for 1637. Total received, 111,643*l*. 15*s*. 1*d*.; outstanding, 84,770*l*. 12*s*. 7*d*. [1 p.]

July 28. 94. Memorandum of Sir William Russell of ship-money received on account of arrears for 1636. Total, 142*l*. 3*s*. 8*d*. [¼ p.]

o o

VOL. CCCXCV.

1638.
July 28.
95. Account of ship-money for 1637, levied and remaining in the hands of the sheriffs. Total, 6,340*l*., which makes the total collected 117,983*l*., which is 33,812*l*. less than was paid in on the 21st July 1637. [1 *p*.]

July 29.
96. John Crane to [the Council]. Recites letter of the 15th inst. (No. 57), wherein he craved an order to receive the remainder of the estimate, which was 11,025*l*. 8*s*. 8*d*., but since that time the Lord Admiral has given order what the winter guard shall be, which will cause a less charge. My desire now is, that I may have order to Sir William Russell for 7,000*l*., to enable me to discharge my credit for what I have done, and to provide victuals for ships to stay out this next winter. [1 *p*.]

July 29.
Sion.
97. Algernon Earl of Northumberland to [Sir John Pennington]. The Earl of Pembroke and Montgomery, Lord Chamberlain, having, on behalf of the Fishing Association, presented to his Majesty, that, notwithstanding the Dutch fishermen employed and lately taken in his busse called the Salisbury were made free denizens, thereby to assure them of his Majesty's protection, and notwithstanding his Majesty's mediation, made by his agent Mr. Gerbier to the Infante Cardinal, on behalf of the said Dutchmen, taken by the Dunkirkers, they still remain in miserable prison, so that two of them are already dead and others lie very sick. His Majesty has thereupon given me order to take some course for their satisfaction. These are, therefore, to require you that whensoever you, or any of the captains under you, encounter any Dunkirk shipping at sea, stay is immediately to be made of such as may give satisfaction for this wrong. Ships of this nature are not to be surprised in harbour or road, and therefore you must have care to caution the captains therein. Concerning the business between the Nicodemus and the Hollander, his Majesty is of opinion that Woolward was a little too forward, and yet does not discommend him; but as things now stand his Majesty will be contented if they make reasonable acknowledgment upon their encounter with his Majesty's ships. You are also to advertise the captains to desist from any further prosecution of the Bull of Amsterdam for this particular. [1¼ *p*.]

July 29.
98. Estimate of the Officers of the Ordnance of a proportion of ordnance and munition appointed to be brought into his Majesty's store, for the 2,000 men designed for Sir Thomas Morton, and for better supply of the magazines, and to be delivered out upon any occasion required by the Master of the Ordnance, according to instructions prescribed by special committee of some of the Lords of the Council. Total, 12,010*l*. 2*s*. 7*d*., of which 8,245*l*. 15*s*. 11*d*. could be supplied out of the stores, and the remainder must be purchased. [12¾ *pp*.]

July 30.
99. Sec. Windebank to Algernon Earl of Northumberland. His Majesty has commanded me to signify to you his pleasure that you order a ship of the lesser rank to transport Mons. Monsigott, an

1638.   VOL. CCCXCV.

envoy from Queen Mother, with his followers, to Rotterdam or other port in Holland. And you are to give private instruction to the captain that shall transport him, not to make any stay in Holland after he shall have landed him, nor to receive any other into his Majesty's ship that shall desire to come from those parts, but to come back immediately, and return to the Downs, or such place as you shall direct. [*Draft.* ¾ *p.*]

July 30. 100. Account of the state of the Fishing Society at this date, showing the loss from the institution of the society in 1633 to the end of 1637, with a Dr. and Cr. account of the state of the society at the latter period. [= 2 *pp.*]

July 30. 101. Estimate of the Officers of Ordnance for pistols, carbines, muskets, bandaliers, and rests to be brought into store, being ordered to be provided by the Master of the Ordnance, according to instructions from a special committee of the Council. Pistols with firelocks are estimated at 3*l.* 10*s.* apiece; carbines, with bolts, swivels, &c., at 2*l.* apiece; muskets at 18*s.* 6*d.* apiece; bandaliers at 3*s.* apiece; rests for muskets at 1*s.* apiece; total, 5,375*l.* [1 *p.*]

July 30. 102. Copy of the same, with an endorsed account, dated the 14th November 1638, of the numbers of the several articles at that time brought in under that estimate. [2 *pp.*]

July 31. The King to [Henry Earl of Holland, Chief Justice in Eyre of
Oatlands. all Forests on this side Trent]. We have sent you a schedule in which are mentioned such number of deer of this season as we are pleased to bestow upon the ambassadors and agents of princes residing with us, with the parks and walks wherein we purpose the said deer shall be killed. We command you to cause your warrants to be directed to the keepers, authorizing them to kill and deliver the said deer. [*Copy. See Book of Orders concerning Forests. Vol. ccclxxxiv., p.* 18. 1 *p.*] *Underwritten,*

> I. *Schedule above alluded to. The ambassadors had each three bucks. They were those of France, Venice, and the States. The agents had two bucks each. They were those of Spain, the Queen of Bohemia, Sweden, Savoy, and Florence. One buck was to be taken from Hyde Park.* [*Copy.* 1 *p.*]

July 31. The same to the same. Similar letter and schedule for deer to be bestowed upon the Lord Mayor, Aldermen, and Recorder of the city of London, 23 in all. [*Copy. Ibid., p.* 20. 1½ *p.*]

July 31. 103. Petition of Robert Whitfield, clerk, to the King. Petitioner has been 23 years incumbent of Liddiard Millicent, Wilts, and he and his predecessors have time out of mind enjoyed common for their cattle, levant and couchant, upon the glebe lands of that church; upon a purlieu in Liddiard aforesaid containing about 230 acres, being now the lands of Sir Anthony Ashley Cooper, his Majesty's ward; and upon another purlieu in Liddiard, being now the lands of Christopher Richmond *alias* Webb, containing about

1638.

VOL. CCCXCV.

550 acres. Sir Anthony and the said Christopher Richmond having enclosed the said purlieus, they and Edward Tucker, the said Sir Anthony's committee, have for two years past refused to suffer petitioner to enjoy his common, and intend to wear him out with suits. Petitioner beseeches, for avoiding suits, (the said parties being so potent in the country as petitioner is hopeless of receiving right there,) a reference to some of the Council to take order for petitioner's relief. [¾ p.] *Underwritten,*

    103. I. *Reference to Archbishop Laud, the Lord Keeper, and the Lord Treasurer, or any two of them, to make such end for the good of the church and petitioner's relief as shall be according to equity. Oatlands, 31st July 1638.* [¼ p.] *Endorsed.*

    103. II. *Appointment, by Archbishop Laud and Lord Treasurer Juxon, of the 25th January next, for hearing this business. 22nd November* 1638. [¼ p.]

July 31.
104. Petition of Lady Theodosia Tressam [Tresham], wife of Sir William Tressam, to the King. Your Majesty having given several commands to Sir William to repay the 4,000*l.* which he had with his wife in marriage, by reason he liveth not with her, and that he should not leave this realm until he had performed the same, yet he is returned the second time into Flanders, without yielding obedience, so that petitioner remains in insufferable distress. Prays command to Sec. Windebank to send royal letters to the Prince Cardinal of Austria to send home Sir William, that he may not live in Flanders, to enjoy so great an estate, without yielding obedience to your Majesty, and upon his return that the said Sir William may remain in the Fleet until he has repaid the said 4,000*l.* [¾ p.]

July 31.
105-6. See "Returns made by the Justices of Peace."

July.
107. The King to his Officers and Sub-searchers at Gravesend. Divers seizures of gold, silver, jewels, and merchandize have been lately made by our officers at Gravesend, which should have been brought to Edward Watkins, our head searcher in the port of London, he being the only person trusted by us for that service, and who has given security to answer our part of all seizures made in the said port and members. The persons addressed are, therefore, upon sight hereof, to deliver to Edward Watkins all such seizures as they have made or shall make. [*Rough draft of a suggested warrant.* 1¾ p.]

July.
108. Petition of the Inhabitants of St. Neots and Eynesbury, co. Huntingdon, to the Council. Complain of the great inconvenience and wrong they suffer by innkeepers and victuallers being restrained from brewing ale and beer, whereby petitioners might any day in the week, or any hour of a day, have four quarts of wholesome small beer for a penny, two for a halfpenny, and one for a farthing, which was a daily comfort to themselves and families. Now they cannot have any small beer for their money, but only on those days the

DOMESTIC—CHARLES I. 581

1638.

Vol. CCCXCV.

brewer tuns his beer, and then it is so bad it does them no good; and if they fill a vessel of three or four gallons, it is so rawly brewed that it dies in the vessel before it be half drank out. Pray the King to license the innkeepers to brew as formerly. [*Signed by* 16 *persons, of whom* 11 *or* 12 *are marksmen. The last name appended is* "Will. Cranwell" *or* "Cromwell." 1 *p.*]

July. 109. Analytical Digest of Facts in controversy between John Barnwell, plaintiff, and Anne, now the wife of Robert Walthew, defendant. The facts arose out of disagreements between the plaintiff, who was a servant of the Countess of Exeter, and Elizabeth his wife, who had been taken away from him by her mother, the said Anne. There had been a decree against the defendant in the Court of Requests, which she had ineffectually endeavoured to get reversed in the King's Bench. [= 2 *pp.*]

[July ?] 110. Supplication of the Nobles, Barons, Burgesses, Ministers, and Commons of Scotland to the Marquess of Hamilton, his Majesty's Commissioner. They are far from any thought of withdrawing themselves from their dutiful subjection and government, which, by descent and under the reign of 107 kings, is most cheerfully acknowledged. Their quietness depends upon the King, as upon God's vicegerent set over them for maintenance of religion and administration of justice, and they have sworn with their means and lives to stand to the defence of the King's person and authority in the preservation of the true religion, laws, and liberties of the kingdom. Pray for the indiction of a free general assembly and parliament. [5 *pp.*]

[July ?] 111. Petition of Robert Heallam and Daniel Field, Collectors of Ship-money for Ware and Tring, co. Hertford, to the Council. Upon the complaint of the sheriff, petitioners have been sent for by warrant, and brought up by a messenger. They have to the uttermost of their power executed their places, and duly paid in all moneys received, and returned the names of defaulters, and are ready to pay all moneys assessed upon them; and this being their chief harvest time, and they sorrowful for having incurred your displeasure, they pray acceptance of their submission and discharge. [½ *p.*]

July. 112–120. See "Returns made by the Justices of Peace."

Vol. CCCXCVI.

ENTRY BOOK of Documents relating to the Council of War, dated between the 26th July 1638 and the 22nd January 1640–1, all which will be found calendared in chronological order.

Vol. CCCXCVII. August 1–31, 1638.

1638.
Aug. 1. 1. Philip Warwick to Sec. Coke. This gentleman has addressed himself in behalf of his Lord [Sir Thomas Roe], for payment of the late bill, signed by Sec. Coke, for his extraordinaries, amounting to 484*l*. The sum warranted by Sir Thomas Roe's privy seal is as follows, which the Lord Treasurer commanded the writer to certify. The privy seal warrants the payment of 6*l*. per diem for his ordinary, and for his extraordinary advance it should be 1,000*l*., to be defalked out of his ordinaries and extraordinaries, and accordingly 1,000*l*. has been issued, leaving but 80*l*. which my Lord has authority to issue. Further advance is now only such sum as you shall certify to be his Majesty's pleasure. My Lord commanded me further to intimate to you that, if you allow the ambassador any sum, my Lord cannot make payment of it without his Majesty's direction to let it be part of those moneys which now come in for other occasions, which must be afterwards supplied out of the ordinary receipts of the Exchequer, which at this time are so low that they will not bear a sum of 500*l*. [1 *p.*]

Aug. 2.
Berwick. 2. Sir James Douglas to Sec. Windebank. After conference with particulars in this town, I found that if his Majesty's letter in my behalf were seconded, declaring that "whereas he had formerly written and had not found the expected effects, this is to require they do not stop me nor my tenants in any part of those grounds until I be legally expelled." I have written to the Duke [of Lenox], who obtained this letter to this effect, and I expect your assistance. Our Scotch business lies over upon expectation of the Marquess of Hamilton's return, whom with they expect all their desires. They are murmuring amongst themselves they must have Leith fortified, and the castle of Edinburgh so kept as it shall not in time coming be hurtful to them; those that are engaged speak great things of their power. If the truth were known they are far short of their ostentation. One thing over-reaches my judgment; to comprehend upon what ground they promise my brother great immunities in matters of religion, and to be confirmed in parliament, if he will suffer those he has interest in to do as they, and subscribe. I should be right prolix if I expressed the foolish liberties some propose to themselves. [2 *pp.*]

Aug. 2.
Oatlands. Henry Earl of Holland, Chief Justice, and Justice in Eyre of the Forests on this side Trent, to the Surveyor, Receiver, and Comptroller of the castle of Windsor. It appears by survey of the decays of Bagshot Lodge, in the bailiwick of Finchampstead within the Forest of Windsor, and by estimate for repairing thereof, that the works will require 11½ loads of timber and 38*l*. 19*s*. 11*d*. in money. You are to cause the said lodge to be repaired according to the said survey and estimate, and we authorize you to take the said proportion of timber out of the timber already cut by virtue of a former warrant, and to issue out of the receipts of the castle of Windsor the

1638.
VOL. CCCXCVII.

requisite money, not exceeding 38*l*. 19*s*. 11*d*. [*Vol. ccclxxxiv., p.* 23. 1 *p.*] *Pre-written,*

 1. *Survey of decays of Bagshot Lodge, with estimate for repairs. By view of Robert Benet, surveyor, Edmond Harrington, comptroller, and workmen, taken* 28*th March* 1637 *by warrant from Henry Earl of Holland, dated* 8*th February* 1636–7. *The lodge is very ruinous, and for repair thereof will ask of timber* 3½ *loads. The charges to sawyers will cost* 1*l*. 10*s*.; *to carpenters,* 2*l*.; *hooks, hinges, nails, and other ironwork for the carpenter,* 1*l*. 10*s*.; *bricks,* 2,000 *at* 17*s. per thousand; lime,* 2 *loads at* 17*s*.; *hair,* 30 *bushels at* 8*d*.; *tiles,* 2,000 *at* 17*s*.; *tile-pine,* 1 *bushel,* 18*d*.; *laths,* 1 *load,* 1*l*. 13*s*.; *lath nails,* 1*l*. 1*s*.; *sand,* 5 *loads, at* 16*d. per load; bricklayers and labourers about* 4*l*. *Also for building a barn of two bays,* 24 *foot by* 16, *to be boarded round for the better defence from wind and weather, will ask of timber* 8 *loads. The charges to sawyers will cost* 3*l*. 6*s*. 8*d*.; *to carpenters,* 5*l*.; *tiles,* 6,000 *at* 17*s. per thousand;* 1 *load of lime,* 8*s*. 6*d*.; *bricks,* 1,000, 17*s*.; *tile pins at* 1*s*. 6*d. per bushel,* 2*s*. 3*d*.; *laths,* 2,000 *at* 14*d. per hundred; lath nails,* ½ *sum,* 7*s*.; *hooks, hinges, nails, and other ironwork,* 40*s*.; *sand,* 3 *loads at* 16*d. per load; bricklayers and labourers,* 2*l*. 5*s*. *Total,* 38*l*. 19*s*. 11*d*. *The timber is already cut and laid at the lodge by virtue of former warrants.* [*Copy. Ibid., p.* 21. 3 *pp.*]

Aug. 3.   3. Attorney-General Bankes to the Council. I have examined the petitions of Edward Heather the elder, Edward Fryer, and Robert Fryer, and other cardmakers, in presence of the wardens and others of the company of Cardmakers, and find that Heather wilfully refused to come into the contract. He now confesses his faults in abusing the officers, who thereupon are content to allow him 20*l*. per annum for two years, and to take him into the contract when the next cardmaker dies, and to take off or seal his 62 gross of cards already made, according to the Lord Treasurer's order. Edward Fryer is willing to make submission, and give security for true dealing for the future, and to accept five gross weekly for one year, and to satisfy Robert Fryer, to which the officers agree. The rest of the petitioners, viz., Jasper Coard, John Hamond, Abel Coard, Philip Pigeon, Margaret Baxter, John Lovell, Edward Heather, and William Smith, being poor men, were persuaded by Edward Fryer and Robert Fryer to subscribe the petition, in hope to get pensions allowed them. They now confess their faults, and offer to submit themselves to the officers. [*Copy.* 1 *p.*]

Aug. 3.
Oatlands.
  4. Sec. Coke to Sir Henry Marten. The letters of reprisal granted to Henley and Polhill were, at the instance of the States' ambassador, and in regard of the conjuncture of the times, suspended by the King's order; nevertheless, by the pressing of some Lords they

1638.

were afterwards set free again, and Henley is charged to have taken a ship within or near our own ports, to the disturbance of trade; and for Polhill, how, without profit to himself, he has destroyed a rich ship, wherein many nations were interested, you will understand by the relation which I send herewith. This again the ambassador has represented to his Majesty, who is so much offended with the miscarriage of these reprisals that he has commanded me to signify his express pleasure, both to the Lord Admiral and yourself, for the further suspending of both the said letters of reprisal. [*Copy.* 1 *p.*]

Aug. 3. 5. Affidavit of Francis Rideing, of Manchester. In June last, according to commission under seal of the soapmakers of London, he having with him his Majesty's proclamation concerning soap, seized prohibited soap of the value of 3*l.*, the owners whereof caused him to be apprehended, and carried before Francis Nevill, justice of peace, near Wakefield, who required him to restore the soap to the owners, the which, for fear of imprisonment, he was forced unto. Shortly after having searched for prohibited soap, he was carried before Edmond Ashton, justice of peace, in Lancashire, to whom he showed his commission and the proclamations, but was committed to the county goal, without the allowance of bail. And William Cooke, a constable in Manchester, has lately, contrary to the proclamation, refused to assist him, but, upon a warrant from Mr. Ashton, committed deponent to prison, being a dungeon for vagrants, where he kept deponent a long space, merely for that he had done his best endeavours in the execution of his office in his Majesty's service. [*Endorsed is a memorandum that the persons complained of had been sent for by warrant.* ⅔ *p.*]

Aug. 3.
Albury.

6. Remembrances of Thomas Earl of Arundel and Surrey for Sir James Bagg, upon his Majesty's pleasure declared concerning Carlisle. That he attend his Majesty, and show him how ready he is for those men and munition to be supplied which he promised. Victuals for 800 men may be suddenly provided in the west. Arms, which must be 500 beyond what Sir James Bagg offers, they must be provided either at Bristol or out of the King's magazine at Hull or Newcastle. The men wanting, who will be above 700, are to be pressed out of Wales, by commission to the Lord President there, by the voice of being sent into Ireland, and so be ready to be transported to Workington, there to expect his Majesty's pleasure. I hold it fit that instantly some quantity of bows with offensive arrows should be poured into our bordering shires of Cumberland, Northumberland, and Westmorland (already used to archery), and their old arms of spear and jack restored. For brown bills I wish 2,000 should be sent thither, which the Earl of Newcastle told me might be spared in the Tower, and some calivers with shot and powder, which might be of great use. All these must move by money, and therefore if his Majesty shall approve, as he declared on Monday last, I beseech him, by one of the Secretaries of State, to give order that moneys be so issued as the King's designs be not lost by advantage of time, upon which others are watchful. [2 *pp.*]

DOMESTIC—CHARLES I. 585

Vol. CCCXCVII.

1638.
Aug. 3/13.
Compostella.
7. Pass granted by the Licentiate Gutierre Falcon de Paços and Junqueras, Greater Cardinal and Penitentiary of the church of Compostella, in which the most blessed body of St. James Zebedee, the only patron of Spain, undoubtedly and miraculously reposes entire under the greater altar, to Robert Puchin [?], Englishman. The person mentioned having personally visited the church of St. James the Apostle, and vowed to visit the shrines of St. Peter and St. Paul and other holy places, is recommended to the alms of the faithful, which blot out sins, that by these and other works of virtue and piety they may attain to the celestial kingdom, and become partakers in the prayers of the holy church of Compostella. [*A form printed on parchment, with a rude but forcible woodcut representing St. James of Compostella.* 1 p.]

Aug. 3. 8. See "Returns made by Justices of Peace."

Aug. 4. Grant to James Levingston, Groom of the Bedchamber, of three-fourth parts of 1,136*l.* 4*s.*, covenanted to be paid to his late Majesty by Viscount Wallingford and Viscount Andover, now Earl of Berkshire, by indenture in the first year of his Majesty, containing a lease of the post fines for a half year's rent reserved upon a former lease of the said post fines made to Viscount Wallingford, by him then surrendered, reserving a fourth part to his Majesty. [*Docquet.*]

Aug. 4. Grant of Incorporation to Sir Theodore de Mayerne, Sir William Brouncker, Dr. Cadiman and others, using the trade of distilling strong water and making vinegar in London and within 21 miles thereof, by the name of master, wardens, assistants, and commonalty of distillers of London, with various customary powers. They are not to be sued upon the statute of 5th Eliz. in case they have used the trade four years last past. All others are inhibited to use this trade within these limits unless they have served seven years apprenticeship. The master, wardens, and assistants are enabled to compose a manuscript of rules for the right making of strong waters and vinegars according to art, which being approved by Sir Theodore de Mayerne and Dr. Cadiman, this company is to follow. They are to have searchers over all who sell these wares, and to examine the materials for making them and the measures, and to destroy unwholesome waters and vinegars. They are also to have search over all brewers for such low wines as they distil and their materials, and finding them musty or unwholesome are to destroy them, but the brewers are not to be impeached in distilling their worts and dregs into low wines. [*Docquet.*]

Aug. 4.
St. James's.
9. Hugh Woodward to Sec. Windebank. I have lately received a letter from Lady Carr, complaining of her unsufferable usage by Sir Robert Carr, who having sold lands to the value of 3,000*l.*, of which he received 300*l.* on Sunday last in the morning, went forth in the afternoon, as it were to take the air, since which she has not seen him, and as she believes he is come to London, to perform some designs of his tending to her further prejudice, leaving her a

1638.

VOL. CCCXCVII.

great family and nothing to maintain them. Lord Danby's opinion was that the reference to the Lords should not be presented until their first meeting after the progress, on account of their much business, and every one's desire of being out of town. Sir Robert is in London, and was at court yesterday. I beseech you, on behalf of this distressed lady, to prevent whatsoever design he may have to his Majesty, in anywise tending to the ruin of her and her children. [*Seal with arms.* 1 *p.*]

Aug. 4. 10. Account of Sir William Russell of ship-money for 1637. Received, 116,340*l*. 15*s*. 1*d*.; unpaid, 80,073*l*. 12*s*. 7*d*. [= 2 *pp.*]

Aug. 4. 11. Account of ship-money levied and remaining in the hands of the sheriffs. Total, 3,440*l*., making the total collected 119,780*l*., being 32,165*l*. less than on the 5th August 1637. [1 *p.*]

Aug. 4. 12. Examination of Margaret Cley, taken before Peregrine Bertie, Sir Anthony Irby, and others. Her uncle, Thomas Stennett, carried her before the Earl of Lincoln, and by the way told her that she had undone her aunt Field, and might never look her in the face any more, and said he would give her some new clothes if she would deny what she had confessed to Lord Willoughby, and deny that her aunt Field had taught her to do any counterfeit tricks, which she was willing to do. The Earl of Lincoln examined her whether Lord Willoughby or any of his servants had beaten her, or used any violence towards her to make that confession. She told the Earl her confession was true. The Earl told her she was a naughty girl, and had wronged her aunt, and so sent her out of the room with her uncle Stennett, who persuaded her, and she promised, to say as he would have her. One of the Earl's men brought her again to the Earl, and then she denied that her aunt had taught her to counterfeit herself possessed, but that she was really possessed, and that Janet Home and Edward South had bewitched her. [*Copy.* ¾ *p.*]

Aug. 4. Examination of Anne Coleson, taken before the same persons. Thomas Stennett, brother to Elizabeth Field, her dame, came and fetched examinant before the Earl of Lincoln, and by the way Stennett desired her to deny what she said before Lord Willoughby, and Elizabeth Field should give her 10*s*., and that she should say that Edward South had given her 2*s*. to accuse her dame, and Jane Thompson had given her 12*d*. to accuse her said dame. The Earl examined deponent, and said she was a naughty girl, and was worthy to be sent to the House of Correction, for that she had caused Margaret Cley to confess that which was not true. After persuasion by Stennett, she said she had done her dame wrong, and denied what she had confessed before Lord Willoughby. The Earl wished her to put her hand to her examination, which she refused to do, though threatened by the Earl to be sent to the House of Correction for not doing it. [*Copy. Written on the same paper as the preceding.* 1 *p.*]

DOMESTIC—CHARLES I. 587

1638.
Vol. CCCXCVII.

Aug. 4.
Oatlands.
Henry Earl of Holland, Chief Justice and Justice in Eyre of Forests on this side Trent, to Richard Batten, messenger of the Chamber. Divers fines imposed by me at the justice seat for the Forest of Essex remain unpaid. You are to repair to the houses of the persons named in a schedule [stated to be] annexed and to demand the fines imposed on them, which, if they refuse to pay, you are to take them into custody, and detain them until they have paid the same. [*Copy. See Vol. ccclxxxiv., p. 24.* ¾ *p.*]

Aug. 4.
13. Assignment by Edmund Butler, of Ballyragget, co. Kilkenny, esquire, to Thomas Harris, of St. Martin-in-the-Fields, tailor, of a lease for seven years granted to Butler by Lawrence Maidwell of the Middle Temple, esquire, of a house on the east side of the arch of the twelve new buildings of William Gifford in High Holborn, being the second house at the east end of the said new buildings, near to Southampton stables, subject to the rent of 45*l.* per annum, reserved in the original lease. [*Copy.* = 2 *pp.*]

Aug. 5.
Oatlands.
14. Order of the King in Council. The Lord Treasurer and Lord Cottington are to consider how far his Majesty's interests may be concerned by having a boom kept at the mouth of Dover harbour, and what duties are required and taken of his Majesty's subjects trading in France, Holland, Flanders, or other foreign parts, where the like booms are kept; also what payments since such boom has been kept at Dover have been taken, to whose use, and by whom paid, and in what manner the keeping of the said boom has been used or abused by those to whom of late times it has been committed. [1⅓ *p.*]

[Aug. 5?]
15. Petition of Styward Trench, Under-sheriff of Middlesex, to the King. There having issued out several warrants from this board for apprehending persons found to be actors or abettors in the notorious riots committed in Holborn in and near petitioner's office, but the messengers, notwithstanding strict command laid upon them by an order stated to be annexed, have not apprehended in seven weeks above two of the said delinquents. Prays order to the Lord Chief Justice of the King's Bench to grant his warrant for apprehending the said delinquents, that they may appear before the commissioners of oyer and terminer at the next sessions. [½ *p.*]

Aug. 5.
Oatlands.
16. Order of the King in Council upon the preceding petition of Styward Trench. It was Ordered that the messengers be straightly charged to use their uttermost diligence to apprehend all those delinquents, whether they be yet remaining in London or gone down into the country, and herein to take the information of the said under-sheriff. [1 *p.*]

Aug. 6.
Pardon to Sir Henry Croke, Clerk of the Pipe, of all offences wherewith he has been charged by an information exhibited in the Court of Star Chamber, and of all other offences by him committed in execution of that place; provided that this pardon shall not

VOL. CCCXCVII.

1638.

extend to discharge him of any debt due to his Majesty, or any accounts of money received. [*Docquet.*]

Aug. 6.

Grant to William Murray, Groom of the Bedchamber, of a yearly rent of 240*l*., with arrearages, reserved to his Majesty, upon letters patent of 28th May last, granted to the Earl of Kinnoul for 30 years of the customs and subsidies of smalts, saffers, and potashes, with forfeitures of the same. [*Docquet.*]

Aug. 6.
Oatlands.

17. Sec. Windebank to Sir Henry Marten. His Majesty having granted letters of reprisal to Henley and Polhill for satisfaction of losses they sustained by subjects of the States of the United Provinces, and finding cause to suspend the execution of those letters for the present, in hope that the States will speedily cause reparation to be made, has commanded me to signify to you that you take present order for suspending the same; and if the ships of Henley or Polhill shall have taken any ships or goods belonging to the subjects of the States, they are to bring them into some ports of England, where they shall understand his further pleasure; and lastly, that the ships of Henley and Polhill, now at sea, be commanded to return into England. And this his Majesty has given in charge as well to Sec. Coke as myself, to the end the business may not receive disturbance by different significations of his pleasure. [*Draft. With an endorsement, from which it appears that a similar letter was written to the Lord High Admiral.* 1 *p.*]

Aug. 6.
Oxford.

18. Sir Nathaniel Brent to Archbishop Laud. I have sent you the ancient decrees of our college, collected out of divers books by the sub-warden of the last year, out of which I trust you will new mould such as will conduce to the better government of this place for the future. The things wherein we have been most "defectuous" are these:—The Master Fellows have used too much neglect in coming to prayers, to meals in the hall, to capitular meetings, accounts, and the like. They have been negligent ever since I came first to the college in all these kinds. But the greatest corruption of our discipline proceeds from two or three of our masters who have lately frequented the company of bachelors and scholars, making them their bedfellows in their chambers, and in the town in inns and alehouses, an abuse not heard of until of late years. Since I heard of it I have much endeavoured to suppress it, but they still offend secretly. Within these few days a Master and a Bachelor, both fellows of the college, were by the proproctor taken together in a drinking school, on a Sunday morning, in sermon time, and some young women have lately been begotten with child where two of our masters frequently resort and sometimes lodge. These things are very scandalous to our college, and I make bold to mention them that you may by injunctions suppress them for hereafter. As I was writing this letter, Mr. Fisher acquainted me that he had newly found, at the end of an old copy of our statutes, some few ordinances which I purpose to send you next week, though, having perused

DOMESTIC—CHARLES I. 589

1638.   VOL. CCCXCVII.

them, I hold them not to be decrees, neither does it appear by whom or at what time they were made. [1 p.]

Aug. 6.
Boston.

19. Sir Anthony Irby to Nicholas. After receiving directions from the Lords, dated the last of June, but which came not to my hands until the 15th July, I went to the assizes, where, speaking with the chief constables and other collectors, I found that very little more money would be paid except I granted out my warrant to distrain, which immediately after my coming home I did, and am now in the midst of that service. I received a warrant of the 5th inst. to appear on the 12th before the council to give account of my proceedings, but under the circumstances stated my absence may rather be a hindrance than furtherance to the service, I have therefore forborne to come, and have sent you this account of my service. Since my being with you, I have received and paid in 220*l*. [*Seal with arms.* $\frac{3}{4}$ *p.*]

Aug. 6.
Oatlands.

The Commissioners for Saltpetre and Gunpowder to the Mayor of Huntingdon, Sir Sidney Montague, Sir John Cutts and [James] Ravenscroft, Justices of Peace for co. Huntingdon. We understand that David Stevenson, saltpetreman for cos. Cambridge, Huntingdon, &c., has much abused the country in divers kinds, and for some of his misdemeanours has lately been indicted in Suffolk. We pray you to examine and certify to us the particulars of his offences, and what was done thereupon against him, whereupon we shall take order for reformation. [*Copy. See Vol. ccxcii., fol.* 83. $\frac{3}{4}$ *p.*]

Aug. 7.
Oatlands.

20. The King to the Officers of the Customs in the port of London. We have given warrant to our Attorney-General for a proclamation to be published for restraint of the importation of latten wire; and whereas many merchants have contracted beyond seas for quantities of the said wire, for the use of the Company of Pinmakers, we authorize you to permit the master of that company to receive the said latten wire until such quantities be expended as they have bargained for abroad, the said master paying the merchants for the same the accustomed rates of these four or five years past. [*Good impression of the signet.* 1 *p.*]

Aug. 7.

21. Copy of the same.

Aug. 7.
Oatlands.

22. Petition of Sir Oliver Nicholas, carver to the Queen, to the King. Many debts, duties, and sums of money grown due to the crown between the beginning of the reign of King James I. and the end of the seventh year of your Majesty, have been concealed or so neglected as to be hardly to be recovered without extraordinary diligence. Prays a moiety of so many of the said debts amounting to 10,000*l*. as by petitioner's means and charge shall be recovered. [$\frac{1}{2}$ *p.*] *Underwritten,*

> 22. I. *Reference to the Lord Treasurer and Lord Cottington to certify their opinions of petitioner's suit. Oatlands, 7th August 1638.* [$\frac{1}{3}$ *p.*] *Endorsed,*

1638.

Vol. CCCXCVII.

22. II. *Report of the Lord Treasurer and Lord Cottington. Petitioner desires by way of gift 10,000l. in debts. The pretence is for service done in the place of cupbearer to your Majesty's father and now of carver to the Queen. There are already divers grants of old debts, but none so near or late as petitioner desires, and besides, it is our duty to inform your Majesty that the particular of debts is one of the heads lately presented to you, and appointed towards the charge of draining the Great Level.* [½ p.]

Aug. 7.

23. Sec. Windebank to the Mayor of Hull. His Majesty, finding it necessary in these stirring times to provide for the safety of that town, being a place of importance, and of the parts near adjoining, and being desirous to understand the true state of the strength thereof, has commanded Captain Legge, his servant, to repair to you, to put in order such things as shall be fit for his Majesty's service and your safety. You are not only to give credit to him in this employment, but also to follow such directions for erecting magazines for munition and victuals, &c., or any other particulars, as he shall think fit, and generally to give him assistance and furtherance in whatsoever he shall direct for the advancement of this great service. [*Draft. It appears from the endorsement that a similar letter was addressed to the mayor of Newcastle-upon-Tyne.* 1 p.]

Aug. 7.

24. The Council to Capt. William Legge, employed by his Majesty to Hull and and Newcastle. Instructions. You are to repair to Hull, and deliver your letters of credit to the mayor. You are to inform yourself of the strength of that town, and give advertisement thereof hither with speed. You are to cause such places as you find fittest to make magazines for corn and munition to be sequestered and prepared for that service. If you find Sir Jacob Ashley there, you are to repair immediately to Newcastle to put that place into a readiness for defence, and to take order for like magazines and preparations as at Hull, proportionably. You are to give advertisements hither from time to time of your proceeding, and upon all important occasions to desire direction, to which purpose order is given to the postmaster to convey packets directed by you. In general you are to take care for providing all such things as you shall judge necessary for securing these two towns and the parts near adjoining. [1½ p.]

Aug. 7.

25. Examination of John Jonson Vander Woolf, who signs himself Jan Jansen Vander Molos, skipper of the Wolf, of Medemblik, taken before George Bagg, lieutenant governor of the fort at Plymouth, and Abraham Biggs, deputy vice-admiral of Devon. Went from Medemblik about seven months since, bound for Cape de Verd. On his return voyage took aboard hides, elephants' teeth, and bees' wax for the West India Company of Holland. In sight of the Lizard, on the 5th August, he met with two English ships, the Recovery and Desire of London, whereof John Wilde and Thomas Harman were captains, who, having his Majesty's letters of reprisal,

1638.	Vol. CCCXCVII.

surprised the Woolf, and brought her into Plymouth upon the 7th inst. [*Endorsed we read,* "13,000 hides, 3,500 wax, 1,009 elephants' teeth." ¾ *p.*]

Aug. 8.	26. Information, unsigned, but apparently given by Edward May, M.D., and endorsed by Archbishop Laud, of words spoken by Mr. Nappier, called Captain Nappier [Napier], a Scottish gentleman, at the lodging of Mrs. Cromewell [Cromwell], near Sherelane [Shire Lane], in St. Clement's parish. Upon occasion of the infirmity of one or two of Mrs. Cromwell's family Dr. May was at her lodging, also about some business of Mrs. Cromwell. Mr. Swadlin, vicar of Aldgate, came in, and was set to write "somethings" in a closet of the same room, where Edward May and Mrs. Cromwell were, with Mrs. Grace Southcott, when Capt. Napier came in to visit Mrs. Cromwell, on behalf of his wife, who was sick. After some discourses, Dr. May asked Capt. Napier (as the manner is) how all matters went, and said he would be glad to hear that all was well in Scotland. "Yea," said Mr. Napier, "we look that your men shortly shall bring our men into England." "What mean you by that?" said Dr. May, and thereupon the paper proceeds as follows:—

"Marry," answered Mr. Napier, "40,000 English are to bring our men in, who are already above 300,000 able men in arms, or well armed." "I hope no such thing," quoth Dr. May. "Yes," said he, "there is a plot;" and after some speeches, he said there was a plot which he knew. "I know the plot," saith he; "I know part of it." Then Mrs. Cromwell asked him if he did not know a Scottish knight lodging in the White Friars, at one Mr. Dillingham's, a tailor's, who lieth exceeding closely there, and hath left his wife and children now in Scotland, to come hither about these businesses, "I believe," saith she; "and no creature cometh at him except one servant, and his cook, and he hath very rich apparel;" with such like other words, to which Mr. Napier answered that there were many good heads writing and busy about these things, &c., and that himself was not here for nothing. Also, he added, that our king might have helped these things in time, but now he cannot help himself, and that there is more in the matter than he knoweth. "Alas! he is made a baby!" and then he said these words, "*Quos Jupiter perdere vult hos dementat.*" To which, while we stood wondering at his free and bold discourse, he subjoined many matters of his own accord concerning the Bishop of Lincoln, and how he is every day almost with him at the Tower, and how that bishop hath more in him than all the rest of the bishops of England, and that if he had been made Archbishop of Canterbury none of these matters had fallen out. Also he freely told that he had a plot to cut short the clergy's revenues, which he summed up, and what they were in value by the year, and what the Archbishop of Canterbury shall have left him yearly, and how much every other bishop and every minister, and how bishops should follow their church callings, and not State matters, and that all the apostles of Christ had not one 100*l.* amongst them. "There is the Lord Treasurer," said he, "who is Bishop of London, but no man can serve God and Mammon;" with many other speeches to like purpose. "But," said Dr. May, "these are Privy Councillors, and you must leave them means to serve the King and State, and to keep foreign correspondence, as is fit for the good of the kingdom. "What means?" said he, "What do they that way bestow?" &c. Some way the Lord of Canterbury was touched obscurely. "Nay; out with it, man!" said Mrs. Cromwell. "I have all this while expected him to come forth, for he is the man that you do not love." Many other speeches there were against the revenues of the clergy and his Majesty's proceedings, who (as he pleased to say) sets up cobbler's sons, and the sons of poor

1638.

Vol. CCCXCVII.

mechanics, to be bishops and privy councillors. "If the King," saith he, "would choose noblemen's younger sons, they would be sensible of honour; but these things shall be reformed, and the Englishmen and ours will join to have a parliament here as well as in Scotland, and there shall not be left in both realms one man that is a papist, although they go to church. We know every papist and his revenues, and where he dwelleth, and going to church shall not serve their turns; they shall all be sent to New England, and they shall have one year's rents to maintain them there."

It is added at the close of the information:—

"This was written in the presence of Mrs. Cromwell and Mrs. Southcott and read twice over unto them, while things were recent; and they said they were true, and moderately set down, as they desired for memory sake. Mr. Swadlin, after the captain's departure, bearing all where he sat, upon the words of Dr. May, came forth; viz., "Many a man hath been laid upon an hurdle for less matters than this, and for concealment." "Yea, that he hath," quoth Mr. Swadlin; "this man speaketh treason confidently." Particulars were repeated, and Mr. Swadlin acknowledged them to be so, touching the principal matters here set down, who remembreth, as I suppose, other things than what are here written."

[*Endorsed by Archbishop Laud as* "Concerning the plot between English and Scottish in this business." 2⅓ *p.*]

Aug. 8. 27. Statement of 37 points of sedition or treason gathered from the speeches of Capt. Napier, above mentioned, with marginal notes of the several witnesses who had deposed to them. In most instances the names of the confirming witnesses are stated thus: "Dr. May," "All agree," or, "Dr. May and the two gentlewomen," but two instances occur in which "Mr. Cromwell" is vouched as an authority. The first instance relates to the suggested appropriation of the lands of the recusants. Mrs. Cromwell asked Napier who should have the surplus after a suggested small payment to the recusant himself; should the King have it? and that Napier answered "No." The margin states, "All agree. Mr. Cromwell saith he said 'No; the Scottishmen.'" The second instance alludes to a statement that the lords of Scotland produced to the Marquess of Hamilton an old law which gave to some lords power to call a parliament, in case the King were a child, or out of the kingdom, or not well advised, or if he went to infringe their liberties or laws. "Dr. May and Mr. Cromwell" are vouched as the authorities for this. [1½ *p.*]

Aug. 8. 28. Statement by Thomas Swadlin, above mentioned, of the words uttered by Capt. Napier. It differs from the preceding in words, but agrees in spirit and generally in meaning. [*Underwritten, a memorandum that,* "Mrs. Cromewell lies at one Mr. Stewart's house in Drury Lane, over against;" *and below that* "Mrs. Southcott." ⅔ *p.*]

Aug. 9.
Gray's Inn. 29. Attorney-General Bankes to Sec. Windebank. I send you the effect of a letter which is to be written for the stay of those men who are to be carried over into Denmark about the making of alum. I think it will be requisite to send a messenger with a warrant for the apprehension of Charles Gray and Frodsham. Frodsham has undertaken to tell the time and place when the warrant

1638.   VOL. CCCXCVII.

shall be executed. This Frodsham acquaints me that the Chancellor's son of Denmark will labour to get men skilful in the alum works from the Pope's alum works at Civita Vecchia, or from Lucas, in Germany, if he fail here, and it were well it were prevented by some letters from the Pope's agent here, and some other letters into Germany. [⅔ p.]

Aug. 9.
Sudbury.
30. [Justices of Peace for Suffolk [unsigned] to the Council.] In obedience to your letters of the 20th June last, we have called such persons as were complained of by John Little, the licensed brewer for Sudbury. They do not deny but that they have offended concerning brewing, but promise hereafter to forbear, refusing to give bond for their conformity, but submitting themselves to your Lordships' mercy, and hoping that paying the same rent as the brewer does they may go on as formerly, which is much desired by the poor people and others of that town and the neighbours adjoining. [Copy. ⅔ p.]

[Aug. 9.]
31. Petition of Inhabitants of Sudbury, Suffolk, to the Council. Petitioners, being licensed inn-keepers and alehouse-keepers, have by brewing beer and ale been enabled to live well and relieve others, and to pay scot and lot, but by being restrained they can have no beer but at 15s. the barrel, no yeast to make their bread but at 3d. the quart, whereas it cost them nothing before, and no grains for swine but at 5d. the bushel; moreover their stock of brewing vessels are all lost to them. Pray the Lords to consider their case. They will willingly give his Majesty a yearly rent for licence to brew. [⅔ p.]

[Aug. 9.]
32. List of the inn-holders and alehouse-keepers in Sudbury, with the yearly rent offered to be paid by each for license to brew. [½ p.]

Aug. 9.
33. Order of the Lord Treasurer and Lord Cottington for payment to Thomas Pott of 9l. 2s. 6d. upon his allowance of 2s. per diem for keeping slughounds for the quarter to Midsummer, 1638. [1 p.]

Aug. 10.
34. Sec. Windebank to James Marquess of Hamilton. I find there has been a miscarriage in a business, which, because it refers to your present negotiation, and reflects upon myself, I crave to give you an account of it, and beg your pardon if I have done amiss, seeing my intentions were far from giving occasion of offence either personal or national. Having too much cause to suspect that some dangerous persons were resorting towards Scotland, I thought it might conduce to his Majesty's service to intercept or interrupt that dangerous intelligence which is too notoriously held between the ill-affected of both nations. To this purpose I gave the postmaster commission to observe such as should pass towards those parts, and to make stay of them, if he found them suspicious, or without warrant from you, the Lord Treasurer of Scotland, the Earl of Stirling, or some of the chief of the Council of either nation. Instead whereof it seems that he made stay of all persons and

VOL. CCCXCVII.

1638.

letters whatsoever, and sent me two great packets of letters which he had intercepted, which I instantly sent back, with charge to dispatch away those that were for Scotland, and to cause those that came from thence to be conveyed to the parties to whom they were addressed, and I superseded his commission. This is the true ground of this business. I have excused it to Colonel Howme, and he professes himself satisfied, and so I beseech you to be. I should hold it a great honour to sacrifice my life for composing these troubles. [*Draft.* 3¼ *pp.*]

Aug. 10.
Burderop.

35. Sir William Calley to Richard Harvey. I thank you for the news in your letter, and for putting me in mind of my promise to write your master a letter, which I thought I had done, but it is the weakness of old age to dote and be forgetful. I have written. [¼ *p.*]

Aug. 10.

36. See "Returns made by Justices of the Peace."

Aug. 11.

37. Copy of Nine Propositions or Articles sent on the 9th inst. by the [Earl of Newport to Sir John Heydon], with answers to the same, all in the handwriting of Sir John. The questions relate principally to the state of the ordnance stores; as, for example, how many pieces of ordnance might be provided to march with an army within a month; provision being required for 16,000 foot, whereof 10,000 were to be musqueteers and 6,000 pikes, what particular stores for such a force were defective, and what the cost of the supply; 12 pieces of ordnance completely mounted and furnished to be shipped next week with all necessary provisions; report the number of pickaxes, shovels, and spades in store; draw a list of all officers requisite to march with a train of artillery with their entertainments; estimate the charge of providing 50 tons of match and 50 tons of lead in shot; consider what shipping will be required to transport the 12 pieces of ordnance with 100 rounds of shot, and to transport 50 tons of match and 50 tons of lead in shot; state in what readiness the train of artillery is, for fitting whereof " I have given direction so long since." Sir John's answers admit the inability of the officers of ordnance to execute many of these requirements, the surveyor being sick, the clerk restrained of his liberty, and one of his clerks absent, the clerk of the deliveries out of town, and his clerk absent, the master gunner dead, the yeoman of the ordnance never present, nor any of the gunners attendant, and the stores for ordnance empty. He sends various lists required. [= 2 *pp.*]

Aug. 11.
London.

38. Sir James Bagg to Sec. Windebank. I have been visited with a fit of the stone, which has confined me to my bed since Monday. Enclosed is the particular I shewed his Majesty, and my Lord of Arundel's remembrance (*see 3rd August inst., No.* 6). His Majesty told me it should go on, and that he would give warrants by you. I am not so well as to prepare them, but will not be wanting in this or any other service. [⅔ *p.*]

1638.
Aug. 11.
Petworth.

Vol. CCCXCVII.

39. Algernon Earl of Northumberland to [Sir John Pennington]. By letter from Sec. Coke I understand of his Majesty's being advertised that divers Scots go from town to town in the Low Countries, and buy up all the pikes, muskets, and others arms they can get, transporting them in Holland bottoms by bills of lading for Hamburgh and other places that way, and being at sea find means to convey them to Scotland. For prevention of that design, upon receipt hereof you are to give order to two good ships, whereof the Entrance to be one, to repair to the mouth of the Maas, and there to search all ships of Holland or the Low Countries or Scotland bound for the northward that may be suspected to carry arms, which if they find they shall seize the ships, and all such Scotchmen as shall be found therein, and cause them to be brought to some safe port of his Majesty's, there to expect his further pleasure. His Majesty has given order to acquaint the States' ambassador herewith, that his masters may take no umbrage, they also professing that they are willing such transportation of arms for Scotland should be hindered by themselves or by us. P.S.—I pray be very careful in keeping this business secret. [¾ p.]

Aug. 11.

40. Examinination of Henry Spier of Reading, clothier, taken at Chichester, before John Pannett, mayor, and Christopher Lewkenor, recorder. Having discourse with William Sanford of that city, innholder, concerning the disorders in Scotland, and the latter saying that the Scots were rogues, rebels, and traitors, examinant said that he hoped the Scots would ere long prove good subjects, also that he said that the wind sometimes blew in the east and sometimes in the west, and that we should have the cart set on his right wheels, and then we should have Sanford calm enough. Further he said that he had heard that there was difference between the King and the merchants. [⅔ p.]

Aug. 11.

41. Account of Sir William Russell of ship-money for 1637. Total paid, 119,038l. 15s. 1d.; remaining, 77,375l. 12s. 7d. [1 p.]

Aug. 11.

42. Account of ship-money for 1637, levied and remaining in the hands of the sheriffs. Total, 3,540l., which makes the sum collected 122,578l., which is 21,464l. less than was paid on the 10th August 1637. [1 p.]

Aug. 13.

43. Petition of Philip Thomas, messenger appointed to attend the Commissioners for Charitable Uses, to the King. Upon inquiry by virtue of your Majesty's commission upon the statute of 43rd Eliz., to discover what goods and money, which hitherto have been given to charitable uses, have been concealed, divers sums of money have been discovered, which may be taken to be within the equity and meaning of the statute. Howsoever, the commissioners dare not inquire further of the same until they be authorized by your Majesty. Petitioner prays a new commission, with power to the commissioners to enquire of all donations for charitable uses, by which means much money will be raised for the poor and other

Vol. CCCXCVII.

1638.

pious uses, and a great revenue to his Majesty, if, for treasurer to receive the same, the King will appoint Sir John Heydon. Petitioner, for his pains and charges, which are great, desires that the commissioners may have power to reward him according to his merit. [1 p.] *Annexed*,

43. I. *Form of the new commission desired by the above petitioner, with appended list of 128 persons who are suggested for commissioners.* [= 2 pp.]

43. II. *Minute of the King's pleasure, signified by Sir Edward Powell, that a new commission should issue forth, with the enlargements desired, and the Attorney or Solicitor General is to prepare the same accordingly. Windsor, 17th August 1638.* [¼ p.]

Aug. 13.
Windsor Castle.

44. Sec. Coke to Sir John Pennington. I send you a packet from the Lord Admiral, wherein you will receive a letter, which I by his Majesty's command wrote unto him, to send ships to lie before the Maas, and to visit vessels suspected to carry arms for Scotland ; but when I had acquainted the States' Ambassador with this resolution, he presented by letter the great apprehension the people of that country would take if men-of-war should lie before their rivers, or visit ships upon their coasts ; whereupon his Majesty, being not willing at this time to give them just offence, who undertake themselves to stop all transportation of arms that way, is now pleased to change that direction, and requires you to employ such ships as the Lord Admiral has appointed, not to lie upon the mouth of the Maas or otherwise upon their rivers or ports, but only to ply to and again at sea and towards Scotland, and there to visit such ships as may justly be suspected to carry arms thither. [1 p.]

Aug. 13.

45. Roger Widdrington to Sec. Windebank. I must suppose you know the whole proceedings of the lords and others sworn to the Covenant in our neighbouring kingdom, and because the matter is of so great importance, and as it appears to us here of so doubtful event, and that it seems not by the carriage thereof hitherto to sort to so quiet and peaceable conclusion as some that dwell more remote, and are not so well acquainted with the humours of that people and manage of that business, may peradventure conceive, my request is, to be held fit to be ranked amongst the number of his Majesty's most loyal subjects, in which point I will not yield to any subject his Majesty has in any of his kingdoms, against whomsoever, domestic or foreign, prince, potentate, or subject, veiled under whatsoever pretext, either of commonwealth or conscience, the ordinary vizards under which rebellions go for the most part masked. I am in years, but not so decrepid that I will seek after a writ of ease to excuse me in his Majesty's service. My abilities are weak, yet they shall not be found a mere nothing in the execution of his Majesty's commands, and such as they are, always shall be faithfully, for the King. I dare not adventure to advise, yet I crave pardon if to you I adventure to wish that these parts of our country and late borders

1638.

VOL. CCCXCVII.

may be looked into, lest a canker neglected may exulcerate and enlarge itself too far, where there is not a timely application of some remedy. P.S.—Believe it, these Lords of the Covenant, for so they are called in Scotland, must, if they be not, as they hope, yielded unto, yield ; and be confident that their power is not by much so great as it is noised, and I wish with all my heart that their obstinacy were not greater than their power, and then they would quickly give over contest against that power they are not able to withstand. There is loyalty, of strength enough, even yet, in that kingdom, if it be rightly used. [*Seal with arms.* 1 *p.*]

Aug. 13.
The White Swan in Cheapside, near Paul's Gate.

46. John Buxton, Sheriff of Norfolk, to Nicholas. I have inclosed a certificate of such chief constables as are most refractory. I conceive the sending for them up by a pursuivant will much advance the service, and put spurs to the rest, who are not so forward as they ought to be. I shall continue, upon the encouragement I have received, to do my uttermost; yet, for that it is a work of time as well as of difficulty, I desire that respite of a further sending for up if moneys do not come in so fast as is expected. I pray you, for the Earl Marshal's better satisfaction, and that he may not repent of his commendation of me at the Board, to let him know what moneys are paid in from henceforward. P.S.—I desire that the messenger sent to fetch up the chief constables would go to Norwich, to my undersheriff, Mr. Beifeild, who will direct him to every of them. [1 *p.*] *Encloses,*

> 46. I. *Certificate that Roger Reignolds and Matthew Stephenson, constables of Blofield hundred, William Moundeford and Jonathan Foster, the like of Walsham hundred, and William Meek, chief constable of Clavering hundred, are in arrear the whole amounts assessed upon their hundreds, and refuse to distrain.* [*Seal with arms.* 1 *p.*]

Aug. 13.
Kedleston.

47. Sir John Curzon, Sheriff of co. Derby, to the same. I have done to the utmost of my power to observe the commands of the Council for the raising the remainder of the ship-moneys, and have got what I could, some by distraining and some by taking away their goods and selling them, and thus have gathered above half that is behind, and have returned it to be paid in the beginning of Michaelmas term, and had no forcible resistance to rescue their goods; but they will not take the surplusage of the moneys again that their goods were sold for, but threaten us hard, which when they begin to do anything I will give an acccount thereof. For the rest of the moneys, if I can get it no other ways, I shall take the course that I have done, that it may be inned at London in the beginning of this term. For the borough towns, I have done my duty frequently to call upon them, and hope it will be ready. [*Seal with arms.* 1 *p.*]

Aug. 13.

48. Christopher Gardyner to his brother, Sir John Heydon. Letter upon astrological matters, principally comments upon statements by De Nuisement respecting the universal spirit, and the manner in which it takes a body. P.S.—Here will be a muster

1638.

very shortly, and my arms are at fault. Let some of your servants direct the bearer to an armourer, to scour and repair them. [*Seal with arms.* 2 *pp.*]

Aug. 13. 49. Certificate [by William Ryley] that Sir John Sedley died this day at Mount Mascall, in North Cray, Kent. He married Elizabeth, sole daughter and heir of Sir John Savile, provost of Eton and warden of Merton College, second son of Henry Savile, of Bradley, co. York, by whom he left surviving, 1, Henry, aged 16; 2, William, aged 8; 3, Elizabeth, aged 17. He lies interred in a family vault on the south side of South Fleet church. [*Draft.* 1 *p.*]

Aug. 13. 50. Certificate of John Carill, Clerk of the Assizes for Cumberland, that at the said assizes held this day before Sir George Vernon and Sir Robert Berkeley, John Pattison, of Hutton John in Cumberland, and Joseph Huddleston and Andrew Huddleston, his sureties, entered into recognizances in certain specified sums for the appearance of the said John Pattison before the Council on the morrow of St. Martin next, to answer to matters objected against him concerning damage done to his Majesty's tenants of Dacre. [¾ *p.*]

Aug. 15.
Whitehall.
51. The Council to Sec. Coke. Upon complaint exhibited by a memorial from the ambassador of Denmark, we took into consideration whether his Majesty should not afford the same favour to the subjects of Denmark as is promised to those of the States of the United Provinces by the 5th article of answer to their ambassadors of the 22nd of February last, the copy whereof we send inclosed, to which in our opinions we inclined; and we pray you to move his Majesty to nominate commissioners according to the said article, and to give directions for such a commission to be issued for the subjects of Denmark and the Low Countries. [*Endorsed is Sec. Coke's note of proposed commissioners.* 1 *p.*]

Aug. 15.
The St. Andrew in the Downs.
52. Sir John Pennington to Sec. Windebank. According to his Majesty's command, signified by you of the 13th, I have sent away the Providence, with Mr. Cole, the messenger, to the Brill. The Sovereign set sail this morning, to ply it up for the Isle of Wight, with the Garland to accompany her. I hope she will prove a brave, stout, serviceable ship. They report that she works very well, and steers exceeding yarely, and I do not see but that she carries her lower tier well for a ship of three tier and a half. [*Seal with arms.* 1 *p.*]

[Aug. 15.] 53. Sir Anthony Weldon to the same. Sir John Sedley is dead, and has, amongst other honourable personages, desired you to be an overseer of his will, and a friend to his disconsolate widow and children, and has left you a legacy of 100*l.* I am entreated by his lady, Sir Edward Hales, and Mr. Crofts, executors with myself, to pray you that if any shall desire anything of his Majesty prejudicial to the heir, and against the orders of the Court of Wards, you will

1638.　　　　　　　　Vol. CCCXCVII.

protect him. I believe none will go any unordinary way, for there is 23,000*l*. to be paid out of the estate in legacies, and two parts of three to pay such legacies and portions. [1 *p*.]

Aug. 15.　54. Sir James Douglas to Sec. Windebank. The insolence of our pretended "zealatours" is such, by and above public treason, they spare not to intercept letters at home. If there be any such thing betwixt this and London by such as have no authority I know not, expecting the best until I have better information. I sent this other inclosed under your protection, not doubting but you can govern the "rouning" as to be careful of your servants letters from all [that] are yours. I have written to Mr. Wilson, to participate all I wrote to you. [1 *p*.]

Aug. 15.　55. Statement in the handwriting of Sir John Heydon of the several officers whose duty it was to see to the provision of the various articles required by an army for fortification, intrenchment, or battery. A duplicate hereof was delivered to the Earl of Newport on the 16th inst., according to his own desire. [1⅔ *p*.]

Aug. 16.
Canonbury.　56. Lord Keeper Coventry to [Sir Thomas Roe]. I received yours of the 21st June, and heard of another of later date by Sir John Finett, but have not received it. I was troubled at your relation in the first, and the more because it lies not in me to contribute anything of worth to ease you in so perplexed an affair, declining so much from those hopes which I perceive you had when I saw you last. But howsoever it happen, I doubt not but your careful endeavours will be rightly understood here, where I have not heard of the least misconceit, and if I had I should not have failed, nor will if I hear hereafter, to serve you with the best offices I may. The businesses you have in hand, as you know, are governed here by his Majesty and his foreign committee, the following whose directions must be your safety, as your timely advertisements must be a prime light to them. I shall heartily pray that things may succeed according to your wishes, which I know to be most sincere towards his Majesty, his sister, and nephews, whose sufferings cannot but trouble them that truly affect the honour and content of the King. If your employment be drawn on into length, as I see you fear, God send you good health to undergo it to our master's advantage. [1 *p*.]

Aug. $\frac{16}{26}$.
Paris.　57. Thomas Lockey, Chaplain to Lord Scudamore, to Archbishop Laud. Having been recommended by your Grace to the service of the Lord Ambassador [Scudamore], in which I have enjoyed all the contentment which my condition could require, and after having finished a competent time therein, intending to take a further voyage into Italy, I desire to return my thanks, thinking it concerned me to look backward before I set forward. [*Seal with arms.* 1 *p*.]

Aug. 16.
Harrogate, near the Spa.　58. James Lord Livingstone of Almond to his cousin, Thomas Livingstone, tailor, over against the New Exchange in the Strand. The extreme rain has so spoiled the waters that it hastens my return to

1638.

Vol. CCCXCVII.

Scotland to-morrow, intending to go to Top[c]liffe. I have left order with Mr. Thomson at Wetherby to be careful of the plate if it come thither. You must enquire after the carriers to whom you delivered it, and if they come not shortly into Scotland let me hear from you, and send the plate with your nephew, Alexander, if he come by sea. Show Dr. Myrene [Mayerne] that I have remained a fortnight at these waters, with little good. I have heard no word out of Scotland since the Marquess's [Hamilton's] arrival. [1 p.]

Aug. 16.
Kensington.

Appointment by Henry Earl of Holland, Chief Justice and Justice in Eyre of Forests on this side Trent, of Gabriel Ludlow as his deputy for choosing foresters, regarders, and other officers of the Forest of Selwood *alias* Zelwood, in the swainmote of that forest. [*Copy. See Vol. ccclxxxiv., p. 25.* ¾ *p.*]

Aug. 17.
Windsor Castle.

59. Sec. Coke to Sir John Pennington. His Majesty having given leave to his resident at Brussels, Mr. Balthazar Gerbier, to come to England for accommodation of his affairs, you are to send one of your ships to Dunkirk road, there to receive him aboard, and bring him to Dover or other fit port. He desires to have 8 or 10 days notice after sending the order for his passage, which I send herewith. [⅔ *p.*]

Aug. 17.

60. Affidavit of John de Marez, Merchant of the Golden Wolf of Medemblik, John Johnson, master of the said ship, and John Jacobson Coy, steersman of the same. They describe the lading of the ship, which consisted principally of hides, wax, ivory, and "glass coral." Off the Lizard they came up with two great ships, and one of them sent a chaloupe to the Wolf, to enquire if they had seen any Turkish pirates. Being answered that they had not, they were told that the master and steersman must come aboard the said ships, with their passport and sea-briefs. They did so, and whilst they were on board the ship of Capt. Harman, the ship of Capt. Wilde boarded the Wolf, beating and ill-using the ship's company, and robbing and rifling the ship. The ship was carried into Plymouth Sound on the $\frac{6}{16}$ August, and the company landed at Plymouth the next day following. [*Copy.* 1⅓ *p.*]

Aug. 17.
Paris.

61. P. C. [?] Lundie to —— Waterhouse. My Waterhouse, my second self, this bearer your servant, or not my son, will give you account of me since my being here. I know my best friend too well to entreat his assistance in what concerns the bearer, and I wish it may prove to the son as to the father, as I think it will do. I never thought I could have envied my son his happiness, but now I do, that he may enjoy my Waterhouse's company. [1 *p.*]

Aug. 18.

62. [Henry Earl] of Holland to Lady Slingsby. Though you will no doubt receive much comfort by the sight and return of your daughter, who does much long to receive your blessing, yet have we a loss in it, for her goodness and behaviour have been visibly expressed to all the world. We hope you will not banish us by her

1638. Vol. CCCXCVII.

stay with you too long from her company that is much esteemed by us. [1½ p.]

Aug. 18. 63. Account of Sir William Russell of ship-money for 1637. Total received, 120,478l. 15s. 1d.; remaining, 75,935l. 12s. 7d. [= 2 pp.]

Aug. 18. 64. Account of ship-money for 1637, levied and remaining in the hands of the sheriffs. Total, 5,514l., which makes the total collected 29,378l. less than on 25th August 1637. [1 p.]

Aug. 18. 65. See "Returns made by Justices of Peace."

Aug. 19. 66. The King to Montjoy, Earl of Newport, Master of the Ordnance. According to an ensuing list, you are to cause to be removed, and brought into the magazine at the Tower, the pieces of brass and iron ordnance in the said list contained. Such as you find serviceable you are to employ upon occasion, and the residue to reduce into such other natures as you shall conceive best. In the list subjoined are mentioned 16 pieces from Landguard Fort, 7 from Rye, 8 from Camber Castle, 9 from Harwich. [1 p.]

[Aug. 19.] 67. Note of the weight of the brass ordnance to be recast; 11 tons 6 cwts. 2 qrs. 25 lbs. [1 p.]

Aug. 20. Warrant to pay 300l. to Anthony Vanden Hennell, with account, for his charges in his Majesty's service in the Low Countries. [*Docquet.*]

Aug. 20. Safe conduct for the said Anthony Vanden Hennell. [*Docquet.*]

Aug. 20. Merton College. 68. Dr. Peter Turner to Archbishop Laud. It may be that Mr. Warden has acquainted your Grace with his late election of officers, as he did with the former election of prosecutors, having gone cross to your pleasure in both. In the election of officers no eye was had to the Founder's statute (as you required), but only to the late practice. It is true Mr. Fisher is not chosen sub-warden again, but his other self is put in his room. The writer complains that the new sub-warden by reason of money transactions is dependent upon Mr. Fisher, is ignorant and incapable in the college accounts, and has an incompatible living. Complains also of Mr. French, who is made superintendent, as a man very illiterate and loose in his conversation, besides that he enjoys, with his fellowship, the Registrar's office, whereupon he might have made way for such as have no means besides their fellowships. Mr. Fisher has entered the act commanded by the Archbishop lamely, and different in words, defective in circumstance and partly in matter. Prays that before the hearing they may have liberty to view the answers of the warden and others, with power to send for the register and account books to their chambers, and that these books may be brought up to the hearing. The Dean of Salisbury has termed the depositions against the warden and sub-warden studied cavils grounded upon malice. If he is to be present at the hearing, requests

1638.

Vol. CCCXCVII.

that the other commissioners may also be called thither, who perchance have examined the complaints with more indifferency. [1⅓ p.]

Aug. 20. 69. See "Returns made by Justices of Peace."

Aug. 21.
Banwell.
70. Certificate of Bishop Pierce of Bath and Wells. The Council by order of 3rd April 1636 referred the examination of differences between Sir Edward Powell and Anthony Earbury, clerk, vicar of Weston, Somerset, to me. I called Mr. Earbury and Robert Powell, solicitor to Sir Edward, and also Thomas Crompton, interested in the same, and after full hearing I found that the petty tithes of the grange of Weston, and of three tenements, lately fallen into the hands of the lord of the manor, were due to the vicar, and thereupon I ordered that the arrearages should be valued by John Culpepper and John Bray, of Weston, and should be paid to Mr. Earbury. Forasmuch as Culpepper and Bray cannot or will not agree about the yearly value of the said tithes, I therefore value the tithes of the said grange at 8*l*. per annum, and the tithes of the three tenements at 50*s*. per annum, for the time past, and I order that the vicar shall be paid the arrears accordingly. [2¼ *pp*.]

Aug. 22.
Canbury.
71. The King to Edward Earl of Dorset, Lord Chamberlain to the Queen, Robert Earl of Ancram, Gentleman of the Bedchamber, William Earl of Stirling, Secretary of State for Scotland, George Lord Goring, Master of the Horse to the Queen, Sir Patrick Acheson, Sir David Cunningham, Sir Henry Gibb, Sir John Michell, Master in Chancery, Sir Henry Spiller, Francis Walsted, Henry Ewer, Clement Spelman, Nathaniel Snape, Francis Dynne, Jasper Manwood, William Smyth, John Woodford, Edward Smyth, William Lockton, Thomas Holford, Humphrey Fulwood, Edward Bardolph, Francis Hanford, William Ewer, John Pulford, Robert Calvert, Henry Pilkington, Thomas Paramore, John Marshall, Robert Pawlett, Richard Kitchin, John Sturton, Jonas Bayley, Ezechiel Turvill, Oliver Lloyd, Arthur Hargell, William Reade, Thomas Read, Richard Taylor, and John Griffith. Commission to inquire of cottages in England, and inmates placed therein, within three years, contrary to the Statute of 31st Elizabeth, by which it was forbidden to any person to erect any cottage for habitation, or to convert any building to be used as a cottage for habitation, unless the said person assign four acres of ground to each tenement to be occupied therewith, upon pain for every offence to forfeit 10*l*., with 40*s*. per month for continuing the same, nor to suffer more than one family to occupy one cottage, upon fine of 10*s*. to the lord of the leet for every month, except cottages erected in cities and market towns, or for workmen in mineral works and quarries. Power is given to the commissioners under this commission to examine constables and others upon oath, and to take compositions, and William Earl Morton is appointed receiver. [*Two skins of parchment.*]

Aug. 22.
Canbury.
72. The same to the same. Commission to inquire of the breach of the laws against the taking of excessive usury, as also against

1638.

VOL. CCCXCVII.

scriveners, brokers, "friperers," and others, for taking greater sums of money for the loan and forbearance of money lent upon bonds and other securities than permitted by law, and against scriveners and others who take greater rewards than are allowed for procuring moneys to be lent, and for making bills and bonds. With power to take compositions to be paid to William Earl Morton, who is appointed receiver. [*Two skins of parchment.*]

Aug. 22. 73. Edward Earl of Dorset to "the Deputy," according to the endorsement. I have received a letter from the Council, which I have inclosed to you, and by which you will understand what is there commanded. [¾ *p.*]

Aug. 23. Thorpe. 74. Henry Herbert to Nicholas at Winterbourne Earls near Salisbury. I made bold to come to your house at Thorpe, you not being at London, from Mr. Herbert, sheriff of Monmouthshire, and not finding you at home acquaint you how the case stands with him. I being his son, and of the Middle Temple, he employed me, and I paid in with the first 1,400*l.*, and this week 70*l.* 10*s.* 3*d.*, which might have been paid before, but we still stayed for the money expected from the mayor of Newport. My father requests you would certify the Lords that he has gathered all that belongs to him, the rest lies upon the mayor, who puts off my father with delays. [*Seal with arms.* 1 *p.*]

Aug. 24. Woodstock. 75. Sec. Coke to Sec. Windebank. The packets to the Lord Chamberlain and to Mr. Comptroller have been delivered. You give notice of Mr. More's death, and that Mr. Norgate is next reversioner in the clerkship of the signet, wherewith I have acquainted his Majesty, who is pleased to accept him, and that he be sworn and admitted according to custom, which I leave to be performed by yourself. [*Endorsed is a memorandum of Sec. Windebank, that he administered to Mr. Norgate the oath of clerk of the signet at his house at Westminster on the 26th, Sir Abraham Williams being present.* ½ *p.*]

Aug. 24. Dover Castle. 76. Sir John Manwood to Sir John Pennington. This day came two gentlemen to me, who came from Holland last night. They report that they saw 3,000 bills, blades, and daggers, and heads for pikes, and they think much powder in barrels, all which were embarked at Amsterdam for Rotterdam, where were to be added 3,000 muskets and many firelocks, all which arms were to be sent presently for Scotland. They talk broad of a difference between England and Scotland. These particulars I have sent to the Court, although I am confident his Majesty has advertisement of them, yet because they concern the King so nigh I thought it my duty to give information of them, as likewise to yourself. [*Seals with arms.* 1 *p.*]

Aug. 25. Woodstock. 77. Philip Earl of Pembroke and Montgomery to the same. Upon my information to his Majesty of injuries our Association had suffered by the Dunkirkers taking again our buss Salisbury,

Vol. CCCXCVII.

1638.

his Majesty gave order for letters of reprisal to be granted by the Lord Admiral, which I understood were directed to you. Three weeks being passed, the winter season drawing on, and nothing done, invites me to call upon you again to expedite that affair, which if it has had no motion by reason of some miscarriage I have again prevailed with the Earl of Northumberland to second his former [see 29th July last, No. 97], which you will receive with these, the speeding whereof I leave to your wonted care. I shall only add, that if our reparation may be made by a merchant, not by a man-of-war, the latter would be more troublesome and less advantageous than the former. You cannot think I write this out of diffidence, or to incite you, but of extreme care that so many of the Association having adventured for my sake, as far as in me lies not any one shall suffer through my default. [Seal with arms. 1 p.]

Aug. 25. 78. Account of Sir William Russell of ship-money for 1637. Total received, 123,010l. 12s. 10d.; unpaid, 73,403l. 14s. 10d. [= 2 pp.]

Aug. 26. Woodstock. 79. Sec. Coke to [Sec. Windebank]. I have received letters from you, with advertisement from Sir John Manwood and from the officers of Melcombe Regis and Weymouth. Concerning the former, directions have been given to Sir John Pennington, and notice received from him that he has disposed ships to give interruption to that passage. For the latter I send a letter to Sir John Pennington to be forwarded by post. One thing more I add by his Majesty's commandment, concerning Sir Robert Carr, at the Earl of Danby's motion, that you are to proceed in that business as his Majesty has already directed you, and not do more therein till you know his further pleasure. [¾ p.]

Aug. 26. 80. Certificate of William Ryley, Bluemantle, that Sir James Bagg, of Saltram, Devon, Governor of Plymouth, died this day at his house in Queen Street, St. Giles's-in-the-Fields, and was buried in St. Martin's-in-the-Fields. He married Grace, daughter of [John] Fortescue, of Were, Devon, by whom he had issue George, his only son and heir, and three daughters: 1, Gertrude, married to Sir Nicholas Slanning, of Hele, Devon, 2, Amy, married to Henry Cary, son of —— Cary, of Cockington, Devon; and 3, Anne, unmarried. [Draft. 1 p.]

Aug. 27. West Ilsley. 81. Bishop Goodman of Gloucester to Sec. Windebank. It was long before the Archbishop acquainted me that I should address myself to you for my answer. Failing to see you at Windsor, it was conceived that in regard of the infection at Westminster, and his Majesty's coming to Woodstock, you would be at your own country house, where I went to attend you, but was disappointed. I entreat you to name your own time and place where I might wait upon you, only wishing that it might be at your best leisure, and in the most private manner, though it be the longer deferred. [Seal with crest. 1 p.]

1638.
Aug. 27.
Merton College.

82. Dr. Peter Turner to Archbishop Laud. Unless you had given me commission when I was last at Lambeth to write to you upon any business concerning our visitation I should not have presumed to interrupt your more weighty affairs. It seems strange to you that by the custom of the college every junior Fellow may command the registers and books of accounts to his chambers. I desire you to consider whether there be any more incongruity in this than that one of the juniors should be chosen sub-warden, as the present warden was, being but regent master. Were it not then a greater incongruity for the senior Fellows to send to a puisne, and to be in danger of a repulse from him? The disdain whereof has made me forbear to send for any of these books, by means whereof many foul practices probably lie concealed. I make no question but Mr. Warden will peremptorily resolve you that there has been no such custom, though he is such a stranger to our college affairs that he knows no more of our customs than he does of St. John's. Before Fisher was sub-warden I never knew it denied to any man. The books which may be of use at the hearing are two college registers, the old and the new, the dean's book, the register of the treasury, the court roll book, the two last bursar's books, two bundles of the present and former warden's accounts. Besides these, if you require that all bonds made to the college may be brought up, a notable piece of knavery may be discovered. [1 p.]

Aug. 28.
Hertford.

83. Edward Laurence, Mayor of Hertford, to Nicholas. I was commanded by the Lords to appear before them 2nd September, or to pay in 55l. assessed upon Hertford. I have paid 40l. to Sir William Russell, being the sum charged within 44s. 2d., as may appear by note stated to be inclosed. The 44s. 2d. is upon men dead and much decayed since the assessment, but I will endeavour to get up as much as I can. The 12l. odd is assessed upon men without the borough, though members of the same, which we have power to assess and demand, but not to distrain; so I return them in charge to the sheriff of the county. I would attend, but am uncertain of the place where the Lords sit, and am not well able to travel. [⅔ p.]

Aug. 28.

84. Opinion of Geoffrey Palmer as to the validity of an assignment of a bond for debt by letter of attorney. If made to a stranger for money it is against law; if to a surety who pays the money for his relief against the principals, it is lawful. [*Copy.* 1 p.]

Aug. 29.
Drury Lane.

85. Sec. Windebank to Sir John Pennington. I received the inclosed letter from Sec. Coke, who desired me to dispatch it away to you. It is to give notice that pirates of Algiers are come lately upon the English coasts, and have pillaged many of his Majesty's subjects, as appears by certificates from Weymouth, Melcombe Regis, and Poole. I doubt not Mr. Secretary has given you order what course to take. I likewise gave Mr. Secretary advertisement of provision of arms made in Holland to be transported into Scotland, which he tells me you have order to intercept. I acquainted his

Vol. CCCXCVII.

1638.

Majesty with the dispatch you gave to Cole, the messenger sent into Holland, and with the advertisement you gave me of the good condition of the great ship, both which were very welcome and pleasing to his Majesty. Excuse me for making use of another hand by reason of indisposition. [1½ p.]

Aug. 29.
London.

86. Order made at the gaol delivery for Newgate held at the Justice Hall in the Old Bailey, London, before Sir Richard Fenn, Edward Earl of Dorset, Sir George Croke, Sir Francis Crawley, Sir Ralph Whitfield, Sir James Cambell, Sir George Whitmore, Sir Nicholas Rainton, Charles Jones, and others, on the trial of Elizabeth Addington, wife of Thomas Addington, for her felonious marrying with Richard Farnham, her former husband being alive. It appeared to this court that she was merely seduced by Farnham's fanatical persuasions that her husband was dead; and taking notice that Farnham is a prisoner in Bethlehem by order of Council, and not so distracted but that he is well able to work, it is the opinion of this Court that he should be carried from Bethlehem to Bridewell, there to be punished for his incontinency, and to be kept at hard labour, and not live idly upon that which may serve for the necessary relief of distracted impotent persons. [1 p.]

Aug. 30.
Woodstock.

87. The King to Sir Edward Powell, Master of Requests. By our commission to divers Lords of the Council and others for removing abuses committed by concealment of donations and legacies bestowed for charitable uses, several gifts are already discovered, which being proffered may not be received, there being not appointed any receiver for the said commission. We appoint you to be our receiver and treasurer for the said commission. [*Impression of the signet attached.* ¾ p.]

Aug. 30.

88. Petition of James Rawson, clerk, vicar of Milton Abbas, Dorset, to the King. The demesnes and manor of Milton Abbas, being part of that dissolved monastery, is worth 2,000*l.* per annum, and the tithes worth 400*l.* per annum, all which is now in the sole possession of John Tregonwell the elder and John Tregonwell the younger, who by their patent are to allow some competent portion for the maintenance of the vicar, who has no other endowment. Petitioner having been incumbent for 20 years, has only received 20 marks, sometimes 16*l.* per annum, and of late 24*l.*, which, with other small church dues, does not amount to 30*l.* Prays reference to the Archbishop of Canterbury and Lord Keeper Coventry, that they may allocate such competent allowance to petitioner and his successors as may enable them to live free from want. [1 p.] *Endorsed,*

    88. I. *Reference as prayed. Woodstock, 30th August* 1638. [¼ p.]

    88. II. *Appointment by the referees of the 30th January next for hearing this business. Woodstock, 24th November* 1638. [¼ p.]

1638.
Aug. 30.
Plymouth.

Vol. CCCXCVII.

89. Nicholas Sherwill, Mayor of Plymouth, to the Council. We received lately information from James Doves and Anthony Prance, mariners, of Turkish men-of-war of Algiers now on the coast, who have taken some of his Majesty's subjects, and are likely to do a great deal of mischief. Examinations stated to be inclosed. [½ p.]

Aug. 30.

90. Archbishop Laud to Sir Nathaniel Brent. I was not willing to trouble you with a letter last week, because of his Majesty's being at Woodstock, and the services there to be attended ; but now, that all things may be in better readiness against the time of hearing, I let you understand the desire of some of the fellows, which to me seems just, especially since, as I am informed, they ask nothing but that which has been anciently and usually accustomed in that college, viz., that they may have the free use of all public registers and accounts of the college, with court-roll books and lease books, &c., which they say were never denied them to peruse at their own chambers for two or three days together, before Mr. Fisher came to be sub-warden. It seems very fit they should at this time see all things, that they may not say that you and the sub-warden have denied them the sight of those things by which they should make their proofs ; for if they allege this at the hearing I must, in justice, assign them the sight of the books, and give time to peruse them, which will cause delay, and perchance more noise than is fit for the business ; neither can I think it fit they should be tied to view them in the sub-warden's chamber, that he may oversee what use soever they make of them in a business of this nature. Therefore I pray let them have the books to view. But to the end that I may be enabled to see the truth as it stands in your registers and other books, these are to require you to bring up with you to the hearing these books following. [*They are described as in Dr. Turner's letter, No. 82.*] For other things I shall give you notice before the hearing, that so at the time of hearing there may be as little impediment as may be. [¾ p.]

Aug. 30.

91. Petition of Francis Thompson to Archbishop Laud. Henry Page, vicar of Ledbury, co. Hereford, has many times used scandalous speeches in the pulpit and elsewhere, more especially upon the fourth commandment. By preaching and otherwise he has, in contempt of the King's declaration concerning the lawfulness of recreation upon Sundays, and in derision of the book set forth by his Majesty, uttered these words, viz.: "Is it not as lawful to pluck at a cart-rope upon the Sabbath day as at a bell-rope? Is it not as lawful for a weaver to shoot his shuttle on the Sabbath day as for a man to take his bow to shoot? And is it not as lawful for a woman to spin at her wheel, or for a man to go to plough or cart, as for a man on the Sabbath day to dance that devilish round?" All which words petitioner will be bound to prove to your Grace and the Court of High Commission. Prays an attachment or letters missive against Mr. Page, to bring him to answer articles. [1 p.] *In the margin,*

91. "*I desire Dr. Merrick to consider of the suggestions of petitioner, and take order for letters missive, if he see cause.* W. CANT." *August 30th*, 1638. [⅙ p.]

Vol. CCCXCVII.

1638.
Aug. 30.
92. Certificate by Philip Thomas that on 13th August inst. he presented a petition to his Majesty for the enlarging of a commission formerly granted concerning charitable uses, and for his Majesty to appoint a treasurer to receive such moneys as should be discovered, wherein Sir John Heydon, being one of the commissioners, was presented for his Majesty's favourable nomination, which petition came to the hands of Sir Edward Powell, Master of Requests, then attending, and upon the 17th of the same month Sir Edward acquainted petitioner that his Majesty had given order to prepare the commission accordingly, but would not signify his further pleasure except the docquet for the commission were new written and himself named for a commissioner, and that Sir John Heydon's name to be treasurer might be left out, which accordingly being done, Sir Edward Powell then signified his Majesty's pleasure touching the commission, but kept the last petition, and will not signify his Majesty's pleasure touching Sir John Heydon's being treasurer other than saying that the said Sir Edward Powell was appointed treasurer and not Sir John Heydon. [⅔ p.]

Aug. 31.
Lease to John Southworth of a messuage called the Bell in Walthamcross Street, Cheshunt, and of other lands there, being parcel of the possessions of Robert late Earl of Salisbury, exchanged with King James, for 21 years, at a rent of 83l. 3s. 10d. and fine of 281l. 4s. [Docquet.]

Aug. 31.
Grant of a prebend's place in Westminster to George Aglionby, D.D., void by the death of Dr. King, and in his Majesty's gift *pleno jure*. [Docquet.]

Aug. 31.
The Downs.
93. Sir John Pennington [to Sec. Windebank]. Yours of the 29th present, with the inclosure, came this morning early to me, in answer whereof there have been two of the fleet to the westward these three weeks, viz., the Leopard and the London, Captains Stradling and Fielding, being commanders, who have already taken away the letters of reprisal from Henley and Polhill's men-of-war, and commanded them in, and are since gone in pursuit of the Turks. I not doubting but they have at least freed the coast of them, notwithstanding, I have two days since, by order from the Lord Admiral, sent two other nimble ships to join with them, viz., the Tenth Whelp and the Greyhound pinnace, with directions to continue there till their victualling be near ended, which will be at least six weeks, and by that time the season itself will free them from our coasts. I have long since sent the Happy Entrance and the Providence to lie upon the coast of Scotland, for intercepting all manner of arms or munition. I am very sorry to hear of your indisposition. P.S.— I have returned Sec. Coke's answer. [1 p.]

Aug. 31.
Sion.
94. Thomas Smith to Sir John Pennington. I will be very careful of all your commands concerning Sir Henry Mainwaring, C. Price, and for the time of the winter convoys beginning, about hastening which I will send you in my next his lordship's answer. The time of Mr. Barlow's coming in, according to his lordship's intention, was

1638.   VOL. CCCXCVII.

very plain in my letters—the time of the ships coming in which were re-victualled, being, as I take it, about the beginning of November. Concerning the city ships, you know we take no notice when they re-victual, nor know I anything of it; but I believe Mr. Barlow will be called in sooner to be put into the execution of Mr. Fleming's place, for we have great complaint of his weakness, and now that Mr. Edisbury is dead the necessity of an able man there will be the greater, especially till a surveyor be appointed, who may be you if you please, for the Lord Admiral asked my opinion of it, and I told him that I thought, unless there were a good addition to the salary, you would not undertake so troublesome a place. I had no commission to say thus much to you; but if you have a stomach to it, pray let me know your mind, and I will strive to be the cook to make ready that dish for you. Here are good sums offered for it, but you shall come free to it. As for Motham, I cannot prevail, though I have done my utmost; peradventure a letter of yours to my Lord may do. Sir W. Russell has written for [John?] Birtby, a clerk in the Navy, but what will be done I know not. As touching the Queen mother's coming hither, it is much noised here, but as it is much against our wills, so she is like to have none of our ships. The businesses are carried so close that I like them the worse. To-morrow the King comes to Oatlands. The Lord Admiral is in perfect health; he came here two days ago, and goes to-morrow to court. [*Margin against the passage relating to the Queen's mother and the following one:* "Of these things not one word to the vulgar." 2½ *pp.*]

Aug. 31.
London.

95. Simon Smith, agent for the Royal Fishings, to Sir John Pennington. Solicits his help in staying 90 weys of Lisbon salt, remainder of 240 weys granted free of the new impost to the Lord Chamberlain by the King. Gives a long account of the present state of the Fishing Society, which he represents as flourishing. They purpose to forsake their station at Lewis. Relates the circumstances of the second capture of the buss "Salisbury," by a Dunkirker, with the ill-usage of her crew. She had been condemned in the Admiralty of Calais, and sold there to Jeronimo Williamson Asheman of Middleburgh, who transferred her, at the price he had paid, to the Fishing Company. Mr. Gerbier had interfered with the Prince Cardinal, but without avail, whereupon the King had authorized the capture of some ship of value by way of reprisals. The immediate execution of this royal order was strongly urged upon Sir John Pennington, and Lawrence Rowe, the bearer of this letter, was sent to him to explain the business. [2 *pp.*]

[Aug. ?]

The King to Lord Chief Justice Finch. The iters which have been lately holden for the Forest of Windsor by Henry Earl of Holland are by the last adjournment to be kept at Windsor Castle upon the 25th instant, and so to be ended or continued until the affairs for that forest shall be settled according to the forest laws. We require you to be there present, and assisting to our said Chief Justice

1638.

Vol. CCCXCVII.

and Justice in Eyre, the better to advise him in such points of law as may fall out before him. [*Copy. It is stated in an underwritten memorandum that a similar letter was written to Judge [Sir William] Jones. See Vol. ccclxxxiv., p. 26.* ¾ *p.*]

[Aug. ?] 96. Justices of Peace of Essex to the Council. In obedience to letter of 31st May upon complaint to you made by Sir Thomas Barrington, touching outrages done in the Forest of Hatfield, Essex, by setting on fire the coppice hedges of Sir Thomas and destroying his wood, conceived to be done by the procurement of Thomas Garratt, John Bernard, and John White. The writers find that Thomas Clarke, a wandering fellow, was harboured by Thomas Garratt and Katherine his wife. Clarke took a firebrand out of Garratt's house, and in half an hour returned back with the news that the coppice was on fire. Garratt and his wife said, "Let them quench it that set it on fire!" and Garratt said, "It was a good turn it was so;" and other circumstances are stated which add to the suspicion against Garratt and his wife. John White, John Casse, and John Bernard stand bound to the next iter for the forest for unlawful cutting of wood. The writers find no cause of offence in Sir Thomas to provoke the said misdemeanours, and suggest that the best way to prevent the like outrages in future is to enable two justices of peace near adjoining the forest to proceed against such offenders. [2 *pp.*]

[Aug. ?] 97. Petition of Lawrence Squibb, James Prager, and Robert Squibb, his Majesty's Officers for Cards, to the Council. State previous complaints of Edward Heather the elder, Edward Fryer, and other cardmakers, a reference in June last to the Attorney General, a hearing before him, and his report calendared under date of 3rd August inst., No. 3. Heather and Fryer utterly refuse to conform, and greatly abuse petitioners, and have sold or concealed great quantities of cards. Pray the Lords to consider the said certificate, and give such order therein as shall seem meet. [¾ *p.*] *Annexed,*

97. I. *Copy of the Attorney-General's certificate above mentioned.* [⅔ *p.*]

[Aug.] 98. [Sec. Windebank?] to Sir Edward Stradling, John Hyde, Michael Parker, and Edward Manering, patentees for the aqueduct from Linchmill pond. His Majesty having granted power to you for bringing water from Linchmill pond, in an aqueduct of brick or stone, for serving London and Westminster, upon information given of the infeasibility of the work, his Majesty took the hearing of the business to himself, and after long debate gave direction for a commission for the better trial of the possibility and utility of the work. The return of which commission his Majesty has seen, and it is entered in the Exchequer. Notwithstanding the proofs of the excessive charges, the small use, and the improbability of its paying his Majesty's rent, he is pleased to hear how you can make good your undertaking, before he proceed to disannul the patent for the lottery

DOMESTIC—CHARLES I. 611

Vol. CCCXCVII.

1638.

granted for that end. He appoints the final hearing for the 26th September, at the court, where he shall be at that time. [*Draft or suggestion.* 1 *p.*]

[Aug.] Note by Nicholas of the names of the Committee of the Council of War, for providing arms, &c. for the army of the north, viz., the Lord Treasurer, the Earl Marshal, the Lord Admiral, Lord Cottington, Mr. Comptroller, and Secs. Coke and Windebank. [*See Vol. cccxcvi., p.* 4. ⅓ *p.*]

[Aug.] 99. See "Returns made by Justices of Peace."

GENERAL INDEX.

A.

A, person so designated, 60.
Abbot, variously spelt ;—
........., George, late Archbishop of Canterbury, 73.
........., Sir Maurice, 165, 204.
Abbot's Cromwell, *see* Cromhall.
.... Ward, *see* Swell, Nether, park.
Abdala, Alcayde Taudar Ben, Ambassador from Morocco, 476.
Abdick and Bulstone, Somerset, hundred, inhabitants of, petition of, 399.
........., ship-money, 156, 398, 407, 433, 486.
Abdy, Alderman of London, 109, 183, 204, 374.
Abeale, Sir John, petition of, 336.
Abele, William Vanden, examination of, 6, 28.
Abell, Alderman, 205.
Abergavenny, Lord, *see* Nevill, Henry.
Abingdon, Berks, 205, 313.
Aboven, Griffith, grant to, 214.
Abridgement, an, book so called, 365.
Aby, co. Lincoln, 170.
........., document dated from, 170.
Acheson, Sir Patrick, commissions to, 602 (2).
Adam or Adams, Elizabeth, petition of, 379.
........., Marcus, 172, 190, 207, 208.
........., Marquis, *see* Marcus.
........., Mr., 305.
........., Robert, 172, 190, 207, 208.
........., William, 235.
Adderley, Salop, 59.
Addington, Surrey, ship-money, 198.
Addington, Elizabeth, 606.
........., Thomas, 606.
Addison, Thomas, petition of, 363.
Admiral, the Lord, 8, 256, 351, 523, 537, 578, 584, 588.
........., ..., reference to, of letter, 565 ; *and see* James, Prince, Duke of York; Percy, Algernon, Earl of Northumberland.
........., ..., late commissioners for executing the office of, commission to, for perfecting unfinished business, 445.

Admirals, late Lord, *see* Villiers, George, late Duke of Buckingham; Howard, Charles, late Earl of Nottingham.
Admirals, all, 290.
........., ..., letters to, 37, 262, 315.
Admiralty, High Court of, 77, 85, 101, 110, 223, 303, 315, 501.
........., ..., order of, 304.
........., ..., commissioners for revision of sentences given in, letter of, 85.
........., ..., Deputy-Registrar of, *see* Wyan, Thomas.
........., ..., encroachments upon jurisdiction of, 222.
........., ..., Judge of, 502. *See* Marten, Sir Henry.
........., ..., King's Proctor, 502.
........., ..., Marshal, *see* Smith, Solomon.
........., ..., ..., letter to, 178.
........., ..., Registrar, 502.
Admiralty, the, Lieutenant of the, *see* Mansell, Sir Robert.
Admiralty, Lords of the, notices of, and casual allusions and references to, *passim*.
........., ..., business to be transacted by, Nicholas's notes of, 24, 94, 159, 174, 182, 194, 228, 243, 261, 266, 373, 487, 501.
........., ..., droits and profits of, 179, 445, 501, 502.
........., ..., instructions of, to Capt. Thomas Ketelby, 241.
........., ..., letters of and appointments by (1637, December), 3, 4 (2), 13 (2), 14, 18, 24 (2), 25 (3), 32, 33, 37, 41, 44 ; (1637, undated) 83, 131 (2), 132 (2) ; (1637-8, January) 138 (2), 139, 142, 159 (2), 160, 162, 166 (2), 170 (2), 174, 175, 194 (3), 195 (3), 202 (4), 213 ; (February) 228 (3), 239, 241, 243 (2), 255. 256 (2), 262 (2), 267, 268 (5), 277, 281 ; (March) 298, 300 (2), 302, 306, 312 (2), 315 (5), 323 (2), 326 (3) ; (April) 341 (2), 343 (2), 344 (6), 371, 373 (2) ; (June) 488, 501, 502, 527 (2), 541 (2).

614 GENERAL INDEX.

Admiralty, Lords of the—*cont.*
........., ..., certificates, orders, and other papers of, 3, 83 (2), 84, 132, 160 (2), 195, 228, 229 (2), 262, 302, 488, 501, 502 (2).
........., ..., letters to, 1, 3, 17, 30 (3), 31, 36, 40, 42, 44, 82, 132, 146 (2), 160, 173, 178, 186, 195, 202, 212, 219, 234 (2), 235, 236 (2), 246, 261, 269, 279, 291, 292, 304, 319 (2), 358, 487.
........., ..., petitions and other papers addressed to, 3 (2), 4 (2), 46, 83 (2), 84 (2), 86 (2), 96, 190, 195 (2), 222, 223, 229, 232, 284, 303, 513, 542.
........., ..., answers to petitions and other applications to, 229.
........., ..., references of petitions, &c. to them, 3, 17.
........., ..., Register of Proceedings of, references to entries in, *passim.*
........., ..., papers relating to appointments to the following offices:—
    Boatswains, 131 (2), 132 (4), 541 (3).
    Carpenter, 132 (2), 541 (4).
    Gunners, 131 (5), 132, 542.
    Lieutenants, 541.
    Pursers, 132, 541, 542 (4).
    Ship-keeper, 131.
    Steward, 542.
Advance, the, of London, 137.
Adventure, the (King's ship), 131 (2), 213, 323.
Æneas, the, of London, 137.
Agas, Edward, petition of, 259.
Agbrigg, co. York, wapentake, 545 (2).
Agersfloate, Holland, 28.
Aglionby, George, D.D., grant to, 608.
Ailston, co. Leicester, 424.
Akeroid, Nathan, 516, 553.
Albans, Earl of, *see* Burgh, Ulick de.
Albury, Surrey, document dated from, 584.
Alcock, Mr., 279 (2).
Aldborough, 347.
Alden, Thomas, 472.
Aldenham, co. Hertford, 355, 392.
Alderbury, Wilts, hundred, 421.
........., constables, letter to, 421.
Alderkirk, co. Lincoln, 426, 428, 444, 465.
Aldermanbury, London, 325.
........., document dated from, 223.
Aldgate, London, 591.
Alehouses, 340, 345 (2), 433 (2).
Aleppo, 103.
........., the King's agent and consul at, *see* Wandesford, John.
Alexander, Henry, petition of, 496.
........., James, 411.
........., Mary, petition of, 496.
........., William, Earl of Stirling, Secretary of State for Scotland, 27, 115, 496, 593.
........., ..., commissions to, 602 (2).
........., ..., letter to, 388.
........., ..., reference to, of petition, 574.

Alexandria, 192, 245, 264.
Alfera, ——, 86.
Alford, Edward, 245.
........., Sir Edward, petition of, 495.
........., John, appointment by, 245.
Alford, co. Lincoln, vicarage, 176.
Algiers, 255.
........., Bashaw of, 255.
........., captives at, 478.
........., ..., petitions on behalf of, 477, 478 (2).
........., ..., proposition for redeeming, 187.
........., "duan" of, 255.
........., pirates, 15, 192, 219, 243, 605, 607.
Alicant, wine of, 41.
Aliens dwelling within three miles of London, new corporation for regulating, 417, 472.
........., ..., officers of, letter of, 19.
........., ..., Provost-Marshal for, 19.
All, John, 185 (2), 213, 214.
Allegiance and supremacy, oaths of, 75, 76, 77, 136, 211, 268, 301, 310, 332, 421, 423, 427, 430, 431 (2), 452, 453, 507, 551 (3), 560, 568, 574.
Allen, John, 424.
........., ..., answer of, 424.
........., Richard, 250.
........., William, petitions of, 368 (2).
Allertonshire, co. York, wapentake, 345.
Allesley, co. Warwick, 539.
Allfarthing, [Surrey], manor, account of wood sold in, 492.
Allhallows, Barking, London, parishioners of, petition of, 67.
.... Church, 67.
Allhallows the Great, London, parson and others of, petition of, 68.
Allibond, Peter, M.A., deposition of, 343.
Allingham, Thomas, 179, 212.
Allington, John, Surveyor of the Customs of the Outports, 99.
Allott, Dr., 507.
All Souls [College], Oxford, document dated from, 348.
Almond, Lord Livingston of, *see* Livingston, James.
Almoner, the King's chief, *see* Curle, Walter, Bishop of Winchester.
Almonry, the King's, two widows, late yeomen's wives of, petition of, 485.
Alms-room, grants of, 6, 214 (2), 409 (2).
Alport, Mr., 265.
Alsop, Bernard, petition of, 71.
Alston, Edward, 233.
Altar, the, "two great books against," 366.
Altingius, Dr., 324 (2).
Alton, Wilts, manor, 253.
Alum works, 33, 97, 593.
........., farmer of, *see* Pindar, Sir Paul.

GENERAL INDEX. 615

Alured, John, 558.
........., ..., bond of, 574.
........., ..., examination of, 558.
........., Mr., secretary to Lord Keeper Coventry, 441.
Alvie, Mr., 76.
Ambassadors, *see* names of the countries they represented, or to which they were sent.
Ambergris, 527.
Ambleside, Westmoreland, returns for, 546, 548.
Ambrose, Dr., 321.
Ambrose, the ship, of London, 137.
America, 33.
"Amigoe, Monsieur," 526.
Amont, Count d', *see* Livingstone, James, Lord Livingstone of Almond.
Amounderness, co. Lancaster, hundred, 544.
Amps, Richard, affidavit of, 391.
Ampthill, co. Bedford, 281.
.... honour, 54.
Amsterdam, 145, 578, 603.
Anabaptists, 166.
Ancheron, Earl of, *see* Ancram, Earl of.
Ancholme, the river, co. Lincoln, 158, 184.
Ancram, Earl of, *see* Ker, Robert.
Andalusia, natives of, 321.
Anderson, Edward, 503.
........., ..., examination of, 504.
........., Sir Henry, letter to, 76.
Andover, Viscount, *see* Howard, Thomas, Earl of Berkshire.
Andover, Hants, 40.
........., document dated from, 452.
........., inhabitants of, memorandum of, 452.
Andrews, variously spelt ;—
........., Edward, brewer, of Reading, petition of, 283.
........., Edward, sheriff of Rutland, letters of, 320, 322, 354, 373.
........., Francis, memorandum of, 521.
........., Henry, Alderman of London, 87, 452.
........., ..., letter of, 161.
........., John, sentence in cause of, 383.
........., Lancelot, Bishop of Winchester, 2, 60.
........., Mrs., 114.
........., Oliver, sentence in cause of, 383.
........., Nicholas, 405.
........., ..., agreement of, 412.
........., Richard, 354.
Angell, John, 424.
Anglesea, archdeaconry, first-fruits, warrant for installing, 147.
Anglesea, Countess of, *see* Villiers, Elizabeth.
Angoulême, Bishop of, her Majesty's almoner, 330 ; *and see* Perron, Jacques du.
Angram, co. York, document dated from, 345.
Ann, Mary, the, 161.
........., ..., owners of, petition of, 260.
Annandale, Earl of, *see* Murray, John.

Anne and Elizabeth, the, 154.
Anne of Denmark, Queen of England, 531.
Anne Royal, the, 209, 446.
Annesley, Arthur, 451.
........., Francis, Lord Mountnorris, 396, 451.
........., ..., answer of, 451.
........., ..., his daughter, 451.
Anson, William, 241.
Antelope, the (ship), 131, 213, 261 (3), 266, 267, 271, 541 (2).
Anthony, William, petition of, 393.
........., servant to Sir Robert Hodgson, 76.
Antinomians, 166.
Antiquitates Britannicæ, extracts from, 288.
Antiquities of England, book of, 130.
Antrim, co., 185.
Antrim, Earl of, *see* Macdonnell, Randal.
Antwerp, 36, 51, 467, 523.
Anwill, Robert, letter of, 298.
........., ..., account of, 299.
........., ..., order concerning, 299.
"Apology of an Appeal," by Henry Burton, 27.
Apothecaries of London, 401.
........., answer to petition of, 358.
Apparition (supposed), 276.
"Appeal to the Throne," by Lady Eleanor Davies, 219.
Applethwaite, Westmoreland, return for, 548.
Appraisers, proposition for office for making appraisements, 179.
Apprentices within three miles of London, corporation for enrolment of, suggested, 98, 417.
Apsley, Sir Allen, deceased, 119, 120 (2), 333.
........., ..., commissioners for passing accounts of, 120.
........., ..., creditors of, petition of, 120.
........., Allen,
........., William,
........., James,   } children of Sir Allen, 120.
........., Lucy,
........., Barbara,
........., John, executor of Sir Allen, petitions of, 119, 120.
........., ..., letter of, 120.
........., Dame Lucy, widow of Sir Allen, 120.
........., Peter, 120.
Apslin, Nathaniel, shipwright, 269.
Arabic books and press, 245, 285.
Arborfield, Berks, ship-money, 348.
Archcliff Bulwark, Dover, 290, 385.
........., account of ordnance in, 350.
Archer, Edward, letter to, 540.
........., James, 399, 415.
........., Mr., parson of All Saints, Hertford, 563.
Archery, 107, 584.

Arches, the, Court of, 38, 65, 77, 81, 183, 200, 240, 248, 259, 264, 275, 365, 411, 426, 499.
........., ..., Register of, extracts from, 376, 563.
Archley, Thomas, articles against, 62.
Armistead, John, certificate of, 490.
Armitage, William, 553.
Armorer, Mr., his Majesty's servant, 315, 323.
Armourers of London, statement by, 532.
Arms, 408, 410, 429, 443, 575, 584. *See also* Musters.
Arms, officers of, 355, 390, 445 (2), 469.
Armstrong, Agnes, 448.
........., Archibald, his Majesty's late jester, 448.
........., James, 448.
Army of the North, the, 611.
Arnold, Andrew, 370.
Arran, Earl of, *see* Hamilton, Charles.
Arscot, Duke of, 493.
Arthur, ——, bailiff, 355.
Artis, Robert, 258.
........., William, 258.
Artlingborough, *see* Irthlingborough.
Arundel, Sussex, 288.
........., rape, 133, 543.
........., ..., ship-money, 92.
Arundel, variously spelt;—
........., Edmund, 168, 169 (2).
........., Thomas, son of Lord Arundel of Wardour, 55.
........., William, son of Lord Arundel of Wardour, 55.
Arundel and Surrey, Earl of, *see* Howard, Thomas.
Arundel House, London, 147, 152.
........., document dated from, 510.
Arundel of Wardour, Thomas, Lord, 198, 408.
........., ..., offer made by, 55.
........., ..., his younger children, 55.
Arwarker, William, 125.
Asgarby, co. Lincoln, 171.
Ash, Essex, *see* Esse.
Ashbourneham, Mr., *see* next entry.
Ashburnham, John, 58, 329, 409.
........., ..., letters of, 40, 145, 562.
........., ..., letter to, 122.
Asheman, Jeronimo Williamson, 609.
Ashen, Essex, *see* Esse.
Ashenden, John, letter to, 201.
Ashenden, co. Buckingham, 564.
Ashford, John, 506.
Ashford, Kent, 133.
Ashley or Asteley, Dorothy, 353.
........., Sir Francis, sheriff of Norfolk, 353, 397.
........., ..., death of, 452.
........., ..., letters of, 220, 289, 395.
........., ..., letter to, 418.

Ashley or Asteley, Lady, 210, 455.
........., ..., petition of, 353.
........., Sir Jacob, 266, 270, 474, 590.
........., ..., letter of, 297.
........., Sir John, licence to, 323.
........., ..., his wife and family, 323.
........., John, father of the above, 323.
Ashmole, Thomas, pardon to, 447.
Ashton, Edmund, 584.
Ashton, co. Northampton, ship-money, 91, 201.
Ashwell, co. Hertford, 371, 372.
Aslin, Richard, 453.
........., Thomas, 71.
Aspinall, Robert, 187.
Aspley, co. Bedford, 377.
Assurance, the, of London, 137.
Assurance, the (King's ship), 243.
Asteley, *see* Ashley.
Aston, Sir Thomas, 41, 158, 423, 461.
........., Walter Lord, English Ambassador in Spain, 271.
........., ..., his secretary, *see* Fanshawe, Mr.
Aston, co. Flint, documents dated from, 312, 407, 429, 507.
Aston-sub-Edge, co. Gloucester, manor, rental of, 492.
Aswardhurn, co. Lincoln, wapentake, ship-money, 257.
Athens, 245.
Atkin or Atkins, Edward, 487.
........., Thomas, sheriff of Middlesex, letters of, 313, 563.
........., Tobias, saltpetreman, 95.
Attorney-General, the, *see* Bankes, Sir John ; Heath, Sir Robert ; Noy, William.
Aubert, Maurice, grant to, 311.
Aubret, Mons., 387.
Audience, Court of, 240, 518, 572.
........., ..., the "Asylum of the Brethren," 573.
Audley, *see* Awdeley.
Aumary, the King's, *see* Almonry.
Austen or Austin, Francis, purser, 132.
........., Susan, 401.
........., John, 325.
........., Richard, petition of, 325.
........., Robert, 325.
........., Thomas, son of Richard, 325.
........., Thomas, pardon to, 16.
........., William, petition of, 113.
Austria, Prince Cardinal of, 580.
Avis, William, 279 (2).
Awbrey, Robert, petition of, 110.
Awdeley or Awdly, Bartholomew, 458.
........., Henry, 489.
........., Hugh, 160, 521.
........., ..., letter of, 486.
........., Stephen, petition of, 23.
........., ..., ..., order on, 23.
Awdley, Essex, 510.

GENERAL INDEX.

Awdry, Godwin, 194, 228.

........., ..., letter and other papers of, 8, 195.

........., ..., letter to, 36.

Awle, John, petition of, 109.

Axminster, Devon, hundred, 136.

Axton, Kent, hundred, 94, 234, 548.

Aylesbury, Sir Thomas, Master of Requests, letter of, 42.

Aylesbury, Bucks, 346 (2).

Aylesford lathe, Kent, 480, 543.

........., west part, 133.

Aynho, co. Northampton, documents dated from, 458, 567.

........., ship-money, 89.

Ayott, St. Lawrence, co. Hertford, document dated from, 492.

Ayre, Robert, examination of, 504.

Ayrie, Adam, 198.

Ayscough, Edward, 335.

........., ..., commission to, 363.

B.

Baber, Edward, bond of, 332.

........., ..., gunpowder-maker, of Bristol, 32.

........., John, of Lincoln's Inn, 179.

Babergh, Suffolk, hundred, 135.

Babington, John, 339.

Bacon, Lady Jane, 34.

........., Lord Chancellor, 128, 215.

........., Mr., mentioned in Dr. Sibthorpe's letter, 535.

........., Mr., of Claydon, 119.

........., Nicholas, 497.

........., Robert, gunner, appointment of, 131.

Badcock, John, 401; *and see* Batcock.

Badd, Thomas, 127 (3).

........., ..., petition of, 127.

........., ..., his sister, 127.

Badgers, licensed, lists of, 171, 340.

Bagg, Capt. George, lieutenant of fort at Plymouth, 28, 590, 604.

........., Grace, Lady (wife of Sir James), 604.

........., Sir James, governor of fort at Plymouth, and Vice-Admiral of South of Cornwall and Devon, 159, 246, 362, 487, 501.

........., ..., his house in Queen Street, 604.

........., ..., letters of, 151, 594.

........., ..., letters to, 501, 502.

........., ..., remembrances for, 584.

........., ..., funeral certificate of, 604.

Bagg, Sir James—*cont.*

........., ..., children of, mentioned in,—
George (the Captain above mentioned), Gertrude, Amy, Anne, } 604.

Baggs, Giles, 357.

Bagley, Richard, petitions of, 239, 389.

........., ..., his son, 239.

Bagnall, [Richard], 95, 487, 501.

........., ..., letter and other papers of, 95, 357, 489.

........., ..., letter to, 95.

Bagot, Hervy, 118.

........., Millicent, 118.

Bagshot Lodge, 582.

........., survey of decays, 583.

Baguley, Hugh, acquittance of, 282.

Bailey, variously spelt;—

........., Andrew, petition of, 247.

........., John, certificate of, 314.

........., Jonas, commissions to, 602 (2).

........., Dr. Richard, Vice-Chancellor of Oxford, 287, 316, 332.

........., ..., letters of, 295, 341, 342.

........., ..., note of moneys disbursed by, 441.

........., Thomas, M.A., presentations to, 315 (2).

........., William, 247.

........., Dr. William (*sic*), 325.

Bailiffs of a town not named, rates made by, vacated, 60.

Bainbridge, Mr., 54.

Baker, Clement, 490.

........., John, prisoner in the Fleet, 174, 185.

........., John, surveyor, 341, 406. *See also* Baker, William.

........., Mary, 213.

........., Thomas, 542.

........., ..., appointment of, 542.

........., Walter, examination of, 15.

........., William, surveyor, 419, 481.

........., ..., bond of, 428. *See also* Baker, John.

........., William, keeper of his Majesty's house at Newmarket, grant to, 425.

Balcarras, Earl of, *see* Lindsay, David.

Baldock, Samuel, 189.

Baldwin, Bartholomew, 398.

........., Thomas, 441, 442.

Bale, Augustine, bond of, 505.

........., Sir John, 65.

Balfour, Robert, Lord Burleigh, 529.

........., Sir William, Lieutenant of the Tower, 266, 270.

........., ..., letter of, 297.

........., ..., letter to, 498.

618 GENERAL INDEX.

Ball, Andrew, 495.
........., Frideswide, 13.
........., Mr., of Northampton, 535.
........., Mr., the Queen's solicitor, 164.
Ballard, William, 463, 470.
Ballasting ships in the Thames, 110, 111 (2).
Bally, Jeremy, 235.
Ballyragget, Kilkenny, 587.
Balmerino, Lord, see Elphinstoun, John.
Balsall, co. Warwick, 76 (2), 77.
Banaster, variously spelt;—
........., Sir Robert, sheriff of co. Northampton, 91, 221.
........., ..., letters and other papers of, 88, 220, 297.
Banbury, Richard, 157, 178, 212.
Banbury, co. Oxford, 365.
........., Countess of, see Knollys, Eliza.
........., Earl of, see Knollys, William.
Bancks, see Bankes.
Bancroft, John, Bishop of Oxford, 69, 313, 332.
........., ..., letter of, 341.
........., ..., letter to, 176.
Banda, Spain, 111.
Bangor, bishopric, 288.
........., ..., first-fruits, warrant for installing, 147.
........., Bishop of, see Roberts, William.
........., court of, 280.
Banister, Sir Robert, see Banaster.
Bankes, variously spelt;—
........., John, account of moneys due to, 339.
........., Sir John, Attorney-General, 10, 41, 43, 44, 55, 76, 87, 88, 92, 98, 103, 109, 113, 116, 117, 120, 124, 144, 148, 153 (2), 155, 159, 163 (2), 165 (2), 170 (2), 185, 188, 190, 193, 196, 207, 213, 220, 224, 225, 240, 241, 250, 252 (2), 254, 283, 293, 295, 318, 319, 328, 335, 338, 355, 357, 370, 383, 388, 397, 399 (2), 411, 416, 417, 431, 436, 450, 464, 472, 473 (2), 483, 488, 501, 512, 514, 517, 519, 520, 529, 531, 537, 552 (2), 556, 589, 596, 610.
........., ..., letters and other papers of, 150, 213, 274, 357, 360, 369, 378, 381, 393, 465, 521, 571, 583, 592, 610.
........., ..., letters to, 34, 58, 101, 116, 143, 155, 156, 166, 170, 190 (2), 283, 319 (2), 478.
........., ..., heads of his argument in Hampden's case, 540 (3).
........., ..., references to, of petitions, 12, 18, 33, 35, 36, 44, 141, 150, 158, 161, 164, 180, 181 (2), 203, 225, 252, 253, 254, 255, 306, 318, 328, 360, 363, 381, 393, 419, 432, 464, 465, 496, 531, 552 (2), 553.
........., Matthew, 333.
........., Mr., 567, 569.
Bankside, London, 272.

Bannier, John, the Swedish General, 122, 146, 264.
Banson, ——, bailiff of Essex, 146.
Banwell, Somerset, 32, 259.
........., document dated from, 602.
Baptism, 63 (2), 74.
Barbadoes, 273.
Barbarini, Cardinal, 467.
Barbary, 20, 499.
........., King of, 276.
........., saltpetre, 8, 24, 25, 97, 223, 242 (2), 276, 499, 509.
Barher, Thomas, grant to, 16.
Barber Surgeons of London, company of, 507.
Barbican, London, documents dated from, 32, 296.
Barbon, Westmoreland, 546.
Barcock, Edward, 163.
........., ..., examination of, 170.
Bardolph, Edward, 94.
........., ..., commissions to, 602 (2).
Bardowe, James, Yeoman of the Queen's Robes, 514 (2).
Bardwell, Suffolk, 183.
Barefoot, ——, 192.
Barillaro, Bartholomew, 554.
Barkeham or Barkham, Sir Edward, 118.
........., ..., reference to, of petition, 119.
........., ..., report of, 119.
........., Robert, 189.
........., ..., petition of, 190.
Barker, Edmond, messenger, petition of, 71.
........., ..., letters to, 178, 406 (2), 450.
........., Edward, petition of, 112.
........., John, petition of, 511.
........., Mr., attorney, 197.
........., ——, 493.
Barkhill, [Salop], 511.
Barking, Essex, 510, 521.
Barkley, Richard, letter to, 210.
Barkston [Ash], co. York, wapentake, 542.
Barley, importation of, 230.
Barloe or Barlow, Thomas, 195.
........., Mr., 608.
Barnaby, Mr., 39.
Barnacle, co. Warwick, 406, 433.
Barnaile, see Barnacle.
Barnard, Thomas, letter of, 550.
Barnard Castle, co. Durham, lordship, 475.
Barnes, Sir William, 48.
........., William, information of, 487.
Barnet, 53, 111.
........., market, 111.
Barnewell or Barnwell, Elizabeth, 581.
........., ..., petition of, 444.
........., John, 444.
........., ... digest of his case, 581.
........., ——, his mother, note of money laid out by, 130.

Barningham, Suffolk, 183 (2).
Barnstaple, Devon, 148.
.... baize, 148.
........., mayor, *see* Doddridge, Pentecost.
..........., ... and corporation of, petition of, 93.
........., ship-money, 93 (3).
Baronet, dignity of, as then granted not descendible, 255.
Barque, the, of Weymouth, 318.
Barre, de la, John, 30, 159, 450.
........., ..., order on petition of, 3.
Barrett, variously spelt ;—
........., Edward, Lord Newburgh, Chancellor of the Duchy of Lancaster, 125, 253, 402, 474, 487.
........., ..., letter to, 283.
........., ..., reference of petition to, 253, 509.
........., John, *see* Borrett, John.
Barrington, Sir Thomas, 610.
Barrington, Somerset, ship-money, 198.
Barrough [Barrow], Maurice, 183 (2).
Barrow, Francis, 288.
........., Isaac, 493.
Barrowcoat, co. Derby, 380.
Barstable, Essex, hundred, 135, 548.
Bartellott, Walter, 88.
Barter, John, letters of, 376, 556.
Bartlam, Henry, 407.
........., Nathaniel, 407.
Bartlett, John, 27 (2), 161.
........., ..., petition of, 26.
........., ..., his father, wife, and children, 27.
Barton, John, 126, 127, 197.
........., ..., his father and sister, 127.
........., Thomas, 297.
........., ..., petition of, 283.
Barty, *see* Bertie.
Barwell, co. Leicester, 567.
Baseley, Richard, 437, 456.
Basingfield, co. Nottingham, 380.
Basingstoke, 474.
.... College, 438.
Baskerville, Sir Simon, 427.
Bassana, Andrea, 345.
Bassett, Francis, Vice-Admiral of North Cornwall, 362.
........., ..., ..., letter to, 502.
........., Thomas, Lieutenant-Governor of Scilly, 270.
........., William, late sheriff of Somerset, 31, 157.
........., ..., letters and other papers of, 89, 147, 151, 157, 175 (2), 179, 314, 389, 407, 486, 488.
........., ..., petition to, 176.
Bastwick, John, M.D., 27, 139, 296.
........., ..., his works, 27, 365.

Batcock or Badcock, John, 401.
........., ..., letter of, 423.
Bateman, Robert, Chamberlain of London, 489.
........., ..., letter to, 422.
Bates, Avis, 263.
........., ..., affidavit of, 263.
........., Francis, 263 (2), 468.
Bath, Edward, 235.
Bath, Somerset, 362.
........., assizes, presentment at, 551.
........., mayor, 362.
.... Forum, Somerset, hundred, 193, 408 (2).
Bath, Order of the, 287.
Bath and Wells, Bishop of, *see* Pierce, William.
Baticala, 307.
Batt, near Berwick, 494.
Battalion *alias* Shotbolt, Philip, agreement of, 314.
Batten, Richard, 430.
........., ..., letter to, 587.
Batts, William, receipt of, 235.
Batty, Patrick, petition of, 282.
Baugh, Edward, 326.
Baxter, Margaret, 583.
........., Robert, 503.
Bay and say makers, *see* Colchester.
Bay Sconce, Kent, 195.
Baylis, Edmond, 384.
Bayly, *see* Bailey.
Baynes, Edward, B.D., 403.
Bayning, Anne, daughter of the Viscount, 556.
........., Paul, Viscount, 523.
........., ..., funeral certificate of, 556.
........., ..., inscription over the grave of, 508.
........., Penelope, Viscountess, 556.
Baynton, Sir Edward, 486.
Bazells (tanned sheep skins), 104.
Beachy Head, 31.
Beadell, Sir Capell, 459.
Beale, Richard, merchant, 386.
........., ..., order on petition of, 188.
........., ..., petition of, 371.
........., Thomas, letter to, 519.
........., Dr. William, 138, 235, 288.
Beane, Edmund, 146, 524, 526.
........., Mr., of Christ Church, 330.
Bear-baiting, 546.
Bearblock, James, 478.
Beaumaris, Anglesea, 112, 140.
Beaver-makers of London, corporation of, 269, 392.
........., ..., petition of, 459.
Beccles, Suffolk, 135.

Becher, Sir William, Clerk of the Council, 48, 108, 188, 291, 450, 515.
........., ..., letters and other papers of, 27, 258, 299, 338, 375, 407.
........., ..., the like to, 129, 322, 498.
........., ..., reference of petition to, 299.
Beck, John, 463, 470.
Beckington, Somerset, churchwardens of, reasons of, 64.
Beconsaw, Sir White, late Sheriff of Hants, 127, 182.
........., ..., letters of, 197, 213.
Becontree, Essex, hundred, 135, 548.
Bedbury, Roger, 421.
........., ... letter of, 421.
Bedford, 310.
........., commissary and official of, see Walker, Walter.
........., St. Paul's, 363.
Bedford, co., 67, 69, 95, 281, 372, 385.
........., Archdeacon of, 569.
........., justices of peace, certificate of, 543.
........., sheriffs, see Boteler, William; Chester, Henry.
........., ship-money, 272, 432, 440.
Bedford, Earl of, see Russell, Francis.
Bedford House, London, documents dated from, 306, 439.
"Bedlam, a counterfeit," 135. See also Bethlehem.
Bedwell, Mr., 245.
Beere, John, 77.
"Beeregar," 318.
Beeston, Thomas, mayor of Portsmouth, memorandum of, 469.
Beetham, Westmoreland, return for, 546.
Begg, Arthur, 464.
Beifeild, Mr., under-sheriff of Norfolk, 597.
Belasys or Belasyse, see Bellasis.
Belcher, Elizabeth, 325.
........., John, 405, 459.
Belgrade, 104.
Belhaven, Viscount, see Douglas, Robert.
Belke, Anne, daughter of Elizabeth, 358, 521.
........., Anne, daughter of Gabriel, deceased, 358, 521.
........., Elizabeth, deceased, 358, 521.
........., Frances, daughter of the last mentioned, 358, 521.
........., Gabriel, deceased, 358, 521.
........., Gabriel, son of Gabriel, deceased, 358, 521.
........., John, deceased, 358, 521, 533.
........., Michael, deceased, 358.
........., Michael, }
........., Thomas, } sons of Gabriel, deceased, 358, 521.
........., Valentine,}
........., William, son of Michael, deceased, 521.
........., ..., petition of, 358.
Bell, Agnes, 447.
........., Capt. Henry, petition of, 291.

Bell, John, 447.
........., ..., petition of, 573.
........., Sir Robert, reference on petition to, 251.
........., Thomas, information of, 259.
Bellarmine, Robert, 60.
Bellasis, Jane, 19, 78.
........., John, 19, 158, 184.
........., ..., statement of his case, 78.
Belley, Robert, 263.
Bellievre, Mons., Ambassador from France, 42.
Bellingham, Sir Edward, 193.
Bempstone, Somerset, hundred, ship-money, 147 (2), 176, 178, 214 (2), 314.
Benagla, Mons., 535.
Bendish, Thomas, 46.
Benediction, the ship, 85, 516.
Benet, see Bennett.
Benfield, John, 43, 172.
........., ..., petitions of, 42, 43.
Bengo, Thomas, 473.
Benlowes, William, junior, 197.
Bennett, variously spelt ;—
........., John, 572.
........., Mr. 226.
........., Robert, surveyor of Bagshot Lodge, 583.
........., Robert, vicar of Hogsthorpe, answer of, 173.
........., Sir Robert, 102, 320.
........., Thomas, 8.
........., William, 205.
Bennington, co. Nottingham, 380.
Benns, James, 541.
Benson, Robert, clerk of the peace for West Riding of co. York, 465.
........., ..., letters of, 433 (2).
Bentley, Essex, 556.
.... church, 556.
.... Hall, 556.
Benwell, Northumberland, 247, 419.
Bere Regis, co. Dorset, 396.
Beresford, Christopher, feodary of co. Lincoln, 144 (2).
........., ..., petition of, 144.
Berkeley, Sir George, letter to, 134.
........., Sir Robert, judge of assize, co. York, 310, 512, 515, 598.
........., ..., letters of, 512, 513.
........., ..., letters to, 135 (2), 136, 345, 433 (2), 544 (3).
........., William, petition of, 203.
Berkhampstead, ship-money, 392.
Berks, co., 13, 64, 95, 181, 373.
........., justices of assize, 89.
........., Archdeacon, 240.
........., sheriffs, 336. See Stonehouse, Sir George; Harrison, Sir Richard.
Berkshire, Earl of, see Howard, Thomas.

Bernard, John, 610.

........., Robert, Recorder of Huntingdon, 138, 194.

........., ..., his chamber at Middle Temple, document dated from, 180.

........., ..., answer of, 180.

........., ..., letter to, 139.

........., Samuel, 288.

Bernard, Duke of Saxe Weimar, 264.

Berrie or Berry, Daniel, 285.

........., ..., Richard, 474.

Berrington, John, 6.

Berrynarbor, Devon, 417.

Bertie, M., letter of, 107.

........., Montague, Lord Willoughby, 10, 151, 421, 586 (2).

........., Sir Peregrine, K.B., 56, 151, 540, 586.

........., Robert, Earl of Lindsey, Lord High Chamberlain, and Lord Lieutenant and Vice-Admiral of co. Lincoln, 10, 57, 85, 129, 151, 170, 214, 241, 362, 522, 540.

........., ..., letters and other papers of, 201, 252, 386, 475.

........., ..., letter to, 501.

........., ..., commission to, 445.

........., ..., reference to, of petition, 56.

........., ..., his works of drainage, calculations respecting, 540.

Berwick-upon-Tweed, 216, 331 (2), 397, 528.

........., document dated from, 582.

........., aldermen of, letter to, 349.

........., bridge and church, minute touching, 115.

........., bailiffs and burgesses, letter of, 456.

........., lecturer, 61.

........., late dissolved garrison, 457.

........., palace, 457 (3).

........., mayor, letters to, 308, 457, 494 ; *and see* Saltonstall, John.

........., vicarage, statement concerning, 60.

........., Recorder, *see* Widdrington, Thomas.

........., the Bound Road near, 309 (2), 331, 332.

Best, Richard, petition of, 355.

........., Rose, 355.

........., Capt. Thomas, letters to, 312, 363.

Bethlehem Hospital, London, 188, 359, 606.

Betton, Dr. David, 78.

Beverage, Mr., 577.

Beverley, co. York, document dated from, 347.

Beville, Sir Robert, letter of, 284.

Bevis, William, 529.

Bewdley, co. Worcester, 116, 394.

Bewick, Robert, sheriff of Northumberland, letters of, 330, 364.

Beynhurst, Berks, hundred, ship-money, 336.

Bible, the Holy, 72, 73, 74, 365.

Bickerstaff, co. Lancaster, manor, 434.

Bickley, Robert, letter of, 323.

Bicknell, [Somerset ?], 516.

Bickton, Roger, petition of, 296.

Bideford, co. Devon, mayor, *see* Saltern, Jonathan.

Bierton, co. Buckingham, 564.

Bigbury Bay, Devon, 270.

Bigg, John, certificate of, 362.

Biggs, Abraham, 590.

........., Thomas, 243.

Bignor, Sussex, 65 (2).

Bilboa, document dated from, 466.

Bill, John, 68, 453.

........., ..., pass for, 481.

Billiard board, the Queen's, 49.

Binfield, Berks, ship-money, 210.

Bing, variously spelt ;—

........., Dr., 169.

........., William, certificate of, 291.

Bingham, co. Nottingham, hundred, 24.

Bingham, John, pardon for manslaughter of, 173.

........., ..., trustee for St. Saviour, Southwark, 415.

Bingley, George, Auditor of Imprest, 139, 333, 488.

........., ..., letters to, 208, 209.

Biondi, Sir Francis, 421.

Birchen Lane, London, 404.

Bird, Thomas, 464, 465.

Birdforth, co. York, wapentake, 345.

Birkenhead, Henry, petition of, 148.

........., Henry, son of the above, 148.

........., Thomas, brother of petitioner, 148.

Birkett, Edward, 39.

Birkhead, Edward, grant to, 1.

Birling, Kent, 111.

Birmingham, 105, 382.

........., plague in, 189.

........., ship-money, 189.

........., sword blades made there, 105.

Birn, Charles, pass to, 185.

Birthy, John, 609.

........., ..., letter of, 323.

Bishbrooke, Rutland, documents dated from, 320, 322, 354, 373.

Bishop, Bartholomew, 395.

........., ..., petition of, 418.

........., Sir Edward, sheriff of Sussex, 92, 124.

........., ..., pass for, 481.

........., Edward, letter of, 221.

........., George, 379.

........., John, petition of, 340.

........., Katherine, petitions of, 16 (2), 17.

Bishop's Castle, Salop, 557.

Bishopsgate Street, London, 110.

Bishop's Itchington, co. Warwick, 437, 474.

Bishopsteignton, Devon, 456.

Bishopstone, [Wilts], 521.

Bishopthorpe, co. York, documents dated from, 172, 310, 332.

Bittadon, co. Devon, 306.
Bitterley, co. Salop, 62.
Bitton, co. Gloucester, ship-money, 178.
Black, Martin, 93.
Blackburn, co. Lancaster, hundred, 136.
Black Rod, the, 445.
Blackfriars, London, 417, 574.
Blackgrove, Joan, 325.
Blackheath, Kent, hundred, 132, 543, 548.
........., Surrey, hundred, 133.
Blackwall, 160, 488.
Blackwell Hall, London, 442.
Blake, Robert, 20, 204, 206, 242.
........., ..., letter of, 329.
........., ..., his wife and children, 329.
........., William, 384.
........., William, bailiff, memorandum of, 452.
........., ———, 500, 538.
Blanche, John, junior, 450.
........., ..., petition of, 350.
........., ———, father of the above, 350, 351.
Blandford Forum, co. Dorset, bailiff, 235.
........., ..., letters to, 211, 417, 485.
........., ..., ship-money, 211, 417, 485.
Blankney, co. Lincoln, 16.
Blatherwick, co. Northampton, 63.
Blechinden, Dr. John, 235.
Blessing, the, of London, 137.
Bletchingly, Surrey, ship-money, 179, 212.
Blewbury, Berks, 131.
Bligh, ———, 500.
Blithe, see Blythe.
Block Islands, North America, 33.
Blofield, Norfolk, hundred, 134, 597.
Blomer, John, 399.
Bloodworth, John, 399.
Bloome, Mr., 367.
Bloomsbury, London, 14, 64.
Blounden, John, 174, 228.
Blount, Montjoy, Earl of Newport, Master-General of the Ordnance, 82, 95, 97, 266, 270, 271, 302 (2), 434, 450, 550, 556, 599.
........., ..., letter of, 297.
........., ..., propositions of, 594.
........., ..., letters and other papers to, 3, 13, 20, 25 (2), 41, 44, 96, 97 (2), 128, 146 (2), 159 (2), 194, 195 (3), 228, 239, 242 (3), 243, 268 (2), 298, 306, 371, 373, 379, 431, 443, 490, 524, 526, 601.
........., ..., his lady, 361.
........., Mr., 577.
Blower, William, 287.
Bludder, Sir Thomas, justice of peace for Surrey, 333.
........., ..., certificate of, 453.
Bludwick, Francis, 487.
Blunden, John, 541.
Blunston, William, 201 (2).

Blunt, ———, 390.
Bluntisham, co. Huntingdon, 447.
Blyth, Northumberland, 397.
Blythe, John, 298.
........., Mr., 228.
........., William, 163.
........., ..., information of, 163.
........., ..., letter to, 505.
Boarstall, co. Buckingham, 564.
Boate, Augustine, 269.
........., Edward, 269.
Boatswains' stores, 30, 162, 166, 236, 237, 255, 262.
Boddam, Peter, licence to, 38.
Boddenham Woods, 480.
Bodenham, Sir Francis, 241, 261.
Bodicote, co. Oxford, 429, 448.
Bodington, John, 423, 425, 443.
Bogan, see Buggins.
Bohemia, Elizabeth, Electress Palatine Dowager, Queen of, 48, 159, 557, 599.
........., ..., letters of, 7, 146.
........., ..., horses for, 315, 323.
........., ..., oysters for, 557.
........., ..., her agent, 579.
........., ..., her sons, 599; *and see* Charles Lewis, Elector Palatine, and Rupert, Prince.
Bolas, Great, Salop, 446.
Bolingbroke, co. Lincoln, 253.
........., inhabitants of, 56.
........., ..., petition of, 55.
Bollaine, see Boulogne.
Bolles, Sir Charles, 176.
Bolley, Robert, 468.
Bolton, division, co. Lancaster, 135, 543.
Bonaventure, the (King's ship), 7, 13, 36.
........., ..., document dated from, 28.
Bonaventure, the Henry (ship), 306.
Bond, Thomas, 349.
Bonner, Ellinor, 363.
........., Thomas, 363.
Bonnington, Francis, 380
........., John, } petition of, 380.
........., Peter, }
........., Ralph, deceased, 380.
Bonyragg, John, see Wragg.
Books, 73, 224; *and see* their respective titles.
........., catalogue of, 123.
........., importation of, 365.
........., ..., licensing, 72.
Booth, Abraham, 228.
Bootwell, Richard, affidavit of, 2.
Boraston, John, 511.
Bordeaux, 45, 173.
Boreman, William, his Majesty's locksmith, warrant to, 147.

Borough, Sir John, keeper of records in the Tower of London, and Garter King at Arms, 389, 469, 510.
........., ..., treatise by, 82.
........., ..., certificate of, 270.
Borough, Devon, 270.
Borrett, John, 185, 213, 240.
Borthwick, —— [?], letters of, 367, 529.
Bosdon, Edward, 335.
........., ..., commission to, 363.
Bosmere and Claydon, Suffolk, hundred, 157.
Bosse, Elizabeth, 340.
Bossiney, Cornwall, mayor, see Wood, Thomas.
........., ship-money, 17.
Boston, co. Lincoln, 10, 26, 214, 253, 347.
........., documents dated from, 28, 138, 139, 267 (2), 307, 563, 589.
........., ship-money, 138 (3), 196, 212.
Bosvile, Sir Leonard, 34.
........., William, order on petition of, 10.
........., ..., grant to, 214.
Boswell, Thomas, 497.
........., Sir William, the King's Ambassador to the United Provinces, letter to, 223.
Boteler, Jane, daughter of Sir Robert, 78.
........., John, Lord, deceased, 78.
........., Sir Robert, deceased, 19.
........., ..., his lady, 19.
........., William, sheriff of co. Bedford, 302.
........., ..., letters of, 272, 432.
Botley, Hants, 411.
Botsone, see Bottisham.
Bottisham, co. Cambridge, 493, 507, 552.
Bott Soham, see Bottisham.
Boughton, Great, co. Chester, 23.
........., ..., document dated from, 23.
........., Kent, hundred, 133, 548.
Boule, the, mansion house near Nether Swell, 351.
Boulogne, 270.
Bourke, Edward, 194.
Bourn, co. Lincoln, 151.
........., ..., estimate of drainage at, 563.
........., ..., Level, 528.
Boustfield, Bartholomew, petition and declaration of, 237, 238.
Bow, Middlesex, 509.
Bow and pike (combined), invention of, 244.
Bowcher, ——, collector of impost at Bristol, 138.
Bowen, Richard, 499.
Bower, Mr., 195.
........., his sister, 195.
Bowers, Thomas, 132.
Bowing during divine service, 62, 64, 157, 240, 363, 539.
Bowker, William, 513.
........., ..., letter of, 487.

Bowles, Leonard, 421.
Bowls, game of, 129.
Bowse, Richard, 473.
........., William, 473.
Bowyer, William, reasons for granting suit of, 238.
........., Sir William, 457.
Boxbury cum Chells, co. Hertford, manor, 19.
Boxley, Kent, 111.
Boyce, Francis, 276.
........., John, 156, 486.
Boyd, Robert, Lord, 529.
Boyerman, John Jacobson, petition of, 85.
Boyles, Thomas, messenger, letter to, 190.
Boynes, Maurice, deceased, 541.
........., Robert, 541.
Brace, Robert, recognizance of, 302.
Brackley, co. Northampton, document dated from, 572.
........., ..., ship-money, 220.
Brackstone, William, 288.
Bradbury, co. Durham, manor, 147.
Braddish, Dr., 396.
Bradgate, Martin, 403.
........., ..., order on petition of, 403.
Brading Haven, [Isle of Wight], 128.
Bradnock, John, 384.
Bradshaw, Capt. Edmund, 206 (2).
........., ..., answer of, 20.
Bradstreet, John, 467.
Braems, see Brames.
Braganza, Duke of, 29.
Braithwell, co. York, manor, 366.
Bramber rape, Surrey, 133, 543 (2).
Bramble, William, 86.
........., ..., objections against, 86.
Brames, variously spelt;—
........., [Arnold], of Dover, 28, 36.
........., Daniel, 178, 315.
........., ..., petition of, 84.
........., James, 151.
Bramhall, John, Bishop of Derry, 538.
........., William, 404, 472, 531.
........., ..., letter of, 538.
Brampton, Moses, letter of, 176.
........., Vincent, 171.
Brampton Bryan, co. Hereford, 249.
Bramshill, Hants, 574.
Bramston, Sir John, Lord Chief Justice of King's Bench, 165, 182, 187, 188, 190, 241, 338, 401, 449, 473, 495 (2), 512, 515.
........., ..., letters and other papers of, 41, 370, 512, 515.
........., ..., the like to, 133, 134 (3), 148, 197, 425, 458, 548 (2).
........., ..., references to, of petitions, 9, 508, 587.

Brand, Mark, 44.
Brandenburgh, Elector of, 291.
Bransby, Thomas, 2.
Brasier, Thomas, petition of, 10.
Bratton, Wilts, 288.
Braughing, co. Hertford, hundred, 135, 545.
Bray, John, 602.
........., Thomas, 421.
........., William, chaplain to Archbishop Laud and prebend of Canterbury, 288, 324, 330.
........., William, gunner, 128.
Braydon, Wilts, forest, 54.
Brazil, 234.
Breames, see Brames.
Brenchley, Kent, ordnance foundry at, 151.
Brensford, Thomas, petition of, 260.
Brent, Sir Nathaniel, vicar-general of the Archbishop of Canterbury, and warden of Merton College, Oxford, 332, 348, 358, 390, 521, 561, 601, 605.
........., ..., his houses at Oxford and London, 343.
........., ..., letters and other papers of, 285, 306, 561, 573, 588.
........., ..., the like to, 71 (2), 73, 570, 607.
Brent, Thomas, 384.
Brent, South, Devon, 288.
Brentford, Middlesex, 393 (2).
Brereton, Sir William, letter of, 375.
Brest, 304.
Brett, variously spelt ;—
........., Jeremy, 128.
........., Richard, 450.
Brewer, John, petition of, 68.
Brewers and brewing, 108 (4), 210 (2), 220, 257, 283, 299, 345, 346, 349, 375, 390, 398, 401, 410, 580, 593 (2).
.... in England and Wales, tables of, 108, 109.
.... of London, company of, 230, 375.
........., letter and petitions of, 222, 250, 251.
Brewing and malting, commissioners for, 210.
........., ..., letters and other papers of, 230, 235 (2), 238.
Brick and tile makers of Westminster, master and wardens of, 107, 338.
........., ..., letter of, 327.
........., ..., petition of, 388.
........., ..., letter to, 332.
........., forms of oaths of freemen, 347 (2).
Brickhill Court, Bucks, 572.
Bride, the ship, 85.
Bridewell, 260, 413, 606
........., keeper of, letter to, 161.
........., Old, 66.
Bridge, William, 184, 201, 212.

Bridgeman, variously spelt ;—
........., John, Bishop of Chester, 158, 172, 360, 377.
........., Sir John, chief justice of Chester, and deputy constable of Forest of Dean, 92, 312, 335 (2).
........., ..., letter of, 199.
........., ..., letters to, 23, 156.
Bridgewater, Somerset, 142, 194, 235, 292, 371.
........., mayor, see Hill, William.
Bridgewater, Earl of, see Egerton, John.
........., Earl of, deceased, see Daubeney Henry.
Briggs, Morton, 178, 221.
........., ..., petition of, 337.
........., Thomas, 235.
........., ..., letter of, 223.
Brigham, Cumberland, 288.
Bright, Susan, 80.
Brigstock, co. Northampton, bailiwick, 318.
Brill, co. Buckingham, 363, 564.
Brill, the, Holland, 323, 598.
Brimon, Francis, petition of, 109.
Bringwood, forest, co. Hereford, 252.
Brinkmary, Levine, passport for, 117.
Briot, Nicholas, 498.
Brissenden, William, letter of, 11.
........., ..., petition of, 86.
........., ..., objections of, 86 (2).
Bristol, 32, 99, 112, 142, 150, 233, 284, 366, 584.
........., documents dated from, 23, 150, 361, 390.
........., Admiralty Court for, 537.
.... cathedral, 259, 360.
........., ..., documents dated from, 32, 449.
........., Chancellor of, see Jones, Dr. Gilbert.
........., corporation, grant to, 537.
........., Custom House, document dated from, 5.
........., ..., duties illegally imposed there, 177.
........., ..., commissioners for examining, 23, 168 (2), 169 (2), 196.
........., ..., ..., letter and papers of, 138, 169.
........., Dean of, see Chetwind, Dr. Edward.
........., Dean and Chapter of, 449.
........., ..., letters of, 32, 259, 361.
........., mayor of, 284.
........., ..., letters to, 32, 231, 437.
........., ..., petition of, 168 (2).
........., ..., ..., order on, 177 ; and see Jones, William.
........., merchants, company of, 169.
........., ship-money, 437.
........., ship-owners, petition of, 96.
........., soapmakers of, see Soapmakers.
........., town clerk, see Dyer, James.

Bristol, St. Augustine's, gatehouse of, 316, 351.
........., Vice Admiralty of, *see* Somerset and Bristol.
........., Bishop of, *see* Skinner, Robert.
........., Earl of, *see* Digby, John.
Bristowe, *see* Bristol.
Britain's Burse, *see* Exchange, the New.
Broad, [Reuben], 37.
Broadhembury, Devon, 218.
Broadlands, [Hants], 145.
Broadwater, co. Hertford, hundred, 544.
Broadwell, co. Gloucester, 351.
Brocas, Thomas, licence for, 427.
........., ..., his wife and family, 427.
Brockett, William, deceased, 125.
........., Sarah, his widow, 125.
........., Thomas,
........., Brian,
........., Frances, } children of the above, 125.
........., Lucy,
........., Margaret,
Brockham, Surrey, 327.
Brockhampton, co. Hereford, 39.
Brodenton, Isabel, 167.
Brogborough park, [co. Bedford], 54.
Broken Wharf, London, the King's storehouse at, 489.
Brome, George, beadle, affidavit of, 2.
Brome, Suffolk, 574.
"Bromedgham blades," 105.
Bromfield, Sir Edward, late lord mayor of London, 39, 161, 188, 193, 371 (2), 374.
........., ..., letters of, 386, 525.
........., ..., reference to, of petition, 374.
Bromfield, co. Denbigh, hundred, 23.
Bromhall, William, 272 (2).
Bromley and Beckenham, hundred, Kent, 132, 543, 548.
Brook or Brooks, variously spelt ;—
........., Ambrose, 105.
........., Bartholomew, 8.
........., Sir Basil, 251.
........., ..., agreement of, 395.
........., ..., petitions of, 53 (2).
........., Lady Frances, 251.
........., John, teller of the Exchequer, 301.
........., ..., affidavit of, 522.
........., John, son of the preceding, 301.
........., Sir John, 151.
........., Lord, *see* Greville, Robert.
........., Robert, rector of Laugharne, 253 (2), 288.
........., Robert, of Westminster, 301.
........., William, 197.
........., ——, guardian to Alexander Stott, 119.
Brothers, William, 555.
Broughton, Sir Edward, letter to, 271.
........., [John], 18, 53.

Brouncker, Sir William, the Queen's physician, 152.
........., ..., account of payments by, 98.
........., ..., certificate of, 515.
........., ..., petition of, 318.
........., ..., grant to, 585.
........., ..., his house at the Old Palace, document dated from, 551.
Brown, variously spelt ;—
........., Edward, 551.
........., Eleanor, 551.
........., Francis, memorandum of, 272.
........., Sir Henry, 143, 182, 370, 473.
........., John, founder of iron ordnance, 3, 24, 151, 159, 450, 535.
........., ..., letter of, 30.
........., ..., petition of, 517.
........., John, of Barking?, 521.
........., ..., information of, 521.
........., Leonard, 90.
........., Mr., mentioned in a letter of John Greaves, 245.
........., Richard, 271.
........., Thomas, of co. Cambridge, 504.
........., Thomas, of Kingston, Surrey, 327.
........., Thomas, in the Star Chamber, 185, 213, 240.
........., William, boatswain, 262.
........., William, messenger, 80.
........., ——, in the Arches Court, 77.
........., ——, of Goldsmith's Row, 155.
Brownescombe, John, 285.
Brownists, 264.
Brownrigg, Dr., 305.
Broxton, co. Chester, hundred, 376.
Broxtow, co. Nottingham, hundred, 24, 422.
Bruce, Lady Magdalen, 162.
........., Thomas, Earl of Elgin, 162.
Bruer, Mrs. 111.
Bruges, George, Lord Chandos of Sudeley, 277.
........., ..., licence to, 30.
........., ..., petition of, 54.
Brune, Sir John, 396.
........., ..., reference of petition to, 396.
Brush, John, 163, 529.
........., ..., examination of, 170.
Brussels, 51, 151, 300, 461, 515, 600.
........., his Majesty's resident at, *see* Gerbier, Balthazar.
Bruton, Somerset, hundred, inhabitants of, petition of, 92.
........., ship-money, 92.
Bryan, Sir Barnaby, 395.
........., ——, 68.
........., ..., his wife, 68.
Bryant, Robert, 313.
Bryce, John, examination of, 504.
Buckby Long, co. Northampton, ship-money 198, 201.

Buckden or Bugden, co. Huntingdon, 71.
........., Bishop of Lincoln's office at, 281.
........., manor of, profits of the Bishop of Lincoln, 115.
Buckeridge, John, Bishop of Ely, 60.
Buckhannon, Walter, 129.
Buckingham, 301, 323, 489.
........., document dated from, 301.
Buckingham, co. 69, 95, 281, 372, 385.
........., archdeaconry of, 67.
........., articles to be inquired of within, 58.
........., official of, see Lambe, Sir John.
........., all ecclesiastical persons within, letter to, 489.
........., archdeacon of, 58, 569.
........., ..., his court, 560.
........., churches in, notes of state of, 564.
........., justices of peace, letter of, 548.
........., ..., certificate to, 543.
........., sheriff, see Chester, Sir Anthony; Denton, Sir Alexander.
........., ship-money, 208, 237, 337, 398.
Buckingham, Duke of, see Villiers, George.
........., Countess of, deceased, see Villiers, Mary.
........., Duchess Dowager of, see Villiers, Katherine.
Buckland, Hants, document dated from, 5.
........., co. Buckingham, 564.
Buckley, Dame Ann, 140.
........., Margaret, petition of, 140.
........., ..., her elder brother, 140.
........., Sir Richard, deceased, 140.
........., Robert, petition of, 140.
........., ..., his elder brother, 140.
Buckram, patent desired for sole making, 106.
Buckwood, co. Lincoln, 405.
Budcheff, John, 276.
Budleigh, West, Devon, hundred, 136, 545.
Bugbrooke, co. Northampton, 191.
Bugden, see Buckden.
Buggins, Richard, 96.
Buildings, new, in and near London, 10 (2), 48, 114 (2), 213, 250, 258, 338, 340, 400, 410, 414, 415, 416, 429, 442.
........., ..., commissioners for, 114, 115, 332, 335, 338, 416, 429, 436, 442.
........., ..., ..., petition to, 46.
Bul, John, petition of, 66,
Bulbeck, co. Cambridge, 506.
Bull, the, of Amsterdam, 578.
Bull, the, Birchen Lane, London, 404.
Bull-baiting, 551.
Bullen, Edward, 288.
Buller, Capt. Richard, 173, 174.
Bullingham, Richard, 468.
Bullock, Toby, 187, 286, 287.
........., ..., his suit in the High Commission, 285, 287.
Bulman, Richard, 506.

Bulmer, co. York, wapentake, 345.
Bulwer, John, 52.
Buncle, George, information against, 63.
Bungay, Suffolk, 135.
Bupton, Wilts, 365.
Burcot, co. Oxford, 489.
Burden, Burdin, or Burdyn, Reginald, 390, 424.
........., letters of, 458, 567.
........., letter to, 226.
Burderop, [Wilts], 169.
........., documents dated from, 14, 25, 29, 169, 176, 352, 365, 444, 446, 447, 460, 488, 489 (2), 506, 528, 537, 564, 594.
Burge or Burges, John, 175, 179.
........., petitions of, 89 (2).
Burges, Elizœus, B.D., archdeacon of Rochester, grant to, 6.
........., Mathias, grant to, 16.
Burgevenney, see Abergavenny.
Burgh, Capt. Christopher, petition of, 122.
........., Ulick de, Earl of St. Alban's, 124.
Burgoyne, John, 421.
........., ..., pass to, 423.
........., Roger, 421, 423.
........., ..., pass to, 423.
Burgundy, 51.
Burian, see St. Burian.
Burkitt, Miles, 191, 364, 536, 572.
........., ..., articles against, 539.
Burlace, Nicholas, 417, 429 (2).
Burlamachi, Philip, 50, 97.
........., ..., letters and other papers of, 33 50, 162, 167, 266 (2), 387.
........., protection to, 442.
Burleigh, Lord, see Balfour, Robert.
Burley, John, 288.
Burling, Sussex, see Birling, Kent.
Burmington, co. Warwick, 343.
Burnaston, co. Derby, 380.
Burnett, John, 64.
Burnham, New, Norfolk, 238.
Burnt Fen, Isle of Ely, 504.
Burr, Peter, 121.
Burrack, co. Cambridge, 56.
Burrell, Mary, widow, petition of, 111.
Burrington, co. Hereford, manor, 252.
Burrish, Edward, 129.
........., Margaret, acknowledgment of, 129.
Burroughs, ———, saltpetreman, 237.
Burse, Britain's, see Exchange, the New.
Bursledon, Hants, ferry, 137.
Burt, Gaspar, 85.
Burton, Henry, 64, 139, 149.
........., Sir Henry, 129.
........., Thomas, 90.
........., Sir Thomas, 538.
........., William, of Merton College, petition of, 438.
Burton in Kendal, Westmoreland, 546.

Burwell, co. Lincoln, 506.
Bury, co. Lancaster, 135 (2).
Bury St. Edmunds, 349.
........., proposed river from the Ouse to, 186, 196, 323.
........., commissioners for, 26.
Buscot, Berks, 476.
Bushell, Thomas, 58, 156.
........., ..., petition of, 536.
........., ..., letter to, 537.
........., William, 165.
Bushton, see Bishopstone.
Butler, Edmund, assignment by, 587.
........., Henry, petitions of, 86, 542.
........., James, Earl of Ormond, 372, 436.
........., Jane, 19.
........., John, 161.
........., Joseph, messenger, report of, 56.
........., Mr., 445.
........., Sir Robert, deceased, see Boteler.
........., Thomas, letters of, 374, 559.
Butter, Nathaniel, report of, 379.
Button, John, late sheriff of Hants, 166.
........., letter and other papers of, 5, 127, 186.
Butts, Timothy, 141.
Buxton, John, sheriff of Norfolk, 238.
........., ..., letter of, 597.
........., ..., letter to, 452.
Byfield, co. Northampton, inhabitants of, petition of, 396.
Byng, see Bing.
Byrch, Mr., 420.
Byron, Sir John, 43, 430.
........., Sir Nicholas, 398.

C.

C. C., see Coggs Court, co. Oxford.
C. J., legal case concerning, 78.
Cables, 4.
Cadbury, North, Somerset, 362.
Caddington, co. Bedford, 363, 448, 473, 480.
........., ..., freeholders of, commissioners for, 448.
.... wood, 473.
Cade, Robert, 248, 497, 513, 519.
Cadiman, Dr., physician to the Queen, petition of, 318.
........., ..., grant to, 585.
Cadiz, 2, 17, 255, 269, 459.

Cæsar, Sir Charles, 382, 498, 573.
........., ..., appointment of, 498.
........., Sir Julius, 496.
........., Mrs., 440.
Cake, Thomas, 147 (2).
........., ..., bond of, 214.
Calais, 50, 569, 609.
........., governor, 493.
........., ships of, 3.
Calandrini, Philip, 50.
........., Pompeio, protection to, 442.
Calceby, co. Lincoln, vicarage, 181.
Calcott, Allen, grant to, 434.
Calehill, Kent, hundred, 133.
Cales, see Cadiz.
Calley, William, letters of, 14, 169, 446, 489, 506, 532.
........., Sir William, 195, 304, 489, 506, 532.
........., ..., his wife, 29, 195, 489, 564.
........., ..., his daughter, 564.
........., ..., letters of, 25, 29, 176, 352, 365, 444, 460, 488, 489, 528, 537, 564, 594.
Calvert, Robert, commission to, 602 (2).
Cambell, Sir James, alderman of London, 606.
........., ..., certificate of, 430.
........., Lady, wife of the above, 25, 460.
Camber Castle, 82, 601.
Cambridge, 167, 305, 362, 372, 423, 568.
........., document dated from, 354.
........., bridge, 193.
........., butt-close, 193.
........., castle, 494, 506.
........., St. Mary's church, 305.
Cambridge, co., 95, 152, 438, 501, 589.
........., constables, letter to, 276.
........., deputy lieutenants of, letter of, 506.
........., Justices of Assize, 232.
........., ..., certificate to, 133, 134.
........., Justices of Peace, certificate and other papers of, 133, 134, 372, 506.
........., Sheriff, 232, 314.
........., ..., reference to, of petition, 233; and see Chicheley, Thomas.
........., ship-money, 232, 314, 577.
........., terre-tenants and inhabitants of, petition of, 232.
........., Vice-Admiral, see Howard, Henry, Lord Maltravers.
Cambridge University, 550.
........., Chancellor of, see Rich, Henry, Earl of Holland.
........., Vice Chancellor, 305.
........., ..., metropolitical visitation of, 70.
........., for Colleges and Halls, see their respective names.
Cambridge, Earl of, see Hamilton, James.
........., Countess, see Hamilton, Mary.
Campbell, John, Earl of Loudoun, 529.
Campden, Viscount, see Noel, Edward.
Campion, Hugh, 492.
........., ..., account rendered by, 492.

Canary Islands, the, 154, 172, 311, 315, 403.
Canary wine, 41.
.... sack, 107.
Canbury, *see* Canonbury.
Canditt, Thomas, letter to, 194.
Candles, exportation of, 525 (2).
Canning, Richard, 492.
Canonbury, documents dated from, 599, 602 (2).
Cansfield, John, petition of, 11.
........, ..., statement concerning, 11.
........, ..., his mother, 11.
Canterbury, 167, 184, 201, 212, 223, 352, 454, 493.
........, document dated from, 407.
........, cathedral, 209, 214, 270, 288.
........, ..., statutes of, 18.
........, ..., close, 209.
........, dean and chapter of, 209.
........, ..., letters of, 60, 270.
........, ..., letter to, 18.
........, mayor, 408.
........, ... and others, order on petition of, 206.
........, ..., ..., letter of, 407.
........, plague, 407.
........, see of, register, extracts from, 569.
........, ship-money, 209, 270.
........, Archbishop of, 40; *and see* Abbot, George; Islip, Simon; Laud, William; Whitgift, John.
........, ..., list of benefices in the presentation of, 69.
Capell, Edward, 262.
Capella Hugonis, *see* Howe, Capell.
Captains of the King's ships, 321, 356, 390.
Captives, English, taken by Turks, *see* Algiers, Morocco, and Sallee.
Caralois or Carolius, ——, a Dutchman, 242.
Cardigan, co., 58.
........, Justices of Great Sessions, letter to, 198.
........, sheriff, *see* Price, Richard; Stedman, John.
........, ship-money, 94, 243.
Cardington, co. Bedford, 550.
Cardmakers' company, of London. 149, 150, 190, 583.
Cards and dice, 270, 288, 381.
........, his Majesty's office for, 190, 357 (2).
........, ..., officers for, 381.
........, petitions of, 149, 322, 610.
........, buying and selling, commissioners for discovery of offenders in, 295, 322, 378,
........, ..., letter of, 326.
........, order of Council concerning, 357.
Cards, foreign, 357 (2).
Careles or Careless, Edward, indictment against, 76.
........, Henry, 488.
........, John, indictment against, 76.

Carew, Sir Edmund, deceased, 46.
........, Lady, widow of the above, 46.
........, Mrs., 478.
........, Thomas, 350, 478.
Carew's Mount, Isle of Wight, 270.
Carey or Cary, Amy, 604.
........, Charles, younger son to the late Lord Hunsdon, 353.
........, ..., petitions of, 309 (2).
........, Henry, 604.
........, Henry, Lord Leppington, 21, 122.
........, Henry, Earl of Dover, petitions of, 57, 458.
........, Horatio, sergeant major, petition of, 250.
........, John, Lord Rochford, 552.
........, John, late Lord Hunsdon, 309.
........, Lucius, Viscount Falkland, 88.
........, ——, of Cockington, Devon, 604.
Carill, John, certificate of, 598.
Carisbrooke Castle, 270.
Carleton, Sir Dudley, Clerk of the Council, 89, 188, 401, 434.
........, ..., letters of, 258, 375, 443.
........, ..., letters to, 16, 31, 32, 34, 140, 146, 349, 363, 515.
........, ..., reference of petition to, 232.
........, Guy, M.A., presentation to, 34.
Carlisle, document dated from, 191.
........, cathedral, 409.
........, remembrances concerning, 584.
Carlisle, Countesses of, *see* Hay, Honora; Hay, Margaret.
........, first Earl of, *see* Hay, James.
........, second Earl of, *see* Hay, James.
Carlton Curlieu, co. Leicester, description of glebe lands, 65.
Carmarthen, late mayor, *see* Thomas, Richard.
........, ship-money, 180.
Carmarthen, co., 292, 442, 508.
........, sheriff, 557.
........, ..., letter of, 302; *and see* Lewen, Rowland; Vaughan, Thomas.
........, ..., ship-money, 180, 302.
Carnarvon, 298.
.... road, 299.
Carnarvon, co., sheriff, 302; *and see* Thomas, William.
........, ship-money, 220.
........, Earl of, *see* Dormer, Robert.
Carne, Edward, 141.
........, William, petition of, 141.
Carnegy, David, Lord, 529.
Carno, co. Montgomery, 459.
Carpenter, Edward, deceased, 84.
........, Mr., brazier, 369 (2).
........, Richard, 235.
........, Joseph, 437.

GENERAL INDEX. 629

Carr, Edward, 200.
........., Leonard, 228.
........., Mr., of London, 334.
........., Mr., of Flaxwell, 257.
........., Philadelphia, 200.
........., Robert, 200.
........., Sir Robert, 269, 553, 585, 604.
........., ..., letter of, 475.
........., ..., licence to, 1.
........., ..., his lady, 269, 585.
........., ..., ..., petitions of, 553, 554.
........., ..., ..., her children, 553.
........., William, 526.
Carriage of timber, saltpetre-liquor, or other commodities for the King's service, 23, 49, 95, 138, 139, 150, 181, 183, 190, 191 (3), 276, 346, 372 (2), 375, 376, 385, 391, 441, 479, 480 (5), 487, 550.
Carrick, Countess of, see Stewart, Elizabeth.
Carriers and the carriage of letters, 22, 143, 150, 171, 177, 183, 194, 216 (2), 284.
Carrington, James, 167.
Carrington, see Cardington.
Carshalton, Surrey, Sheppard Close, 129.
Carswell, Thomas, 349.
Carter, George, messenger, warrants to, 149, 199, 406.
........., Giles, indenture of, 351.
........., Henry, certificate of, 446.
........., Richard, petition of, 120.
........., William, 327.
Carteret, Capt. George, of the Antelope, 356.
........., Sir Philip, warrants to, 442, 475.
Cartmel, co. Lancaster, liberty, 543.
Cartwright, John, 89.
Cashio, co. Hertford, hundred, 134, 392, 544.
Casse, John, 610.
Cassel, 47.
Cassilis, Earl of, see Kennedy, John.
Castell, William, 436.
Casterton, Westmoreland, return for, 546.
Castile soap, 113, 142, 161, 292.
Castle, William, 248, 497, 513, 519.
Castle Bytham, co. Lincoln, statement as to tithes of, 69.
Castle Tavern, the, St. Clement Danes, London, 139.
Castlehaven, Countess of, see Touchet, Anne.
Castle Rising, Norfolk, ship-money, 220.
Castles and forts, 28, 81 (2), 94, 121, 194, 195 (3), 220, 242, 271, 282, 290, 302, 325.
Castlon, John, petition of, 52.
Castro, Don Juan de, see Hogan, Thomas.
Catesby, George, information against, 64.
Cathedral not named, legal case of difference between the dean and treasurer, 158, 159.
Cathedrals, 221.
........., mayors and others to attend service in, 62.
Cathedral service preached against, 60.

Caulkers, 157; and see Shipwrights.
Cavalry of England and Wales, proposals for reformation of, 81, 250.
Cave, Mr., 322, 354.
........., Sir Richard, 47.
Cavendish, Elizabeth, Countess of Devonshire, 336.
........., William, Earl of Newcastle, Lord-Lieutenant of co. Nottingham, 81, 361, 584.
........., ..., letter of, 494.
........., ..., letters to, 244, 494.
........., ..., commission to, 434.
Caversham, co. Oxford, 424.
Caythorpe, co. Lincoln, 34.
Cecil or Cecill, Anne, daughter of Earl of Salisbury, afterwards Countess of Northumberland, 34.
........., Edward, Viscount Wimbledon, Governor of Portsmouth, 266, 451, 459, 460, 463.
........., ..., letters of, 81, 463.
........., Elizabeth, Countess of Exeter, 581.
........., Mary, daughter of Thomas, Earl of Exeter, deceased, 340.
........., Robert, Earl of Salisbury, 496, 608.
........., Thomas, Earl of Exeter, 340.
........., William, Earl of Exeter, 326, 572.
........., ..., letter of, 500.
........., William, Earl of Salisbury, 34, 404.
........., ..., letter of, 530.
........., ..., his two sons, 315.
Chadborne, Bryan, 359 (2).
........., ..., examination of, 359.
Chadwick, James, petition of, 68.
Chafford, Essex, hundred, 135, 548.
Chafin, Richard, 370.
Chalfont St. Giles, co. Buckingham, 560, 563.
Chalkwell, Essex, 296.
Chaloner, Sir Thomas, 434.
Chamber, the Privy, Treasurer of, see Uvedale, Sir William.
........., sewers of the, petition of, 467.
Chamberlain, the Lord, 52, 112, 213, 452, 609. See Herbert, Philip, Earl of Pembroke and Montgomery.
Chamberlaine, Abraham, petition of, 516.
........., Edward, petition of, 345.
........., John, 426.
........., Richard, 160.
Chambers, Dr. [James], 20.
........., [Richard?], 512, 563.
Chambre, Calcot, order on petition of, 164.
........., Calcot, deceased, 164.
Chancery, Court of, 66, 79, 183, 204, 215 (2), 231, 233, 238, 255, 261, 342, 363, 368, 388, 475, 476, 495, 500.
........., ..., Clerk of the Patents in, see Wolseley, Sir Robert.
........., ..., escheators of, 141.
........., ..., Master in, see Rich, Sir Charles.

Chancery, Court of—*cont.*
.........., ..., Registrar, *see* Washington, Sir Lawrence.
.........., ..., six clerks of, *see* Six Clerks.
Chancery Lane, London, 115.
Chandos, Lord, *see* Bruges, George.
Chapel Royal, the, 333.
.........., master of the children, *see* Day, Thomas.
Chapman, Christopher, 235.
.........., Mr., of Claydon, 119.
.........., William, of Tetbury, letter of, 317.
.........., ..., his brother, 317.
.........., William, of Shelton, statement of, 87.
Charing Cross, 53, 116, 397, 401, 431, 450.
.........., proposal for laying water-pipes between Temple Bar and, 113.
Charitable Uses, Commissioners for, *see* Pious Uses.
Charity, the, of Southampton, 341.
Charles I., notices of, and references and allusions to, *passim.*
.........., assertion that he was a Catholic, 14, 473.
.........., warrant for his masquing apparel, 19.
.... goes aboard the Sovereign of the Seas, 32, 166.
.... was consulted concerning Admiralty business, 94, 266, 271, 356.
.........., mathematical instruments made for, 121, 122, 282.
.........., sermon preached before, 166.
.........., ecclesiastical state of parishes of Norwich laid before, 167.
.........., letters or papers "apostiled," or otherwise answered by, 171, 182, 197.
.........., his desire to increase the knowledge of the Eastern languages, 285.
.........., interest felt by him in questions connected with ship-money, 274, 297, 443.
.........., money, jewels, and plate of, alleged to be concealed, 98.
.........., pictures bought of Rubens, 488.
.........., statues agreed to be purchased of Le Sueur, 518.
.........., commissions of, 363, 434, 445, 602 (2).
.........., grants of, 1 (2), 6 (4), 16 (2), 19, 22, 29, 34, 37, 39 (3), 142, 147, 148, 160, 173, 193, 200, 203, 214 (5), 236, 309, 311 (3), 315 (2), 323 (8), 400 (3), 409 (2), 410, 422, 427 (2), 434 (2), 441, 442, 447 (3), 454 (3), 466, 475, 476, 498, 526, 527, 537, 585 (2), 588, 608 (2.)
.........., letters of, 18, 20, 34, 40, 56 (2), 58 (2), 74, 101 (3), 116, 117, 123, 128, 168 (2), 193, 196, 197 (2), 198, 231, 236, 247, 277, 283, 306, 309, 319, 351, 353, 377, 425 (2), 427, 428, 457, 463, 482, 484, 494, 498, 514, 527, 537, 559, 574, 579 (2), 580, 589 (2), 601, 606, 609.
.........., letters patent of, 11, 19, 29.

Charles I.—*cont.*
.........., pardons granted by, 16, 173, 214, 447, 498, 587.
.........., protections granted by, 79, 311, 442.
.........., warrants, privy seals, and fiats of, 1 (2), 19 (2), 29, 37, 39, 41, 42 (2), 147 (2), 148 (2), 152 (3), 173 (4), 174 (3), 179, 192, 201, 203 (3), 236, 309, 315, 409 (3), 418, 424, 425 (2), 427 (2), 428, 435 (5), 441 (2), 442 (2), 447, 475, 476 (4), 514 (4), 517 (2), 576, 577 (2), 601 (2).
.........., orders of, 49, 258, 461 (3), 462 (3).
.........., ..., in Council, 15, 26 (2), 27, 28, 60, 177 (4), 184, 196 (4), 285, 347, 397 (3), 410, 416 (3), 417, 528, 587 (2).
.........., letters, petitions, and other papers addressed to, *see* the names of the writers.
.........., his lands and revenues as Prince of Wales, 158.
.........., ..., Commissioners of, 53.
.........., ..., ..., their clerk, *see* Tipper, Robert.
.........., ..., ..., ..., order of, 227.
.........., ..., ..., ..., house or office of, Fleet Street, London, document dated from, 227.
.........., his almoner (chief), *see* Curle, Walter, Bishop of Winchester.
.........., his avery, 376.
.........., ... barber, *see* Davies, Thomas.
.........., ... barges, master of, *see* Warner, Nowell.
.........., ... bedchamber, instruments for, 122
.........., ... late bit-maker, *see* Shackspeare, John.
.........., ... chapel, 208.
.........., ..., dean of, 208.
.........., ... closet, 208.
.........., ..., clerk of, 208; *and see* Steward, Dr. Richard.
.........., ... distiller of sweet herbs, *see* Middleton, Henry.
.........., ... drummers, certificate of, 22.
.........., ... equerries, 7, 38.
.........., ... footmen, 464.
.........., ... game, preservation of, 37.
.........., ... garden at Whitehall, 39.
.........., ... granary, 35.
.........., ... horses, 476.
.........., ... houses in London, water supply of, 410, 514.
.........., ... jeweller, *see* Duart, James.
.........., ... jewels, *see* Jewels.
.........., ... kitchen, 279.
.........., ... library, keeper of, *see* Middleton, Henry.
.........., ... locksmith, *see* Boreman, William.
.........., ... music, master of, *see* Laniere, Nicholas.
.........., ... musicians, confirmation of charter to, 514.
.........., ... physician, *see* Mayerne, Sir Theodore.

GENERAL INDEX.

631

Charles I.—*cont.*
........., his printing house, 73.
........., ... progress in 1638, 173, 202, 203 (2), 523, 558.
........., ..., provisions for, estimate of, 537.
........., ... revenues (casual), 97, 334, 362, 371, 421, 435, 439, 441, 452, 469, 498.
........., ... serjeants-at-arms, 1, 22, 39.
........., ... servants of the household, 409.
........., ..., names of, 339.
........., ... sewer, 35.
........., ... slughounds, 593.
........., ... stables, 30, 35, 49 (2), 173, 376, 441.
........., ..., surveyor of, *see* Wethered, Francis.
........., ... trumpeters, 174 (3).
Charles, Prince, subsequently Charles II., 121 (2), 208, 225, 315, 357, 361, 421, 500.
........., ..., knighthood of, 510.
........., ..., ..., notes upon, 486.
........., ..., ..., fees of, 445 (2).
........., ..., commission to the Earl of Newcastle to take charge of, 434.
........., ..., concealed lands belonging to, offer to discover, 58.
........., ..., his Attorney-General, *see* Lane, Richard.
........., ..., his revenues, 500.
........., ..., ..., Receiver-General, *see* Cunningham, Sir David.
........., ..., ..., auditor, *see* Harbord, Sir Charles.
........., ..., his servants, list of, 50.
........., ..., his Groom of the Stole, *see* Cavendish, William, Earl of Newcastle.
........., ..., his tutor, 361; *and see* Duppa, Brian, Bishop of Chichester.
Charles Lewis, Elector Palatine, *see* Palatinate.
Charles, the, (ship,) 213, 291.
........., ... of London, 137, 213.
Charlewood, Edward, 327.
Charlton, co. Worcester, document dated from, 344.
Charnock, Richard, 161.
Chart and Longbridge, Kent, hundred, 133.
Charter House, London, 245, 484 (2).
........., document dated from, 308.
........., feoffees and commissioners of, letter to, 484.
........., revenues and lands of, lords and governors of, petition to, 308.
Charterhouse in Sculcoates, co. York, 574.
Chatham, 3, 30, 192, 202 (2), 246, 269, 279, 290, 291.
........., documents dated from, 261 (2), 460.
........., chest at, *see* Chest, the, at Chatham.
Chatillon, General, 493.
Chatterton, William, petition of, 120.
Cheadle, Ann, 140.
........., Thomas, 140.

Cheadle, co. Stafford, 511.
Cheam, Surrey, 512.
Cheapside, London, 46, 155.
........., document dated from, 597.
Cheeswick, Devon, document dated from, 430.
Cheham, *see* Cheam.
Chellaston, co. Derby, 497.
Chelmorton, co. Derby, particulars of premises in, 409 (2).
Chelmsford, 470.
Chelsea, Middlesex, 521.
.... Manor, 526.
.... Place, 526.
........., ship-money, 336.
.... House, document dated from, 475.
Cheltenham, 210.
Chenies, co. Buckingham, 363.
Chensford, *see* Chelmsford.
Cheshunt, co. Hertford, the Bell, in Waltham-cross Street, lease of, 608.
Chest at Chatham, Commissioners for, 373.
Chester, Sir Anthony, sheriff of co. Buckingham, 208, 398.
........., Henry, late sheriff of co. Bedford, 440.
........., Robert, *see* Henry.
........., Sir Robert, 391.
Chester, *otherwise* West Chester, 52, 231, 441, 461, 466, 471.
........., documents dated from, 158, 363, 377.
.... Castle, 363, 462.
...., document dated from, 376.
.... Cathedral, 462.
........., Chief Justice, 501; *and see* Milward, Sir Thomas.
........., Dean and Chapter, 377.
........., Exchequer Court, 471.
........., Mayor, *see* Throppe, Thomas.
........., ..., and others, letters of, 158, 377.
........., ..., ..., letter to, 185.
........., stone called the Gloverstone, 364; *and see also* Gloverstone.
........., ship-money, 27, 158, 363, 377.
Chester, Bishop of, 462; *and see* Bridgeman, John.
Chester, co., 148, 362, 441, 461, 492, 498, 501.
........., Judges of Assize, 28, 158, 186, 377, 462.
........., ..., letter of, 363.
........., Justices of Peace, 158, 174, 344, 375.
........., ..., letters of, 375, 423.
........., nobility and others of, letter of, 423.
........., prothonotary and clerk of the Crown, 148.
........., Sheriffs, *see* Cholmondeley, Thomas; Delves, Sir Thomas.
........., ship-money, 41, 44, 158, 186, 190, 265 (2), 300, 451, 462 (2).
........., Vice-Admiral, *see* Stanley, William, Earl of Derby.
Chesterfield, document dated from, 186.

Chetwind or Chetwynd, Dr. Edward, Dean of Bristol, letter of, 32.
........., Philip, 145.
Chevreuse, Duchess of, 7, 13, 28, 538.
........., Duke of, Ambassador Extraordinary from France, 201.
Chew, John, petition of, 394.
Chewton, Somerset, hundred, ship-money, 89 (2), 175, 179, 314.
Cheynell, Francis, 306.
........., ..., letter to, 306.
Chicheley, Henry, 430.
........., [Thomas], Sheriff of co. Cambridge, 577.
Chichester, 595.
........., document dated from, 548.
........., Dean, see Steward, Dr. Richard.
........., diocese, 65.
........., Mayor, see Pannett, John.
........., Recorder, see Lewkenor, Christopher.
........., rape, 133, 543, 548.
........., Bishop, see Duppa, Brian; Montagu, Richard.
Chichester, Edward, Viscount, Vice-Admiral for Ulster, 364.
........., ..., letter to, 501.
........., Henry, 285.
Chideock, Dorset, 445.
Chidley Sir George, 429.
Chieveley, co. Cambridge, hundred, 134.
Child, John, 46, 178, 185.
........., ..., petition of, 205.
........., ..., ..., order on, 205.
Chilford, co. Cambridge, hundred, 133.
Chilworth, Surrey, the King's powder mills at, 46, 150, 160, 488.
Chingford, Essex, rate for ship-money made at, 64.
Chipping Norton, co. Oxford, ship-money, 266.
Chirbury, Salop, 59.
.... hundred, ship-money, 312.
Chishall Magna, Essex, 411.
Chiswick, Middlesex, ship-money, 90.
"Choare, Lord," 526.
Cholmondeley, Thomas, Sheriff of co. Chester, letters and other papers of, 199, 265 (2), 300, 451.
Christ Church, London, 402 (2), 485.
........., parishioners of, statement and certificate of, 485, 488, 492.
........., Canterbury, document dated from, 270.
........., Oxford, deanery, 59.
........., ..., Dean and Chapter, order of, 70.
........., ..., statements of their rights, 70 (2).
Christchurch, Hants, 293.
Christ's Hospital, London, 413, 442.
........., steward, see Wickins, William.
"Christian, the poor doubting," (book,) 366.
Christmas wife, 63.
Chrysostom, St., works of, 341.

Chudleigh, Sir George, 430.
........., letter of, 218.
Chudleigh, Devon, 456.
Church, persons fined for not going to, 135.
Church, Percy, Groom of the Chamber, petitions of, 12, 123.
........., Randolph, petition of, 238.
Church Aston, Salop, 446.
Churchill, co. Oxford, 470 (2).
Churching of Women, 382.
Churchman, William, 64.
Ciena, see Sienna.
Cinque Ports, Admiralty, serjeant of, see Jacob, John.
........., castles in, 290.
........., Judge of, see Rives, Dr. Thomas.
........., Lord Warden of, 94, 527, 569. See Howard, Theophilus, Earl of Suffolk.
........., ..., petition of, 93.
Civil Law, Doctors of, certificates of, 238, 293.
Civita Vecchia, 593.
Clackclose, Norfolk, hundred, 134.
Clapp, ——, 500.
Clapthorne, George, reference to, of petition, 251.
Clare, Countess Dowager of, see Holles, Anne.
........., first Earl of, see Holles, John.
........., second Earl of, see Holles, John.
Clare Hall College, Cambridge, 193.
Clarendon Park, Wilts, 55, 506.
Clarington Park, see Clarendon Park.
Clark, see Clerk.
Clavering hundred, Norfolk, 597.
Clavering, Mr., 76.
........., Ralph, 490.
Claverton, Somerset, documents dated from, 314, 486, 488.
Clay, Richard, petition of, 46.
........., ..., widow, 487.
Clay, North, co. Nottingham, hundred, ship-money, 24, 43, 184.
........., South, co. Nottingham, hundred, ship-money, 24, 43, 184.
Claydon, Suffolk, 119.
Claypole, John, 201, 297.
Clayton, Dr. Ralph, minister of Stanton Lacy, 326, 338, 473.
Clee, Thomas, letter to, 509.
Clement, Robert, 44.
Clements, Mr., merchant of London, 160.
Clements Inn, London, 429, 436.
........., document dated from, 212.
.... Fields, 442.
Cleobury Mortimer, co. Salop, 511.
Clergy, ship-money paid by, see Ship-money.
Clerk, variously spelt;—
........., Edward, Groom of the Queen's Bedchamber, 123.
........., Edward, of Fenny Compton, 437.
........., George, petition of, 284.

GENERAL INDEX. 633

Clerk, variously spelt—*cont.*
........., Hamlet, 508.
........., Henry, 542.
........., John, 487.
........., ..., certificates of, 386, 453.
........., Lewis, 386.
........., Matthew, of Alderkirk, 426, 428, 444.
........., ..., petition of, 465,
........., ..., bond of, 466.
........., ..., minute of his discharge, 466.
........., Matthew, of Bitterley, articles against, 62.
........., Mr., 183, 228.
........., Mr., of Eastcot, 518.
........., Michael, pass to, 185.
........., Samuel, constable, letter of, 346.
........., Dr. Samuel, 191, 395, 535, 572.
........., ..., letter of, 518.
........., ..., letter to, 123.
........., ..., his proceedings in the diocese of Peterborough, 157.
........., Thomas, post of London, 51.
........., Thomas, creditor of Sir Allen Apsley, petition of, 120.
........., Thomas, rector of Mappowder, 396.
........., ..., letter of, 568.
........., Thomas, of the forest of Hatfield, 610.
........., Valentine, Groom of the Queen's Privy Chamber, petition of, 123.
........., William, petition of, 163.
........., ..., pardon to, 163.
........., ..., his wife and family, 163.
Clerkenwell, London, 162, 399.
........., document dated from, 558.
........., churchwardens and others of, answer of, 386.
.... Green, document dated from, 20.
Cleveland, Earl of, *see* Wentworth, Thomas.
Cley, Margaret, 586.
........., ..., examination of, 586.
Cleypoole, John, 201, 297.
Cliff, bailiwick, 318.
Clifford's Inn, London, 385.
Clifton, Gervase, 558.
........., ..., statement of, 558.
Clifton, co. York, manor, 366.
Clincard, Gabriel, 228.
Clink, the, (prison,) 75.
........., liberty, inhabitants of, petition of, 113.
Clinton, Theophilus, Earl of Lincoln, 586 (2).
Clitherow, Sir Christopher, 165, 520, 549.
........., William, 447.
Clobery, Oliver, 406, 417.
........., William, letter to, 8.
........., ..., letter and other papers of, 276, 478, 499 (2), 516.
Cloth and clothiers, 54, 104, 135, 142, 153, 164, 176, 218 (3), 411, 433, 553.
Clothier, Richard, 473.

Cloyden, *see* Claydon.
Clutterbooke, Thomas, 110.
Coaker, Robert, 359.
........., ..., information of, 359.
"Coal from the Altar, the," book, 62, 366.
Coale, John, 235.
Coals and coal trade, 47, 108, 227, 239, 247, 295, 347, 387, 394, 395, 397 (3), 401, 419, 422, 436, 489, 490, 501. *See also* Collieries, corporation of ship-masters for, 95.
Coard, Abel, 583.
........., Jasper, 583.
"Coat" cards, 150.
Cobb or Cobbe, Abraham, petition of, 239, 240.
........., Mr., 40.
Cobden, William, 133.
Cobham, John, the elder, letter of, 489.
........., William, 489, 505.
Cockaine, William 204.
Cocke, Hugh, pass for, 419.
Cock-fighting, 447.
Cockington, Devon, 604.
Coffland, Daniel, 555.
........., Mary, petition of, 555.
Cogan, Henry, letter of, 42.
Coggeshall, Essex, 235.
Coggin, John, petition of, 66.
Coggs, co. Oxford, documents dated from, 265, 303, 333, 420, 566.
Coggs Court, co. Oxford, document dated from, 520.
Coghill, Henry, 355.
........., ..., answer of, 392.
........., Mr., 296.
Coin, transportation of, 50.
........., information concerning, 50.
........., proposition concerning, 112.
........., manufacture of, 498.
Coke, Sir Edward, deceased, 2.
........., George, Bishop of Hereford, 59.
........., ..., his vicar-general and other officers, 59.
........., ..., reference to, of petition, 511.
........., John, letter to, 418.
........., Sir John, Secretary of State, and one of the Comptrollers General of the Posts, allusions and references to, *passim.*
........., ..., letters and other papers of, 12 (2), 38, 49, 82, 128, 130. 223, 242 (3), 257, 271, 278, 297, 341, 361, 408, 443, 451, 583, 596, 600, 603, 604.
........., ..., letters and other papers to, 51, 52 (2), 82, 139, 140, 274, 300, 301, 329, 361, 375, 394, 445, 475, 499, 531, 582, 598.
........., ..., references to, of petitions, 4, 5, 204, 451, 509, 511.
........., Sir Robert, 469.
........., Thomas, 178.
........., Walter, letter to, 312.

Coker, William, 210.
Colchester, 125, 137, 281, 341, 347, 557.
........, English bay and say-makers of, petition of, 104 (2).
........, ..., order on, 104.
........, Mayor, 557.
........, ..., letter to, 419.
........, Mayor and Aldermen, petition of, 47.
........, ship-money, 419.
........, St. Runwald, 69.
Coldham, John, 105.
Coldharbour, London, 417.
Coldingham, co. Berwick, 334.
Cole, variously spelt;—
........, Mary, 510, 522.
........, ..., examination of, 514.
........, ..., informations against, 521.
........, ..., her daughter, 522.
........, Mr., messenger, 598, 606.
........, Richard, 542.
........, Samuel, certificate of, 314.
........, Thomas, petitions of, 51 (2).
Cole Island, North America, 33.
Colebeach, Thomas, parson, articles against, 62.
Coleherbert, see Coldharbour.
Coleman Street, London, ward, return for, 114.
Coleridge, Devon, hundred, 134.
Coles, Edward, 197.
Coleson, Anne, examination of, 586.
Colkett, Robert, 91.
Collard, Thomas, letters of, 346, 435.
........, ..., his daughter, 346, 435.
Colleton, Anna, letter to, 15.
........, ..., her husband, 15.
Collieries, 247, 387, 419.
Collins, George, his Majesty's late gunpowder maker, deceased, 14, 46.
........, Increased, captain of Moate's Bulwark, Dover, particular and other papers by, 290, 350.
........, Richard, of Lubenham, letter of, 357.
........, Richard, late clerk of Stationers' Company, 379.
........, Sarah, widow, 14.
........, ..., petition of, 46.
........, William, 115.
........, ——, 125.
Collis, William, mayor of Northampton, 395.
........, ..., letter of, 394.
Colne, co. Huntingdon, manor, 447.
Colne, the river, 557.
Colston, Thomas, 169, 231 (2).
Colt, George, 526.
Colthurst, William, 3.
Coltman, Mr., 357.
Comber, Dr., 305.
Combes, John, 88.
........, ..., petition of, 88.
........, Thomas, petition of, 232.

Comfort Point, Virginia, castle, 323.
........, ..., ..., Captain of, see Morrison, Capt. Richard.
Commerce of England, damage to, by employment of ships under privilege of the King of Poland, 102.
Common Garden, see Covent Garden.
Common Pleas, Court of, 65, 76, 207, 223, 229, 270, 465, 512, 519.
........, ..., Justices of, 181, 223, 464.
........, ..., ..., letters and warrants to, 19, 148, 179, 236.
........, ..., Lord Chief Justice of, see Finch, Sir John.
........, rule in a cause in, 413.
........, filazer of, office of, 447, 573.
........, Treasury of, 532.
Common Prayer Book, 63, 69.
"Commoners Defence, the," case entitled, 159.
Commons, House of, late clerk of, see Wright, John.
Communion, the, 62, 64, 69, 74, 324, 363, 373, 539.
........, table, 64 (2), 67, 69, 157, 240, 248, 518, 536, 572.
Compostella, Spain, document dated from, 585.
........, St. James's church, 585.
Compter, the, in Wood Street or the Poultry, 119, 126, 359.
........, the, Southwark, 187.
........, ..., keeper, see Lindsey, James.
Compton, Sir Henry, 299.
........, John, 359, 372.
........, Nicholas, 257.
........, Walter, father of William, 372.
........, William, 359, 372.
Compton Abdale, co. Gloucester, 361.
Compton Dando, Somerset, 358, 386, 395.
Con, Mons., 62, 535.
Conception, the, of Dunkirk, 28; see also St. John, the, of Dunkirk.
Coneygarths near Berwick, 494.
Coneo, Signor, 62, 535.
Confession to a priest, 305.
Confidence, the, of London, 268.
Congham, William, 418.
........, ..., letter of, 418.
Congleton, co. Chester, 404, 472, 531, 538.
........, Mayor and others, petition of, 272.
Coningsby, variously spelt;—
........, Lieut.-Col. Francis, surveyor of ordnance, list by, 26.
........, Sir Thomas, sheriff of co. Hertford, letters and other papers of, 244, 355, 392.
........, ..., certificate to, 545.
Conisborough, co. York, 57.
Conliffe, John, 454.
Connant, Benjamin, petition of, 43.
Connaught, 502.
Connocke, Richard, 200.

GENERAL INDEX. 635

Conquest, Edmund, 155, 188.
........., Richard, petition of, 5.
Constant Reformation, the, or the Reformation, which see.
Constantinople, 103, 245, 255, 264, 361.
Consulage, Strangers', 102.
Conventicles, 382.
Convertive, the, 170, 237, 243, 261 (3), 266, 268, 271, 284, 356.
Convicts, transportation of, 400.
Conway, Edward, second Viscount Conway and Killultagh, 105, 421.
........., ..., letters to, 121, 144.
Cook, variously spelt;—
........., Amy, 424.
........., John, 453, 487.
........., Lambard, petition of, 123.
........., ..., his father, 123.
........., ..., his wife, 123.
........., Mrs., nurse, petition of, 365.
........., ..., her daughter, 365.
........., Richard, son of Capt. William, 446.
........., Richard, of Devonshire, 210.
........., Robert, 228.
........., Thomas, of the Isle of Ely, 504.
........., ..., examination of, 504.
........., Thomas, of London, petition of, 10.
........., Thomas, of Chishall Magna, 411.
........., Capt. William, master attendant of the Navy, 1, 36.
........., ..., letter of, 446.
........., William, constable, 584.
Cookes, Edward, 288.
Cookham, Berks, ship-money, 210.
Cooper, Sir Anthony Ashley, 579.
........., Thomas, certificate of, 463.
........., Thomas, bailiff of co. Northampton, 91.
........., ..., information of, 198.
........., William, petition of, 426.
Coopers, Wine, of London, company of, petition of, 45.
........., ..., ..., order on, 149.
Copehall, see Cople.
Cople, co. Bedford, 550.
........., ..., ship-money, 302.
Copley, William, 131.
Copper mines, 58.
Coppinger, John, 469.
Copple, William, appointment of, 131.
Copthorne, Surrey, hundred, 133, 543.
Corbet, variously spelt;—
........., Sir John, 59, 404.
........., Robert, sheriff of co. Montgomery, 490.
........., Simon, 149, 172.
Cordage, 30, 86, 262, 284.
........., account of expended, 30.
Cordall, Mr., 5.

Cordeliers, Friars, 448.
Cordewell, Samuel, the King's gunpowder maker, 14, 25, 46, 95, 97, 150, 160, 228, 242, 262, 348, 396, 488, 502, 509, 510, 527.
........., letter to, 23.
Corles, Richard, petition of, 141.
Corn, 32, 111, 112, 256, 551.
........., scarcity of, 156, 222, 303, 320.
........., transportation of, 112 (2), 156 (2), 278 (2), 279.
Cornbrough, co. York, 574.
Cornbury [co. Oxford], document dated from, 269.
Cornet Castle, Guernsey, 149.
Cornish, Abraham, 109.
........., Henry, 325.
........., ..., reference of petition to, 325.
Cornwall, 43, 95, 98, 130, 142, 156, 292, 353, 496, 502.
........., Vice-Admiral of South, see Bagg, Sir James.
........., ..., of North, see Bassett, Francis.
Cornwall, Sarah, petition of, 248.
........., ..., her children, 249.
........., Thomas, 248.
Cornwallis, Sir Frederick, bond of, 574.
Cororion, co. Carnarvon, 218.
Correction, House of, 473 ; and see Middlesex.
Corrie or Cory, George, grant to, 475.
........., Thomas, letter of, 548.
Cosin, Dr. John, 263.
........., letter of, 305.
"Cotcher houses," 176.
Cotchett, Gawen, deceased, 32.
........., Priscilla, 32.
Cotes, Mr., 424.
Cottages, commission to inquire of those erected without four acres of land being assessed to each, 602.
Cottesloe, co. Buckingham, hundred, 543, 548.
Cottingam, ——, letter to, 12.
Cottington, Francis, Lord, Chancellor of the Exchequer, and Master of the Court of Wards and Liveries, 4, 15, 44, 55, 75, 85, 118, 120, 144, 148, 153, 169, 227, 239, 241, 253, 266, 267, 272, 283, 298, 301, 378, 384, 387, 389, 402, 403, 409 (4), 440, 533, 575, 587, 611.
........., ..., letters and other papers of, 141, 144, 239, 294, 322, 346, 455, 461, 515, 519, 522, 525, 533, 576, 590, 598.
........., ..., the like to, 42, 98, 109, 168, 369, 445, 574.
........., ..., references to, of petitions, 5, 12, 16, 33, 35, 44, 141, 144 (2), 149, 204, 227, 233, 239, 248, 252, 345, 346, 354, 355, 366, 373, 477, 492, 496, 509, 520, 525, 552, 553, 554, 589.
........., ..., list of deeds of lands of, 131.
Cotton, Sir Thomas, letter of, 284.
........., ——, young, 441.

Cottrell, John, petition of, 98.
Council, the, notices of, and casual references and allusions to, *passim.*
.........., letters of, (1637, December) 15, 26, 30, 44 (2). (Undated) 76, 82, 97; (1637-8, January) 143, 146, 149 (2), 151, 155 (3), 156 (4), 161 (2), 166 (2), 171, 172 (5), 174, 177, 178 (7), 179, 184 (3), 185 (4), 189, 190 (3), 193, 196, 198, 199, 201 (5), 206, 207 (2), 208, 209 (4), 210 (6), 211 (6), 212 (5); (March) 295, 326 (2); (April) 385; (May) 398 (2), 400 (3), 403, 405, 406 (9), 410, 417, 418, 419, 422 (4), 423, 427, 428 (2), 433 (2), 434, 436, 437 (8), 440, 442, 443 (2), 446 (3), 450 (2), 452, 458, 459 (4), 462, 467, 472, 478, 479 (4), 480 (7), 485; (June) 538; (August) 590, 598.
.........., orders of, 7, 10, 22, 23, 42, 76, 80, 102, 148, 149 (3), 153 (4), 154 (4), 155, 164 (2), 165 (3), 166, 171 (2), 176, 183 (3), 184 (2), 185, 187 (2), 188 (5), 189 (4), 205, 206, 207 (3), 208 (2), 260 (2), 273, 281, 293 (2), 296, 299, 357, 368, 384, 397, 401 (3), 402 (4), 403 (6), 404 (3), 405 (2), 406, 408, 416, 422, 436 (4), 437, 442 (2), 448 (4), 449 (6), 450 (3), 462, 463, 469, 470 (4), 471 (3), 472 (4), 473 (2), 531.
.........., orders of, when the King present, 15, 26 (2), 27, 28, 60, 177 (4), 184, 196 (4), 347, 397 (3), 410, 416 (3), 417 (2), 454, 461 (3), 462 (3), 528, 587 (2).
.........., Nicholas's notes of proceedings of, 399.
.........., references to, of petitions, 272, 295, 374, 396, 509.
.........., reference from, of petition, 27.
.........., book of Councillors present at meetings, 148.
.........., inventory of books of acts of, 482.
.........., letters and petitions to, *see* the names of the writers.
.........., Chest, 351, 482, 515.
.........., Clerks of, 208, 256, 461.
.........., ..., list of papers delivered to, 224.
.........., Register, drafts and minutes for entries on, 142, 151, 190 (2), 199 (2), 201, 206, 208 (2), 212 (6), 398 (4), 405 (2), 410, 417 (4), 419, 423 (2), 425, 429, 430, 333, 435 (2), 440 (3), 443, 444 (3), 450, 452, 456, 459 (2), 463, 465, 466, 467, 474, 481 (4.)
Council Chamber, 40.
.........., ..., books in, 515.
.........., ..., keepers of, *see* Ravenscroft, George; Railton, William.
Counter, the, (prison,) *see* Compter, the.
Countrey or Country, John, 262.
.........., Jonathan, 30.
Couper, Lord, *see* Elphinstone, James.
Court, the, 21, 162, 289, 338, 339, 349, 357, 388, 467, 474, 559, 571, 586, 603, 611.
.........., list of Lent preachers at, 235.

Court, order of the King for government of, 49.
.........., postmaster of, *see* Poole, Richard.
.........., deputy postmaster of, *see* Wytton, John.
Courteen, William, deed of, 351.
.........., petition of, 3.
Covell, Mr., 126.
Covenant, the new, (book,) 366.
Covenanters, the, *see* Scotland.
Coveney, co. Cambridge, 494.
Covenham, St. Mary, co. Lincoln, 66.
Covent Garden, London, 6, 21, 114, 487.
Coventry, Francis, 440.
.........., ..., his wife, 440.
.........., Thomas, Lord, Lord Keeper, 22, 58, 106, 116, 128, 141, 150, 208, 225, 292, 297 (2), 312, 342, 350, 362, 380. 384, 474, 484, 486, 491, 497, 508, 511 (2), 517 (2), 536, 553, 557, 563, 574, 606.
.........., ..., letters of, 274, 435, 599.
.........., ..., orders and other papers of, 41, 141, 182, 183 (3), 205, 206, 362, 404, 405 (3), 455, 477, 478, 606.
.........., ..., letters and other papers to, 138 (2), 142, 174, 175, 215, 274, 283, 343, 344 (5), 351, 370, 408, 481, 486.
.........., ..., references to, of petitions, 12, 141, 174, 227, 250, 253, 255, 293, 309, 342, 350, 362, 373, 380, 461, 477, 484, 495, 508, 552, 553, 554, 574, 580, 606.
.........., ..., his lady, 491.
.........., ..., his secretary, *see* Alured, Mr.
.........., Thomas, letter of, 440.
Coventry, 539.
.........., King's free school at, 73.
.........., mercers of, petition on behalf of, 73.
.........., St. Michael's church, 305.
Cowdall, Henry, boatswain, 262.
.........., ..., petition of, 284.
Cowell, Dr., 567.
.........., ..., his Interpreter, 567.
Cowley, Samuel, 125.
Cowper, William, certificate of, 424.
Cowthery, William, of Strathfield Turgis, petition of, 474.
.........., William, of Basingstoke, 474.
Cox, variously spelt;—
.........., John, 396.
.........., Ralph, information of, 333.
.........., Richard, 393.
.........., Sarah, 376, 499.
.........., Thomas, 63.
.........., William, letter of, 418.
Coxall, Richard, answer of, 170.
Coy, John Jacobson, 600.
Coytmore, Robert, 183.
Crabb, John, the elder, examination of, 504.
Craddocke or Cradock, Mr., 3.
.........., Walter, 186.
Craft, William, memorandum of, 317.
Cramborne, 506.

Cramer, ——, Alderman of London, 87.
Cramond, Elizabeth, Viscountess, 34, 162.
Cranborne Chase, 55.
........., ..., rangers and others of, warrant to, 476.
........., Wood, 268, 320.
Crane, Sir Francis, late Chancellor of the Order of the Garter, 256, 429.
........., John, Victualler of the Navy, or Surveyor of Marine Victual, 24, 36, 142, 184, 208, 243, 256, 268, 302, 312, 319 (2), 333, 344, 358, 361, 479, 502 (2).
........., ..., letters of, 160, 278, 279, 294, 301, 565, 578.
........., ..., other papers of, 85, 209, 312, 565.
........., ..., order for, 228.
........., ..., letters to, 278.
........., ..., warrant to, 192.
........., ..., his children, 301.
........., Mrs., sister to Endymion Porter, 129.
........., dame Mary, widow of Sir Francis, 256.
Cranfield, Lionel, Earl of Middlesex, 435.
........., petition of, 372.
Cranford, co. Northampton, 249, 264.
Cranham Hall, Essex, 510, 514.
Cranston, William, Lord, 529.
Cranwell or Cromwell, William, 581.
Crathorne, Ralph grant to, 447.
Craven, William, Lord, 424, 505.
Crawley, Sir Francis, Justice of Common Pleas, 448, 606.
........., ..., his argument in Hampden's case, 540.
........., ..., letters to, 135, 546.
Cray, North, Kent, 598.
Crediton, Devon, 472.
........., hundred, 136, 545.
Creech, Giles, petition of, 166.
Creed, Thomas, 71.
Creeton, co. Lincoln, statement of changes in the tithes of, 69.
Creswell, Emanuel, 247.
Creswick, Francis, 231 (2).
Crettall, John, 111.
........., Richard, letter of, 111.
Crewe, John, 164.
Crewkerne, Somerset, rectory, 253.
Crimes, Commissioners for foul, 505.
Crippes or Crips, Adam, 107.
........., Capt., 99.
Crispe, Capt., 183.
........., John, petition of, 61.
........., Nicholas, petitions of, 254 (2), 516.
........., ..., certificate of, 478.
Crocker, Samuel, 223.
Croft or Crofts, Cicely, deceased, late maid of honour to the Queen, 247, 419.
........., Henry, order in cause of, 383.
........., John, 172, 221.

Croft or Crofts, Mary, 346.
........., Mr., 159, 598.
Croke, Sir George, Justice of the King's Bench, 182, 370, 443, 473, 495, 606.
........., ..., argument of, in Hampden's case, 541 (2).
........., ..., letter of, 512.
........., ..., letters to, 133, 134 (3), 548.
........., Sir Henry, Clerk of the Pipe, 557.
........., ..., pardon of, 587.
........., Sir John, Sheriff of co. Dorset, letter of, 317.
........., ..., letter to, 210.
Cromer, Norfolk, 3.
Cromhall, co. Gloucester, 316, 351.
Crompe, James, letter to, 518.
Crompton, Thomas, of Weston, Somerset, 479, 602.
........., Thomas, executor to Lady Vanlore, 271, 496.
........., ..., ..., exceptions by, 455.
Cromwell, variously spelt;—
........., Sir Henry, 308.
........., Mr., 592.
........., Mrs., 591, 592 (2).
........., Sir Oliver, letter of, 369.
........., William, 581.
Crook, Westmoreland, hundred, 546.
Crookehorne, see Crewkerne.
Crosby, Sir Pierce, 520.
........., ..., petitions of, 432, 519.
........., Sir Walter, 432.
Croshaw, Richard, deceased, 372, 435.
Crosland, Thomas, petitions of, 80 (2).
........., his wife and children, 80.
Cross [Leonard], messenger, 75.
........., ..., letter to, 194.
........., Thomas, 428.
Cross Keys tavern, [Covent Garden,] London, 21.
Crosseley, Adam, grant to, 434.
Crossing, Thomas, Mayor of Exeter, letter of, 411.
Crosthwaite, Westmoreland, return for, 546.
Croston, co. Lancaster, vicarage, information concerning, 60.
Crow, Edward, 506.
........., Sir Sackville, Ambassador to Turkey, 103, 122, 303.
........., ..., letter of, 103.
........., ..., warrant to, 303.
Crown, the, manuscripts concerning succession to, 21.
........., clerk of, 41, 208.
Crown Office, the, 208, 536.
Crowne, Edmund, letter of, 556.
........., Joan, letter of, 516.
........., ..., letter to, 516.
........., ..., her husband, 516.
........., ..., William, petition of, 363.

Crowther, Richard, 8.
Croydon, co. Cambridge, 391.
........., Surrey, 327, 570.
Crumwell, see Cromhall.
Cufaud, Francis, 384, 399.
Cull, John, 192.
Cullompton, Devon, 218.
Culpeper, John, 602.
........., Sir William, Sheriff of Sussex, letter of, 88.
Cumberland, co., 58, 362, 501, 584, 598.
........., Sheriff, see Dacre, Sir Thomas.
........., ship-money, 191 (2).
........., Vice-Admiral, see Howard, Theophilus, Earl of Suffolk.
Cundall, Arthur, memorandum touching, 48.
Cunningham, [D ?], letter of, 99.
........., Sir David, Receiver-General of the Prince of Wales's revenue, 99, 510.
........., ..., demise to, 392.
........., ..., commissions to, 602 (2).
Curle, Walter, Bishop of Winchester, 288.
........., ..., letter and other papers of, 64, 205.
........., ..., reference to, of petition, 318.
Curry Mallett, Somerset, 407.
Curzon, Sir John, sheriff of co. Derby.
........., ..., letters of, 327, 412, 597.
Cusse, Henry, 486, 521.
Custom House, London, 2, 24, 25, 99 (2), 101, 123, 154, 260.
Customs, the, 44, 50, 105, 149, 201, 214, 252, 310, 366, 378, 403, 588.
........., farmers and officers of, 99 (2), 242, 409.
........., ..., letters and other papers of, 22, 38, 106, 204, 327.
........., ..., the like to, 42, 106, 203, 262, 403, 409, 422, 476, 589 (2).
........., of the out-ports, Surveyor of, see Allington, John.
Cutlers, the, of London, letter of, 105.
Cutterice or Cutteris, John, 374, 482.
........., letters of, 445, 515.
Cutts, Sir John, letter to, 589.
Cyril, Patriarch of Constantinople, 264.

D.

Dack, Roger, petition of, 229.
........., ..., ..., order on, 229.
Dacorum, co. Hertford, hundred, 392.
Dacre, Randal ?, Lord, 309, 353.
........., Sir Thomas, Sheriff of Cumberland, letter of, 191.
Dacre, Cumberland, 598.
Dacres, Mr., deceased, see Dacre, Randal, Lord.
Dade, Henry, L.L.D., bailiff of Ipswich and judge of the Vice-Admiralty of Suffolk, letter of, 139.
Dadford, George, 470.
Dalby, Gerrard, gunner, appointment of, 131.
........., John, 23.
Dale, Anne, 471.
........., John, deceased, 409.
........., William, 409.
Dalhousie, Earl of, see Ramsay, William.
Dalkeith, 529.
Dallison, Mr., 475.
Dallygood, John, 372.
Dalton, Joseph, late mayor of Hertford, 356.
Damerham, [Wilts], 530.
Danbury, [Essex], document dated from, 146.
Danby, Earl of, see Danvers, Henry.
Daniel, Anne, petition of, 117.
........., ..., letter to, 117.
........., Capt. Charles, 117.
........., Edward, 270.
........., Mr., parson, 563.
Danske, Stephen, 269.
Dantzic, 3, 31.
........., sturgeon, 444.
Danvers, Henry, Earl of Danby, Governor of Guernsey, 149, 271, 324, 448, 586, 604.
........., ..., letters of, 269, 475.
........., ..., his Lieutenant, see Darell, Capt. Nathaniel.
........., ———, brother to William Calley, 169, 506.
Darcy, Sir Francis, Justice of Peace for Middlesex, certificate of, 431.
........., Thomas, Earl of Rivers, 186.
........., ..., his Lady, 186.
Darell or Darrell, Marmaduke, 507.
........., Sir Marmaduke, 226, 333.
........., Capt. Nathaniel, Lieutenant to the Earl of Danby, Governor of Guernsey, 149.
........., Sir Sampson, deceased, 333.
Darmstadt, landgrave of, 47.
Dart, ——, 500.
Dartford, Kent, 31, 548.
........., ship-money, 197.
Dartmouth, 149, 245.
Darton, Sir John, petition of, 458.
Daubeney, Henry, Earl of Bridgewater, 275.
........., ..., his Countess, 275.

Davenant, John, Bishop of Salisbury, 304, 420, 434.
........., ..., letter of, 408.
........., ..., letter to, 211.
........., Mary, petition of, 359.
........., William, 359, 360.
Davenport, Sir Humphrey, Chief Baron of the Exchequer, 449, 471, 495.
........., ..., warrant of, 148.
........., ..., reference to, of petition, 9.
........., William, 427.
........., ..., agreement of, 314.
Daventry, co. Northampton, 536.
........., ship-money, 220.
Davey, William, petition of, 258.
........., ..., his father and son, 258.
Davies, variously spelt;—
........., Lady Eleanor, 219, 554.
........., ..., her "Appeal to the Throne," 219.
........., Evan, late sheriff of co. Radnor, petition of, 322.
........., Henry, warrant to, 179.
........., Hugh, 382, 383.
........., John, 460.
........., Philip, petitions of, 239, 240.
........., Robert, 163.
........., ..., petition of, 96.
........., ..., information of, 163.
........., Thomas, his Majesty's barber, letter of, 263.
........., ..., answer to allegations of, 468.
........., William, 340.
Davison, variously spelt;—
........., David, petition of, 109.
........., Mr., 489, 532.
........., ——, 24.
Daw, William, 271.
Dawes, Sir Abraham, 54, 149, 360.
........., ..., grant to, 19.
........., ..., reference to, of petition, 306.
........., ..., petition of, 458.
Dawson, Thomas, 395, 397.
Day, Cyprian, petition of, 164.
........., George, grant to, 409.
........., Thomas, master of the children of the Chapel Royal, certificate of, 22.
........., Thomas, ship-carpenter, 541 (2).
Deal Castle, 291.
Dean or Deane Forest, co. Gloucester, 53 (2), 54, 254, 400, 531.
........., ironworks in, 53, 54, 254.
........., farmers of, 168.
........., ..., petition of, 18.
........., new farm of, proposition for taking, 53.
Dean, Little, co. Gloucester, 287.
........., inhabitants of, letters of, 286, 287.
Deane, John, affidavit of, 349.
Dean's Yard, Westminster, 434.
Deare, Pierce, 141.

Dearing, ——, 500.
Dee, Francis, Bishop of Peterborough, 157, 206, 533.
........., ..., collector of tenths in his diocese, see Lambe, Sir John.
Deer, 579.
........., proclamation touching, 163.
........., schedules of, bestowed upon ambassadors and others, 579 (2).
Deering, Charles, 298.
Defiance, the, 132, 182, 243.
Delamain, Richard, petitions of, 121 (2), 282.
Delate, John, 496.
Delbridge, John, 93.
........., Richard, 93.
Delegates, Court of, 77 (3), 84.
........., registrar of, 84; and see Fielding, George.
Delft, 110, 365.
Deliverance, the, of Ipswich, 298.
Dell, William, Secretary to Archbishop Laud, 65, 69, 138, 238.
........., ..., letter to, 142.
Delves, Sir Thomas, late sheriff of co. Chester, 199.
........., ..., letters of, 41, 44.
De Merito, book by Bishop Morton, of Durham, 263.
Demi-casters, hats so called, 106.
Demry, Henry, petition of, 239.
Denbigh, document dated from, 387.
Denbigh, co., justices of peace, letter to, 271.
........., sheriff, see Morris, Edward.
........., ship-money, 92, 387 (3).
Denbigh, Earl of, see Fielding, William.
Denford, co. Northampton, plague in, 91.
........., ship-money, 91.
Denham, Sir John, Baron of the Exchequer, 274.
........., ..., letter of, 274.
Denison, Dr. Stephen, 324, 325.
Denization, grant of, 410.
Denmark, 592, 598.
........., ambassador from, 598.
Denn, Walker, pardon to, 173.
Dennington, Suffolk, 248, 497, 519.
Denny, Edward, Earl of Norwich, deceased, 340.
........., Honora, daughter of Edward, Earl of Norwich, 340.
........., Mary, Countess of Norwich, death of, 321.
........., ..., funeral certificate of, 340.
Denton, Sir Alexander, Sheriff of co. Buckingham, 337, 567.
........., ..., letter of, 237.
........., ..., licence to, 6.
........., ..., his lodging in Princes Street, document dated from, 237.
De Nuisement, ——, writer on astrology, 597.
Depositions, proposal of an examiner in every county, for taking, 78.

Deptford, 139, 292, 480.
........., documents dated from, 33, 314, 577.
"Deputy, the," letter to, 603.
Deputy Lieutenants, all, letter to, 257.
Derby, document dated from, 180.
........., bailiffs and burgesses, 155.
........., ..., letter of, 180.
........., mayors, see Mellor, Henry; Hope, John.
........., plague in, 180.
........., ship-money, 91 (2), 180.
Derby, Earl of, see Stanley, William.
........., Countess Dowager of, see Stanley, Alice.
Derby, co., 125, 152, 179.
........., Justices of Assize, 413.
........., Justices of Peace, 413.
........., Sheriff, see Curzon, Sir John.
........., ship-money, 327, 412, 494, 597.
........., Deputy Lieutenants, 494.
........., ..., letter of, 494.
........., Lower peak, 98.
........., Higher peak, 98, 112.
Derby [West], co. Lancaster, hundred, 136 (2), 546.
........., ..., manor, 282.
Derling, Richard, grant to, 400.
Dervold, co. Hereford, forest, 252.
Desire, the, of London, 590.
Desmond, Earl of, see Fielding, George.
........., the late Earl, see Preston, Richard.
Devereux, Dorothy, daughter of Walter, Earl of Essex, 556.
........., Robert, Earl of Essex (temp. Eliz.), 263.
........., Robert, Earl of Essex (1603–1646), 414.
........., Walter, Earl of Essex (temp. Eliz.), 241, 556.
Devizes, Wilts, mayor, certificate of, 137.
Devon, co., 43, 95, 98, 130, 142, 156, 176, 292, 306, 362, 430, 439 (3), 445, 449, 501, 512.
........., brethren of the Merchant Adventurers Company residing in, 176.
........., Justices of Peace, certificates and letters of, 136 (2), 137, 218, 545.
........., ..., letters and other papers to, 210, 218.
........., Lord Lieutenant, see Russell, Francis, Earl of Bedford.
........., Sheriffs, see Rolle, Dennis; Wise, Thomas.
........., ship-money, 2, 93, 235.
........., Vice-Admirals, see Seymour, Sir Edward; Bagg, Sir James.
Devonshire, Countess of, see Cavendish, Elizabeth.
Dewell, Henry, Surveyor to his Majesty for the Highways, letter of, 341.
........., Humphrey, 8.
Diamond, the, of London, 3, 137.

Dice, 149.
........., Commissioners for discovery of offenders in buying and selling unsealed, 295; and see Cards.
Dicker, John, 285.
Dickson, Joseph, 259.
........., Richard, of Kinnell, 529.
........., Richard, of co. Warwick, 405, 459.
........., Robert, 397.
Dieppe, 19, 83, 94, 117, 244, 261, 277, 315, 326, 330, 493, 569.
Dieu Repulse, the, see Repulse, the.
Digby, George, Lord, 162, 309.
........., John, Earl of Bristol, letter of, 175.
........., ..., his son, 175.
........., Sir Kenelm, report of, 192.
Digges, Sir Dudley, Master of the Rolls, 155, 174.
........., ..., reference to, of petition, 174.
Dillingham, Mr., 591.
Dillon, William, LL.D., 201.
........., ..., petition of, 65.
........., ..., list of witnesses in cause of, 65.
Dimock, Henry, 506.
Dinely, John, 147.
Dingley, Sir Edward, Sheriff of co. Worcester, letter of, 344.
........., John, 198, 201.
Dingley, co. Northampton, 206.
Dinham, Lady, 77.
Dinnington, see Dennington.
"Direction, the," book so termed, comments upon, 62.
Disafforesting lands, Commissioners for, 424.
Discovery, the, ship, 160.
Distiller of sweet herbs and waters, the King's, office of, grant of, 39.
Distillers of London, master, wardens, assistants, and commonalty, 585.
Dixon, Ann, 140 (2), 146.
........., Edward, 325.
........., ..., reference to, of petition, 325.
........., John, 140.
........., ..., petition of, 140.
........., Richard, petitions of, 368 (2), 379.
Doctors' Commons, London, 238, 313, 382.
........., documents dated from, 158, 159.
........., ..., Steward of, 79.
Dodd, variously spelt;—
........., Dr., dean of Ripon, 287.
........., John, petition of, 362.
Doddington, co. Chester, document dated from, 41.
Doddridge, Pentecost, late Mayor of Barnstaple, petitions of, 93 (2).
Doding, ——, 242.
Dodington, Alice, petition of, 128.
........., Sir Francis, 416.
........., ..., petition of, 128.
Dolben, William, 280.

GENERAL INDEX.

Doleman, Ann, 384, 399.
........., Thomas, 384.
Dollars, transportation of, 149.
Dolman, Mr., 336.
Dolphin, the, merchant ship, 213.
Don, the river, 57.
Dones, Samuel, petition of, 120.
Donington, co. Leicester, document dated from, 577.
........., co. Warwick, 288.
Donne, John, petition of, 25.
........., [John], dean of St. Paul's, father of the above, 25.
Dorchester, 62, 574.
........., burgesses of, memorandum of, 439.
........., ship-money, 210 (2).
Dore, Mr., 501.
........., William, 175, 179.
Dorington, Mr., 75.
Dormer, Robert, Earl of Carnarvon, account of fees paid on his creation as Viscount and Earl, 50.
Dorset, co., 142, 284, 292, 445, 501.
........., Justices of Peace, letter of, 118.
........., sheriff, 169, 238. *See* Croke, Sir John; Freke, John; Trenchard, Sir Thomas.
........., ..., letter to, 210.
........., ship-money, 4, 169, 317.
........., Vice-Admiral, *see* Howard, Theophilus, Earl of Suffolk.
........., Countess of, *see* Sackville, Mary.
........., Earl of, *see* Sackville, Edward.
Dorset House, Salisbury Court, Fleet Street, London, 34.
........., documents dated from, 34, 321, 356, 361, 474.
Dorton, co. Buckingham, 564.
Doughtie, Thomas, 116.
Douglas, Sir Archibald, 582.
........., ..., letter of, 554.
........., Capt., 458.
........., Lady Eleanor, 554.
........., Sir George, 527.
........., James, 530.
........., Sir James, 457, 494.
........., ..., letters of, 61, 582, 599.
........., ..., minutes by, 324, 349.
........., James, Viscount Drumlanrig, 529.
........., Margaret, 435.
........., ..., her husband, 435.
........., Robert, Viscount Belhaven, 274, 409.
........., ..., letter of, 270.
........., William, Earl of Morton, 152, 602, 603.
Dove, Robert, M.A., presentation to, 203.
Dover, Alexander, 263.
........., Samuel, 501.

Dover, 19, 36, 45, 50, 75, 151, 173, 234, 269, 277, 326, 361, 569, 600.
........., documents dated from, 290 (2), 291, 556.
........., boom across the harbour's mouth, 527, 569, 587.
........., ..., keeper of, *see* Manwood, Sir John.
........., harbour, 282, 527, 569, 587.
........., ..., Commissioners for, 569.
........., ..., ..., certificate of, 569.
........., King's prison at, keeper of, *see* Reston, John.
........., mayor and jurats of, 569.
.... pier, 223.
.... road, 330.
........., searchership, 100 (8), 129, 451.
Dover Castle, 81, 282, 290.
........., documents dated from, 558, 569, 603.
........., inventory of ordnance in, 352.
........., particular of defects in, 290.
........., Lieutenant of, 569; *and see* Manwood, Sir John.
Dover, Earl of, *see* Carey, Henry.
........., John, haberdasher, 155, 161.
Dover Merchant, the (ship), 137.
Doves, James, 607.
........., Capt. Samuel, 487, 488.
Dowdeswell, Richard, petition of, 495.
Dowell, Jo[hn], letter of, 5.
Downame, John, petition of, 68.
Downes, John, 281, 336.
........., Roger, 471.
........., ..., letter of, 481.
........., Thomas, report of, 379.
Downham, co. Cambridge, 503.
Downham, Dr., 338.
Downing, ——, 242.
Downs, the, 86, 155, 223, 268, 444, 482, 493, 579.
........., documents dated from, 3, 15, 17, 31, 36, 44, 173, 202, 234, 246, 269, 304, 499, 598, 608.
Dragon, the, ship, 306.
Drapers, Corporation of New, 11.
Draycot, co. Wilts, 195 (1).
........., document dated from, 195.
Drayton Parslow, co. Buckingham, 564.
Dreadnought, the, 170, 243, 541 (2).
Drope, ——, 458.
Drumlanrig, Viscount, *see* Douglas, James.
Drummond, Sir David, General-Major to the Queen of Sweden, 130.
Drury, Sir Anthony, 238.
........., Jeremy, 159.
........., William, 92.
Drury Lane, 442, 592.
........., document dated from, 605.
Drywood, George, petition of, 458.
Duart, James, his Majesty's jeweller, account of moneys due to, 173.

Dublin, 468.
.... Castle, 401.
Dubois, John, 222, 223.
Ducie, Sir Richard, late sheriff of co. Gloucester, 165.
........., ..., letter to, 211.
Duck, Dr. Arthur, Chancellor of London, 78, 90, 187, 287, 326, 332, 348, 379.
........., ..., letters and other papers of, 158, 238, 341.
........., ..., petitions to, 71, 73.
Duddeley, Sir Robert, 77.
........., Katherine and other daughters of the above, petition of, 77.
Duels, 213.
Duke's Place, London, 417.
Dukeson, Richard, 399.
Dunblane, Bishop of, see Wedderburn, James.
Duncombe, George, 360, 451.
........., ..., grant to, 19.
........., Henry, petition of, 318.
........., William, 214.
Dunkirk, the, 3, 6, 15, 18, 28 (2), 36, 44, 102, 151, 234, 246, 270, 296, 300, 304, 444, 482, 493, 499, 569, 600.
Dunkirkers, the, 6, 8, 17, 28, 36, 44, 76, 151, 174, 202, 234, 246, 262, 266, 270, 296, 329, 499, 578, 603, 609.
Dunmow, Essex, park, 425.
Dunn, Thomas, 409.
Dunning's Alley, Without Bishopsgate, London, 163.
Dunsmore, Lord, see Leigh, Francis.
Duppa or Dupper, Alexander, 384, 399, 473.
........., Brian, Bishop of Chichester and tutor to the Prince, 70, 361.
........., ..., presentation to, 444.
........., ..., reference on petition to, 555.
........., Capt. James, 220, 349.
........., ..., letters and other papers of, 108, 230, 235 (2), 238, 271, 346, 349.
Durham, documents dated from, 274, 475.
........., Bishop, see Morton, Thomas; James, William.
.... Castle, document dated from, 294.
........., Chancellor, 475.
........., Dean and Chapter, 60, 61.
........., ..., petition of, 250 (2).
........., Mayor, see Heighington, John.
........., prebends, 61.
........., ship-money, 294.
Durham, co., 346, 362, 501.
........., Justices of Assize, 387.
........., Vice-Admiral, see Howard, Theophilus, Earl of Suffolk.
Durham House, Strand, 402.
........., document dated from, 42.
Durie, Gilbert, 61.
Dursley, co. Gloucester, document dated from, 142.
Dury, John, 263.

Dutch East India Company, 263.
Dwarfs, the Queen's, 49.
Dyer, James, town clerk of Bristol, 138.
........., ..., letter of, 23.
........., Katherine, Lady, 200.
........., Mary, grant to, 200.
Dyers, 130.
Dymoke, Charles, petition of, 9.
Dynes, John, 91.
Dynne, Francis, 335.
........., ..., commissions to, 363, 602 (2).
Dyott, Sir Richard, 382.

E.

Eadmer, extract from chronicle of, 288.
Earbury, Anthony, 602.
Earith, co. Huntingdon 447.,
Earl's fen, part of Wildmore fen, 55.
Ears, loss of, punishment, 491.
Eason, Richard, 427.
East, John, petition of, 128.
Eastcot, co. Northampton, 518.
East Country Merchants, see Eastland Merchants.
East fen, co. Lincoln, 55.
East India Company, 153, 228, 262, 307, 488, 502 (2).
........., letters to, 19, 509.
........., their storehouse at Blackwall, 160.
........., their ships, 19, 279.
........., ..., saltpetre, 19, 228, 262, 263.
East Indies, 15, 18, 19, 36.
........., fleet for, commander of, see Weddell, Capt. John.
Eastland Merchants, 549.
........., petitions of, 112, 334.
........., ..., orders on, 149, 153.
........., letter to, 514.
........., master of, see Clitherow, Sir Christopher.
East Smithfield, the King's manor of, 479.
Eaton, Garrod, letter to, 271.
........., Jarrett, 23.
........., Prestwick, letter of, 19.
Eccleshall Castle, co. Stafford, document dated from, 351.
Ecclesiastical Commission, see High Commission.
Ecton, co. Northampton, 64.

Eden, Dr. Thomas, Master of Trinity Hall, Cambridge, and Chancellor of Ely, letter of, 316.
Edgborough, see Edisbury.
Edinburgh, 308, 331, 524, 525, 529, 554.
........., documents dated from, 159, 324, 349, 529.
.... castle, 352, 529, 534, 582.
........., Weigh House in, 524.
Edisbury, Kenrick, Surveyor of the Navy, 175, 228, 333, 344.
........., ..., death of, 609.
........., ..., letters of, 36, 82, 131, 162, 249, 261, 269, 311, 460, 542.
........., ..., letters to, 132, 363.
........., ..., his wife, 311.
Edithweston, co. Rutland, 390.
Edmondes, Sir Thomas, Treasurer of the Household, 333, 421, 427, 521.
Edmonds, Robert, petition of, 68.
Edmund Hall, Oxford, 198.
Edward II., 565.
.... III., 45.
.... IV., 357.
.... VI., 60, 114, 118, 226, 253, 413, 452, 478.
Edwards, David, 199, 296, 312, 335.
........., ..., petitions of, 335 (2).
........., Evan, baron of the Exchequer at Chester, 471.
........., James, 4 (2).
........., John, the elder, 296, 312.
........., ..., note of his charges, 301.
........., John, the younger, 296, 312.
........., John, of Weston Patrick, 381, 400, 406, 435, 452.
........., Mr., justice of peace at Northampton, 395.
........., Renatus, girdler, 155, 161.
........., Richard, 370, 383, 399.
........., Robert, searcher at Dover, in reversion, 100.
........., Robert, [of Huntingdon?], certificate of, 513.
........., Thomas, constable of Flint castle, grant to, 400.
........., Thomas, of Rorington, Salop, 199, 296, 312, 335.
........., ..., petitions of, 335 (2).
........., William, builder, letter of, 176.
........., William, of Rorington, 199, 296, 312, 335.
........., ..., petition of, 335 (2).
........., ——, of Salop, 434.
Edwardstone, Suffolk, 233.
Edwinstree, co. Hertford, hundred, 134, 545.
Effingham, Surrey, hundred, 133, 543.
Egerton, John, Earl of Bridgewater, Lord President of Wales, letters of, 32, 296.
........., Peter, 404.
........., Sir Rowland, 370.
Egerton, Kent, 224.

Egham, 560.
Egleton, Robert, 346.
Eglinton, Earl of, see Montgomery, Alexander.
Egmont, Count of, 493.
.... his son, 493.
Eight Hundred, Holland, Swineshead or Swinstead, Fen, near Boston, 57, 476, 522 (2), 528, 553.
........., adventurers in drainage of, statement of shares to be raised by, 151 (2).
Ekins, Thomas, 245.
Ekyns, John, grant to, 447.
Elbridge, Giles, 231 (2).
Elcho, Lord, see Wemyss, David.
Eldinge, Edward, 132, 541.
Elector Palatine, see Palatinate.
Elgin, Earl of, see Bruce, Thomas.
Eliot, variously spelt;—
........., David, 160.
........., Sir William, letter of, 348.
........., ..., letter to, 527.
Elizabeth, Queen of Bohemia, see Bohemia.
........., Queen of England, 49, 60 (2), 69, 81, 105, 197, 241, 247, 250, 252, 263, 287, 328, 366, 380, 448, 452, 467, 469, 560, 585, 595.
Elizabeth Castle, Jersey, 442, 475.
Elizabeth Islands, North America, 33.
Ellesdon, Anthony, Mayor of Lyme Regis, certificate of, 429.
Elliott or Ellyott, see Eliot.
Elmbridge, Surrey, hundred, 133, 543.
Elmes, John, 214, 241.
Elphinstone, James, Lord Coupar, 529.
........., John, Lord Balmerino, 529.
........., W., letter of, 159.
Elston, co. Nottingham, 470 (2).
Eltham [Kent], 15, 67.
Eltham, Statutes or Articles of, observations on, 49 (2).
........., the old book of, 515.
Eltonhead, Ralph, 111.
Ely, 503.
........., Bishop of, see Buckeridge, John; White, Francis; Wren, Matthew.
........., bishopric, warrant for installing first fruits of, 435.
........., ..., homage of Bishop Wren on appointment, 483.
........., Dean and Chapter, congé d'elire to, 311.
........., Chancellor of, see Eden, Dr. Thomas.
........., Isle of, 362, 471, 493, 501.
........., ..., Judges of Assize and Judge of, 232.
........., ..., Justices of Peace, letter of, 503.
........., ..., ship-money, 232.
........., ..., the Great Level in, 56, 152, 438, 471.
Emerson, Francis, saltpetreman, 228, 344, 375, 501.
........., ..., letter and other papers of, 23, 376.

Emerson, Thomas, 147.
Emery, James, 480.
........., Richard, petition of, 224.
Emildon, Northumberland, 343.
Emott, William, 76, 77.
Ems, Mr., 145.
Emsworth, Hants, 293.
Endfield, co. Stafford, see Enville.
Enfield, Middlesex, 391, 487.
........., Chase, 487.
........., Commissioners for newly erected cottages in, 487.
........., manor, 498.
........., ship-money, 87.
Engine for working mills, 16.
England, Church of, 21, 63, 67, 224, 277, 287, 305, 306, 377, 382, 477, 534, 573.
English Popish Ceremonies, Scotch book so called, 365.
Enmore, Somerset, document dated from, 377.
Enrolments, Clerk of the, charges against, 77.
Entrance, the (ship), see Happy Entrance.
Enville, co. Stafford, 540.
Epping, Essex, 160, 190, 191.
.... Forest, 328.
Epsom, Surrey, 327.
Erith, Kent, 1, 166.
Erle, Sir Walter, 396.
........., ..., letter of, 568.
........., ..., reference on petition to, 396.
Ermington, Devon, hundred, 137.
Erpingham, South, Norfolk, hundred, 544.
Erskine, Thomas, Earl of Kelly, warrant to, 435.
Esse alias Ash [Essen alias Ashen?], Essex, 181.
Essex, 95, 153, 155, 175, 182, 337, 362, 441, 501, 505, 557.
........., brewers of, petition of, 108.
........., ..., list of, 108.
........., ..., incorporation of, 311.
........., Commissioners for brewing in, 108.
........., forest of, 587.
........., Justices of Assize, letter to, 548 (2).
........., Justices of Peace, 235, 460.
........., ..., letters and returns of, 135, 136, 548 (2), 549, 610.
........., ..., letter to, 480.
........., Sheriff, 207, 210, 470; see Luckyn, Sir William; Mildmay, Sir Humphrey.
........., ship-money, 146, 185, 208.
........., Vice-Admiral, see Rich, Robert, Earl of Warwick.
Essex, Earl of, see Devereux, Walter.
Essex House, Strand, 162.
Essington, William, agreement of, 176.
Estcourt, Sir Giles, 205, 211.
Estimates, Navy, 146 (2).
........., Ordnance, 32, 155, 170, 320 (2), 367, 522, 523, 535, 578, 579 (2).

Eton College, former provost of, see Savile, Sir Henry.
Etwall, co. Derby, 380.
Evans, John, 521.
Eveleigh, ——, 500.
Evelyn, John, late gunpowder maker, 96, 126, 163, 170, 480, 529.
........., Mr., 480.
Everard or Everett, Clement, 372.
........., ..., certificate of, 386.
........., Dr., 166.
........., Edward, information of, 139.
Eversholt, co. Bedford, 432.
Everton, co. Lancaster, manor, 282.
Everts, John, indictment against, 76.
Every, Henry, 77.
Evesham, co. Worcester, 156.
Ewecross, co. York, wapentake, 134.
Ewens, Francis, 53.
Ewer, Henry, commission to, 602 (2).
........., William, commission to, 602 (2).
Ewry, grooms and sergeants of the, 263.
Exacted fees, Commissioners for, 80.
........., request of, 77.
Examiner, proposal for establishment of one in every co., 78.
Exchange, and see Royal Exchange.
........., the old, 20.
........., the new, 402, 599.
........., office of, 247.
Exchange, the, ship, 137, 213.
........., the, of Southampton, 232, 243, 262.
........., ..., names of crew, 232.
Exchequer, the, 12, 16, 17, 34, 38, 44, 45, 58, 79, 82, 87, 97, 100, 116, 120, 123, 128 (2), 130, 149, 165, 171, 180, 182, 189, 196 (2), 204, 214, 227, 231, 239, 245, 260 (2), 267, 271, 283, 292, 301 (3), 303, 309, 317, 325, 334, 362, 366, 369, 371, 383, 384, 385, 400, 419, 421, 424, 429, 435, 439, 441, 452, 469, 477, 483 (2), 492, 495, 498, 562, 582, 610.
........., account of money paid out to purveyors, 227.
........., auditors of, 6, 148.
........., notes of assignments of moneys to be received, 221, 371, 575.
........., writ and orders of, 257, 258 (2), 359, 372, 483.
........., Barons of, 248, 434, 487, 492 (2).
........., Chamber, 115, 471, 559.
........., Chancellor of, see Cottington, Francis Lord.
........., Chief Baron, see Davenport, Sir Humphrey.
........., ..., the late, see Walter, Sir John.
........., officers of, 6, 9, 115.
........., letters and warrants to, 20, 148, 152 (3), 303 (2), 309, 476.
........., Remembrancer of, 359; see Fanshaw, Sir Thomas.
........., ..., account of duties of office, 98.
........., treasurer of, warrant to, 428.

GENERAL INDEX. 645

Exchequer, Under Treasurer of, warrants to, 39, 428, 574.
Exeter, 114, 142, 148, 176, 283, 404.
........, document dated from, 411.
........, Officers of Customs at, letter to, 434.
........, close, 114.
........, diocese, 562.
........, Mayor, letter to, 434, *and see* Crossing, Thomas.
........, division of authority in, notes of inconveniences arising from, 114.
........, brethren of the Merchant Adventurers Co. in, 164, 176, 185, 218.
........, Bishop of, *see* Hall, Joseph.
........, ship-money, 93, 456.
Exeter College, Oxford, Regius Professor of Divinity and Rector of, *see* Prideaux, Dr. John.
........, ..., and others of, certificate of, 282.
Exeter, Earl of, *see* Cecil, William.
........, Earl of, the late, *see* Cecil, Thomas.
Exminster, Devon, 472.
........, ..., hundred, 456.
Exmoor Forest, Devon and Somerset, 55.
Expedition, the, King's pinnace, 186, 213, 237, 243, 356, 535.
Exping, *see* Epping.
Export of un-customed goods, proposed office for prevention of, 43.
Extill, Nathaniel, 381, 405.
Eyhorne, Kent, hundred, 137.
Eynesbury, co. Huntingdon, inhabitants of, petition of, 580.
Eynesford, Norfolk, hundred, 544.
Eyres, Lady, 182.

F.

Fairfax, Sir Ferdinando, 433.
........, Thomas, 433.
........, William, 162.
Falcon de Paços and Janqueras, Gutiere, pass of, 585.
Faldoe, William, letter to, 433.
Falkland, Viscount, *see* Carey, Lucius.
Falkner, Lyon, 320.
Familists, 166.
Fanchau, *see* Fanshawe.
Fane, Mildmay, Earl of Westmoreland, 14, 42.
Fanshawe, Mr., Secretary to the English Ambassador in Spain, 31, 271.

Fanshawe, Sir Thomas, Remembrancer of Exchequer, 539.
........, ..., certificate of, 488.
Farbeck, Thomas, petition of, 468.
Fareham, Hants, ship-money, 126, 127 (4).
Faringdon, Berks, document dated from, 574.
Farlsthorpe, co. Lincoln, 167.
........, document dated from, 167.
Farmer, Sir Hatton, *see* Fermor, Sir Hatton.
Farmery, Dr., 129.
Farnaby, John, certificate of, 492.
Farnham, Richard, 188, 606.
Farren, Peter, churchwarden of All Saints, Northampton, 157.
........, petition of, 248.
Farrington, Lionel, 11, 74.
........, statement concerning, 11.
Farrow, Ambrose, 506.
........, William, B.D., presentation to, 400.
Fathers, John, 296.
Faunt, Sir William, 54, 126.
...., his three daughters, 126.
........, George, executor and nephew of Sir William, petition of, 126.
Fausbrooke, Mr., minister of Cranford, 249.
Fautrait or Fawtrart [Peter], 138.
........, petition and other papers of, 272, 273, 280.
Faversham, Kent, hundred, 133, 548.
Fawkes, Michael, 403.
Fearne, Sir John, 336.
Feasey, Walter, 203.
Featley, Dr. Daniel, 324.
........, ..., deed of, 399.
Fees which might be granted without concurrence of Parliament, 131.
........, Commissioners for, 114, 148.
........, ..., reference to, of petition, 148.
Felgate, William, 85.
........, ..., petition of, 109.
Fell, Samuel, D.D., dean of Lichfield, 168, 352.
Felons' goods, grant of, 98.
Feltham [Middlesex], 131.
Fen or Fenn, Edward, clerk to Sir William Russell, 91, 115, 313.
........, ..., letters of, 527, 557, 572.
........, Edward, ship-owner, 44.
........, Richard, afterwards Sir Richard, Lord Mayor of London, 606.
........, ..., letters and other papers of, 357, 369, 507, 563.
........, ..., the like to, 161 (2), 369, 472.
Fenchurch Street, London, document dated from, 468.
Fenner, Edward, 224.
........, ..., junior, petition of, 224.
........, John, 224.
Fenny Compton, co. Warwick, 437 (2), 456.
.... Stanton, co. Huntingdon, 420.

Fens, draining, in co. Cambridge, 56 (2), 438, 493, 504.
........., ..., Carmarthen, 292.
........., ..., Glamorgan, 292.
........., ..., Lincoln, 5, 10, 12, 26, 55, 56, 57, 151, 152, 158, 252, 253 (2), 438, 475, 522, 540, 556, 563, 572, 590.
........., ..., Norfolk, 438, 566.
........., ..., Northampton, 438.
........., ..., Nottingham, 12, 253.
........., ..., Pembroke, 292.
........., ..., Suffolk, 438.
........., ..., York, 12, 253.
........., popular tumults in the, 493, 500, 503, 504, 506, 571, 572.
Fenton, co. Nottingham, 326.
........., documents dated from, 327, 443.
........., co. Huntingdon, manor, 447.
Fenwick, George, 310.
........., ..., his books, 172.
........., Robert, letter to, 456.
Ferentz, Thomas, or Sir Thomas, Mons., or Colonel, 7, 47.
........., ..., letter of, 29.
Fermor, Sir Hatton, 395.
Férnefold, Sir Thomas, 156, 185.
Ferrabasco, Mrs., 63.
Ferrers, Edward, 403.
........., ..., petition of, 508.
........., Sir Henry, 508.
........., ..., petition of, 380.
........., Jane, deceased, 380.
........., Judith, 380, 509.
........., Thomas, deceased, 380, 508.
........., William, the elder, deceased, 380, 508.
........., William, the younger, deceased, 380, 508.
Ferris, Mr., 85.
Fessant, Mr., 197.
Fesse, see Fez.
Fetter Lane, London, the Naked Boy in, 445.
Fez, 117.
........., English Consul at, see Penn, Giles.
Field, Daniel, petition of, 581.
........., Elizabeth, 586.
........., Robert, M.A., presentation to, 16.
........., ——, aunt to Margaret Cley, 586 (2).
Fielding, George, Earl of Desmond, 435.
........., ..., petition of, 366.
........., George, Registrar of the Court of Delegates, letter to, 85.
........., Mary, 431.
........., Capt. Richard, 608.

Fielding, William, Earl of Denbigh, Master of the Great Wardrobe, 431.
........., ..., account of, 329.
........., ..., note of his employments at sea, 390.
........., ..., warrants to, 30, 174, 409, 427, 435, 441, 514, 577 (2).
Fiennes, William, Viscount Say and Sele, 206.
........., James, 164.
Fifehead, co. Dorset, 316.
... ., vicar of, 352.
Filder, Mr., 505.
Filgrove, co. Buckingham, 275.
Fillingham, Richard, 201 (2).
Filo [Filey?] co. York, bridge, 17.
........., harbour and light for, 17, 371.
........., pier, 17.
Finch, Edward, certificate of, 488.
........., James, 65.
........., Sir John, Lord Chief Justice of Common Pleas and Chief Judge of the Western Circuit, 65 (2), 173, 274 (2), 384, 401, 408, 449, 465, 474, 495 (2), 574.
........., ..., letters and other papers of, 41, 229, 408, 412, 455.
........., ..., argument in Hampden's case, 541.
........., ..., letters and other papers to, 148, 222, 412, 425, 480, 519, 609.
........., ..., references to, of petitions, 9, 354, 495.
Finchampstead, Berks, 582.
Fines to his Majesty, to be paid by suitors after judgment, warrants for rating, 148, 236.
Finett, Sir John, 599.
Finnimore, Henry, 453 (2), 487, 488, 510, 513 (3), 515 (2).
Firbank, Westmoreland, return for, 546.
Fire insurance, 392.
Fire-engines, 338, 392.
Fires, proposition for prevention of, 392, 393.
First fruits, 147, 435.
Fishborne, Richard, deceased, 426.
Fisher, Sir Edward, 492.
........., Capt. John, muster-master of the city of London, grant to, 29.
........., Luke, statement respecting will of, 78.
........., Martin, indictment against, 76.
........., Mr., 478.
........., Mr., sub-warden of Merton College, 390, 438, 562, 570, 573, 588, 601, 605, 607.
Fishermen, see Thames.
Fishing, Society and Associations for, with their councils or other governing bodies, 101, 143, 204, 260, 578, 603, 609.
........., ..., account of the state of, 579.
........., ..., certificates of, 8 (7).
........., ..., letter of, 109.
........., ..., defaults in subscriptions to, 4.
........., ..., passes of, 419 (2).

Fishings, proposition for ordering the, 112.
........., the Royal, 609.
Fishlake, co. York, 57.
Fison, Mr., 107.
FitzGeoffrey, Henry, 340.
FitzGerald, Edmund, 34.
........., George, Earl of Kildare, 309.
FitzHarris, ——, 432.
FitzHerbert, John, 542.
FitzWilliam, Humphrey, 551.
........., John, Lord, 89.
........., Walter, 335.
........., ..., request of, 99.
........., ..., letter to, 363.
Flags, 82, 265.
Flamborough Head, co. York, 17, 371.
........., ..., lights at, 25, 371.
Flamsteed, Mr., information by, 64.
Flanders, 137 (2), 291, 493, 511, 554, 580, 587.
Flats, the (at mouth of the Thames), 202.
Flaxwell, wapentake, co. Lincoln, ship-money, 257.
Fleckney, co. Leicester, 357.
Fleet, the, 128.
........., sent out in 1636, 208.
........., sent against the Turks at Sallee, see Sallee.
........., sent out in 1637, 83, 160, 182 (2), 390.
........., sent out in 1638, 24, 146, 159, 162, 174, 182 (2) 194, 212, 228, 262, 266, 268 (2), 290, 291, 356, 373 (2), 410, 428, 444, 474, 578.
........., Admiral of, see Percy, Algernon, Earl of Northumberland.
........., Vice-Admiral of, see Pennington, Sir John.
........., Rear-Admiral of, 356.
Fleet, the (prison), 10, 27, 42, 43, 105, 124, 126, 189 (2), 206, 207, 218, 220, 283, 284, 322, 378, 400, 469, 477, 569, 580.
........., tower chamber of, 123.
........., warden of, 189, 480.
........., ..., warrants to, 149, 156, 166, 172, 174, 185 (2), 206, 207, 326 (2), 398 (2), 400 (2), 406 (2), 418, 428, 467, 480.
........., ..., his deputy, see Ingram, James.
Fleet Street, London, 6, 34, 236, 565.
........., ..., document dated from, 227.
Fleetwood, Sir Gerard, 186.
........., Sir Miles, Receiver of the Court of Wards, 374, 402.
........., ..., warrant to, 428.
........., Sir Paul, 131.
........., Sir Richard, 131.
Flegg, East, Norfolk, hundred, 134.
........., West, Norfolk, hundred, 134.

Fleming, Dennis, Clerk of the Navy, 175, 195, 344, 609.
........., John, letter to, 524.
........., John, Lord, 529.
........., Lady Margaret, certificate touching, 431.
Flendish, co. Cambridge, hundred, 134.
Fletcher, John, purser, 132.
........., Mr., 97.
Flint castle, constable of, see Edwards, Thomas.
........., ship-money, 92.
Flint, co., 148, 441.
........., Justices of Peace, petition of, 92.
........., Prothonotary and Clerk of the Crown for, 148.
........., sheriff, see Whitley, Thomas.
........., ship-money, 92, 312, 407 (2), 429, 485, 507.
Flitton, co. Bedford, 363.
Florence, 31, 467, 579.
Floyd, Dr., 23.
........., Lewis, 370.
........., Richard, 23.
Fludd, ——, 241.
Fluellin, Eleanor, 276.
Flushing, 82.
Flute, Thomas, 159, 222.
........., ..., petition of, 222.
........., ..., ..., abstract of, 223.
Fly, William, 293.
Foard, John, evidence of, 288.
........., Sarah, evidence of, 288.
........., Thomas, agreement of, 176.
Folkingham sessions, co. Lincoln, inhabitants of, petition of, 211.
........., ship-money, 211.
Folkstone, 93.
Folwell, Henry, petition of, 364.
Fonthill, Wilts, 131,
Foord, John, petition of, 393.
Foote, ——, 393.
Foots Cray, Kent, document dated from, 132.
Forhench, Charles, M.A., affidavit of, 549.
Force, Duke de la, 493.
Ford, Emmanuel, 210.
........., Richard, 449.
Forehoe, Norfolk, hundred, 546.
Foreign Churches in England, viz. ;—
........., Walloon congregation, Norwich, remonstrance of, 356.
Foreign occurrents, books of, 444.
Forests, book of orders concerning, 289.
Forests and Woods, see their respective names.
Forman, Richard, order in cause of, 383.
Forrester, George, Lord, 529.
Forster, Ann, petition of, 18.
........., George, 18.
........., William, 345.
Fort, Robert, 275.
........., Roger, 275 (2).

648 GENERAL INDEX.

Fortescue, Anthony, 224.
........., ..., petition of, 117.
........., Grace, 604.
........., Edmund, petition of, 43.
........., John, petition of, 229.
........., ..., order on, 229.
........., [John] of Were, Devon, 604.
........., Mr., of Somercotes, 482.
Fortifications, 599.
........., proposed general charge for, 81.
........., engineers of, 121 (2).
........., principal engineer for, see Paperill, John.
Forts, see Castles.
Fortune, the (pink), 213.
........., the, of Hoorn, 85.
........., the, of London, 239. Ship
Fortune, Richard, petition of, 264.
Foster, Jonathan, 597.
........., Mr., 577.
........., Thomas, 333.
........., William, 336.
........., ———, 488.
........., ———. 187.
Fotherby, Edward, 488.
........., W , receipt of, 160.
Fountnay, Julian, petitions of, 7, 38.
Fowke, Anthony, 540.
........., Thomas, certificates of, 301, 323.
Fowl, Wild, 363.
Fowling, Robert, 77.
Foxe, [Charles,] 23, 168.
........., ..., letter and other papers of, 138, 169.
........., Lieut., 321, 356.
Foxholes, co. York, 288.
Foxton, John, 309, 331.
........., ..., information of, 331.
........., ..., letter to, 309.
Foxton, co. Cambridge, 372.
Frampton, Thomas, 4.
France, 3, 7, 19, 29, 36, 45, 50, 81, 85, 96, 106, 117, 122, 136, 246, 261, 277, 300, 304, 315, 321, 326, 330, 484, 493, 530, 535, 551, 558, 564, 587.
........., Ambassadors from, 201, 278, 523, 579 ; and see Bellievre, Mons.; Chevreuse, Duke of.
........., English Ambassador in, see Sydney, Robert, Earl of Leicester.
........., embargo in, 3, 18, 45, 173, 234.
........., King of, 117, 201.
........., fleet and ships of, 6, 262, 266, 290, 304, 516.
........., salt of, 217.
........., wines of, 41 (2), 42, 106, 107, 461.
........., ..., merchants of, trading in, memorial of, 106.
........., ..., petitions of, 106 (2).

Franchis or Franqui, John Nicholas de, brief in a cause of, 554.
Francis, Mal[achi?], fees and charges of, 340.
........., David, petition of, 52.
........., ..., his father, 52.
"Francisco, the Italian mountebank," 130 (2).
Franck, Sir Leventhorpe, 120.
........., Dame Lucy, 120.
Francklyn, ———, searcher, 99.
Franklyn, James, Keeper of Newgate, 512.
Freebridge Lynn, Norfolk, hundred, 134.
........., Marshland, Norfolk, hundred, 134.
Freeholders, book of, in every county, 425.
Freeman, Catherine, 338.
........., Edward, 437.
........., Sir Ralph, one of the Masters of the Requests, letter of, 42.
........., Ralph, 119.
........., ..., paper of, 119.
........., ..., reference to, of petition, 119.
Freere or Freer, Henry, letter of, 346.
........., Thomas, 467.
Freeze, James, 384, 399, 473.
Freke, John, formerly sheriff of co. Dorset, 4.
........., ..., letter of, 169.
........., Richard, 88 (2).
French, John, 194.
........., Robert, 232, 304.
........., ———, of Merton College, Oxford, 562, 601.
Frere, Thomas, 371, 431.
Frewen, Dr. Accepted, 287.
........., ..., letter of, 425.
........., ..., letter to, 438.
........., Dr. Richard, 325.
Friesland, East, 47.
"Frissell," ———, in a list of Scottish covenanters, 529.
Frizell, James, 255.
........., William, 51.
........., ..., bond of, 145.
Frodsham, Edward, 443, 444, 450.
........., ———, 592.
Frome, Selwood, Somerset, 131.
........., Whitfield, co. Dorset, ship-money, 210 (2), 238.
Fromonds, Bartholomew, 512, 513.
........., ..., his wife, 512.
Fryar or Fryer, Edward, 322, 381 ? 583, 610.
........., Robert, 270, 322, 381 ? 583.
Fuel which yields no smoke, 490.
Fulbert, George, certificate of, 551.
Fulford, Sir Francis, 396, 574.
........., ..., letter of, 568.
........., ..., reference on petition to, 396.
Fulham House, Middlesex, document dated from, 522.
Fulke, Peirce, 370.
Fuller, Christopher, 406 (2).

GENERAL INDEX.

Fullerton, Sir James, 447.
Fulmer, Bucks, 507.
Fulwood, Anthony, 201 (2).
........., Humphrey, 487.
........., ..., commissions to, 602 (2).
........., Roger, 376.
........., ..., petition of, 498.
Funeral certificates, 34, 340, 431, 500, 556, 598, 604.
Furley, Joan, indictment against, 76.
........., Thomas, indictment against, 76.
........., William, indictment against, 76.
Furlong, James, 431.
Furness, co. Lancaster, liberty, 543.
Fursman, John, 441.
Fyfield, Essex, 172, 190, 207, 220.

G.

Gage, George, governor of the Soapmakers Company of Westminster, 71, 369.
........., Lady Penelope, 162.
Gaire, ———, 500.
Gallard, John, 267.
Gallas, ———, 264.
Galloway, see Galway.
Galway, 194.
Games, Catherine, 78.
........., Hoe, statement relative to the wardship of, 78.
........., John, deceased, 78.
........., Sir John, 78.
Gamon, Giles, 363.
Gandy, John, 288.
Ganner, Paul, 539.
Garbler, office of, 114.
Gardener, variously spelt ;—
........., Christopher, letters of, 9, 29, 41, 597.
........., Thomas, Recorder of London, letters of, 400, 481.
Gare, ———, 191, 536, 539.
Gariney, Lieut. John, petition of, 250.
Garland, the, 213, 598.
Garnier, Mons. Jean, 118, 261.
........., Louis, 261.
Garrard, Humphrey, answer of, 167.
Garratt or Garret, Katherine, 610.
........., Thomas, deceased, 98.
........., Thomas, 610.
........., William, soapmaker, 105.
........., William, stationer, petition of, 298.

Garraway or Garway, Henry, 553.
........., John, 370.
........., William, 41, 109, 183, 204.
........., ..., petition and other papers of, 3, 192.
Garret, see Garratt.
Garsley, Jeremy, 473, 480 (2).
Garter, order of, 287, 486, 537.
........., ..., Chancellor of, grant of pension to, 214; and see Roe, Sir Thomas.
........., ..., feast of, 353.
........., ..., Knight of, installation of Prince Charles as, 445 (3).
Garthorpe, co. Lincoln, 368, 370.
Gartsyde, John, 167.
Garway, see Garraway.
Garwood, Thomas, the younger, certificate of, 463.
Gascogne wine, 41.
Gascoigne, Sir William, (temp. Henry IV.,) 81.
Gasset, Robert, 452.
Gatcombe, [Somerset,] document dated from, 418.
Gatcombe, Isle of Wight, 446.
Gatehouse Prison, Westminster, 117, 224, 291, 556.
........., ..., keeper of, warrants to, 437, 442, 443.
Gates, Timothy, letter, letter to, 210.
Gaudy, William, petition of, 283.
Gawen, Katherine, 458.
........., William, 458.
Gayner, Thomas, 85.
Gayney, ———, mate of the Swiftsure, 37.
Geddes, John, account of, 38.
Gelasius, patriarch of Alexandria, 264.
Geneva, 71.
Gentile, Charles, account of moneys due to, 329.
........., ..., warrant to, 424.
Gentlemen Pensioners, Board of, petition of, 233.
George, hundred, see St. George.
George, the, ship, 403.
Gerard, see Gerrard.
Gerbier, Balthazar, the King's agent in Brussels, 461, 578, 600, 609.
........., ..., receipt of, 515.
Germany, 7, 130, 226, 526, 534, 593.
........., Emperor of, 47, 51.
Gerrard, variously spelt ;—
........., Francis, 560.
........., ———, Alderman of London, 87.
Gery, Mr., 567.
Gibb, Sir Henry, commissions to, 602 (2).
Gibbes, variously spelt ;—
........., Captain William, petition of, 250.
........., Dr. William, certificate of, 75.

Gibbes, variously spelt—*cont.*
........., William, proposed Commissioner respecting abuses by porters, 319.
........., ——, of Merton College, 562.
Gibbins, Eleanor, petition of, 283.
Gibbon, John, 403, 515.
........., ..., petitions of, 16 (2), 17, 517, 533.
........., ..., order on petition of, 515.
Gibson, Sir John, 33.
........., Mr., 226.
Giffard, variously spelt ;—
........., George, 466.
........., ..., letter of, 466.
........., John, note by, 395.
........., Dr. John, certificate of, 75.
........., William, 587.
Giffords Manor, Suffolk, 181.
Gift of God, the, of London, 110.
Giggen, John, Mayor of Wareham, memorandum of, 441.
Gilbert, Anne, petition of, 562.
........., Robert, senior, 506.
........., Thomas, order in cause of, 383.
........., William, 562.
Giles, Edward, petition of, 23.
........., ..., ..., order on, 23.
........., Walter, bond of, 505.
Gilkes, William, 365.
Gill, ——, a poor widow, 155, 161.
Gilling, East, co. York, wapentake, 345.
........., West, co. York, wapentake, 345.
Gillingham, Kent, 1, 304, 329, 421.
Gilpin, Randolph, 183.
Gipps, Mr., 567.
Gladding, Richard, 21, 22.
Gladman, Ralph, petition of, 111.
Glamorgan, co., 292.
Glanford Brigg, co. Lincoln, 157.
Glanville, Sir Francis, 430.
Glapwell, co. Derby, 494.
Glass, 23, 153, 154.
Glaziers, Company of, 153.
Gleane, Matthew, 498.
Gleaners of corn in the night, 135.
Glemham, Sir Thomas, 556.
Glemham Hall, Suffolk, 556.
Glendon House, co. Northampton, 249.
Glenn, co. Leicester, 424.
Gloucester, 187, 372.
........., Archdeacon of, *see* Robinson, Dr. Hugh.
........., Common Council, orders of, 286 (5).
........., corporation of, extracts from their minute books, 286, 287.
........., mayor and others, letters to, 286 (2), 287.
........., King James's Hospital, 286.
........., Margaret's Hospital, 286.

Gloucester, St. Bartholomew Hospital, 187, 285, 286 (4), 287.
........., ..., Commissioners to survey orders at, 286.
........., ..., ..., names of, 286.
........., ..., ..., report of, 286.
Gloucester, co., 156, 502.
........., Judges of Assize, 362.
........., Justices of Peace, 210.
........., ..., letter to, 210.
........., Sheriff, *see* Ducie, Sir Richard ; Leigh, William ; Pointz, Sir Robert.
........., ship-money, 9, 165, 184, 337.
........., Vice-Admiral, *see* Guise, Sir William.
........., Bishop of, *see* Goodman, Godfrey.
Glover, Alexander, 221.
........., Richard, petition of, 68.
Glovers of London, papers relating to their incorporation, 104, 338 (3).
Gloverstone, co. Chester, 363.
........., ship-money, 27, 158, 186, 231, 377, 423, 462.
Goates, William, examination of, 503, 504.
Goche, Henry, D D., petition of, 511.
Godalming, Surrey, 126, 405.
........., hundred, 133.
Godbeare, Anne, 363.
Godbold, Mr., 497.
Goddard, Anthony, grant to, 434.
........., Henry, letter of, 261.
........., William, 427.
Godfrey, William, boatswain, 174, 541.
........., ——, 145.
Godley, Surrey, hundred, 133.
Godmanchester, co. Huntingdon, ship-money, 11.
Godney, William, information of, 521.
Godolphin, Sir Francis, Governor of Scilly, 151, 266, 270, 540.
........., ..., letters of, 260, 261.
........., ..., letter to, 498.
........., Francis, 362.
Godstone, Surrey, 163.
Godwin, Paul, report of, 276.
Gogney, Mr., 510.
Gold, transportation of, 153.
........., ..., information concerning, 50.
.... thread or wire, *see* Thread.
Golden Fleece, the (ship), 137.
Golden Wolf, the, or Wolf (ship,) 84, 590, 600.
Goldsmith's Row, Lombard Street and Cheapside, London, 155, 161 (2), 330.
Golsbery, Austin, 144.
Golsborough, Nicholas, letter to, 201.
Gomeldon, William, bill of, 329.
Gomersall, Grace, 516, 553.
........., Thomas, 553.
Gooch, Thomas, 453.
Goodcole, Henry, 399.
Goodfellow, Edward, 482.

GENERAL INDEX. 651

Goodman, Godfrey, Bishop of Gloucester, 287.
........., ..., letter of, 604.
........., Robert, 333.
Goodrick, Sir Henry, 433.
Goods, lost, office for discovery of, 19.
Goodson, George, 398.
Goodwin, variously spelt :—
........., Gartwright *alias* Sanders, 264.
........., Patrick, letter of, 378.
Goodyeare, John, letter of, 257.
Goold, John, letter of, 265.
Gore, William, 110.
Goree, 82.
Gorges, Edward, Lord, petition of, 252.
Goring, Colonel, 474.
Goring, George, Lord, Master of the Horse to the Queen, 103, 141, 422.
........., ..., commissions to, 602 (2).
........., ..., petition to, 99.
........., ..., warrants to, 303, 418.
........., Sir William, 88.
Gorpdet, Mons. de, Ambassador from the States, 178.
Gorway, William, 359.
........., ..., information of, 359.
Gosselin, Peter, 350, 450.
Gotha, 47.
Gotte, Morris, statement of, 391.
Gonbard, David, 306.
Gouge, Barnaby, 199, 201 (2).
........., Dr. William, 325.
Gough, Henry, 247.
Gower, Stanley, charge against, 249.
Grace, the, of Weymouth, 298.
Grafton, the honor or park of, 374, 428, 518.
Graham, James, Earl of Montrose, 529.
Graienunce, John, *see* Gray, John.
Grancester, *see* Grantchester.
Grange, Mary, 125.
........., William, 125.
Grant, John, letter of, 37.
Grantchester Mills, co. Cambridge, 343.
Grantham, Lady Lucy, petition of, 81.
........., Sir Thomas, 81.
Grantham-cum-Socâ, co. Lincoln, ship-moncy, 212.
Grasmere, Westmoreland, return for, 546.
Graunt, John, letter of, 430.
........., Winter, 472.
Gravenhurst, Nether, co. Bedford, ship-money, 272.
Graves, John, 82.
Gravesend, 147, 178, 194, 195, 388, 449, 482, 580.
........., officers and sub-searchers of, letter to, 580.
Graveship, Nether, Westmoreland, 370.
........., return for, 547.
Gray, Charles, 592.
........., John, messenger, 481, 512, 513.
........., ..., order on petition of, 187.

Gray, John, of Milton Ernest, 417, 429, 440.
........., ..., bond of, 440.
........., John, vicar of North Somercotes, letter of, 482.
Grayrigg, Westmoreland, return for, 546.
Gray's Inn, London, 21, 229, 376, 464, 538.
........., document dated from, 592.
Great Level, co. Lincoln, 5, 152, 253, 471, 475, 571, 572, 590.
........., adventurers for draining, petition of, 252.
........., commissioners for letter of, 571.
........., ..., reference on petition to, 253.
Greaves, John, letter of, 245.
........., ..., his brother, 245.
Greece, 264.
Greek Church, the, 264.
.... printing type, 72.
Green, variously spelt ;—
........., Charles, deceased, 128.
........., Charles, bookseller, petition of, 257.
........., Gougb, 23.
........., John, brother to Richard, 35.
........., John, of Lamerton, 331.
........., John, constable of Towcester, 561.
........., Richard, petition of, 35.
........., Simon, 35.
........., William, of co. Lincoln, 201.
........., William, of London, 443.
Greencloth, the, 222, 312, 376, 401.
........., ..., officers of, 226, 258, 368, 398, 466, 467, 520, 531.
........., ..., ..., letters and certificate of, 375, 467, 510.
Greenfield, William, 133.
Greenhoe, South, Norfolk, hundred, 544.
Greenstead, Essex, 185.
Greenwax, 152.
........., farmers of, 152.
Greenwich, 48, 113, 162, 282, 309, 461, 538, 550, 571.
........., documents dated from, 465, 467, 494, 495, 496 (3), 497, 499, 505, 508, 509 (3), 517 (3), 518, 520 (2), 527, 528, 532, 533, 536, 552 (2), 553 (2), 554, 557, 558, 559.
Gregge or Grigg, Edward, 381, 449.
........., ..., bond of, 458.
........., Michael, paymaster for the repair of St. Paul's, 422.
........., ..., letter to, 422.
........., ——, 102.
Gregory, Francis, 436.
........., John, 432.
Gregory XIII., Pope, 264.
Gresford [co. Denbigh], rectory, 253.
Gresham College [London], 245.
........., document dated from, 245.
Gresham, John, 481.
Grestmere, *see* Grasmere.
Grenville, Sir Richard, petition of, 129.

Greville, Robert, Lord Brooke, 144.
Grey, Anne, Countess of Stamford, 9.
........., Henry, Earl of Stamford, 9, 56.
Greyhound, the (pinnace), 213, 608.
Griffin, William, 437.
Griffith, variously spelt ;—
........., Sir Edward, 206.
........., John, commissions to, 602 (2).
........., John, Vice-Admiral of North Wales, letter to, 502.
........., Roger, 23.
........., Thomas, 400.
........., Dr. William, letter to, 201.
........., William, late serjeant-at-arms, 22.
........., William, of Westminster, information of, 139.
........., William, of co. Carnarvon, 218, 288.
Grigge, see Gregge.
Grigson, William, 331 (2).
Grills, ——, 500.
Grimes, Agnes, 448.
........., William, 448.
Grimmer, Mr., curate, Wickham, 493.
Grimsby, Great, co. Lincoln, ship-money, 2, 212.
........., ..., mayor, see Hollis, Gervase.
Grimshoe, Norfolk, hundred, 544.
Grimstone, Harbottle, justice of peace for Middlesex, 469.
........., ..., certificate of, 507.
........., Sir Harbottle, certificate of, 549.
Grinewige, see Greenwich.
Grinstead, Sussex, 480.
Grise, Nicholas, 129 (2).
Groningen, 324.
Grosse, ——, 500.
Grosthead [Grossetête], Robert, Bishop of Lincoln (1234-1253), 339.
Grove or Groves, Elizabeth, petition of, 283.
........., Hugh, letter to, 95.
........., John, 283.
........., ——, stationer, 155, 161.
Grovely [Wood], Wilts, 55, 506.
Grover, Jason, carrier, 22, 171, 217, 297.
........., ..., petitions of, 217, 284.
Groyne, the, 6, 7, 13, 28 (2), 278, 554.
Groyne fleet, the, see Spain, fleet of.
Guard, the King's, clerk of the check of, answer by, 394.
Guard Chamber, the, Whitehall, 521.
Guernsey, 270, 278, 350, 450.
........., governor of, see Danvers, Henry, Earl of Danby.
........., ..., his lieutenant, 351, 450; and see Darell, Capt. Nathaniel.
........., King's Free School, 448.
Guest, ——, 384.
Guildford, Surrey, 490.
........., document dated from, 348.
........., ship-money, 198, 420.
Guildhall, London, 109.

Guilserland, on the borders of Scotland, 558.
Guinea merchants, 417.
Guise, John, 383, 384.
........., William, 383, 384.
........., Sir William, Vice-Admiral, co. Gloucester, letter to, 502.
Gulliford, ——, 351.
Gunnell, Reignold, letter to, 406.
Gunners, 13 (2), 128, 146.
Gunpowder, 46, 96, 97, 243, 408, 499, 528, 529.
........., carriage of, see Carriage for the King's service.
........., commissioners for, see Saltpetre.
........., consumption of, 9, 25 (2), 26, 160.
........., embezzlement of, 163, 170, 348, 505.
........., foreign, 85.
........., transportation of, 444.
.... maker, the King's, 25. See Cordewell, Samuel.
........., ..., late, see Collins, George; Evelyn, John.
........., papers relating to manufacture of, 12 (2), 32, 94, 95 (2), 96 (6), 97, 150, 160, 170 (2), 502.
........., ..., report touching, 242 (3).
........., the like to sale of, 5, 8, 9, 20, 36, 85, 95, 96 (2), 126, 146 (2), 159, 163, 194, 195, 228, 284, 288, 371, 379, 431, 443, 489, 490, 524, 526.
.... magazines, propositions concerning, 195.
Gunpowder treason, the, 522.
Gunstone, Mr., 14.
Gutstring makers, petition of, 22.
........., certificates respecting, 22 (2).
Gutteridge, William, 463.
Guy, Leonard, 303, 304, 307.
........., ..., information of, 298.
........., William, 469.
Guylett, John, 261.
........., Richard, 261.
Gwynn, Richard, 78.
........., Dr. Thomas, 78 (2).
Gyfford, see Giffard.
Gylden, George, letter to, 179.
Gyles, see Giles.

H.

Hackhurst, see Hawkhurst.
Hackwell, Mr., Justice of Peace of co. Bucks, 346.
Hacon, Hubert, 458.
........., John, 458.
Haddenham, co. Cambridge, 493.
Hadleigh, Suffolk, plague in, 157.
Hadnett, John, 198.
Haggar, Thomas, 390, 391 (4).
........., ..., his wife, 391.
Hague, the, 82, 147.
........., documents dated from, 7, 29, 146.
Hails, see Hales.
Hales, Sir Edward, 598.
........., John, answer of, 167.
........., Mr., letter to, 129.
Halford, Jane, petition of, 79.
........., Mr., 554.
........., Richard, petition of, 79.
........., ..., letter of, 390.
........., Thomas, 390.
Haling, see Hayling.
Hall, Bartholomew, marshal of the Marshalsea, and his wife, 48.
........., John, 145.
........., Joseph, Bishop of Exeter, letter of, 218.
........., ..., petition to, 218.
........., Robert, 261.
........., Thomas, 429, 448.
........., Valentine, 363.
Hallikeld, co. York, wapentake, 345.
Hallingbury Magna, Essex, 464.
........., ship-money, 213, 224.
Halsey, Dr. James, 288.
Halstead, Lawrence, agreement of, 176.
Ham, West, Essex, 287.
Hambleton, Col., 71.
Hamburgh, 449, 483, 595.
........., English ambassador sent to a congress at, 47.
........., other ambassadors at, 7.
........., Merchant Adventurers of, 110.
........., ..., Court of, 110.
........., ships of, 3, 269.
........., treaty at, 7, 29, 47, 146.
........., Venetian ambassador at, 7.
Hamby, Richard, 329.
........., ..., account by, 130.
Hamhaw, Surrey, 348, 406, 480, 527.
Hamilton, Alexander, 48.
........., Colonel Hugo, letter to, 367.
........., Colonel James, 270, 302.
........., ..., letter of, 297.

Hamilton, James, Marquess of, and Earl of Cambridge, Master of the Horse, Steward of Hampton Court, and his Majesty's Commissioner in Scotland, 37, 98 (2), 100, 173, 431, 490, 521, 524, 529, 534, 575 (2), 582, 592, 600.
........., ..., letters of, 394, 415.
........., ..., letters and other papers to, 476, 526, 581, 593.
........., John, warrant to, 425.
........., Mary, Marchioness of, and Countess of Cambridge, funeral certificate of, 431.
........., ..., ..., herald's proclamation at her interment, 431.
........., ..., ..., fees paid on, 469.
........., ..., inscription on her coffin, 431.
........., ..., her children
    Charles, Earl of Arran,
    James,
    William, } 431.
    Anne,
    Susan.
........., Robert, 101.
........., Sir William, 499.
Hammersley, Sir Hugh, 110.
Hamond, Francis, petition of, 90.
........., John, 583.
Hampden, John, 337.
........., ..., his case respecting ship-money, papers relating to, 540.
Hampson, Thomas, 173.
Hampton [Bishop, co. Hereford], 39.
Hampton and Claverton, liberty, Somerset, ship-money, 193.
Hampton Court, 162, 376, 442.
........., ..., documents dated from, 131, 559.
Hanaper, the, 208.
Hanbury, Sir John, Sheriff of co. Northampton, 192.
........., ..., letters of, 294, 364.
........., ..., return of, 220.
Hanchett, ——, 146.
Hancock, ——, mercer, 73.
Hanford, Francis, commission to, 602 (2).
Hang, East, co. York, wapentake, 345.
........., West, co. York, wapentake, 345.
Hangings, see Tapestry.
Hanham, West, co. Gloucester, 178.
Hannam, Thomas, 156.
Hans[lip?], ——, 458.
Hanslope, co. Buckingham, manor, 374.
Hanson, Francis, 167.
Hants, 95, 104, 175, 460, 502.
........., Judges of Assize, reference on petition to, 474.
........., Justices of Peace, letter to, 480.
........., sheriffs, 127 (3), 411. See Beconsaw, Sir White; Button, John; Oglander, Sir John; Whithed, Richard.
........., ship-money, 5, 166, 182, 186, 197, 198, 213, 293, 307 (2), 320, 367 (2), 381, 505.

Hants, Vice-Admiral, *see* Weston, Jerome, Earl of Portland.
Hanworth, Middlesex, 131.
Happing, Norfolk, hundred, 134.
Happy Entrance, the, 213, 608.
Harbert, Edward, letter of, 179.
Harbie or Harby, Clement, late tin farmer, 452.
........., ..., widow and orphans of, petition of, 204 (2).
........., ..., ..., references of, letters of, 319, 320.
........., Sir Job, 50, 204, 329.
........., ..., petition of, 83.
........., John, 173.
........., Sir John, 39, 452.
Harbingers, the Gentlemen, presentment of, 202.
Harbord, Sir Charles, the King's Surveyor-General and Auditor of the Prince's revenue, 99, 111, 153, 168, 254 (2), 333, 571.
........., ..., letter of, 35.
........., ..., letter to, 318.
........., ..., references to, of petition, 35, 153, 253.
Hardenburch, Capt. Daniel, 84.
........., ..., prize brought in by, statement concerning, 84.
Harding, John, 441.
........., Mr., 559.
........., Thomas, 405.
........., ..., petition of, 342.
........., ..., ..., referees of, appointment by, 342.
Hardinge Castle, co. Flint, 96.
Hardware, Thomas, 453.
Hardwick, John, 105.
Hardwicke, co. Buckingham, 564.
Hargell, Arthur, commissions to, 602 (2).
Harlech Castle, co. Merioneth, office of constable of, 236.
Harleston [Norfolk], 235.
Harleton, co. Cambridge, 391 (2).
Harley, Sir Robert, 249, 498.
Harlow, Essex, hundred, 172 (2), 186, 207, 220, 548.
Harman, Edmund, 468.
........., Nicholas, petition of, 336.
........., Capt. Thomas, 590, 600.
Harmwood, Thomas, petition of, 83.
Harnham, Wilts, bridge, 524.
........., St. Nicholas, document dated from, 523.
Harrington, Edmond, 583.
........., Thomas, petition of, 509.
........., ..., his father, 509.
Harris, variously spelt ;—
........., Alexander, saltpetreman, 237.
........., ..., petitions of, 95, 273.
........., ..., letter to, 95.
........., Alexander, prisoner in Fleet, petition of, 126.

Harris, Dr., 206.
........., George, petition of, 396.
........., Henry, farmer of paper mills, petition of, 108.
........., Lieutenant Henry, petition of, 250.
........., Lewis, under-sheriff of co. Oxford, 88, 199, 232, 234, 235.
........., ..., letters of, 278, 304.
........., ..., declaration of, 232.
........., ..., ..., answer to, 235.
........., Sir Paul, late sheriff of Salop, 199, 296, 301, 311, 335.
........., ..., statement by, 335.
........., Richard, of London, information concerning, 114.
........., Richard, of Salop, petition of, 311.
........., Robert, 426, 465.
........., Thomas, of Witney, co. Oxford, 313.
........., Thomas, of St. Martin's-in-the-Fields, 587.
........., ——, petition of, 128.
Harrison, variously spelt ;—
........., Christian, 283.
........., Edward, 220.
........., John, farmer of customs, letter to, 204.
........., Mr., of Mortlake, 460.
........., Mr., minister of South Somercotes, 374.
........., Nicholas, 406 (2).
........., Sir Richard, late sheriff of Berks, 102, 211, 239 (3), 336, 348, 389.
........., Thomas, petition of, 283.
Harrogate near the Spa, document dated from, 599.
Harrow-on-the-Hill, Middlesex, 560.
Harston, co. Cambridge, 372.
Hart, Richard, 453, 487, 513.
........., William, affidavit of, 495.
Hartismere, Suffolk, hundred, 157.
Hartlib, Samuel, 264.
Hartpury, co. Gloucester, Millgrove close, 359, 372.
Harvey, Edmund, 119.
........., Jerome, letter of, 182.
........., Sir John, governor of Virginia, petition of, 509.
........., Richard, constable of Abdick and Bulstone, 407, 486.
........., Richard, servant to Endymion Porter, 36.
........., ..., letter of, 468.
........., ..., letters to, 14, 25, 29, 34, 169, 176, 182, 195, 346, 349, 352, 358, 365, 367, 376, 377, 386, 395, 396, 424, 430, 435, 444, 445 (2), 446, 447 (2), 460, 466, 467, 482, 488, 489 (2), 506, 515, 516, 528 (2), 530, 532, 537, 559, 564, 569, 594.

Harvey, Roger, 516.
........., ..., letters of, 367, 396, 424, 445, 447, 516.
........., ..., his relations, 445, 447.
........., Ursula, 516.
........., Dr. William, certificate of, 2.
........., ——, 435.
Harwich, 347, 601.
........., mayor, 235.
........., ..., letter to, 210.
........., ship-money, 210, 419.
Harwood, Mr., 182.
Haryes messuage, Essex, 464.
Haslemere, Surrey, 133.
Haslopp, William, 454.
Hastings, George, Earl of Huntingdon, deceased, 577.
........., Henry, Earl of Huntingdon, 126.
........., ..., letter of, 577.
........., ..., petition of, 54.
........., ..., his late wife, 54.
Hastings, Sussex, mayor, 557.
........., Rape, 133, 549.
Hastler, Edward, petitions of, 65 (2).
........., Richard, information of, 521.
Hatch, John, petition of, 90.
Hatchway, Ann, 325.
Hatfield, Essex, 207.
.... Forest, Essex, 610.
Hatfield, Herts, 492.
.... Chase, co. York, 404, 464.
........., draining, 57.
........., partners in draining, petitions of, 12, 16 (2), 253, 533.
........., ..., order of, 515.
Hatfield, co. Nottingham, hundred, ship-money, 24, 43, 184.
Hatherleigh, co. Devon, 512.
Hats and caps, 106, 392, 460.
........., proclamation respecting, 269.
Hatte, Anthony, 489.
Hatton, Christopher, 560.
........., Lady Elizabeth, 156, 353.
........., ..., her family, 156.
Haughton, Robert, petition of, 120.
Havefrith, see Havering.
Haverfordwest, ship-money, 288.
Havering, Essex, 328.
Havre de Grace, 260.
Haward, Thomas, petition of, 98.
........., Mr., clerk of the Petty Bag Office, 556.
Hawett, Thomas, 431.
Hawkhurst, Kent, 111, 423.
Hawkins, John, 247.
........., Mark, 245.
........., Mr., clothier, 447.
........., Mr., mentioned by Isaac Pennington, 498.
........., Stephen, petition of, 250.

Hawkins, William, of Westminster, 245.
........., William, of Ilchester, 271.
........., ——, 151.
Hawnes, co. Bedford, 550.
Hay, Sir George, late Chancellor of Scotland, 454.
........., George, Earl of Kinnoul, 588.
........., ..., grant and demise to, 454.
........., Honora, Countess of Carlisle, deceased, first wife of James, first Earl of Carlisle, 340.
........., James, first Earl of Carlisle, 115, 340.
........., ..., trustees of, petition of, 492.
........., James, second Earl of Carlisle, 321, 340.
........., ..., petition of, 492.
........., Sir James, 129 (2).
........., John, Lord Yester, 529.
........., Lucy, Countess of Carlisle, widow of James, first Earl of Carlisle, grant to, 309.
........., Margaret, Countess of Carlisle, 340.
........., Lady S., letters of, 129 (2).
........., Lady Sidney, letter of, 129.
........., William, 192.
Hay and straw, office for weighing, 472.
Hayles, co. Gloucester, monastery, 128.
Hayling, Hants, documents dated from, 29, 41.
Haynes, Thomas, 441.
Haytor, Devon, hundred, 136.
Haywood, see Heywood.
Head, Henry, 379, 437, 440.
Headlam, William, 407.
Heale, Mr., 179.
Heallam, Robert, return of, 476.
........., ..., petition of, 581.
Hearn, Mr., 297.
Hearne, William, late bailiff of Godmanchester, 11.
Heath, Isaac, 552.
........., Sir Robert, sergeant, formerly Attorney-General and late Lord Chief Justice of the Common Pleas, 9, 274, 458.
........., ..., question submitted to, 410.
........., Sarah, 264.
Heather, Edward, the elder, 583, 610.
Heathfield, Henry, 240.
... ., Mr., of Minehead, 276.
Heaward, William, 567.
........., ..., letter of, 424.
Hebb, Andrew, petition of, 379.
Hebditch, Edward, 276.
........., Richard, 275.
Heckington, co. Lincoln, document dated from, 257.
Heddington, Wilts, 200.
Heidelberg, 325 (2).
Heighington, John, mayor of Durham, 294.

Heiley, Jasper, messenger, 15, 493, 556.
........., ..., letters and other papers of, 15, 30, 56, 513.
........., ..., letter to, 572.
Hell Gates, North America, 33.
Hellyer, Ralph, bill of, 515.
Helsington, Westmoreland, 370.
........., return for, 547.
Hemingham, Mrs., 540.
Hempson, Mr., 291.
Hempstead, Essex, 456.
Henchman, Dr., 304, 524.
Henden, Sergeant Edward, 136, 436.
Henderson, Alexander, 529.
........., Mr., minister of Brentford, 393.
Hendley, Sir Thomas, sheriff of Kent, answer of, 87.
Heneage, Sir Thomas, 241.
Henhurst, Kent, manor, 311.
Henlei, Mr., 78.
Henley [George], 82, 84, 300, 454, 583, 588, 608.
........., ..., reasons touching, 83.
Henley, co. Oxford, 489.
Henman, Allen, 423.
........., pass to, 423.
Hennage, Sir George, 201 (2).
Hennell, Anthony Vanden, warrant to, 601.
........., ..., safe-conduct for, 601.
Hennys, Hugh, 131.
Henrietta, the, 159, 262, 542 (3).
Henrietta Maria, Queen, 33, 55, 74, 75, 99, 101, 152, 164, 202, 203, 208, 213, 243, 259, 289, 333, 357, 394, 447, 466, 473, 506, 510, 512, 521, 523 (2), 531, 537, 566.
........., letter to, 75.
........., petition to, 115.
........., her almoner, see Perron, Jacques du, Bishop of Angoulême.
........., attorney, 517. See Herbert, Edward.
........., billiard board, 49.
........., carver, see Nicholas, Sir Oliver.
........., chamber, grooms of, petitions of, 50, 123.
........., council, 229.
........., dogs, 49.
........., dwarfs, 49.
........., embroiderer, see Gentile, Charles.
........., equerry, see Garnier, Mons. Jean.
........., grooms, 203, 514 (2), 538.
........., horses, 476.
........., rich beds for her lying in, 329, 424.
........., maid of honour, 247.
........., marriage expenses, 226.
........., marriage portion, 162, 167.
........., master of the horse, see Goring, George Lord.
........., monkeys, 49.
........., physicians, see Brouncker, Sir William; Cadiman, Dr.; Mayerne, Sir Theodore.

Henrietta Maria, Queen—cont.
........., robes, groom of, 514 (2).
........., Receiver-General, see Wynn, Sir Richard.
........., saddles and other provisions for a progress, estimate for, 537.
........., servants, 118, 261, 409, 514 (2).
........., solicitor, see Ball, Mr.
........., stables, 441, 577 (2).
........., treasurer, see Wynn, Sir Richard.
........., yeoman of the leash, 80.
........., secretary and master of requests to, see Wintour, Sir John.
Henrietta Maria, the (ship), 170.
Henry IV., 81.
Henry VI., 250, 263 (2).
Henry VII., 564.
Henry VIII. 60, 70, 77, 162, 256, 468, 511, 531, 560.
........., Prince, son of James I., 434.
Henshawe, Edward, petition of, 411.
........., Rebecca, petition of, 411.
Henslowe, Philip, 415.
Henton, Somerset, ship-money, 193.
Hepthrow, Roger, 522.
........., ..., examination of, 522.
Heralds, see Borough, Sir John; Ryley, William.
Herbert, Sir Charles, 31, 58, 329, 556.
........., ..., reference to, of petition, 153.
........., Edward, Lord Herbert of Chirbury, 162.
........., ..., letter to, 373.
........., Edward, the Queen's attorney, 172, 213.
........., Gerrard, see Wright.
........., Henry, letter of, 603.
........., Philip, Earl of Pembroke and Montgomery, Lord Chamberlain of the Household, Lord Warden of the Stannaries, High Steward of the Duchy of Cornwall, Vice-Admiral of South Wales, and Lord Lieutenant of Kent, 18, 53, 173, 213, 338, 343, 362, 408, 416, 474, 521, 578, 603.
........., ..., his Fishing Association, 109.
........., ..., letters and petition of, 353, 500, 515, 603.
........., ..., letters to, 341, 501.
........., ..., reference to, of petitions, 18.
........., ..., his secretary, see Oldisworth, Michael.
........., William, sheriff of co. Monmouth, 603.
........., William, Earl of Pembroke, 53.
Hercules, the, 83.
Hereford, document dated from, 233.
.... Cathedral, 59, 70.
........., Dean and Chapter, 59.
........., Dean and Canons, particular by, 70.
........., diocese, 38.
........., mayors, 233, 235. See Symonds, Thomas; Walle, Walter.
........., ..., names of, 325.

GENERAL INDEX. 657

Hereford—*cont.*
........., plague, 92.
........., ship-money, 13, 233.
........., Bishop, *see* Coke, George.
Hereford, co., justices of peace, petition of, 92.
........., ..., return to, 544.
........., plague in, 92.
........., sheriff, *see* Lingen, Henry; Vaughan, Roger.
........., ..., petition of, 92.
........., ship-money, 92, 233, 507.
Herne, Kent, 40, 44, 182.
Herne, John, justice of peace for Middlesex, return by, 162.
........., ..., letter of, 332.
........., Mr., barrister, 399.
........., Nicholas, 188.
Heron, Arthur, 183.
........., Sir Edward, 151, 540.
........., John, 369.
........., ..., petition of, 308.
Herrick, Sir William, 89.
Herrings, 109, 494.
........., exportation of, 20, 460.
Herriotts, co. Radnor, 53.
Herstmonceaux *alias* Hurst Mounsey, *see* Hurstmonceaux.
Hertford, 392, 545.
........., document dated from, 605.
........., mayor, letter to, 210; *and see* Lawrence, Edward.
........., ..., late, *see* Dalton, Joseph.
........., mills, 403.
........., ship-money, 210, 356, 605.
........., All Saints, 563.
........., St. Andrew's, 403.
Hertford, co., 69, 95, 281, 372, 385.
........., Lord Lieutenant, 244.
........., justices of assize, letter and return to, 134, 545.
........., justices of peace, returns of, 134 (2), 135 (2), 136, 544 (2), 545 (3).
........., ..., petition and return to, 134, 390.
........., plague in, 135.
........., registrar, 563.
........., sheriff, 392, 527, 581, 605. *See* Coningsby, Sir Thomas.
........., ship-money, 88, 244, 355, 392, 527.
Hertford, hundred in that co., 135, 545.
Hervey, Giles, of the Society of Jesus, certificate of, 321.
Hesse, 47.
........., Frederick, Landgrave of, deceased, 29.
........., the Landgravine of, 7, 29.
Hester, William, 105.
Heveningham, Sir Walter, 360.
Heversham, Westmoreland, return for, 547.
Hewes, William, clerk of the check, 438.
Hewett, Sir John, sheriff, co. Huntingdon, letters of, 246, 420, 565.
Heyborne, co. Durham, 130.

Heyburn, William, 398.
Heydon, Sir John, Lieutenant of the Ordnance, 3, 12, 25, 121 (2), 208, 266, 282, 303, 410, 518, 575, 596, 608.
........., ..., letter and other papers of, 209, 297, 594, 599.
........., ..., letters and other papers to, 9, 29, 41, 498, 594, 597.
Heyes, John, 3.
Heyghley, [co. Montgomery], documents dated from, 365, 490.
Heylin, Dr. Peter, 64.
Heyward, Mark, 521.
........., ..., examination of, 522.
........., William, 554.
Heywood, Peter, justice of peace for Middlesex, 139 (2), 142, 397, 436, 448.
........., ..., letters and other papers of, 401, 453, 551, 560, 568.
........., Dr. William, 235, 399, 416.
Hickman, William, 406, 433, 440.
Hicks, Thomas, petition of, 116.
Hieron, Mr., counsellor, 217.
Higgins, John, return of, 87.
........., ——, 418.
High Commission Court, 10, 26, 32, 63 (2), 64, 65, 66, 67 (2), 73, 74, 78, 80, 126, 142, 145, 167, 224, 229, 231, 233, 238, 240, 244, 248, 249, 259, 287, 296 (2), 313, 314, 364, 368, 379, 412, 492, 532, 536, 555, 607.
........., articles exhibited against accused persons, 13, 62, 63 (2), 64, 219, 285 (2), 338, 382, 539 (2).
........., ..., answers to, 339, 382.
........., brief in, 65.
........., sentences in, 240, 383, 497.
........., orders of, 382, 383, 497.
........., judges in, notes of opinions of, 513.
........., ..., letter of, 519.
........., register, extract from, 13, 187.
........., registrars, 187, 244, 248; *and see* Knight, Mr.
........., ... office, 272.
........., commissioners, 19, 27, 66, 244, 360.
........., ..., letters to, 231 (2).
........., ..., petitions to, 71 (2).
High Holborn, London, 587.
........., inhabitants of, petition of, 107.
Higham, Thomas, grant to, 214.
Higham-Ferrers, co. Northampton, ship-money, 220.
Higham Gobion, co. Bedford, 19.
Highways, surveyor of, 419; *and see* Dewell, Henry.
Higney, co. Huntingdon, 308 (2), 369.
........., Isle of, 308, 369.
Hildiard, Christopher, petition of, 443.
Hildick, the river, 55.
Hill, Capt. Anthony, 452.
........., ..., pass for, 459.
........., John, letter of, 219.

T T

Hill, Lady, her almshouses, 133.
........., Mr., connected with the draining of Bourne Level, particular by, 528.
........., Mr., [of Tewkesbury?] 317.
........., Peter, 245.
........., Samuel, letter to, 428.
........., Thomas, petition of, 66.
........., William, mayor of Bridgewater, memorandum of, 371.
........., William, clerk, petitions of, 280 (2).
........., William, auditor of the Exchequer, 6.
........., William, junior, son of the last mentioned, 148.
........., ..., grant to, 6.
........., ——, stationer, a widow, see Gill, ——.
Hill alias Hull, co. Gloucester, 239.
Hillesdon, co. Buckingham, 567.
Hillington, see Hillesdon.
Hilton, Edward, 395, 398.
........., Henry, information of, 130.
Hilton, co. Durham, 130, 147.
Hinckley, co. Leicester, 458.
Hinde or Hynde, John, affidavit of, 495.
........., William, [of North Somercotes?], 2.
........., William, of Southwark, petition of, 113.
Hingham, Norfolk, 259.
Hinton, Somerset, rate so called, 89.
Hinward, Mr., 349.
Hippisley, Richard John, captain of Sandgate Castle, certificate of, 291, 369.
Hitchin, co. Hertford, 545.
........., ..., hundred, 135, 424 (3), 545.
Hitchins, Bartholomew, 379.
Hobart, Sir Miles, deceased, 54, 309, 480.
Hobbard, see Hobart.
Hobbes, Edward, 361, 449.
........., ..., petition of, 360.
Hobby, Alice, 128.
........., Mary, 128.
........., William, the elder, 128.
........., William, the younger, 128.
Hobson, Lancelot, 154.
Hockin or Hocking, Christopher, 285, 430, 439 (2), 449.
........., William, 405, 430, 439 (2), 449, 512.
........., ..., petition of, 439.
Hoddesdon, co. Hertford, plague in, 135.
Hodges, Anthony, indenture of, 351.
........., Henry, late sheriff of Somerset, 92, 222, 377, 398, 408.
........., ..., letter of, 151.
........., Mr. [of Shipton Moyne], 142.
........., ..., his son, 142.
Hodgkinson, Mr., 74.
Hodgson, Edward, receipt of, 489.
........., Elizabeth, 170.
........., Nicholas, recognizance of, 366.
........., Sir Robert, 130.
........., ..., his servant Anthony, 76.
........., Thomas, 467.

Hodson, Sir Robert, see Hodgson.
Hoe, Stephen, 189.
Hogan, Thomas, of the order of St. Francis, calling himself Don Juan de Castro, examination of, 230.
Hoggate, Edward, 156.
Hoggestone, co. Buckingham, 564.
Hogsthorpe, co. Lincoln, 167, 173.
Holborn, London, 107, 154, 188, 258, 538, 587; see also High Holborn.
Holborne, Robert, reply to Solicitor-General Littleton in Hampden's case, 540.
Holdernesse, Roger, 373.
........., late Earl of, see Ramsay, John.
Holdsworth, Dr. Richard, 325.
Hole, ——, 500.
Holford, Thomas, commissions to, 602 (2).
Holiland, Hercules, 328.
Holland, 4, 50, 104 (3), 110, 246, 474, 530, 579, 587, 603, 605.
........., ambassador from, 82, 300, 315, 361; and see Joachimi, Sir Albertus.
........., ships and fleets of, 6, 15, 28, 83, 202, 234, 246 (2), 262, 266, 300, 304, 315, 361, 499, 578, 595.
........., ..., Admiral, see Tromp, Martin Harpenson.
........., ..., Vice-Admiral, 234.
........., West India Company of, 590.
Holland, Henry, petition of, 73.
Holland, co. Lincoln, 211, 307, 479.
Holles, Anne, Countess Dowager of Clare, 353, 354, 455.
........., Denzil, 353.
........., ..., letter to, 530.
........., Dorothy, 353.
........., John, first Earl of Clare, 353.
........., John, second Earl of Clare, 353, 442, 445.
........., ..., his mansion in Drury Lane, 442.
Hollingbourne, Kent, 288.
Hollings, Katherine, petition of, 553.
........., Roger, petition of, 516, 553.
Hollis, Gervase, late mayor of Great Grimsby, 2.
Hollond, John, letter of, 33.
Holman, Michael, 101, 152.
........., Richard, 101, 152.
Holme, Westmoreland, return for, 547.
Holmes, Dr., instructions for articles against, 63.
Holne, Devon, 136.
Holsworthy, co. Devon, 512.
Holt, co. Denbigh, 23.
Holt, Edmund, attorney-at-law, 395, 397.
........., Edward, executor of Richard, Viscount Molineux, 389, 481.
........., John, petition of 120.
........., [Thomas], 321.
Holy Island, Northumberland, fort, 80, 575.
Holyrood Chapel, Edinburgh, 529.

GENERAL INDEX. 659

"Holy Table, Name, and Thing, &c.," book so entitled, 339, 365.
Homage, fines for respite of, 152.
Home, James, Earl of, 529.
........., Janet, 586.
Honiton, co. Lincoln, 288.
Honywood, Mr., 146.
........., Sir Robert, his lady and three children, pass for, 481.
Hood, Paul, D.D., petition of, 61.
........., ..., schedule of injuries, 61.
Hooke, Capt., deceased, 323.
........., Humphrey, 85.
........., Thomas, 85.
........., ———, 174.
Hooper, Mr., 159.
Hoorn, Holland, 85.
Hope, George, 205.
........., John, mayor of Derby, petition of, 91.
........., ..., letter of, 180.
........., Sir Thomas, 554.
Hope, the, of Dantzic, 3.
Hopkins, Anthony, petition of, 369.
........., John, 382.
........., Richard, 198.
Hopton, Sir Arthur, 271.
........., Sir Richard, 507.
Hopton-in-the-Hole, Salop, 62.
Hore, Robert, petition of, 114.
Horfield, co. Gloucester, manor, 316, 351.
Horncastle, co. Lincoln, soke, inhabitants of, petition of, 90.
........., ship-money, 90.
Hornchurch, Essex, ship-money, 463, 470.
Horne, John, petition of, 200.
........., Robert, Bishop of Winchester, (1561-1580), 469.
Horneck, ———, one of the Prince Palatine's gentlemen, 7, 47.
Horpury, co. Gloucester, 372.
Horse, the (sandbank), 202.
Horse, master of the, 531, 549. See Hamilton, James, Marquess of.
Horses, exportation of, 44.
Horsleydown, Surrey, 137.
Horth, Thomas, 347.
........., ..., proposition by, 347.
Horton, Capt. Roger, 203.
Hosier Lane, London, 359.
Hoskyns, Sergeant John, letter to, 452.
Hosskisse, Richard, petition of, 311.
Houghton Conquest, Beds, 5.
.... Guildable, Beds. 5.
Houlderness, Roger, 357.
Houlton, James, 359.
........., ..., information of, 359.
Hound Street co. Warwick, 367
........., document dated from, 182.
Hounstert or Houndstret, see Hound Street.

Hour-glass makers, petition of, 23.
........., ..., orders on, 23, 154.
House, Thomas, 346.
Household, the royal, barbers for, 263, 468.
........., beer for, 222, 250, 375, 401.
........., bills of fare of, 521, 530.
........., books concerning, kept in the Council Chamber, 515.
........., composition from the cos. for provision for, 89, 258.
........., diets served in the, 510.
........., officers of, warrant to, 428.
........., ..., fees payable to, on knighthood of Prince Charles, 445.
........., list of papers concerning, 256.
........., statutes of Eltham, for regulation of, 49 (2), 515.
........., orders of Charles I. for regulation of, 49.
........., notes by Nicholas of proceedings of a committee for revising the regulations of, 142, 147, 162, 202, 256, 549.
........., orders and resolutions of the committee above mentioned, 143, 256, 368, 376, 443, 466 (2), 520, 531, 549.
........., presentments and other papers prepared for the information of the said committee, 202, 203 (2), 216, 301, 312, 339, 394, 423, 467, 485.
........., cofferer of, 421, 520, 531.
........., ..., reference of petition to, 467.
........., comptroller, 402; and see Vane, Sir Henry.
........., Lord Steward, 258, 468.
........., treasurer, 258, 402, 421, 575; and see Edmondes, Sir Thomas.
........., Vice-Chamberlain, see Jermyn, Sir Thomas.
Houses in London occupied by many families, 114.
Housman, John, 443 (2).
Hovell, ———, of Bottisham, 493.
Howard, Anne, wife of William Lord Howard of Effingham, funeral certificate of, 500.
........., Charles, Earl of Nottingham, 362.
........., ..., letter to, 501.
........., Charles, late Earl of Nottingham, 321, 500.
........., Sir Charles, letter of, 348.
........., ..., letter to, 527.
........., Elizabeth, 500.
........., Elizabeth, Countess Dowager of Suffolk, letter to, 559.
........., Sir Francis, 11.
........., ..., letter of, 349.
........., Henry, Lord Maltravers, 147, 362.
........., ..., letter to, 501.
........., ..., petition of, 252.
........., John, 327.
........., Lady Mary, 118 (2).

T T 2

Howard, Theophilus, Lord Howard of Walden, and afterwards second Earl of Suffolk, Lord Warden of the Cinque Ports, and Lord Lieutenant of Essex, 83, 84, 152, 324, 401.

........, ..., letter and other papers of, 81, 281, 282, 296.

........, ..., order on complaint of, 80.

........, ..., letters to, 493, 501, 558, 559.

........, Thomas, license to, 454.

........, Thomas, late Earl of Suffolk, 362, 559.

........, Thomas, Earl of Arundel and Surrey, Earl Marshal, 18, 204, 213, 241, 260, 266, 338, 349, 355, 445, 452, 515, 574, 594, 597, 611.

........, ..., letters and other papers of, 115, 143 (2), 205, 389, 435, 510, 584.

........, ..., letter to, 117.

........, ..., reference to, of petitions, 10 (2), 18, 164, 193, 251, 373, 496.

........, Thomas, Earl of Berkshire, formerly Lord Howard of Charleton and Viscount Andover, 20, 79, 152, 186, 236, 282, 314, 326, 430, 585.

........, ..., letter to, 128.

........, Sir William, 118 (2).

........, William, Lord Howard of Effingham, eldest son of Charles Earl of Nottingham, 500.

Howdenshire, co. York, division of, 137.

Howe Capell *alias* Capella Hugonis [How Caple], co. Hereford, 288.

Howe, George, letter of, 143.

........, ..., letter to, 37.

Howlet, William, 105.

Howme, *see* Hume.

Howson, Mr., 438.

........, William, 503.

Howston, John, petition of, 366.

Hoy, ——, 123.

Hubbock, Mr., 424.

Huberley, Francis, 473.

Huchens, Joseph, *see* Hutchinson.

Huddleston, Andrew, 598.

........, John, 598.

Hudson, John, answer of, 181.

........, Nicholas, 154, 188, 258.

Hulbert, George, justice of peace for Middlesex, 139 (2), 142, 397, 540.

........, ..., certificate of, 401.

Hull, Thomas, 126.

Hull, 323, 347, 557, 584, 590.

........, documents dated from, 225, 323.

........, mayor, 323. *See* Watkinson, James.

........, ..., letter to, 590.

........, plague, 225, 323, 348.

Hull, co. Gloucester, *see* Hill.

Humanes, Conde de, 230.

Humber, the river, light at mouth of, 25.

Humbleyard, co. Norfolk, hundred, 546.

Hume, Colonel, 594.

........, James, 288.

Humfrey, Sir Edmund, certificate of, 140.

Huncks, Lady Katherine, letter of, 121.

Hungary, 104.

Hungerford, Sir Edward, 205.

........, Walter, 476.

Hunsley Beacon, co. York, division, 137.

Hunt, Jonas, petition of, 91.

........, Mrs., 567.

Huntingdon, 138, 181, 276, 426, 438, 500, 513.

........, documents dated from, 500, 571.

........, mayor, 138.

........, ..., letters and papers of, 139, 180.

........, ..., letter to, 589.

........, recorder, *see* Bernard, Robert.

Huntingdon, co., 67, 69, 95, 139, 152, 372, 438, 442, 589.

........, constables, letter to, 276.

........, alehouse keepers, names of, 340.

........, justices of peace, letter of, 545.

........, ..., letters to, 459, 589.

........, judges of assize, letter to, 545.

........, sheriff, 246.

........, ..., letter to, 459; *and see* Hewett, Sir John.

........, ship-money, 246, 420, 565.

Huntingdon, Earl of, *see* Hastings, George; Hastings, Henry.

Huntington, co. Hereford, hundred, ship-money, 87 (2).

Hunton, Francis, 185 (2), 213.

........, Mordecai, 201 (2).

........, William, deceased, 486, 521.

........, ..., his children, 486.

Huntspill, Somerset, 214.

Hurst, William, 372.

........, ..., certificate of, 385.

Hurst, Berks, 239.

Hursthourne-Tarrant, Hants, ship-money, 186.

Hurstmonceaux, Sussex, 288.

Huse, Michael, 50.

Hussey, Sir Edward, sheriff of co. Lincoln, 267.

........, ..., letter to, 212.

........, ..., petition of, 90.

........, Richard, 85, 315.

Hutchinson, Joseph, 139 (2).

........, ..., examination of, 142.

Huttoft, co. Lincoln, 167.

Hutton, Sir Richard, justice of Common Pleas, 443.

Hutton-John, Cumberland, 598.

........, New,⎫
........, Old, ⎬ Westmoreland, returns for, 547.
........, Roof,⎭

Hutton, Somerset, 212, 214.

Hyde, John, letter to, 610.

........, Sir Lawrence, 480.

........, Nathaniel, 381.

........, ..., acquittance of, 451.

........, Robert, recorder of Salisbury, 489.

GENERAL INDEX.

Hyde Park, 579.
........., new lodge, 441.
Hygate, Thomas, petition of, 98.
Hynde, *see* Hinde.
Hythe, Kent, 93.

I.

Ibbitt, ——, 391.
"Ignatius his conclave," pamphlet alleged to have been written by John Donne, Dean of St. Paul's, 25.
Ilchester, Somerset, 271.
Ilsley West, Berks, document dated from, 604.
Images in churches, 67.
Imbercourt, document dated from, 443.
Import or export, illegal, grant of benefit due to his Majesty thereon, 35.
Imposts, 23.
Impressment of ships for the King's service, 3 (2), 4.
Imprests, auditors of the, 120, 170, 229.
........., ..., letters of, 358, and *see* Bingley, George.
Ince, John, 409 (4).
Industry, the, ship, 83.
Infante, the Cardinal, Governor of the Low Countries, 578, 609.
Informations, Commissioners at, in the High Commission, 68.
Inglish, Mr., 367.
Ingmanthorpe, co. York, 355.
Ingram, James, Deputy Warden of the Fleet, 124.
Inkberrow, co. Worcester, plague, 145.
Inner Temple, the, 464.
Innes or Innis, Capt. Robert, grant to, 19.
........., R[obert], his lodging at Clerkenwell green, document dated from, 20.
........., ..., letter of, 20.
Innkeepers, 410.
Insley, ——, 458.
Interest on money, proposition for limiting, 112.
Inventions, 79, 108, 113, 128, 236, 238, 244, 282, 340, 395, 418, 482, 490.
Ipswich, Suffolk, 22, 119, 137 (4), 139, 140 (2), 171, 177, 217, 278, 284, 297, 298, 347.
........., documents dated from, 139, 157.
........., bailiffs of, 140 (2).
........., ..., letter to, 146; and *see* Dade, Henry.
........., ship-money, 200.

"Ipswich, News from," book printed in Dutch and French, 365.
Irby, Sir Anthony, Sheriff of co. Lincoln, 211, 465, 479, 586.
........., ..., letters and other papers of, 28, 138 (3), 140, 220, 267 (2), 307, 426, 589.
........., ..., letters to, 196, 212, 257.
........., ..., petitions to, 90, 337.
Ireland, 9, 170, 217, 230, 242, 263, 299, 361, 366, 372, 401, 427, 436, 449, 509, 525 (2), 534, 563, 584.
........., ferriage, office of, 8.
........., Marshal and Water Bailiff of, *see* Smith, Robert.
........., ships employed for guard of the coast, 24, 159, 174, 178, 194, 228 (2), 241, and *see* Ninth Whelp, the; Swallow, the.
........., Admiral of, *see* Ketelby, Capt. Thomas.
........., Chief Remembrancer of the Exchequer, office of, 539.
........., Lord Deputy, *see* Wentworth, Thomas, Viscount.
Ireland, Gilbert, 27, 231, 363.
........., Peter, 435.
Ireton, John, 6.
Irish soldiers in Spanish service to be sent to Brazil, 234.
Iron, 395, 418, 482.
Ironside, Mr., a minister, 62.
Ironworks in Forest of Dean, *see* Dean, Forest of.
Irthlingborough, co. Northampton, ship-money, 91.
Isack, Samuel, petition, 114.
Isaled, co. Denbigh, hundred, 387.
Isleworth, new park of Richmond so called, 131.
Islington, 130, 162.
........., the Maidenhead in, 324.
Islip, Adam, 379 (2).
........., Simon, Archbishop of Canterbury (1351), 70.
Issayndre, co. Cardigan, division, ship-money, 198, 243.
Istleworth, *see* Isleworth.
Italy, 31, 130, 187, 245, 467, 535, 599.
Ivara, Martin Lopez de, 555.
Iver, co. Buckingham, parishioners of, certificate of, 418.
Ives, John, information of, 504.
Ivy Bridge, Westminster, 404.
Ivye, Nicholas, petition of, 309.
Izaack, Thomas, 558.

J.

Jackson, Benjamin, 262.
........., Dr., 76.
........., Henry, bill in cause of, 227.
........., ..., plea and demurrer to, 228.
........., John, 310.
........., Joseph, grant to, 11.
........., Miles, 231 (2).
........., Oliver, 420.
........., Sir Robert, 457.
........., ..., letter and instruction to, 456, 457.
........., Simon, 552.
........., Thomas, 228.
Jacob, John, sergeant of Admiralty of the Cinque Ports, 84.
........., Sir John, 401.
........., Lucas, 263.
Jacobson, Philip, petitions of, 16 (2), 17.
Jago, Thomas, 245.
James I., 35, 45, 49, 54, 58, 60 (2), 74, 101, 106, 115, 130, 144, 147, 152, 153, 200, 221, 227, 252, 263, 264, 283, 293, 339, 342, 360 (2), 365, 393, 434, 447, 457, 464 (2), 484 (2), 485, 496, 518, 531, 537, 556, 571, 585, 589, 590, 608.
James, Prince, Duke of York, appointed Lord High Admiral, 351.
James, Gerance, 138, 272.
........., Henry, Mayor of Totnes, certificate of, 421.
........., William, Bishop of Durham (1606-17), 475.
James, the, King's ship, 170, 243.
........., the, merchant ship, 85.
Jane Ann and Judith, of London (ship), 137.
Jarrow Slake, near the Tyne, 250, 407.
Jarvis, Dr., 189.
........., Peter, 56.
Jason, Frances, petition of, 218 (2).
........., her daughters and son, 218.
........., Robert, 149, 151, 155, 165, 166, 188, 189, 218.
Jay, Thomas, 122.
........., ..., petition of, 252.
........., Sir Thomas, Justice of Peace for Middlesex, 122.
Jeffes, George, 437, 446, 456.
........., Thomas, 437, 456.
........., William, 437.
Jegges, Robert, 8.
Jemmat, John, minister, of Berwick, 216.
........., ..., letter to, 528.
Jenkins, Sir Robert, 325.
........., ..., reference to, of petition, 325.
Jennings, variously spelt ;—
........., Alexander, 406.
........., Sir John, K.B., 94, 448.
........., Thomas, 109.

Jennison, John, 440.
........., ..., petitions of, 439, 440.
........., William, 439.
Jenoure, Francis, 160.
Jenyns, see Jennings.
Jepson, Sir John, 480.
Jeremy, the, of London, 222.
Jermyn, Henry, 266, 271, 447.
........., ..., petition of, 35.
........., ..., his father, 35.
........., Thomas, letter and another paper of, 4, 158.
........., Sir Thomas, Governor of Jersey and Vice-Chamberlain of the Household, 271, 324.
........., ..., letter of, 557.
Jersey, 270, 273, 278, 280, 298, 299.
........., Governor of, see Jermyn, Sir Thomas.
........., Lieutenant Governor, 299.
........., spinners, 206.
........., Elizabeth Castle, 442, 475.
Jerusalem, Knights of St. John of, 206.
Jerves, Thomas, petition of, 55.
Jervis, Peter, 99.
Jervoise, Sir Thomas, 182.
........., ..., protection to, 311.
Jesuits, 75, 321, 325, 450, 535.
........., list of certain, apprehended, 76.
Jewel, the, ship, 15, 31, 36.
Jewel House, the, Master of, 531.
Jewels, redemption of those of the King pawned in Holland, declaration concerning, 50.
........., concealed, 98.
........., money due for, 173.
Joachimi, Sir Albertus, Ambassador from Holland, 84.
........., ..., letter to, 84.
Jobson, John, 268.
........., ———, 122.
John, King of England, 118.
John, the, of London, 159.
John, David ap, 387.
Johnson, variously spelt ;—
........., Archibald, 529.
........., Edward, of St. Martin's in the Fields, 366.
........., Edward, Commissioner for cards and dice, 295.
........., Edward, trumpeter, 174.
........., ..., warrant to, 174.
........., George, petition of, 54.
........., Humphrey, 257, 258.
........., John, Master of the Golden Wolf, affidavit of, 600 ; and see Molos, Jan Jansen vander.
........., John, rector of St. Mary Matfellon, Whitechapel, deed of, 399.
........., John, son of Simon, 212.
........., Magdalen, writ to, 257, 258 (2).
........., Richard, 143, 166.

GENERAL INDEX.

Johnson, variously spelt—*cont.*
........., Simon, pass for, 212.
........., ..., his wife, 212.
........., William, boatswain, 131.
........., William, bailiff, petitions of, 368, 370.
........., ——, Walker's man, 458.
Johnston, *see* Johnson.
Jones, Charles, 606.
........., Dr. Gilbert, Chancellor of Bristol, 179, 316.
........., Humfrey, 218.
........., Ignatius, *see* Inigo.
........., Inigo, Surveyor of his Majesty's works and Justice of Peace for Middlesex, 319, 376, 422, 441, 442 (2), 518.
........., ..., letters and other papers of, 64, 298, 318 (2), 332, 514.
........., ..., commission to, 363.
........., Robert, 243.
........., Thomas, of Shrewsbury, minutes touching, 306, 337.
........., Thomas, of Tidcombe, Devon, 288.
........., William, Mayor of Bristol, letter of, 150.
........., William, printer, 72, 74, 180.
........., William, of Ratcliffe, ropemaker, petition of, 4 (2).
........., Sir William, Justice of King's Bench and Judge of Assize for co. Monmouth, 241, 491, 515.
........., ..., letter of, 512.
........., ..., appointment of, 515.
........., ..., letter to, 610.
Jonson, *see* Johnson.
Joyce, Martin, 214, 241.
........., William, petition of, 340.
Joyner, Leonard, messenger, warrant to, 98.
........., Mr., 53.
Juby, William, 238.
Judges and other officers, letters to, 74, 425.
Judith, the, of London, 389.
........., ..., owners of, petition of, 388.
Juell, ——, his daughter, 346.
Juring, William, 268.
Jurors, issues of, 98.
Justices of Peace, returns made by, 132, 133, 134, 135, 136, 137, 542.
........., letters and other papers to, 156, 257, 389.
"Justification of Separation," book by Robinson, 366.
"Juvenilia," alleged to have been written by John Donne, 25.
Juxe, Edward, deceased, 174 (2).
Juxon, William, Bishop of London and Lord Treasurer, 4, 44, 52, 69, 75, 99 (2), 100 (2), 120, 144, 148, 153, 159, 169, 195, 215, 225, 227, 228, 233, 252, 254, 266, 271 (2), 272, 278, 281, 298, 299, 302, 326, 342, 361, 362, 376, 378, 380, 381, 387, 402 (2), 403, 425, 474, 477, 484, 485, 487, 497, 518, 533, 552, 558, 571, 575, 582, 583, 587, 591, 611.

Juxon, William, &c.—*cont.*
........., ..., letters and other papers of, 141, 183 (2), 206, 239, 354, 362, 397, 404 (2), 405 (2), 427, 455 (2), 461, 515, 519, 522, 525, 533, 575, 576, 580, 590, 593.
........., ..., the like to, 14, 35, 39, 42, 73, 101, 143, 168, 301, 369, 409, 435, 445, 481, 574.
........., ..., references to, of petitions, 3, 5, 12, 16, 33, 35 (2), 44, 149, 193, 227, 239, 248, 250, 252, 253 (2), 254, 281, 310, 342, 354, 355, 362, 366 (2), 380, 397, 427, 477 (2), 484, 492, 496, 509, 511, 518, 525, 552, 553, 554, 565, 580, 589.
........., ..., references by, of petitions, 35, 141, 233.
........., ..., his Chancellor, *see* Duck, Dr. Arthur.

K.

Keane, Charles, 288.
Kedleston, co. Derby, documents dated from, 327, 597.
Keeling, Mr., 563.
Keeper, the Lord, *see* Coventry, Thomas, Lord.
........., the late Lord, *see* Williams, John, Bishop of Lincoln.
Keier, John Paterson, grant to, 410.
Kellam, Bartholomew, notes respecting, 123.
Kellick, John, 179.
Kelly, Earl of, *see* Erskine, Thomas.
Kelmarsh, co. Northampton, documents dated from, 294, 364.
Kempsford, co. Gloucester, ship-money, 211.
Kendal, Westmoreland, ward, 546.
........., ..., park, 370.
Kenilworth Castle, 77.
Kennedy, John, Earl of Cassilis, 529.
Kennington, Surrey, 131.
Kensbere, *see* Kentisbeare.
Kensham, George, letter to, 123.
........., ..., his daughter, 123.
Kensington, document dated from, 600.
Kent, 42, 87, 95 (2), 98, 155, 175, 362, 385, 441, 442, 492, 502, 557.

Kent—*cont.*
........., Justices of Peace, 460.
........., ..., returns and letters of, 132, 133 (4), 135 (2), 136, 137, 543 (4), 546, 548 (4), 549, 550.
........., ..., letter to, 479.
........., Lord Lieutenant of, *see* Herbert, Philip, Earl of Pembroke and Montgomery.
........., muster-master of, 29.
........., sheriff, letters to, 197, 209. *See* Hendley, Sir Thomas.
........., ship-money, 87, 197.
........., Vice-Admiral, *see* Walsingham, Sir Thomas.
Kentisbeare, Devon, 218.
Kentmere, Westmoreland, return for, 547.
Ker, Charles, Lord, licence to, 466.
........., Robert, Earl of Ancram, gentleman of the Bedchamber, 122, 154, 172, 466, 552.
........., ..., letter of, 213.
........., ..., commissions to, 602 (2).
........., ..., grant to, 527.
........., William, Earl of Lothian, 529.
Kersey, Suffolk, plague in, 157.
Kesteven, co. Lincoln, ship-money, 211, 212, 267, 307, 479.
Ketelby or Kettleby, Capt., Thomas, admiral of ships employed on the coast of Ireland, 194, 228.
........., ..., appointment as Admiral, 228.
........., ..., instructions to, 241.
........., ..., his lieutenant, *see* Owen, Capt. Richard.
........., Thomas, lieutenant in the Swallow, appointment of, 541.
Ketton, co. Rutland, 468 (2).
Key, Thomas, 506.
Keyme, Henry, messenger, 238.
........., ..., warrants to, 437 (2).
Keystou, co. Huntingdon, 261.
Keyworth, co. Nottingham, 380.
Kildare, Earl of, *see* FitzGerald, George.
Killfoord, co. Denbigh, manor and park of, 158.
Killigrew, Cicely, deceased, 247, 419.
........., Mr., 512.
........., Sir Peter, petition of, 496.
........., Thomas, 12.
........., ..., petitions of, 9, 247, 419, 517, 552.
........., ..., warrant to, 147.
........., Sir William, 151, 540.
........., ..., affidavit of, 522.
........., ——, 88.
Killington, Westmoreland, return for, 547.
.... Firbank, Westmoreland, return for, 547.
Killingworth, *see* Kenilworth.
Kilmorey, Viscount, *see* Needham, Robert.
Kilns, newly invented, 128, 314.
........., ..., proclamation concerning, 236.
Kilsby, co. Northampton, 61.
Kilvert, [Richard,] 37, 171, 323.

Kinaston, Thomas, 468; *and see* **Kynaston**.
Kinder, Philip, 16.
King, Bartholomew, 249.
........., Dr., 608.
........., John Nicholas, grant to, 410.
........., Matthew, 179.
........., Sarah, 249.
........., Thomas, petition of, 411.
........., William, 22.
........., ..., statement of, 21.
........., ..., petition of, 122.
Kingham, co. Oxford, 470.
King's Bench, the Court of, 80, 166, 225, 238, 377, 385, 389, 412, 447, 449, 500, 508, 581.
........., ..., Justices, 214.
........., ..., ..., warrant and letters to, 148, 197, 236; *and see* Berkely, Sir Robert; Croke, Sir George; Jones, Sir William.
........., ..., ..., reference on petition to, 508.
........., ..., letter of, 512.
........., ..., Lord Chief Justice, 587. *See* Bramston, Sir John.
King's College, Cambridge, Provost and others of, letter to, 193.
King's Evil, the, 506.
King's Lynn, Norfolk, 252, 347, 480, 566.
........., ..., recorder, *see* Paulett, Francis.
........., ..., ship-money, 220.
Kingsmill, William, 186.
King's Norton, co. Worcester, 384.
King's Printers, proclamations, books, &c. printed by, 208.
........., notes on the establishment of, 74.
........., their printing house, 73.
Kingsthorpe, co. Northampton, document dated from, 518.
........., ..., ship-money, 560.
Kingston, co. Nottingham, 380.
Kingston, Earl of, *see* Pierrepont, Robert.
Kingston-upon-Hull, *see* Hull.
Kingston-upon-Thames, 179, 327, 479, 550, 567.
........., three masters of, memorandum of, 498.
........., ship-money, 420.
........., hundred, 133, 543.
Kinnell, [Perthshire,] 529.
Kinnoul, Earl of, *see* Hay, George.
Kirby Kendal, Westmoreland, return for, 547.
Kirby Park, co. Lincoln, *see* Kirkby.
Kirdford, Sussex, 133.
Kirk, variously spelt :—
........., George, gentleman of the robes, 49 (3).
........., ..., letter of, 559.
........., ..., warrant to, 19.
........., Mr., 56.
Kirkby, Roger, sheriff of co. Lancaster, 149.
........., ..., certificate of, **146.**

GENERAL INDEX.

Kirkby Park, co. Lincoln, 44.
Kisby, Roman, examination of, 504.
Kitchin, Richard, commissions to, 602 (2).
Kite, Mr., 144.
.........., ..., his sister, 144.
.........., ..., ..., her children, 144.
Knaptoft, co. Lincoln, 400.
Knaresborough, waters, 526.
Knight, George, 110.
.........., Mr., registrar of the High Commission, 145, 370 (2), 536.
.........., ..., reference of petition to, 224.
.........., ——, 509.
Knightbridge, Richard, M.A., petition of, 574.
Knighting kings' children, observations concerning, 287.
Knightley, Hugh, 163.
.........., ..., examination of, 170.
.........., Robert, 520.
.........., ..., his daughter, 520.
.........., Samuel, 271.
.........., Thomas, petition of, 396.
Knighton, Richard, petition of, 91.
Knightsbridge, Middlesex, 341.
Knock, Thomas, 494.
Knockfergus, 85.
Knollys, Eliza, Countess of Banbury, 321, 326.
.........., Sir Henry, 333, 510.
.........., Sir William, Comptroller of the Household, 468.
.........., William, Viscount Wallingford, and afterwards Earl of Banbury, 181, 585; and see Knowles.
Knott, Thomas, of Exeter, agreement of, 176.
.........., Thomas, of Alderkirk, 426, 428, 444, 465.
Knowles, Sir Robert, petition of, 181.
.........., ..., his sons, 181.
.........., William, eldest son of the above, 181; and see Knollys.
Knowleton, Richard, 487.
.........., ..., affidavit of, 391.
Knowsley Barn, co. Lancaster, 225.
Knoyle Episcopi or Magna, Wilts, 37, 143, 232.
Kt., Mr., see Knight, Mr.
Kyme, Henry, messenger, 323, 325, 460.
.........., ..., petition of, 93.
.........., ..., letters to, 160, 172, 302, 373.
.........., Mrs., note of, 78.
.........., ..., her husband, 78.
Kyme, co. Lincoln, 151.
.... Eau and Bourne, estimate of drainage to be done in, 563.
Kynaston, Sir Edward, 388.
.........., ..., letter to, 277.
.........., ..., letter of, 388.
.........., Sir Francis, 277, 388.
.........., ..., petition of, 388.
.........., Samuel, 288; and see Kinaston.
Kynnesman, Richard, 333.

L.

La Croix, see Moore, George.
Lady, the, (ship,) of London.
Lake, Dr., 390.
.........., Dr., of Leicester, letter to, 401.
.........., Edward, letter of, 554.
.........., John, certificate of, 94.
Lakenheath, Suffolk, 503.
Lamaghi, Messrs., letter to, 535.
Lamb or Lambe, Henry, licence to, 323.
.........., ..., order on petition of, 26.
.........., ..., names of persons who will attend at Whitehall on behalf of, 186.
.........., Sir John, official to the archdeacon of Buckingham, and Dean of the Arches, 11, 27 (2), 69, 72, 78, 81, 123, 130, 180, 187, 226, 238, 247, 248, 249, 287, 339, 341, 342, 358, 365, 369, 377, 379, 383, 413, 491, 498, 513, 516, 561, 569.
.........., ..., letters and other papers of, 38, 40, 69, 72 (2), 114, 182, 233, 298, 313, 314, 332 (2), 341, 342, 382, 418, 498, 516, 521, 533, 563, 567, 570.
.........., ..., the like to, 2, 45, 67 (2), 68 (5), 71, 73, 79, 80, 99, 191, 219, 249, 275, 285, 316, 317, 323, 326, 354, 357, 369, 390, 424, 458, 492, 518, 535, 554, 567, 571, 572, 577.
.........., ..., references to, of petitions, 10, 11, 25, 32, 145, 167, 180, 200 (2), 224, 238, 240 (2), 245, 248 (2), 249, 257, 259 (2), 264, 275, 280 (2), 281 (2), 293, 296, 298, 308, 313, 314, 364, 369 (2), 370, 377, 379 (2), 382, 411, 412, 426 (2), 444, 460, 468, 491, 506, 516, 560, 562.
.........., ..., appointed to gather tenths in diocese of Lincoln, 45.
.........., Peter, petition of, 99.
.........., William, 99.
Lambard, John, 521.
Lambell, Mr., 107.
Lambert, Thomas, letter to, 37.
Lamberton, co. Berwick, 331 (3), 349.
.........., ..., document dated from, 308.
Lambeth, Father, 15.
Lambeth, 145, 280, 281, 341, 399, 453, 555, 561, 570, 605.
.........., document dated from, 382, 383 (2), 438, 453, 489, 497 (2).
.........., parishioners, letter of, 410.
Lambrigg, Westmoreland, 547.
Lampreys, 112.
.........., transportation of, 110, 142, 143, 471.
Lancaster, 123.
.........., ship-money, 146.
Lancaster, co., 159, 171 (2), 362, 431, 442, 501, 584.
.........., badgers licensed, list of, 340.
.........., justices of assize, letters to, 135 (2), 136, 544 (3).

Lancaster, co.—cont.
........., justices of peace, letters and other papers of, 135 (2), 136 (6), 543 (2), 544 (4), 546.
........., ..., certificates to, 543, 544.
........., sheriff, see Kirkby, Roger.
........., vice-admiral, see Stanley, William, Earl of Derby.
Lancaster, duchy, 498, 531.
........., ..., court of, 79, 253, 458, 487.
........., ..., chancellor of, see Barrett, Edward, Lord Newburgh; May, Sir Humphrey.
Lancaster, house of, 241.
........., Lanckton, Christopher, 487.
Landen, Sir Philip, deceased, 56.
Landguard Fort, Suffolk, 601.
Lane, Mr., 249.
........., Richard, Attorney-General to Prince Charles, and recorder of Northampton, 427, 518, 536.
........., ..., letter of, 418.
........., ..., letters to, 394, 463.
........., ..., appointed the Earl of Holland's deputy in Forest Courts, 484.
........., ——, glazier, 91.
Laney, Dr. Benjamin, 235.
Langar, co. Nottingham, 288.
Langbaine, [Dr. Gerrard,] provost of Queen's College, Oxford, 390.
Langbaugh, co. York, wapentake, 345.
Langdale, Westmoreland, 546.
Langdon, Westmoreland, return for, 547.
Langhorne, [William,] letter to, 468.
Langley, Timothy, 105.
Langport, Somerset, 157.
Langston, Elizabeth, 276.
........., Francis, sergeant at arms, grant to, 22.
........., John, 384.
Langthorn, Christopher, 453.
Langton, Mr., 151.
Laniere, Clement, 472.
........., Nicholas, master of the King's music, certificate of, 22.
Lanvuda, see Llanvedw.
Lascelles, variously spelt ;—
........., Elizabeth, petition of, 469.
........., ..., ..., order on, 470.
........., George, late sheriff of co. Nottingham, certificate of, 430.
........., George, father of the next mentioned, 469, 470.
........., John, petition of, 469.
........., ..., ..., order on, 470.
Lasham, Hants, 469.
Latch, Mr., 556.
Latham, Mr., 247.
Lathum, Mr., 219.
........., Ralph, 507.
........., Thomas, 147.
Latten wire, 589.
Latton, Essex, 417, 430, 437, 443.

Laud, William, Archbishop of Canterbury, 20, 47, 59, 61, 62, 63, 68 (2), 69, 70, 72, 73, 78, 115, 141, 142, 187, 225, 231, 241, 245, 259, 267, 269, 276, 285, 289, 317, 326, 338, 342, 350, 360, 362, 363, 380, 384, 401, 412, 441, 442, 463, 474, 484, 497, 511 (2), 521, 523, 524, 534, 535, 553, 591, 604, 606.
........., ..., letters of, 102, 286, 306, 315, 438, 453, 489, 519, 571, 607.
........., ..., other papers of, 38, 45, 59, 60, 167, 182, 183 (3), 205 (2), 206, 404 (2), 405 (4), 427, 455 (2), 477, 478, 491, 580, 606.
........., ..., letters to, 32, 37, 38, 40, 44 (2), 60, 64, 67, 157, 229, 231, 270, 295, 305, 316, 380, 348, 351, 370, 409, 425, 481, 561 (2), 563, 567, 573, 588, 599, 601, 605.
........., ..., other papers to, 298, 426.
........., ..., petitions to, 10, 25, 32, 37, 51, 66 (3), 67 (2), 71, 73 (3), 74, 80, 126, 145, 166, 180, 200 (2), 224 (2), 237, 239, 240 (2), 244, 247, 248 (3), 257, 258, 259, 264, 274, 280 (3), 281, 298, 296, 298, 313 (2), 341, 342, 358, 364, 368 (2), 370, 377, 379 (2), 389, 411 (2,) 426 (2), 438, 444, 460, 468, 491, 505, 516, 550, 555, 560, 562, 607.
........., ..., articles of, respecting vicarages, answers to, 167 (3), 170, 173, 176, 181.
........., ..., references to, of petitions, 5, 141, 250, 253, 318, 342, 350, 354, 362, 380, 397, 461, 477, 484, 511, 552, 553, 554, 580, 606.
........., ..., answers and references by, on petitions, 10, 25, 32, 141, 145, 167, 180, 200 (2), 224 (2), 238, 248 (2), 249, 257, 258, 259, 264, 275, 280 (2), 281 (2), 293, 296, 298, 313, 314, 362, 370, 379, 411, 426 (2), 427, 444, 460, 468, 491, 506, 509, 516, 550, 555, 560, 562, 607.
........., ..., list of benefices in the presentation of, 69.
........., ..., notes of presentations to livings procured by, 287.
........., ..., his attorney, see Lambe, Sir John.
........., ..., chaplain, see Bray, William.
........., ..., secretary, see Dell, William.
........., ..., vicar-general, see Brent, Sir Nathaniel.
Laugharne, co. Carmarthen, rectory, 253, 288.
Laurence, see Lawrence.
Lavender, Henry, examination of, 504.
Law, John, evidence of, 288.
........., Peter, information of, 331.
Lawes, Thomas, 481.
Lawharne, see Laugharne.
Lawrence, Edward, mayor of Hertford, letter of, 605.
........., Mr., a priest, 187.
........., Sir John, petition of, 336.
........., Dr. Thomas, 235.

Lawrence, ——, of Shoreham, 279 (2).
Lawson, George, 59, 337.
Layer, John, statement of, 372.
Lea, *see* Lee.
Lead mines, 125, 458.
.... ore, 458.
........., ..., farmer of the King's right to the pre-emption of, office of, 98 (2).
Leadenhall Street, London, 313.
Leader, William, 314.
Leading Hall, *see* Leadenhall.
Leake, Henry, petition of, 113.
Leakey, Alexander, 276.
........., Elizabeth, 276.
........., Old Mr., 276.
Leaming or Leamon, Anthony, 444, 482.
Leate, Captain, 478.
........., Huett, petition of, 255.
........., Nicholas, 255.
........., Richard, 255.
Leather, 104, 338 (3), 366.
Leau, Jacob de, petition of, 50.
Leaver, John, petition of, 145.
Ledbury, co. Hereford, 63, 607.
Leddoze, Thomas, petition of, 86.
Ledesham, Mary, 309.
........., Richard, 309.
Lee, variously spelt;—
........., Dorothy, 15.
........., ..., examination of, 14.
........., Henry and Company, petition of, 311.
........., Hugh, 226.
........., John, 285.
........., Mr., servant to Lord Darcy, 186.
........., Robert, of London, 270.
........., Robert, of Gravesend, 449; *see also* Leigh.
Leedes, Sir John, 278.
........., ..., letter of, 278.
........., ..., letter to, 279.
Leek, Squire, 326.
Lefever, Thomas Fountaine, petition of, 250.
Le Fountaine, Francis, petition of, 250.
Leger, John, 386.
Legge, Capt. William, 590.
........., ..., letter to, 590.
Leicester, 401, 424, 567.
........., documents dated from, 271, 289, 424.
........., archdeaconry of, 323.
........., castle, document dated from, 554.
........., commissary of, 323.
........., mayor, *see* Morfin, Daniel.
........., St. Mary's, 563.
Leicester, co., 67, 69, 179, 199, 345, 458.
........., forest, the King's late, 54.
........., ..., lieutenant of, statement of the profits of, 54.
........., sheriff, 370. *See also* Roberts, Sir Richard.
........., ship-money, 289.

Leicester, Earl of, *see* Sydney, Robert.
Leigh, Francis, Lord Dunsmore, 78.
........., Thomas, 471.
........., Sir Thomas, late sheriff of co Warwick, 77.
........., ..., letter to, 440.
........., William, formerly sheriff of co. Gloucester, 9, 184.
........., *see also* Lee.
Leigh, Surrey, 327.
Leigh cum Spelhurst, [Speldhurst?,] co. Kent, 34.
Leighton, co. Lancaster, 398, 410.
Leighton, Mr., 416.
Leimpster, *see* Leinster.
Leinster, 363, 501.
Leith, 582.
Leitrim, Lord, *see* Sherard, Henry.
Leke, Thomas, 75.
........., petition of, 75.
Lemens, John Baptista van, 5.
Lemmond, the, of London, 17.
Lempster, *see* Leominster and Leinster.
Lenning, ——, 525.
........., ..., his son, 526.
Lennox, Duke of, *see* Stuart, James.
........., Duchess, *see* Stuart, Mary.
Lent and other fasting days, observance of, 171.
Lent preachers at court, list of, 235.
Lenthall, Sir Edmund, 46.
........., Sir John, 197.
........., Mr., 359, 372, 559.
Leominster, 233.
Leopard, the, 213, 291, 608.
Leppington, Lord, *see* Carey, Henry.
Lesley, variously spelt;
........., General, 529.
........., John, Earl of Rothes, 529.
........., Col. John, 83.
........., Col. Lodowick, petitions of, 113 (2).
L'Espert, Peter, petition of, 117.
........., ..., his wife, 117.
L'Estrange, Sir Hamon, letter to, 418.
Letchford, Mr., 528.
........., Sir Richard, petition of, 336.
........., ... his daughters, 281, 336.
Letts, William, servant to Sir John Lambe, letter of, 249.
Levant Company, the, memorials of, 102.
........., ..., petition of, 103.
Levens, Westmoreland, return for, 547.
Leveret, James, 161.
Levinston or Levingston, *see* Livingstone.
Levison, Lady Katherine, petition of, 77.
........., Sir Richard, petition of, 77.
Lewen or Lewin, George, 406, 417.
........., Rowland, sheriff of co. Carmarthen, letter of, 180.
........., William, order on petition of, 293.
Lewes, Sussex, 536.
........., rape, 133.

Lewes or Lewis, Hugh, 100 (2).
........., ..., application of, 100.
........., Robert, 448.
........., Thomas, petition of, 164.
Lewis, the, merchant ship, 213, 291, 297, 300 (2).
Lewis, Isles of, 8, 419, 609.
Lewkenor, Christopher, recorder of Chichester, 595.
Ley, James, late Earl of Marlborough and lord treasurer, 54, 227 (2).
........., Mrs., 346.
........., Philip, 346.
Leyden, 245.
Leyland, co. Lancaster, hundred, 136.
Libels, and profane or seditious speeches and publications, 14, 25, 71, 140, 143, 241 (2), 259, 359 (2), 362, 406, 448, 459, 473 (2), 510, 521, 522, 550, 591.
Licenses to go abroad, see Passes.
Lichfield, document dated from, 305.
........., cathedral, 219.
........., ..., close, 219.
........., dean, 316, 352. See Fell, Samuel.
........., ..., and chapter, 352.
........., president and chapter of, letter to, 168.
........., town clerk, see Noble, Michael.
........., the Angel at, 219.
Lichfield and Coventry, Bishop of, see Wright, Robert; Morton, Thomas.
........., diocese, 315.
Liddell, variously spelt ;—
........., Thomas, mayor of Newcastle-upon-Tyne, 227, 436.
........., letter of, 76.
Liddiard Millicent, Wilts, 579.
Lide, Henry, justice of peace of Westminster, 448.
........., ..., certificate of, 423.
Liens, John, petition of, 57.
Light, Robert, saltpetreman, petition of, 96.
Lightfoot, John, 333.
........., Mr., 260, 374.
Lights or lighthouses, 17, 25, 371.
Lile, see Lilly.
Lillingstone Lovell, co. Oxford, document dated from, 232.
Lilly, [Charles], his Rules, (book,) 366.
Limehouse, 115, 137.
Linchmill pond, 610.
Lincoln, 95, 151, 181, 189, 307.
........., document dated from, 530.
........., bishopric, estimate and calculations of the revenue of, 114, 115 (2).
........., cathedral, 60, 61, 468.
........., diocese, 38, 45, 69, 315, 339, 377.
........., ..., commissioners for visitation of, notes of, 363, 564.

Lincoln—cont.
........., ecclesiastical court, 66.
........., ..., registrars, see Pregion, John; Pregion, Philip.
........., ..., apparitor for, 571.
........., ship-money, 211.
........., vicars of, the four old, petition of, 61.
........., Bishops of, 281, 339 ; and see Grosthead, Robert; Sutton, Oliver; Williams, John.
Lincoln, co., 12, 28, 55, 57, 69, 95, 152, 201, 214, 253, 324, 438, 501, 532.
........., constables, letter to, 276.
........., judges of assize, letter to, 479.
........., commissioners for sewers, letters to, 56, 157.
........., feodary, see Beresford, Christopher.
........., sheriffs, 212; and see Hussey, Sir Edward; Irby, Sir Anthony; Norton, Sir Walter.
........., ..., letter to, 26.
........., ship-money, 26, 28, 90, 211, 212 (2), 220, 267 (2), 307, 426, 479, 589.
........., under-sheriff, see Wyatt, Perkins.
........., Earl of, see Clinton, Theophilus.
........., Vice-admiral, see Bertie, Montagu.
Lincoln College, Oxford, 343.
Lincoln's Inn, London, 163, 179, 181, 188, 464.
.... Fields, 115.
Lindsay, David, Earl of Balcarras, 529.
........., John, Lord, 529.
........., Capt. Thomas, petition of, 79.
Lindsey, Earl of, see Bertie, Robert.
........., James, keeper of the Counter prison, 187.
........., Robert, 425.
Lindsey, co. Lincoln, 211, 307, 479.
Liney, John, 235.
Ling, ——, 22.
Lingen, Henry, 188, 405.
........., Henry, sheriff of co. Hereford, letter of, 507.
Linton, Mr., 21.
Lion's Whelp, the First, 170, 186, 237, 243 (2), 373, 410.
........., ..., the Second, 131 (2), 234, 246.
........., ..., the Third, 131 (2), 243.
........., ..., the Fifth, 132.
........., ..., ..., loss of, 86, 542.
........., ..., the Eighth, 213.
........., ..., the Ninth, 33, 178, 194, 228, 241.
........., ..., the Tenth, 213, 608.
Lion's Whelps, the, 356.
Lippencott, Francis, 77.
........., ..., petitions of, 283, 284.
Lipsius, annotations of, 71.
Lisbon, 86.
........., castle, 89.
........., salt, 609.

Lisle, Capt. Edmund, deceased, 345.
........., Lawrence, 295.
........., Nicholas, lieutenant of Walmer Castle,
........., ..., letter and another paper of, 291 (2), 344, 345.
Lisley, John, petition of, 91.
Lisney, John, letters to, 423, 443, 446, 459.
Lister, Dr. Matthew, certificate of, 17.
"Litany," by John Bastwick, 27.
Litchfield, Margaret, 167.
Litharge, 309.
Little, John, 593.
Littlecote, Wilts, 169.
........., document dated from, 349.
Little Dean, co. Gloucester, document dated from, 287.
Little and Lesness, Kent, hundred, 132, 197, 543, 548.
Littleport, co. Cambridge, 494, 503 (2).
Littleton, Adam, justice of Chester, 335.
........., ..., letter of, 199.
........., Sir Edward, Solicitor-General, 117, 220, 254, 297, 335, 393, 399, 405, 417, 450, 459, 464, 472, 531, 540, 596.
........., ..., letters and other papers of, 60, 203, 351.
........., ..., letters to, 101, 116, 204.
........., ..., references to, of petitions, 180, 203, 242, 253, 306, 351, 531.
........., Sir Edward, late sheriff of co. Stafford, petition of, 90.
........., John, 399.
........., Mr. 420.
Liturgy of the church of England, the, 305, 342.
Liverpool, ship-money, 146.
Livingstone, James, groom of the bed-chamber, petition of, 36.
........., ..., grant to, 585.
........., James, Lord Livingstone of Almond, 529.
........., ..., letter of, 599.
........., ..., letter to, 526.
........., Thomas, 526.
........., ..., letter to, 599.
........., ..., his nephew Alexander, 600.
Lizard, the, Cornwall, 15, 590, 600.
Llambedrocke, [Llambedrog,] co. Carnarvon, 288.
Llanidloes, co. Montgomery, plague in, 490.
Llanrhaiadr in Kinmerch, co. Denbigh, 280 (2).
Llanvair [co. Monmouth?], 280.
Llanvedw, co. Glamorgan, 65.
Lloyd, Griffin, 441.
........., Hugh, 418.
........., John, 280.
........., Sir Marmaduke, justice of Chester, 335.
........., ..., letter of, 199.
........., Oliver, 472.
........., ..., grant to, 16.
........., ..., commissions to, 602 (2).
........., Richard, 555.

Lloyd, Thomas, affidavit of, 311.
Locke, John, letters of, 358, 377.
Locker, ———, 334.
Lockey, Thomas, chaplain to Lord Scudamore, letter of, 599.
Locking, Somerset, 176, 179.
Lockton, William, commissions to, 602 (2).
Lockwood, Francis, deceased, 147.
Loes, Suffolk, hundred, 544.
Loftus, Sir Adam, vice-admiral of Leinster, letter to, 501.
........., Sir Robert, 363.
Logwood, 154, 172, 213, 403 (3), 483 (2).
Lombard Street, London, 155, 325, 328, 330.
London, references and allusions to, *passim*;—
........., documents dated from, 36, 37, 147, 151, 152, 197, 313, 329, 354, 395, 401, 431, 434, 478, 482, 499, 508, 515, 531, 557, 571, 594, 606.
........., for streets and other places in, mentioned or referred to, *see* the names of those streets or places.
........., aldermen of, court of, 374 (2), 472, 507.
........., aliens dwelling within, *see* Aliens.
........., apprentices, *see* Apprentices.
........., archdeacon, reference to, of petition, 426.
........., archdeacon's court, 426.
........., chamber, 284, 392, 393, 459, 464.
........., chamberlain, 77, and *see* Bateman, Robert.
........., citizens of, letter of, 56.
........., coals for, 57.
........., common council, order of, 116.
........., companies of, *see* their respective names.
........., fire-engines, 338, 392.
........., fires in, propositions for prevention of, 392.
........., houses divided, *see* Houses.
........., merchant adventurers of, *see* Merchant Adventurers of England.
........., merchants and ship-owners of, 20.
........., ..., petition of, 553; *see also* Portugal and Spain,
........., muster-master, *see* Fisher, Capt. John.
........., ..., office of, licence for erection of, 29.
........., oaths administered in, fees on, 77.
........., plague, 31, 70, 338, 340, 358.
........., residence in prohibited, 2, 17, 34, 156, 162, 432.
........., riots, 209, 333, 338.
........., ship-money, 87, 271, 386, 512, 563.
........., streets, encroachments upon, 116.
........., water supply, 164, 340, 369, 610.
........., ships contributed by, for the King's service, 142, 291, 297, 339, 352, 390, 609.
........., ..., committee for, 165, 291, 352.
........., ..., ..., letter to, 300.

London—*cont.*
.........., soapmakers society of, *see* Soapmakers.
.........., Lord Mayor, and Lord Mayor and others, 87, 112, 114, 116, 338, 512, 551, 579.
.........., ..., letters and other papers of, 113, 357, 507, 563.
.........., ..., letters and other papers to, 155, 171, 209, 256, 273, 330, 422 (2).
.........., Lord Mayors for previous year, *see* Clitherow, Sir Christopher.
.........., Lord Mayor for 1636-7, 161; *and see* Bromfield, Sir Edward.
.........., ..., for 1637-8, *see* Fenn, Sir Richard.
.........., recorder of, 165, 269, 579, *see* Gardiner, Thomas.
.........., sheriffs of, 48, *and see* Atkin, Thomas; Rudge, Edward.
.... and surrounding parishes, tithes of, 386, 399, 400, 403, 410, 413 (4), 414 (7), 415 (3), 416 (2), 463.
London, the, ship, 291, 300 (2), 608.
London, Bishop of, *see* Juxon, William.
London House, 355.
.........., ..., documents dated from, 11, 16, 35.
London, John, 221, 477.
London, Little, co. Cambridge, 504.
Londonderry, the Londoners' plantation in, 509.
.........., Bishop of, *see* Bramhall, John.
Long, Felix, 25, 169, 176, 461, 489, 532.
.........., ..., letter of, 530.
.........., George, justice of peace for Middlesex, 556.
.........., ..., letters and other papers of, 22, 162, 332, 452, 558.
.........., Mr., 559.
.........., Richard, 138.
.........., Robert, 151.
.........., ..., letter of, 56.
.........., ..., affidavit of, 522.
.........., Thomas, 409.
.........., Walter, 409.
Long Acre, London, 10, 46, 340.
.........., ..., document dated from, 169.
.........., ..., inhabitants of, certificate of, 46.
Long Island, America, 33.
Lord of misrule, 63.
Lorraine, Duke of, and others of the house of, 117, 223, 224.
Lort, Henry, petition of, 112.
Losse, Don Lopes de, general of the Spanish fleet, 6.
Lothian, Earl of, *see* Ker, William.
Lotteries, 71.
Loubnome, *see* Lubenham.
Louche's Buildings, near Clement's Inn, 429.
Loudoun, Earl of, *see* Campbell, John.
Loughborough, co. Leicester, 577.

Louis XI. of France, 564.
Love, the, of London, (Flemish built,) 44, 137.
.........., the, of London, 137.
Lovell, George, 203.
.........., John, 583.
Low or Lowe, George, deputy of the Merchant Adventurers Company, residing in London, agreement of, 176.
.........., Mr., prisoner, 86.
.........., ——, 183.
Low Countries, the, 2, 51, 81, 212, 281, 315, 323, 341, 398, 456, 459, 481, 484, 522, 595, 598, 601.
.........., ..., information of things observed in, 365.
Lowder, Richard, 319.
Lowen, John, 404.
Lowndes, Robert, 30.
Lowne or Lownes, Anthony, boatswain, petition of, 86.
.........., ..., ..., order on, 262.
Lowth, Simon, 206.
Lubenham, co. Leicester, document dated from, 357.
Lucas, ——, of Essex, 185.
.........., ——, connected with alum works, 593.
Luckyn, Sir William, sheriff of Essex, letter of, 185.
Lucy, Lady Constance, 186.
Luddington, Henry, 201 (2).
Ludgershall, co. Buckingham, 564.
Ludlow, Salop, 62, 296, 326, 335 (2).
.........., castle, 505.
.........., ..., document dated from, 199.
Ludlow, Gabriel, 600.
.........., Henry, senior, 433, 443, 474.
.........., Henry, junior, 443.
.........., Sir Henry, 385.
.........., Mr., 515.
Luke, Sir Samuel, petition of, 550.
Lullingston Park, Kent, 479, 550.
Lumley, Martin, warrant to, 476.
Lund, Thomas, 62.
Lundie, P. C. [?], letter of, 600.
Lunenburg, Duke of, 47.
Lunenis, Dr., preacher of Heidelberg, 325.
Lunningston, *see* Lullingston.
Lupton, Westmoreland, return for, 547.
Lutterworth, 458.
Luttrell, Edward, 346, 435.
.........., ..., his wife, 346, 435.
Lydd, Kent, 93.
Lyddell, *see* Liddell.
Lydney, co. Gloucester, 74.
Lyford, William, 288.
Lyham, Robert, 495.
Lyle, Thomas, 130.

Lyme Regis, co. Dorset, 349.
........., ..., document dated from, 429.
........., ..., mayor, *see* Ellesdon, Anthony.
Lyndhurst, Hants, 426.
Lynn, *see* King's Lynn.
Lynne, William, 125.
Lyons, John, 522.
Lyon's Inn, London, 270.
Lyte, Thomas, 271.
Lyttleton, *see* Littleton.
Lytton, Sir William, 88.

M.

Maas, the, (river,) 595, 596.
Mabank, John, 327.
Mabb, Edward, petition and propositions of, 392.
Maccube, John, 399.
Macdonnell, Randal, Earl of Antrim, 524, 574.
Mace, Elizabeth, 361.
........., Thomas, examination of, 361.
Mackay, Donald, Lord Reay, 309.
Mackworth, Sir Henry, 241.
Maddington, Wilts, 205.
Madeira, 478.
Madeley, co. Stafford, 431, 433.
Madlendyke and Madlenfield, near Berwick, 494.
Madrid, 466.
........., document dated from, 31.
Maesland Sluis, Holland, 341.
Magdalen College, Oxford, *see* St. Mary Magdalen.
Maiden Bradley, Wilts, 385, 539.
........., ..., parishioners of, petition of, 412.
Maidstone, 42, 343, 480.
........., document dated from, 550.
........., assizes, document dated from, 133.
........., hundred, 137.
Maidwell, Lawrence, 587.
Maie, Anthony, 411.
........., Edward, 411.
........., Joan, 411.
........., Thomas, 411.
Mainstone, Salop, 59.
Mainwaring, Sir Arthur, 320, 367.
........., Sir Henry, 7, 608.
........., ..., letter of, 542.
Majorca, 192.
Malabar, 307.

Malaga, 31.
.... wine, 41.
Malby, Alice, order on petition, 296.
........., Thomas, 296.
Malcolm, Henry, 13.
Maldon, Essex, 235, 557.
........., bailiffs of, letter to, 211.
........., mayor, 557.
........., ship-money, 211, 419, 572.
Malet or Malett, John, late sheriff of Somerset, 89, 92, 222, 398.
........., ..., letters of, 151, 377.
........., ..., letter to, 418.
........., Mr., 530.
Mallory, Thomas, Dean of Chester, 377.
........., William, 433.
Mallowes, Stephen, petition of, 113.
Malt, inventions for making and drying, 79, 128, 236, 238.
Malting and brewing, 220, 222, 230.
........., commissioners for, 210.
Maltravers, Lord, *see* Howard, Henry.
Maltsters, 230.
.... in England and Wales, tables of, 108, 109.
Man, Alexander, petition of, 464.
........., Capt., 160.
........., Samuel, report of, 379.
Manchester, 584.
........., ship-money, 146.
.... College, 20.
........., late warden of, *see* Murray, Richard.
........., Earl of, *see* Montagu, Henry.
........., division of, co. Lancaster, 136.
Manering, Edward, letter to, 610.
Manley, Sir Richard, 333, 510.
Manners, Lady, 15.
Manning, Edward, grant to, 147.
Manningtree, Essex, 310.
Mansbridge, Hants, hundred, 411.
Mansell, Sir Robert, lieutenant of the Admiralty, 23 (3), 138, 153, 154.
........., ..., warrant for payment to, 343.
Mansergh, Westmoreland, return for, 547.
Manshead, co. Bedford, hundred, 543.
Manuscripts, purchase of, 21.
Manwood, Jasper, 335.
........., ..., commissions to, 363, 602 (2).
........., Sir John, lieutenant of Dover Castle, 352, 604.
........., ..., letter and other papers of, 290 (2), 291, 493, 558, 569 (2), 603.
........., ..., letters to, 291, 527.
........., ..., reference to, of petition, 251.
Maperley, ——, searcher, 99, 272.
Marbach, 47.
Marcellus, *see* Marseilles.
March, George, pass for, 465.
........., Richard, 465.
Marez, John de, affidavit of, 600.

Margaret, the, of Yarmouth, 397, 401, 422, 436, 453, 490.

........., ..., owners of, petitions of, 397, 401.

Margate road, 474.

Margetts, George, petition of, 109.

Maria, the, 159, 542.

Marigold, the, of Weymouth, 86.

Mariners, *see* Seamen.

Marke, Paul, petition of, 117.

Markes, John, 396.

Market, the deputy clerk of, objections against, 103.

Market Deeping, co. Lincoln, 10.

Marlay, John, mayor of Newcastle-upon-Tyne, 490.

........., ..., letter of, 406.

Marlborough, 447.

Marlborough, Earl of, deceased, *see* Ley, James.

Marque, letters of, 455, *see also* Reprisal, letters of.

Marrall, Mr., 374.

Marriott, John, printer, 25.

Marseilles, 260.

Marsh, Gabriel, 122.

........., Judith, petition of, 122.

........., Stephen, of Islington, examination of, 324.

........., Stephen, of Hants, 197, 213.

........., Thomas, of Barnet, 111.

........., Thomas, of Ipswich, 298.

Marshal, the Earl, *see* Howard, Thomas, Earl of Arundel and Surrey.

Marshall, Hamlet, D.D., 61 (2).

........., John, commissions to, 602 (2).

........., William, 14, 15.

Marshalsea, the, 12, 110, 314, 393.

........., Marshal, *see* Hall, Bartholomew.

... ., prisoners in, certificate of, 48, 314.

Marshes, *see* Fens.

Marston, North, co. Buckingham, 564.

........., Fleet, co. Buckingham, 564.

Marten or Martin, Dr., son of Sir Henry, 151, 524.

........., Edward, letter to, 385.

........., Sir Henry, Judge of the Court of Admiralty, 8, 83, 84 (2), 110, 160, 175, 222, 243, 339, 455, 516 (2), 517, 537.

........., ..., letters and other papers of, 82, 222, 300, 301, 361, 557.

........., ..., letters to, 151, 155, 583, 588.

........., ..., notes of orders to, 535.

........., ..., reference to, of petitions, 361.

........., John, order in cause of, 383.

........., Nicholas, letters of, 349, 386, 395.

... ., Roger, 83.

........., William, 370.

Martin, *see* Marten.

Martin's [Martha's] vineyard, North America, 33.

Marwood, George, 433.

Marwood, Devon, *see* Merwood.

Mary, the, ship, 83.

Mary, the, of London, 137, 477, 478.

Mary, Princess of England, 226.

........., her servants, 50.

Mary, Queen of England, 49, 263, 466.

Mary de Medici, Queen-mother of France, 259, 579.

........., her coming to England, 609.

........., envoy from, *see* Monsigott, Mons.

Mary and Dorothy, the, of London, 339.

Mary Margaret, the, (ship), 77.

Maryborough, Ireland, 389.

Mason, John, *see* Reynolds.

........., Mr., master of fence, death of, 523.

........., Richard, 405, 459.

........., Dr. Robert, chancellor of Winchester, 487, 502, 524, 555.

........., ..., letter to, 446.

........., Samuel, 106.

........., William, information of, 359.

Masques, 1, 19, 329.

Massam, John, petition of, 293.

Massey or Massie, Ralph, 384, 538.

........., Richard, 66 (2), 129.

........., Judith, 66, 129.

Massingberd, John, 153.

Master, James, 184, 201, 212.

Masterman, Ralph [?], petition of, 61.

Matchett, ——, 228.

Mathera, *see* Madeira.

Matthew, the ship, 291, 300 (2).

Matthew, ——, 500.

Maud, Richard, letter of, 176.

Mauleverer, Thomas, 433.

Maunsell, Dame Dorothy, widow, petition of, 508.

........., Sir Walter, 508.

Maurice, Landgrave, and his sons by a second wife, 47.

Maurodd, William, petition of, 464.

Maxton, Mr., 475.

Maxwell, James, 20, 160.

........., ..., agreement of, 395.

........., Robert, deceased, 1.

May, Adrian, grant to, 173.

........., Edward, M.D., 592.

........., ..., information given by, 591.

........., Sir Humphrey, chancellor of the duchy of Lancaster, 44.

........., Lady Judith, 162.

........., Richard, grant to, 173.

Mayerne or de Mayerne, Sir Theodore, first physician to both their Majesties, 17, 600.

........., ..., letters and other papers of, 318, 431, 526.

........., ..., grant of incorporation to, 585.

Mayflower, the (ship), 137.

........., the, of London, 444, 482.

GENERAL INDEX.

Maynard, Sir John, 425.
........., William, Lord, 425.
Mayne, Richard, petitions of, 283, 284.
Mayo, Humanitas, messenger, 298.
........., ..., letters to, 190, 295.
........., John, 556.
........., Thomas, messenger, 512.
Mayors and others, letters to, 150, 156, 161 (2), 257, 281, 585.
Measie, Juliana, indictment against, 76.
Meautys, Thomas, clerk of the Council and muster-master general of England, 94, 187, 256.
........., ..., letters and other papers of, 109, 375.
........., ..., letters to, 285, 306.
Medcalfe, Oswald, cook, 155, 161, 357.
........., ..., petition of, 272.
........., ..., ..., order and reference on, 272.
Medemblik, 590, 600.
Medney, Norfolk, ship-money, 152.
Medway, the, 160, 281, 480.
Meek, William, 395, 397, 597.
Meene, Joshua, 405.
........., ..., agreement of, 412.
Melcombe Regis, co. Dorset, 86, 296, 435, 604, 605.
........., Mayor, see Michell, Henry.
Meldrum, Sir John, 17.
Melksham, Wilts, 195.
........., document dated from, 8.
Mellor, Henry, Mayor of Derby, letters of, 91, 180.
Melton, co. York, 368.
Melton Constable, Norfolk, document dated from, 289.
Mennes, Capt. John, captain of Walmer Castle and of the ship the Nonsuch, 344.
........., ..., certificate of, 345.
........., ..., letter and instructions to, 366, 428, 456.
Meppen, 47.
Mercer, Alice, 185.
Mercers [Company] of London, 60.
........., petitions of, 216, 426.
Merchandize, suggestion of measures to prevent the false making of, 105.
Merchant Adventurers Company of England, 102, 164, 176 (2), 185, 218 (2), 449, 527.
........., remonstrance of, 218.
........., their deputy at Rotterdam, 102.
........., ..., at London, see Low, George.
.... of Hamburgh, 110.
........., ..., Court of, 110.
Merchants and ship owners of London, allegations in answer to a petition of, 460.
........., answer of, 494.
Mercury, the (ship), 3, 4, 41, 137.
Mere, hundred, Wilts, 539.
Meredith, Edward, letter to, 271.

4.

Meredith, Mr., 23.
Merhonour, the, 24, 30, 131 (2), 182, 194, 202, 243.
Meridale, ——, 400.
Merioneth, co., Sheriff, see Nanney, Hugh.
........., ship-money, 287, 328, 329, 466.
Merrick, Dr., reference on petition to, 607.
Merry, Sir Thomas, 333, 510.
Merton College, Oxford, 245, 285, 306, 316, 438, 561 (2), 570, 573, 588, 598, 601, 605, 607.
........., documents dated from, 306, 316, 561, 601, 605.
........., Commissioners for visitation of, 342, 348, 602.
........., ..., letter of, 341.
........., ..., orders of, 341.
........., ..., ..., notes thereon, 342.
........., ..., note of allegations forgotten, 390.
........., questions, concerning, propounded to Archbishop Laud, 298.
........., statutes, 332, 570, 588.
........., ..., extract from, 70.
........., fellows of, certificate of, 306.
........., warden, see Brent, Sir Nathaniel.
........., ..., articles to be enquired of, 332 (2).
........., ..., letter to, 453.
........., sub-warden, see Fisher, Mr.
........., Bodley's chest at, 341.
........., Read's chest at, 341.
Mervin, Sir Henry, 82, 195, 356.
........., Richard, 288.
Merwood alias Marwood, Devon, 203.
Messengers of the Chamber, 338.
........., warrants to, 97, 326, 327, 400, 467, 488.
........., list of, 342.
Methley, co. York, 516.
Meverell, Ottowell, physician, 188.
Mewe, Richard, 364.
Mews, the, St. Martin's-in-the-Fields, 341, 376.
Mexborough, co. York, 57.
Michelgrove, Sussex, 92.
Michell, Henry, Mayor of Weymouth and Melcombe Regis, certificate of, 435.
........., Sir John, 411.
........., ..., commissions to, 602 (2).
Micklethwaite, Paul, D.D., master of the Temple, 288, 462.
........., ..., petition of, 45.
Mickleton, co. Gloucester, manor, rental of, 492.
Middleburgh, 84, 609.
Middlecote, William, 201 (2).
Middlesex, 46, 48, 95 (2), 98, 175, 443.
........., official to the Archdeacon of, 68.
........., Court of Sessions for, order of, 74.

U U

Middlesex, House of Correction, 473.
........, ..., governor of, letter to, 185.
........, justices of peace, 139 (2), 146, 393.
........, ..., return of, 162.
........, ..., letter to, 459.
........, quarter sessions, orders of, 426 (2).
........, lord lieutenants, see Rich, Henry, Earl of Holland ; Sackville, Edward, Earl of Dorset.
........, sheriff, 46, 48, 87, 90, 205 (2), 314, 336, 429, 442.
........, ..., letter to, 436 ; and see Atkin, Thomas.
........, under-sheriff, 538 ; and see Trench, Styward.
........, ship-money, 46, 313, 314.
Middlesex, Earl of, see Cranfield, Lionel.
Middle Temple, London, 587, 603.
........, document dated from, 186.
........, benchers and gentlemen of, letter to, 463.
Middleton, Alexander, 407, 486.
........, Henry, grants to, 39 (3).
........, Robert, 398, 410.
........, ..., bond of, 410.
........, Thomas, of Steynton, co. Pembroke, 287, 398.
........, Thomas, of Leighton, co. Lancaster, 398, 410.
........, Sir Thomas, 23.
........, Sir William, governor of the New River Company, 293.
Middleton, Westmoreland, return for, 547.
Midney, Somerset, ship-money, 157, 178, 212.
Milandre, Mons., 7, 47, 146.
Milbrook, Hants, 45.
Mildenhall, Suffolk, 323, 504.
Mildmay, Sir Anthony, 500.
........, Sir Henry, Master of the Jewel House, 77, 147.
........, ..., letter of, 560.
........, Sir Humphrey, Sheriff of Essex, 208, 505.
........, ..., letter of, 146.
Milk Street, London, 145.
Miller, Edward, 436.
........, George, 240.
........, Katherine, 436.
........, Sir Thomas, Chief Justice of the Marches of Wales and Judge of Chester, letter to, 344.
Millgrove in Horpury, co. Gloucester, 372.
Milliner's hill, 327.
Millington, Mr., 467.
Mills, William, of Hamhaw, 406.
........, William, of Newcastle, 228 (2).
Milner, Thomas, certificate of, 314.
Milton, Kent, 449.
........, Fort, 194.
........, hundred, 133, 548.

Milton Abbas, co. Dorset, 396, 568, 574, 606.
........, document dated from, 568.
........, monastery, 396, 606.
Milton Ernest, co. Bedford, 417, 429, 440.
Milverton, Somerset, hundred, ship-money, 156, 398.
Milward, Agnes, 447.
........, John, D.D., 447.
........, Sir Thomas, Justice of Chester, 363, 376.
........, ..., letter of, 375.
Mimms, North, co. Hertford, documents dated from, 244, 355.
Minch, Richard, 283.
Mincing Lane, London, 91.
........, ..., documents dated from, 1, 30, 36, 42, 132, 186, 234 (2), 236 (2), 269, 279, 290, 358, 441, 542.
........, meeting house of the Officers of the Navy at, 41.
Minehead, Somerset, 276.
Mines, surveyors general of, 58.
Minety, Wilts, 54.
Minories, the, London, 9, 282.
Minorites, see Minories.
Mint, London, the, 128, 498.
........, document dated from, 43.
........, court held in, 161.
........, officers of, 42, 43.
........, ..., letter of, 42.
........, ..., petitions of, 161, 427.
Misselden, Edward, 102.
Mitchell, ——, boatswain, 249.
Mitford, Norfolk, hundred, 546.
Moate's Bulwark, Dover, particular of defects in, 290.
........, account of ordnance expended, 350.
........, Captain of, see Collins, Increased.
Moctree, co. Hereford, Forest, 252.
Mogridge, John, petition of, 80.
Mohun, John, Lord, 168, 177, 196.
........, ..., statement by, 169.
........, Reignold, 185.
........, Warwick, letter and other papers of, 138, 169.
Molos, Jan Jansen vander, examination of, 590 ; see also Johnson, John.
Molyneux, Cecil, 225, 481.
........, Marie, Viscountess, widow of the 1st Viscount, 183, 481.
........, ..., petition of, 224.
........, ..., her children, 224, 481.
........, Richard, 1st Viscount, deceased, 224, 389, 481.
........, Richard, 2nd Viscount, 481.
Momford, Nicholas, 136.
Moncrieff, Thomas, letter of, 13.
Money, Ambrose, 418.
........, ..., letter of, 418.
Money, comparative value of, 82.
........, transportation of, 291.

GENERAL INDEX. 675

Moneyers, his Majesty's, 142.
........., petitions of, 42, 43.
........., ..., answer to, 42.
........., ..., order on, 42.
Monington, Richard, letter of, 373.
........., ..., his wife, 373.
Monmouth, 334.
Monmouth, co., sheriff, see Herbert, William.
........., ship-money, 603.
Monsigott, Mons., envoy from the Queen Mother of France, 578.
Monson, Sir John, 158.
........., ..., minute concerning, 61.
........., William, Viscount, 198.
Montacute, Somerset, document dated from, 31.
Montagu, variously spelt ;—
........., Edward, Viscount Mandeville 162.
........., Henry, Earl of Manchester, Lord Privy Seal, 55, 106, 115, 141, 154, 204, 254, 362, 380, 402, 474, 484, 495, 497, 516, 517 (2).
........., ..., letter and other papers of, 143, 353, 397, 404, 405, 427, 455.
........., ..., the like to, 141, 365.
........., ..., reference to, of petitions, 4, 5, 9, 141, 164, 193, 204, 251, 255, 309, 318, 362, 380, 397, 427, 484, 495, 509, 520, 554.
........., ..., his children, 365.
........., Richard, Bishop of Chichester, afterwards Bishop of Norwich, 444 (2), 519.
........., ..., letter of, 330.
........., ..., royal assent and other papers relating to his appointment to Norwich, 425, 444.
........., Sir Sidney, 297, 565.
........., ..., letter to, 589.
Montgomery, Alexander, Earl of Eglinton, 529.
........., Sir Edward, 500.
........., Hugh, Lord, 529.
Montgomery, co., ship-money, 92, 365, 490.
........., sheriff, see Corbett, Robert ; Newton, John.
Montgomery, hundred in co., 459.
Montifaul, Mons., 261.
Montrose, Earl of, see Graham, James.
Moodie, John, 409.
Moon, the, King's ship, 243.
Moor, variously spelt ;—
........., Edward, 105.
........., Gabriel, petition of, 67.
........., George, called La Croix, letter of, 75.
........., Ja., letter of, 345.
........., John, indenture of, 351.
........., Marmaduke, order on petition of, 401.
........., ..., letter to, 423.
........., Mr., 603.
........., Ralph, petition of, 23.
........., ..., orders on, 23, 154.
........., Robert, of Croydon, 327.

Moor—cont.
........., Robert, of Charter House, 484.
........., ..., petition of, 484 (3).
Mordaunt, Elizabeth, Countess of Peterborough, 500.
........., John, Earl of Peterborough, 500.
........., Henry, Lord Mordaunt,⎫
........., John,   ⎬ children of the above, 500.
........., Elizabeth,   ⎪
........., Anne,   ⎭
Moreclack, see Mortlake.
Moreclack, John, 57.
Morecock, Robert, 541.
Morecroft, Ferdinand, certificate of, 440.
........., George, 470, 475.
Morfin, Daniel, Mayor of Leicester, certificate of, 271.
Morgan, Blanche, 188, 405.
........., Edmond, petition of, 120.
........., Henry, 188, 405.
........., Turberville, 100 (2), 451.
........., ..., applications of, 100 (3).
........., ..., statement respecting, 129.
........., Sir William, 32.
Morehead, Arthur, 448.
........., Mr., 530.
Morhead, William, 367.
Morinus, John Baptist, 9.
Morison, see Morrison.
Morlaix, France, 388, 411, 422, 434.
Morland, Austin, 238 (2).
Morley, Mr., coal contractor, 347, 397, 401, 453.
Morley House, 464.
.... park, 464.
Morley, co. York, wapentake, 545 (2).
Morley and Monteagle, Elizabeth, Lady, see Parker, Elizabeth.
........., William and Henry, Lords, see Parker, William ; and Parker, Henry.
Morocco, 20 (2), 116.
........., Ambassador from, 20, 294, 321, 356 ; and see Abdala, Alcayde Tauda Ben.
........., King or Emperor of, 20, 204, 206, 321, 476.
........., Queen of, 20.
........., English consul at, see Penn, Giles.
Morriloy, Mr., merchant, 235.
Morris, Edward, Sheriff of co. Denbigh, letter of, 387.
........., Richard, 393 (2).
Morrison, variously spelt ;—
........., Dr., letter to, 201.
........., Capt. Richard, appointment of, 323.
Morse, Anthony, 13.
........., ..., his late wife, 13.
........., ..., his present wife, 13.
........., Henry, 75.
Mortlake, Surrey, 173.
........., inhabitants, petition of, 460.
Mortlock, John, 506.

U U 2

Morton, Earl of, *see* Douglas, William.
Morton, John, of St. Andrew's, Holborn, 366.
........., John, saltpetreman, 385, 386, 488.
........., ..., petition of, 371.
........., ..., information of, 372.
........., Mr., minister of St. Saviour, Southwark, 415.
........., Robert, 441.
........., Thomas, Bishop of Lichfield and Coventry, and afterwards Bishop of Durham, 61, 539.
........., ..., his book, *De Merito*, 263.
........., ..., letter of, 294.
........., ..., letter to, 263.
........., Sir Thomas, 575.
........., ..., estimate of ordnance for, 578.
Moseley, Maurice, 281, 336.
Mosse, Clement, 507.
Mostin or Mostyn, Anne, widow, 370.
........., Richard, petition of, 218.
........., Thomas, 370.
Motcombe, co. Dorset, document dated from, 317.
Motham, 609.
Mott, John, 191.
........., ..., certificate of, 191.
Mould, Anthony, warrant to, 427.
Moundeford, Sir Edmund, 186.
........., William, 597.
Mount Mascall, in North Cray, Kent, 598.
Mountebank, an Italian, 130.
Mountnorris, Lord, *see* Annesley, Francis.
Mousdale, Thomas, information of, 487.
"Mouth of the Poor," book so called, 128.
Moxon, James, 365.
Moyle, Robert, 76.
........., Walter,⎫
........., John, ⎬ sons of the above, 76.
........., Robert,⎭
........., Samuel, 288.
"Much-a-vile, a," 63.
Muchelney, Somerset, ship-money, 157, 178, 212, 314.
Mulgrave, Earl of, *see* Sheffield, Edmund.
Mumby, co. Lincoln, vicarage, 167.
........., documents dated from, 167.
Munck, ——, 358.
Munster, Lord President of, 194.
Murden, grounds so called in Nether Swell, co. Gloucester, 351.
Murford, Nicholas, letters of, 113, 147, 152.
Murray, John, Earl of Annandale, 20, 198, 360.
........., ..., petition of, 360.
........., Mungo, 360, 526.
........., ..., grant to, 19.
........., Richard, D.D., deceased, 20, 360.
........., William, 231.
........., ..., grants to, 476, 588.
........., ..., petition of, 241.
Murrell, Mr., 445, 515.

Mursley, co. Buckingham, 564.
Muscadel wine, 41.
Muscovia Merchant, the, of Woodbridge, 137.
Muscovy ducks, 31.
.... Company, 106.
Museum Minervæ, regent and professors of, petition of, 70.
...., propositions concerning, 70.
Musgrave, Nathaniel, 449.
Musters, 9, 81, 94, 195, 597.
........., papers relating to those for the following counties :—
    Devon, 285, 306, 417.
    Kent, 48.
    Lancaster, 410.
    Lincoln, 201, 386.
    Nottingham, 81.
Mutcheney, *see* Muchelney.
Mynne, George, 183, 452.
........., Sir Henry, 213, 241 (2).
........., ..., his wife, 241.
........., Mr., 53 (2).
........., Capt. Nicholas, petition of, 130.
........., Thomas, 201.
Myrene, Dr., *see* Mayerne.

N.

Nanney, Hugh, sheriff of co. Merioneth, 287,
........., ..., letters of, 328, 329, 466.
Nantwich, co. Chester, ship-money, 199.
Napier or Nappier, Capt., 21.
........., ..., information of words spoken by, 591.
........., ..., statement of points gathered from the speeches of, 592.
........., ..., statement of words uttered by, 592.
........., ..., his son, 21.
Naples, 51, 467,
Narrow Seas, the, 279.
........., ..., ships of Vice-Admiral of, *see* the Swiftsure and the St. Andrew.
Nassaburgh, co. Northampton, hundred, ship-money, 89.
Natland, Cumberland, return for, 547.
Naunton, Lady Penelope, 556.
........., Penelope, daughter of, 556.
........., Sir Robert, deceased, 345, 556.

Navy, the, commissioners for, *see* Admiralty, Lords of.
........., abuses in, 86 (2).
........., captains in, their pay, 195.
........., flags for, 265.
........., offices in to be granted during pleasure, 256.
........., papers relating to appointments in, (1637, July to December,) 131, 132 ; (1638, January to June,) 541, 542.
........., the four principal officers of, allusions and references to, *passim*,
........., ..., their meeting house in Mincing Lane, London, 42.
........., ..., to be commissioners of peace, 175.
........., ..., letters and other papers of, 1, 30 (2), 42, 146 (2), 186, 195, 219, 234, 236 (2), 261, 279, 290, 291, 292, 319, 358, 441.
........., ..., letters to, 4 (2), 11, 14, 24, 82, 131 (2), 132 (2), 160, 162, 166 (2), 202 (4), 213, 237, 243, 255, 261, 262, 267, 268 (2), 300, 312, 315, 323, 541 (2).
........., ..., references to, of petitions, 229.
........., ..., salaries and fees of, 82, 182, 219, 234 (2), 290.
........., clerk of the Navy, 160, 195. *See* Fleming, Dennis.
........., comptroller of the Navy, 82 ; *and see* Palmer, Sir Henry.
........., purveyor of timber to the Navy, *see* Robins, James.
........., masters attendant, 131.
........., master shipwrights, their pay, 195.
........., surgeons' wages, 33.
........., surveyor of, 1, 82, 609 ; *and see* Edisbury, Kenrick.
........., treasurer of, *see* Russell, Sir William.
........., victualler, *see* Crane, John.
........., victuallers (former), *see* Apsley, Sir Allen ; Bludder, Sir Thomas; Darrell, Sir Marmaduke; Darrell, Sir Sampson.
........., petty officers, 146.
........., ..., wages paid to, 33.
Naylor, James, letter to, 406.
Neale or Neile, Joseph, 197.
........., Richard, archbishop of York, 61, 235.
........., ..., "my house at Bishopthorpe," document dated from, 310.
........., ..., letters of, 172, 310, 332.
........., ..., letters to, 211, 231 (2).
Needham, Robert, Viscount Kilmorey, 59.
Nepper, *see* Napier.
Netherlands, the, 484, 493.
Neve, Augustine, certificate of, 340.
........., Francis, 357.
........., ..., letter of, 330.
Neville, Lady Frances, late wife of Sir Thomas, 251.
........., Francis, 584.

Neville, Henry, Lord Abergavenny, petition of, 251.
........., ..., his younger children, 251.
........., Henry, son of Henry Lord Abergavenny's eldest son, 251 (2).
........., Richard, 341, 343.
........., Sir Thomas, deceased, eldest son of Henry, Lord Abergavenny, 251.
Newark, co. Nottingham, document dated from, 326.
........., ..., mayor, *see* Thompson, Launcelot.
........., ..., ..., late, 186.
........., ..., ship-money, 89, 186, 282, 326, 430.
........., ..., hundred, ship-money, 24, 43, 184.
Newark, Viscount, *see* Pierrepont, Henry.
Newburgh, Lord, *see* Barrett, Edward.
"New Canaan," book so entitled, 257.
Newcastle-upon-Tyne, 47, 113, 153, 217, 227, 257, 347, 387, 397, 401, 422 (2), 453, 584, 590.
........., document dated from, 349.
........., brewers, fellowship, names of, 108.
........., burgesses, 227 (2).
........., ..., plea and demurrer of, 228.
........., mayor, 227 (3), 257, 490. *See* Liddell, Thomas ; Marlay, John.
........., ..., letter to, 590.
........., ..., plea and demurrer of, 228.
........., ... and others, petitions of, 334, 406.
........., merchants and others trading to, 397.
........., ..., petition of, 295.
........., merchant adventurers of, 449, 527.
........., plague, 76, 154, 334.
........., ship-money, 334.
Newcastle, Earl of, *see* Cavendish, William.
Newce, William, 369.
New College, Oxford, 206, 231.
........., ..., documents dated from, 277, 354.
Newcombe, *see* Newcomen.
Newcomen, Thomas, indictment against, 69.
........., ..., ..., ..., opinion on, 69.
Newdigate, Henry, 179.
New England, 33, 88, 257, 356, 411 (2), 536, 592.
New England Company, 411.
New Exchange, *see* Exchange.
New Forest, Hants, the, 145.
Newfoundland, 232, 243, 262, 341.
........., ships employed to, warrant to stay, 37.
Newgate, 75, 122.
.... prison, 21, 54, 110, 119, 220, 359, 400, 481, 512.
........., ..., keeper of, letter to, 207 ; *and see* Franklyn, James.
........., gaol delivery for, order at, 606.
Newhaven, Sussex, 111.
Newhaven, in France, *see* Havre de Grace.
Newington, Thraces and Thrognolls in, 343.

Newington, Middlesex, inhabitants of, petition of, 461.
Newington South, co. Oxford, 398, 448.
Newington, Surrey, 399.
........., ..., churchwardens of, authority to, 415.
........., ..., parishioners of, authority of, 415.
Newland, Berks. 348.
Newland, Robert, 197.
Newman, Richard, 341, 343.
........., William, petition of, 120.
........., ——, vicar of Fifehead, Dorset, 316.
Newmarket, 9, 37, 279, 388, 391, 499, 506.
........., documents dated from, 269, 271, 272, 277, 278, 281, 293, 295, 297, 506.
........., his Majesty's house at, keeper of, see Baker, William.
Newnham, co. Gloucester, 287.
Newport, co. Monmouth, mayor, 603.
Newport Pagnel, co. Buckingham, 66, 363.
Newport, Earl of, see Blount, Montjoy.
New River, 487.
.... Company, of London, clerk of, 293.
...., governor of, see Middleton, Sir William.
Newstead, Harber, 374.
Newton, Francis, 512.
........., ..., petitions of, 75, 450.
........., John, of Salop, 312.
........., John, sheriff of Montgomery, and formerly sheriff of Salop, letters of, 365, 490.
........., Mr., of Northampton, 535.
........., Mr., of Queen Street, 388.
........., William, petitions of, 163, 181.
Newton, co. Cambridge, 372.
Newton, near Brecon, 78.
Newtown, co. Montgomery, plague in, 490.
Nibbs, Maria, indictment against, 76.
Nicholas, Betty, sister to Edward next mentioned, 524.
........., Edward, clerk of the Council, secretary to the Admiralty, allusions and references to, *passim*,
........., ..., his house at Thorpe, 603.
........., ..., warrant to pay him moneys, 170, 343.
........., ..., answer to a petition of, 486.
........., ..., letters of, 4, 8 (2), 36, 38, 95 (7), 96 (2), 122, 231, 237, 304, 324, 407, 523.
........., ..., his notes of Council business, 399, 611.
........., ..., the like of business to be transacted by Lords of the Admiralty, 24, 94, 159, 174, 182, 194, 228, 243, 261, 266, 373, 487, 501.
........., ..., the like of committee for the Royal Household, 142, 143, 147, 162, 202, 256, 549.
........., ..., the like of the Council of War, 270, 302.

Nicholas, Edward—*cont.*
........., ..., other minutes, drafts and memoranda of, 9, 85 (2), 88, 96, 102, 103 (2), 131, 219, 299, 482.
........., ..., reports, notes, and other papers of, relating to ship-money, 87, 88, 197, 386.
........., ..., letters to, (1637, December,) 5, 8, 13, 23, 31, 33, 36, 40; (Undated,) 37, 86, 131, 132 (2); (1637-8, January) 139, 145, 151, 152, 162, 173, 175 (3), 179 (2), 182, 185, 186, 197, 201, 213 (4); (February,) 222, 233, 234 (2), 237, 243, 244, 246, 249, 261, 265 (2), 266, 267, 269, 278 (2); (March) 289 (2), 290, 293, 294 (2), 297, 300, 302, 303, 304, 307 (3), 311, 312, 313, 314 (2), 317, 320 (2), 322, 327 (2), 329, 330, 333; (April) 344, 348, 354 (2), 355, 364 (2), 365, 367, 373, 377, 379, 381, 389; (May) 394, 407, 408 (2), 412, 418, 420 (4), 429, 432, 434 (2), 439, 441, 443 (2), 446, 451, 456, 460, 463, 466, 467; (June) 486, 489, 490, 505, 507, 510, 515, 520, 523, 527, 528, 541, 542; (July) 557, 558, 560, 562, 565, 566, 572; (August) 589, 597 (2), 603, 605.
........., ..., reference of accounts to, and appointment thereon, 232.
........., ..., reference to, of petition, 299.
........., ..., servant Francis, see Smith, Francis.
........., ...; wife, 304.
........., Edward, the younger son of Edward above mentioned, 31, 145, 304, 329, 421, 558.
........., John, father of Edward first above mentioned, letters of, 31, 304, 329, 420, 434, 558.
........., John, son of Edward first above mentioned, 31, 145, 329, 421, 558.
........., Dr. Matthew, brother of first mentioned Edward, 31, 122, 145, 329.
........., ..., letter of, 523.
........., ..., his wife, 558.
........., Richard, petition of, 90.
........., Sir Oliver, carver to the Queen, petition of, 589.
........., Susanna, mother of Edward first above mentioned, 524, 558.
Nicholl, Richard, pardon to, 498.
Nicholls, Arthur, petition of, 71.
........., ..., causes of his complaint, 72.
........., John, 323.
........., ..., certificate of, 301.
Nicholson, Mr., 280.
Nicolson, Thomas, 288.
Nicodemus, the, (ship,) 131, 132, 213, 268, 542, 578.
Nicolaldi, Don John de, resident ambassador from Spain, 85.
........., Don Michael, 85.
Nicoll, William, 43, 172.
........., ..., petitions of, 42, 43.
Noake, Sir, (clergyman,) 535.

Noble, Marie, articles against, 219.
........., Michael, town clerk of Lichfield, 219.
Noel, Edward, Viscount Campden, 241, 384.
........., Thomas, petition of, 384.
Nonconformists, see Puritans.
Nonsuch, the King's ship, 132, 159, 213, 366, 428, 541.
Nonsuch palace, Surrey, 435.
Nook, Northumberland, 397.
Norberie, Thomas, 342.
Nordway alias Nordwell, Hugh, 65.
Norfolk, 95, 152, 153, 216, 357, 438, 441, 460, 492, 501.
........., justices of assize, letter to, 134 (2), 548.
........., justices of peace, 238.
........., ..., letter and certificates of, 134 (4), 544 (2), 546.
........., ..., letters to, 480, 544.
........., sheriff, see Asteley, Sir Francis; Buxton, John.
........., under-sheriff, see Beifield, Mr.
........., ship-money, 89, 220, 289, 395, 397, 597.
........., vice-admiral, see Howard, Henry, Lord Maltravers.
Norgate, Edward, letter of, 230.
.... Mr., 603.
........., Thomas, boatswain, 30, 262.
Normancross, co. Huntingdon, hundred, 284, 545.
Norrill, see Northill.
Norris, Edward, 327.
........., Sir Francis, formerly sheriff of co. Oxford, 232.
North, Sir Dudley, 151.
........., Edward, 80.
........., Roger, Lord Treasurer of the Household, 468.
........., Sir Roger, 186.
North, the Council of, or of York, 79, 80, 225.
........., ..., reference to, of petition, 11.
........., ..., president of, see Wentworth, Thomas, Viscount.
........., ..., vice-president, 75, 225; and see Osborne, Sir Edward.
Northampton, 364, 385, 535.
........., documents dated from, 191, 394.
........., heath, 518.
........., mayor, 418, 518. See Collis, William.
........., plague in, 394, 395, 418, 428, 518.
........., recorder, see Lane, Richard.
........., ship-money, 220.
........., All Saints, 157, 248, 518.
Northampton, co., 50, 95, 152, 345, 372, 385, 438, 518, 519.
........., justices of peace, 92.
........., ..., letter to, 427.
.. .., ship-money, 92, 198, 220 (2), 294, 297, 336, 337, 345, 364 (2).
........., sheriffs, 91, 336. See Hanbury, Sir John.

Northborough, co. Northampton, 201.
Northcott, Devon, the barton of, 346.
Northill, co. Bedford, 550.
Northop, co. Flint, 52.
Northumberland, 216, 362, 584.
........., documents dated from, 330, 364.
........., plague in, 330, 365.
........., sheriff, see Bewick, Robert; Widdrington, Sir William.
........., ship-money, 213, 330, 364.
........., vice-admiral, see Howard, Theophilus, Earl of Suffolk.
Northumberland, Earl of, see Percy, Algernon.
........., Countess of, see Percy, Anne.
Norton, Sir Daniel, 64.
........., Francis, petition of, 393.
........., ..., particulars of grievances of, 393.
........., Sir Gregory, 299, 407, 450.
........., John, 73, 379.
........., ..., petitions of, 73 (2).
........., Sir Richard, 474.
........., ..., warrant to, 476.
........., Sir Walter, late sheriff of co. Lincoln, 28, 505.
Norton Ferris, Somerset, hundred, inhabitants of, petition of, 92.
........., ..., ship-money, 92, 175, 179, 314, 539.
Norton, St. Philip, Somerset, liberty of, ship-money, 152, 193, 408.
Norwich, 15, 143, 289, 383, 442, 480, 569, 597.
........., bishopric of, 425, 444.
........., chancellor, 259.
........., guildhall, 220.
........., mayor, 177, 442. See Sumpter, Robert.
........., ... and others of, letters of, 150, 548.
........., merchants of, trading in stuffs, petitions of, 216 (2).
........., ..., reasons of, 217.
........., ministers, order on petition of, 177.
........., parishes, ecclesiastical state of, laid before the King, 166.
........., ship-money, 220.
........., carriage of letters from and to, 143, 150, 177, 183, 216 (3), 217, 284.
........., Walloon congregation at, petition of, 356.
........., bishop, 177, 356; and see Montagu, Richard; Wren, Matthew.
Norwich, Countess of, deceased, see Denny, Mary.
........., Earl of, deceased, see Denny, Edward.
Nottingham, documents dated from, 24, 244.
Nottingham, co. 12, 81, 253, 267.
........., deputy lieutenants of, letter of, 244.
........., justices of peace, 43, 184.
........., ..., letter of, 24.

Nottingham, lord lieutenant of, see Cavendish, William, Earl of Newcastle.
........., sheriffs, 24, 186. See Lascelles, George; Thornhaugh, Sir Francis.
........., ship-money, 43, 159, 184, 186, 327, 430, 437, 443, 462.
........., under-sheriff, see Webster, James.
Nottingham, Earl of, see Howard, Charles.
Nowell, Henry, 395, 406, 440, 444.
Noy, William, Attorney-General, deceased, 16, 22, 346, 351, 419, 436.

O.

Oakely, John, 459.
Oakes, John, 73.
........., Nicholas, 73.
........., ..., petition of, 73.
Oakham, 241.
Oakley, co. Buckingham, 564.
Oath, ex officio, legality questioned, 2.
Oaths, various, note of fees for administering, 77.
Oatlands, Surrey, 129, 282, 502, 523, 609.
........., documents dated from, 131, 579, 580, 582, 583, 587 (3), 588, 589 (4).
Ockendon, Essex, 522.
Odiham, Hants, ship-money, 198.
Odsey, co. Hertford, hundred, 134, 391, 545.
Offices which might be created without concurrence of Parliament, notes of, 131.
Officiall, William, 90.
Offington, Sussex, 245.
Offley, John, 431.
........., ..., pass for, 433.
........., Sir John, 431.
Oglander, Sir John, sheriff of Hants, 166.
........., ..., letters of, 293, 307 (2), 320, 367 (2), 381, 505.
Ogle, Sir John, 427.
........., ..., petitions of, 16 (2), 17.
........., ———. 343.
Ogmore, co. Glamorgan, manor, 498.
Okehampton, Devon, 169.
Okely, Richard, letter to, 201.
Old Bailey, London, 114, 218.
........., justice hall in, 606.
Old Jewry, London, document dated from, 389.

Oldam or Oldham, John, 142.
........., ..., information against, 63.
Oldfield, Philip, 469.
Oldham, co. Lancaster, 542.
Oldisworth, Michael, secretary to the Earl of Pembroke and Montgomery, 408, 515.
........., ..., letter of, 48.
........., ..., letter to, 48.
........., ..., warrant to, 1.
Oldland, co. Gloucester, ship-money, 178.
Old Palace Yard, Westminster, 116.
Oliver, Nicholas, gunner, appointment of, 131.
........., Thomas, brief on his behalf, 288.
........., Vincent, 498.
Olney, Bucks, 68.
Oneby, Humphrey, 235.
........., letter of, 223.
Ongar, Essex, hundred, 172, 548.
Oniate et de Villa Mediana, Condé de, ambassador from Spain, 456, 493, 555.
........., ..., pass for, 434.
Onsloe, George, 495.
Opinions, legal, 60, 69, 158.
Orange, Henry Frederick, Prince of, 8, 47, 281, 341, 493, 511, 523, 557.
Orchard [Portman,] Somerset, 287.
........., document dated from, 222.
Ordnance, officers of, 13, 25, 256, 268, 271, 278, 404, 450, 509, 550, 594.
........., ..., letters and other papers of, 25 (2), 97, 272 (2).
........., ..., letter to, 223.
........., accounts and estimates, 32, 151, 170, 320 (2), 350 (2), 367, 502, 503, 522, 523 (2), 535, 578, 579 (2), 601.
........., ..., other papers relating to, 228, 243, 344, 345, 550, 594.
........., warrants for owners of merchant ships to be allowed to purchase, 3, 41, 44, 159, 239, 268, 298, 306.
........., iron, transportation of, 3, 31.
........., founder's store for sale of, in East Smithfield, 41, 44, 239.
........., surveyor, see Coningsby, Lieut. Col. Francis.
........., lieutenant, 270. See Heydon, Sir John.
........., Master-General, 256, 578, 579; and see Blount, Montjoy, Earl of Newport.
Ordnance Office, London, 105, 260, 302, 325.
........., documents dated from, 32, 170, 272, 367, 502, 503, 522.
Ormes, John, 506.
Ormond, Earl of, see Butler, James.
Orson, Elizabeth, 424.
Orton, John, 440.
Osbaldiston, Lawrence, [Lambert?], 339.
Osbolston, Lambert, clerk, petition of, 37.
Osborne, Dr., 524.
........., Sir Edward, Vice-President of the Council of the North, letter of, 439.
........., ..., reference to, of petition, 11.

GENERAL INDEX. 681

Osborne, Sir Peter, 266, 271.
Ottery St. Mary, co. Devon, 77, 210.
Ouchterlony, Sir James, deceased, 80.
........., Lady, 24, 25.
Ouse, the river, 26, 196, 310, 323.
Oved, John, 156.
Oven to bake bread, new invention of, 79.
Overbury, Sir Nicholas, 492.
Overton, Wilts, manor, 253.
Owen, Evan, deceased, 39.
........., John, 193.
........., Rice ap Evan ap, 459.
........., Capt. Richard, of the Ninth Whelp, 194.
........., ..., letter to, 228.
........., William, grant to, 236.
Owens, Dr., 280.
Oxenbridge, Dr. Daniel, certificate of, 2.
........., Sir Robert, 384.
Oxenhall, co. Gloucester, 385.
Oxford, 72, 142, 286, 295, 333, 343, 407, 441, 561, 564.
........., documents dated from, 278, 325, 342, 561, 573, 588.
........., Bishop of, 471; *and see* Bancroft, John.
........., Carfax, conduit in, 295.
........., ship-money, 266.
........., Star Inn, the, 273.
Oxford, co., 54, 95, 181.
........., constables of, warrant to, 273.
........., sheriffs, *see* Norris, Sir Francis; Penyston, Sir Thomas; Walter, William; Wentworth, Sir Peter.
........., ship-money, 88 (2), 252 (3), 234, 235 (3), 265, 273, 278, 303, 333, 337, 394, 420, 510, 566.
........., under-sheriff, 510.
Oxford University, 69, 475, 550, 573.
........., Chancellor of, *see* Laud, William, Archbishop of Canterbury.
........., ..., power of, 287.
........., Vice-Chancellor, 425, 438. See Bailey, Dr. Richard.
........., metropolitical visitation of, 70.
........., heads of houses in, letter of, 295. For the several colleges and halls, *see* their several names.
Oxney, Kent, hundred, 548.
Oxton, Thomas, mayor of St. Alban's, returns of, 91, 134.
Oysters, exportation of, 155, 281, 341, 557.
........., report on the causes of the scarcity of, 557.

P.

P. J., letter of, 528.
P. T., (printer,) 58.
Package, scavage, balliage, and portage, offices of, 113.
Packer, Mr., 524.
Pack-horses, 217.
Packington, Sir John, 427.
........., pass to, 428.
Paddington, Middlesex, ship-money, 91.
Page, Henry, 607.
........., ..., statement of, 63.
........., Mr., 226.
........., ..., Nicholas, petition of, 79.
Paine, variously spelt ;—
........., Edward, 111.
........., Mr., 246.
Palace Yard, Westminster, 48 ; *and see* Old Palace Yard.
Palacio, Don Juan de, 456.
Palatinate, the, 2.
........., Charles Louis, the Elector Palatine, 7, 29, 146, 324, 360, 418, 535.
........., ..., his departure from England, 82, 86 (2).
........., ..., letter of, 47.
Palfreman, Walter, 285.
Palmer, Andrew, letter of, 42.
........., Geoffrey, opinion of, 605.
........., George, 487, 513 (2).
........., ..., certificate and letter of, 453 (2).
........., Sir Henry, Comptroller of the Navy. 175, 344, 449, 523.
........., ..., letters of, 82, 234.
........., ..., letter to, 363.
........., Sir James, 277.
........., ..., warrant to, 173.
........., ..., grant to, 498.
........., Lady, letter to, 277.
........., ..., her children, 277.
........., ..., her father, 277.
........., Mr., 121.
........., Sir Roger, 333, 510.
Palmers *alias* Rawlies, Suffolk, a tenement, 181.
Pangbourne, Berks, 357.
Pannett, John, mayor of Chichester, 595.
Panting, Mr., vicar of St. Michael's, Coventry, 305.
Panton, Edward, petition of, 250.
[Panzani], Signor Gregorio, 61.
Paper-mills, 108.
Paperill, John, lieutenant-colonel, principal engineer for fortifications, 385.
Papworth, Thomas, certificate of, 424.
........., William, certificate of, 424.
Paradice, Thomas, appointment of, 542.
Paramore, Thomas, commissions to, 602 (2).
Parens, Herman, grant to, 410.

682 GENERAL INDEX.

Parham, Sussex, 481.
Paris, 162, 167, 264, 387, 499.
........., documents dated from, 376, 599, 600.
........., parliament of, arrêt of, 117, 223.
Paris Garden, liberty, inhabitants, petition of, 113.
Parker, Charles, son of William, Lord Morley and Monteagle, petition of, 464.
........., Elizabeth, Lady Morley and Monteagle, petition of, 464.
........., Henry, Lord Morley and Monteagle, petition of, 464.
........., Michael, letter to, 610.
........., John, stationer, report of, 379.
........., John, of Covent Garden, information against, 114.
........., Sir Philip, sheriff of Suffolk, account by, 200.
........., Thomas, son of Henry, Lord Morley and Monteagle, 464.
........., Thomas, 119.
........., Walter, 284.
........., William, of London, petition of, 99.
........., William, of co. Lincoln, 2.
........., William, Lord Morley and Monteagle, 464.
........., William, son of the last above mentioned, 464.
Parkhurst, Sir William, 295.
........., ..., letters of, 42, 230.
Parkinson, William, 62.
Parks, Thomas, petition of, 53.
Parliament, 215, 247, 251.
........., members, fee for administering oath to, 77.
........., notes of offices which might be created, and fees granted without the concurrence of, 131.
........., Sutton's Act of, extract from, 484.
Parliament Stairs, Westminster, 48.
Parman, William, petition of, 283.
Parneholt, Hants, 447.
Parr, John, 223.
Parrat, Mr., list by, 89.
Parrett, John, 50.
Parsons, Henry, 412.
Partridge, James, letter of, 176.
........., Robert, deceased, 125.
........., Robert, son of the last above mentioned, petition of, 125.
........., Rose, mother of the foregoing, 125.
Pasfield, George, 298, 302, 304 (2), 307, 312.
........., ..., petition of, 303.
Paslowe, Amias, 285.
Passenham, co. Northampton, document dated from, 297.
Passes or licences to quit the kingdom, 1, 30, 117, 212, 398, 423 (2), 428, 433, 452, 459.
Paston, Clement, petition of, 75.
........., ..., his father, 75.
Pastorne, see Paston.

Patience, the, 298, 302, 303, 304.
Patney, Wilts, manor, 253.
"Pattern of Catechistical Doctrine," book so entitled, 298.
Pattishall, co. Northampton, 285, 364, 518, 539, 572.
........., ship-money, 285.
Pattison, John, 598.
Paul, Robert, 167.
Paulerspury, co. Northampton, rectory of, 138, 229, 272, 273, 280, 288.
Paulett or Powlett, variously spelt;—
........., Lord Charles, 474.
........., Lord Edward, 569.
........., Francis, recorder of Lynn Regis, report to, 566.
........., John, Lord, petition and letter of, 79, 197.
........., ..., letter to, 4.
........., Mr., 524.
........., Robert, 168, 535.
........., ..., letter and other papers of, 138, 169.
........., ..., commission to, 602 (2).
........., ———, 23.
Paulspurry, see Paulerspury.
Paunsford, Walter, 464, 465.
Pawlett, see Paulett.
Pawling, Andrew, 267, 271, 301, 317, 325, 334, 362, 371, 383, 385, 421, 429, 435, 439, 441, 452, 469, 498.
Pawlsbury, see Paulerspury.
Paxford, Richard, application of, 226.
Pay, Nicholas, 333.
Payne, variously spelt;—
........., George, 415.
........., Thomas, 72, 180.
........., ..., petition of, 74 ; and see Paine.
Peachy, Hugh, letters to, 417, 438.
Peacock, Mr., letter to, 56.
Peard, Roger, brief on behalf of, 339.
Pearl, the ship, 300.
Pearse, Gregory, petition of, 111.
Pecke, Robert, 259.
Peebles, John, grant to, 6.
Pellet, William, 65.
Pelsant, Margaret, 219.
Pember, Walter, return of, 87.
Pemberton, Sir Lewis, petition of, 538.
Pembroke, ship-money. 288.
........., co., 32, 112, 156, 292.
........., justices of peace, 112.
........., sheriff, see Phillips, Thomas.
........., ship-money, 288.
Pembroke, Earl of, see Herbert, William.
Pembroke and Montgomery, Earl of, see Herbert, Philip.
Pembroke Hall, Cambridge, 437.
Pembroke, the ship, 298.
Penance performed, 68, 275, 276, 424, 463, 572.
Pendennis Castle, Cornwall, 496.

Penford, ——, 127.
Penkevill, ——, 192.
Penn or Penne, Giles, his Majesty's consul at Sallee, warrant to, 42.
………, ……, petition of, 116.
………, ——, 468.
Pennare, William, 3.
Pennington, Isaac, letters of, 498, 508.
………, ……, accounts of, 34 (2).
………, Capt. Sir John, 28, 34, 37, 151, 195, 262, 266, 268, 271, 428, 604.
………, ……, appointed Vice-Admiral of the Fleet, 366.
………, ……, letters and other papers of, 3, 15, 17, 31, 36, 44, 173, 202, 234, 246, 269, 291, 304, 499, 598, 608.
………, ……, letters to, 7, 13, 19, 83, 175, 244, 261, 277, 315, 321, 323 (2), 326 (2), 330, 356, 361, 366, 444, 474, 482, 498, 508, 523, 578, 595, 596, 600, 603 (2), 605, 608, 609.
………, ……, his ship, 361. *See* the St. Andrew and the Swiftsure.
………, ……, his nephew, 321, 356.
………, Thomas, 34.
Pennington, the (ship), of London, 137.
Penniston, Anthony, petition of, 53. *See also* Penyston.
Penny, William, 80.
Pensford, Somerset, documents dated from, 358, 377.
Penteland, Northumberland, 343.
Penyston, Sir Thomas, sheriff of co. Oxford, letters and other papers of, 265, 273, 303, 333, 394, 420, 520, 566.
………, ……, his house at Coggs, document dated from, 303.
………, ……, his lady, 520. *See also* Penniston.
Percival, variously spelt;—
………, Capt. Anthony, papers of, 290, 350 (2).
………, ……, Sir Philip, 165.
Percy, Algernon, Earl of Northumberland, 34, 213, 243, 309, 356, 441, 501, 574, 596, 604, 608, 609, 611.
………, ……, appointed high admiral of England, 321, 326, 445.
………, ……, his house at Salisbury Court, documents dated from, 366 (2).
………, ……, letters and other papers of, 330, 366 (2), 474, 578, 595.
………, ……, instructions of, 428.
………, ……, letters and other papers to, 82, 578, 588.
………, ……, his sickness, 428, 523, 609.
………, Anne, Countess of Northumberland, funeral certificate of, 34.
………, Anne,⎫
………, Dorothy,⎬ daughters of the said
………, Elizabeth,⎪ Countess, 34.
………, Katherine,⎭
Perkins, Francis, petition of, 75.
………, ——, 337.

Perron du, Jacques, her Majesty's almoner, Bishop of Angoulême and abbot of St. Taurin and Lyre, 330.
………, ……, acquittance of, 461.
Perrott, Lady Dorothy, 556.
………, Penelope, 556.
………, Sir John, *see* Sir Thomas.
………, Sir Thomas, 556.
Persall, John, petition of, 520.
……… ……, his wife and children, 520.
………, Sir John, 520.
Persia, 511.
Persons un-named, 530.
………, letters and other papers of, 61, 71, 78, 81, 98, 519, 524 (3) 533, 535.
………, letters to, 56, 130, 519, 529, 533, 556.
Pescod, Mr. 329.
………, Nicholas, petition of, 495.
Peter and Andrew, the, (ship,) 4.
Peterborough cathedral, 409.
………, diocese, 206, 533.
………, ……, visitation of, 157.
………, ship-money, 220.
………, Bishop, *see* Dee, Francis.
………, chancellor and commissaries, substitutes of, proceedings of, 157.
………, Countess of, *see* Mordaunt, Elizabeth.
………, Earl of, *see* Mordaunt, John.
Peterston manor, 259.
Petherton, North Somerset, forest, 36.
………, South, 275, 276.
Petre, Mr., 521, 522.
Pett, Peter, the younger, 175, 269.
………, Capt. Phineas, 30, 202 (2), 291.
Petty, Laurence, 467.
………, Mr. 245.
Petty Bag Office, the, 87, 556.
Petworth, Sussex, 34, 444.
………, document dated from, 595.
Pevensey, Sussex, rape, Downish division, 135.
Peverell, cos. Nottingham and Derby, honour of, grant of, 422.
Pews or seats in churches, 308, 317, 577.
Peyto, Sir Edward, 71.
Peyton, Sir John, 89.
………, Lady, 89.
Phalsbourg, Princesses of, 223.
Phelipps *see* Phillips.
Phelps, Thomas, 450, 452, 463 (2).
Philip, the, of London, 311, 315.
Phillips, variously spelt;—
………, Augustine, 83, 84, 454.
………, Edward, 314.
………, Fabian, 292.
………, Francis, auditor for cos. Northampton and Rutland, 148, 256, 368, 376, 510.
………, ……, letter of, 312.
………, ……, warrant to, 50.

Phillips, John, grant to, 148.
........., Mr., 407.
........., Phillis, 405, 459.
........., Richard, of co. Warwick, 405, 459.
........., Richard, of London, 118, 119 (2).
........., Robert, 181.
........., ..., statement of, 391.
........., Sir Robert, 271.
........., ..., letter and other papers of, 31, 276.
........., Susanna, 181.
........., Thomas, sheriff of co. Pembroke, 288.
........., ——, 53.
Philpot, Henry, 79.
........., Sir John, 7, 79 (2).
Phipps, Edmund, petition of, 108.
........., John, 240.
........., Mary, 240.
Physicians, College of, London, 2, 399.
........., ..., answer of, 358.
........., ..., ..., order in Council as to, 401.
Piccadilly Hall, 410.
Piccolomini, General, 558.
Pichonotti, Francisco Maria, 554.
Pickering, Mr., 510, 514, 521, 522.
........., William, of co. Derby, order in cause of, 383.
........., William, of Salop, 473 (2).
........., ..., articles against, 338.
........., ..., petition of, 45.
Pickering Lythe, co. York, wapentake, 345.
Piether, Isaac, 259.
Piddletown, co. Dorset, 396.
Pierce, William, Bishop of Bath and Wells, 32, 69, 89, 92, 398, 433.
........., ..., letters and other papers of, 151, 275, 276, 378, 602.
........., ..., letter to, 156.
........., ..., his registrar, statement of, 275.
Pierrepont, Henry, Viscount Newark, 434.
........., ..., pardon to, 16.
........., Robert, Earl of Kingston, 380.
........., William, sheriff of Salop, letters of, 266, 326, 423, 434.
........., ..., letter to, 446.
"Piety, the Practice of," book, 365.
Pigeon, Philip, 583.
Pigge, John, certificate of, 386.
Pigott, John, 126, 163 (2), 170, 529.
Pilchards, 112.
Pilkington, Dr., late archdeacon of Leicester, 323.
........., Henry, commission to, 602 (2).
Pimme, John, 162.
Pinck, Dr., 206.
Pinckney, Leonard, 453, 487, 513.
........., ..., letter of, 515.
........., ..., letter to, 138.
........., Mr. 575.

Pincombe, ——, 500.
Pindar, Sir Paul, farmer of the alum works, 109.
........., ..., petition of, 97.
Pine, John, 407.
Pinke, Nicholas, 469.
Pinmakers, poor distressed, petition of, 107.
........., company, 107, 589.
........., ..., hall of, 107.
Pinnaces for the Navy, 82.
Pinner, Middlesex, ship-money, 90.
Pinson, William, 382.
........., ..., articles against, 382.
........., ..., answer of, 382.
........., ..., his wife, 382, 383.
Pious uses, commissioners for, 61.
........., new commission for, 595, 596 (2), 606, 608.
........., ..., receiver and treasurer, see Powell, Sir Edward.
Pipe, clerk of the, see Croke, Sir Henry.
Pipe-staves, 24, 502.
Pirates, and proceedings with a view to the suppression of piracy, 15, 17, 43, 83 (2), 103, 110, 600, 605; see also Algiers, Barbary, Sallee, and Turks.
Pitcairn, Mr., 78.
Pitchcott, co. Buckingham, 564.
Pitman, John, certificate of, 156.
Pitney, Somerset, hundred, ship-money, 156.
Pitt, ——, cousin to John Nicholas, senior, 31.
Pitts, Edward, 474.
........., Elizabeth, 63.
Pix, trial of the, 43.
Plague, the, supposed to be identical with the spotted fever, 395.
........., means adopted for its prevention, 108, 144, 389, 411, 422, 428.
Plantations, the King's, 203.
Plays, 546. See also Masques.
Pleadall, Mr., 287.
Please, Richard, 285.
Pleydell, ——, 192.
Plomesgate, Suffolk, hundred, 544.
Plowden, Sir Edmond, 469.
Plucknett, George, 441.
Plucknett, Somerset, 445.
Plumstead, Great, Norfolk, 444.
Plusher, Simon, 222, 223.
Plymouth, 28, 85, 151, 270, 290, 591, 600.
........., documents dated from, 6, 607.
........., governor, see Bagg, Sir James.
........., lieutenant-governor, see Bagg, Capt. George.
........., harbour, 6.
........., mayor, 379; see Sherwill, Nicholas.
........., ship-money, 379.
Plymouth Sound, 269, 600.
........., ..., document dated from, 28.

Plympton, Devon, 572.
........., mayor, 572.
Plymtree, Devon, 218.
Pocklington, William, constable, 186, 430, 437.
Pococke, Mr., 245.
Poe, William, 473.
Poem, 25.
Pointall, Mr., 257.
Pointz, Sir Robert, sheriff of co. Gloucester, 337.
........., ..., letters to, 178, 211.
Poland, 7, 153.
........., ambassador from, 117.
........., King of, 7, 102.
........., Queen of, 7.
"Polanders," ships so called, 102.
Pole, Periam, demise to, 142.
Poley, Edmund, letter of, 157.
Polhill, Nicholas, 84 (2), 454, 583, 588, 608.
........., ..., letter of, 84.
Pollard, Col., 306.
........., [Sir Hugh?], Baronet, 430, 512.
........., Ralph, mayor of St. Albans, certificates of, 94, 544.
........., ———, 503.
Pomerania, 264.
Ponte, the river, 557.
Pool, the, of the Thames, 422.
Poole, John, 172.
........., Sir John, letter to, 210.
........., Mr., 515.
........., Richard, postmaster of the Court, 341.
........., Richard, receiver of saltpetre, accounts rendered by, 396.
........., ..., letters to, 95, 237.
........., Richard, clerk, of Shrewsbury, 58, 337.
........., Thomas, 172, 190, 207.
Poole, Dorset, 605.
Poore, Henry, Viscount Valentia, 299, 407.
Pope, Henry, 176.
........., Hugh, 435, 514.
........., John, 406.
........., Robert, 214.
........., ..., petition and certificate of, 147, 176.
Pope, the, 3, 10, 390, 474, 535, 593, see Gregory XIII.
Popham, Alexander, 365.
........., Edward, 384.
........., Sir Francis, 461, 495, 496.
........., John, deceased, 176.
........., ..., his funeral, 169, 176.
........., ..., his father, brother, and wife, 176.
Portell, John, 270.

Porter, Charles, 130.
........., Endymion, groom of the bedchamber, 36, 38, 78, 145, 152, 327, 358, 367, 371, 372, 434, 445, 466 (2), 468, 482, 492 (2), 559.
........., ..., accounts of, 129, 492.
........., ..., agreements of, 292, 395.
........., ..., petitions of, 17, 55, 255.
........., ..., letters of, 467, 528, 569.
........., ..., letters to, 53, 147, 374.
........., ..., his servant, see Harvey, Richard.
........., ..., styled "Sir Endymion," 358, 377.
........., George, trumpeter, 174.
........., ..., warrant to, 174.
........., George, son of Endymion Porter, 556.
........., John, petition of, 99.
........., Mrs., " good old," 29, 445.
........., Olive or Olivia, wife of Endymion, letter to, 556.
........., ..., bills of, 327.
........., Thomas, 514.
........., ..., information of, 510.
Porters of London, abuses committed by, 319 (3).
Portington, William, lieutenant of the horse for Middlesex, petition of, 46.
Portland, Earls of, see Weston, Jerome; Weston, Richard.
........., Countess of, see Weston, Frances.
........., Countess Dowager of, see Weston, Frances.
Portland, Isle of, 64, 290, 298, 318.
Portman, Sir William, sheriff of Somerset, letters of, 222, 354, 398.
........., ..., letters to, 433, 479.
Portsdown, hundred, Hants, 567.
Portsea, Isle of, 567.
........., inhabitants of, petition of, 566.
Portsmouth, 86, 160, 195, 242, 243, 262, 269, 278, 279 (2), 290, 291, 293, 307, 321, 356, 361, 367, 408, 469, 480.
........., ..., documents dated from, 381.
........., clerk of check at, see Steventon, William.
........., fortifications, 81.
........., governor, 566; and see Cecil, Edward, Viscount Wimbledon.
........., master-shipwright for, 202.
........., mayor, see Beeston, Thomas.
........., under victualler, see Holt, [Thomas].
Portugal, 29.
........., merchants of London trading to, petition of, 103.
Post-horses, abuse respecting, 269, 390, 391 (3), 421.
Postmasters General, 51, 239, 421, 551, see Coke, Sir John; Windebank, Sir Francis.
........., the late, see Stanhope, Charles and John, Lords.

Postmasters, 421 (2), 434.
........., foreign, 51; *and see* Witherings, Thomas.
Posts, 22, 52 (3), 53 (2), 150, 171, 177, 183, 217 (2), 238, 257, 278, 297, 391 (6), 394, 421, 515, 551, 576; *see also* Carriers.
Potashes, 101, 184.
Pott, Thomas, 593.
........., ..., petition of, 44.
Potter, Elizabeth, information of, 259.
........., Dr. [Christopher ?], 343, 425, 438.
Poulett, *see* Paulett.
Poulter, Thomas, 514.
........., ..., examination of, 522.
Poultney, Mr., 567.
........., Mrs., 567.
Poulton, co. Lancaster, 544.
Povey, Justinian, 333.
Powell, Cadwallader, 62, 339.
........., Charles, of Bristol, 360, 361, 449.
........., Charles, of Dover, 129.
........., Edmund, letter to, 201.
........., Edward, letter of, 323.
........., Sir Edward, Master of Requests, 403, 436, 455 (2), 497, 575, 596, 602, 608.
........., ..., letter to, 606.
........., John, letter to, 201.
........., Dame Mary, 403, 436, 455 (2), 497.
........., ..., petition of, 575.
........., ..., her mother, 403; *and see* Vanlore, Dame Jacoba.
........., Richard, of Pattishall, 572.
........., ..., articles against, 285.
........., Richard, verderer of Shotover Forest, 564.
........., Robert, Roman Catholic, 321.
........., Robert, solicitor, 602.
........., Thomas, warrant to, 435.
........., Sir Thomas, 23.
........., William, petition of, 107.
........., Sir William, letter to, 201.
Power, John, lease to, 6.
Powle, Henry, 336.
Powlett, *see* Paulett.
Powter, Thomas, *see* Poulter, Thomas.
Poyner, Richard, 385.
Poynter, John, 426.
Poyntz, Edward, 306.
"Practice of Piety," book, 145.
Prance, Anthony, 607.
Pratt, Griffin, 346.
Pregion, John, deceased, registrar of the diocese of Lincoln, 67.
........., Philip, son of the above, and registrar of the diocese of Lincoln, letter of, 67.
........., ..., his mother and her eight children, 67.
Prentice, Robert, petition of, 125.
........., Sarah, petition of, 125.

Presteigne, co. Radnor, inhabitants of, 322.
........., ..., petition of, 321.
........., plague in, 321, 322 (2).
........., ship-money, 311, 321, 322 (2).
Prestland, Paul, petition of, 10.
Prestmasters, 236, 290, 292.
Preston, Dr. [John], books of, 366.
........., Richard, late Earl of Desmond, 372, 435.
........., Samuel, 189.
Preston Pans, 101.
........., Patrick, Westmoreland, return for, 547.
........., Richard, Westmoreland, return for, 547.
Prettyman, Sir John, letter to, 210.
Prevost, Sebastian, petition of, 112.
Price, Capt. Charles, 608.
........., ..., letter to, 440?.
........., George, 420.
........., Richard, sheriff of co, Cardigan, petition of, 94.
........., William, groom of the Chamber, 188, 258.
........., ..., order on petition of, 154.
Prichard, Edward, 235.
Prideaux, Denys, 288.
........., Dr. John, Regius Professor of Divinity, and rector of Exeter College, Oxford, 325 (2).
........., ..., certificate of, 282.
........., Sir Thomas, letter to, 210.
Prielove, Amos, 172, 186, 207.
Priests, *see* Roman Catholics.
Prigeon, John, the elder, 170.
Prince, Edward, 388.
........., ..., affidavit of, 389.
........., ..., petition of, 389.
Prince Royal, the (ship), 24, 30, 37, 182, 192, 194, 202, 460, 480.
Princess Street, [London], document dated from, 237.
Printers and Printing, 71, 72, 73, 172, 180, 200, 245.
........., commissioners for, petition to, 73.
.... of London, Society of, 71; *see also* the King's printers.
........., decree of Star Chamber for regulating, 72 (2).
........., notes upon the power of the Crown in regulating, 74.
Printers' Hall, the, clerk of, 72.
Priors Marston, co. Warwick, 437 (2), 456.
........., churchwarden and others, certificate of, 446.
Priske, Degory, 527.
Prisons, *see* Clink, Compter, Fleet, Gatehouse, Marshalsea, Newgate, and White Lion.
Pritchard, Christopher, 39.
Privy Chamber, gentlemen of, petition of, 216.
Privy Seal, keeper of, *see* Montagu, Henry, Earl of Manchester.

Privy Seals, warrant to discover moneys still in the hands of the collectors, 442.
Prize ships, 28 (2), 160, 296, 590, 600.
........., taken by foreign vessels sold in English ports, 6.
Proclamations, 39, 163, 236, 269, 532.
........., order concerning payment for, 208.
Proger, James, petitions of, 149, 322, 610.
Prosperous, the, of London, 137.
........., the, of Exeter, 411, 434.
Proudfoot, Mark, petition of, 525.
Providence, the, (pinnace,) 86 (3), 213, 244, 261, 361, 535, 598.
Providence, the, of London, 444, 482, 608.
Prust, ——, 500.
Prynne, William, 27, 64, 71, 123, 139 (2), 142, 240, 296.
........., ..., his man, see Wickens, Nathaniel.
........., ..., account of his voyage to Jersey, 298.
Pryor, John, 363.
Prythergh, Richard, letter of, 363.
Publow, Somerset, document dated from, 395.
Puchin, Robert, 585.
Pulford, John, 11.
........., ..., commissions to, 602 (2).
........., ..., statement concerning, 11.
........., Thomas, 271.
Pulham, co. Dorset, 511.
Pulman, William, 268.
Purbeck, Isle of, 385.
Purfleet, [Essex,] the King's fee-farm mills at, information concerning, 57.
Puritans and Nonconformists, 2, 62, 166, 192, 231, 518, 534, 572.
........., letter to, 13.
Purlieus, the, near Havering, Essex, 328.
Pursefield, near Lincoln's Inn, London, 163, 181.
Putney, document dated from, 266.
Pwlford, Thomas, 507.
Pyborne, John, 467.
Pye, Nicholas, messenger, warrant to, 172.
........., Sir Robert, 123, 201, 461.
........., ..., letters of, 574 (2).
........., ..., letter to, 575.
Pyle, Lady, 365.
Pym, John, letter of, 571.
Pyne, John, 486.

Q.

Quadring, Sir William, 307.
Quarilis, see Quarles.
Quarles, John, 575 (3), 576 (2).
........., Sir Robert, his walk near Havering, 328
Quarmby, co. York, 80.
Quarrendon, co. Buckingham, 564.
Quarry Hill, Hants, 480.
Queenborough, Kent, 366.
Queenhithe, London, 357.
Queeniborough, co. Leicester, 226.
Queen Street, London, 388.
........., St. Giles's-in-the-Fields, 604.
Queen's College, Oxford, provost of, see Langbaine, Dr. Gerard.
Questwood, Mark, 268.
Quitville, John de, 350.

R.

Raby, co. Durham, lordship, 475.
Radcliffe, Susan, *alias* Bright, 80.
Radfield, co. Cambridge, hundred, 133.
Radley, Berks, document dated from, 348.
Radnor, co. 311.
........., justices of peace, letter of, 322.
........., sheriff, see Davies, Evan.
........., ship-money, 322.
Raffe, William, 468.
Ragley House, co. Warwick, 144.
Ragusa, 104.
Railton, William, keeper of the Council Chamber, 41, 53, 467.
Rainbow, the, 170, 243.
Rainsborough, Capt. William, 195, 249, 268.
........., ..., letter and another paper of, 132, 187.
........., ..., letters to, 312, 363.
Rainton, Sir Nicholas, justice of peace for Middlesex, 87 (2), 259, 606.
Ralph, William, 263 (2).
Ramsay, John, late Earl of Holdernesse, 484.
........., William, Earl of Dalhousie, 529.
Ramsbury, Wilts, 304.
Ramsden, Sir John, late sheriff of co. York, 19.
Ramsey, co. Huntingdon, 308 (2), 369 (2).
........., document dated from, 369.

Randall, James, 34.
Randy, Nicholas, 188.
Ransford, Sir Garrett, petition of, 124.
Raphelengius, ——, 245.
Rashleigh, Jonathan, 185.
Ratcliff, Middlesex, 4, 115, 273, 311.
Rates, book of, 366.
Raven, William, 512.
Ravenscroft, George, 212.
........., James, justice of peace for co. Huntingdon, letter to, 589.
Rawleigh, Dr., 288.
Rawley, Edward, 9.
Rawlies, a tenement in Suffolk, 181.
Rawlin, Mr., 44.
Raworth, Robert, petition of, 71.
Rawson, James, 568.
........., ..., petitions of, 396, 606.
........., ..., acknowledgment of, 574.
........., Nehemiah, 10, 214, 405, 406.
Rea, Joseph, deputy-bailiff of Westminster, petition of, 94.
........., Lancelot, 210.
Read, variously spelt;—
........., Andrew, 288.
........., Edward, 239.
........., Foulke, letter of, 144.
........., Oliver, 406, 417.
........., Robert, secretary to Sec. Windebank, 74, 537, 574.
........., ..., letter of, 467.
........., ..., petition of, 123.
........., ..., letters to, 61, 99, 328, 574.
........., ..., grant and warrant to, 6, 147.
........., Thomas, commissions to, 602 (2).
........., ..., letter of, 492.
........., Sir Thomas, 88.
........., W., letter of, 226.
........., William, commissions to, 602 (2).
Reading, 126, 283, 376, 489, 595.
........., brewers of, petition of, 283.
........., Abbey Mills, 283.
........., St. Giles's Mills, 283.
Reay, Lord, see Mackay, Donald.
Records in the Tower of London, keeper of, see Borough, Sir John.
Recovery, the ship, 213.
........., the, of London, 590.
Recreations on the Lord's day, 63, 240, 377, 560, 563, 607.
Reculver, Kent, church, an ancient sea mark, 40, 44.
Recusants, 75, 241, 310, 332, 338, 363, 426, 439, 445, 592.
........., petition of, 74.
........., papers concerning, 74 (5).
........., revenues, commissioners for, 439.
........., ..., petition to, 11.
........., ..., reference on petition to, 440.

Redbourn, co. Hertford, plague in, 134.
Redford, ——, 500.
Redlands, co. Gloucester, 452, 459.
Red Lion, the, (King's ship), 229.
........., ..., sale of, 18, 202.
Redmore Fenn, Isle of Ely, 504.
Redriffe, see Rotherhithe.
Reed, see Read.
Reeresoun, Capt. John, statement of abuses committed by, 361.
Reeve, Hugh, petition of, 285.
........., Richard, evidence of, 288.
........., Roger, petition of, 491.
Reformation, the, in England, 64.
Reformation, the, or the Constant Reformation (King's ship), 213, 228, 291, 541.
........., the, merchant ship, 213.
Regimorter, Capt. ——, 178.
Reigate, ship-money, 198.
........., hundred, 546.
Renton, John, 331 (3), 349.
........., ..., letters of, 308, 309.
Reprisal, letters of, papers relating to, 83 (2), 84, 300, 583, 588, 590, 604, 608, 609. See also Marque, letters of.
Repulse, the, 131 (2), 243.
Requests, Court of, 79, 183, 231, 495, 517, 581.
........., ..., masters of, to the King, see Aylesbury, Sir Thomas; Powell, Sir Edward.
........., ..., master of, to the Queen, see Wintour, Sir John.
Reston, John, keeper of the King's prison at Dover, petitions of, 83, 84.
Reston, South, co. Lincoln, 386.
Revell, ——, 68.
Revenues, casual, due to the King, 97, 334, 362, 371, 421, 435, 439, 441, 452, 469, 498.
Review, commission of, never granted in cause of defamation, 238, 293.
Reynell or Reynoll, Adam, 111.
........., Sir Thomas, 558.
Reynolds, John, alias Mason, 178, 221.
........., Roger, 395, 397, 597.
........., Samuel, 235.
........., William, 6.
Reyser, Nicholas, petition of, 124.
Rhé, Isle of, 3, 430.
Rhenish wines, 106.
Rhine, the, 264.
Ribbesford, co. Worcester, 511.
Ricaut or Richaut, Peter, 4, 109, 260, 508.
........., ..., letter of, 482.
Rich, Sir Charles, master in Chancery, letters to, 332, 333.
........., Henry, Earl of Holland, Chief Justice and Justice in Eyre of the Forests on this side Trent, Chancellor of the University of Cambridge, and Lord Lieutenant of Middlesex, 44, 113, 124, 129, 247, 583, 609.

Rich, Henry, Earl of Holland—*cont.*
   ...., ..., letters and other papers of, 19, 256, 318, 320, 332, 430, 484, 518, 519, 563, 582, 587, 600 (2).
   ...., ..., the like to, 209, 447, 501, 579 (2).
   ...., ..., his deputy in the Forest Courts, *see* Lane, Richard.
   ...., ..., his two eldest sons, 19.
   ...., ..., reference to, of petition, 254.
   ...., Robert, Earl of Warwick, 8, 162, 362.
   ...., Sir Robert, 115, 295.
Richard II., 565.
Richard III., 357.
Richards, Henry, petitions of, 179, 180.
Richardson, John, letter of, 475.
   ...., ..., his grandchild, 475.
   ...., Matthew, 11.
   ...., Mr., 441.
   ...., William, vicar of Garthorpe, 368, 370, 379, 491.
   ...., William, letter of, 97.
Richaut, *see* Ricaut.
Richbell, Thomas, letter to, 201.
Richmond, Surrey, park, 131, 270, 274.
   ...., document dated from, 270.
   .... House, 274.
Richmond *alias* Webb, Christopher, 573.
Riddell, Mr., 227.
   ...., Sir Peter, 227, 419, 517.
   ...., Sir Thomas, 227.
   ...., ..., letter of, 349.
Rideing, Francis, affidavit of, 584.
Rider, Henry, 490.
Ridge, Mr., alderman of London, 520.
Ridges, Thomas, petition of, 66.
Ridler, Walter, 286, 287 (3).
Rigby, George, clerk of the peace for co. Lancaster, lists certified by, 171 (2).
   ...., Hugh, 363.
   ...., ..., petitions of, 27, 231.
Rigge, Robert, 127 (2).
   ...., ..., petitions of, 126, 127 (2).
Riley, William, certificate by, 500.
Ring, Christopher, 357.
Riots, 57, 198, 209 (2), 309, 333, 338, 349, 384, 493, 503, 506, 587.
Ripon, deanery, 287.
Ripplingham, Thomas, 49 (2).
   ...., William, 49.
Risdon, Thomas, 488.
Rishworth, Francis, *see* Rushworth, Francis.
Risley, William, 292.
Rively, Lewis, 481.
Rivers, Earl of, *see* Darcy, Thomas.

Rives or Ryves, Bruno, 377.
   ...., ..., petition of, 389.
   ...., Dr. Thomas, the King's Advocate, and Judge of the Admiralty of Cinque Ports, 174, 450.
   ...., ..., letters and other papers of, 59, 173, 351.
   ...., ..., reference to, of petitions, 351, 460.
Roade, co. Northampton, 189.
Roane, Dr., 418, 577.
Robbins, *see* Robins.
Robert, Prince, *see* Rupert, Prince.
Roberts, Dr., vicar of Enfield, 87.
   ...., Fulke, 370.
   ...., Sir Richard, sheriff of co. Leicester, letter of, 289.
   ...., Thomas, 398, 448.
   ...., Sir Walter, 369.
   ...., ..., certificate and petitions of, 40, 136, 251.
   ...., William, Bishop of Bangor, 148, 288, 315.
   ...., William, of Monmouth, certificate of, 334.
   ...., William, of co. Derby, order in cause of, 383.
Robes, office of, orders for regulation of, 49 (2).
   ...., ..., commissioners to inquire as to observance of, report of, 49.
   ...., clerk of, *see* Thelwall, Sir Bevis.
   ...., gentleman of, 49 (2); *and see* Kirke, George.
Robins, variously spelt ;—
   ...., Henry, 176, 179, 212.
   ...., ..., bond of, 214.
   ...., James, purveyor of timber, 480.
   ...., John, 323.
   ...., ..., his wife, 323.
   ...., Richard, petition of, 336.
Robinson, Dr. Hugh, archdeacon of Gloucester, letter of, 142.
   ...., John, boatswain, 132 (2).
   ...., John, vicar of Sunninghill, petitions of, 350 (2).
   ...., ..., ..., order on, 478.
   ...., ..., his "Justification of Separation," 366.
   ...., John, of Newcastle, 228.
   ...., Mr., 577.
   ...., Peter, pass to, 398.
   ...., Richard, petition of, 107.
Rochdale, co. Lancaster, 136, 544.
Roche Forest, Somerset, 303.
Roche, Cornwall, 288.
Rochelle, 6, 173, 276.
   .... wine, 41.
Rochester, 489.
   ...., archdeaconry, 6.
   ...., bishopric, 173, 288.
   .... Cathedral, 6.

Rochester, Bishop of, *see* Warner, John.
Rochford, Essex, 99.
........., hundred, 123.
Rochford, Lord, *see* Carey, John.
Rockingham Forest, co. Northampton, 318, 430, 485.
........., commissioners for compounding for offences against the forest laws, 355.
........., hundreds within, constables of, letter to, 354.
Rockley, Ellen, 102.
........., Thomas, answer of, 167.
Rodborne Cheney, Wilts, 13.
Rodeney or Rodney, Sir Edward, Vice-Admiral of Somerset, 362.
........., ..., letter of, 179.
........., ..., letter to, 502.
........., George, 194.
Roe, variously spelt ;—
........., George, 445.
........., Lawrence, 609.
........., Mr., proctor in the Court of Arches, 264.
........., Mrs., 445.
........., Sir Thomas, Chancellor of the Garter, 24, 241, 241, 255, 582.
........., ..., his family, 48.
........., ..., grant to, 214.
........., ..., letter and report of, 192, 263.
........., ..., letters to, 7, 29, 47, 146, 599.
Roebuck, the (King's pinnace), 37, 170, 213, 237, 542.
Rogers, Hester, 46.
........., John, gardener at Nonsuch, 435.
........., John, constable, co. Denbigh, 23.
........., John, clerk, 46.
........., John, of Wolverhampton, articles against, in High Commission Court, 382.
........., Mr., vicar of Bere Regis, 396.
Rokeby, William, petition of, 17.
........., ..., his wife and children, 17.
Rolewright, William, letter to, 194.
Rolfe, ——, a scrivener, 384 (2), 538.
Rolle, Dennis, late sheriff of Devon, 2.
Rolls, Master of the, 174; *and see* Digges, Sir Dudley.
Roman Catholics, 15, 16, 75 (2), 129, 230, 277, 450, 510, 592.
........., priests and others arrested or prosecuted, 75 (3), 123, 147, 187, 511.
........., ..., list of, 76.
Romball, Robert, affidavit of, 491.
Rome, 64, 185, 264, 338, 423, 428, 433, 452, 465, 467, 474, 481.
........., documents dated from, 467, 499.
........., alum of, 33.
........., St. Peter's, 585.
........., ..., document dated from, 321.
........., St. Paul's, 321, 585.
Romney, Kent, 93.

Rooker, William, 179, 212.
Rookes, George, 100 (2), 451.
........., ..., letter of, 85.
........., ..., answer to allegation of, 100.
........., ..., paper concerning, 100.
........., Robert, 328.
........., ..., his father, 328.
........., Thomas, 100 (2).
........., ..., statement by, 100.
........., ..., paper concerning, 100 (2).
........., William, 328.
Roos, Christopher, 355.
........., Richard, 355.
........., Robert, 355.
........., Rose, 355.
Rorington, Salop, ship-money, 199, 335.
Rosden, William, 61 (2).
Rose, the Mary (King's ship), 243, 373 (2), 410.
........., ..., (merchant ship,) 3, 4, 137.
Rose, William, order in cause of, 383.
Rosemary Lane, London, 273.
Roslingworth, 386.
Rosse, Mr., 125.
........., Rose, 125.
Rotherford, James, 66.
........., ..., his wife and children, 66.
Rotherhithe, 137, 298, 417.
Rothes, Earl of, *see* Leslie, John.
Rothwell, co. Northampton, 572.
........., document dated from, 249.
........., hundred, ship-money, 88.
Rotterdam, 84, 102, 365, 449, 535, 579, 603.
Rouen, 45.
Rous, Sir John, 497, 519.
Rowden, John, 221.
........., ..., petition of, 477.
Rowe, *see* Roe.
Rowell, John, 526.
Rowell, co. Northampton, *see* Rothwell.
Rowse, Humphrey, order on petition of, 187.
Royal or Old Exchange, London, 20, 204.
Royal Merchant, the (ship), 4.
Roydon, Essex, 172.
Royston, 269, 391 (3).
........., inhabitants of, petition of, 390.
Royston, Giles, affidavit of, 391.
Rubens, Sir Peter Paul, 34, 36, 434, 467, 488.
Ruddle, John, 399.
Rudge, Edward, sheriff of London, letter of, 563.
Rudyard, Sir Benjamin, 421.
Rugge, Walter, 449, 514.
Rumboll, Adam, 411.
Rumney, George, 299.
Rupert, Prince, son of Elizabeth, Queen of Bohemia, 82.
Ruscomb, Berks, ship-money, 349.

Rushcliffe, co. Nottingham, hundred, 24.
Rushden, co. Northampton, 81.
Rushforth, John, letter to, 457.
Rushworth, Francis, 157.
........., ..., petition of, 248.
Russell, Edward, 365.
........., Francis, license to, 37.
........., Francis, Earl of Bedford, Lord Lieutenant of Devon, 5, 340, 429, 438, 439 (2), 449, 462 (2), 493, 501, 571, 572.
........., ..., letters of, 285, 306, 429, 430, 439, 512.
........., ..., petition of, 252.
........., ..., letter to, 501.
........., ..., reference to, of petition, 153.
........., George, 487.
........., Margaret, daughter of the Earl of Bedford, 340.
........., Robert, chandler, 20, 146.
........., Thomas, letter and other papers of, 453 (2).
........., Sir William, Treasurer of the Navy, 18, 40, 82, 88, 94, 138, 160, 169, 175, 177, 179, 180, 195, 197, 202, 204, 208 (2), 210, 221, 233, 235, 246, 249, 262, 265 (2), 267, 269, 278, 289, 290, 294, 297, 304, 307, 313, 320, 327, 344, 354, 367 (2), 381, 407, 417, 419, 420, 423, 437, 449, 456, 462, 520, 565. 578, 605, 609.
........., ..., his clerk, see Fenn, Edward.
........., ..., accounts of ship-money, 4, 5, 14, 26, 45, 144, 145, 196 (2), 208, 209 (3), 246 (3), 265 (2), 276, 277 (2), 294, 303, 314, 327 (2), 354, 352, 364, 373, 386, 413 (2), 431, 444, 460, 488, 505, 516, 527, 537, 564, 577 (2), 586, 595, 601, 604.
........., ..., letters and other papers of, 91, 115, 139, 292, 314, 379, 577.
........., ..., letters to, 184, 363, 410.
........., ..., warrant for his pay, 344.
........., ..., receipts of, for ship-money, 2 (2), 4, 9, 11, 13, 19.
........., Sir William, baronet, license to, 37.
Russia, 4.
.... Company, 106.
Rustorff, ———, 7.
Rutland, co., 50, 95, 519, 563.
........., constables, letter to, 276.
........., sheriff, see Andrewes, Edward.
........., ship-money, 320, 322, 354, 373.
Rutland, Joseph, petition of, 106.
Rutter, John, 391.
........., ..., affidavit of, 391.
Ruxley, Kent, hundred, 132, 543, 548.
Ryce, John, 286.
Rydall, Westmoreland, 546.
Rye, Sussex, 163, 435, 601.
.... pier, 94.
Ryedale, co. York, wapentake, 345.
Ryehill, Essex, ship-money, 172, 207.

Ryley, William, petition and propositions of, 392 (2).
........., William, Bluemantle, certificate and other papers of, 34, 263 (2), 340, 431, 598, 604.
Ryther, Robert, 473.
Ryves, see Rives.

S.

S. T., 114.
Sackville, Edward, Earl of Dorset, Lord Chamberlain to the Queen, and one of the lord lieutenants of Middlesex, 85, 151, 204, 208, 241, 254, 266, 338, 362, 380, 402, 408, 474, 516, 540, 606.
........., ..., letters and other papers of, 12, 33, 115, 143 (2), 353, 603.
........., ..., the like to, 209, 282, 315, 445, 447, 602 (2).
........., ..., references to, of petitions, 9, 10 (2), 56, 255, 380.
........., Mary, Countess of Dorset, 315, 555.
Sacomb, co. Herts, 19.
Sadleir, Robert, 94.
Sainthill, Peter, warrant to, 203.
"Saint's Spiritual Strength," (book,) 366.
St. Albans, Herts, 111, 376, 392, 544.
........., liberty, 134, 544.
........., mayors, 235, 356.
........., ..., letter to, 211; and see Oxton, Thomas; Pollard, Ralph.
........., ship-money, 91, 94, 211, 356.
St. Anderos, see Santander.
St. Andrew, the, 17, 213, 279, 366, 474.
........., documents dated from, 499, 598.
St. Andrew's, Holborn, 162, 366, 481, 495.
St. Andrew's priory, Scotland, 39.
St. Augustine, 60.
St. Augustine, lathe, Kent, 135, 549.
St. Barbe, Mr., 145.
St. Bartholomew's, London, 417.
.... hospital, 258.
...., governors of, 154, 188.
...., the Great, London, 190.
St. Borian alias Burian, see St. Burian.
St. Botolph without Bishopgate, London, 313.
........., Aldgate, 505.
St. Brelade's, Jersey, 273.
St. Bride's, Fleet Street, London, 6.
St. Burian, Cornwall, deanery, 288.

St. Chad, Shrewsbury, church, 58.
.........., ..., ..., account of revenues of, 59.
St. Chrysostom, works edited by Sir Henry Savile, 71.
St. Clement Danes, London, 139, 167, 399, 404, 495.
.........., churchwardens, letter of, 414.
.........., parishioners, authority of, 414.
.........., churchyard, 142.
St. Dennis, the, 213, 474.
St. Dunstan's-in-the-West, London, 507, 566.
St. Elmund's Bury, Suffolk, plague in, 157.
St. Etheldred, Suffolk, liberty, 544.
St. Francis, superior of order, 230.
St. George, Sir George, Vice-Admiral of Connaught, letter to, 501.
St. George, the, (King's ship,) 86, 170, 213, 237, 279, 291.
St. George, hundred, Dorset, ship-money, 210.
St. George's, Southwark, 399.
.........., parishioners, petition of, 413.
St. George's Fields, Southwark, 113.
St. George's feast at Court, 357.
St. Giles, Mr., 343.
St. Giles-in-the-Fields, London, 107, 332, 399, 416 (3).
.........., churchwardens and vestrymen, letter of, 414.
.........., parishioners, answer of, 400.
.... ship-money, 178 (2), 205.
.........., ..., assessors and collectors, petition of, 46.
.........., ..., list of defaulters, 46.
St. Gregory's, London, papers relating to arrangement between the parishioners of, and those of Christchurch, 402, 485.
St. Ives, co. Huntingdon, 310.
St. James, Clerkenwell, 399.
St. James's church, Compostella, Spain, 585.
St. James's Palace, Westminster, 490.
.........., documents dated from, 396, 494, 516, 585.
.... park, 148.
St. John, Anne, daughter of the next mentioned. 500.
.........., John, Lord, of Bletsoe, deceased, 500.
.........., Sir John, 121.
St. John, of Dunkirk, (ship,) 6. *See also* Conception, the.
.........., of Agersfloate, (ship,) 28.
St. John Street, London, 130.
St. John's College, Oxford, 184, 288, 441, 605.
... ., Cambridge, 292, 507.
.........., president and others of, petition and letter of, 307, 354.
.........., library, 308 (2), 354.
.........., president, *see* Spell, Thomas.
St. Katherine, Tower Hill, London, 505.
St. Katherine Creechurch, London, churchwardens, petition of, 68.
St. Lawrence, Old Jury, London, 145.

St. Leger, Anthony, 24.
.........., ..., petition of, 2.
.........., Barbara, wife of the above, petition of, 2.
.........., Sir Warham, 2.
St. Leonard, Shoreditch, 399.
.........., parishioners, petition of, 413.
St. Lucar, 3 (2), 17, 223, 269, 304.
St. Malo, 270.
St. Margaret's, Southwark, 415.
St. Margaret's, Westminster, 399.
.........., churchwardens, letter of, 414.
St. Martin, Mons. de, 261.
St. Martin's-in-the-Fields, Westminster, 68, 145, 166, 298, 341, 366, 399, 406, 419, 450 (2), 452, 481, 528, 587, 604.
.........., churchwardens, letter of, 414.
.........., inhabitants, order on petition of, 404.
.........., late overseers, certificate of, 526.
.........., vestry, names of persons who have compounded with, 540.
St. Martin's Lane, London, document dated from, 263.
St. Mary Magdalen, Southwark, 415.
St. Mary Magdalen College, Oxford, document dated from, 425.
St. Mary Matfellon, Whitechapel, 399.
.........., churchwardens, letter of, 414.
.........., parishioners, authority of, 414.
St. Mary, Newington, 399.
St. Mary, Overy, priory, 415
St. Mary's, Scilly Islands, garrison of, 130.
St. Mary's Creek, Chatham, 1.
St. Neots, co. Huntingdon, 310.
.........., inhabitants, petition of, 580.
.........., ship-money, 246.
St. Nicholas [at Wade], Kent, 40, 44.
St. Olave's, Southwark, 116, 399.
.........., parishioners, petition of, 413.
St. Omer, 493, 558.
St. Paul, tapestry illustrative of the history of, 173.
St. Paul's Cathedral, London, 461, 551, 552, 597.
.........., repairs, 20, 157, 233, 275, 284, 306, 318, 360, 393 (2), 422 (2), 426, 442, 459, 463, 489, 567.
.........., ..., paymaster for, 422.
.........., ..., accounts respecting, 64.
.........., ..., commissioners for, letter to, 459.
.........., Dean, late, *see* Donne, John.
.........., ..., present, *see* Winniffe, Thomas.
.........., Dean and Chapter, 473, 480.
.........., ..., petition of, 551.
.........., sailors in ships that brought stone for repairs, exempted from impressment, 64, 298.
St. Paul's Cray, Kent, 240.
St. Peter, the, of Rotterdam, 535.
St. Peter, the, (ship,) 124.
St. Peter's College, Cambridge, document dated from, 305.

St. Peter's, Westminster, see Westminster Abbey.
St. Saviour's, Southwark, 399.
........., churchwarden and vestry, letter of, 415.
St. Sepulchre's, London, 359.
St. Sebastian, document dated from, 19.
St. Stephen's, Cornwall, 296.
St. Thomas, Southwark, 400, 426.
........., parishioners, letter of, 413.
St. Thomas the Apostle, hospital of, 413.
Salcey forest, co. Northampton, 374, 430, 484, 518.
........., officers of, letter to, 256.
Salesbury, Foulk, 466.
Salford, hundred, co. Lancaster, 135 (2), 544.
........., co. Warwick, 288.
Salisbury, Wilts, 55, 274, 421, 495, 523, 576, 603.
........., document dated from, 408.
........., assizes, presentment at, 576.
........., Dean, 601.
........., deanery, 287.
........., recorder, see Hyde, Robert.
........., Three Swans at, 421.
........., St. Edmund's churchyard, 211.
Salisbury, Bishop of, see Davenant, John.
Salisbury Court, Fleet Street, London, 34, 138.
...., documents dated from, 330, 366 (2).
Salisbury House, London, document dated from, 530.
Salisbury, Earl of, see Cecil, William.
........., ..., the late, see Cecil, Robert.
Salisbury New, see Salisbury.
Salisbury, the, (buss,) 578, 604, 609.
Sallee, 116, 321, 390.
........., governor, 321.
........., the King's consul at, see Penn, Giles.
........., the late expedition against, 82, 86, 116.
Salop, co., 18, 95.
........., sheriff, 337; see Corbett, Robert; Harris, Sir Paul; Newton, John; Pierrepont William.
........., ..., letter to, 446.
........., ship-money, 199, 266, 301, 311, 423, 434, 490.
Salt, 101, 113, 147, 217, 609.
Saltern, Jonathan, mayor of Bideford, memorandum of, 383.
Saltmakers of Great Yarmouth, see Yarmouth, Great.
Saltonstall, John, mayor of Berwick-upon-Tweed, 61 (2), 331 (3).
........., ..., letter of, 456.
........., ..., letter to, 349.
Saltoun, Lady, see Stewart, Ann.
Saltpetre, 8, 24, 25, 95 (2), 150, 159, 194, 223, 228, 242, 243, 348, 371, 375, 487 (2), 489, 499, 501, 502, 509 (2), 529.

Saltpetre, deputies for, 237.
........., ..., petitions of, 95 (2); and see saltpetremen; and also their respective names.
........., receiver of, see Poole, Richard.
Saltpetre and gunpowder, commissioners for, 237.
........., ..., letters and other papers of, 14, 19, 20, 23, 96, 146 (2), 150, 228, 242, 262, 263, 371, 379, 431, 443, 488, 490, 502, 505, 509 (2), 524, 526.
........., ..., the like to, 95 (2), 96 (2), 273, 284, 371, 489.
........., ..., register book, entry in, 510.
Saltpetremakers and saltpetremen, 95 (7), 97, 242. 276.
........., ..., complaints against, 24, 37, 143, 174, 232, 344, 372 (2), 375, 376, 385, 551, 589.
........., ..., complaints by, 23 (2), 138, 139, 159, 180, 357, 375, 376.
........., ..., petitions of, 95 (2).
........., ..., proportions to be supplied by, and amounts brought in, 396.
Saltram, Devon, 604.
Samford, Mr., 164.
........., Thomas, petition of, 218.
Samon, John, indictment against, 76.
Sampford, Great, Essex, 406.
Sampson, Abraham, 30.
........., Samuel, 519.
.... ——, of Holborn. 538.
Sampson's Place, formerly Simpson's Place, document dated from, 554.
Samuel, Sir Richard, 191, 536.
Sanders, Anthony, 345.
........., Gartwright, see Goodwin.
........., Sir Thomas, 346.
........., ——, drugster, 155, 161.
Sandgate Castle, Kent, 291, 369.
........., captain of, see Hippesley, Richard John.
Sandham, see Sandown.
Sandhurst, Berks, ship-money, 348.
Sandiford, Thomas, 143, 166.
Sandis, Henry, 474.
Sandown Castle, Isle of Wight, 270, 291.
Sandwich, 93.
Sandy, Sir Miles, the elder, letter of, 493.
........., ..., the younger, letter to, 493.
Sandypoint, North America, 33.
Sanford, William, 595.
Sankey, Clare, 431.
........., Richard, the elder, 431.
Santander, 278.
Sardinia, 192.
Sarnesfield, co. Hereford, 373.
........., document dated from, 373.
Saunders, Carew, petition of, 110.
........., Francis, articles against, 63.
........., Mrs., 90.
........., Valentine, 407, 450.
........., ..., petition of, 299.

Savage, Henry, pardon to, 16.
........, John, Viscount, 471.
........, Mr., 375.
Savile, Elizabeth, 598.
........, Henry, 598.
........, Sir Henry, 71, 570.
........, John, teller of the Exchequer, letters to, 13, 129, 270, 424.
........, Sir John, 598.
Savoy, 579.
........, the, London, 399, 404, 459.
........, churchwarden and vestry, certificate of, 415.
Sawyer, Sir Edmund, 102, 170, 256, 348, 368, 376, 488, 510.
........, ..., letters and other papers of, 312, 336, 424.
........, ..., brief of money received by, 64.
........, Francis, petition of, 92.
Saxby, John, 156.
Saxby, co. Lincoln, 158, 184, 368.
Saxe, Duke of, 122.
Say, Edward, 436.
Say and Sele, Viscount, see Fiennes, William.
Sayre, Nicholas, 503.
........, information of, 503.
Scandaret, Mr., one of her Majesty's servants, 7, 13, 15, 28.
Scarle, South, co. Nottingham, 61.
Scilly Islands, 363.
...., fortification of, 260, 270 (2), 278, 297, 302.
...., governor of, see Godolphin, Sir Francis.
...., lieutenant-governor, see Bassett, Thomas.
...., St. Mary's, garrison of, 130.
Scoble, ——, 500.
Scortreth, George, answer of, 176.
Scotch Arms, the, (sign) Westminster, 516.
.... coal, 395.
Scotland, 8, 101, 113, 217 (2), 367, 409, 419, 435, 447, 573, 599.
........, papers and references concerning the rebellion in, 21, 124, 357, 365, 523, 524, 528, 529, 533, 535, 554, 558 (2), 561, 564, 582, 591, 593, 595 (2), 596, 597, 603, 605, 608.
........, arms of, see "Scotch."
........, council of, 115, 525.
........, ..., letter to, 101.
........, covenant, the, 529, 534, 596.
........, covenanters, 362, 597.
........, ..., commissioners and assessors appointed by, minutes of business of, 349 (2).
........, ..., ..., resolutions of, 324 (2).
........, last parliament in, book on proceedings of, 365.
........, proclamation to people of, 532.

Scotland, nobles and commons of, supplication of, 581.
........, freights between London and, proposed office to confirm bargains for, 476.
........, Lord Chancellor of, 101.
........, ..., the late, see Hay, Sir George.
........, Lord Treasurer, 101, 593.
........, King's commissioner, see Hamilton, James, Marquess of.
........, Secretary of State, see Alexander, William, Earl of Stirling.
Scotland Yard, Westminster, 332.
...., new sewer in, names of contributors to, 114.
Scott, David, letter to, 437.
........, Col. James, petitions of, 113 (2).
........, Sir James, grant to, 466.
........, Richard, petition of, 52.
Scottish men, secret of state concerning, 21.
........, news, unknown writer of, 27 (2).
Scras, Tuppin, 495.
Scray, lathe, Kent, upper division, 133, 543.
Scriveners, 101.
.... and brokers, late commission for, 152.
Scudamore, John, Viscount, ambassador to France, 599.
........, ..., his chaplain, see Lockey, Thomas.
Sculcoates, co. York, 574.
Seacroft, co. York, 465.
Seagood, ——, 442.
Seale, Henry, printer, 25.
Seals, leaden, invention of, 11.
Seaman, Capt. Edmund, 11, 86.
........, objections against, 86.
Sea-mark, ancient, 40, 44.
Seamen, impressment of, 243, 292, 323, 449.
........, ..., abuses in, 236.
........, ..., exemptions from, 64, 262, 315, 341.
........, void of employment, proposal for registering, 2, 3.
Seamour, see Seymour.
Searle, John, 324.
Seaton, Lady, 367.
........, Zachary, petition of, 377.
Seaward, Humphrey, brief on behalf of, 77.
Secretaries of State, see Coke, Sir John; Windebank, Sir Francis.
Seatonn, Scotland, 529.
Sedcole, John, 160, 186, 191 (2), 194, 200.
........, ..., petition and other papers of, 190, 191.
........, ..., his father, 191.
Sedgmoor, King's, Somerset, 55.
Sedgwick, Westmoreland, return for, 547.
Seditious and libellous speeches, see Libels.

Sedley, Lady Elizabeth, 598 (2).
........., Sir John, funeral certificate of, 598.
........., Henry, ⎫
........., William, ⎬ children of the above, 598.
........., Elizabeth, ⎭
Selby, William, grandson of Sir William, 387.
........., Sir William, petition of, 387.
Selside and Whitwell, Westmoreland, return for, 547.
Selwood, John, 179.
Selwood, *alias* Zelwood forest, Somerset, 303, 600.
Selwyn, Jasper, 163, 170, 528.
........., ..., examination of, 529.
Senior, John, 2.
Sergeant, Robert, 19.
Sergeant's Inn, Fleet Street, 515.
Sermon, notes for on text, "*Per me reges regnant,*" 60.
Servants, suggested office for registering their licences to depart from service, 193.
Sessions, William, 470 (2), 475.
Seven Stars, the, (ship), 243.
Seven Stars, the, Fleet Street, London, 565.
Severne, Thomas, 131 (2).
Sewers, commission or commissioners of, 16, 189.
........., ..., for co. Cambridge, 152.
........., ..., Isle of Ely, 152.
........., ..., for co. Huntingdon, 152, 438.
........., ..., ..., Kent, 40.
........., ..., ..., Lincoln, 56, 152, 157, 184, 214.
........., ..., ..., Norfolk, 152.
........., ..., ..., Northampton, 152.
........., ..., ..., Suffolk, 152.
........., ..., ..., Sussex, 40.
........., ..., ..., York, 57, 404, 515, 533.
Seymour, Edward, 412.
........., ..., affirmation of, 385.
........., Sir Edward, vice-admiral of Devon, 151, 245.
........., ..., letter of, 218.
........., ..., letter to, 501.
........., Thomas, 186.
Seyr, Richard, 363.
Shackspeare, John, deceased, 30.
........., Mary, widow of John, warrant to, 30.
Shadwell, Middlesex, 115.
........., Upper, 38.
Shadwell, Thomas, 309.
Shaftesbury, 257, 576.
Shaftoe, Robert, 228.
Shamblehurst, Hants, ship-money, 186.
Shangton, co. Leicester, 63.
Shapcott, Thomas, brief on behalf of, 77.
........., Urith, 77 (2).
Sharnford, co. Leicester, 567.
Sharpe, George, constable, 186, 430, 437.

Sharpey, Sir Robert, petitions of, 125 (2).
Shavington, co. Chester, Holy Trinity church, 59.
Shaw, William, junior, 322 (2), 326 (3), 378 (2).
........., ..., bond of, 298.
Sheares, William, printer, 25, 298.
Shearsby, co. Leicester, 219.
Sheen, Surrey, 376.
........., his Majesty's mews at, 173.
........., late monastery of, 274.
Sheeres, Mr., servant to Lady Rivers, 186.
Sheffield, Edmund, Earl of Mulgrave, vice-admiral for co. York, letters to, 353, 501.
Sheldon, Dr. Gilbert, 235, 332.
........., ..., letters of, 341, 348.
Sheldwich, Kent, 358, 521.
Shelley, Edward, bond of, 481.
........., Sir John, petitions of, 33, 92.
........., ..., his son, deceased, 33.
........., ..., ..., wife and child of, 33.
........., Lady ———, her house at Islington, 130.
Shelton, [co. ———], 87.
Shepherd, variously spelt;
........., Alice, 185.
........., Mary, 68.
........., Richard, 68.
........., Thomas, justice of peace for Middlesex, 107.
........., William, bill of, 329.
Sheppey, Isle of, 133, 548.
Shepway, Kent, lathe, 543, 548.
Sherard, Abigail, Lady, 213, 241.
........., William, Lord of Leitrim, 213, 241 (2).
Sherborn, co. Dorset, 288.
........., document dated from, 175.
Sherelane, *see* Shire Lane.
Sheriffs of England and Wales, 26, 87, 208.
.... accounts of ship-money in hands of, 5, 26, 246, 265, 277 (2), 294, 303, 314, 334, 352, 364 (2), 373, 387, 413, 431, 460, 488 (2), 505, 516, 527, 537, 564, 578, 595, 601.
........., ..., order of council touching, 207.
........., letters to, 38, 150, 437.
........., list of, 437 ; *and see* under the names of the several counties.
Sherley, Henry, 124.
........., Thomas, 3.
Sherman, Mr., 48.
........., ..., his father, 48.
Sherwill, Nicholas, mayor of Plymouth, letters of, 6, 607.
Sherwood, Mr., letter to, 113.
Sheylor, Thomas, petition of, 240.
Shields, 76, 113.
........., North, 257, 258.
Shillitoe, Elizabeth, petition of, 465.
........., George, 465.

Ship unnamed, list of crew, 85.
........., the great, *see* Sovereign of the Seas.
.... carpenters, 228.
.... caulkers, *see* Shipwrights.
.... masters, certificate of, 3.
Ship-money, 40, 69, 523.
........., papers relating to, 87 (2), 208, 233, 283, 297, 540.
........., *see* names of the places mentioned in the calendar in connexion with.
........., paid by the clergy, 5, 26, 44, 91, 146, 209, 220 (2), 265 (2), 266, 267, 270, 287, 288, 307, 329, 344, 377, 387, 407, 423, 462.
........., preached against, 285.
........., fleet set out with the amount received, *see* Fleet.
........., Nicholas's reports and other papers concerning, 87, 88, 197.
........., ships furnished by the city of London, 142.
........., accounts of, 4, 5 (2), 14, 26, 45, 88, 139, 144, 196 (2), 208, 209 (3), 246 (4), 265 (4), 276, 277 (3), 294 (2), 303 (2), 314 (2), 327 (2), 334 (2), 352 (2), 364 (2), 373 (2), 386, 387, 413 (3), 431 (2), 444, 460 (2), 488 (2), 505 (4), 516 (2), 527 (2), 537 (2), 564 (2), 577 (2), 578, 586 (2), 595 (2), 601 (2), 604.
........., receipts given for ship-money, 2 (2), 4.
........., sum charged upon the counties and towns for 1636-7, 87.
........., order in council concerning returns by sheriffs, 26.
Ship-owners, certificate of, 3.
Ship timber for the Navy, 42.
Shipp, Thomas, 506.
Ships, lists of, 82, 186, 339.
........., merchants, hired or impressed for the King's service, and those furnished by the city of London, 3 (2), 4, 82, 83, 139, 142, 165, 186, 194, 212, 232, 291, 294, 297, 300 (2), 339, 352, 390, 609.
........., money paid for freight of, commission for enquiry into, 170.
........., convoyed by King's ships, 83, 482, 608.
........., void of employment, proposal for registering, 2, 3.
........., the King's, 4, 9, 13 (2), 24, 186, 226, 279, 320.
........., ..., .ists of, 182, 339, 390.
Shipton Meyne, co. Gloucester, 63.
Shipwright, the (ship), of London, 137.
Shipwrights, 174, 194.
.... forbidden to serve foreign powers, 268.
Shipwrights' company of London, 262.
........., master and wardens of, letter of, 175.
........., ..., letter to, 268.
........., order concerning, 195.

Shipwrights of the Navy, or the King's master shipwrights, 30, 175, 186, 194, 202.
........., petition of, 195.
Shire Lane in St. Clement's parish, London, 591.
Shirley, Lady Dorothy, petition of, 124.
........., ..., her children, 124.
........., Sir Henry, 124. *See also* Sherley.
Shoard, Edward, 539.
Shoreditch, London, 399, 413.
Shoreham, 278, 279 (2).
Shotbolt, Philip, *see* Battalion.
Shotover Forest, co. Oxford, officers of, letter to, 564,
Shottesbrook, Berks, ship-money, 336.
Shrewsbury, 225.
........., bailiffs and others, letter to, 58.
........., mayor, 306, 337.
........., school, 338.
........., ship-money, 266, 423.
........., town clerk, 225.
........., St. Chad's, 337.
Shute, Josias, 325.
Sibbes, Dr., books of, 366.
Sibthorpe, Dr. Robert, 458.
........., ..., his proceedings in the diocese of Peterborough, 157.
........., ..., letters of, 535, 572.
Sidmonton, Hants, ship-money, 186.
Sienna, 31.
Signet, clerk of the, letters and other papers to, 18, 256, 510, 575.
Sigswick, *see* Sedgwick.
Silkmen of London, company of, petition of, 305.
Silsoe, co. Bedford, 363.
Silver, 58, 156, 536.
........., foreign imported, privy seal for raising duty on, 514.
........., transportation of, 153.
Simcocks, Thomas, 123.
Simonson, Mr., 343.
Simpson, Christopher, 445.
Simpson's Place, *see* Sampson's Place.
Sims, Robert, 359.
Sinclair, John, Lord, 529.
"Sion, Guide unto," book, 366.
Sion, abbess of, 60.
Sion House, Middlesex, 34.
........., ..., documents dated from, 578, 608.
Six clerks of the court of Chancery, petition of, 174.
Skelsmergh and Patton, co. Westmoreland, return for, 547.
Skelton, Gilbert, 76.
Skill, John, 406, 456.
Skillington, co. Lincoln, 426.
Skingle, John, 107.

GENERAL INDEX. 697

Skinner, Robert, Bishop of Bristol, 32, 315, 351, 568.
........., ..., letter of, 409.
........., ..., statement by, 315.
........., ..., letter to, 259.
Skippon, Luke, M.A., presentation to, 214.
Skipton, co. York, document dated from, 433.
Skipwith, Henry, 577.
........., William, 2.
Skirbeck, co. Lincoln, soke or wapentake, inhabitants of, petition of, 337.
........., ..., ship-money, 337.
Skreenes, Essex, 424.
Skyers, co. York, 17.
Skyrack, co. York, wapentake, 542.
Slaney or Slany, John, 463, 470.
........., Humphrey, petition of, 254, 516.
........., ..., certificate of, 478.
Slanning, Lady Gertrude, 604.
........., Sir Nicholas, 604.
Slater, William, 90.
Sleaford, 267, 553.
........., document dated from, 475.
.... and Folkingham, sessions, co. Lincoln, 267, 479.
........., inhabitants of, petition of, 211.
Sleddale, Long, Westmoreland, return for, 547.
Sleigh, John, letter to, 456.
........., Mr., 331.
Slingsby, Capt., 356.
........., Edmund, 363.
........., Lady, letter to, 600.
........., ..., her daughter, 600.
........., Sir William, 198, 319.
Smart, John, 405.
........., ..., agreement of, 412.
Smeeth, Richard, 90.
Smethe, S., certificate of, 463.
Smith, variously spelt ;—
........., Anne, warrant to, 201.
........., David, 504.
........., Sir Charles, 74.
........., Christopher, deceased, 201.
........., Edward, commissions to, 602 (2).
........., Frances, 235.
........., Francis, suspected priest, 513.
........., ..., petition of, 511.
........., Francis, Nicholas's man, 185, 482.
........., Francis, commissioner concerning abuses in timber imported, 335.
........., ..., commissions to, 363.
........., Francis, of Balsall, indictment against, 76.
........., Humphrey, 176.
........., ..., petition of, 313.
........., John, in High Commission Court, petition of, 80.
........., John, of Rushden, 81.
........., John, assumed name, 530.
........., Joseph, petition of, 99.

Smith, Mary, of Warmingham, 292.
........., Mary, in High Commission court, petition of, 80.
........., Mr., of Salisbury Court, 138.
........., Richard, 409.
........., Richard Alleyne, 363.
........., Robert, messenger and marshal and water-bailiff of Ireland, 326.
........., ..., letters to, 194, 373.
........., Robert, relator in the Star Chamber, petition of, 552.
........., Simon, letter of, 609.
........., Solomon, letters to, 315 (2).
........., Thomas, ballaster of ships, 111.
........., ..., petitions of, 110, 111.
........., Thomas, of Brentford, 393 (2).
........., Thomas, of Dorset House, 428.
........., ..., letters of, 321, 356, 361, 608.
........., Thomas, of co. Oxford, 448.
........., William, cardmaker, 583.
........., William, commissions to, 602 (2).
........., ——, mercer of Lombard Street, London, 328.
........., ——, alderman of London, 87, 375.
Smithfield, East, London, see East Smithfield.
Smithick, Robert, deceased, 203.
Smyth, see Smith.
Snape, Nathaniel, justice of peace for Middlesex, 319.
........., certificate of, 421.
........., ..., commissions to, 602 (2).
Snelling, Lawrence, 240.
........., Richard, warrant to, 1.
........., Thomas, bond of, 298.
Snow, Anne, information of, 522.
........., Mr., 446.
Soame, see Soham.
Soap, 105, 184, 196, 203, 233, 292, 374, 450.
........., propositions for preventing making unserviceable, 105.
Soapmakers of Bristol, 142, 292.
........., master, wardens, and others, petition of, 105.
Soapmakers of London, society of, 39, 105, 196, 203, 260 (2), 299, 467, 584.
........., ..., letters of, 370, 525.
........., ..., proclamation touching, 39.
........., ..., governor, 260. See Bromfield, Sir Edward.
Soapmakers, the Western Hard, 142, 292.
Soapmakers of Westminster, late company of, 39, 299, 526.
Soham, co. Cambridge, 56.
Soldiers, 234, 430, 584.
.... maimed, 64, 385, 412.
.... from abroad, 134 ; see also Volunteers.
Solicitor-General, see Littleton, Sir Edward.
Somercotes, North, co. Lincoln, 482.
........., ..., documents dated from, 374, 482, 559.

Somercotes, North, co. Lincoln—*cont.*
..........., ..., marshes, 482.
..........., ..., measurement of banks of, 2.
..........., ..., account touching, 38.
..........., South, co. Lincoln, 374, 482.
Somerleyton, Suffolk, 123.
Somers, John, deceased, 542.
Somerset, 142, 156, 292, 362, 412, 447, 502.
..........., judges of assize, 399.
..........., justices of peace, letter of, 378.
..........., ..., brief of cause of, 539.
..........., sheriffs, letters to, 156, 193, *see* Bassett, William; Hodges, Henry; Malet, John; Portman, Sir William.
..........., ship-money, 89, 93, 147, 179, 222, 354, 377, 389, 398, 418, 486, 488, 539.
Somerset and Bristol, vice-admiralty, 179.
..........., vice-admiral, *see* Rodney, Sir Edward.
Somerset House, London, 14, 15, 213, 333, 410.
..........., ..., document dated from, 576.
Somerset Yard, London, 14.
Somerset, Thomas, Viscount Somerset of Cashel, letter and other papers of, 531.
Somersham, co. Huntingdon, manor, 447.
..........., ..., soke, 35 (2).
Somes, Dr. Thomas, 264.
Sommers, Nicholas, 349.
Sonning, Berks, hundred, ship-money, 348 (2).
Sopham, co. Cambridge, 56.
Souldern, co. Oxford, 342, 405.
"Soul's Humiliation," book, 366.
South, Edward, 586 (2).
Southampton, 232, 262, 279 (2), 341, 495.
Southampton stables, near High Holborn, 587.
Southampton, Earl of, *see* Wriothesley, Thomas.
Southbrooke wood, 268, 320.
Southcott, Sir George, 98.
..........., Mrs. Grace, 591, 592.
..........., Nicholas, grant to, 292.
..........., Sir Popham, grant and demise to, 142, 292.
Southells, John, 258.
Southern, Thomas, 492.
Southfleet, Kent, 598.
Southrey, Norfolk, 152.
Southwark, 95, 109, 113, 137, 187, 237, 392, 399, 413 (3), 454.
..........., document dated from, 431.
..........., ship-money, 198, 420.
Southworth, John, lease to, 608.
Sovereign of the Seas, the Royal, 1, 36, 85, 122, 146, 166, 174, 182, 192, 213, 262, 291, 357.
..........., ..., visited by the King, 32, 166.
..........., ..., trial of, 598, 606.
..........., ..., ordnance for, 151, 517.
..........., ..., ..., estimates for, 32, 367, 522, 523, 535.
..........., ..., ..., inscription and device on, 367.
..........., ..., certificate of charge of, 146.

Sovereignty of the Seas, treatise on the, by Sir John Borough, 82.
Spain, 3 (2), 81, 102, 122, 130, 187, 192, 230, 234, 291, 426, 456, 467, 493, 533, 555, 579, 585.
..........., ambassador extraordinary, *see* Oniate, Condè de.
..........., ambassador from, 75, 230, 295, 426, 493; *and see* Nicolaldi, Don John de.
..........., ..., his chaplain, *see* Hogan, Thomas.
..........., English ambassador to, *see* Aston, Walter, Lord.
..........., ..., his secretary, *see* Fanshawe, Mr.
..........., King of, 28, 29, 44, 51, 230, 434, 499, 554.
..........., fleet of, 6 (2), 15, 18, 28, 270, 304.
..........., ..., general of, *see* Losse, Don Lopes de.
..........., ..., plate, 17.
..........., merchants of London trading to, petition of, 103.
..........., wines of, 107.
Spanish cloth, 164, 176, 218 (2), 537.
..........., makers of, petition of, 218.
Sparrow, Robert, 119.
Sparsholt, Hants, ship-money, 198.
Spearman, Nicholas, petition to, 229.
..........., ..., ..., order on, 229.
Spell, Thomas, president of St. John's College, Cambridge, 354.
Spelman, Clement, commissions to, 602 (2).
Spencer or Spenser, Arnold, 11.
..........., ..., petition of 310.
..........., Benjamin, 400, 413.
..........., Sir Edward, 393.
..........., Henry, Lord, 277.
..........., John, petition of, 110.
..........., ———, 45.
Spier, Henry, examination of, 595.
Spiller, Sir Henry, justice of peace for Middlesex, 115, 319, 416, 442.
..........., ..., commissions to, 363, 602 (2).
Splinter, the, betwixt Gravelines and Dunkirk, 44, 270, 304, 499.
Spoon, silver, taken on admission to company of weavers, 454.
Sports, book of, 63, 240, 377, 560, 563.
Spranger, George, 191.
Sprott, Mr., 329.
Squibb, Lawrence, 6, 562.
..........., ..., petitions of, 149, 322, 378, 610.
..........., ..., grant to, 160.
..........., Robert, petitions of, 149, 322, 610.
Squier, John, 399.
Stafford co., Sheriff, *see* Littleton, Sir Edward.
..........., ship-money, 90.
Stafford, barony of, notes on descent of, 118 (2).
..........., Edward, Duke of Buckingham, (temp. Hen. VIII.,) 118.

Stafford, Henry, Lord, deceased in 1637, 117, 118.
........., ..., his mother, 118.
........., ..., his sister Mary, 117, 118.
........., Henry, Lord, (temp. Edw. VI.,) 118.
........., ..., his son Richard, 118.
........., ..., his grandson Roger, 118.
........., Robert, Lord, (temp. King John,) 118.
........., Roger, Lord, questions on his title, 118.
........., Sir Thomas, 50, 151, 540.
........., Thomas, 236.
........., William, 63.
Staincliffe and Ewecross, co. York, wapentake, 134.
Staine, co. Cambridge, hundred, 134.
Stainton, Westmoreland, return for, 547.
Staltone, John, 325.
Stamford, Countess of, see Grey, Anne.
........., Earl of, see Grey, Henry.
........., co. Lincoln, 63, 322.
........., ship-money, 212.
Stamford, St. Mary's, 563.
Stamper, Richard, 288.
Stanborough, Devon, hundred, 134.
Standeven, Allfeires, 328.
Standish, Sir Ralph, 193.
Stane, William, 172, 186, 207.
Stanford, Anthony, agreement of, 395.
........., ..., petition of, 418.
........., Charles, Lord, 52, 238.
........., ..., petition of, 51.
........., ..., his mother, 51.
Stanhope, Dr., 62.
........., John, Lord, father of Charles, 51 (2).
........., Michael, letter of, 401.
Stanlake, co. Oxford, 287.
Stanley, Alice, Countess Dowager of Derby, 55.
........., Charlotte, Lady Strange, 481.
........., Edward, license to, 434.
........., James, Lord Strange, 183, 225 (2), 481.
........., William, Earl of Derby, 28, 158, 186, 231, 362, 377.
........., ..., letter of, 363.
Stanley Regis, co. Gloucester, 68.
Stannary Courts, 500 (2).
Stannaries, warden of, see Herbert, Philip, Earl of Pembroke and Montgomery.
Stanton, Dr., 567.
........., Thomas, 568.
Stanton Lacy, Sàlop, 338.
Stanwell, Middlesex, 377, 389.
Staploe, co. Cambridge, hundred, 134.

Star Chamber, 16, 34, 37, 45, 54, 62, 66, 73, 79, 92, 100, 109, 111, 114, 126, 127, 149, 153, 156, 170, 188, 196, 200, 215 (3), 224, 231, 308, 338, 339, 345, 358, 366, 393, 396, 401, 409, 416, 427, 432, 433, 436, 451 (2), 483 (2), 491, 496, 500, 514, 519, 520, 552, 558, 587.
........., documents dated from, 189 (2), 192, 214, 241, 371, 384, 406 (3).
........., orders of, 72 (2).
........., bill in, 227.
........., lists of causes to be heard in, 185, 213, 240, 370, 383, 399, 473.
........., Sec. Windebank's notes of causes heard in, 185, 192, 214, 241, 384 (2), 399, 473.
........., the Inner, documents dated from, 176, 182, 183 (3), 189, 205 (2), 206 (2), 207 (2), 208 (2), 293, 384, 401 (2), 402 (2), 403 (2), 404 (2), 405 (3), 469, 470 (3), 471, 473, 474.
Starch, 190, 220.
........., notes on the receipts from an imposition upon, 101.
Starchmakers Company, 109, 552.
........., information as to the state of, 105.
Starkeys, John, 417, 430, 437, 442.
Start, the, 270.
States, the, or Holland, or the United Provinces, 47, 300, 361, 456, 523, 598.
........., ambassador to, 361, see Boswell, Sir William.
........., ... from, 84, 86, 159, 315, 361, 455, 579, 583, 595, 596 ; and see Joachimi, Sir Albertus ; Gorpdet, Mons. de.
States General, the, 85.
........., ..., letter of, 84.
Stationers Company, 71, 72, 73 (2), 145, 379, 567.
........., wardens of, 257 (2).
Stationers Hall, 567.
Statute Office, the, 124.
Statutes, Clerk of the office of, 173.
Staveley (three hamlets), Westmoreland, return for, 547.
Staverton, Thomas, 274.
Stebbranck, Susan, 119.
........., ..., petitions of, 118, 119.
........., ..., various relations of, 119 (2).
........., Thomas, petitions of, 118, 119.
Stebunheath, see Stepney.
Steckland, see Strickland.
Stedman, John, Sheriff of co. Cardigan, letter of, 243.
Steil, Jaon Janson, 281, 341.
Stennett, Thomas, 586 (2).
Stepney alias Stebunheath, Middlesex, patentees for sale of tobacco in, license of, 38.
Sterne, Edmund, statement of, 391.
Stevenson, variously spelt ;—
........., David, saltpetreman, 139, 180, 194, 372, 453, 589.
........., ..., letters of, 138, 276.

Stevenson, variously spelt—*cont.*
........., Matthew, 395, 397, 597.
........., Richard, 359.
........., William, prisoner in York castle, 211, 310, 332.
Steventon, variously spelt ;—
........., Thomas, 163.
........., ..., examination of, 170.
........., [William], clerk of the check at Portsmouth, 307, 321.
Steward or Stewart, Ann, Lady Saltoun, petition of, 9.
........., ..., her children, 9.
........., [Elizabeth?], Countess of Carrick, petition of, 122.
........., George, grant to, 466.
........., Mr., 592.
........., Dr. Nicholas, 78.
........., Dr. Richard, dean of Chichester and clerk of the closet, 524.
........., ..., deed of, 365.
........., ..., letters to, 173, 305.
........., Thomas, 186.
........., Capt. Walter, 195.
........., ..., letter of, 13.
........., ..., brief of proofs against, 554.
........., ..., notes on examination of, 426.
........., Sir William, grant to, 466; *see also* Stuart.
Steyning, Sussex, 279.
Steynton, co. Pembroke, 287.
Stile, Sir Humphrey, reference on petition to, 251.
Stilton, co. Huntingdon, 52.
Stirling, Earl of, *see* Alexander, William.
Stockdale, Leonard, petition of, 552.
Stockdell, Edward, letters to, 417, 480.
Stockenden, house so called, in Surrey, 125.
Stockton, Wilts, manor, 253.
Stockwell, Car[ew?], information of, 560.
Stoddart, Sir Nicholas, 124.
Stoke, co. Nottingham, 282.
Stoke Edith, co. Hereford, 405.
Stoke juxta Guildford, Surrey, ship-money, 198.
Stoke Mandeville, co. Buckingham, 564.
Stoke Milborough, Salop, 172.
Stoke park, co. Northampton, 256.
Stokenham, Devon, 288.
Stone, Benjamin, 105.
........., John, in Star Chamber, 214, 241.
........., John, of North Cadbury, 362.
........., Mr., 510.
........., Thomas, 444, 482.
Stonehouse, Sir George, sheriff of Berks, letters of, 89, 348.
........., ..., letter to, 210.
........., Sir James, 404.
Stoner, ——, a lecturer, 536.
Stornoway, Scotland, harbour, 101.
Stort, Thomas, bill of, 427.

Stott, Alexander, 119.
........., David, 119.
........., ..., petition of, 119.
........., ..., warrant to, 172.
Stoughton, Nicholas, sheriff of Surrey, letter of, 420.
........., Roger, 161.
Stoughton, Sussex, document dated from, 420.
........., co. Leicester, 249.
Stour, the river, 310.
Stow, Suffolk, hundred, 157.
Stowe, Richard, 235.
Stracey, Robert, order on petition of, 207.
Stradling, Sir Edward, 369.
........., ..., letter to, 610.
........., Capt. Henry, 36, 608.
........., ..., letter of, 28.
........., ..., examination before, 28.
Straits, the, 3 (2), 83, 139, 304.
Strancke, *see* Stranke.
Strand, London, the, 14, 15.
........., document dated from, 367.
Strange, Lord, *see* Stanley, James.
........., Lady, *see* Stanley, Charlotte.
Strangers, congregations of, *see* "Foreign Churches in England."
Strangers, proposed office for registering names of, 203.
Strangers born using trades in England, Commissioners for, order of, 104.
........., ..., petitions to, 104 (2).
Stranke, variously spelt ;—
........., Robert, 228, 344, 375.
........., ..., letter and other papers of, 23, 376.
Stratfieldsaye, Hants, South End farm in, 474.
Stratfield Turgis, Hants, 474.
Stratford, Robert, letter of, 385.
Stratford, [Essex,] document dated from, 490.
Stratford Loughton, Essex, 191.
Stratton, Long, Norfolk, 235.
Strechley, William, 417, 485.
Streete, Humphrey, 111.
Stretthay, John, reasons for granting suit of, 238.
Strickland, Walter, 551.
Strickland, Kettle, Westmoreland, return for, 547.
........., Roger, Westmoreland, the like, 547.
Strode, Sir John, 215 (3).
........., Sir Richard, petitions of, 215 (3).
Stroud, William, 93, 198.
........., Sir William, 430.
Stuart, James, duke of Lennox, 39, 274, 278, 574, 582.
........., ..., pretended speech of, 564.
........., ..., his secretary, *see* Webb, ——.
........., John, 334.
........., Mary, Duchess of Lennox, 574.
Studley, John, 266.
Stuffs, 206, 514, 553.
Sturrilaw burn, near Berwick, 331.

Sturton, John, commissions to, 602 (2).
........., Mr., 445.
Styles, Matthew, B.D., 402.
Sudbury, Suffolk, 310, 383, 593.
........., document dated from, 593.
........., inhabitants of, petition of, 593.
........., list of inn holders and alehouse keepers in, 593.
........., St. Gregory's church, 383.
........., St. Peter's chapel, 383.
Sudeley, Lord Chandos of, see Bruges, George.
Sueur, Hubert le, sculptor, agreement of, 518.
Suffolk, 95, 152, 153, 157, 438, 492, 495, 501, 589.
........., justice of peace, returns of, 135 (2), 544, 593.
........., sheriff, 91, 314, see Parker, Sir Philip.
........., ..., return to, 544.
........., ship-money, 91, 200, 314.
........., Vice Admiral, see Tollemache, Sir Lionel.
Suffolk, Earl of, see Howard, Theophilus.
........., ..., the late, see Howard, Thomas.
Suffolk House, London, document dated from, 296.
Suger, Richard, 384.
Sulke, John, 3, 31.
Summers, John, deceased, 542.
Sumpter, Robert, mayor of Norwich, letters of, 150, 548.
"Sunday, no Sabbath," book, 62.
Sunderland, 347, 397.
Sunninghill, Berks, 350, 478.
........., ship-money, 89, 210.
.... park, 350.
Supremacy, oath of, see Allegiance.
Surplice, 62, 64, 240, 249.
Surrey, 95 (2), 98 (2), 104, 175, 431, 441, 442, 460.
........., justices of assize, letters to, 133 (2), 546.
........., justices of peace, certificates of, 133 (3), 136, 543, 546 (2).
........., ..., letters to, 480, 528, 543.
........., sheriff, 179, see Stoughton, Nicholas; Vincent, Sir Anthony.
........., ..., warrant to, 203.
........., ..., ship-money, 179, 198, 420, 479.
Surveyor-General, the, see Harhord, Sir Charles.
Sussex, 33, 95, 98, 362, 441, 501, 536.
........., justices of assize, certificates to, 133, 135.
........., justices of peace, certificates of, 133 (5), 135 (2), 136, 543 (3), 546, 548, 549.
........., ..., letter to, 480.
........., sheriff, see Culpeper, Sir William; Bishop, Sir Edward.
........., ship-money, 88 (2), 293.
........., Vice Admiral, see Howard, Charles, Earl of Nottingham.

Sutterton, co. Lincoln, 288.
Sutton, Henry, 572.
........., Oliver, Bishop of Lincoln, (A.D. 1280,) 468.
........., Thomas, founder of the Charter House, extract from his Act of Parliament, 484.
Sutton, co. Bedford, 421.
........., co. Hereford, document dated from, 507.
........., co. Nottingham, 380.
Sutton at Hone, Kent, lathe, 133, 548.
Sutton Marsh, co. Lincoln, 58 (2).
Sutton-cum-Buckingham, prebend of, [in the cathedral of Lincoln,] opinion on title to, 60.
Sutton's Hospital, see Charter House.
Swadlin, Thomas, vicar of Aldgate, 591.
........., ..., statement by, 592.
Swaffham, Norfolk, 506.
Swallow, the, 33, 178, 194, 228, 241, 541.
........., the, of Colchester, 137.
Swallowfield, Berks, 240.
Swalman, Dr. Geoffrey, official to the archdeacon of Middlesex, 68, 389.
........., ..., letter to, 377.
Swan, Thomas, indictment against, 76.
Swan, the, ship, 4.
........., the, of Flushing, prize ship, 170, 213.
........., the, of Weymouth, 318.
Swanbourne, co. Buckingham, 564.
Swane, John, 94.
Swansea, 115.
Sweden, 7, 29, 122, 264, 367, 579.
........., King of, 325.
........., Queen of, her General Major, see Drummond, Sir David.
Sweet, ——, 500.
"Sweet Waters," 537.
Swell, Nether, co. Gloucester, 351.
........., park and other grounds, 351.
........., Inferior, see Swell, Nether.
Swetman, Lawrence, see Swettnam.
Swettnam, Lawrence, 6, 562 (2).
Swiftsure, the, 37, 279.
........., documents dated from, 3, 15, 17, 31, 36, 44, 173, 202, 234, 246, 269, 304.
Swinton, co. York, 551.
Swords, manufacture of, 105.
Sydenham, Devon, document dated from, 456.
Sydney, Robert, Earl of Leicester, English Ambassador in France, 76, 77, 244, 387.
Sykehouse, co. York, 57.
Sykes, Nathaniel, saltpetreman, 191, 200.
........., ..., petition of, 95.
........., ..., letter to, 95.
Symbarbe, see St. Barbe.
Symes, ——, 404.
Symmes, Edward, 119.
Symmons, Matthew, information of, 365.

Symonds, Henry, petition of, 23.
........., ..., order on, 23.
Symonds, Richard, 249.
........., Thomas, of London, 204, 319, 320, 329.
Symonds, Thomas, mayor of Hereford, certificate of, 325.
Symons, Mr., 528.

T.

T. G. [?], letters of, 533, 535.
"Tabies" and other like stuffs, privy seal for levying subsidy and impost on, 514.
Tacitus, annals of, 71.
Taddington see Tarrington.
Tadley, Hants, 433, 443, 474.
Talbot, Thomas, 25, 80, 250.
Talboys, Mrs., 317.
........., Richard, 317.
........., Thomas, 317.
Talboys Woods, Essex, 464.
Taliaris, co. Carmarthen, document dated from, 302.
Tallow, export of, 525 (2).
Talworth, Surrey, 133.
Tammies and other stuffs, 206.
Tandridge, Surrey, hundred, 546.
Tanner, John, orders on petition of, 154, 171.
Tapestry, 173.
Tarrington, co. Hereford, 405.
Tartaro, Mr. or Mons., 183, 394, 481.
Taunton, Somerset, 276.
........., documents dated from, 367, 424, 430, 445, 447.
Taverner, Philip, B.A., 282.
........., Robert, messenger, letters to, 184, 405, 406, 437.
Taverns, 107 (2).
Tavistock alias Tawstock in diocese of Exeter, rectory of, 214.
Taylor, variously spelt;—
........., Arthur, 507.
........., Francis, messenger, petition of, 119.
........., ..., warrant to, 172.
........., George, 207.
........., John, the King's agent in Germany, note of payments to, 526.
........., ..., account relating to, 537.

Taylor, Joseph, petition of, 99.
........., Richard, commissions to, 602 (2).
........., Thomas, 259.
........., William, 201, 220.
........., ..., petition of, 221.
Taynton, co. Oxford, 351.
"Teats and Varlets," (on cards) 149, 190.
Teignbridge, Devon, hundred, 136.
Tempest, Thomas, opinion of, 527.
Temple, George, 308, 309, 331 (2), 332.
........., ..., information of, 332.
........., Thomas, 308, 309, 331 (2), 332.
........., ..., information of, 331.
Temple, the, London, 462.
........., church, London, 45, 462.
........., master, see Micklethwaite, Paul.
........., manor, 45. See also Middle Temple and Inner Temple.
Temple, Bar, 167, 236.
........., ..., proposal for laying water-pipes between Charing Cross and, 113.
Temple Chelfin, co. Hertford, manor, 19.
Tempsford, co. Bedford, 123.
Tenby, co. Pembroke, 288.
Tendring, Essex, hundred, 549.
Tenths, 45, 533.
........., accounts of, 38, 69.
Terrill, { Charles, Thomas, William, } pass for, 435.
Terwhitt, Robert, petition of, 164.
Tetbury, co. Gloucester, 317.
........., document dated from, 317.
Tewkesbury, co. Gloucester, 156.
........., bailiffs and others, 317.
Teynham, Kent, hundred, 133, 548.
Thame, co. Oxford, 235.
Thames, the, 36, 41, 83, 103, 110 (2), 113, 124, 139, 147, 160, 161, 164, 192, 276, 281, 298, 340, 347, 385, 389 (2), 404, 422, 480 (2).
........., encroachments upon, information concerning, 115.
........., fishermen, petition of, 109.
........., ..., order on, 471.
........., ..., complaint of, 110.
........., shipwrights of, see Shipwrights.
Thaxted, Essex, ship-money, 419.
Thelwall, Sir Bevis, clerk of the Great Wardrobe, 49 (3).
........., ..., information of, 49.
........., ..., petition of, 128.
Theobald, Sir George, 270.
Theobalds, Herts, 328, 391, 523.
........., ..., documents dated from, 477 (2), 511 (3), 515, 530, 565, 567.
Thetford, Norfolk, ship-money, 220, 395.
Theydon Mount, Essex, 288.
Thirsk, co. York, document dated from, 346.

Thomas, Sir Anthony, 10, 26, 138 (2), 196, 214.
........., ..., petitions of, 253, 374.
........., David, 370.
........., Mary, petition of, 180.
........., Philip, messenger to the commissioners for charitable uses, petition of, 595.
........., Philip, information of, 139.
........., Philip, certificate of, 608.
........., Richard, late mayor of Carmarthen, 180.
........., Walter, petition of, 115.
........., William, sheriff of co. Carnarvon, return of, 220.
Thompson, variously spelt;—
........., Francis, petition of, 607.
........., Jane, 586.
........., John, servant to Lord Keeper Coventry, 491.
........., John, of Newcastle, 228.
........., John, ship-master, 101.
........., John, sailor, 160.
........., Launcelot, mayor of Newark, letter and another paper of, 267, 326.
........., ..., his son, 326.
........., Maurice, 406, 417.
........., Mr., 600. See also Tomson and Thompson.
Thornbury, co. Hereford, 39.
Thorne, Abraham, appearance of, 142.
........., Rachel, information of, 259.
Thornhaugh, variously spelt;—
........., Sir Francis, sheriff of Notts, 89, 186.
........., ..., letters of, 159, 327, 443.
........., ..., letters to, 326, 462.
Thornhill, Edward, saltpetreman, 372, 373, 424, 488.
........., ..., petition of, 95.
........., ..., answer of, 385.
........., ..., letter to, 95.
........., Thomas, saltpetreman, 24, 37, 143, 243.
........., ..., letter of, 235.
Thornhurst, Dame Barbara, 2.
........., ..., petition of, 2.
........., Sir Thomas, deceased, 2 (2), 3 (2).
Thornton, co. York, 11.
Thornton, Thomas, 42, 43.
........., William, letter of, 212.
Thorogood, George, 463, 470.
Thorpe, Surrey, chapel, 318.
Thraces [manor?] in Newington, 343.
Thread, gold and silver, 163 (2).
Thredling, Suffolk, hundred, 544.
Thriplow, co. Cambridge, 372.
Throgmorton, Sir Baynham, letter of, 53.
Thrognolls [manor?] in Newington, 343.
Throppe, Thomas, mayor of Chester, letter of, 158.

Thurgarton a-Leigh, co. Nottingham, hundred, 24, 422.
Thurloe, John, statement of, 391.
Thwing, George, 447.
Thynne, Sir Thomas, 2.
........., petition of, 2.
........., Mrs., her servant Robert, 14.
Tias, Robert, petition of, 49.
........., ..., his father and grandfather, 49.
Tibballs, see Theobalds.
Tiberstreet, part of Aldenham, Herts, 392.
Tidcombe, Tiverton, Devon, 288.
Tide, Bartholomew, 488.
Tiehall, Essex, 424.
Tieson, Bastion, 315.
Tilbury Fort, 195.
Tilbury Hope, 1, 209, 389.
........., ..., document dated from, 446.
Tilney, Richard, 474.
Tilsworth, co. Bedford, ship-money, 432.
Timber, imported, surveyorship of, 334.
........., ..., commission as to frauds practised in, 363.
........., land carriage of, for the Navy, 87, 346, 441, 479, 480 (6), 550.
........., purveyors of, orders for redress of, abuses of, 368.
........., for the Navy, payment for, 42.
Tin, 201, 500.
........., farmers, the, petition of, 83.
Ting, John, 172, 190, 207 (2), 220.
Tinmouth, co. Durham, see Tynemouth, Northumberland.
Tintagell, Cornwall, mayor, see Wood, Thomas.
........., ship-money, 17.
Tintinhull, Somerset, hundred, ship-money, 31, 314.
Tipper, Robert, 227.
........., William, 58.
Tisted, East, Hants, 476.
Titchborne, John, D.D., 32 (2), 172.
........., John, son of the above, 32, 172.
........., John, mentioned in Sir William Calley's letter, 25, 176.
........., John, son of Robert, 32.
........., Nevill, 32.
........., ..., petition of, 172.
........., Priscilla, wife of Dr. John, 172.
........., ..., petition of, 32.
........., Sir Richard, 7 (2), 38, 79 (2).
........., ..., protection to, 79.
........., ..., petition of, 193.
........., Robert, 32.
........., Sir Walter, deceased, 7, 79 (2).
Tithes, 405, 461, 477, 478, 481, 602; and see "London and surrounding parishes."
Tiverton, co. Devon, 218.
Tixover, co. Rutland, 468 (2).

T'Kint, Capt., 535.
Tobacco, 14, 99 (2), 405, 449.
........., commissioners for, 103, 449, 458.
........., ..., letters of, 381 (2).
........., license to sell, 38.
........., licenses, office of receiver of revenue of, 141.
Tobacco pipe makers company, petition of, 393.
Tobin, James, 481.
Tokeley, Capt. Robert, 159, 488.
Tollemache, Sir Lionel, 497.
........., ..., letter to, 501.
Tolson, John, 90.
Tomaso, Prince, 493, 558.
Tomes or Toms, Robert, 89, 91.
........., ..., information of, 198.
Tompkins, Edward, 437, 474.
........., Nathaniel, 111.
Tompson, Dr., 307.
........., Elizabeth, 498.
Tomson, John, of Balsall, indictment against, 76.
........., John, in Star Chamber, 241.
Toovey, Mr., 458.
Topcliffe, 600.
Toppe, John, letter of, 143.
........., ..., letter to, 37.
Torrington Magna, Devon, 405, 449, 512.
........., document dated from, 385.
........., mayor, memorandum of, 385.
Totnes, Devon, 421.
........., mayor, see James, Henry.
Tottenham, Middlesex, document dated from, 408.
........., the Bull in, 487.
Tottenham, Betteris, letter of, 123.
Tottie, Samuel, 2.
Totton, John, letter to, 312.
Touchet, Anne, countess of Castlehaven, 384.
........., George, petition of, 136.
........., ..., his father, 136.
Tour and Tassis, Count de la, bill concerning, 51.
Tournour, Timothy, letter of, 452.
Towcester, co. Northampton, 395, 518, 536, 561.
Tower of London, 67, 96 (2), 465, 509, 584, 591, 601.
........., records in, keeper of, see Borough, Sir John.
Tower Dock, London, 509.
Tower Street, London, 379, 431, 524.
........., document dated from, 265.
Towns, encroachments upon the streets of, 116.
Trade, commissioners or committee for, 410.
........., letter of, 94.
........., ..., reference on petition to, 530.

Trafford, Mr., magistrate of co. Denbigh, 23.
........., Mr., of Newington, 343.
Trafford, co. Northampton, 396.
Trained-bands, 9, 77, 94, 195, 209, 242, 284, 494 (2) ; *and see* Musters.
........., account of numbers of, 241.
Trankmore, Robert, 82.
Treasurer, the Lord, *see* Juxon, William, Bishop of London.
........., late Lords, *see* Ley, James, Lord Marlborough ; Weston, Richard, Earl of Portland.
Treasury, the late Lord Commissioners of, 50, 162, 253, 281.
Tredway, Francis, 107.
Tregonwell, John, the elder, 396, 568, 574, 606.
........., John, the younger, 396, 568, 574, 606.
Treherne, John, 415.
Trench, Styward, under-sheriff of Middlesex, petition of, 587.
........., ..., order on, 587.
Trenchard, Sir Thomas, late sheriff of co. Dorset, letter of, 169.
Trenchfield, Capt., 160.
Trent, Council of, extract from review of the, 390.
Trepelo, Ann, 123.
Treport, France, 117.
Tresham, Theodosia, Lady, 1.
........., ..., petitions of, 511, 580.
........., Sir William, 511 (2), 580.
........., ..., letters of, 328, 457.
........., ..., letter to, 1.
Tressam, *see* Tresham.
Trevena, Cornwall, mayor, *see* Wood, Thomas.
........., ..., ship-money, 17.
Trevillian, Thomas, 507.
Trevor, Sir Thomas, baron of the Exchequer, 87, 158, 241, 447.
........., ..., letter of, 424.
........., ..., notes of his argument in Hampden's case, 541.
Tribert, Francis, 350, 450.
Trigg, ——, of London, 2.
Trinder, John, 192.
Tring, co. Hertford, ship-money, 581.
Trinity College, Cambridge, 6.
Trinity Hall, Cambridge, document dated from, 316.
........., ..., master of, *see* Eden, Dr. Thomas.
Trinity House, Ratcliffe, and Deptford Stroud, 15, 132, 166, 312.
........., ..., documents dated from, 237, 319.
........., ..., officers of, 1, 80, 174, 236, 262, 302.
........., ..., ..., letters and certificates of, 132, 237, 319, 541.

Trinity House, officers of—*cont.*
........., ..., letters to, 13, 25, 371.
Trinity House Certificates, 137.
Tristram, ——, 500.
Triumph, the, 170, 182, 243, 279.
Tromp, Martin Harpenson, admiral of the Holland fleet, 202, 234.
Troops for foreign service, 83, 130, 328, 457.
Trotman, Edward the elder, 335, 553.
........., commission to, 363.
Troutbeck, Westmoreland, return for, 548.
Trowell, Joan, 436.
........., Richard, 436.
Troy [House, co. Monmouth], 373.
Trussell, Edward, lease of, 6.
Tubney, Berks, 425.
Tucker, Edward, 580.
Tuderley, Hants, *see* Tytherley.
Tugfall's Alley near the Scotch Arms, Westminster, 516.
Tunbridge, 299.
Tunis, 192, 255.
........., captives in, petition of their wives and children, 478.
Tunstead, Norfolk, hundred, 134.
Tunsteed, Richard, 409.
........., Thomas, 409.
.... Hall, co. Derby, particulars of, 409 (2).
Turkey, 20, 42, 102, 103, 206.
........., Grand Signior, 103.
........., English ambassadors to, 103; *and see* Crow, Sir Sackville; Wyche, Sir Peter.
Turkey Company, the, 15, 103, 255.
........., ..., letter to, 285.
"Turkish History," fourth part, 379 (2).
Turks, 103, 192, 478 (2), 600, 607, 608.
Turner, variously spelt;—
........., John, 179, 212.
........., Dr. Peter, professor of geometry in Oxford, and fellow of Merton College, 70, 607.
........., ..., letters of, 316, 561, 601, 605.
........., ..., letter to, 245.
........., Richard, clerk to the company of barber surgeons, 507.
........., Richard of Caddington, 473, 480 (2).
........., Thomas, deed of, 399.
........., ——, plaintiff in cause in Stannary Court, 500.
........., ——, servant to Sir John Lambe, 390.
Turney, ——, 442.
Turvill, Ezechiel, commissions to, 602 (2).
Tutchen, Anthony, letter to, 312.
Twinhill, documents dated from, 346, 435.
Twisden, Margaret, 219.
Twisse, Thomas, petition of, 476.
Twyford, Hants, ship-money, 186.

Twysden, Charles, letter of, 305.
........., Sir Roger, letter of, 299.
Tyeth, Isaac, order on petition of, 132.
Tymbrell, ——, of Portsmouth, 321.
Tyne, the river, 227, 250, 406, 407.
........., commissioners for conservancy of, 407.
........., ..., letter to, 406.
Tynemouth, Northumberland, 288.
Type for printers, 72, 245.
........., Greek, 72.
Tyringham, Anthony, 274.
........., Edward, 274.
........., John, petition of, 274.
........., Sir Thomas, deceased, 274.
Tyringham, co. Buckingham, 275.
Tyrrell, Sir John, uncle to the Sir John next mentioned, 182, 370, 473.
........., ..., his lady, 370.
........., Sir John, 143, 370, 473.
........., ..., order on petition of, 182.
........., Thomas, 402.
........., ..., petition of, 374.
Tytherley, Hants, document dated from, 182.

U.

Uchayndre, co. Cardigan, division, ship-money, 198, 243.
Uckfield, Sussex, 135.
........., document dated from, 519.
Uffculme, Devon, 218.
Ufford, co. Northampton, 288.
Ufton, Berks, 75.
Ulster, 362, 501.
Ulverstone, co. Lancaster, division, 136.
Underbarrow, Westmoreland, return for, 547.
Underhill, William, in Court of Exchequer, 359, 372.
........., ——, 122.
Undermilbeck, Westmoreland, return for, 548.
Unicorn, the, (King's ship,) 3, 83, 170, 186, 243 (2), 542.
Union, Francis, bond of, 481.
United Provinces, the, 455, 588.
........., ambassador of, 178.
Universities, the, *see* Cambridge and Oxford.
........., the Archbishop of Canterbury's right to visit metropolitically, 70.
Uphill, Somerset, 179.
Upnor Castle, Kent, 195.
Upper levels of Kent and Sussex, Commissioners of Sewers and owners of, petition of, 40.

706 GENERAL INDEX.

Uppingham, co. Rutland, 320.
Upshire, William, pass for, 419.
Usury, commission to inquire of taking excessive usury, 602.
Uvedale, Richard, 495.
........., Sir William, Treasurer of the Chamber, warrants to, 41, 174 (2), 203, 212.

V.

Vale Royal, co. Chester, documents dated from, 199, 265, 300, 451.
Valencia, Capt. Philip, 28.
Valentia, Viscount, see Poore, Henry.
Valentine, Thomas, petition of, 560.
........., ..., entry of appearance of, 563.
Valliet, John, 238.
Vanduren, Marcellis, petitions of, 16 (2), 17.
Vane, Sir Henry, Comptroller of the Household, 15, 85, 195, 258, 266, 387, 448, 456, 474, 499, 521, 523, 575 (2), 603, 611.
........., ..., letter and other papers of, 226, 242 (3), 528.
........., ..., ..., the like to, 5, 445, 475, 542.
........., ..., his late embassy to Germany, 226.
........., ..., reference to, of petitions, 250, 309, 496.
........., George,} sons of Sir Henry, 474;
........., Walter, } pass to, 456.
Vanguard, the, 170, 194, 228, 237, 243, 541 (2).
Van Haesdonk, John, 492.
Vanley, ——, 507.
Vanlore, Jacoba Lady, wife of the late Sir Peter, 455, 496, 575.
........., Jane, deceased, daughter of the late Sir Peter, 380.
........., Mary, daughter of Sir Peter, deceased 496, 497.
........., Sir Peter, deceased, 380, 496 (2), 575.
........., ..., his grandchildren, 496.
........., Sir Peter, son of the above, 403, 455 (2), 496.
........., ..., petition of, 496.
........., ..., his children, 497.
Van Notten, Anne, pass for, 459.
........., James, 459.
Vassall, Samuel, answer of, 104.
Vaughan, George, 78.
........., John, 459.

Vaughan, Roger, sheriff of co. Hereford, letter of, 233.
........., Thomas, late sheriff of co. Carmarthen, 180.
........., Sir Walter, 78, 302.
Vaux, Mr., 448.
Venice, 7, 21, 467.
........., ambassador from, 579.
........., glass from, 129.
Venison, 579 (2).
........., proclamation touching, 163.
Verani, Giovanni Michaele, safe-conduct for, 427.
Verd, Cape de, 590.
Vere, Horace, Lord, of Tilbury, deceased, 128.
........., Mary, Lady, widow of the above, 128.
Verhagen, John, examinations of, 6, 28.
Vermuyden, Sir Cornelius, 16.
........., ..., petitions of, 12, 253.
Vernatti, Sir Philiberto, petitions of, 5, 16 (2), 17.
........., ..., ..., order on, 515.
........., ..., letter to, 482.
Verney, Sir Edmund, 329.
........., ..., petition of, 97.
Vernon, George, grant to, 193.
........., Sir George, Justice of Common Pleas, 598.
........., ..., letters to, 134, 135 (2), 136, 544 (3).
........., Sir Robert, 122.
Veynall, Richard, deceased, 325.
Vicarages, answers to Archbishop Laud's articles concerning, 167 (3), 170, 173, 176, 181.
Vice-Admirals, 268.
........., accounts of, 326, 445, 487, 501.
........., letters to, 262, 281, 341 (2), 501, 502.
........., note of those who have not accounted in Admiralty, 362.
Vicke, John, 365.
Victory, the, 213, 356, 554.
Victualler of the Navy or Surveyor of Marine Victuals, see Crane, John.
Victualling Office or House, Tower Hill or East Smithfield, 479.
........., commissioners for survey of, letter of, 333.
Victualling ships, 3, 24, 36, 85, 160, 184, 209, 228, 229, 256, 262, 266, 268, 279, 291, 294, 301 (2), 304, 312 (2), 319 (2), 361, 502 (2), 523, 565 (2), 578, 609.
Villiers, Elizabeth, Countess of Anglesea, 421.
........., George, the late Duke of Buckingham, 21, 265, 321, 431, 445, 501, 532.
........., Godfrey, 468.
........., Katherine, Duchess Dowager of Buckingham, 167, 574.
........., Mary, daughter of the late Duke, 574.
........., Mary, Countess of Buckingham, deceased, 431.
........., William, Viscount Grandison, 421.

Vincent, Sir Anthony, late sheriff of Surrey, account of, 198.
........., ..., letter to, 479.
........., Francis, letter to, 95.
........., John, 529.
Vintners, of London, Company of, 45, 149.
Violet, Thomas, 153.
Virginia, 273, 323, 509.
........., governor of, *see* Harvey, Sir John.
Visitations, ecclesiastical, 59, 157, 239, 240, 280, 285, 292, 316, 317, 341 (2), 363, 377, 418, 434, 554, 564, 568, 569.
........., commissioners for, 332.
........., ..., letter of, 341.
........., Archbishop Laud's claim to visit the Universities, 70, 317.
Volunteers for foreign service, 83, 130, 328, 457.
Vow, Leonard, 199.
Vows, theological treatise upon, by Mr. White, of Dorchester, 62.

W.

W. E., *see* Worseley, Edward.
Waddesdon, co. Buckingham, 564.
Wade, William, petition of, 396.
Wadham College, Oxford, 69, 574.
Wagget, Roger, 157, 178, 212.
Wainright, ——, pursuivant, 123.
Waistcoat, John, 445.
Wake, Lionel, junior, 467.
........., ..., his lodging, document dated from, 34.
........., ..., letters and other papers of, 34, 36, 434, 488.
Wakefield, 584.
Wakeham, John, 270.
Wakeman, Mr., 182.
........., Richard, certificate of, 52.
Wakes, 546.
Walden, Essex, 146, 372.
Walden, King's, co. Hertford, 492.
Wale, John, purveyor of timber, 42.
........., ..., certificate of, 87.
Wales, 12, 156, 434, 584.
........., Lord President of, 92, 335, 584; *and see* Egerton, John, Earl of Bridgwater.
........., Marches of, 280, 394.
........., ..., chief justice of, *see* Miller, Sir Thomas.

Wales, Council of, 79, 326, 335, 508.
........., ..., letters to, 23, 156.
........., North, 71, 92, 249, 400, 502.
........., South, 92, 95, 362, 501.
Walker, George, 62.
........., John, 219.
........., Mr., 458.
........., Susan, 219.
........., Walter B. L, 339.
........., ..., letter of, 323.
........., William, 560.
Wall, William, 483.
........., ..., petition of, 483.
Walle, John, 13.
........., Walter, formerly mayor of Hereford, 13.
Waller, Francis, affidavit of, 411.
........., ..., petition of, 411.
........., Thomas, 363.
........., Sir William, grant to, 447.
Wallingford, Viscount, *see* Knollys, William.
Wallingford, Berks, 235, 489.
Wallingford House, near Charing Cross, 431.
Walloon Congregation at Norwich, petition of, 356.
........., weavers, 530 (2).
Walmer Castle, 291 (2), 344, 345.
........., document dated from, 291.
........., Captain of, *see* Mennes, John.
........., Lieutenant of, *see* Lisle, Nicholas.
Walpole, Norfolk, 566.
Walpole, Henry, bond of, 426.
Walrond, William, letter of, 378.
Walsham, Norfolk, hundred, 134, 597.
Walsingham, Sir Thomas, Vice-Admiral of Kent, 362.
........., ..., letters of, 34, 48.
........., ..., letters to, 48, 502.
Walsoken, Norfolk, 566.
Walsted, Francis, commissions to, 602 (2).
Walter, Sir John, the late Lord Chief Baron of the Exchequer, 158, 447, 475.
........., Peter, petition of, 61.
........., William, 325.
........., ..., reference on petition to, 325.
........., William, justice of peace for co. Oxford, 470, 475.
........., William, sheriff of co. Oxford, 278, 304.
........., ..., letters of, 88, 510.
........., ..., account of, 88.
........., ..., his brother Killigrew, 88.
Waltham, Essex, 340.
........., half-hundred, 548.
Waltham, co. Hertford, 51.
Waltham Cross Street, Cheshunt, 608.
Waltham Hall, document dated from, 185.
Waltham, White, Berks, ship-money, 336.
Walthew, Ann, digest of her case, 581.
........., Robert, 581.

Walton, see Woodwalton.
Walton in Marshland, Norfolk, 566.
Walworth, co. Durham, 439, 440.
Wandesford, John, the King's agent and consul at Aleppo, letter to, 571.
........., Rowland, 464.
Wandsor, see Windsor.
Wangford, Suffolk, hundred, 135.
Wanstead, Essex, document dated from, 560.
Wapping, London, 115, 137, 268.
........., documents dated from, 132, 175.
........., ship-building at, 137.
.... Street, 115.
.... Wall, 115, 514.
Wappingthorn, Sussex, document dated from, 279.
War, Council of, 81, 250, 271, 324.
........., ..., entry book of documents relating to, 581.
........., ..., names of, 266.
........., ..., orders of, 270 (2), 302 (2).
........., ..., ..., list of, 325.
........., ..., committee of, for providing arms for army of the North, names of, 611.
........., ..., minutes of their proceedings, 271.
........., ..., Nicholas's notes of business touching, 270, 302.
........., ..., reference to, of petition, 250.
Ward, Ann, 133.
........., Elizabeth, 133.
........., John, of London, 443.
........., [John], of Dennington, 248, 519.
........., ..., sentence against, 497, 513.
........., Robert, 235.
........., Sergeant, 436.
........., Thomas, 201 (2).
........., William, of Allesley, articles against, 539.
........., William, partly concerned in draining, agreement of, 292.
........., William, of London, information against, 114.
Warden, Cicely, certificate of, 191.
Wardour, Sir Edward, clerk of the Pells, 200.
........., ..., certificate of, 301.
........., ..., petition of, 90.
........., Edward, 200.
........., Mary, grant to, 200.
Wardour, co. Wilts, estate of the Lord Arundel, offered for sale to the King, 55.
Wardrobe, the Great, 49.
........., clerk of, 49; and see Thelwall, Sir Bevis.
........., master of, warrants to, 174, 409, 427, 435, 441, 514, 577 (2); and see Fielding, William, Earl of Denbigh.
........., list of articles purchased for, 327.
........., commission for regulation of office of, report of, 49.

Wards and Liveries, Court of, 79, 80, 123, 124, 144, 574, 598.
........., certificate of receipts and payments of, 421.
........., order of, 431.
........., attorney of, 252.
........., ..., reference to, of petition, 381.
........., clerks of, 160.
........., master of, see Cottington, Francis, Lord.
........., ..., the late, see Naunton, Sir Robert.
........., receiver, see Fleetwood, Sir Miles.
Ware, co. Hertford, 391.
........., ship-money, 576, 581.
........., plague in, 135.
Wareham, Dorset, 441.
........., mayor, see Giggen, John.
........., manor, 441.
Waresley, co. Huntingdon, documents dated from, 246, 420, 565.
Wargrave, co. Berks, 288.
Warham Sconce, 195.
Warham, William, Archbishop of Canterbury, (1504-1532,) 288.
Warkworth, co. Northampton, ship-money, 201, 220.
Warmingham, co. Chester, 292.
Warne, Edward, 238.
........., Robert, 238.
Warner, John, of Hamhaw, 348, 527.
........., ..., son of, 348.
........., John, Bishop of Rochester, 168, 288, 352.
........., ..., restitution of temporalities of see of Rochester, 173.
........., Nowell, master of the King's barges, 110, 471.
........., ..., articles against, 110.
........., ..., referees of a petition of, orders of, 143 (2).
........., ..., petition of, 204.
Warnford, Hants, 287.
Warnham, Sussex, 479, 550.
Warren, John, petition of, 68.
........., ——, 359.
Warrington, co. Lancaster, 123, 136.
Warwick, co., 58, 95, 156, 179, 501.
........., judges of assize, letter to, 459.
........., justices of peace, letter to, 76.
........., sheriff, see Leigh, Sir Thomas.
........., ..., letter to, 189.
........., ship-money, 189, 440.
Warwick, Earl of, see Rich, Robert.
Warwick, Philip, letter of, 582.
Warwick Lane, London, 259.
Washington, Sir Lawrence, registrar of the Court of Chancery, 143.
Wastell, Clement, letter to, 201.
Watchfield, Westmoreland, ship-money, 370.
Wate, Thomas, 201.

Water supply, 113 (3), 164, 213, 340, 369, 410, 514.
Waterhouse, ——, letter to, 600.
Waterworth, Thomas, letters to, 178 (2), 212, 406.
Watkins, Dr., 458.
........., David, petition of, 23.
........., ..., ..., order on, 23.
........., Edward, 580.
........., John, 449.
........., William, grant to, 442.
Watkinson, James, mayor of Hull, 324.
........., ..., letter of, 225.
Watson, Francis, 446.
........., John, 437.
........., Thomas, petition of, 111.
........., ——, 433.
Watton-at-Stone, co. Hertford, 288.
Watts, Thomas, of Long Buckby, co. Northampton, 198, 201.
........., Thomas, of Westerham, 235.
Wavertree, co. Lancaster, manor, 282.
Wayland, Norfolk, hundred, 544.
Wayte, Thomas, 99.
Weale, Samuel, 164.
Wear [Gifford], Devon, 604.
Weaskete, see Waistcoat.
Weatherheard, George, petition of, 115.
Weavers, 528, 537.
........., of London, company of, 528.
........., confirmation of their charters, 454, 537 (2).
........., petition of, 530.
........., indenture between the King and, 454.
........., foreign, in London, note of number of, 530.
Webb, Benedict, 183.
........., Christopher, see Richmond.
........., Thomas, clothier, petitions of, 67, 244.
........., Thomas, messenger, letters to, 190, 295.
........., ——, secretary to the Duke of Lennox, letter to, 550.
Webster, James, under-sheriff of co. Nottingham, letter of, 186.
Weckherlin, [George Rudolph,] 82, 117, 224, 300.
........., ..., letter to, 85.
Weddell, Capt. John, commander of the fleet to the Indies, letter to, 306.
Wedderburn, James, Bishop of Dunblane, 529.
Weedon, John, 342.
Weekes or Weeks, Henry, warrants to, 441, 442.
........., John, 235.
........., Thomas, 264.
Weights and measures, 104.
Weimar, Duke William of, 47.
Welbeck, Richard, petition of, 283.
Welch, Thomas, letter to, 201, 437.

Weldon, Sir Anthony, letter of, 598.
........., ..., paper on ship-money by, 233.
........., Robert, letter of, 191.
Welles, John, 91.
........., Thomas, 201.
........., ..., petition of, 91.
Wellingborough, co. Northampton, 458.
Wellingham, George, letter to, 19.
Wellow, Somerset, document dated from, 398.
........., hundred, ship-money, 151, 193, 408.
Wells, Somerset, 486.
........., documents dated from, 151, 275, 278.
........., cathedral, 276, 378, 403.
........., sub-deanery of, 315.
........., ship-money, 354, 378, 398, 403.
Wells Ducis, Norfolk, quay, 418.
Wells Forum, Somerset, hundred, ship-money, 378, 403.
Welsh *alias* Wood, Thomas, examination of, 361.
Wemyss, David, Lord Elcho, 529.
........., John, Earl of Wemyss, 529.
Wenlock, Salop, document dated from, 221.
........., mayor of, letter to, 177.
........., ship-money, 177, 221, 337.
........., the Clees at, 337.
Wentworth, Henry, petition of, 109.
........., Sir John, 123.
........., Sir Peter, formerly sheriff of co. Oxford, 232 (2), 278.
........., ..., letter and other papers of, 234, 235 (3).
........., ..., letter to, 427.
........., Thomas, Viscount, Lord Deputy of Ireland and Vice-Admiral of Munster, 16, 159, 164, 178, 242, 401, 432, 439, 525, 534, 575.
........., ..., letters to, 8, 24, 34, 194, 198, 309, 326, 501.
........., Thomas, Earl of Cleveland, list of his debts, 130.
........., Thomas, Lord Wentworth, list of his debts, 130.
West, Henry, 214, 241.
........., John, 189.
........., Richard, petition of, 108.
........., ——, woodmonger, 453.
Westbeare Forest, Hants, 447.
West Country Merchants, report on petition of, 192.
West India Company, 29.
........., of Holland, 590.
Westerham, Kent, 235.
Western Circuit, judges of assize for, letter to, 211.
Western Islands of Scotland, 102.
Westgate, Kent, hundred, ship money, 209.
Westminster, casual allusions and references to, *passim*—
........., documents dated from, 4, 7, 8 (2), 13, 18, 36, 40, 42, 201, 231, 236, 244, 261, 304, 324, 332, 351, 377, 425, 432, 438, 444, 445, 467, 484, 523, 556.

Westminster, apprentices, 209.
........., brewers of, 108, 490.
........., courts held there, 500.
........., free school, 221 (2).
.... Hall, courts held there, 77.
........., justices of peace and others of, letters of, 6, 332.
.... Palace, painted chamber, 389.
........., plague in, 114, 604.
........., prebends, 608.
........., ship-money, 94.
........., tumults in, 209.
........., water-pipes to be laid between Temple Bar and, proposal for, 113.
........., water supply, 164, 213, 610.
........., Sun tavern, 555.
Westminster Abbey, 431, 500.
........., ..., cloisters, 16.
........., ..., close, 221 (2).
........., ..., sub-dean and prebendaries of, petition of, 221.
........., ..., commissioners for, petition to, 67.
Westmoreland, co., 362, 501, 584.
........., justices of peace, letter of, 546.
........., Vice-Admiral, see Howard, Theophilus, Earl of Suffolk.
Westmoreland, Earl of, see Fane, Mildmay.
Weston, Frances, Countess of Portland, 447.
........., Frances, Countess Dowager of Portland, 425.
........., Henry, letter to, 527.
........., Jerome, Earl of Portland, Governor of the Isle of Wight and Vice-Admiral of Hants, 266, 272, 424, 447.
........., ..., letters to, 324, 502.
........., Mr., 467.
........., Richard, Earl of Portland, late Lord Treasurer, 9, 116, 123, 227, 233, 477, 559.
........., Sir Richard, Baron of the Exchequer, 142, 292, 407.
........., ..., argument in Hampden's case, 540.
........., ..., letters to, 135, 546.
........., Simon, merchant, 266.
........., Sir Simon, 219.
........., ..., his lady, 219.
........., Thomas, 424.
Weston, Somerset, 602.
........., ship-money, 479.
Weston Patrick, Hants, 381, 400, 406, 435, 452.
Weston Turville, co. Buckingham, 564.
Westover, Hants, documents dated from, 40, 562, 574.
Westrop, Thomas, bond of, 574.
West's Wharf, Charing Cross, 401, 453.
Westwood, Jonathan, 504.
Westwood, co. Worcester, 428.
Wetherby, co. York, 600.
Wethered, Francis, surveyor of his Majesty's stables, warrant to, 173.

Wetwang, co. York, opinion and statement as to the King's title to the prebend of, 59 (2).
Weymouth, Dorset, 86, 296, 298, 318 (2), 604, 605.
........., mayor, see Michell, Henry.
Weymouth, William, deceased, 131.
Whalley, Ralph, 179, 236.
........., ..., his daughters, 179, 236.
........., ..., his brother, 236.
........., William, 179, 236.
Wharton, Sir Michael, 158, 184.
........., "Old," letter of, 2.
........., John, (probably the same person as the preceding,) petition of, 569.
........., ..., his wife, 569.
Whatman, Thomas, 539.
........., ..., petition of, 412.
Wheat, see Corn.
Wheatley, Thomas, petition of, 66.
Wheeler, Henry, letter to, 194.
Wheler, Francis, 384.
Whelpmore Fen, Isle of Ely, 503 (2).
Wherwell, Hants, ship-money, 198.
Whetstone, Young, 17.
Whichcote or Whichcott, Charles, brief on behalf of, 339.
........., Samuel, petition of, 225.
Whineates, Peter, order in cause of, 383.
........., Richard, the like, 383, 497.
Whippe, Robert, 169.
Whitaker, Francis, petition of, 66.
........., Lawrence, Clerk Extraordinary of the Council and justice of peace for co. Middlesex, 107, 115, 319, 349, 397, 416 (2), 436, 538.
........., ..., letters and other papers of, 230, 332, 401, 427, 429, 453.
........., ..., the like to, 363, 450.
Whitbourne, co. Hereford, document dated from, 38.
Whitby, Daniel, 288.
........., Thomas, 81.
Whitby Strand, co. York, wapentake, 345.
Whitchurch, co. Buckingham, 564.
White, Francis, Bishop of Ely, judgment of, 59.
........., ..., death of, 311.
........., Henry, 514, 549.
........., John, 610.
........., Mr., in Sir John Pennington's fleet, 321.
........., Mr., of Dorchester, treatise by, 62.
........., Richard, 424.
........., William, 288.
Whitechapel, 399, 414.
Whitefriars, London, 417, 591.
Whitehall, 39, 148, 162, 166, 186, 213, 321, 394, 410.
........., documents dated from, *passim*.
........., masque at, 1.
.... Palace, 490.
.... gate, 333.
...., riot near, 333, 338.

White Lion Court, near Fleet Street, London, 6.
.... Prison, Southwark, 203.
White Swan, the, in Cheapside, near Paul's Gate, document dated from, 597.
Whitfield, Sir Ralph, 136, 606.
........., Robert, clerk, petition of, 579.
........., Serjeant, 254, 274, 481.
Whitgift, John, late Archbishop of Canterbury, 2.
Whithed, Richard, late sheriff of Hants, letter and other papers of, 182, 198.
Whitland Abbey, co. Carmarthen, 452.
.... Wood, co. Carmarthen, 452.
Whitledg, William, memorandum of, 317.
Whitley, Seuce [Susey?], petition of, 374.
........., Thomas, sheriff of co. Flint, letters and other papers of, 312, 407, 429, 485, 507.
........., Thomas, of London, 374.
Whitmore, Sir George, alderman of London, 606.
........., ..., letter of, 161.
........., Sir Ralph, 168.
........., Capt. Thomas, 58.
........., ..., letter to, 482.
........., Thomas, counsellor at law, petition of, 505.
Whitney, Francis, 556.
........., Geoffrey, 79.
........., Henry, petition of, 79.
Whittlesey, co. Cambridge, landowners of, 471.
Whittlesford, co. Cambridge, hundred, 133.
Whittlewood Forest, co. Northampton, 430, 484, 518.
Whitwell and Selside, *see* Selside.
Whorwood, Lady, 200.
Wicken, co. Cambridge, 56, 506.
Wickens or Wickins, Nathaniel, servant to William Prynne, 71.
........., William, steward of Christ's Hospital, 488, 492.
Wickham, co. Cambridge, 493.
Wickham, Edward, 205, 231.
........., William, 205, 231.
........., William formerly Bishop of Winchester, 206, 231.
Wickhams, of Swalcliffe, the family, claim to be regarded as of kin to William of Wickham, 231.
Widdrington, Roger, letters of, 349, 596.
........., Thomas, recorder of Berwick, letter to, 456.
........., Sir William, sheriff of Northumberland, his house at Blankney, 16.
........., ..., letters of, 16, 213, 349.
........., ..., letters to, 15 (2), 30 (2).
Widdrington, Northumberland, document dated from, 213.
Widford, co. Gloucester, 288.
Wigan, 360 (2).
Wigan, Frederick, 324.

Wight, Isle of, 31, 33, 270, 271, 272, 278, 293, 502, 598.
........., ..., documents dated from, 293, 307 (2), 320, 367 (2), 505.
........., ..., Governor and Vice-Admiral, *see* Weston, Jerome, Earl of Portland.
........., ..., ship-money, 307; *and see* Hants.
Wight, Mary, certificate of, 521.
Wigley, Thomas, indictment against, 76.
Wigston Magna, co. Leicester, 411.
Wilburton, co. Cambridge, document dated from, 493.
Wilde or Wild, Capt. John, 590, 600.
........., Mr., letter to, 238, 271, 346.
Wilden, co. Bedford, 417, 429.
Wildman, Martha, petition of, 124.
Wildmore Common, co. Lincoln, 90.
.... Fen, co. Lincoln, 9, 55, 90.
Wilford, Father John, 467, 500.
Wilford, Suffolk, hundred, 544.
Wilkinson, Edward, 80.
........., Mary, petition of, 10.
........., Richard, gunner, 131, 268, 542.
........., William, petition of, 10.
Willes, ——, 192.
William, the, ship from the East Indies, 15, 31.
.... and Thomas, the, 213.
William or Williams, Sir Abraham, 349, 603.
........., ..., letter of, 230.
........., Christopher, brief on behalf of, 77.
........., George, 214.
........., John, witness in the Bishop of Lincoln's case, letter to, 201.
........., John, prisoner in Newgate, petition of, 54.
........., ..., his wife and children, 54.
........., John, of London, letter of, 15.
........., John, Bishop of Lincoln, 21, 37, 61 (3), 62 (2), 65 (2), 66, 67, 115, 173, 176, 201, 218, 281, 308 (2), 323, 563, 571, 591.
........., ..., answer of, to articles in High Commission, 339.
........., ..., petition of, answer to, 57.
........., ..., information against, 170.
........., ..., charges against, in Star Chamber, 339.
........., ..., commissioners to exercise episcopal jurisdiction during suspension of, 69.
........., Morgan, 65.
........., Paul, 526.
........., Thomas, 185.
........., William, 110.
Williamson, Sir Joseph, 60.
........., Mr., 458.
Willis, Richard, 335.
........., ..., commission and letters to, 363, 518, 519.
Willmer, John, petition of, 328.
........., Sir William, 396.

Willoughby, Henry, 144.
..........., ..., letter to, 37. *See also* Willoughby, William.
..........., Sir Henry, petition of, 152.
..........., Sir John, 152.
..........., Lord, *see* Bertie, Montagu.
..........., Mr., merchant of London, 160.
..........., Sir Robert, 118.
..........., ..., his lady, 118 (2).
..........., ..., his tenants, certificate of, 118.
..........., William, 144.
Willoughby in-the-Marsh, co. Lincoln, 167.
Willow, Mr., 424.
Wills, Richard, petition on behalf of, 73.
Wilmot, Charles Viscount, 266.
Wilse, Mr., 286, 287.
Wilson, Felix, 377, 389.
..........., Francis, 467.
..........., George or Goodridge, 201, 220.
..........., ..., petition of, 221.
..........., Mr., 599.
..........., ———, 503.
Wilton, Robert, 238.
Wilts, 75, 228, 412.
.... assizes, presentment at, 576.
..........., justices of peace, 480.
Wiltshire, John, 417, 429.
Wimberley, Mr., 58.
..........., Gilbert, 399.
Wimbledon, Viscount, *see* Cecil, Edward.
Wimpole, co. Cambridge, 430.
Winch, Richard, 424.
Winchelsea, Sussex, 93.
Winchendon, Upper, co. Buckingham, 564.
Winchester, 274, 469.
..........., documents dated from, 274.
..........., bishopric, 64.
.... Castle, 447.
.... College or School, 206, 231, 421, 558.
.... Consistory Court, surrogate of, letter to, 446.
..........., dean and chapter, petition of, 253.
..........., diocese, chancellor, *see* Mason, Dr. Robert.
..........., mayor, 367.
..........., ship-money, 367 (2), 381, 386.
..........., Bishop, *see* Andrewes, Lancelot; Curle, Walter; Horne, Robert; Wickham, William.
Windebank, Christopher, son of the Secretary, letters of, 31, 467, 499.
..........., Sir Francis, Secretary of State, and one of the Comptrollers-General of the Posts, allusions and references to, *passim*.
..........., ..., his house at Westminster, 603.
..........., ..., letters of, 1, 7, 13, 34, 130, 156, 244, 257, 261, 277, 285, 341, 435, 438, 444, 456, 572, 578, 588, 590, 593, 605, 610.
..........., ..., other papers of, 51, 69, 143, 319, 426, 443, 455, 515, 533.

Windebank, Sir Francis—*cont.*
..........., ..., letters and other papers to, 4, 15, 16, 19, 20, 28, 31, 50, 51, 52 (3), 53, 55, 61, 70, 81, 98, 141, 159, 162, 172, 253, 266 (2), 269, 271, 274, 277, 278, 290, 291, 294, 296 (2), 297, 319, 320, 354, 387, 388, 389, 394 (2), 400, 443, 445, 451, 457, 467, 475 (2), 481, 490, 499 (2), 513, 557, 558, 559, 571, 582, 585, 592, 594, 596, 598 (2), 599, 603, 604 (2), 608.
..........., ..., notes of causes heard in the Star Chamber, 185, 192, 214, 241, 384 (2), 399, 473.
..........., ..., references to, of petitions, 5, 16, 141, 164, 193, 204, 250, 251, 255, 354, 373, 496, 509, 520, 536.
..........., ..., his gifts to the repair of St. Paul's, 489.
..........., ..., his secretary, *see* Read, Robert.
..........., John, son of the secretary, letters of, 277, 354.
..........., Thomas, son of the secretary, 123.
Winder, George, 416 (2).
Windermere, Westmoreland, return for, 548.
Windham, Mr., 375.
Windsor, 235, 424, 468, 489, 510, 604.
..........., documents dated from, 141, 596.
.... Castle, 609.
...., documents dated from, 596, 600.
...., and honour of, receiver and comptroller of, letters to, 320, 582.
..........., dean, 24, 373, 445; *and see* Wren, Dr. Christopher.
.... Free Chapel, 247.
.... Forest, 332, 582, 609.
.... Great Park, 320.
..........., ..., survey of, 268.
..........., poor knights, 445.
..........., Old, 268.
Wine cask, commissioners for licensing, 375, 401.
..........., ..., letter of, 398.
Wines, 45, 54, 107, 214.
..........., prizing, order touching, 41.
..........., customs upon, farmers of, account of, 327.
..........., warrant to, 42.
Wingate, Mr., 448.
Wingfield, Edward Maria, answer of, 261.
..........., Sir James, 261.
Winkfield, Richard, pass to, 398.
Winlaton, co. Durham, 387.
Winniffe, Thomas, Dean of St. Paul's, 473, 480.
..........., ..., petition of, 551.
Winter, John, grant to, 214; *and see* Wintour.
Winterbourne, Wilts, 304.
..........., late fire at, 31.
Winterbourne Earls, Wilts, 603.
Wintour, Sir John, Secretary and Master of Requests to the Queen, 53, 74.
..........., ..., warrant to, 428.
..........., Lady Mary, 74.

Winwick, co. Lancaster, 136.
Wire, Forest of, Salop, 511.
Wirehill [co. Salop], 511.
Wisbeach, co. Cambridge, 78.
Wisdom, Richard, petition of, 126.
........., ..., his wife, 126.
Wise, Thomas, sheriff of Devon, letters and other papers of, 235, 456.
Wiseman, Diana, 213, 241.
........., Sir Richard, 213, 241, 416, 436, 440.
........., ..., notes of his case in the Star Chamber, 491 (2).
........., Lady Susan, 213, 241.
Wispington, co. Lincoln, 181.
Witchalse, John, 456.
Witcherley, Daniel, 301.
Witches, 20, 586 (2).
Witchingham, Norfolk, document dated from, 330.
With, Thomas, 298.
Witham, the river, 55.
Withering, Thomas, ship-owner, 239.
Witherings, Thomas, postmaster for foreign services, 22, 51 (2), 52 (2), 53, 143, 171, 177, 183, 216, 217, 271, 284, 297.
........., ..., petition of, 217.
Witherslack, Westmoreland, return for, 547.
Withins, Christopher, petition of, 67.
........., ..., his wife, 67.
Witney, co. Oxford, church, 176, 313.
........., ship-money, 266.
........., White Hart, the, 273.
Wittam, Anna, 65.
Wittersham level, Kent and Sussex, commissioners of sewers and owners of lands, petitions of, 40, 251.
Wittlesford, co. Cambridge, 372.
Woburn, co. Bedford, 363.
Woely, Mary, petition of, 313.
........., Richard, 313.
Woking, Surrey, 16.
........., hundred, 133.
Wokingham, Berks, ship-money, 348.
Wolf, the, (ship,) or Golden Wolf, of Medemblik, 84, 590, 600.
Wolffen, John Gaspar, letter and petition of, 50, 108, 490.
Wolley, Edward, 59.
Wolrich, Robert, 538.
Wolseley, Sir Robert, clerk of the patents, petition of, 80.
Wolstenholme, Sir John, farmer of customs, 1, 109, 120, 148.
........., ..., letter of, 204.
Wolverhampton, 247, 382 (2).
Wolveton, co. Dorset, document dated from, 169.
Wolvin, Thomas, petition of, 88.
Wonersh, Surrey, ship-money, 49.
Wonford West, Devon, hundred, 136, 545.

Wood, variously spelt;
........., Ambrose, 89.
........., Dr. Andrew, B.D., 238.
........., Dr. Basil, 63, 78, 159.
........., ..., opinion of, 158.
........., Josias, 172, 186, 207, 220.
........., Thomas, of Compton Abdale, see Welsh, Thomas.
........., ..., mayor of Bossiney, Trevena, and Tintagell, ship-money rate made by, 18.
Woodbevington, co. Warwick, 288.
Woodbridge, Suffolk, 137, 347.
Woodcock, Richard, affidavit of, 556.
Woodend in Copehall, [Cople?] co. Bedford, 550.
Woodfall, Richard, 437, 456.
Woodfine, Edward, 143, 166.
Woodford, John, commissions to, 602 (2).
Woodhall, [co. Lincoln?,] 130.
........., document dated from, 569.
Woodham, John, 198, 201.
........., Walter, Essex, 248.
Woodkeeper, Richard, 107 (2).
Woodom, see Woodham.
Woodroffe, Edmund, messenger, letter to, 295.
Woods, John, certificate of, 478.
Woodstock, co. Oxford, 394, 604, 607.
........., documents dated from, 603 (2), 604, 606 (3).
........., manor court at, 436.
........., House, 95.
Wood Street, London, 119, 126, 476.
Woodwalton, co. Huntingdon, 308 (2), 369.
Woodward, Hugh, letter of, 585
........., Richard, 468.
Woolf, John Johnson Vander, examination of, 590,
Woolfe, Richard, letter to, 184.
Woolhouse, Mr., 412, 494.
Woolner, [Benjamin,] 17.
Woolstaple Stairs, Westminster, 6.
Woolward, [Capt?,] 578.
Woolwich, 30, 103, 192, 269, 479, 480, 550.
........., ships building at, 202.
Wootton, see Wotton.
Wootton Underwood, co. Buckingham, 564.
Worcester, 214, 337.
........., prebend of, see Steward, Richard.
Worcester, co., 156.
........., feodary, see Chamberlaine, Edward.
........., sheriff, 527. See Dingley, Sir Edward.
........., ship-money, 344, 527.
Worfield, Jo., auditor, 333, 488.
Workington, Cumberland, 584.
Works, office of his Majesty's, Scotland Yard, London, 332, 368.
........., officers of, 335, 410.
........., surveyor of, 410.

Z Z

Worlaby, co. Lincoln, 158, 184.
Wormstead, Lawrence, examination of, 504.
Worpson [?], Launcelot, see Thompson, Launcelot.
Worseley or Worsley, Edward, letters of, 12 (2), 13.
........., Dame Frances, 128.
........., Sir Henry, 128.
........., Mr., 446.
........., Thomas, petition of, 283.
Worsop, John, 26.
Wotton or Wootton, Richard, 233.
........., William, 214.
........., ..., letter to, 507.
Wotton, Thomas, Lord, and his lady, 229.
Wotton, Surrey, hundred, 133.
Wragg, alias Bonywragg, John, 400.
Wray, Joseph, 228.
Wrecking and wrecks, 33, 44, 179, 245, 269.
Wren, Dr. Christopher, dean of Windsor and Wolverhampton, and registrar of the Order of the Garter, 24, 37, 143, 247, 373.
........., ..., his dovecot, estimate of repairs, 232.
........., Matthew, Bishop of Norwich, afterwards Bishop of Ely, 317, 330, 412.
........., ..., act of homage by, 483.
........., ..., order of, 183, 405.
........., ..., petition to, 356.
........., ..., his visitation articles, 568.
Wrenham, Capt. Francis, petition of, 57.
........., ..., particulars of his case, 58.
Wrexham, co. Denbigh, document dated from, 375.
Wright, Ezekiel, B.D., petition of, 248.
........., alias Herbert, Gerard, agreement of, 292.
........., Henry, 8.
........., Hugh, 475.
........., James, 8.
........., John, late clerk of the House of Commons, heirs or executors of, letter to, 247.
........., Mr., of Madrid, 31.
........., Richard, Justice of Peace for Surrey, certificate of, 431.
........., Robert, incumbent of Dennington, deceased, 497, 519.
........., Robert, Bishop of Lichfield and Coventry, 59, 219, 316, 409.
........., ..., letter to, 315.
........., ..., letters of, 351, 540.
........., Thomas, 311.
........., William, 417, 430, 437, 442.
........., ——, Alderman of London, 374.
........., ——, 482.
Wrightinton, Edward, letter of, 481.
Wriothesley, Thomas, Earl of Southampton, 162.
........., John, 174, 541.
........., ——, 482.
Write, see Wright.

Wroughton, Sir George, 486.
Wyan, Thomas, deputy registrar of the Admiralty, letters of, 222, 307.
........., ..., letters to, 33, 170, 343.
Wyatt, Parkins, under-sheriff of co. Lincoln, 28.
........., William, 506.
Wyche, George, letter of, 466.
........., ..., letter to, 466.
........., Sir Peter, Ambassador to Turkey, 103.
Wymondham, Norfolk, 405, 412.
Wynne, variously spelt;—
........., Hugh, 65.
........., John, 23.
........., Maurice, 244.
........., Sir Richard, treasurer and receiver general to the Queen, 77, 152.
........., ..., grant to, 441.
........., Robert, letter of, 195.
Wytton, John, deputy postmaster of the Court, petition of, 51.

Y.

Yardley, Ralph, 188.
Yardley, co. Hertford, 314.
Yarmouth, Great, Norfolk, 22, 171, 177, 217, 284, 347, 401, 436, 453, 460.
........., ..., bailiffs of, letter of, 134.
........., ..., ..., petition of, 217.
........., ..., fishermen and herring traders of, 494.
........., ..., ..., allegations of, 20.
........., ..., saltmakers of, corporation of, 147, 152.
........., ..., salt manufacture at, 113, 217.
........., ..., ship-money, 220.
Yarmouth, Isle of Wight, castle, 270.
Yarnfield, Somerset, 385, 412, 539.
Yaxley, co. Huntingdon, 453, 488, 515.
........., document dated from, 487.
Yelford, co. Oxford, St. Nicholas, 288.
Yeo, Robert, 430, 512.
........., ..., account of, 439.
Yester, Lord, see Hay, John.
Yonge, Francis, bond of, 505.
........., Thomas, 483.
........., ..., petition of, 483.
York, Mr., 15.
York, 226, 310, 441.
........., castle, keeper of, 310.

GENERAL INDEX.

York, cathedral, 62.
........, dean and chapter, petition of, 62.
........, council of, *see* North.
........, ..., president of, *see* Wentworth, Thomas, Viscount.
........, ..., vice-president, *see* Osborne, Sir Edward.
........, Archbishop of, *see* Neile, Richard.
........, James, Duke of, 315, 537, 555.
........, ..., appointment as Lord High Admiral, 351.
York, co., 12, 14, 17, 80, 226, 253, 323, 501.
........, deputy-lieutenants, petition of, 97.
........, judges of assize, 211.
........, ..., letter of, 134.
........, justices of peace, returns of, 137 (2), 542, 545 (2).
........, ..., letters of, 346, 347.
........, ..., letter to, 134.
........, sheriff, 246. *See* Ramsden, Sir John.
........, ship-money, 19, 246, 348.
........, Vice-Admiral, *see* Sheffield, Edmund, Earl of Mulgrave.
........, East Riding, 137 (2), 225.
........, ..., justices of peace, letter of, 247.
........, North Riding, 225, 345.
........, ..., justices of peace, letter of, 346.

York, West Riding, 225, 433.
Young, Patrick, 72.
........, Robert, printer, 116.
........, ..., petition of, 200.
........, Thomas, clerk of the signet in Scotland.
........, ..., letter to, 554.
Ysairon or Yss Aioron, *see* Issayndre.
Ywchairon or Ywich Ayron, *see* Uchayndre.

Z.

Zacharie or Zachary, Francis, 516.
Zealand, Holland, 110, 178.
........, ..., court of Admiralty of, 84 (2).
Ziegenhain, 47.
Zouch, Sir Edward, and his lady, 451.
........, James, 16, 446.
........, ..., petition and other papers of, 396, 451.
........, ..., his wife, 451.

ERRATA.

Page 191, line 40, *for* Sir Miles Burkitt *read* Miles Burkitt.
Page 267, line 1, *for* Launcelot Worpson? *read* Launcelot Thompson.
Pape 287. The paper next to No. 48, is numbered 48 A.

LONDON:
Printed by GEORGE E. EYRE and WILLIAM SPOTTISWOODE,
Printers to the Queen's most Excellent Majesty.
For Her Majesty's Stationery Office.

Lightning Source UK Ltd.
Milton Keynes UK
UKHW051844111219
355217UK00007B/98/P